1 2 7
8 10 12 13

Cost and Managerial Accounting

Ronald V. Hartley (Ph. D., University of Illinois at Urbana-Champaign) is Professor of Accounting at Bowling Green State University, where he has taught since 1965. He was Visiting Professor of Accounting at the University of Texas at Austin in 1978–1979. Professor Hartley has taught undergraduate Cost Accounting courses for 23 years. His articles have appeared in *The Accounting Review, The Journal of Accounting, Taxation for Accountants, The Mid-Atlantic Journal of Business,* and *Management Accounting.* Professor Hartley has also written another text, *Operations Research: A Managerial Emphasis* (Goodyear, 1976) and the chapter "Quantitative Methods," in Miller and Mead's *CPA Review Manual,* Fifth Edition (Prentice-Hall, 1979). His research interests are management accounting topics, especially as they relate to optimization techniques. Currently, he is an associate editor of *Decision Sciences.* He has been secretary/treasurer of the Management Accounting section of The American Accounting Association.

Cost and Managerial Accounting

Second Edition

Ronald V. Hartley

Bowling Green State University

Allyn and Bacon, Inc.

BOSTON · LONDON · SYDNEY · TORONTO

Series Editor: Richard Carle
Production Editor: Peter Petraitis
Editorial/Production Services: Harkavy Publishing Service
Interior/Cover Designer: David Ford
Cover Coordinator: Linda Dickinson

Library of Congress Cataloging-in-Publication Data

Hartley, Ronald V.
  Cost and managerial accounting.

  Includes bibliographies and index.
  1. Cost accounting. 2. Managerial accounting.
I. Title.
HF5686.C8H2725   1986   657'.42   85-22914
ISBN 0-205-07789-7

Material from Uniform CPA Examination Questions, Copyright © 1958, 1959, 1964, 1965, 1966,
1967, 1968, 1969, 1970, 1971, 1972, 1973, 1974, 1975, 1979, 1980, 1981, 1982 by the American Institute
of Certified Public Accountants, Inc., is reprinted (or adapted) with permission.

Material from the Certificate in Management Accounting Examinations, Copyright © 1972, 1973,
1974, 1975, 1976, 1977, 1978, 1979 by the National Association of Accountants, is reprinted (or
adapted) with permission.

Printed in the United States of America.
10 9 8 7 6 5 4 3 2   90 89 88 87

Contents

Preface

The management accountant performs a dynamic and important role in the operation of any organization, be it manufacturing, retail, service, or nonprofit. This role is not that of a passive, financial police officer, but of an active initiator and catalyst. The top priority of any accounting system is to provide information to management. Accountants first help the organization to be successful; then they turn to the job of reporting the success to interested "external" parties. This book covers material that is important to all accountants, regardless of their chosen specialties. Public accountants, for example, audit cost data. They need to have a good understanding of cost methods in order to give an informed opinion. Well-trained and imaginative cost and management accountants can make valuable and creative contributions to top management in all types of organizations.

Approach

Cost and managerial accounting courses are offered in a variety of ways. Recognizing that no book can perfectly meet the needs of everyone, I have tried to provide substantial flexibility, along with some depth and integration. These are somewhat contradictory goals, and the book naturally reflects my own biases regarding what are reasonable objectives for a college course. Any instructor, however, should be able to use the book for a course that meets his or her specific objectives. For example, for those who wish to enrich the quantitative aspect of the course, the chapters in Part 5 provide a variety of topics. An MBA-type course can be designed by omitting some of the chapters that get into the details but are not crucial for understanding the results.

This book recognizes the value of both theory and practice. Being able to do accounting without really understanding the whys and wherefores can be dangerous, especially when faced with a new situation. At the same time, understanding theory without knowing how to apply it is of little value, at least outside the classroom. The many demonstration examples and self-study problems (with solutions) throughout the book are designed to demonstrate the practical application of cost/managerial principles. The student can further enhance his or her skills by working through the problems at the end of each chapter. There are many elementary, intermediate, and challenging problems in each chapter.

I have tried to present the material in this book in a logical order and in clear, understandable language. Some ideas in cost accounting no doubt appear difficult to the student encountering them for the first time, but a reasonably careful reading should put most students on the road to understanding. I happen to think that the cost accounting process is of itself interesting. I cover it early in the book (and in my own course) and use several strategies to illuminate its importance. I stress, for instance, the significant role of cost accounting data in evaluating employee performance. Once students see that cost is often an input to performance evaluation, the "nuts and bolts" of costing suddenly take on new interest. My goal is to have students begin to think independently about measuring and determining costs in a manner that is fair to management, employees, shareholders, and the public. In this way I try to establish the social and economic importance of cost accounting.

Organization

The book is divided into five parts. Part 1 introduces terminology, the basic concepts of cost flows, flexible budgeting, and financial statements.

In Part 2, the basic cost accounting systems are explored. The major topics are job order, process costing, standard costing, and variable costing. Subtopics include spoilage, service department accounting, joint-cost accounting, and applications to nonmanufacturing entities. While the emphasis is on the systems, there is ample discussion of the implications of the data for planning, decision making, and performance evaluation.

Part 3 closely examines planning and decision-making topics. Such subjects as budgeting, CVP analysis, relevant data, and capital budgeting lend themselves to a comprehensive one-semester course or second course.

Control is the theme of Part 4. How can the accounting system provide information that is fair both to the superior and to the subordinate, and that will motivate the subordinate to achieve the goals established by the superior?

Part 5 covers a number of quantitative topics. Included for the first time is a discussion of the use of electronic spreadsheets and decision support systems. As mentioned earlier, the instructor can pick and choose from these topics, depending on course needs.

Changes in This Edition

Past users of this book will see immediately the biggest of six changes I have made. Most of the quantitative material has been pulled out of various chapters and assembled in the new Part 5. In some cases, particular techniques have been retained where they were in the first edition (such as the use of matrix algebra in allocating service department costs), but are marked as optional.

Second, self-study problems and their solutions have been added to all but the first chapter.

Third, there is a new chapter on the application in cost/managerial accounting of the revolutionary electronic spreadsheets and decision support systems.

Fourth, the standard cost chapter has been split (now Chapters 5 and 6), and material on the establishment of responsibility for standard cost variances has been moved into the second, Chapter 6, from the first edition's Chapter 18.

Fifth, several advanced topics have been eliminated from this edition.

Finally, over 200 new problems have been added, most of them being of the basic variety so that students can "get their feet wet" before plunging into the more challenging problems.

Supplementary Materials

The Solutions Manual contains detailed solutions to every problem in the text. A separate Instructor's Resource Manual contains helpful suggestions for using the book, detailed analyses of the text problems, demonstration materials for in-class use, and an extensive multiple-choice examination bank. The Student Study Guide contains key concepts for each chapter and a variety of review-type questions and exercises.

Acknowledgments

I would be remiss if I did not acknowledge, in an admittedly small way, the significant contributions that others have made to this project. First, E.E. Ray, former professor of accounting at Ohio University, challenged me to think about the topics in this book and led me to understand them in an enormously interesting way. Even though he is no longer with us, I know he is aware of his impact.

All the people who contributed directly to the manuscript in the review of both the first and second editions were not revealed to me. It is helpful to have input from others; it seems that whatever you write is frequently better understood by yourself than by those who are more independent. Thanks to all who helped in this way.

Many others contributed to this edition indirectly through the discussions I have had with them. Among them are Norm Eckel, Wayne Johnson, Bob Patton, Jim Sullivan, and my own students.

Rich Carle, Senior Editor at Allyn and Bacon, must also be thanked for his continuing interest and confidence in the project. He is a facilitator and a catalyst. I am indebted to Bowling Green State University for providing resources. For permission to use selected problems, I thank The Institute of Management Accounting and The American Institute of Certified Public Accountants.

Much thanks goes to my wife Judy and my children Karen and Daryl, who were understanding of the responsibilities of the project and accepted the demands which it placed on the family. I am also indebted to my mother and father, who sacrificed so that their children could ultimately have economic resources in an abundance they themselves could not have had even if their sacrifice had not been made.

I welcome any and all comments from users.

R.V.H.

Cost and Managerial Accounting

Part 1 Introductory Materials

CHAPTER 1

The Role of Cost and Managerial Accounting

Accounting, like many other disciplines, encompasses several functional areas. These areas include financial accounting, tax accounting, auditing (both external and internal), cost accounting, and managerial accounting. These various areas of accounting do not exist as independent entities but are related to each other, just as the accounting discipline itself is related to several other disciplines. The purpose of this book is to examine cost and managerial accounting.

When using the book you should be prepared to learn *how* to apply various principles and *why* they are appropriate. Each situation encountered in practice will be unique. If the practitioner or user does not understand the reason for the basic principles of cost/managerial accounting, adapting them to new situations will prove difficult. That is, knowing how to perform some accounting procedure does you no good unless you know when to use it.

This book is intended for both preparers and users of accounting data. If you are going into accounting as a profession, you will need to have a good understanding of cost and management accounting principles regardless of the specific area of accounting you choose. Cost accounting supplies data for all types of external reports. Thus you will need to understand this area of accounting if you are involved in the external reporting function for a firm or if you are associated with the company's auditing firm. It is not possible to be an objective evaluator of cost accounting data unless you understand the principles of cost accounting. Tax reporting also uses cost data. Thus, if you go into the tax area you will need to be knowledgeable of cost accounting methods. Obviously, if you join the controller's staff of a company, cost accounting will be used daily.

Cost and management accounting must also be understood by many allied professionals. For example, production managers, marketing managers, and engineers need to appreciate the meaning of cost data in making many of their decisions. Managers who are in positions of evaluating personnel that report to them will need to be able to interpret the cost data that will inevitably be part of the evaluation of those personnel.

As will be seen throughout this book, it is not always obvious what is meant by "cost." Likewise, it is not always clear which cost should be used for any given purpose. The only thing that is always clear is that the same cost figure *cannot* be used (correctly) for any and all purposes. Because of this, all accountants and several allied professionals must study this discipline carefully.

This introductory chapter establishes a framework for the remaining course of study. First, the general functions of cost and managerial accounting are explained and placed in perspective with its various users. Second, a section is devoted to an examination of the factors influencing the design of a cost/managerial accounting system. The final section establishes the organizational environment surrounding the cost/managerial function as well as the professional and other bodies related to the area.

Functions of Cost and Managerial Accounting

It is appropriate to begin by considering the nature of cost and managerial accounting. Some consider these two areas to be synonymous and to encompass the provision of data needed by the firm's managers for making decisions and reporting to owners. Others distinguish cost accounting from managerial accounting by defining cost accounting as the theories and procedures for determining the inventory costs and the cost-of-goods-sold figure for financial reporting purposes. Those who separate the areas refer to managerial accounting as the theories and procedures for supplying the data needed by internal users. There is no desire, here, to create a semantic controversy. The two areas do not have clear territorial boundaries, thus the title *Cost and Managerial Accounting*.

As *conventionally* used, cost accounting implies the process of determining how the costs that have been assigned to a given accounting period will be assigned to the various cost objectives with which the firm was involved during the accounting period. (Cost objectives are entities for which a cost determination is desired.) For example, some people hold the view that financial accounting theories govern the amount of depreciation to be recognized in any given accounting period. On the other hand, the assignment of depreciation to the various cost objectives (such as the units produced) would be within the realm of cost accounting.

It is not a particularly significant, or desirable, distinction to associate cost accounting only with the external reporting function. There are at least two good reasons to support this. First, it is absolutely necessary to understand the differences in the data requirements of various users and the limitation of using data for a purpose that was not intended. By simultaneously considering the needs of all end-users of cost accounting data one can more easily highlight these differences and establish a solid criteria for what is appropriate for the circumstances. Second, it may be that certain concepts have applicability to multiple uses. If so, it is more efficient to explore the potential of these concepts in one course of study rather than in multiple courses.

It is generally agreed that cost/managerial accounting serves four functions: (1) external financial reporting, (2) the managerial function of decision making, (3) the managerial function of planning, and (4) the managerial function of control. The remainder of this section considers, in more detail, the role of accounting with respect to these four functions. This classification scheme is not ideal because the functions are not independent of each other. Nevertheless, the four functions provide a focus to guide the discussions in this text.

FINANCIAL REPORTING. From an historical perspective, the first demand placed upon cost/managerial accounting was that of cost determination for financial reporting. That is, the accounting system is expected to accumulate the figures pertaining to the cost of manufactured product and other objectives, such as the cost of operating a given geographical or product line segment of the firm. This requires an understanding of how to trace the flow of costs to the various objectives that benefit from the incurrence of the costs. Such a function is of the nature of "score-keeping" in that the costs are actual recorded costs that are assigned to a variety of objectives in order to determine accounting income.

Cost accounting is important for income determination, for inventory evaluations, and for making and evaluating pricing decisions. Part II of the book emphasizes this function and is done by exploring the various cost accounting systems that can be used. Although they will not be defined here, the systems include job order, process cost, standard cost, and direct costing. Other topics discussed in Part II include accounting for spoilage, accounting for departments that provide services within a firm, and accounting for multiple products that emerge from a single production operation.

Management accountants, of course, are involved in more than just the cost accounting aspect of financial reporting. In a survey done by Lander and others, the responding practicing management accountants indicated significant involvement in the preparation of balance sheets, income statements, and funds statements. The involvement was reported to be either preparation or review of the statements, and extended beyond the inventory and cost-of-goods-sold components.[1]

DECISION MAKING. Within an organization there is a cycle of related activities that all need information. The cycle begins with decision making, continues with the making of plans to implement decisions, and concludes with the evaluation of the results (control). Each of these managerial responsibilities will be examined with a view toward establishing the role of the cost/managerial accountant.

Decision making is the process of determining whether to commit resources to a given purpose. Decisions can be of many types: recurring, one-time, firm-wide, departmentally based, those that have short-run impacts, those that have long-run impacts, and so forth. In the survey cited in footnote 1, it was revealed that the following are the areas with which management accountants are most frequently involved:[2]

1. Long-range strategic planning
2. Allocation of company resources
3. Financing alternatives
4. Personnel
5. Management information systems

---

[1]Gerald H. Lander, James R. Holmes, Manuel A. Tipgos, and Marc J. Wallace, *Profile of the Management Accountant* (New York: National Association of Accountants, 1983), pp. 25–38.
[2]Ibid., p. 52.

6. Offering new products or services
7. Discontinuing products or services
8. Marketing strategy
9. Production scheduling

Further, decision makers are characterized by the different styles they use in making decisions and their different levels of knowledge. Each type of decision will most likely require a different kind of information. Also, the data required may be both historical and projected. Thus, it is difficult to generalize about the system needed to satisfy this demand on cost/managerial accounting.

There are some common characteristics, however. The "costs" upon which decisions should be based must be **incremental** costs. These are the additional costs that will be incurred as a result of making the decision to accept some course of action. Sometimes these are called **differential** or **marginal** costs. On some occasions, historical data may be used, without adjustment, to project incremental costs. On other occasions, the historical data may need to be modified to reflect conditions that will be different than those that existed at the time the historical costs were collected. On yet other occasions, historical costs may be of no help whatsoever in estimating incremental costs.

The usefulness of cost/managerial accounting to the decision-making process depends on how well it can be adapted to the changing requirements of decision problems. For historical data, this means that the system must be designed to be flexible. Of course, increased flexibility results in a higher cost of operating the system. Thus, some consideration must be given to the benefit per dollar of increased cost. A flexible system would be one that permits data to be classified in different ways for different purposes. It is impossible to foresee all possible future uses of accounting data. When unforeseen needs arise, data may have to be analyzed differently than for the foreseen needs. The adequacy of these analyses is dependent on how data have been aggregated (summarized) in the system. If too much aggregation has taken place, it may be impossible to "sort it out" and regroup if for other needs. Because of this possibility it is imperative to include accounting professionals in the decision-making process. By doing this, the firm's accountants will have a maximum chance to prepare for the ultimate data requirements and can then be of maximum usefulness in generating historical data.

To provide projected data, the system of collection must be different. Such data do not originate with completed exchange transactions that result in an accounting entry. This aspect of the system entails monitoring external data and processing those data into a form usable by the firm. Projected data may be based on historical data but modified to reflect anticipated future conditions.

A significant amount of *two*-way communication is necessary with the users of the data. The user needs to understand the limitations of accounting and to provide some assumptions on which the accountant can proceed. Part III of the book emphasizes the role of accounting with respect to this as well as the planning function. Topics include budgeting, cost-volume-profit analysis, the determination of decision-relevant data, and capital budgeting.

PLANNING. **Planning** is the process of implementing the managers' decisions. It includes the organization of personnel, the assignment of duties, the coordination of the progress, and the projection of cash and income flows in order to anticipate problems before their occurrence. The controller of the firm will likely have direct responsibility for the latter aspect. This is known as budgeting. Like the support of decision making, planning will need projected data. Thus, most of what was said about the support of decision making is equally applicable to this function.

CONTROL. When a firm expands, there is an increased need for a formalized control system. **Control** is the process of ensuring that objectives are achieved. To accomplish this, current actions must be monitored and data collected. The data should then provide feedback to both the employee and the supervisor so that they may compare achievements against some norms. Control is facilitated by organizing firms into subunits, or small groups of people, with a designated supervisor. These subunits are called **responsibility centers.** The supervisors may also be organized into groups, with supervisors from a higher stratum of the organization.

Now consider *part* of the control system: the collection of data about performance. Within the manufacturing function, for example, there will be responsibility centers that are held accountable for performing various tasks. Actual costs are collected for each responsibility center and then compared with the expected costs given the accomplishments of the period. If the actual costs are significantly above the expectations, an explanation will be sought. This is not the only type of control that will be in place. These are called accounting controls and will only be part of a good control system. Other types of controls will be discussed in Part IV of the book. For example, internal auditing is part of the overall control system.

SUMMARY OF THE FUNCTIONS OF COST/MANAGERIAL ACCOUNTING AND BOOK ORGANIZATION. The four functions discussed above are summarized in Exhibit 1.1 and shown in concert with the related activities of the firm's managers. The exhibit shows the parallel activities in the order they occur. That is, management makes decisions, formulates plans for implementing the decisions, evaluates those responsible for implementing the decisions, and reports to the shareholders and other interested external parties. Along side each of these managerial activities is a brief description of the accountant's function.

The third column of Exhibit 1.1 is a reference to the topic coverage in this book. Two things should be explained. First, the book begins in Part II with a discussion of the accountant's role in the last step of the managerial process. This should not be considered to be "out of order." The book is exploring the accounting process, not the management process. Discussing the reporting role of accounting is a prerequisite to gaining a proper perspective to understanding the accountant's role in the other areas. Second, note that Chapters 5 and 6 are, in effect, useful in two areas of the accounting function. These chapters are on standard costing, which is a cornerstone for control. However, the topic is also a cornerstone for discussing

Exhibit 1.1   Management Functions and the Role of the Cost and Management Accountant

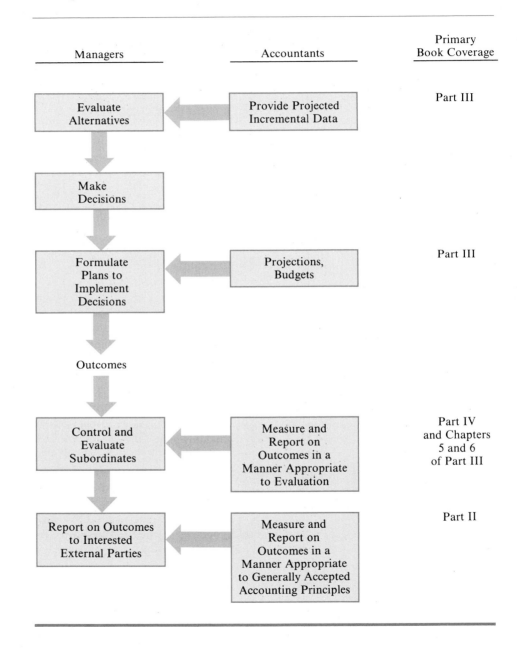

Managers	Accountants	Primary Book Coverage
Evaluate Alternatives	Provide Projected Incremental Data	Part III
Make Decisions		
Formulate Plans to Implement Decisions	Projections, Budgets	Part III
Outcomes		
Control and Evaluate Subordinates	Measure and Report on Outcomes in a Manner Appropriate to Evaluation	Part IV and Chapters 5 and 6 of Part III
Report on Outcomes to Interested External Parties	Measure and Report on Outcomes in a Manner Appropriate to Generally Accepted Accounting Principles	Part II

the design of accounting systems. Part II of the book is a study of cost/managerial accounting information systems. Thus, the topic was included in Part II but is also important in Part IV. The flow of the book, then, is:

Part   I—Introductory materials
Part   II—Systems to support reporting function
Part III—Topics in support of decision making and planning
Part IV—Topics in support of control
Part   V—Quantitative support topics

Factors Influencing the Design of a Cost/Managerial Accounting System

In this section there is an examination of some additional factors that are important to the overall organization and design of the cost/managerial accounting system. First, there is a discussion of some possible philosophical approaches to designing the system. Second, there is an examination of the possible business units that can be served by cost/managerial accounting and the impact that their differences can have on the system.

POSSIBLE APPROACHES TO DESIGNING A COST/MANAGERIAL ACCOUNTING SYSTEM. There are three possible approaches that can be used in designing an accounting system: the historical communication, user-decision model, and information evaluation approaches.[3] The approach that has been, and perhaps continues to be, the dominant method is the **historical communication** approach. Although this approach recognizes that there are multiple uses of data, system design decisions are guided by the goal to produce a single set of summary data that can be used reasonably well by *all* interested parties. To create maximum usefulness for each user, this approach carefully establishes the rules of information processing, communicates them to all users as clearly as possible, and uses them consistently. It is assumed that if users understand the rules of information processing, they will see what adjustments are needed to adapt the data to their own needs and will be able to make the adjustments themselves. In practice, systems that use this approach as their focus have information processing rules that, generally, are heavily influenced by financial reporting standards and by rules governing the determination of taxable income.

A second approach is that of the **user decision** model. Although there is some earlier evidence of this approach, its impact was not serious until around 1960. An information system designed via the user decision model approach attempts to provide data that are appropriate for the intended use. The success of designing such a system is dependent on several things. First, the user of the specific data must be known. It is also necessary to know the user's style, the user's cognitive

---

[3]For a more thorough discussion of these approaches see the American Accounting Association's "Report of the Committee on Concepts and Standards—Internal Planning and Control," *The Accounting Review Supplement* (1974), pp. 79–96; or Joel S. Demski and Gerald A. Feltham's *Cost Determination: A Conceptual Approach* (Ames, Iowa: The Iowa State University Press, 1976), Chapter 1.

makeup, the type of action to be taken, and the existing knowledge of the user. This approach assumes that only when all of the above are known can relevant data be collected and communicated to the user.

The **information evaluation** approach has been proposed as a third alternative, and it explicitly recognizes that information generation has a cost. It is guided by the principle that the benefit of generated information should exceed the cost of providing it. Neither the cost nor the benefits of information are likely to be capable of precise measurement. However, it is important to consider both and their relationships with each other.

The information evaluation approach needs to be explored further. As with the input for any other decision, the input needed to make a decision about an information-gathering system will require estimates. In estimating the cost of the system, factors to be considered include design costs, length of time the system will be used, the cost of operating the system, and the cost of maintaining the system. Benefits will be more difficult to measure. In this approach to systems design it is not sufficient to rely solely on the user's desires. The critical questions are results-oriented. For example, the end-users may think a particular system or piece of information will improve their decision quality. But, will it in fact improve the quality, and, if so, by how much? Even if the quality of the decision is improved it may not be of a sufficient magnitude to offset the added cost of generating the information. The specifics of measuring benefits are not always clear. There are some general principles from the field of statistical decision theory that are useful as a starting point. Some of these principles are discussed in Chapter 25.

DEPENDENCE ON TYPE OF BUSINESS UNIT SERVED. Another variable that affects cost/managerial accounting systems is the type of business unit being served. For our purpose business units are classified as (1) manufacturing organizations, (2) profit-oriented retail and service organizations, and (3) nonprofit organizations.

A **manufacturing** firm, of course, converts materials, which it purchases, into another desired product through the use of labor and machines. Even within this category of business units there are differing characteristics that cause differences in the accounting system. Some firms' production may be geared to customer specification. For example, Lockhead Aircraft and McDonnell Douglas Corporation produce much of the equipment needed by the U.S. Defense Department, which is usually special (custom) ordered. Most jobs done by large printing companies are also custom orders. In these cases, each order has one or more attributes that are different from those of any other order processed by the firm. Since each order differs as to the amount and kind of material and labor required, the accounting system must be designed to treat each job as a separate cost-collection entity. Such systems are called *job order* systems and are discussed in more detail in Chapter 3.

Other firms, such as a furniture company, may produce a variety of standard products; that is, the product requirements are relatively constant. However, the firm may choose to produce only one or a few of their products at a time. This may be necessary when the demand does not justify a separate production line for each product. When production lines are shared, the machinery and processes will have to be set up to meet the requirements of the product being produced. In such cases it would be impractical to adjust the production processes frequently, and thus production of a given item is scheduled in batches. In these situations the products are still manufactured in batches; thus, a job order system is applicable.

A third category of manufacturing firms consists of those whose products' demand and plant capacity are such that the products are manufactured in a continuous stream. Automobile companies, appliance manufacturers, and petroleum processors are examples of these types of companies. Under these circumstances a job order system is not practical. The products are not produced in batches and, therefore, there is no *job* entity to which costs can be assigned. Thus the cost/managerial accounting system will differ in many ways from that of a job order system. In these cases, the firm will probably use a *process cost* accounting system. Process cost accounting is introduced in Chapter 4.

Regardless of whether a job order or process cost system is used, a firm may elect to assign manufacturing costs at a *predetermined* rate rather than prorate actual costs. This is known as a *standard cost* system and is discussed in Chapters 5 and 6.

A given firm may have a system that is a combination of the aforementioned ones. For example, some of the production may be accounted for on a job order basis and some on a process cost basis. A machine tools manufacturer, for example, may have several standard products (tools used by many firms) and also produce special ordered products. Process costing could be used for the first type of production and job order costing for the second. Also, some of the manufacturing costs may be accounted for using an actual cost philosophy and some using a standard cost philosophy. For example, a publishing company may be able to account for the materials needed in producing books at a standard cost. However, the editing and typesetting labor may not be capable of being standardized because they will vary significantly from one type of book to another. (Typesetting a mathematics book differs greatly from typesetting a history book because of the mathematical notation.) The appropriate combination depends on the nature of the manufacturing processes and on the objectives that the firm has for its accounting system.

The preceding discussion centered on an overview of the systems used for product cost determination. However, it is important to recognize that products are not the only entities for which a cost determination is needed. There may be, for example, a need to know the cost of operating a particular department within the firm, the cost of operating in a particular geographic region, the cost of implementing a particular project, the cost of developing a new product, the cost of implementing a given contract, or any number of other entities. If a cost accounting system is strictly product–cost-oriented, then it will not be of maximum service to all of its users.

The second classification of firms mentioned earlier is that of **profit-oriented retail** and **service organizations.** These would include department stores, food stores, accounting firms, banks, medical clinics, and restaurants. Such organizations, of course, do not *manufacture* a product and, therefore, their cost determination requirements are different. But this does not mean that cost/managerial accounting is irrelevant to such firms. These firms also have cost questions similar to those posed in the previous paragraph. The principles of cost determination do not change just because the firm is of the service type. For example, when a consulting firm determines the cost of one of its engagements, it should use the same basic principles that a manufacturing firm would use in determining the cost of completing one of its production jobs.

Nonprofit organizations include governmental units, universities (in spite of what you might think when you pay your fees), hospitals, and charitable organizations. These organizations also need good cost information. In judging effectiveness of their operations, nonprofit organizations will have different criteria from profit-oriented organizations, but this does not affect the applicability of cost determination principles. Some examples of costs that may be valuable to know include the cost of processing a welfare case, the cost of an imprisonment, the cost of a rehabilitation, the cost of operating summer school, the cost of offering a course, and the cost of raising and administrating the funds of a charitable organization.

To summarize this section, there are many factors that influence the particular form of a cost/managerial accounting system. A few of these have been discussed here in order to provide an overview of the subjects examined in this book. Other factors will be introduced later.

The Cost/Management Accounting Environment

To provide further overview of the cost and management accounting profession it is useful to consider its place within an organization and the various professional external organizations that aid and affect it.

INTERNAL ORGANIZATION. Firms are conventionally organized in such a way that the authority and responsibility for certain decisions are delegated. The company president, for example, cannot personally make all of the decisions that must be made in an organization. Thus many of the decisions are delegated to others. For example, there may be a vice-president of manufacturing, a vice-president of marketing, and a vice-president of finance. Each of these vice-presidents may further delegate a portion of their duties.

A representative organization chart for a manufacturing firm is shown in Exhibit 1.2. As you review that chart, take particular note of the vice-president of finance and the organization under that area of responsibility. This is where the accounting function is "housed." In the remainder of this section there will be a brief description of the specific duties of the controller, the treasurer, and the director of internal auditing.

Exhibit 1.2   Representative Organization Chart

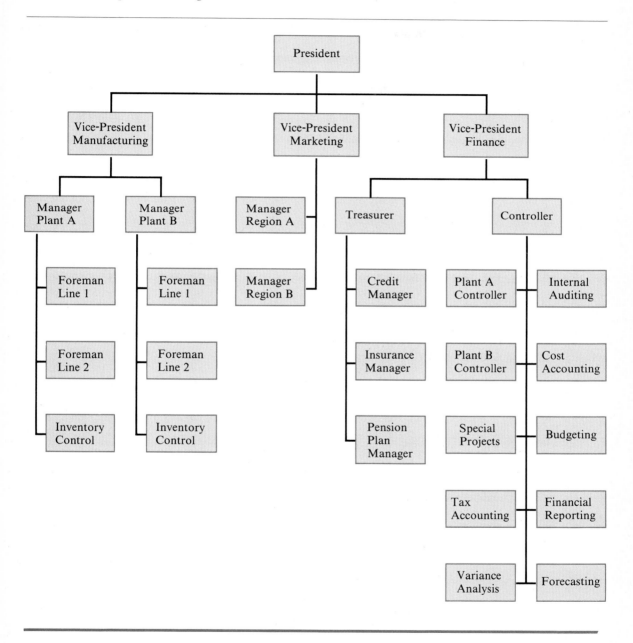

Also note the organization under the vice-president of manufacturing. It is somewhat common for each of the various plants under the vice-president of manufacturing to have a plant controller. When this is the case, it would be advisable for these controllers to report to the corporate controller, not the plant manager. This is the way it was shown in Exhibit 1.2. The reason for this is to ensure independence of the plant controller from the plant manager and to facilitate consistency of accounting throughout the organization. Without an independence from the plant manager, the plant controller could be placed under extreme pressure to account for the activities of the plant in ways that are favorable to the plant but will not portray the "correct picture" to top management. An alternative to this arrangement is sometimes found. The plant controller might report to the plant manager and coordinate activities through the corporate controller. This arrangement has the advantage of making the plant controller seem less of a "spy" on the activities of the plant and more of a confidant.

Now consider, briefly, the function of the controller. First, the controller serves the firm in an advisory capacity rather than in a decision-making capacity. This does not mean that controllers never make decisions. Although they do not make policy decisions for the firm, they do make decisions about the policies of the accounting system.

The **controller's** primary duty is to design, install, and operate the entire accounting system, including the cost/managerial accounting subsystem. In some firms, the controller may be responsible for the entire management information system, which would include such subsystems as production and inventory control, marketing research, and personnel records in addition to the accounting subsystem. Typically, however, the controller is only concerned with the accounting portion of the total system. In cases where controllers are not responsible for the entire system, they should be involved in the development of the nonaccounting system in order to provide coordination and input.

Outputs of the accounting system include various financial statements, both internal and external. These would obviously be the responsibility of the controller and would include internal reports as well as external reports to the shareholders, the Securities and Exchange Commission (SEC), the Internal Revenue Service (IRS), and others. Thus, the controller needs to be knowledgeable of the rulings and regulations of the Financial Accounting Standards Board (FASB), the SEC, and the IRS. If the firm is involved with U.S. government contracts, the controller will also need to be knowledgeable of the rulings of the Cost Accounting Standards Board (CASB). (The SEC, IRS, FASB, and CASB are described later in this section.)

The controller typically is also responsible for coordinating the budgeting system of the firm. This includes setting budget formats and reporting dates, and providing data needed by the functional areas in submitting their budgets. Related to this, the controller is expected to analyze the variances between the actual result and the budgeted figures and to aid department managers in understanding the meaning of the variances.

Finally, the controller is given the responsibility of developing an internal control system to aid in protecting the firm's assets. This may be delegated to a **director**

of internal auditing. (Sometimes it will be found that the director of internal auditing will report directly to the vice-president of finance rather than to the controller.) The responsibility consists of identifying various types of transactions that will occur, dividing the processing of these transactions into segments, and determining which individual will be responsible for each segment. The controller is also responsible for organizing the firm's internal auditing division, which will provide some insurance that the internal control system is working. Further, internal auditors may do operational audits. This entails an evaluation of how well management is making their decisions. That is, given the actual conditions that occurred, an operational audit asks if management made the best decision.

In contrast to the controller, the **treasurer** is the money manager. The treasurer's tasks include arranging for raising capital through shareholders, banking institutions, and so forth. The treasurer also arranges for short-term borrowing and supervises the investment of cash in order to minimize loss from idle funds. A treasurer is responsible for the credit and collections function of the firm and is likely to be responsible for the firm's insurance program.

The treasurer's function is not explained in as much depth because the subject of this book is more properly classified as controllership. But enough information has been provided to distinguish between the roles of these two important positions in a business.

EXTERNAL ORGANIZATIONS RELATED TO MANAGEMENT ACCOUNTING. There are a variety of external organizations with which the management accountant must deal and which may be of assistance to the personnel of a firm's accounting department. These organizations are discussed in this section.

Four organizations have already been mentioned. The **Financial Accounting Standards Board (FASB)** is a private, independent board created by the American Institute of Certified Public Accountants. It has been given the responsibility for determining the standards to be used by firms when reporting to the public. Obviously, in carrying out its external reporting duties, the firm's accountants must be knowledgeable of the FASB standards.

The **Internal Revenue Service (IRS)** is very well known and, of course, is responsible for collecting the taxes imposed by the U.S. Congress. There are many rules and regulations of the IRS that must be known by the controller's staff in order to ensure that the firm does not pay more taxes than it is obliged to pay under the law.

The **Securities and Exchange Commission (SEC)** is another branch of the U.S. government. It has the responsibility of ensuring that individuals who trade in the stock of publicly held companies have access to neutral and fair financial data on which to base their trading decisions.

The **Cost Accounting Standards Board (CASB)** was created by the U.S. Congress to establish rules to be used in determining the cost of certain types of contracts that are made with the government. Simply put, the CASB was to establish accounting rules in order to give the government some insurance that the cost charged to them for a cost-plus contract was a "fair" cost. If you become associated with a firm that does business with the U.S. government, you may have to become very familiar with the CASB rules. The CASB no longer exists but its rules are enforced by the Government Accounting Office.

The remaining organizations to be highlighted here are in the form of professional support groups. These include the Financial Executives Institute, the National Association of Accountants, the Institute of Internal Auditors, and the Planning Executives Institute. The **Financial Executives Institute (FEI)** is an organization of corporate vice-presidents of finance and controllers. It has a research foundation that sponsors studies of problems with widespread interest. Further, it publishes a monthly magazine, *FE: The Magazine for Financial Executives*.

The **National Association of Accountants (NAA)** is a professional organization open to all managerial accountants and any others that have an interest in management accounting. It publishes a monthly magazine, *Management Accounting*. The NAA has also established the Institute of Management Accounting, which conducts a program of certification for management accountants. This is done through an examination and the meeting of certain experience requirements. Upon passing the examination and meeting the experience, a Certificate of Management Accounting (CMA) is awarded. This can be used to "validate" your management accounting knowledge if such validation is important to either you or your employer. Many of the problems in this book are adapted, with permission, from the CMA exam.

The **Institute of Internal Auditors (IIA)** is a professional organization open to all who are interested in internal auditing. The IIA also sponsors a validation process. When completed you are awarded a Certificate of Internal Auditing (CIA). This organization, also, publishes a monthly magazine, *Internal Auditing*.

The **Planning Executives Institute (PEI)** is a group for those who are involved in a firm's planning activities. It publishes a magazine, *Managerial Planning*.

Each of the four professional organizations described above have local chapters that hold monthly meetings to discuss topics of interest to the group. In addition, annual national meetings are held in order to broaden the experiences of members. Some of these associations sponsor continuing education programs for members.

Summary

This chapter provides a general overview of cost/managerial accounting. It has been noted that it serves four managerial functions: financial reporting, decision-making, planning, and control. These four functions are present in all types of organizations, whether they be manufacturers, retailers, service organizations, or nonprofit organizations. Cost/managerial accounting is of equal importance to all of these entities. However, because of the massive data collection problems caused by the need for cost determination in a manufacturing firm, there will be more discussion devoted to manufacturers in this book.

You should be aware that the nature of the data needed from an organization's information system depends on the function being served and on the type of entity it is. The remainder of the book expands on specifics of these differences.

Also be aware that there are different philosophical approaches that can be used in designing an accounting system. There is the historical communication approach, the user decision model approach, and the information evaluation approach. These approaches were discussed in their pure forms. In any given situation all three approaches may influence the actual system design.

Finally, you were introduced to the organizational environment of cost/management accounting. You should understand how cost/management accounting fits into an organization's structure and be aware of the various external groups that effect or aid internal accountants in performing their jobs.

At the end of each chapter summary you will find a list of key terms and concepts that were introduced in the chapter. In addition to being discussed in the chapter, these terms are defined in the glossary at the end of the book. Key terms in this chapter are the following:

Decision making
Planning
Control
Responsibility accounting
Historical communication approach
Decision model approach
Information evaluation approach
Controller
Treasurer
Financial Accounting Standards Board (FASB)
Security and Exchange Commission (SEC)
Internal Revenue Service (IRS)
Cost Accounting Standards Board (CASB)
Financial Executives Institute (FEI)
National Association of Accountants (NAA)
Institute of Internal Auditors (IIA)
Planning Executive Institute (PEI)

References

American Accounting Association. "Committee Report on Managerial Accounting," *The Accounting Review Supplement* (1970): 1–8.

————. "Report of the Committee on Concepts and Standards—Internal Planning and Control," *The Accounting Review Supplement* (1974): 79–96.

Anthony, R.N. "The Rebirth of Cost Accounting," *Management Accounting* (October 1975): 13–16.

Demski, J., and Feltham, G. *Cost Determination: A Conceptual Approach.* Ames, Iowa: Iowa State University Press, 1976.

Garner, S.P. *Evolution of Cost Accounting to 1925.* Tuscalossa, Ala.: University of Alabama Press, 1954.

Half, R. "Do Management Accountants Have an Image Problem?" *Management Accounting* (August 1980): 10–13.

Kaplan, R.S. "The Evolution of Management Accounting," *The Accounting Review* (July 1984): 390–418.

Lander, G.H., Holmes, J.R., Tipgos, M.A., and Wallace, M.J. *Profile of the Management Accountant.* New York: National Association of Accountants, 1983.

McFarland, W.B. *Concepts for Management Accounting.* New York: National Association of Accountants, 1966.

National Association of Accountants. *Statements on Management Accounting: Definition of Management Accounting,* Statement Number 1A. New York: National Association of Accountants, 1981.

———. *Statements on Management Accounting: Objectives of Management Accounting,* Statement Number 1B. New York: National Association of Accountants, 1982.

———. *Statements on Management Accounting: Standards of Ethical Conduct for Management Accountants,* Statement Number 1C. New York: National Association of Accountants, 1983.

Sheldahl, T.K. "Toward a Code of Professional Ethics for Management Accountants," *Management Accounting* (August 1980): 36–40.

Problems

1-1. "'Management accountant' is a high-class name for a bookkeeper." Comment.

1-2. "If management accountants were licensed by the state, as are CPAs, lawyers, and doctors, they would have a better public image." Comment.

1-3. "Our company is unique, not manufacturing per se; we don't have a need for management accountants. We are processors." Comment.

1-4. "Cost accounting will be of no use to you if you go into public accounting." Comment.

1-5. "Historical cost data are of no use to the decision-making function." Comment.

1-6. "Data generated to satisfy generally accepted accounting principles will be sufficient for all purposes." Comment.

1-7. At a staff meeting, one of the marketing managers indicated that most of the firm's competitors had recently lowered the sales price on one of the firm's products. She asked whether the company could lower the per unit price to the market price of $10 and still earn a profit. The accountant in charge of external reporting indicated that the cost in the latest month was $10.50 per unit. Evaluate the pros and cons of using the $10.50 "cost" to help with the pricing question.

1-8. In evaluating the managers of the various departments of its store, the Dudson Department Store uses cost per unit as one measure. This is computed by taking the invoice cost of the units sold plus a variety of operating costs, such as clerk salaries, and allocated building costs, divided by the number of units sold. In comparison with last month, the average cost per pair of shoes sold in the Men's Shoe Department increased from $35 to $38. Enumerate the pros and cons of this cost for evaluating the performance of the manager of the department.

1-9. The local electric company proposes to the State Board of Utilities to increase the electric rates charged to the consumers. The only defense was that the community had been very successful in an "Efficient Energy Program," and had reduced consumption by a significant amount.

Required:

1. How can the company's reason be defended?
2. As a consumer of electricity, what would be your reaction?

1-10. In organizations it is common to refer to the various officers as having *line* or *staff* authority. Line officers are responsible for the main functions of the business, whereas staff officers provide advice to the line officers.

Required:

1. Would the controller's department be line or staff?
2. Can you identify a possible staff function not listed in Exhibit 1.2?

1-11. The manager of a division of which you are controller has asked that you arrange for dating invoices 12/2 19x1 for items that will be shipped to customers in 19x2. The manager wants to increase his 19x1 sales so that his performance evaluation report will look better. What would you do?

1-12. What are the advantages of having a plant controller report directly to the corporate controller? To the plant manager?

1-13. The examination for a CIA places more emphasis on decision-making techniques and models than the CPA exam. Explain why this is so.

1-14. You are about to vote in your first election. One item on the ballot is a school levy that would increase the property tax rates. The school board has provided the following items in support of the need for the levy.

1. The state increased the mandated minimum teacher salary levels by 10%. The school had been operating at a minimum that was 15% above the previous state minimums.
2. The population base of the community has been increasing in the past several years. Thus, there are more students and, therefore, more teachers needed.
3. For the reason cited in number 2, the utilities (heat and light) have been increasing.
4. Due to inflation, operating costs (electric, gas, gasoline, etc.) are increasing.
5. It is felt that the English classes have too high a student-to-teacher ratio. To reduce the ratio, it will be necessary to hire more English teachers.

Required:

Comment on the validity of the above arguments from a cost standpoint.

CHAPTER 2

Cost Concepts, Cost Behavior, Systems, and Reporting

To understand cost/managerial accounting, you must understand a variety of cost concepts. It is useful, then, to preface the study of the accountant's specific functions with a discussion of these basic concepts. This is done in the first two sections of this chapter. The first section reviews the accounting concept of cost. The second section reviews a variety of cost classifications.

Further, all functions of cost/managerial accounting assume an ability to identify the way costs behave. Whether the accountant does the analysis personally or relies on someone else, a need still exists to understand how cost behavior can be identified. The third section identifies several needs for specifying cost behavior patterns and identifies a variety of tools that can be used to determine the behavior.

Section four provides an overview of accounting systems. In this section there is a demonstration of how accountants design their data collection systems in order to supply data for the many different requests received by them for information.

The final section reviews the external reporting of the results of a manufacturing firm. A manufacturer's statements are contrasted with those of nonmanufacturing firms.

The Cost Concept

A cost/managerial accountant is frequently asked to determine the cost of some item, project, or proposal. You should be aware, however, that "cost" does not have a unique meaning. In fact, the term "cost" probably should not even be used without a modifier. In this section we explore a variety of concepts that will help you refine your understanding of the term.

COST VERSUS EXPENSE VERSUS LOSS. In a financial accounting sense, **cost** normally refers to the sum of the necessary outlays made in order to acquire an asset and to make it ready for its intended use. For example, the cost of merchandise purchased for resale is its invoice price, plus shipping cost, plus receiving and handling costs, less purchase discounts. That is, the cost of merchandise is not just the invoice price charged by the supplier. Consider a second example. The cost of a stamping machine to be used in the production of automobiles is the sum of its invoice price, shipping charges, installation costs, and the cost of adjusting and testing the equipment before using it.

Stated alternatively, the cost of an asset, such as the stamping machine, is the value of the assets given in exchange at the time of its acquisition. In such an exchange, the *total* assets do not change but their *form* does change. In this example, one asset, cash, is exchanged for another asset, a stamping machine. The accounting cost of the stamping machine is equal to the value of the asset exchanged, the cash.

An asset can be viewed as a "bundle" of utility or service potential waiting to be used. There are a variety of ways in which this service potential may expire. For example, as the asset is used, a portion of the service potential is consumed. Likewise, if an asset is sold or exchanged for another asset, the utility or service potential of the first asset expires. Finally, the service potential of an asset may expire because the asset is accidentally destroyed (fire, for example) or becomes obsolete.

An **expense** is defined as the expired cost resulting from a *productive* usage of an asset. That is, as a portion of the service potential of an asset is consumed, a part of its cost is reclassified as an expense. These expenses are then matched against the revenues that they helped to generate. In contrast, a **loss** is an expired cost resulting from a decline in the service potential of an asset that generated *no benefit* to the firm (the fire loss or obsolescence, for example). In this event, the cost is also reclassified but as a loss. Of course, there is no revenue against which it can be matched. More will be said later about the problems of accounting for expired service potentials when the cost attachment concept is reviewed.

HISTORICAL VERSUS REPLACEMENT VERSUS OPPORTUNITY COST. The cost/managerial accountant must not only use historical costs but also replacement costs and opportunity costs. **Historical cost** is the actual outlay made at the time an asset is acquired. If $10,000 was paid for a stamping machine acquired in 19x1, then its historical cost is $10,000. It is the type of cost conventionally accounted for in financial accounting. In contrast, **replacement** (current) cost is the outlay that would have to be made if the asset were to be replaced. If the firm would have to pay $13,000 for a similar stamping machine today, then its replacement cost is $13,000. In cost/managerial accounting, replacement cost will often be more relevant than historical cost.

To introduce the **opportunity cost** concept, note that taking some action will normally preclude taking certain other actions. For example, the cost of studying on Saturday night is the sacrifice of not going to a football game or to a social event. Using a resource to produce one product precludes its use in producing another product. The satisfaction, or gain, of the activity foregone is an opportunity cost of the act chosen. If there are two or more mutually exclusive actions foregone, then the opportunity cost of the act chosen is the highest satisfaction or gain that was precluded.

To summarize, historical cost is a *past* expenditure. Replacement cost is an anticipated *current* expenditure, and opportunity cost is a *foregone* profit or satisfaction.

SPECIFIC TYPES OF HISTORICAL COSTS. Next consider the general types of historical costs incurred by most firms. Costs may be classified into product costs and period costs. **Product costs** are those assigned to the products that the firm manufactures. They become an expense when the product to which they were assigned is sold. In contrast, **period costs** are costs that are treated as expenses in the accounting period in which they are incurred. There is no attempt to trace them to the product. To illustrate, the tires of an automobile are product costs and the automobile manufacturing company's advertising cost is a period expense. The latter is treated as a period expense by accountants because it is very difficult to assign to a specific product.

The product costs of a manufacturing firm are often difficult to determine. Before proceeding with specific topics in this area, let us review the components of a manufacturer's product costs. Product costs, for these firms, will consist of manufacturing costs only. **Manufacturing costs** include only those costs that can be directly identified with the production function. Selling costs are excluded because they are incurred to market the product, not to produce it. General administrative expenses, such as the salaries of the executives whose duties are not exclusively manufacturing-related, are not included because of the difficult task of determining how much expense was incurred for the benefit of manufacturing.

Manufacturing costs are further categorized into direct material, direct labor, and manufacturing overhead. **Direct material** refers to items that become a physical part of the finished products and can be conveniently traced to them. **Direct labor** consists of the wages paid to those employees whose tasks are such that they are *physically* engaged in the actual production process as opposed to support activities, such as supervision, cleanup, and production accounting. **Manufacturing overhead** consists of all other manufacturing costs, that is, those that are neither direct material nor direct labor. By definition, manufacturing overhead consists of production costs that cannot be physically and conveniently traced to the products. Each of these cost concepts will be discussed in more detail in Chapter 3. Exhibit 2.11 (p. 43) illustrates how these costs are reported to compute product costs.

CONCEPT OF COST ATTACHMENT. The concept of **cost attachment** is very important for understanding an accounting system. Thus, let's consider this concept in a manufacturing environment. A manufacturing firm takes some combination of materials and converts them into a finished product. In this conversion process, additional expenditures are incurred in the form of labor and overhead. Now consider what happens.

As materials are put into production, they lose their utility *as a raw material*. But this does not imply the incurrence of an expense. An expense is not recognized at this point because the utility of the total asset package has not been reduced. The utility of the raw material is now incorporated into the finished product. Thus, instead of creating a "raw material expense," the production process is viewed as an exchange of assets. In a sense, what has happened is no different from a transaction where cash is exchanged for materials. In a production situation, material (and other resources) is exchanged for a finished product. Thus, accountants say that the cost of the materials "attaches" as part of the cost of the finished product. Consequently, the cost of this effort is assigned to the finished units containing the raw materials so that it can be deferred until the units are sold. (Sometimes the assignment of cost to an asset is referred to as *capitalizing* the cost.) By this type of accounting, there is a *matching* of the costs with the revenue they produce.

Similarly, cash is exchanged for direct labor and some of the manufacturing overhead items. As these resources are used in production, they lose their utility as direct labor and as other assets. But they help create utility in the finished product and thus, again, their costs attach to the output rather than being considered as expenses. That is, in a manner similar to materials, labor and overhead are exchanged for a finished product.

When the finished product is sold, the sum of all these individual utilities that are incorporated into the finished goods cease to have future utility and are said to expire. Then the cost of the finished goods flows to an *expense* account, which is normally called "cost of goods sold." The word "cost" in this account title is unfortunate but conventional. It is unfortunate in that much care has been taken to carefully distinguish between a cost and an expense. (Expense is an expired cost, and the above account should be "expense of goods sold.") As explained earlier, the cost attachment process has the effect of deferring the efforts (expenses) of producing a product until the accomplishment (revenue) is recognized.

Other Concepts and Definitions

In addition to the concept of accounting cost, there are other concepts with which the cost/managerial accountant must be familiar. In this section, the following additional concepts are reviewed:

1. Variable versus fixed costs.
2. Committed versus programmed costs.
3. Cost objectives.
4. Direct versus indirect costs.
5. Separable versus joint costs.
6. Controllable versus noncontrollable costs.

VARIABLE VERSUS FIXED COST. To account for and estimate costs properly, we need to determine how they behave. That is, we must determine what factor(s) causes a cost to be incurred and the specific relationship between this factor(s) and the cost. Fundamental to this are the meanings of fixed and variable cost.

A cost is said to be **variable** with respect to a specific factor if the total amount of the cost incurred changes in direct proportion to changes in that factor. (See Exhibit 2.1.) For example, direct material used is variable with respect to production because an increase in production results in a proportional increase in the total direct material cost. Sales commissions are variable with respect to units *sold* but not necessarily with respect to units produced. Production and sales are not always the same. Thus an increase in sales will result in an increase in sales commissions, but an increase in production will not.

More realistically, it may be found that the variable cost does not remain constant over all units of the causal factor. It is typical for some inefficiencies to occur at both the lower and upper extremes of activity. In such a case we will find that

Exhibit 2.1   Behavior of a Strictly Variable Cost

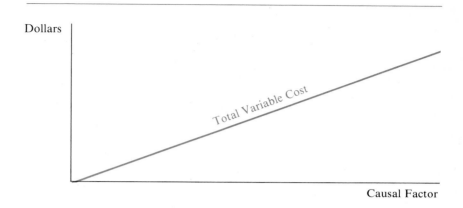

the cost will increase at a decreasing *rate* near the lower levels of activity, at a constant rate over the middle of the range, and at an increasing rate near the upper extreme. This behavior is depicted in Exhibit 2.2.

In Exhibit 2.2, note that the cost behavior is approximately linear between the points *a* and *b*. So long as the activity is in this range, a simple linear, or straight, line will be appropriate in estimating the costs. Most firms operate in a range

Exhibit 2.2   Real Behavior of a Variable Cost

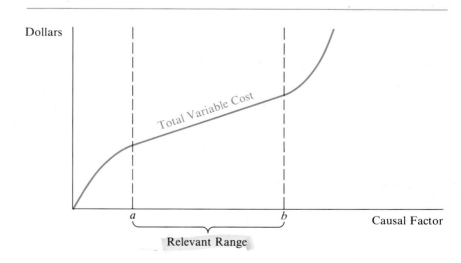

where linear expressions are accurate enough. Such a range is called the **relevant range.** So long as management is interested in the cost behavior for levels of activity in this range, accountants can feel relatively safe in using simplistic relationships for estimating costs. But they must recognize that this is what is being done and be prepared to use alternative techniques for activity levels outside this range.

Costs are said to be **fixed** with respect to some factor if they do not change in direct proportion with that factor. For example, salaries of the production supervisors are fixed with respect to production. Over some relatively wide range of production volume, a company will still need the same level of supervisory support and these salaries will not change. Note the definition did not indicate these costs would never change as the factor changes. For example, if production needs increased enough that another production shift had to be added, then supervisory salaries would increase, but in a step fashion. Technically, these are called **step-fixed costs.** The behaviors of fixed costs and step-fixed costs are depicted in Exhibit 2.3.

As a final point, it should be noted that a given cost could be **mixed**; that is, it could include both a fixed and a variable component. For example, an electric company's billing rate might be a flat charge per month that is independent of consumption, plus a rate per unit in excess of the minimum. This is shown in graph A of Exhibit 2.4. Graph B in Exhibit 2.4 shows a second type of mixed cost. Telephone costs, for example, have a fixed rental per month plus long distance toll charges. For zero activity the toll charges will be zero but will increase as activity increases. Later in the chapter, some methods are explored that will enable mixed costs to be analyzed into their fixed and variable amounts.

Exhibit 2.3   Fixed Cost Behavior

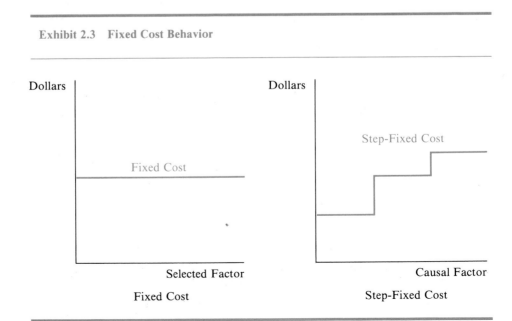

Fixed Cost

Step-Fixed Cost

Exhibit 2.4   Examples of Mixed Costs

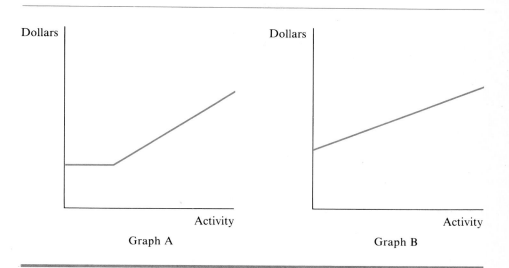

COMMITTED VERSUS PROGRAMMED COSTS. In the previous subsection, costs were classified into variable and fixed. Fixed costs can be further classified as either committed or programmed (sometimes called discretionary) costs. This classification is based on the degree to which a firm is "locked into" the asset or service that is generating the fixed cost. **Committed costs** cannot be avoided in the short run. For example, the salaries of the top echelon of management may represent a committed cost if, by policy, the executives would not be released unless the firm is completely liquidated. Likewise, depreciation on plant and equipment is committed because these facilities cannot be easily changed in the short run.

In contrast, **programmed,** or **discretionary,** costs are not as permanent. Some fixed costs can be eliminated rather easily by managerial decree. One example of a programmed cost is advertising. This cost can be avoided or reduced in the short run, if desired by management. The salaries of the lower echelons of management may, by policy, be programmed. These distinctions are important to the cost control and planning functions of cost/managerial accounting. For example, short-run decisions might be made using data that exclude committed costs since committed costs cannot be eliminated in the short run.

COST OBJECTIVES. Many discussions of cost will center on the concept of a cost objective. Thus, it is important to understand how this concept is used. **A cost objective** constitutes some entity for which it is desired to collect cost data. The following are illustrative:

1. A product.   *thing you are costing*
2. A special contract.

3. An area of responsibility within the firm, such as the assembly department or the controller's department.
4. A division of the firm.
5. A given project, past or proposed.
6. A geographical market area served by the firm.
7. Some activity of the firm, such as that of producing and holding inventory.
8. A function, such as the personnel, sales, manufacturing, or administrative function.

Obviously, a firm may have many different cost objectives that are of simultaneous interest. Data may need to be constructed in a different manner for each objective. Further, a given item of cost may be assigned to several different cost objectives.

DIRECT VERSUS INDIRECT COSTS. Now that the meaning of a cost objective has been discussed, it is possible to distinguish between direct and indirect costs. Costs are **direct** with respect to a given cost objective if they can be conveniently traced to that objective. For example, materials actually included in a finished product are a direct product cost. The foreman's salary is direct with respect to his or her department although, in many cases, it is not a direct product cost.

Indirect costs cannot be traced to a single cost objective. This is not to imply that the objective did not benefit from the incurrence of the cost. It just means that there is no physical relationship that ties the cost directly to the objective. For example, depreciation on the factory building is an indirect product cost. Depreciation is the portion of the original cost of the building assigned to the current period. This period's production benefits from the existence of the building and, therefore, from the depreciation. However, it is not possible to directly trace the benefit to the produced units. In accounting for indirect costs, the accountant faces two difficult questions: (1) should they be allocated to an objective, and (2) if so, how should they be allocated? Both of these issues are discussed in later chapters.

SEPARABLE VERSUS JOINT COSTS. These two cost terms are conventionally used in production situations where there are multiple products produced from a common input. For example, the processing of soybeans yields oil and meal. The results are unavoidable. **Joint costs** are those costs incurred in a single manufacturing process and up to the point where two or more products resulting from the process become separately indentifiable. These situations are called joint product situations and are explored in Chapter 10.

Separable costs are the costs incurred after the separation of the joint products and for the exclusive benefit of one of the products. For example, after soybeans are processed to obtain soybean oil and soybean meal, additional production costs may be incurred to further process each product. Once separated, these additional processing costs can be traced directly to a specific product. That is, they are separable.

CONTROLLABLE VERSUS NONCONTROLLABLE COSTS. In implementing the control function, a cost/managerial accountant must carefully consider who has control over the various costs. If controllability is not carefully considered, then accounting reports can have an undesirable motivational impact. Controllability is typically determined from the standpoint of a particular division of the firm. However, the organization of most firms is such that controllability is not completely traceable to a single individual within the firm.

With this in mind, **controllability** is defined as the existence of a significant degree of influence on the incurrence of the cost. In some cases this influence may be solely that of one individual. Frequently, however, several members of the organization will be able to exert influence on some policy or action that results in a cost incurrence. Then the accountant will have a difficult time establishing responsibility for the cost incurrence. For example, a particular production manager may be a member of a group of executives charged with making a recommendation on the acquisition of a new machine. In this situation, the decision is a group decision and the responsibility is not solely that of the production manager. Therefore, controllability is not a clear issue although it is clear the production manager is *partly* accountable for the outcome of the decision. If little or no influence can be exerted by a particular segment of the firm, then the cost would be considered **noncontrollable** by the segment.

The distinction between controllable and noncontrollable is also dependent on time. In the short run, fewer items are controllable than in the long run. However, given a long enough period of time, there is no cost that cannot be influenced by someone in the firm. Therefore, in the long run all costs are controllable.

The Need for a Knowledge of Cost Behavior and Methods of Determination

Although all of the cost concepts discussed in the previous sections are important, the fixed-variable distinction may be the most important. Thus, this classification is explored in more detail. Before considering *how* to make distinctions between fixed and variable costs in practice, you need to understand *why* they should be made. An example will be used to illustrate the importance of knowing cost behavior for supporting (1) the cost determination function in financial reporting, (2) the decision-making and planning function, and (3) the control function.

SUPPORT OF COST DETERMINATION. A very practical reason for knowing how costs behave is that some of the cost systems discussed in Chapters 3 through 7 assume an ability to separate costs into fixed and variable categories. Both the standard and the variable (direct) costing systems make this assumption. Let us briefly explore why those systems that require the fixed-variable classification came into being. In doing so, it will be more obvious why it is necessary to understand cost behavior.

Consider a system that ignores the distinction between fixed and variable costs. Such a system, called an "actual cost system," allocates *all* of the costs incurred during a period to the actual output of the period. However, such a system leads to some problems. Consider the case of the Five Alarm Chili Factory. In 19x1 the firm manufactured 20,000 cases and incurred a total manufacturing cost of $100,000. In

19x2 production decreased to 10,000 cases and manufacturing cost to $70,000. The average cost of production was $5.00 per case in 19x1 ($100,000 ÷ 20,000) and $7.00 per case in 19x2 ($70,000 ÷ 10,000). If these unit costs are used to arrive at the inventory value for financial statement purposes, the accountant may have trouble justifying the difference. Recall that an asset represents a future service potential. The 19x2 inventory in the preceding example cannot be said to have more service potential than the 19x1 inventory. Accountants have the responsibility of assigning costs to the assets owned by the firm. They must monitor these costs for consistency and reasonableness. An actual cost system may, over time, produce inventory costs that would send misleading "signals" to users of the information. In the above case, the service potential added by the production process is approximately the same in both 19x1 and 19x2. However, the accounting system used shows the cost in 19x2 to be greater than in 19x1.

The cause of the problem in the preceding case is the way fixed costs were accounted for. Suppose an analysis reveals that Five Alarm's costs consisted of fixed costs of $40,000 and variable costs of $3 per case. This cost behavior can be described by an equation:

$$y = 40,000 + 3x \qquad\qquad (2\text{-}1)$$

where: y = total cost
        x = cases of chili produced

You can verify that equation (2-1) yields the costs incurred in 19x1 and 19x2:

19x1: $y = 40,000 + 3(20,000) = 100,000$
19x2: $y = 40,000 + 3(10,000) = 70,000$

Now it can be seen that the *average fixed* cost per unit was $2.00 in 19x1 ($40,000 ÷ 20,000) and $4.00 in 19x2 ($40,000 ÷ 10,000). If one of the goals of a cost accounting system is to generate approximately the same inventory cost when the units require similar work effort, then it is necessary to know what the fixed costs are so that they can be accounted for in an appropriate manner. Also, the basic nature of fixed costs has caused some accountants to favor a system that assigns no fixed cost to production: the variable (direct) cost system. Obviously, then, there is a need for an ability to isolate the fixed costs in order to implement these types of systems.

SUPPORT FOR DECISION MAKING AND PLANNING. As discussed in Chapter 1, decision making and planning is future-oriented, and costs relevant to these activities must be projected costs. To project the costs of certain actions or decisions, it is necessary to know how the costs behave, or react, with respect to the variables of the decision situation. As a start it is useful to look at the way costs appear to have behaved in the past.

To illustrate, reconsider the Five Alarm Chili Factory. Suppose that the firm is budgeting a production of 8,000 units in 19x3. For cash planning purposes they need to know the anticipated costs. How would these costs be projected? If average total costs ($5.00 in 19x1 and $7.00 in 19x2) are all that are available, then how would total costs for 19x3 be projected? The average cost is dependent on the volume and there is no direct information about a volume of 8,000 units. Of course, if the behavior was known to be as described in equation (2-1), the forecast would be easier.

Obviously, forecasting is not as simple as described here, but a case has been made for determining the variables affecting cost incurrence and the relationship between each of the variables and the total cost. Also, there are many decision situations that could benefit from such knowledge, including contract bidding, project evaluation, price acceptability, operations research models (such as linear programming, inventory modeling, queueing models, and simulation), operating budgets, and capital budgeting.

SUPPORT OF CONTROL. The control function can also benefit from the knowledge of fixed and variable costs. First, fixed costs may not be as controllable as variable costs. Second, preparing meaningful budgets is not possible without the fixed-variable cost dichotomy. For example, in the case of the Five Alarm Chili Factory, a 19x3 budget of $56,000 for 8,000 units (8,000 × $7.00 average in 19x2) is not attainable. The attainable amount is $64,000 from equation (2-1), 40,000 + (3 × 8,000), and the $56,000 is a result of budgeting the costs using an incorrect behavior pattern. Such a budget is called a **flexible budget** since it is adjusted to be appropriate for a given volume level. That is, a flexible budget is one that varies with the activity levels as opposed to being constant, or fixed. If you were the manager, you probably would be somewhat upset with the $56,000 budget when you compared your actual costs of producing 8,000 units with your budgeted costs. The comparison might imply that you incurred more costs than justified, which, of course, is not the case. An example of a flexible budget for this case is as follows:

	8,000 Cases	10,000 Cases	20,000 Cases
Fixed Costs	$40,000	$40,000	$ 40,000
Variable costs at $3 per case	24,000	30,000	60,000
	$64,000	$70,000	$100,000

In summary, there are many reasons for knowing how costs behave. In the remainder of this section a variety of ways of acquiring this knowledge will be examined.

METHODS OF ESTIMATING COST RELATIONSHIPS. This section continues with a discussion of selected methods the accountant can use in analyzing cost behavior. The methods to be discussed are engineering estimates, scattergraphs, the high-low approach, and regression analysis.

An additional preface to the discussion is warranted. In reality, cost incurrence may be a function of many variables. For example, the overhead cost incurred in operating the milling department might be a function of direct labor hours, direct labor dollars, machine hours, orders processed, weather conditions, employee morale, general economic conditions, and, perhaps, other variables.

In practice it may not be possible to consider all possible independent variables and, further, the relationship between the variable to be predicted and causal variables may not be linear. The first limitation is the result of two factors. First, it may not be possible to identify all of the variables affecting cost incurrence. Second, even if all variables could be identified, the cost of including them all in the analysis may be greater than the benefit. Thus, the analysis is simplified by selecting a *subset* of the variables to be included in the estimating equation. The variables selected to be in the subset will depend on a variety of factors including the objectives of the analysis. The second problem will be solved either by tolerating a linear approximation of a nonlinear relationship or by using some nonlinear functional form.

Now consider the specifics of selecting an appropriate estimating equation. First, it is necessary to identify the potentially relevant variables. Then the general form of the relationship must be selected: that is, linear or some specific nonlinear form. Third, it is necessary to have data and a mechanism for processing them in order to estimate the relational equation. Finally, there must be some evaluation methods to assess the adequacy of the results. With this background the aforementioned methods of estimation will be examined.

ENGINEERING METHOD. The engineering method is so named because it was first implemented by industrial engineers. This approach is one whereby various physical inputs are estimated. For example, material input can be estimated by analyzing product blueprints and specifications. Labor input can be estimated through time-and-motion studies. If the variables of the estimating equation are the volumes of each product produced, then the rate of increase in the cost per unit of the product is determined by pricing the derived inputs using current cost rates.

This method will estimate the actual costs incorrectly if there is no allowance for natural and unavoidable waste and for normal inefficiency. That is, the method is not based on past recorded experience that would automatically include these unavoidable costs. Further, there is nothing inherent in the method itself that entails an evaluation of its reliability. That is, there is no way to express the strength of the stated relationship and no way to assess the probable error that might be contained in an estimate that results from the use of the equation.

SCATTERGRAPHS. If it is hypothesized that there is only one relevant independent variable, then a scattergraph analysis might be used to separate a mixed cost into its fixed and variable components. To do such an analysis we simply graph the actual observations that have been collected and then visually estimate the behavior.

To illustrate this and other techniques in this chapter, let us assume that the Delaware Drill Company has collected the overhead costs for one of its departments over the last five months as well as the direct labor hours worked in that department. The department assembles ten different models of drills. These data are presented in Exhibit 2.5 and plotted in Exhibit 2.6. It is conventional to use the *y*-axis (the vertical axis) for the dependent variable (costs in this case) and the *x*-axis (the horizontal axis) for the independent variable (direct-labor hours in this case).

**Exhibit 2.5   Delaware Drill
Company Illustrative Data**

Month	Overhead Costs	Direct Labor Hours
1	$ 32,457	2,416
2	29,570	2,324
3	30,057	2,354
4	27,176	1,840
5	28,062	1,892

Exhibit 2.6   Scattergraph of Overhead Data

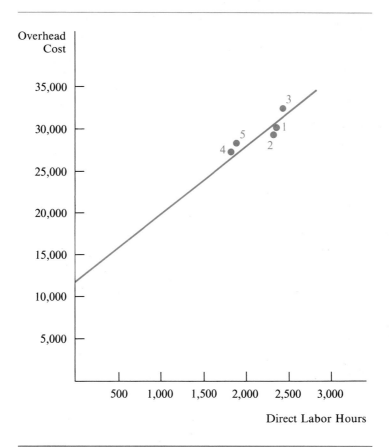

Visual inspection of a scattergraph is a starting point in determining if it is reasonable to assume a linear relationship between the dependent and independent variable. Although there are only five observations in our example, the plot in Exhibit 2.6 appears to be linear. When a relationship is linear it is of the form:

$$y = a + bx \tag{2-2}$$

where: y = dependent variable
        x = independent variable
        a = intercept
        b = slope

The line in Exhibit 2.6 represents an arbitrary visual construction of a good line. The fit is reasonable in that some of the observations are above and some below the line. You should note that it intercepts the cost axis at approximately $12,000. To determine the slope of the line, two points can be used. For example, use (0, $12,000) and one other point on the line, say (2,354, $30,057), which is point number 1 in Exhibit 2.6 and approximately on the line. These two points could be substituted into the high-low method discussed in the next section in order to estimate the variable cost rate.

Many other lines can be fit to the data that are as reasonable as the one in Exhibit 2.6. The scattergraph only permits a rough estimate of the behavior and has no test for the goodness of the fit of the line. However, this method does have usefulness. First, a plot of the data indicates whether the relationship is approximately linear. Of course, in the preceding example the sample is so small that there may still be no justification in assuming that the relationship is linear. However, such an assumption is made here for illustrative purposes.

Second, a scattergraph indicates if there are atypical observations in our sample. Atypical observations are those that are grossly out of line. For example, if there was an observation of (2,100, $50,000) in the preceding sample, it would be necessary to question what happened. Maybe there had been a measurement error or maybe some unusual and nonrecurring phenomena took place during the period of the observation. In either case, the observation probably should not be allowed to affect the estimating equation. Thus, the atypical case may need to be excluded from the sample. You are advised to plot the data even if you are going to use some other method in determining the parameters of the equation. Doing so will enable you to justify the use of a particular form of relationship and to construct an appropriate sample.

HIGH-LOW METHOD. The **high-low method** makes use of *two* observations in constructing the estimating line. However, intelligent use of the high-low method dictates that we not automatically select the observations with the highest and lowest values recorded for the independent variable. If either of these extreme observations appear to be atypical, they should be excluded in favor of a representative observation.

Continuing with the data of the Delaware Drill Company we find that in month 1 the direct-labor hours were 2,416 and that this is the highest recorded level of activity. In Exhibit 2.6 this point does not appear atypical so it will be used as a high point. Month 4's direct labor of 1,840 hours was the lowest recorded activity level and also appears to be typical.

The high-low method assumes that the costs are linearly related to the measure of activity, that is, in the form of equation (2-2). The values of *a* and *b* are determined as follows. Let C_H and C_L be the costs at the selected high and low points, respectively. Also, let x_H and x_L be the activity level at the respective points. If we can assume a linear relationship, then *b*, the variable cost *per unit of activity,* can be determined as follows:

$$b = \frac{C_H - C_L}{x_H - x_L} \qquad (b = \text{the rate at which costs increase}) \qquad (2\text{-}3)$$

Exhibit 2.7 will help explain. Exhibit 2.7 is a plot of some hypothetical data. Points I and II have been selected as the low point and high point, respectively. The cost at point I is C_L and the activity level is x_L. The cost and activity level at point II are C_H and x_H, respectively. Now, examine equation (2-3). In the numerator, the equation computes the difference in cost of the high point compared with the low point. This is labeled as "Numerator" in Exhibit 2.7. If there are any fixed costs,

Exhibit 2.7   Graph to Illustrate High-Low Method

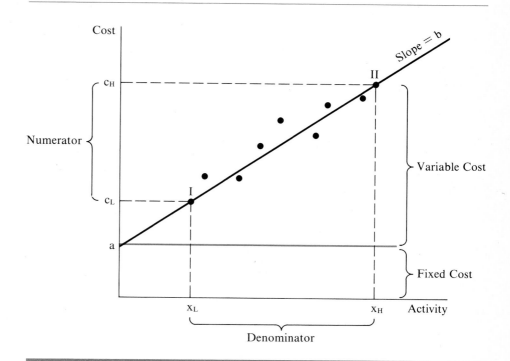

they would be included in both C_H and C_L. When deducting C_L from C_H, the fixed costs cancel out and therefore are not included in the difference (the numerator).

Only variable costs remain in the numerator of 2-3 and the result is the increase in those costs attributable to the difference in the activity levels $(x_H - x_L)$. Dividing the change in variable costs by the change in activity levels gives the *rate* of change in variable costs. This is the slope of the line in Exhibit 2.7. For our example:

$$b = \frac{C_H - C_L}{x_H - x_L} = \frac{32,457 - 27,176}{2,416 - 1,840} = \frac{5,281}{576} = 9.1684 \qquad (2\text{-}3')$$

The value of *a* in equation (2-2) is determined as follows when using the high-low method. Again consider Exhibit 2.7. The total costs are being estimated by the diagonal line. The fixed costs are represented by the level line. At either the high or low point the total costs are known. Deduct the variable costs from the total costs to get the fixed costs. The variable costs can be deduced by multiplying the rate, *b*, by the volume associated with the point being used to determine the fixed costs. Thus:

$$a = C_H - b(x_H) \text{ or } a = C_L - b(x_L) \qquad (2\text{-}4)$$

In our example:

$$a = C_H - bx_H = 32,457 - 9.1684(2,416) = 10,306.14 \qquad (2\text{-}4')$$

You can verify that using the second form of equation (2-4) will yield the same value of *a*. Thus, the high-low method results in the following estimating equation:

$$y = 10,306.14 + 9.1684x \qquad (2\text{-}5)$$

The disadvantage of this method is that most of the information is ignored in constructing the line and there are no *formal* ways of evaluating the "goodness" of the result. The next method to be discussed, regression analysis, overcomes this problem and also provides some measures of the quality of the estimating equation.

Accountants will frequently need to analyze cost data that have been recorded during periods of *inflation*. That is, if the same physical volume of a resource is acquired in two periods where the prices have been different, then the cost analysis should take this into consideration. Before doing the analyses, you should adjust for the effects of price changes.

To illustrate, suppose the following five years of data are available:

Year	Direct Labor Hours	Overhead Cost	Comment
19x1	4,000	$60,000	
19x2	1,000	49,500	Low volume
19x3	3,000	66,500	
19x4	5,000	86,515	High volume
19x5	2,000	73,205	

A casual examination of the recorded data will reveal that some factor other than the volume of direct labor hours is influencing the costs. The cost of 3,000 hours in 19x3 is higher than the cost of 4,000 hours in 19x1. This factor could be inflation.

Upon further examination, it has been found that the inflation rate during each of the years was 10%. Now, before using the high-low method to analyze the cost behavior, you will need to adjust the selected months to a common price level. Because the most likely use of the analysis will be to forecast future costs, it will make sense to adjust the recorded costs forward to the most recent year's price levels. Start with the "high" observation in 19x4. If price levels rose by 10% during 19x5, in comparison with 19x4, then the physical resources consumed in 19x4 would have had a cost that was 10% higher if they were purchased in 19x5. Thus:

Adjusted 19x4 costs = $86,515 × 1.10 = $95,167

The resources used in 19x2, the low year, would have cost 110% more in 19x3, 121% more in 19x4 (110 × 1.10), and 133.1% more in 19x5 (121 × 1.10). Thus:

Adjusted 19x2 costs = $49,500 × 1.331 = $65,885

The high-low analysis would use the adjusted costs:

$$b = \frac{\text{High cost} - \text{Low cost}}{\text{High volume} - \text{Low volume}} = \frac{95,167 - 65,885}{5,000 - 1,000} = \$7.32$$

The intercept of the high-low line could then be found using the adjusted cost of either of the two points. Using the high observation, 19x4:

$a = 95,167 - 7.32(5,000) = \$58,567$

In terms of year 5 price levels, the estimating equation is:

$y = 58,567 + 7.32x$

When using the above estimating equation, you must remember that it is in terms of year 5 price levels. If you anticipate additional price changes in future years, you must account for them in using the above results. For example, suppose the budgeted direct labor hours for 19x6 are 2,500. Then:

Estimated overhead (19x5 prices) = 58,567 + 7.32(2,500) = $76,867

If the price levels are expected to increase by 8% in 19x6, then the adjusted estimate is:

Adjusted estimate = $76,867 × 1.08 = $83,016

REGRESSION ANALYSIS. Simple linear regression (sometimes called **least squares** analysis), like the high-low method, assumes that the estimating line is of the form in equation (2-2). That is, it is assumed there is a *single* independent variable and the relationship between it and the dependent variable is *linear*. In this section there is a brief review of what linear regression is and of how the accountant can use it in analyses. Chapter 23 considers the technical aspects of the tool.

The basic idea of regression is very simple. As with the scattergraph and high-low methods, the objective is to construct a good fitting line through the data points of the sample. However, unlike the other methods, regression is based on some mathematical principles that ensure a best fitting line. The definition of a "best" fitting line and the technical issues of regression analysis are deferred to Chapter 23. To use regression it is necessary for the analyst to have data about the variable to be predicted, overhead cost in the Delaware Drill Company, and the variable to be used as a predictor, direct labor hours in this case. It is necessary for the analyst to select the variables and provide "clean" data to be used in some complex equations. Rather than just using two of the observations, regression analysis can use all that are available.

Many commercially available computer software packages can be used to do the mathematics required to find the best fit. For Delaware Drill, such a package would indicate that overhead costs should be estimated as follows:

$$y = 15,180.60 + 6.59699x \tag{2-6}$$

That is, variable overhead would be estimated at $6.59699 per direct labor hour. Subject to some restrictions as described in Chapter 23, the fixed component of overhead would be estimated at $15,180.60. In comparison with the high-low results of equation (2-5), you can see the equation is quite a bit different. That is, the high-low results are significantly removed from the best fit. As will be discussed in Chapter 23, regression analysis generates a set of statistics that can be used to evaluate the adequacy of the regression equation.

At this point in the book do not be concerned about the specifics of regression analysis. Just keep in mind that it is a potentially useful tool when it is necessary to analyze cost behavior.

Overview of Accounting Systems

As an additional preface to the study of cost accounting systems that will be used to collect some of the data requested of accountants, let us preview the process of "designing" the system. First, compare the basic cost flow systems of a merchandising firm and a manufacturing firm. For now, assume that the *only* requirement of the manufacturing firm's cost/managerial system is product cost determination and that there are only two products in its line. Remember in Chapter 1 it was pointed out there are several functions to be served by cost/managerial accounting. It will be easier to discuss the data collection process if the functions are limited. Thus, we will start with a simple system and then proceed toward a system that attempts to simultaneously meet some of the several needs identified in Chapter 1.

COST DETERMINATION. Exhibit 2.8 shows the flow of costs for the merchandising firm, and Exhibit 2.9 shows the flow for the manufacturing firm. (A perpetual inventory system is assumed in both cases.) Before considering the flowcharts in detail, you should note two factors. First, Exhibit 2.9 illustrates one

Exhibit 2.8   Cost Flow for Merchandising Firm

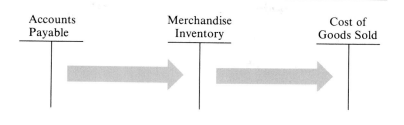

Exhibit 2.9   Product Cost Flow for a Manufacturing Firm Only Interested in Product Cost Determination

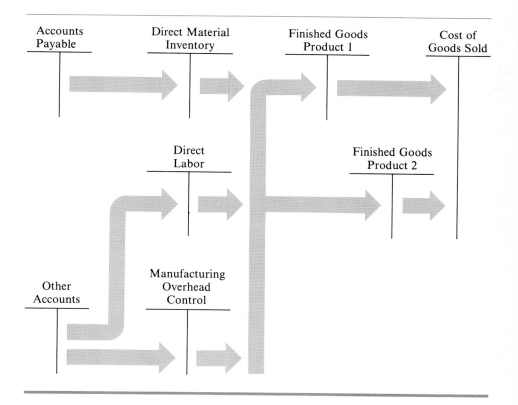

stage in the evolutionary development of manufacturers' systems. It is *not* the form that would be expected in a modern firm. (A modern form will be illustrated after a basic system is considered.) Second, the flows can be interpreted as a representation of the debits and credits that would be involved. A flow originating on the right side of an account is a credit; one terminating on the left side is a debit.

The product cost flow for a merchandising firm is rather straightforward. The invoice costs flow into the inventory account. When sold, these same costs flow into cost of goods sold. Granted, there may be a problem of which costs flow into cost of goods sold and this will be dependent on whether a FIFO (first-in, first-out), LIFO (last-in, first-out), or weighted average cost flow assumption is made. In contrast, the manufacturing firm's product cost flow is more complex. The cost of the manufactured products is the sum of several inputs. Determining this cost is more involved than just referring to an invoice in a file, as is the case in a merchandising firm. Exhibit 2.9 shows the product cost flow for a firm that produces two products. As indicated, the firm is only interested in cost determination.

Consider Exhibit 2.9 in more detail. For several reasons there are intermediate collection points, or accounts, for the material, labor, and manufacturing overhead cost components in a manufacturing firm. First, direct material is, itself, an inventory. Thus, the purchase of direct material does not constitute an expense. If the items are unused at the end of a period, they should be considered an asset. Second, for a variety of reasons it may be desirable to know the amount of the total labor and manufacturing overhead incurred during the period. Making future projections of these costs will be easier if the amounts are known by function. Envision, if you will, the hopelessness of projecting future costs if all you knew was the total amount of all manufacturing costs in each of the last several years. Where would you start on such an assignment? Thus, these costs are initially recorded in a labor and overhead account so that various analyses can be done in future periods. Furthermore, it would be impractical to trace manufacturing costs to the various products each time there is an original transaction with parties outside the firm. Therefore, several individual transactions are aggregated in appropriate accounts and then periodically distributed to the products.

CONTROL. As noted in Chapter 1, firms organize themselves into responsibility centers in order to facilitate control. It was also indicated there that to facilitate control, costs are collected for each responsibility center in order that they might be compared with the expected cost levels as one element of control.

Exhibit 2.10 depicts, in general, how the dual demands of product cost determination and control are managed in the accounting system. Assume there are only two responsibility centers, each with an in-charge foreman. The responsibility centers are referred to as Departments 1 and 2. Further, assume the firm manufactures two products. Each of the products requires some work in each of the departments. The work is completed in Department 1 before the products are transferred to Department 2. For example, Department 1 may be a sheet metal production department and Department 2 an automobile fender stamping department. The numbers on some of the flows of Exhibit 2.10 are reference indexes to facilitate the discussion.

Exhibit 2.10   Manufacturing Firm's Cost Flow Modified to Include Control Requirements

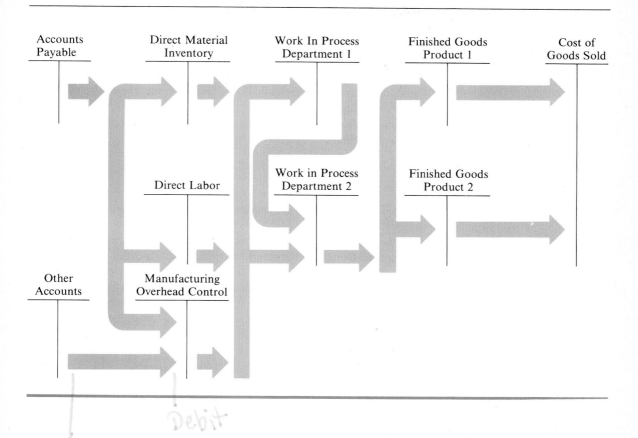

First the basic costs used by each department (material, labor, and overhead) are assigned to each responsibility center (as a debit to their respective work in process accounts). The flows labeled 1 and 2 depict this assignment. Of course, to support these flows, some raw data must be collected about the actual usage of material by each department and the actual labor devoted to each. Likewise, it will be necessary to find some acceptable way of assigning overhead costs to the two departments. By collecting these costs according to responsibility centers, you provide data for evaluating those in charge of each area. Just how this is done will be discussed in detail later in the book. For now, suffice it to say that the actual costs recorded on the debit side of each responsibility center account will be compared with the budgeted costs allowed for the center. Major deviations of the actual from the budget would be cause for an investigation.

Remember that the system in Exhibit 2.10 has a dual purpose. Now that a means of cost control has been provided, it is necessary to accumulate the total cost of producing the products. Since the products require services in each department, the costs assigned in Department 1 are transferred to Department 2 when the products are finished by Department 1 (flow #3). Department 2 becomes accountable for the costs added in Department 1 and assigned to Department 1's finished production as well as for the material, labor, and overhead charged directly to the department. From Department 2, the costs flow into finished product inventory accounts. Of course, to be able to transfer costs to two different finished product accounts, you must organize the record keeping in a manner that will permit the identification of costs by product as they flow through the responsibility center accounts. These flows are labeled 4 and 5. In this manner, then, the system in Exhibit 2.10 will simultaneously fulfill the two objectives of product cost determination and control. A self-study problem at the end of the chapter will require you to trace the actual flow of costs through this simple system.

Financial Statements of a Manufacturing Firm

The general overview provided by this chapter concludes with a review of a manufacturing firm's financial statements. They differ somewhat from those of other types of firms. These statements are reviewed in this section in order to contrast them with the statements of nonmanufacturing firms and in order to preview the end-product of a cost accounting system. This section also is a connecting link between what the profession has conventionally labeled "financial" and "cost" accounting. Typically, financial accounting textbooks give much less consideration to cost determination than to cost *reporting,* given that costs have been determined. The cost accounting chapters of this book will deal with the principles of cost determination, but it is useful to review what will be done with them in external reporting.

Exhibits 2.11 and 2.12 are a manufacturer's financial statements that are typical of those prepared for external reporting purposes. It should not be assumed, however, that these statements are the only reports or that they are the important ones for internal reporting. Further, they appear in more detail than might be found in a firm's *published* report. However, they do demonstrate the differences in financial reporting of a manufacturing firm and a merchandising firm.

Assume that the Bulkman Model Train Company produces only HO-type engines. Exhibit 2.11 is a statement of the company's cost of goods manufactured during 19x1. Of course a nonmanufacturing firm does not have need for such a statement. This is the major difference in the reporting for these types of companies. A retailer, for example, need only look at its merchandise purchasing activity in order to determine the cost of its sales. However, a manufacturer must "purchase" several resources (material, production labor, and other supporting resources) and combine them in the production effort to get the product it sells. Because many activities are needed by a manufacturer to get to the point of sale, the cost of goods manufactured statement is needed to summarize the cost of all of the efforts.

Several things should be noted about the cost of goods manufactured statement. Note that it has four principal sections. The first three sections entail an accounting

Exhibit 2.11   Bulkman Model Train Company Cost of Goods Manufactured Statement for the Year Ended December 31, 19x1

Direct material used:			
Materials inventory, January 1, 19x1		$ 1,000	
Purchases	$50,000		
Freight in	4,000		
Total	$54,000		
Purchase discounts	1,200	52,800	
Cost of materials available		$53,800	
Less materials inventory,			
December 31, 19x1		3,000	$ 50,800
Direct labor			70,000
Manufacturing overhead:			
Factory supervisory salaries		$15,000	
Indirect labor		5,000	
Depreciation—factory building		4,000	
Depreciation—factory equipment		7,000	
Power		8,000	
Indirect supplies		9,000	48,000
Current cost of manufacturing			$168,800
Add work in process, January 1, 19x1			8,000
Costs to be accounted for			$176,800
Less work in process, December 31, 19x1			10,000
Cost of goods manufactured			$166,800

Exhibit 2.12   Bulkman Model Train Company Income Statement for the Year Ended December 31, 19x1

Sales		$300,000
Cost of goods sold:		
Finished goods inventory, January 1, 19x1	$ 20,000	
Cost of goods manufactured (Exhibit 2.11)	166,800	
Cost of goods available for sale	$186,800	
Finished goods inventory, December 31, 19x1	15,000	171,800
Gross margin		$128,200
Selling and administrative expenses:		
Sales commissions and salaries	$ 12,000	
Administrative salaries	50,000	
Advertising	10,000	
Depreciation expense—general office building	8,000	80,000
Net income before income taxes		$ 48,200

for the three costs of manufacturing: direct material, direct labor, and manufacturing overhead. Note that the direct material section is similar to the cost-of-goods-sold section of a retail concern. That is, the cost of material used is determined as:

Cost of Material Used = Beginning Material Inventory + *Net* Purchases − Ending Material Inventory

The direct labor section consists of one item representing the 19x1 wages earned by employees while they were physically working on the product. The items in manufacturing overhead represent production costs that cannot be *directly* traced to the output. Of course, for a single product firm all costs would have been incurred for the production of one product. But, in general, there will be multiple products, in which case a direct tracing would be impossible.

The fourth section of the statement is an adjustment for the work-in-process inventories. **Work-in-process** inventory represents the cost of production started but unfinished at the date of the inventory. Beginning work-in-process inventory represents the cost of the work done last period on units that were not entirely completed until the current period. The sum of the costs in the first three sections is the total production costs incurred during the current year. The sum of current production costs and beginning work-in-process inventory represents the total costs to be assigned to the output of the current period. This total will be allocated to the units completed and to the ending work in process. In later chapters there will be a discussion of the various methods that can be used in making the allocation. After the cost of the ending work in process is determined, it is deducted from the total costs to determine the cost of the units actually finished in this period.

Bulkman's income statement is presented in Exhibit 2.12 and is similar to one for a retail concern. Note in the cost-of-goods-sold section that the output of the cost of goods manufactured statement is used in lieu of the "purchases" account that is common to a retailer. **Finished goods** is the cost of completed but unsold units and is an adjustment needed to determine the cost of goods sold. Also, note that selling and administrative expenses are treated as period expenses, that is, deducted in the period of incurrence. Similar to those of a retail concern, these expenses are considered impossible to assign as a cost of the product.

Also note another difference between a manufacturer and a retailer. Three inventory accounts (materials, work in process, and finished goods) are present in the manufacturer's system. These are all needed by a manufacturer in order to account for physical inventories that are in various states of completion. A retailer has need for only one type of inventory account. This is the merchandise inventory account that accumulates the purchased, but unsold, stock.

Summary

The purpose of this chapter was to review various cost concepts, examine cost behavior, and introduce methods of determining cost behavior. Further, the basic idea of a cost accounting system was introduced and the financial statements of a manufacturer were reviewed. You should now be familiar with a variety of cost terms. Their meanings will be expanded in the chapters that follow. You should especially start to appreciate the need for distinguishing between fixed and variable costs. Be sure you understand the scattergraph and the high-low method. Be aware, also, that regression analysis is a more sophisticated way of analyzing cost behavior.

At this point you should also be able to create a cost/management accounting system that will collect data needed in the functions of product cost determination and cost control. But remember that the collection of historical costs will not serve all purposes. Finally, you should be able to prepare and interpret the financial statements of a manufacturing firm.

Key terms for this chapter include:

Cost
Expense
Loss
Historical cost
Replacement cost
Opportunity cost
Direct material
Direct labor
Manufacturing overhead
Variable cost
Fixed cost
Step fixed cost
Mixed cost
Committed cost   –Pg 37
Programmed (discretionary) cost
Cost objective — the thing you are costing
Direct cost – Pg 20
Indirect cost
Separable cost
Joint cost
Controllable cost
Noncontrollable cost
Flexible Budget
High-low method
Regression analysis
Work in process
Finished goods

SELF-STUDY PROBLEM ONE. At the end of this and the remaining chapters there are one or more self-study problems. The purpose of these problems is to allow you to work a reasonably comprehensive problem that emphasizes the major points of the chapter. A detailed solution is provided in a follow-up section to give you complete and immediate feedback. It is suggested that you work these problems without reference to the solution. Doing this will increase your independence and enable you to solve problems without reference to the book.

For the first self-study problem of this chapter, consider the Tennessee Saw Company. For a variety of planning and control questions it desires to have a flexible budget prepared for a variety of volumes. Although the company produces several different hand saws, it is reasonably sure its overhead cost is a function of labor hours. Following are some actual data for the last two months:

Direct labor hours	20,000	35,000
Supervision	$40,000	$40,000
Power costs	$10,000	$17,500
Other overhead	$30,000	$41,250

Required:

1. Use the high-low method to separate each of the three costs into their fixed and variable portions.
2. Prepare a flexible budget that includes the costs at volumes of 20,000, 35,000, 50,000, 75,000, and 100,000 direct labor hours.

Solution to Self-Study Problem One

1. Based on what is given it is obvious that supervision is a fixed cost. It is $40,000 for each of the listed volumes. For power costs:

$$b = \text{variable rate} = \frac{\$17,500 - \$10,000}{35,000 - 20,000} = \frac{\$7,500}{15,000} = \$0.50$$

$$a = \text{fixed} = \$17,500 - 0.50(35,000) = 0 \text{ or}$$
$$= \$10,000 - 0.50(20,000) = 0$$

Thus, power cost is strictly a variable cost. For other overhead:

$$b = \frac{\$41,250 - \$30,000}{35,000 - 20,000} = \frac{\$11,250}{15,000} = \$0.75$$

$$a = \$41,250 - 0.75(35,000) = 15,000 \text{ or}$$
$$\$30,000 - 0.75(20,000) = 15,000$$

Thus, other overhead is given by $[\$15,000 + 0.75 \times (\text{direct labor hours})]$.

2. The flexible budget can be constructed using the results from part 1.

Direct labor hours	20,000	35,000	50,000	75,000	100,000
Supervision	40,000	40,000	40,000	40,000	40,000
Power costs at $0.50 per hour	10,000	17,500	25,000	37,500	50,000
Other					
Fixed	15,000	15,000	15,000	15,000	15,000
Variable at $0.75 per hour	15,000	26,250	37,500	56,250	75,000
Total	$80,000	$98,750	$117,500	$148,750	$180,000

(handwritten margin notes:)
$C = a + bx$
component + component
Cost you are = fixed cost + Variable cost (units)
analyzing
$C = a + bx$
fixed cost (units)
component

SELF-STUDY PROBLEM TWO. The Zimmerman Company manufactures pencils. Following are accounts from its year-end adjusted trial balance and other information.

	January 1	December 31
Inventories		
Finished goods	$20,000	$30,000
Work in process	8,000	7,000
Wood inventory	2,000	3,500
Lead inventory	1,000	1,500
Eraser inventory	1,500	2,500
Wood purchases		40,000
Lead purchases		45,000
Eraser purchases		35,000
Payroll costs		
Production line workers		50,000
Maintenance crew		15,000
Factory supervision		30,000
Sales salaries		55,000
Inventory handling		10,000
Property taxes*		5,000
Depreciation*		40,000
Machine repairs (parts)		12,000
Power costs (for machines)		8,000
Income taxes		42,000

*The factory occupies 80% of the building square footage.

Required:

Prepare the statement of cost of goods manufactured.

Solution to Self-Study Problem Two

Zimmerman Company
Statement of Cost of Goods Manufactured

Material used		
Wood		
Beginning inventory	$ 2,000	
Purchases	40,000	
	$42,000	
Ending inventory	3,500	$ 38,500
Lead		
Beginning	$ 1,000	
Purchases	45,000	
	$46,000	
Ending inventory	1,500	$ 44,500

Erasers

Beginning inventory	$ 1,500	
Purchases	35,000	
	$36,500	
Ending inventory	2,500	$ 34,000
Total material used		$117,000
Direct labor		
Production line workers		50,000
Manufacturing overhead		
Maintenance crew	$15,000	
Supervision	30,000	
Inventory handling	10,000	
Property taxes (0.8 × $5,000)	4,000	
Depreciation (0.8 × $40,000)	32,000	
Machine repair parts	12,000	
Power costs	8,000	111,000
Current cost of manufacturing		$278,000
Add: Beginning work-in-process inventory		8,000
		$286,000
Less: Ending work-in-process inventory		7,000
Cost of goods manufactured		$279,000

Notes:

1. Finished goods would be included in the cost-of-goods-sold statement, not the cost-of-goods-manufactured statement.
2. Sales salaries, 20% of the property taxes, 20% of the depreciation, and the income taxes are operating expenses and will appear on the income statement.

SELF-STUDY PROBLEM THREE. The third self-study problem for this chapter assumes the production situation represented in Exhibit 2.10. Its purpose is to have you think through the details of cost flow for a manufacturer.

Assume the following items have been incurred by a firm whose system is identical to that in Exhibit 2.10. That is, it produces two products, each of which requires processing in two production departments.

Material issued to production	$100,000
Direct labor for the factory	200,000
Depreciation on factory equipment	20,000
Other factory overhead	80,000

An analysis of the use of the above resources by department is as follows:

	Department 1	Department 2
Material	60%	40%
Labor	70	30
Overhead	70	30

Work-in-process inventories are as follows:

	Department 1	Department 2
Beginning	$3,000	$6,000
Ending	7,000	5,000

Finished goods inventories were:

	Product 1	Product 2
Beginning	$10,000	$ 6,000
Ending	20,000	25,000

The cost of product 1 sold during the period totaled $320,000.

Required:

Copy the flowchart from Exhibit 2.10 and determine the amounts of each of the cost flows represented by the paths of the exhibit. You may not be able to determine some of the amounts based on the data given.

Solution to Self-Study Problem Three

Exhibit 2.13 contains the solution to this problem (in thousands). The following comments explain the solution.

1. The beginning balance for the two WIP and two finished goods accounts have been entered.
2. Note the flow of costs out of material—$60,000 to Department 1, representing 60% of the total material issued, and $40,000 to Department 2, representing 40%.
3. Likewise, note the distribution of the direct labor account, $140,000, or 70%, to Department 1 and $60,000, or 30%, to Department 2.
4. Note that the depreciation of $20,000 and other overhead of $80,000 have both been entered in Manufacturing Overhead for the period. In a manufacturing firm, depreciation on production facilities is considered as an overhead item, not a depreciation expense for the period.
5. Since the ending WIP inventory of Department 1 is $7,000, this means the cost of the goods finished and transferred to Department 2 is $266,000 ($273,000 total less $7,000).
6. The total cost to be accounted for in Department 2 is $402,000. Since Department 2's ending inventory is $5,000, that means the cost of its finished production was $397,000 ($402,000 − $5,000).
7. Now trace the cost of product 1 sold, $320,000, back to the Finished Goods account. The cost of product 1 finished this period can be forced out:

Beginning Finished Goods (Product 1)		Cost of Product 1 Sold
+	=	+
Cost of Product 1 finished		Ending Finished Goods (Product 1)

$10,000 + x = $320,000 + $20,000
x = $340,000 − $10,000 = $330,000

8. The cost of product 2 completed can now be computed using the results in comment 7 and comment 6.

Cost of product 2 finished = Cost of all production finished −
    Cost of product 1 finished
= $397,000 − $330,000 = $67,000

9. Now the cost of product 2 sold can be computed:

Beginning inventory	$ 6,000
Cost of goods finished	67,000
Cost of goods available	73,000
Ending inventory	25,000
Cost of goods sold	$48,000

Exhibit 2.13   Solution to Self Study Question Three

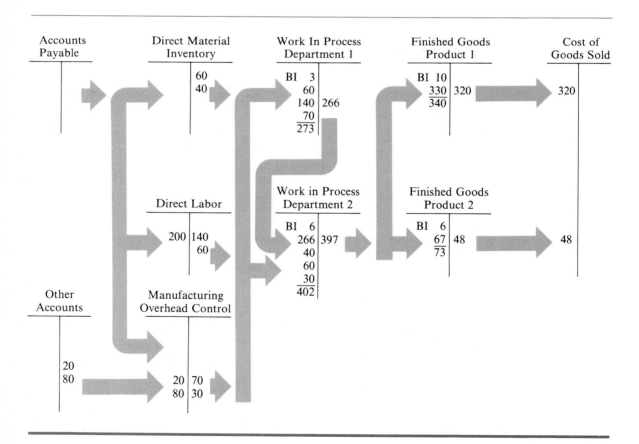

References

Bulloch, J., Keller, D.E., and Vlasho, L. *Accountants' Cost Handbook*. New York: John Wiley & Sons, 1983.

Davidson, S., and Weil, R.L. *Handbook of Cost Accounting*. New York: McGraw-Hill, 1978.

National Association of Accountants. *Statements on Management Accounting: Management Accounting Terminology,* Statement Number 2. New York: National Association of Accountants, 1983.

Problems

2-1. Using Definitions. Several situations that involve some of the following cost concepts appear below:

1. Committed cost.
2. Joint cost.
3. Controllable cost.
4. Direct cost.
5. Fixed cost.
6. Historical cost.
7. Indirect cost.
8. Opportunity cost.
9. Programmed cost.
10. Replacement cost.
11. Separable cost.
12. Noncontrollable cost.
13. Variable cost.

Indicate the concept that most specifically identifies the cost concept in each situation:

1. The A Company has noticed that when its volume is *up* its actual manufacturing cost per unit is *down*. Identify the cost that would cause this.
2. The B Company owns a warehouse for which it received an offer to rent by the C Company. B Company refused the offer because it wanted to use the warehouse to store inventory during the peak production times. They included the rental offer in the storage costs. Identify this cost.
3. Company D, in computing the cost of operating its three production divisions, had difficulty in determining how to prorate the production manager's salary among the divisions. Identify the cost.
4. If Company D, in number 3, had established manufacturing, marketing, research and development, and administration as four cost objectives for a particular analysis, then which concept would describe the production manager's salary?
5. Company E was trying to decide if a particular stamping machine should be replaced. The depreciation expense on the old machine was ignored in the decision. Identify the ignored cost.
6. Identify the cost whose average per unit remains relatively constant over a wide range of volume.
7. Company F's management approved an advertising budget for 19x2 in the amount of one million dollars. In doing so they stated it was an experimental venture. Identify this cost.
8. Company G also approved a one million dollar advertising budget, taking the position that in the next five years they would continue this commitment in order to keep pace with the competition. Identify this cost.
9. In preparing a report on the Assembly Department for performance evaluation, the H Company excluded the building depreciation applicable to the Assembly Department. Identify the excluded cost.

10. Which of the listed concepts best describes the basis on which a manufacturing firm will carry its inventory for financial statement purposes?

2-2. Using Basic Definitions. The Morgan Company has two profit centers, called Division A and B. For various reports the company needs to classify certain costs as (1) fixed (F) or variable (V) with respect to sales volume (production and sales volume are approximately the same), (2) if fixed, then either committed (C) or programmed (P), (3) direct (D) or indirect (I) with respect to Division A, and (4) controllable (CN) or noncontrollable (N) in the long run by the manager of Division A.

The company's job description manual contains the following: the company vice-president is responsible for the acquisition of building facilities for the entire company; the division managers are responsible for the acquisition of equipment, the employment of personnel under them, and local advertising.

Consider the following eleven items:

1. President's salary.
2. Direct advertising in the geographical area served by Division A.
3. Depreciation on Division A's factory equipment (straight line).
4. The company president employed a management consultant to aid the Division A manager in a reorganization.
5. Sales staff's commissions for Division A.
6. National advertising benefiting both divisions. The separate benefits cannot be measured.
7. Rent of factory building occupied by Division A.
8. The transportation of raw material for Division A.
9. Division A's engineers—when they are not busy with normal work they are assigned by the division manager to a special project that requires several years research.
10. Air conditioning of Division A's buildings. The decision to air condition the buildings was made by the Division A manager.
11. All sales are on account, and the home office assumes the responsibility of collecting the accounts of both divisions. The XYZ Collection Agency has been retained for this job. The rate is a fixed percentage of accounts collected and has been constant for several years. The bad debt rate is the same in both divisions. Classify the collection agency's fee.

Required:

Set up a work sheet to classify these items. Your headings should be:

Case	(1) F or V	(2) C or P	(3) D or I	(4) CN or N

2-3. Functional Cost Classification. Classify the following items of cost of the Crunchy Potato Chip Company as:

Direct Material (DM)   Selling & Administrative (S&A)
Direct Labor (DL)   Other (O); If other, explain.
Manufacturing Overhead (MOH)

1. Potatoes.
2. Depreciation on peeling machine.

3. Cooking oil.
4. Salt.
5. Wages of peeling machine operator.
6. Repair of the cooking vat.
7. Potato chip bags.
8. Shipping boxes—reusable.
9. Controller's salary.
10. Production manager's salary.
11. Advertising.
12. Lubricants for the machinery.
13. Gasoline for the delivery truck used to ship potato chips.

2-4. CPA Problem: Determining Cost Behavior. Select the graph that best matches the following factory cost or expense data. The vertical axes of the graphs represent *total* dollars of expense and the horizontal axes represent annual production. In each case the zero point is at the intersection of the two axes. The graphs may be used more than once.

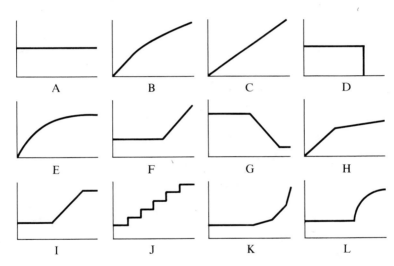

1. Depreciation of equipment, where the amount of depreciation charged is computed by the machine hours method.
2. Electricity bill—a flat fixed charge, plus a variable cost after a certain number of kilowatt hours are used.
3. City water bill, which is computed as follows:

First 1,000,000 gallons or less	$1,000
Next 10,000 gallons	0.003 per gallon used
Next 10,000 gallons	0.006 per gallon used
Next 10,000 gallons	0.009 per gallon used
etc.	

4. Cost of lubricant for machines, where cost per unit decreases with each pound of lubricant used (for example, if one pound is used, the cost is $10,00; if two pounds are used,

the cost is $19.98; if three pounds are used, the cost is $29.94; with a minimum cost per pound of $9.25).

5. Depreciation of equipment, where the amount is computed by the straight-line method. When the depreciation rate was established, it was anticipated that the obsolescence factor would be greater than the wear-and-tear factor.

6. Rent on a factory building donated by the city, where the the agreement calls for a fixed fee payment unless 200,000 man-hours are worked, in which case no rent need be paid.

7. Salaries of repairmen, where one repairman is needed for every 1,000 hours of machine hours or less (that is, 0 to 1,000 hours requires one repairman; 1,001 to 2,000 hours requires two repairmen, etc.).

8. Social security taxes for the year, where the labor force is constant in number throughout year (average annual salary is $30,000 per worker).

9. Cost of raw material used.

10. Rent on a factory building donated by county, where agreement calls for rent of $100,000 less $1 for each direct labor hour worked in excess of 200,000 hours, but minimum rental payment of $20,000 must be paid.

2-5. Basic Problem on Flexible Budgeting. The Lopez Company produces one product requiring raw material X. Each unit requires three pounds of material X, which costs $4 per pound. Each unit also needs five labor hours. Labor costs $10 per hour. At a volume of 10,000 units the following overhead costs would be incurred:

Supervisory salaries	$ 50,000
Building depreciation	100,000
Factory supplies	30,000
Power costs	40,000

Required:

Prepare a flexible budget of manufacturing costs for volumes of 5,000, 10,000, and 20,000 units.

2-6. Flexible Budgeting. The Trammel Company has prepared the following flexible budget:

	20,000 units	50,000 units
Material	$ 60,000	$150,000
Labor	100,000	250,000
Depreciation	85,000	85,000
Indirect labor	70,000	160,000
Power costs	40,000	100,000
Supervision*	50,000	50,000
Total	$405,000	$795,000

*The capacity of having one eight-hour shift per day is 60,000 units. More than one shift is possible. Supervision costs per shift would be the same.

Required:

Extend the flexible budget to volumes of 70,000, 100,000, and 150,000 units.

2-7. Basic Problem on Determining Cost Behavior. The Brazil Company manufactures one product. During 19x4, 20,000 units were produced and the following costs were incurred.

Material (variable)	$100,000
Labor (variable)	60,000
Supervision (fixed)	35,000
Depreciation (fixed)	20,000
Power costs (variable)	10,000

For 19x5, it is estimated that the *unit* variable costs and *total* fixed costs would be the same as in 19x4.

Required:

1. If Brazil is planning to produce 25,000 units in 19x5, how much would you estimate its costs would be?
2. What would be your estimate of the costs if Brazil planned to produce 15,000 units in 19x5?

2-8. Using Statements to Project Position. The Bair Company has prepared the following income statement representing its actual results for 19x1 (its first year of operation).

Bair Company
Income Statement
for the Year 19x1

Sales (10,000 units)		$400,000
Cost of goods sold		
Cost of production (15,000 units)		
Direct material	$ 30,000	
Direct labor	75,000	
Variable overhead	45,000	
Fixed overhead	90,000	
Total	$240,000	
Ending inventory (5,000 units)	80,000	160,000
Gross margin		$240,000
Selling and administrative expenses		
Sales commissions (5% of sales dollars)	$ 20,000	
Other variable sales expenses	50,000	
Fixed selling and administration	40,000	110,000
Net income		$130,000

During 19x2 the Bair Company is projecting sales at 12,000 units and production at 18,000 units. The sales price will increase to $42. All cost behavior patterns are expected to be the same as 19x1 and, except where indicated, are a function of the appropriate unit volume, not dollar volume.

Required:

Project the 19x2 income using a formal statement. The ending inventory will be carried at the average cost of production in 19x2.

2-9. Projecting Income When There are Multiple Products. The Redville Company has prepared the following income statement for 19x1 operations:

	Product A	Product B
Sales (22,000 of A; 30,000 of B)	$1,100,000	$600,000
Cost of goods sold		
Beginning inventory (1,000 of A; 2,000 of B)	30,000	32,000
Cost of production (30,000 of A; 30,000 of B)		
Direct material	180,000	60,000
Direct labor	300,000	150,000
Variable overhead	300,000	150,000
Fixed overhead	200,000	100,000
Cost of goods available	$1,010,000	$492,000
Ending inventory (9,000 of A; 2,000 of B)	294,000	30,667
Total	$ 716,000	$461,333
Gross margin	$ 384,000	$138,667
Selling and administrative		
Sales commissions (5% of sales dollars)	$ 55,000	$ 30,000
Fixed	103,529	56,471
Total	$ 158,529	$ 86,471
Net income	$ 225,471	$ 52,196

Manufacturing overhead costs have been allocated to the products on the basis of direct-labor dollars. Fixed selling and administrative costs were allocated to the products on the basis of sales. Inventories are carried at the average current cost of production.

During 19x2 Redville is projecting both product A and B sales at 25,000 units. Production is scheduled at 20,000 units of A and 32,000 units of B. Sales prices, but not costs, are expected to increase by 10% during 19x2.

Required:

Project the 19x2 income using the format above.

2-10. Estimating Cost Behavior with High-Low Method: Basic. The Bolivia Company is a warehousing company that buys from manufacturers and sells to retailers. One of its major costs is telephone expense. Bolivia is reasonably sure these costs vary with its total sales revenue. It would like to know how much of this cost is fixed and how much is variable. You have been asked to help them based on the following information:

	Telephone Expense	Sales Revenue
January	$2,800	$30,000
February	$2,450	$25,000
March	$3,450	$45,000
April	$2,500	$28,000

Required:

1. Use the high-low method to derive an estimating equation for telephone expenses in the form:

   $y = a + bx$

2. What if Bolivia's estimated sales revenue for May is $30,000. Using the results from part 1, estimate Bolivia's telephone expense for May.
3. Comment on your results, especially as they compare to the actual data recorded during the four months listed above.

2-11. Using High-Low When There Are Atypical Observations. The Argentina Company produces one product and is in need of a way to estimate its total manufacturing overhead. It has some actual data and is reasonably sure the incurrence of overhead cost is related to direct-labor hours. Following are the available data:

Month	Overhead Cost	Direct-Labor Hours
1	$ 8,500	2,000
2	25,000	4,000
3	9,550	2,500
4	10,500	3,000
5	8,650	2,100
6	6,000	1,500
7	9,400	2,400
8	8,800	2,200

Required:

1. Use month 2 and month 6 as the high and low months and derive the cost-estimating equation using the high-low method.
2. Plot the above data.
3. Based on your plot in part 2, revise your high-low estimating equation. Compare your equation with the one from part 1.

2-12. High-Low, Scattergraph, and Regression. The Reggie Company produces a delectable candy bar that is especially popular in California. The company has been in operation for six months and realizes that there is a problem in estimating the overhead costs. The data, to date, are:

Month	Production	Overhead Cost
1	100	$ 1,200
2	200	1,500
3	300	2,250
4	200	1,750
5	300	2,300
6	400	2,700
Total	1,500	$11,700

As a staff accountant in the controller's office you are trying to determine how best to estimate the costs and are considering the high-low and regression methods.

Required:

1. Prepare a scattergraph of the data.

2. Determine the high-low estimating equation.
3. It can be shown that the regression equation is:

$$y = 631.82 + 5.2727x$$

Estimate the overhead cost for volumes of 350 units, 200 units, and 400 units.

2-13. Examination of "Strange" Behavior. The Catfish Company has conducted cost studies on two of its overhead items. Regression analysis and a high-low study produced somewhat the same results, and the analyst is having some difficulty in interpreting them. Thus, for purposes of this problem, only two sets of points are presented for each of the costs:

	Item A		Item B	
Observation	Cost	Volume	Cost	Volume
1	$ 7,000	1,000	$34,000	1,000
2	17,000	2,000	28,000	2,000

Required:

1. Find the estimating equation for item A. Provide a possible explanation for your results.
2. Find the estimating equation for item B. Provide an explanation for your results. Suggest some costs that might behave according to your results.

2-14. Inflation, Cost Behavior, and Decisions. The HL Company is a custom order manufacturer and has been in operation for five years. It is now early 19x6 and a decision has to be made on whether to accept a particular contract at the customer's bid of $970,000.

The contract in question would require 15,000 labor hours costing $200,000 (19x6 wage rates). This represents approximately half of the firm's labor capacity. The material for the contract is estimated at $300,000 (19x6 prices).

It is your task to estimate the overhead attributable to the contract. You have the following overhead data as recorded in the accounts:

	Direct Labor Hours	Overhead Cost
19x1	10,000	$300,000
19x2	12,000	374,000
19x3	30,000	847,000
19x4	20,000	665,500
19x5	25,000	878,460

Required:

1. Estimate the *variable* overhead that would be incurred as a result of accepting the contract. (The fixed overhead is irrelevant to this case because it is estimated that the plant will be idle at least 15,000 hours unless this contract is accepted.) Overhead is correlated with direct labor hours.
2. Would you recommend the acceptance of the contract? Why?

3. Now suppose you determine the above overhead data are affected by inflation. In fact, all overhead has been increasing at an annual rate of 10% and is expected to continue to increase at that rate. Repeat part 1.
4. Based on your results in part 3 would you recommend the acceptance of the contract? Why?

2-15. Cost and Its Role in Pricing Decisions. The Softalk Company is an association of computer consultants. Currently they are preparing to bid on a consulting project for the U.S. Department of Agriculture (USDA). The USDA will allow a profit of 10% based on cost. Further, they will allow costs to be determined as the average total cost of providing the service. Softalk will determine the average total cost as follows:

1. Determine the total cost for the period.
2. Determine the total consulting hours for the period.
3. Determine the average as item one divided by item two.

In talking with the officials of Softalk you determine they can estimate their annual costs, y, as a function of consulting hours, x, with the following equation:

$$y = 200,000 + 15x$$

There are three cases that Softalk would like to consider for the coming year:

	Case 1	Case 2	Case 3
Projected consulting hours for USDA	3,000	3,000	3,000
Projected consulting hours for other clients	2,000	5,000	1,000
Total projected consulting hours	5,000	8,000	4,000

Required:

1. For each of the three cases, what would be the allowable billing rate per consulting hour on the USDA project?
2. Comment on your results in part 1 giving consideration to the dependency of the billing rate on the volume of consulting hours.
3. In talking further with the Softalk officials, you find there are some who feel that the cost-estimating equation was acceptable for volumes around 5,000 consulting hours. However, they feel that the variable costs are a larger percentage of the total costs than implied in the equation $y = 200,000 + 15x$. Specifically, they feel the following equation is more "accurate":

$$y = 75,000 + 40x$$

   a. Verify that both equations yield the same results at a volume of 5,000 consulting hours.
   b. Repeat part 1 using this proposed equation.
   c. Compare your results in part 3b with those in part 1 and explain why the variation among the three cases is different.

2-16. Decisions with "Nonlinear" Cost Behavior. The Gamble Company produces one product and is having difficulty determining the optimal volume at which to operate. Following is a flexible budget at four possible volumes of operation.

	Volume			
	10,000	20,000	30,000	40,000
Material	$ 20,000	$ 40,000	$ 60,000	$ 80,000
Labor	30,000	55,000	90,000	130,000
Supervision	5,000	6,000	6,000	10,000
Depreciation	40,000	40,000	40,000	40,000
Other overhead	30,000	93,000	167,000	234,000
Total	$125,000	$234,000	$363,000	$494,000
Cost per unit	$12.50	$11.70	$12.10	12.35

One of the managers, Ms. Jean, contends that the firm should operate at a volume of 20,000 units. Her reasoning is that the average total cost is the smallest at that volume and, therefore, the profit per unit is the highest. A second manager, Mr. Roberts, contends that the firm should operate at the highest volume possible so long as the selling price exceeds the average cost. The sales price is $13 and thus he contends the volume should be 40,000 units.

The company can sell any number of units up to 40,000 at the $13 price. Assume that the four volumes are the only ones to be considered.

Required:

Who do you agree with, Ms. Jean or Mr. Roberts? If you agree with one of them, why? If you agree with neither, what volume do you recommend and why?

2-17. Cost Flowchart. Using Exhibit 2.10 as a model, prepare a flowchart of the accounting system for the Main Spark Company that produces spark plugs as follows. Spark plugs are assembled in Department C using metal spokes, which are produced in Department A; insulation material, which is produced in Department B; and miscellaneous other materials. All materials must be requisitioned from the storeroom. After the assembly, the spark plugs are transferred to Department D, which does the labeling and packaging. Departments A, B, C, and D are all responsibility centers that are controlled, in part, by comparing their actual costs with budgeted costs. In producing spokes and insulation, both Departments A and B require raw materials. All materials are centrally accounted for. Likewise, all labor and overhead costs are centrally collected and then distributed to the departments benefiting from their incurrence.

2-18. Cost Flows with Amounts. The Seaver Company produces one product, and its manufacturing process is organized into three responsibility centers: Departments A, B, and C. The product requires work in all three centers. During its *first* month of operation the company purchased materials totaling $25,000. Materials costing $15,000, $3,000, and $1,000 were issued to Departments A, B, and C, respectively.

Department A started 15,000 units of the product, and during the first month it transferred 12,000 units to Department B. (The balance was in the ending work-in-process inventory.) Department B transferred 10,000 units to Department C. Department C transferred 8,000 units to Finished Goods, and 5,000 units were sold. The materials are added at the very beginning of production in each department. That is, as soon as Department B receives units from Department A, it adds the materials to be added in Department B.

Required:

Prepare a flowchart that traces the dollars disbursed for material from accounts payable to cost of goods sold. Indicate the dollar amount of material cost that would have been transferred along each path of the flowchart during the first month.

2-19. Cost Flows with Amounts: Backward Reasoning. The Rose and Bench Company produces two products: fielder's gloves and catcher's mitts. All direct materials are accounted for in a single control account. At the start of the year the direct material inventory amounted to $2,000. The ending direct material inventory amounted to $5,000. There was no beginning finished goods inventory.

The following information about ending finished goods and cost of goods sold is available:

	Fielder's Gloves—Finished Goods Inventory	Catcher's Mitts—Finished Goods Inventory	Cost of Goods Sold
Direct materials	$4,000	$9,000	$35,000
Units:			
Fielder's gloves	2,000 units	—	10,000 units
Catcher's mitts	—	3,000 units	5,000 units

Costs are assigned at a unit cost equal to the total costs divided by the production for the period.

Both products are processed through a sequence of three responsibility centers: Department A, Department B, and Department C. Sixty percent of the direct material is used in completing the activities in Department A, thirty percent is added in Department B, and the remainder is added in Department C. There were no beginning or ending inventories in any of these departments.

Required:

1. Prepare a flowchart that traces the material cost from accounts payable to cost of goods sold.
2. Enter the beginning direct materials inventory in the appropriate account of your flowchart. Then, using the data given, indicate the dollar amount of material cost that would have been transferred along each path of your flowchart.

2-20. Classification of Items in Financial Statements. The following prototype statements are for a manufacturing firm. The sections are labeled A through G.

Cost of Goods Manufactured

A. Direct material used   xxx
B. Direct labor   xxx
C. Manufacturing overhead   xxx
   Total current product costs   xxx
D. Inventory adjustment(s)   xxx
   Cost of goods manufactured   xxx

Statement of Income

E. Sales	xxx
F. Cost of goods sold	xxx
Gross margin	xxx
G. Selling and administrative	xxx
Net income	xxx

Number an answer sheet from 1 through 20. Next to the corresponding number place the letter of the section in which the following items would be included. If the item does not belong in any of the above sections, place an X beside the number. If the item should be deducted within the chosen section, indicate this by circling the letter.

The items listed are for an automobile manufacturer.

1. Custodial supplies for the factory.
2. Plant manager's salary.
3. Ending work-in-process.
4. Transportation in on transmissions.
5. Nuts and bolts used on automobiles.
6. Wages of the door mounters.
7. Wages of the forklift operator who moves materials from receiving dock to storage area.
8. Beginning finished goods inventory.
9. Plant controller's salary.
10. Corporate controller's salary.
11. Purchase of a drill press needed to bore mounting holes.
12. Ending raw materials inventory.
13. Transportation out.
14. Purchase discounts on transmissions.
15. Depreciation on plant building.
16. Warranty expense on automobiles.
17. Customer rebates.
18. Tires.
19. Wages of the paint sprayers.
20. Depreciation on the drill press.

2-21. Financial Statements. Consider the following data for the Griffey Company:

	January 1, 19x1	December 31, 19x1
Inventories:		
Finished goods	$50,000	$40,000
Direct material	10,000	12,000
Work in process	25,000	18,000
Advertising expense		80,000
Controller's salary		45,000
Delivery expense		90,000
Depreciation (see note)		100,000
Direct labor		200,000
Factory equipment purchased in 19x1		900,000
Indirect labor		30,000

Miscellaneous general and administrative expense	40,000
Other manufacturing costs	20,000
Production manager's salary	35,000
Purchase discount on materials	10,000
Direct material purchases	100,000
Sales	1,000,000
Sales salaries	90,000
Supplies expense (factory)	15,000

Note: The depreciation is comprised of $50,000 on the factory building, $30,000 on factory equipment, and $20,000 on the general offices.

Required:

Prepare a statement of cost of goods manufactured and an income statement for 19x1.

2-22. Manufacturing Statement with Multiple Departments. The Driessen Company produces one product, and its factory is organized into three departments for control purposes. The following data have been collected:

	January 1, 19x1	December 31, 19x1
Inventories:		
Materials	$80,000	$ 70,000
Work in process—Department A	20,000	10,000
Work in process—Department B	40,000	50,000
Work in process—Department C	50,000	45,000
Finished goods	60,000	50,000
Materials purchased		100,000
Total direct labor		800,000
Total manufacturing overhead		900,000

Required:

1. Prepare a statement of the cost of goods manufactured in 19x1 for the firm as a whole.
2. Suppose separate statements are required for each department. What additional information would you need to prepare the statements?

2-23. CPA Problem—Cost of Goods Manufactured. The Helper Corporation manufactures one product. You have obtained the following information for the year ended December 31, 19x3, from the corporation's books and records:

a. Total manufacturing cost added during 19x3 (sometimes called "cost to manufacture") was $1,000,000.
b. Cost of goods manufactured was $970,000.
c. Total factory overhead costs added to work in process equaled 75% of the direct labor cost and 27% of the total costs placed into production.
d. Beginning work-in-process inventory, January 1, was 80% of ending work-in-process inventory, December 31.

Required:

Prepare a statement of the cost of goods manufactured during 19x3. Show as much detail as possible.

2-24. Finding the Missing Values. Following are two cases involving the cost of goods manufactured and sold. Supply the missing values.

	Case 1	Case 2
Inventories, 1/1/x1		
Raw material	$ 5	$ 7
Work in process	10	18 [a]
Finished goods	12	22
Inventories, 12/31/x1		
Raw material	3	8
Work in process	8	20 [a]
Finished goods	14	24
Raw materials purchased	45	61
Current cost of goods manufactured		
Material	47	60
Labor	50	100 [b]
Overhead	23	40 [b]
Total cost of goods manufactured	122	202
Cost of goods sold	120	200

[a]The ending work in process is equal to 90% of the beginning work in process.

[b]Overhead was applied at a rate equal to 40% of direct labor and, in this case, was equal to two-thirds of the material cost.

(handwritten annotations in margin: 5, 43, 50, 240%, 40%, 200+x-24=, (22+x-14=120, x=12)

2-25. Mind-Expanding Questions. The following questions are designed to start you thinking about some of the issues we will discuss in subsequent chapters.

1. Suppose that in order to produce all the units that are demanded, the A Company had to work overtime. The employees normally earn $8 per hour but are paid $12 per hour for overtime. Would you consider the entire $12 per hour as direct labor? Why?
2. Company B gives each of its employees a three-week paid vacation. Would you consider the vacation pay earned by direct laborers to be direct labor during the weeks the employees were on vacation? Why?
3. Certain employees of Company C are on a guaranteed minimum wage plan. During a given period these employees were paid for forty hours each even though they only worked thirty hours. Would you consider all of the wages paid to these employees in this period to be direct labor? Why?
4. During 19x1 Company D produced 1,000 units of its product and incurred $10,000 of fixed production costs. One unit was unsold at year-end and had $10 of fixed cost assigned to it for inventory purposes. During 19x2 the company produced 500 units, incurred $10,000 of fixed cost, and assigned $20 of fixed cost to the one unit remaining in inventory at the end of 19x2. Someone has asked you why the one unit in 19x2 is more valuable than the one in 19x1. Explain. Should this phenomenon be permitted to happen? Why?
5. After doing some processing on a batch of units, Company E discovers that 10% of them are defective. Of course, materials, labor, and overhead have been expended on the defective units. How would you account for these units that are unrepairable and have no value?

2-26. Cost Flowchart for Firm That Produces Parts Needs for Its Final Products. The Amox Company manufactures and sells two computers, the Pear and the Bartlett. Each computer requires boards and chips. Amox also manufactures these two parts.

Boards are manufactured in a two-step process. Department A1 does the first step and Department A2 the second. Chips only require a one-step operation and that is done in Department B.

Department F1 does the assembling of both computers. Pears require five boards and three chips. Bartletts require four boards and four chips. After assembly in Department F1 the computers are transferred to Department F2 for testing and packing. Separate finished goods inventory accounts are maintained for each salable product.

A materials control account is maintained. Materials are needed by all five departments and they are issued directly to the departments as needs arise.

Required:

1. Construct a flowchart representing the flow of material cost for the Amox Company. Ignore labor and overhead.
2. Now assume the following data:

	1/1x1	1/31/x1
	(000 omitted)	
Inventories		
Materials	$ 3	$ 4
Department A1	2	1
Department A2	5	12
Department B	10	9
Department F1	0	0
Department F2	0	0
Finished goods—Pears	40	0
Finished goods—Bartletts	0	30

Also assume that the company processed the same quantity of Pears and Bartletts through Departments F1 and F2. Further, material was issued to the production departments as follows (000 omitted):

A1—$50   A2—$100   B—$125   F1—$26   F2—$10

Enter the appropriate cost flow on each path of your flowchart constructed in part 1. Assume Pears and Bartletts require the same amount of additional material per unit in both of the finishing departments, F1 and F2.

Part 2   Systems to Support Reporting Function

CHAPTER 3

Job Order Systems

In Chapter 1 three classes of manufacturing firms were identified. Two of these, the custom manufacturer and the manufacturer that produces standard products in batches, were identified as potential users of a job order system. Before considering the components of a job order system, we will first examine the characteristics that are associated with a potential user. Then we will discuss the details of determining the cost of materials used, the cost of direct labor, and the accounting for manufacturing overhead. The last section will be a comprehensive problem that illustrates the integration of the various principles.

The accountant has to be knowledgeable not only of the principles of cost accounting, but also of its procedures. Thus, this chapter will be a blending of theory and of the details of collecting raw data. Although the discussion of the details will assume a physical record system, we emphasize that a computerized system will most likely be used in practice. The record keeping can be programmed for computer implementation. Instead of accounts, ledgers, and file cabinets, such a system would have memory disks and tapes, central processing units, machine readable input, and computer output. To understand the computer processing, one is aided in having a physical representation of the system.

The purpose of a job order system is to collect the cost of each job and, in turn, provide data for a variety of purposes. For example, the data would be used in financial reporting. That is, the cost system would generate the cost-of-goods-sold figure and the cost of the inventories. It might also be used as a basis for bidding on similar jobs in the future and for evaluating the responsibility centers that worked on the job.

Situations Served by a Job Order System

Let's consider the type of situation for which a job order system might be useful. A familiar type of manufacturer is the building contractor. Each job that a building contractor does is unique, easily identified, and can serve as a cost objective. Sometimes these jobs are referred to as custom orders. Thus, job order costing would be the natural type of system to use. Additional examples of this type of manufacturer include shipbuilders, aircraft manufacturers, heavy equipment manufacturers, crop farmers, and book publishers. Similar to the building contractor, each of the latter manufacturers produce a readily identifiable product that can serve as a cost objective.

If a firm produces one of its standard products in readily identifiable batches, then the batches can serve as cost objectives for a job order system. For example, a furniture manufacturer may be able to produce more Danish modern furniture per year than is demanded, and so Danish modern may share a production line with colonial style furniture. The sharing would not be in the form of simultaneous production but, instead, a batch of Danish modern followed by a batch of colonial. Between batches, the production line may have to be halted while equipment is reset for the next style. Because of these breaks, it is possible to identify easily the batches and treat them as separate jobs. Other examples of this kind of production scheduling might include manufacturers of fabric, clothing, and toys, as well as certain food processors.

A firm's product line may be such that only part of its production is suitable for a job order system. As stated earlier, there is no conceptual problem with mixing basic system ideas in order to create a custom system that meets the specific needs of the firm.

For our purposes a system is defined as the method of collecting, processing, and presenting data. Of necessity, the systems described in this book are general in nature. For specific cases it will be necessary to abstract from the general in order to provide for unique demands. Before discussing the system, some preliminary observations are necessary. First, the nature of the inventory accounts is considered and then there is an examination of the various manufacturing cost elements.

THE INVENTORY ACCOUNTS.   Most manufacturing firms have three types of inventories and, hence, three types of inventory accounts. The **materials** inventory represents materials that have been purchased for future use in the production process. Usually there is a control account representing the total materials inventory, and then some type of subsidiary record that accounts for each individual type of material. Sometimes the control account includes materials that are indirect to the production of the product. Indirect materials include such items as custodial supplies, machine lubricants, polishing supplies, welding supplies, cutting blades, drill bits, light bulbs, and work clothing. The materials account is sometimes called **stores,** especially if it is to be a control account for both direct and indirect materials.

The second type of inventory is **work in process.** As its name implies, this inventory represents the cost of units or jobs that are not entirely complete. Work-in-process accounts are usually maintained for each responsibility center within the production area. If these accounts are maintained on a perpetual basis, they serve the dual purpose of accounting for the partially completed units and for collecting costs that are needed to evaluate the performance of the responsibility center. That is, all of the center's activity for the period will be recorded in its work-in-process account.

Finally, the **finished goods** account contains the cost of production that has been finished, but not sold. Like the materials inventory, this account may be a control account for a variety of different products. If so, subsidiary accounts must be maintained for each finished product.

CLOSER EXAMINATION OF THE MANUFACTURING COST ELEMENTS (MATERIALS, LABOR, AND OVERHEAD). In Chapter 2 **direct materials** were defined as those that are a physical part of the finished products and can be conveniently traced to them. Let us briefly expand upon this definition. Some materials may become a physical part of the finished product, but tracing them to the production may not be practical because of their immateriality with respect to total costs. Examples include glue used in furniture production, machine screws and rivets used in the manufacture of equipment, nails in the construction of a house, and the paint for automobiles. In specific cases, judgment must be used in determining what will be considered direct and what will be indirect. Earlier in the section we listed several examples of materials that were obviously indirect. Those types of materials plus those that are not conveniently traced will become a part of the manufacturing overhead.

The meaning of **direct labor** as defined in Chapter 2 also needs to be expanded. Again, convenient traceability to the job or product is the key. For employees whose entire responsibility consists of actual work on the product, there is little problem in classification. But what if an employee's time is divided between production work and general cleanup work, for example? Then, the wage for production time is direct, and the wage for cleanup is indirect. As another example of this kind of problem, consider employees that are under a guaranteed wage contract, that is, wages are paid whether work is done or not. Only the wages for time actually spent on production should be considered direct. If such employees are idle and not working on any jobs, that time should be classified as indirect labor and included in overhead cost. In other words, it is not sufficient to classify the workers themselves as direct or indirect. The accountant must, instead, classify time spent on the job as direct or indirect.

The third element in a job order system is **manufacturing overhead.** In the discussion of direct material and direct labor, many items were identified that are classified as manufacturing overhead. In addition to those items, overhead would include the following: depreciation expense, rent, property taxes and insurance on the production plant, production supervisory salaries, maintenance cost for machinery, energy costs, safety costs, material handling, material inspection, shift differential costs, overtime premiums, social security taxes, vacation pay, and holiday pay.

The last five items deserve some additional discussion. Shift differentials are wage premiums paid to induce people to work the less desirable shifts, for example, the 11:00 P.M. to 7:00 A.M. shift. Overtime premiums are inducements to work more than the contracted number of hours, for example, more than forty hours per week. In either of these cases, it is *not* appropriate to charge these extra labor costs to just the units that were actually worked on during the time for which the premiums are being paid. The units produced during this time received the same amount of benefit from the production effort as the other units, so the premiums should be averaged over the entire production. This can be accomplished by including them in overhead costs. As will be seen later, overhead is accounted for in a way that considers problems like this one. A different treatment can be justified in cases where a particular job is the only reason for working overtime. Then, there is justification for charging that job with the overtime premium. Justification of this treatment is possible even if the particular job was actually completed in regular time and other "normal" jobs were shifted to overtime to meet a special schedule or deadline.

Social Security is a retirement wage that is paid by the federal government and financed by a tax on both the employee and employer. The employer's share of the tax is an operating expense of the firm. Social security taxes paid on manufacturing salaries and wages are production costs. However, these costs are not incurred uniformly over the calendar year. For each employee there is a maximum amount of each year's salary that is subject to the tax. Thus, the firm's social security tax is not likely to be as high late in the year as it is in January.

Now compare two production jobs: one worked on before the employee's earnings went above the maximum and one after. Should social security taxes be charged to the first job and not to the second? Many would argue that to do so is unjustified and that such a cost should be averaged over the entire year's production rather than over the production that was done before reaching the wage limits of social security. If this is considered to be a more equitable treatment, then it can be accomplished by accounting for social security tax as an overhead item.

Vacation and holiday pay are obviously disbursed during periods of employee nonproductivity, but these wages were earned while the employees were working, not when they were on vacation. Again, these costs should be prorated in some manner to all jobs worked on during the year. Thus, it is conventional to consider them overhead costs. Later, you will see how these actually get charged to the jobs.

So far we have not discussed how material, labor, and manufacturing overhead costs are actually determined and assigned. In the next section we present and discuss a flowchart that will help you understand how material and labor are accounted for in the job order system. Assignment of the manufacturing overhead costs will be discussed separately.

THE FLOWCHART AND DOCUMENT SUPPORT. Let's examine the flow of costs and supporting documents for a *general* job order system. The text will be illustrated with a set of flowcharts that you should use to guide you through the discussion. Before you consider the first flowchart there is an essential document whose purpose you should understand. Central to the working of this system is the **job card** or its equivalent. A detailed job card is illustrated in Exhibit 3.1. For each job a card is maintained for the purpose of accumulating the amount of material and labor that are directly incurred in completing the job. Further, a share of the estimated manufacturing overhead cost will be computed and added to the direct costs. At the end of an accounting period the balance in work in process should equal the sum of the balances accumulated on the job cards for the jobs that are

Exhibit 3.1   Job Cost Card

JOB COST CARD

Job No. __331__

Job Description: __Orange Crushing Machines__

Quantity: ____10____

Date Started   __1/23__
Date Finished   _____

MATERIALS

Date	Req #	Department	Part No.	Quantity	Price	Total
1/23	43402	Casting	5165-N	100 lbs.	$2.00	$200.00

LABOR

Date	REF	Department	Description	Hours	Rate	Total
1/24		Casting		16	$5.00	$80.00

OVERHEAD

Department	Basis	Hours	Rate	Total
Casting	Direct Labor	16	$4.00	$64.00

SUMMARY

	Total	Per Unit
Material	200.00	20.00
Labor	80.00	8.00
Overhead	64.00	6.40
Total	344.00	34.40

incomplete at that point. These job cards are actually subsidiary accounts to the work-in-process account. This relationship is shown in Exhibit 3.2 by indicating the job cards as support to the work-in-process account. The job cards are the only source to determine the amount of cost to transfer from work in process to finished goods (representing the cost of production finished during the period, called the

Exhibit 3.2   Materials Cost Flow

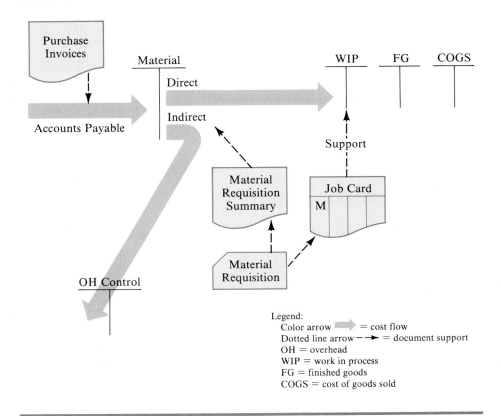

cost of goods manufactured) and from finished goods to cost of goods sold (representing the cost of goods sold during the period).

If the system is computerized, then each job would have to be given a designated storage space. Within that space a status code should be included that indicates whether the job is still in process, finished but not sold, or sold. Further, there would have to be provision for a mechanism of determining which jobs were finished during the period. The mechanics for this should be worked out in consultation with competent systems analysts and programmers.

It is also worthwhile to point out that there may be two or more responsibility centers within the factory. If so, the job card may be designed to accumulate the costs of each center.

The remainder of the discussion is directed toward the specifics of accounting for the material, labor, and overhead. For material, follow the flowchart in Exhibit

3.2 as the discussion proceeds. First, consider the document support for purchases. The source document that provides the cost of materials purchased is the purchase invoice that is originated by the supplier. Perhaps a special journal, such as the purchase (voucher) register, will be used to collect the purchase transactions. If so, then summary entries can be made periodically to record the acquisitions in the material control account.

Next, consider the use of material. In order to ensure that materials are used appropriately, they should be centrally controlled. That is, they should be kept in a storeroom and obtained through a storeroom clerk with proper authorization. When materials are needed for a particular job, the production foreman in charge of the job initiates a **materials requisition.** As you can see in Exhibit 3.3, a requisition should provide a variety of data including the part number and quantity requested. The department (responsibility center) making the request should be identified as well as the number of the job on which the materials will be used. As you can see in the flowchart of Exhibit 3.2, the requisition provides the information for the materials section of the job card. The requisition should be signed only by an authorized representative of the production center receiving the material. This signing acknowledges the acceptance of responsibility for the material by the individual signing the requisition and releases the storeroom clerk of that responsibility. This is all part of what the accountant calls internal control.

Periodically, the material requisitions are summarized by the accounting department. A material requisitions summary is illustrated in Exhibit 3.4. It lists the individual requisitions, classifies the cost by department if there are multiple departments, and also classifies the cost as direct or indirect within the department. (This classification is initially indicated on the materials requisition form.) The column totals of this form provide data for a summarizing journal entry reflecting the actual use of the material during the period. Exhibit 3.2 shows only

---

Exhibit 3.3   **Materials Requisition**

MATERIALS REQUISITION

Date 1/23   Req # 43402

Part No.	Quantity	Price	Total
5165-N	100 lbs.	$2.00	$200.00

Job # 331   Dept. Casting
  (I if indirect)

Foreman: _____

Exhibit 3.4   Materials Requisition Summary

MATERIALS REQUISITION SUMMARY
Period:_____

	Casting Department		Assembly Department	
Req #	Direct	Indirect	Direct	Indirect
43402	200.00			

one work-in-process account. However, there may be multiple production departments, and, if so, the requisition summary would provide the data about the amount of materials used by each department.

Now consider the accounting for labor and its flow of costs in Exhibit 3.5. This accounting begins with the clock cards, sometimes called in-out cards, that are maintained by the employees. Such a card is not separately illustrated, but it merely indicates the employee's name, social security number, and the daily check-in and checkout times. A reading of the in-out times at the end of the week indicates the total number of hours worked.

From this information the accounting department can prepare a payroll sheet. As can be seen in the illustrative payroll sheet in Exhibit 3.6, the first computation is the determination of each employee's total or gross wages. From this amount, the various withholdings are deducted. The deductions include such things as income tax, social security, union dues, employee bond purchases, and so forth. Using the totals from the payroll sheet, a summary journal entry can be made. A "payroll" account will be used to record the total *gross* wages. Gross wages are the earnings before withholdings. The gross wages, not the net wages, are the costs to the firm. Withholdings are made to pay employee expenses in behalf of the employee. A payroll account is set up as a temporary holding account until an analysis can be performed to determine what manufacturing accounts should be charged with labor costs and how much should be charged. Such an entry, in general form, is:

Payroll	xxx
Withholding Tax Payable	xxx
Social Security Tax Payable	xxx
Union Dues Payable	xxx
Accrued Payroll	xxx

The payroll sheet does not indicate whether the labor was direct or indirect, which department benefited from the labor, or which job benefited. For product

Exhibit 3.5   Labor Cost Flow

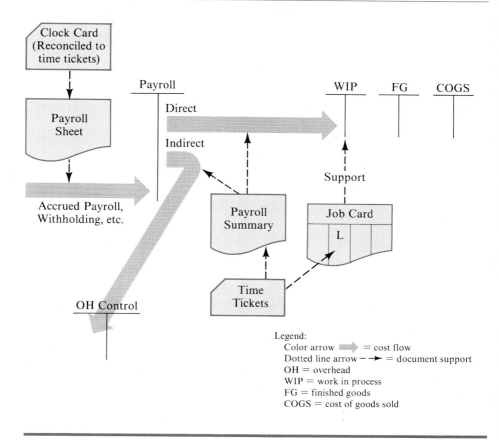

Legend:
Color arrow ⟹ = cost flow
Dotted line arrow – –▸ = document support
OH = overhead
WIP = work in process
FG = finished goods
COGS = cost of goods sold

cost determination, the payroll account must be classified into direct and indirect labor and, if there are multiple departments, by department. The basic source document to accomplish this is the time ticket (illustrated in Exhibit 3.7). Time tickets are maintained by the individual workers, indicating the jobs on which they worked and the amount of time spent on each. If some of their time was spent on indirect activity, this should also be noted. To provide some insurance of accuracy, the time tickets should be approved by the employee's supervisor. Further, this document should be reconciled to the employee's clock card to verify that the total hours agree.

Using the time tickets, a payroll analysis can be done to determine how the payroll costs should be distributed. This analysis is not illustrated but would be organized in a manner similar to the materials requisition summary. It would be done so as to permit a journal entry dividing the total payroll into direct and indirect, and the separation of both types of labor according to departments. If the firm had

Exhibit 3.6 Payroll Sheet

PAYROLL SHEET

Period: Week of 1/24

Name	Social Security No.	Hours	Rate	Gross	Withholding: With-holding Tax	Withholding: Social Security Tax	Withholding: Bonds	Withholding: Other	Net
J. Doe	999-99-9999	40	$5	$200	$20	$14	0	0	$166
M. Due	888-88-8888	40	$10	$400	$80	$28	$100	0	$192

Casting and Assembly Departments, then the entry to allocate the payroll account, set up when the wages were paid, is of the form:

WIP—Casting Department	xxx
WIP—Assembly Deaprtment	xxx
Manufacturing Overhead—Casting	xxx
Manufacturing Overhead—Assembly	xxx
Payroll	xxx

Exhibit 3.7 Time Ticket

TIME TICKET

Name: J. Doe No. ______

SS # 999-99-9999 Date 1/24

Pay Code ______

Job No. or Indirect	Out	In	Time	Department	Foreman Signature
331	4pm	8am	8	Casting	

Finally, you should note in Exhibit 3.5 that the time tickets provide the raw data for determining each job's labor cost.

To complete the flow of costs, turn to Exhibit 3.8. First, note that actual overhead costs incurred during the accounting period are shown flowing into overhead control. Also note that overhead is being transferred from overhead control to work in process (WIP) using a rate. We will soon learn how this rate is derived and why it is used. Generally it is not acceptable to assign overhead to the work-in-process account based on the actual costs incurred. The reasons for this have been alluded to earlier and will also be more fully developed very shortly. This application rate is also used on the job cost card.

Further discussion of "overhead application" will be deferred until the next section so that the discussion of the flowchart can be completed. Exhibit 3.8 shows that the job card is the source of information for determining the cost of finished goods and the transfer from WIP to finished goods. Likewise, the job card is the

Exhibit 3.8   Overhead Cost Flow and Flow of Finished Production

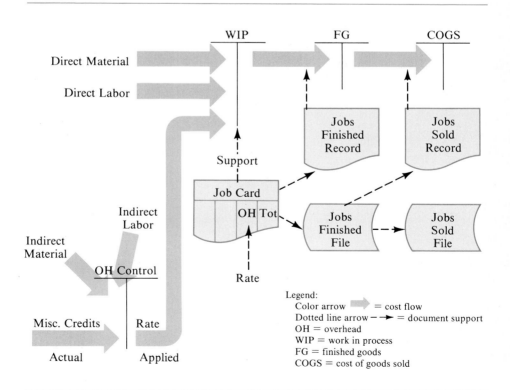

Legend:
Color arrow ➡ = cost flow
Dotted line arrow – ➤ = document support
OH = overhead
WIP = work in process
FG = finished goods
COGS = cost of goods sold

source of data for cost of goods sold determinations. For your convenience, the flowcharts of Exhibits 3.2, 3.5, and 3.8 have been merged into Exhibit 3.9 (see below).

By now you should be aware of the importance of conveying to the workers and managers that their cooperation is needed in collecting accurate data. The completion of material requisitions and time tickets is apt to be considered as an impediment to or, perhaps, even harassment on the job. Obtaining cooperation is not an easy task for the accountant. Among other things, the accountant must gain respect from workers and managers. Respect can be enhanced by acquiring a working knowledge of the problems in the factory and by monitoring the equity of the way the data are used in the evaluation function.

Exhibit 3.9   Job Cost Flow

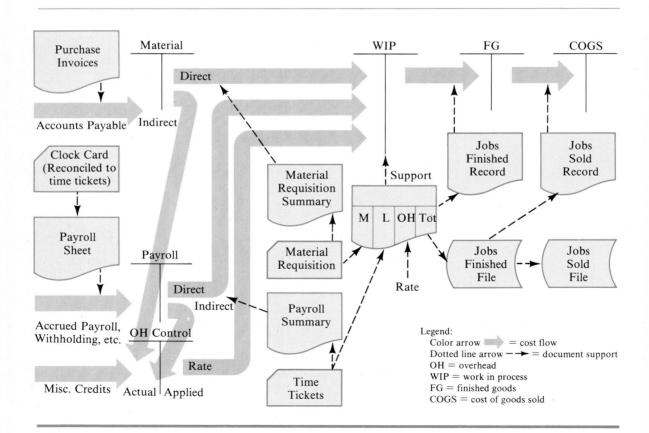

Legend:
Color arrow = cost flow
Dotted line arrow --► = document support
OH = overhead
WIP = work in process
FG = finished goods
COGS = cost of goods sold

Accounting for Overhead

As has been discussed, manufacturing overhead costs represent items that benefit production only in an indirect way. We now come to the important problem of how these costs should be assigned to the output (the jobs). Keep in mind that some of these indirect costs are variable with respect to output, and others are fixed. Another problem involves the seasonal aspect of some of the costs. For example, heating costs are incurred only in the winter and, as discussed earlier, vacation pay and social security taxes tend to be seasonal. In this section, we will examine the assignment of manufacturing overhead to jobs by a **predetermined application rate.** That is, the rate is determined before the start of the accounting period and before the knowledge about what the actual overhead costs will be. A variety of issues related to determining the application rate will be discussed. Then we will consider whether a plant-wide rate or a departmental rate should be used. Finally, the accounting mechanics of using an overhead rate will be illustrated.

NEED FOR A RATE. There are several reasons for using a predetermined rate in assigning overhead to jobs. First, there is the problem of fixed costs. An important question is whether all of the fixed costs of the period should be prorated to the jobs produced that period. This makes sense if the plant was operating near capacity. But what if it operated significantly below capacity? In such a case jobs would be assigned a greater amount of fixed costs than if the plant were working at capacity because the fixed costs are the same regardless of the volume of production. For example, the plant has to be heated in the winter whether it is operating at 60% or 95% of capacity.

Fixed costs represent the costs of having a capacity to produce. A given job will consume the same amount of that capacity regardless of the amount of capacity needed to support the actual production of the period. Thus, the benefit received by a given job is independent of the total number of jobs in production for a given period and many accountants would argue that the costing mechanism should be designed to assign a fixed cost that is independent of volume. This can be accomplished by first estimating the fixed costs of the forthcoming period and then determining an application rate that will be used throughout that period. Note carefully that estimated, not actual, costs are being used, since this rate is being determined before any jobs are produced.

To have a rate, as discussed above, implies there is a divisor. The divisor will be some appropriate measure of production activity that is readily measurable and associated with every job. For example, direct labor hours may be used as a measure of activity. The fixed overhead rate will be equal to the estimated fixed costs divided by some specific value for the selected activity measure. (This will be developed in more detail shortly.) Then, the costs assigned to a job using the predetermined rate will only depend on the amount of production activity required for the job and will be independent of the number of other jobs that happened to be scheduled into the same period.

Seasonal costs raise a similar issue. These costs are not a function of the type of volume or jobs processed. They are due to other factors. Yet it is not practical to produce without incurring them. The production process benefits from their incurrence, but the benefit cannot be measured by just averaging the actual amount of cost incurred in a short period (say a month) over the production of the period. Doing this is justified only if the selected period were relatively long. For example, if a yearly period were selected, then the *actual* overhead rate for all of the jobs completed during the year would yield a relatively good measure of benefit from seasonal costs. This is not practical, however. In most cases firms need to know the cost of a job relatively soon after it is completed. Actually, in some cases the sales price of the products produced in the job may be dependent on the cost (a cost-plus contract, for example). As with fixed overhead, the solution is to estimate these costs at the beginning of the year and prorate them over some appropriate measure of activity. This entire procedure is examined in the next section.

ESTABLISHING THE MANUFACTURING OVERHEAD RATE. Exhibit 3.10 contains a listing of the steps needed to derive an overhead rate. Each of these steps is discussed in this section but first we preview the problem. The overhead rate should be established by first estimating, or budgeting, the overhead costs for the period (usually a year). As indicated in Chapter 2, costs cannot be properly budgeted unless their different behaviors are taken into consideration. The end result of this proess is an estimate of the *total* fixed overhead costs and the *rate* at which variable overhead costs will increase with increases in activity. That is, a *flexible budget,* as discussed in Chapter 2, must be prepared and, mathematically, is of the form:

$$y = F + Vx$$

Exhibit 3.10   The Overhead Rate Determination Process

In order to derive a predetermined overhead rate it is necessary to do the following (not necessarily in the order listed).

1. Select a method of measuring production activity. This measure should be related to overhead incurrence.

2. Construct a flexible overhead budget formula using the activity measure(s) as independent variable(s).

3. Select a specific point on the activity scale to use as a divisor activity level (theoretical capacity, practical capacity, normal activity, or expected activity).

4. Determine rate:
   Total overhead rate =
     Variable overhead rate (from flexible budget)
     + Fixed rate
   Fixed rate = $\dfrac{\text{Budgeted Fixed Cost}}{\text{Divisor Activity}}$

---

where F is the total fixed overhead costs; V, the variable overhead rate; x, the measure of activity; and y, the total cost.

There are a variety of ways the flexible budget can be determined. These were introduced in Chapter 2 (scattergraph, high-low method, and regression analysis). Such studies may have to be done only for the costs that are mixed (containing both fixed and variable components). Other cost behaviors may be obvious. For example, straight-line depreciation is a fixed cost. The final result of such an analysis will be an estimate of total fixed overhead costs and an estimated variable overhead rate.

Before doing the flexible budget, as the first task in computing the overhead rate, select an overall way to measure production activity. In measuring activity, a factor must be selected that can be easily associated with production. Further, this factor should have some causal relationship with the incurrence of overhead. If multiple products that have vastly different material and labor requirements are being manufactured, using the sum of all of the units produced is inappropriate. For example, a publishing firm would not be justified in measuring activity by adding the number of copies of all the different books produced this period. A 1,000-page book and a 100-page book cannot be considered as equivalents.

In a production setting it is typical to consider the following as candidates for overall measures of activity: direct-labor hours, direct-labor dollars, and machine hours. For example, if it takes fifteen minutes of labor to assemble the 1,000-page book and five minutes for the 100-page book, then the production of one of each of the books would mean twenty minutes of activity. Adding the minutes is an overall measure of activity because the relative efforts are considered. It is perhaps not appropriate to measure the activity, in this case, as two books.

If no relationship can be demonstrated between a possible factor and the amount of overhead, there is no justification in using it as a measure of activity. For example, if a particular production process is highly mechanized, then it is likely that there will be little correlation between direct-labor hours and overhead. At first glance, it might appear that two of these overall measures of activity, direct-labor hours and direct-labor dollars, are the same. However, there are generally multiple labor rates within the firm. Consider two jobs that need the same total labor hours but one uses a larger proportion of the higher labor rate than the other. Applying overhead as a function of direct-labor dollars will result in the first job receiving a larger amount of overhead than the second job. Applying overhead on an hourly basis results in the same amount. Different amounts could be justified only to the extent that variable overhead is a function of labor dollars. Fringe benefits, for example, may have a tendency to vary with labor dollars, but the use of supplies may not. In short, the problem of selecting an activity measure must be given serious thought and analysis.

The flexible budgeting process, as discussed in Chapter 2, explicitly yields a rate at which variable overhead cost can be assigned to a job. Costs must be separated into fixed and variable elements. Variable costs increase at a constant rate per unit of activity and this rate of incurrence is also the rate at which variable overhead should be assigned to the jobs. If some activity causes overhead to be incurred at a given rate, then that activity should be assigned the cost it caused.

There is no causal association that can be used in assigning fixed overhead costs to the jobs. Whatever is done is somewhat arbitrary. It is normal, however, to derive a predetermined fixed overhead rate by first selecting, as a divisor, a specific point on the scale of activity used to explain the incurrence of variable overhead. There are four possible points that can be considered: theoretical capacity, practical capacity, normal activity, and current expected activity. One of these points should be chosen, called the **divisor activity,** and then used to determine the rate at which fixed overhead will be assigned:

$$\text{Fixed overhead application rate} = \frac{\text{Budgeted fixed costs}}{\text{Divisor activity}}$$

Theoretical capacity, stated in terms of the chosen measurement unit, is the volume of activity that is possible if both people and machines worked *continuously.* It assumes that people do not need breaks and that machines do not need repair time. Further, it assumes that all output that would result has a market and will be sold. If a plant is operating *less* than three eight-hour shifts, a question arises as to whether theoretical capacity should be based on a twenty-four-hour day or on the number of shifts that are capable of being staffed with the current personnel. Generally, the latter premise is more defensible, but the accountant would have to exercise some judgment. For example, if the estimated lives of machines are based on one eight-hour shift per day and supervisory personnel are sufficient for one shift, then one shift should be used to compute practical capacity. The concept of a capacity is needed for fixed-cost allocation and capacity should be measured consistent with the makeup of these costs. Theoretical capacity is *never used,* but it does provide a convenient benchmark for discussing the other concepts.

Practical capacity differs from theoretical capacity in that it recognizes people and machines will not normally be productive all of the time. It will be computed as theoretical capacity reduced by an allowance for a reasonable amount of nonproductive time. For example, assume that our plant could employ fifty full-time direct laborers. The plant will work one eight-hour shift per day for each of the 250 working days in the year. Swing workers are employed to cover personal absences and vacations. The figure of fifty represents full-time equivalent employees. Employees are on the job from 8:00 A.M. to 5:00 P.M. and, including the lunch hour, are given 1.5 hours of break time during the day. The lunch hour will not be included in the eight-hour compensation base. Interruptions in production time due to machine failures average 1,000 hours per year. The practical capacity, measured in terms of labor hours, is as follows:

Theoretical capacity 50 × 8 × 250		100,000
Less reasonable downtime		
Compensated breaks 50 × 0.5 × 250	6,250	
Unavoidable machine-caused downtime	1,000	7,250
Practical capacity		92,750

This concept still assumes that all output that results from operating at the practical level could be sold.

Normal activity is the level at which the firm must typically operate in order to produce the average demand that can be expected for its products. Usually it will be computed by averaging the activity level of the last four or five years and adjusting that average for significant trends that can be anticipated over the next four or five years. The theory of normal activity as the divisor for the fixed cost component of the overhead rate is that facilities were acquired to support the actual average demand. Practical capacity may be larger than the normal activity because of the desire to have some flexibility in meeting peak demands. According to this theory, the fact that the firm could operate at a level above the average demand is immaterial. The fixed costs should be averaged over the demand that was anticipated at the time of building a plant and of training supervisory personnel to conveniently meet that demand.

Current expected activity is the level at which the firm reasonably expects to operate during the next year. If this concept is used and if the actual activity has a tendency to make large swings from one year to another, then the rate at which fixed costs are assigned will change dramatically from year to year. Those who believe that production should be assigned a relatively constant cost from year to year are forced to reject this concept. (Of course, price level changes may cause unit cost changes from year to year, but this is another problem.)

Theoretically, most accountants prefer to use either the concept of practical capacity or of normal activity. Normal activity is usually preferred to practical capacity unless, due to anticipated growth, practical capacity was deliberately created to be greater than the capacity currently needed. For example, at the time of the last capacity expansion it might have been determined that it was optimal to add all the planned expansion at that time rather than in phases. In such a case, there is no justification for charging the cost of added but currently unneeded facilities to the current production. There is no way to justify any benefit accruing to the current production from the existence of these facilities that temporarily are in excess of the current needs. Further, the market is not going to absorb the expansion costs through higher product prices.

To illustrate and compare the different divisor activity concepts, continue the example started in the discussion of practical capacity. Suppose that the firm had averaged 80,000 labor hours during the past five years and, due to an expected one-year downturn in demand, plans to operate at 70,000 hours in the coming year. The following flexible budget has been prepared.

	Theoretical Capacity	Practical Capacity	Normal Activity	Expected Activity
Direct-labor hours	100,000	92,750	80,000	70,000
Fixed overhead costs	$ 742,000	$ 742,000	$ 742,000	$ 742,000
Variable overhead costs	500,000	463,750	400,000	350,000
Total	$1,242,000	$1,205,750	$1,142,000	$1,092,000

As you can confirm, the variable overhead rate is $5 per hour (variable cost ÷ direct labor hours). Since the variable overhead is expected to be incurred at the rate of $5 per hour it would be logical to assign $5 of variable overhead for each direct-labor hour spent on a particular job.

Possible fixed overhead rates would be as follows:

Base	Computation	Rate
Theoretical capacity	$742,000 ÷ 100,000	$ 7.420
Practical capacity	$742,000 ÷ 92,750	8.000
Normal activity	$742,000 ÷ 80,000	9.275
Expected activity	$742,000 ÷ 70,000	10.600

Which fixed overhead rate should be chosen? Since it is not even practical to operate at 100,000 hours, the $7.42 rate would not come close to assigning all of the fixed overhead costs. If the rate based on expected activity is chosen, $10.60, it will likely permit the assignment of most of the fixed overhead for the period. Further, it does represent the most likely "average fixed cost" for the current period. However, neither of these arguments makes any sense as a defense of how fixed costs should be assigned to the jobs worked on during the period. The utility of the production facilities accruing to a given job is not increased as a result of operating at lower levels of activity. As explained earlier, using the expected activity level can lead to fluctuations in the fixed overhead rate over time. The utility accruing to two comparable jobs, one done in a low-volume year and one in a high-volume year, is the same. Thus, the results that are possible under the expected activity concept cannot be defended.

As explained earlier, the choice is really limited to a rate based on practical capacity or on normal activity. Without additional facts, it is not possible to present a defense of one over the other. In summary, then, use one of the following rates:

	Practical Capacity	Normal Activity
Fixed	$ 8.00	$ 9.275
Variable	5.00	5.000
Total	$13.00	$14.275

PLANT-WIDE VERSUS DEPARTMENTAL RATES. In a firm that has multiple responsibility centers there is the additional issue of whether a single overhead rate will be used in all departments or whether one will be developed for each center. Generally, there are enough differences among departments to justify separate rates.

To illustrate the problem, assume that two jobs require work in two departments. Both departments feel that direct-labor hours would be the factor most strongly correlated with overhead incurrence. The establishment of the departmental and plant rates is demonstrated in Exhibit 3.11. Suppose Job #1 requires 150 hours in Department A and 50 hours in Department B. Job #2 requires 50

Exhibit 3.11   Overhead Rates for Departmentalized Firm

	Department A	Department B	Plant
Budgeted fixed overhead	$60,000	$480,000	$540,000
Direct labor hours at normal activity	10,000	12,000	22,000
Fixed overhead rate	$6.00	$40.00	$24.55
Variable overhead rate	4.00	10.00	7.27*
Total overhead rate	$10.00	$50.00	$31.82

---

*Total variable cost at normal:

Department A $ 4 x 10,000	$ 40,000
Department B $10 x 12,000	120,000
Total	$160,000
Total direct labor hours	22,000
Average variable cost per hour	$7.27

hours in Department A and 150 in B. It is clear that if the plant-wide rate is used, then both jobs would receive an identical overhead cost allocation of $6,364 (200 × $31.82). If departmental rates are used, the following results are obtained:

	Department A @ $10	Department B @ $50	Total
Job #1	$1,500	$2,500	$4,000
Job #2	500	7,500	8,000

Note that Job #1 is allocated a larger amount of overhead with the plant-wide rate than with departmental rates ($6,364 versus $4,000). This is because the plant-wide rate implicitly assumes that all jobs require a relatively constant proportion of work in each department and that this proportion is equal to the ratio of the department's budgeted direct-labor hours to the total budgeted direct-labor hours. For example, if Job #3 requires 91 hours in Department A and 109 in Department B, then using individual departmental rates yields an allocation of $6,360 [(91 × $10) + (109 × $50)]. This, of course, is virtually the same allocation that is given by the firm-wide rate. But note that the ratio of Department A to Department B hours is the same for this job as at normal activity. (At normal activity the ratio of A's hours to the total is 10,000 ÷ 22,000 or 45.45%. Job #3 requires 200 hours, 45.45% of which is in Department A.)

The preceding example should suggest one criterion to be applied in making the decision about the type of rate structure to use. That is, if the relative demands placed upon the departments vary significantly from job to job, then a departmentalized rate structure should be used. An additional factor that would favor a departmentalized rate structure is the need to use different variables to achieve the best overhead allocation system in each department. For example, if one department is highly labor-oriented and another is highly mechanized, then overhead will have to be assigned on two different measures in order to properly estimate the relative benefit. Of course, the cost of having a more elaborate system will have to be balanced with the benefits.

Finally, it should be noted that multiple allocation bases *within* the same department may be necessary. For example, some situations may demand that people-related costs be allocated using a different base than would be used for building-related costs. Allocating both types of cost using the same base will not ensure equitable results.

AN ILLUSTRATION OF OVERHEAD ACCOUNTING. To illustrate the accounting mechanics for overhead on a predetermined basis, consider the Osborne Company. Osborne manufactures a variety of telephones on a contract basis. The phones are produced according to customer specification and are accounted for in lots. Although several departments are identified, it is felt that a plant-wide rate is appropriate. The budgeted overhead costs for a normal activity of 100,000 direct-labor hours are given in Exhibit 3.12. Since the company experiences some fluctuations in demand, they expect to have both idle time costs as

Exhibit 3.12   Overhead Budget for Osborne Company for Normal Activity of 100,000 Direct Labor Hours

	Fixed	Variable Rate
Indirect supplies	——	$0.10
Indirect labor	$ 10,000	0.40
Supervisory salaries	100,000	——
Social security taxes	5,000	0.45
Pension payments	10,000	——
Health care costs	20,000	——
Overtime premiums	——	0.15
Idle time costs	5,000	——
Vacation pay	40,000	——
Depreciation—plant and equipment	70,000	——
Property taxes	22,000	——
Property insurance	18,000	——
Repairs and maintenance	2,000	0.05
Power costs	10,000	0.40
Material handling	——	0.75
Total	$312,000	$2.30
Normal activity	100,000	
Overhead rates	$3.12	$2.30
Total rate	$5.42	

well as overtime costs. As you can see, the overhead rate is $5.42 per direct-labor hour.

As jobs are completed, the direct-labor hours incurred are determined from the time tickets. Then each job is charged $5.42 per hour for the overhead costs. For example, if Job #382 incurred 200 labor hours, it would be charged with $1,084 of overhead. This is known as the **applied overhead.** In most cases, the total overhead applied during the year will not be the same as the actual overhead costs incurred. Suppose that during the year the contracted jobs required a total of 90,000 direct-labor hours and that the actual overhead incurred totaled $523,000. Following are the summary entries for the year's activity with respect to overhead:

Incurrence of Actual

Manufacturing overhead	523,000	
Accounts payable and other accounts		523,000

Application Using Predetermined Rate

Work in process (90,000 × $5.42)	487,800	
Manufacturing overhead		487,800

As can be seen, there is a debit balance of $35,200 remaining in the manufacturing overhead account at the end of the year ($523,000 - $487,800). This is called underapplied, or unabsorbed, overhead, and there is an issue of how it should be disposed. Obviously, the underapplied overhead represents the excess of actual costs over those that were applied to the jobs during the year. (Note that there might have been the reverse situation: overapplied, or overabsorbed, overhead.) Deciding what to do with over-underapplied overhead is not easy because there are several contributing reasons for its existence. This problem arises again in Chapters 5 and 6 when standard costs and variances are discussed. At that point there will be a complete discussion of the possible methods of accounting for such "variances." Here it will suffice to say that the common solution is to close the balance of the manufacturing overhead account to the cost-of-goods-sold account.

An Integrative Problem on Job Order Costing

In order to "tie" this chapter together it will be useful to discuss an integrative problem. Assume that the Rossford Company produces custom-engineered machines. Regardless of the particular order, however, every machine must be worked on by each of two departments, A and B. Further, the nature of the work is such that a machine must be processed in Department A and then transferred to Department B for completion. Separate departmental overhead rates are used. Both departments can demonstrate that direct-labor dollars are significantly correlated with overhead incurrence. Separate overhead accounts are maintained for each department. The 19x2 rates were developed in late 19x1 as follows:

	Department A	Department B
Budgeted overhead (total)	$1,680,000	$480,000
Direct-labor *dollars* at normal activity	1,200,000	600,000
Total overhead rate per direct-labor dollar		
$1,680,000 ÷ 1,200,000	1.40	
$480,000 ÷ 600,000		0.8

Two jobs, #108 and #109, were still in process at the *beginning* of 19x2. Their job cards are in Exhibit 3.13. The records show that $100,000 worth of material and supplies were acqured by Rossford during January 19x2. An analysis of the material requisitions by jobs and departments is found in Exhibit 3.14.

Checks totaling $140,000 were issued to plant employees for net wages earned during January. The payroll summary for January shows gross manufacturing wages of $200,000, federal income taxes withheld of $40,000, social security taxes withheld of $10,000, and union dues withheld of $5,000. January 31 fell in midweek (Friday is payday) so that some wages earned were still payable.

The January time tickets are summarized in Exhibit 3.15. It shows labor classified by department and job.

During January the actual overhead incurred in Department A totaled $125,000 *exclusive* of indirect material and indirect labor. In Department B the actual overhead was $25,000 *exclusive* of indirect material and labor.

Exhibit 3.13   Rossford Company Job Cards for Unfinished Jobs at January 1, 19x2

	Job 108[a]	Job 109[b]
Department A		
Material	$ 5,000	$10,000
Labor	10,000	10,000
Overhead	13,000[c]	13,000[c]
Department B		
Material	10,000	0
Labor	20,000	0
Overhead	16,000	0
Total	$74,000	$33,000

[a]Completed in Department A; not yet complete in Department B.

[b]Not yet complete in Department A.

[c]Based on 19x1 rates.

Exhibit 3.14   Rossford Company Analysis of Materials Requisitions for January 19x2

	Department A	Department B	Total
Job 110	$10,000	$ 2,000	$ 12,000
Job 111	50,000	10,000	60,000
Job 112	10,000	0	10,000
Total Direct	$70,000	$12,000	$82,000
Indirect	15,000	5,000	20,000
Total	$85,000	$17,000	$102,000

Following are the summarizing journal entries needed to record January's activity. Also refer to Exhibit 3.17 to visualize the cost flow.

Stores Acquisition:

Stores	100,000	
Accounts payable		100,000
For materials acquired during January		

Labor Incurred:

Payroll	200,000	
Witholding tax payable		40,000
Social security tax payable		10,000
Union dues payable		5,000
Accrued payroll		145,000
For wages earned during January		

Exhibit 3.15   Rossford Company Analysis of Time Tickets for January 19x2

	Department A	Department B	Total
Job 108	$ 0	$ 2,000	$ 2,000
Job 109	1,000	10,000	11,000
Job 110	80,000	30,000	110,000
Job 111	30,000	7,000	37,000
Job 112	10,000	0	10,000
Total Direct	$121,000	$49,000	$170,000
Indirect	20,000	10,000	30,000
Total	$141,000	$59,000	$200,000

Payment of Wages:

Accrued payroll	140,000	
Cash		140,000

For payroll checks issued during January. (Note that $5,000 is payable at the end of January.)

Materials and Supplies Used:

Work in process—Department A	70,000	
Work in process—Department B	12,000	
Manufacturing overhead—Department A	15,000	
Manufacturing overhead—Department B	5,000	
stores		102,000

For materials used during January (from Exhibit 3.14). (Note that there must have been a beginning balance in stores.) *100,000 requisitioned less 102,000.*

Allocation of Payroll:

Work in process—Department A	121,000	
Work in process—Department B	49,000	
Manufacturing overhead—Department A	20,000	
Manufacturing overhead—Department B	10,000	
payroll		200,000

For allocation of labor cost during January (from Exhibit 3.15)

Additional Overhead Incurred:

Manufacturing overhead—Department A	125,000	
Manufacturing overhead—Department B	25,000	
Accounts payable and other accounts		150,000

For additional overhead incurred during January

Overhead Application:

Work in process—Department A	169,400	
Manufacturing overhead—Department A		169,400

$121,000 × 1.40; to apply Department A's overhead.

Work in process—Department B	39,200	
Manufacturing overhead—Department B		39,200

$49,000 × 0.80; to apply Department B's overhead.

At January 1, 19x2, Job #108 was finished in Department A but still in process in Department B. Also, Job #109 was still in process in Department A. During January, Jobs #108, #109, and #110 were completely finished. At January 31, Job #111 still required some processing in Department B, and Job #112 required additional processing in Department A, as well as complete processing in Department B. Thus, Jobs #109, #110, and #111 were completed in Department A during this period, and the following entry is necessary:

Transfer from Department A to Department B:

Work in process—Department B	359,400	
Work in process—Department A		359,400

(The amount for this entry is derived in Exhibit 3.16.)

Exhibit 3.16   Rossford Company Amounts To Be Transferred from Departments January 31, 19x2

	From Department A to B			
Item	*109*	*110*	*111*	*Total*
Beginning cost	$33,000	$ 0	$ 0	$ 33,000
Material—19x2	0	10,000	50,000	60,000
Labor—19x2	1,000	80,000	30,000	111,000
Overhead—19x2 (140%)	1,400	112,000	42,000	155,400
Total	$35,400	$202,000	$122,000	$359,400

	From Department B to Finished Goods			
Item	*108*	*109*	*110*	*Total*
Beginning cost				
(including Dept. A)	$74,000	$ 0	$ 0	$ 74,000
January costs:				
Dept. A cost to B[a]	0	35,400	202,000	237,400
Dept. B material	0	0	2,000	2,000
Dept. B labor	2,000	10,000	30,000	42,000
Dept. B overhead (80%)	1,600	8,000	24,000	33,600
Total	$77,600	$53,400	$258,000	$389,000

[a]See first section of this schedule.

During January, Jobs #108, #109, and #110 were completed in Department B and:

Transfer from Department B to Finished Goods:

Finished goods	389,000	
Work in process—Department B		389,000

(The amount for this entry is derived in Exhibit 3.16.)

Although there are other entries that might be made if this were the last month of the period, the preceding entries complete the accounting for January. In problem 3-7 you will be asked to perform additional analyses of this case.

Summary

This chapter has been an examination of the job order system. A job order system is just one of several possible cost systems that might be considered in accounting for production costs. For companies that have their production organized into batches, a job order system is likely to be the most applicable. At this point you should have a better understanding of the flow of data through a cost accounting system. The system examined here has the job card as the central source of the

Exhibit 3.17   Summary of Cost Flow for Rossford Case

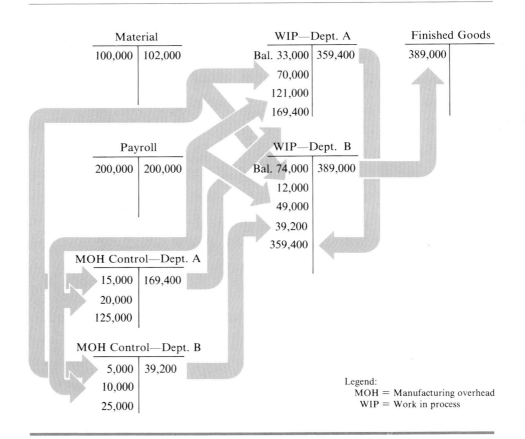

		Material		
100,000	102,000

Material		WIP—Dept. A		Finished Goods	
100,000	102,000	Bal. 33,000	359,400	389,000	
		70,000			
		121,000			
		169,400			

Payroll		WIP—Dept. B	
200,000	200,000	Bal. 74,000	389,000
		12,000	
		49,000	
		39,200	
		359,400	

MOH Control—Dept. A	
15,000	169,400
20,000	
125,000	

MOH Control—Dept. B	
5,000	39,200
10,000	
25,000	

Legend:
MOH = Manufacturing overhead
WIP = Work in process

data. Other systems use a different mechanism to determine the cost flow but they are based on the same principles and use some of the same documents discussed here when accounting for the material and labor costs.

It is also important at this point that you understand the principles of overhead allocation. These will continue to be used in later chapters. It should be clear that cost accounting is more than a *process* of assigning costs. To be useful, cost allocations must withstand some test of economic reasonableness. If they cannot meet these tests, then the costs are merely numbers that cause the system to balance. To provide a useful service, professional accountants must use judgment that is developed through an understanding of the theory and of the practical problems of the firm they are serving. With regard to overhead accounting, this chapter has taken the first step toward developing a theory.

Vocabulary terms introduced in this chapter include:

Job order system
Job card
Stores
Work in process
Finished goods
Direct material
Direct labor
Materials requisition
Time ticket
Payroll sheet
Predetermined overhead rate
Flexible budget
Divisor activity
Theoretical capacity
Practical capacity
Normal activity
Current expected activity
Applied overhead
Over-under applied (absorbed) overhead

SELF-STUDY PROBLEM. The Ozark Company manufactures different models of a product in lots. Therefore, a job cost system is used. Direct-labor cost is considered to be a fair basis for the overhead rate. On January 1, 19x4, it was estimated that during 19x4 $300,000 would be incurred for direct labor and $180,000 for overhead. The following information is presented to you:

Inventories	January 1, 19x4	June 30, 19x4
Direct material	$10,000	$14,000
Work in process	A	B
Finished goods	5,000	3,000

The payroll summary for the period January 1, 19x4 to June 30, 19x4 is:

Employee	Gross	Withholding Tax	Social Security Tax	Union Dues	Net
W.A. Johnson	$10,000	$1,000.00	$ 500.00	$100.00	$ 8,400
H. Donley	12,000	1,000.00	600.00	100.00	10,300
E. Bomeli	2,000	200.00	100.00	100.00	1,600
	$24,000	$2,200.00	$1,200.00	$300.00	$20,300

Johnson worked only on job 205, Donley only on 204, and Bomeli only on 201. The job cost sheets for the jobs worked on this period are as follows:

	No. 201*	No. 204*	No. 205	Total
Material added in 19x3	$ 3,000	0	0	$ 3,000
Labor added in 19x3	5,000	0	0	5,000
Overhead applied in 19x3	2,500	0	0	2,500
	$10,500			
Added in 19x4				
Material	$ 1,000	$7,000	$4,000	$12,000
Labor	C	D	E	F
Overhead	G	H	I	J

*Jobs 201 and 204 were completed by June 30, 19x4.

Required:

1. Based on all the information provided, determine the missing amounts labeled A through J.
2. Prepare entries for the following. If you should find it impossible to prepare any of the requested entries, indicate so and explain why.

   a. The acquisition of material during the first half of 19x4. Assume all material is purchased on account and that indirect material is accounted for in a supplies control account.
   b. The incurrence of direct labor in the first half of 19x4 and the recording of the checks issued to employees. The net direct labor accrued at January 1 was $1,000 and zero at June 30.
   c. The recording of manufacturing overhead items incurred during the first half of 19x4.
   d. The transfer of material, labor (if not transferred in part b), and overhead into production during the first half of 19x4.
   e. The cost of the goods completed during the first half of 19x4.
   f. The sale of products during the first half of 19x4 at 150% of their cost. All sales were made on account.

Solution to Self-Study Problem

1. A = $10,500; the beginning WIP account would have a balance equal to the cost on the job cards of the uncompleted jobs at the beginning of the period.
   B: See below.
   C = $2,000; Bomeli's *gross* wages since he worked only on job 201 and no one else worked on that job.
   D = $12,000; Donley's *gross* wages.
   E = $10,000; Johnson's *gross* wages.
   F = C + D + E = $24,000
   G = $1,200; overhead rate = 60% of direct-labor dollars ($180,000 ÷ 300,000). Thus, 2,000 × 0.60.
   H = $7,200; 0.60 × $12,000
   I = $6,000; 0.60 × $10,000
   J = G + H + I = $14,400
   B = $20,000; Cost of job 205 (the only uncompleted job at the end of the period) = $4,000 + E + I = $4,000 + $10,000 + $6,000.

2. a. Direct material   16,000
       Accounts payable   16,000

       Beginning inventory + purchases =
         used (material added in 19x4)
         + ending inventory
       10,000 + Purchases = 12,000 +
         14,000
       Purchases = 26,000 − 10,000

b. *Incurrence:*   24,000
       Payroll
         Witholding tax payable   2,200
         Social security tax payable   1,200
         Union dues payable   300
         Accrued payroll   20,300
       From the payroll summary.
       Payment
       Accrued payroll   21,300
         Cash   21,300

Have to pay this period's net plus the beginning balance of accrued payroll less the
ending balance of accrued payroll.

c. Impossible—There is no information given about the actual overhead incurred during the period. The information available is for the *applied* overhead.

d. Work in process   50,400
         Direct material (given)   12,000
         Payroll (from payroll)   24,000
         Manufacturing overhead   14,400
         Applied overhead = item J.

e. Finished goods   40,900
         Work in process   40,900
         Job 201
           19x3 costs $10,500
           19x4 costs
             Material (given)   1,000
             Labor (item C)   2,000
             Overhead (item G)   1,200 $14,700
         Job 204
             Material (given) $ 7,000
             Labor (item D)   12,000
             Overhead (item H)   7,200   26,200
           Total $40,900

f. Cost of goods sold   42,900
         Finished goods   42,900

Cost of goods sold = Beginning finished goods + Jobs finished (from part e) −
Ending finished goods
5,000 + 40,900 − 3,000 = 42,900

       Accounts receivable   64,350
         Sales   64,350
       42,900 × 1.50

3-1. Material Accounting in a Job Order System. The Hooper Wire Company uses job order costing to account for its custom orders. Two production departments have been established. The following data are available at the end of January:

Beginning stores inventory	$50,000
Ending stores inventory	$30,000
Materials issued during January:	
To Department I	
Direct	$80,000
Supplies	10,000
To Department II	
Direct	$70,000
Supplies	$20,000

Required:

1. Prepare the journal entry to record the purchase of stores during January.
2. Prepare the journal entry to record the issue of stores to production during January.

3-2. Labor Accounting in a Job Order System. Continue with the Hooper Wire Company of problem 3-1. During January the following labor-related data were recorded:

Beginning accrued payroll	$ 25,000
Ending accrued payroll	$ 28,000
Factory wages earned during January	$200,000
Income tax withholding rate	21%
Social Security tax rate (matched by employer)	8%
Analysis of factory wages	
Department I	
Direct	$ 90,000
Indirect	$ 20,000
Department II	
Direct	$ 80,000
Indirect	$ 10,000

Required:

1. Prepare the entry to record the incurrence of labor for January.
2. Prepare the entry to record the checks issued to employees during January.
3. Prepare the entry to allocate January's payroll costs.

3-3. Overhead Accounting in a Job Order System. Continue with the Hooper Wire Company in problem 3-1. Overhead is applied on a predetermined basis. Following are some budget data:

	Department I *labor intensive*	Department II *mechanized*
Practical capacity for the year		
Machine hours	500,000	600,000
Direct-labor hours	1,000,000	3,000,000

Budgeted fixed = Fixed overhead appl. rate
Divor activity

Normal yearly activity		
Machine hours	400,000	500,000
Direct-labor hours	900,000	250,000
Expected activity for year		
Machine hours	300,000	400,000
Direct-labor hours	700,000	200,000
Budgeted fixed costs at expected activity	$4,000,000	$6,000,000
Budgeted variable costs at expected activity	$3,500,000	$4,000,000

Forcast

Department II is highly mechanized whereas Department I is labor intensive. The actual data for January are:

	Department I	*Department II*
Actual direct-labor hours	60,000	22,000
Actual machine hours	30,000	40,000
Actual fixed overhead	$400,000	$500,000
Actual variable overhead	$160,000	$310,000

Required:

1. Record the actual overhead for January.
2. Record the overhead charged to the jobs during January.
3. Compute the over-underapplied overhead for January.

3-4. Classifying Labor Costs in a Job Order System. The NCR Company uses a job order system. The following payroll costs have been incurred in February for one of its production departments:

Direct-labor hours incurred (including 9,000 overtime hours)	80,000
Regular wage rate per hour	$10
Overtime hourly rate	$15
Idle time hours paid (included in the 80,000)	1,000
Vacation hours paid (not included in the 80,000)	1,200

Required:

Prepare the entry to allocate the payroll account at the end of February.

3-5. Overhead Accounting Over Several Years. The Fanasonic Company's overhead data for the last four years follow:

	19x1	*19x2*	*19x3*	*19x4*
Budgeted fixed overhead	$300,000	$300,000	$300,000	$300,000
Budgeted variable overhead	$200,000	$300,000	$240,000	$260,000
Actual fixed overhead	$301,000	$302,000	$299,000	$298,000

Actual variable overhead	$185,000	$310,000	$245,000	$260,000
Expected activity (direct-labor hours)*	100,000	150,000	120,000	130,000
Actual activity (direct-labor hours)	90,000	160,000	121,000	129,000
Normal activity (direct-labor hours)	125,000	125,000	125,000	125,000

*As estimated at the beginning of the year.

Required:

1. If Fanasonic uses expected activity as its divisor activity for overhead applications, at what rate would it have applied overhead in each of the last four years?
2. Repeat part 1 but assume Fanasonic uses normal activity as its divisor activity.
3. Compare and comment on the results you obtained in parts 1 and 2.

this includes
F/oh + v/oh

3-6. Basic Problem on Job Costing. The following list contains several transactions and items of the Build-to-Order Company. A job order system is in use, and the factory is not departmentalized. The manufacturing overhead rate is $3.00 per direct-labor hour. You are to prepare the journal entries for these items.

1. Materials and supplies costing $100,000 were purchased on account.
2. Wages totaling $100,000 were earned during the month. Assume income taxes averaging 15% and social security taxes averaging 7% are withheld.
3. The accrued payroll at the beginning of the month was $10,000, and at the end of the month it was $5,000. Prepare the entry for the payroll checks issued during the month.
4. Property taxes on the factory plant and equipment of $5,000 were paid during the period.
5. Health insurance costs amounted to $20,000 during the period. Of this amount, 75% was for factory personnel and 25% for other personnel.
6. Depreciation on the factory plant and equipment totaled $60,000 for the month.
7. Materials put into process were as follows:

Job 1	$10,000
Job 2	20,000
Job 3	30,000
Supplies	12,000

8. Payroll analysis reveals:

Job 1	2,500 hours @ $8	$20,000
Job 2	3,750 hours @ $8	30,000
Job 3	5,000 hours @ $8	40,000
Idle time	300 hours @ $8	2,400
Indirect labor	1,900 hours @ $4	7,600

9. Summary entry for the overhead applied during the month.

10. Jobs 1 and 2 were finished during the month.
11. Job 1 was sold for $70,000.

3-7. Analyses of Case in Text. Reconsider the Rossford Company case in the last section of the chapter. The following questions are designed to help you summarize the solution of that case.

Required:

1. Prepare the job cost sheets that will verify the ending balances in the two WIP accounts.
2. Considering that this is the first month of the year, what would you recommend be done with the ending balance in the manufacturing overhead control account?
3. Prepare a statement of cost of goods manufactured for the month in as much detail as permitted by the data.

3-8. Cost Classification. The cost of goods manufactured and sold statement is depicted in the following form:

A. Materials used.
B. Direct labor.
C. Manufacturing overhead.
D. Inventory adjustment to obtain cost of goods manufactured. *add beg WIP / less ending WIP*
E. Inventory adjustment to obtain cost of goods sold. — *add beg fin goods / less end fin goods*

The Toledo Fish Scale Company produces a variety of scales in lots using two production departments: molding and assembly. A job order system with a predetermined overhead rate is used. The following list includes a variety of items. By using the letters associated with the sections of the preceding statement you are to indicate the section in which each of the items would be included. If an item is to be deducted within a section, indicate this by circling the letter. Should an item not be properly included on the cost of goods manufactured and sold statement indicate this with the letter X.

1. Materials inventory at beginning of period.
2. Advertising.
3. Employer social security taxes paid on wages earned by direct laborers in molding department.
4. Finished goods inventory at end of period.
5. Commissions paid to manufacturer's agent in selling the scales.
6. Custodial supplies for the factory.
7. Purchase of highly sensitive springs used in the scales.
8. Freight on the purchase in number 7.
9. Assembly foreman's salary.
10. Freight paid on delivery of scales to customers.
11. Work-in-process inventory at end of period.
12. Idle time paid to workers that are normally direct laborers in the assembly department.
13. Depreciation on equipment in molding department.
14. Depreciation on equipment for the general administrative offices.
15. Dividends paid on stock voluntarily purchased by factory employees.
16. Labor in molding department to rework items failing inspection (normal occurrence).
17. New long-lived equipment purchased for the molding department.

18. I.M. Lazy earns a regular wage of $6 per hour as a direct laborer in the molding department. Last week he worked forty-five hours and earned $285:

40 hours @ $6	$240
5 hours @ $6	30
5 hours @ $3	
(overtime premium)	15
Total	$285

The overtime resulted from general conditions. Classify the $30.
19. Classify the $15 in number 18.
20. Shift differentials paid to direct laborers of the molding department working the night shift.
21. Company logo decals put on each scale.

3-9. Basic Problem. From the following data prepare all journal entries (from acquisition of material, labor, and overhead to the sale of the finished product). Prepare them in logical sequence. Ignore payroll taxes and assume a job order system.

Material purchased	$ 4,000	Material used	$ 3,000
Direct wages paid	24,000	Direct wages earned	
Overhead paid	13,000	during month @ $4	
Factory depreciation	3,000	per hour	20,000
Beginning work in		Budget for overhead at	
process	0	capacity	240,000
Ending work in process	8,000	Direct-labor *hours* at	
		capacity	80,000

All finished jobs were sold at 120% of cost.

3-10. Job Order and Nonmanufacturing Firm. The M & M Heating and Air Conditioning Company installs furnaces and air conditioners in houses and commercial buildings. Each installation is designed according to the physical properties of the building. During the current month M & M worked on two jobs:

	John Doe Residence	*Button's Night Club*
Material and equipment	$2,000	$30,000
Labor	500	10,000

Overhead has been charged at a predetermined rate of 10% of material and equipment used on the job.
   Events of the month include the following:

1. Purchased material and equipment for $40,000.
2. Payroll for labor was $12,000. M & M did not have enough jobs to keep installers busy during the month.

3. Other costs for the period were:

Truck Cost	$1,500
Shop cost	1,200
Showroom cost	800
Installation inspection cost	1,000
Advertising	1,300

Required:

1. Prepare the journal entries for the month.
2. What is the overapplied or underapplied overhead for the month?

3-11. Computation and Allocation of Payroll. The Carlton Manufacturing Company uses a job cost system. The nature of the work in Department 2 is such that a group bonus plan is used to determine the employee's wages. There are three people employed in Department 2. In addition to the regular rate per hour, the employees receive a bonus if their production exceeds a standard amount. The amount of the bonus is computed by first determining the percentage by which the group's weekly production exceeds the standard production. One-half of this percentage is then applied to a wage of $4.00 to determine an hourly bonus rate. Each person in the group is paid, as a bonus, this rate applied to their total hours worked during the week. The standard rate of production before a bonus can be earned is 200 pieces per man-hour. Time and a half is paid for time in excess of 40 hours a week. Production for the week was 28,800 pieces. Employee's records reveal:

Employee	Hours Worked	Regular Rate
A	40	$6.00
B	36	6.00
C	44	5.00

Required:

1. Compute the rate of the bonus for the week.
2. Compute the gross pay for A, B, and C for the week.
3. Prepare all entries relating to the payroll for the week. Assume that income taxes withheld average 10% and that the social security rate is 7% for both employee and employer.

3-12. Reconstructing Accounts. Several accounts, including some data, follow. Note that some beginning and ending balances have been provided. When other items are shown in the accounts, the account title given is the other account that was involved in the entry. For example, the 90,000 debit to Accounts Payable—Stores was also credited to Cash.

Stores (Direct and Indirect)

Bal., 1/1	13,000	
Bal., 1/31	20,000	

Accounts Payable—Store

Cash	90,000	Bal., 1/1	4,000
		Bal., 1/31	1,000

Accrued Payroll

Cash	110,000	Bal., 1/1	10,000
		Bal., 1/31	20,000

Work in Process

Bal., 1/1	15,000		
Bal., 1/31	10,000		

Manufacturing Overhead

Cash	100,000	Applied	143,000
Accum. Depr.	20,000		

Finished Goods

Bal., 1/1	25,000		
Bal., 1/31	30,000		

Cost of Goods Sold

343,000		

Payroll (Direct and Indirect)

Withholdings from payroll checks average 20% of gross wages. Overhead is applied at 110% of direct-labor cost.

Required:

Copy these accounts and amounts onto your own work sheet. Then reconstruct the transactions that must have occurred during the period and record them into your accounts. Be sure to cross-reference your amounts.

3-13. Construction of Overhead Rate. The Schmidt Company produces several products on a job order basis. During the last five years the following facts about its overhead have been collected:

Year	Direct-Labor Hours	Total Supplies	Total Indirect Salaries	Total Other Overhead
19x3	30,000	$6,000	$10,000	$15,700
19x4	26,000	5,200	10,000	14,700
19x5	24,000	4,800	10,000	14,200
19x6	20,000	4,000	10,000	13,200
19x7	30,000	6,000	10,000	15,700

During the five-year period, which is considered by the company to be its business cycle, the same basic facilities were available. Assume that price changes during the five years were so insignificant as not to affect the cost relationships. The company operates two shifts of 10 employees each. Each employee works 40 hours per week and is granted a two-week vacation each year. Paid holidays total 10. Rest periods total 3 hours per week per employee. During 19x8 it is anticipated that there will be a strike against the company that probably will last for two weeks. A total of 400 hours will be spent by the 20 employees in making normal and necessary repairs.

Required

1. Compute the overhead rate using practical capacity. Show fixed and variable components.
2. Compute the overhead rate using normal activity. Show fixed and variable components.

3-14. Construction of Overhead Rate When There Is Inflation. The McGraw Company produces tugboats in a variety of sizes. For 19x5 it is trying to establish its predetermined overhead rate. The rate will be established by projecting from historical data that is known to be influenced by inflation. It is felt that, production-wise, the last four years are representative of the expected future demand. The following data are available:

	Machine Hours	Variable Overhead	Fixed Overhead
19x1	10,000	$18,182	$36,281
19x2	15,000	30,000	38,095
19x3	12,000	26,400	40,000
19x4	17,000	41,140	42,000

The items in both the variable and fixed overhead categories are essentially well-behaved except for inflation, which has been a relatively constant rate. There is no reason to expect next year's inflation rate to be any different than experienced in the past. Because of the presence of depreciation in the fixed overhead, it is expected that a different rate will be found there than for variable overhead.

Required:

Using the expected 19x5 prices, determine the fixed and the variable overhead rate for the McGraw Company. Assume that normal activity is used as the capacity concept.

3-15. Determining Appropriate Activity Measure and Overhead Rate. The Luzinski Company produces long-playing records and has several different recording companies as clients. Since each order is separately identifiable, a job order accounting system is in use. Two departments are utilized, and the following overhead budget data at normal activity are available for the *year* 19x1 as well as the actual overhead cost for January 19x1:

	Overhead Budget for 19x1 at Normal Activity	January Actual Overhead
Department A		
Fixed	$240,000	$22,000
Variable	200,000	21,000
Department B		
Fixed	$360,000	$29,000
Variable	300,000	17,000

During January two jobs were in production, #419 and #420. The following is a summary of some of the data from their respective job cost sheets.

	Job #419		Job #420	
	Department A	Department B	Department A	Department B
Direct labor	$36,000	$5,000	$12,000	$14,000
Direct-labor hours	8,000	1,000	2,000	3,000
Machine hours	1,600	8,000	1,000	4,000

The estimates of the departmental direct labor dollars, direct-labor hours, and machine hours at normal activity are also provided in the following table.

	Department A Volume at Normal	Department B Volume at Normal
Direct-labor dollars	$500,000	$240,000
Direct-labor hours	100,000	50,000
Machine hours	30,000	200,000

The manager of Department A feels that his department's overhead is most likely to be caused by direct-labor hours. The manager of Department B feels her department's overhead is more closely related to machine hours.

Required:

1. Assuming a good cost accounting system (one that assigns a relatively constant cost to production), what is the overhead cost for job #419?
2. During January the company recieved an invitation from a regular customer to bid on a job that, if won, would be produced in February. The job was estimated to require $50,000 of material and the following:

	Department A	Department B
Direct-labor dollars	$25,000	$11,000
Direct-labor hours	5,000	2,000
Machine hours	1,000	7,000

How much overhead would you include in the bid?

3. In addition to the items just mentioned in part 2, what other costs should be considered in making the bid? Think about general items, not about specific costs a record company might incur.

3-16. Understand Overhead Application. The Bowa Company applies overhead to its jobs on the basis of a predetermined overhead rate. The rate is established as the estimated manufacturing overhead at normal activity divided by the direct-labor hours at normal activity.

During 19x5, a total manufacturing overhead of $335,000 was incurred. As a result of applying overhead at a rate of $7.00 per direct-labor hour, the ending balance in the Manufacturing Overhead Control account was $55,000 (debit). The activity in 19x5 was 80% of the normal activity.

Required:

1. How many direct-labor hours were worked during 19x5?
2. How much overhead was budgeted at normal activity?
3. If the overhead budgeted for the actual direct-labor hours incurred during 19x5 was $330,000, then how much of the $7.00 rate is due to variable costs?
4. What would you do with the $55,000 balance in manufacturing overhead control at the end of the year?

3-17. Analyzing a Job Cost System Where There Are Multiple Departments. The Katt Company manufactures castings according to customer specification. Two responsibility centers are used: molding and grinding. After work is completed in the molding department the job is transferred to the grinding center for completion.

Factory overhead in each department is charged to the jobs on the basis of the direct-labor dollars incurred on the job. During February of the current year the underapplied factory overhead in the molding department totaled $5,000. The factory overhead was $4,000 over-applied in the grinding department. Separate overhead accounts are maintained for each department.

Four jobs were worked on during February (#331, 332, 333, and 334). Jobs #331, 332, and 333 were finished, and #334 is still in molding at the end of February. The following data are from the job cards:

	#331 Molding	#331 Grinding	#332 Molding	#332 Grinding	#333 Molding	#333 Grinding	#334 Molding	#334 Grinding
January:								
Material	$10,000	$ 500	$5,000	0	0	0	0	0
Labor	20,000	2,000	8,000	0	0	0	0	0
Overhead	10,000	4,000	4,000	0	0	0	0	0
February								
Material	0	1,500	1,000	$4,000	$20,000	$10,000	$ 5,000	0
Labor	0	3,000	1,000	8,000	10,000	20,000	20,000	0
Overhead	0	A	B	C	D	E	F	0

Both direct and indirect materials are accounted for in the stores' control account. The February 1 balance of stores was $12,000 and the February 28 balance is $15,000. During February indirect material amounting to $400 was issued to the molding department and $600 to grinding.

Withholding and social security taxes amount to 20% of the employees' wages. During February $10,000 of wages were classified as indirect, and these were equally distributed between the two departments.

Required:

1. Determine the overhead amounts that are missing in the schedule and labeled A through F.
2. Prepare the entry for the purchase of stores during February.
3. Assume that a payroll account is used to record all labor as it is incurred. (See part 5 for the entry to allocate the payroll account.) Prepare the entry to record the incurrence of the February payroll.
4. Prepare the entry to record the usage of all materials and supplies during February.
5. Prepare the entry to allocate the payroll account.
6. Record any other actual overhead incurred during February that was not recorded in parts 4 and 5.
7. Prepare the entry to apply the overhead for February.
8. Prepare the entry to record the transfer of jobs from the molding to the grinding department during February.
9. Prepare the entry to record the cost of jobs delivered during February.

3-18. Alternative to 3-17. The Eagle-Raider Company processes a variety of customer orders utilizing two production departments. The following data pertain to February of 19x1, the second month of its fiscal year. All orders require processing in each department and it must be done in sequence: Department 1, then Department 2.

The books are closed annually; thus, the manufacturing overhead accounts have beginning balances representing the overapplied or underapplied overhead in January. Overhead is applied on the basis of direct-labor dollars in both departments.

The stores' account is used for all direct materials and factory supplies. Likewise, the payroll account is a temporary collection account for all factory wages, direct and indirect.

Following are some relevant data:

A. Balances at February 1, 19x1:

Stores	$ 8,000	Finished goods	$30,000
WIP—Dept. 1	20,000	MOH—Dept. 1 (debit)	1,000
WIP—Dept. 2	18,000	MOH—Dept. 2 (credit)	500

B. Balances at February 28, 19x1:

Stores	$10,000	Finished goods	$24,000
WIP—Dept. 1	15,000	MOH—Dept. 1 (debit)	2,000
WIP—Dept. 2	25,000	MOH—Dept. 2 (debit)	1,500

C. Analysis of ending WIP inventory in Department 2:

means they should appear on debit side

$1 per hour

	Material	*Labor*	*Overhead*	*Total*
Added in Dept. 1	$4,000	$3,000	$ 3,000	$10,000
Added in Dept. 2	3,000	4,000	8,000	15,000
Total	$7,000	$7,000	$11,000	$25,000

2/ per hour of

D. The total direct labor in February was $200,000. Analysis reveals 60% was incurred in Department 1 and 40% in Department 2.
E. Direct materials issued to Department 1 totaled $50,000 during February.
F. Factory supplies issued during February totaled $15,000: $10,000 to Department 1 and $5,000 to Department 2.
G. Indirect labor amounted to $8,000 in Department 1 and $7,000 in Department 2.
H. The cost of goods sold amounted to $580,000 in February.

Required:

1. Set up T-accounts for stores, payroll, manufacturing overhead—Dept. 1, manufacturing overhead—Dept. 2, WIP—Dept. 1, WIP—Dept. 2, finished goods, and cost of goods sold. Enter any of the data in items A–H that are appropriate.
2. Reconstruct the remaining entries for February.

3-19. Case Involving Problems with Bidding on Jobs. The Lonborg Company is a manufacturer of a variety of specialty products that are produced to customer specification. The normal procedure in this industry is for potential suppliers to be invited to submit a competitive bid on each job. For the most part, Lonborg's business is obtained through this bidding mechanism. Recently, the competition has increased, and Lonborg has had difficulty in winning enough bids to keep production running near capacity. They cannot afford many more months like the last one when one of their production departments was operating at approximately 10% of capacity.

Because Lonborg's typical job can require different combinations of extremely diverse work, the company has been organized into two different departments, A and B. The bidding activity for the last month is summarized in the table:

Job #	Hours in Department A	Hours in Department B	Direct-Labor Hours Estimated	Overhead in Bid	Won or Lost
1	8,000	2,000	10,000	$27,500	Lost (6th)
2	2,000	8,000	10,000	27,500	Won
3	10,000	0	10,000	27,500	Lost (3rd)
4	0	10,000	10,000	27,500	Won
5	5,000	5,000	10,000	27,500	Lost (2nd)

The numbers in the parentheses of the last column indicate the relationship that Lonborg was to the winner of the job.

As can be seen, Department A was only scheduled for 2,000 hours of work last month; it has a monthly capacity of 20,000 hours. Also, Department B was scheduled for 18,000 hours of work, which was near to its capacity of 20,000 hours per month. Management is perplexed because this type of utilization has been experienced for the past several months: Department A virtually idle and Department B close to capacity.

When you were asked to advise on the situation you discovered that a predetermined overhead rate was being used, based on practical capacity. Its derivation is as follows:

Budget at Yearly Practical Capacity

Factory fixed costs	$ 360,000
Factory variable costs	960,000
Total	$1,320,000
Total direct-labor hours at practical capacity	480,000
Overhead Rate	$2.75

Additional analysis reveals that one-third of the company's fixed costs, if allocated using fair schemes, would be allocated to Department A and, at capacity, Department A would incur 25% of the total variable costs.

Required:

Discuss a probable cause of Lonborg's problem. If necessary, devise an alternative bidding scheme and recompute the overhead that you would have included in the bid for the five jobs mentioned.

3-20. Billing Rates in Hospital. It has been the practice of General Hospital to bill all of its patients at $100 per day plus drugs. This rate was set to recover the hospital's cost based on normal operations.

Following are the costs at normal operating levels:

Administrative salaries	$ 500,000
Physicians	3,000,000
Nursing staff	4,000,000
Supplies	1,500,000
Patient meals	2,000,000
Other overhead	1,000,000

General measures its activity using patient-days. At normal levels the patient-days are as follows:

Surgical	70,000
Maternity	40,000
Psychiatric	10,000

An analysis of personnel time allocation reveals the following:

	Surgical	*Maternity*	*Psychiatric*
Physicians	80%	10%	10%
Nurses	40	40	20

Required:

1. Show how the $100 per day billing rate was derived.
2. A new controller argues that separate billing rates should be used for surgical, maternity, and psychiatric. Assume:

a. Administrative salaries should be allocated to the three areas on the basis of a simple average of the percentage of time physicians spend in the department plus the percentage of time spent by nurses.
b. Supplies are strongly related to nurses' time.
c. Other overhead is allocated on the basis of a simple average of the percentage of time nurses spend in the department plus the percentage of patient days incurred in the department.
d. Compute the three billing rates.

3. Comment on the relative merits of the two ways of computing billing rates.

3-21. Selecting a Concept of Capacity. The McBride Company is facing a conceptual problem concerning its bidding strategy on the custom jobs that its potential customers submit for bid. The overhead cost behavior has been identified as a fixed component of $400,000 monthly plus variable costs at $3.00 per direct-labor hour. A problem has developed within the management team as to what rate to use for fixed costs in constructing a bid.

Ms. Pat Practical suggests a $4.00 per hour base because the practical capacity has been computed at 100,000 direct-labor hours. She reminds the other managers of the decision four years ago to expand capacity at a level that was above the increased needs at that time. That is, capacity at that time was sufficient to support 60,000 direct-labor hours per month. Orders requiring 80,000 direct-labor hours could have been accepted if there was capacity. Since it was felt that demand was going to continue to increase, the decision was made to increase capacity by 40,000 direct-labor hours. Certain efficiencies of construction were obtained by building the capacity all at once rather than in stages.

Mr. Norm Normal is advocating a $5.00 per direct-labor hour rate based on the normal activity of the two years immediately preceding last year (80,000 direct-labor hours). He reminds the group that this concept was used the last three years and he does not see any reason to change.

Ms. Tricia Peckta reminds all that for some reason volume dropped off last year and her reading of the market's view of the McBride Company is that volume will continue to be down during the next year. She advocates a rate of $8.00 per direct-labor hour based on expected activity of 50,000 direct-labor hours. "After all," she says, "fixed costs must be recovered before there is a profit."

Required:

Discuss the pros and cons of each argument. What position would you advocate? Why?

3-22. Inflation and Job Order Costing. The Flate Company manufactures a variety of products using optimal run sizes. Thus a job order system is used. Currently, the controller's department is trying to determine the manufacturing overhead rate that will be used during 19x3. Following is a summary of the recorded data for 19x1 and 19x2.

	19x1	19x2
Total factory overhead	$300,000	$440,000
Production		
Product A (units)	5,000	4,000
Product B (units)	1,000	7,000
Product C (units)	7,000	1,000
Total	13,000	12,000
Direct-labor hours	20,000	30,000
Machine hours	7,000	9,500

The average activity for 19x1 and 19x2 represents Flate's normal activity. At practical capacity the company can generate 40,000 direct-labor hours and 13,000 machine hours. During 19x3 the expectation is that 28,000 direct-labor hours and 9,000 machine hours will be incurred.

Required:

1. Based on the above data, determine the overhead budget formula to be used for estimating costs during 19x3. Justify all assumptions you make.
2. Based on the estimating equation you determined in part 1, determine the overhead rates to be used in 19x3. Show separate fixed and variable overhead rates. Justify all assumptions.
3. What is the expected total overhead to be incurred in 19x3?
4. Now the company economist informs you that the costs in 19x2 were 10% higher than in 19x1. (For simplicity, assume *all* cost items were subject to the *same* inflation rate.) Further, it is felt that the costs in 19x3 will be 10% higher than in 19x2. Recompute the budget formula to be used in 19x3.
5. Based on the new information in part 4, recompute the fixed and variable overhead rates to be used in 19x3.

3-23. Applying Job Order Princples to a Nonmanufacturing Situation. The Philadelphia Consulting Group is a firm of management consultants. The firm's personnel consists of seniors, managers, and partners as follows:

	Number	Average Compensation	Billable Hours per Year*
Seniors	25	$12,000	1,800
Managers	18	18,000	1,500
Partners	10	60,000	1,000

*Billable hours are hours available to the clients. In determining this, adjustments are made for general research time, administrative duties, client relationship activities, etc. Each member of the firm would be working a normal 2,000 hours per year (8 hours × 5 days × 50 weeks).

Other costs that are incurred by the firm consist of office facility cost, secretarial costs, report generation, travel, and entertainment. These costs are estimated at $820,000 per year. It has been decided to bill the other costs to the client using an hourly rate. After personnel and other costs have been determined for a given engagement, the in-charge partner will add on a fair profit.

Required:

1. Develop the hourly billing rates for the firm (that is, the total rate at which each type of personnel will be billed). These rates should not include profit.
2. Assume that we are bidding on a job from a potential client that has the following time estimates:

	Employee-Days
Seniors	20
Managers	10
Partners	5

How much cost would be included in the bid?

3. Comment on the potential weaknesses of the overhead allocation scheme developed in part 1.

3-24. Error Correction in a Job Order System. The Soft Sofa Company is a furniture manufacturer. Because of the different styles that they produce they use a job order accounting system. During an audit the items in the following list were discovered and need to be considered as to their disposition. You are to indicate any adjustments or corrections that are necessary in the general accounts. If there is no entry required to the general records, indicate this by writing "No Entry." Each of the items should be regarded as independent of the others, and it should be assumed in each case that any other pertinent recordings have been made correctly based on the source document that was processed, unless it is stated otherwise. The books are not yet closed.

The company's predetermined overhead rate is $2.00 per direct-labor hour. Perpetual inventory systems are in use.

1. It is discovered that $1,000 of direct materials have been charged to the wrong job cost card. Both jobs have been completed but not yet sold.
2. It is discovered that an error was made in adding the direct-labor hours on the job cost sheet of a certain job that has now been completed and sold. The dollar amount of direct labor was added correctly, but the hours were overstated by 100.
3. The cost of job #103 in the amount of $3,200 was transposed as $2,300 when preparing the job's finished record, which is used for the entry reflecting the cost of finished units. Job #103 has been sold.
4. The accounts payable clerk misread an invoice for 100 units of material X. It was entered in the accounts payable register as $2,020 instead of $2,200. The 100 units were subsequently used on job #321, which has been finished but not sold.
5. Material requisition #121, which was for material on job #425, was misread and entered in the materials requisition summary as $250 instead of the correct amount of $520. Job #425 is finished but not sold. The material requisition summary is used to prepare the summary entry for the cost of materials used.
6. A time ticket, which is used to distribute daily wages to the various tasks performed, was incorrectly prepared for Helen Restalot. The amount of 20 hours (at $6.00) was erroneously indicated as direct labor for job #325. Actually it was indirect labor. Job #325 is still in process. The time ticket has been completely processed.
7. Factory supplies in the amount of $400 have not yet been expensed although they have been used on job #325 according to the foreman. Factory supplies are accounted for in store's control.

CHAPTER 4   **Process Cost Accounting**

Chapter Overview

In Chapter 3 we examined the job cost system, which is appropriate for situations where production is grouped into identifiable jobs. When products are produced continuously, a job system is impractical. For example, if a given production line is devoted to the assembly of one type of automobile day-in and day-out, there is no natural set of units that can be treated as a job. If production is continuous, the accounting system will need to use the individual produced unit as the cost objective rather than a job. That is, the costs of a given time period are accumulated and then assigned to the units that were produced in that period. In that sense, then, the unit becomes the cost objective. A **process cost system** accumulates production costs according to responsibility centers rather than batches and then assigns the cost of each center to the products processed by that center. In this chapter there is an examination of a system that, primarily, assigns costs based on an *average actual* rate. Chapter 5 will examine the system known as standard costing, where costs are assigned on a predetermined basis rather than on an average actual basis.

This chapter begins with a general overview of the process cost system. Then the concept of *equivalent production* is considered. After exploring the equivalent unit concept, an accounting format for this system is developed: the process cost report. This is followed by some illustrative cases and an evaluation of the system.

Overview of Process Cost System

Before examining the details, let us review the basic flow of costs for a process cost system and look at the document flow differences between this system and the job order system. It must be emphasized that process costing is a system designed primarily for cost determination. Because of the nature of the production process for which this system is intended (continuous production versus custom-ordered in a job order system), the data are less likely to be used for pricing decisions. This is not to say that process costing data are always irrelevant for decision making and control. It is just that the *main* thrust of these systems is cost determination. The system should be viewed from this perspective and not as a system that is intended to provide data for *all* possible uses.

At this point you should review the flowchart in Exhibit 4.1, which is a reproduction of the one in Exhibit 2.10. The flowchart found there is representative of

Exhibit 4.1   **Cost Flow for Typical Manufacturer That Might Use Process Costing**

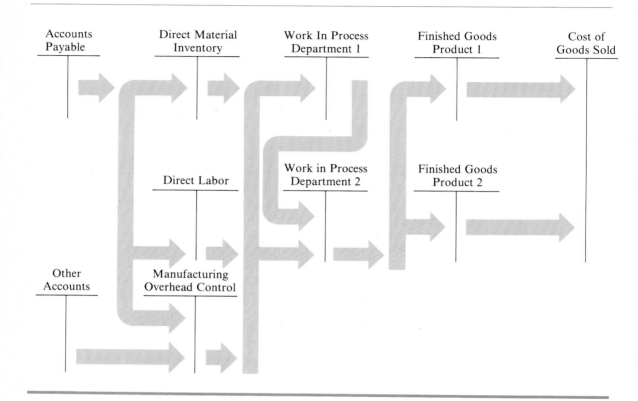

a process cost system where there are two responsibility centers within the production area. Keeping Exhibit 4.1 in mind will help orient you as the accounting details are discussed.

Process costing, like job order, is concerned with tracing the three elements of cost (material, labor, and overhead) to the production. As will be seen, it accomplishes this goal using different procedures. Consider some of the differences. First, note that there are some differences between process costing and job order costing with respect to the content and flow of supporting documents. These are summarized in Exhibit 4.2. There are no job cost cards since production in these cases cannot be identified by "job." In accounting for material, the flow into various departments is supported by material requisitions, but only the requesting department will be indicated on the requisition since there are no identifiable jobs. Labor analysis is approximately the same as with a job order system except that, in most cases, time tickets are not maintained. In continuous production situations, employees will probably be assigned to a specific department (responsibility center) where all of their work will be done. Thus, there would be no reason to ask

---

Exhibit 4.2   Differences between Process Costing and Job Order Costing

---

	Job Order	*Process Costing*
Purpose	For production done in batches or for custom orders	For continuous production situations
Focus of the accounting process	Job cost card	Department account and process cost reports
Source documents		
Material acquisition	Invoice	Invoice
Material use	Material requisition	Material requisition
Labor incurrence	In-out card	In-out card
Labor allocation	Time ticket	Employee assignment
Overhead incurrence	Invoices	Invoices
Overhead allocation	Rate	Actual for period averaged over production of period unless "normal" system is used, then use a predetermined rate

---

for a time analysis unless there is a need to divide the wages of an individual employee into direct and indirect portions.

The discussion in this chapter assumes that the total actual costs are prorated over the production of the period. In the process of determining total costs for a specific department it will be found that some costs have been incurred for the benefit of several departments. For example, the depreciation of the manufacturing plant jointly benefits all production departments but is not directly traceable to any of them. Thus, it will be necessary to develop a means of prorating the depreciation, and other such costs, to the departments in a manner that approximates the benefit received. The allocation of common costs among the benefited departments is common to all cost accounting systems and deserves separate attention. Chapter 9 is devoted to this and related issues. An allocation of costs among departments is independent of the issue considered here which is, given the department's costs, how to assign them to the products manufactured by the department.

The Need for an Equivalent Unit

If all the effort and costs in a given department were devoted to a single product *and if* there were no partially completed units at the beginning or end of the period, then the assignment of the department's cost would be simple. Frequently, however, there are partially completed inventories and/or multiple products.

PARTIALLY COMPLETED UNITS. When units are worked on during the accounting period but are unfinished at the reporting date, the manufacturing cost per unit cannot be computed by using the total units as a divisor. To do so would say that each unit received the same benefit during the period regardless of its state of completion.

When there are some units that have only been partially completed during the period, it is necessary to measure the work effort of these units in a way that is comparable to the effort required for a completely finished unit. The **equivalent unit** is such a concept and represents the fractional part of a whole unit that would result from the total effort expended to date on the partially finished unit. For example, if one unit were 75% completed this period, the equivalent work amounts to 0.75 whole units. If 200 units are all 75% completed this period, the work effort expended is equivalent to 150 whole units (200 × 0.75).

To further illustrate, assume that material, labor, and overhead are all continuously incurred throughout the processing in Department A and that the department's total cost for January was $18,400. During January, 10,000 potential units of product were started in Department A. However, only 8,000 were completed and the remaining 2,000 units were 60% complete at January 31. It is common to refer to the above sets of units as layers. That is, all units that are at the same stage of completion are grouped together and referred to as a layer. The equivalent production is arrived at by taking the number of units in the layer multiplied by the percentage completion:

Units finished 8,000 × 1.0	8,000
Ending inventory 2,000 × 0.6	1,200
Equivalent production	9,200

Since the total cost of the department was $18,400, the cost per equivalent unit is $2.00 ($18,400 ÷ 9,200). Now, each *equivalent unit* of work would be assigned a cost of $2.00. Thus:

Cost of finished units 8,000 × $2.00	$16,000
Cost of ending inventory 1,200 × $2.00	2,400
Total	$18,400

PROBLEMS CAUSED BY DIFFERENT COST BEHAVIORS. The discussion so far assumed all costs are incurred as a continuous stream throughout the production process. In reality, costs are incurred in a variety of patterns. For example, costs might be incurred at specific points in the process, or continuously throughout some portion of the production interval rather than throughout the entire interval. Materials may be put in at the very beginning of the process, or at the very end (packing cases), or at other points. If the production process is largely mechanical, labor might be incurred, for example, only during the first and last 10% of the process. As you can see, there is a possibility for the existence of a large number of different cost behaviors.

If each unit is to be assigned its prorated share of each cost, the different cost behaviors must be accounted for separately. This means that all costs that occur according to the same pattern or behavior should be pooled (collected) together and allocated over the *equivalent units* computed for that pool (a group of collected costs). To illustrate assume that:

1. Material *X* is added at the beginning of the process.
2. Material *Y* is added when production is 75% complete.
3. Labor and overhead costs are added continuously throughout production. From this point on, these two costs will be referred to as conversion costs. If overhead is correlated with labor, then the two costs can be collected into a single pool. These combined costs are called **conversion costs** because they represent expenditures needed to *convert* materials into a finished product.

Further, assume there was no beginning work-in-process inventory, that 8,000 units were finished and 2,000 units were 60% completed at the end of the month. Since there are three cost behavior patterns, three equivalent production figures must be computed:

Equivalent Units for Assigning

	Material X Cost	Material Y Cost	Conversion Costs
Finished	8,000	8,000	8,000
Ending inventory	2,000[a]	0[b]	1,200[c]
Equivalent units	10,000	8,000	9,200

[a] All material *X* has been added; $2,000 \times 100\%$.

[b] No material *Y* will be added until the production is 75% complete; $2,000 \times 0\%$.

[c] Equivalent units $= 2,000 \times 60\%$.

The costs per equivalent unit would then be the total cost in each category divided by the respective equivalent units.

ACCOUNTING FOR COST TRANSFERRED FROM PRIOR DEPART-MENT. Normally the cost of producing a product must be accounted for as it passes through a sequence of production departments. Thus, we need to examine how, in process costing, the product costs of one department will be accounted for in the subsequent departments of the sequence.

The collective costs transferred from Department A can be treated as if they were raw materials purchased by Department B and *added at the beginning of processing* in B. Department B views this as a raw material but not one that came directly from the store's inventory. For example, assume that Department A produces motors that are used in the production of hair dryers. Department B assembles the hair dryers using one motor from Department A for each unit. During the current period Department A incurred $15,000 material cost, $25,000 labor cost, and $10,000 overhead to produce 30,000 motors. All of these motors were transferred to Department B. Department B needs the motors at the beginning of its production process. In effect, Department B has used 30,000 motors that can be viewed as being "purchased" from Department A at a "price" of $50,000. The $50,000 is the sum of the material, labor, and overhead costs assigned by Department A's accounting system to the motors transferred to Department B.

Once the motors leave Department A there normally is no reason to maintain their costs in the separate pools (material, labor, and overhead) that were needed in making A's cost assignment. As processing is completed in Department B, B's costs are added to those of A. Then the collective costs representing the processing in *both* A and B are merged into one figure for purposes of transfer to Department C. The mechanics will be illustrated via the case problem discussed later in this chapter. There is one important thing to remember, however. The accumulated costs incurred in a previous department can be treated by the subsequent department as if the units had been purchased from an outside supplier at a price equal to the costs transferred.

WEIGHTED AVERAGE EQUIVALENT UNIT METHOD. You will note that the discussion and illustrations of the previous subsections never considered the possibility of a work-in-process inventory at the beginning of the accounting period. In this and the next section two alternative ways of assigning costs will be considered for the more realistic situation where there is a beginning work-in-process inventory. If a beginning work-in-process inventory exists, then there must have been some costs assigned to it in the *previous accounting period*. These costs can either (1) remain attached to the specific units in the beginning inventory or (2) be averaged with the current costs in determining the unit cost to be used this period. The first concept is used in the FIFO cost method and the second in the weighted average method.

Theoretically, we cannot demonstrate that one of these methods is superior to the other. Both methods will be discussed, but no preference is given.

If the weighted average concept is used, you will need to know the amount from *each* cost behavior pool (material or conversion cost, for example) that was assigned *last period* to the beginning inventory. To reflect the different cost behaviors properly, you need to compute a weighted average cost for each pool. This average is the sum of the current *and* the beginning inventory cost identified with the pool divided by some appropriate measure of activity.

To illustrate, assume the following information about the KRH Company. KRH's only product is a decorative wooden candle holder. In Department A, two separate pieces of wood are cut, bored, sanded, and attached together. After this is done the holders are sent to Department B, where they are stained, varnished, and packed into protective shipping cartons. Cost and inventory data in Department A for January 19x1 are:

WIP—Department A

Bal. 1/1/x1 (1,000 units)	3,645[a]	To Department B	10,000 units[b]
Material			
(for 11,000 units)	22,000		
Conversion costs	41,000		
	66,645		

[a]Beginning inventory contained 1,000 potential units. Material was 100% complete at January 1 and conversion was 25% complete. Last month (December), $2,120 of material costs was assigned and $1,525 of conversion costs for a total of $3,645.

[b]There are 2,000 units in Department A's ending inventory. These units are 100% complete as to material and 25% as to conversion costs.

Since the various costs of the beginning inventory (material and conversion costs) will be added to the current material and conversion costs, all 10,000 *finished* units can receive a full share of the combined costs. That is, the weighted average method removes the costs from the beginning inventory and reallocates it through the average cost per unit. The beginning inventory is finished at the end of the period and is treated the same as all other finished production in the sharing of these total costs. For the weighted average method, the equivalent unit (EU) computation is:

$$EU = \text{Units finished} + \text{Equivalent units in ending inventory} \qquad \text{(4-1)}$$

Thus:

	Materials	Conversion Costs
Units finished	10,000	10,000
Ending inventory (100% for material and 25% for conversion costs)	2,000	500
Equivalent units	12,000	10,500

Combining the costs from the beginning inventory with the current costs and dividing by the equivalent production yields the average unit costs:

$$\text{Material/unit} = \frac{\$2,120 + \$22,000}{12,000} = \$2.01$$

$$\text{Conversion cost/unit} = \frac{\$1,525 + \$41,000}{10,500} = \$4.05$$

January's total cost per unit = $2.01 + $4.05 = $6.06

When prorating the current period's costs between the units finished and the ending work in process inventory, the unit costs derived above will be used as follows:

Cost of units finished 10,000($2.01 + $4.05)		$60,600
Cost of ending inventory		
Material 2,000 × $2.01	$4,020	
Conversion costs 500 × $4.05	2,025	6,045
		$66,645

As you can see, the total cost assigned is equal to the total cost recorded in the WIP account.

MODIFIED FIFO. With the FIFO inventory method, costs once assigned to a layer remain attached until it is sold. In a production situation, the beginning WIP inventory in each department is treated as one layer and all other items processed by the department during the period as a second layer. The costs assigned to the beginning WIP during the last period would remain attached to those units rather than being combined with the current period's costs. This means that *last period's* work must be excluded in computing the equivalent production that will be used to allocate the cost of the current period.

Before discussing a method of computing the equivalent production for the FIFO method, we need to define a new term, the **units started and finished.** Started and finished units are those placed into production by a given department during the current period and transferred out before the end of the same period. Since all work of the department has been performed on these units during the current period, they each would receive a full share of the department's current costs. In the previous example, 11,000 units were started and all but 2,000 were finished. Thus, 9,000 units were started and finished. Another way of looking at it is to note that 10,000 units were finished, but 1,000 of these units were started in the previous period. Again, 9,000 were started and finished. Units started and finished can be computed by *either* of the following equations (the results are the same):

Started and finished = Units started   (4-2a)
                  − Units in ending inventory

Started and finished = Units finished   (4-2b)
                  − Units in beginning inventory

Since the beginning work-in-process inventory was finished during the period, it also should be allocated some of the current period's costs. Likewise, the ending work-in-process should be assigned a share. Adding the three layers together, the equation for total equivalent units (EU) for the FIFO method is:

EU = EU *to complete* beginning WIP + Units started and finished   (4-3)
    + EU in ending WIP

The equivalent units of work done on the beginning WIP during the current period is given by:

EU *to complete* beginning WIP $= (1 - p)U$ (4-4)

where

$p =$ percentage of completion of the work in process inventory at the
beginning of the period, and
$U =$ units in beginning WIP.

Equation (4-4) is explained as follows. First, it is conventional to state the percentage completion of an inventory *at the time* of the inventory. Thus, if a beginning inventory is said to be 40% complete, this means it was 40% complete at the beginning of the period. The remaining 60% would have to be done in the current period. The percentage of the total work effort done last period on the beginning inventory is denoted as p in equation (4-4). Therefore, the remaining work $(1-p)$ must be done this period. Multiplying the units, U, by the percentage of work done this period gives the equivalent units of work performed on the beginning inventory this period. To illustrate, suppose 12,000 units are in the beginning inventory, 40% complete with respect to labor. Then for labor the equivalent units are:

EU to complete beginning WIP $= (1 - 0.4)12{,}000 = 7{,}200$ (4-4')

Using the example of the previous section you should note that when using the FIFO method the $3,645 (the cost of the beginning inventory) will remain attached to the units in the beginning WIP. Thus only the *current* costs will have to be allocated. The cost per unit will be computed using the following equivalent units:[1]

---

[1]An alternative way to compute FIFO equivalent units is as follows:

Units finished	xx
EU in ending WIP	xx
	xx
Less EU of work done last period	
on the beginning WIP	xx
Equivalent units	xx

Note that this method is the same as the weighted average method except for the last step. The effect of the last step is to remove last period's work from the total, leaving only the work done this period. For the example:

	Materials	Conversion Costs
Units finished	10,000	10,000
Ending inventory	2,000	500
	12,000	10,500
Less EU of work done last period		
on the beginning WIP		
Material 1,000 × 1.00	1,000	
Conversion costs 1,000 × 0.25		250
Equivalent units	11,000	10,250

	Materials	Conversion Costs
Beginning inventory*	0	750
Started and finished		
(11,000–2,000)	9,000	9,000
Ending inventory (100% for material and 25% for conversion costs)	2,000	500
Equivalent units	11,000	10,250

*Since the beginning WIP was completed as to material at the beginning of the period, no material would have been added this period. However, the remaining 75% of the conversion work would have been done in the current period.

The current costs would be allocated using the following unit costs:

$$\text{Material/unit} = \frac{\$22,000}{11,000} = \$2.00$$

$$\text{Conversion cost/unit} = \frac{\$41,000}{10,250} = \$4.00$$

The costs are assigned to the finished units as follows. First, the beginning inventory cost of $3,645 remains attached to the units that were in the beginning inventory and are now finished. To complete these units, 750 equivalent units of work was done this period at a cost of $4.00 per unit. The remainder of the units finished had all of their work done this period at a total cost of $6.00 ($2.00 for material and $4 for labor). Thus:

Cost of finished production:		
Beginning inventory finished this period		
Cost assigned last period	$3,645	
Cost to complete 750 × $4.00	3,000	$ 6,645
Units started and finished 9,000 × $6.00		54,000
Total cost of finished production		$60,645

The cost of Department A's ending work-in-process inventory is:

Material 2,000 × $2	$4,000
Conversion costs 500 × $4	2,000
Total cost of ending inventory	$6,000

As you can see, a total of $66,645 ($60,645 + $6,000) has now been assigned, which equals the total debits in the WIP account.

It should be explained why this method is called *modified FIFO*. If the idea of FIFO is carried out to the "letter of the law" in a multiple-department firm, there would be an excessive number of inventory layers. In the preceding example two layers are being transferred out of Department A: the layer represented by the units in the beginning inventory and the layer represented by the units started and finished. *Conventional* FIFO would require that these two layers be separated in Department B. If so, the units transferred out of Department B would contain three layers; the two from A and a third representing the beginning work-in-process inventory of Department B. Maintaining these many separate layers is not practical or useful. Thus, the *entire group* of units being transferred to Department B will be treated as one layer with one average cost per unit in that department even though it was treated as two layers in Department A. This is the modification that is conventionally made to the FIFO concept.

The Process Cost Report and Case Problem

In order for accountants to keep the data organized and to report the information resulting from a process cost system to management, a convenient format is needed. Each firm will have its own form but for our purposes a four-part report is used:

1. Section A—Units schedule
2. Section B—Cost to be accounted for
3. Section C—Equivalent unit and unit cost computation
4. Section D—Cost assignment

The purpose of Section A is twofold. First, it is necessary to report the total units for which each department was accountable during the period. Normally, this will be the beginning inventory plus the units started (or transferred in) during the period. Second, a report is needed on what happened to the units for which the department was accountable. This includes the ending inventory, units transferred out, and other items to be discussed later.

Section B is a formal presentation of the debits to the work-in-process account during the period. The format of this section depends on whether weighted average or modified FIFO is used. The purpose of Section C is to show the details of the equivalent unit and unit cost computations. Section D shows the calculation of the cost assigned to each layer. Continuing with the KRH Company example, this report will now be illustrated.

In addition to the information about Department A of the KRH Company, assume the following data about Department B. Except for packing cases, no additional material is needed.

WIP—Department B

Bal. 1/1/x1 (1,000 units)	7,950[a]	To Finished Goods	(9,000 units)[b]
Conversion costs	26,500		
Packing cases	9,000		
From Department A	?		

[a]Beginning inventory contained 1,000 potential units, complete with respect to Department A's cost ($5,950) but only 75% complete as to conversion costs in Department B ($2,000). Packing cases are put in at the very end of the production in Department B.

[b]The ending WIP inventory in Department B contained 2,000 units that were 25% complete with respect to conversion costs.

Exhibit 4.3 is a cost report for Department A using the weighted average method. The content of this report has been developed in earlier sections and are summarized here. You should refer to Exhibit 4.3 as its contents are discussed. First, consider Section A. The units to be accounted for consist of the beginning inventory plus the units started. For the data, see Department A's WIP account and the accompanying notes on page 121. This is also the source of the data for the units accounted for.

Exhibit 4.3   KRH Company Department A Cost Report (using weighted average) for January 19x1

A. Units schedule
    To be accounted for:
       Beginning inventory (material, 100%;
          conversion costs, 25%)   1,000
       Units started   11,000
       Total units to be accounted for   12,000
    Units accounted for:
       To Department B   10,000
       Ending inventory (material, 100%;
          conversion costs, 25%)   2,000
       Total units accounted for   12,000

B. Costs to be accounted for:

	Material	Conversion Costs	Total
Beginning inventory	$ 2,120	$ 1,525	$ 3,645
Current costs	22,000	41,000	63,000
Total costs to be accounted for	$24,120	$42,525	$66,645

C. Equivalent units and unit cost computation:

	Material	Conversion Costs
Finished in this department	10,000	10,000
Ending inventory (2,000 × percentage completion)	2,000	500
Equivalent units	12,000	10,500
Costs (from schedule B)	$24,120	$42,525
Cost per equivalent unit	$2.01	$4.05

D. Cost assignment
    To Department B [10,000 × ($2.01 + $4.05)] $60,600
    Ending inventory
       Material (2,000 × $2.01) $4,020
       Conversion costs (500 × $4.05)   2,025   6,045
    Total costs assigned $66,645

The source of the data for Section B is also the WIP account and the analysis provided in the footnote to that account. Note that two cost pools have been formed corresponding to the two different cost behaviors. Since the weighted average method is being used, the material and conversion costs assigned last month to the beginning work in process have been added into their respective cost pools. The total of each of these pools will be allocated over the units of work as computed by the weighted average method. Section C is a summary of the equivalent unit computation previously explained on page 121.

In Section D, note that the unit cost of the items transferred to Department B is just the sum of the material cost per equivalent unit and the conversion cost per equivalent unit. Likewise, the ending inventory cost is found by using the respective equivalent units (from Section C) and unit cost figures (also in Section C). Finally, note the total cost assigned in Section D is equal to the total cost to be accounted for in Section B. This provides some checks on the mechanical accuracy of the cost allocations.

Exhibit 4.4 is the cost report for Department B. Several things should be noted:

1. Units started in Department B are equal to units finished in Department A because Department B is taking each candle holder and doing additional work. See Exhibit 4.3 for the number of units transferred out of Department A. For Department B's inventory data, see the WIP account on page 125.
2. The $60,600 of *current* Department A cost transferred into Department B (see Section B of Exhibit 4.4) is equal to the cost assigned to the finished production in Department A's report (see Section D of Exhibit 4.3). The other cost data in Section B are found in B's WIP account.
3. There are three cost behaviors in Department B and, therefore, three cost pools and equivalent unit computations. The three behaviors are: (1) Department A's cost at the *beginning* of B's production, (2) conversion costs added *continuously* throughout the process, and (3) packing cases added at the *end* of the process.
4. You can use the percentage completion and inventory data in Section A to verify the equivalent unit computation in Section C. Note the packing case equivalent unit computation shows zero units for the ending work-in-process inventory because the packing cases are not added until the end of manufacturing.
5. The separate material and conversion cost incurred in Department A have been merged together as one pool ($60,600) in Department B.
6. Note and study the cost assignments in Section D. All of the data needed for the assignments come from Section C.

Exhibit 4.5 demonstrates a reporting format for the modified FIFO method. The example used is Department A of the KRH Company. This permits an easy comparison of modified FIFO with weighted average. In comparison with Exhibit 4.3 several things should be noted. First, Section A is the *same* as in Exhibit 4.3. In Section B of Exhibit 4.5 you will observe that the cost of the beginning inventory, $3,645, is *not pooled* with the current costs. Likewise, the beginning inventory layer is separately maintained when computing the cost of finished production in Section D. This treatment is consistent with the FIFO concept. Third, note the equivalent unit section, C, is as discussed on page 124. Further, note that only the current costs are used to determine a unit cost. This is because the FIFO concept

Exhibit 4.4   KRH Company Department B Cost Report (using weighted average) for January 19x1

A. Units schedule
   To be accounted for
   Beginning inventory (Department A
   costs, 100%; conversion costs, 75%;
   packing cases, 0%)   1,000
   From Department A (units finished in
   Department A)   10,000
   Total units to account for   11,000
   Units accounted for
   To finished goods   9,000
   Ending inventory (Department A costs, 100%;
   conversion costs, 25%; packing cases, 0%)   2,000
   Total units accounted for   11,000

B. Costs to be accounted for:

	Department A Costs	Conversion Costs	Packing Cases	Total
Beginning inventory	$ 5,950	$ 2,000	0	$ 7,950
Current costs	60,600*	26,500	9,000	96,100
Total costs to account for	$66,550	$28,500	$9,000	$104,050

C. Equivalent units and unit cost computation

	Department A Costs	Conversion Costs	Packing Cases
To finished goods	9,000	9,000	9,000
Ending inventory (2,000 × percentage completion)	2,000	500	0
Equivalent units	11,000	9,500	9,000
Costs (from Schedule B)	$66,550	$28,500	$9,000
Cost per equivalent unit	$6.05	$3.00	$1.00

D. Cost assignment
   To finished goods [9,000 × ($6.05 + $3 + $1)] $ 90,450
   Ending inventory
   Department A (2,000 × $6.05) $12,100
   Conversion costs (500 × $3.00)   1,500   13,600
   Total costs assigned $104,050

*From Schedule D of Exhibit 4.3.

Exhibit 4.5   KRH Company Department A Cost Report (using modified FIFO) for January 19x1

A. Units schedule
   To be accounted for
   Beginning inventory (material, 100%;
      conversion costs, 25%)   1,000
   Units started   11,000
   Total units to be accounted for   12,000
   Units accounted for
   To Department B   10,000
   Ending inventory (material, 100%;
      conversion costs, 25%)   2,000
   Total units accounted for   12,000

B. Costs to be accounted for
   Beginning inventory $ 3,645
   Material   22,000
   Conversion costs   41,000
   Total costs to be accounted for $66,645

C. Equivalent units and unit costs (for current costs)

	Material	Conversion Costs
Beginning inventory 1,000 × (1 − percentage completion at January 1)	0	750
Started and finished (11,000 − 2,000)	9,000	9,000
Ending inventory 2,000 × percentage completion at January 31	2,000	500
Total equivalent units	11,000	10,250
Current costs (from Schedule B)	$22,000	$41,000
Cost per equivalent unit	$2.00	$4.00

D. Cost Assignment
   To finished goods
   Beginning inventory
      Prior period costs (from Schedule B) $3,645
      Cost to complete (750 × $4)   3,000 $ 6,645
   Started and finished [9,000 × ($2.00 + $4.00)]   54,000
   Cost of finished production $60,645
   Ending inventory
      Material (2,000 × $2) $4,000
      Conversion costs (500 × $4)   2,000   6,000
   Total costs assigned $66,645

leaves the beginning inventory cost assigned to the units in the beginning inventory. Thus, only the current costs have to be allocated. Note carefully the difference in the method of cost assignment in Section D as compared to weighted average. First, the beginning WIP inventory had $3,645 of cost assigned to it last period. It was completed this period and the cost of the *current period's work* (750 equivalent units of conversion) is computed using the *current unit cost*. Second, the units started and finished this period, 9,000 units, receive a cost assignment at a rate equal to the sum of the current unit cost figures. The total cost of the beginning inventory is combined with the cost of the 9,000 units to get the cost of finished production for the period. Finally, the method of costing the ending WIP inventory is identical to that used in Exhibit 4.3. In problem 4-6 you are asked to prepare a cost report for Department B using the FIFO concept.

Evaluation of a Process Costing System Based on Actual Costs

At this point it is appropriate to consider the weaknesses of the process cost system. The major problems are a result of the system being constructed around the averaging of actual costs and are of two types. First, the conversion costs will include both actual fixed and variable costs. You should consider what happens in process costing when there are large changes in volume from one period to another. Second, there is a possibility that the variable costs will be affected by inefficient uses of resources, and this yields results that are hard to defend. That is, inefficiency increases costs, which, in turn, will be included in the cost of the product. But, inefficiency does not add utility to the product and it may be hard to defend the higher cost.

To facilitate a discussion, the KRH Company problem of the previous section will be extended to a second month. Following is the February work-in-process account for Department A. Note that the beginning inventory figure resulted from using the weighted average method in January (see Exhibit 4.3).

WIP—Department A			
Balance, 2/1/x1		To Department B	(4,000 units)
(2,000 units)	$ 6,045*		
Material	8,040		
Conversion cost	34,740		
	$48,825		

*Both the beginning and ending inventories were 25% complete as to conversion costs at their respective dates and material was 100% complete.

The ending inventory contains 2,000 units.

The weighted average equivalent production figures are 6,000 for material (4,000 + 2,000) and 4,500 for conversion costs (4,000 + 0.25 × 2,000). Thus, unit cost figures to be used during February are determined as follows:

	Material	Conversion Costs
Beginning inventory (from Exhibit 4.3)	$ 4,020	$ 2,025
Current costs	8,040	34,740
Total	$12,060	$36,765
Equivalent units	6,000	4,500
Cost per equivalent unit	$2.01	$8.17

Using these data, the following cost assignments are made:

To finished goods [4,000 × ($2.01 + $8.17)]		$40,720
Ending inventory		
Material (2,000 × $2.01)	$4,020	
Conversion costs (500 × $8.17)	4,085	8,105
Total		$48,825

Now compare these results with those for January. Note that the conversion cost per unit is more than twice that used in January ($8.17 versus $4.05). Further, the work-in-process inventory, which is the same size and at the same percentage completion as January's inventory, will be carried at a cost that is $2,060 higher than last month's ($8,105 − $6,045). Can this be defended? If accounting is viewed as an activity that is guided by economic principles, then a defense is difficult. The 2,000 units in February's ending inventory did not receive any greater benefit from the production process than the 2,000 units in January's inventory. If cost assignments should reflect relative benefits, then clearly something is wrong with the results.

A major source of this problem is that the monthly conversion costs consist of some fixed costs. Suppose a cost analysis reveals that fixed overhead costs are $30,750 per month. Then the variable conversion costs were $10,250 in January ($41,000 − $30,750) and $3,990 in February ($34,750 − $30,750). It should now be obvious why February's cost per unit was higher than January's. The process costing system discussed in this chapter averaged the fixed costs over a smaller amount of work in February causing the unit cost figure to increase.

What can be done to avoid such a problem in the context of process costing? The answer is a predetermined fixed overhead rate. A normal rate would be determined by the method described in the job order chapter. If fixed costs were assigned to work in process by a predetermined rate times the number of equivalent units for the conversion costs, then the debit to work in process would be only for the *applied* fixed overhead, not the actual. The equivalent unit should be for this period's work and, therefore, would have to be measured by the modified FIFO computation rather than the weighted average. Since weighted average regroups the work done on the beginning inventory into the total work denominator, using the weighted average equivalent units as a base for overhead application would result in some effort being assigned costs twice. If overhead is applied using a predetermined rate, then the system is usually referred to as **normal cost-ing.** Such a system will be used in problem 4-15.

The inefficient use of resources causes a problem similar to that just described. If material, labor, or overhead is incurred at a rate greater than normally needed, the process cost system discussed here will just include such costs in the unit fig-ures and thus inflate inventories. It is questionable that the affected production receives a greater benefit. Another problem arises if some of the production is spoiled. In Chapter 8 there will be an explanation of different kinds of spoilage and various ways of accounting for it.

Summary

With this chapter, you should have further enhanced your understanding of cost flow. Also, you should understand the idea of an equivalent unit since it will be needed in later chapters. Further, you should know how to compute the weighed average and modified FIFO equivalent production figures. Finally, be sure you understand how costs are assigned to inventories and completed production in a process cost system. In Chapter 8 process costing will be explored further by con-sidering how to account for the cost of spoiled production.

Process costing uses a unit of output as the cost objective. If such a system uses average actual cost as the unit cost, then the chances are great that the resulting product costs will vary from period to period, and this is not defensible. To avoid the phenomenon of fluctuating unit costs, a standard cost system may be used or, at least, a normal cost version of process costing (one that uses a predetermined fixed overhead rate).

Key terms and concepts for this chapter include:

Process cost system
Equivalent unit
Conversion costs
Weighted average equivalent unit method
Modified FIFO equivalent unit method
Units started and finished
Process cost report
Normal costing

SELF-STUDY PROBLEM. The purpose of this self-study problem is to have you apply the concepts of the chapter to a situation that is representative of some mod-ern-day manufacturers. With the advent of robotics, some manufacturing pro-cesses require very little human labor.

The Fisk Company uses one process to make its one product. Thus, a process cost system is in use. Because of the mechanization it has been found that over-head is more closely related to machine hours than labor hours. Robots and machines are used throughout the entire process, whereas direct labor is only needed during the last 25% of the process and then jointly with the robots and machines. The overhead cost must therefore be separated from the labor costs in applying them to the product. One unit of finished product is made by combining

2 gallons of *X* (put in at the beginning of the process) with 3 gallons of *Y*, which is constantly added as the processing is performed.

The production and cost records for January show the following:

Beginning inventory: 400 units, all 25% complete	$ 15,104*
Cost of material *X* added this period	108,000
Cost of material *Y* added this period	168,000
Overhead costs for this period	224,000
Cost of labor this period	54,000
Transferred to finished goods: 5,000 units	?
Ending inventory: 800 units, all 87.5% complete	?

*The beginning inventory costs are analyzed as follows:

Material *X*	$ 7,420
Material *Y*	3,114
Overhead	4,570
	15,104

Required:

1. Assume the weighted average method is used. What is the cost of the 800 units in the ending inventory?
2. Determine the cost of the ending inventory assuming the modified FIFO method is used.

Solution to Self-Study Problem

1. First, it is necessary to identify the different types of cost behavior. There are three:
   1. Material *X* at *beginning* of the process.
   2. Material *Y* and overhead *continuously* throughout the process.
   3. Labor continuously throughout the *last 25%* of processing. In the accounting which follows, material *Y* and overhead will be kept separate even though they are both incurred continuously throughout production.

Second, compute the equivalent units for use in assigning costs:

	Material X	Material Y and Overhead	Labor
Units finished	5,000	5,000	5,000
Ending inventory			
800 × 1.0	800		
800 × 0.875		700	
800 × 0.5*			400
	5,800	5,700	5,400

*Labor is needed in the last 25% of the process. That is, it is used starting at the 75% point and then continuously until the units are finished. The following should help you visualize the process where the shaded area represents the labor done on the ending inventory this period:

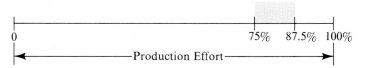

The percentage of the total labor done on the ending inventory, then, is:

$$\frac{87.5 - 75.0}{100.0 - 75.0} = \frac{12.5}{25.0} = 50\%$$

Now, the cost per unit can be computed:

	Material X	*Material Y*	*Labor*	*Overhead*
Beginning inventory	$ 7,420	$ 3,144	0	$ 4,570
Current costs	108,000	168,000	$54,000	224,000
Total	$115,420	$171,114	$54,000	$228,570
Equivalent units	5,800	5,700	5,400	5,700
Cost per unit	$19.90	$30.02	$10.00	$40.10

Finally, the cost of the ending inventory is:

Material X	800 × $19.90	$15,920
Material Y	700 × $30.02	21,014
Labor	400 × $10.00	4,000
Overhead	700 × $40.10	28,070
		$69,004

2. To answer question 2, first compute the FIFO equivalent units:

	Material X	*Material Y* and Overhead	*Labor*
Beginning inventory			
400 × 0.0	0		
400 × 0.75		300	
400 × 1.00[a]			400
Started and finished			
5,000 − 400	4,600	4,600	4,600
Ending inventory (same as weighted average)	800	700	400
Total	5,400	5,600	5,400

[a]Since the beginning inventory was 25% complete at the beginning of January, it had all of its labor added during January because labor is not needed until the last 25% of the process.

The *current* costs per equivalent unit are:

Material X $108,000 ÷ 5,400 = $20.00

Material Y $168,000 ÷ 5,600 = $30.00

Labor $ 54,000 ÷ 5,400 = $10.00

Overhead $224,000 ÷ 5,600 = $40.00

The cost of the ending inventory is:

Material X	800 × $20	$16,000
Material Y	700 × $30	21,000
Labor	400 × $10	4,000
Overhead	700 × $40	28,000
		$69,000

Problems

4-1. Basic Process Costing with No Beginning Inventories. The Kansas Can Company produces standard quart containers for sale to other manufacturers. A process cost system is used to account for the manufacturing costs. During November the following data were collected:

Costs	
Material used	$ 87,000
Conversion costs	$191,800
Production data	
Beginning work-in-process inventory	0 units
Ending work-in-process inventory	4,000 units
Percentage completion of ending work-in-process inventory	
Material	100%
Conversion costs	60%
Units finished during November	25,000

Required:

1. Prepare the November process cost report.
2. Prepare any journal entries that are implied by the process cost report.

4-2. Basic Process Costing with Beginning Inventories (Weighted Average). The Idaho Hoe Company manufactures garden hoes using one production department. A process cost system is used to account for its manufacturing costs. During October, the following data were collected:

Costs	
Material used	$115,500
Conversion costs	$ 93,021
Production Data	
Beginning work-in-process inventory	2,000 units
Percentage completion of beginning work-in-process inventory	
Material	100%
Conversion costs	40%

Costs assigned to beginning work-in-process inventory in September	
Material	$ 6,650
Conversion costs	$ 2,109
Ending work-in-process inventory	5,000 units
Percentage completion of ending work-in-process inventory	
Material	100%
Conversion costs	30%
Units finished during October	30,000

Required:

1. Assume Idaho Hoe uses the weighted average method of assigning costs. Prepare its process cost report for October.
2. Prepare any journal entries that are implied by the process cost report.

4-3. Basic Process Costing with Beginning Inventory (FIFO). Reconsider the Idaho Hoe Company's activities for October as described in problem 4-2. Now assume that it uses the modified FIFO method of accounting for its costs.

Required:

1. Prepare its process cost report for October.
2. Prepare any journal entries that are implied by the process cost report.

4-4. Basic Problem on Equivalent Units. Following are descriptions of three process cost cases:

Case A: In a given department material X is added at the beginning of the process. The beginning inventory contained 2,000 units, each of which was 25% completed at the beginning of the month. Units finished during the month totaled 15,000. There is an ending inventory of 3,000 units, one-third complete. Conversion costs are incurred uniformly throughout the process.

Case B: Assume that material Y is added at an even rate throughout a particular process and that material Z is added when the process is 50% complete. Conversion costs are incurred uniformly throughout the process. Additional data are:

Beginning inventory:	5,000 units, 40% complete
Ending inventory:	4,000 units, 75% complete
Units started:	19,000

Case C: Department II is the second department in a chain of departments. The following production data are available:

Received from Department I:	100,000 pounds
Transferred to Department III:	76,000 pounds
Ending inventory:	24,000 pounds
Beginning inventory:	0

In this department additional material is added to the work received from the preceding department. Three distinctly different types of materials are used at three points:

Material A is added at the beginning of the process.
Material B is added when the process is 25% completed.
Material C is added when the process is 75% completed.

Labor and factory overhead are incurred at a uniform rate throughout the manufacturing process in this department. Examination of the unfinished work discloses that:

1/4 was 7/8 completed.
1/2 was 1/2 completed.
1/4 was 1/6 completed.

Required:

1. For each case just described, compute the weighted average equivalent units of work for each type of cost behavior.
2. Repeat part 1 using the modified FIFO concept.

4-5. Basic Process Costing with Multiple Cost Behavior. The Koenig Company assembles dishwashers in a one-step operation and uses process costing to account for its production costs. The dishwasher frames are needed at the start of the process, the control units at the 75% point, and the cover at the 95% point. Other materials are accounted for as one pool and are used uniformly throughout the process, as is labor and overhead. Following are inventory data for July:

	Beginning	Ending
Work in process (units)	4,000	2,000
Percentage completion	25%	80%
Cost		
Frames	$106,000	?
Other materials	25,000	?
Labor	20,000	?
Overhead	10,000	?
Finished goods (units)	10,000	14,000

During July 50,000 dishwashers were started into production. The following costs were charged to production:

Frames	$2,000,000
Control units	1,593,000
Covers	780,000
Other materials	1,315,000
Labor	1,052,000
Overhead	526,000

Required:

1. What is the per unit costs at which each of the six items should be charged during July if the weighted average equivalent unit method is used?
2. Continuing part 1, what is the entry to record July's finished production?
3. What is the per unit costs at which each of the six items should be charged during July if the modified FIFO equivalent unit method is used?

4-6. Finish Example Started in Text. The KRH Company problem was used as a demonstration in this chapter. Exhibits 4.3 and 4.4 are the January cost reports for the two departments using the weighted average concept, whereas Exhibit 4.5 contains Department A's report using the modified FIFO method.

Required:

Prepare Department B's cost report using modified FIFO.

4-7. Basic Problem Requiring a Process Cost Report (Weighted Average). The Rice Company produces one product in a one-step process. Material *A* is needed in producing the product. Of the total quantity of *A* needed, one-half is added at the beginning of processing, and the remaining half is added when processing is 75% complete. Following is the work-in-process account for January 19x1:

Work in Process

Beginning inventory (3,000 units, 1/3 complete)	$ 5,810*	To finished goods (10,000 units)†
Material *A*	22,050	
Conversion costs	30,000	

*Material, $3,030; conversion costs, $2,780.

†The ending WIP inventory contained 4,000 units, 25% complete.

Required:

Prepare January's process cost report assuming the weighted average inventory method is used.

4-8. Basic Problem Requiring a Process Cost Report (Modified FIFO). Reconsider the Rice Company case in problem 4-7. Prepare a process cost report assuming the modified FIFO inventory method is used.

4-9. Two Departments; Weighted Average (This problem is continued in the Chapter 5 problems). The Yaz Company produces one product through two processes and uses process cost accounting. For the current month the following report has been prepared for Department A (material is added at the beginning of the process):

Yaz Company
Department A
Process Cost Report for October 19x1

A. Units schedule
        To account for

Beginning inventory (75% complete)	4,000
Units started	18,000
Total units to account for	22,000

Accounted for
   Transferred to B   20,000
   Ending inventory (50% complete)   2,000
      Total units accounted for   22,000

B. Costs to be accounted for:

	Material	Conversion Costs	Total
Beginning inventory	$ 40,110	$ 24,800	$ 64,910
Current costs	190,890	174,700	365,590
Total costs to be accounted for	$231,000	$199,500	$430,500

C. Equivalent unit and unit cost computation:

	Material	Conversion Costs
Transferred to B	20,000	20,000
Ending inventory	2,000	1,000
Equivalent units	22,000	21,000
Costs	$231,000	$199,500
Unit cost	$10.50	$9.50

D. Cost assignment
   Transferred to B: 20,000($10.50 + $9.50) $400,000
   Ending inventory
     Material: 2,000 × $10.50 $ 21,000
     Conversion costs: 1,000 × $9.50 $ 9,500   30,500
       Total costs assigned $430,500

You have the following information about Department B. First, you know that labor and conversion costs are incurred continuously throughout the process. Second, Department B adds some additional material when the work is 50% complete. Finally, the following data are available:

Beginning work-in-process inventory
  Units: 9,000 (conversion 75% complete)
    Costs: Department A $188,700
         Material—Department B   18,000
         Conversion costs in Dept. B   20,000
                         $226,700

Current costs added
  Material—Department B $ 32,000
  Conversion costs—Department B   58,000
Ending work-in-process inventory: 4,000
units (conversion 25% complete)

Required:

Prepare a schedule computing the cost of the units finished during October in Department B and the cost of its ending work-in-process inventory. Department B also uses the weighted average method.

4-10. Process Costing with Multiple Departments. Maxe Company manufactures a liquid fertilizer that is sold in 15-gallon containers. The production occurs as follows:

1. Chemical A is produced in Department A.
2. Chemical B is produced in Department B.
3. The fertilizer is produced in Department C using 3 gallons of chemical A, 5 gallons of chemical B, and 7 gallons of water as follows. For each container, the 3 gallons of chemical A are added at the beginning of the mixing in Department C. When the mixing is 25% complete, a gallon of chemical B is added. Two additional gallons of chemical B are added when the mixing is 50% complete and the final two gallons of B are added when the mixing is 75% complete. The 7 gallons of water are added continuously throughout the mixing process. Also, labor and overhead occur continuously throughout the process. At the end of processing in Department C the fertilizer is put into 15-gallon containers and sent to the warehouse.
4. The mixing takes place in batches but a process cost system is used since the product is always the same.

The following costs were charged to Department C during January 19x1:

1. From Department A: 60,000 gallons of chemical A; $80,000.
2. From Department B for chemical B used; $49,200.
3. Water; $8,450.
4. Labor; $76,050.
5. Overhead; $57,460.
6. Containers; $18,750.

Inventories in Department C were as follows:

1. January 1: A batch of 3,000 containers, 70% complete with respect to mixing. The cost assigned last month was $34,000.
2. January 31: Two batches as follows:
   a. 6,000 containers, 40% complete with respect to mixing.
   b. 2,000 containers, 80% complete with respect to mixing.

Required:

Prepare Department C's cost report. The modified FIFO method is used.

4-11. Using Process Cost Reports of Prior Departments to Prepare Report for a Subsequent Department. The Morris Company manufactures a chemical product in a three-step operation. Each step is accomplished in a separate production department. You are the accountant for Department II.

In Department II one barrel of chemical *X*, which is produced in Department I, is added at the beginning of the process for each container of output. Then for each container two barrels of chemical *Y* are gradually added during the first 30% of the processing. Another barrel of chemical *Y* is added entirely when processing is 50% complete. Conversion costs are incurred uniformly throughout the process.

Following is *February's* cost assignment schedule for Department I.

To Department II
  Beginning inventory
    Prior period costs $ 12,460
    Cost to complete
      Material   0
      Conversion costs $2,000 \times 0.6 \times \$4.50$ 5,400
      Total $ 17,860
  Started and finished $43,000(\$3.98 + \$4.50)$ 364,640 $382,500
  Ending inventory
    Material $4,000 \times \$3.98$ $ 15,920
    Conversion costs $4,000 \times 0.5 \times \$4.50$ 9,000   24,920
  Total costs assigned $407,420

January's cost assignment schedule for *Department II* is as follows:

To Department III
  Beginning inventory
    Prior period costs $ 63,760
    Cost to complete
      Conversion costs $5,000 \times 0.7 \times \$4.05$ 14,175
      Total $ 77,935
  Started and finished
    $30,000(\$8.45 + \$3.10 + \$4.05)$ 468,000 $545,935
  Ending inventory
    Chemical X $6,000 \times \$8.45$ $ 50,700
    Chemical Y $6,000 \times 2/3 \times \$3.10$ 12,400
    Conversion costs $6,000 \times 0.4 \times \$4.05$ 9,720   72,820
  Total costs assigned $618,755

During the current period the cost of chemical Y added in Department II totaled $131,200 and the current conversion costs totaled $164,205. At the end of February there are two batches in process; one of 9,000 containers, 15% complete, and a second consisting of 3,000 containers, 70% complete.

Required:

Prepare February's entire process cost report for Department II. The modified FIFO method is used.

4-12. Adapted CPA Problem; Two Departments; Both Inventory Methods; Increase in Volume. The Crews Company produces a chemical agent for commercial use. The company accounts for production in two cost centers: (1) Cooking and (2) Mix-Pack. In the first cost center, liquid substances are combined in large cookers and boiled. After the batch is cooked, it is transferred to Mix-Pack, the second cost center. The batch then has a quantity of alcohol added equal to the liquid measure of the batch. Following this, the batch is mixed and bottled in one-gallon containers.

Material is added at the beginning of production in each cost center, and labor is added equally during production in each cost center. The modified FIFO method is used in the Cooking department and the weighted average method in the Mix-Pack department.

The following information is available for the month of October:

	Cooking	Mix-Pack
Work in Process, October 1		
Materials	$ 996	$ 114
Labor	100	60
Overhead	80	48
Prior department cost	0	426
Month of October		
Materials	$39,600	$15,276
Labor	10,050	16,000
Overhead	8,040	12,800

Inventory and production records show that Cooking has 1,000 gallons, 40% processed, on October 1 and 800 gallons, 50% processed, on October 31; Mix-Pack had 600 gallons, 50% processed, on October 1 and 1,000 gallons, 30% processed, on October 31.

Production reports for October show that Cooking started 40,000 gallons into production and completed and transferred 40,200 gallons to Mix-Pack and Mix-Pack completed and transferred 80,000 one-gallon containers of the finished product to the distribution warehouse.

Required:

1. Prepare a process cost report for the Cooking department
2. Prepare a process cost report for the Mix-Pack department.

4-13. CPA Problem, Acquired Inventory, FIFO Method. Bisto Corporation manufactures valves and pumps for liquids. On December 1, 19x4, Bisto paid $25,000 to the Poplen Company for the patent of its watertight valve. Bisto planned to carry on Poplen's procedure of having the valve casing and parts cast by an independent foundry and doing the grinding and assembling in its own plant.

Bisto also purchased Poplen's inventory of the valves at 80% of its cost to Poplen. The purchased inventory was comprised of the following:

	Units
Raw material (unfinished casings and parts)	1,100
Work in process	
Grinding (25% complete)	800
Assembling (40% complete)	600
Finished valves	900

Poplen's cost accounting system provided the following unit costs.

	Cost per unit
Raw materials (unfinished casings and parts)	$2.00
Grinding costs	$1.00
Assembling costs	$2.50

Bisto's cost accounting system accumulated the following costs for the month of December that do not include the cost of the inventory purchased from Poplen.

Raw material purchases (casings and parts for 5,000 units)	$10,500
Grinding costs	$ 2,430
Assembling costs	$ 5,664

Bisto's inventory of watertight valves at December 31, 19x4, follows:

Raw material (unfinished casings and parts)	2,700
Work in process:	
Grinding (35% complete)	2,000
Assembling (one-third complete)	300
Finished valves	2,250

No valves were spoiled or lost during the manufacturing process.

Required:

Prepare the process cost reports using modified FIFO.

4-14. Process Costing with Intermediate Inventories; Material Added at Different Points.
The Meyer Company produces one of its products, ZAP, in a three-step process. Department I produces one of the component parts for ZAP, XL1. Department II assembles ZAP, which requires 3 units of XL1 and 1 unit of ZY, which is purchased from an outside supplier. Department III paints and crates the finished product.

In Department II, ZAP is assembled as follows. One unit of XL1 is needed at the beginning of the process. When the process is 50% complete the other 2 units of XL1 are added. Part ZY is added when production is 75% complete. Labor and overhead are incurred uniformly throughout Department II.

Department I and II are not completely synchronized. Thus an inventory of part XL1 is maintained. The XL1 inventory account for the current period is as follows:

XL1 Inventory

Beginning inventory		To Dept. II (177,000 units)
(5,000 units)	15,520	
From Dept. I		
(180,000 units)	601,200	

Department II started the current period with a beginning inventory of 6,000 ZAPs. They were 60% complete and had a cost of $87,480 assigned to them in the previous period. At the end of the period there were two layers of inventory with different percentages of completion as follows:

Layer 1 (9,000 units)	25% complete
Layer 2 (12,000 units)	80% complete

Department II transferred 50,000 units of ZAP to Department III during the current period.

The cost of part ZY used this period in Department II totaled $310,000 and conversion costs amounted to $466,000.

The FIFO inventory method is used by the Meyer Company in all departments and inventory accounts.

Required:

Prepare a complete process cost report for Department II.

4-15. Process Costing with a Predetermined Overhead Rate. Reconsider the KRH Company problem in the chapter and assume that January's activity in Department A was at the normal level. Also consider the overhead analysis on page 131.

Required:

1. Assume that a predetermined fixed overhead rate is to be used. Determine this rate using the principles of rate setting discussed in Chapter 3.
2. Reconstruct the debit side of Department A's work-in-process account for February assuming that fixed costs are assigned to production using the predetermined fixed overhead rate.
3. Prepare the entries to account for the incurrence and application of February's fixed overhead.
4. Recompute the cost of the units transferred to Department B during February and the ending work-in-process inventory assuming that the predetermined overhead rate is used. Compare your results with those for January and with those on page 131.

4-16. Evaluation of Process Costing. The Evans Company produces a single product using a single production center. The modified FIFO method is used to apply actual production costs, and the work-in-process data for January and February are presented in the accompanying account:

Work in Process			
Balance, 1/1/x1	0	To finished goods (20,000 units)	$240,000.00
Materials	$ 50,000.00	Balance, 1/31/x1	
Conversion costs	225,000.00	(5,000 units, 50%)	35,000.00
	$275,000.00		$275,000.00
Balance, 2/1/x1	$ 35,000.00	To finished goods (7,500 units)	$130,500.00
Materials	16,500.00	Balance, 2/28/x1	
Conversion costs	135,000.00	(5,000 units, 50%)	56,000.00
	$186,500.00		$186,500.00
Balance, 3/1/x1	$ 56,000.00		

Ms. Bosox is a very astute manager and notes that February's physical inventory is the same as January's but that its cost is considerably higher. She asks for an explanation and you have been assigned the task. To date, your investigation has revealed the following facts:

1. The monthly fixed conversion costs amount to $90,000.

2. Materials cost the same in February as in January but were used at a greater rate per unit than in January. February's rate of usage was 10% higher than January's. Material is added at the beginning of the process.

Required:

1. Verify the cost assignments for both months.
2. Reconcile the two ending inventory costs. The following items need to be considered:
   a. Difference due to the rate at which fixed costs are allocated.
   b. Difference due to the change in material costs.

4-17. Variety of Analytical Problems. Following are some cases in process costing that require analysis.

1. The R Company uses weighted average process costing. In one department, 12,000 units were finished this period, and the ending inventory was 30% complete with respect to conversion costs. The total conversion cost of $50,880 was to be allocated at $4.00 per equivalent unit. How many whole units were in the ending inventory?
2. The E Company also uses process costing. During the current period, Department B, the second department, started with 3,000 units in WIP, finished 15,000 units, and ended with 4,000 units in process. Using the weighted average method, Department B assigned Department A's cost at a rate of $4.00 per unit this period. During this period Department A transferred $64,300 of cost to Department B. What was the amount of Department A's cost included in Department B's beginning work in process?
3. The D Company finished 15,000 units of its only product during February 19x1. The ending WIP inventory consisted of 5,000 units, 20% complete. Using the weighted average method, material costs were assigned at a rate of $3.00 per unit and conversion costs at $5.00 per unit during February. The actual cost of material added during February totaled $48,400. In January, material costs were assigned at $2.90 per equivalent unit and conversion costs at $4.80. Material is added at the beginning of processing. The beginning WIP inventory was 25% complete. How many units were in the beginning WIP inventory?
4. Continuing with the case in part 3, what is the amount of conversion costs added during February?

4-18. Reconstruction of Process Cost Report When There Are Multiple Departments. The Lynn Company produces one product in a three-step process. Each step is the responsibility of a different department. Weighted average process costing is used in all departments. In Department A, the first department, 3,000 units were in process at November 1, 19x1. These units were 20% complete. During November, 12,000 units were started in Department A. Material is added at the beginning of processing in Department A. The ending work-in-process inventory consisted of 2,500 units, 40% complete. During November, the weighted average cost of material was $4.98 and conversion costs were $10.00 per unit.

Department C, the third department, began November with 2,500 units, 20% complete. Additional material is added at the end of processing in this department. During November, 14,000 units were finished, and the ending inventory contained 3,500 units, 80% complete. The cost of the product transferred into Department C during November totaled $300,000.

Department B's beginning inventory was 20% complete and had a total cost of $87,750 assigned to it in October. Its ending inventory was two-thirds complete and consisted of

3,000 units. During November, Department A's costs were charged at a rate of $15.00 per unit in Department B. No additional material is added in Department B.

Required:

Completely reconstruct Department B's process cost report. Be sure to include all four sections with the same detail as in Exhibit 4.1. (That is, show the costs of the beginning inventory, current costs added, and all other detail.)

4-19. Process Cost with Departments for Part Production and for Assembly. The Eckersley Company produces a single product as follows. Part A is produced in Department I and part B in Department II. In both departments, the needed materials are required at the beginning of the process. The final product is completed in Department III. For each finished unit, 2 units of part A are added at the beginning of the processing in Department III, and 3 units of B are required when processing is 50% completed. Selected data from the records as they appear on June 30 are shown in the accompanying accounts:

Department I			
Beginning inventory (16,000 units, 25% complete)	$ 26,050	To Department III (30,000 units)	
Material added during June	28,800		
Conversion costs	64,600		
	$119,450		

Department I's ending WIP inventory consists of two layers:

Layer 1: 8,000 units, 75% complete with respect to conversion costs.
Layer 2: 2,000 units, 100% complete with respect to all costs.

Department II		
	To Department III (57,000 units)	$142,500

Department III			
Beginning inventory (4,000 units, 25% complete)	$25,400	To finished goods (17,000 units)	
Conversion costs during June	$14,875		

Department III's ending inventory contains 2,000 units, 75% complete.

Required:

1. Prepare Department I's process cost report for June. Use the method that is permitted by the data.
2. Prepare Department III's process cost report for June.

CHAPTER 5 **Standard Cost Systems**

*Chapter
Overview*

In the previous two chapters we have discussed cost accounting systems that primarily are actual cost-oriented. The output of actual cost systems is not particularly useful when management evaluates performance. To truly evaluate performance, management needs a base for comparison. For an actual cost system, the performance of previous years is typically used as the comparative base or the benchmark. However, the results of a previous year may contain inefficiencies or efficiencies that should not be included in a comparative base. If last year's performance was inefficient and if it is used as a benchmark in evaluating this year's performance, then the inefficiency would be implicitly condoned. Conversely, if last year's performance was efficient, then using it as a benchmark could be considered as too demanding. Workers might not be motivated to improve because, in effect, their performance would just increase the standard by which they are evaluated.

To provide a more useful evaluation mechanism a *standard cost* system should be considered. If proper standards of performance are established, then they can be used as a better comparative base for control purposes. As a by-product, proper standards may enable better forecasting of the financial impact from various courses of action. All of this is to suggest that a standard cost system serves many purposes. Thus, the discussion of this system could be included in several different parts of this book. The purpose of Part II is to cover all of the accounting systems and, therefore, standard costing systems must be discussed in this part of the book.

After exploring the nature and applicability of standard costs we will consider the standard-setting process. Then variances between actual and standard will be defined, calculated, and interpreted. Finally, we will consider the application of standards where there are work-in-process inventories, multiple products, and multiple departments. It should be noted early that even though the applications in this chapter are to manufacturing situations it is possible to use a standard cost system in nonmanufacturing firms. In Chapter 6, we will continue this subject and consider how standards can be incorporated into the accounting system, how to use them in evaluating performance, and how the variances should be accounted for at year-end. Other topics in standard costs are discussed in Chapters 8, 17, and 18.

Nature and Applicability of Standard Costs

Before we can adequately depict the nature of standard costs, some terms need to be defined. First, successful organizations and individuals have goals, or targets, toward which they work. **Goals** are desired achievements and are normally accompanied with a plan of action for their fulfillment. In working toward these goals, individual efforts may be classified as effective or ineffective, and as efficient or inefficient. For example, a firm may have a goal of being one of the top two firms in its industry as measured by total sales. **Effectiveness** is a measure of the extent to which a goal was accomplished. Effectiveness in the above example is rather easy to measure. Was the firm one of the top two as measured by sales? On the other hand, **efficiency** is a measure of the relationship between the resources used (the input) and the accomplishment achieved (the output). To measure efficiency in the above example the ratio of sales to costs (or net income to sales) could be compared with the industry average. Of course, it would be preferred for the firm to be both effective and efficient. However, depending on the nature of the goal, an organizational unit may be effective and inefficient or ineffective and efficient. Parenthetically, it should be noted that in cases where profit of a given magnitude is the goal, then effectiveness and efficiency become intricately meshed.

Although a very important topic, the analysis of effectiveness will be delayed until a later chapter. The methods of analyzing effectiveness variances are such that they have no implications for the record-keeping system. The discussion is delayed since the thrust of this part of the book is to explore the various cost accounting systems that can be used.

Accounting **standards,** then, are carefully predetermined amounts of resources that are expected to be consumed in accomplishing some objective. Obviously, a comparison of the actual resources consumed with the expected consumption for a given accomplishment, or output, will be *a* measure (not *the* measure) of efficiency. (Other types of efficiency variances are also important and will be discussed in later chapters since they have no implications for the accounting system.) The usefulness of standards is dependent on many variables including the "tightness" with which the standards are set and the behavioral makeup of the people on whom they are imposed.

Deferring, for a moment, the specifics of setting standards, let us consider some of the possible guiding philosophies. On one end of the spectrum there are **theoretical standards.** This concept has no compassion for the frailties of people or equipment. It assumes that the material content physically contained in finished production is all that should have been used. But it is not practical, for example, to expect the cloth actually contained in a dress to be all that is consumed in its production. Some waste will be a necessity. In computing labor time allowances, theoretical standards do not allow downtime for employee work breaks or for equipment repairs. In short, this concept assumes that both people and machinery work at *peak* efficiency 100% of the time and that it is possible to produce with no waste. Such a concept would generate a very tight standard and one that could never be attained. Studies have shown that excessively tight standards are typically counterproductive in motivating efficient performance.[1]

---

[1] See A.C. Stedry and E. Kay, "The Effects of Goal Difficulty on Performance: A Field Experience," *Behavioural Science,* November 1966, pp. 459–470. This is discussed further in Chapter 17.

At the middle of the spectrum is the philosophy of **currently attainable standards.** As the name implies, the standards are set so that they can be achieved with an acceptable level of performance. Allowances are made for normal and unavoidable material wastage. In computing time allowances, the time for work breaks and machine repairs are incorporated in the time allowed per unit of output. It is not possible to be very definitive about the precise meaning of attainable because that is so dependent upon the circumstances. Nevertheless, you should understand the difference in the philosophies of attainable and theoretical standards. To be current simply means that prices and technological capabilities are constantly monitored so that standards can be updated to reflect the changes in these conditions.

In addition to providing better motivation and better benchmarks for efficiency evaluations, currently attainable standards will provide information that is more useful to budgeting. Attainable standards are the only type that will reasonably reflect the actual results for various projected courses of action. If tight standards are used for budgeting, then actual resource consumption will be underestimated.

One other type of standard that needs to be mentioned is the system of **basic standards.** This type of system is implemented by setting standards and then revising them only very *infrequently.* Such a system has no long-run planning or control value, and all that can be said for it is that it simplifies the record keeping for production and inventory costs.

Now consider the type of situation where standard costing would be the more useful cost accounting system. If practicality and cost are ignored, then we might argue that a standard system is preferred to an actual-based system, regardless of the type of activity whose cost needs to be controlled (manufacturing, selling, or administrative) or regardless of the type of firm. However, the standard setting process, which is considered in more detail in the next section, is not an effortless, cost-free endeavor.

The practical acceptability of standards increases as the activity being controlled becomes more repetitive. For example, it is usually worth the cost to develop and monitor standards for a product that is produced continuously (such as automobiles) or for some nonproduction activity that is performed day after day (such as the shipping of the product). It is impractical to develop a full set of standards for custom orders (such as a space shuttle) or for other one-time, unique activities. In a sense, then, almost any production activity that lends itself to actual process cost accounting, as discussed in the last chapter, might better be served by standard costing. In these situations, having a benchmark (the standard) to compare with actual performance can give management valuable information. The comparison of the actual with the standard enables management-by-exception. That is, management needs to give attention only to those areas where there is a significant variation between the actual and the standard.

In closing this section it should be noted that a cost system does not have to be all standard or all actual. For those activities that lend themselves to standards a firm should use them. Job order costing discussed in Chapter 3 is an example of this blending of accounting techniques because overhead was allocated using a predetermined rate.

Setting Standards

In a manufacturing setting, the process of establishing standards depends on whether *price standards* or *quantity standards* are being set and on whether the standards are for material, labor, or overhead. Starting with material quantity standards there will be an examination of each of these processes. The accountant may initiate a **material quantity** study by determining the physical material content of a product and may rely on an engineer's analysis of the product's requirements. If appropriate, an allowance for normal material spoilage and/or waste should be included in the standards. If spoilage and waste are not accounted for in this manner, then the variance between the actual and the standard will contain some unavoidable usage. More will be said about this in Chapter 8.

A **standard price for material** depends on the desired grade or quality of material to be used, the suppliers to be used (if supplier reliability is an issue), the quantity to be purchased (if there are quantity discounts available), shipping costs, anticipated price changes during the period of time a particular standard price is to be in effect, and perhaps other variables. Since the grade of material and reliability of the supplier are variables, it is obvious that the standard price is not necessarily the lowest one available. When quantity discount arrangements are available, the firm may want to use economical order quantity models (see Chapter 22), with quantity discount features, to determine the optimal order size. In turn, the standard price would be equal to the one corresponding to the optimal size.

Price changes during the period present a problem. Theoretically, the standards should be changed any time there is a price change in the market. For practical reasons, a company may not want to make such a revision more than once of year.[2] If this is the case and if such changes can be reasonably anticipated, then the standard price might be determined by weighting each price by the length of time it will be in effect and summing the results. For example, if the price is estimated to be at $10 for three months and at $11 for nine months, then the standard price could be set at $10.75:

$$\frac{(3 \times \$10) + (9 \times \$11)}{12}$$

With this procedure some of the month-to-month variations between actual and standard prices would really be uncontrollable and must be allowed for in explaining the variance. At year-end, the variations due to market price changes would cancel out *if* the changes had been forecast correctly.

Labor time standards are somewhat more difficult to determine because they directly involve people. Taking an average of past times may build exceptional efficiencies or inefficiencies into the base. Also, there may be learning involved so that the past is not a good expectation for future production. The solution to this is to use time-and-motion studies and learning curves. Time-and-motion analyses deal

---

[2]Some of the potential difficulty of changing standards may be eliminated for firms that have data base management systems. The general idea of these systems is to have a *single* source of data for all uses. Thus the price of material can be changed in the data base and accomplish the change for all future uses of the data.

with how best to time an activity; they cover such things as methods of dividing the total job into subparts for observation and procedures that make allowance for possible deliberate slowdowns by employees if they know that their work is being timed. After determining the actual time, it may also be necessary to add a factor for work breaks and other unavoidable nonproductive time. Again, this will be explored more in Chapter 8.

With the existence of labor contracts, the task of determining **labor rate standards** may appear to be easy. But you must recognize that most firms will have different rates that are a function of skill and/or seniority. If so, then management must determine how many different labor classifications they want to use in a standard cost system. It may not be practical to have as many classes of labor as there are rate classes. If a particular classification encompasses several labor rates, then the question becomes one of determining how to combine them. Presumably, the weighting would be according to the anticipated proportions of each type of labor to the total in the class. For example, if a product is estimated to require five labor hours in a given class where two hours are provided by employees earning $6.00 per hour and three by employees earning $8.00, then the combined rate would be $7.20 per hour [(2/5)$6.00 + (3/5)$8.00]. In this kind of situation a price variance may be attributable to a difference between the actual mix of labor and the anticipated mix. For example, if the five hours needed for a given unit turns out to actually be one hour at the $6.00 rate and four at the $8.00 rate, then the actual labor rate for that unit is higher than $7.20.

The establishment of **overhead rates** is the same process as discussed in Chapter 3 for determining a normal overhead rate in a job costing system. That is, a measure of activity must be selected that is related to the incurrence of overhead and then a decision must be made about a concept of capacity to be used. These procedures will not be discussed again, and you are referred back to Chapter 3 if you need a review. However, there is something else that does need to be explored.

Standards have been defined as carefully predetermined amounts of resources that are expected to be consumed in accomplishing some objective. The behavior of *variable* costs is such that we can estimate them as the product of the standard rate per unit and the planned output (rate × output). However, fixed overhead *should not be* estimated in this way. Fixed overhead costs represent a quantity of resources that are expected to be consumed regardless of the achieved output. However, there has been a case made for assigning them to production at a constant amount per unit represented by the fixed overhead rate. Thus, the fixed overhead rate *does not* represent a rate of incurrence—just the rate of assignment. In turn, *it is not* appropriate to estimate the expected fixed cost at an amount equal to the fixed overhead rate multiplied by the output. The expected fixed cost is equal to the budgeted amount used in getting the rate. The implication of these observations will be explored in the next section.

Material Variances and Their Meanings

In this *and the next two* sections the variances that occur between the standard cost for given output of the period and the actual cost of obtaining that output are identified and explained. To be useful, the total variance must be analyzed in such a way that management can determine some specific courses of action to reduce or eliminate such variances in the future. For example, it is not very useful to tell management that the actual total cost of production this period was $2,000,000 and the standard cost was $1,800,000. It will be more informative if there is an indication of which cost items are out of line in the current period.

As a beginning analysis of the $200,000 total variance in the example above, it can be classified into variances related with material, labor, and overhead. Then if there are different types of material the total material variance can be classified according to each type. Likewise, the total labor variance can be analyzed according to the class of labor. Further, overhead variance can be classified according to each functional item such as indirect labor, supplies, power, and so forth. Additional data are provide by analyzing each of the material variances into price and quantity components, each labor class variance into rate and efficiency components, and each overhead variance into noncontrollable and controllable. The controllable overhead variance can also be classified into efficiency and spending variance. (These terms will be more carefully defined later in this section.) Exhibit 5.1 summarizes this analysis.

Now consider an example that will illustrate the variance computations. The E.E. Ray Company manufactures several products including a children's game known as Headache. The standard cost of producing one copy of the game is given in Exhibit 5.2. During January 19x1, 90,000 copies of the game were produced and 80,000 copies were sold. The actual resources consumed are itemized in Exhibit 5.3. Using these data the results for the period will be analyzed.

In a standard cost system, the amount of material *allowed* for the current period's production is called the standard material cost. This is also the amount that would be assigned to the output and traced through the accounting system if a standard cost accounting system is used. There will usually be a difference between the standard material cost allowed for production and the actual cost of materials purchased during the period. It is useful to management to analyze this difference. Knowledge of these components will help identify proper managerial responses to the performance of the period. First, note that:

$$\text{Standard quantity of material allowed} = \text{Standard quantity per unit of output} \times \text{Output for the period} \qquad (5\text{-}1)$$

$$\text{Standard material cost allowed} = \text{Standard quantity of material allowed} \times \text{Standard price per unit of material} \qquad (5\text{-}2)$$

The actual cost of material purchased during the current period can be expressed as:

$$\text{Actual cost of materials purchased} = \text{Actual units of material purchased} \times \text{Actual price per unit of material}$$

Exhibit 5.1   Classification of Standard Cost Variances

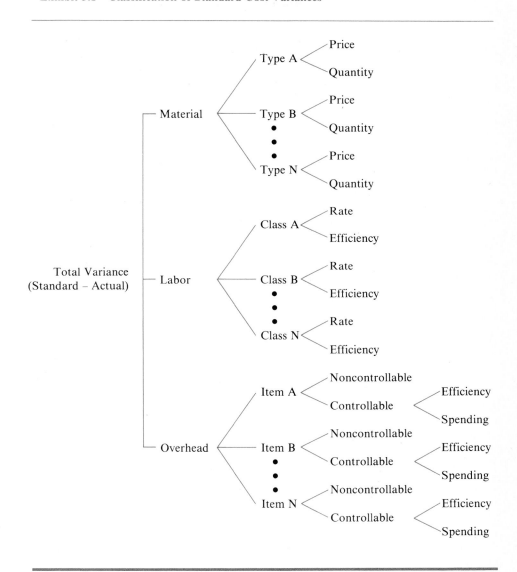

Exhibit 5.4 is a representation of the analysis. Note that unit costs are represented on the vertical axis and unit quantities on the horizontal. The entire rectangle (cell A + B + C + D) represents the actual cost of materials purchased during the period. The three shaded areas (A, C, D), collectively, represent the difference between the standard material cost allowed, or area B (the white area),

---

Exhibit 5.2   E. E. Ray Company Standards for the Headache Game as of January 1, 19x1

Material:		
Cardboard for box: (4 square feet @ $0.25)		$1.00
Paper: (5 square feet @ $0.10)		0.50
Labor (1/2 hour @ $6.00)		3.00
Overhead:		
Variable (1/2 hour @ $0.80)[a]	$0.40	
Fixed: (1/2 hour @ $0.20)[b]	0.10	0.50
Total standard cost per unit		$5.00

---

[a]Analysis has shown that variable overhead is related highly with direct labor hours. Thus, overhead is being assigned to this and all other products produced by E. E. Ray on the basis of labor hours.

[b]The fixed overhead rate of $0.20 was determined as a result of a budgeted fixed production cost for the year of $120,000 divided by a *normal capacity* of 600,000 direct labor hours. Assume that the $120,000 will be incurred at an even rate throughout the year.

and the actual cost of materials purchased. But only cells A and C represent variances. The figure reveals that the material purchased during the period exceeds the quantity used, which, in turn, exceeds the standard quantity allowed. Likewise, the actual cost per unit is greater than the standard cost.

The standard cost of material allowed is represented in the unshaded cell of Exhibit 5.4 (cell B). Numerically, this cost is given by equation (5-2). If the material inventory is maintained *at the standard cost,* then cell D is the dollar change in

---

Exhibit 5.3   E. E. Ray Company Actual Data For the Month of January 19x1

Headache games produced	90,000 units
Headache games sold	80,000 units
Cardboard purchased and used: (370,000 square feet @ $0.24)	$ 88,800
Paper purchased: (500,000 square feet @ $0.12)	$ 60,000
Paper used	440,000 sq. ft.
Labor: (46,000 hours @ $6.10)	$280,600
Variable overhead	$37,030
Fixed overhead	$10,100

Exhibit 5.4   Material Variance Analysis

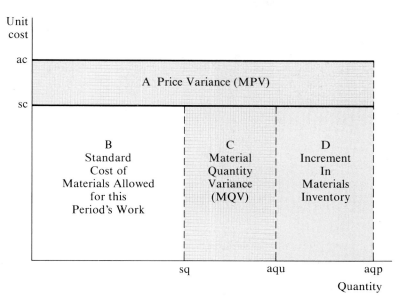

Notation:
     ac = *a*ctual *c*ost per unit of material
     sc = *s*tandard *c*ost per unit of material
     sq = *s*tandard *q*uantity of material
          allowed for this period's output
    aqu = *a*ctual *q*uantity of material *used*
          in production this period
    aqp = *a*ctual *q*uantity of material
          purchased this period

Variances:
    MPV = (sc − ac)aqp
    MQV = (sq − aqu)sc

the raw material inventory during the current period. This is simply an increase (or decrease) in the firm's assets, *not a variance*. Numerically, the amount of the change is:

$$
\begin{array}{l}
\text{Change in} \\
\text{materials} \\
\text{inventory}
\end{array}
=
\left[
\begin{array}{l}
\text{Actual} \\
\text{quantity} \\
\text{purchased}
\end{array}
-
\begin{array}{l}
\text{Actual} \\
\text{quantity} \\
\text{used}
\end{array}
\right]
\begin{array}{l}
\text{Standard} \\
\times \text{ cost} \\
\text{per unit}
\end{array}
$$

As indicated, the cells labeled A and C represent variances. The **material price variance** represents the effect of the actual cost *per unit of material* (not the cost per unit of the product) differing from the standard cost per unit. Cell A of Exhibit 5.4 represents the price variance, which is computed as follows:

$$
\begin{array}{l}
\text{Material} \\
\text{price} \\
\text{variance}
\end{array}
=
\left[
\begin{array}{l}
\text{Standard cost} \\
\text{per unit of} \\
\text{material}
\end{array}
-
\begin{array}{l}
\text{Actual cost} \\
\text{per unit of} \\
\text{material}
\end{array}
\right]
\begin{array}{l}
\text{Actual quantity} \\
\times \text{ of material} \\
\textit{purchased}
\end{array}
\qquad (5\text{-}3)
$$

This equation has been abbreviated in Exhibit 5.4. Further, all of the variance expressions in this book have been devised so that a positive variance is favorable (F) and a negative variance is unfavorable (U). The material price variances (MPV) for the example problem are:

MPV (cardboard) = ($0.25 − $0.24)370,000 = $ 3,700 F

MPV (paper)   = ($0.10 − $0.12)500,000 = $10,000 U

Consider an alternative to the price variance in equation (5-3). For reasons to be discussed in the next chapter, some accounting systems are set up to isolate the material price variance only when materials are *used* rather than when they are purchased. If so, the materials inventory should be carried at *actual unit costs*. Then, the portion of cell A directly above cell D in Exhibit 5.4 (vertically extend cell D) would be included in materials inventory rather than in the price variance. In this case, the price variance is:

$$
\begin{array}{l}
\text{Material} \\
\text{price} \\
\text{variance}
\end{array}
=
\left[
\begin{array}{l}
\text{Standard cost} \\
\text{per unit of} \\
\text{material}
\end{array}
-
\begin{array}{l}
\text{Actual cost} \\
\text{per unit of} \\
\text{material}
\end{array}
\right]
\begin{array}{l}
\text{Actual quantity} \\
\times \text{ of material} \\
\textit{used}
\end{array}
\qquad (5\text{-}3a)
$$

In the example problem this variation would not make any difference for cardboard because purchases and usage are the same. However, for paper:

MPV (paper) = ($0.10 − $0.12)444,000 = $8,800 U

Conceptually, the first method is preferred because a price variance occurs at the time of purchase, not at the time of use. Therefore, why wait until sometime after a purchase to recognize the variance? As will be seen later, the reasons for delaying recognition are practical and due to multiple uses of accounting data and to the desire to introduce some simplifications into the system.

Now that the material price variance has been computed, what does it indicate? Does it mean that the purchasing officer of the firm was doing a good job of acquiring cardboard and a bad job of acquiring paper? Be careful in drawing these conclusions and try to ensure that such a conclusion is not automatically drawn by others. All this variance indicates is that a difference occurred between the actual and the standard. It is not behaviorally desirable to establish the responsibility for a variance by mere association. The purchasing officer is probably in the best position to explain the variances but he or she cannot automatically be given the credit or the blame.

Good or bad performance of the purchasing officer, of course, may be part of the explanation of a price variance. Other reasons include inappropriate standards and acts of other personnel. In the latter category, you might find, for example, that the production department did not give sufficient lead time to acquire a certain material, and, to prevent delay, the purchasing officer decided to use non-standard procurement procedures. Assuming a delay in production would have had a large opportunity cost, such a decision could be justified. In this case, the responsibility for the variance is actually the production department's.

Next, consider the **material quantity variance.** This is represented by cell C of Exhibit 5.4 and is due to a difference between the standard allowance, given the output, and the actual consumption for material for the period. The computation can be inferred from Exhibit 5.4:

$$
\begin{matrix} \text{Material} \\ \text{quantity} \\ \text{variance} \end{matrix} = \begin{bmatrix} \text{Standard} & & \text{Actual} \\ \text{quantity} & - & \text{quantity} \\ \text{allowed} & & \text{used} \end{bmatrix} \times \begin{matrix} \text{Standard} \\ \text{cost per} \\ \text{unit} \end{matrix} \tag{5-4}
$$

The unit quantity difference is converted into dollars by using the standard cost because the dollar measurement of this variance should not be a function of price fluctuations (these are accounted for in the price variance). In our example the standard quantities allowed for the current period's production are given by using equation (5-1):

Cardboard: 4 × 90,000 = 360,000 square feet

Paper: 5 × 90,000 = 450,000 square feet

Note that *production,* not sales, was used to obtain the standard quantity allowed. This is because production represents the output of the manufacturing process and thus measures the activity for which material is consumed. The quantity variances (MQV) for the example are:

MQV (cardboard) = (360,000 − 370,000)$0.25 = $2,500 U

MQV (paper)   = (450,000 − 440,000)$0.10 = $1,000 F

In seeking an explanation for material quantity variances the accountant would start with the production manager. Again, this does not mean that the production manager is at fault; only that he or she is in the best position to explain it. The fault, for example, could be due to the purchasing agent's failure to acquire the proper grade of material which, in turn, caused wastage to be greater than anticipated. Thus, it is emphasized once more that the accountant needs to be cautious in seeking reasons for the variances and needs to take some precautions to ensure that others involved in this process are also cautious.

An alternative way to portray the material variances is by a "spread sheet" approach. This is illustrated in Exhibit 5.5 using the preceding data for the paper content of the Headache game. A spread sheet begins with the total purchases of material on the left and ends with the standard material cost for this period's output on the right. The difference in these two amounts is explained by the change in inventory, the material price variance, and the material quantity variance. In the spread sheet these three differences can be obtained by comparing the adjacent columns of the work sheet. You should take particular note of the four columns in

Exhibit 5.5   Spread Sheet Analysis of Material Variances

Actual Cost of Purchases	Standard Cost of Purchases	Standard Cost of Material Used	Standard Cost of Material Allowed This Period
Actual Quantity Purchased at Actual Costs	*Actual Quantity Purchased at Standard Costs*	*Actual Quantity Used at Standard Costs*	*Standard Quantity Allowed at Standard Costs*

For paper in E. E. Ray case:

500,000	500,000	440,000	450,000
×	×	×	×
0.12	0.10	0.10	0.10
60,000	50,000	44,000	45,000

	Material Price Variance		Inventory Change		Material Quantity Variance	

10,000 U*	+ 6,000	1,000 F*

For alternative method of recognizing price variance

Actual Cost of Purchases	Actual Cost of Material Used	Standard Cost of Material Used	Standard Cost of Material Allowed This Period
Actual Quantity Purchased at Actual Cost	*Actual Quantity Used at Actual Cost*	*Actual Quantity Used at Standard Cost*	*Standard Quantity Allowed at Standard Cost*

500,000	440,000	440,000	450,000
×	×	×	×
0.12	0.12	0.10	0.10
60,000	52,800	44,000	45,000

	Inventory Change		Material Price Variance		Material Quantity Variance	

+ 7,200	8,800 U*	1,000 F*

*Note that in this spread sheet, positive variances are unfavorable and negative are favorable. This is the opposite of the equations used elsewhere.

the spread sheet. The first two are actual quantities of material purchased multi-plied, respectively, by the actual cost per unit and the standard cost per unit. The last two are actual quantity used and standard quantity allowed multiplied, in both cases, by the standard cost per unit.

Finally, consider a potential problem that might arise with respect to the inter-pretation of material variances. Since there will typically be two managers involved in the control of material costs, you might encounter the following type of argument. The purchasing officer might argue that the unfavorable price variance was higher than it should be because the production manager used material inefficiently. That is, if the production department had used the standard amount of material, then the purchasing agent would have needed to acquire a smaller quantity and would have avoided some of the price variance. Thus, the argument suggests there is a **joint price-quantity variance.** Implicit in the argument for a joint responsibility is that the purchasing agent *did not* have any control over the price paid. If this is the case, and it may well be, then can the purchasing officer be held accountable for *any* of the price variance? That is, no one should be held responsible for the price variance in this case. If the purchasing officer does have control over the prices paid, he or she could have avoided the price variance on the inefficiently used material by acquiring those units at the standard price. If an agent could have avoided the variance by his or her own action, there is no case to be made for joint responsibility. In short, there is no good case for computing a joint variance.

There are some accountants, however, who would argue that the price variance should be divided into a pure price variance and a joint price-quantity variance. The **pure price variance** would be a function of the standard quantity allowed for the achieved output so that it would not be affected by production inefficiencies. To illustrate, consider Exhibit 5.6. (The variances are still the cells labeled A and C.)

If one wants to argue for the possibility of a joint price-quantity variance, then the price variance will have to be isolated at the time when the units are used. If it is measured when they are purchased, there is no way of knowing whether it is a pure or a joint variance. Thus, the material inventory will be carried at actual prices. Cell A_1 would be the pure variance and cell A_2 the joint variance. The *total* price variance is given by equation (5.3a) and can be divided between pure and joint variance as follows:

$$\text{Pure material price variance} = \left[\begin{array}{c}\text{Standard cost} \\ \text{per unit of} \\ \text{material}\end{array} - \begin{array}{c}\text{Actual cost} \\ \text{per unit of} \\ \text{material}\end{array}\right] \times \begin{array}{c}\text{Standard} \\ \text{quantity} \\ \text{allowed}\end{array} \quad (5\text{-}5)$$

$$\text{Joint price quantity variance} = \left[\begin{array}{c}\text{Standard cost} \\ \text{per unit of} \\ \text{material}\end{array} - \begin{array}{c}\text{Actual cost} \\ \text{per unit of} \\ \text{material}\end{array}\right] \quad (5\text{-}6)$$

$$\times \left[\begin{array}{c}\text{Actual} \\ \text{quantity} \\ \text{used}\end{array} - \begin{array}{c}\text{Standard} \\ \text{quantity} \\ \text{allowed}\end{array}\right]$$

Both of the equations are abbreviated in Exhibit 5.6. Note that the pure price variance cannot be affected by inefficient use of materials.

Exhibit 5.6   Material Variances if Price Variance Is Divided Into a Pure and Joint Component

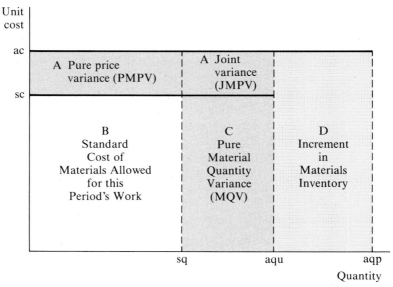

Notation:
ac = *a*ctual *c*ost per unit of material
sc = *s*tandard *c*ost per unit of material
sq = *s*tandard *q*uantity of material
      allowed for this period's output
aqu = *a*ctual *q*uantity of material *used*
      in production this period
aqp = *a*ctual *q*uantity of material
      purchased this period

Variances:
PMPV = (sc − ac)sq
JMPV = (sc − ac)(aqu − sq)
MQV = (sq − aqu)sc

Labor Variances

The variance between the standard labor cost allowed for the current output and the actual labor cost incurred can be analyzed in a manner similar to material. First, compute the hours allowed:

| Standard labor hours allowed | = | Standard hours allowed per unit of output | × | Output for period | (5-7) |

As with material, note that the standard hours allowed are a function of production. Direct labor would be needed to support production activity, not the sales activity. Then:

$$
\begin{array}{l}
\text{Labor} \\
\text{rate} \\
\text{variance}
\end{array}
=
\left[
\begin{array}{l}
\text{Standard} \\
\text{labor rate} \\
\text{per hour}
\end{array}
-
\begin{array}{l}
\text{Actual} \\
\text{labor rate} \\
\text{per hour}
\end{array}
\right]
\times
\begin{array}{l}
\text{Actual} \\
\text{labor} \\
\text{hours}
\end{array}
\qquad (5\text{-}8)
$$

$$
\begin{array}{l}
\text{Labor efficiency} \\
\text{(quantity)} \\
\text{variance}
\end{array}
=
\left[
\begin{array}{l}
\text{Standard} \\
\text{labor hours} \\
\text{allowed}
\end{array}
-
\begin{array}{l}
\text{Actual} \\
\text{labor} \\
\text{hours}
\end{array}
\right]
\times
\begin{array}{l}
\text{Standard} \\
\text{labor rate} \\
\text{per hour}
\end{array}
\qquad (5\text{-}9)
$$

For the E.E. Ray example find the data in Exhibits 5.2 and 5.3 and verify:

Standard labor hours allowed $= (1/2) \times 90{,}000 = 45{,}000$

Labor rate variance $= (\$6.00 - \$6.10)46{,}000 = \$4{,}600$ U

Labor efficiency variance $= (45{,}000 - 46{,}000)\$6.00$
$$= \$6{,}000 \text{ U}$$

Labor variances can also be depicted using the spread-sheet approach. Again, actual labor costs are on the left and applied on the right. The two variances result from comparing the extremes with the standard cost of the actual hours:

Actual labor	Standard cost of actual hours	Applied labor
Actual hours at actual rate	Actual hours at standard rate	Standard hours at standard rate

$$
\underbrace{\qquad\qquad}_{\substack{\text{Labor} \\ \text{rate} \\ \text{variance}}}
\underbrace{\qquad\qquad}_{\substack{\text{Labor} \\ \text{efficiency} \\ \text{variance}}}
$$

$(+ = \text{unfavorable}; - = \text{favorable})$

Overhead Variances

As indicated in Exhibit 5.1, overhead variances can be classified as noncontrollable or controllable. Such a classification is called the **two-variance system.** The **controllable overhead variance** is the portion of the variance for which there is some cause to say it could have been avoided with better performance. It is computed as the difference between the total budget (fixed plus variable) *at the standard level of activity* (not the actual level) and the total actual overhead:

$$
\begin{array}{l}
\text{Controllable} \\
\text{overhead} \\
\text{variance}
\end{array}
=
\begin{array}{l}
\text{Budgeted cost} \\
\text{for standard} \\
\text{activity level}
\end{array}
-
\begin{array}{l}
\text{Actual} \\
\text{overhead} \\
\text{cost}
\end{array}
\qquad (5\text{-}10)
$$

Note that the first term is the *budgeted* cost at the standard activity level. The budget would be a flexible budget. That is, the variable cost is adjusted to be appropriate for the activity level. The fixed costs would be at a constant amount and would not vary with activity.

This variance is based on the premise that both the activity level and the rate of cost incurrence per unit of activity can be controlled. To further explain, consider Exhibit 5.7. Assume that in a multiple product environment, where several products are being produced, it has been found that direct-labor hours is the best explanatory variable of overhead incurrence. As depicted in Exhibit 5.7, the output of the products cause direct-labor hours to be incurred and, in turn, direct-labor hours cause variable overhead costs to be incurred. Fixed overhead is shown but with no causal variables that are related to activity levels. Now, *if*:

1. direct-labor hours are incurred at the planned rate for all products, and
2. variable overhead is incurred at the planned rate per direct-labor hour, and
3. fixed costs are incurred at the planned rate,

then controllable overhead variance will be zero. But, one or more of these three conditions may not be present.

Exhibit 5.7   Relationship of Overhead Incurrence and Production Activity

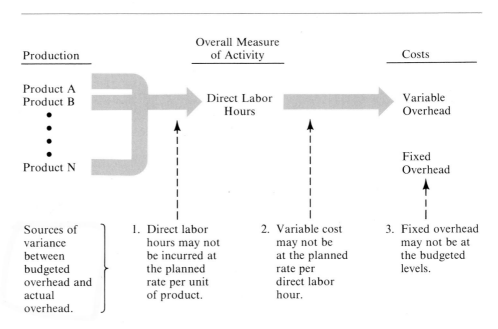

How does equation (5-10) include all three elements? By basing the variable costs in the budget on *standard* activity levels, variations from item 1 will be included. The budget will not include any overhead that would be caused by the actual labor hours being different from the standard. However, any additional costs caused by the difference would be included in the actual overhead cost. Variations from item 2 are incorporated as a result of budgeting the variable costs at the *planned rate* of incurrence (the standard rate per hour). The third variation is included since the flexible budget would include fixed costs at the planned amount. Again, this variance is computed on the assumption that each of the three sources listed in Exhibit 5.7 can be controlled by someone in the production area. Of course, the extent to which this will be true is dependent on the circumstances and must be assessed by the accountant.

For the example problem the controllable overhead variance is:

Budgeted fixed cost per month = (1/12) × $120,000	$10,000
Budgeted variable costs at standard hours = $0.80 × 45,000	36,000
Total budget at standard hours	$46,000

Actual overhead cost = $10,100 + $37,030 = $47,130

Controllable variance = $46,000 − $47,130 = $1,130 U

As you can see, a portion of this variance is due to fixed overhead ($100; budget of $10,000 less actual of $10,100) and a portion due to variable ($1,030; budget of $36,000 less actual of $37,030).

The noncontrollable variance is due to the difference between the amount of *applied* and *budgeted* fixed cost. The variance is also part of the variance system that is discussed next. Thus, its discussion is deferred.

Overhead variance analysis will likely be more useful if the controllable variance is further detailed. The classification system discussed next corresponds to the three sources of variation detailed in Exhibit 5.7 and the *courses of action needed to eliminate* the future incurrence of the variance.

The four variance system has two variances for variable overhead and two for fixed. An analysis of variable overhead parallels the material and labor costs. Consider Exhibit 5.8. Dollars are plotted on the vertical axis and the activity level on the horizontal axis.

In the four variance system, the variable overhead portion of controllable variance is divided into an efficiency and a spending component. First, consider the **variable overhead efficiency** variance. Since variable overhead costs are applied on the basis of an overall measure, such as direct-labor hours or machine hours, and since a prerequisite for this measure of activity is correlation with cost incurrence, then an increase (or decrease) in the activity level from the standard amount allowed will cause an increase (or decrease) in the variable overhead costs. This is reflected in Exhibit 5.8 by noting that as the activity level moves from the standard level to the actual level, it is expected that the variable cost will move to

Exhibit 5.8   Representation of Variable Overhead Variance Analysis

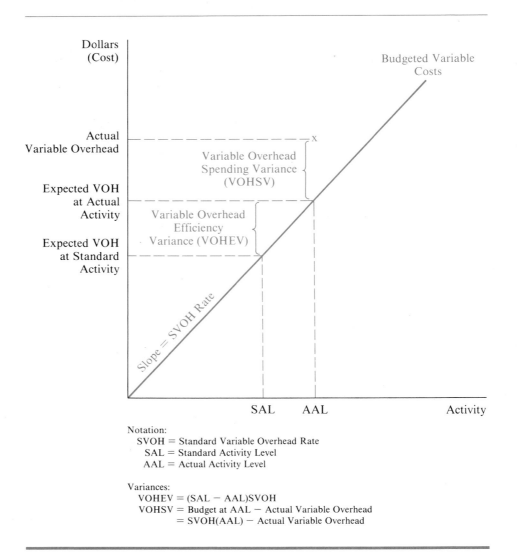

Notation:
SVOH = Standard Variable Overhead Rate
SAL = Standard Activity Level
AAL = Actual Activity Level

Variances:
VOHEV = (SAL − AAL)SVOH
VOHSV = Budget at AAL − Actual Variable Overhead
= SVOH(AAL) − Actual Variable Overhead

a higher level. This increase in the expected cost to be incurred is called the variable overhead efficiency variance because it is caused by inefficiency (or efficiency) in the variable being used to measure activity. Thus:

$$\begin{matrix} \text{Variable overhead} \\ \text{efficiency} \\ \text{variance} \end{matrix} = \begin{bmatrix} \text{Standard} & & \text{Actual} \\ \text{activity level} & - & \text{activity} \\ \text{allowed} & & \text{level} \end{bmatrix} \times \begin{matrix} \text{Standard} \\ \text{variable} \\ \text{overhead rate} \end{matrix} \qquad (5\text{-}11)$$

This variance is due to source number one as identified in Exhibit 5.7.

The second variable overhead variance is the spending variance. Note that the variable overhead efficiency variance assumes that variable costs will increase (or decrease) at a rate equal to the standard variable overhead rate. However, the actual rate of overhead incurrence with respect to the overall measure of activity may differ from the predetermined rate. For example, supplies may have been purchased at a different unit cost than planned. Also physical supplies might be consumed at a different rate per unit of activity than planned. This can happen if supplies consumption is not *perfectly* correlated with the overall measure of activity. *Perfectly* correlated variables are rare in practice. Both of these variations would be included in the variable overhead spending variance and similar phenomena could occur with respect to all variable overhead items. These variances are called **spending variances** and correspond to item two in Exhibit 5.7. As you can see in Exhibit 5.8, variable overhead spending variance is computed as:

$$\begin{matrix}\text{Variable} \\ \text{overhead} \\ \text{spending} \\ \text{variance}\end{matrix} = \begin{matrix}\text{Variable costs} \\ \text{budgeted at} \\ \textit{actual} \text{ activity} \\ \text{levels}\end{matrix} - \begin{matrix}\text{Actual} \\ \text{variable} \\ \text{overhead}\end{matrix} \qquad (5\text{-}12)$$

These two variances are now illustrated via our example. The budgeted variable overhead at actual labor hours is $36,800 ($0.8 × 46,000).

$$\text{VOH efficiency variance} = (45,000 - 46,000)\$0.80 = \$800 \text{ U} \qquad (5\text{-}11')$$

$$\text{VOH spending variance} = \$36,800 - \$37,030 = \$230 \text{ U} \qquad (5\text{-}12')$$

This analysis would suggest that $800 of the controllable variable overhead variance could be eliminated by using direct-labor hours more efficiently. The remaining $230 of the $1,030 variance can be corrected by getting the variable overhead rate per direct-labor back in line with the planned rate. As mentioned earlier, the actual overhead rate per labor hour could differ from the planned rate for two basic reasons. First, the prices that are actually paid may differ from the planned prices. Second, the rate of physical consumption of the resources (supplies, indirect labor, and so forth) may differ from the planned rate. *The latter is not accounted for by the efficiency variance.* The variable overhead efficiency variance is due to the actual activity being different than the standard activity, and not due to a variance in the consumption rate per unit of activity.

To elaborate on the meaning of the variable overhead spending variance assume, for simplicity, that there is only one item in E.E. Ray's variable overhead, factory supplies. Further, the budgeted supplies cost at the normal activity level of 600,000 direct-labor hours was:

100,000 boxes @ $4.80/box = $480,000

As you can see, such a budget for supplies would yield the variable overhead rate of $0.80 per direct-labor hour as stated in Exhibit 5.2:

$$\text{Variable overhead rate} = \frac{\$480,000}{600,000} = \$0.80$$

Further, there is an implicit rate at which supplies are expected to be consumed. If 100,000 boxes are anticipated when direct-labor hours are 600,000, then it is expected that one-sixth of a box of supplies will be used for each direct-labor hour incurred:

$$\text{Supplies rate/direct-labor hour} = \frac{100,000 \text{ boxes}}{600,000 \text{ hours}} = \frac{1}{6}$$

It was stated in Exhibit 5.3 that the actual variable overhead for the period was $37,030. Suppose this represented 7,666.67 boxes of supplies at a price of $4.83 (7,666.67 × $4.83 = $37,030). In this case, the variable overhead spending variance of $230 (see [5-12']) is due to supplies being acquired at a price different from the planned price ($4.83 versus $4.80). The rate of supplies consumed per actual direct-labor hour is at the planned level:

$$\frac{7,666.67}{46,000} = \frac{1}{6}$$

Consider a second case. Suppose the $37,030 was the result of using 7,714.58333 boxes, which cost $4.80 each (7,714.58333 × $4.80 = $37,030). The variable overhead spending variance is still $230. Since the price paid per box is at the planned level, $4.80, the source of the variance has to be the rate at which the supplies were used. Obviously the rate per hour is greater than 1/6.[3]

The above cases show that the variable overhead spending variance can be due to a combination of price variances and rate of consumption variances. Either of these variations will cause the dollar amount of supplies per direct-labor hour to be different than planned. Carefully note the second case. It is tempting to say the variation in that case is variable overhead efficiency variance. *It is not* and you must remember what the efficiency variance represents. It is the increase (decrease) in overhead costs that is expected as a result of the overall activity level (direct-labor hours in this case) being above (below) the standard level. If the activity level is above the standard level, the variable overhead efficiency variance is the increase in costs caused by the extra direct-labor hours and has nothing to do with the rate of overhead per direct-labor hour.

The elaboration on the spending variance has been included to help you better understand the meaning of the variance. In turn, you should be better able to explain these variances to management and help them take appropriate preventative actions.

Finally, consider the variance analysis of fixed overhead items. As indicated earlier, fixed costs do not behave according to a rate of incurrence *per unit* of activity. However, a standard cost system does use a rate of application. Consider Exhibit 5.9. Note that the vertical axis is *total* cost.

---

[3]It should be noted that in the case of less than perfect correlation there are offsetting errors in the variable overhead efficiency variance and the variable overhead spending variance. If overhead is not perfectly correlated, then the efficiency variance will not be as high as computed. Then the offsetting result would be that the rate of resource consumption per unit of activity will be lower than the budgeted rate and cause the overhead spending variance to be lower.

Exhibit 5.9   Fixed Overhead Variance Analysis

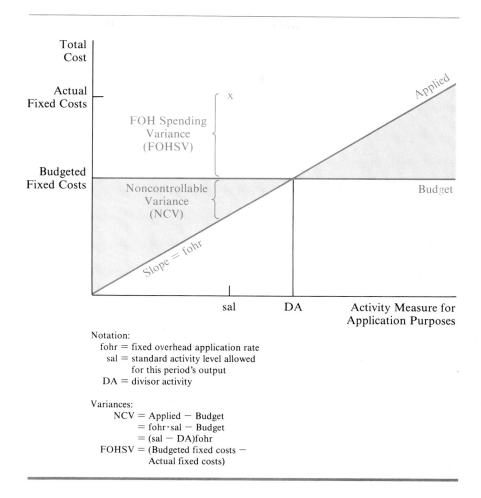

Notation:
    fohr = fixed overhead application rate
    sal = standard activity level allowed
            for this period's output
    DA = divisor activity

Variances:
    NCV = Applied − Budget
        = fohr·sal − Budget
        = (sal − DA)fohr
    FOHSV = (Budgeted fixed costs −
            Actual fixed costs)

Again, there are two components of the total fixed overhead variance. First, there is the **noncontrollable variance.** When fixed costs are assigned at a constant rate determined by use of a divisor activity, then the applied fixed costs will equal the budgeted fixed costs only if the activity level is equal to the divisor. This is the point where the budget line and the applied line intersect in Exhibit 5.9. If the firm does not operate at the divisor level, then the fixed overhead costs applied will not equal the *budgeted* fixed costs. The noncontrollable variance is just the portion of the budgeted fixed costs not applied (underapplied) or the amount applied in excess of the budget (overapplied). That is:

Noncontrollable variance = Applied fixed − Budgeted fixed   (5-13)

For the example, January's noncontrollable variance is:

Noncontrollable variance = 45,000 × 0.20 − (1/12)(120,000) = $1,000 U

Note that the fixed cost is applied on the basis of *standard* hours allowed.

Sometimes the noncontrollable variance is called the **volume variance.** That is, there will be a variance if the volume of activity is not equal to the divisor activity. Further, there is an alternative way to compute this variance. First, note that:

Applied fixed overhead = Application rate × Standard activity level

Since:

Application rate = Budgeted fixed costs ÷ Divisor activity

then:

Budgeted fixed costs = Application rate × Divisor activity

Therefore:

Noncontrollable variance = (Application rate × Standard activity level − Application rate × Divisor activity)

Factor out the application rate:

$$\text{Noncontrollable (volume) variance} = \left[\text{Standard activity level} - \text{Divisor activity} \right] \times \text{Application rate} \tag{5-13a}$$

Let us further explore the noncontrollable, or volume, variance. If the divisor activity is normal or expected activity, it may be found that this variance is either negative, representing underapplied fixed costs, or positive, representing overapplied. If a normal activity is used, then, depending on the accuracy of the forecast, it should be found that the sum of the noncontrollable variance over several years approaches zero. That is, if the divisor activity used is actually the normal (or the average), then the underapplications should be approximately equal to the overapplications. This provides some support for *not* closing out this variance at year-end and for taking it forward as a deferred charge or credit. However, in practice it will be found that this variance is closed annually.

If practical capacity is used as the divisor activity, then the noncontrollable variance should never be positive. If it were, that means the firm is working *above* practical capacity. Use of practical capacity will tend to be more indicative of idle facilities than will use of normal activity as the divisor. However, accountants should not do anything to encourage *needless* production that might be scheduled just to eliminate a negative noncontrollable variance. If such a variance is anticipated to continue into the long run, then some consideration should be given to either making some productive use of idle facilities or to reducing capacity.

As shown in Exhibit 5.9, the actual fixed costs will not necessarily be equal to the budgeted amount. This difference is called **fixed overhead spending variance** and is computed as:

$$\text{Fixed overhead spending variance} = \text{Budgeted fixed costs} - \text{Actual fixed costs} \tag{5-14}$$

The fixed overhead spending variance is the third item of Exhibit 5.7. For Jaunary of the illustrative case, the budgeted fixed costs are $10,000 ($120,000 ÷ 12 months). Thus:

Fixed overhead spending variance = $10,000 − $10,100

$$= \$100 \text{ U}$$

It may not always prove possible or practical to separate *actual* overhead costs into fixed and variable amounts. If so, then it will not be possible to compute *separate* spending variances for fixed and variable overhead. (In equations 5-12 and 5-14, note that actual costs are needed by category in order to complete the computations.)

Alternatively, in these cases, the two spending variances can be combined. In equation 5-12 note that the first component is the budgeted variable overhead at the actual activity level. Summing the budgeted variable costs at actual activity and the budgeted fixed costs and calling the result the total budget at actual activity, the total overhead spending variance can be computed as:

$$\begin{array}{l} \textit{Total} \text{ overhead} \\ \text{spending} \\ \text{variance} \end{array} = \begin{array}{l} \text{Total overhead} \\ \text{budget at} \\ \textit{actual} \text{ activity} \end{array} - \begin{array}{l} \text{Total actual} \\ \text{overhead} \\ \text{costs} \end{array} \qquad (5\text{-}15)$$

The budget would be a flexible budget of the form $y = a + bx$ where a is the fixed cost; b, the variable rate; and x, the measurement of activity. Note that x, in this case, would be the actual activity, not the standard activity allowed.

Exhibit 5.10 is a spread-sheet summary of the overhead variance accounting. The overhead analysis of the E.E. Ray case is included for illustrative purposes. As with the material and labor spread sheets, the overhead variances can be computed by comparing the adjacent columns. Column one should be obvious. The second column is a flexible budget at *actual* levels, whereas column three is a flexible budget at *standard* levels. Column four is total applied costs (not budgeted).

In the last three sections there was a discussion of the variances from standard that can be computed to help management in striving for an efficient operation. Keep in mind that these variances are just messages and cannot be used for evaluation in a *carte blanche* manner. This will be further explored in Chapter 6.

Standards When There Are Work-in-Process Inventories

In the previous sections the examples did not involve any partially completed production. Such a possibility is introduced here. Suppose that the E.E. Ray Company had the following inventories:

	January 1	January 31
Work in process (games)	10,000	20,000
Percentage completion		
Cardboard	100%	100%
Paper	80%	30%
Labor	60%	40%

Exhibit 5.10   Spread Sheet Analysis Of Overhead Variances

Total Actual Overhead	*Budget at Actual Activity*	*Budget at Standard Activity*	*Applied*
Actual fixed + actual variable	*Budgeted fixed + actual activity at standard variable rates*	*Budgeted fixed + standard activity at standard variable rates*	*Standard hours at standard total rates*
$10,100	$10,000	$10,000	45,000
+	+	+	×
$37,030	46,000 × $0.8	45,000 × $0.8	$1.00
$47,130	$46,800	$46,000	$45,000

Spending Variance	Efficiency Variance	Noncontrollable Variance
$330 U	$800 U	$1,000 U

Controllable Variance (Two-Way Method)	Noncontrollable Variance
$1,130 U	$1,000 U

Further, assume that 90,000 games were still finished during January. How would the variance analysis be done in this case?

The standard allowance for material and labor will still be based on the accomplishment, or output, for the month. The output during January would be the FIFO equivalent production. FIFO, you will recall from Chapter 4, measures only the work done in the current period. This is what is needed for determining how much material and labor the production department should have used during the period. To evaluate efficiency as measured by resources used this period, we need to compare the actual with the standard allowed for this period's output. Thus, the equivalent units and standard allowances are:

	Cardboard	*Paper*	*Labor*
Beginning inventory	0	2,000	4,000
Started and finished (90,000–10,000)	80,000	80,000	80,000
Ending inventory	20,000	6,000	8,000
Equivalent units	100,000	88,000	92,000
Standard per unit (from Exhibit 5.2)	4	5	0.5
Standard allowance	400,000	440,000	46,000

The above values would be used as called for in the variance analysis. Specifically, they would be needed in the computation of the material quantity variance, the labor efficiency variance, the variable overhead efficiency variance, and the noncontrollable variance.

The overhead spending variance is:

OHSV = $47,750 − $46,000 = $1,750 F

4. The variable overhead efficiency variance is computed using equation (5-11):

VOHEV = (40,000 − 41,000)$0.25 = $250 U

5. The noncontrollable variance is computed using equation (5-13a):

NCV = (40,000 − 50,000)0.75 = $7,500 U

References

Dopuch, N., Birnberg, J.G., and Demski, J. "An Extension of Standard Cost Variance Analysis," *The Accounting Review* (July 1967): 526–536.

Manes, R.P. "The Expense of Expected Idle Capacity," *Management Accounting* (March 1969): 37–41.

Solomons, D. "Standard Costing Needs Better Variances," *NAA Bulletin* (December 1961): 29–39.

Problems

5-1. Determining Standard Material Allowed. The JM Company manufactures one product for which the standard material allowance is 4 pounds per unit. During the current period, 40,000 units of the product were sold. The beginning finished goods inventory was 500 units and the ending finished goods inventory was 2,000 units.

Required:

What is the standard quantity of material allowed for the period?

5-2. Determining Standard Labor Quantities When There Are Work-in-Process Inventories. The LP Company's only product is allowed 6 labor hours per unit. During the current period 100,000 units were finished, including 15,000 units from the beginning work-in-process inventory, which were 30% complete at the start of the period. There is an ending work-in-process inventory of 20,000 units, 60% complete. Labor is added uniformly throughout the period.

Required:

What is the standard quantity of labor allowed for the period?

5-3. Standard Labor Allowed When There Are Multiple Products. The LW Company produces two products. Following are some data for the current period:

	Product #4	Product #2B
Beginning work-in-process inventory (units)	6,000	10,000
Percentage completion for labor	25%	40%
Ending work-in-process inventory (units)	3,000	15,000
Percentage completion for labor	30%	60%
Units finished	40,000	70,000
Units sold	42,000	65,000
Labor allowed per unit	5 hours	3 hours

Required:

How many labor hours are allowed for this period's work?

5-4. Labor Rate Variance. The AT Company has three classes of labor but uses just one labor rate for its standard costing system. The labor standard for the product produced this period was 9 hours at $12.111 and was determined as follows:

Class 1	3 hours @ $15	$ 45
Class 2	2 hours @ $12	24
Class 3	4 hours @ $10	40
	9 hours	$109

Rate = $109 ÷ 9 hours = $12.111.

During the current period, 10,000 units of the product were produced. The following labor cost was incurred:

Class 1	32,000 hours @ $15	$ 480,000
Class 2	19,000 hours @ $12	228,000
Class 3	39,000 hours @ $10	390,000
	90,000	$1,098,000

Required:

Compute the labor rate variance for the period.

5-5. Understanding Relationships between Budgeted and Applied Fixed Overhead. The HJ Company applies fixed overhead at a rate of $7 per direct-labor hour. This rate was established using a divisor activity of 200,000 labor hours per year. During the current year 50,000 units of their only product was produced. Each unit is allowed 3 labor hours. Actual labor hours totaled 155,000. Actual fixed costs totaled $1,300,000.

Required:

What is the budgeted fixed overhead for the period?

5-6. Basic Variance Analysis. Reconsider the E.E. Ray Company problem whose standards are stated in Exhibit 5.2. During February 19x1 the company produced 101,000 copies of the Headache game and sold 105,000 copies. The following data were noted:

Cardboard purchased: (450,000 square feet @ $0.245)	$110,250
Cardboard used	410,000 square feet
Paper purchased: (440,000 square feet @ $0.11)	$ 48,400
Paper used	490,000 square feet
Labor: (49,000 hours @ $6.05)	$296,450
Variable overhead	$ 40,000
Fixed overhead	$ 9,800

Required:

Prepare a complete variance analysis showing two variances for each material, two for labor, and four for manufacturing overhead. The January 19x1 data are in Exhibit 5.3 and should also be considered.

5-7. Variance Analysis. The Garvey Company uses a standard cost system where overhead is applied on the basis of labor hours and fixed overhead rates are established on the basis of normal activity. At a normal production level of 12,000 units of its only product, 36,000 standard direct-labor hours would be required, and the following costs would be applied to production:

Direct material	$144,000
Direct labor	108,000
Variable factory overhead	18,000
Fixed factory overhead	36,000

During August 19x2, 38,800 direct-labor hours were actually needed to produce a total of 13,000 finished units. The actual costs of this production included $120,280 for direct labor, $19,700 for variable factory overhead, and $36,000 for fixed factory overhead.

Required:

1. Compute the direct-labor rate variance. Is it favorable or unfavorable?
2. Compute the direct-labor efficiency variance. Is it favorable or unfavorable?
3. Compute the variable overhead spending variance. Is it favorable or unfavorable?
4. Compute the variable overhead efficiency variance. Is it favorable or unfavorable?
5. What is the budgeted fixed factory overhead for August 19x2?
6. What is the applied fixed factory overhead for August 19x2?
7. Compute the noncontrollable (volume) variance.

5-8. Overhead Rate Determination. The LA Dodge Company produces ten different products. Each of these products requires processing in the assembly department. You have drawn the assignment of determining the factory overhead rates in this department for 19x2. It has already been decided that direct-labor hours will be used as the measure of activity and that the divisor volume will be measured on the basis of normal activity.

During the last five years, the average standard labor hours used in meeting production schedules totaled 100,000. The average actual hours totaled 105,000. The company economist has forecasted the average demand for labor during the next five years at a figure that is 10% higher than the past five years.

Using a variety of sources, you have compiled the following cost estimates at direct-labor volumes of 50,000 and 100,000 hours:

	50,000 Hours	*100,000 Hours*
Factory Depreciation		
(Equipment and Building)	$100,000	$100,000
Indirect Labor	60,000	110,000
Indirect Material	155,000	305,000
Power	125,000	225,000
Supervisory Salaries*	150,000	300,000

*An activity of 0 to 74,999 hours could be managed with one shift; 75,000 to 150,000 hours would required two shifts

Required:

Prepare a schedule showing the computation of the 19x2 overhead rates for the assembly department. Organize your schedule to display both fixed and variable components. (Assume that all cost behaviors follow a linear pattern.)

5-9. Detailed Overhead Analysis. The D. Baker Company prepared the following overhead budget for a normal monthly activity of 100,000 direct labor hours:

Variable Costs:		
Indirect material	$ 30,000	
Indirect labor	40,000	
Power	20,000	
Other	100,000	$190,000 1.90/m.
Fixed Costs:		
Depreciation	$ 50,000	
Supervision	70,000	
Other	40,000	160,000 1.60/m.
Total		$350,000

During March the output produced should have required 80,000 direct-labor hours. The actual direct-labor hours employed totaled 82,000 hours and cost $500,200 (the standard labor rate was $6.00 per hour). The following actual overhead costs were incurred:

Variable Costs:		
Indirect material	$25,000	
Indirect labor	32,000	
Power	16,400	
Other	83,000	$156,400
Fixed Costs:		
Depreciation	$50,000	
Supervision	72,000	
Other	39,000	161,000
Total		$317,400

Required:

Prepare an itemized schedule analyzing the March manufacturing overhead. Include the following columns: Applied, Budgeted at Standard Hours, Budgeted at Actual Hours, Actual Costs, Total Variance, Efficiency Variance, Spending Variance, and Noncontrollable Variance.

5-10. Using Various Standard Cost Concepts To Derive Selected Results. The Lopes Company's *total* overhead rate is $2.00 per direct-labor hour based on normal volume. Total budgeted overhead for 3,000 and 7,000 labor hours per month is $8,500 and $14,500, respectively. During June 19x3 the actual manufacturing overhead was $9,000, the actual labor hours totaled 3,000, and 3,200 standard hours were allowed for June's production.

Required:

1. What is the variable overhead rate per hour?
2. What is the budgeted fixed overhead at 3,000 labor hours?
3. What is the budgeted fixed overhead at 4,000 labor hours?
4. What is the normal activity per month?
5. What is the applied total overhead for June 19x3?
6. Compute the *total* overhead variance for June 19x3.
7. Analyze the total overhead variance for June 19x3 into three components.

5-11. Graph the Material Variance (Including the Joint Price-Quantity Variance). Assume that the material price variance is measured according to equation (5-3a). The following questions request you to prepare some graphs. Plot unit costs on the vertical axis and quantities on the horizontal axis.

Required:

1. Assume that the actual cost per unit exceeds the standard and that the actual quantity used exceeds the standard quantity allowed. Show a graph using the following notation to label the indicated areas:

A = standard material cost for the period
B = material quantity variance
C = material price variance

2. Repeat part 1 but assume that the material price variance is to be divided into a pure and a joint variance and labeled as:

C = pure price variance
D = joint price-quantity variance

3. Now assume that the actual cost per unit exceeds the standard cost but that the actual quantity used is less than the standard quantity allowed. Prepare a graph that displays the standard material cost, the material quantity variance, the pure price variance, and the joint price-quantity variance.
4. Repeat part 3 except assume that the actual cost per unit is less than the standard cost, whereas the actual quantity used exceeds the standard allowed.

5-12. Interpreting a Graph of the Overhead Variances. Consider the case where overhead is applied on the basis of direct-labor hours. Exhibit 5.11 on page 180 depicts various relationships concerning total (fixed and variable) overhead incurrence, expectations, and application.

Required:

1. Identify the meaning of the following: a. Line (b, k); b. Line (b, n); c. Line (a, m); d. Line (c,d); e. Line (d, e); f. Line (e, f); g. Line (g, j); h. Line (h, i); i. Line (i, j).
2. Using the graphical notation, how would you depict the total overhead applied?

5-13. Interpreting Overhead Variances. The Yeager Company applies overhead on the basis of direct-labor hours. One item included in factory overhead is supplies. It is estimated that a half-unit of supplies is needed per direct-labor hour. A unit of supplies costs $2.00. To produce one unit of the finished product, 2 hours of labor are needed.

During the current period 210 hours of labor were needed to produce 100 units of the finished product. In doing this 101 units of supplies were used at a cost of $2.00.

Required:

1. What must be true to justify the use of direct-labor hours as the base of applying overhead?
2. How much of the overhead efficiency variance is due to supplies?
3. How much of the overhead spending variance is due to supplies?

5-14. Interpreting Overhead Variances. The Cey Company's product required ten direct-labor hours at $8.00 per hour. In developing the manufacturing overhead budget, supplies

---

Exhibit 5.11   Graph of Overhead Variances

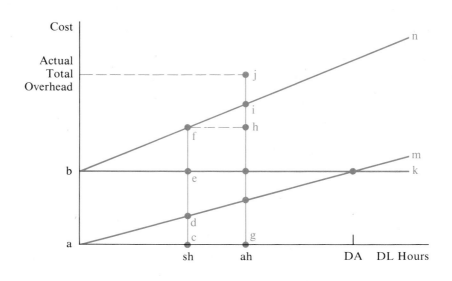

Notation:
   sh = standard hours allowed
   ah = actual hours
   DA = divisor activity

---

were budgeted at $0.20 per labor hour. (Assume this results from the estimate of one $2.00 box of supplies for every ten labor hours.) During the current month 10,000 units were produced. The payroll records show 101,000 direct-labor hours were employed.

Required:

1. For the month just cited, is it possible for the overhead efficiency variance due to supplies to be zero? If yes, what would the actual number of boxes used have to have been if the actual price per box were $2.00. If no, why?
2. For the month just cited, is it possible for the spending variance due to supplies to be zero if the actual cost per box were $2.02? If yes, what actual quantity would have to have been used? If no, why?

5-15. Alternative to Problems 5-13 and 5-14. The Ahful Company produces 67 different products. Many of these products require processing in the Forming Department. At the beginning of 19x1 an overhead budget was prepared for the Forming Department. Selected items from the budget are as follows:

Divisor Activity	100,000 direct-labor hours
Supplies 25,000 boxes @ $8	$200,000
Overhead rate for supplies	$2 per direct-labor hour

During November of 19x1 the Forming Department produced 800 units of product #13 and 600 units of product #29. The standard labor hour allowances per unit are 4 and 10 for product #13 and #29, respectively.

Required:

1. Under what condition in the above situation, if any, would there be a supplies component of an unfavorable variable overhead efficiency variance. State a specific case, if there is one, and calculate the amount of the variance.
2. Under what condition in the above situation, if any, would there be an unfavorable variable overhead spending variance attributable to supplies if supplies were purchased at a cost of $8 per box. State a specific case, if there is one, and calculate the amount of the variance.
3. Suppose actual labor for the period was 500 over the standard. The variable overhead rate is $4 and a variable overhead efficiency variance of $2,000 resulted. The plant accountant stated that overhead cost would have been $2,000 less if production had been efficient. What assumption did the plant accountant make?
4. Suppose that an inspection revealed 50 units of product #13 were damaged and had no salvage value. This damage occurred as a result of poor performance by the workers and is part of the total manufacturing cost variances. What specific variances would include the resources wasted on these units?

5-16. Graphical Understandings of Overhead Accounting. Consider the graph of a firm's total manufacturing overhead as depicted in exhibit 5.12. During the current period the output was such that the standard machine hours allowed were 8,000 but 10,000 machine hours were used. Overhead is applied on the basis of machine hours.

Required:

(Show all calculations and justify your answers.)

1. What divisor activity (numerical amount) did the firm use in constructing its overhead application rate?
2. How much overhead (fixed and variable) was applied during the current period?
3. What was the overhead efficiency variance for the period?
4. Lubricants are variable and were budgeted at one gallon per 5,000 machine hours. The standard cost per gallon was $50. In this period the actual usage averaged 1.1 gallons per 5,000 hours and cost $51 per gallon
   a. What is the lubricant component of the overhead efficiency variance computed in part 3?
   b. What is the lubricant component of the overhead spending variance?

5-17. Standard Costs Contrasted to a Process Cost System. Reconsider Department A in problem 4-9. Assume, now, that a standard cost system is to be used and that the standards have been established as follows:

Material	2 units @ $5.00	$10.00
Labor	1 hour @ $6.00	6.00
Variable overhead	1 hour @ $3.00	3.00
Fixed overhead	1 hour @ $1.00*	1.00
Total		$20,00

*Established using 20,000 direct-labor hours as the divisor activity.

Exhibit 5.12   Graph for Problem 5-16

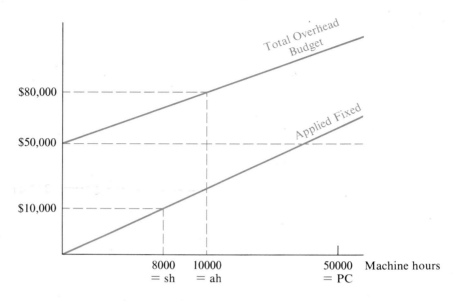

where: sh = standard machine hours
ah = actual machine hours
PC = practical capacity

The $190,890 of material represented 37,800 units of material used. (There was no change during the month in materials inventory.) The conversion costs have been analyzed as follows:

Labor 17,000 hours @ $6.00	$102,000
Variable overhead	52,700
Fixed overhead	20,000
Total	$174,700

Required:

1. Compute the material price variance for Department A. Is it favorable or unfavorable?
2. Compute the material quantity variance for Department A. Is it favorable or unfavorable?
3. Compute the labor efficiency variance for Department A. Is it favorable or unfavorable?
4. Compute the overhead efficiency variance for Department A. Is it favorable or unfavorable?
5. Compute the overhead spending variance for Department A. Is it favorable or unfavorable?

6. Compute the noncontrollable (volume) variance for Department A. Is it favorable or unfavorable?
7. Compute the standard cost of the ending work-in-process inventory for Department A.
8. In general, what would cause the difference in the cost of the inventory computed in part 7 and the cost computed in problem 4-9?

5-18. Variance Analysis with Step Fixed Costs. The T. John Company applies overhead costs to its several products on the basis of direct-labor hours. Its fixed manufacturing overhead behaves in the following step manner:

Volume	Fixed Costs
0 to 34,999 hours	$140,000
35,000 to 70,000 hours	250,000

The normal volume of activity has been 50,000 direct-labor hours.

Required:

1. Compute the fixed overhead rate based on normal activity.
2. Construct a graph showing the budgeted and applied fixed cost.
3. Using equation (5-13) and the budgeted fixed costs for the *achieved* output, compute the noncontrollable (volume) variance for each of the following volumes:
   a. 20,000 standard direct-labor hours.
   b. 28,000 standard direct-labor hours.
   c. 30,000 standard direct-labor hours.
   d. 40,000 standard direct-labor hours.
   e. 50,000 standard direct-labor hours.
   f. 60,000 standard direct-labor hours.
4. Repeat part 3 using equation (5-13a). Did you get different results? If so, explain why.
5. Now assume that 36,000 hours of work were used to achieve an output that should have required only 34,000 standard hours. The actual fixed manufacturing cost was $250,000.
   a. What is the applied fixed overhead?
   b. What is the budgeted fixed overhead?
   c. What is the total variance due to fixed cost?
   d. Using equation (5-13) and the budgeted fixed costs for the achieved output, analyze the total variance into spending and noncontrollable components.
   e. Repeat part d using equation (5-13a).
   f. Considering your results in parts d and e, which do you find to be more defensible? Why?

5-19. Joint Price-Quantity Variance. The Fancy Faucet Company is a major producer of faucets. The standard cost of one of the materials, stainless steel, is $2.00 per pound. The company maintains its stainless steel account at *actual* prices. The FIFO method is used in costing the stainless steel issued to production.

The company had an inventory of 8,000 pounds of stainless steel at the beginning of 19x7 with a cost of $15,500. During 19x7, 652,000 pounds of stainless steel were purchased for $1,369,200. The ending inventory was 10,000 pounds at $21,000. The standard quantity of stainless steel allowed for this period's output is 651,000 pounds.

Required:

1. Assuming that a joint price-quantity variance is to be computed (see part 2), compute the pure material price variance that will be recognized during 19x7. Is it favorable or unfavorable?
2. Compute the joint price-quantity variance for 19x7. Is it favorable or unfavorable?

5-20. Using Standard Cost Relationships to Find Unknowns. The following two cases are based on a standard cost system, and they should be considered independently. Compute and enter the appropriate amounts in the blank spaces of each case. The data refer to the activities for an entire year. When computing variances, indicate whether they are favorable or unfavorable by writing either F or U after the variance.

		Case A	*Case B*
1.	Standard material cost per finished unit (3 units of material in both cases)	1. $10.00	$21.00
2.	Standard labor cost per finished unit (2 hours of labor in both cases)	2. _____	8.00
3.	Total overhead per finished unit (applied on labor hours)	3. _____	_____
4.	Total standard cost per finished unit	4. $25.00	$40.00
5.	Normal activity (labor hours)	5. 20,000	_____
6.	Fixed overhead costs at normal activity	6. $60,000	$20,000
7.	Variable overhead rate/labor hour	7. $1.00	$5.00
8.	Units finished (assume no WIP inventory)	8. 9,000	_____
9.	Actual labor hours worked	9. 22,000	_____
10.	Standard labor hours allowed	10. _____	_____
11.	Total overhead applied to product	11. _____	_____
12.	Budgeted fixed costs at actual hours	12. _____	_____
13.	Budgeted variable costs at actual hours	13. _____	_____
14.	Total budget at actual hours	14. _____	_____
15.	Actual total overhead costs	15. $89,000	_____
16.	Total overhead variance	16. _____	$12,000 U
17.	Noncontrollable variance	17. _____	_____
18.	OH spending variance (total)	18. _____	_____
19.	OH efficiency variance	19. _____	_____
20.	Labor efficiency variance	20. _____	$ 8,000 U
21.	Standard cost of finished production	21. _____	$600,000

5-21. Working Backward in a Multiple Product Case; Entries. The Wretched Wrench Company makes two products and uses a standard cost system. *Overhead is applied on the basis of direct-labor hours* using normal activity. Both products make use of a common raw material. The following standards have been established:

	Common Wrench	Metric Wrench
Materials @ $2.00/unit of raw material	$ 6.00	$ 8.00
Labor @ $3.00 per hour	6.00	9.00
Total overhead (fixed and variable)	12.00	18.00
Total standard cost/finsished unit	$24.00	$35.00

The total overhead behaves in a linear manner, and the following budget data for *total* factory overhead are available:

Direct-Labor Hours	Total Overhead Cost
220,000	$1,240,000
160,000	1,120,000

During the current year the following data were collected:

	Common Wrench	Metric Wrench
Beginning finished goods inventory	2,000 units	4,000 units
Sales	28,000 units	41,000 units
Ending finished goods inventory	4,000 units	3,000 units
Actual costs were:		
Material purchased and used:		
255,000 units @ $2.05		$522,750
Direct labor: 185,000 hours @ $3.00		555,000
Variable overhead		375,000
Fixed overhead—same as budget		?

All inventories are maintained at standard and there are no work-in-process inventories at either the beginning or end of the period.

Required:

1. What is the variable overhead rate per hour?
2. What is the fixed overhead application rate per hour?
3. What is the budgeted fixed overhead cost for the actual hours incurred this period?
4. What is the normal activity?
5. Prepare an analysis of material variances in as much detail as possible.
6. Prepare an analysis of labor variances in as much detail as possible.
7. Prepare an analysis of overhead variances in as much detail as possible.

5-22. Working Backward. You have the following data:

1. Fixed overhead rate—$2.00 per direct-labor hour.
2. Total overhead applied in April—$120,000.
3. Practical capacity (divisor activity) in April—25,000 direct-labor hours.
4. Total overhead spending variance in April—$5,000 F.
5. Variable overhead budgeted for April's actual labor hours—$86,000.
6. Overhead efficiency variance in April—$6,000 U.

Required:

1. What is the amount of fixed overhead budgeted for April?
2. What is the actual *total* overhead incurred in April?
3. What is the noncontrollable (volume) variance in April?
4. What is the variable overhead rate per direct labor hour?
5. How many actual labor hours were incurred in April?

5-23. Comprehensive Problem Covering Process Costing and Standard Costing. The Friday Company produces two products, lawn mowers and snow blowers. Four responsibility centers are utilized: Departments I, II, III, and IV. Department I produces a small pulley that is needed for both products. Department II assembles, balances, and tests both products using one production line for each. When finished by Department II, lawn mowers are transferred to Department III for finishing, labeling, and packaging and snow blowers are transferred to Department IV.

Department II's activities differ depending on the product and are summarized as follows:

Lawn Mowers: At the beginning of the process two pulleys are needed. Labor is needed during the first 10% of processing and again in the last 10%. Motors are added when processing is 50% complete. Overhead is a function of machine hours, which are incurred uniformly throughout Department II.

Snow Blowers: At the beginning of the process three pulleys are used. Labor is needed during the first 20% of processing and again in the last 10%. Like lawn mowers, motors are added when processing is 50% complete and overhead is a function of machine hours.

Inventory and production data for October are as follows:

	Department I Pulleys	Department II Lawn Mowers	Department II Snow Blowers	Dept. III	Dept. IV
Beginning inventory (units)	4,000	5,000	6,000	2,000	4,000
Percentage completion	30%	40%	60%	30%	40%
Ending inventory (units)	10,000	8,000	2,000	4,000	3,000
Percentage completion	40%	95%	15%	50%	20%
Transferred out (units)	170,000	?	?	28,000	39,000

Department II's standards have been established as follows:

	Lawn Mowers	Snow Blowers
Pulleys (2, 3) @ $20	$ 40	$ 60
Motors (1, 1) @ $30	30	30
Labor (1, 1/2) @ $10 per hour	10	5
Variable overhead		
5 machine hours @ $6	30	
$1\frac{2}{3}$ machine hours @ $6		10
Fixed overhead		
5 machine hours @ $3	15	
$1\frac{2}{3}$ machine hours @ $3		5
	$125	$110

In Department I all costs are added uniformly and the current costs totaled $3,628,800 during October. Department I's beginning inventory, if assigned a cost using actual process costing, would have been $26,940.

Some of the actual costs incurred in Department II during the current period are:

Motors purchased 80,000 @ $31	$2,480,000
Actual variable overhead	$1,428,000
Actual fixed overhead (same as budgeted for October)	$750,000
Motors used	73,500
Actual machine time	240,000 hours
Actual labor time ($10.20 per hour)	50,000 hours

Required:

1. If FIFO actual process costing is used in Department I what is the cost per equivalent unit (in Department I) during October?
2. If weighted average actual process costing is used in Department I what is the cost per equivalent unit (in Department I) during October?
3. Assume FIFO actual costing is to be used in Department II. (Note carefully that this requirement refers to Department II.) Compute all divisors that will be needed to derive unit cost data giving *careful consideration to the way the actual cost data have been collected.*
4. Assume that a standard cost system is in use. Compute all material-type variances for which the *Department II manager* will be asked to explain.
5. Assume that a standard cost system is in use. Prepare a four-way analysis of Department II's overhead variances.

CHAPTER 6

Standard Cost Systems—Additional Topics

Standard costing is a very important topic for the management accountant. As such, there is more material than is practical for one chapter. In this chapter several additional topics are considered.

First, the methods of incorporating standards into the system of accounts are considered. The second section will discuss the procedures of accounting for the variances from standards when reports must be generated to satisfy external needs. Finally, it is important for controllers and their staffs to understand how to help management in using standards as a behaviorally effective control device. Thus, a section on the control implications of variances is included.

Accounting Systems with Standards

This section illustrates the systems aspects of standard costing. As you might imagine, the possible variations in systems are almost infinite and depend on the nature of the firm and its expectation of the accounting system. The first variation that will be explored is one that might be considered the most preferred from a theoretical viewpoint. In this system *all* inventory accounts (material, work in process, and finished goods) are maintained at *complete* standards. That is, only standard costs (standard quantities at standard unit costs) are permitted to enter the inventory accounts. After exploring the general nature of this system, we will see its operation illustrated using an example that differs from the one in the previous chapter in that it contains *partially completed production* and applies overhead on the basis of machine hours. Following that, there is an examination of other variations for the system and their justifications.

BASIC FLOWCHART FOR PREFERRED SYSTEM. The major distinction among the different standard cost accounting systems is primarily one of isolating the variances at different points in the accounting process. Except for one case, which is discussed later, the magnitude of the variances are the same. A system whereby all inventory accounts are maintained at complete standard is the one that isolates all variances at the *earliest possible point* within the accounting process. However, this is not always practical as will be discussed later.

Exhibit 6.1 is a flowchart of this system. To help in discussing the figure, every flow is uniquely represented by a two-number index referring to the point from which the amount is taken and the point to which it goes. Also, the flow is constructed assuming all of the variances are *unfavorable*. A favorable variance will just flow to the credit side of the account instead of the debit side.

With the system explored here, the materials price variance would have to be isolated at the time of purchase because the material inventory is maintained at standard. This variance would be computed according to equation (5–3) and is represented by the flow (1 to 5) in the flowchart. Materials would be debited with the standard cost of the quantity acquired (1 to 6). A direct-labor account has been included in this system and is a temporary holding account for the *actual* direct labor incurred. It would be composed of the net pay (2 to 7) and the amount withheld from the employees for such things as withholding (income) taxes, social security, union dues, insurance, and so forth (3 to 7). As the actual overhead is incurred, it is charged to the manufacturing overhead control account (4 to 8).

During the period, materials are issued to production. However, under this system, only the *standard* amount of material is charged to work in process (9 to 18). The material quantity variance, as measured by equation (5–4), is recognized at this point (9 to 12). Likewise, only the standard labor cost is charged to work in process via (10 to 19), and the two variances are recorded (10 to 13) and (10 to 14), using the results in equations (5–8) and (5–9). Finally, overhead is applied using the *total* (fixed plus variable) overhead rate (11 to 20). This will leave a balance in the manufacturing overhead control account representing the total overhead variance. The variance can be analyzed into the various components discussed in the last chapter, efficiency via equation (5–11), spending via (5–12) and (5–14), and noncontrollable via (5–13). These are then recorded in their respective accounts, flows (11 to 15), (11 to 16), and (11 to 17).

The transfer from work in process to finished goods would be made at the *standard cost per finished unit* (21 to 22). Any ending work-in-process inventory would be carried at the standard cost per equivalent unit contained in the inventory. The transfer from finished goods to cost of goods sold (23 to 24) would also be at standard. The only thing that remains is the ultimate disposition of the variances. This will be discussed in a later section of this chapter.

ILLUSTRATION. To illustrate the system consider the following example. The Fenzel Company produces one product. One department is used, and the standards are in Exhibit 6.2. Production and inventory data for 19x2 are presented in Exhibit 6.3.

In Exhibit 6.4 there is a computation of the equivalent units for material, labor, and overhead. Recall that equivalent units are needed to measure the current work accomplished. These results are multiplied by the respective allowances per finished unit to obtain the standard quantities allowed.

Exhibit 6.1   Flow Chart of a Standard Cost System

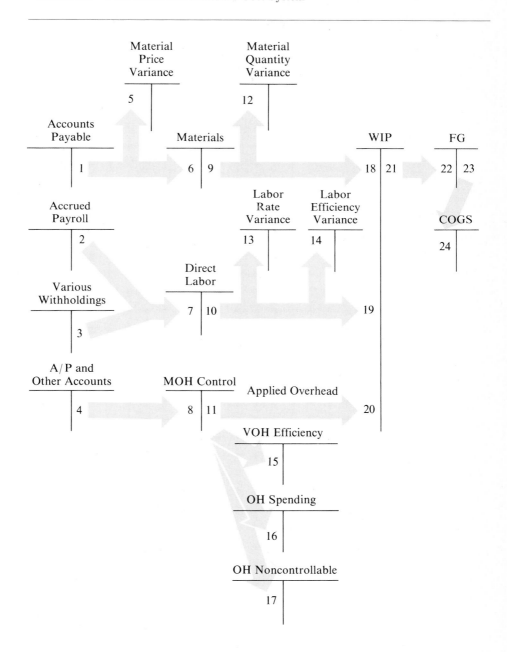

Exhibit 6.2   Fenzel Company Product Standards as of
January 1, 19x2

Material (2 units @ $4.00)	$ 8.00
Labor (1 hour @ $6.00)	6.00
Variable overhead: (4 machine hours @ $5.00)	20.00
Fixed overhead: (4 machine hours @ $2.00*)	8.00
Standard cost per finished unit	$42.00

*Studies revealed that machine hours provided a better explanation of
overhead than direct labor hours. Consequently, the budgeted fixed costs of
$70,000 per year is to be assigned on the basis of 35,000 machine hours at
normal capacity.

Exhibit 6.3   Fenzel Company Production and Inventory Data for
the Year Ended 12/31/x2

Material Inventory 1/1/x2	0
Work in process	
At 1/1/x2, 100% completed with respect to material, 25% with respect to labor and 75% with respect to machine time	1,000 units
At 12/31/x2, 100% completed with respect to material, 50% with respect to labor and 100% with respect to machine time	2,000 units
Started this year	9,000 units
Finished this year	8,000 units
Finished goods	
At 1/1/x2	2,000 units
At 12/31/x2	1,000 units
Sold this year (at $60 per unit)	9,000 units
Actual data for 19x2	
Material purchased (25,000 units @ $4.01)	$100,250
Material used	17,100 units
Labor (8,960 hours @ $6.25)	$56,000
Machine hours used	36,000 hours
Variable overhead	$183,375
Fixed overhead	$71,000

Exhibit 6.4   Fenzel Company Determination of Standard Quantities for the Year 19x2

	Material	Labor	Overhead
Equivalent units			
Beginning inventory	0	750	250
Started and finished	7,000	7,000	7,000
Ending inventory	2,000	1,000	2,000
Total	9,000	8,750	9,250
Allowance per whole unit	2	1	4
Standard allowed for 19x2 work	18,000	8,750	37,000

Exhibits 6.2, 6.3, and 6.4 contain all the basic information needed to analyze the variances and to prepare the entries. It is suggested that you construct a flowchart similar to Exhibit 6.1 and enter the amounts as you reason through the following entries. Your results can be checked by the flowchart at the end of the section. The variance analysis is done as part of the entries.

Material Purchases

Materials Inventory (25,000 × $4.00)	100,000	
Material price variance ($4.00 − $4.01) 25,000	250	
Accounts payable		100,250

Material Transferred to Production

Work in process (18,000 × $4.00)	72,000	
Material quantity variance		
(18,000 − 17,100) $4.00		3,600
Materials Inventory (17,100 × $4.00)		68,400

(Note that work in process is debited with the standard material quantity (from Exhibit 6.4) at the standard price per unit of material.)

Labor Incurrence
(Assume withholdings are 20% of gross pay.)

Direct labor	56,000	
Accrued payroll (80%)		44,800
Withholdings (20%)		11,200

Labor Application

Work in process (8,750 × $6.00)	52,500	
Labor rate variance ($6.00 − $6.25) 8,960	2,240	
Labor efficiency variance (8,750 − 8,960) $6.00	1,260	
Direct labor		56,000

(Note that work in process is debited with the standard labor hours (from Exhibit 6.4) at the standard rate per hour.)

Overhead Incurrence

Manufacturing overhead control		
($183,375 + $71,000)	254,375	
Accounts payable and other accounts		254,375

Overhead Application

Work in process [37,000 × ($5.00 + $2.00)]	259,000	
Manufacturing overhead control		259,000

(Note that work in process is debited with the standard machine hours (from Exhibit 6.4) multiplied by the total overhead rate.)

Before doing the overhead variance analysis, note that machine hours are being used as the measure of activity in this problem. Then:

Overhead Variances
(Note the overhead applied exceeds actual.)

Manufacturing overhead control		
(259,000 credits − $254,375 debits)	4,625	
Overhead spending variance*	4,375	
Overhead efficiency variance		
(37,000 − 36,000)$5.00		5,000
Noncontrollable variance [Using equation		
(5–13a): (37,000 − 35,000) $2.00]		4,000

---

*Variable : $5(36,000) − $183,375	$3,375 U (See equation (5-12).)	
Fixed: ($70,000 − $71,000)	1,000 U (See equation (5-14).)	
Total	$4,375	

Finished Production

Finished goods ($42.00 × 8,000)	336,000	
Work in process		336,000

Note that the beginning balance in work in process would have been $30,500:

Material: 1,000 × 1.00 × 2 × $4.00	$ 8,000
Labor: 1,000 × 0.25 × 1 × $6.00	1,500
Total overhead: 1,000 × 0.75 × 4 × $7.00	21,000
	$30,500

The ending balance would be $78,000:

Material: 2,000 × 1.00 × 2 × $4.00	$16,000
Labor: 2,000 × 0.50 × 1 × $6.00	6,000
Total overhead: 2,000 × 1.00 × 4 × $7.00	56,000
	$78,000

A summary of the work in process account follows:

Work in Process

Inventory, 1/1/x2	$ 30,500	To finished goods	$336,000
Material	72,000	Inventory, 12/31/x2	78,000
Labor	52,500		
Overhead	259,000		
	$414,000		
			$414,000
Inventory, 1/1/x3	$ 78,000		

Units Sold

Cost of goods sold (9,000 × $42)	378,000	
Finished goods		378,000
Accounts Receivable (9,000 × $60)	540,000	
Sales		540,000

Each of these entries has been entered in a flowchart similar to Exhibit 6.1. Check your understanding of the cost flow by referring to Exhibit 6.5. The disposition of the variances are considered in the next section.

DISCUSSION OF OTHER SYSTEM VARIATIONS. This section concludes with a brief discussion of some of the possible variations in a standard cost accounting system. One variation involves the accounting for the acquisition of materials. Since financial reporting principles and the IRS, in effect, require an actual cost accounting, it is possible to reduce the variance disposition problems by keeping the materials account at actual. (Technically, standards are permitted if the results are not materially different from an actual system.) If this is done, then the materials account will not need to be adjusted to actual cost at the end of the period. For this variation, material price variance would be a function of usage (see equation [5–3a]) and the price variance account would shift to the right of the materials account in the flowchart of Exhibit 6.1. In this system some of the price variance will not be isolated in the period of incurrence. However, if material inventory changes are small, the problem is insignificant.

A second variation may arise as a result of not knowing the actual output at the time of using material and incurring labor. For example, when 5,000 units of material are issued to production, it is not known how many units of finished product will result. If the output is unknown, then the standard quantity of material allowed cannot be computed. Further, if it is not possible to wait until the end of an accounting period to make the transfers into work in process, then work in process cannot be debited on the basis of the standard quantity. Standard prices and rates could still be used, but not standard quantities. In this case the material price variance would be accounted for as before (or in the manner of the preceding par-

Exhibit 6.5 Summary of Fenzel Company

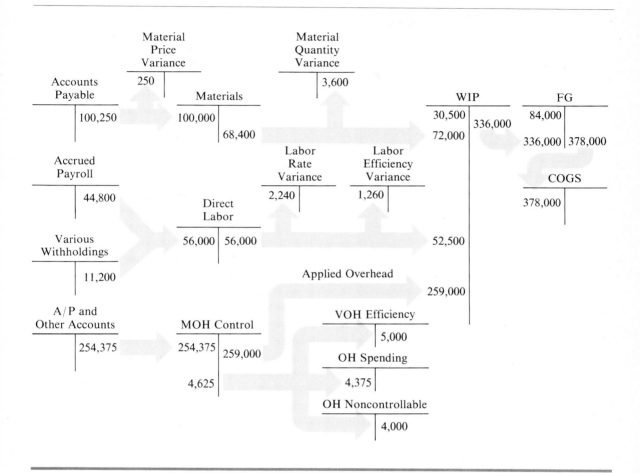

agraph) as would the labor rate variance. However, the material quantity and labor efficiency variances would be created by a transfer out of work in process and, in the flowchart, the accounts would be located between work in process and finished goods. Obviously, the output is known when making the transfer to finished goods, and then it is possible to measure the quantity type variances.

Another system variation is that of debiting work in process at actual quantities times actual prices. Then all variances would be isolated out of work in process. Yet another variation involves accounting for some items at standard and others at actual. In summary, the type of system you find or devise will depend on the situation and expected usages of the data.

Year-End Disposal of Cost Variances

There are a variety of ways in which the standard cost variances can be disposed at the end of the year and different methods are acceptable for the various reporting requirements. First, there are three basic ways of accounting for the variances: (1) treat them as is and show them as charges against the current period's income, (2) treat them as additions to cost of goods sold by closing them into that account, or (3) prorate them to inventories (materials, work in process, and finished goods) and cost of goods sold using some equitable prorating scheme. Accounting principles, the IRS, and the CASB (Cost Accounting Standards Board) require the third treatment but will permit method 2 if it does not produce a result that is materially different from method 3. Let us examine the rationale and mechanics of each of these methods.

Method 1 is the preferred treatment for *internal purposes*. It makes no sense to generate all of the variances and then account for them in such a way that their effect cannot be noticed. A general reporting format for internal reporting is illustrated in Exhibit 6.6. Under method 1 the variances would be shown on the income statement as separate items. In the closing process they would be closed directly into the Revenue and Expense (Income Summary) account.

For both internal and external purposes, method 3, the prorating scheme, cannot be defended from a theoretical standpoint. The utility of the inventories is not increased when there are inefficiencies and idle time. Would not the act of adding some of these losses to the cost of inventories imply additional utility? We would argue here that if the standards are *current* and *attainable* there is no better cost for the inventories than the standard costs. There are other considerations, however, which will be discussed momentarily.

The FASB, IRS, CASB and perhaps others require inventories to be assigned a cost based on *actual* outlays. The reason for this is objectivity. Standard costs are not objective, by accounting definitions, in that they are not established as a result of an exchange transaction between two independent parties. Thus, the external reporting standards would require that the standard cost results be adjusted to an actual cost basis. If standards were permitted for external reporting it would be possible for management to manipulate the reported income by manipulating the standard costs. Theoretically, this means that method 3 must be used for external reporting. At a miniumum, the method actually used for external reporting must produce results that are very similar to method 3.

The Fenzel case of the previous section will be used to illustrate how proration would be accomplished. To arrive at an approximation of an actual cost basis, it is normally acceptable to assume the variances can be prorated on a basis that measures the *current work* content of the affected assets and expenses. That is, it is assumed that the various units produced contributed to the standard cost variances in an amount equal to the work effort needed to produce the units.

In measuring the work effort at least three questions need to be answered. First, in the event there are ending *work-in-process* inventories, how is the effort contained in those units going to be measured in comparison to the whole units produced this period? Of course, the answer is to use the equivalent unit. More

---

Exhibit 6.6   Format for Internal Reporting Standard Cost Variance

---

Sales		xxx
Standard cost of sales		
Material	xxx	
Labor	xxx	
Overhead	xxx	xxx
Standard gross margin		xxx
Deduct (add) unfavorable (favorable)		
variances from standard		
Material price variance	xxx	
Material quantity variance	xxx	
Labor rate variance	xxx	
Labor efficiency variance	xxx	
Variable overhead efficiency		
variance	xxx	
Variable overhead spending		
variance	xxx	
Fixed overhead spending variance	xxx	
Noncontrollable variance	xxx	xxx
Adjusted gross margin		xxx
Selling and administrative costs		xxx
Net income		xxx

---

specifically, the FIFO equivalent unit should be used. Only the *current* period's work effort could have contributed to the current period's variances.

The second question is what cost flow assumption to make with regard to inventory accounting, FIFO or LIFO? This question is relevant because of the need to answer the question of where the current period's work effort is located. FIFO would say that the cost of last period's output was the cost of the first units to be sold. Therefore, the cost of the units in cost of goods sold would, in part, be last period's production costs and, in part, this period's. Under the FIFO cost flow assumption only some of the units in cost of goods sold would be assigned a share of this period's variances. On the other hand, if LIFO is assumed, then the last units produced are considered to be the first units sold. Then, the units in ending inventories would contain the units that were in the beginning inventories. If so, some of the ending inventory units should not be assigned any of this period's variance.

The third question is relevant to multiple-product situations. If there are multiple products then the question is how to measure the dissimilar work effort in an equivalent manner. The answer is to use the standard quantities of material allowed as a basis for prorating material variances, the standard labor allowed to prorate the labor variances, and so forth.

Now consider the specifics of the Fenzel case. Only one product is being produced so it is not necessary to be concerned about the third question listed above. However, the solution posed here will use standard quantities in order to illustrate the mechanics that would be needed when making a variance allocation in a multiple-product setting.

Let's consider the allocation of the labor variances first. There are work in process inventories in this case so question one is relevant. In Exhibit 6.4, the standard hours allowed for the period was computed to be 8,750. As discussed earlier, it is assumed for this purpose that each unit of work effort contributed equally to the incurrence of labor variances ($2,240 for rate and $1,260 for efficiency). In order to prorate the two variances it is next necessary to determine what accounts contain the current work effort of 8,750. Some of this will be in ending work in process, some in ending finished goods, and some in cost of goods sold.

Because the FIFO cost flow assumption was made, the ending inventories will consist of current work efforts. As shown in Exhibit 6.4, 1,000 equivalent units of labor work effort are in the ending work in process. This means that there are 1,000 standard labor hours (1,000 × 1) contained in the ending work in process. Where are the remaining 7,750 standard labor hours located? There are 1,000 units in the ending finished goods inventory and, therefore, 1,000 labor hours. The remaining 6,750 standard labor hours are assigned to units that are now in cost of goods sold. In summary, then, the labor variances should be allocated as follows:

	Labor Hours	Ratio for Labor Variances
Work in process	1,000	100/875
Finished goods	1,000	100/875
Cost of goods sold	6,750	675/875
	8,750	

Next, consider the overhead variances. Overhead was best related to machine hours in this case and, thus, the overhead variances should be allocated in proportion to the standard machine-hour content in each of the three relevant accounts. Exhibit 6.4 indicates there are 2,000 equivalent units of overhead effort in the ending work in process. Therefore, there are 8,000 standard machine hours in that inventory (2,000 × 4 machine hours per unit). The 1,000 units in ending finished goods inventory represent 4,000 standard machine hours. The remaining 25,000 machine hours (37,000 − 8,000 − 4,000) are associated with units in cost of goods sold. In summary:

	Machine Hours	Ratio for Overhead Variances
Work in process	8,000	8/37
Finished goods	4,000	4/37
Cost of goods sold	25,000	25/37
	37,000	

Finally, consider the material variances. Because the price variance was isolated at the time of purchase there is an additional inventory, raw materials, that should share in the variance. Further, the price variance should be assigned to the affected accounts on the basis of the *actual* units of material that will be assigned to each. It was the actual units purchased that created the price variance, not the standard. If the material quantity variance is prorated first, then it will be known how many actual units of material are assigned to each account. That is, the standard quantity plus the account's share of an unfavorable material quantity variance (or less the account's share of a favorable material quantity variance) is the actual quantity of material assigned.

Thus, first consider the material quantity variance. The equivalent unit computation in Exhibit 6.4 indicates the total amount of work done for the period. There were 9,000 equivalent units of work for material representing 18,000 standard units of material. Therefore the material quantity variance ($3,600 favorable) should be allocated over this base. With a FIFO assumption, the equivalent work of material for the period is assigned to the various layers using the following logic. Since there are 2,000 units of equivalent work in the ending WIP inventory, it represents 4,000 standard units of material. Next, the 1,000 equivalent units in ending finished goods represents 2,000 standard units. The balance, then, must be in cost of goods sold. A summary follows, along with the ratio of the quantity variance to be assigned to each layer:

	Standard Material	Ratio for Material Quantity Variance
Work in process	4,000	4/18
Finished goods	2,000	2/18
Cost of goods sold (forced)	12,000	12/18
	18,000	

Finally, consider the price variance. The 25,000 units of material purchased this period represents the total base over which the price variance should be allocated. The current location of these units can be determined by considering the following. First, the material quantity variance represents 900 units. The material quantity variance is converted to dollars by using the standard cost of $4.00 per unit. Thus a $3,600 favorable variance indicates that the actual consumption was 900 units *below* the standard, $3,600 ÷ $4. Since the variance is favorable, the standard allowances should be adjusted *downward* to arrive at the actual material content assigned to each account. The ratios used in allocating the material quantity variance will also be used to allocate the 900 units among the layers. Thus:

	(1) Standard Material for Current Work	(2) Quantity Variance Adjustment*	(3) = (1) − (2) Actual Material Assigned	(4) Ratio for Price Variance
Material	——	——	7,900†	79/250
Work in process	4,000	200	3,800	38/250
Finished goods	2,000	100	1,900	19/250
Cost of goods sold (Current)	12,000	600	11,400	114/250
		900	25,000	

*900 × ratios for material quantity variance proration.
†See Exhibit 6.3 to compute the actual units of material in the ending materials inventory: Beginning materials inventory + Purchases − Materials used = 0 + 25,000 − 17,100.

Using the preceding four sets of ratios, a complete schedule of variance allocation can now be prepared. This is done in Exhibit 6.7. It is possible to stop at the working paper level with this adjustment or a firm may actually close the variance accounts into the four accounts that are to receive allocations using the amounts in Exhibit 6.7.

One last observation is needed before leaving this topic. External accounting does not advocate a complete actual cost system. If the firm were operating at a very low volume and had to allocate a large noncontrollable variance, for example, over a small production, then it is possible that the total cost would exceed the net realizable value of the inventory. Financial accounting principles would require the application of the lower of cost or market inventory method and, in turn, would recognize a loss on the reduction of inventory to market. Thus, financial accounting ensures an economically defensible inventory figure by this means rather than through a standard costing mechanism.

You can certainly imagine the burden of the prorating scheme when there are multiple material inventories and multiple departments. Since this allocation would only be done annually, it would be normal for the inventories to constitute a small proportion of the total output for the period and, in turn, would receive a small share of the variances. Under these circumstances, method 2 would yield *approximately* the same results as method 3 with much less effort. In most cases, this will be an acceptable compromise. For the example, method 2 would result in the total favorable variance of $4,475 (see Exhibit 6.7) being deducted from the standard cost of goods sold in comparison with $2,711 as derived in Exhibit 6.7 using method 1.

Exhibit 6.7   Fenzel Company Schedule of Variance Allocation

	Total	Materials Rate	Materials Amount	WIP Rate	WIP Amount	FG Rate	FG Amount	COGS Rate	COGS Amount
Labor variances	3,500	—	—	$\frac{100}{875}$	400	$\frac{100}{875}$	400	$\frac{675}{875}$	2,700
Overhead Variances	(4,625)	—	—	$\frac{8}{37}$	(1,000)	$\frac{4}{37}$	(500)	$\frac{25}{37}$	(3,125)
Materials quantity Variance	(3,600)	—	—	$\frac{4}{18}$	(800)	$\frac{2}{18}$	(400)	$\frac{12}{18}$	(2,400)
Materials price Variance	250	$\frac{79}{250}$	79	$\frac{38}{250}$	38	$\frac{19}{250}$	19	$\frac{114}{250}$	114
Total variances	(4,475)		79		(1,362)		(481)		(2,711)
Standard cost*			31,600		78,000		42,000		378,000
Adjusted cost			31,679		76,638		41,519		375,289[+]

*The balances as can be computed from the accounts in Exhibit 6.5.

[+]Plus any variance that would have been allocated to inventories in previous year.

The Control Implications of Variances

Many times in Chapter 5 there were warnings about the problems of interpreting the variances of a standard cost or other type of performance evaluation system. This section synthesizes those observations from a behavioral perspective. Further, there is a hypothetical situation that illustrates an approach to determining the share of the variances for which each manager is accountable.

SYNTHESIS OF VARIANCE INTERPRETATION PROBLEMS. Variances result from both performance fluctuations and from other factors that are beyond the control of the individual and/or the unit of the firm being evaluated. If the latter factors are not identified and taken into consideration during the evaluation review, then considerable damage can be done to the relationship among the firm's personnel. When managers suspect that variances caused by factors that are not within their control are still being considered in their evaluation, there is a tendency for them to reject the standards. That is, company goals will not be accepted as personal goals. Accountants must be very cautious when interpreting variances if they desire to avoid the impairment of company goals. In this section there is a discussion of various techniques that will help accountants to avoid being dysfunctional.

First, recognize that *work processes are random processes*. Material and labor consumption will not be exactly the same each time a particular operation is performed. Thus, it must be realized that standards are average consumptions. Actual observations should be expected to vary around the average. If variation is a normal occurrence, then performance is acceptable as long as it is in some interval around the standard. The width of this range may be arbitrarily set or established through a statistical procedure. The latter will be introduced later in the book.

Second, recognize that the *accounting for actual performance is subject to measurement error.* Many forms and individuals are relied upon to collect the data. Thus, there is opportunity for misclassification and other errors. Ironically, accountants may be able to increase the credibility of their reports if they acknowledge to others the possibility that some of the variance could be due to human error in the accounting process.

Third, remember that the *activity measures used to assign indirect costs probably are not perfectly correlated wtih the incurrence of those costs*. For example, assume the overhead is being assigned at $5.00 per direct-labor hour. When variable overhead is applied or budgeted at the $5.00 per-hour-rate established, there is an implicit assumption of perfect correlation between overhead and labor hours. Obviously, perfect correlation is not likely to occur in an actual situation (only in textbooks). The effect of less than perfect correlation should be considered in interpreting both the variable overhead spending and efficiency variances. The spending variance is affected because of the error in measuring the relationship between overhead and labor hours. That is, it is not reasonable to expect the variable overhead cost to vary at a rate of exactly $5 per direct-labor hour. The efficiency variance is affected by that error and also by the probable lack of perfect correlation between the firm's output and the overall measure of its output, direct-labor hours in this case. That is, if output is being measured by direct-labor hours, do not expect labor hours to vary *exactly* with output. Further, variable overhead is not expected to vary exactly with direct-labor hours. Thus, there are two basic types of random variation that affect the efficiency variance.

Fourth, recognize that the *variances may not represent the total opportunity cost of inefficiencies or the gain of efficiency. If a resource is limited,* its inefficient use, for example, will create a cost equal to the asset's out-of-pocket cost and also will prevent it from being used in some alternative way. The gain from the alternative is another cost that may be frequently overlooked in a conventional variance analysis.

There are other factors that perhaps should be considered in interpreting variances. The four mentioned, however, should be sufficient to indicate the need for a careful interpretation.

ILLUSTRATION OF ESTABLISHING RESPONSIBILITY FOR VARIANCES. To illustrate the process of properly establishing accountability for variances, consider the Myles Company, which produces only one product. Assume that overhead is applied on the basis of labor hours. The following cost standards (variable costs only) have been established:

Direct material (3 units @ $4)	$12.00
Direct labor (2 hours @ $5)	10.00
Variable overhead (2 hours @ $3)	6.00
Total variable cost	$28.00

During the current period, 20,000 units of the product were finished, 65,000 units of material were purchased and used (average price was $3.47), and there were 45,000 direct-labor hours incurred at a rate of $5.10 per hour. The actual variable overhead cost for the period was $140,000.

Exhibit 6.8 is a variance report for the current period. One of the assistant controller's duties is to seek explanations for the variances and assess who is responsible. She has determined the following additional data:

1. The production of the 20,000 units was scheduled uniformly throughout the period. During the last half of the period the purchasing agent made a decision, on his own, to purchase a substandard material at $3.00 per unit. He did this because the price of the regular material increased to $4.10. Based on follow-up inquiries, the controller estimates that it takes 3.4 units of the substandard material to produce one finished unit.
2. The substandard material is more difficult to work with. Inquiry reveals that 2.2 hours of labor would be needed to finish one unit of the finished product.

As a revision of the initial report, the assistant controller decided to determine the portion of each variance that is assignable to the purchasing agent and to the production manager. The material price variance is favorable and should be attributed to the purchasing agent. Although he will be credited with this variance, the purchasing agent should also be charged for some portion of the unfavorable effi-

Exhibit 6.8   Myles Company Variance Report

	Applied	Actual Cost	Total Variance	Price Rate or Spending	Quantity or Efficiency
Direct material	$240,000[a]	$225,550[b]	$14,450	$34,450	($20,000)
Direct labor	200,000[c]	229,500[d]	(29,500)	(4,500)	(25,000)
Variable overhead	120,000[e]	140,000[f]	(20,000)	(5,000)	(15,000)
Total	$560,000	$595,050	($35,050)	$24,950	($60,000)

[a] $12 × 20,000   [b] $3.47 × 65,000

[c] $10 × 20,000   [d] $5.10 × 45,000

[e] $6 × 20,000   [f] Given

ciency variances incurred by the production department as a result of the decision to purchase substandard material. If the purchasing agent's share of those variances does not exceed the favorable price variance, then the purchasing agent's decision can be justified from a financial point of view. However, it is also necessary to consider the effect of the decision on product quality, which may have an effect on sales.

To determine the share of the material quantity variance actually attributable to the production department, it is necessary to recognize that the quantity standard was too tight in the last half of the period during which one-half of the total output was produced. Thus, the revised standard quantity would be as follows:

First 10,000 units:	10,000 × 3.0	30,000
Second 10,000 units:	10,000 × 3.4	34,000
Total		64,000

Then the production department's share of the material quantity variance should be computed using the revised standard and the actual quantity of 65,000 units:

(Revised standard − Actual quantity) Standard material cost
= (64,000 − 65,000) 4 = $4,000 U

The difference between the standard quantity of material allowed via the original standard and the revised standard should be charged to the purchasing agent. This is legitimate because his decision is the reason for some of the excess usage of material. The amount chargeable to him is:

(Original standard − Revised standard) Standard material cost
= (20,000 × 3 − 64,000) 4 = $16,000 U

The labor efficiency variance should be prorated in the same way as the material quantity variance. Revising the standard hours of work allowed for production, yields:

First 10,000 units:	$10,000 \times 2.0$	20,000
Second 10,000 units:	$10,000 \times 2.2$	22,000
Total		42,000

The labor efficiency variance attributable to the production department is:

(Revised standard − Actual hours) Standard labor rate
$(42,000 - 45,000)\, 5 = \underline{\$15,000}$ U

Again the difference between the original and revised labor standard should be charged to the purchasing agent since it was his decision that resulted in the need for increased labor. This amounts to $10,000:

(Original standard − Revised standard) Standard labor rate
$(20,000 \times 2 - 42,000)\, 5 = \underline{\$10,000}$ U

Based on the available information, the labor rate variance should be assigned to the production manager. This only means he is responsible for explaining why it exists; it may or may not be his fault.

The revision is not yet done. If overhead and labor hours are correlated, as the overhead rate implies, then some of the overhead efficiency variance is also attributable to the purchasing agent. Using the original and revised standards from the labor analysis:

To production:

(Revised standard − Actual hours) Variable overhead rate
$= (42,000 - 45,000)\, 3 = \underline{\$9,000}$ U

To purchasing:

(Original standard − Revised standard) Variable overhead rate
$= (40,000 - 42,000)\, 3 = \underline{\$6,000}$ U

The variable overhead spending variance, like the labor rate variance, should be assigned to the production manager for explanation. Exhibit 6.9 is a summary of the revisions.

As you can see in Exhibit 6.9, the purchasing agent's favorable price variance was not completely offset by the unfavorable production variances attributed to him. Whether his decision was good depends on the product quality implications. Another factor not yet considered is the savings that resulted from the avoided increase in the price of the regular material. Actually, making the decision about using an alternative material is a relevant costing problem and will not be analyzed here.

Summary

In this chapter three additional topics related to standard costing have been discussed. You should now be able to incorporate standards and variances into an accounting system. In order to support external reporting requirements you have seen how to allocate the variances back to the inventory and cost-of-goods-sold accounts in order to approximate an actual cost system. Third, there was a discussion of the various factors that contribute to variances and of the factors that you

---

Exhibit 6.9   Myles Company Revised Variance Report

	Total	Purchasing	Production
Material price variance	$ 34,450	$34,450	0
Material quantity variance	(20,000)	(16,000)	$ (4,000)
Labor rate variance	(4,500)	0	(4,500)
Labor efficiency variance	(25,000)	(10,000)	(15,000)
Overhead efficiency variance	(15,000)	(6,000)	(9,000)
Overhead spending variance	(5,000)	0	(5,000)
Total	$(35,050)	$2,450	$(37,500)

---

should consider in establishing the responsibility for the variances. The "procedures" in the latter section are only representative since each situation is context dependent. There were no critical new key words introduced in this chapter.

SELF-STUDY PROBLEM. The Sweet Candy Company manufactures one type of candy and uses a standard cost system. At the beginning of the current year standards were established as follows:

Requirements for One Batch

Sugar (20 pounds @ $2)	$ 40
Other materials (70 pounds @ $3)	210
Labor (5 hours @ $12)	60
Variable overhead (5 hours @ $4)	20
Fixed overhead (5 hours @ $3)	15
	$345

During the current period 19,000 batches were completed. Actual resources used consisted of the following:

Actual sugar purchased (450,000 pounds @ $1.97⅔)	$ 889,500
Actual sugar used	415,000 pounds
Other material purchased and used (1,400,000 pounds @ $3)	$4,200,000
Labor (102,250 hours @ $12)	$1,227,000
Variable overhead	$ 413,075
Fixed overhead (equal to budget)	$ 375,000
Beginning inventories	
Sugar	0
Other materials	0
Work in process (100% complete with respect to all materials, 30% complete with respect to conversion costs)	3,000 batches
Finished goods	1,000 batches

Ending inventories

Sugar	35,000 pounds
Other materials	0
Work in process (100% complete with respect to all materials, 47.5% complete with respect to conversion costs)	4,000 batches
Finished goods	2,000 batches

In addition to the above it has been discovered that at the beginning of the period 110,000 pounds of grade B sugar were purchased at $1.75 per pound and used in production. The purchasing agent did this without consulting with production and assumed it would cause no problems. The standards are based on grade A sugar. The remaining 340,000 pounds of sugar purchased was grade A at a cost of $2.05 per pound. In order to meet the company's sweetness standards, the sugar content of the candy had to be increased by 10% over that needed if grade A sugar was used. Except for the 10% extra, the production on which grade B sugar was used turned out to be efficient with regard to sugar usage.

When production made use of grade B sugar it was necessary to use 5% more labor. During the period 1,500 overtime hours were used. The $6 per hour overtime premium was charged to variable overhead. The overtime, in part, is due to the extra 5% labor needed for production when using the grade B sugar.

Required:

1. Compute all of the manufacturing cost variances using the beginning-of-year standards.
2. For each of the variances, how much, if any, should be the responsibility of the purchasing agent?
3. Ignore the issue of whether inventories are material. Prorate the standard cost variances in order to adjust the standards to an actual basis for external reporting. The quantity variances incurred because of grade B sugar will be allocated over all units, not just those produced with grade B sugar. You may assume a FIFO cost flow.

Solution to Self-Study Problem

1. Because of the WIP inventories, it will be necessary to compute equivalent units in order to determine the standard quantity of material and labor required.

	Material	Labor
Beginning inventory	0	2,100
Started and finished (19,000 − 3,000)	16,000	16,000
Ending inventory	4,000	1,900
	20,000	20,000
Standards		
Sugar 20,000 × 20	400,000	
Other materials 20,000 × 70	1,400,000	
Labor 20,000 × 5	100,000	
MPV		
Sugar (2.00 − 1.97⅔) 450,000	$10,500 F	
Other material (3.00 − 3.00) 1,400,000	0	

MQV

Sugar (400,000 − 415,000) 2	$30,000 U
Other material (1,400,000 − 1,400,000)	0

LRV (12 − 12) 102, 250   0

LEV (100,000 − 102,250) 12 $27,000 U

Variable overhead efficiency variance
  (100,000 − 102,250) 4 $ 9,000 U

Variable overhead spending variance
  ($4.00 × 102,250) − 413,075 $ 4,075 U

Fixed overhead spending variance
  (375,000 − 375,000)   0

Noncontrollable variance
  (100,000 × 3 − 375,000) $75,000 U

2. The 110,000 pounds of grade B sugar first used would be the equivalent of 100,000 pounds of grade A sugar (110,000 ÷ 1.1). Thus, it was used for the first 5,000 batches (100,000 ÷ 20). In computing the revised standards against which to evaluate the production manager's performance you should use a different rate for the first 5,000 equivalent units of production from that for the last 15,000 units. The purchasing agent should be held accountable for the difference between the original and the revised standard.
    Variance for which purchasing agent is responsible:

MPV (all)		$10,500 F
MQV		
Original standard	400,000	
Revised standard		
[110,000 + 20 (20,000 − 5,000)]	410,000	
Difference	10,000	
Standard cost	2	$20,000 U
LEV		
Original standard	100,000	
Revised standard		
(5,000 × 5 × 1.05) + (15,000 × 5)	101,250	
Difference	1,250	
Standard cost	12	$15,000 U
Variable overhead efficiency variance		
Original standard	100,000	
Revised standard (from above)	101,250	
Difference	1,250	
Variable overhead rate	4	$ 5,000 U
Variable overhead spending variance		
Extra hours needed because of grade B		
sugar 5,000 × 0.05 × 5	1,250	

Inefficient hours after allowing for wrong grade of sugar; (actual hours − revised standard) = (102,250 − 101,250). These hours could have been avoided if production had been efficient. If so, then these 1,000 hours would not have been needed and no overtime

premium would have been needed. Thus the
purchasing agent cannot be held accountable
for overtime premium that could have been
avoided.*

	1,000	
Overtime hours attributed to grade B sugar	250	
Overtime premium	6	
Overtime cost attributable to purchasing		$ 1,500 U

*Removing these 1,000 hours from the responsibility of the purchasing agent assumes that production had no scheduling problems that caused overtime. In other words, overtime was caused solely because the total hours needed during the period exceeded a 40-hour week.

3. The basis for allocating the MQV is:

	Standard Material	Percentage
Ending work in process 20 × 4,000	80,000	20%
Ending finished goods 20 × 2,000	40,000	10
Cost of goods sold (balance)	280,000	70
Total standard (from part 1)	400,000	

The basis for allocating the price variance on sugar is the actual quantity purchased, which would be allocated among the accounts as follows:

	Standard Material	MQVᵃ	Adjusted Material	Percentage
Stores	—	—	35,000	350/4,500
Work in process	80,000	3,000	83,000	830/4,500
Finished goods	40,000	1,500	41,500	415/4,500
Cost of goods sold (balance)	280,000ᵇ	10,500	290,500	2,905/4,500
	400,000	15,000	450,000ᶜ	

ᵃAllocated using ratios for MQV. The total is from the MQV computation in part 1.

ᵇThis figure would have to be reduced by the beginning inventory of sugar if there was one. With a FIFO cost flow assumption, the beginning inventory of sugar would be used first. However, it did not contribute to *this* period's price variance.

ᶜThis column must add to material purchased this period.

Basis for all other variances:	Standard Hours	Percentage
Work in process 5 × 1,900	9,500	9.5%
Finished goods 5 × 2,000	10,000	10.0
Cost of goods sold (balance)	80,500	80.5
Total standard (from #1)	100,000	

Variance allocation:
To stores
  MPV 350/4,500 × 10,500   (817)
To work in process
  MPV 830/4,500 × 10,500   (1,937)
  MQV 0.20 × 30,000   6,000
  Conversion cost variances
    0.095 (27,000 + 9,000 + 4,075 + 75,000)   10,932   14,995
To finished goods
  MPV 415/4,500 × 10,500   (968)
  MQV 0.10 × 30,000   3,000
  Conversion cost variances
    0.10 (27,000 + 9,000 + 4,075 + 75,000)   11,508   13,540
To cost of goods sold
  MPV 2,905/4,500 × 10,500   (6,778)
  MQV 0.70 × 30,000   21,000
  Conversion cost variances
    0.805 (27,000 + 9,000 + 4,075 + 75,000)   92,635   106,857

References

Atkinson, J.W. *An Introduction to Motivation.* Princeton, N.J.: D. Van Nostrand, 1964.

Lawler, E.E. *Motivation in Work Organizations.* Monterey, Calif.: Brooks Cole Publishing Co., 1973.

Stedry, A.C., and Kay, E. "The Effects of Goal Difficulty on Performance: A Field Experiment," *Behavioural Science* (November 1966): 459–470.

Problems

6-1. Journal Entries for a Standard Cost System. Reconsider the E.E. Ray Company in Chapter 5 and its results for the month of January (Exhibit 5.3).

Required:

Prepare the journal entries to reflect January's activity.

6-2. Journal Entries for a Standard Cost System. Reconsider the data in problem 5-6.

Required:

Prepare the journal entries to reflect February's activity.

6-3. Variance Analysis and Entries. The Fenzel Company reviewed its standards at the beginning of 19x3 and found that no changes were needed (see Exhibit 6.2). In 19x3 the following data were recorded and should be used in addition to that of Exhibits 6.2 and 6.3:

Work in process:
  Started this year   10,000 units
  At 12/31/x3, 100% completed with respect to
    material, 20% with respect to labor, and 60%
    with respect to machine time   4,000 units

Finished goods inventory, 12/31/x3	1,000 units
Actual data for 19x3	
Material purchased (15,000 units @ $4.02)	$ 60,300
Material used	21,000 units
Labor (8,000 hours @ $6.30)	$ 50,400
Machine hours used	34,000 hours
Variable overhead	$172,000
Fixed overhead	$ 70,000

Required:

1. Compute the material, labor, and overhead variances using the same variance system as used in the chapter.
2. Prepare the journal entries to reflect the results during 19x3.

6-4. Entries in a Standard Cost System. Consider the data for the Sweet Candy Company in the self-study problem for this chapter.

Required:

Prepare the journal entries to reflect the results during the period as given in the self-study problem.

6-5. Comprehensive Standard Cost Problem with Entries. The North Company produces two products, A and B. Both products are started in Department ABC. After processing in Department ABC, product A is transferred to Department DEF for finishing, and product B is transferred to Department GHI.

For each product, raw material is put into processing at the beginning of production. Both products use the same raw material. There is some direct labor required in Department ABC, but the process is primarily a machining operation. Thus, overhead is applied on the basis of machine hours.

Raw material price variance is isolated at the time of purchases and therefore raw material inventory is carried at standard prices. *Actual* material units and labor hours are transferred into work in process at *standard prices*. Overhead is charged to work in process on the basis of standard machine hours. Work-in-process inventories are carried at standard costs. Thus, the material quantity and labor efficiency variances are established at the end of the period when the cost of production is transferred from work in process to finished goods. Other variances are established in the usual manner.

For overhead purposes the divisor activity has been established at 1,200,000 machine hours *per year*. The standards were the same in February as in January. The actual machine hours in February were 89,000. A manufacturing overhead control account and a partial work in process account for February are included.

Manufacturing Overhead Control

Actual Fixed	$205,000	Applied	$450,000
Actual Variable	275,000		
	$480,000		

Work in Process—ABC

Inventory, January 31		To Dept. DEF(10,000 units)	
Product A	0		
		To Dept. GHI (21,000 units)	
Product B (1,000 units)	29,500*		
		Inventory, February 28	None
Material (actual quantity)	177,500		
Labor (actual quantity)	151,500		
Overhead (standard quantity	450,000		
	808,500		

*The standard cost of the January 31 inventory was as follows:

Material was 100% complete	$ 5,000	
Labor was 75% complete	4,500	
Overhead based on machine hours; machine hours 100% complete	20,000	
Cost at January 31	$29,500	

A partial list of standards follows. Based on the preceding information you are asked to complete this list in part 1.

		Product A			*Product B*	
Material	3 units	@ $2.50 = $7.50	_____units	@ $2.50 =	_____	
Labor	1/2 hour	@ $6.00 = 3.00	_____hours	@ $6.00 =	_____	
Overhead based on machine hours						
Variable	1 hour	@ $3.00 = 3.00	_____hours	@ $3.00 =	_____	
Fixed	1 hour	@ $2.00 = 2.00	_____hours	@ $2.00 =	_____	
Total per unit		$15.50			_____	

Required:

1. Complete the preceding standards list for product B.
2. Prepare the entry (or entries) to transfer the units finished in Department ABC during February. Do not set up variances at this time.
3. How many units of raw material are allowed for February's production?
4. Compute the material quantity variance.
5. Compute the standard labor hours allowed for February's production.
6. Compute the labor efficiency variance.
7. Compute the variable overhead efficiency variance.
8. Compute the overhead spending variance.
9. Compute the noncontrollable (volume) variance.
10. Considering your answer to part 2, prepare the entry to adjust the work-in-process account to a zero balance at February 28.
11. Prepare the entry closing the manufacturing overhead control account into the variance accounts.

6-6. Basic Problem on Prorating Labor Variances. The Strawberry Company uses one material in the production of its only product. Inventory data are:

Beginning of period	
Materials	12,000 pounds
Work in process (100% complete with respect to	
material, 40% complete with respect to labor)	20,000 units
Finished goods	0
End of period	
Materials	15,000 pounds
Work in process (100% complete with respect to	
material, 70% complete with respect to labor)	35,000 units
Finished goods	0
During the current period the following activity	
occurred:	
Material purchased	171,000 pounds @ $4.05
Production started	80,000 units
Production finished	65,000 units
Material used	168,000 pounds
Labor cost	423,300 hours @ $11

Required:

1. The standard labor cost for Strawberry's product is 5 hours @ $10 or $50 per unit. Compute the labor rate and labor efficiency variance.
2. Allocate the labor rate and labor efficiency variance to inventories and cost of goods sold in order to meet external reporting requirements.
3. What is the adjusted labor cost of Strawberry's ending work-in-process inventory?

6-7. Comparison of Standard Costing and Actual Process Costing When Labor Variance Is Allocated. Assume that the Strawberry Company of problem 6-6 uses actual process cost accounting.

Required:

1. Using FIFO process costing, how much of the actual labor cost of $4,656,300 (423,300 × $11) would be assigned to the ending work-in-process inventory?
2. Compare your results in part 1 with the results in part 3 of problem 6-6.

6-8. Basic Problem on Prorating Material Variances. Reconsider the Strawberry Company problem stated in 6-6. Assume the standard cost for material is 2 pounds at $4.00, a total of $8 per unit.

Required:

1. What is the standard cost of material in the ending work-in-process inventory?
2. What is the material price variance for the period based on the actual quantity purchased?
3. What is the material quantity variance for the period?
4. How much of the material quantity variance should be allocated to the ending work-in-process inventory in order to adjust the standards to an actual cost system?

5. How much of the material price variance should be allocated to the ending work-in-process inventory in order to adjust the standards to an actual cost system?

6-9. Standard Costing and Process Costing Compared When There Are Material Variances. Reconsider the material accounting for the Strawberry Company of problems 6-6 and 6-8. Assume the actual per unit cost of the beginning materials inventory was also $4.05. Then, under an actual process cost system the cost of materials issued to production would be $680,400 (168,000 × $4.05).

Required:

1. What would be the material cost of the ending work-in-process inventory using process cost accounting?
2. Compare your results in part 1 with the *adjusted* standard cost of the work in process inventory in problem 6-8.

6-10. Prorating Labor Variances When There Are Multiple Products. The Darling Company produces two products. The labor standards are as follows:

	Televisions	Stereos
Labor hours	20	30
Inventory data include		
Beginning work in process	3,000	5,000
Labor completion	30%	40%
Ending work in process	6,000	4,000
Labor completion	20%	55%
Beginning finished goods	10,000	2,000
Ending finished goods	8,000	7,000

During the period 32,000 television sets were sold and 45,000 stereos. Labor hours total 2,500,000, at an average cost of $13 per hour. The standard labor rate was $12 per hour.

Required:

1. Compute the labor variances for the period.
2. Allocate the labor variances to the inventories and cost of goods sold.

6-11. Comprehensive Problem on Prorating Variances. The Sutton Company uses a standard cost system to account for its manufacturing costs. During the current year they had a contract with the U.S. Defense Department to supply 10,000 units of its product. The Cost Accounting Standards Board requires the variances to be prorated to inventories and cost of goods sold.

All inventories are maintained at complete standard, and the following data are available:

Inventory data (units)	
Materials at 1/1/x1	0
Materials at 12/31/x1	10,000
Work in process at 1/1/x1	0
Work in process at 12/13/x1 complete as to	
material, 25% complete as to labor	4,000
Finished goods at 1/1/x1	2,000
Finished goods at 12/31/x1	5,000
Units sold (includes the defense contract)	50,000

Standards per unit

Material (2 units @ $4.00)	$ 8.00
Labor (6 hours @ $5.00)	30.00
Variable overhead (6 hours @ $2.00)	12.00
Fixed overhead (6 hours @ $3.00)	18.00
Total	$68.00

Selected trial balance data at 12/31/x1

Materials	$	40,000
Work in process		92,000
Finished goods		340,000
Cost of goods sold		3,400,000
Material price variance (credit balance)		10,034
Material quantity variance (debit balance)		5,700
Labor rate variance (debit balance)		4,000
Labor efficiency variance (debit balance)		10,000
Overhead spending variance (debit balance)		12,000
Overhead efficiency variance (debit balance)		4,000
Noncontrollable variance (debit balance)		24,000

Required:

1. Prepare a schedule of variance allocations.
2. What would be the adjusted manufacturing cost of the defense contract?

6-12. Variance Proration with Multiple Products. At the end of 19x1 the Pendleton Company discovers it must allocate the variances from standard to inventories and cost of goods sold in order to satisfy external reporting requirements. Pendleton produces two products with standards as follows:

	Cabinets	*Bookshelves*
Material (@ $5/foot)	$ 10	$20
Labor (@ $10/labor hour)	50	30
Overhead (@ $15/labor hour)	75	45
	$135	$95

During 19x1 the following sales and production occurred:

	Cabinets	*Bookshelves*
Unit sales	26,000	28,000
Units transferred to finished goods	20,000	23,000

On January 1, 19x1, there were 20,000 units of raw material on hand, whereas 25,000 units are on hand on December 31, 19x1. Inventory data on the two products are:

	Cabinets	Bookshelves
Work in process, January 1	10,000 units	5,000 units
Percentage completion		
Material	100%	100%
Conversion costs	40%	60%
Work in process, December 31	8,000 units	7,000 units
Percentage completion		
Material	100%	100%
Conversion	70%	50%
Finished goods, January 1	6,000 units	9,000 units
Finished goods, December 31	0 units	4,000 units

The variances were as follows:

Material price variance (based on actual quantity purchased)	$28,744 F
Material quantity variance	13,600 U
Conversion cost variances	71,400 U

Assume a FIFO cost flow

Required:

1. What is the standard labor hours allowed for 19x1's output?
2. Prepare a schedule allocating the conversion cost variances. Separate work-in-process, finished goods, and cost-of-goods-sold accounts are maintained for the two products.
3. What is the standard quantity of material allowed for 19x1's output?
4. Prepare a schedule allocating the material quantity variance.
5. How many units of raw material were purchased in 19x1?
6. Prepare a schedule allocating the material price variance.

6-13. CMA Problem on Establishing Responsibility for Cost Variances. The Felton Company manufactures a complete line of radios. Because a large number of models have plastic cases, the company has its own molding department for producing the cases. The month of April was devoted to the production of the plastic case for one of the portable radios, Model SX76. The molding department has two operations, molding and trimming. There is no interaction of labor in these two operations. The estimated labor cost for producing ten plastic cases of model SX76 is as follows:

Molders	0.50 hrs. @ $6.00 =	$3.00
Trimmers	0.25 hrs. @ $4.00 =	1.00
		$4.00

During April, 70,000 plastic cases were produced in the molding department. However, 10% of these cases (7,000) had to be discarded because they were found to be defective at final inspection. The purchasing department had changed to a new plastic supplier to take advantage of a lower price for comparable plastic. The new plastic turned out to be of a lower quality and resulted in the rejection of completed cases.

Direct-labor hours worked and direct-labor costs charged to the molding department are as follows.

Direct Labor Charged to the Molding Department

Molders	3,800 hours @ $6.25 =	$23,750
Trimmers	1,600 hours @ $4.15 =	$ 6,640
Total labor charges		$30,390

As a result of poor scheduling by the production scheduling department, the supervisor of the molding department had to shift molders to the trimming operation for 200 hours during April. The company paid the molding workers their regular hourly rate even though they were performing a lower rated task. There was no significant loss of efficiency caused by the shift. In addition, the supervisor of the department indicated that 75 hours and 35 hours of idle time occurred in the molding and trimming operations, respectively, as a result of unexpected machinery repairs required during the month.

Required:

1. The monthly report that compares actual costs with standard cost of output for the month of April shows the following labor variance for the molding department:

Actual labor for April	$30,390
Standard labor cost of output	
(63,000 × $4.00/10)	25,200
Unfavorable labor variance	$ 5,190

   This variance is significantly higher than normal, and management would like an explanation. Prepare a detailed analysis of the unfavorable labor variance for the molding department that shows the variance resulting from (1) labor rates, (2) labor substitution, (3) material substitution, (4) idle time, and (5) operating efficiency.
2. The supervisor of the molding department is concerned with the large variances charged to her department. She feels that the variances due to labor substitution and change in raw materials should not be charged to her department. Does the supervisor have a valid argument? Briefly justify your position.

6-14. CMA Problem; Adjusting for Uncontrollable Variances. The Lenco Co. employs a standard cost system as part of its cost control program. The standard cost per unit is established at the beginning of each year. Standards are not revised during the year for any changes in material or labor inputs or in the manufacturing processes. Any revisions in standards are deferred until the beginning of the next fiscal year. However, in order to recognize such changes in the current year, the company includes planned variances in the monthly budgets prepared after such changes have been introduced.

The following labor standard was set for 100 units of one of Lenco's products effective July 1, 19x1, the beginning of the fiscal year.

Class I labor	4 hours @ $ 6.00	$24.00
Class II labor	3 hours @ $ 7.50	22.50
Class V labor	1 hour @ 11.50	11.50
Total for 100 units		$58.00

The standard was based upon the quality of material that had been used in prior years and what was expected to be available for the 19x1–x2 fiscal year. The labor activity is performed by a team consisting of four persons with Class I skills, three persons with Class II skills, and one person with Class V skills. This is the most economical combination for the company's processing system.

The manufacturing operations occurred as expected during the first five months of the year. The standard costs contributed to effective cost control during this period. However, there were indications that changes in the operations would be required in the last half of the year. The company had received a significant increase in orders for delivery in the spring. There were an inadequate number of skilled workers available to meet the increased production. As a result, the production teams, beginning in January, would be made up of more Class I labor and less Class II labor than the standard required. The teams would consist of six Class I persons, two Class II persons, and one Class V person. This labor team would be less efficient than the normal team. The reorganized teams work more slowly so that only 90 units are produced in the same time period that 100 units would normally be produced. No raw materials will be lost as a result of the change in the labor mix. Completed units have never been rejected in the final inspection process as a consequence of faulty work; this is expected to continue.

In addition, Lenco was notified by its material supplier that a lower quality material would be supplied after January 1. One unit of raw material normally is required for each good unit produced. Lenco and its supplier estimated that 5% of the units manufactured would be rejected upon final inspection due to defective material. Normally, no units are lost due to defective material.

Required:

1. How much of the lower quality material must be entered into production in order to produce 42,750 units of good production in January with the new labor teams? Show your calculations.
2. How many hours of each class of labor will be needed to produce 42,750 good units from the material input? Show your calculations.
3. What amount should be included in the January budget for the planned labor variance due to the labor team and material changes? What amount of this planned labor variance can be associated with (1) the material change and (2) the team change. Show your calculations.

6-15. Determining Responsibility for Variance. The Holzer Company produces wood products. Variable overhead is applied on the basis of labor hours, and fixed overhead costs may be ignored in this problem. A particular product had the following standards established:

Grade B Lumber	2 square feet @ $1.00	$ 2.00
Labor	3 hours @ $4.00	12.00
Variable overhead	3 hours @ $2.00	6.00
Total		$20.00

During the current period 12,000 units of the product were produced. The following costs were incurred:

Lumber purchased and used: 25,200 square feet	$ 27,940
Labor: 38,000 hours @ $4.00	152,000
Variable overhead	76,000

Since the purchasing officer and the production manager have their bonuses tied to the standard cost variances, it is necessary to carefully study the meaning of each variance. After talking to all people involved, you determine the following facts:

1. The production of 12,000 units was accomplished in three equal batches of 4,000 units.
2. The production manager did not give the purchasing officer ample lead time to order the lumber for batch 1. To prevent delay the purchasing officer purchased grade A lumber, which was available at a nearby dealer. This was a justifiable decision by the purchasing officer.
3. Grade B lumber was purchased for batch 2. The purchasing officer did not buy in optimal lot sizes, however.
4. In an attempt to reduce his variance, the purchasing officer purchased grade C lumber for batch 3.
5. Following is a detailed schedule of the actual lumber purchased and used:

Grade	Quantity (sq. ft.)	Price	Total
A	7,000	$1.30	$ 9,100
B	8,200	1.20	9,840
C	10,000	0.90	9,000
	25,200		$27,940

6. Depending on the grade of lumber used, the amounts of lumber and labor allowed for the product are as follows;

Grade	Quantity Allowed (sq. ft.)	Labor Allowed (hours)
A	1.50	3
B	2.00	3
C	2.75	4

Required:

1. Compute the variances that would be reported by using the standards established at the beginning of the period.
2. Analyze each of the variances in part 1 to determine the amount attributable to the purchasing officer and to the production manager.

6-16. Alternative to Problem 6-15. The Moyer Company produces two products, A1 and B2. There is a common production line, and this necessitates the use of a batch-scheduling arrangement. An EOQ model was used to select the optimal size of each run. As a result, product A1 is normally produced in runs of 100 units each and B2 in runs of 200. Based on these run sizes, the standard hours allowed per unit were developed as follows:

	Product A1	Product B2
Set up time per run (hours)	60	20
Production time per run (hours)	500	560
Tear down time per run (hours)	40	20
Total hours per run	600	600
Lot size (units)	100	200
Standard time per unit	6	3

During October, the production department completed three runs (13, 14, and 15). Run 13 was not originally scheduled. It was done as a favor to the marketing department that needed a rush job for 50 units of product A1 ordered by a preferred customer. Run 14 was a normal run for product B2, and 15 a normal run for product A1. In total, 150 units of A1 were produced during October and 200 units of B2. The accounting department prepared the following performance report based on 1,500 standard hours [(150 × 6) + (200 × 3)]. Note in the performance report that overhead is applied on the basis of direct-labor dollars.

	Standard	Actual	Variance
Direct-labor hours	1,500	1,700	(200)
Direct-labor dollars at			
$5 per hour	$ 7,500	$ 8,500	($1,000)
Variable overhead			
Supplies (10%)	$ 750	$ 850	($ 100)
Indirect labor including			
fringes (20%)	1,500	1,800	(300)
Fringes on direct labor (5%)	375	425	(50)
Power (3%)	225	250	(25)
Other (6%)	450	500	(50)
Total	$ 3,300	$ 3,825	($525)
Total conversion costs	$10,800	$12,325	($1,525)

In discussing this report with the production manager you became aware that he was disturbed with its implications. First, he felt it was unreasonable to use the per unit labor standard on run 13. He pointed out that set-up and tear-down time is independent of the size of the run. The set-up and tear-down labor is accounted for as direct labor. Further, there was a machine breakdown while run 15 was on the line. The production manager had requested the maintenance department to do preventive maintenance on this machine during September. Due to inefficiencies in the maintenance department, this was never done. As a result, production incurred 100 hours of idle labor waiting on crisis repairs. These hours were still considered as direct-labor hours in the accounting system. In short, the production manager feels he is not responsible for all of the variance in his performance report.

Required:

Prepare a revised performance report. In addition to the three columns of this report, add columns for "Marketing's Responsibility," "Maintenance's Responsibility," "Balance To Be Explained," "Efficiency Variance," and "Spending Variance."

6-17. Alternative to 6-16. Merritt Company produces three standard products (A1, B2, and C3) in lots of variable sizes. The standards currently being used for these products in Department 1 (where overhead is applied on the basis of direct-labor hours) are as follows:

	A1	B2	C3
Material	2 @ $20 = $ 40	3 @ $20 = $ 60	6 @ $20.00 = $120
Direct labor	7 @ $12 = 84	5 @ $12 = 60	8 @ $12.75 = 102
Variable overhead	7 @ $ 5 = 35	5 @ $ 5 = 25	8 @ $ 5.00 = 40
Fixed overhead	7 @ $ 3 = 21	5 @ $ 3 = 15	8 @ $ 3.00 = 24
	$180	$160	$286

The labor standard is a composite of various skill levels. Specifically, the labor rates were established as follows:

	A1	B2	C3
Skill level I	2 @ $15 = $30	2 @ $15 = $30	3 @ $15.00 = $ 45
Skill level II	3 @ $12 = 36	1 @ $12 = 12	4 @ $12.00 = 48
Skill level III	2 @ $ 9 = 18	2 @ $ 9 = 18	1 @ $ 9.00 = 9
	7 @ $12 = $84	5 @ $12 = $60	8 @ $12.75 = $102

The fixed overhead rate was established using a practical capacity of 2,240 direct-labor hours per reporting period.

During the current reporting period, consisting of 20 working days, the following production (listed in the order in which it occurred) took place:

Job #	Product	Units	Days	Standard Material	Actual Material	Standard Labor	Actual Labor
117	A1	70	5	140	140	490	500
118	B2	40	2	120	120	200	220
119	C3	30	3	180	230	240	300
120	A1	70	5	140	140	490	500
121	B2	80	5	240	240	400	440
				820	870	1,820	1,960

The actual costs for the reporting period consisted of:

Material	$18,000
Direct labor	23,505
Variable overhead	10,388
Fixed overhead	6,750

In following up on the variances you discover the following:

1. The materials needed for job #117 arrived late because the purchasing agent did not allow ample lead time. To compensate, the production manager scheduled overtime during the first week of the period. Overtime hours totaled 40. The premium was charged

to manufacturing overhead but overtime was not budgeted for in the $5 variable overhead rate. Also, there was 30 hours of idle time charged to manufacturing overhead that was not anticipated in the original budget.

2. The materials needed for job #118 were acquired via a rush order. This job was scheduled after the normal time of informing the purchasing agent. In order to get the units on time the purchasing agent used a different supplier and paid $23 per unit for the material.

3. The standards for product C3 do not reflect the fact that there is normally a 20% spoilage rate on this product. Spoilage is not detected until the end of processing.

4. The materials needed for job #120 arrived late because of problems attributable to the supplier. The purchasing agent claims to have done all he could to ensure proper delivery. Overtime hours totaled 40 during the third week. There were 30 idle hours, and both the overtime and idle time were charged to manufacturing overhead.

5. During the fourth week of the period the factory supervisor shifted three of the skill level I employees to help with some problems in Department III. Not only was Department I left short-handed, they had to use a different labor mix in producing product B2. The actual mix of labor per unit for the week was:

Skill level I	1.0
Skill level II	2.5
Skill level III	2.0
	5.5

It should be clear that in explaining the variances of Department I, the responsibility must be shared by four parties:

The production manager
The purchasing agent
The accounting system (for inappropriate accounting)
The factory supervisor

Required:

1. Using the current standards compute the material price variance.
2. How much of the variance in part 1 is attributable to each of the four parties listed above?
3. Using the current standards compute the material quantity variance.
4. How much of the variance in part 3 is attributable to each of the four parties listed above?
5. Using the current standards the labor rate variance is:

$$\text{LRV} = \text{Standard rate} \times \text{Actual hours} - \$23,505$$
$$\text{Standard rate} \times \text{Actual hours} = 12\,(500 + 220 + 500 + 440) + 12.75\,(300) = 23,745$$
$$\text{LRV} = 23,745 - 23,505 = \$240 \text{ F}$$

How much of the labor rate variance is attributable to each of the four parties listed above?

6. Using the current standards the labor efficiency variance is:

$$\text{LEV} = (490 - 500)\,12 + (200 - 220)\,12 + (240 - 300)\,12.75 + (490 - 500)\,12 + (400 - 440)\,12 = \$1,725 \text{ U}$$

How much of the labor efficiency variance is attributable to each of the four parties listed above?

7. Using the current standards the variable overhead spending variance is

   VOHSV = 5 (1,960) − 10,388 = $588 U

   How much of the variable overhead spending variance is attributable to each of the four parties listed above?

CHAPTER 7

The Variable (Direct) Costing System

In the last four chapters substantial effort was devoted to solving the problems caused by the existence of fixed costs. In this chapter there is a discussion of a system that avoids the problem of fixed cost allocation but, in turn, has its own set of problems.

Variable (direct) costing is not acceptable for any external financial reporting requirement: FASB, SEC, or IRS. (The reasons for this will be explained later.) However, if internal benefit can be established, the external requirements should not be a deterrent to the use of variable costing unless the cost of implementing the system exceeds the benefit. The merits of variable costing are attributed to the fact that it accounts for costs in a manner that parallels a firm's cost behavior and, presumably, provides management with better information for their decisions. This presumption will be closely examined in this chapter.

The discussion starts with a definition of variable (direct) costing. Then the mechanics will be illustrated and contrasted with the full absorption methods discussed in the previous chapters. Full absorption, you should recall, assigns a share of all manufacturing costs to production, both variable and fixed. As part of the illustration there is an introduction of the contribution margin reporting format that typically accompanies a variable (direct) costing system. With this background you will be better able to follow the analysis of the system's alleged pros and cons. Following this analysis there is a comparative examination of the full absorption and variable (direct) costing methods over time. The chapter ends with a consideration of the working-paper adjustments that will be needed to derive full absorption statements from a variable costing system.

Definition

Two terms, direct and variable, have been used to identify the concept to be explained in this chapter and, as will be seen, neither represents a completely adequate description. The variable (direct) costing system was originated in response to the following type of situation. Suppose that, in comparison to 19x1 sales volume, 19x2 sales are up. However, 19x2 net income is lower than 19x1, and management is puzzled as to why. Analysis reveals that 19x2 production was considerably *below* the 19x2 sales. The result, of course, is a decline in the inventory. Under full absorption costing the effect of this is to release against 19x2's revenue an amount of fixed cost that is greater than the amount incurred during 19x2.

This is due to the fixed costs of preceding periods, which have been included in the beginning inventory and released when the inventory was reduced. To help illustrate consider Exhibit 7.1.

In Exhibit 7.1 it is assumed that 19x2's sales are double 19x1's. The variable costs amount to $25 per unit and fixed costs are assigned to production at a rate equal to $25 per unit. In 19x1 assume that the firm operated at the divisor activity used in determining the fixed overhead rate (6 units). Thus, there would be no noncontrollable variance. For illustrative purposes, assume that the firm did not produce any units in 19x2. That is, the firm produced enough in 19x1 to supply the demand in both 19x1 and 19x2. In 19x2 the noncontrollable variance (unabsorbed fixed cost) would be equal to the budgeted fixed costs (6 units × $25) and is an added cost of the period. The comparative bar charts show how the situation described in the previous paragraph could occur. Variable and assigned fixed costs constitute the same percentage of revenue in both years. However, in 19x2 the noncontrollable variance is charged against revenue so that the net income in 19x2 is smaller than 19x1 in spite of the increased sales. This phenomenon can be explained from an accounting standpoint, but it is difficult to gain an understanding from the nonaccountant. As a result of this type of situation, variable (direct) costing was proposed.

Variable (direct) costing, then, does not assign any fixed cost to production (including ending work in process and finished goods inventory). All fixed manufacturing costs are accounted for as a period cost rather than a product cost. That is, these costs are charged as an expense of the period in which they are incurred. As a result of this treatment, units produced during the current period are assigned only the variable manufacturing costs (direct material, direct labor, and variable manufacturing overhead).

Using direct costing as the term to identify this concept might imply that only the direct product cost (direct material and direct labor) are assigned to production. Thus, some have suggested the use of the term variable costing. This is better but you should not infer that all variable costs are assigned to production. Variable selling and administrative costs are still considered period expenses.

From this point forward variable costing will be used to identify this concept of income determination. Variable costing can be used with a job order, process, or standard cost system. It is *not an alternative* to one of these systems but a modification. That is, the question of how to account for fixed manufacturing overhead is independent from the question of whether to use a job order or process cost system and from whether or not to use standards. Exhibit 7.2 summarizes and compares the treatment of various costs in the full absorption and variable costing system.

Illustration and Contrast with Full Absorption Costing

An example will now be introduced that will help differentiate the treatment of fixed cost in a full absorption and variable costing system. In addition to examining

Exhibit 7.1   Illustration of Situations Where Full Absorption
Net Income Is Smaller When Sales Are Higher

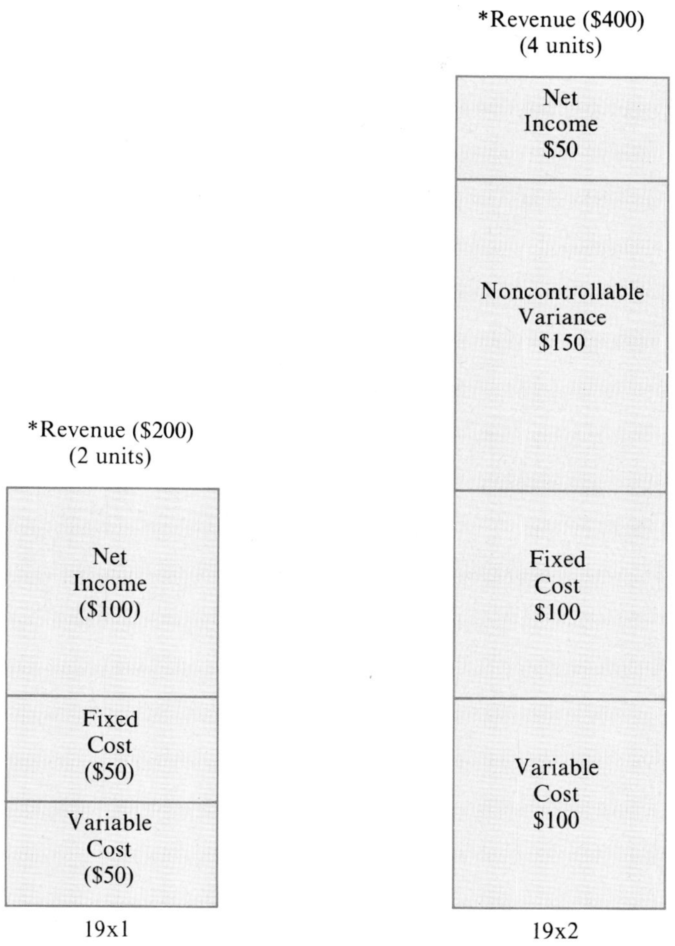

*Revenue ($400)
(4 units)

| Net Income $50 |
| Noncontrollable Variance $150 |
| Fixed Cost $100 |
| Variable Cost $100 |

*Revenue ($200)
(2 units)

| Net Income ($100) |
| Fixed Cost ($50) |
| Variable Cost ($50) |

19x1   19x2

*The entire bar graph represents revenue. The partitions represent the portion of
revenue that is "consumed" by the costs or remains as net income.

the comparative treatments, the contribution margin format of income reporting
will be introduced. Further, there is a reconciliation of the income difference that
will result when both concepts are applied to the same situation. Last, there is consideration of modifications that will be needed to convert the systems discussed in
the previous chapters into their variable costing counterparts.

**Exhibit 7.2   Summary and Comparison of Accounting for Costs
Full Absorption versus Variable Costing**

	Full Absorption		Variable Costing	
	Product Cost	Period Cost	Product Cost	Period Cost
Direct material	x		x	
Direct labor	x		x	
Variable manufacturing overhead	x		x	
Fixed manufacturing overhead	x			x
Variable selling and administrative		x		x
Fixed selling and administrative		x		x

A FULL ABSORPTION COST EXAMPLE. To provide a reference point for comparison, a full absorption cost example is introduced in this subsection. Assume that the Harrison Company produces one product and uses a standard full cost system whereby overhead is applied on the basis of direct-labor hours. Labor hours at normal activity total 100,000. The following standards are in effect:

Direct material	3 units @ $4.00	$12.00
Direct labor	2 hours @ $3.00	6.00
Variable overhead	2 hours @ $4.00	8.00
Fixed overhead	2 hours @ $5.00	10.00
Total		$36.00

Assume the product sells for $40.00, the variable selling expenses amount to $0.50 per unit sold, and the fixed selling and administrative costs total $15,000.

Consider the full absorption income computation under three different conditions. These conditions involve various combinations of production and sales, as indicated in the first two lines of Exhibit 7.3. It is assumed that the beginning inventory is sufficient to permit sales to exceed production in any given case. Further, it is assumed that the standards used in the previous period were the same as those used in the current period; therefore, the unit costs of the beginning and ending inventories are the same. Finally, assume the firm did not incur any variable cost variances. If they had, they would be shown as adjustments to cost of goods sold or prorated to inventories and cost of goods sold depending on the situation.

Now, refer to Exhibit 7.3 and be sure you understand the results for each case. Note the noncontrollable (volume) variance. Remember that this is the under/

[handwritten: Applied fixed − (Budgeted fixed (100m units)) (100m units) × 2 hours ×$5 + ($55.00 × 229) = 100M]

Exhibit 7.3   Harrison Company Comparative Cases Full Absorption Costing

	Case 1	*Case 2*	*Case 3*
Sales (units)	40,000	50,000	40,000
Production (units)	40,000	30,000	50,000
Sales @ $40	$1,600,000	$2,000,000	$1,600,000
Cost of goods sold			
Standard cost @ $36	$1,440,000	$1,800,000	$1,440,000
Noncontrollable (volume)			
variance*	100,000	200,000	0
Total	$1,540,000	$2,000,000	$1,440,000
Gross margin	$ 60,000	$ 0	$ 160,000
Selling and administrative			
Variable @ $0.50	$ 20,000	$ 25,000	$ 20,000
Fixed	15,000	15,000	15,000
Total	$ 35,000	$ 40,000	$ 35,000
Net income	$ 25,000	$ (40,000)	$ 125,000

*Noncontrollable variance = Applied fixed − Budgeted fixed
                = Standard hours × Fixed rate − Budgeted fixed
Standard hours allowed = 2 × Production
Budgeted fixed costs = Fixed rate × Divisor activity
              = $5 × 100,000 = $500,000
Thus noncontrollable variance for:
  Case 1: 80,000 × 5 − 500,000
  Case 2: 60,000 × 5 − 500,000
  Case 3: 100,000 × 5 − 500,000

[handwritten: 200   50 ×3=150]

over-applied fixed overhead and is based on production, not on sales. Also compare case 2 with case 1. Case 2's sales are greater than case 1's and, yet, the net income is $65,000 lower. Imagine a manager's reaction to this kind of news if cases 1 and 2 represented years 1 and 2, respectively. Further note that case 3's sales are the same as case 1's. Yet, the net income of case 3 is $100,000 greater than case 1's. Observe from this comparison that it is *possible* to manipulate income by merely manipulating production. That is, production can simply be increased at the end of the year in order to increase net income. Managers and accountants must be alert to this possibility under full absorption costing in order to prevent some dysfunctional results. This will be explored later.

VARIABLE COSTING COUNTERPART. The full absorption cases have demonstrated the potential problems that might occur with that method of computing income. Now examine how these cases would be reported under variable costing. Before considering the variable costing system it is necessary to introduce and define the contribution margin reporting format. The **contribution margin** of one unit is the difference between its sales price and its *total* variable costs (manufacturing, selling, and administrative). This margin represents the rate at which the product *contributes* to the firm's fixed costs and profits. An income statement prepared in a **contribution margin format** is one that groups costs according to behavior (variable versus fixed) rather than according to a functional classification. In skeletal form the statement is:

Sales	xx
Less variable costs	xx
Total contribution margin	xx
Less fixed costs	xx
Net income	xx

Exhibit 7.4 represents a recasting of the three cases of Exhibit 7.3 into a variable costing result. Several things should be noted. First, the net income for case 1 is the same under variable costing as under full absorption costing. In general, the two methods will report approximately the same net income if production and sales are the same. A difference between the two methods will occur only if there has been a change in the inventories. This is due to the fact that the amount of fixed cost that will be charged against the current period's income under full absorption costing is a function of both production and sales. An excess of production over sales will result in some fixed costs of the current period being capitalized (assigned to the inventory) and deferred to be charged against a future period's revenue. Variable costing would release *all* of this year's fixed cost against this year's revenue. Full absorption costing divides the fixed cost between the units sold and the inventory. Thus, in this situation full absorption costing will charge a smaller amount of fixed costs against this period's revenue than variable costing.

Exhibit 7.4   Harrison Company Comparative Cases Variable Costing

	Case 1	Case 2	Case 3
Sales (units)	40,000	50,000	40,000
Production (units)	40,000	30,000	50,000
Sales @ $40	$1,600,000	$2,000,000	$1,600,000
Variable costs			
Manufacturing @ $26	$1,040,000	$1,300,000	$1,040,000
Selling @ $0.50	20,000	25,000	20,000
Total	$1,060,000	$1,325,000	$1,060,000
Contribution margin	$ 540,000	$ 675,000	$ 540,000
Fixed costs			
Manufacturing	$ 500,000	$ 500,000	500,000
Selling and administrative	15,000	15,000	15,000
Total	$ 515,000	$ 515,000	$ 515,000
Net income	$ 25,000	$ 160,000	$ 25,000

The result is that full absorption income will be higher than variable costing income.

An excess of sales over production results in opposite effects. In the latter case there is an inventory decline. With a decline in inventory the fixed costs released against revenue under full absorption costing will be greater than the fixed costs incurred during the period. Again, variable costing would charge only the current period's fixed cost against income. Because of the greater amount of fixed costs released under full absorption costing it will yield a lower income than variable costing.

 A second observation in comparing Exhibits 7.3 and 7.4 is that variable costing results in an income that moves in the same direction as sales and is totally independent of production. Note that with variable costing, the income in case 1 and 3 are the same even though production volume is 10,000 units higher in case 3. In case 2 the sales volume is higher and so is the net income. Some would consider this type of result to be desirable and, thus, an advantage of variable costing.

Third, be sure you understand the derivation of the amount of fixed manufacturing cost deducted in Exhibit 7.4. Remember that the fixed overhead application rate for full absorption costing was derived as:

$$\text{Fixed overhead application rate} = \frac{\text{Budgeted fixed costs}}{\text{Normal activity}}$$

Thus, the budgeted fixed costs are \$500,000:

$$
\begin{aligned}
\text{Budgeted fixed cost} &= \text{fixed overhead application rate} \\
&\quad \times \text{ normal activity} \\
&= \$5.00 \times 100,000
\end{aligned}
$$

RECONCILING THE DIFFERENCES. Earlier in this section we indicated that the reason for the difference between full absorption costing and variable costing income is an inventory change. To further explain this, consider an exact reconciliation of the two income figures. A general form of the reconciliation is:

Variable costing income	xx
Less fixed costs in full absorption	
beginning inventories	xx
Total	xx
Add fixed costs in full absorption	
ending inventories	xx
Full absorption costing income	xx

Exhibit 7.5 is helpful to explaining the reconciliation between the two income figures. Frame one shows what happens to one unit that is in the beginning inventory. It is sold during the year and the assigned cost (variable cost only under variable costing and variable plus fixed under full absorption) is deducted against its revenue. As you can see in frame one, the variable costing income would be higher

Exhibit 7.5   Graphical Illustration of Reconciliation of Variable Costing with Full Absorption Costing

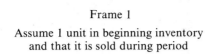

Frame 1

Assume 1 unit in beginning inventory
and that it is sold during period

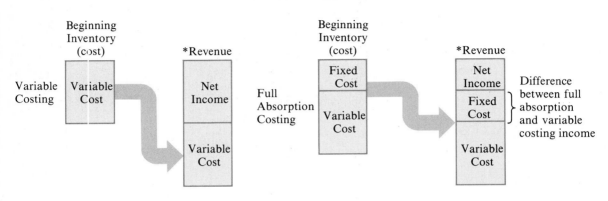

Frame 2

Assume 1 unit in ending inventory

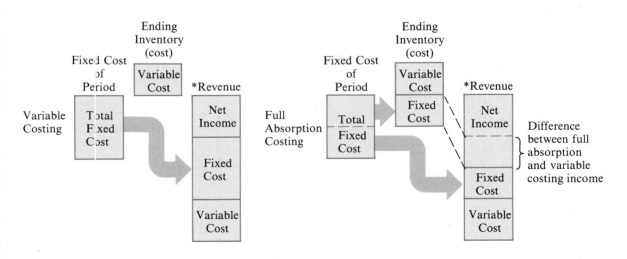

*The entire bar graph represents revenue. The partitions represent the portion of
revenue that is "consumed" by the costs or remains as net income.

than the full absorption costing income in an amount equal to the fixed costs assigned to the beginning inventory. Thus, to reconcile, the fixed costs assigned to the beginning inventory must be deducted from the variable costing income to approach full absorption costing income.

Frame two of Exhibit 7.5 assumes one unit of the period's production remains in the ending inventory. Variable costing would assign no fixed cost to it whereas full absorption costing would. Thus, the amount of fixed cost released against revenue would be different. Again the difference in income is equal to the fixed cost assigned to the ending inventory. As you can see in frame two, the fixed cost assigned to the ending inventory under full absorption costing would have to be added to the variable costing income in order to reconcile to full absorption income.

Observe that *if* there is only one type of inventory *and if* the unit fixed cost is the same in both the beginning and ending inventories, then the reconciliation can be shortened to:

Variable costing income	XX
Add (deduct) increase (decrease) in	
inventory × fixed cost rate	XX
Full absorption costing income	XX

This shortened form can be used in our example because of the assumption that last period's standards were the same as this period's. Exhibit 7.6 contains the reconciliation for each case of the example.

The example of this section is simplified because there was only one product, no work-in-process inventories, and a constant standard cost. Some of the problems

---

Exhibit 7.6   Harrison Company Reconciliation of Variable and Full Absorption Costing Income

	Case 1	Case 2	Case 3
Variable costing income	$25,000	$160,000	$ 25,000
Add (deduct) increase (decrease) in inventory at fixed overhead rate/unit			
Case 1: 0 × $10	0		
Case 2: (20,000) × $10		(200,000)	
Case 3: 10,000 × $10			100,000
Full absorption costing income	$25,000	$(40,000)	$125,000

at the end of the chapter will require you to extend the ideas discussed here to situations that have multiple products and work-in-process inventories, as well as to actual cost systems that result in changing unit costs.

MODIFICATIONS OF PREVIOUSLY DISCUSSED SYSTEMS. It was mentioned earlier that variable costing represented a modification that might be incorporated into any of the systems that were discussed in the previous four chapters. The modifications are uniform and, primarily, entail the classification of overhead costs into fixed and variable. In all systems, the fixed overhead would be accounted for in a *separate account.* Whether there are fixed overhead accounts for each department or just a single account for the entire plant would depend on the possible information needs to be satisfied. For the computation of variable costing income, the fixed overhead account(s) would be directly closed to the revenue and expense summary account. In systems where overhead is applied with a predetermined rate it is necessary to establish only a variable overhead rate and apply only variable costs.

Pros and Cons of Variable Costing

The cost accounting literature is abundant with discussions of variable costing. Space does not permit an inclusion of all the arguments, but this section is an examination of the major arguments for and against this system. First, there is an evaluation of the system from both an internal and external reporting perspective. As this evaluation progresses it will become evident that the variable costing-full absorption issue is not an either/or issue. Therefore, the section is concluded with an examination of an alternative income concept that may be preferable for internal purposes.

INTERNAL USAGE—AN EVALUATION. Internally, the major argument for variable costing is that it provides *better data* for managers to use in making decisions. Good decisions are dependent on being able to predict cost behavior. Full absorption costing was not designed with internal decision making in mind and has a tendency to disguise true cost relationships. Its practice of applying fixed costs may give the illusion that they are variable. If full absorption cost data are all that are available, then it is possible that a decision maker might project cost increases and decreases at a rate equal to the unit cost assigned to production. This implicitly assumes that fixed costs change proportionately with volume. As volume changes, it may well be that fixed costs do change, but they probably do not change at a rate equal to the linear fixed overhead application rate used in full absorption costing. By accounting for fixed costs as a period cost there is a reduction in the likelihood that they will be used in erroneous ways to make decisions. That is, with variable costing, decision makers will probably be more careful in analyzing the way fixed costs change in response to proposed courses of action.

Second, if a standard cost system is modified to the variable costing concept, then the possibility of a *noncontrollable (volume) variance is eliminated.* Not only is this variance uncontrollable in the short run, it is hard to explain. Many accountants, as well as many nonaccountants, have some trouble understanding why a firm could expect certain manufacturing costs to be incurred but plan not to apply them as product costs.

A third possible advantage of variable costing is that it *corresponds to the typical cost-volume-profit analysis*. These analyses are discussed later in this book and entail studies to determine the volume of activity that must be achieved in order to accomplish some profit goal. The correspondence between variable costing income and cost-volume-profit analysis is a result of variable costing income being a function only of sales volume. Recall that full absorption costing income is a function of both sales and production volume. It will be made clear in a later chapter that variable costing must be used in computing income in order for there to be a correspondence between the reported income and cost-volume-profit analysis. Whether or not this correspondence is absolutely desirable is debatable and will be further explored later in this section.

A final advantage relates to a possible *improvement in performance measurement and evaluation* that results from using variable costing. To the extent that performance measurement and evaluation is associated with income, it is desirable that the income measurement process reflect "true" income. As was seen in the previous section, full absorption income can be managed to a certain extent in the short run. Suppose a given manager is evaluated, in part, via the full absorption costing income measure and that he or she does, in fact, deliberately increase inventories for the sole purpose of increasing his or her yearly income. In this situation the accounting system can be considered an accomplice to the misrepresentation of "true" income for the current period.

There is no disagreement that the use of variable costing eliminates the possibility of improving the appearance of one's performance through judicious production scheduling. However, you should not jump to the conclusion that all increases in inventory are designed to manipulate income for the personal gain of a manager. There may be some situations where the decision to change inventory levels will result in benefits to the firm. If there are situations such as these, then a manager's performance rating should be higher if he or she decided to change inventory levels than if the decision was not to change them. Conventional variable costing will not distinguish between manipulative situations and valid situations. In the last part of this section some valid reasons for short-run inventory changes will be examined. There will also be a discussion of an alternative to full absorption and variable costing that will reflect the impact of such a decision in the income number to be used for evaluation purposes.

In short, the advantages of variable costing are:

1. Provides better data in that it follows the fixed-variable behavior.
2. There is no noncontrollable (volume) variance.
3. Income corresponds to cost-volume-profit analysis.
4. Will, perhaps, provide an income number that is better for evaluating managerial performance.

In the previous discussion, some of the possible internal disadvantages of variable costing were unavoidably discussed or inferred. Now consider the counterarguments. First, consider the support of the decision-making function. It is clear that variable costing can lead to *better data for short-run marginal decisions.* For these types of decisions, the marginal, or incremental, cost associated with the decision is frequently given by the variable cost. For some short-run decisions the incremental cost may not be limited to variable cost, however. Further, many decisions have long-run implications. The relevant cost for the long run is definitely *not limited to variable costs.* For example, long-run pricing strategies that ignore fixed costs are suicidal. Some would argue that full absorption costs are more in line with the long run. It must be pointed out, however, that data from a full absorption system still needs to be augmented when making long-run decisions. For example, selling and administrative costs must be attributed to various actions. Full absorption costing, per se, does not provide this type of information.

In response to the above charge it should be noted that data for decision making must be collected and presented in a manner that most closely portrays the actual patterns of behavior. It is assumed that an experienced manager will know and understand the various situations and, in turn, will adjust his or her data needs accordingly. With the variable costing format, the cost behavior is not disguised and will better enable proper analysis. Although variable costing is not the ultimate system it is generally an improvement over full absorption costing.

A second disadvantage of variable costing is that it *requires a classification of costs into fixed and variable pools.* Doing the classification entails a cost. To be able to justify the increased costs of data collection and generation, it is necessary to show that the benefits justify the cost. Further, the classification may not be clear cut. That is, it may not always be obvious which costs are fixed and which are variable.

One final concern will be considered. Why should the income figure for performance evaluation only be a function of sales when sales is not the only function of the business? *When the situation involves legitimate differences between production and sales why not let these differences affect income?* Additional comments about this will be deferred until the conclusion of this section.

In summary of the cons:

1. All decisions are not short-run, marginal decisions. Thus, variable costing data may not be adequate for all decisions.
2. Classifying costs into fixed and variable may be difficult and costly to do.
3. Sales is not the only function of a business and it is not clear that sales should be the only variable to affect net income.

EXTERNAL USAGE—AN EVALUATION.   In defense of using variable costing for external reporting we find two major arguments. To introduce the first, note that fixed manufacturing costs represent the cost of having production capacity. For example, depreciation is a cost of having equipment and buildings, and supervisory salaries are costs related to the human component of capacity. One argument for external reporting via variable costing is that the *capacity costs should be*

at the end of the year its gone!

allowed to expire as the capacity expires. Since capacity expires with the lapse of time, it follows that the fixed costs should be treated as period costs. That is, the capacity to produce this period expires whether or not it is used. It cannot be stored and, thus, why should the fixed costs be "stored" through the inventory costing mechanism?

A second argument is related to the first. That is, *assets should not be assigned costs incurred during the current period if such incurrence cannot be shown to avoid a future cost incurrence.* There is no question that the act of producing for inventory this period will avoid an incurrence of variable production costs next period when the item is sold. But what about the fixed cost that would be assigned to the units in inventory under full absorption cost? Will there be any future fixed cost avoided by producing that item this period? The answer to this is normally "no." If no, how can it be argued that the fixed costs should be inventoried? If an asset's cost can be thought of as an avoided future cost, then it may be hard to argue for the assignment of fixed costs to inventory.

The counterargument to these views is the one advocated by bodies that establish external reporting requirements. The argument is based on the matching concept. The *matching concept* states that when revenues, the accomplishments, are recognized, all of the expenses related to that revenue should also be recognized. These expenses would be for the collective efforts needed to achieve the accomplishments. Since capacity is needed to make possible the production of inventory, *a share of the capacity cost should be assigned to the inventory and matched against the revenue when it is realized.* To do otherwise violates the matching concept. The matching concept continues to be an integral part of accounting theory. For this reason, then, full absorption costing must be used for external reporting.

≥ OVERCOMING SOME PROBLEMS WITH FULL ABSORPTION AND VARIABLE COSTING. When evaluating the relative internal usefulness of variable and full absorption costing, it became obvious that a constant application of either concept would, in certain cases, be at variance with the ideal. If it is argued, for example, that variable costing should *always* be used, then what are the implications for the following situations?

1. Next period's expected demand for the product exceeds next period's production capacity. Would not an inventory buildup be justified? Suppose a manager recognizes the situation and produces inventory in the current period. Under variable costing the manager's current income would be the same as if the additional units were not produced. (Remember that variable costing income is a function of sales only.) Thus, the variable costing income concept will not provide any short-run incentive for avoiding the lost profits of not producing this period for next period's demand. Of course, if in these situations managers elect to produce this period, their income next period under variable costing will be higher than if the decision was not to produce extra inventory. More will be said on this later.

2. Next period's variable manufacturing cost per unit is expected to be higher than this period's. Again, would not an inventory buildup be desirable if the savings of producing now are not offset by increased holding costs for inventory?

These situations may create some problems when accountants are requested to provide income data to be used in evaluating managerial performance. For example, suppose managers receive a bonus based on some type of income number. If the income number is based on the variable costing concept, then a manager may have a legitimate complaint that his or her current bonus will be less than it should be. A counterargument might be that their income will be higher next year and, therefore, the bonus will be received at that time. Of course, the manager would be deprived of the bonus for one year, which does have an opportunity cost. Further, the manager may be promoted or transferred to another division, in which case their successor would be the one to receive the bonus. Depending on the magnitude of the amounts this can be a serious problem. In the event that the amount is material, let's consider what can be done to ensure an equitable treatment.

Remember that the situation posed here is an *internal* problem. As such, the management accountant is not bound by the conventional external reporting principles of accounting. Thus it will not be necessary to adhere to the realization principle that, generally, requires an exchange between two independent parties as a condition of revenue recognition. In this case, the profits saved by producing in the current period could be recognized as income of the current period. The Harrison Company in Exhibit 7.4 will be used to illustrate a possible solution.

Consider case 3 of Exhibit 7.4. Assume the beginning inventory was zero and the production capacity is 60,000 units yearly. Further, suppose that next year's demand is estimated at 70,000 units, which is 10,000 units greater than capacity. Thus, the firm has avoided an opportunity cost on each of the 10,000 units added to inventory this period. That is, if 10,000 units had not been produced this period the maximum sales next period would have been 60,000 units even though the demand is estimated to be 70,000 units. The major reason financial accounting requires an exchange transaction as a condition of revenue recognition is objectivity. Internally, objectivity does not need to be ensured in the same way as in financial reporting. If there is reasonable assurance (as opposed to certainty) that next year's demand will be 70,000 units, then there is no reason, for internal purposes, that revenue of the 10,000 units in inventory, along with their cost, cannot be recognized in the current period. If so, the opportunity cost avoided will be equal to the difference between the revenue of the 10,000 units and their cost and will be recognized in the current period. In certain cases, this might be a more equitable treatment than waiting to next period to recognize the sale.

As a modification to the above case assume that the projected demand next year is for 68,000 units. If this is the case, an opportunity cost is being avoided only on the first 8,000 units of the 10,000-unit inventory. Thus, for internal purposes it may be desirable to recognize the revenue and cost of an additional 8,000 units in the current period.

Consider one final example. Again assume case 3 from Exhibit 7.4. Suppose next year's variable manufacturing cost per unit is forecast to increase to $28.00 and there will be no inventory-holding cost. Since the current variable manufacturing cost is $26.00 ($12 for material, $6 for labor, and $8 for variable overhead) there is a $2.00-per-unit savings of producing now. Thus, the 10,000 units in the ending inventory have cost $20,000 less than if they were produced next year. This $20,000 savings could be recognized this period with the following adjustment:

Inventory	20,000	
Gain from early production		20,000

With the above adjustment the inventory is carried into the next period at a higher value than would be given by the variable costing system. When the units are actually sold next period the rest of the income on these units would be recognized. The important aspect is that gains resulting from this period's decisions are recognized in this period. Again, recognize that these suggestions are being made for internal purposes only. Obviously, these income computations are dependent upon some subjective estimates and, hence, will never be acceptable for external reporting. But, internally, dependence upon estimates should not be considered as an absolute deterrent to its usage. Being a professional entails the acceptance of a responsibility for making judgments of this nature.

Examination of Different Costing Methods over Time

The differences between variable and full absorption costing income are strictly timing differences. That is, in the long run, the total net income will be the same under either method. (This assumes that tax rates and other expenses that might be a function of income remain constant over time.) To illustrate this and to provide some data illustrative of the direction and magnitude of these differences, let us examine a hypothetical case over time.

The DJH Company was organized in 19x1 to produce a single product. Its accounting system is basically an actual cost system, but a predetermined fixed manufacturing overhead rate is used. The fixed overhead application rate of $4.00 per unit was established using an expected normal production of 50,000 units. In order to isolate the yearly differences in income that are due to the selection of a costing system, it will be assumed that the actual variable costs were incurred at the same *rate* in each year and that the actual fixed costs were always the same as budgeted. Any noncontrollable (volume) variance under full absorption costing will be closed to cost of goods sold. Exhibit 7.7 contains the production, sales, and cost data for 19x1 through 19x4. The sales price is $10.00 per unit. Selling and administrative costs will be ignored in this example.

The full absorption incomes are computed in Exhibit 7.8. Note the treatment of fixed costs in the cost-of-sales schedule. The fixed costs would be applied at $4.00 per unit, and in years when production was not at the normal of 50,000 units there would be an adjustment to the cost of goods sold for the noncontrollable (volume) variance. Because of the assumptions that were made about the year-to-year cost behavior, the predetermined overhead rate, and the accounting for noncontrollable (volume) variance, all units in inventory are carried at $6.00 (the variable cost of $2.00 plus the fixed rate of $4.00).

Exhibit 7.7   DJH Company Data for 19x1 through 19x4

	19x1	19x2	19x3	19x4
Production (units)	50,000	50,000	40,000	40,000
Sales (units)	40,000	40,000	50,000	50,000
Ending inventory (units)	10,000	20,000	10,000	0
Variable costs	$100,000	$100,000	$ 80,000	$ 80,000
Fixed costs	$200,000	$200,000	$200,000	$200,000

Exhibit 7.9 contains the variable costing income computations. Everything there should be self-explanatory. Note that the four-year income total is the same as given by full absorption costing. This is due to the fact that the 19x4 inventory is at zero units and all timing differences have canceled against each other.

Finally, note that in years when production exceeded sales, variable costing income was less than full absorption income. Again, this is due to the fixed cost deferral mechanism of full absorption costing. Likewise, in years when production was less than sales, variable costing income exceed full absorption income. This is due to the extra fixed costs released by full absorption costing. The relationship between the income figures is summarized as follows:

Exhibit 7.8   DJH Company Full Absorption Income Statements for the Years 19x1 through 19x4

	19x1	19x2	19x3	19x4	Total
Sales	$400,000	$400,000	$500,000	$500,000	$1,800,000
Cost of sales (from below)	240,000	240,000	340,000	340,000	1,160,000
Gross margin	$160,000	$160,000	$160,000	$160,000	$ 640,000

Cost of Sales

	19x1	19x2	19x3	19x4
Beginning inventory	0	$ 60,000	$120,000	$ 60,000
Variable costs	$100,000	$100,000	$ 80,000	$ 80,000
Applied fixed costs @ $4	200,000	200,000	160,000	160,000
Total	$300,000	$300,000	$240,000	$240,000
Cost of goods available	$300,000	$360,000	$360,000	$300,000
Ending inventory @ $6	60,000	120,000	60,000	0
Unadjusted cost of goods sold	$240,000	$240,000	$300,000	$300,000
Noncontrollable (volume) variance	0	0	40,000	40,000
Cost of sales	$240,000	$240,000	$340,000	$340,000

Exhibit 7.9   DJH Company Variable Costing Income Statements for the Years 19x1 through 19x4

	19x1	*19x2*	*19x3*	*19x4*	*Total*
Sales	$400,000	$400,000	$500,000	$500,000	$1,800,000
Variable manufacturing costs (from below)	80,000	80,000	100,000	100,000	360,000
Contribution margin (exclusive of selling and administrative costs	$320,000	$320,000	$400,000	$400,000	$1,440,000
Fixed costs	200,000	200,000	200,000	200,000	800,000
Net income (exclusive of selling and administrative costs	$120,000	$120,000	$200,000	$200,000	$ 640,000

Variable Manufacturing Costs

	19x1	*19x2*	*19x3*	*19x4*
Beginning inventory	0	$ 20,000	$ 40,000	$ 20,000
Variable manufacturing costs incurred	$100,000	$100,000	$ 80,000	$ 80,000
Variable cost of goods available	$100,000	$120,000	$120,000	$100,000
Ending inventory @ $2	20,000	40,000	20,000	0
Variable manufacturing costs expensed	$ 80,000	$ 80,000	$100,000	$100,000

If Production > Sales,
  then: Variable costing income < Full absorption costing income
If Production < Sales,
  then: Variable costing income > Full absorption costing income
If Production = Sales,
  then: Variable costing income = Full absorption costing income

⋛ WORKING-PAPER ADJUSTMENTS TO CONVERT TO FULL ABSORP-
TION COSTING. If it is agreed that variable costing methods will provide management with better information on a day-to-day basis, then we should *insist* on
such an accounting system. Since variable costing is not permitted for external
reporting, we must be prepared to meet the external requirements by adjusting the
variable costing records. These requirements can be met via working-paper
adjustments rather than by keeping two sets of records. Using the example of the
previous section, we will now illustrate how this can be accomplished.

Assume that the DJH Company is keeping its books on a *variable costing basis*.
At the end of 19x1, the fixed cost account has a balance of $200,000. To obtain
equivalent full absorption results, this account must be distributed to appropriate
accounts. That is, the inventory and cost-of-goods-sold accounts must be increased
for an appropriate share of the fixed costs. Since the full absorption rate is $4.00

per unit and since full absorption costing would not have a noncontrollable (volume) variance in 19x1, the following working-paper adjustment is needed for 19x1:

Finished goods inventory (4.00 × 10,000)	40,000	
Cost of goods sold ($4.00 × 40,000)	160,000	
Fixed Costs		200,000

Now consider 19x2. So that the year-end adjustment is simpler, a working-paper reversing entry will be made at the beginning of 19x2 in order to return the inventory to its variable cost. The offsetting debit will be to retained earnings because the two costing methods resulted in different incomes that will be reflected in retained earnings after the closing process in 19x1. Thus at the beginning of 19x2 make the following working-paper entry:

Retained earnings	40,000	
Finished goods inventory		40,000

At the end of 19x2 the fixed cost account must again be distributed. There are now 20,000 units in inventory and, before adjustments, they are carried at variable cost. Thus:

Finished goods inventory ($4.00 × 20,000)	80,000	
Cost of goods sold ($4.00 × 40,000)	160,000	
Fixed costs		200,000
Retained earnings		40,000

The credit to retained earnings reflects the fact that at the beginning of 19x2 there was an accumulated difference in income of $40,000 between the two systems. Of course, at the end of 19x2 there is an accumulated difference of $80,000 (see the income statements in Exhibits 7.8 and 7.9). But the income differences due to the activities of 19x2 will not affect retained earnings until *after* the closing process for 19x2.

At the beginning of 19x3 reverse the entry on finished goods inventory in order to return to variable costing:

Retained earnings	80,000	
Finished goods inventory		80,000

Since full absorption costing would have a noncontrollable (volume) variance in 19x3, and since it represents underapplied fixed cost, it needs to be considered in making the year-end adjustments. Of course, this variance is to be closed to cost of goods sold so that the adjustment of this account consists of two components:

Applied fixed costs (50,000 × 4)	$200,000
Noncontrollable (volume) variance	
(see Exhibit 7.8)	40,000
Total	$240,000

The adjusting entry, then, is:

Finished goods inventory ($4 × 10,000)	40,000	
Cost of goods sold (see preceding computation)	240,000	
Fixed costs		200,000
Retained earnings		80,000

Again, note that the adjustment to retained earnings reflects the accumulated differences in income at the *beginning* of 19x3.

Finally, for 19x4 make the reversal entry for finished goods inventory:

Retained earnings	40,000	
Finished goods inventory		40,000

Since the 19x4 ending inventory is zero, it needs no adjustment. The adjustment to cost of goods sold would be the same as in 19x3. Thus:

Cost of goods sold	240,000	
Fixed costs		200,000
Retained earnings		40,000

Note there would be no reversal at the beginning of 19x5 since all of the differences between the two concepts have now canceled out. You can imagine that the adjusting process might be more complicated for more involved situations. However, the principles would be the same.

Summary

Variable costing is an alternative system that many accountants consider as an improvement over conventional systems. Its advantages are due to the parallelism between cost behavior and the reporting of costs. Fixed costs are reported as lump sums rather than being averaged into the unit costs.

At this point you should understand the implications of variable costing for job, process, and standard costing. You should also know what is meant by contribution reporting. Further, it was established that both variable costing and full absorption costing are sometimes inadequate. Finally, you should understand the adjustments needed to convert a variable costing system into full absorption.

Terms introduced in this chapter with which you should be familiar include:

Variable costing
Contribution margin
Contribution margin reporting format

SELF-STUDY PROBLEM. Consider the following 19x3 *full absorption* income statement for the Garner Company where overhead has been applied on the basis of direct-labor hours.

Sales (5,000 units)		$200,000
Cost of goods sold at standard		
Direct material	$40,000	
Direct labor (2 hours/unit)	30,000	
Total overhead (fixed + variable)	40,000	110,000
Standard gross margin		$ 90,000
Variances		
Noncontrollable variance =		
(Standard hours − Divisor activity) x		
Fixed overhead rate =		
(20,000 − 30,000)$1.50	$15,000	
Material quantity variance	2,000	$ 17,000
Actual gross margin		$ 73,000
Selling and administrative expenses		
Variable	$20,000	
Fixed	$10,000	30,000
Net income		$ 43,000

The beginning inventory of the finished product totaled 2,000 units and was recorded at the standard full absorption cost.

7000 left in inv.

Required:

1. How many units were produced during 19x3?
2. What is the standard cost per finished *unit* (not per hour) for: (a) direct material, (b) direct labor, (c) variable overhead, and (d) fixed overhead.
3. What is the standard full absorption cost of the ending finished goods inventory?
4. What is the standard cost of the ending finished goods inventory under variable costing principles?
5. Recast the preceding statement into a variable costing format. You may show the variable cost of sales rather than beginning inventory plus production costs less ending inventory.
6. Prepare an adjusting entry to convert the variable costing accounts to full absorption costing accounts.

Solution to Self-Study Problem

1. Each unit requires 2 labor hours. According to the noncontrollable variance computation, 20,000 standard labor hours were allowed for 19x3's production. (Remember that standard allowances are based on production.) Thus, 10,000 units were produced.
2. a. From cost of goods sold
        Standard material cost = 40,000 ÷ 5,000 = $8.00
    b. From cost of goods sold
        Standard labor cost = 30,000 ÷ 5,000 = $6.00

c. From cost of goods sold

Total overhead = 40,000 ÷ 5,000	$8.00
Fixed overhead (from noncontrollable variance)	
$1.50 × 2 hours	3.00
Variable overhead per unit	$5.00

d. From above: $3.00

3. Units in ending inventory
   Beginning inventory + Production (answer 1) − Sales
   2,000 + 10,000 − 5,000 = 7,000
   Cost = 7,000($8 + $6 + $5 + $3) = $154,000

4. 7,000($8 + $6 + $5) = $133,000

5.

Sales		$200,000
Variable cost		
Material 5,000 × $8	$40,000	
Labor 5,000 × $6	30,000	
Variable overhead 5,000 × $5	25,000	
Material quantity variance	2,000	
Selling and administrative	20,000	117,000
Contribution margin		$ 83,000
Fixed costs		
Manufacturing (from noncontrollable variance)		
30,000 × $1.50	$45,000	
Selling and administrative	10,000	55,000
Net income		$ 28,000

6.

Finished goods inventory (7,000 × $3)	21,000	
Cost of goods sold (5,000 × $3)	15,000	
Noncontrollable variance	15,000	
Fixed costs		45,000
Retained earnings		6,000

Since there was 2,000 units in the beginning inventory the cumulative earnings under full absorption costing would be higher than under variable costing to the extent of the fixed costs that would be assigned to the beginning inventory.

References

Ferrara, W.L. "Relevant Costing: Footnote to a Controversy," *Management Accounting* (January 1970): 45–47.

Fess, P.E., and Ferrara, W.L. "The Period Cost Concept for Income Measurement—Can It Be Defended?" *The Accounting Review* (October 1961): 598–602.

Green, D. "A Moral to the Direct Costing Controversy," *The Journal of Business* (July 1960): 281–226.

Horngren, C.T., and Sorter, G.H. "'Direct' Costing for External Reporting," *The Accounting Review* (January 1961): 84–93.

Sorter, G.H., and Horngren, C.T. "Asset Recognition and Economic Attributes—The Relevant Costing Approach," *The Accounting Review* (July 1962): 391–399.

Staubus, G.J. "Direct, Relevant or Absorption Costing," *The Accounting Review* (January 1963): 64–74.

7-1. Understanding the Relationship between Variable and Full Absorption Costing. The KM Company has prepared the following budget for one of its products:

	Annual Fixed Costs	Variable Cost per Unit
Direct material	——	$10
Direct labor	——	20
Manufacturing overhead	$30,000	5
Selling expenses	$20,000	2
Administrative expenses	$40,000	0
	$90,000	$37

The normal production volume of this product is 5,000 units. During the current year 4,000 units were produced, 3,000 units were sold, and 1,000 units remained in ending inventory. KM uses a predetermined overhead rate.

Required:

1. What is the cost of the ending inventory using variable costing?
2. What is the cost of the ending inventory using full absorption costing?

7-2. Basic Problem Comparing Full Absorption and Variable Costing. The Stargell Company uses an actual cost system. Following are some data at December 31, 19x1:

All beginning inventories	$ 0
Ending inventory of raw material	$ 1,000
Ending inventory of finished goods	400 units
Ending work-in-process inventory	0
Raw material purchased	$16,000
Direct-labor costs	$10,000
Variable factory overhead	$ 5,000
Fixed factory overhead	$ 8,000
Variable selling and administrative costs	$ 7,000
Fixed selling and administrative costs	$ 9,000
Units completed this period	4,000 units
Units sold this period	3,600 units
Selling price	$20.00 per unit

Required:

1. Prepare a full absorption costing income statement.
2. Prepare a variable costing income statement.
3. Prepare a reconciliation of the two income figures you obtained in the first two parts.

7-3. Basic Problem on Variable Costing. Following is an income statement prepared in conformance with full absorption costing principles applied to actual costs:

Parker Company
Income Statement
for Year Ended December 31, 19x1

Sales			$400,000
Cost of goods sold			
Inventory, 1/1/x1		0	
Production costs for 50,000 units			
Direct material	$100,000		
Direct labor	75,000		
Variable factory overhead	25,000		
Fixed factory overhead	$ 50,000		
Total	$250,000		
Inventory, 12/31/x1 (10,000 units)	50,000	200,000	
Gross margin			$200,000
Selling and administrative expenses			
Variable	$100,000		
Fixed	40,000	140,000	
Net income			$ 60,000

Required:

Prepare, in detailed form, a contribution margin income statement using variable costing principles. Be sure to show the ending inventory as part of the income statement.

7-4. Using Knowledge of Variable-Full Absorption Relationships. At a particular date you have the following inventory information for the same firm but prepared on two different bases, variable costing and full absorption costing:

	Method A	*Method B*
Beginning inventory	$100,000	$ 80,000
Ending inventory	$120,000	$105,000

Required:

1. Which of the above methods, A or B, must have been variable costing? Why?
2. What is the dollar difference between the net income of variable costing versus full absorption costing? Assume that any noncontrollable variance under full absorption costing will be closed to cost of goods sold.

7-5. Adapted CMA Problem. The S.T. Shire Company uses variable costing for internal management purposes and absorption costing for external reporting purposes. Thus, at the end of each year financial information must be converted from variable costing to absorption costing in order to satisfy external requirements.

At the end of 19x1 it was anticipated that sales would rise 20% the next year. Therefore, production was increased from 20,000 units to 24,000 units to meet this expected demand. However, economic conditions kept the sales level at 20,000 units for both years.

The following data pertain to 19x1 and 19x2:

	19x1	19x2
Selling price per unit	$ 30	$ 30
Sales (units)	20,000	20,000
Beginning inventory (units)	2,000	2,000
Production (units)	20,000	24,000
Ending inventory (units)	2,000	6,000
Unfavorable labor, materials, and variable overhead variances (total)	$ 5,000	$ 4,000

Standard variable costs per unit for 19x1 and 19x2:

Labor	$ 7.50
Materials	4.50
Variable overhead	$ 3.00
	$15.00

Annual fixed costs for 19x1 and 19x2 (budgeted and actual):

Production	$ 90,000
Selling and administrative	$100,000
	$190,000

The overhead rate under absorption costing is based upon practical plant capacity which is 30,000 units per year. All variances and underabsorbed or overabsorbed overhead are taken to cost of goods sold.

Required:

1. Present the income statement based on variable costing for 19x2.
2. Present the income statement based on absorption costing for 19x2.
3. Explain the difference, if any, in the net income figures. Give the entry necessary to adjust the book figures to the financial statement figure, if one is necessary.

7-6. Adapted CPA Problem Comparing Full Absorption and Variable Costing; WIP Inventories. Norwood Corporation is considering changing its method of inventory valuation from standard absorption costing to standard variable costing and has engaged you to determine the effect of the proposed change on the 19x1 financial statements.

The corporation manufactures Gink, which is sold for $20 per unit. Marsh is added before processing starts, and labor and overhead are added evenly during the manufacturing process. Production capacity is budgeted at 110,000 units of Gink annually. The standard costs per unit of Gink are:

Marsh, 2 pounds	$3.00
Labor	6.00
Variable manufacturing overhead	1.00
Fixed manufacturing overhead	1.10

Inventory data for 19x1 follows:

	Units	
	January 1	*December 31*
Marsh (pounds)	50,000	40,000
Work in process		
2/5 processed	10,000	
1/3 processed		15,000
Finished goods	20,000	12,000

During 19x1, 220,000 pounds of Marsh were produced and 230,000 pounds were transferred to work in process. Actual fixed manufacturing overhead during the year was $123,000. There were no variances between standard variable costs and actual variable costs during the year.

Required:

1. Prepare a schedule presenting the computation of equivalent units of production for material, labor, and overhead.
2. Prepare a schedule presenting the computation of the number of units sold.
3. Prepare a schedule presenting the computation of the standard unit costs under variable costing and absorption costing.
4. Compute the noncontrollable (volume) variance. Note that overhead is being applied on the basis of a unit of product rather than on the basis of direct-labor hours.
5. Prepare comparative income statements using standard variable costing and standard absorption costing.
6. Reconcile the variable cost income with the full absorption income.

7-7. Comparison of Variable and Full Absorption Costing in a Standard Cost System; WIP Inventories. The Blyleven Company keeps its accounts on a standard variable costing basis. Overhead is assigned on the basis of labor hours and the standard *full absorption* cost of one unit is as follows:

Material	2 units @ $3.00	$ 6.00
Labor	3 hours @ $6.00	18.00
Overhead	3 hours @ $3.00	9.00
Total		$33.00

If the company operates at normal activity of 120,000 direct-labor hours and sells all that it produces, it is estimated that the following costs would be incurred:

	Manufacturing Overhead	*Selling and Administrative*
Fixed	$144,000	$ 80,000
Variable	216,000	120,000

During 19x7, 36,000 units of the finished product were sold at a price that yielded a $50 per unit *contribution margin*. The beginning WIP inventory consisted of 5,000 units, 80% complete as to conversion costs. The ending WIP inventory consisted of 4,000 units, 50% complete. Material is added at the beginning of processing. The beginning finished goods inventory contained 5,000 units, the ending 2,000 units. Assume that all costs were incurred as anticipated in the budget.

Required:

1. Prepare a complete income statement (starting with sales) using the variable costing principle.
2. Prepare a complete income statement using the full absorption costing principle.
3. Reconcile the variable costing income to the full absorption costing income. The standards were the same in 19x6 as in 19x7.
4. Prepare the working paper adjustments for 19x7 to convert the accounts to full absorption costing.

7-8. Deriving Relationships for Variable-Full Absorption Costing Comparisons. The Moreno Company began operations in 19x1 and uses actual costs in its accounting system. An overhead rate is not used. During 19x1 and 19x2 the cost behavior was considered to be identical and the following data are available:

	19x1	*19x2*
Production (units)	100,000	50,000
Sales (units)	80,000	65,000
Selling price	$5.00	$5.00
Total manufacturing costs	$300,000	$200,000
Total selling and administrative cost	$100,000	$ 85,000

Required:

1. Assuming the FIFO inventory method is used, prepare a schedule showing the cost of goods sold in 19x2 under full absorption costing principles.
2. Prepare an income statement for 19x2 using full absorption costing principles.
3. Prepare an income statement for 19x2 using variable costing principles.
4. Reconcile the 19x2 net income computed with the two concepts in parts 2 and 3.
5. Assuming the accounts were maintained on a variable costing basis, prepare the 19x2 working-paper adjustments to convert to full absorption costing.

7-9. Deriving Data for Variable Costing Statements Using Data from Two Years. The Dempster Company manufactures a single product, SDC, and uses a standard full absorption cost system. The standards have remained the same during 19x1 and 19x2. All variances are closed to cost of goods sold. During 19x1 production exceeded sales by 2,000 units. Following are the 19x1 and 19x2 full absorption income statements.

	19x1	*19x2*
Sales @ $50 per unit	$500,000	$1,250,000
Cost of goods sold		
Direct material	$ 50,000	$ 125,000
Direct labor	100,000	250,000
Variable overhead	80,000	200,000
Fixed overhead applied	40,000	100,000
Variable cost variances	10,000 U	(8,000) F
Noncontrollable variance	72,000 U	22,000 U
Total	$352,000	$ 689,000
Gross margin	$148,000	$ 561,000
Selling and administrative—total	$ 50,000	$ 95,000
Net income	$ 98,000	$ 466,000

Required:

1. Determine the divisor activity (in units) that must have been used in determining the overhead rates.
2. How many units were produced (not sold) in 19x2?
3. Recast the 19x2 income statement using variable costing concepts.
4. Reconcile the difference between the 19x2 variable costing income and the full absorption costing income.

7-10. Variable Costing with Multiple Products. The Candlelara Company produces two products, regular candles and decorative candles. Overhead is applied on the basis of labor hours. The full absorption standards per dozen are as follows:

	Regular	*Decorative*
Direct material	$ 2	$12
Direct labor @ $5 per hour	10	20
Variable overhead @ $1.00 per hour	2	4
Fixed overhead @ $2.00 per hour	4	8
Total	$18	$44

The summary results for 19x2, using full absorption costing, are as follows:

Sales (detailed as follows)		$6,700,000
Cost of goods sold (detailed as follows)		4,822,000
Gross margin		$1,878,000
Selling and administrative		
Fixed	$350,000	
Variable	500,000	850,000
Net income		$1,028,000

The detail of the sales and cost of sales figures are as follows:

	Regular	Decorative	Total
Beginning inventory (units)	8,000	10,000	
Production (units)	50,000	100,000	
Total	58,000	110,000	
Ending inventory (units)	6,000	20,000	
Sales (units)	52,000	90,000	
Sales price	$25.00	$60.00	
Sales (dollars)	$1,300,000	$5,400,000	$6,700,000
Sales (units)	52,000	90,000	
Standard cost per unit	$18.00	$44.00	
Standard cost	$ 936,000	$3,960,000	$4,896,000
Controllable variance (variable costs)			26,000
Noncontrollable variance (favorable)			(100,000)
Cost of sales			$4,822,000

Required:

1. Prepare an income statement using variable costing principles.
2. Reconcile the variable costing income to the full absorption income.
3. Assuming the accounts are maintained on a variable costing basis, prepare the 19x2 working-paper adjustments to convert to full absorption costing.

7-11. Variable Costing with Multiple Products. The Due-It-Right Company maintains its accounts on a standard variable costing basis. For the most recent period the following variable costing income statement was prepared:

	Product A	Product B	Total
Sales (A @ $50; B @ $90)	$2,000	$9,000	$11,000
Variable costs			
Manufacturing			
Beginning inventory (A @ $29; B @ $50)	$ 145	$ 500	$ 645
Current production (A @ $30; B @ $52)	1,140	5,460	6,600
Available	$1,285	$5,960	$ 7,245
Ending inventory (A @ $30; B @ $52)	90	780	$ 870
Variable manufacturing costs	$1,195	$5,180	$ 6,375
Selling expenses	200	500	700
Total variable costs	$1,395	$5,680	$ 7,075
Contribution margin	$ 605	$3,320	$ 3,925
Fixed costs			
Manufacturing (equal to budget)			$ 2,000
Selling and administrative			1,000
Total			$ 3,000
Net income			$ 925

Overhead rates are based on *practical capacity,* which is 1,000 labor hours. All standard costs were revised at the beginning of the current period to reflect current costs. Product A requires 3 labor hours and product B 7 hours.

Required:

1. What is the fixed overhead rate per direct-labor hour that would be used for full absorption costing?
2. What is the current total full absorption cost for products A and B (per unit)?
3. What is the noncontrollable variance under full absorption costing for the period?
4. Assuming the budgeted fixed costs last year were the same as this year, prepare the entry to convert the variable costing accounts to full absorption costing.
5. Assuming the budgeted fixed manufacturing costs were $1,900 last year, prepare the entry to convert the variable costing accounts to full absorption costing.

7-12. Working Backward to Derive Results. The Tanner Company uses variable costing and has reported a net income in 19x3 of $20,000. Had standard full absorption costing been used, the net income would have been reported as $15,000. The *beginning* finished goods inventory contained 3,000 units. Its cost under variable costing was $54,000. By full absorption principles its cost would have been $60,000. The standard material cost is $10 per unit and labor is $5 per unit.

Required:

1. How many units are in the *ending* finished goods inventory? Assume that there is no WIP inventory (beginning or ending).
2. What would be the amount of overhead included in the cost of the ending finished goods inventory under *variable costing?*

7-13. Income as an Evaluation Tool. The Three Rivers Company has two divisions producing the same product for distribution in different geographical regions. Both divisions have been experiencing the same cost behavior pattern. During 19x1 the following data were recorded:

	Eastern	Western
Units in beginning inventory	4,000	4,000
Units produced	38,000	50,000
Total available	42,000	54,000
Units sold	40,000	40,000
Units in ending inventory	2,000	14,000

Both divisions have a production capacity of 50,000 units, a variable manufacturing cost of $10 per unit, fixed manufacturing costs of $100,000 per year, and fixed selling and administrative costs of $20,000 per year. The product sells for $20 per unit. Both divisions assigned fixed production costs at a rate based on practical capacity.

Required:

1. Prepare the 19x1 full absorption cost income statements for both divisions.
2. Prepare the 19x1 variable costing income statements for both divisions.

3. Suppose you are the manager of the Western Division, and the projected sales level for *each* division in 19x2 is 64,000 units. How would you feel about being compared with the manager of the Eastern Division in 19x1 using the variable costing income figures as the basis of comparison? How would you feel about being compared using the full absorption costing incomes as the basis?

4. Continue the assumption from part 3 and compute the 19x2 income for both divisions using (a) full absorption costing and (b) variable costing.

5. Continue part 3 but suppose you are the supervisor over the Western Divison manager. There is a year-end bonus tied to the reported income. At the end of 19x1, the Western Division manager was promoted to another job. Comment on the relative fairness to the promoted manager of applying the bonus system to full absorption costing income as opposed to variable costing income.

6. Now suppose you are the manager of the Eastern Division and the projected sales level for each division in 19x2 is 40,000 units. How would you feel about being compared using full absorption costing income as the basis?

7. Considering the various situations raised in this problem, evaluate the potential of the alternative income concept discussed in this chapter.

7-14. Income Measurement for Performance Evaluation. A summary of the activities of the Ott Company for 19x1 follows:

19x1

Beginning inventory	10,000 units
Production in 19x1	400,000 units
Sales in 19x1	350,000 units
Practical capacity	500,000 units
Costs for 19x1	
Variable manufacturing	$2,800,000 $7/unit
Variable selling and administrative	1,400,000
Fixed manufacturing	2,000,000 $4/unit
Fixed selling and administrative	1,000,000
Sales price per unit	$25.00

Fixed costs would be assigned at a predetermined rate under full absorption costing. Assume last year's cost per unit is the same as in 19x1.

Required:

1. Suppose next year's sales are estimated to be less than 500,000 units. What would the income be under (a) full absorption costing, (b) variable costing, and (c) the alternative concept discussed in the chapter?

2. Suppose next year's sales are estimated to be in excess of 600,000 units. What would the income be under (a) full absorption costing, (b) variable costing, and (c) the alternative concept discussed in the chapter?

7-15. Income Measurement for Performance Evaluation. The HSFF Company produces two products, and the following data are available at the end of the year:

	Product A	Product B
Beginning inventory	10,000 units	24,000 units
Current year's production	400,000 units	200,000 units
Current year's sales	340,000 units	220,000 units
Labor hours required per unit	2	3
Sales price per unit	$20	$35

Current year's data	
Practical capacity (hours needed to operate plant at full capacity)	2,000,000 hours
Variable manufacturing costs (all are a function of labor hours)	$4,900,000
Variable selling and administrative (function of sales dollars)	$2,465,000
Fixed manufacturing	$4,000,000
Fixed selling and administrative	$2,000,000

Required:

1. Assume that next year's sales for products A and B are forecast at 400,000 and 300,000 units, respectively. What is the net income by (a) full absorption costing, (b) variable costing, and (c) the alternative concept discussed in the chapter?
2. Assume that next year's sales for products A and B are forecast at 400,000 and 470,000 units, respectively. What is the net income by (a) full absorption costing, (b) variable costing, and (c) the alternative concept discussed in the chapter?

7-16. Alternative Income Measurement and Working-Paper Adjustments. The Fausnaugh Company produces several products. Overhead was felt to be strongly related to direct-labor hours. At annual normal activity levels, 100,000 direct-labor hours are incurred. The relationship between overhead (OH) and labor (DLH) was confirmed using a high-low analysis. Specifically, the estimating equation for monthly costs is:

$$OH = 20,000 + 3(DLH)$$

During the last two months, only one product was produced, DJH. Product DJH requires 2 labor hours. For the current month the activity for product DJH is summarized as:

Beginning inventory	1,000 units
Production	3,500 units
Available	4,500 units
Sales	4,000 units
Ending inventory	500 units

Product DJH sells for $27 per unit. Exclusive of overhead the variable production costs total $15 per unit. Variable selling costs are $2 per unit and fixed selling costs amount to $5,000 monthly.

The actual fixed overhead for the current month was $21,000. There were no variable cost variances. No fixed cost variances have been recorded on the books.

Required:

1. The books are maintained on a variable costing basis. Prepare the working-paper adjusting entry to convert the accounts to full absorption costing.
2. Suppose the practical capacity of the plant is also 100,000 direct-labor hours annually. Further, suppose that the sales forecast for next month is 4,700 units of DJH. What is the net income by (a) full absorption costing, (b) variable costing, and (c) the alternative concept discussed in the chapter?

7-17. Variable Costing and a Job Order System. Reconsider the Luzinski Company in problem 3-15. Assume that job #419 was the only job sold in January. Its material cost was $30,000, and it was sold for $200,000. Ignore selling and administrative costs.

Required:

1. Prepare the January income statement using variable costing principles and assuming variances resulting from overhead application are prorated to inventories and cost of goods sold.
2. Repeat part 1 but assume that variances are closed to cost of goods sold.

7-18. Variable Costing and a Process Cost System. Reconsider the Evans Company in problem 4-16. Continue the assumption of an actual process cost system but assume variable costing is to be used.

Required:

Reconstruct the work in process account as it is found in problem 4-16.

7-19. Variable Costing and a Standard Cost System. Reconsider the E.E. Ray Company in problem 5-6. Note the budgeted fixed costs are $120,000 yearly (see Exhibit 5.2).

Required:

Prepare all journal entries for the *overhead* component of manufacturing cost assuming a variable costing system. Be sure to record all variances that would be appropriate to this system. (Note that you are not being asked to prepare the entries for material and labor.)

7-20. Working-Paper Adjustments When Standard Costs Are Changing. The Tekulve Company uses a standard variable costing system to account for its only product. Annually the standards are revised to reflect current prices and technology. The standard and budgeted fixed costs for 19x1 through 19x3 were as follows:

	19x1	*19x2*	*19x3*
Standard cost/unit			
Direct material	$10	$11	$12
Direct labor	20	23	25
Variable overhead	15	17	18
Total	45	51	55
Budgeted fixed costs	$80,000	$90,000	$106,000

Following are the production and sales data:

	19x1	19x2	19x3
Ending work in process	1,000	0	0
Percentage completion	25%	—	—
Units started into production	8,000	10,000	12,000
Units sold	5,000	12,000	13,000

Material is added at the beginning of processing, and conversion costs are incurred continuously throughout the process. If full absorption costing were to be used, the fixed overhead costs would be applied at a rate based on normal yearly activity of 10,000 units. The FIFO inventory flow will be used for units that are carried at different standards. Assume there were no variances from standard and that the actual fixed costs equaled the budget.

Required:

Prepare the working paper adjustments to convert the accounts to full absorption costing. Assume the noncontrollable (volume) variance will be shown separately rather than as part of cost of goods sold.

7-21. A Comprehensive Review Problem. The Madlock Company maintains its accounts on a standard variable costing basis. Direct material is also maintained at standard. The following data are available at the year end 12/31/x4:

	Product A	*Product B*
Standards		
Material @ $5	$10 (2 units)	$15 (3 units)
Labor @ $8	32 (4 hours)	24 (3 hours)
Variable overhead @ $5	20 (4 hours)	15 (3 hours)
Total	$62	$54

	Product A	*Product B*
Finished goods, 1/1/x4	1,000 units	3,000 units
Finished goods, 12/31/x4	2,000 units	1,000 units
Sales during 19x4	19,000 units	32,000 units

Direct material inventory, 12/31/x4	20,000 units
Normal activity (in direct-labor hours)	200,000 hours
Budgeted fixed costs	$680,000
Material price variance	$ 15,000 U
Labor rate variance	$ 17,000 U

There are no variances, other than the two listed, and there were no beginning or ending work-in-process inventories. In 19x3 there were no variances and the company worked at normal activity.

Required:

1. Determine the standard quantity of direct material allowed for 19x4's production.
2. Determine the standard labor hours allowed for 19x4's production.
3. Determine the *standard* full absorption cost of the finished goods inventory.
4. For purposes of converting the accounts to full absorption costing, compute the noncontrollable (volume) variance.
5. Prepare the adjusting entry to distribute the fixed cost account in order to convert to *standard* full absorption costing.
6. Prepare a schedule allocating the material price, labor rate, and noncontrollable variance to direct materials, finished goods—A, finished goods—B, and cost of goods sold.

CHAPTER 8

Spoilage and the Cost Accounting System

Chapter Overview

Inherent in many production processes is the problem of spoiled units. Although spoilage should be minimized, completely eliminating unacceptable production may be impossible. Thus, the accountant must be knowledgeable of possible accounting methods for spoiled units.

In this chapter we will discuss the meaning of spoilage and distinguish between abnormal and normal spoilage. A proper accounting for spoilage depends on two factors: (1) the type of spoilage, and (2) the type of cost accounting system in use. Thus, for each of the three basic cost systems a section will be devoted to the problem of accounting for spoilage. Shrinkage is another form of spoilage that occurs in certain production processes. An optional section is devoted to a discussion of the modifications needed in the accounting process when there is shrinkage. We conclude this chapter with a discussion of possible accounting treatments in situations where the spoilage has a scrap value.

Definitions and Concepts

Before distinguishing between abnormal and normal spoilage, we need to discuss the meaning of spoilage itself. In practice it is common for some accountants to distinguish between spoilage and waste and for some to use the terms interchangeably. For our purposes **spoilage** will be defined as the portion of the firm's finished, or partially finished, product that is damaged or defective. These units would be detected by a quality control inspection and would not be saleable as a regular product unless it is possible to correct the defects with some rework. In contrast, **waste** may refer to either of two things. First, waste can mean the loss of a resource (input) during the process of production. That is, waste is the loss of an input before it becomes part of the potential output. Second, it is common to consider the unwanted, but unavoidable, residues of production as waste.

To illustrate the definitions, first consider the situation where a product has been produced but fails the quality control inspection at the end of the processing. Assume that it is not possible or desirable to correct the defective units. Then the accountant would consider these units as spoilage. The cost of the spoilage would include some labor and overhead in addition to the materials physically contained in the units.

Examples of the first meaning of waste include materials that are damaged before being put into production, and labor hours that are idle and unproductive. The second kind of waste includes cuttings in steel manufacturing, ashes and nuclear waste in power generation, bones in meat processing, and sludge in petroleum and chemical processes.

In practice, any of the foregoing situations may have other aspects that will have to be considered. For example, the spoiled units may have a scrap value, may be capable of recycling, may be capable of being reworked, or may have a disposal cost in addition to the lost production costs. Each of these aspects are also possible for tangible waste items. Of course, waste of intangible resources, such as lost labor hours, would not have salvage values, disposal costs, and so forth. The accounting for situations where these are possibilities will be considered after the basic cases are discussed.

ABNORMAL SPOILAGE. As alluded to earlier, there are two types of spoiled production: abnormal and normal. **Abnormal spoilage** is that which is avoidable with better performance and would include units damaged in industrial accidents as well as damage in excess of a normal amount. In the latter case the distinction between abnormal and normal spoilage is partly a matter of judgment. Nevertheless, the implication of abnormal spoilage is that it could have been avoided with better performance.

NORMAL SPOILAGE. Because of human and mechanical frailties, it is not always realistic to expect there would never be any spoilage. Production in a glass factory is not going to be without some breakage, even with the best of performance. Thus, **normal spoilage** is *expected* and, from a practical standpoint, *unavoidable* damage. Because of the unavoidable characteristic it seems clear that its cost should be viewed and disposed of differently from the cost of abnormal spoilage.

GUIDING CONCEPTS. Regardless of the accounting system in use, the basic concepts of accounting for the two types of spoilage are the same. Before examining the specifics of the various systems, let us explore some of these concepts.

Abnormally spoiled production has the same *economic characteristics* as a fire loss, a theft, or obsolescence. That is, there is a consumption or expiration of resources with no resulting benefit. Thus, there is no justification for assigning the cost of these spoiled units to the good units of production. The utility of the good units is not increased as a result of the abnormal spoilage. Further, the firm cannot expect to recover these costs in an efficient, competitive market place. Thus, the cost of such units should be considered a loss for the accounting period.

Normal spoilage is different. If, as a practical matter, it is unavoidable, then spoilage cost is just as necessary to the production process as material, labor, and overhead. Given that such costs are necessary for the creation of good production, they should be assigned to the good output. Consider an alternative justification.

Spoilage can, perhaps, be avoided by incurring the cost of an improved manufacturing process. However, it may be less costly to incur the spoilage. In either case, there is an unavoidable cost that can be defended as being inventoriable.

An issue related to spoilage accounting is the control and elimination of spoilage. With the attention given to the success and growing reputation of Japanese manufacturing, this has become a concern of very high interest. It is Japanese philosophy to totally eliminate defects.[1] To help control this, the information system may need to create some additional ways of reporting data. For example, the Japanese monitor the percentage of their production that makes it all the way through the manufacturing process without any rework. Many American firms do not even collect information such as this, let alone attempt to control the defects.[2]

It is not the purpose of this chapter to discuss ways in which spoilage and rework costs can be reduced. Instead, it is our purpose to discuss how to account for such costs when they do occur.

Accounting for Spoilage in a Process Cost System

The principles of accounting for spoilage are perhaps most easily understood in the context of process cost accounting. Thus, we will start with that system. As in Chapter 4, we continue the assumption that the system is entirely based on actual costs. The discussion will be divided into three topics: accounting for abnormal spoilage, accounting for normal spoilage by the method of "omission," and accounting for normal spoilage by the method of "recognition and reassignment."

ABNORMAL SPOILAGE. In a process cost system, accounting for abnormally spoiled units is not much different than accounting for inventory. To account for abnormally spoiled units it is necessary to identify, at the point of detection, the percentage completion of the units with respect to each cost behavior. The cost of such spoilage will be treated as a loss. Thus, the total equivalent production used for computing average costs must include the number of equivalent units of work expended on the spoiled units from the time they were started in production until the time they were detected and removed. By including these units of work as part of the total equivalent production, the total recorded manufacturing costs will be allocated to both the good units and the abnormally spoiled units. Using the resulting unit costs, the abnormal spoilage loss can be computed in the same way as the cost of the ending inventory.

To illustrate, assume that the Carle Company uses the weighted average version of process cost in accounting for the actual costs of its casting department. The following data are availabe for the month of April:

---

[1]See Robert H. Hayes, "Why Japanese Factories Work," *Harvard Business Review* (July–August 1981), pp. 57–66.

[2]See Robert S. Kaplan, "Measuring Manufacturing Performance: A New Challenge for Managerial Accounting Research," *The Accounting Review* (October 1983), p. 690.

Beginning inventory (100% complete as to material, 25% as to conversion)		4,000 units
Cost of beginning inventory (material of $6,400 and conversion of $36,920)		$ 43,320
Units started during April		16,000
Material added during April		$ 24,160
Conversion costs added during April		$322,432
Units finished during April		17,100
Ending inventory (100% complete as to material, 75% as to conversion)		2,000 units
Spoilage (100% complete as to material and 80% complete as to conversion when detected)		900 units

Exhibit 8.1 is the process cost report for April assuming that the spoilage is abnormal. Sections A and B should be obvious. Note the inclusion of abnormal spoilage in the equivalent unit computation of section C. Since the spoiled units are identified when production is 80% complete, conversion costs equal to only 80% of a completed unit would have been incurred. Also note the determination of the abnormal spoilage cost in section D. The journal entry transferring costs out of the Casting Department for April would be:

Abnormal spoilage loss	14,767.20	
Finished goods	344,188.80	
Casting department		358,956.00

If modified FIFO process costing is used, then an assumption is needed with respect to the beginning inventory. The need for an assumption can best be explained by examining the FIFO equivalent unit computation. Recall that with FIFO the beginning inventory is treated as a separate layer. Consequently, the equivalent amount of work done *this period* on the beginning inventory depends on how many, if any, of the units in the beginning inventory were spoiled during the period. The common assumption made is that all units in the beginning inventory are finished as good output regardless of whether they were or were not. In other words, it is commonly assumed that all spoilage comes from the units started during the current period. This assumption is reflected in the manner in which the units started and finished are computed. Note that the units furnished, 17,100, are free of spoilage. Likewise, note that if all 4,000 units in the beginning inventory are deducted in deriving the started and finished layer then it is implicitly assumed that all spoilage is from the started layer. The FIFO equivalent production for the Carle problem, then, is:

	Material	*Conversion Costs*
Beginning inventory	0	3,000
Started and finished (17,100 − 4,000)	13,100	13,100
Ending inventory	2,000	1,500
Abnormal spoilage	900	720
Equivalent units	16,000	18,320

The current material cost of $24,160 would be averaged over 16,000 equivalent units and the current conversion of $322,432 over 18,320 units. These unit costs would then be used in assigning the costs to the various layers including the abnormal spoilage.

Exhibit 8.1   Carle Company Casting Department Process Cost Report for April 19x1 (spoilage is abnormal; weighted average)

A. Units schedule
   To be accounted for

Beginning inventory (conversion 25% complete)	4,000
Started	16,000
Total	20,000

   Units accounted for

Finished	17,100
Ending inventory (conversion 75% complete)	2,000
Abnormal spoilage (conversion 80% complete)	900
Total	20,000

B. Costs to be accounted for

	Material	Conversion Costs	Total
Beginning inventory	$ 6,400	$ 36,920	$ 43,320
Current costs	24,160	322,432	346,592
Total	$30,560	$359,352	$389,912

C. Equivalent units and unit cost computation

	Material	Conversion Costs
Units finished	17,100	17,100
Ending inventory	2,000	1,500
Abnormal spoilage	900	720
Equivalent units	20,000	19,320
Costs	$30,560	$359,352
Cost per equivalent unit	$1.528	$18.60

D. Cost assignment

To finished goods [17,000 ×		
($1.528 + $18.60)]		$344,188.80
Ending inventory		
Material (2,000 × $1.528)	$ 3,056.00	
Conversion costs (1,500 × $18.60)	27,900.00	30,956.00
Abnormal spoilage		
Material (900 × $1.528)	$ 1,375.20	
Conversion costs (720 × $18.60)	13,392.00	14,767.20
Total		$389,912.00

ACCOUNTING FOR NORMAL SPOILAGE BY THE METHOD OF OMISSION. As indicated earlier, normal spoilage may be treated in one of two ways in a process cost system. The first method omits the normally spoiled units when computing equivalent production. Since the total costs incurred would include the resources used on the normally spoiled units, excluding the spoiled units from the equivalent unit computation has the effect of averaging their costs over the good units. This is the most commonly used method but there are some theoretical deficiencies that will be explored after an illustration.

The illustration will be accomplished by changing the facts in the Carle Company problem. Instead of the 900 units being abnormal spoilage, assume they are normal spoilage and that they will be accounted for in the manner suggested previously. Exhibit 8.2 contains the results. In section C of Exhibit 8.2 you should observe that the normal spoilage has been omitted. Also note that the unit costs are higher than those in Exhibit 8.1 and that the costs of finished production and ending inventory are higher. This reflects the absorption of the normal spoilage cost into the cost of the good units (which is desired).

Now consider the conceptual problems with accounting for normal spoilage by the omission method. The **omission method** assigns normal spoilage costs to the layers (finished units and ending inventory) in a proportion equal to the equivalent unit content of the various layers to the total equivalent production. On the surface this may not appear objectionable. However, it should be noted that a layer may share in spoilage costs even if it has not been subjected to an inspection. This is the case with the ending inventory of the casting department in the example. It is 75% complete, and the spoilage is detected when the production is 80% complete. Thus, it might be argued that if there is spoilage in the ending inventory layer of 2,000 units it has not yet been identified. If not, then one might ask why the ending inventory should be assigned any of this period's normal spoilage cost. The argument would continue by suggesting the normal spoilage costs of the period should be assigned only to the good units that passed the inspection point during the period. This is the thrust of the recognition and reassignment method that is discussed in the next subsection.

Before considering the alternative treatment, let's consider some defenses for the method of omission. Even though this method does assign spoilage costs to units that have not been subjected to an inspection, it does so only at a rate per equivalent unit of work done during the current period. Thus, if the rate of normal spoilage is relatively constant from period to period, then the total amount of spoilage cost that is ultimately assigned to a unit in this period's uninspected ending inventory is approximately the same as a unit that was entirely completed this period. The only difference is that some of the spoilage is assigned to the ending inventory during the current period and some during the next period. Thus, this method may not be technically correct, but given the assumed circumstances, it will produce results that are consistent with the alternative method to be discussed later. Furthermore, it is computationally less involved than the alternative method.

ACCOUNTING FOR NORMAL SPOILAGE VIA RECOGNITION AND REASSIGNMENT. If a more technically correct method of accounting for normal spoilage is desired, then one must:

1. Include the normally spoiled units in the equivalent unit computation.
2. Assign a cost to the normally spoiled units in the same manner as ending inventory or abnormal spoilage.
3. Allocate the normal spoilage costs as computed in part 2 to those good units that passed the inspection point during the period. The mechanics of doing this are dependent on whether the weighted average or the modified FIFO method is used and on the status of the beginning and ending inventories with respect to the inspection point. Some of these mechanics will now be explored.

Exhibit 8.2   Carle Company Casting Department Process Cost Report for April 19x1 (spoilage normal; accounted for by omission; weighted average)

A. Units schedule

To be accounted for	
Beginning inventory (conversion 25% complete)	4,000
Started	16,000
Total	20,000
Units accounted for	
Finished	17,100
Ending inventory (conversion 75% complete)	2,000
Normal spoilage (conversion 80% complete)	900
Total	20,000

B. Costs to be accounted for

	Material	Conversion Costs	Total
Beginning inventory	$ 6,400	$ 36,920	$ 43,320
Current costs	24,160	322,432	346,592
Total	$30,560	$359,352	$389,912

C. Equivalent units and unit cost computation

	Material	Conversion Costs
Units finished	17,100	17,100
Ending inventory	2,000	1,500
Normal spoilage (omitted)	---	---
Equivalent units	19,100	18.600
Costs	$30,560	$359,352
Cost per equivalent unit	$1.60	$19.32

D. Cost assignment

To finished goods [17,100 × ($1.60 + $19.32)]		$357,732
Ending inventory		
Material (2,000 × $1.60)	$ 3,200	
Conversion costs (1,500 × $19.32)	28,980	32,180
Total		$389,912

Let us again use the Carle Company's casting department as an illustration. Sections A, B, and C of the cost report would be the same as in Exhibit 8.1 except all references to abnormal spoilage should be changed to normal spoilage. The cost of normal spoilage is computed in section D of Exhibit 8.3 to be $14,767.20. This is a new section that is recommended when spoilage is accounted for by the **recognition and reassignment method.** Only step 3 of the above procedure needs elaboration. That is, how should the normal spoilage be allocated? In this case, the units in the beginning inventory would have been subjected to an inspection this period. With the recognition and reassignment method, no spoilage cost would have been assigned to this layer last period and all good units from the layer should share in this period's normal spoilage cost. Likewise, the ending inventory has not been inspected and should not share in this period's spoilage. Thus, all of the normal spoilage cost of $14,767.20 should be assigned to the finished units bringing their total cost to $358,956 ($344,188.80 + $14,767.20).

Note that, in this example, it is *unfair* to compare this result with the cost of finished goods derived in Exhibit 8.2 ($357,732) because we used the same beginning inventory *cost* for both normal spoilage illustrations. Obviously, if a given method

---

Exhibit 8.3   Carle Company Process Cost Report for April 19x1 (spoilage normal; recognized and reassigned; weighted average)

Schedules A, B, and C same as in Exhibit 8.1

D. Normal Spoilage
   Cost

Material (900 × $1.528)		$ 1,375.20
Conversion costs (720 × $18.60)		13,392.00
Total		$ 14,767.20

   Allocation Percentages

	Units	Per Cent
Finished goods	17,100	100%
Ending inventory	0	0
Total	17,100	100%

E. Cost assignment
   Finished goods

Material and conversion [17,100 × ($1.528 + $18.60)]		$344,188.80
Spoilage (1.00 × $14,767.20)		14,767.20
Total		$358,956.00
Ending inventory		
Material (2,000 × $1.528)	$ 3,056	
Conversion costs (1,500 × $18.60)	27,900	
Spoilage	0	30,956.00
Total		$389,912.00

has been used consistently over time, then the beginning inventory cost would have been different for each method. If this had been built into the example, it might be expected that the two results would have been closer.

For the recognition and reassignment method there are four basic cases that might arise, as indicated in Exhibit 8.4. First, consider the accounting for normal spoilage in each of these cases where the weighted average method is being used. The preceding case is an example of case 1. Case 2 differs from case 1 in that the ending inventory will share the spoilage cost proratably with the finished units. For example, if the finished production included 8,000 units and the ending inventory 2,000 units that had passed the inspection point, then 20% of the normal spoilage cost would be assigned to the ending inventory.

Case 3 is slightly different from case 1 in that a spoilage cost would have been assigned last month to the beginning inventory. Under the weighted average concept of costing, this spoilage cost would be pooled with the current spoilage cost. The combined pool would then be prorated over the appropriate number of units. However, in case 3 the finished production would be the only absorbing layer. (The ending inventory has not been inspected.)

Case 4 is the most involved case. Like case 3, the beginning inventory would have a spoilage cost that would have to be pooled with the cost of the current spoilage. Then the *pooled spoilage cost* would be prorated to finished goods and ending inventory in a manner similar to case 2. For example, assume the beginning inventory had $2,000 of spoilage assigned to it last period. Then in the normal spoilage section (section D of Exhibit 8.3), the $2,000 would be added to the current spoilage, $14,767.20. This total would be prorated between the two layers per previous discussions.

Cases 3 and 4 also entail a slight modification to section B of the process cost report. The spoilage carried forward in the beginning inventory should be accounted for with a separate entry in a spoilage cost column. No current spoilage could be shown in this new column because it is not computed until section D. Further, the spoilage cost would result from reclassifying costs accounted for as material and conversion in section B. The cost must be included only *once* in section B.[3]

The four basic cases in Exhibit 8.4 could also occur with the FIFO method. The difference is in the treatment of the costs of the beginning inventory. The assumption is still made that the beginning inventory was completed without the loss of any units. Any costs assigned last period, including spoilage loss, would remain attached to these specific units. Of course, with this spoilage method, the beginning inventory would have had spoilage cost assigned to it last period only if it had passed the inspection point last period. Thus, in cases 1 and 2 the units in the beginning inventory would be assigned a pro rata share of the current period's

---

[3]The explanation assumed that *all* units in inventory were at the *same* point of completion at the time of taking inventory. Of course, in reality some units may have just been started, some may be half finished, and some may be nearly finished. Depending on the degree of precision that is desired and the added cost of achieving the precision, the inventory in these cases may need to be viewed as two or more layers.

Exhibit 8.4   Normal Spoilage Cases (NI = Not Inspected; I = Inspected)

	Case 1	Case 2	Case 3	Case 4
Status of beginning inventory at start of period	NI	NI	I	I
Status of ending inventory at end of period	NI	I	NI	I

spoilage cost. In cases 3 and 4, the beginning inventory would not receive any of the spoilage costs.

Accounting for Spoilage in a Standard Cost System

As pointed out in Chapter 5, one purpose of a standard cost system is to help detect and control inefficiency. By definition, abnormal spoilage is a type of inefficiency in that its occurrence results in a needless consumption of resources. The resources allowed for a given period's accomplishments, the standard, would be a function of the good output. Thus, abnormally spoiled units *would not* be reflected in the amount of resources (material, labor, and so forth) allowed for the production of the period. Nevertheless, when abnormal spoilage occurs, resources are consumed. The material contained in the abnormally spoiled units would be reflected in the material quantity variance. Likewise, labor hours consumed by the abnormal spoilage would be included in the labor efficiency variance, and the overhead efficiency variance would be similarly affected.

As pointed out previously, if the standard costing system is implemented in accordance with Chapters 5 and 6, then the abnormal spoilage loss is contained in three variances. The spoilage would provide an explanation (not a justification) for the existence of part of each of these variances. In some cases, it might be necessary to isolate the total cost of the abnormal spoilage.[4] If so, then each of the variances can be appropriately reduced and the amount due to the spoilage charged to a loss account. The amount remaining in the variance accounts would then be subjected to the usual analysis to identify the reasons for their occurrence.

Since normal spoilage is an unavoidable occurrence, there is a strong case for arguing that it should be anticipated and included in the standard allowances per unit of good output. If the standards *do not* reflect these unavoidable spoilages, then each reporting period part of the variance analysis effort would have to be devoted to identifying the portion of the variances that are uncontrollable. This is

---

[4]For example, if the variances must be prorated to inventories and cost of goods sold for external reporting, it *would not be appropriate* to prorate the portion of the variances due to abnormal spoilage. Abnormal spoilage must be considered a period cost, not a product cost, even for external reporting.

a time-consuming and inefficient process. Thus, the accounting for normal spoilage really takes place in the process of constructing the standards.

To illustrate, assume that one of the Gilman Company's products requires two pounds of material that is put in at the beginning of production. (This is the actual physical content of material needed in the finished product, not the amount that must be started into production.) In the process of preparing the material, 3% is wasted even when there is acceptable performance. The product also requires three hours of labor. Laborers are allowed thirty minutes of break time for each of eight hours on the job. (The break time is not included in the three hours of production time.) After production is 80% complete, an inspection is made. When performance is acceptable there is an average failure rate equal to 5% of the total units passing the inspection point. Assume the unacceptable units have no salvage value. In summary:

Material	2 pounds
Labor	3 hours
Material wasted in preparation	3%
Break time	30 minutes per 8-hour day
Inspection point	80%
Normal failure rate at inspection	5%

First consider the establishment of the material quantity standard. There are two basic ways of including such a cost in the standard. First, if it is convenient to monitor the actual usage of material, then that which is identified as normal spoilage can be tagged as indirect material and charged to overhead. In this approach, the overhead rate would be constructed to include the estimated spoilage. Then the material contained in normal spoilage would be excluded from the actual *direct* material used and, therefore, excluded from the quantity variance. Of course, to properly implement this system it would be necessary to constantly monitor material requisitions in order to classify the material as being used in good output as abnormal spoilage, or as normal spoilage.

A second accounting method is to include a spoilage allowance in the material quantity standard rather than in the overhead rate. Although there are alternative ways to do it, perhaps the easiest way to demonstrate how this can be done in our example is to trace what happens to a 100,000-pound batch of material (this weight was arbitrarily selected). The following schedule shows the computation of the expected number of *good* units that should result from the processing of 100,000 pounds:

Beginning weight	100,000 pounds
Less preparation wastage (3%)	3,000 pounds
Usable material	97,000 pounds
Production possible, 97,000 ÷ 2 pounds per unit	48,500 units
Less units failing inspection (5%)	2,425 units
Good units expected	46,075 units

Thus, the expectation is that 100,000 pounds of material will result in 46,075 good units of production. The material used per good unit is 2.1704 pounds, 100,000 ÷ 46,075. The standard quantity allowed for a given period will be computed as the number of good units times 2.1704 pounds.

The labor standard is slightly more complicated in our example due to the fact that the spoilage is not fully complete with respect to labor at the time of its detection. Again, there are two options. First, the work break time and time spent on normal spoilage could be considered as indirect labor and classified as manufacturing overhead. Then, the estimated nonproductive time would be included in the overhead rate. As a second accounting alternative, the labor hour standard could be adjusted upward to allow for the work breaks and time spent on normal spoilage. If this treatment is selected, then the labor *time* will not have to be classified as direct or indirect; only the labor force will need to be classified. To implement such a procedure, note that laborers are actually working 93.75% of the time (7.5 hours ÷ 8 hours). How many hours must be employed in order to have the 3 hours needed to complete one *whole* unit? Let x be the total hours employed in order to get 3 productive hours. Then:

$$3 = 0.9375x$$

$$x = 3 \div 0.9375 = 3.2$$

Again, there are other ways to determine the labor hours per good unit but the following is rather straightforward. Let us arbitrarily assume a batch of 100 units of the product is started. Such a batch would be expected to yield 95 good units since the spoilage rate is 5%. The total labor hours expected for the batch, *including break time,* is:

For good units	95 × 3.2	304.0
For spoiled units	5 × 3.2 × 0.8*	12.8
Total		316.8

*The inspection occurred when labor was 80% completed.

The labor hours per good unit is 3.33473, 316.8 ÷ 95, and thus becomes the standard allowance per unit of output.

Accounting for Spoilage in a Job Order System

In a job order setting, the cause of the spoilage would have to be unrelated to a specific job if it is to be classified as abnormal. For example, suppose some electrical malfunction resulted in a machine failure while a specific job was being produced and caused 100 units to be unacceptable. Further, suppose it was reasonable to expect the operator of the machine to notice the effect of the power outage and to prevent the spoilage. In such a circumstance, the spoilage is not due to any specific characteristics of the job and is preventable. Therefore, it should be accounted for as abnormal spoilage. If the cause of the spoilage is inherent to a specific job and not preventable, then the spoilage should be charged to that job and, in effect, would be considered as normal.

As an example of a job-related characteristic that might cause spoilage to be classified as normal instead of abnormal, consider the following. Suppose it is conventionally acceptable to have a tolerance for the borings on a particular motor head of ± 2 millimeters. With such a tolerance it is reasonable to expect 3% of the heads to be rejected even when there is good performance. The current job, however, has a tolerance of ± 0.5 millimeters. This increases the rejection rate to 9%. The additional 6% spoilage can be considered normal to this particular job even though, in general, it is not normal.

To illustrate the accounting for *abnormal spoilage,* suppose that 100 units of a particular product were being processed in a given job lot. The total material, labor, and overhead for this job totaled $25,000. At the inspection point it was determined that 10% of these units were defective. The defective units have no salvage value or any costs of disposal. Further investigation revealed that the cause was not normal and not job related. The entry would be:

Finished goods	22,500	
Spoilage loss	2,500	
Work in process		25,000

Since 10% of the production was abnormally lost, 10% of the costs originally assigned to this job should be accounted for as a loss.

Our definition of normal spoilage does not necessarily imply that it will occur at a constant rate. However, if it does occur at a constant rate, a proper accounting for normal spoilage can be achieved simply by treating the accumulated costs of each job (less any abnormal spoilage) as the cost of the good units on the job. If the rate of normal spoilage occurrence is not constant, then the accounting will be more involved. All jobs should be charged with a pro-rata share of normal spoilage. Charging the job that currently is in process when the loss occurs will not achieve this result if the spoilage rate is not constant. In these cases normal spoilage should be included in the variable overhead budget and thus the variable overhead rate. Then there will be a proration of spoilage via the application rate.

If spoilge is applied via the overhead rate, the cost of the actual normal spoilage should be charged to the manufacturing overhead control account when incurred. To illustrate the accounting procedures, when normal spoilage does not occur at an *even* rate, suppose the Petry Company is a job coster and usually operates at 100,000 labor hours, of which an average of 10,000 is spent on items that are considered normal spoilage. Laborers earn $5 per hour. Thus, the costs at 100,000 hours should be averaged over 90,000 hours since these are the hours expected to result in good production. As discussed earlier, normal spoilage costs are legitimate costs of good production. The overhead rate is derived as follows and includes the cost of the material and labor to be incurred in the spoiled production:

Material on normally spoiled items	$ 40,000
Labor on normally spoiled items (10,000 hours)	50,000
Other variable overhead	360,000
Total	$450,000
Divisor activity	90,000
Overhead rate per hour	$5.00

Other variable overhead is the *total* expected to be incurred at normal activity. Fixed costs have been excluded from the example so that the noncontrollable (volume) variance does not influence the results.

Now suppose that in January the company operated at 8,000 *total* hours. In this month, however, the normal spoilage consumed 500 labor hours (included in the 8,000). That is, the actual spoilage rate was somewhat below normal in January. For this example, assume that the material and labor were incurred in the same proportion as budgeted above: a rate of $4 of materials to $5 of labor. Since spoilage is being charged to the jobs by the overhead rate, the 500 hours should be excluded from the 8,000 hours when computing the direct costs of the jobs. Thus the WIP entries for January would be summarized as:

Work in process	105,000	
Direct labor (7,500 × 5)		37,500
Direct materials (4/5 × 37,500)		30,000
Manufacturing overhead (7,500 × $5 rate)		37,500

Now let us consider the accounting for the actual overhead *incurred* during January. First, assume that the other overhead is being incurred at the anticipated rate (this is assumed so that the results will be free of other influencing factors). Note that in the overhead rate derivation the other variable overhead is expected to be $360,000 when the actual direct-labor hours are 90,000. Thus, the other variable overhead costs are expected to be incurred at a rate of $4.00 per direct-labor hour. Because of the assumption, the *actual other overhead* for January is $30,000; 7,500 × $4.00. The entry for this is:

Manufacturing overhead	30,000	
Miscellaneous credits		30,000

To finish the accounting for January, we now must consider the material and labor incurred on the 500 units of production that were detected as normal spoilage. These costs represent additional overhead costs incurred during the period. Thus:

Manufacturing overhead	4,500	
Direct labor 500 × 5		2,500
Direct material $2,500 × 4/5		2,000

The summarized manufacturing overhead and WIP accounts are as follows:

Manufacturing Overhead			
January		January	
Actual—other	30,000	Applied	40,000
Normal spoilage, from			
Direct labor	2,500		
Direct material	2,000		

Work in Process			
January		January	
Material	30,000	To finished goods	105,000
Labor	37,500		105,000
Applied overhead	37,500		
	105,000		

A final situation that should be considered in a job order system is the possibility that spoilage is in excess of the normal due to some characteristic of the job itself. For example, the quality standards on the job might have been contracted higher than normal. In this case, it is justifiable to charge the costs of the abnormal spoilage to the specific job.

⩾ Shrinkage and Accretion

Some processes entail raw materials that may evaporate or shrink while in production. This is referred to as **shrinkage** and should be contrasted with spoilage. With spoilage the materials still exist; they just are not acceptable. If shrinkage occurs, the material physically disappears. Shrinkage often occurs in processes that involve liquid products. If production is accounted for via a liquid measurement such as gallons or liters, then shrinkage presents a problem. Ending volume and beginning volume will not be the same. If shrinkage occurs gradually, then the actual volume of work-in-process inventories is neither in terms of the beginning nor the ending volume. In an actual cost system the unit cost figures will be determined as a ratio of costs to units produced. If the current work is measured by simply adding the *unadjusted* volumes of the various layers of production, then there will be a lack of equivalence. Without an adjustment, partially completed production will be assigned costs at an excessive rate because the implicit assumption is that it was completed without additional shrinkage. Thus, there are two types of equivalence problems: a volume equivalence and a work equivalence.

To illustrate the accounting for shrinkage in a process cost system, assume the following situation. The Crystal Chemical Company, in processing one of its products, must start 100 pounds of a certain chemical for each 80 pounds of finished production. *All of the chemical is added at the start of processing.* A 20% evaporation (based on beginning weights) takes place gradually throughout the process. In terms of *actual* weights at the point of the measurements, the following production statistics from April are available:

Beginning inventory (75% complete)	21,250 pounds
Started (cost $2.00 per pound)	110,000 pounds
Finished	80,000 pounds
Ending inventory (25% complete)	33,250 pounds
Cost assigned to beginning inventory	$100,000

| Current conversion costs | $252,000 |
| Curent material costs | $220,000 |

Assume the FIFO method is used.

Before the equivalent amount of work can be computed, it will be necessary to convert all of the weights to a common reference point. Using ending, or net, weights will be the most convenient. That is, each of the layers should be adjusted to the weights they are expected to produce at the end of processing. This can be done as part of schedule A in the typical process cost report. First, consider the beginning inventory. Since it was 75% complete at April 1, its weight at that point would be 15% less than its starting weight (0.75×0.2). Remember that the shrinkage rate is based on beginning weight. Thus, the weight at April 1 is 85% of the beginning weight, B:

$$21,250 = 0.85B$$

$$B = \frac{21,250}{0.85} = 25,000$$

The ending weight, E, would be 80% of the beginning weight. Thus:

$$E = 0.8B$$

$$E = 0.8 \times 25,000 = 20,000$$

The ending weight of the pounds started this month would be 88,000, $110,000 \times 0.8$. The final weight of the ending inventory can be derived the same way as the beginning inventory:

$$33,250 = 0.95B \text{ (weight reduction to date} = 0.25 \times 0.2 = 0.05)$$

$$B = \frac{33,250}{0.95}$$

$$E = 0.8B = 0.8\left(\frac{33,250}{0.95}\right) = 28,000$$

These data are summarized in section A of Exhibit 8.5

Note in section C of Exhibit 8.5 that the equivalent units were computed using the net weights, not the actual weights. This includes the equivalent units for conversion costs whereby the percentage completions were applied to the net weight. Also, note the cost assignment was completed using the equivalent amount of work as measured by net weight.

Accretion is a volume gain due to the natural production process. The process of allowing for it would be the same as for shrinkage. The only difference is that the ending weight would be greater than the beginning weight.

In a standard cost system, shrinkage and accretion would be accounted for through the standards themselves. If standards were to be used in the preceding example, we would state that each pound of output would have to have a material input of 1.25 pounds ($1 \div 0.8$). The only implementation problem would be in

Exhibit 8.5   **Crystal Company Process Cost Report (FIFO) for Month of April 19x1**

A. Units schedule (using net weight)
   Pounds to be accounted for
   Beginning inventory [conversion 75% complete;
   $(21,250 \div 0.85) \times 0.8$]   20,000
   Started $110,000 \times 0.8$ 88,000
   Total   108,000
   Pounds accounted for
   Finished   80,000
   Ending inventory [conversion 25% complete;
   $(33,250 \div 0.95) \times 0.8$]   28,000
   Total   108,000

B. Costs to be accounted for

	Total
Beginning inventory	$100,000
Material	220,000
Conversion costs	252,000
Total	$572,000

C. Equivalent unit and unit cost computation

	Material	Conversion Costs
Beginning inventory	0	5,000
Started and finished	60,000	60,000
Ending inventory	28,000	7,000
Equivalent units	88,000	72,000
Current costs	$220,000	$252,000
Cost per equivalent unit	$2.50	$3.50

D. Cost assignment
   Finished goods
   Beginning inventory

Prior period costs		$100,000
Current conversion costs ($5,000 \times \$3.50$)		17,500
Total		$117,500
Started and finished [$60,000 \times (\$2.50 + \$3.50)$]		360,000
Total		$477,500
Ending inventory		
Material ($28,000 \times \$2.50$)	$70,000	
Conversion costs ($7,000 \times \$3.50$)	24,500	94,500
Total		$572,000

computing the standard input for a partially completed inventory. The adjustment here would be similar to what was done previously. In fact, since FIFO was assumed, the equivalent units of work in section C represents the base for computing the standard allowances. For material, we would allow an input of 100,000 pounds, 1.25 × 88,000. For labor we would allow an amount equal to 72,000 times the labor rate per finished pound. No other changes would be needed.

≥ Accounting for Rework, Scrap Value, and Recycling

In the previous sections, it was assumed that spoilage had no value. But what if spoilage did have some type of value to the firm? There are several possible situations. First, the spoilage may be such that with some reworking it can be made acceptable. Second, it may be possible to sell the spoiled units at some scrap value. A third possibility is that the materials involved in the spoilage could be recycled into a usable material. In this section we will examine each of these basic situations.

REWORK. When spoiled units, whether abnormal or normal, can have their damage corrected, they are called **rework.** If units are reworked, the only loss is the cost of reworking. Depending on the situation, the cost of units may either be left in work in process until reworked or transferred to a separate account such as reworkable inventory. Then if the spoilage is abnormal, the material, labor, and overhead needed in the reworking would be charged to spoilage loss rather than to work in process. Upon completion of the rework, the original cost of the items would be transferred to finished goods. This treatment would be the same for all of the accounting systems discussed in this book.

Likewise, when normal spoilage can be reworked, the loss is limited to the rework cost. The accounting for these costs would be according to the principles of accounting for spoilage as outlined in the sections for each of the systems.

In a process cost system, the rework cost may be charged to work in process. If so, it will be averaged over the units produced this period. Alternatively, these costs could be kept separate and then proratably assigned to the units passing the inspection point during the current period.

If a standard cost system is in use, then the rework costs for normal spoilage should be incorporated into the standards. To illustrate, suppose that 5% of the production will not meet specifications. The units requiring rework are not identified until the completion of all processing. *Before rework* costs are considered, the standard costs per unit are:

Material	3 units @ $4	$12.00
Labor	4 hours @ $5	20.00
Variable overhead	4 hours @ $3	12.00
Fixed overhead	4 hours @ $2	8.00
Total		$52.00

Assume that, on the average, the rework will require one additional unit of material and one additional labor hour. For a hypothetical batch size of 100 units, the following resources would be consumed:

Material
    Original processing (100 × 3)   300
    Rework (100 × 0.05 × 1)   5
      Total for 100 units   305
Labor
    Original processing (100 × 4)   400
    Rework (100 × 0.05 × 1)   5
      Total for 100 units   405

Thus, the standard quantity of material is 3.05 units per finished product and the standard labor hours allowed per unit is 4.05.

In a job order system it will be necessary to estimate the normal rework cost rate. This estimate would be included in the overhead budget and, therefore, in the overhead rate.

SCRAP VALUE. When the spoilage can be sold, it is considered to have a **scrap value.** If this value is *very* small, it is common to treat the recovery value as miscellaneous income or as a reduction of manufacturing overhead rather than as a reduction in applied costs. Practicality and judgment must be used in deciding if this accounting is proper. If the value is of more than minor significance, then it should be treated as a reduction in applied costs. For such cases the treatments parallel the previous discussions of this chapter.

The scrap value of abnormal spoilage can be accounted for as a reduction in the spoilage loss. For example, assume that Carle's spoilage in Exhibit 8.1 could be salvaged for $1,146. Then, the cost of the scrap inventory would be equal to the market value, and the $14,767.20 originally assigned to the abnormal spoilage would now be divided as follows:

Abnormal spoilage loss	13,621.20	
Scrap inventory	1,146.00	
Work in process		14,767.20

When the scrap inventory is sold, cash would be debited and the inventory credited.

The scrap value of normal spoilage, if material in amount, should be offset against the production costs assigned to the spoiled units before averaging the spoilage cost over the good units.

In a process cost system that omits normal spoilage in the equivalent unit computation, it would generally be appropriate to offset this scrap against the material cost *before* computing a cost per equivalent unit. Presumably, the scrap value of spoilage would be due to the material. Assuming the Carle Company's spoilage is normal and still has a scrap value of $1,146, section C of Exhibit 8.2 would be modified as follows:

	Material	*Conversion Costs*
Equivalent units	19,100	18,600
Costs		
Material ($30,560 − $1,146)	$29,414	
Conversion		$359,352
Cost per equivalent unit	$1.54	$ 19.32

Then section D would be:

D. Cost assignment

Finished goods [17,100 × ($1.54 + $19.32)]		$356,706
Ending inventory		
Material (2,000 × $1.54)	$ 3,080	
Conversion costs (1,500 × $19.32)	28,980	32,060
Scrap inventory		1,146
Total		$389,912

If the normal spoilage is being recognized and reassigned, as in Exhibit 8.3, then the scrap value would be deducted from the normal spoilage cost of $14,767.20 in section D. The net spoilage cost of $13,621.20 would then be allocated according to the percentages in section D. The only remaining modification would be the inclusion of the scrap inventory in section E.

To account for scrap value in a standard cost system requires careful analysis. Because of this, there may be more motivation to account for scrap value as other income or as an adjustment to cost of goods sold. Another possible treatment would be to budget the scrap value of the normal spoilage as a "negative cost" in establishing the overhead rate.

If the scrap is of a material value, then it may be desirable to exercise better control than is possible through the preceding suggestions. To illustrate a process for doing this, reconsider the Gilman Company Case. Incorporation of scrap into the standard will entail a reduction of the cost to be net of scrap recovery value. Assume that the standard price per pound of material is $9.215. Further, assume that any wasted materials (both those wasted in preparation and those contained in the spoiled units) can be salvaged at a standard price of $2.3478 per pound. Recall that 100 pounds of input are expected to produce 46.075 acceptable units of the finished product. Since each of these units actually contain 2 pounds of material, the expected wastage per 100-pound batch would be 7.85 pounds, 100 − (2 × 46.075). Thus, the net cost would be:

Material cost (100 × $9.215)	$921.50
Less scrap (7.85 × $2.3478)	18.43
Total net cost	$903.07
Good units	46.075
Net cost per unit	$ 19.60

Although $19.60 is the correct net standard cost of materials, it is not a complete statement of a standard in the sense of a quantity times a price. For example, in applying the standards, what is the proper price to use in evaluating the purchasing function? Although it is possible to convert the $19.60 to some unit cost (divide by 2.1704 pounds allowed per unit, for example), the result is not relevant to the *purchasing* function. Why should the expected acquisition cost be lowered as a result of scrap value? Further, assuming a price and determining the standard quantity per unit implied by a net cost of $19.60 will produce a result that is not useful to controlling the amount of material going into production.

A solution to this dilemma is to state the net material cost as two separate components. To do this, note the expected scrap per finished unit is 0.1704 pounds, 7.85 ÷ 46.075. Earlier the expected consumption of material was computed to be 2.1704 pounds per finished unit. Thus, the material standard per unit of good output should be expressed as:

Material used (2.1704 × $9.215)	$20.00
Less scrap (0.1704 × $2.3478)	0.40
Net material cost	$19.60

To illustrate the usage of the standard, assume that during April the Gilman Company produced 46,075 good units. The actual material purchased and used amounted to 101,000 pounds. These materials were acquired at a cost of $9.30 per pound. The scrap recovered during the month totaled 8,850 pounds, and it was sold at $2.30 per pound. The entry for the material purchased would include a debit to materials at the standard acquisition cost of $9.215 per unit:

Materials (101,000 × $9.215)	930,715	
Material price variance		
($9.215 − $9.30)101,000	8,585	
Accounts payable		939,300

The standard net material cost for 46,075 units is $903,070, 46,075 × $19.60, and this is the amount for which work in process should be debited. The scrap inventory should also be debited for the standard recovery value of $20,778, 8,850 × $2.3478. The standard amount of materials allowed for the production is 100,000 pounds, 46,075 × 2.1704. Since 101,000 pounds were used there must have been more spoilage than normal.[5] In computing the material quantity variance we need to consider the *economic impact* of the inefficiency. Although these materials had a standard acquisition cost of $9.215, they can be salvaged at a standard recovery value of $2.3478. Therefore, the loss, at standard rates, is $6.8672 per pound. The material quantity variance should be computed using this standard loss per pound. The entry for the month's consumption of material is:

---

[5]It has been assumed that the actual material content in each unit of the finished product did not vary from the amount called for in the product specification (2 pounds as stated on page 269).

Work in process (46,075 × $19.60)	903,070	
Scrap inventory (8,850 × $2.3478)	20,778	
Material quantity variance		
(100,000 − 101,000)6.8672	6,867	
Materials (101,000 × 9.215)		930,715

The scrap was not sold at the standard rate and a salvage rate variance could be established:

Cash (8,850 × $2.30)	20,355	
Rate variance on scrap sales		
(2.3478 − 2.30)8,850	423	
Scrap inventory	20,778	

For a job order system, the scrap value should be estimated when budgeting the overhead. Inclusion of this item in the budget would reduce the overhead rate.

RECYCLING. **Recycling** of wastage is just a special case of scrap value. If the wastage can be recycled, it obviously has value even though that value cannot be established in any kind of external market. Examples include the glass industry where production breakage can be remelted and formed again, and the various metal manufacturers whose spoilage can also be reused. Once it is decided how to value the spoilage, the treatment would be similar to that of scrap value as discussed in the previous section.

There are many possible circumstances that may be encountered. For example, the recovered material may be of the same general form and quality as newly purchased raw material. If so, then the recovery value would just be the original cost of the material, and this cost would be transferred back into materials inventory. The loss, in this case, would be confined to the conversion cost incurred when processing the spoiled units.

In other circumstances, such as recovered aluminum, the spoilage may have a different value than the original raw material (bauxite in the case of aluminum). For aluminum production, the conversion costs of processing recaptured waste will be *less* than processing bauxite. In cases such as this, it will be necessary to determine the cost savings of not having to process an appropriate amount of raw materials to achieve the same results as processing the recaptured scrap. This cost saving would then be assigned to the recaptured material and thus reduces the loss.

Summary

Spoilage can be a significant cost and needs to be controlled carefully. In a competitve market a firm cannot expect to recover excessive spoilage through increased sales prices. Even in a noncompetitive market, business ethics suggest that the customer should not be charged for avoidable waste. As suggested throughout this chapter, unavoidable waste is a legitimate cost of production. However, in making the judgment as to what is unavoidable, accountants and managers must be careful. A close and critical evaluation of the production and supporting processes needs to be made in order to ensure that we really know what is unavoidable. A good starting point for making the judgment might be to ask the question, "If the sales price is cost plus profit, would I be willing to pay for this loss if I were the customer?"

In this chapter you should have learned how to account for normal and abnormal spoilage under each of the basic accounting systems. Further, the problems of accounting for shrinkage, rework costs, scrap values, and recycling were explored. It has not been feasible to discuss every possible situation but the ones considered here should provide you with the principles on which to develop your own solutions.

Now terms introduced and discussed in this chapter with which you should be familiar include:

Spoilage
Waste
Abnormal spoilage
Normal spoilage
Omission method of accounting for normal spoilage
Recognition and reassignment method of accounting for normal spoilage
Shrinkage
Accretion
Rework
Scrap value
Recycling

SELF-STUDY PROBLEM. Assume that a firm produces only one product. Its assembly and packing department adds material at the beginning of the process and conversion costs uniformly throughout the process. A quality control inspection is made when production is 75% complete in the assembly and packing department. The company uses process cost accounting and the recognition and reassignment method for normal spoilage accounting. The following data are available for the current month:

Unit data

Beginning inventory—layer 1 (40% complete)	5,000
Beginning inventory—layer 2 (80% complete)	8,000
Ending inventory—layer 1 (70% complete)	2,000
Ending inventory—layer 2 (90% complete)	3,000
Units started	40,000
Normally spoiled units	1,000
Abnormally spoiled units	1,500

Cost data

Beginning inventory—layer 1		
Material	$11,000	
Conversion cost	$11,000	$ 22,000

Beginning inventory—layer 2		
Material	$15,000	
Conversion cost	33,000	
Normal spoilage	1,100	49,100
Materials added this period		80,000
Conversion costs added this period		215,375

Required:

1. Assume the modified FIFO equivalent unit method is used. Prepare a process cost report.
2. Assume the weighted average equivalent unit method is used. Prepare a process cost report.

Solution to Self-Study Problem

1. The complete solution to part 1 is contained in Exhibit 8.6. The following comments will help you understand the solution.

   Schedule A

   1. Note that the inventory is at different stages of completion and each is listed separately.
   2. The percentage completion for the spoiled units is the point at which they are inspected and determined to be defective.
   3. The units finished must be forced so that the units accounted for add to 53,000.

Exhibit 8.6   Self-Study Problem Solution to Part I

A. Units to be accounted for	
Beginning inventory (40%)	5,000
Beginning inventory (80%)	8,000
Started	40,000
	53,000
Units accounted for	
Ending inventory (70%)	2,000
Ending inventory (90%)	3,000
Finished (forced)	45,500
Normal spoilage (75%)	1,000
Abnormal spoilage (75%)	1,500
	53,000
B. Costs to be accounted for	
Beginning inventory—layer 1 ($11,000 + $11,000)	$ 22,000
Beginning inventory—layer 2 ($15,000 + $33,000 + $1,100)	49,100
Material	80,000
Conversion costs	215,375
Total	$366,475

C. Equivalent units and unit costs

	Material	Conversion Costs
Beginning inventory—layer 1	-0-	3,000
Beginning inventory—layer 2	-0-	1,600
Started and finished (45,500 − 5,000 − 8,000)	32,500	32,500
Ending inventory—layer 1	2,000	1,400
Ending inventory—layer 2	3,000	2,700
Normal spoilage	1,000	750
Abnormal spoilage	1,500	1,125
Equivalent units	40,000	43,075
Current costs	$80,000	$215,375
Cost per unit	$2.00	$5.00

D. Normal spoilage

Cost

Material 1,000 × $2	$2,000	
Conversion costs 750 × $5	3,750	$5,750

Allocation percentages

Finished goods

Beginning inventory—layer 1	5,000		
Beginning inventory—layer 2	-0-		
Started and finished	32,500	37,500	92.59%
Ending inventory—layer 1		-0-	
Ending inventory—layer 2		3,000	7.41
		40,500	100.00%

E. Cost assignment

To finished goods

Beginning inventory—layer 1

Prior period costs	$22,000	
Cost to complete		
Conversion costs 3,000 × $5	15,000	$ 37,000

Beginning inventory—layer 2

Prior period costs	$49,100	
Cost to complete		
Conversion costs 1,600 × $5	8,000	57,100
Started and finished 32,500($2 + $5)		227,500
Normal spoilage 0.9259($5,750)		5,324
Total		$326,924

Ending inventory—layer 1

Material 2,000 × $2	$4,000	
Conversion costs 1,400 × $5	7,000	11,000

Ending inventory—layer 2

Material 3,000 × $2	$ 6,000	
Conversion costs 2,700 × $5	13,500	
Normal spoilage 0.0741($5,750)	426	19,926

Abnormal spoilage

Material 1,500 × $2	$ 3,000	
Conversion costs 1,125 × $5	5,625	8,625
		$366,475

Schedule B

Since FIFO is being used all costs assigned to this period's beginning inventory, including normal spoilage cost, would remain attached to those units.

Schedule C

1. Note that in computing the started and finished units all units contained in the beginning inventory were deducted from the units finished. In the case of layer 1, this assumes that all 5,000 units were finished (the conventional assumption) regardless of whether they were.
2. Since the recognition and reassignment approach is to be used in accounting for normal spoilage, the equivalent units for normal spoilage have been included.

Schedule D

1. First, the normal spoilage cost is determined using the equivalent units and the unit costs all of which are determined in schedule C.
2. To assign the normal spoilage cost, allocation ratios must be derived. All *good units* passing the inspection point *this period* should share the cost.
3. Layer 1 of the beginning inventory passed the inspection point this period. Because of the assumption in computing started and finished units all 5,000 units have to be put into the allocation base.
4. Layer 2 of the beginning inventory did not pass the inspection point this period.
5. All units started and finished this period had to pass the inspection point.
6. The first ending inventory layer has not yet been inspected. Layer 2 has.

Schedule E

1. The cost of finished goods would include the completed cost of both beginning inventory layers, the cost of the units started and finished, and a percentage of normal spoilage cost. Both the percentage and the normal spoilage cost were computed in schedule D.
2. Note that ending inventory layer 2 was allocated a share of the normal spoilage cost.
3. Note the computation of the cost of the abnormal spoilage.

2. Exhibit 8.7 contains the solution to part 2. Comments follow.

Schedule B

1. Since this is the weighted average method the costs of the beginning inventories must be pooled with the current costs.
2. Note the column labeled "Spoilage." The normal spoilage cost assigned last period to layer 2 is placed in the spoilage column. This is added to the current normal spoilage cost (in Schedule D) and the total normal spoilage is then allocated to the appropriate units.

Schedule C

1. Remember that with the weighted average method all units finished, regardless of when they were started, are included in the equivalent units.

Schedule D

1. Again, note the cost computation. Normal spoilage costs carried forward in the beginning inventory are added to the current normal spoilage to arrive at the total. The current normal spoilage is computed using the equivalent units and unit cost data in section D.

Exhibit 8.7   Self-Study Problem Solution to Part 2

A. Same as Schedule A in Exhibit 8.6

B. Costs to be accounted for:

	Material	Conversion Costs	Spoilage	Total
Beginning inventory				
Layer 1	$ 11,000	$ 11,000		$ 22,000
Layer 2	15,000	33,000	$1,100	49,100
Current	80,000	215,375	*	295,375
Total	$106,000	$259,375	$1,100	$366,475

*Computed in Schedule D.

C. Equivalent units and unit costs

	Material	Conversion Costs
Finished	45,500	45,500
Ending inventory—layer 1	2,000	1,400
Ending inventory—layer 2	3,000	2,700
Normal spoilage	1,000	750
Abnormal spoilage	1,500	1,125
Total	53,000	51,475
Costs	$106,000	$259,375
Cost per unit	$2.00	$5.0388

D. Normal spoilage

Cost		
From prior period		$1,100
Current		
Material 1,000 × $2		2,000
Conversion costs 750 × 5.0388		3,779
Total		$6,879
Allocation percentages		
Finished	45,500	93.8%
Ending inventory—layer 2	3,000	6.2
Total	48,500	100.00%

E. Cost assignment

Finished goods		
Direct cost 45,500 × ($2.00 + $5.0388)		$320,268
Normal spoilage 0.938(6,879)		6,453
Total		$326,721
Ending inventory—layer 1		
Material 2,000 × $2	$4,000	
Conversion costs 1,400 × $5.0388	7,054	11,054
Ending inventory—layer 2		
Material 3,000 × $2	$ 6,000	
Conversion costs 2,700 × $5.0388	13,605	
Normal spoilage 0.062(6,879)	426	20,031
Abnormal spoilage		
Material 1,500 × $2	$ 3,000	
Conversion costs 1,125 × $5.0388	5,669	8,669
Total		$366,475

2. Consider the allocation percentages. Since the costs of the beginning inventory, including normal spoilage, are repooled under the weighted average method, then all units finished during the period should share in the normal spoilage cost.
3. Any ending inventory units that have passed the inspection point should also share in the normal spoilage cost.

References

Hayes, Robert H. "Why Japanese Factories Work," *Harvard Business Review* (July–August 1981): 57–66.

Kaplan, Robert S. "Measuring Manufacturing Performance: A New Challenge for Managerial Accounting Research," *The Accounting Review* (October 1983): 686–705.

Problems

8-1. Basic Problem Covering Spoilage in a Process Cost System. In its Department II, the Belanger Company has prepared the following data for April 19x1:

Beginning inventory	4,000
Units started	40,000
Units to account for	44,000
Units finished	36,000
Ending inventory	6,000
Normal spoilage	2,000
Units accounted for	44,000

The company uses process cost accounting and accounts for normal spoilage by computing its cost and then reassigning it to the appropriate good units. Department II adds material X as soon as the partially completed products are transferred from Department I. Material Y is added at the midpoint of production. An inspection is made when production is 75% complete. The normal spoilage cost for the current period has been computed to be:

Department I cost	2,000 × $5.00	$10,000
Material X	2,000 × $2.95	5,900
Material Y	2,000 × $9.00	18,000
Conversion costs	1,500 × $4.00	6,000
		$39,900

Required:

1. Assuming the beginning inventory was 90% complete at the beginning of the period and the ending inventory was 80% completed, assign the normal spoilage cost. Assume the modified FIFO method is used.
2. Assuming the beginning inventory was 90% complete at the beginning of the period and the ending inventory was 50% complete, assign the normal spoilage cost. Assume the modified FIFO method is used.
3. If the normal spoilage had a scrap value indicate how you would account for it in the context of this problem.

8-2. A Basic Problem with Spoilage in Process Costing. The May Company produces its product in a one-step operation. Material A is added at the beginning of the process, and packing supplies are used at the end of the process. Spoilage is detected when production is 3/5 complete. During March enough material was started to complete 12,150 units. Normal spoilage is accounted for by the *omission method*. The *FIFO method* is used. Following is an incomplete work in process account.

Work in Process			
Beginning inventory (2,000, 1/4)	5,000	To finished goods (10,000 units)	
Material A	23,000	Normal spoilage (650 units)	
Packing supplies	11,000	Ending inventory (3,000, 1/3)	
Conversion costs	32,400		
	71,400		

Required:

1. Prepare the process cost report.
2. Assume the spoilage had a scrap value of $1.00 per unit (due to its material content only; that is, no value is obtained from conversion) and is to be inventoried at its sale value. What is the cost of the ending work in process under these conditions?

8-3. Examination of Treatment of Spoilage in a Variety of Cases. The following work in process account reflects the operations of the Dauer Company's Department I for April 19x2:

Department I			
Inventory, 4/1/x2 (4,000 units)	28,000	To Department II (20,000 units)	
Material	36,000	Normal spoilage (2,000 units)	
Conversion costs	203,700	Inventory, 4/30/x2 (2,000 units)	

All material is added at the beginning of the process. The beginning inventory was 50% complete with respect to conversion costs at April 1. The $28,000 of cost consists of $8,000 for material and $20,000 for conversion. The ending inventory is 70% complete with respect to conversion.

The recognition and reassignment method is used to account for spoilage, and the modified FIFO method is used to account for inventories.

Required:

1. Assume that spoilage is detected when production is 80% complete. What is the cost of the units transferred to Department II?
2. Assume that spoilage is detected when production is 60% complete. What is the cost of the units transferred to Department II?

3. Assume that spoilage is detected when production is 40% complete and that the beginning inventory cost was $31,000 (including $8,000 for materials, $20,000 for conversion, and $3,000 for normal spoilage). What is the cost of the units transferred to Department II?

8-4. Variety of Spoilage Cases with Weighted Average. Reconsider problem 8-3 but assume that the weighted average method is used to account for inventories. Retaining the assumption about the method of accounting for spoilage repeat the requirements of problem 8-3.

8-5. Completing a Process Cost Report When There Is Spoilage. The PKL Company uses weighted average process costing to account for its product. It typically experiences some spoilage and occasionally some abnormal spoilage. In producing the product material is needed at the start of processing and conversion costs are incurred continuously throughout processing. An inspection is made when processing is 80% complete. Units failing inspection are removed from the production line. Following is schedule A of PKL's current process cost report.

A. Units schedule
   Beginning inventory
      Layer 1 (40% complete)   5,000
      Layer 2 (90% complete)   3,000
   Started   42,000
      Total   50,000
   Ending inventory
      Layer 1 (30% complete)   2,000
      Layer 2 (90% complete)   1,000
   Finished   46,200
   Normal spoilage   500
   Abnormal spoilage   300
   Total   50,000

Required:

Assume that normal spoilage is accounted for by the method of recognition and reassignment and that the costs to be accounted for are as follows:

	Material	Conversion Costs	Spoilage	Total
Beginning inventory				
Layer 1	$ 14,000	$ 13,000	0	$ 27,000
Layer 2	8,400	17,550	$250	26,200
Current	127,600	259,490	——	387,090
Total	$150,000	$290,040	$250	$440,290

Finish the process cost report.

8-6. Process Costing When There Are Two Inspection Points. CB Company uses process costing to account for one of its products, JAS, that makes exclusive use of Department ASOR. Conversion costs are incurred uniformly throughout Department ASOR. Product

JAS needs two raw materials, X and Z. Material X is put in at the beginning of processing in Department ASOR and material Z when processing is 55% complete. Since material Z is expensive an inspection is done before it is added. Another inspection is made before product JAS is packaged for sale.

Inspection #1 is done when processing is 50% complete. At normal efficiencies, 2% of the units inspected at station #1 are found to be defective and removed from the production line. When spoilage exceeds this percentage the excess is accounted for as abnormal spoilage.

Inspection #2 is done when processing is 90% complete. The normal failure rate at this station is 1% and amounts in excess of this are also accounted for as abnormal spoilage.

At the beginning of the current period, two layers of product JAS were in process:

Beginning WIP		
Layer 1 (20% complete)		4,000 units
Cost		
Material X	$ 7,900	
Conversion	$ 3,300	$11,200
Layer 2 (70% complete)		2,000 units
Cost		
Material X	$ 3,950	
Material Z	17,000	
Conversion	5,775	$26,725

During the current period 56,000 additional units were started into production.

The good units finished during the period totaled 56,030. The ending WIP inventory of JAS consisted of 3,000 units, 60% complete. The inspector at station #1 informs you that her crew rejected a total of 2,000 units during the current period.

Department ASOR's current costs of production include:

Material X	$108,460
Material Z	516,870
Conversion costs	225,560

The ASOR department uses modified FIFO and accounts for normal spoilage by the method of omission.

Required:

Prepare the process cost report for Department ASOR.

8-7. Comprehensive Process Cost Problem with Spoilage. The Palmer Company has two producing departments. Part #X2L is produced in Department A and is used in Department B. As the parts are completed in Department A, they are immediately transferred to Department B where they are held in inventory until they are needed. Until needed they are accounted for in a separate parts inventory account.

To make one unit of finished product, the production process in Department B is as follows: two units of raw material X are put in at the beginning of the process. When the processing is 50% complete one unit of X2L is added. Two additional units of X2L are added when the processing is 75% complete. Labor and overhead costs are incurred evenly throughout the process.

It is normally expected that some of the X2L parts are broken in assembly. In addition to this, it is normal that some of the finished units test unacceptable at the end of process B and are scrapped. However, during the current period an abnormal industrial accident caused 12,000 potential finished units to be destroyed when they were 70% complete.

The beginning work-in-process inventory contains 5,000 potential finished units, 25% complete. These units had $11,000 of material X cost and $5,000 of conversion costs assigned to them. There were 13,000 units of X2L on hand at the beginning of the period and they cost $12,000.

During the current period 160,000 units of X2L costing $150,000 were transferred from Department A. The cost of the 112,000 units of material X used was $107,000. The 112,000 units represented 56,000 potential units started. The labor and overhead cost totaled $262,000.

During the period 40,000 finished units were transferred to the warehouse. The ending work in process contained 7,000 units, 4,000 of which were 80% complete and 3,000 units which were 60% complete. The ending X2L inventory contains 16,000 units and are from the 160,000 units transferred into Department B during the current period.

Required:

Assuming normal spoilage is accounted for by the method of omission, prepare a process cost statement for Department B. The weighted average method is used.

8-8. Working Backward To Determine Needed Information. You are the controller for the Weaver Company. One of your staff accountants prepared a cost assignment schedule for the March activities of Department I. You know the FIFO method was used. Following is his report:

Finished production			
Beginning inventory, 5,000 units,			
partially complete* as to material,			
40% complete as to conversion:			
Prior period costs:			
Material		$ 10,800	
Conversion		3,350	
Total		$ 14,150	
Cost to complete:			
Material	$ 2,000		
Conversion	9,000	11,000	
Completed cost of beginning inventory		$ 25,150	
Started and finished (20,000 units)		100,000	$125,150
Ending inventory (4,000 units)			
Material†		$ 4,000	
Conversion†		3,000	7,000
Abnormal spoilage (1,000 units)			
Material†		$ 2,000	
Conversion†		1,500	3,500
Total costs accounted for			$135,650

*This is less than 100% but the staff accountant forgot to include the percentage.

†Percentage completion was not provided by the staff accountant.

Required:

1. Determine the cost of material added to the process during the current period.
2. Determine the conversion costs added to the process during the current period.
3. Compute the equivalent production figures for the weighted average method.
4. Compute the unit costs for material and conversion costs if the weighted average method is to be used.

8-9. Spoilage and Weighted Average Process Costing. The Quacker Company produces Trubles in a single process. In this process three units of material A are processed and added to two units of B in order to make one Truble. Material A is all put in at the beginning of the process, and material B is added when the processing is 75% complete.

There is an inspection made when the production is 50% complete and it has been found that normally 5% of the units *passing the inspection point* are defective. Occasionally spoilage exceeds 5%, and defective units in excess of 5% are accounted for as abnormal spoilage.

At October 1, the in process inventory consisted of 300 potential Trubles that were 1/3 complete. They had $3,000 of material A cost and $800 of conversion costs assigned to them. The October 31 in-process inventory has 500 units and was 40% complete. The following costs were charged to production during October:

Material A (30,000 units)	$110,300
Material B (18,000 units)	18,000
Conversion costs	85,600
Total	$213,900

During October 9,000 units were finished. The Quacker Company uses the *weighted average method* of accounting for its inventories. Normal spoilage is accounted for by the recognition and reassignment method.

Required:

Prepare the process cost report.

8-10. Process Costing; Spoilage with Recovery Value. The O.I. Quit Company produces product XYZ in a two-step process. Raw material A is put in at the beginning of the *melting* process. Then the units are transferred to the *forming* process where material B is added at the halfway point. *One unit of XYZ requires 1/2 pound of melted A.* Due to the nature of raw material A there is some breakage in the forming process. However, material A can be reused; thus, any breakage is returned to raw material inventory and reused in the melting process. This spoilage is detected when forming is 75% complete and is immediately removed from production. When the breakage is remelted, material B is cooked out as a waste ingredient.

Due to the nature of the production process as just described, the spoilage (both normal and abnormal) has value. Thus the company transfers the spoilage back to raw material inventory at a value measured by the average cost of raw material A transferred to forming during the current period. No conversion costs (of either process) or material B costs are included in this value since they must be incurred again when the material is reprocessed. The latter costs are handled as in conventional spoilage cases. Assume FIFO is used in both processes.

Data for the melting process are as follows:

Quantity schedule		
Beginning inventory (40% complete)		10,000 pounds
Started		40,000
Pounds to be accounted for		50,000
Transferred to forming		46,000
Ending inventory (50% complete)		4,000
Pounds accounted for		50,000
Cost to be accounted for		
Beginning inventory		
Material	$20,000	
Conversion	4,200	$ 24,200
Material added		80,000
Conversion		66,000
Total		$170,200

Following are some data regarding the forming process:

1. Beginning inventory—8,000 units of XYZ, 75% complete, $40,000.
2. Units finished—80,000.
3. Ending inventory—8,000 units, 25% complete.
4. Normal spoilage—8,000 units
5. Current costs: material B, $91,200; conversion, $158,000.

Required:

1. Prepare the process cost report for the melting process. The unit of measurement is pounds. Due to the nature of the recovery value of spoilage, it is recommended that the material A cost be maintained separately from conversion costs throughout this and all subsequent departments.
2. Prepare a process cost report for the forming process. Production activity is measured in units of XYZ. Assume the beginning inventory was completed without spoilage. You will need to compute the scrap value of material A. Normal spoilage is accounted for by the omission method.

8-11. Establishing Standards When There Is Spoilage: One of the staff accountants of the Martinez Company was given the assignment to develop the standards for one of its products. The product requires processing in two departments, A and B. Material X is added at the beginning of processing in Department A and material Y at the beginning of Department B's process. Variable costing is used. You are reviewing the standard costs per unit of each department's output, which are presented as follows:

Department A

Material X (2 units @ $4)	$ 8
Labor (3 hours @ $7)	21
Variable overhead (3 hours @ $5)	15
	$44

Department B

A's output (2 units @ $44)	$ 88
Material Y (3 units @ $2)	6
Labor (4 hours @ $10)	40
Variable overhead (4 hours @ $6)	24
	$158

Upon questioning the staff accountant you find that normal spoilage was not considered in these standards. Spoilage is detected by an inspection that takes place when processing is 75% complete in Department B. It is normal for 3% of the units inspected to be defective.

Required:

1. Assuming the spoilage has no recovery value, prepare a schedule of adjusted standards that reflect the spoilage in quantity allowances for material and labor hours.
2. Assuming that the spoilage can be recycled to recover material X, prepare a schedule of adjusted standards. Material X's recovery value is equal to its original cost.

8-12. Spoilage in a Standard Cost System. Arlene Company has been having some problems controlling the costs of producing one of its products, ZIP. In developing the standards for ZIP the only factor considered was the quantity of material and labor actually needed for a unit of ZIP. There was no consideration given to the usual and unavoidable spoilage that occurs in the production process. The standards that have been used are as follows:

Direct material	5 units @ $ 7	$ 35
Direct labor	10 hours @ $12	120
Overhead	10 hours @ $20	200
Total		$355

Considering several opinions from the involved managers it is reasonable to expect ZIP to be spoiled at a rate of 15% due to its peculiar characteristics. The spoilage can be detected when processing is 80% complete. Production managers have continually complained that this fact is ignored in computing the variances for which they are responsible.

For example, in January of the current year production started 10,000 units of ZIP and finished 8,500 good units. There were no beginning or ending WIP inventories. The variance report indicated an unfavorable material quantity variance of $52,500 and an unfavorable efficiency variance of $144,000. Production claims they were not that inefficient. The actual material issued totaled 50,000 units and the actual labor hours employed amounted to 97,000. All material is added at the beginning of the process and labor is added uniformly.

Required:

1. Consider January's results.
   a. Show how the two variances reported in January were derived.
   b. Evaluate production's claim and recompute the standards and variances if you deem it necessary.
2. Now assume that January's results were identical to those reported above except that only 8,000 good units were produced. What would you report as the material quantity and labor efficiency variance?

3. Suppose that in February another 10,000 units were started (no beginning WIP inventory) and that 1,000 units, 60% complete, were still in process at the end of the month. Assume that the good units produced totaled 7,650. Actual material used amounted to 50,000 units and labor totaled 93,300 hours. What would you report as the material quantity and labor efficiency variance?

8-13. Alternatives for Incorporating Spoilage into Standards. The Flanagan Company produces a single product, SO. Product SO is such that is impossible to avoid spoilage in production. The spoilage cannot be detected until all production is complete. The average spoilage rate is equal to 10% of inspected production. If spoilage is *not* incorporated into the allowances, product SO requires 2.7 pounds of material and 1.8 hours of labor. The firm normally operates at a practical capacity of 100,000 labor hours producing 50,000 *good* units of product SO.

Material will cost $10 per pound and labor $8 per hour. Exclusive of any of the material and labor contained in spoilage, the variable overhead at full capacity is budgeted at $677,500. The accounting system is a standard variable costing system.

Required:

1. Assume the spoilage is to be accounted for by increasing the material and labor allowances on a good unit to include the loss of resources on spoilage. Prepare a schedule presenting the standard cost of one unit of SO.
2. Assume the spoilage is to be included in the variable overhead rate. Prepare a schedule presenting the standard cost of one unit of SO.
3. Assume that during the current year, 50,000 good units were produced, 150,000 pounds of material were purchased and used, and labor hours totaled 100,000. Further, assume that material cost $10 per pound, labor $8 per hour, and variable overhead (exclusive of spoilage) totaled $677,500. Prepare comparative entries for the month using (a) the standards determined in part 1, and (b) the standards determined in part 2.
4. Assume the same facts as in part 3 except that the output was 49,000 units. This means the spoilage rate was above normal. Prepare comparative entries using the two sets of standards.

8-14. Extension of Problem 8-13 to Multiple Products. Reconsider problem 8-13, but now assume Flanagan can produce product K in addition to product SO. Product K is also subject to spoilage that, as is the case with SO, cannot be detected until all processing is complete. The average rate of spoilage is 5% for product K. Exclusive of spoilage, product K requires 3.8 pounds of material and 4.75 hours of labor. Product K is budgeted at 10,000 good units and product SO at 25,000 good units. This budget exhausts the labor capacity and is the optimal combination based upon the projections of contribution margins and available resources.

Required:

1. Assume the spoilage is to be accounted for by increasing the material and labor allowances of the good units to include the loss of resources on spoilage. Prepare a schedule showing the standard cost of one unit of each of the products.
2. Assume the spoilage is to be included in the variable overhead rate. Prepare a schedule presenting the standard cost of one unit of each of the products.
3. Why are your standard costs in part 1 different from those in part 2? Which set of standards would you prefer from a theoretical standpoint? Why?

8-15. Spoilage with Scrap in Standard Cost System. Reconsider the Gilman Company problem as modified on pages 278–280 in the scrap subsection. During May, 41,467 good units were produced. The actual material purchased and used totaled 89,000 pounds, and the acquisition price was $9.20 per pound. The scrap recovered during May amounted to 6,069 pounds, and it was sold for $2.35 per pound.

Required:

Prepare all entries for materials and scrap during May.

8-16. Spoilage in a Job Order System. The Oriole Company produces a variety of products in lots of a predetermined optimal size. The nature of the materials and products are such that spoilage is unavoidable. During 19x1 and 19x2 material and labor prices have remained constant at $8 and $6, respectively. The prices are expected to be the same during 19x3.

Following are the data from 19x1 and 19x2. A review of those results indicated that material wastage, idle time, and spoiled production were all at the rate that was expected.

	19x1	19x2
Material purchased and issued	100,000 units	150,000 units
Direct-labor hours (including idle time and time spent on spoiled production	200,000 hours	250,000 hours
Material spoilage (including content in spoiled production)	1,000 units	1,500 units
Idle time and time spent on spoiled production	10,000 hours	12,500 hours
Overhead cost (excluding material spoilage and unproductive labor time)		
Material ordering and receiving	$ 69,900	$ 74,850
Material handling	128,600	174,100
Material storeroom	140,000	140,000
Fringe benefits	332,500	$380,000
Supervision	285,000	285,000
Depreciation	570,000	570,000
Indirect labor	190,000	237,500
Indirect supplies	95,000	118,750
Other overhead	177,500	186,250

The Oriole Company uses two overhead rates; one for material related items and one for items whose benefits are related to labor (including depreciation and indirect supplies). At practical capacity the current material-processing capacity is 200,000 units yearly and direct-labor capacity is 300,000 hours. Both of these figures are before wastage and spoilage.

Required:

1. Assuming the Oriole Company wants to include normal spoilage in overhead, determine the two overhead rates to be used during 19x3. Show separate components for fixed and variable costs.

2. During April 19x3, job #707 was processed. The engineering department indicated that if there was no wastage, 9,800 units of material and 19,000 hours of labor would be needed. Upon completion it was discovered that 10,000 units of material and 20,000 hours of labor were consumed. The differences were considered normal. Prepare the entries for this job to reflect the total material and labor used and to apply the overhead.
3. During May 19x3, job #34 was processed. The engineering estimates for this job included 5,000 units of material and 10,000 hours of labor. Actual consumption included 6,000 units of material and 11,500 labor hours. Abnormal conditions caused 500 units of the extra material and 500 extra labor hours. Prepare the entries for this job to reflect the total material and labor used and to apply the overhead.

8-17. Problem When There Is Shrinkage. The Stone Company manufactures product Neyt from a liquid substance called Voda. Process 2 is an evaporation process in which the Voda loses 30% of its original weight at a uniform rate. Occasionally there is some abnormal spoilage that can be detected at the midway point of process 2. When discovered, the damaged goods are immediately removed from the process. Assume that the beginning inventory is completed without abnormal spoilage. Following is the process-2 account for March:

Process 2

Beginning inventory		To process 3 (3,150 pounds)
(540 pounds,		Ending inventory (720 pounds,
1/3 complete)	3,400	2/3 complete)
From process 1 (5,000		
pounds)	17,500	
Direct labor	15,000	
Overhead	20,000	
	55,900	

Required:

Assuming that the weights are the actual weights at the specified point in the process, prepare a process cost report using FIFO.

8-18. Comprehensive Problem Involving Spoilage in a Standard Cost System. The Singleton Company is a very advanced company and has entirely converted its production processes to mechanical operations. The wages and salaries of the few personnel involved are considered indirect costs.

Two products are produced, A and Z. Both require processing in each of two departments. The standards are as follows:

	Product A		Product Z	
	Department I	*Department II*	*Department I*	*Department II*
Material @ $5.00	2 units*	0	4 units	0
Packing cartons @ $2.00	0	1	0	1
Machine hours	4 hours*	2 hours	3 hours	1 hour

*The engineering estimate called for material content of 1.9 units and machine hours of 3.8. However, an inspection is made at the end of production in Department I. Even with *good performance,* 5% of the units fail inspection and must be destroyed at no salvage value. Thus, the standards have been adjusted so that the good output absorbs the resources wasted on the units failing inspection.

Separate overhead rates are used in Departments I and II. The divisor activities are measured in machine hours and are 200,000 and 100,000 hours for Departments I and II, respectively. In Department I, one eight-hour shift equates to 100,000 machine hours on a yearly basis. The department normally operats two complete shifts, but in a given year the activities may entail more or less than two shifts. The only cost affected by this is the supervisory salaries (it is a step-fixed cost).

A flexible manufacturing overhead budget for Department I is provided as follows:

	100,000 hours	*200,000 hours*
Supervisory salaries (step-fixed)*	$ 50,000	$100,000
Depreciation	50,000	50,000
Power (semivariable)	100,000	150,000
Indirect supplies and labor (variable)	200,000	400,000
	$400,000	$700,000

*$50,000 for 0 to 100,000 hours; $100,000 for 100,001 to 200,000 hours.

For Department II the total fixed manufacturing overhead at divisor activity is $100,000 and the variable is $50,000.

Following is a schedule of units to account for, and the units accounted for during the current year:

	Department I		*Department II*	
	Product A	*Product Z*	*Product A*	*Product Z*
To account for				
Beginning inventory	0	0	0	1,000[a]
Units started	19,000	20,000	18,000	20,000
	19,000	20,000	18,000	21,000
Accounted for				
Transferred out	18,000	20,000	18,000	19,000
Failed inspection	1,000	0	0	0
Ending inventory	0	0	0	2,000[b]
	19,000	20,000	18,000	21,000

[a]40% completed with respect to machine hours at start of year; 100% completed with respect to prior department's cost.

[b]60% completed with respect to machine hours at end of year; 100% with respect to prior department's cost.

Actual data are itemized as follows:

	Department I	*Department II*
Materials purchased and used	116,100 @ $5.10	0
Packing cartons purchased and used	0	37,500 @ $2
Machine hours	130,000 hours	73,000 hours
Variable overhead	$331,000	$36,500
Fixed overhead	$205,000	$98,000

The company maintains *all* inventories at standard cost and transfers cost into work in process at complete standards.

Required:

1. Prepare a schedule of the *total* standard cost per unit for each product (that is, through both departments). Show subtotals for processing in each department. Show separate rates for fixed and variable overhead.
2. Prepare the entry to record the purchase of materials and packing cartons.
3. Prepare the entry to record the actual overhead incurred this period. (A separate overhead control account is maintained for each department.)
4. Prepare the entry to record the standard material and overhead costs transferred *into* Department I during the year and to record the material variances. Only one WIP— Department I account—is maintained and it serves as a control account over both products.
5. Prepare the entry to record the overhead and packing carton costs transferred *into* Department II during the year and to record the packing carton variances. Again, only one WIP—Department II account—is maintained and serves as a control account.
6. Prepare the entries transferring costs from Department I to Department II and from Department II to finished goods control.
7. Prepare the entry to close the balances of the manufacturing overhead accounts of Department I into the appropriate overhead variance accounts. You need *not* do this for Department II.
8. The foreman of Department I states, "I had no material quantity variance this period. I am allowed 1.9 units per unit of A and 4 units per unit of Z. This adds to 116,100 units, which equals the quantity used." She presents the following:

A 19,000 units started 1.9   36,100
B 20,000 units started at 4.0   <u>80,000</u>
                                     <u>116,100</u>

If you do not agree, then explain to the foreman why you disagree.

CHAPTER 9

Allocation of Indirect Costs

Indirect costs have been defined previously as those that cannot be unequivocally traced to a given cost objective. In previous chapters, we have considered only one class of these costs: those departmental costs that are indirect with respect to the production of the department. However, some of the costs assigned to a given department may be indirect with respect to that department. We have not yet examined how costs that jointly benefit several departments will be assigned. In this chapter there will be a consideration of these additional issues in the accounting for indirect costs.

Many of the problem areas of accounting are due to the need to allocate. For example, in financial accounting the amount of depreciation recognized each year is the result of an allocation process: the allocation of the original cost to the time periods benefited. In cost accounting, the objectives of cost allocations are generally something other than a time period: products and departments, for example. This chapter will begin by considering how to allocate costs that are indirect to the various responsibility centers within the firm. Additionally, the concept of a service department, as opposed to a production department, will be introduced. The costs of operating a service department are indirect with respect to production departments and, in turn, create another allocation problem. Allocation methods for such cases will also be discussed in this chapter. The issues explored here have implications for overhead rate computations, and a section will be devoted to rate construction under these circumstances. Finally, there will be a brief consideration of the treatment of allocated costs for control purposes.

Need for and Types of Allocation

Like many other aspects of cost accounting, there are multiple purposes that may be served by the allocation process. Thus, it is possible that one allocation system may not adequately serve all possible uses. But in devising an allocation system it is necessary to give consideration to the possible uses *and* to cost effectiveness. Because of cost, it may not be possible to design an allocation system that is optimal for *all* uses. Some compromises have to be made, and as a result the accountant must guard against possible misuses by those who rely on accounting data. Also, the accountant must be alert for the possible need to revise a particular system. As data requirements change, procedures that were once considered cost ineffective may become justifiable. With this in mind, let us examine, in general, some of the needs for cost allocation.

A primary need for cost allocation is to determine inventory costs and, in turn, net income. As with the assignment of departmental costs to its output, this aspect of the cost allocation sytem should be designed to attach costs according to the benefits received by the cost objectives and/or commensurate with the level of costs caused by the objective.[1] Even if the *final* cost objectives for the cost allocations are the finished products, it usually will not be feasible to measure *directly* the benefit that the output will receive from certain costs. For example, the benefit that a given product receives from factory building depreciation is hard to measure directly. We are likely to achieve more defensible results if we first measure the benefit received by the departments sharing the building, then measure the interdepartmental benefits, and, finally, measure the benefit a given product received from the services of each of the producing departments.

A second need for cost allocations is to aid in the setting and evaluation of sales prices and in determining a cost for negotiated cost-plus contracts. Such contracts are typical in business relationships with government agencies. In fact, many of the rules of the Cost Accounting Standards Board establish limits on how such allocations may be made. The content of this chapter is within the framework of the CASB rules. Here, too, it will be found that benefit received is considered to be the preferred criterion for a proper allocation.

Third, planning and decision making can benefit from an allocation process. Indirect costs are not limited to fixed costs. Some costs may, in general, vary with the total volume of output. When making decisions, it is necessary to estimate the total cost impact of the various alternatives. If cost allocation schemes are carefully thought out with a view toward decision making, then some useful data may result from the allocation process. For decision-making purposes it is desirable to establish a cause-effect relationship. If such a relationship can be established and if benefit received is according to the causal relationship, then there will be congruence for the first three possible uses of an allocation system.

Finally, control processes can be enhanced by good allocation systems. That is, cost allocations may help to motivate managers to monitor these costs and to direct them toward certain corporate goals. It is easy to envision that inefficiency by one department may cause other departments to incur added costs. Good allocation systems will enhance the estimation of the *total* economic consequences of the inefficiency. As we will see later, however, cost allocations have the potential for creating havoc among departmental managers. Accountants can minimize the dysfunctional consequences by exercising vigilance over the usage of the data.

Before considering the specific techniques of cost allocation, it is helpful to develop an overview of the cost flows. You can follow this discussion with the aid of Exhibit 9.1. As costs are incurred, it is common to record them in functional (object-of-expenditure) accounts such as supervisory salaries, supplies, depreciation, and so forth. After this initial recording, the costs enter the allocation system

---

[1]See James M. Fremgen and Shu S. Liao, *The Allocation of Corporate Indirect Costs* (New York: National Association of Accountants, 1983), p. 48, for a confirmation of this intent in practice.

Exhibit 9.1   Flowchart of an Expanded Cost System

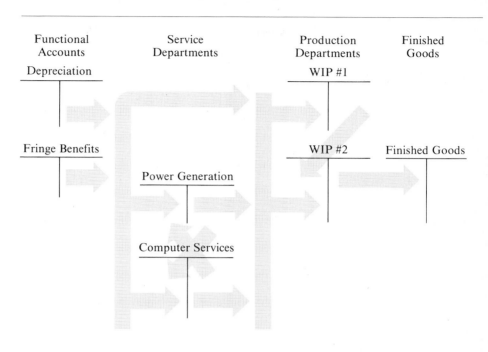

Functional Accounts	Service Departments	Production Departments	Finished Goods
Depreciation		WIP #1	
Fringe Benefits		WIP #2	Finished Goods
	Power Generation		
	Computer Services		

that has been designed to best serve the needs of the firm. The design of this system is centered around cost objectives: purposes for which cost data are desired. Production departments and final products are the two cost objectives that were the subjects of earlier chapters. However, there will generally be responsibility centers, known as **service departments,** that provide products and services consumed entirely within the firm. Controlling these activities is just as important as controlling the activities that are directly involved with the firm's marketable output. Examples of activities that might be the responsibility of service departments include power generation, material purchasing, material receiving, material handling, repair and maintenance, personnel services, and computer services.

Depending on the organizational structure of the firm's responsibility centers, a cost recorded in a functional (object-of-expenditure) account may either be directly traceable to a given department or require an allocation among several departments. In the next section some guiding principles and illustrations of this type of allocation will be provided.

Once allocations of the foregoing type are made, the accountant must then consider how the service activities are to be charged to the various users of the service departments. The costs of these services are only recoverable through the sales price of the final products. Through the financial accounting concept of matching efforts with accomplishments, accountants can justify the allocation of such costs to production departments and, in turn, to their outputs. If implemented properly, this process will also provide data for control and evaluation purposes. The user departments are, in effect, buying services from the providing departments and the users should be expected to account for the acquired services. Thus, a section of the chapter will be directed toward the special problems created by the need to allocate service department costs.

After the service department costs have been allocated, the total costs will be physically contained in the production department accounts. In the previous chapters, we have discussed how to proceed at this point. That is, the next step would be to allocate the costs to the units produced in each department.

In summary, the costing mechanics occur in the following steps:

1. Functional (object-of-expenditure) classification.
2. Allocation of functional accounts to service and production departments.
3. Service department allocation.
4. Allocation of production department costs to products.

With this general overview let us now examine the details of steps 2 and 3.

Allocation of Functional Accounts

Before becoming too involved in the allocation process, certain terminology should be clarified. Specifically, the idea of *cost pools* should be explored. The CASB defines an **indirect cost pool** as "a grouping of incurred costs identified with two or more cost objectives but not identified specifically with any final cost objective."[2] Although the CASB's rules are limited to certain negotiated government contracts, this definition is reflective of the way the cost pool concept is used in general cost accounting. It should be understood that an indirect cost pool may refer to a collection of costs that benefit two or more departments (service and/or production), to a particular department's costs, or to a subset of costs within a given department. One reason for pooling costs is that it facilitates the allocation process. However, certain requirements should be met.

Presumably, cost pools will be collections of homogeneous items. That is, the items will have something in common. If the homogeneous characteristic is appropriate, then one can justify giving each item in the pool similar treatment. Obviously, there are many possibilities for the common thread. For example, all of the costs of generating power have a common purpose. But the object of the cost *is not necessarily* the appropriate characteristic on which to construct pools for allocation purposes. For allocation purposes, a homogeneous indirect cost pool is one whereby each item in the pool has the same beneficial or causal relationship with the cost objectives to which the pool will be allocated. As will be seen later, it is not necessarily appropriate to allocate *all* of the costs of power, or any other service department, on the same basis.

---

[2]*Federal Register,* Vol. 38, No. 214, November 7, 1973, p. 30732.

A final term to be explained is **general factory overhead.** This is a term that is frequently used to refer to costs that benefit the several departments within the production area. Costs that are directly traceable to the factory but not to any specific department within the factory might include building depreciation, property taxes, property insurance, and general supervision.

The process of assigning the functional accounts to departments should, in general, proceed as follows: *To move something from T to T.*

1. Any costs that can be specifically associated with a given department can obviously be directly assigned. For example, the accounting system for indirect materials and indirect labor should indicate the department that actually utilized these resources.
2. The remaining items should be assigned according to some surrogate measure of causation and/or benefit. Those items that can be allocated on the same basis may be pooled together and allocated as a group. Exhibit 9.2 is a schedule of items that might fall into this category, along with some suggestions of possible allocation bases.

These ideas will be incorporated into an example later in the chapter.

Allocation of Service Department Costs

This section is devoted to a discussion of the issue of allocating service department costs. In some ways, this process of cost accounting parallels that of product costing. The major difference is that a service is being assigned a cost. A service, of course, does not have any physical properties.

After examining some general guidelines two problems are considered. The first is the issue of whether it is appropriate to allocate all of the costs of a service department using the same basis. Fixed and variable costs do not necessarily have homogeneous properties for allocation purposes. We explore why this is so and examine a preferred assignment method in a section on dual base distribution. Additionally, it is possible that service departments provide services to each other as well as to production departments. This is known as the reciprocal services

---

Exhibit 9.2   Representative Indirect Departmental Costs and Possible Allocation Bases

Item	*Possible Allocation Bases*
Building depreciation	Square footage, cubic footage
Heat and light	Cubic footage, square footage
Factory superintendency	Number of employees, total payroll, total labor hours
Base telephone cost	Number of telephones, number of employees
Insurance on building and contents	Sum of (1) pro rata share of building and (2) insurable value of equipment contained in department

problem, and there will be an examination of a variety of ways to allocate the costs of service departments under these circumstances.

GENERAL GUIDELINES. Three general guidelines should be considered in allocating service department costs. First, the allocation system should assign costs according to the *benefit received and/or the degree of causation.* In some cases, the allocation base may be obvious. For example, if power is produced internally by a service department and *metered* out to other departments, then prorating power costs according to the meter readings would be a reasonable approach. On the other hand, it may not be obvious what base should be used for allocating the cost of a personnel services department (to handle insurance claims, retirement counseling, and so forth). Number of employees per department might seem reasonable as an allocation base. However, one department may be more accident prone than another. If so, using the number of employees as the base for allocation will shift some of the costs caused by the accident-prone department to other departments. (This assumes that the variable cost of operating such a department is significant.) Under these circumstances, it may be necessary to consider the number of cases from each department as the allocation base. To do this implies that data would have to be collected concerning the home department of each employee who used personnel services. Even then, it might be argued that some cases require more time of the personnel service workers than others and/or that certain costs vary as a function of the number of cases while others vary as a function of the consultation time. From this scenario, it can be seen that selecting an allocation base entails a conflict between achievement of fairness and the cost of maintaining additional statistics. Exhibit 9.3 list various service departments and suggests some possible bases.

A second guideline for service department allocation is that *inefficiencies of the sevice department should not be passed through to the user departments.* From a costing standpoint, the inefficiently used resources provide no benefit to other departments or to the various outputs. Further, from a control standpoint, the allocation of inefficiencies may be dysfunctional. The user departments will not generally have authority over the department providing the service and they will be resentful about the implied responsibility for controlling the inefficiency. This guideline implies that standard costing should be used in service department accounting. Services should be charged at a standard rate, and differences between actual and standard should be isolated as variances of the service department.

Finally, the allocation system should be designed in such a way that the service department cost charged to one department is *independent of the level of activity of all other user departments.* The benefit received from a given function, as has been discussed before, is not dependent upon the total amount of service generated during a given period. Further, a department manager will find it hard to understand why he or she was charged a higher cost this month than last month when the utilization of the service department remained constant.

Exhibit 9.3   **Possible Allocation Bases for Service Departments**

Service	*Possible Allocation Bases**
Power department	Kilowatt hours used, number of machines
Repairs and maintenance	Number of machines, number of repair calls, repairman hours
Materials ordering	Direct material dollars, number of orders initiated
Materials receiving	Direct material dollars, number of orders, volume, weight
Materials handling	Direct material dollars, number of requisitions
Personnel services	Number of employees, number of cases
Engineering services	Direct labor hours, direct labor dollars

---

*To the extent that any of the services of these departments are provided to nonmanufacturing departments (such as sales or general administration), then some of their costs should be assigned to the nonmanufacturing areas. As with other nonmanufacturing costs, the portion of the service department costs assigned to the nonmanufacturing areas would be treated as period costs, not product costs.

DUAL BASE DISTRIBUTIONS. A service department will incur both fixed and variable costs in performing its functions. As with a production department, the fixed costs represent a capacity cost or a cost of being ready to serve. Presumably, a service department's capacity is geared to some type of normal or practical collective usage on the part of the user departments. On the other hand, its variable cost represents the cost of meeting the collective actual demand. If it is likely that the relative demand among the user departments will fluctuate over time, then using a single allocation base to distribute both the fixed and variable cost of the service department will violate the third guideline of the preceding section.

When fluctuating relative demand is a possiblity, then we can avoid the problems of costing services at different rates each period by using a **dual distribution base.** Stated simply, this means that fixed costs should be assigned based on the demand of the service department's output by each user department when the users operate at *capacity,* and the variable costs should be assigned according to the *actual service provided.* The dual base method would be needed in order to assign costs according to causation.

The specific base for fixed cost allocation should be established in a manner congruent with the planning of the service department's capacity. That is, there should be an estimate of the percentage of the constructed capacity that was provided to meet capacity levels of each user department. Of course, if all departments are simultaneously operating at capacity levels, then allocation of the fixed costs based

on actual usage would result in an appropriate assignment. Also, if all departments were operating at levels below normal activity but at *constant relative rates*
with respect to each other, then an allocation of the fixed costs according to actual
utilization rates would result in appropriate assignments. In short, for firms whose
departmental activities are generally synchronized, using a dual base is not necessary. This might be the case in assembly-line operations where all departments
tend to react the same way in any situation.

Of course variable costs should always be allocated according to actual usage
since they would be expected to fluctuate with usage. Thus, each user department
would be charged with a portion of these costs approximating the amount it caused
to be incurred.

As with standard variable (direct) costing, a dual-based system would require a
fixed-variable classification of costs. Doing this, of course, would also benefit the
planning and control processes. The possible benefits would have to be compared
with the cost of supporting such a system.

RECIPROCAL SERVICES.   When service departments provide **reciprocal services** to each other there will be additional allocation problems. Consider Exhibit
9.4. The service departments are denoted S_1, S_2, and S_3, and the production
departments as P_1 and P_2. Service department S_1 not only provides services to S_2
and S_3 but also is serviced by those two departments. Of course, after allocating
S_1's cost to S_2, S_3, P_1, and P_2, its account would contain a zero balance. But after
the costs of S_2 and S_3 are distributed, S_1's account would contain additional costs

Exhibit 9.4   Illustration of Reciprocal Services

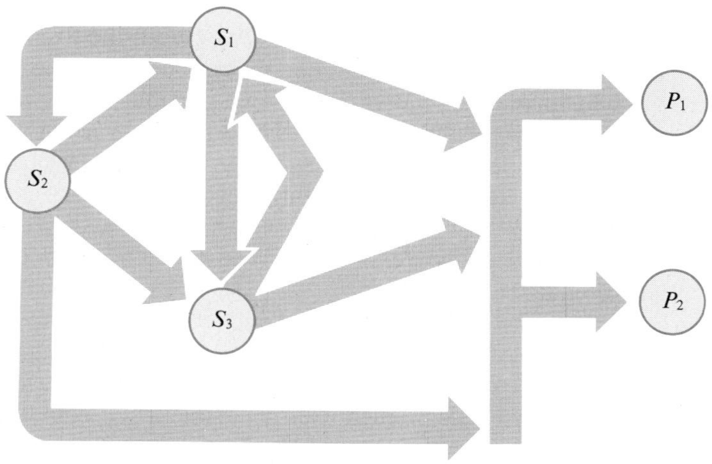

reflecting the services provided to the other two service departments. This process would continue in a circular fashion and would require several iterations to complete the assignment. There are three basic ways of making the allocation in order to avoid the iterative process. In this section we discuss the direct allocation method, the step method, and the method of reciprocal equations. To make the latter method more practical from a solution standpoint, a separate section is devoted to the matrix algebra approach of solving the reciprocal equations.

As a medium for illustrating each of these methods, consider the data in Exhibit 9.5 which represent the activities of May for the Sansing Company. The Sansing Company has the departmental structure of Exhibit 9.4. Assume that all departments operated at the normal levels planned for at the time the service departments' capacities were established. Thus, a single-based distribution will be appropriate in this case.

If a **direct allocation** method is used, then the allocation problems of reciprocity are avoided by *ignoring* the services provided to other service departments. That is, all service department costs will be directly assigned to the production departments only, and according to each *production department's* relatively usage of the service department. For example, Department S_1 provided 40,000 units of service to Department P_1 and 30,000 units to P_2. Thus, its cost of $92,400 will be allocated 4/7 to P_1 and 3/7 to P_2. Note that the services to S_2 and S_3 are ignored. Exhibit 9.6 contains the results of the direct allocation method.

The problem with the direct allocation method is that the cost of the ignored services to the other service departments may not be assigned according to the degree of causation. Consider Department S_1. The cost of the 30,000 units provided by S_1 to Departments S_2 and S_3 have, in effect, been assigned to the production departments at the rate of 4/7 and 3/7. In reality, the ignored service directly benefits the other service departments, which, in turn, served the production departments in proportions different from 4/7 and 3/7. This may produce undesirable results depending on how the data might be used and on the decision or control model's sensitivity to the data.

Exhibit 9.5   Sansing Company Report on Activities for May 19x1

| | Units of Service Acquired From | | | Costs |
| | Department S_1 | Department S_2 | Department S_3 | Prior to |
Department				Service Costs
S_1	0	20,000	45,000	$ 92,400
S_2	10,000	0	0	184,800
S_3	20,000	40,000	0	138,600
P_1	40,000	100,000	15,000	400,000
P_2	30,000	40,000	90,000	500,000
Total	100,000	200,000	150,000	$1,315,800

Exhibit 9.6   Sansing Company Allocation of Service Costs Via Direct Allocation for May 19x1

	Department S_1	Department S_2	Department S_3	Department P_1	Department P_2
Costs prior to allocation	$ 92,400	$184,800	$138,600	$400,000	$500,000
Allocation					
S_1 $(\frac{4}{7}, \frac{3}{7})^a$	(92,400)			52,800	39,600
S_2 $(\frac{10}{14}, \frac{4}{14})^a$		(184,800)		132,000	52,800
S_3 $(\frac{15}{105}, \frac{90}{105})^a$			(138,600)	19,800	118,800
Total	0	0	0	$604,600	$711,200

^{a}Allocation ratios to the production departments.

A second scheme that can be used is the **step method.** This method accounts for some of the reciprocal services, but not all. It is a system whereby some department is selected to be the first one allocated. A pro-rata share of the cost of the selected department should be allocated to the departments that it serviced. Then a second department is chosen. Its cost, including those allocated from the first department, would then be allocated to all departments it serviced except the one first allocated. This process is continued until all service costs have been assigned. Note that the allocations are done so that departments whose costs have been *previously* assigned do not absorb any costs of the department being allocated. In this way, the problems of reciprocity can be avoided.

There is more than one scheme for selecting the order in which the departments will be allocated. Suggestions consist of first allocating the department that serves the greatest number of other service departments or the one that provides the greatest collective percentage of output to other service departments. Any suggestion is somewhat arbitrary. Perhaps the latter will result in the smallest error, but that depends on the situation. Using this approach for the Sansing Company does not resolve the order of distribution since all three departments provided 30% of their total service to other service departments. Using the first approach eliminates S_3 but does not select between S_1 and S_2. In Exhibit 9.7 we have used the order S_1, S_2, S_3. Note that all four departments using S_1's services shared its cost. Further, note that S_1 was excluded from S_2's allocation and that the cost allocated from S_2 was $194,040, the original $184,800 plus the $9,240 of cost from S_1. Further, note that this method allocated more cost to Department P_2 than the direct allocation method and, of course, less to Department P_1.

Although more involved mathematically, the **method of reciprocal equations** simultaneously considers all of the services and is the technically correct method. In this approach a set of equations is formulated to solve for the total amount of

Exhibit 9.7   Sansing Company Allocation of Service Costs Via Step Method for May 19x1

	Department S_1	Department S_2	Department S_3	Department P_1	Department P_2
Costs prior to allocation	$ 92,400	$184,800	$138,600	$400,000	$500,000
Allocation					
S_1 (10, 20, 40, 30)^a	(92,400)	9,240	18,480	36,960	27,720
S_2 ($\frac{40}{180}, \frac{100}{180}, \frac{40}{180}$)^a	0	(194,040)	43,120	107,800	43,120
S_3 ($\frac{15}{105}, \frac{90}{105}$)^a	0	0	(200,200)	28,600	171,600
Total	0	0	0	$573,360	$742,440

^{a}The figures inside the parenthesis are the allocation ratios for computing the cost assignment to the respective departments.

cost of operating each of the service departments *after* all allocations have been made. Using the solution to these equations, we can then independently allocate each department to all user departments.

Let S_1, S_2, and S_3 by the *postallocation* costs for the three service departments. In expressing S_1, for example, it is $92,400 *plus* a share of the costs in Departments S_2 and S_3. Referring to Exhibit 9.5, it can be seen that S_1 should absorb 10% of S_2's cost (20,000 ÷ 200,000) and 30% of S_3's (45,000 ÷ 150,000). Thus, the equation for S_1 is:

$$S_1 = 92,400 + 0.10S_2 + 0.30S_3 \qquad (9\text{-}1)$$

In a similar manner determine equations for S_2 and S_3:

$$S_2 = 184,800 + 0.10S_1 \qquad (9\text{-}2)$$

$$S_3 = 138,600 + 0.20S_1 + 0.20S_2 \qquad (9\text{-}3)$$

The three equations must now be simultaneously solved for S_1, S_2, and S_3. Substituting equations (9-2) and (9-3) into (9-1) gives:

$$S_1 = 92,400 + 0.1(184,000 + 0.1S_1) \qquad (9\text{-}4)$$
$$+ 0.3(138,600 + 0.20S_1 + 0.20S_2)$$

Expanding the last two terms of (9-4) results in:

$$S_1 = 92,400 + 18,480 + 0.01S_1 + 41,580 \qquad (9\text{-}5)$$
$$+ 0.06S_1 + 0.06S_2$$

Combining terms and substituting the right-hand side of equation (9-2) for S_2 we have:

$$S_1 = 152,460 + 0.07S_1 + 0.06(184,800 + 0.10S_1) \qquad (9\text{-}6)$$

This reduces to:

$$S_1 = 152,460 + 0.07S_1 + 11,088 + 0.006S_1 \qquad (9\text{-}7)$$
$$= 163,548 + 0.076S_1$$

Thus:

$$0.924S_1 = 163,548 \qquad (9\text{-}8)$$
$$S_1 = 177,000$$

Now substituting the solution to S_1 into equation (9-2) gives the value of S_2:

$$S_2 = 184,800 + 0.10(177,000)$$
$$= 202,500$$

Finally, substituting the values of S_1 and S_2 into (9-3):

$$S_3 = 138,600 + 0.20(177,000) + 0.20(202,500)$$
$$= 214,500$$

Now the service department costs are allocated using the solutions to S_1, S_2, and S_3, which represent the amounts for each of the departments *after* the allocations have been made. Exhibit 9.8 contains the results. Note, for example, that $177,000, the solution to S_1, is the amount allocated out of Department S_1 and that the allocation percentages are according to the relative consumptions as given in Exhibit 9.5. Further, note that after the costs of S_2 and S_3 have been allocated, there is a zero balance in S_1. The results of the first two allocations are also in Exhibit 9.8 for ease in comparing the systems.

Exhibit 9.8   Sansing Company Allocation of Service Costs Via Reciprocal Equations for May 19x1

	Department S_1	Department S_2	Department S_3	Department P_1	Department P_2
Costs prior to allocation	$ 92,400	$184,800	$138,600	$400,000	$500,000
Allocations:					
S_1 (10, 20, 40, 30)[a]	(177,000)	17,700	35,400	70,800	53,100
S_2 (10, 20, 50, 20)[a]	20,250	(202,500)	40,500	101,250	40,500
S_3 (30, 0, 10, 60)[a]	64,350	0	(214,500)	21,450	128,700
Total	0	0	0	$593,500	$722,300
Total costs using the methods discussed earlier					
Direct allocation (from Exhibit 9.6)				$604,600	$711,200
Step allocation (from Exhibit 9.7)				$573,360	$742,440

[a]The percentage usage rates for assigning costs to the consuming departments.

≥ Reciprocal Allocations via Matrix Algebra

When there are many service departments with complex reciprocal relationships, the mechanics of solving the simultaneous equations are imposing. However, many firms have access to computer installations with software packages that can invert matrices. If you have access to a matrix inversion routine, then the reciprocal equations can be solved easily using matrix algebra. In this section we will discuss this approach but without getting involved with the mechanics of inverting a matrix.

To implement a matrix algebra solution it is necessary to put the reciprocal equations into a standard order. That is, all variables should be collected in an identical order on the left side of each equation. Rearranging equations (9-1), (9-2), and (9-3) into standard order we have:

$$1.00S_1 - 0.10S_2 - 0.30S_3 = 92,400$$

$$-0.10S_1 + 1.00S_2 + 0.00S_3 = 184,800$$

$$-0.20S_1 - 0.20S_2 + 1.00S_3 = 138,600$$

The second step is to write the system of equations in matrix format. This is done by forming a matrix of coefficients (call it A), a column matrix of variables (call it X), and column matrix of constants (call it C). Then, the system in matrix form is:

$$AX = C \tag{9-9}$$

For this problem the matrix system is:

$$\begin{bmatrix} 1.0 & -0.1 & -0.3 \\ -0.1 & 1.0 & 0.0 \\ -0.2 & -0.2 & 1.0 \end{bmatrix} \begin{bmatrix} S_1 \\ S_2 \\ S_3 \end{bmatrix} = \begin{bmatrix} 92,400 \\ 184,800 \\ 138,600 \end{bmatrix}$$

Refer to the inverse of matrix A as A^{-1} (read as A inverse). A^{-1} is a matrix that when multiplied by matrix A will result in a product that is an identity matrix (a matrix denoted as I with all diagonal elements equal to one and every other element equal to zero). If A^{-1} exists, then:

$$A^{-1}A = I \tag{9-10}$$

Assuming it exists, premultiply both sides of equation (9-9) by A^{-1}:

$$A^{-1}AX = A^{-1}C \tag{9-11}$$

Thus, using the property in (9-10):

$$IX = A^{-1}C \tag{9-12}$$

When any matrix is multiplied by the identity matrix, I, the product is just the original matrix. Thus, to solve for the matrix of unknowns, premultiply the constant matrix by the inverse of the matrix of coefficients:

$$X = A^{-1}C \tag{9-13}$$

For the Sansing Company problem it can be shown that the inverse of A is:

$$\begin{bmatrix} 1.0 & -0.1 & -0.3 \\ -0.1 & 1.0 & 0.0 \\ -0.2 & -0.2 & 1.0 \end{bmatrix}^{-1} = \begin{bmatrix} \dfrac{1,000}{924} & \dfrac{160}{924} & \dfrac{300}{924} \\ \dfrac{100}{924} & \dfrac{940}{924} & \dfrac{30}{924} \\ \dfrac{220}{924} & \dfrac{220}{924} & \dfrac{990}{924} \end{bmatrix}$$

Using the results in (9-13), we have:

$$\begin{bmatrix} S_1 \\ S_2 \\ S_3 \end{bmatrix} = \begin{bmatrix} \dfrac{1,000}{924} & \dfrac{160}{924} & \dfrac{300}{924} \\ \dfrac{100}{924} & \dfrac{940}{924} & \dfrac{30}{924} \\ \dfrac{220}{924} & \dfrac{220}{924} & \dfrac{990}{924} \end{bmatrix} \begin{bmatrix} 92,400 \\ 184,800 \\ 138,600 \end{bmatrix} = \begin{bmatrix} 177,000 \\ 202,500 \\ 214,500 \end{bmatrix}$$

Remember that when multiplying two matrices, the element in row i, column j of the product matrix is a sum of the products of corresponding elements from *row i* of the first matrix and *column j* of the second matrix. Thus:

$$S_1 = \frac{1,000}{924} \times 92,400 + \frac{160}{924} \times 184,800 + \frac{300}{924} \times 138,600$$

$$= 177,000$$

$$S_2 = \frac{100}{924} \times 92,400 + \frac{940}{924} \times 184,800 + \frac{30}{924} \times 138,600$$

$$= 202,500$$

S_3 would be determined by using the third row of A^{-1}. As you can see, the results are the same as the solution found by using the reciprocal equations method because this is just another way to solve the equations.

Implication for Overhead Rate Construction

The procedures discussed in the preceding two sections are just as applicable to constructing a predetermined overhead rate as to accounting for actual costs. If predetermined rates are constructed with care, they will not only provide for a better cost assignment but also be useful for planning, decision making, and control. There are two keys to good rate construction. First, there should be a distinction between fixed and variable costs at each level of accumulation. Second, the basis used to allocate costs at each level must, as closely as possible, reflect causation. If these two principles can be closely adhered to, then the resulting rates will be reflective of the benefit accruing to the final product and of the marginal or incremental, cost of production.

In practice there are several complications. First, causal relationships are not easy to disclose. A variety of analyses can help identify correlated variables, but that does not resolve all issues. Second, costs that are variable with respect to the output of a service department may not be variable with respect to the output of a production department. For example, variable personnel service costs may be a function of the number of cases served, but the cases served may not be a function of production. In this case, the personnel services costs that were variable when charged out of the service department would have to be treated as a fixed cost in the production departments. The real problem arises when there is a moderate amount of correlation between the service department output and the production department output. In practice, you will find it conventional to assume either perfect correlation or no correlation in these cases. With moderate correlation some of the variances will be uncontrollable by the various managers. At this time, however, variance analysis procedures have not been advanced to a point that is sophisticated enough to analyze such phenomena. Further, it is possible that the benefit of such an analysis would not be worth the cost.

It is constructive to consider an illustration of the preceding situation. This will allow us to demonstrate the procedures of establishing and using standards when there are reciprocal services. Consider the Lee Company that has two service departments, power and maintenance, and two production departments, P_1 and P_2. The two production departments were asked to provide a variety of information about their activities at normal levels. After top management reviewed the projections, the data were submitted to the two service departments along with a request to estimate their activities needed to support the production departments at normal levels. Since there were reciprocal services between the two departments, the managers had to coordinate their reports closely. Exhibit 9.9 is a summary of the data that resulted from this process.

For simplicity, assume there are only two pools of general factory overhead: a building-related cost pool and a supervision cost pool. In both pools the costs are considered to be fixed. The building-related pool includes items such as building depreciation, property taxes, insurance, and building repairs. The latter are not performed by the maintenance department. Supervision includes the plant manager's salary, the plant controller's salary, the general factory office secretaries' salaries, and general factory office supplies. The total amounts of each of these pools are:

Building-related $500,000
Supervisory $320,000

With the data available in Exhibit 9.9 it would be most reasonable to use factory floor space for allocating the building-related pool. This is done in Exhibit 9.10. Selecting the base for allocating the supervision pool is more difficult. Although

Exhibit 9.9   Lee Company Data at Normal Activity

	Power Department	Maintenance Department	Department P_1	Department P_2	Total
Factory floor space (square feet)	10,000	15,000	25,000	50,000	100,000
Direct labor hours	—	—	1,000,000	400,000	1,400,000
Machine hours	—	—	200,000	500,000	700,000
Number of employees	10	40	500	250	800
Kilowatt hours of power	10,000	30,000	60,000	210,000	310,000
Maintenance hours	2,000	0	2,000	6,000	10,000
Direct traceable costs					
Fixed	$44,000	$65,800	$514,600	$455,600	$1,080,000
Variable	$196,000	$245,000	$271,000	$413,000	$1,125,000

the number of employees appears to be the most reasonable, it is not clear that the department benefit of the factory controller's salary, for example, is a function of the size of the department's labor force. But compromises such as this must, inevitably, be made when allocating indirect cost pools. Number of employees is used as the base for allocating this pool in Exhibit 9.10.

The next allocations that need to be made are the total fixed costs of the service departments. These include both their internal fixed cost and those previously allocated in the preceding process. Note from Exhibit 9.10 that the total fixed costs to be allocated are $98,000 and $156,800, respectively. Kilowatt hours would be used for power. Note in Exhibit 9.9 that power provides some service to itself. This cost, of course, must also be absorbed by the user departments. Thus, omit the 10,000 kilowatts from the total and allocate the costs 10% to maintenance (30,000 ÷ 300,000), 20% to P_1 (60,000 ÷ 300,000), and 70% to P_2 (210,000 ÷ 300,000). Maintenance would be allocated on the basis of maintenance time. The reciprocal equations to distribute the service department costs to each other, where E represents electrical power and M represents maintenance, are:

$$E = 98,000 + 0.2M \tag{9-14}$$

$$M = 156,800 + 0.1E \tag{9-15}$$

It can be shown that the solution to (9-14) and (9-15) is:

$$E = 132,000$$

$$M = 170,000$$

The allocations of the service department fixed costs are also made in Exhibit 9.10.

Exhibit 9.10   Lee Company Allocations of Fixed General Factory Overhead Pools and Service Department Fixed Costs for Purpose of Fixed Overhead Rate Construction

	Power Department	Maintenance Department	Department P_1	Department P_2	Total
Direct fixed costs	$44,000	$ 65,800	$514,600	$455,600	$1,080,000
Allocation of general overhead					
Building related (10, 15, 25, 50)[a]	50,000	75,000	125,000	250,000	500,000
Supervision $(\frac{1}{80}, \frac{4}{80}, \frac{50}{80}, \frac{25}{80})$[a]	4,000	16,000	200,000	100,000	320,000
Total fixed	$98,000	$156,800	$839,600	$805,600	$1,900,000
Allocation of service departments					
Power (10, 20, 70)[a]	(132,000)	13,200	26,400	92,400	0
Maintenance (20, 20, 60)[a]	34,000	(170,000)	34,000	102,000	0
Total	0	0	$900,000	$1,000,000	$1,900,000

[a]The percentage usage rates for the consulting departments.

Since Department P_2 is highly mechanized it was decided to base its overhead rate on machine hours. Department P_1's rate is based on labor hours. The fixed overhead application rates are:

Department P_1: $900,000 \div 1,000,000 = \$0.90$

Department P_2: $1,000,000 \div 500,000 = \$2.00$

As long as the *expected* fixed costs remain the same, the allocations in Exhibit 9.10 represent the charges that should be made to each department. If actual building-related costs differ from $500,000, the difference should be treated as a fixed overhead budget variance rather than being assigned to the service departments. Of course, unavoidable differences should eventually be reflected in the allocations. Likewise, a variation in a service department's fixed costs is a spending variance which should remain as its responsibility. The amounts allocated represent a normal cost which is free of inefficiencies over which the receiving departments have no control.

Now that the fixed costs have been incorporated into the overhead rate, let us consider the variable cost. Variable cost standards, of course, will have to be constructed on a unit cost basis. As volume changes, the total cost assigned must be changed. The variable costs expected at normal activity can be allocated in the same way as the fixed costs. Those results are then used to determine a variable rate for billing the services of the power and maintenance departments.

Exhibit 9.11 contains the allocations of total variable costs at normal activity. To determine the allocations just solve (9-16) and (9-17), which are similar to (9-14) and (9-15) except for the direct cost component:

$$E = 196,000 + 0.2M \qquad (9\text{-}16)$$

$$M = 245,000 + 0.1E \qquad (9\text{-}17)$$

Solving simultaneously yields:

$$E = 250,000$$

$$M = 270,000$$

The standard billing, or costing, rates can now be determined for power and maintenance by using the preceding solutions for E and M. When power is scheduled to operate at 300,000 *net* kilowatt hours, it is estimated that its *total* variable cost will be $250,000. Therefore, each kilowatt hour should be billed at $0.83\frac{1}{3}$ ($250,000 \div 300,000). Further, each maintenance hour should be billed at $27.00 ($270,000 \div 10,000).

To illustrate that the rates will work "properly," assume all departments are *operating at normal and at standard.* The variable overhead costs are accounted for in the following accounts and indicate that all costs are assigned either to user departments or to the products.

Power Department

Actual direct variable	196,000	To maintenance (0.83 1/3	
From maintenance	54,000	× 30,000)	25,000
		To Dept. P_1 (0.83 1/3	
		× 60,000)	50,000
		To Dept. P_2 (0.83 1/3	
		× 210,000)	175,000
	250,000		250,000

Maintenance Department

Actual direct variable	245,000	To power (27 × 2,000)	54,000
From power	25,000	To Dept. P_1 (27 × 2,000)	54,000
		To Dept. P_2 (27 × 6,000)	162,000
	270,000		270,000

Department P_1

Actual direct variable	271,000	Applied	
From power	50,000	1,000,000 × 0.375	375,000
From maintenance	54,000		375,000
	375,000		

Exhibit 9.11   Lee Company Allocation of Variable Costs for Purpose of Variable Overhead Rate Construction

	Power Department	Maintenance Department	Department P_1	Department P_2	Total
Direct variable costs	$196,000	$245,000	$271,000	$413,000	$1,125,000
Power[a]	(250,000)	25,000	50,000	175,000	0
Maintenance[a]	54,000	(270,000)	54,000	162,000	0
Total	0	0	$375,000	$750,000	$1,125,000
Normal volume					
Direct labor hours			1,000,000		
Machine hours				500,000	
Variable overhead rate			$0.375	$1.50	

[a]Allocated using the same percentages as were used in allocating the fixed costs in Exhibit 9.10.

Department P_2			
Actual direct variable	413,000	Applied	
From power	175,000	500,000 × 1.50	750,000
From maintenance	162,000		750,000
	750,000		

The purpose of this section was to provide a relatively complete insight to overhead rate construction and some of the problems that might be encountered. Some of the end-of-chapter problems will ask you to experiment with these standards in different cases.

Treatment of Allocations for Control Purposes

Although we will explore it more fully later in the book, we should briefly mention the relationship of cost allocations to the control process. Much of what was done in this chapter was directed toward cost determination, although the last section may be useful for planning and decision making. For these purposes there is an attempt to measure benefit and/or discover causation. As has been mentioned before, the central theme for good control is to hold managers responsible only for costs over which they can exert some influence. This may mean, then, that the allocated fixed general factory overhead should not be considered in evaluating departmental managers. Further, the allocated fixed costs of operating service departments will quite likely be uncontrollable by other departmental managers. For that matter, the fact that certain costs can be directly identified with a department, whether fixed or variable, *is not* prima facie evidence of controllability.

In Chapter 17, there is a discussion of responsibility accounting and performance evaluation. There you will find an integrated discussion of these problems, including some recommendations for implementation. As with many other aspects of management accounting you will find that the accountant must develop a keen sense of professional judgment in dealing with these issues.

Summary

In this chapter we have completed our examination of the cost accounting process. Two major concepts were discussed. First, you should now understand the goals, problems, and mechanics of allocating indirect costs. Also, you should understand how to construct overhead rates when there are a variety of indirect costs and reciprocal relationships.

Again, you must be cautioned to keep in perspective the purpose of the allocation system discussed here. Primarily, this chapter was oriented toward reporting purposes. A lot of what was done in this chapter will not be particularly relevant to making decisions and controlling operations.

New terms with which you should be familiar are:

Service departments
Cost pool
General factory overhead
Dual distribution base
Reciprocal services
Direct allocation method
Step method
Reciprocal equation allocation method

SELF-STUDY PROBLEM. Consider the following problem from a CMA exam. Barrylou Corporation is developing departmental overhead rates based upon direct-labor hours for its two production departments—Molding and Assembly. The Molding Department employs 20 people and the Assembly Department employs 80 people. Each person in these two departments works 2,000 hours per year. The production-related overhead costs for the Molding Department are budgeted at $200,000 and the Assembly Department costs are budgeted at $320,000. Two service departments, Repair and Power, directly support the two production departments and have budgeted costs of $48,000 and $250,000, respectively. The production departments' overhead rates cannot be determined until the service department's costs are properly allocated. The following schedule reflects the use of the Repair Department's and Power Department's output by the various departments.

	Department			
	Repair	*Power*	*Molding*	*Assembly*
Repair hours	0	1,000	1,000	8,000
KWH	240,000	0	840,000	120,000

Required:

1. Calculate the overhead rates per direct-labor hour for the Molding Department and the Assembly Department using the direct allocation method to charge the production departments for service department costs.

2. Calculate the overhead rates per direct-labor hour for the Molding Department and the Assembly Department using the reciprocal allocation method to charge the production departments for service department costs.

Solution to Self-Study Problem

1. First allocate the service department costs to the production departments. With the direct method, the services provided to other service departments are ignored. Thus, Repair costs would be allocated 1/9 to Molding and 8/9 to Assembly:

Molding: (1/9)$48,000 = $5,333

Assembly: (8/9)$48,000 = $42,667

Power costs would be allocated as follows:

Molding: (84/96)$250,000 = $218,750

Assembly: (12/96)$250,000 = $31,250

The total overhead budgets, normal activities, and departmental overhead rates are as follows:

	Molding	*Assembly*
Direct costs of department	$200,000	$320,000
From repair department	5,333	42,667
From power department	218,750	31,250
Total overhead costs	$424,083	$393,917
Normal activity		
Molding: 20 × 2,000	40,000	
Assembly: 80 × 2,000		160,000
Rate per direct labor hour	$10.602	$ 2.462

2. To allocate the service department costs define:

R = postallocated costs in the Repair Department

P = postallocated costs in the Power Department

Then:

$R = 48,000 + 0.20P$

$P = 250,000 + 0.10R$

Note that total repair hours are budgeted at 10,000 (1,000 + 1,000 + 8,000) and that 10% of them benefit the Power Department (1,000 ÷ 10,000). Likewise, the total KWHs budgeted are 1,200,000 (240,000 + 840,000 + 120,000) and that 20% benefit the Repair Department (240,000 ÷ 1,200,000). Solve the two equations by substituting the second one into the first one:

$R = 48,000 + 0.20(250,000 + 0.10R)$

$0.98R = 98,000$

$R = 100,000$

Substitute R into the equation for P:

$P = 250,000 + 0.10(100,000) = 260,000$

The budgets and rates are as follows:

	Molding	Assembly
Direct costs of department	$200,000	$320,000
From repair department		
(1,000 ÷ 10,000)$100,000	10,000	
(8,000 ÷ 10,000)$100,000		80,000
From power department		
(840,000 ÷ 1,200,000)$260,000	182,000	
(120,000 ÷ 1,200,000)$260,000		26,000
Total costs	$392,000	$426,000
Normal activity (from part 1)	40,000	160,000
Overhead rate	9.80	$2.6625

References

Fremgen, J.M., and Liao, S.S. *The Allocation of Corporate Indirect Costs,* New York: National Association of Accountants, 1983.

Ijiri, Y. "An Application of Input-Output Analysis to Some Problems in Cost Accounting," *Management Accounting* (April 1968): 49–61.

Kaplan, R.S. "Variable and Self-Service Costs in Reciprocal Allocation Models," *The Accounting Review* (October 1973): 738–748.

Thomas, A.L. "Useful Arbitrary Allocations," *The Accounting Review* (July 1971): 472–479.

Williams, T.H., and Griffin, C.H. "Matrix Theory and Cost Allocations," *The Accounting Review* (July 1964): 671–678.

Zimmerman, J.L. "The Costs and Benefits of Cost Allocations," *The Accounting Review* (July 1979): 504–521.

Problems

9-1. Basic Problem on Indirect Cost Allocation. The Angel Company produces one product that requires processing in both Department A and Department B. There are two support departments: Power, and Material Handling and Security (MH&S). The company follows the practice of pooling its overhead costs into three categories:

1. Payroll oriented
2. Building oriented
3. Machine oriented

During 19x1 the following factory overhead items were recorded:

Employer's social security tax	$ 2,000
Lubricants and general parts	2,000
Vacation pay	4,000
Mechanics' wages	3,000
Building depreciation	12,000
Pension expense	4,000
Property taxes	8,000

The following additional information is available:

	Power Department	MH&S Department	Department A	Department B
Floor space (square feet)	1,000	2,000	4,000	3,000
Number of employees	20	30	100	50
Total wages	$25,000	$25,000	$ 90,000	$ 60,000
Number of machines	10	5	20	15
Labor hours	5,000	5,000	9,000	6,000
Material and supplies used	$10,750	$26,325	$100,000	$200,000
Number of calls for MH&S service	0	0	2,000	8,000
KWH of electricity used	0	1,000	6,000	3,000

Required:

1. Determine the amount of each overhead pool.
2. Allocate each overhead pool on the best available base. Indicate what base you are using.
3. Allocate the service department's total cost.

9-2. CPA Problem on Service Department Allocation. During the month of November the expenses of operating the power service department amounted to $9,300, of which $2,500 was considered a fixed cost.

Schedule of Horsepower

	Producing Departments		Service Departments	
	A	B	X	Y
Needed at capacity production	10,000	20,000	12,000	8,000
Used during the month of November	8,000	13,000	7,000	6,000

Required:

1. What dollar amounts of the power service department expense should be allocated to each producing and service department?
2. What are the reasons for allocating the costs of one service department to other service departments as well as to producing departments?
3. Justify the base (or bases) that you used in making the allocation.

9-3. Problems with Cost Allocation. The Downing Company produces its own power and has created a service department with the responsibility for this function. There are two production departments, A and B. The budget for the power department contains a monthly fixed cost of $300,000 and a variable rate of $2 per unit of power. The power department costs have been allocated according to actual usage, and the results for January, February, and March were as follows:

	January	February	March
Units of power used			
Department A	100,000	50,000	100,000
Department B	50,000	50,000	50,000
Cost assignment			
Department A	$400,000	$250,000	$420,000
Department B	200,000	250,000	210,000
Total Power Cost	$600,000	$500,000	$630,000

Both departments operated at capacity during January and March.

At the quarterly management review meeting, Department B's manager complained that his usage of power remained constant but he was assigned a different cost each month. Both department managers complained about the increased costs of March in comparison to January even though consumptions were the same.

Required:

1. Identify possible reasons for the occurrence of the identified fluctuations in cost assignments.
2. Propose a different cost assignment system and prepare a schedule of cost assignments using your proposal.

9-4. Determining and Correcting Problems with Allocation System. The Heckel-Jeckel Company has two production departments—A and B. Both of these departments are serviced by service Department S. Some unhappiness has arisen about the way the company has been charging the costs of Department S to Departments A and B. The last two months of data are summarized below and highlight the problem.

Department S's costs were $580,000 in January and $380,000 in February. During these two months, S's output was 100,000 and 60,000 "units" of service, respectively. The service was provided as follows:

	January	February
To Department A	40,000	40,000
To Department B	60,000	20,000

In January Department A was charged $232,000 for services from S and in February $253,333. The manager of Department A complained that he consumed 40,000 units in each month but was charged in excess of $21,000 more in February than in January.

Required:

1. Show how the costs were allocated in both January and February.
2. Based on the allocation method evidently used, explain to the manager of Department A why there could be a difference in the amount charged to his department for identical consumption amounts.
3. Assuming that all three departments operated at capacity in January, distribute both January's and February's costs using the dual based method.
4. State specific demand levels by Departments A and B for Department S's services such that A and B would receive identical cost allocations using either an actual consumption based method or a dual based method. The demand levels you select must be below capacity and above zero. Show that the allocations for your chosen demand levels would be identical. The additional facts in question 3 can be assumed to be in effect.

9-5. Direct Allocation Method When There Are Reciprocal Services. The Tanana Company has two service departments and two production departments. In January the costs incurred by service departments S_1 and S_2, before any distribution of their costs, were $3,030 and $2,000, respectively. The relative utilization of the service departments was as follows:

User Department	Supplying Department S_1	S_2
S_1	—	20%
S_2	10%	—
P_1	30	40
P_2	60	40

Required:

Prepare a cost allocation schedule using the direct method.

9-6. Problem 9-5 Using Step Method. Reconsider the Tanana Company in problem 9-5. Prepare a cost allocation schedule using the step method (Distribute S_2 first, then S_1.)

9-7 Problem 9-5 Using Reciprocal Equation Method. Reconsider the Tanana Company in problem 9-5. Prepare a cost allocation schedule using the reciprocal equation method.

9-8 Problem 9-5 Using Matrix Algebra. Reconsider the Tanana Company in problem 9-5. It can be shown that the inverse to the appropriate matrix for the equation in problem 9-7 is:

$$\begin{bmatrix} \dfrac{100}{98} & \dfrac{20}{98} \\[2ex] \dfrac{10}{98} & \dfrac{100}{98} \end{bmatrix}$$

Show that the solution using this matrix is the same as in problem 9-7.

9-9. More Involved Problem with Reciprocal Services. BG Company has organized its production department into six responsibility centers. Three of them, S_1, S_2, and S_3, are service departments and the remaining three, P_1, P_2, and P_3, are production departments. The service departments provide services to the production departments as well as to each other.

During the current period the direct variable costs of operating the service departments were as follows:

S_1—$189,050
S_2— 94,525
S_3— 283,575

The percentage of the services provided to each department was as follows:

		From	
To	S_1	S_2	S_3
S_1	0%	20%	10%
S_2	5	0	20
S_3	10	15	0
P_1	20	25	30
P_2	30	35	20
P_3	35	5	20

Required:

Distribute the service department costs using the direct method.

9-10. Problem 9-9 Using Step Method. Reconsider problem 9-9. Distribute the service department costs using the step method. Use the order S_3, S_2, and S_1.

9-11. Problem 9-9 Using Reciprocal Equations Method. Reconsider problem 9-9.

Required:

1. Set up the simultaneous equations to be used in the reciprocal equations method. Define S_1, S_2, and S_3 to be the postallocated costs.
2. The solution to the equations in part 1 is:

S_1 = 257,500
S_2 = 174,500
S_3 = 335,500

Using this solution distribute the service department costs.
3. Construct the matrix that would have to be inverted to solve the equations in part 1 by the matrix algebra approach.

9-12. Allocation of Service Departments When Reciprocal Services Exist. The Ryan Company's production function is divided into six responsibility centers: two production departments and four service departments. During May 19x4, all departments operated at full capacity, and the service department outputs were allocated as follows:

Units from Department

To Department	S_1	S_2	S_3	S_4
S_1	100	500	0	300
S_2	700	0	0	600
S_3	800	1,000	0	600
S_4	600	0	1,000	0
P_1	1,000	2,500	8,000	900
P_2	1,800	6,000	11,000	600
	5,000	10,000	20,000	3,000

Before distributions, the service departments' costs were as follows:

S_1	\$237,035
S_2	142,221
S_3	94,814
S_4	47,407

Required:

1. Distribute the costs using the direct method.
2. Distribute the costs using the step method in an order determined by:
   a. Percentage of services provided to other services departments.
   b. Number of other service departments serviced.
3. Write the equations that would be needed if the reciprocal equation method is to be used. In the equations, permit some of S_1's cost to be *assigned back to itself*.
4. It can be shown that the inverse needed to solve the equations in part 3 by the matrix algebra method is:

$$
\begin{bmatrix}
\dfrac{98900}{94814} & \dfrac{5000}{94814} & \dfrac{550}{94814} & \dfrac{11000}{94814} \\[2mm]
\dfrac{16420}{94814} & \dfrac{95740}{94814} & \dfrac{1050}{94814} & \dfrac{21000}{94814} \\[2mm]
\dfrac{20040}{94814} & \dfrac{10600}{94814} & \dfrac{95980}{94814} & \dfrac{23320}{94814} \\[2mm]
\dfrac{12870}{94814} & \dfrac{1130}{94814} & \dfrac{4865}{94814} & \dfrac{97300}{94814}
\end{bmatrix}
$$

Distribute the service department costs using the reciprocal method.

9-13. Distributions of Costs Using Reciprocal Equation Method. The Grich Company produces its products in a two-step process (Department A and Department B). The company is serviced by three service departments—power, repair, and general office. During January the company operated at full capacity. The costs of operating the service departments were:

Power	$3,790
Repair	6,600
General Office	4,890

The usage rates when operating at full capacity are given in the following schedule:

		Supplying Department		
		Power	*Repair*	*General Office*
Percentage of service				
supplied to:	Power	——	3%	0%
	Repair	10%	——	0%
	Office	4%	7%	——
	A	36%	60%	70%
	B	50%	30%	30%

Required:

Prepare the distribution entries for the service departments' cost using the reciprocal equation method.

9-14. Dual Based Distributions When There Are Reciprocal Services. The Baylor Company has two service departments that incurred the following costs during May 19x4:

	Maintenance	*Power*
Fixed	$ 3,000	$ 9,500
Variable	7,500	3,000
Total	$10,500	$12,500

The service departments serviced each other as well as two production departments, A and B. The relative consumptions of maintenance and power at normal capacity and at the actual level of operation for May are as follows:

	At Capacity		May's Actual	
	Maintenance	*Power*	*Maintenance*	*Power*
To: Maintenance	——	20%	——	50%
Power	10%	——	20%	——
Department A	70	30	50	30
Department B	20	50	30	20

Required:

Distribute the service departments' costs using the best method possible with the data that are given.

9-15. Basic Problems on Establishing Overhead Rates When There Are Service Departments. Exclusive of power costs, the budget for Department III of the Ford Company shows the following items for 120,000 yearly direct-labor hours at practical capacity:

Fixed	$16,000
Variable	$18,000

Department III uses 50% of the power when the company operates at practical capacity. Power costs at practical capacity are:

Fixed $16,000
Variable $12,000

Required:

1. Prepare a complete budget for Department III, and compute the fixed and variable overhead rate.
2. Prepare a schedule of costs that Department III would be *expected* to incur during a month when 8,000 direct-labor hours are used.
3. What is the *applied* overhead for a month in which the output is allowed 8,000 labor hours. Assume the practical capacity for the month was 10,000 hours.

9-16. Determining Standard Costs When There Are Reciprocally Related Service Departments. The Bengal Company produces several products and has its production divison divided into five responsibility centers: service departments S_1, S_2, and S_3, and production departments P_1 and P_2. Each year the standard costs are revised to reflect current conditions. You are to aid in that process.

Each department has been requested to provide you some data under the assumption that *all* departments will be operating at normal activity levels. Data from the three service departments are summarized as follows:

	S_1	S_2	S_3
Fixed costs	$49,750	$99,500	$199,000
Variable costs	49,750*	99,500*	$199,000*

*You have confirmed that the fixed and variable costs are expected to be the same at normal activity.

When all departments are working at normal levels, the service departments' outputs will be distributed as follows:

		G, supplies From	
To	S_1	S_2	S_3
S_1	—	5%	0%
S_2	10%	—	0
S_3	20	15	—
P_1	30	50	70
P_2	40	30	30

Department P_1 provided you the following data. Overhead is most closely correlated with direct-labor hours (*L*). At normal activity levels, 100,000 direct-labor hours would be incurred. *Exclusive of service department costs,* Department P_1 estimates its overhead (*OH*) using the following function of direct labor:

$$OH = 172,975 + 6L$$

In addition to the above, you have data about the production requirements of product A, which is processed in Department P_1. Each unit *started* requires 6.44 pounds of material and 27.6 hours of labor. However, it is *normal* for 8% of the units started not to pass the quality control inspection at the end of processing in Department P_1. Material costs $5 per pound and labor $8 per hour.

Full absorption costing is used and the service department costs are to be allocated using the reciprocal equation method.

Required:

1. Assume that all departments do operate at normal activity and that the service departments' costs are as budgeted. Write the equations to distribute the service departments' fixed costs. Do not solve.
2. Assume the solution to your equations in part 1 is:

$S_1 = \$55,000$
$S_2 = \$105,000$
$S_3 = \$225,750$

Prepare a supported standard full absorption schedule of producing one good unit of product A in Department P_1.

9-17. Working with Results of Chapter Case on Overhead Rate Construction. Reconsider the Lee Company problem discussed on pages 313–317. Assume that the rates established there are valid for the year described as follows. The building related and supervisory costs are incurred as budgeted. The following schedule summarizes the year's results:

	Power Department	Maintenance Department	Department P_1	Department P_2	Total
Direct-labor hours			600,000	400,000	1,000,000
Machine hours			120,000	600,000	720,000
Kilowatts of power used	10,652	31,593	36,000	252,000	330,245
Maintenance hours used	2,131	0	1,200	7,200	10,531
Direct fixed cost	$ 45,000	$ 65,000	$514,600	$455,600	$1,080,200
Direct variable cost	$208,800	$258,000	$162,600	$495,600	$1,125,000

Required:

1. Verify that the variable costs per unit of power and per maintenance hour are the same as the budgeted rates. Also verify that for Department P_1 the ratio of direct-labor hours to machine hours is the same as in the budget.
2. Prepare the accounts for power, maintenance, overhead—Department P_1, and overhead—Department P_2. In each case post the amounts of all entries during the year that affect the accounts. Be sure to apply the production department overhead.
3. Explain any balances remaining in the accounts at the end of the year. Assume that the actual direct-labor hours in Department P_1 and actual machine hours in P_2 were both equal to the standard allowances.

9-18. Problem 9-17 Reconsidered When There Are Inefficiencies. Assume the same facts as problem 9-17 except that the year's results are as follows:

	Power Department	Maintenance Department	Department P_1	Department P_2	Total
Direct-labor hours			580,000*	410,000	990,000
Machine hours			120,000	600,000*	720,000
Kilowatts of power used	11,000	32,000	36,000	252,000	331,000
Maintenance hours used	2,200	0	1,200	7,200	10,600
Direct fixed cost	$ 45,000	$ 65,000	$514,600	$455,600	$1,080,200
Direct variable cost	$208,530	$265,000	$162,600	$495,600	$1,131,730

*Equal to standard allowed for this period's output.

Required:

Repeat parts 2 and 3 of problem 9-17.

9-19. Allocating Costs for a Regulated Utility. The Natural Gas Company is permitted to classify its customers into groups and charge each group a different rate per CCF (hundred cubic feet) based on the characteristics of the group. Natural has classified its customers into three groups:

1. Residential
2. Nonmanufacturing business
3. Manufacturing

A large percentage of Natural's costs are fixed. Their fixed costs include pipeline costs, pumping station costs, and storage well costs. These facilities are designed to meet peak demands. Natural's variable costs are primarily the cost of the gas itself.

The following demand statistics for gas are available:

	Average Demand	Maximum Demand	Expected Current Demand
Residential	20,000 CCF	30,000 CCF	15,000 CCF
Nonmanufacturing business	40,000	55,000	45,000
Manufacturing	80,000	125,000	90,000

*This is the highest from the past five years.

The estimated costs for the current year are:

Fixed	$84,000
Variable	67,500

Required:

1. Assume that all customers are to be considered as one class. What rate per CCF would Natural charge if:
   a. All costs were averaged over the expected current demand?
   b. The fixed costs were averaged over the average demand and variable over the expected current demand?

    c. The fixed costs were averaged over the maximum demand and variable over the expected current demand?

2. Assume that the fixed costs are to be allocated among the three groups on the basis of maximum demand. What would the *total* rate per CCF be for each group if:

    a. The fixed costs are billed based on the average demand?

    b. The fixed costs are billed based on the estimated current demand?

3. Comment on the relative "fairness" of the rates developed in parts 1 and 2.

CHAPTER 10

Accounting for Joint Costs

Until now it has been assumed in this book that each of the firm's products could be manufactured independently of all others. Although situations have been encountered where several products share facilities and resources, the implicit assumption has been that such an arrangement was at the option of the firm and not of physical necessity. When the nature of the raw materials and/or the production requires joint processing of two or more products through part of the manufacturing cycle, then we have a joint product situation.

A familiar joint production process is that of petroleum products. Crude oil is the raw material that is put into a cracking process, the joint process, and results in gasoline, heating oil, diesel fuel, kerosene, and other products. Other examples of joint production include the chemical, meat packing, cotton, wood products, and extractive ore industries.

There are a variety of ways to account for costs in a joint product situation. Depending on several factors, the output of such a process may either be referred to as a main product or a by-product. In this chapter we will distinguish between these two classifications and discuss a variety of ways to account for each. After examining the basic accounting methods, some complications will be considered. For example, there is consideration of the possibility that production must go through a series, or chain, of joint processes. That is, a beginning raw material is converted into two or more identifiable products in one process. Then one of the outputs is further processed into two or more products in a subsequent process. As with the preceding chapters, the *prevailing theme here is cost determination.* Many of the procedures discussed will generate unit costs that are not marginal costs. Therefore, the results of the accounting *will not* be useful for decision making and control. The final section of the chapter considers this limitation in more detail.

Definitions

The output of a joint process will consist of a combination of main and by-products. Making a distinction between the two types of products is a matter of *judgment and materiality.* In this section some guidelines for making such a distinction are discussed. These guidelines need to be understood because the accounting process depends on the type of product.

Joint products can be classified into major, or main, products and minor products. The distinction between them is that "major" products are those that have a relatively large volume of output and/or sales dollars. Note that the criteria give consideration to both physical and dollar volume. A product which is produced in a quantity that is small relative to total output may still be considered a main product if it results in a sales dollar volume that is relatively large. This also means that some of the output might be considered a by-product at one point in time but a main product at another point. Such a change in classification could be the result of technological or economic circumstances that increased the value of the product.

Obviously the question of whether the output or revenue of a product is relatively large becomes a matter of judgment. There is no mandate for a firm to classify a product either way. As you will see later, however, there is more careful attention given to measuring the cost benefit for a main product than for a by-product. Thus, in making the decision some consideration must be given to the added cost of accounting for output as a main product relative to the benefits of a better cost allocation.

It should also be understood that the output from a joint process is not always fixed. That is, it may be possible to change the manufacturing process so that a relatively larger quantity of a given product can be obtained. For example, in processing crude oil it is possible to increase or decrease the amount of gasoline that is obtained. In fact, this is done. Prior to the winter season gasoline production is reduced in order to obtain a larger quantity of heating oil. The possibility of changing the proportions of output presents some problems for the costing system. Some of these problems will be discussed as we proceed.

One other definition that needs to be understood is that of a **split-off point.** This is the point in the manufacturing process where the products become separately identifiable. Of course, some of the products may still have to go through additional processing before they are marketable. The importance of the split-off point is that the variable costs that are incurred after that point can be directly traced to specific products.

Accounting for Main Products

Several systems for allocating joint costs are in use. In this section we will examine four basic ways of accomplishing the allocation. These methods are known as (1) the units method, (2) the weighted average method, (3) the net realizable value method, and (4) the net realizable value less normal profit method.

THE UNITS METHOD.   Cost allocation via the **units method** is very simple. The total costs incurred in the joint process (material, labor, and overhead) are allocated to the various products produced in the joint process according to the ratios of their physical measurement. Before discussing the implications of this method, let us consider an illustration.

Assume that the Nevares Company manufactures products A, B, and C by processing a raw material known as Ingrediente. The processing is done in Department I. Although this is not a complex situation, it is a good habit to flowchart joint product cases in order to visualize the process. The flowchart for this simple case is in Exhibit 10.1

At Nevares the production process is such that for every 11,000 pounds of Ingrediente put into Department I, 4,000 pounds of A, 2,500 pounds of B, and 3,500 pounds of C are obtained. The remainder, 1,000 pounds, is waste for which there is no value. Each batch of 11,000 pounds of Ingrediente processed through Department I costs $226,300.

In this case, a pound is the physical measurement unit. Thus, using the units method, 40% of the joint cost would be allocated to product A since the number of pounds of A obtained is 40% of the total number of *good* pounds resulting from the batch. The complete cost allocation is found in Exhibit 10.2.

It should be noted that this allocation method resulted in *identical costs per pound* for each product. In turn, this implies that the benefit accruing to a pound of each product is identical. Identical benefits will accrue only if the products are homogeneous. To assess the adequacy of the results, it is necessary to determine the homogeneity between the various products involved. For this situation it is common to use unit sales prices as the measure of homogeneity. That is, if the unit sales prices of the joint products are relatively close to each other, then the products would be considered homogeneous and the units method would be acceptable to most accountants.

Another argument for measuring homogeneity by unit sales prices is that the market recognizes different production costs and benefits through the sales price it is willing to pay for the product. Obviously, cost of production is not the only factor that influences the price. Thus, we must be careful not to go to extremes in

---

Exhibit 10.1   Nevares Company's Joint Production Process Basic Case

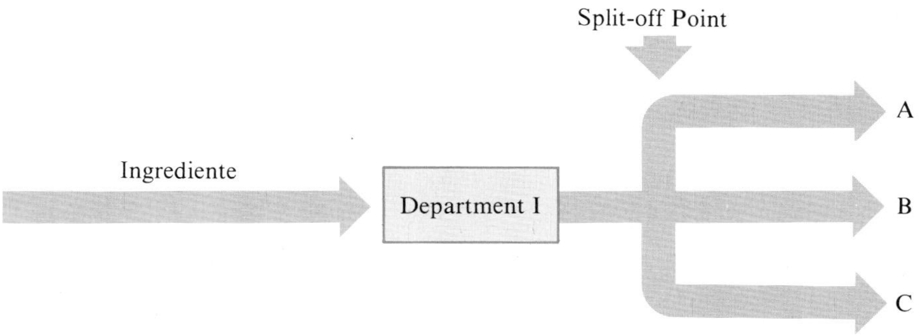

Exhibit 10.2   Nevares Company Allocation of Joint Costs
Using Units Method

Product	Pounds	Ratio	Allocated Joint Costs	Cost per Pound
A	4,000	40%	$ 90,520	$22.63
B	2,500	25	56,575	22.63
C	3,500	35	79,205	22.63
	10,000	100%	$226,300	

using sales prices as the measure of homogeneity. But for the moment, let us assume that this is an appropriate measure and that the unit sales prices are:

Product A $ 50.00
Product B   100.00
Product C   80.00

Then, the units method generates the following gross margins:

	Product A	Product B	Product C
Sales price	$50.00	$100.00	$80.00
Cost of production	22.63	22.63	22.63
Gross margin	$27.37	$ 77.37	$57.37
Gross margin percentage	54.74%	77.37%	71.71%

These results may be hard to defend; that is, each of the products shared the facilities but have different gross margin percentages. The other three methods of allocating joint costs provide a mechanism to account for the costs if the products lack homogeneity.

WEIGHTED AVERAGE METHOD.   In the case of a lack of homogeneity among products, one solution is to use a weighting scheme, the **weighted average method.** That is, before computing the ratios needed for the cost allocations, the volume of output for each product is multiplied by a weight that adjusts for the collective difference among the products. Sometimes these weights may be based on some important physical characteristics of the output. For example, Griffin suggests that petroleum products be weighted according to their gravity.[1] In other cases, the weights may be the result of expert judgment resulting from a general consideration of all the relevant characteristics of the product.

---

[1]Charles H. Griffin, "Multiple Product Costing in Petroleum Refining," *The Journal of Accountancy* (March 1958), pp. 46–52.

To illustrate, let us continue with the Nevares case. Suppose that giving consideration to a variety of factors, including the sales price, the size of the unit, the labor time needed to process the product *beyond* the split-off point, and others, the following weights are to be used:

Product A   5
Product B   3
Product C   1

Using these weights, the costs are allocated in Exhibit 10.3.

The weighted average method generates unit costs for the products that are related to each other in a *proportion equal to the weights assigned to the products.* Note that A's cost per pound is five times C's and B's is three times C's. Of course, with this method the gross margin ratios would vary from product to product, but this is not undesirable. Presumably, the reason a weighted average scheme would be used is that factors in addition to sales price must be considered when measuring benefit from the joint process accruing to the products. Because of this it would not be expected that the gross margins be proportional to the sales prices. The major disadvantage of the method is the establishment of the weights. Since the weights must frequently be the result of a judgmental process, they could be difficult to defend in any objective way.

NET REALIZABLE VALUE METHOD.   In its basic form the **net realizable value (NRV) method** is a specific version of the weighted average method. *The weights are equal to the "value" of the products at the split-off point.* Thus, this method assumes that homogeneity is achieved by giving consideration *only* to the net realizable values. In addition to being called the NRV method, it is also referred to as the **relative sales value method** and, when processing is required beyond the split-off point, as the **hypothetical market value method.** Using the sales prices introduced earlier and assuming all products are sold at the split-off point, the NRV joint cost allocation is found in Exhibit 10.4.

Exhibit 10.3   Nevares Company Allocation of Joint Costs Using Weighted Average Method

Product	Pounds	Weight Factor	Weighted Output	Ratio	Allocated Joint Cost	Cost per Pound
A	4,000	5	20,000	200/310	$146,000	$36.50
B	2,500	3	7,500	75/310	54,750	21.90
C	3,500	1	3,500	35/310	25,550	7.30
			31,000		$226,300	

Exhibit 10.4   Nevares Company Allocation of Joint Costs Using Net Realizable Value Method

Product	Pounds	Market Price	Market Value	Ratio	Allocated Joint Cost	Cost per Pound
A	4,000	$ 50	$200,000	20/73	$ 62,000	$15.50
B	2,500	100	250,000	25/73	77,500	31.00
C	3,500	80	280,000	28/73	86,800	24.80
			$730,000		$226,300	

Note in Exhibit 10.4 that the costs per unit are in *proportion to the sales prices.* Thus, the NRV method generates the same gross margin percentage for all products. For each product the assigned cost is 31% of the sales price and the gross margin is 69%.

Now that the basic methods have been established, we are prepared to expand the accounting to more involved cases. First let us assume that it is *not possible* to sell the products at the split-off point. Each product must be subjected to some type of additional processing in order to make it marketable. In this situation there are costs other than the joint costs. Further, there is a problem in determining the "value" of the products at the split-off point. Assuming that the additional processing for product A, B, and C is done in Departments II, III, and IV, respectively, then the situation is depicted in Exhibit 10.5. The cost figures included in

Exhibit 10.5   Nevares Company's Joint Production Process All Units Requiring Additional Processing

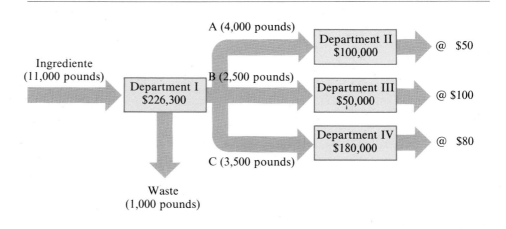

the flowchart are the costs of operating each department in order to completely process an *original batch size of 11,000 pounds* of Ingrediente.

If additional processing is required beyond the split-off point, then it is *not* logical to argue that the split-off value of the products is equal to the final sales value. Certainly the additional processing beyond the split-off point adds value and must be considered in determining the product's value at the split-off point. *The NRV method infers the split-off values by subtracting the costs beyond the split-off point from the final market value of the products.* The ratios needed to allocate the joint costs are computed using these implicit net realizable values. Those costs beyond the split-off point are referred to as *separable costs* because they can be identified with one specific product. Exhibit 10.6 derives the cost allocation.

Note that the NRV column is derived by subtracting the separable costs from the total market value of the current production. Then, the allocation ratios are the respective NRV's divided by the total net realizable value.

Unlike the original case, the NRV method in this case does not generate the same gross margin rates for each product. To illustrate, note that the separable cost per pound is $25.00 for product A ($100,000 ÷ 4,000), $20.00 for B ($50,000 ÷ 2,500), and $51.429 for C ($180,000 ÷ 3,500). The gross margin rates are as follows:

	Product A		Product B		Product C	
Sales price		$50.000		$100.00		$80.000
Cost of production:						
Joint cost	$14.144		$45.26		$16.164	
Separable cost	25.000	39.144	20.00	65.26	51.429	67.593
Gross margin		$10.856		$ 34.74		$12.407
Gross margin rate		21.72%		34.74%		15.51%

The different gross margin rates are due, in part, to an inherent assumption of the NRV method. *It assumes that the work done beyond the split-off point contributes nothing to profits.* Exhibit 10.6 shows that the NRV of product B, for example, is $200,000 at the split-off point. Thus, the implication is that the additional work beyond the split-off only increases the sales value by $50,000 (from $200,000 at the split-off point to $250,000 after processing in Department III). Therefore the assumption is that this effort adds nothing to profits; the *increase in the product's "sales value" is equal to the separable costs.*

It may be more logical to argue that the product's profit is earned over the entire span of production rather than just during the joint span. If so, then the joint costs must be allocated a different way. This is the topic of the next section. Regardless of this apparent lack of logic, the NRV method continues to be *widely used.* Thus, before examining the next method there are some additional issues that need to be considered when using the NRV method.

First, it is possible for there to be more than one alternative use for the products that emerge from the joint process. For example, the products might *either* be sold at the split-off point *or* processed further. In this case it is normally agreed that the

Exhibit 10.6   Nevares Company Allocation of Joint Costs Using NRV Method Case Where All Products Require Additional Processing

Product	Pounds	Market Price	Market Value	Separable Costs	NRV	Ratio	Allocated Joint Cost	Joint Cost per Pound
A	4,000	$ 50	$200,000	$100,000	$100,000	25%	$ 56,575	$14.144
B	2,500	100	250,000	50,000	200,000	50	113,150	45.260
C	3,500	80	280,000	180,000	100,000	25	56,575	16.164
			$730,000	$330,000	$400,000		$226,300	

NRV will be the actual market value at the split-off point. If the product *must* be processed further, then there would be no actual market value at the split-off point and it is necessary to deduce a market value as was done previously. *However, when a market exists for the product as it is found at the split-off point, there is no reason to use the surrogate measure of that value.* Most accountants would argue that the market value at split-off should be used for the joint cost allocation even if the optimal course of action is to process the product further. That is, the fact that management may not elect to sell at the intermediate market does not change the fact that there is a market for the product at that point. So long as a market exists there is a measure of the worth of such products at the split-off.

To illustrate, assume that the Nevares Company has two options for product B. It can be sold at the split-off point for $40 per pound or processed further as previously depicted in Exhibit 10.5. Assuming that *Department III's cost is variable,* the prudent course of action would be to further process product B. The separable cost of $50,000 per batch represents a cost of $20 per pound. Thus, with an additional expenditure of $20 per pound, a product can be produced that has a sales price of $100: a contribution of $80 per pound. In contrast, the contribution per pound is equal to the split-off sales price of $40 if the product is sold immediately after processing in Department I. Thus, additional processing will contribute $40 per pound more than a sale at the split-off point. However, for purposes of allocating the costs of Department I, we are interested in the value created by the processing in that department. In the case of product B this value is $40 per pound. Assuming all other factors the same as in Exhibit 10.5, the joint cost allocation would be as found in Exhibit 10.7. Note in Exhibit 10.7 that the NRV of product B is equal to its intermediate market value, whereas product A's and product C's NRV is derived as the market value after additional processing less the separable costs.

When there are alternatives at the split-off point, it should be further argued that the allocation of the joint costs be independent of the action taken. If this independence exists, then decisions about which alternative is to be selected will

Exhibit 10.7   Nevares Company Allocation of Joint Costs Using NRV Method Case Where Some Products May Be Sold at Split-off or Further Processed

Product	Pounds	Relevant Market Price	Market Value	Relevant Separable Costs	NRV	Ratio	Allocated Joint Costs	Joint Cost per Pound
A	4,000	$50	$200,000	$100,000	$100,000	1/3	$ 75,434	$18.858
B	2,500	40	100,000	—	100,000	1/3	75,433	30.173
C	3,500	80	280,000	100,000	100,000	1/3	75,433	21.552
					$300,000		$226,300	

be correct *even if they are based on the cost obtained from the allocation.*[2] In the preceding case, for example, if the decision maker knows that product B will receive an allocation of $30.173 per pound from Department I regardless of what is done with B, he or she would rationally choose the option that had the greatest contribution *beyond* the split-off point. This will be explored in more detail in Chapter 14.

There is a final issue to be considered. It is possible that the NRV at the split-off point will be negative. For example, suppose product C could not be sold at the split-off point and required an expenditure of $297,125 per batch in Department IV to make it marketable at $80 per pound.[3] Then the NRV would be − $17,125, $280,000 − $297,125. It does not make sense to contend that a product has negative value at the split-off point. Further, if the negative NRV was used in the joint cost allocation scheme, the products with positive net realizable values would be allocated joint costs *exceeding* the amount actually incurred. To help illustrate the issue let's go ahead and allocate the joint costs using the situation in Exhibit 10.5 (product B having no market at the split-off) and the preceding modification:

Product	NRV	Ratio	Joint Cost
A	$100,000	35.351%	$ 80,000
B	200,000	70.703	160,000
C	(17,125)	(6.054)	(13,700)
	$282,875		$226,300

If the NRV method is implemented without an adjustment, then, in effect, some of the costs that are *specifically* identified with product C will be shifted to products

---

[2]This should not be construed as an argument for allocating costs to obtain decision-making data. It is just an anticipation of the possibility that data derived for cost determination purposes may be used for other purposes.

[3]The action implied here is *less costly* than disposing of the product.

A and B. In the preceding schedule, $13,700 is shifted and represents a subsidy to product C. Although not the case here, an unmodified use of the NRV method could result in a subsidy that is large enough to cause a decision maker to direct that product C be processed further even when it cannot be economically justified.

Because of the problems of justifying the results, most accountants would argue that product C, in this case, has a zero value at the split-off point. The NRV of products A and B would be the same as previously discussed. Consequently, the joint cost would be allocated one-third to product A, two-thirds to B, and zero to C. With this modification there would be no subsidy, and thus better decisions would result if the data are used for that purpose.

NET REALIZABLE VALUE LESS NORMAL PROFIT METHOD.   As indicated earlier, the NRV method implicitly assumes that all profits are earned in the joint process and none in the processing beyond the split-off point. If management does not desire to have this kind of result, then the **net realizable value less normal profit method** should be considered. This method *assigns the total profits of all production proratably to each dollar of cost incurrence regardless of where it is incurred.* To illustrate, consider the Nevares case where all products must be further processed (see Exhibit 10.5). The results are in Exhibit 10.8 and derived as follows. First compute a ratio of total production cost (joint and separable) to total ending market value. This ratio is an average cost ratio per dollar of sales. Subtracting the average cost ratio from 100% gives an average profit ratio. The total market value of each product is reduced by the average profit computed as the rate times the market value. Then reducing this result by the separable costs will yield a figure that represents the share of joint cost to be allocated to that product.

Exhibit 10.8   Nevares Company Joint Cost Allocation Using the NRV Less Normal Profit Method

Product	Pounds	Market Value	Normal Profit[a]	Separable Costs	Joint Cost Allocation[b]	Joint Cost per Pound
A	4,000	$200,000	$ 47,589	$100,000	$ 52,411	$13.103
B	2,500	250,000	59,486	50,000	140,514	56.206
C	3,500	280,000	66,625	180,000	33,375	9.536
		$730,000	$173,700	$330,000	$226,300	

[a]Market value × Normal profit rate where:
  Normal profit rate = 1 − (Joint costs + Separable costs) ÷ Total
         market value
      = 1 − [($226,300 + $330,000) ÷ $730,000]
      = 1 − 0.76205
      = 0.23795

[b]Market value − Normal profit − Separable cost

As indicated, this method does generate a gross profit margin that is the same for all products. To demonstrate, consider the following *per unit* data:

	Product A		Product B		Product C	
Sales price		$50.000		$100.000		$80.000
Cost of production						
Joint cost	$13.103		$56.206		$ 9.536	
Separable cost	25.000	38.103	20.000	76.206	51.429	60.965
Gross margin		$11.897		$ 23.794		$19.035
Gross margin rate		23.79%		23.79%		23.79%

Similar gross margin rates may not be a desirable characteristic. We would not expect to find such a characteristic among independently produced products.

Accounting for By-Products

As defined earlier, a by-product is one of minor value. Because of the insignificance of by-products, they are accounted for in ways that are simpler than the main product methods. There are two major classifications of by-product accounting methods and several variations within each classification.

The simplest way of accounting for by-products is to only *recognize their revenue at the point of sale* by recording the sales price as revenue. With this method *no costs are assigned* to the by-products. To illustrate, let us now assume that the 1,000 pounds classified as waste in the Nevares case can be sold at some nominal value. Refer to this output as product D and classify it as a by-product. The sales price is $2.00 per unit. For illustrative purposes, assume that only one batch of Ingrediente was processed during 19x1 and that 800 pounds of product D were sold. Using this version of by-product accounting, the 19x1 revenue would include $1,600 from the sales of product D. Since this method assigns no cost to by-products, the 200 units in inventory would not be recognized on the financial statements.

There are three other variations of this method. Rather than be included in the firm's revenue, the sales of the by-product can be treated as *other income*, or as a *reduction of the cost of sales* of major products, or as a *reduction of the cost of production* of the major products. The first two variations are just locational preferences on the income statement and would generate the same net income as the method of including the sales in total revenue. The third variation would have implications for the cost of the ending inventory of the major products. Since the latter option reduces cost of production, there would be a pro rata reduction in the inventory of major products. In the Nevares case, the $226,300 production cost in Department I would be reduced by $1,600 to $224,700. The $224,700 would then be allocated by one of the cost allocation methods discussed in the previous section.

In the process of selling by-products there may be some distribution costs. The treatment of these costs provides yet another dimension in the accounting for by-products. One alternative is to account for these costs as a part of the total selling and administrative costs. That is, they are *pooled with all other selling and administrative costs* and the pool is deducted against total revenues. A second treatment is to net the selling and administrative costs specifically associated with the by-products *against the by-product revenue*. The two treatments of distribution costs combined with the four possible treatments of the revenue result in eight possible accounting methods within this classification of by-product accounting.

The second major variation of by-product accounting is one that assigns a portion of the production costs to the by-products as they are produced. That is, the costs of the joint process are assigned *both to the main products and to the by-products*. There are at least two variations of this method. The first variation assumes there is to be *no profit recognized* from the sales of by-products. With this method, the sales price would be assumed to *just be sufficient* to recover the production cost and the distribution cost. To determine the amount of the joint process's cost to be assigned to the by-product, just reduce the by-product's sales price by the distribution costs.

Continuing the Nevares case as an illustration, assume that the cost of selling product D totals $0.50 per pound. If no profit is to be recognized, then the production cost would be assigned at $1.50 per pound ($2.00 − $0.50). Since 1,000 pounds were produced in 19x1, $1,500 of Department I's cost would be assigned to product D. The balance of Department I's cost, $224,800 ($226,300 − $1,500), would then be allocated to the main products using an acceptable allocation method. If 800 pounds were sold in 19x1, then the following items must be accounted for:

Revenue (800 × $2.00)	$1,600
Cost of sales—product D	
(800 × $1.50)	1,200
Selling costs (800 × $0.50)	400
Inventory (200 × $1.50)	300

The inventory, of course, would be given the same treatment as any other inventory. There are some options, however, for the first three items. Each of these items could be given the same treatment as any other product; that is, including by-product revenue with total revenue, by-product cost of sales with total cost of goods sold, and by-product selling costs with selling and administrative costs. Alternatively, the cost of sales and selling costs could be netted against the revenue and the result shown as other income. However, no profit is recognized in this variation so the net amount included in other income would be zero.

A final variation is to *recognize some normal profit* from the sales of by-products. This profit rate may be arbitrarily selected and need not be the same rate as recognized on main products. Suppose the Nevares Company wanted to recognize profits on by-products at the rate of 10% of sales. With a $2.00 sales price, this amounts to $0.20 per pound. Then, the amount of Department I costs assigned is $1.30 per pound. Now it would be assumed that the by-product's sales price is just sufficient to cover the production costs, the distribution costs, and the profit. That is, the $2.00 sales price would be reduced by the selling cost of $0.50 and the profit of $0.20. In this way, then, the manufacturing cost is forced out. For 19x1, a total production cost of $1,300 would be assigned to product D. Again, the balance of Department I's cost of $225,000 ($226,300 − $1,300) would be assigned to the main products. The revenue from the sales of D would be accounted for by one of the methods discussed in the preceding paragraph.

Since there are so many by-product methods, they have been summarized for your convenience in Exhibit 10.9. The methods are numbered according to the order in which they were discussed. Since a by-product's economic impact is small, there is little theoretical preference of one method over the others. Thus, there is little value in attempting to support one of the methods over the other.

≳ Chain Joint Processes

One final situation involving joint products needs to be discussed: **chain joint processes.** As defined earlier, a chain joint process is one where there are multiple split-off points. That is, one of the products of a joint process becomes an input into another joint process, which, in turn, has multiple products as an output. To

---

Exhibit 10.9   Summary of By-Product Accounting Methods

Method Number	Consideration Given To			Accounting for Sales Price				Accounting for Costs of Production		Accounting for Selling Costs	
	Sales Only	Production; No Profit	Production; Profit	Revenue	Other Income	Decrease COGS*	Decrease COGM†	COGS*	Netted	S&A**	Netted
1	✓			✓						✓	
2	✓			✓							✓
3	✓				✓					✓	
4	✓				✓						✓
5	✓					✓				✓	
6	✓					✓					✓
7	✓						✓			✓	
8	✓						✓				✓
9		✓		✓				✓		✓	
10		✓			✓				✓		✓
11			✓	✓				✓		✓	
12			✓		✓				✓		✓

*Cost of goods sold

†Cost of goods manufactured

**Selling and administrative

account for the costs of the joint processes it is necessary to apply the joint cost allocation system repetitively. The mechanics will be illustrated in this section.

Let us modify the Nevares Company problem. These modifications are incorporated in Exhibit 10.10. Product C, in this modification, cannot be sold but must be further processed in Department IV. As a result, product C is split into two products, D and E. Product D can be sold at the split-off point for $80 per pound. Product E must go through additional processing via Department V. The 3,500 pounds of C that result from processing an 11,000 pound batch of Ingrediente will produce 1,500 pounds of D and 2,000 pounds of E. It will cost $20,000 to process this volume of E through Department V. Note also that the Department I and IV costs per batch are different from the original example. The joint cost method to be used is the NRV method.

Although not absolutely necessary, it is convenient to work through the allocation of the joint costs in reverse order. Thus, first consider Department IV. The cost of $174,000 is not the total joint cost of processing product C. Some of Department I's cost will be allocated to Department IV. However, the fact that the total joint cost of Department IV is not yet known does not stop us from computing the cost sharing ratios via the NRV method. These are shown in section A of Exhibit 10.11.

Next, consider Department I and note section B of Exhibit 10.11. The market value of products A and B are easily determined. Product C has a market value only through the sale of products D and E. In section A of Exhibit 10.11 note that the *total* market value is $310,000 per 3,500 pound batch of product C. Further, the separable costs of product C consist of $174,000 in Department IV and $20,000 in Department V. Although the $174,000 cannot be separately identified with respect to products D and E, there is no question about its separability with respect to

---

Exhibit 10.10   Nevares Company Chain Joint Processes

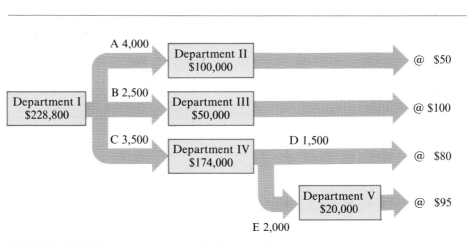

Exhibit 10.11   Modified Nevares Company Problem

A. Cost Allocation Ratios—Department IV

Product	Pounds	Market Price	Market Value	Separable Cost	NRV	Ratio
D	1,500	$80	$120,000	—	$120,000	12/29
E	2,000	95	190,000	$20,000	170,000	17/29
			$310,000	$20,000	$290,000	

B. Department I Cost Allocation

Product	Pounds	Relevant Market Price	Market Value	Separable Cost	NRV	Ratio	Joint Cost Allocation
A	4,000	$ 50	$200,000	$100,000	$100,000	100/416	$ 55,000
B	2,500	100	250,000	50,000	200,000	200/416	110,000
C	3,500	—	310,000[a]	194,000[b]	116,000	116/416	63,800
			$760,000	$344,000	$416,000		$228,800

C. Department IV Cost Allocation

Product	Ratio[c]	Allocation of Department I's Cost Assigned to Department IV	Allocation of Department IV's Cost	Total
D	12/29	$26,400	$ 72,000	$ 98,400
E	17/29	37,400	102,000	139,400
		$63,800[d]	$174,000	$237,000

[a]From Section A; total market value.

[b]Department IV cost + Department V cost.

[c]From Section A.

[d]From Section B.

product C. The NRV of product C is its ultimate market value of $310,000 less the separable cost of $194,000.

In section B of Exhibit 10.11 the Department I cost to be allocated to product C has been computed: $63,800. This cost is a joint cost to products D and E and should be allocated according to the ratios in section A. All of Department IV's costs are allocated in section C of Exhibit 10.11. A cost summary is provided in Exhibit 10.12.

Summary

Joint costs create problems whenever they occur, but they are particularly troublesome when their benefits extend to multiple products that result from a single production effort. In this chapter we have discussed various methods of accounting for joint costs. This accounting depends on whether the output is classified as a main product or by-product and on the characteristics of the situation.

Exhibit 10.12   Nevares Company Cost Summary Chain Joint Process Cost

	Product A	Product B	Product D	Product E	Total
Department I	$ 55,000[a]	$110,000[a]	$ 26,400[b]	$ 37,400[b]	$228,800
Department II	100,000				100,000
Department III		50,000			50,000
Department IV			72,000[b]	102,000[b]	174,000
Department V				20,000	20,000
	$155,000	$160,000	$ 98,400	$159,400	$572,800

[a]From Exhibit 10.11, Section B.

[b]From Exhibit 10.11, Section C.

At this point you should be comfortable with the purpose and mechanics of the net realizable value approach. Although other methods were discussed, the NRV approach is the one most commonly used. Theoretically, we might prefer the NRV less normal profit approach because it assumes that each of the production processes contribute to the final profit. However, this method has not been generally accepted in practice.

Several by-product accounting methods were explained. Further, we examined the NRV methods when there are two or more joint processes. The problems of joint costs in the context of decision making, planning, and control will be explored in more detail later in this book.

The new terms introduced in this chapter that you should be familiar with include:

Main products
By-products
Split-off point
Units method of allocating joint costs
Weighted average method of allocating joint costs
Net realizable value method of allocating joint costs
Relative sales value method
Hypothetical market value method
Net realizable value less normal profit method
Chain joint processes

SELF-STUDY PROBLEM. The Doherty Company processes raw material X23 in Department I to obtain three products: A and B, which are considered main products, and C, which is considered a by-product. Material X23 is added at the beginning of processing and conversion costs are incurred uniformly throughout the process. One batch of 10,000 pounds of X23 yields the following:

A   3,000 pounds
B   6,000 pounds
C   1,000 pounds

Product A can either be sold at the split-off point for $20 per pound or processed further in Department II at a total cost of $8 per pound. The output from Department B is called product D and is sold at $30 per pound.

Product B must be further processed in Department III. The output, product E, is sold at $15 per pound.

Product C is sold at $1.00 per pound. The selling and administration costs total $0.20 per pound. Product C is assigned a cost so that a zero profit will be recognized.

In the current period all departments began with no inventories in process. *Three* batches (10,000 pounds each) were started in Department I. Two were completed. The third is 75% complete at the end of the period.

All of product A, except for 500 pounds, was processed through Department II to obtain product D. The 500 pounds is in an intermediate inventory. There is no ending work in process inventory in Department II. All pounds of D produced were sold.

Department III started all but 1,000 pounds of product B. These 1,000 pounds are in an intermediate inventory. All but 600 pounds of the 11,000 pounds started in Department III were finished. The 600 pounds are 50% complete in Department III. Seven hundred (700) pounds of product E are in finished goods inventory. Department III's costs are incurred uniformly.

All but 300 pounds of product C produced this period were sold. The following production costs were incurred during the period:

Department I $30,000 for X23 and $275,000 for conversion
Department II $8 per pound
Department III $53,500

Required:

1. Flowchart the current period's activity.
2. Determine the cost of Department I's ending WIP inventory.
3. Considering your answer to number 2, assign the remainder of Department I's cost to products A, B, and C. The net realizable value method is used for main products.
4. Determine the cost of the ending inventories for products A, B, C, and E.

Solution to Self-Study Problem

1. The flowchart is contained in Exhibit 10.13.
2. Using units of X23, compute the equivalent units of activity in Department I.

Exhibit 10.13   Flowchart for Self-Study Problem The Doherty Company

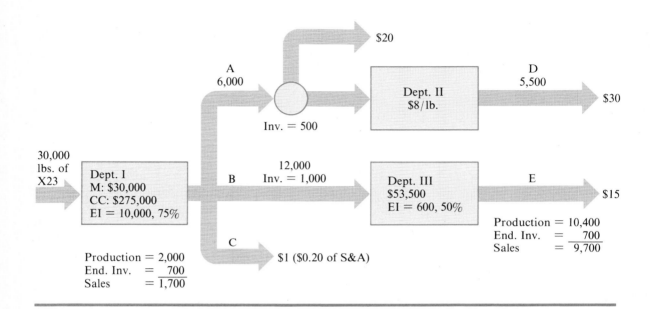

	Material	Conversion Costs
Started and finished	20,000	20,000
Ending inventory (100% for material and 75% for conversion costs)	10,000	7,500
Total	30,000	27,500
Current costs	$30,000	$275,000
Cost per unit	$ 1.00	$ 10.00
Ending inventory cost:		
Material 10,000 × $1.00	$10,000	
Conversion cost 7,500 × $10.00	75,000	
Total	$85,000	

3. The total costs to be transferred out of Department I are:

Total current costs ($30,000 + $275,000)	$305,000
Cost of Department I's ending inventory	85,000
Balance to transfer out	$220,000

Next, determine the cost of the by-product, product C. The production cost per unit must be $0.80—$1.00 selling price less $0.20 selling costs—since zero profits are to be recognized on by-products. Thus the 2,000 units of C produced this period would be assigned $1,600:

C: 2,000($1.00 − $0.20) = $1,600

This leaves $218,400 of Department I cost to allocate between products A and B, $220,000 − $1,600.

Following is the schedule to allocate the $218,400 using the NRV method.

Product	Pounds[a]	Relevant Price	Market Value	Separable Cost	NRV	Joint Costs
A	6,000	$20[b]	$120,000	—	$120,000	$109,200
B	12,000	15[c]	180,000	$60,000[d]	120,000	109,200
					$240,000	$218,400

[a]Note that the total output of Department I this period must share in this period's cost. Even though fewer pounds were processed further and/or sold, all 6,000 pounds of A and 12,000 of B benefited from the costs incurred this period in Department I.

[b]Product A has a market value at the split-off point. Use it as the relative value at that point.

[c]Sales price of product D, which is made from product B.

[d]The $53,500 incurred in Department III yielded benefits, on a relative basis, to all 11,000 units worked on this period; not just the 10,400 units completed. Find the cost per equivalent unit and then use it to project the cost of processing 12,000 units through Department III. (It is necessary to find the cost of 12,000 units since all of these units benefited from the cost in Department I, which we are trying to allocate.)

	Conversion Costs
Started and finished	10,400
Ending inventory (50%)	300
Total	10,700
Current costs	$53,500
Cost per unit (53,500 ÷ 10,700)	$5.00

Projected cost of 12,000 units = 12,000 × $5.00 = $60,000

Summary of cost allocation in Department I

Department I ending inventory (from part 1)	$ 85,000
To product C produced this period	1,600
To product A produced this period	109,200
To product B produced this period	109,200
Total	$305,000

4. Cost of ending inventories:

Product A (intermediate inventory) 500 × ($109,200 ÷ 6,000 pounds)	$9,100
Product B (intermediate inventory) 1,000 × ($109,200 ÷ 12,000 pounds)	9,100
Product C (by-product) 300 × $0.80	240
Product E 700 × (Product B cost + Conversion cost in Department II [determined in part 3, footnote d]) 700 × ($109,200 ÷ 12,000 + $5.00)	9,870

References

Griffin, C.H., "Multiple Products Costing in Petroleum Refining," *The Journal of Accountancy* (March 1958): 46–52.

Hartley, R.V. "Decision Making When Joint Products Are Involved," *The Accounting Review* (October 1971): 746–755.

Louderback, J.G. "Another Approach to Allocating Joint Costs: A Comment," *The Accounting Review* (July 1976): 683–685.

Moriarity, S. "Another Approach to Allocating Joint Costs," *The Accounting Review* (October 1975): 791–795.

Thomas. A.L. *Allocation Problem: Part II.* Sarasota, Fla.: American Accounting Association, 1974; 163–174.

Weil, R. "Allocating Joint Costs," *American Economic Review* (December 1968): 1342–1345.

Problems

10-1. Basic Problem on Joint Cost Accounting. The Texas Oil Company is a processor of crude oil. For each barrel of crude oil processed in the cracking department, 30 gallons of gasoline, 10 gallons of kerosene, and 15 gallons of diesel fuel are obtained. The variable cost of purchasing and processing crude oil totals $30 per barrel. During the current period 30,000 barrels of crude oil were processed. At the end of the current period the inventory consisted of 100,000 gallons of gasoline, 15,000 gallons of kerosene, and 50,000 gallons of diesel fuel. Gasoline sells at $0.80 per gallon, kerosene at $0.50, and diesel fuel at $0.70.

Required:

1. Determine the variable cost of the ending inventories using the units method for allocating the joint costs.
2. Determine the variable cost of the ending inventories using the net realizable value method of allocating the joint costs.

10-2. Basic Joint Cost Problem with Options at the Split-Off. In January the Ferrara Company processed 20,000 pounds of raw material through their joint process, Department I, at a total cost of $23,000. Two products, A and B, were obtained from that process in the following volumes:

A—12,000 pounds   B—8,000 pounds

Output A can either be sold at the split-off point or processed further. Due to a capacity limitation in Department II only 10,000 pounds of product A were further processed to produce product C. The remaining 2,000 pounds of product A were sold as is for $5 per pound.

In producing product C, $30,000 of costs were incurred in Department II. During the current period 8,000 pounds of product C were sold at $10 per pound.

Product B has to be processed further to obtain product D. During January all 8,000 pounds of product B were processed in Department III at an additional cost of $32,000. Of these pounds, 7,000 were sold at $8 per pound.

Required:

Use the NRV method to allocate joint costs and then determine the cost of the ending inventories of products C and D.

10-3. By-Product and Main Products with Options at Split-Off. The Illini Company makes three products from one common input. Process I is the joint process, and every 10 gallons of input yields 6 gallons of X, 3 gallons of Y, and 1/2 gallon of Z. The remaining 1/2 gallon is a waste product with no market value. Product X requires further processing in Process II at an average cost of $2.00 per gallon. It is then sold at $20 per gallon. Product Y is sold at the split-off point at $10 per gallon. Product Z, after further processing in Process III (at $0.50 per gallon), is sold at $1.00 per gallon. The selling expenses associated with Z are negligible, and the company desires to cost product Z so as to report a profit of 10% on its sales. During the current period 100,000 gallons of input was processed through Process I (assume no inventories), and the total operating costs in process I were $1,007,000.

Required:

1. Determine the amount of Process I cost to be assigned to by-product Z.
2. Determine the amount of joint costs to be assigned to X and Y using the relative sales value approach.
3. Determine the amount of joint costs to be assigned to X and Y using the NRV less normal profit approach.

10-4. Adapted CPA Problem on Basic Joint Product Costing. Miller Manufacturing Company buys zeon for $0.80 a gallon. At the end of processing in Department I, zeon splits off into products A, B, and C. Product A is sold at the split-off point, with no further processing. Product B and C require further processing before they can be sold; product B is processed in Department 2, and product C is processed in Department 3. Following is a summary of costs and other related data for the year ended June 30, 19x3.

	Department		
	1	*2*	*3*
Cost of zeon	$96,000	——	——
Direct labor	14,000	$45,000	$ 65,000
Manufacturing overhead	10,000	21,000	49,000

	Products		
	A	*B*	*C*
Gallons sold	20,000	30,000	45,000
Gallons on hand June 30, 19x3	10,000	——	15,000
Sales in dollars	$30,000	$96,000	$141,750

There were no inventories on hand at July 1, 19x2, and there was no zeon on hand at June 30, 19x3. All gallons on hand at June 30, 19x3, were complete as to processing. There were no manufacturing overhead variances. Miller uses the relative sales value method of allocating joint costs.

Required:

Prepare a schedule showing the cost of sales of each product and the cost of each ending inventory.

10-5. Basic Joint Products Problem with Volume Gain. The Fremgen Company processes a raw material through a joint process, Department I, to obtain two products, A and B. Both of these products must be further processed in order to make them marketable. Product A is processed further in Department II and product B in Department III.

During the current period $34,500 of cost was incurred in Department I to process 10,000 barrels of raw material. This yielded 4,000 barrels of product A, which were processed through Department II at an additional cost of $12,000. Product A was then sold at $8.00 per barrel.

The yield of product B this period was 6,000 barrels. In processing this product in Department III, 1,000 barrels of water were mixed with product B in order to dilute it to a usable product. The total output was 7,000 barrels and each barrel was sold at $9.00. Additional costs in Department III totaled $14,000 for the period.

Required:

Use the NRV method to allocate Department I's costs to products A and B.

10-6. Joint Products with a Volume Gain. Bibler Company processes peanuts into peanut butter and peanut oil. The normal volume of peanuts that can be processed per month is 30,000 pounds. Including the cost of peanuts the variable cost per pound in the crushing process is $0.60. The monthly fixed costs for the crushing department is $5,000.

The crushing process yields 70% "paste," 20% oil, and 10% waste. The paste is mixed with butter in the mixing department to obtain peanut butter. A pound of paste is mixed with 0.2 pounds of butter to obtain 1.2 pounds of peanut butter. Including the butter, the variable cost of processing a pound of peanut butter in the mixing department is $0.25. (Note, this is per pound of peanut butter, not per pound of paste.) The mixing department's fixed cost is $2,100 per month.

The oil must be pasteurized and bottled. The variable cost of bottling amounts to $0.45 per pound. Bottling's fixed costs are $700 per month.

Peanut butter sells for $1.40 per pound and peanut oil for $1.62 per pound.

Required:

1. Use the net realizable value method to determine the amount of joint costs that would be assigned to the output from a 30,000-pound batch.
2. Use the net realizable value less normal profit method to determine the amount of joint costs that would be assigned to the output from a 30,000-pound batch.

10-7. CPA Problem on Main and By-Product Accounting. In its three departments Amaco Chemical Company manufactures several products:

1. In Department 1 the raw materials amanic acid and bonyl hydroxide are used to produce Amanyl, Bonanyl, and Am-Salt. Ananyl is sold to others who use it as a raw material in the manufacture of stimulants. Bonanyl is not salable without further processing. Although Am-Salt is a commercial product for which there is a ready market, Amaco does not sell this product, preferring to submit it to further processing.
2. In Department 2 Bonanyl is processed into the marketable product, Bonanyl-X. The relationship between Bonanyl used and Bonanyl-X produced has remained constant for several months.
3. In Department 3 Am-Salt and the raw material Colb are used to produce Colbaynl, a liquid propellant that is in great demand. As an inevitable part of this process Demanyl is also produced. Demanyl was discarded as scrap until discovery of its usefulness as a catalyst in the manufacture of glue; for two years Amaco has been able to sell all of its production of Demanyl.

In its financial statements Amaco states inventory at the lower of cost (on the first-in, first-out basis) or market. Unit costs of the items most recently produced must therefore be computed. Costs allocated to Demanyl are computed so that after allowing for packaging and selling costs of $0.04 per pound no profit or loss will be recognized on sales of this product.
Certain data for October 19x2 follow:

Raw Materials:

Used	Pounds Cost	Total Cost
Amanic acid	6,300	$5,670
Bonyl hydroxide	9,100	6,370
Colb	5,600	2,240

Conversion Costs (labor and overhead):

	Total Cost
Department 1	$33,600
Department 2	3,306
Department 3	22,400

Products:

	Pounds Produced	Inventories, Pounds September 30	October 31	Sales Price per Pound
Amanyl	3,600			$ 6.65
Bonanyl	2,800	210	110	
Am-Salt	7,600	400	600	6.30
Bonanyl-X	2,755			4.20
Colbaynl	1,400			43.00
Demanyl	9,800			0.54

Required:

Prepare for October 19x2 the schedules listed. Supporting computations should be prepared in good form. Round answers to the nearest cent.

1. Cost per pound of Amanyl, Bonanyl, and Am-Salt produced—relative sales value method.
2. Cost per pound of Amanyl, Bonanyl, and Am-Salt produced—units method.
3. Cost per pound of Colbanyl produced. Assume that the cost per pound of Am-Salt produced was $3.40 in September 19x2 and $3.50 in October 19x2.

10-8. Joint Products; Inventory in Subsequent Department. The Longhorn Company processes crude oil in Department I. During the current period the following costs were incurred in Department I to obtain 20,000 barrels of product A and 30,000 barrels of product B:

Direct material	$ 50,000
Direct labor	150,000
Variable overhead	75,000
Fixed overhed	53,000
	$328,000

Product A could be sold at the split-off point for $5 per barrel or processed in Department II at an additional cost of $4 per barrel and then sold for $10 per barrel. During the current period all 20,000 barrels of A were processed in Department II. There was an ending inventory of 5,000 barrels of A.

Product B must be processed further in Department III. The following information from the current period is available about Department III:

Barrels Processed	*Costs*
31,000*	$310,000

*There were 1,000 barrels from the previous period's production of Department I processed in this period.

There is an ending inventory of 1,000 barrels of product B. The selling price of product B is $20 per barrel.

Required:

Determine the cost of the ending finished goods using the net realizable value method to allocate the joint costs.

10-9. NRV Less Normal Profit Method. The Bee Gee Chemical Company produces chemicals A and B from raw material X. One hundred gallons of X yields 80 gallons of A and 20 of B as a result of processing it in Department I. Product A requires further processing in Department II and then is sold at $15 per gallon. Product B is sold at the split-off point for $11.25 per gallon. The following additional data are available:

	6/1/ × 1	*6/30/ × 1*
Department I:		
Gallons in Department I inventory	0	100
Percentage completion of		
conversion costs	—	50%
Cost of material X added in June		
(1,100 gallons)	$2,200	$2,200
Conversion costs in June		$3,150
Department II:		
Gallons in Department II inventory	0	200
Percentage completion of		
conversion costs	—	25%
Conversion costs in June		$5,200
Finished goods inventories:		
Product A	0	100
Product B	0	50

Required:

Using the net realizable value less normal profit method, prepare a schedule to support the entry transferring the cost of completed production out of Department I.

10-10. Comprehensive Main and By-Product Problem. The Findley Company is a manufacturer of chemicals. Their production involves the mixing of several ingredients in Department I, which results in three products being siphoned off at the end of the processing. During the current month a batch of 10,000 barrels was processed in Department I. This processing resulted in product A at the rate of 30% of input, product B at 40%, product C at 25%, and waste at 5%.

Product A can be sold as is for $12 per barrel or processed further in Department II. There is neither volume gain nor loss in this department and the resulting product, product D, can be sold at $20 per barrel. During the current period the company converted all available product A into product D at a total cost of $15,000 in Department II. There were no beginning or ending inventories in this department.

Product B is not marketable as is. It must go through two additional processes in Departments III and IV. More chemicals are immediately added in Department III which increase the volume by a factor equal to 20% of the original volume started in Department III. There is no volume change when product B is further processed in Department IV. After the additional processing, product B can be sold at $25 per barrel.

During the current period the total direct cost of operating Department III was $28,000. There were no beginning or ending inventories.

Department IV started the period with an inventory of 2,000 barrels, 40% complete. It had been assigned a cost of $25,000 in the previous period, including $9,000 of Department I cost, $11,500 from Department III, and $4,500 from Department IV. Its ending inventory consisted of 1,000 barrels, 70% complete. The direct costs for the period totaled $38,000. Equivalent units are computed using the FIFO method.

Product C is also not marketable at the split-off point. It must be further processed in Department V. After that it can either be sold at $35 per barrel or processed further in Department VI to obtain product E. At a normal volume of 10,000 barrels started in

Department I the yield averages an additional cost of $10 per barrel to process in Department VI. Then, product E is sold at $40 per barrel. During the current period, Department VI was used for another purpose and product C was sold immediately after the processing in Department V. The total direct costs incurred by Department V were $37,500.

Department I's operating costs for the period total $58,000. In addition, the waste had to be disposed of at a cost of $0.80 per barrel. The sales volume for the month was as follows:

D—3,500 barrels   B—5,000 barrels   C—2,500 barrels

Required:

Use the relative sales value method to determine the allocation of Department I costs to the various products that resulted from the processing in Department I.

10-11. Comprehensive Problem; Main, By-Product, Inventory, and Spoilage. The Champagne Cheese Company produces three grades of cheese: A, B, and C. Grades A and B are considered main products and sell for $9 and $7 per pound, respectively. Grade C is a by-product and sells for $1 per pound. The company does not recognize any profit on its by-product. (Selling expenses are negligible.)

Raw material X is put into Department I, the joint process. Grade A cheese requires further processing in Departments II and III before being sold. Grade B is processed further in Department IV, and Grade C requires additional processing in Department V. The company uses the net realizable value method in assigning joint costs.

The following data about the five departments are available:

	Department I	Department II	Department III	Department IV	Department V
Cost of material added in January (added at beginning of processing)	$190,000	$40,000	0	0	0
Conversion costs added in January	265,000	31,000	$38,500	$69,000	$3,485
Inventory, 1/1/x1 (pounds)	0	0	0	2,000	0
Percentage completion of conversion in 1/1/x1 inventory	—	—	—	25%	—
Inventory, 1/31/x1 (pounds)	0	0	0	3,000	0
Percentage completion of conversion in 1/31/x1 inventory	—	—	—	One-third	—

During January 91,000 pounds of raw material X were put into Department I. It yielded 50,000 pounds of A, 35,000 pounds of B, and 5,000 pounds of C. Due to unusual circumstances, one batch of 1,000 gallons of X was defective but was not detected until production was complete.

Required:

Prepare a combined journal entry to transfer out the appropriate amount of Department I's cost during January. Prepare supporting schedules. (The modified FIFO equivalent unit method is used.)

10-12. Problem 10-11 Using NRV Less Normal Profit Method. Reconsider problem 10-11 but assume that the conversion cost added during January in Department V was $1,000 instead of $3,485.

Required:

Prepare the required journal entry for Department I assuming the net realizable value less normal profit method is used.

10-13. Joint Products with Inventories in Joint Process. The Falcon Company produces three products from a single raw material input. One unit of raw material X processed in Department I yields 2 boxes of A (sales value, $5 per box), 1 gallon of B (sales value, $6 per gallon), and 1/2 pound of C (sales value, $0.20 per pound). Before product A can be sold, it requires further processing in Department II. Material Y is added at the start of the processing in Department II but does *not* increase the number of boxes. Likewise, products B and C require further processing in Departments III and IV, respectively.

Product C is a by-product and is accounted for so that it yields a zero profit. Selling and administrative costs average $0.02 per pound for product C. The following data concerning the four departments are available:

	I	II	III	IV
Material cost	$105,000	$60,000	0	0
Conversion cost	61,000	40,000	$91,800	$1,150
Beginning inventory	1,000 units	0	400 gallons	0
Percentage completion;				
beginning inventory	20%	—	25%	—
Cost of beginning inventory	$ 6,750	—	$ 1,000	—
Ending inventory	500 units	0	300 gallons	0
Percentage completion;				
ending inventory	40%	—	One-third	—

During the current month, 30,000 units of raw material X were put into Department I. The modified FIFO system is used in accounting for the various departmental costs.

Required:

Assume the net realizable value method is used in accounting for joint costs. Support and prepare the entry transferring the appropriate current costs out of Department I.

10-14. Comprehensive Problem Over Several Chapters. The Cleve and Brown Company produces two products, X and Z. The manufacturing begins by putting a raw material, S, into a separating process, Department A. For each 10,000 units of S started the company obtains 2,000 units of X and 8,000 units of Z. Product X can be sold as is for $10 per unit. Product Z requires additional processing in two additional processes, Departments B and C. The incremental *standard* cost in Department B is $30 per unit (including labor) and is $20 per unit in Department C (including labor) or a total of $50 per unit beyond Department A. After this additional processing, product Z can be sold at $100 per unit. During the current period 10,000 units of S were processed by Department A.

The company also produces its own power. Thus, in addition to the product responsibility centers, the company has a Power Department. A standard cost system is in use. In this problem you will be asked to consider the labor cost only. The flowchart in Exhibit 10.14 is

Exhibit 10.14   Cleve and Brown Company Labor Cost Flow

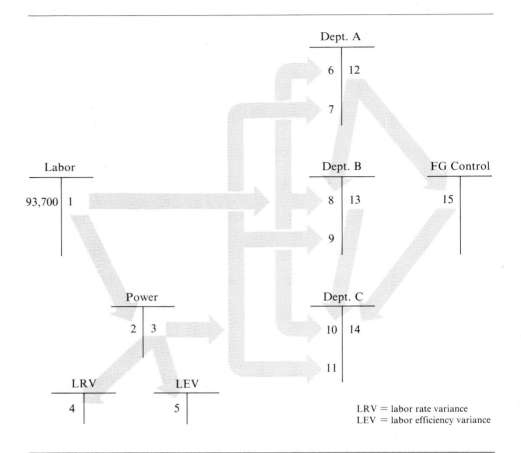

for the labor component and assumes that all three production departments incurred no labor variances during the current period. (The numbers are to aid in the identification of the various cost flows.)

The payroll records reveal that the total labor of $93,700 was incurred and attributable as follows:

Department A	$30,000
Department B	18,000
Department C	24,000
Power Department	21,700
	$93,700

The standards in the Power Department allows 3,333.33 labor hours per 10,000 kilowatt hours at a standard cost of $3.00 per labor hour. During the current period 20,000 KWH of power were generated and metered out as follows:

Department A	12,000 KWH
Department B	6,000 KWH
Department C	2,000 KWH

The actual labor charged to Power totaled 7,000 hours.

Beginning inventories were zero in all three production departments. Likewise, there were no ending inventories except in Department C where 2,000 units were partially complete at the end of the period. Labor was 25% complete.

The power costs were accounted for as an overhead cost in each of the production departments. In all three cases, overhead is applied on the basis of labor hours.

All references to labor in the questions below are to be interpreted as *total* labor, not just direct labor.

Required:

1. What is the labor cost flow from:
   a. 1 to 2?
   b. 1 to 6?
   c. 1 to 8?
   d. 1 to 10?
2. What is the labor cost flow from:
   a. 3 to 4?
   b. 3 to 5?
   c. 3 to 7?
   d. 3 to 9?
   e. 3 to 11?
3. Assuming that the relative sales value method is used for the allocation of joint costs, what is the labor cost flow from:
   a. 12 to 15?
   b. 12 to 8?
4. What is the labor cost flow from:
   a. 13 to 10?
   b. 14 to 15?

10-15. Process Costing with Main and By-Products. The Ohio Company produces three products from one input. For each barrel of Glop put into the separation process (Department A) the company normally obtains 20 gallons of Why, 30 gallons of Zee, and 5 gallons of Bypo. Why and Zee are accounted for as main products and Bypo as a by-product.

Product Why can either be sold at the split-off point for $4.00 per gallon or processed in Department B to produce Whynot. Each gallon of Whynot requires one gallon of Why and can be sold at $8.00

Zee must be further refined in Department C. Then it can be sold at $20 per gallon. There is no loss of volume in Department C when Zee is processed.

Bypo sells for $1.00 per gallon. Subsequent to its transfer from Department A, a cost of $0.80 per gallon is incurred on the packaging, selling, and administrative costs. Bypo is to be assigned production costs so that it will show an income of zero dollars.

During January 900 barrels of Glop were started in Department A. The company has decided to process all output of Why in order to make Whynot. The weighted average method is used in all departments. Following are the production and cost data for each department. The percentage completions apply to all departments. During January one batch of 50 barrels of Glop was abnormally spoiled and had no value (not even as Bypo). This was detected only after *all* processing was complete. There was no normal spoilage.

	Department A	Department B	Department C
Beginning inventory	100 barrels	1,000 gals.	0
Material cost (100%)	$310	——	——
Conversion cost (25%)	150	$250	——
Prior department (100%)	——	210	——
Ending inventory	200 barrels	0	0
Material cost (100%)	?	——	——
Conversion cost (75%)	?	——	——
Abnormal spoilage	50 barrels	——	——
Glop cost (current)	$2,690	——	——
Conversion cost (current)	4,600	$15,750	$410,000

Required:

1. Prepare a complete process cost report for Department A. On this statement determine the *total* cost to be transferred *out* of Department A. This figure need not be detailed as to where it will be transferred. See parts 2 and 3 for this.
2. How much of the cost to be transferred out of Department A will be assigned to Bypo? Show support.
3. How much of Department A's cost will be transferred to Department B and to Department C? Show support and assume the relative sales value method is used.

10-16. Chain Joint Processes. The Bobcat Company markets four products: C, D, E, and G. To obtain these products, material X is processed in Department I to obtain intermediate products A and B. Product A must then be processed in Department II to obtain C and D. Likewise product B must be further processed in Department III to obtain E and F. Product F is not marketable in the form resulting from Department III and requires additional processing in Department IV to obtain product G.

For each 1,000 pounds of X, 300 pounds of A and 700 pounds of B are obtained. The variable cost of processing a 1,000-pound batch of X in Department I is $10,640. It costs $1,400 to process a 300-pound batch of A in Department II and this results in an output of 200 pounds of C and 100 pounds of D.

In Department III there is a weight loss of 100 pounds to obtain an output of 300 pounds of E and 300 of F. Department III incurs cost at the rate of $9,000 per 700-pound batch. When the 300 pounds of F are processed through Department IV, 200 pounds of additional material are added. Including the additional material, the cost of processing a batch of F is $6,000.

The sales prices of the various products are as follows:

| C | $20 per pound | E | $40 per pound |
| D | $30 per pound | G | $48 per pound |

Required:

Using the net realizable value method to allocate the joint costs, determine the total cost of each of the products that are obtained from a 1,000-pound batch of raw material X.

10-17. Chain Processes with Negative NRV. Reconsider the Bobcat case in problem 10-16. Instead of the sales prices used there, assume the following:

| C | $40 per pound | E | $50 per pound |
| D | $60 per pound | G | $ 4 per pound |

Further, assume that it would cost more than $6,000 to destroy 300 pounds of product F. Thus, it has been decided to process them through Department IV.

Required:

Using the net realizable value method to allocate the joint costs, determine the total cost of each of the products that are obtained from 1,000-pound batch of raw material X.

10-18. Adapted CPA Problem on Chain Processes. The Harrison Corporation produces three products: Alpha, Beta, and Gamma. Alpha and Gamma are main products, whereas Beta is a by-product of Alpha. No joint costs is to be allocated to the by-product. The production processes for a given year are as follows:

1. In Department I, 110,000 pounds of raw material Rho are processed at a total cost of $120,000. After processing in Department I, 60% of the units are transferred to Department II, and 40% of the units (now Gamma) are transferred to Department III.
2. In Department II, the material is further processed at a total additional cost of $38,000. Seventy percent of the units (now Alpha) are transferred to Department IV, and 30% emerge as Beta, the by-product, to be sold at $1.20 per pound. Selling expenses related to disposing of Beta are $8,100.
3. In Department IV, Alpha is processed at a total additional cost of $23,660. After this processing, Alpha is ready for sale at $5 per pound.
4. In Department III, Gamma is processed at a total additional cost of $165,000. In this department, a normal loss of units of Gamma occurs which equals 10% of the *good output* of Gamma. The remaining good output of Gamma is then sold for $12 per pound.

Required:

Prepare a schedule showing the allocation of the $120,000 joint cost between Alpha and Gamma using the relative sales value approach. The net realizable value of Beta should be treated as an addition to the sales value of Alpha.

10-19. Involved Chain Process Problem. The Austin Company processes raw material Y by subjecting it to a secret separation procedure in Department I. Each 100 gallons of Y produces 50 gallons of A and 40 gallons of B. The remaining 10 gallons are considered to be waste with no value. The Department I variable cost totals $7,500 per batch.

Product A must be processed through Department II at a variable cost of $7,800 per 50 gallon batch. This process further separates output A into 30 gallons of product C and 20 gallons of D. After additional processing in Department III at a variable cost of $3,500 per 30 gallon batch, product C is converted into 25 gallons of product F and sold at $500 per gallon. The remaining 5 gallons are waste.

The 40 gallons of product B that results from processing a batch in Department I is converted to product E in Department IV. Department IV's variable cost is $1,200 per batch. Then, product D from Department II is mixed with product E to obtain product G. Although product D could be sold at the Department II split-off point for $200 per gallon, studies have shown that using it for product G is more profitable. Department V does the mixing using 1 gallon of D and 2 gallons of E for every container of G. Since a 100-gallon batch of Y yields 20 gallons of D and 40 gallons of E, the output of Department V is 20 containers of G per batch started in Department I. The variable mixing cost in Department V is $5,000 per batch, and product G sells for $1,000 per container.

Required:

Using the net realizable value method, determine the total variable cost of the 25 gallons of F and 20 containers of G that result from 100 gallons of material X.

CHAPTER 11

Cost Accounting Applied to Nonmanufacturing Costs

The previous chapters have considered the major issues in cost accounting. There are a number of other secondary issues that must also be considered. For example, cost accounting principles can be potentially applied to accounting for selling, general, and administrative services of any type of organization whether it be manufacturing, retail, service, or nonprofit. Some of these applications will be explored here. Further, the costing of products and services are sometimes prescribed by a variety of government regulations. The regulations we emphasize are primarily in the nonmanufacturing cost area. Therefore, we have elected to delay the coverage of some of these regulations until this chapter.

The first section concentrates on the possible uses of cost accounting in the area of selling, general, and administrative expenses. All firms incur these types of expenses, and the discussion will be broad enough to include any type of profit-oriented organization. Because of the special needs of manufacturing, retail and service, and nonprofit organizations, a section is devoted to each in order to explore their unique cost accounting requirements.

Costing of Selling, General, and Administrative Services

In this section we explore the possibilities of extending the principles of cost accounting to the area of selling, general, and administrative services. As in previous chapters, remember that the theme in Part II of this book is cost determination. We begin by considering cost determination situations in which the selling, general, and administrative data are needed on other than an aggregated, or total basis. Then we consider some of the techniques used to allocate these costs in obtaining data relevant to those needs.

NEED FOR SELLING, GENERAL, AND ADMINISTRATIVE COST BY SEGMENT. Under generally accepted accounting principles, selling, general, and administrative (SGA) costs are treated as *period* costs. Thus, they are not allocated to output for inventory costing and income determination purposes. However, inventory costing is not the only need that must be served by cost accounting. Financial accounting standards require industrial and geographical **segment**

reporting, which, in turn, requires an allocation of certain SGA costs. Further, product price setting and analysis requires a consideration of total costs, including SGA costs. Some contracts are cost-plus-profit contracts where cost includes a share of the SGA costs. Finally, the Robinson-Patman Act requires that firms be able to cost-justify any price differentials that may exist among purchasers of products that are of like grades and quantities. Frequently these differentials will be due to SGA costs. Each of these requirements are briefly considered in this subsection.

In December 1976 the Financial Accounting Standards Board issued *FAS Statement Number 14,* entitled "Financial Reporting for Segments of a Business Enterprise." This reporting requirement was imposed as a direct result of the widespread trend of business enterprises to diversify their operations. The Board's feeling was that a diversified firm can be better evaluated if there are data provided about the portion of the firm's total sales, profits, and assets that are attributable to each of its major segments. The Board's conclusion is based on the premise that changing conditions affect various industries differently. Of course, this premise is a major reason that firms want to diversify. Through diversification a firm attempts to minimize the fluctuation of its income by selecting segments that respond differently to a variety of economic conditions.

Much of *FAS Standard 14* is not appropriate for discussion in this text. However, the standard does require an allocation of operating costs including SGA costs and, for this reason, its basic requirements are examined. A firm must classify its products and services into industrial lines. If a given line is a significant portion of the firm, then it must be separately reported in the published statements. Criteria for classifying a segment as significant are included in *FAS Standard 14.* Similarly, if there are operations in foreign countries, there must be a classification of the firm's activities by geographic area and a separate reporting on each one that is significant. Going into the details of the criteria is not essential for our purposes, but it might be beneficial to consider how some selected companies are complying with this requirement. Exhibit 11.1 lists several companies and the segments on which they reported in recent annual statements.

FAS Standard 14 does not provide any specific guidelines for the allocation of operating expenses among the segments except that the allocations should be made on a reasonable and consistent basis. The Board felt it was not appropriate for it to devise any *specific* rules and procedures for the necessary allocations. It was thought that an accountant with knowledge of the situation could better make these judgments. For purposes of this standard, operating expenses include all those expenses that relate to revenue but exclude, among others, general corporate expenses, interest expense, and income taxes. General corporate expenses include corporate officers' salaries, general legal expenses, and shareholder costs. As to the segment allocation of the manufacturing component of operating expenses, the previous chapters should provide sufficient guidelines. In the next section we consider some possible techniques of allocating SGA costs.

A second need for segmenting SGA costs is for *price determination and/or analysis.* If there is any kind of competition in the marketplace, cost is only one of sev-

---

Exhibit 11.1   Representative Examples of Compliance with
FASB Standard on Segment Reporting

Owens-Illinois, Inc.

Industrial Segments	*Geographical Segments*
Packaging Products	United States
Food and Beverage Service	Other Western Hemisphere
Other	Europe

Gulf Oil Corporation

Industrial Segments	*Geographical Segments*
Petroleum	United States
Exploration and Production	Canada
Refining and Marketing	Europe
Chemicals	Other
Minerals	

E. I. due Pont de Nemours

Industrial Segments	*Geographical Segments*
Chemicals	United States
Plastics	Europe
Speciality Products	Other
Fibers	

Dow Chemical Company

Industrial Segments	*Geographical Segments*
Chemicals/Metals	United States
Plastics/Packaging	Europe/Africa
Bioproducts/Consumer Products	Canada
	Pacific
	Latin America
	Brazil

---

eral factors that must be considered in the pricing decision. When conditions are competitive, prices will be a function of the type of market, the relationship between supply and demand, the relationship between demand and price, the firm's present market strategy, the firm's cost structure, and other factors. Even if the price is determined entirely by the market, management will need to know the behavior of total costs in order to determine if it wants to continue to compete for a share of the demand. Pricing is a decision-making activity and is included in discussions in later chapters. The purpose of discussing this type of decision here is that, occasionally, the price is *cost plus* a profit. The prices of the output of regulated industry are cost-related prices that usually must be approved by some regulatory commission. (Natural gas, electricity, and transportation are examples.) Also cost-plus-profit prices are frequently the base for contracts with various government agencies when the products or services are not openly traded in the market. That is, there are some situations where the cost must be determined before the price can be set. As with previous chapters, keep in mind the purpose of our present mission; do not proceed with the impression that a full cost is needed for every purpose.

TECHNIQUES OF ALLOCATION. Given there is a valid reason for allocating SGA costs to a given cost objective, how should it be done? Although it is difficult to gather evidence to support it, there is a suspicion that these allocations are frequently made on *grossly arbitrary* bases. Of course, in the final analysis, a carefully chosen base may still be considered by some critics to be arbitrary. However, it might be argued that there are degrees of arbitrariness.

If there is a general rule for allocating SGA costs, it would have to be of the same nature as discussed in previous chapters. That is, any cost allocation should measure, to the maximum extent possible, the relative benefit accruing to the objectives receiving a share of the costs. Further, the cost allocated to one segment should be as independent as possible of the activities of all other segments that will share the cost.

Ideally, the data collection process will permit an identification of those SGA costs that directly and singularly benefit one segment. Costs that can be identified in this way need not be allocated. For example, if advertising is product oriented, then its cost would clearly benefit and be assignable to only one industrial (product) segment for segment reporting purposes. On the other hand, if advertising is directed toward achieving firm identification and loyalty, then direct tracing to specific products is impossible.

After isolating the directly traceable items accountants face the question of whether to allocate the remaining common costs and, if so, how. As an empirical starting point, let us consider some of the results of a very extensive study done for the Financial Executive's Institute by Richard Vancil.[1] In this 1979 study, firms were surveyed on a variety of matters related to the problems of decentralization, including how certain SGA costs were allocated. Of the companies having research and development functions that served several organizational units, 23% reported allocating their costs on a project (actual usage) basis, 9% on the basis of sales, 8% on the basis of operating costs, 25% on a combination basis (part on actual usage and part on an allocation scheme), and 29% did not allocate.[2] Other selected service costs and allocation techniques include:[3]

---

[1] Richard F. Vancil, *Decentralization: Managerial Ambiguity by Design* (Homewood, Ill.: Dow Jones-Irwin, 1979).

[2] Vancil, p. 218.

[3] Vancil, p. 250

Advertising

22%—Actual usage
14 —Allocated on sales
13 —Estimated usage
28 —Not allocated

Finance and Accounting

21%—Estimated usage
20 —Allocated on sales
10 —Allocated on some cost basis
27 —Not allocated

Electronic Data Processing

34%—Actual usage
20 —Estimated usage
12 —Allocated on sales
13 —Not allocated

Corporate Planning Department

23%—Allocated on sales
12 —Allocated on some cost basis
37 —Not allocated

Fremgen and Liao did a similar study in 1983. They asked firms how a variety of SGA expenses are allocated for each of four purposes:

1. Performance Evaluation
2. Cost-Based Pricing
3. Decision Analysis
4. Financial Reporting

Thirty of the 123 firms that responded used a single allocation basis for *all* expenses for *all* four purposes. For example, eight firms used sales as the basis of allocating all SGA costs for all purposes. Seven used net assets and five used total direct expenses for all allocations.[4]

Being separated from the situations surrounding the need for methods of allocating the SGA costs, it is difficult to evaluate the merits of any company's procedures. In general, however, you need to exercise caution to avoid some potential pitfalls. You will note that sales revenue was frequently used as a base for allocating several of the aforementioned costs. This, however, may be more representative of a segment's ability to bear the cost than of benefit received or degree of causation. For example, sales do not cause advertising; instead, advertising *may* cause sales.

To illustrate the potential impact of using sales as the allocation base, consider the following case. The Snively Company reports on three individual product segments. The results for 19x8 and 19x9 are contained in Exhibit 11.2 where sales salaries *are allocated on the basis of sales dollars.* The salesmen are responsible for marketing all of the firm's products. During 19x8 the activities of the three segments were approximately the same as in previous years and their relationship to each other reflected reasonably well the relative effort that had been put forth by the sales staff. However, in 19x9 some of the products in segment B became increasingly harder to sell. This was due to increasing competition and the shift of the market to lower-quality versions of the products, a market in which the company had elected not to compete.

---

[4]James M. Fremgen and Shu S. Liao, *The Allocation of Corporate Indirect Costs* (New York: National Association of Accountants, 1983), p. 50.

Exhibit 11.2   Snively Company Income Statement by Segment for the Year Ended 12/31/x8 and 12/31/x9

		19x8		
	Segment A	*Segment B*	*Segment C*	*Total*
Sales	$500,000	$300,000	$50,000	$850,000
Variable costs	250,000	180,000	35,000	465,000
Contribution margin	$250,000	$120,000	$15,000	$385,000
Fixed costs				
Sales salaries	$100,000	$ 60,000	$10,000	$170,000
Other—direct traceable	60,000	30,000	3,000	93,000
Total fixed	$160,000	$ 90,000	$13,000	$263,000
Net income	$ 90,000	$ 30,000	$ 2,000	$122,000
		19x9		
	Segment A	*Segment B*	*Segment C*	*Total*
Sales	$500,000	$150,000	$200,000	$850,000
Variable costs	250,000	90,000	140,000	480,000
Contribution margin	$250,000	$ 60,000	$ 60,000	$370,000
Fixed costs				
Sales salaries	$100,000	$ 30,000	$ 40,000	$170,000
Other—direct traceable	60,000	30,000	3,000	93,000
Total fixed	$160,000	$ 60,000	$ 43,000	$263,000
Net income	$ 90,000	$ 0	$ 17,000	$107,000

Simultaneously, the products in segment C caught the attention of the market. Having been a leader in the development of those products, the Snively Company faced almost no competition during 19x9. Thus, with very little additional sales effort, the sales quadrupled in comparison with 19x8. However, the allocation method used for sales salaries makes it appear that the sales effort for segment C products also quadrupled. In fact, there was a shifting of effort during 19x9 to segment B's products in an attempt to meet the competition.

It should be obvious in this case that revenue is not a good allocation base for the 19x9 salaries. What might be done instead? It might be necessary to poll the sales staff to see if some consensus can be determined about the relative effort expended in marketing the products of each segment. Obviously this may not result in a totally objective base, but it will be more relevant than the sales base. It is important that accountants avoid letting objectivity be the sole criterion for the selection of accounting procedures. You must always be alert to the reasonableness of the results, and this depends on the purpose for which the allocation is needed. As an alternative to polling the sales staff, sampling techniques could be used. To do this a sample of the staff would be selected and asked to keep detailed time analyses of how their efforts are expended. From this sample, allocation ratios could be derived.

Costing SGA Services in a Manufacturing Firm

As indicated in the introduction to this chapter, a section is being devoted to each general type of organization (manufacturing, retail and service, and nonprofit) and the potential applicability of cost accounting to their nonmanufacturing activities. For a manufacturing firm, we examine two unique problems of accounting for SGA costs. First to be considered is the accounting for and control of order-getting and order-filling costs. Second, the Robinson-Patman Act is discussed in terms of its implications for cost accounting.

ACCOUNTING FOR ORDER-GETTING AND ORDER-FILLING COSTS. **Order-getting costs** are represented by such broad classes of activities as advertising, sales salaries and commissions, sales promotions, and marketing research. In contrast, **order-filling costs** are incurred to fulfill the sale and include such items as warehousing costs, transportation and delivery costs, and order processing costs. The cost accounting techniques needed to effectively control these classes of costs are different from those needed to control manufacturing costs.

Order-getting costs do not represent activities that are repetitive and standardized. Efficiency and effectiveness of order-getting costs efforts *cannot* be measured by determining the amount of input that should have been expended in order to obtain the output (sales). Standards based on output would imply that order-getting costs are caused by sales volume when, in effect, the relationship is reversed. Even if a standard costing system were capable of being constructed for order-getting activities, it would likely lead to dysfunctional results. For example, advertising could be managed to look more effective by promoting easy-to-sell products. The ratio of advertising to sales dollars would be lowered by such an action. However, this may not be the action that management intended to be induced by a control system.

Controlling order-getting costs requires a system that differs from those suggested for controlling manufacturing costs. Following are some considerations that should be incorporated into the design of such a system. When planning order-getting efforts, there should be a forecast of their anticipated benefits such as the expected increase in profits. Then efficiency and effectiveness would be measured by comparing the actual results with those anticipated. In doing this, the accountant will be faced with many problems that require professional judgment. For example, in projecting and computing profits there will be many cost items that would be questionable inclusions. Should the variable or full absorption costing approach be taken? This can only be answered in the context of the situation.

Other factors that complicate the evaluation of order-getting costs include different market response rates to order-getting efforts and time lags between efforts and results. The response rate of a market simply translates as the change in sales resulting from an additional unit of sales effort. This change is, in part, a function of the product, geographical area, general economic conditions, and the current state of market saturation. A time lag is the elapsed time between effort and results. When evaluations are based on data from a short period of time, a lagged market response is critical in the sense that the effort expended by the marketing staff is underevaluated.

Now, consider the other type of sales costs. Since order-filling costs are caused by sales, using a predetermined standard allowance may prove useful in certain situations. That is, it may make sense to determine the resources that should have been used in filling the orders of the period. However, unlike factory workers, office workers are more likely to regularly shift their efforts from one function to another. Thus, accounting for their time is very difficult. Even though standards are conceptually desirable in controlling order-filling costs, they may prove impractical. Again, each situation will have to be carefully evaluated to assess the practicality of standards.

IMPLICATIONS OF ROBINSON-PATMAN ACT. The Federal Trade Commission is responsible for enforcing the Robinson-Patman Act which requires firms to be able to justify price differentials that might be made to purchasers of like products. The purpose of this regulation is to prevent firms from using price differentials that would lessen competiton or create monopolies and that would injure, destroy, or prevent competition. Since the act refers to like products, it would be reasonable to assume that any cost differentials would generally be due to non-manufacturing costs. Thus, if price differentials among customers are anticipated, the selling and administrative costs will need to be accounted for in an appropriate way in order to justify the differences.

There are few pronouncements and precedents to guide a firm in meeting the requirements of the Robinson-Patman Act. What little that does exist suggests that to be in compliance a firm must generally be able to show differentials by individual products, not by groups of products. Also, for showing compliance, a grouping of customers is allowed only if the group is homogeneous. Further, fixed costs must be assigned and the compliance assessed in terms of a total cost. In enforcing the act, the Federal Trade Commission (FTC) has never allowed cost differentials to be proven by looking at differences in marginal costs. If economies of scale do occur as a result of increased activity, the FTC has argued that all customers should benefit, not just the last customer. Thus, it is generally necessary to show that cost differentials are due to avoided costs associated with specific methods of processing the order (SGA costs).

Allocating joint costs on the basis of sales is not acceptable to the FTC. This is circular reasoning. With such an allocation scheme the difference in price would itself lead to a cost justification. The customer paying the smaller price will be charged with less cost when allocations are based on sales.

Further, a cost study is more convincing if it is done prior to the sale rather than after. A study done prior to setting prices suggests that forethought was given to setting a differential. A postsale study has the appearance of trying to defend an action already taken. In gathering acceptable evidence it may be necessary to require salespeople to account for their time by customer. Then the fixed costs of supervision and occupancy can be allocated on the basis of salespeople's time. Space does not permit any additional discussion of the implications of the Robinson-Patman Act.[5]

Applications to Retail and Service Organizations

In recent years, there has been increasing attention given to applying cost accounting to nonmanufacturing firms. In this section consideration is given to retail and service organizations. These organizations have some needs that are the same as those of a manufacturing firm and others that are different. We explore these differences and a possible system that is very useful in accounting for the cost of operating this type of organization.

NEEDS OF RETAIL AND SERVICE ORGANIZATIONS. Of course, retail organizations differ from manufacturers in that they do not produce the products they sell. Thus they have no need for an elaborate system that determines the cost of readying their products for sale. Under conventional accounting techniques, all labor and overhead costs of a retail firm are treated as period selling and administrative expenses. Service organizations, of course, do not handle any type of physical product. Even though they can be viewed, in a broad sense, as producing the services they sell, these services are not inventoriable. Conventionally, then, the labor and overhead costs of service organizations are also accounted for as period expenses. In short, retail and service organizations do not have the visible, readily identifiable cost objective that is characteristic of manufacturers: the produced product. Even though financial accounting systems accumulate these costs as period expenses, there are objectives for which an allocation of costs is needed.

Some of the needs for allocating costs in retail and service organizations are identical to those in manufacturing organizations: sales price analyses, cost-plus contracts, rate justifications (for regulated firms), and a variety of decisions. So long as a given activity can best be served by data that reflect the fair share of the costs that benefited the activity, the principles of allocation discussed to this point in the book still apply. There is nothing to be gained by discussing them again.

It is instructive, however, to sample some of the cost needs of these nonmanufacturing business firms. Retail organizations need to know cost behaviors in order to make intelligent decisions about markups over the invoice prices of the items they sell. Banks must know the cost of providing various services in order to evaluate their service charges and the profitability rate of both the customer and the service. This might be accomplished by establishing various responsibility centers within the bank and, in turn, a standard cost rate per unit of the center's output. Responsibility centers might include electronic data processing, proof machine operators, tellers, mortgage administration, and so forth. Then each service would

---

[5]For an expanded discussion, see Herbert F. Taggart, *Cost Justification, Michigan Business Study,* vol. 14, no. 3 (Ann Arbor: Bureau of Business Research, University of Michigan, 1959).

be analyzed as to the amount of effort extended by each responsibility center. Using the time required in each center and the standard rates, a total cost of the service could be estimated.

Insurance companies must know the cost of issuing and maintaining a policy in addition to the probable payout that will occur. Real estate developers need to know the cost of their various projects and how much should be attributed to each unit within the project. Fast food chains need to know the cost of preparing a hamburger for sale; sports organizations, the cost of putting an athletic team on the field; stock brokerage houses, the cost of servicing an account; accounting firms, the cost of assigning a senior to the audit; and so forth.

Although the form of costing for nonmanufacturing business organizations may be different, its substance is the same as for a manufacturer. The difference is that the cost objective is something other than a product. Further, quality control in a service organization must be different since there is no physical product that can be inspected. Measuring the quality of professional services is a much less precise endeavor.

In regulated businesses there are other concerns. Regulated businesses must meet the requirements of their allied regulatory bodies. Various state and federal utility commissions have cost accounting rules that must be complied with when telephone, gas, and electric companies make a rate request. That is, they must cost justify the prices they charge. Railroads, pipeline companies, motor carriers, and bus lines are governed by the Interstate Commerce Commission. When working for a regulated company, it is necessary to carefully observe the rules by which it is governed.

ATTRIBUTABLE COST AS A POSSIBLE BASIS FOR A COST SYSTEM.   For manufacturing firms, accounting systems tend to be product or job oriented. There are fewer reasons for such an orientation in a service organization. Exceptions to this include consulting and accounting firms that would have identifiable jobs. When there is no product or job, some suggest that attributable cost be the prevailing theme in designing a cost accounting system.[6] **Attributable costs** are those costs that will be eliminated if the service or product is eliminated and if enough time is allowed to make the necessary adjustments to permit their elimination. This concept is not synonymous with the typical fixed-variable dichotomy. Although fixed costs do not change with most changes in volume, they are likely to change when volume goes to *zero*. For example, a salaried salesperson that is employed only to sell life insurance would represent a cost that is attributable to the life insurance line of the company. If the life insurance line is discontinued, then the salesperson's salary is eliminated.

Determining the attributable cost frequently is not as easy as this illustration. For example, each of a broker's insurance agents may market all types of insurance

---

[6]For an expanded discussion of this concept, see Gordon Shillinglaw, "Concept of Attributable Cost," *Journal of Accounting Research,* Spring 1963, pp. 73–85, or John Dearden, "Cost Accounting Comes to Service Industries," *Harvard Business Review,* September–October 1978, pp. 132–140.

lines. If so, there would be no direct association of agents with lines and it would be difficult to treat a given agent's salary as an attributable cost of a specific line of insurance. In these cases, the personnel manager may have to be asked to determine the feasibility of realigning agent assignments so there could be a reduction of total staff if a segment of the firm were to be eliminated. Given these realignments, attributable cost would equal the reduction in salaries that would be experienced if the hypothetical discontinuation took place.

As a result of a process such as that just described there would certainly be many costs that would not change. For example, if the size of the staff was strictly a function of the geographical territory to be covered and not of the mix of services being marketed, then a discontinuation of a service would not permit the elimination of any salaries. The remaining costs would be considered as common to the several services as opposed to attributable. For many purposes, there would be no information or benefit of allocating the common costs. The advantage of basing a system on the attributable cost concept is that costs would be collected according to the amount that would be avoided if a particular segment were to be eliminated. Such a system would readily provide the economic impact of such a decision.

To illustrate, consider the Coverall Insurance Company. It deals in three lines of insurance: life, property, and automotive. For organizational purposes, the area served by Coverall is divided into four regions: East, West, North, and South. If management were interested in the amount of agent's salaries attributable to each insurance line, then the regional managers would have to respond to the following questions. If the life (or property, or automotive) insurance line were to be discontinued, then what reduction in agent staff size could you realize?

Assume the following summarizes the response to these questions:

	Current Number of Agents	Reductions in Agents if Discontinued		
		Life	Property	Automotive
East	3	0.5	1	0.5
West	4	2	1.5	1
North	5	1	0.5	1.5
South	2	0.5	1	0.25

To operationalize the measurement of attributable cost, consider the life insurance line. For simplicity, assume all agents earn $20,000 annually. The Eastern and Southern regional managers would now have to respond to another question. Is it possible to achieve a reduction of one-half of an agent? Perhaps it is possible if one of the agents is willing to work on a part-time basis. If not, then the reductions achievable through the singular action of each of the two managers are, realistically, zero.

Should part-time agent help be impossible, then is there any possibility that the Eastern and Southern regions could share an agent? If so, then an agent in one region could be released and one from the other region be given redefined duties that include both regions. Depending on the answers to these questions, the agents' salaries attributable to the life insurance line ranges from $60,000 (3 $\times$ $20,000) to $80,000 (4 $\times$ $20,000). A similar line of reasoning would be necessary for the other two lines.

As another note on this illustration, observe that the figures for the Eastern region *imply* that a reduction of two agents could be realized if *all three* lines were discontinued. Really, the reduction would be three and the difference is due to the fact that the three questions, about each insurance line, were answered independently of each other. Alternatively stated, the agents presumably are performing some functions that have common benefits to the three lines.

Finally, the figures for the Western region add to 4.5. Of course, there are only four agents. A possible explanation for this result is that the Western region currently has some slack. That is, due to an inability to secure part-time help, a fourth full-time agent had to be employed even though his/her *full-time* services were not needed.

Applications to Nonprofit Organizations

Nonprofit organizations constitute the third grouping toward which we want to direct your attention concerning cost accounting applications. Nonprofit organizations would include federal, state, and local governments; hospitals, universities, public schools, voluntary health and welfare agencies, charitable organizations, religious organizations, art museums, and orchestras. Such organizations do not operate in an environment where profit performance is the system that regulates the efficient allocation of resources. That is, they do not attract capital based on the promise of a return. It would seem that both the managers of such organizations and society at large would place premiums on knowing how the resources were used; that is, on knowing the costs. Ironically, we find that cost accounting is much less developed in nonprofit organizations than elsewhere.

Several factors have inhibited the development of cost accounting in nonprofit organizations. First, the absence of a benefit-based pricing mechanism for the services provided by nonprofit organizations results in a lessening of the need to collect the costs of providing the service. The benefactors of government services, for example, frequently are not those who paid the taxes. This is one reason we have government: to provide services to those who need them but are not in a position to foot the entire bill themselves. The services may even be "free" to the benefactors. Even though the services may not be "priced" on the basis of cost, there is still a need for the provider of the "capital" and "revenue" (the public) to know the cost of providing the services so they may evaluate the administrators and do cost-benefit analyses. For this reason there should be increased attention given to nonprofit cost accounting.

Another impediment to the development of cost accounting is the emphasis on budgetary and dollar accountability required by law. The legal reporting requirements for many nonprofit organizations are very different from those for profit-motivated firms. These requirements necessitate accounting systems that track dollar expenditures with a view toward showing they are within the budgetary authority of the administrator. For example, asset acquisitions are treated as claims against the budget of the period of purchase, and no depreciation is recognized in future periods. Legal requirements include the establishment of funds and accounting for expenditures therefrom. But a given project may be completed using resources from two or more funds. In such a case, there would be no natural way to show the cost of the project. Such an accounting system varies from the principles of cost accounting by a greater degree than the external financial accounting requirements of a profit-motivated firm. Satisfying the diverse data needs is a potentially more costly proposition for nonprofit organizations than for profit-oriented firms; thus the impediment.

Finally, many are of the opinion that it makes no sense or difference what it costs to provide the service. What is the value of maintaining health, of preserving a life, of educating a child, of mending a broken mind, of a four-lane interstate highway, of military strength, or of the esthetics of art? Obviously, there are no easy answers to these questions. Some might argue that cost should be no consideration; life is important and must be saved at *any* cost. This is a hard argument to refute, but, still, there are needs for cost information. Resources are limited, and there must be trade-offs. Even though *another* kidney machine might save one additional life per year, the resources it requires might be better used elsewhere; for example, another nurse in the intensive care unit that might help save thirty lives per year. Making decisions on the commitment of resources without knowledge of the costs is irresponsible.

Organizations that depend on the voting public for their funds are beginning to experience the problems of not knowing the cost. Taxpayers are increasingly unwilling to sign blank checks. In effect, they are saying, "Tell us what you are doing and what it is costing. Only then will we consider voting tax increases." This is a reasonable request and one that many school boards, for example, may not be prepared to provide.

A further need for cost is to have a measure of efficiency. The public may be willing to pay to maintain their health but may not be willing to pay for two x-rays when one would have been sufficient. Unfortunately, establishing standards for nonprofit organizations is not as easy as for manufacturing firms and, thus, monitoring efficiency is more difficult.

Some nonprofit organizations have third-party payers (such as health insurance companies) that make reimbursements on a cost-based system. In these cases there is no choice but to comply with the reporting requirements imposed upon them, and they must be able to justify their billings.

Regardless of the aforementioned considerations, costs must be considered. In fact, they may become the base for setting the rate at which services are billed. The following is an illustrative example. Suppose a hospital is faced with the problem of setting the billing rate for its operating room. Some of the costs incurred in the operating room will be fixed and some variable. A user of the operating room should expect to pay for a "fair share" of the fixed costs as well as for the incremental costs resulting from their use of the facility. The concept of a dual-based distribution, discussed in Chapter 9, could be used in developing the billing rate.

To illustrate, suppose the estimated fixed costs are $80,000 per year. By definition, these costs are the costs of having the ability to serve and are not directly related to any short-run measure of activity. Thus, any prorating scheme can be considered fair by some and arbitrary by others. However, there is probably consensus that the user should expect to share in such costs. One possible scheme might be to build the rate to include a given amount of fixed cost per hour of operating room use. Just as in overhead costing, the hospital would have to decide how many hours to use as a divisor: practical capacity or normal activity, for example. Practical capacity might be considered as 8,760 hours per year (24 hours per day × 365 days). However, it is unlikely that the operating room could be scheduled to have 100% utilizaton. Suppose the average utilization is 5,000 hours per year. Thus, the fixed component of the billing rate might be established at $16 per hour of usage ($80,000 ÷ 5,000).

A "fair" billing rate would also include a charge for the variable costs that resulted from a particular patient's usage of the room. Ideally, these costs would be billed in such a way as to give consideration to the specific requirements of each operation. Some operations might require more medical supplies than others, for example. If so, the billing rate should reflect the factors that must be considered in accounting for the costs of a nonprofit organization.

There is much room for innovation and improvement in cost accounting for nonprofit organizations. The purpose of this section has been to familiarize you with some of the basic differences and to establish some basis for thought on how nonprofit organizations can be served by cost accounting.

In this chapter we have provided the framework for extending cost accounting to nonmanufacturing organizations. It was seen that even though these firms had no products, they still have objectives that require a cost determination. Further, it was learned that performance evaluation is much more difficult because a standard resource consumption is hard to measure for nonmanufacturing activities.

You should now be familiar with the new concepts introduced in this chapter which include:

Segment reporting
Order-getting costs
Order-filling costs
Attributable costs

SELF-STUDY PROBLEM. The Dayna Company produces products for sale in two industries: automotive and heavy truck. For simplicity, assume four products: truck drive trains, car frames, truck axles, and car transmissions. Following are some data for 19x0:

	Truck Drive Trains	Car Frames	Truck Axles	Car Transmissions
Sales	$100,000	$150,000	$200,000	$ 550,000
Standard manufacturing cost (percent of sales)				
Material	20%	30%	25%	15%
Labor	10	5	10	15
Variable overhead	8	4	8	12
Applied fixed overhead	10	5	10	15
Assets attributable to product line (book value)	$600,000	$500,000	$900,000	$1,000,000
Relative sales effort*	5	3	6	7

*The sales force has been surveyed concerning their perceived effort relative to each product. In the survey, the salespeople were to use a base figure of 5 as the effort needed to obtain $1,000 of truck drive train sales and then rate the other products relative to the base. These data represent the consensus of the sales force.

The actual total costs for 19x0 as recorded in the accounts are:

Materials	$213,300
Manufacturing labor	102,800
Manufacturing overhead	
Variable	92,160
Fixed	130,000
Sales salaries	48,000
Institutional advertising	80,000
Research and development	60,000
General corporate expenses	20,000
Interest expense	10,000
Fixed overhead noncontrollable (volume) variance	10,000 U*
Income tax rate	40%

*Unfavorable.

Required:

Prepare an income statement to conform with the segment reporting requirements of *FAS Statement Number 14.* (You may assume that both segments meet the significance criteria of the standard.) Select and *defend* the most appropriate allocation bases available.

Solution to Self-Study Problem

The car frames and car transmissions constitute the Automotive Divison, whereas the truck drive trains and truck axles constitute the Truck Divison.

	Automotive	Truck	Total
Sales ($150,000 + $550,000), ($100,000 + $200,000)	$700,000	$300,000	$1,000,000
Cost of sales:			
Material[a]	$137,700	$ 75,600	$ 213,300
Labor[b]	77,100	25,700	102,800
Variable overhead[c]	69,120	23,040	92,160
Fixed overhead[d]	97,500	32,500	130,000
Total	$381,420	$156,840	$ 538,260
Gross margin	$318,580	$143,160	$ 461,740
Selling and general expenses			
Sales salaries[e]	$ 34,400	$ 13,600	$ 48,000
Institutional advertising[f]	56,000	24,000	80,000
Research and development[g]	42,000	18,000	60,000
Total	$132,400	$ 55,600	$ 188,000
Segment income	$186,180	$ 87,560	$ 273,740
General corporate expenses			
General			$ 20,000
Interest expense			10,000
Total			$ 30,000
Income before income tax			$ 243,740
Income tax @ 40%			97,496
Net income after tax			$ 146,244

[a]Allocated on basis of standard material cost:
Automative

$$\frac{0.3(150,000) + 0.15(550,000)}{0.2(100,000) + 0.3(150,000) + 0.25(200,000) + 0.15(550,000)}(213,300)$$

Truck: $\dfrac{0.2(100,000) + 0.25(200,000)}{197,500}(213,300)$

[b]Allocated on basis of standard labor cost:
Automative:

$$\frac{0.05(150,000) + 0.15(550,000)}{0.10(100,000) + 0.05(150,000) + 0.10(200,000) + 0.15(550,000)}(102,800)$$

Truck: $\dfrac{0.10(100,000) + 0.10(200,000)}{120,000}102,800$

[c]Allocated on basis of standard variable overhead costs:
Automative:

$$\frac{0.04(150,000) + 0.12(550,000)}{0.08(100,000) + 0.04(150,000) + 0.08(200,000) + 0.12(550,000)}(92,160)$$

Truck: $\dfrac{0.08(100,000) + 0.08(200,000)}{96,000}(92,160)$

[d]Allocated on basis of standard fixed overhead cost:
Automative:

$$\frac{0.05(150,000) + 0.15(550,000)}{0.10(100,000) + 0.05(150,000) + 0.10(200,000) + 0.15(550,000)}(130,000)$$

Truck: $\dfrac{0.10(100,000) + 0.10(200,000)}{120,000}(130,000)$

[e]Allocated on basis of weighted sales effort:
Automotive: $\dfrac{3(150) + 7(550)}{5(100) + 3(150) + 6(200) + 7(550)}(48,000)$

Truck: $\dfrac{5(100) + 6(200)}{6,000}(48,000)$

[f]Allocated on basis of sales: 70% to automotive and 30% to trucks.

[g]Allocated on basis of sales. May not be best way but no other method is apparent.

References

American Accounting Association. "Report of the Committee on Accounting Practices of Not-for-Profit Organizations," *The Accounting Review Supplement* (1971): 80–163.

Black. H.A., and Edwards, J.D. (eds.). "Part 6—Cost and Managerial Accounting for Other Economic Entities," *The Managerial and Cost Accountant's Handbook.* Homewood, Ill.: Dow Jones-Irwin, 1979.

Dearden, J. "Cost Accounting Comes to Service Industries," *Harvard Business Review* (September–October, 1978): 132–140.

Fremgen, J.M., and Liao, S.S. *The Allocation of Corporate Indirect Costs.* New York: National Association of Accountants, 1983.

Rappaport, A., and Lerner, E.M. *Segment Reporting for Managers and Investors.* New York: National Association of Accountants, 1972.

Shillinglaw, G. "Concept of Attributable Cost," *Journal of Accounting Research* (Spring 1963): 73–85.

Taggart, H.F. *Cost Justification, Michigan Business Studies,* vol. 14, no. 3. Ann Arbor: Bureau of Business Research, University of Michigan, 1959.

Vancil, R.F. *Decentralization: Managerial Ambiguity by Design.* Homewood, Ill.: Dow Jones-Irwin, 1979.

Problems

11-1. Allocating Sales Salaries. The Wilcox Company has to report on three product segments. Salesmen sell all three lines. During the current period sales salaries totaled $500,000. Sales by segment were:

Segment 1	$1,200,000
Segment 2	500,000
Segment 3	800,000

A survey of the salesmen revealed that the effort per $100,000 of sales in each of the segments to be:

Segment 1	1
Segment 2	5
Segment 3	2

Required:

1. Allocate sales salaries to the segments using sales dollars as the basis.
2. Allocate sales salaries to the segments using sales effort as the basis.
3. Comment on the relative merits of your results.

11-2. Role of Depreciation in Setting Hospital Billing Rate. The Wood Memorial Hospital was constructed in 19x1 at a cost of $10,000,000. It had an estimated useful life of 50 years. Price levels in 19x8, the current year, are 40% higher than 19x1. The emergency room occupies 10,000 square feet of the total of 200,000 square feet. In a typical year the hospital will handle 100,000 cases including 4,000 emergency cases.

Required:

1. Suppose that there is no anticipation of any "outside funds" being available to help replace the facility 43 years from now. Determine two different depreciation rates that could be included in the emergency room billing rate for 19x8.

2. Under what circumstances could you defend each of the rates in part 1?
3. Under what circumstances could you defend *no depreciation* in the hospital's billing rates?

11-3. Adapted CMA Problem Requiring Analysis of Selling Costs. The Scent Company sells men's toiletries to retail stores throughout the United States. For planning and control purposes the Scent Company is organized into twelve geographic regions with two to six territories within each region. One salesman is assigned to each territory and has exclusive rights to all sales made in that territory. Merchandise is shipped from the manufacturing plant to the twelve regional warehouses, and the sales in each territory are shipped from the regional warehouses. National headquarters allocates a specific amount at the beginning of the year for regional advertising.

The net sales for the Scent Company for the year ended September 30, 19x4, totaled $10 million. Costs incurred by national headquarters for national administration, advertising, and warehousing are summarized as follows:

National administration	$250,000
National advertising	125,000
National warehousing	175,000
	$550,000

The results of operations for the South Atlantic Region for the year ended September 30, 19x4, are presented in the accompanying schedule.

Net sales		$900,000
Cost and expenses:		
Advertising fees	$ 54,700	
Bad debt expense	3,600	
Cost of sales	460,000	
Freight out	22,600	
Insurance	10,000	
Salaries and employee benefits	81,600	
Sales commissions	36,000	
Supplies	12,000	
Travel and entertainment	14,100	
Wages and employee benefits	36,000	
Warehouse depreciation	8,000	
Warehouse operating costs	15,000	753,600
Contribution		$146,400

The South Atlantic Region consists of two territories—Green and Purple. The salaries and employee benefits consist of the following items:

Regional vice-president	$24,000
Regional marketing manager	15,000
Regional warehouse manager	13,400
Salesmen (one for each territory with all receiving the same salary base)	15,600
Employee benefits (20%)	13,600
	$81,600

The salesmen receive a base salary plus a 4% commission on all items sold in their territory. Bad debt expenses has averaged 0.4% of net sales in the past. Travel and entertainment costs are incurred by the salesmen calling upon their customers. Freight out is a function of the quantity of goods shipped and the distance shipped. Thirty percent of the insurance is expended for protection of the inventory while it is in the regional warehouse, and the remainder is incurred for the protection of the warehouse. Supplies are used in the warehouse for packing the merchandise that is shipped. Wages relate to the hourly paid employees who fill orders in the warehouse. The warehouse operating costs account contains such costs as heat, light, and maintenance.

The following cost analyses and statistics by territory for the current year are representative of past experience and expected future operations.

	Green	Purple	Total
Sales	$300,000	$600,000	$900,000
Cost of sales	$184,000	$276,000	$460,000
Advertising fees	$ 21,800	$ 32,900	$ 54,700
Travel and entertainment	$ 6,300	$ 7,800	$ 14,100
Freight out	$ 9,000	$ 13,600	$ 22,600
Units sold	150,000	350,000	500,000
Pounds shipped	210,000	390,000	600,000
Salesmen miles traveled	21,600	38,400	60,000

Required:

1. The top management of Scent Company wants the regional vice-presidents to present their operating data in a more meaningful manner. Therefore, management has requested the regions to separate their operating costs into the fixed and variable components of order getting, order filling, and administration. The data are to be presented in the following format:

	Territory Costs		Regional	Total
	Green	Purple	Costs	Costs
Order Getting				
Order Filling				
Administration				

Using management's suggested format, prepare a schedule that presents the costs for the region by territory with the costs separated into variable and fixed categories by order-getting, order-filling, and administrative functions.

2. Suppose the top management of Scent Company is considering splitting the Purple Territory into two separate territories (Red and Blue). From the data that have been presented, identify what data would be relevant to this decision (either for or against) and indicate what other data you would collect to aid top management in its decision.

3. If Scent Company keeps its records in accordance with the classification required in part 1, can standards and flexible budgets be employed by the company in planning and controlling marketing costs? Give reasons for your answer.

11-4. CPA Problem Applying Standards to Order-Filling Costs. Engler Corporation's actual and standard marketing costs for the month of January 19x6 are:

	Budget at Standard Cost	*Actual Operations*
Sales	$750,000	$750,000
Direct distribution costs		
Selling	$ 12,000	$ 15,000
Shipping salaries	7,000	9,450
Indirect distribution costs		
Order filling	17,250	21,500
Other	2,100	2,500
Total costs	$ 38,350	$ 48,450

Additional data:

1. The company sells a single product for $10 per unit.
2. Shipping salaries and indirect distribution costs—other are allocated on the basis of shipping hours.
3. January shipping hours data follow:

	Hours
Budgeted	3,500
Standard operating level	4,400
Actual	4,500

4. Order-filling costs are allocated on the basis of sales and are comprised of freight, packing, and warehousing costs. An analysis of the amount of these standard costs by unit order size follows:

Unit-Volume Classification	*Order Filling Standard Costs Classified by Unit Order Size*			
	1–15	*16–50*	*Over 50*	*Total*
Freight	$ 1,200	$ 1,440	$ 2,250	$ 4,890
Packing	2,400	3,240	4,500	10,140
Warehousing	600	720	900	2,220
Total	$ 4,200	$ 5,400	$ 7,650	$17,250
Units sold	12,000	18,000	45,000	75,000

Required:

1. Compute and analyze variances from standard cost for (a) shipping salaries and (b) indirect distribution costs—other. Use the two-variance method. The analysis should compare actual and standard costs at the standard operating level.
2. Management realizes that the distribution cost per unit decreases with an increase in the size of the order and, hence, wants to revise its unit sales prices upward or downward on the basis of the quantity ordered in proportion to the allocated freight, packing, and warehousing standard costs. Management assumes that the revised unit prices will

require no changes in standards for sales volume, the number of units sold in each order size classification, and the profit per unit sold.

a. For each unit volume classification, prepare a schedule computing the standard cost per unit for each order filling cost: freight, packing, and warehousing. Use the format in number 4 above for this schedule.

b. Prepare a schedule computing the revised unit sales prices for each unit-volume classification.

11-5. Comprehensive Problem on Cost Allocation for Segment Reporting. The Sullivan Company produces and markets four products. Applying the rules of *FAS Statement #14,* it will be required to report on two industrial segments and two geographical segments. Industrial segment A consist of products 1 and 2 and segment B consists of products 3 and 4. The geographical segments are the "U.S. Market" and the "Foreign Market." All four products are sold in both geographical territories. However, product 1 is produced exclusively by foreign divisions and product 4 exclusively by U.S. divisions. The manufacturing division transfers these products to the marketing division at cost. Other than this the products sold in each geographical market are produced by divisions within the market.

During the current year the following sales (in thousands) were recorded:

	U.S. Trade	Foreign Trade
Product 1	$200	$100
Product 2	300	400
Product 3	500	600
Product 4	800	700

Actual recorded production costs are reported below. These costs are for all items produced by divisions within the geographical territory and include costs for those items transferred to other segments.

	U.S. Divisions	Foreign Divisions
Material	$330	$140
Labor	370	260
Variable overhead	270	155
Fixed overhead	280	200

There were no beginning or ending inventories.

At standard, the ratios of the production costs to sales are as follows:

U.S. Divisions (percentages are with respect to U.S. sales prices)

	Product		
	2	3	4
Material	15%	10%	15%
Labor	20	15	15
Variable overhead	20	10	10
Fixed overhead	5	20	10

Foreign Divisions (percentages are with respect to U.S. sales prices)

	Product		
	1	*2*	*3*
Material	20%	10%	5%
Labor	30	25	10
Variable overhead	10	15	10
Fixed overhead	15	10	15

The U.S. prices on products 1 and 4 are both 10% higher than the foreign prices.
Other costs (in thousands) recorded by the U.S. and foreign segments are:

	U.S. Divisions	*Foreign Divisions*
Sales salaries	$170	$340
Salaries of corporate officers that are only responsible for segment activities	200	100

The sales salaries recorded in each segment are in support of that segment's activities. On
a product-by-product basis, the salesmen in both segments agree on the following indexes
of relative sales effort to obtain $1,000 worth of sales:

Product 1	5	Product 3	2
Product 2	3	Product 4	7

Corporate costs include $200,000 of central management salaries and $250,000 of income
taxes.

Required:

1. Prepare the geographical segment income statements. It can be shown that the labor,
   variable overhead, and fixed overhead allocated to the U.S. segment is $313, $211, and
   $233, respectively. You will need to do the remaining allocations. Be sure to support your
   allocations.
2. Prepare the industrial segment income statements. It can be shown that the labor, variable overhead, and fixed overhead allocated to industrial segment 1 is $256, $153, and
   $111, respectively. You will need to do the remaining allocations.

11-6. CPA Problem Involving Cost Allocation to Determine Taxes. Thrift-Shops, Inc.
operates a chain of three food stores in a state that recently enacted legislation permitting
municipalities within the state to levy an income tax on corporations operating within their
respective municipalities. The legislation establishes a uniform tax rate that the municipalities may levy, and regulations providing that the tax is to be computed on income derived
within the taxing municipality after a reasonable and consistent allocation of general overhead expenses. General overhead expenses have not been allocated to individual stores previously and include warehouse, general office, advertising, and delivery expenses.

Each of the municipalities in which Thrift-Shops, Inc. operates a store has levied the corporate income tax as provided by state legislation, and management is considering two plans for allocating general overhead expenses to the stores. The 19x9 operating results before general overhead and taxes for each store were as follows:

| | Store | | | |
	Ashville	Burns	Clinton	Total
Sales, net	$416,000	$353,600	$270,400	$1,040,000
Less cost of sales	215,700	183,300	140,200	539,200
Gross margin	$200,300	$170,300	$130,200	$ 500,800
Less local operating expenses				
Fixed	$ 60,800	$ 48,750	$ 50,200	$ 159,750
Variable	$ 54,700	64,220	27,448	146,368
Total	$115,500	$112,970	$ 77,648	$ 306,118
Income before general overhead and taxes	$ 84,800	$ 57,330	$ 52,552	$ 194,682

General overhead expenses in 19x9 were as follows:

Warehousing and delivery expenses		
Warehouse depreciation	$20,000	
Warehouse operations	30,000	
Delivery expenses	40,000	$ 90,000
Central office expenses		
Advertising	$18,000	
Central office salaries	37,000	
Other central office expenses	28,000	83,000
Total general overhead		$173,000

Additional information includes the following:

1. One-fifth of the warehouse space is used to house the central office, and depreciation on this space is included in other central office expenses. Warehouse operating expenses vary with the quantity of merchandise sold.
2. Delivery expenses vary with distance and number of deliveries. The distances from the warehouse to each store and the number of deliveries made in 19x9 were as follows:

Store	Miles	Number of Deliveries
Ashville	120	140
Burns	200	64
Clinton	100	104

3. All advertising is prepared by the central office and is distributed in the areas in which stores are located.

4. As each store was opened, the fixed portion of central office salaries increased $7,000, and other central office expenses increased $2,500. Basic fixed central office salaries amount to $10,000, and basic fixed other central office expenses amount to $12,000. The remainder of central office salaries and the remainder of other central office expenses vary with sales.

Required:

1. For each of the following plans for allocating general overhead expenses, compute the income of each store that would be subject to the municipal levy on corporation income:

   Plan 1. Allocate all general overhead expenses on the basis of sales volume.

   Plan 2. First, allocate central office salaries and other central office expenses evenly to warehouse operations and each store. Second, allocate the resulting warehouse operations expenses, warehouse depreciation, and advertising to each store on the basis of sales volume. Third, allocate delivery expenses to each store on the basis of delivery miles times number of deliveries.

2. Management has decided to expand one of the three stores to increase sales by $50,000. The expansion will increase local fixed operating expenses by $7,500 and require ten additional deliveries from the warehouse. Determine which store management should select for expansion to maximize corporate profits.

11-7. Adapted CPA Problem on Controlling Selling Costs. In recent years marketing costs of the Avey Company have increased more than other expenditures. For more effective control the company plans to provide each local manager with an income statement for his or her territory showing monthly and year-to-date amounts for the current and the previous year. Each sales office is supervised by a local manager; sales orders are forwarded to the main office and filled from a central warehouse; billing and collections are also centrally processed. Expenses are first classified by function and then allocated to each territory in the following ways:

Function	*Basis*
Sales salaries	Actual
Other selling expenses	Relative sales dollars
Warehousing	Relative sales dollars
Packing and shipping	Weight of package
Billing and collections	Number of billings
General administration	Equally

Required:

1. Discuss the effectiveness of the Avey Company's comparative income statements by sales territories as a tool for planning and control. Include in your answer additional factors that should be considered and changes that might be desirable for effective planning by management and evaluation of the local sales managers.

2. Compare the degree of control that can be achieved over production costs and marketing costs and explain why the degree of control differs.

3. Criticize the Avey Company's allocation and/or inclusion of (a) other selling expenses, (b) warehousing expenses, and (c) general administration expenses.

11-8. CMA Problem Requiring Product Line Analysis. The Justa Corporation produces and sells three products. The three products, A, B, and C, are sold in a local market and in a regional market. At the end of the first quarter of the current year, the following income statement has been prepared:

	Total	Local	Regional
Sales	$1,300,000	$1,000,000	$300,000
Cost of goods sold	1,010,000	775,000	235,000
Gross margin	$ 290,000	$ 225,000	$ 65,000
Selling expenses	$ 105,000	$ 60,000	$ 45,000
Administrative expenses	52,000	40,000	12,000
Total	$ 157,000	100,000	$ 57,000
Net income	$ 133,000	$ 125,000	$ 8,000

Management has expressed special concern with the regional market because of the extremely poor return on sales. This market was entered a year ago because of excess capacity. It was originally believed that the return on sales would improve with time, but after a year no noticeable improvement can be seen from the results as reported in the preceding quarterly statement.

In attempting to decide whether to eliminate the regional market, the following information has been gathered:

	Products		
	A	B	C
Sales	$500,000	$400,000	$400,000
Variable manufacturing expenses as a percentage of sales	60%	70%	60%
Variable selling expenses as a percentage of sales	3%	2%	2%

Product	Sales by Markets	
	Local	Regional
A	$400,000	$100,000
B	300,000	100,000
C	300,000	100,000

All administrative expenses and fixed manufacturing expenses are common to the three products and the two markets and are fixed for the period. Remaining selling expenses are fixed for the period and separable by market. All fixed expenses are based upon a prorated yearly amount.

Required:

1. Prepare the quarterly income statement showing contribution margins by market.
2. Assuming there are no alternative uses for the Justa Corporation's present capacity, would you recommend dropping the regional market? Why or why not?
3. Prepare the quarterly income statement showing contribution margins by products.

4. It is believed that a new product can be ready for sale next year if the Justa Corporation decides to go ahead with continued research. The new product can be produced by simply converting equipment presently used in producing product C. The conversion will increase fixed costs by $100,000 per quarter. What must be the minimum contribution margin per quarter for the new product to make the changeover financially feasible?

11-9. CPA Problem on Hospital Cost Accounting. The administrator of Wright Hospital has presented you with a number of service projects for the year ending June 30, 19x2. Estimated room requirements for inpatients by type of service are:

Type of Patient	Total Patients Expected	Average Number of Days in Hospital		Percent of Regular Patients Selecting Types of Service		
		Regular	Medicare	Private	Semiprivate	Ward
Medical	2,100	7	17	10%	60%	30%
Surgical	2,400	10	15	15	75	10

Of the patients served by the hospital, 10% are expected to be Medicare patients, all of whom are expected to select semiprivate rooms. Both the number and proportion of Medicare patients have increased over the past five years. Daily rentals per patient are $40 for a private room, $35 for a semiprivate room, and $25 for a ward.

Operating room charges are based on man-minutes (number of minutes the operating room is in use multiplied by number of personnel assisting in the operation). The per manminute charges are $0.13 for inpatients and $0.22 for outpatients. Studies for the current year show that operations on inpatients are divided as follows:

Type of Operation	Number of Operations	Average Number of minutes per Operation	Average Number of Personnel Required
A	800	30	4
B	700	45	5
C	300	90	6
D	200	120	8
	2,000		

The same proportion of inpatient operations is expected for the next fiscal year, and 180 outpatients are expected to use the operating room. Outpatient operations average 20 minutes and require the assistance of three persons.

The budget for the year ending June 30, 19x2, by departments, is:

General services	
Maintenance of plant	$ 50,000
Operation of plant	27,500
Administration	97,500
All others	192,000
Revenue-producing services	
Operating rooms	68,440
All others	700,000
	$1,135,440

The following information is provided for cost allocation purposes:

	Square Feet	Salaries
General services		
Maintenance of plant	12,000	$ 40,000
Operation of plant	28,000	25,000
Administration	10,000	55,000
All others	36,250	102,500
Revenue-producing services		
Operating room	17,500	15,000
All others	86,250	302,500
	190,000	$540,000

Basis of allocations:

Maintenance of plant—salaries
Operation of plant—square feet
Administration—salaries
All others—8% to operating room

Required:

Prepare schedules showing the computation of:

1. The number of patient days (number of patients multiplied by average stay in hospital) expected by type of patients and service.
2. The total number of man-minutes expected for operating room services for inpatients and outpatients.
3. Expected gross revenue from routine services.
4. Expected gross revenue from operating-room services.
5. Cost per man-minute for operating-room services assuming that the total man-minutes computed in part 2 is 800,000 and that the step method of cost allocation is used (allocate in the following order: plant maintenance, plant operation, administration, and other).

11-10. Cost Determination for an Airline. Ohio International Airways is attempting to cost its flight 666. Flight 666 is from Boston to New Orleans. The plane assigned to 666 completes its route as flight 680 from New Orleans to Los Angeles and then as flight 700 from Los Angeles to Boston. The flight times and flight preparation times are as follows:

Flight	Preflight Preparation Time	Air Time
666	1 hour	4 hours
680	1 hour	2 hours
700	1 hour	5 hours

The remaining time (10 hours) is used for daily maintenance and to cover unpreventable delays in meeting the schedule.

The pilot of flight 666 earns $100,000 annually, the co-pilot earns $50,000, and the engineer $35,000. Five flight attendants are assigned to this flight and they earn an average of

$20,000 annually. One eight-person crew is assigned to flights 666 and 680, which constitutes an 8-hour day. On the second day of the crew's rotation it is assigned to other flights that return them to Boston. This schedule is repeated on days 3 and 4 of their rotation, and the crew is off 2 days. It takes three crews, with staggered days off, to keep this schedule. Each crew is given a total of 41 days of vacation and holidays. Rotating crews are scheduled to cover these periods. You may assume all crew salaries are the same and that there are 365 days of flight.

Airport landing fees are $1,000 per flight and depreciation on the type of plane used on flight 666 is $80,000 per year. Fuel costs $1.30 per gallon and consumption averages 700 gallons per flight hour.

The entire crew must be on board during the preflight preparation time. In addition this preparation requires three flight mechanics, each earning $25,000 yearly. Each works 1,920 hours yearly. A major overhaul of the plane engines must be done every 400 flight hours at a cost of $10,000 per occurrence.

Required:

Considering only those costs mentioned above, determine the daily full absorption cost of flight 666.

Part 3   Topics in Support of Decision Making and Control

CHAPTER 12

The Master Budget

Part II of the book (Chapters 3 through 11) concentrated on cost determination systems. With this chapter we change our orientation from cost determination to the accountant's role in the support of the decision making and planning function. It was impossible in earlier chapters to completely avoid a discusssion of planning and control data requirements. However, we wanted to organize the book in a way that would emphasize the three major responsibilities of the management accountant. It is appropriate to initiate Part III of the book by discussing the master budget. This budget summarizes financial plans for repetitive activities that must be implemented by effective managers, and they provide a means of coordinating all of the efforts of the firm.

We begin this chapter by considering the nature of a master budget and the needs it can fulfill. Further, we examine the process of preparing a budget. It is necessary to study this because the controller will generally be responsible for initiating and coordinating the input from the several members of an organization. Following the introduction to the budget process, there is a comprehensive problem demonstrating the procedures, data needs, assumptions, uses, and organization of the budget process. The final section will be a general introduction to the implementation problems and follow-up uses of budgets.

The Need for and Nature of a Master Budget

A master budget is a catalyst that facilitates the creation of the type of environment necessary for the accomplishment of many objectives. In this section we explore the needs of a well-managed firm that can be served by a master budget and also preview its components and their relationships.

Budgeting is the process of quantifying a plan of action into a formal, written, financial description of the activities involved. The **master budget** is a set of interrelated budgets that serves as a basic framework for describing an organization's plans in financial terms.

The budget process encourages all managers to plan in specific terms. Organizations need more than general goals in order to be effectively managed. The budgeting process is one way to create an environment that requires the translation of general goals into specific plans. Also, most well-managed firms subject the proposed specific plans to a *critical evaluation* giving consideration to feasibility in the context of the limited resources available.

As a result of the advanced planning necessary for the budgetary process, management will be *forewarned about various problems* that might occur. For example, due to the peaks and valleys in cash flow, a firm may face a temporary *shortage of cash*. The budget process will enable management to anticipate this before it occurs and gives them the opportunity to arrange short-term financing. By having time to prearrange for this temporary need, financing costs may be less than if arrangements were made in a crisis. Similarly, the type of planning needed for budgeting permits a production schedule resulting in *less costly inventory levels*. Further, there may be cyclical demands for products that could put *strains on the capacities* of certain resources (labor, material availability, storage capability, and so forth). Knowing in advance that these types of problems are going to occur will enable much better solutions.

When there are two or more people involved in managing a business there is need for *coordination*. Although budgets are not the only way to achieve coordination, they are of major importance to fulfilling the objective. For example, it is rather obvious that the production and marketing departments must be coordinated in their efforts. Further, various divisions of the firm may be competing for the same limited resources. If so, there must be some planning for the allocation of resources. To provide input for these decisions, many firms require divisional plans and budgets. Based on these budget presentations, and on the divisions' credibility as established by their ability to perform as promised in previous periods, corporate management determines a course of action for the firm.

Behaviorally, we know that we are better motivated if we have specific targets to strive for. Budgets can provide these *targets*. For example, the firm may establish a target for a certain amount of profit or a given return on investment. Targets such as these must then be translated into specific sales levels and cost budgets. In turn, these budgets imply targets for each subdivision of the firm. If each operational level meets its specific goals, then the corporate objectives will be met. However, care must be exercised in analyzing differences between the budget and actual results because the realized conditions may differ from the planned. It is not desirable to create an environment that encourages meeting the budget just for the sake of meeting it. Most would agree that the budget should encourage the achievement of targets only to the extent that those targets continue to reflect a proper course of action.

Subject to these last comments, a budget represents *input into the evaluation process*. At the end of the period a budget can represent a good benchmark against which to compare the actual results. If the actual conditions do not vary significantly from the assumed conditions at the beginning of the period, then differences between the budget and the actual will represent areas where management performed better or worse than anticipated.

The budgeting process is outlined in Exhibit 12.1 Since the *final* result of this process is a forecast of the organization's ending financial position, it is necessary to start with a beginning position. Also needed at the beginning of the process are budget assumptions, sales forecasts, and various operating strategies. **Budget assumptions** are critical to the process. They include assessments of economic and industrial conditions and the impact of these conditions on the firm. With respect to forecasting, there are several techniques that can be used. Before constructing the budget, a forecasting method must be selected, and the results must be com-

Exhibit 12.1   The Master Budget

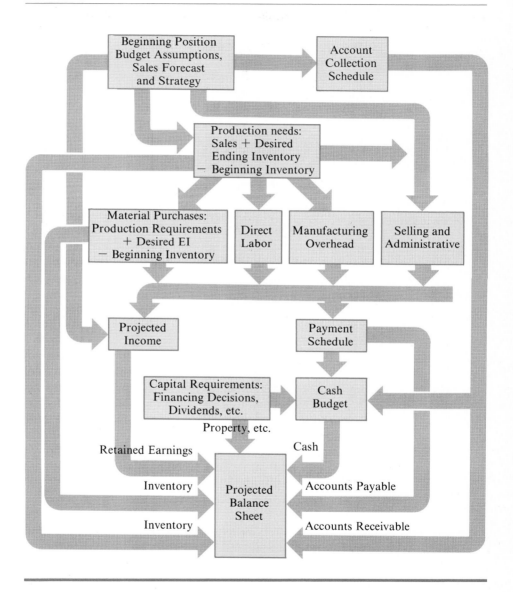

piled. Other questions that must be answered before preparing a budget include a forecast of the pattern followed by customers in paying their bills, the length of the lead time needed to produce a product or purchase raw material, the way production and manpower are scheduled, the behavior pattern of costs, and many others.

Strategy would include product mix planning in situations where resources do not permit the fulfillment of all sales levels, advertising and marketing plans, capital and asset acquisitions, and others.

The assumptions, forecasts, and strategies are extremely important inputs and require careful consideration. Although it is difficult to simulate the development of these inputs in a textbook, we do consider them as we proceed. As you can see in the flowchart, these inputs form the basis for the *entire* budget. It seems obvious, then, that the quality of the budget depends on the quality of the assumptions, forecasts, and strategies.

As a result of the sales forecast, a **sales budget** can be constructed. This budget is not illustrated here because it is simply a schedule of the volume of sales on a product-by-product basis. Additionally, the budgeted sales prices per unit might be shown and the total planned revenue.

If the firm is a manufacturing firm, it is necessary to prepare a **production budget**—to plan for production levels needed in meeting the anticipated sales. Note that the total units needed during any period are given by the sum of the expected sales level and the desired ending inventory. The portion of these needs that must be produced during the period is the total need reduced by the beginning inventory of the finished product. Production budgeting can be further complicated by the way in which production is to be scheduled within the period and by the lead time requirements. This will be explored as part of the example in the next section.

After the production budget is prepared, it is then possible to project (budget) the material purchases, labor needs, and overhead costs. **Material budgets** take the same form as production budgets and are subject to considerations of such things as optimal order quantities and lead time requirements.

The sales forecast is also the basis for projecting cash receipts. This is done using an account collection schedule. An account collection schedule provides input to the cash budget and to the projected balance sheet (discussed below).

In the flowchart it has been assumed that variable selling and administrative costs are a function of both sales and production. It is not necessary to accept this assumption; it may well be that these costs are a function of only sales. Obviously selling expenses would be a function of sales only, but administrative costs could be a function of both.

The cash payment schedule recognizes that expenses of a period may not be equal to the period's cash outflow; thus it also provides accounts payable data for the balance sheet. The **cash budget,** as used here, is a summary of all the expected cash flows (receipts and payments). As you can see in the flowchart, all of the aforementioned items are incorporated into the projected income statement and balance sheet. In the next section there is an example of the budgetary process.

The Budget Process

To illustrate the complete budget process let us consider the Oakes Company, which manufactures two types of kitchen cabinets, wall cabinets and under-the-counter cabinets (called base cabinets). Its beginning statement of financial position on January 1, 19x2, is found in Exhibit 12.2. Various budget assumptions are found in Exhibit 12.3 including the sales forecast for the first quarter. Carefully examine all of the assumptions. We will refer to them as we proceed.

The production budgets for both products are contained in Exhibit 12.4. These budgets follow the general form mentioned earlier: sales needs, plus desired ending inventory, less beginning inventory. The "Total" column is for the three months combined. Carefully note that the ending inventory in the "Total" column is the same as March's ending inventory (March and the three-month period have the same ending date). Further, the beginning inventory in the "Total" column is the same as January's beginning inventory (January and the three-month period have

---

Exhibit 12.2   Oakes Company Statement of Financial Position January 1, 19x2

Assets

Current			
Cash		$ 600,000	
Accounts receivable (net)		1,275,000	
Finished goods inventory			
Wall Cabinets (8,000 × $62)		496,000	
Base Cabinets (5,000 × $54)		270,000	
Materials inventory (35,000 feet × $5)		175,000	$ 2,816,000
Property, Plant and Equipment			
Land		$1,400,000	
Buildings and equipment	$8,000,000		
Less accumulated depreciation	1,500,000	6,500,000	7,900,000
Total assets			$10,716,000

Equities

Current Liabilities			
Accounts payable		$500,000	
Accrued payroll		400,000	
Property taxes payable		216,000	
Bonds payable, 2/15/x2		400,000	
Dividends payable, 1/31/x2		900,000	$ 2,416,000
Long-Term Liabilities			
Bonds payable, 2/15/x3		$ 400,000	
Bonds payable (after 19x3)		3,200,000	3,600,000
Total liabilities			$ 6,016,000
Stockholders' Equity			
Common stock		$3,000,000	
Retained earnings		1,700,000	4,700,000
Total equities			$10,716,000

Exhibit 12.3   Oakes Company Budget Assumptions First Quarter, 19x2

---

1. *Sales forecast (units):*

	Sales Price	January	February	March	April
Wall Cabinets	$70	10,000	20,000	20,000	20,000
Base Cabinets	85	20,000	30,000	10,000	20,000

2. *Standard Costs:*

	Wall Cabinets	Base Cabinets
Material		
Wall Cabinets (2 feet @ $5)	$10	
Base Cabinets (3 feet @ $5)		$15
Direct labor		
Wall Cabinets (4 hours @ $8)	32	
Base Cabinets (3 hours @ $8)		24
Variable manufacturing overhead		
Wall Cabinets (4 direct labor hours @ $3)	12	
Base Cabinets (3 direct labor hours @ $3)		9
Fixed manufacturing overhead		
Wall Cabinets (4 direct labor hours @ $2)	8	
Base Cabinets (3 direct labor hours @ $2)		6
Total	$62	$54

3. *Divisor activity* is 120,000 direct-labor hours per month.

4. *Lead time* requirements:
   Wall Cabinets   2 weeks
   Base Cabinets   1 week
   Materials   10 days
   Production and sales occur uniformly throughout the month.

5. *Desired ending inventory* at March 31 for raw materials:
   40,000 feet.

6. *Selling and administrative expense* function:
   S&A = $60,000 + $2(Wall Cabinet sales) + $4(Base Cabinet sales)

7. *Accounts receivable collection pattern:*
   a. All sales are on account.
   b. 50% are collected in month of sale.
   c. 30% are collected in first month following sale.
   d. 18% are collected in second month following sale.
   e. 2% are uncollectible.
   If customers pay in month of sale they receive a 1% discount for prompt payment.

8. *January 1, 19x2 accounts receivable aging:*
   Originating in November, 19x1 $395,000
   Originating in December, 19x1   880,000

9. *Cash payment patterns and related information:*
   a. Materials and supplies; 50% in month of purchase; balance in following month.
   b. The current work force is sufficient for 120,000 direct-labor hours per month. Oakes will maintain a stable work force by paying idle time when work requires less than 120,000 hours and utilizing overtime at time and a half when work exceeds 120,000 hours.
   c. Payroll (direct, indirect, idle time, and overtime) is paid as follows: 75% in month of employment; 25% in following month.
   d. Vacation pay is charged to manufacturing overhead as incurred. The annual vacation pay is estimated at $705,600. In the past, 30% of the total vacations have been taken during July, 30% during August, 13% during December, and the balance evenly throughout the remainder of the year. The disbursement is made in the month of vacation.
   e. Property taxes are paid during the year following the year of assessment. The first half is due on March 31; the second half on July 31.
   f. Insurance is prepaid in semiannual installments on January 1 and July 1. Since there will be no prepayment at year-end, interim prepayments are charged to manufacturing overhead.
   g. All remaining overhead requiring cash (the selling expenses and the administrative expenses) are paid as incurred.

10. *Land* costing $1,000,000 has been purchased with payment scheduled on January 20, 19x2.

11. *Equipment* costing $800,000 will be purchased and paid for on March 31, 19x2. It replaces old equipment costing $500,000. The old equipment will be fully depreciated on March 31 and has no salvage value.

12. *Short-term borrowing* with the local bank can be made in multiples of $100,000 at an interest rate of 12%. Payments are to be in multiples of $100,000. Borrowing takes place at the beginning of the month in which funds are needed; repayments at the end of the month. Interest on the balance outstanding at the beginning of the month is payable at the end of the month.

---

the same starting date). Each month the ending inventory of wall cabinets is established in an amount equal to 50% of next month's sales. This is due to the lead-time requirement stated in budget assumption number 4. If the lead time is two weeks and if we assume February's sales and production occur uniformly during the month, then the demand during the first half of the month will have to be supplied from production scheduled during January. Similarly for base cabinets, the lead time is one week, and one-fourth of February sales must be in inventory at the end of January. (Of course the firm may elect to schedule its production in alternative ways. If so, the ending inventories would have to be planned for in a different way from that suggested here.) March's ending inventories are the appropriate percentages of April sales. Finally, the ending inventory for January becomes the beginning inventory for February and so forth. The January beginning inventories are those on the January 1 statement of financial position in Exhibit 12.2.

The next budget discussed is for the material purchasing requirements and is found in Exhibit 12.5. First it is necessary to compute the amount of material needed for the scheduled production of each product. The standard material allowances are given in budget assumption number 2. (Note that we are assuming each product uses the same type of material.) Multiply these standards by the scheduled production requirement in Exhibit 12.4. Since the lead time on material purchases is ten days (assumption number 4), the ending inventory is targeted at one-third of next month's total material needs. (This assumes a thirty-day month, a uniform scheduling of production over the month, and a uniform purchasing rate of materials.) Budget assumption number 5 is the source of March's ending inventory. (Technically the ending inventory should be based on the production scheduled for April which would depend, in part, on May's forecasted sales.) Again, January's beginning inventory is from Exhibit 12.2. Finally, the dollar amount for raw material purchases is derived using the per foot price of material.

The direct-labor budget is contained in Exhibit 12.6 and should be self-explanatory. Exhibit 12.7 is the manufacturing overhead budget. Cost analyses have been done for each item to determine their behaviors. These analyses generated the variable rates in the rate column and the fixed costs in the fixed cost section. Direct-labor hours represent the best available surrogate measure of activity. Note that the monthly budgeted fixed cost is $240,000. Dividing the budgeted fixed costs

---

Exhibit 12.4   Oakes Company Production Budget (in units) First Quarter, 19x2

		Wall Cabinets		
	January	*February*	*March*	*Total*
Sales needs	10,000	20,000	20,000	50,000
Desired ending inventory	10,000	10,000	10,000	10,000
Total needs	20,000	30,000	30,000	60,000
Beginning inventory	8,000*	10,000	10,000	8,000
Production requirement	12,000	20,000	20,000	52,000

		Base Cabinets		
	January	*February*	*March*	*Total*
Sales needs	20,000	30,000	10,000	60,000
Desired ending inventory	7,500	2,500	5,000	5,000
Total needs	27,500	32,500	15,000	65,000
Beginning inventory	5,000*	7,500	2,500	5,000
Production requirement	22,500	25,000	12,500	60,000

*From Exhibit 12.2

Exhibit 12.5   Oakes Company Raw Material Purchasing Requirements First Quarter, 19x2

	January	February	March	Total
Needed to support production				
For Wall Cabinets				
(production* × 2 feet)	24,000	40,000	40,000	104,000
For Base Cabinets				
(production* × 3 feet)	67,500	75,000	37,500	180,000
Total	91,500	115,000	77,500	284,000
Desired ending inventory (one-third of next month's requirement	38,334	25,834	40,000	40,000
Total needs	129,834	140,834	117,500	324,000
Beginning inventory	35,000†	38,334	25,834	35,000
Purchasing requirements (feet)	94,834	102,500	91,666	289,000
Cost per foot	$5	$5	$5	$5
Purchasing requirements (dollars)	$474,170	$512,500	$458,330	$1,445,000

*From Exhibit 12.4.

†From Exhibit 12.2.

Exhibit 12.6   Oakes Company Direct-Labor Requirements First Quarter, 19x2

	January	February	March	Total
Budgeted production of Wall Cabinets (Exhibit 12.4)	12,000	20,000	20,000	52,000
Labor requirement per Wall Cabinet (budget assumption 2)	4	4	4	4
Needed for Wall Cabinets	48,000	80,000	80,000	208,000
Budgeted production of Base Cabinets (Exhibit 12.4)	22,500	25,000	12,500	60,000
Labor requirement per Base Cabinet (budget assumption 2)	3	3	3	3
Needed for Base Cabinets	67,500	75,000	37,500	180,000
Total labor hours needed	115,000	155,000	117,500	388,000
Labor cost per hour	$8	$8	$8	$8
Total labor cost	$924,000	$1,240,000	$940,000	$3,104,000

Exhibit 12.7   Oakes Company Manufacturing Overhead Budget First Quarter, 19x2

	Rate*	January	February	March	Total
Expected direct-labor hours	—	115,500	155,000	117,500	388,000
Variable costs					
Supplies	0.200	$ 23,100	$ 31,000	$ 23,500	$ 77,600
Indirect labor	0.400	46,200	62,000	47,000	155,200
Idle time and overtime					
premium	0.505	58,328	78,275	59,337	195,940
Vacation pay	0.490	56,595	75,950	57,575	190,120
Repairs	0.300	34,650	46,500	35,250	116,400
Material handling	0.150	17,325	23,250	17,625	58,200
Power	0.750	86,625	116,250	88,125	291,000
Other	0.205	23,677	31,775	24,088	79,540
Total	3.000	$346,500	$465,000	$352,500	$1,164,000
Fixed costs*					
Supervision		$ 70,000	$ 70,000	$ 70,000	$ 210,000
Clerical		30,000	30,000	30,000	90,000
Depreciation		90,000	90,000	90,000	270,000
Property taxes		20,000	20,000	20,000	60,000
Insurance		10,000	10,000	10,000	30,000
Other		20,000	20,000	20,000	60,000
Total		$240,000	$240,000	$240,000	$ 720,000
Total		$586,500	$705,000	$592,500	$1,884,000

*These amounts are based on cost analyses and are being given to you for the first time.

by the divisor activity of 120,000 labor hours (assumption number 3) we obtain the fixed overhead rate of $2.00 per hour which was used in deriving the full absorption standard costs.

An analysis of selling and administrative costs, in the form of a relational equation, is given in budget assumption number 6. This equation is used to project these expenses as found in Exhibit 12.8. (Note that the case varies from the flowchart in that selling and administrative costs are a function of sales only.)

A pattern of collecting customer accounts is outlined in budget assumption number 7. These percentages are used to forecast cash inflows in Exhibit 12.9. To estimate the cash flows from the beginning accounts receivable use the aging schedule in assumption number 8 along with the collection pattern. Since accounts receivables are stated net of bad debts, the beginning receivables from November would be collected in full during January. The beginning receivables would also include 48% of December sales. Since the pattern has been to collect 30% of a month's sales in the next month, 30/48 of the December layer would be collected during

Exhibit 12.8   Oakes Company Selling and Administrative Expense Budget First Quarter, 19x2

	January	February	March	Total
Wall Cabinet sales	10,000	20,000	20,000	50,000
Variable rate	$2	$2	$2	$2
Total	$20,000	$40,000	$40,000	$100,000
Base Cabinet sales	20,000	30,000	10,000	60,000
Variable rate	$4	$4	$4	$4
Total	$ 80,000	$120,000	$40,000	$240,000
Total variable	$100,000	$160,000	$80,000	$340,000
Fixed	60,000	60,000	60,000	180,000
Total	$160,000	$220,000	$140,000	$520,000

Exhibit 12.9   Oakes Company Schedule of Collections on Account First Quarter, 19x2

	Total	January	Collected in February	March	Collectible After 3/31/x2	Bad Debts
Beginning accounts receivable	$1,275,000	$ 945,000[a]	$ 330,000	0	0	0
January sales						
($70 × 10,000 + $85 × 20,000)	2,400,000	1,188,000[b]	720,000	$ 432,000	0	$ 48,000
February sales						
($70 × 20,000 + $85 × 30,000)	3,950,000	0	1,955,250[b]	1,185,000	711,000	79,000
March sales						
($70 × 20,000 + $85 × 10,000)	2,250,000	0	0	1,113,750[b]	1,080,000	45,000
Total	$9,875,000	$2,133,000	$3,005,250	$2,730,750	$1,791,000	$172,000

[a]Collection from November sales $395,000
  Collection from December sales, 30/48 × $880,000   550,000

    Total $945,000

[b]Cash net of discounts:

	Sales	Collected in Month of Sale (50%)	Sales Discount	Net
January	$2,400,000	$1,200,000	$12,000	$1,188,000
February	3,950,000	1,975,000	19,750	1,955,250
March	2,250,000	1,125,000	11,250	1,113,750
			$43,000	

January. The balance would be collected in February. Since the collection pattern is critical to reliably estimating cash flows, we need to consider how it might be determined. Of course we could rely on an estimate from the credit department. If the credit department's estimates prove too erroneous, then other analyses might have to be considered.

The cash discounts offered for the timely payment of accounts are computed in footnote b of Exhibit 12.9. These discounts must be deducted from the gross accounts collected in order to project cash inflow. Further, they must be deducted in the income statement to arrive at net sales.

Next, all of the expenses need to be analyzed to determine the timing of their associated cash disbursements. This is done with the use of the various payment patterns outlined in number 9 of the assumptions. The disbursements schedule is contained in Exhibit 12.10. Only a few of these items merit discussion. The idle time and overtime items are being *averaged* in the overhead application rate, and these averages indicate nothing about the actual rates of cash flow. To compute the estimated cash disbursements during the months covered by the budget, compare the estimated direct-labor time needs from Exhibit 12.6 with the available hours of the stable work force (120,000 hours). Idle time would be accounted for at $8 per hour and overtime *premium* at $4. In the case of overtime we need only consider the premium because the base of $8 is included in the direct labor figures.

Likewise, vacation pay is being smoothed through the overhead rate; thus the rate does not reflect the cash flow. The actual amount incurred would be derived from the facts in assumption 9-d. July, August, and December account for 73% of the vacations. The 27% balance would be taken at the rate of 3% per month during the remaining nine months. Thus, the cash outflow for vacation pay would be estimated at 3% of the total budgeted amount of $705,600. (Note that differences between the expense and the disbursement will be reflected in the overapplied or underapplied overhead.)

One-half of the accrued property taxes on January 1, 19x2, would be paid during March; these are actually 19x1 expenses. The first-quarter 19x2 tax expense is equal to the amount estimated in Exhibit 12.7 and would be added to the liability. The insurance expense per month (from Exhibit 12.7) is $10,000 and, therefore, the semiannual installment due in January would amount to $60,000. (See assumption 9-f.) Finally, note that depreciation represents an expense that does not require a cash disbursement.

In Exhibit 12.11 the expected activity in the cash account has been summarized. Most of that schedule should be obvious. Remember that short-term financing is to be in multiples of $100,000, and that interest must be paid at the end of the month for principal outstanding during the month.

The projected statement of income is contained in Exhibit 12.12. It is based on standard full absorption cost principles. Any overapplied or underapplied overhead will be retained in the manufacturing overhead account until the end of the year. Remember that one of the purposes of applying overhead is to smooth cyclical costs over the entire year's production.

The budget process concludes with the projected (often called pro forma) ending statement of financial position (Exhibit 12.13). Ending inventory quantities are

Exhibit 12.10   Oakes Company Cash Payments Schedule—Operating Items First Quarter, 19x2

			Payment during		Payable After 3/31/x2
	Total	January	February	March	
Accounts payable, 1/1/x2	$ 500,000	$ 500,000	0	0	0
Materials (Exhibit 12.5)					
January purchases	474,170	237,085	$ 237,085	0	0
February purchases	512,500	0	256,250	$ 256,250	0
March purchases	458,330	0	0	229,165	$229,165
Supplies (Exhibit 12.7)					
January	23,100	11,550	11,550	0	0
February	31,000	0	15,500	15,500	0
March	23,500	0	0	11,750	11,750
Accounts payable, 3/31/x2					$240,915
Accrued payroll, 1/1/x2	400,000	400,000	0	0	0
Direct labor (Exhibit 12.6)					
January	924,000	693,000	231,000	0	0
February	1,240,000	0	930,000	310,000	0
March	940,000	0	0	705,000	235,000
Indirect labor (Exhibit 12.7)					
January	46,200	34,650	11,550	0	0
February	62,000	0	46,500	15,500	0
March	47,000	0	0	35,250	11,750
Idle time and overtime premium					
January (120,000 − 115,500)8	36,000	27,000	9,000	0	0
February (155,000 − 120,000)4	140,000	0	105,000	35,000	0
March (120,000 − 117,500)8	20,000	0	0	15,000	5,000
Accrued payroll, 3/31/x2					$251,750
Vacation pay					
January	21,168	21,168	0	0	0
February	21,168	0	21,168	0	0
March	21,168	0	0	21,168	0
Property taxes payable, 1/1/x2	216,000	0	0	108,000	108,000
Property tax expense first quarter of 19x2	60,000	0	0	0	60,000
Property taxes payable, 3/31/x2					$168,000
Insurance	60,000	60,000	0	0	0
Repairs	116,400	34,650	46,500	35,250	0
Material handling	58,200	17,325	23,250	17,625	0
Power	291,000	86,625	116,250	88,125	0
Supervision	210,000	70,000	70,000	70,000	0
Clerical	90,000	30,000	30,000	30,000	0
Other	139,540	43,677	51,775	44,088	0
Selling and Administrative	520,000	160,000	220,000	140,000	0
Total	$7,702,444	$2,426,730	$2,432,378	$2,182,671	$660,665

Exhibit 12.11   Oakes Company Cash Budget First Quarter, 19x2

	January	February	March	Total
Beginning balance	$ 600,000	$ 89,270	$ 245,142	$ 600,000
Operating receipts				
(Exhibit 12.9)	2,133,000	3,005,250	2,730,750	7,869,000
Total cash available	$2,733,000	$3,094,520	$2,975,892	$ 8,469,000
Disbursements				
Operating				
(Exhibit 12.10)	$2,426,730	$2,432,378	$2,182,671	$ 7,041,779
Dividends				
(Exhibit 12.2)	900,000			900,000
Bonds				
(Exhibit 12.2)		400,000		400,000
Land				
(Assumption 10)	1,000,000			1,000,000
Equipment				
(Assumption 11)			800,000	800,000
Total	$4,326,730	$2,832,378	$2,982,671	$10,141,779
Cash balance before				
financing	$(1,593,730)	$ 262,142	$ (6,779)	$(1,672,779)
Short-term borrowing	1,700,000*		100,000	1,800,000
Repayment of short-				
term borrowing		0+		
Interest	17,000	17,000	18,000	52,000
Ending balance	$ 89,270	$ 245,142	$ 75,221	$ 75,221

*A loan of $1,600,000 would be sufficient to cover the cash shortage. However, interest will have to be paid at the end of the month and borrowing $1,600,000 would not be sufficient to also pay $16,000 interest. Thus, it will be necessary to borrow $1,700,000.

+A repayment could be made at the end of February. However, another loan is needed at the beginning of March. Thus, rather than retiring debt and immediately renewing it, the cash balance will just be carried into March.

those projected in other budgets and are included at standard costs. Land has been increased from the January 1 value to reflect the anticipated acquisition. Building, equipment, and accumulated depreciation amounts were derived as follows:

	Buildings and Equipment	Accumulated Depreciation
January 1 balance	$8,000,000	$1,500,000
Acquisition	800,000	
Depreciation for the		
quarter (Exhibit 12.7)		270,000
Replaced equipment	(500,000)	(500,000)
March 31 balance	$8,300,000	$1,270,000

The short-term loan payable, from Exhibit 12.11, is $1,800,000. Overapplied overhead is included in the statement of financial position because March 31 is an

---

Exhibit 12.12   Oakes Company Projected Statement of Income First Quarter, 19x2

Sales (Exhibit 12.9):		
($2,400,000 + $3,950,000 + $2,250,000)		$8,600,000
Less: Bad debt expense (Exhibit 12.9)	$ 172,000	
Sales discounts (Exhibit 12.9)	43,000	215,000
Net sales		$8,385,000
Cost of goods sold (at standard)		
Wall Cabinets 50,000 × $62	$3,100,000	
Base Cabinets 60,000 × $54	3,240,000	6,340,000
Gross margin		$2,045,000
Selling and administrative (Exhibit 12.8)	$ 520,000	
Interest expense (Exhibit 12.11)	52,000	572,000
Projected net income		$1,473,000

---

interim date. Such balances are allocated only at year-end. The amount can best be explained by constructing the expected status of the manufacturing overhead account using the data in Exhibit 12.7 and adjusting for the way idle time, overtime premium, vacation pay, and insurance is paid.

Manufacturing Overhead			
Estimated debits for quarter		Variable and fixed applied	
Supplies	77,600	during quarter (388,000	
Indirect labor	155,200	labor hours @ $5)	1,940,000
Idle time and overtime	196,000[a]		
Vacation pay	63,504[b]		
Repairs	116,400		
Material handling	58,200		
Power	291,000		
Other variable	79,540		
Supervision	210,000		
Clerical	90,000		
Depreciation	270,000		
Property taxes	60,000		
Insurance	60,000[c]		
Other fixed	60,000		
	1,787,444		
Overapplied	152,556		
	1,940,000		1,940,000

[a]See Exhibit 12.10: $36,000 + $140,000 + $20,000; charged to overhead as incurred.

[b]See Exhibit 12.10: 3 × $21,168; charged to overhead as incurred.

[c]Charged to overhead as incurred.

Exhibit 12.13   Oakes Company Projected Statement of Financial Position March 31, 19x2

Assets

Current			
Cash (Exhibit 12.11)		$ 75,221	
Accounts receivable (Exhibit 12.9)		1,791,000	
Finished goods inventory			
Wall Cabinets (10,000 × $62)		620,000	
Base Cabinets (5,000 × $54)		270,000	
Materials inventory (40,000 × $5)		200,000	$ 2,956,221
Property, Plant and Equipment			
Land ($1,400,000 + $1,000,000)		$2,400,000	
Buildings and equipment	$8,300,000		
Less accumulated depreciation	1,270,000	7,030,000	9,430,000
Total assets			$12,386,221

Equities

Current Liabilities			
Accounts payable (Exhibit 12.10)		$ 240,915	
Accrued payroll (Exhibit 12.10)		251,750	
Property taxes payable (Exhibit 12.10)		168,000	
Bonds payable, 2/15/x3		400,000	
Short-term loans and interest payable		1,800,000	$ 2,860,665
Long-Term Liabilities			
Bonds payable			3,200,000
Total liabilities			$ 6,060,665
Deferred Credits			
Overassigned manufacturing overhead			152,556
Stockholders' Equity			
Common Stock		$3,000,000	
Retained earnings ($1,700,000 + $1,473,000)		3,173,000	6,173,000
Total equities			$12,386,221

The retained earnings increases by the estimated income for the period. This completes the statement of financial position, as well as the master budget. Several issues were not given an in-depth consideration and will be considered in the remaining section and some later chapters.

Implementation and Follow-up Uses of Budgets

Of equal importance to the budget process are its implementation and its use in performance evaluation. By implementation we mean the process of gathering input about the assumptions, limitations, and plans. Does all of this input originate with the top level of management who then communicates it down to their subordinates? Or is there input from all levels of management with some give-and-take to reach a mutually agreed-upon base for constructing the budget? The first style is an **authoritarian budget style** and the latter is a **participatory budget style.**

Generally, it is felt that a participatory style is better, and there are some studies that support this.[1] If all levels of management have participated in the budget development, then they are more likely to internalize them; that is, adopt them as their personal goals. Participation may originate as a request from top management for a proposal of next year's plans by seeking proposals from various areas within their divisions. After the "downward" requests reach their end, then proposals flow up through the organizational chain of command. At each major point of responsibility, the plans would be evaluated, coordinated, defended, and accepted or rejected. At each level full participation would involve the manager and his or her first-line subordinates. When the lowest responsibility level comes to a united front, then the plan is forwarded up the line where the process is repeated. When this has been done at all levels, the corporate plan is communicated throughout the organization. In the control section of this book, the behavioral implications of budgets will be examined in greater depth.

Follow-up uses of budgets are primarily for the purpose of control. That is, at the end of the budget period both the manager and the subordinate will be interested in how the actual results compare with the budget. At times this comparison can result in an explosive situation. As with standard cost variance analysis, accountants must be very careful in placing blame. Variations from the budget may be due to noncontrollable factors such as an unanticipated turndown in the economy.

When performance is evaluated by comparing actual costs with budgeted costs, it is essential to adjust the budget to a level representative of actual output. Such budgets are called *flexible budgets* and are ones where the variable costs are adjusted to correspond to the achieved output. The budget in Exhibit 12.7 is a flexible budget in that the expected costs each month were adjusted to be in line with the expected activity. The only difference for performance evaluation at the end of the period is that actual outputs are used as the base of constructing the budget.

Appropriate uses of budgets in a control situation are more than a comparison with the actual results. For certain levels of management there is profit responsibility rather than cost responsibility. Variances from standard cost only partially explain why budgeted profits were not achieved. When there is profit responsibility there is implied control over both costs and sales volume. Profit variance analysis will be examined in a later chapter but we want to establish now that it is more sophisticated than merely detailing the reasons why actual results varied from the

[1]For example, see: Selwyn Becker and David Green, Jr., "Budgeting and Employee Behavior," *Journal of Business* (October 1962), pp. 392–402, and Andrew C. Stedry, "Budgeting and Employee Behavior: A Reply," *Journal of Business* (April 1964), pp. 195–202.

plan. That is, the accounting function should carefully guard against leaving the impression that management seeks conformance with plans. Effective managers will strive for budget and control systems that encourage and reward the adherence to optimal strategies *given those conditions that actually occur.* Further, effective managers will do more than react to unfavorable events; they will also recognize the achievement or betterment of goals. This area provides room for improvement, both on the part of management and accounting, and warrants an expanded discussion at a later point.

Summary

This chapter covered many aspects of the operating budget. You should now have a working knowledge of the master budget: its components, problems, and data needs. The selection of a rather complex multiple-product problem to demonstrate the budget process was deliberate. You should now be better able to comprehend what occurs in actual budgeting environments.

New key terms introduced in this chapter include:

Operating budget
Master budget
Budget assumptions
Sales budget
Production budget
Material budget
Cash budget
Authoritarian budget style
Participatory budget style

SELF-STUDY PROBLEM. The Texas Implement Company produces two products—A and B. Each of these products requires a particular kind of transistor. Product A requires two transistors per unit and product B requires three per unit.

The strategic planning group has forecasted the expected sales (in units) for the first three months of next year. These data and the December actual sales are:

	Product A	Product B
December (actual)	10,000	5,000
January (forecast)	11,000	6,000
February (forecast)	5,000	5,000
March (forecast)	8,000	10,000

The controller has asked you to prepare an estimate of the cash required for the purchase and handling of the transistors and you have acquired the following additional data:

1. Transistors cost $10 each.
2. Since the lead-time period from the supplier is around 15 days, the ending inventory of transistors is maintained at 50% of next month's total production requirements.
3. The December 31 inventories include 18,000 transistors, 3,000 units of product A, and 1,000 units of product B.

4. The production time on each product is about 1 week. Thus the company wants to maintain its ending finished goods inventories at 25% of next month's forecasted sales.
5. In the production of products A and B there is damage to some of the transistors. The damaged transistors have no value and are disposed of when damaged. The rate of spoilage equals 5% of the total transistors *issued* to production.
6. Product A sells for $50 and product B for $75.
7. Transistors are paid for in the month of purchase. Transportation costs average $0.10 per transistor. Storage costs total $0.24 per unit per year including $0.12 for the lost interest that could have been earned on the investment in the transistor inventory. Storage costs are to be computed on the average of beginning and ending inventory.

Required:

Prepare a detailed schedule(s) estimating the cash disbursements in January for the purchase, transportation, and storage of *transistors*.

Solution to Self-Study Problem

To solve this problem you have to define, for yourself, what has to be done. Let's expand as follows:

$$
\begin{aligned}
\text{Cash disbursements} = \ &\text{Cash for purchase} &&(1)\\
&+ \text{ Cash for transportation} &&(2)\\
&+ \text{ Cash for storage} &&(3)
\end{aligned}
$$

To determine (1) and (2) we need to determine the number of transistors that are planned for purchase in January:

$$
\begin{aligned}
\text{Transistor purchases} = \ &2 \text{ (January production of A)} &&(1a)\\
&+ 3 \text{ (January production of B)} &&(1b)\\
&+ \text{ January spoilage} &&(1c)\\
&+ \text{ Desired ending inventory} &&(1d)\\
&- \text{ Beginning inventory} &&(1e)
\end{aligned}
$$

The desired ending inventory is equal to 0.50 times the total transistors needed in February. The latter would be computed in the same way as above.

Now start at the end of this logic and work back. First, let's do January's and February's production:

| | January | | February | |
	A	*B*	*A*	*B*
Sales needs	11,000	6,000	5,000	5,000
Desired Ending Inventory				
0.25 × Next Month's Sales	1,250	1,250	2,000	2,500
Total needs	12,250	7,250	7,000	7,500
Beginning inventory	3,000	1,000	1,250	1,250
Production	9,250	6,250	5,750	6,250

Now find the transistors needed (before spoilage) by multiplying by the transistors per unit. Then compute the spoilage allowance, which is 5% of gross:

Net = Gross − 0.05 × Gross or
Net = 0.95 × Gross or
Gross = Net ÷ 0.95

	January	*February*
For A:		
2 × 9,250; 2 × 5,750	18,500	11,500
For B:		
3 × 6,250; 3 × 6,250	18,750	18,750
	37,250	30,250
Needed with spoilage:		
37,250 ÷ 0.95	39,210	
30,250 ÷ 0.95		31,842

January's purchases can now be computed. Items (1a), (1b), and (1c) will total to 39,210: the gross purchases. Item (1d) is 0.50 of February's needs (31,842). Item (1e) is given. In summary:

Gross needs for January	39,210
Desired Ending Inventory (0.5 × 31,842)	15,921
Total	55,131
Less beginning inventory	18,000
Total purchases	37,131

Cash disbursement items (1) and (2) are obvious. Consider item (3), cash for storage costs. The storage rate is $0.24 per unit per year but it includes $0.12 representing lost interest. The latter is an absence of a cash inflow, not a cash outflow. Since the requirements are for cash disbursements, the relevant unit cost is $0.12 ($0.24 − $0.12). Further, the requirements are for one month's cash outflow. The $0.12 is an annual rate, and the monthly rate is $0.01. Finally, the storage cost is to be computed on the simple average of the beginning and ending inventory, 18,000 and 15,921 units, respectively.

In summary:

Cash Required for:	
Purchases 37,131 × $10	$371,310
Transportation 37,131 × $0.10	3,713
Storage 0.01[(18,000 + 15,921)/2]	170
Total cash outflow	$375,193

References

Becker, S., and Green, David Jr., "Budgeting and Employee Behavior," *Journal of Business* (October 1962): 392–402.

Stedry, A., "Budgeting and Employee Behavior: A Reply," *Journal of Business* (April 1964): 195–202.

Welsch, G.A. *Budgeting: Profit Planning and Control*. Englewood Cliffs, N.J.: Prentice-Hall, 1976.

Problems

12-1. Adapted CMA Problem on Basic Budgeting. Einhard Enterprises has a comprehensive budgeting program. Proforma statements of earnings and financial position are prepared as the final step in the budget problem. Einhard's projected financial position as of June 30, 19x2, is presented below. Various $19 \times 2 - \times 3$ master budget schedules, based upon the plans for the fiscal year ending June 30, 19x3, also appear below.

All sales are made on account. Raw material, direct labor, factory overhead, and selling and administrative expenses are credited to vouchers payable. Federal income tax expense is charged to income taxes payable. The federal income tax rate is 40 percent.

Einhard Enterprises
Proforma Statement of Financial Position
as of June 30, 19x2
($000 omitted)

Assets

Cash	$ 800
Accounts receivable	750
Direct material inventory	506
Finished goods inventory	648
Total Current assets	$ 2,704
Land	$ 1,500
Property, plant, and equipment	11,400
Less accumulated depreciation	(2,250)
Total long-term assets	$10,650
Total assets	$13,354

Liabilities and Equity

Vouchers payable	$ 1,230
Income taxes payable	135
Notes payable (due $12/30/\times 2$)	1,000
Total liabilities	$ 2,365
Common stock	$10,200
Retained earnings	789
Total liabilities and equity	$13,354

Sales Schedule in Units and Dollars

Units Sales	Selling Price per Unit	Total Sales Revenue
2,100,000	$16	$33,600,000

Production Schedule in Units and Dollars

Production in Units	Cost perUnit	Total Cost of Manufacturing
2,110,000	$12.00	$25,320,000

Raw Material Purchases Schedule in Units and Dollars

Purchases in Pounds	Cost per Pound	Total Purchase Cost
4,320,000	$2.75	$11,880,000

Two pounds of raw material are needed to make one unit of finished product.

Direct Labor Schedule in Units and Dollars

Production in units	Direct-Labor Cost per Hour	Total Direct-Labor Cost
2,110,000	$8	$8,440,000

Each unit requires one-half hour of direct-labor time.

Manufacturing Overhead Schedule in Dollars
(expected activity level—1,055,000 direct-labor hours)

Variable expenses	$2,954,000*
Depreciation	600,000
Other fixed expenses	1,721,000*
Total manufacturing overhead	$5,275,000

*All require cash expenditures. The manufacturing overhead rate is $5.00 per direct-labor hour: ($5,275,000 ÷ 1,055,000).

Selling and Administrative Expense Schedule in Dollars

Selling expenses	$2,525,000
Administrative expenses	2,615,000
Total	$5,140,000

All selling and administrative expenses require the expenditure of cash.

Beginning Inventory Schedule in Units and Dollars

	Quantity	Cost per Unit	Total Cost
Direct material	184,000 pounds	$ 2.75 per lb.	$506,000
Finished goods	54,000 units	$12.00 per unit	$648,000

Cash Receipts and Disbursements Schedule ($000 omitted)

Cash balance 7/1/x2 (estimated)	$ 800	
Cash receipts		
Collection of accounts receivable	33,450	
Total cash available		$34,250

Cash disbursements
   Payment of vouchers payable

Direct material	$11,900	
Direct labor	8,400	
Manufacturing overhead	4,650	
Selling and administrative expenses	5,200	
Total vouchers payable	$30,150	
Income taxes	1,100	
Purchase of equipment	400	
Cash dividends	820	
Total cash disbursement		32,470
Excess cash		$ 1,780
Financing		
Repayment of note payable 12/30/x2	$ 1,000	
Interest expense	50	
Total financing cost		$ 1,050
Projected cash balance 6/30/x3		$ 730

Required:

Construct a proforma statement of financial position for Einhard Enterprises as of June 30, 19x3.

12-2. Basic Problem on Production Budget. The Stegdub Manufacturing Company wants to maintain its finished goods inventory at a minimum level of 25% of the next month's budgeted sales. The capacity of Stegdub's plant is 50,000 units per month. The January 1, 19x4, inventory of finished goods is 25,000 units. Sales forecasted for 19x4 follow:

January	45,000 units
February	60,000 units
March	36,000 units

[handwritten: 39 m needed in Jan 54 m " " Feb]

Required:

Prepare a budget showing the number of units that will need to be produced during January and February in order to meet the company's requirements. Show separate budgets for each of the two months.

12-3. Cash Disbursements Budget; Continuation of Problem 12-2. The Stegdub Company, from problem 12-2, is also interested in budgeting the cash disbursements. To aid in this, you are provided the December 19x3 actual income statement. December 19x3 was a typical month in terms of the cost behavior.

Sales (at $10 per unit)		$400,000
Manufacturing cost of sales		
Variable	$240,000	
Fixed (including depreciation of $10,000)	60,000	300,000
Gross margin		$100,000
Selling expense (including variable expense		
equal to 10% of sales)	$ 50,000	
General expense (fixed)	10,000	60,000
Net income		$ 40,000

All manufacturing costs of producing a product are paid in the month following its production. Selling and general expenses are paid in the same month in which they are incurred.

Required:

Prepare a schedule of estimated cash disbursements for February 19x4.

12-4. Cash Budgeting When Multiple Products Are Purchased. The Simmons Company buys and sells two products, A and B. The purchase lead time for product A is one week and it is two weeks for product B. Purchases are paid for as follows:

—70% of a month's purchases are paid for in the month of purchase.
—30% of a month's purchases are paid for in the month following purchase.

The company's credit department reports the following experience with respect to the collection of sales revenue:

1. 20% of the sales are by cash transactions.
2. The credit sales are 80% of total sales and are collected as follows:
   a. 2% of these are bad debts; never collected.
   b. 8% are collected in the second month after sale.
   c. 40% are collected in the first month after sale.
   d. 50% are collected in the month of sale:
      i. 60% of these sales qualify for a 3% cash discount for prompt payment.
      ii. The remaining 40% of these collections are not entitled to a cash discount and are collected in full.

Product A is marked up at one-third above cost, whereas product B is marked up at two-thirds of cost. At January 1, 19x2, the cash balance was $9,000. Following are some actual and forecasted unit sales data as well as the per-unit purchase prices. The actual sales in November and December 19x1 were equal to the budgeted sales.

Product	Purchase Price	Nov.	Dec.	Jan.	Feb.	March
A	$15	1,000	1,200	1,300	1,000	800
B	18	500	600	500	700	600

Required:

Prepare a statement of the forecasted January 31, 19x2, cash balance assuming there are no other receipts and disbursements except for those mentioned above.

12-5. Planning Material Purchases When There Are Quantity Discounts. The Plan Ahead Company buys its raw material from a supplier who bills as follows: If the quantity purchased per month is 200,000 units or more, the unit price is $0.95 for all units. For quantities less than 200,000, the price is $1.00 per unit for all units.

Production requirements for January and February are 180,000 and 179,000 units, respectively. *Minimum* ending inventories are set at 30,000 and 46,000 units, respectively. There will be 15,000 units on hand at January 1. The warehouse capacity is 50,000 units.

Required:

Prepare a purchase budget for January and February giving consideration to the fact that the company wants to minimize the costs of its materials.

12-6. Cash Budgeting When Multiple Products Are Produced. The Fremont Company produces and sells a particular kind of heavy-duty industrial machine, the Hulk. The Hulk requires three units of part 341, which the firm also manufactures. All of the part 341s needed for a Hulk must be produced and on hand before a Hulk can be started. That is, it is not possible to produce a Hulk and its 341s simultaneously. Part 341 has a limited operational life and requires frequent replacement. Thus, Fremont also does considerable business in the part replacement market.

The manufacturing process of both the Hulk and part 341 requires a special metal whose purchase must be carefully scheduled. Each part 341 requires two pounds of this metal and, in addition to the three 341s, the Hulk machine requires one pound of the metal for other components.

For budgeting purposes, Fremont divides the year into thirteen periods of four weeks each (a total of twenty working days per period). The estimated sales demand for the Hulk and for replacement parts during the next four periods are as follows:

	Period 1	*Period 2*	*Period 3*	*Period 4*
Hulk	8,000	5,000	10,000	6,000
Part 341 replacement	10,000	20,000	32,400	25,000

At the beginning of period 1, 2,000 Hulks, 5,000 units of part 341, and 7,000 pounds of the special metal will be on hand.

Part 341 requires a production lead time of eight working days. The Hulk's production lead time is four working days. When purchasing the metal, a ten-day lead time must be allowed.

The Hulk sells for $1,000 and part 341 is sold at $100 per unit.

Required:

Prepare a schedule(s) estimating the amount of metal that should be purchased during period 1.

12-7. Adapted CMA Problem on Budgeting and Scheduling Material Purchases. The Press Company manufactures and sells industrial components. The Whitmore Plant is responsible for producing two components referred to as AD-5 and FX-3. Plastic, brass, and aluminum are used in the production of these two products.

Press Company has adopted a thirteen-period reporting cycle in all of its plants for budgeting purposes. Each period is four weeks long and has twenty working days. The projected inventory levels for AD-5 and FX-3 at the end of the current (seventh) period and the projected sales for these two products for the next three four-week periods are presented in the accompanying schedule.

	Projected Inventory Level (in units) End of Seventh Period	*Projected Sales (in Units)*		
		Eighth Period	*Ninth Period*	*Tenth Period*
AD-5	3,000	7,500	8,750	9,500
FX-3	2,800	7,000	4,500	4,000

Past experience has shown that adequate inventory levels for AD-5 and FX-3 can be maintained if 40% of the next period's projected sales are on hand at the end of a reporting period. Based on this experience and the projected sales, the Whitmore Plant has budgeted production of 8,000 AD-5 and 6,000 FX-3 in the eighth period. Production is assumed to be uniform for both products within each four-week period.

The raw material specifications for AD-5 and FX-3 are as follows:

	AD-5	*FX-3*
Plastic	2.0 lb.	1.0 lb.
Brass	0.5 lb.	—
Aluminum	—	1.5 lb.

Data relating to the purchase of raw materials are presented as follows.

	Purchase Price per pound	*Standard Purchase Lot (in pounds)*	*Reorder Point (in pounds)*	*Projected Inventory Status at the End of the Seventh Period (in pounds)*		*Lead Time in Working Days*
				On Hand	*On Order*	
Plastic	$0.40	15,000	12,000	16,000	15,000	10
Brass	0.95	5,000	7,500	9,000	—	30
Aluminum	0.55	10,000	10,000	14,000	10,000	20

The sales of AD-5 and FX-3 do vary from month to month. However, the safety stock incorporated into the reorder point for each of the raw materials is adequate to compensate for variations in the sales of the finished products.

Raw material orders are placed the day the quantity on hand plus on order falls below the reorder point. Whitmore Plant's suppliers are very dependable so that the given lead times are reliable. The outstanding orders for plastic and aluminum are due to arrive on the tenth and fourth working days of the eighth period, respectively. Payments for all raw material orders are remitted in the month of delivery.

Required:

Whitmore Plant is required to submit a report to corporate headquarters of Press Company summarizing the projected raw material activities before each period commences. The data for the eighth period report are being assembled. Determine the following items for plastic, brass, and aluminum for inclusion in the eighth period report:

1. Projected quantities (in pounds) of each raw material to be issued to production.
2. Projected quantities (in pounds) of each raw material ordered and the date (in terms of working days) the order is to be placed.
3. The projected inventory balance (in pounds) of each raw material at the end of the period.
4. The payments for purchases of each raw material.

12-8. Adapted CPA Problem on Selected Budgeting Concepts. The Dilly Company marks up all merchandise at 25% of the gross purchase price. All purchases are made on account with terms of 1/10, net/60. Purchase discounts, which are recorded as miscellaneous income, are always taken. Normally, 60% of each month's purchases are paid for in the month of purchase, whereas the other 40% are paid during the first ten days of the first month after purchase. Inventories of merchandise at the end of each month are kept at 30% of the next month's projected cost of goods sold.

Terms for sales on account are 2/10, net/30. Cash sales are not subject to discount. Fifty percent of each month's sales on account are collected during the month of sale, 45% are collected in the succeeding month, and the remainder are usually uncollectible. Seventy percent of the collections in the month of sale are subject to discount, whereas 10% of the collections in the succeeding month are subject to discount.

Projected sales data for selected months follow:

	Sales on Account—Gross	Cash Sales	Total Sales
December	$1,900,000	$400,000	$2,300,000
January	1,500,000	250,000	1,750,000
February	1,700,000	350,000	2,050,000
March	1,600,000	300,000	1,900,000

Required:

1. Compute the projected cost of the inventory at the end of December.
2. Compute the projected gross purchases for January.
3. Compute the projected payments to suppliers during February.
4. Compute the projected sales discounts to be taken by customers making remittances during February.
5. Compute the projected collections from customers during February.

12-9. **Adapted CMA Problem on Cash Budgeting.** The Barker Corporation manufactures and distributes wooden baseball bats. The bats are manufactured in Georgia at its only plant. This is a seasonal business, with a large portion of its sales ocurring in late winter and early spring. The production schedule for the last quarter of the year is heavy in order to build up inventory to meet expected sales volume.

The company experiences a temporary cash strain during this heavy production period. Payroll costs rise during the last quarter because overtime is scheduled to meet the increased production needs. Collections from customers are low because the fall season produces only modest sales. This year the company concern is intensified because of the rapid increases in prices during the current inflationary period. In addition, the sales department forecasts sales of less than one million bats for the first time in three years. This decrease in sales appears to be caused by the popularity of aluminum bats.

The cash account builds up during the first and second quarters as sales exceed production. The excess cash is invested in U.S. Treasury bills and other commercial paper. During the last half of the year the temporary investments are liquidated to meet the cash needs. In the early years of the company, short-term borrowing was used to supplement the funds released by selling investments, but this has not been necessary in recent years. Because costs are higher this year, the treasurer asks for a forecast for December to judge if the $40,000 in temporary investments will be adequate to carry the company through the month with a minimum balance of $10,000. Should this amount ($40,000) be insufficient, he wants to begin negotiations for a short-term loan.

The unit sales volume for the past two months and the estimate for the next four months are:

October (actual)	70,000
November (actual)	50,000
December (estimated)	50,000
January (estimated)	90,000
February (estimated)	90,000
March (estimated)	120,000

The bats are sold for $3 each. All sales are made on account. One-half of the accounts are collected in the month of the sale, 40% are collected in the month following the sale, and the remaining 10% in the second month following the sale. Customers who pay in the month of the sale receive a 2% cash discount.

The production schedule for the six-month period beginning with October reflects the company's policy of maintaining a stable year-round work force by scheduling overtime to meet production schedules:

October (actual)	90,000
November (actual)	90,000
December (estimated)	90,000
January (estimated)	90,000
February (estimated)	100,000
March (estimated)	100,000

The bats are made from wooden blocks that cost $6 each. Ten bats can be produced from each block. The blocks are acquired one year in advance so they can be properly aged. Barker pays the supplier one-twelfth of the cost of this material each month until the obligation is retired. The monthly payment is $60,000.

The plant is normally scheduled for a forty-hour, five-day work week. During the busy production season, however, the work week may be increased to six ten-hour days. Workers can produce 7.5 bats per hour. Monthly output during regular time is 75,000 bats. Factory employees are paid $4.00 per hour (up $0.50 from last year) for regular time, and time and one-half for overtime.

Other manufacturing costs include variable overhead of $0.30 per unit and annual fixed overhead of $280,000, including depreciation of $40,000. Selling expenses include variable costs of $0.20 per unit and annual fixed costs of $60,000. Fixed administrative costs are $120,000 annually. All fixed costs are incurred uniformly throughout the year.

The controller has accumulated the following additional information:

1. The balances of selected accounts as of November 30, 19x4, are as follows:

Cash	$ 12,000
Marketable securities (cost and market are the same)	40,000
Accounts receivable	96,000
Prepaid expenses	4,800
Accounts payable (arising from raw material purchase)	300,000

Accrued vacation pay	9,500
Equipment note payable	102,000
Accrued income taxes payable	50,000

2. Interest to be received from the company's temporary investments is estimated at $500 for December.
3. Prepaid expenses of $3,600 will expire during December, and the balance of the prepaid account is estimated at $4,200 for the end of December. Of the amount expiring, 50% is applicable to fixed manufacturing overhead and the balance to administrative expenses.
4. Barker purchased new machinery in 19x4 as part of a plant modernization program. The machinery was financed by a twenty-four-month note of $144,000. The terms call for equal principal payments over the next twenty four months with interest paid at the rate of 1% per month on the unpaid balance at the first of the month. The first payment was made May 1, 19x4.
5. Old equipment, which has a book value of $8,000, is to be sold during December for $7,500.
6. Each month the company accrues $1,700 for vacation pay for plant employees by charging fixed manufacturing overhead and crediting accrued vacation pay. The plant closes for two weeks in June when all plant employees take a vacation.
7. Quarterly dividends of $0.20 per share will be paid on December 15 to stockholders of record. Barker Corporation has authorized 10,000 shares. The company has issued 7,500 shares, and 500 of these are classified as treasury stock.
8. The quarterly income taxes payment of $50,000 is due on December 15, 19x4.

Required:

1. Prepare a schedule that forecasts the cash position at December 31, 19x4. What action, if any, will be required to maintain a $10,000 cash balance?
2. Without prejudice to your answer in part 1, assume Barker regularly needs to arrange short-term loans during the November-to-February preiod. What changes might Barker consider in its methods of doing business to reduce or eliminate the need for short-term borrowing?

12-10. Estimating Cash Receipts under a Cycle Billing System. The Ace Bicycle Company is a wholesale distributor of bicycles. They have installed a cycle billing system whereby each of four groups of customers is billed every four weeks but on a staggered basis so that only one group is billed during a given week. A group is billed for the purchases for the four-week period ending with the week before the billing week. For example, the group billed in week 6 would be billed for their purchases in weeks 2, 3, 4, and 5.

The merchandise is marked up so that the gross margin is equal to *20% of sales.* The actual sales in a given week are generally divided equally among the four groups. The billing terms entitle the customer to a 2% discount if paid within one week of the billing. Experience has shown that:

1. 60% of the customers pay in the first week following the billing.
2. 20% of the customers pay in the second week following the billing.
3. 10% of the customers pay in the third week following the billing.
4. 5% of the customers pay in the fourth week following the billing.

For purposes of this problem refer to the first week in February as week 1, the second week as week 2, and so forth. Although the company has been doing business for some time, you are asked to consider sales activity beginning in week 1. The budgeted *cost of sales* totals $16,000 each for weeks 1, 2, 3, and 4 and $32,000 each for weeks 5, 6, 7, and 8.

Required:

1. Prepare a schedule showing when the sales of weeks 1 through 8 would be billed. Use three column headings: "Week," "Total Sales," and "Amount Billed in Week Number." Under the later heading, include ten columns for weeks 1 through 10.
2. Using the results of the schedule in part 1, estimate the cash collections in week 9.

12-11. Projected Income When There Is Inflation and a Standard Cost System. The Detroit Lion Company has established a standard cost system. Although there were some variances in 19x1, a review of the quantity standards indicated that they were reasonable and will not be changed in 19x2. Action is being taken to control these areas better, and it is reasonable to believe that the controllable variances will be substantially eliminated in 19x2. *However, the company is expecting inflation to cause 10% increases in selling prices and the cost of resources acquired during 19x2.* Following is the 19x1 income statement.

Detroit Lion Company
Income Statement
for the Year Ended 12/31/x1

Sales (6,000 units)			$60,000
Cost of sales:			
Beginning finished goods inventory			
(3,000 units)		$20,700	
Production costs for 5,000 units at standard:			
Direct material	$12,000		
Direct labor	15,000		
Variable overhead	4,500		
Fixed overhead applied	3,000	34,500	
Standard cost of goods available		$55,200	
Ending finished goods inventory			
(2,000 units)		13,800	41,400
Standard gross margin			$18,600
Variances			
Variable cost variances		$ 1,200 U	
Noncontrollable (volume) variance*		1,800 U	3,000
Actual gross margin			$15,600
Selling and administrative expenses:			
Sales commissions		$ 2,400	
Other variable selling expenses		600	
Depreciation on office building		500	3,500
Net income			$12,100

*The overhead is applied on the basis of labor hours. At standard, there is one hour allowed per unit. In 19x1 the *fixed* rate was established as follows:

Factory depreciation	$3,200
Other fixed costs	1,600
Total	$4,800
Divisor activity	8,000 hours
Fixed overhead rate	$ 0.60

Assume the standard hours allowed for the 19x1 activity totals 5,000. Also assume that work-in-process inventories are always zero. Sales commissions are based on *sales dollars* but all other items behave as a function of the appropriate *unit* volume. The office building is being depreciated by the straight-line method over twenty years. During 19x2 the company plans to sell 9,000 units and to increase the ending inventory of finished goods to 3,000 units.

Required:

1. Using the divisor activity and adjusting for price level changes, determine the fixed overhead rate for 19x2.
2. Using the format of the 19x1 statement, prepare a projected income statement for 19x2.

12-12. Adapted CPA Problem Involving Budget for Construction Firm. David Construction, Inc. builds heavy construction equipment for commercial and government purposes. Because of two new contracts and the anticipated purchase of new equipment, the management needs certain projections for the next three years. You have been requested to prepare these projections.

You have acquired the following information from the company's records and personnel:

1. David Construction uses the completed-contract method of accounting whereby construction costs are capitalized until the contract is completed. Since all general and administrative expenses can be identified with a particular contract, they also are capitalized until the contract is completed.
2. David's December 31, 19x3, balance sheet follows:

Assets		
Cash		$ 72,000
Due on contracts		——
Cost of uncompleted contracts in excess of billings		——
Plant and equipment	$2,800,000	
Less accumulated depreciaton	129,600	2,670,400
Total		$2,742,400
Liabilities and Stockholders' Equity		
Loans payable		——
Accrued construction costs	$ 612,400	
Accrued income tax payable	65,000	
Common stock ($10 par value)	500,000	
Paid in capital	100,000	
Retained earnings	1,465,000	
Total	$2,742,400	

3. Two contracts will be started in 19x4—contract A and contract B. Contract A and contract B are expected to be completed in December 19x5 and December 19x6, respec-

tively. No other contracts will be started until after contracts A and B are completed. All other outstanding contracts had been completed in 19x3.

4. Total estimated revenue for contract A is $2,000,000 and for contract B, $1,500,000. The estimated cash collections per year follows:

	19x4	*19x5*	*19x6*
Contract A	$ 800,000	$1,200,000	$ ——
Contract B	300,000	450,000	750,000
	$1,100,000	$1,650,000	$750,000

5. Estimated construction costs to be incurred per contract, per year, follow:

	Contract A	*Contract B*
19x4	$ 720,000	$ 250,000
19x5	1,000,000	400,000
19x6	——	650,000
	$1,720,000	$1,300,000

6. Depreciation expense is included in these estimated construction costs. For 19x4, 10% of the estimated construction costs represent depreciation expense. For 19x5 and 19x6, 15% of the estimated construction costs represent depreciation expense. The cash portion of these estimated construction costs is paid as follows: 70% in the year incurred and 30% in the following year.

7. Total general and administrative expenses (not included in construction costs) consist of a fixed portion each year for each contract, and a variable portion that is a function of cash collected each year. For the two prior years, cash collected and total general and administrative expenses (based on one contract each year) were as follows:

	Cash Collected	Total General and Administrative Expenses
19x3	$1,350,000	$27,250
19x2	1,180,000	24,700

These general and administrative expenses all represent cash expenses and are paid in the year incurred.

8. Dividends are expected to be distributed as follows:
   19x4 Stock—10% of common shares outstanding (estimated fair market value is $15 per share).
   19x5 Stock split—2 for 1 (par value to be reduced to $5 per share).
   19x6 Cash—$1.00 per share.

9. David will acquire a new asset in 19x5 for $700,000 and plans to pay for it that year.

10. When the cash balance falls below $70,000, David obtains short-term loans in multiples of $10,000. For purposes of this problem, *ignore interest on short-term loans and ignore any repayments on these loans.*

11. Assume income taxes are paid in full the following year.

Required:

1. Prepare projected income statements for each of the calendar years 19x5 and 19x6 (when contracts are to be completed). The income tax rate is 40%, and the company uses the same methods for accounting and tax purposes.
2. Prepare cash budgets for each of the calendar years 19x4, 19x5, and 19x6. The budgets should follow this format:

Cash (beginning of year) $
Plus: collections
Less: disbursements (enumerated)
Plus: borrowing (if any)   _____
Cash (end of year)   =======

12-13. Adapted CMA Problem: Budget for a Nonprofit Organization. United Business Education, Inc. (UBE) is a nonprofit organization that sponsors a wide variety of management seminars throughout the United States. In addition it is heavily involved in research into improved methods of educating and motivating business executives. The seminar activity is largely supported by fees and the research program from member dues.

UBE operates on a calendar-year basis and is in the process of finalizing the budget for 19x8. The following information has been taken from approved plans that are still tentative at this time.

Seminar Program

Revenue—The scheduled number of programs should produce $12,000,000 of revenue for the year. Each program is budgeted to produce the same amount of revenue. The revenue is collected during the month the program is offered. The programs are scheduled so that 12% of the revenue is collected in each of the first five months of the year. The remaining programs, accounting for the remaining 40% of the revenue, are distributed evenly through the months of September, October, and November. No programs are offered in the other four months of the year.

Direct Expenses—The seminar expenses are made up of three segments:

1. Instructors' fees are paid at the rate of 70% of the seminar revenue in the month following the seminar. The instructors are considered independent contractors and are not eligible for UBE employee benefits.
2. Facilities fees total $5,600,000 for the year. They are the same for each program and are paid in the month the program is given.
3. Annual promotion costs of $1,000,000 are spent equally in all months except June and July when there is no promotional effort.

Research Program

Research Grants—The research program has a large number of projects nearing completion. The other main research activity this year includes the feasibility studies for new projects to be started in 19x8. As a result, the total grant expenses of $3,000,000 for 19x8 is expected to be paid out at the rate of $500,000 per month during the first six months of the year.

Salaries and Other UBE Expenses

Office Lease—Annual amount of $240,000 paid monthly at the beginning of each month.

General Administrative Expenses (telephone, supplies, postage, etc.)—$1,500,000 annually or $125,000 a month.

Depreciation Expense—$240,000 a year.
General UBE Promotion—Annual cost of $600,000, paid monthly.
Salaries and Benefits—

Number of Employees	Annual Salary Paid Monthly	Total Annual Salaries
1	$50,000	$ 50,000
3	40,000	120,000
4	30,000	120,000
15	25,000	375,000
5	15,000	75,000
22	10,000	220,000
50		$960,000

Employee benefits amount to $240,000 or 25% of annual salaries. Except for the pension contribution, the benefits are paid as salaries are paid. The annual pension payment of $24,000, based on 2.5% of salaries (included in the total benefits and the 25% rate), is due April 15, 19x8.

Other Information

Membership Income—UBE has 100,000 members, each of whom pays an annual fee of $100. The fee for the calendar year is invoiced in late June. The collection schedule is as follows.

July	60%
August	30%
September	5%
October	5%

Capital Expenditures—The capital expenditures program calls for a total of $510,000 in cash payments to be spread evenly over the first five months of 19x8.
Cash and Temporary Investments—At January 1, 19x8, they are estimated at $750,000.

Required:

1. Prepare a budget of the 19x8 cash receipts and disbursements for UBE, Inc.
2. Prepare a cash budget for UBE, Inc. for January and the first six months of 19x8.
3. Using the information you developed in parts 1 and 2, identify two important operating problems of UBE, Inc.

12-14. Alternative to 12-13; CMA Problem. The Triple-F Health Club is a nonprofit, family-oriented health club. The club's Board of Directors is developing plans to acquire more equipment and expand the club facilities. The Board plans to purchase about $25,000 of new equipment each year and wants to begin a fund to purchase the adjoining property in four or five years. The adjoining property has a market value of about $300,000.

The club manager, Jane Crowe, is concerned that the Board has unrealistic goals in light of its recent financial performance. She has sought the help of a club member with an accounting background to assist her in preparing a report to the Board supporting her concerns.

The club member reviewed the club's records, including the cash basis income statements presented below. The review and discussion with Jane Crowe disclosed the additional information which follows the statement.

Statement of Income (Cash Basis)
for Years Ended October 31
($000 omitted)

	1980	1979
Cash revenues		
Annual membership fees	$355.0	$300.0
Lesson and class fees	234.0	180.0
Miscellaneous	2.0	1.5
Total cash received	$591.0	$481.5
Cash expenses		
Manager's salary and benefits	$ 36.0	$ 36.0
Regular employees' wages and benefits	190.0	190.0
Lesson and class employee wages and benefits	195.0	150.0
Towels and supplies	16.0	15.5
Utilities (heat and light)	22.0	15.0
Mortgage interest	35.1	37.8
Miscellaneous	2.0	1.5
Total cash expenses	$496.1	$445.8
Cash income	$ 94.9	$ 35.7

Additional Information
- Other financial information as of October 31, 1980
  - —Cash in checking account, $7,000.
  - —Petty cash, $300.
  - —Outstanding mortgage balance, $360,000.
  - —Accounts payable arising from invoices for supplies and utilities that are unpaid as of October 31, 1980, $2,500.
- No unpaid bills existed on October 31, 1979.
- The club purchased $25,000 worth of exercise equipment during the current fiscal year. Cash of $10,000 was paid on delivery and the balance was due on October 1 but has not been paid as of October 31, 1980.
- The club began operations in 1974 in rental quarters. In October of 1976 it purchased its current property (land and building) for $600,000, paying $120,000 down and agreeing to pay $30,000 plus 9% interest annually on November 1 until the balance was paid off.
- Membership rose 3% during 1980. This is approximately the same annual rate the club has experienced since it opened.
- Membership fees were increased by 15% in 1980. The Board has tentative plans to increase the fees by 10% in 1981.
- Lesson and class fees have not been increased for three years. The Board's policy is to encourage classes and lessons by keeping the fees low. The members have taken advantage of this policy and the number of classes and lessons have grown significantly each year. The club expects the percentage growth experienced in 1980 to be repeated in 1981.

- Miscellaneous revenues are expected to grow at the same percentage as experienced in 1980.
- Operating expenses are expected to increase. Hourly wage rates and the manager's salary will need to be increased 15% because no increases were granted in 1980. Towels and supplies, utilities, and miscellaneous expenses are expected to increase 25%.

Required:

1. Construct a cash budget for 1981 for the Triple-F Health Club.
2. Identify any operating problem(s) that this budget discloses for the Triple-F Health Club. Explain your answer.
3. Is Jane Crowe's concern that the Board's goals are unrealistic justified? Explain your answer.

12-15. **Adapted CMA Problem: Modeling the Budgeting Process.** Over the past several years, the Programme Corporation has encountered difficulties estimating its cash flows. The result has been a rather strained relationship with its banker.

Programme's controller would like to develop a means by which she can forecast the firm's monthly operating cash flows. The following data were gathered to facilitate the development of such a forecast.

1. Sales have been and are expected to continue increasing at 0.5%.
2. 30% of each month's sales are for cash; the other 70% are on open account.
3. Of the credit sales, 80% are collected in the first month following the sale and the remaining 20% are collected in the second month. There are no bad debts.
4. Gross margin on sales averages 25%.
5. Programme purchases enough inventory each month to cover the following month's sales.
6. All inventory purchases are paid for in the month of purchase at a 2% cash discount.
7. Monthly expenses are: payroll—$1,500; rent—$400; depreciation—$120; other cash expenses—1% of that month's sales. There are no accruals.
8. Ignore the effects of corporate income taxes, dividends, and equipment acquisitions.

Required:

Using the preceding data, develop a mathematical model the controller can use for her calculations. Your model should be capable of calculating the monthly operating cash inflows and outflows for any specified month.

12-16. CMA Problem: Budgeting When There Are Variances. Rein Company, a compressor manufacturer, is developing a budgeted income statement for the calendar year 19x2. The president is generally satisfied with the projected net income for 19x1 of $700,000 resulting in an earnings per share figure of $2.80. However, next year he would like earnings per share to increase to at least $3.

Rein Company employs a standard absorption cost system. Inflation necessitates an annual revision in the standards as evidenced by an increase in production costs expected in 19x2. The total manufacturing cost for 19x1 is $72 per unit produced.

Rein expects to sell 100,000 compressors at $110 each in the current year (19x1). Forecasts from the sales department are favorable and Rein Company is projecting an annual increase of 10 percent in unit sales in 19x2 and 19x3. This increase in sales will occur even though a $15 increase in unit selling price will be implemented in 19x2. The selling price increase was absolutely essential to compensate for the increased production costs and operating expenses. However, management is concerned that any additional sales price increase would curtail the desired growth in volume.

Standard production costs are developed for the two primary metals used in the compressor (brass and a steel alloy), the direct labor, and manufacturing overhead. The following schedule represents the 19x2 standard quantities and rates for material and labor to produce one compressor.

Brass	4 pounds @ $5.35/pound	$21.40
Steel alloy	5 pounds @ $3.16/pound	15.80
Direct labor	4 hours @ $7.00/hour	28.00
Total prime costs		$65.20

The material content of the compressor has been reduced slightly, hopefully without a noticeable decrease in the quality of the finished product. Improved labor productivity and some increase in automation have resulted in a decrease in labor hours per unit from 4.4 to 4.0. However, the significant increases in material prices and hourly labor rates more than offset any savings from reduced input quantities.

The manufacturing overhead cost per unit schedule has yet to be completed. Preliminary data are as follows:

	Activity Level (units)		
Overhead Items	100,000	110,000	120,000
Supplies	$ 475,000	$ 522,500	$ 570,000
Indirect labor	530,000	583,000	636,000
Utilities	170,000	187,000	204,000
Maintenance	363,000	377,500	392,000
Taxes and insurance	87,000	87,000	87,000
Depreciation	421,000	$ 421,000	$ 421,000
Total overhead	$2,046,000	$2,178,000	$2,310,000

The standard overhead rate is based upon direct-labor hours and is developed by using the total overhead costs from the above schedule for the activity level closest to planned production. In developing the standards for the manufacturing costs the following two assumptions were made.

1. The cost of brass is currently at $5.65 per pound. However, this price is historically high and the purchasing manager expects the price to drop to the predetermined standard early in 19x2.
2. Several new employees will be hired for the production line in 19x2. The employees will be generally unskilled. If basic training programs are not effective and improved labor productivity is not experienced, then the production time per unit of product will increase by fifteen minutes over the 19x2 standards.

Rein employs a LIFO inventory system for its finished goods. Rein's inventory policy for finished goods is to have 15% of the expected annual unit sales for the coming year in finished goods inventory at the end of the prior year. The finished goods inventory at December 31, 19x1, is expected to consist of 16,500 units at a total carrying cost of $1,006,500.

Operating expenses are classified as selling, which are variable, and administrative, which are all fixed. The budgeted selling expenses are expected to average 12% of sales revenue in 19x2, which is consistent with the performance in 19x1. The administrative expenses in 19x2 are expected to be 20% higher than the predicted 19x1 amount of $907,850.

Management accepts the cost standards developed by the production and accounting department. However, they are concerned about the possible effect on net income if the price of brass does not decrease, and/or the labor efficiency of new employees does not improve as expected. Therefore management wants the budgeted income statement to be prepared using the standards as developed but to consider the worst possible situation for 19x2. Each resulting manufacturing variance should be separately identified and added to or subtracted from budgeted cost of goods sold at standard. Rein is subject to a 45% income tax rate.

Required:

1. Prepare the budgeted income statement for 19x2 for Rein Company as specified by management. Round all calculations to the nearest dollar.
2. Review the 19x2 budgeted income statement prepared for Rein Company and discuss whether the president's objectives can be achieved.

CHAPTER 13

Cost-Volume-Profit Analysis

Decision makers typically face a variety of uncertainties and ask a variety of "what-if" questions. **Cost-volume-profit (CVP) analysis** can be a useful simplification of the relationships and will help forecast the results of taking certain actions. CVP is an analysis of the effect on net income of changes in sales volume, costs, and selling prices.

In this chapter, we first discuss the various types of decision-making environments that can benefit from CVP analysis. Second, we consider the technique as it applies to a single-product situation. A third section will cover CVP analysis when multiple products are involved because the analysis in these situations is different. In the last two sections we will discuss the implementation of CVP analysis in situations that are either uncertain or nonlinear.

Situations Where CVP Analyses Are Useful

It is obvious that profits are a function of prices, costs, and volume of activity. Further, prices, costs, and volume are related to each other: volume is a function of price, and cost is a function of volume. There are several decisions for which these interrelationships must be considered.

For example, the manager's problem may be such that it is useful to know the break-even volume. **Break-even** is the volume that must be achieved so there is zero profit. This volume is used as a benchmark in the following way. Typically, the demand for the product is uncertain, and the decision maker will only have a vague perception of the uncertainty. But the decision maker may have a strong enough perception of the odds of being on either side of the benchmark so that a decision can be made. By providing a reference point the accountant has made it easier for the decision maker to use a subjective assessment of the situation.

Another similar case is the need for knowing the volume necessary to achieve a target profit. For example, the target return on investment might be 15%. Knowing the investment, this can be converted to a target dollar profit that must be achieved. Then CVP analysis can be used to estimate the necessary volume. Again, the decision maker can use the result as a benchmark and assess the probability of achieving the target.

A third application of CVP analysis is to estimate the impact of changes in the product's sales price. Price and demand are known to be related. The specifics of the case will govern the exact form of the relationship. Elasticity of demand is a major determinate of the form, but, in the final analysis, it cannot be stated with any degree of precision. Because of this, there will be uncertainties about the impact of a pricing decision on profits. Nevertheless, CVP analysis can provide data to help answer questions of which the following is representative: If price is lowered by 5%, by how much must volume increase in order for income to be 3% higher than last year?

Another example where CVP analysis can be used is in the evaluation of the impact of advertising. For example, if advertising is increased by $500,000, by how much must volume increase so that return on sales will increase from 6% last year to 7% this year? There are an endless number of situations that may benefit from CVP analysis. The preceding cases are representative and should provide you with a general impression of the possibilities.

CVP Analysis for a Single Product

We begin the technical discussion by considering the CVP model in single-product situations. First the assumptions and definitions are stated. Then, the break-even analysis will be developed for two cases: well-behaved fixed costs and step-fixed costs. Next the methodology will be extended to that of achieving target profits, both before and after income taxes. Finally the results will be used to analyze some situational cases.

ASSUMPTIONS AND DEFINITIONS. As implied earlier, the conventional CVP analysis may be a simplification of reality and is built on a set of assumptions. Among them are the following:

1. *Profits are assumed to be a linear function* of revenues, costs, and volume. More simply, revenue is assumed to be a straight-line function of volume whereby every unit change in volume will change total revenues by the same amount. In reality, of course, revenues may not change at a constant rate. That is, it may not be possible to increase demand unless prices are lowered. Such a possibility will be ignored in this section. Further, costs are assumed to be a straight-line function of volume and to consist of the usual components: fixed and variable. Of course, costs could be a nonlinear function of volume. Again, this will be ignored in this section. When profits are computed as the difference between two straight-line functions, then the difference must be a straight line (or linear).

2. *Inventories are assumed to remain constant.* If full absorption accounting is used to determine net income, it is known that a change in inventories will result in fixed costs being released against revenue in an amount different from that incurred during the accounting period. In general, then, these circumstances would result in reported profits being different from the amount estimated in a CVP analysis. Alternatively, it may be assumed that variable (direct) costing is used to calculate income.

3. The linearity assumption just stated (number 1) may be realistic so long as *volume is in the relevant normal range.* If so, then an alternative to assumption number 1 is to assume that the volume resulting from a CVP analysis is within that range. Should the resulting volume be outside the relevant range, then the conclusions will be subject to greater estimation error. This is the explanation for the accountant's revenue and cost curves being

at variance with the economist's curves. To illustrate, consider Exhibit 13.1. The curve shown is typical of the economist's *cost* curve. The solid portion of the curve is relatively linear and representative of the accountant's cost curve. As you can see, if projections are to be made for volumes between point *a* and point *b,* the accountant's curve would yield a solution that is not significantly different from the economist's curve.

4. It is assumed that the *time value of money is not important.* If, for example, the CVP analysis extends across several time periods, the assumption is that the dollar flows of each year can be added together. Actually, in such a case it would be more justifiable to treat a dollar received in 19x6, for example, to be of less value than one received in 19x1. However, the time value of money in CVP analysis is ignored until Chapter 16.

Keeping these assumptions in perspective, let us define some variables and parameters that will be convenient in a CVP analysis. Define:

S = sales price *per unit*
V = variable cost *per unit* (including manufacturing, selling, and administrative costs)
F = fixed costs for the period (including manufacturing, selling, and administrative costs)
T = marginal income tax rate
I = target after tax income (a specific dollar amount)
R = the target *ratio* of income to sales (that is, a percentage)
x = volume of activity (measured in units)

These definitions can be used to develop selected CVP models. As this is done, keep in mind that the emphasis is on a general method of doing CVP analysis. The

Exhibit 13.1   Relationship between Accountant's and Economist's Cost Curves

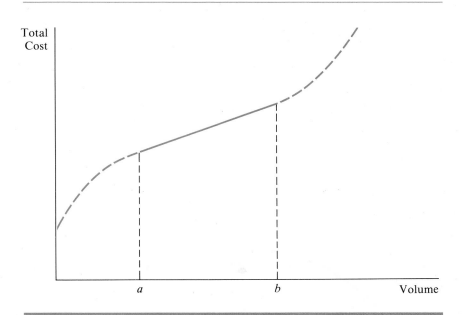

equations that result should not be used indiscriminately. The results are useful only if the assumptions on which they were based are realistic for the situation. When the assumptions are not met you will need to develop your own results.

BREAK-EVEN. For the introductory exercise, assume data are available for S, V, and F (that is, the unit sales price, the unit variable cost, and total fixed costs) and management is interested in determining a break-even volume. That is, the target income, I, is zero. Since inventories are assumed to be constant, the taxable income would also be zero at break-even volume and there is no need to be concerned about income taxes. The model for accounting income determination is:

$$\text{Sales} - \text{Variable costs} - \text{Fixed costs} - \text{Income taxes} = \text{Income} \qquad \textbf{(13-1)}$$

Using the definitions of the previous subsection, the sales at a volume of x units is Sx, and the variable costs are Vx. Define x_0 as the point on the volume interval where break-even is achieved (that is, the x where profits are zero). Then equation (13-1) becomes:

$$Sx_0 - Vx_0 - F - 0 = 0 \qquad \textbf{(13-2)}$$

Factoring out x_0 and adding F to both sides:

$$(S - V)x_0 = F \qquad \textbf{(13-3)}$$

Solving for x_0

$$x_0 = \frac{F}{S - V} \qquad \textbf{(13-4)}$$

Exhibit 13.2 is a graph of the CVP relationships. The first graph simply plots total revenue and total costs. The *difference* between the two lines is profit (or loss). Break-even occurs at the point where revenue equals costs; that is, where the two lines intersect. The x axis is labeled x_0 at this point and denotes the break-even volume. The second graph in Exhibit 13.2 portrays profit only. The slope of the line in the second graph is the contribution margin $(S - V)$. At a zero volume losses would be equal to the fixed costs.

Reflection on equation (13-4) and the second graph in Exhibit 13.2 indicates that if each unit's *contribution* toward fixed costs and profits is $S - V$, then the break-even volume occurs at the volume given by the ratio of fixed costs to the contribution margin per unit. To illustrate, suppose that the following data pertain to the Eckel Company's product:

Sales price per unit	$ 90
Variable manufacturing cost per unit	30
Fixed manufacturing cost per month	15,000
Variable selling and administrative cost per unit	20
Fixed selling and administrative cost per month	5,000

Exhibit 13.2   Graph of CVP Model

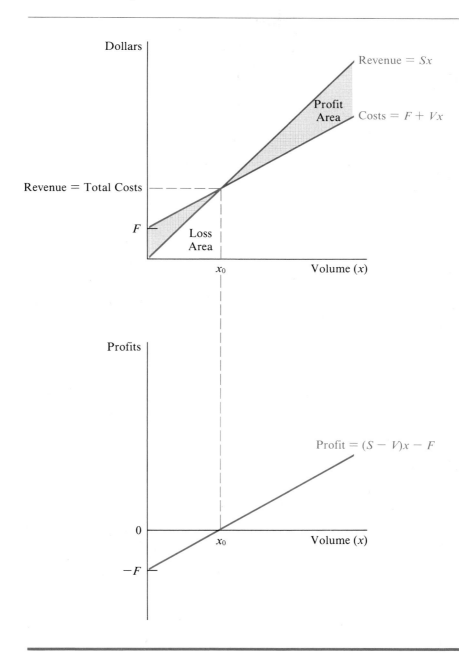

Then the monthly break-even volume is:

$$x_0 = \frac{15,000 + 5,000}{90 - (30 + 20)} = \frac{20,000}{40} = 500 \text{ units}$$

A concept related to the break-even point is the *margin of safety*. The margin of safety is the difference between some planned-for (budgeted) volume and the break-even point. This a safety factory in that it represents the amount by which actual sales can fall below the planned sales and still avoid incurring a loss.

ACHIEVING A TARGET INCOME.   In this section there is a consideration of a variety of cases where management's goal is to achieve some target income. It will be seen that these targets can be expressed in a variety of ways, and each will require a different approach in doing the CVP analysis.

First, assume that the target income has been expressed as a *specific dollar amount; I,* in the preceding definitions. Note, also, that the target, I, was defined to be after income taxes. Define x_i to be the point on the volume interval where the target income is achieved. Then:

$$Sx_i - Vx_i - F - T(Sx_i - Vx_i - F) = I \tag{13-5}$$

Note the income tax component of equation (13-5). Obviously it is assumed that the *taxable* income is equal to accounting income. In general this is an acceptable assumption. (Of course there may be differences between accounting and taxable income. For example, straight-line depreciation might be used for the accounting income computation and an accelerated rate for taxable income. However, APB Opinion number 11 requires deferred tax accounting whereby the tax expense of the period would be computed on the basis of accounting income and any difference between the tax expense and the tax paid would be accumulated in a balance sheet account. Thus, the tax *expense* would be as indicated in equation (13-5).) Therefore, multiplying the accounting income by the marginal tax rate, T, gives the income tax expense.

To solve for x_i, the volume that will produce an income of I, first factor out the quantity $(Sx_i - Vx_i - F)$ in equation (13-5):

$$(Sx_i - Vx_i - F)(1 - T) = I \tag{13-6}$$

Divide both sides by $(1 - T)$, add F to both sides, and factor out x_i:

$$(S - V)x_i = F + \frac{I}{(1 - T)} \tag{13-7}$$

Now the solution to x_i is obvious:

$$x_i = \frac{F + [I/(1 - T)]}{(S - V)} \tag{13-8}$$

Note that in the final result, the after-tax income, I, is adjusted to an equivalent pretax figure before the volume computation is made (note the bracketed term in equation [13-8]). For example, if the marginal tax rate, T, is 40% and the target after-tax income, I, is $60,000, then the pretax income, call it I_{pt}, would have to be such that:

$$I_{pt} - 0.4I_{pt} = 60,000$$

Solving:

$$I_{pt} = \frac{60,000}{(1 - 0.4)} = 100,000$$

To illustrate, return to the Eckel Company case and assume the tax rate and target after-tax income are 40% and $60,000, respectively. Then:

$$x_i = \frac{20,000 + 60,000/(1 - 0.4)}{(90 - 50)} = \frac{120,000}{40} = 3,000$$

There are occasions when the target income is stated as a *percentage of sales*. For example, suppose the Eckel Company wants to know the volume at which after-tax income will equal 10% of total sales volume. In cases such as this, the target income is not a directly specifiable dollar amount. Remembering the definition of R (a target income ratio) in an earlier section, the accounting income model to determine this volume is:

$$(Sx_i - Vx_i - F)(1 - T) = RSx_i \tag{13-9}$$

Note the right-hand side of (13-9). Total sales are given by Sx_i. Multiplying this total by the target percentage yields the target after-tax income.

To solve for x_i, first divide both sides by $(1 - T)$ and then add F to both sides:

$$Sx_i - Vx_i = RSx_i/(1 - T) + F \tag{13-10}$$

Now subtract the first term on the right from both sides of (13-10) and factor out x_i:

$$[S - V - RS/(1 - T)]x_i = F \tag{13-11}$$

Dividing both sides by the term in brackets:

to find # of units it take to reach a certain % of sales.

$$x_i = \frac{F}{S - V - RS/(1 - T)} \tag{13-12}$$

For the Eckel Company target just stated, (13-12) yields:

$$x_i = \frac{20,000}{90 - 50 - (0.1)(90)/(1 - 0.4)}$$

$$x_i = \frac{20,000}{40 - 9/0.6} = \frac{20,000}{40 - 15} = \frac{20,000}{25} = 800$$

To verify that 800 units is correct, consider the following income statement:

Sales (800 × $90)		$72,000
Variable costs (800 × $50)	$40,000	
Fixed costs	20,000	60,000
Taxable income		$12,000
Income taxes at 40%		4,800
After-tax income		$ 7,200

Note that the ratio of after-tax income to sales is 10%.

The final problem to be considered requires an entirely different approach. Consider the case where the fixed costs behave in a step manner. Rather than being $20,000 over all volumes, suppose the behavior of Eckel's fixed cost is as follows:

Activity Range	Fixed Costs
0–399	$11,000
400–549	14,000
550–999	18,000
1,000–1,999	32,000
2,000 and over	40,000

Assuming the variable cost behavior is the same as before, at what volume must the firm operate in order to earn a *pretax* income of $10,000? There is no simple formula to determine this. Instead, an iterative, or step-by-step, process must be used.

Before considering the specific problem just stated, it will be helpful to graphically illustrate the problem. In *general,* the CVP graph for a step-fixed cost problem is found in Exhibit 13.3. The total cost line differs from Exhibit 13.2 and reflects the step increments in fixed costs. Except for the break points, the slope of the line is still equal to the variable cost rate.

As you can see in Exhibit 13.3, the revenue might not intersect the total cost line in every activity range. Further, there may be intersections in more than one range. Of course, if the cost data from the Eckel problem are plotted it could be observed which ranges contained intersections. Then it would be possible to solve the equations for the volume(s). For more complex problems and/or the need to incorporate such a behavior into a computer routine, a process other than graphing is needed. In lieu of a plot, the following process can be used.

To solve the problem without benefit of a graph, start by assuming that the target can be met in the first activity range. If this is possible, then the volume would be given by using equation (13-8). Recognizing that $I/(1 - T)$ is the *pretax* income the results are:

$$\text{Trial value of } x_i = \frac{11{,}000 + 10{,}000}{(90 - 50)} = 525$$

Exhibit 13.3   Illustration of CVP Analysis with Step-Fixed Costs

---

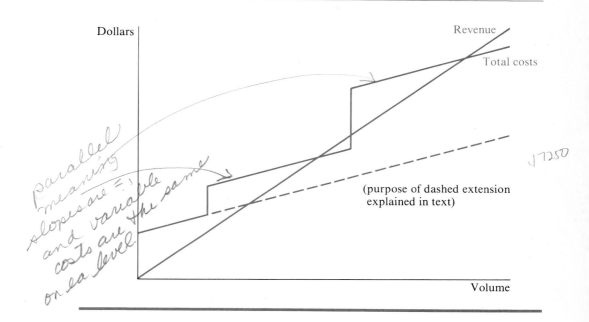

(handwritten notes: parallel meaning = slopes are =) and variable costs are the same on a level)

(handwritten: ↓7250)

(purpose of dashed extension
explained in text)

A $10,000 profit *cannot* be achieved at a volume of 525 units because this volume is in the range whereby fixed costs will be $14,000, not $11,000 as assumed in the trial. In terms of the graph in Exhibit 13.3, the preceding result is the intersection of the extended line (dashed line) and the revenue line.

Since this result was not feasible, assume the required volume is now in the second range. If so, then:

$$\text{Trial value of } x_i = \frac{14{,}000 + 10{,}000}{(90 - 50)} = 600$$

Again, this volume is not feasible. That is, a volume of 600 will result in a fixed cost of $18,000, not $14,000 as was assumed.

This procedure is continued until a feasible answer is found. Assume that the goal can be achieved in the third range. Then:

$$\text{Trial value of } x_i = \frac{18{,}000 + 10{,}000}{(90 - 50)} = 700$$

A volume of 700 is consistent with the assumption and is feasible. This, then, represents the *minimum* volume at which a $10,000 pretax profit can be realized.

However, as stated earlier, there is a possibility that the target can be achieved at more than one point. For example, test this possibility in the fourth range:

$$\text{Trial value of } x_i = \frac{32,000 + 10,000}{(90 - 50)} = 1,050$$

This point, also, is consistent with the assumption and is feasible. There is no feasible solution in the last range; *all* points in that range will return an income in excess of $10,000. Any situation containing step-fixed costs could be adapted to the type of analysis suggested here.

SELECTED "WHAT-IF" CASES. There are many decisons that can benefit from the information that results from CVP analyses. But not all of them will be consistent with the forms discussed in the previous subsection. There will now be an examination of a cross-section of cases to illustrate a general approach to such situations.

First, return to the Eckel Company's *original* cost behavior and suppose they operated last month at a 3,000-unit level and earned the amount estimated for that level: $60,000 after taxes (result of the case discussed on page 437). In order to increase income, a proposal has been made to increase advertising by $15,000 simultaneously with lowering the sales price to $85 per unit. What volume level must be achieved in order to increase income by 5% over last month?

The analysis would be as follows. Since last year's after-tax income was $60,000, this month's target, I, is $63,000, $60,000 \times 1.05$. The fixed costs, F, are now $35,000 ($20,000 original + $15,000 advertising), and S is $85. Equation (13-8) can be applied to yield:

$$x_i = \frac{35,000 + 63,000/(1 - 0.4)}{85 - 50} = \frac{140,000}{35} = 4,000$$

The planners would now have to assess whether the combined actions will result in an increase of 1,000 units or more.

As a second case, suppose the Eckel Company operated last month at the 800-unit level and achieved the target income of 10% on sales as estimated in the second example of the previous subsection (see page 437). Currently, a cost-plus-5% defense contract is being considered. The government will allow fixed manufacturing, administrative, and selling costs to be added to the contract at a rate given by a monthly divisor activity of 1,000 units. The contract is for 400 units. How many total units, including the defense contract, must be sold to maintain the income at 10% of sales.

This case is a bit more difficult in that it will be necessary to do the analysis in two phases. First, we must assess the impact of the contract. Its sales price is a function of its assigned cost. Further, some of these assigned costs will reduce the amount of fixed costs that must be absorbed by the remaining business. Also, the contract's income contributes to the target. To assess the impact of the contract, note the variable cost per unit is still $50 and the assignable fixed cost totals $20 per unit ($20,000 divided by the divisor activity of 1,000). Thus, for the contract, the company would realize the following income:

Sales price 400 × ($50 + $20) × 1.05		$29,400
Variable cost 400 × $50	$20,000	
Fixed cost assigned 400 × $20	8,000	28,000
Contribution to income before tax		$ 1,400
Tax @ 40%		560
Contribution to income after tax		$ 840

Since the income goal is stated as a percentage of sales, none of the previous results, including equation (13-12), applies. The latter equation is not appropriate because the units are not all earning profits at the same rate. Instead, let us return to the basic accounting income model. Define x as the volume that must be sold *in addition* to the defense contract. Then reduce the fixed costs by the $8,000 recovered through the contract; the remainder of $12,000 must be recovered by the additional units. The income computation should include the $840 to be earned by the contract. Since the left-hand side of the following equation represents after-tax income, it should be set equal to 10% of sales (contract sales plus additional sales). Thus:

$$0.6(90x - 50x - 12,000) + 840 = 0.1(29,400 + 90x)$$
$$24x - 7,200 + 840 = 2,940 + 9x$$
$$15x = 9,300$$
$$x = 620$$

or $(1-T)(Sx_1 - Vx_1 - F) = RSx_1$

If the contract for 400 units is accepted, then an additional 620 units must be sold so that income will equal 10% of sales. Verification can be made as follows:

Sales		
Contract	$29,400	
Other 620 × $90	55,800	$85,200
Variable costs 1,020 × $50	$51,000	
Fixed costs	20,000	71,000
Net income before taxes		$14,200
Taxes at 40%		5,680
Net income after taxes		
(equal to 10% of sales)		$ 8,520

As a final case let's now examine how CVP analysis can be used in a situation involving inflation and labor negotiations. Continue with the Eckel Company case and assume the original variable manufacturing costs consist of the following:

Direct material	$ 5.00
Direct labor (2 hours @ $5)	10.00
Variable overhead (2 hours @ $7.50)	15.00
Total	$30.00

Indirect labor amounts to 20% of the variable overhead. The fixed manufacturing overhead includes union-covered salaries and wages amounting to 40% of the total fixed manufacturing overhead.

Next month material costs will increase by 10% over the current cost, and the firm is also negotiating with its labor union which is bargaining for a 10% wage increase. Direct laborers and the indirect laborers referred to are the only laborers covered by the union contract. In preparation for the labor negotiations, management wants two analyses:

1. First, by how much must the selling price of the product be increased in order to continue earning monthly after-tax profits of $60,000 when the volume is 3,000 units?
2. Assume the material price increase will be passed on to the consumer by increasing the sales price. So that prices will not also have to be increased to recover the increase in labor costs, management wants to know what productivity gain must be achieved by the direct-labor work force and still maintain the $60,000 after-tax income level with a volume of 3,000 units? That is, what reduction in labor hours per unit must be achieved so that the increase in labor rates will not increase the sales price?

To answer question 1 it is necessary to first recompute the variable cost rate:

Original variable cost/unit		$50.00
Increase due to:		
Direct material 0.1 × $5	$0.50	
Direct labor 0.1 × $10	1.00	
Variable overhead 0.1 × 0.2 × $15	0.30	1.80
New variable cost/unit		$51.80

Also, recompute the fixed costs:

Original fixed cost	$20,000
Increase due to salary increase:	
0.1 × 0.4 × $15,000	600
New fixed cost	$20,600

Let s be the new selling price. Then for a volume of 3,000 units the revenue and variable costs are:

Revenue = 3,000s
Variable costs = 3,000 × $51.80

The profit can be computed as:

$$[3,000s - 51.80(3,000) - 20,600](1 - 0.4) = 60,000$$

Solving:

$$3,000s - 155,400 - 20,600 = 100,000$$
$$3,000s = 276,000$$
$$s = \$92$$

That is, the sales price would have to be increased by $2.00 per unit in order to continue earning $60,000 at a volume of 3,000 units. Alternatively, this result can be derived by noting the variable cost per unit will increase by $1.80. The $600 increase in fixed cost averaged over the 3,000 units represents the remaining $0.20 of the required increase in the price.

To answer the second question, let h be the revised labor hours per unit. With this proposal the new selling price will be $90.50 because the material increase is to be passed through to the consumer. The new direct-labor rate per hour is $5.50. The original indirect labor was 20% of the $7.50 per hour variable overhead rate. This amounts to $1.50 per direct-labor hour and a 10% increase would raise it to $1.65. Let's make the assumption that the incurrence of indirect-labor hours is highly correlated with direct-labor hours so that if there is a productivity gain in direct-labor hours there will be a related decrease in indirect-labor consumption. That is, total variable indirect-labor cost will be $1.65h. Since indirect labor accounted for $1.50 of the original $7.50 overhead per hour, the remainder is $6.00, and this, too, is assumed to be highly correlated with direct-labor hours. Thus, the new variable manufacturing cost per unit is the *sum* of the following:

Material	$5.50
Direct labor	5.50h
Variable overhead	7.65h
Variable selling and administrative	20.00

In order for labor increases to be offset by productivity gains as stated in question 2, h would have to satisfy the following:

$$[3,000(\$90.50 - 25.50 - 13.15h) - 20,600](1 - 0.4) = 60,000$$

Divide both sides by $(1 - 0.4)$ and solve:

$$271,500 - 76,500 - 39,450h - 20,600 = 100,000$$
$$74,400 = 39,450h$$
$$h = 1.885931559 \text{ (not rounded in order to minimize future error)}$$

Of course, if the direct-labor work force did manage to lower the average from two hours to the value just computed and if the firm did not increase its total output, then the *total* wages would not increase; in fact they would decrease. The idea of productivity gains would be that the employees earn more but *also* produce more. Thus, assume the laborers continue to work a total of 6,000 hours (3,000 units times the original hours per unit of 2), but average 1.885931559 hours per unit. Then production would be 3,181.45 units (6,000/1.885931559): an increase of 181.45 units over the output from the original 6,000 hours. Of course, if the firm did not change the sales price, its profits would increase as well as the employees' wages. In a macro sense, this would not be inflationary because more units would be available for customer consumption. This case will be explored further in problem 13-15.

CVP Analysis When There Are Multiple Products

For a multiple-product firm, CVP analysis can be more complicated, depending upon the situation. Should the case require a marginal analysis for a single product or project, then the modifications are slight. First, it is necessary to identify the fixed costs that are attributable (directly traceable) to the product or project. Fixed costs that are common to several of the firm's segments would be excluded from the analysis. Then, the marginal analysis would be concerned with the segment's contribution toward its attributable cost.

If the CVP analysis is to be made for the firm as a whole, then there are additional assumptions and approaches to be considered. A multiple product analysis is dependent upon the product mix. The mix refers to the relative quantity of each product in relation to the total volume of all products. For example, if the typical mix in a three-product case is 5 to 2 to 1 for products *A, B,* and *C,* then to be a *constant* mix a volume of 8,000 units of *A* must be accompanied by sales of 3,200 of *B* and 1,600 of *C.* As you can see in the example, the sales volume of *A* is 5 times that of *C* and *B*'s volume is 2 times that of *C.* For these cases, it is typical to assume the product mix is constant or, at least, that the rate of contribution to profits from the product mix is constant. The latter is a weaker assumption and could be satisfied even if the former is not. For example, if products *B* and *C* contributed to profits at an identical rate per unit, then the contribution of a 5 to 2 to 1 package is the same as a 5 to 1 to 2 package.

Another problem is caused by the need for an equivalent measure for activity. Obviously, volume cannot be measured as the sum of each product's output. There are two basic solutions to the equivalence problem. The activity can either be measured by sales dollars or by a common unit such that each unit will consist of the proportionate mix of each of the products.

To illustrate the first option mentioned, define:

D = the sales dollars that are needed to achieve a desired objective
p = percentage representing the ratio of the firm's variable cost to sales

Also, *F, I,* and *T* will be defined the same as in the previous section. Then the accounting profit model of revenue less variable expenses, fixed costs, and income taxes is:

$$(D - pD - F)(1 - T) = I \qquad \qquad (13\text{-}13)$$

Note that the total variable cost in (13-13) is determined as the product of the cost ratio, *p,* and the sales dollars, *D.* The activity variable in this model is *D* and you should satisfy yourself that:

$$D = \frac{F + I/(1 - T)}{1 - p} \qquad \qquad (13\text{-}14)$$

To illustrate, assume that the Ritts Company sells three products. From past data it has been noted that the ratio of variable costs to sales has always been approximately 60%. Fixed costs are $200,000, the marginal tax rate is 30%, and the target after-tax income is \$140,000. In order to achieve this target, sales must be at \$1,000,000:

$$D = \frac{200,000 + 140,000/(1 - 0.3)}{1 - 0.6} = \frac{400,000}{0.4} = \$1,000,000$$

Again, in making this analysis the mix of products was assumed to remain constant.

A second way to analyze such a situation is to define a new unit of measurement that is a group of the products constructed according to the anticipated mix. Then the approach of the previous section can be used. To illustrate, assume the following additional information about the Ritts Company:

Product	Sales Price/Unit	Variable Cost/Unit	Mix Ratio
A	\$ 50	\$40	5
B	60	25	2
C	130	50	1

The group is a combination of the products *A, B,* and *C* with an arbitrary total content, but with the assumed mix. For example, the group could consist of 8 total units with a mix of 5, 2, and 1 units of products *A, B,* and *C,* respectively. Or, the group could be defined to consist of 40 units: 25 units of *A,* 10 of *B,* and 5 of *C.* If the first grouping is used, then the sales price of the redefined unit is \$500 (\$50 × 5 + \$60 × 2 + \$130 × 1). The variable cost of the group is computed in a similar way and amounts to \$300 (\$40 × 5 + \$25 × 2 + \$50 × 1).

In terms of the new unit of measurement, the volume needed for an after-tax income of \$140,000 is determined by using equation (13-8):

$$x_i = \frac{200,000 + 140,000/(1 - 0.3)}{500 - 300} = \frac{400,000}{200} = 2,000$$

$$X_1 = \frac{F - [I/1-T]}{Salespr - V_c}$$

This means that the respective outputs must be:

A: 2,000 × 5 = 10,000
B: 2,000 × 2 = 4,000
C: 2,000 × 1 = 2,000

Given the group as defined, note that the variable cost ratio is 60%, the same as assumed earlier when sales dollars were used to measure activity. Thus the total sales dollars of the preceding output schedule should be equal to the previously determined sales volume. You should verify that this is the case.

Yet another way to do certain analyses when there are multiple products is to use linear programming and and other mathematical programming models. Within the context of these models it is possible to answer various "what-if" questions. Linear programming is considered in more detail in Chapter 22.

≥ CVP Analysis under Uncertainty

Until now it has been assumed that the actual values of the variables of a CVP analysis were exactly as predicted. However, many variables defy precise prediction. For example, it is impossible to exactly forecast the volume demanded or the variable cost per unit. In the language of uncertainty, variables that are likely to assume any of several possible values are called *random variables*. That is, the realized values of such variables are out of our control.

To analyze a situation that has uncertain outcomes, it is necessary to be able to state the possible values that have a chance of being the observed value of the random variable. Further, it must be possible to express the probability that each of these values will be the realized outcome. Obviously, both of these processes involve subjectivity and should be made by those who are in positions to offer informed judgments. Although space does not permit its exploration, there is an emerging science of eliciting such judgments.[1] In many uncertain situations, we all have inclinations as to the odds of an event occurring but are only infrequently asked to express them in any tangible way. Assuming that it is possible to deduce the preceding types of information about the random variables of a CVP analysis, we will now explore how the data could be used.

The presumption here is that there will be greater confidence in estimates of the various components of the income calculation than in estimates of income itself. To assess the probabilities of achieving various income levels *without* the aid of a probabilistic CVP model, one has to simultaneously process his or her uncertainties about volume, variable cost per unit, fixed cost levels, and other variables. Such a request will likely result in an overload of the human data processing capability and also in a lower level of confidence about the assessments. Instead, it would be more desirable to seek informed judgments about the rudimentary components of the income calculation and then mechanically process these judgments to deduce assessments about income.

Let us now introduce some details. To operationally define a random variable its probability distribution must be known. That is, the possible outcomes and their associated chance of occurrence must be known. Using the Eckel Company as an example, let us now assume there is uncertainty that the variable cost will actually be $50 per unit. Instead assume that our expectations are as follows:

Range	Probability
$35 to $40	0.02
$40 to $45	0.13
$45 to $55	0.70
$55 to $60	0.13
$60 to $65	0.02
	1.00

---

[1]For example, see G.R. Chesley, "Elicitation of Subjective Probabilities: A Review," *The Accounting Review* (April 1975), pp. 325–335.

The notation "$35 to $40⁻" means a range from $35 to, but not including, $40. The values in each of the ranges are equally likely to occur, and the percentage of the time that the occurrence will be **in the range** is indicated in the probability column.

The preceding distribution is graphically portrayed in Exhibit 13.4. A distribution has been selected that will permit an easy demonstration of the basic idea of CVP analysis under uncertainty. The example should not be construed as a realistic one. In fact, it may be possible to use one of the various distributions that are studied in statistics: the normal, triangular, log normal, or gamma, for example.

Once its probability distribution has been stated, it is possible to determine the expected value of a random variable. The **expected value** is the average value that would result from repeated observations from the distribution. Although not a generalized method, the expected value of the random variable in Exhibit 13.4 can be computed by adding a set of elements each of which is a product of the range's probability and midpoint. The midpoints of the variable cost ranges are $37.50, $42.50, $50, $57.50, and $62.50. The expected variable cost can be shown to be $50:

$$\text{Expected variable cost} = 37.50(0.02) + 42.50(0.13) + 50(0.07) \\ + 57.50(0.13) + 62.50(0.02) = 50$$

Exhibit 13.4   Probability Distribution for Variable Cost

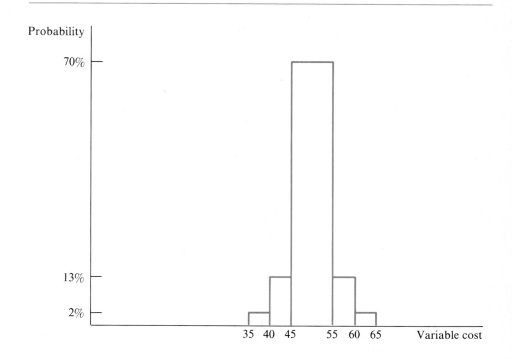

The expected value can be computed in this way because of the equal likelihood of every value within a group range.

As additional data for Eckel's revised problem, assume the following distributions for demand and fixed costs:

Demand		Fixed Costs	
Range	*Probability*	*Range*	*Probability*
400–500⁻	0.02	$18,500–$19,000⁻	0.02
500–600⁻	0.13	19,000– 19,500⁻	0.13
600–800⁻	0.70	19,500– 20,500⁻	0.70
800–900⁻	0.13	20,500– 21,000⁻	0.13
900–1,000	0.02	21,000– 21,500	0.02
Expected value = 700		Expected value = $20,000	

For each of the distributions, a form has been assumed that is symmetrical, identically distributed around the mean. Each of these distributions can be thought of as approximately normal. Of course, the normal distribution is a continuous bell-shaped curve, not a step-type function as portrayed in Exhibit 13.4. In the following analysis, it has also been assumed, unrealistically, that the random variables are *independent* of each other. If simulation is used to analyze the problem, this assumption *does not* need to be made.

Assuming the sales price of the product is $90 per unit and using the *expected values* of the three random variables, the *expected income, E(I),* can be computed as:

$$E(I) = (\$90 - \$50)700 - 20,000 = \$8,000$$

The expected values of the three random variables have been used exactly as if they were deterministic. However, it is very unlikely that all three of them will *simultaneously* realize their expected values. Thus, the likelihood of an $8,000 income is extremely small. If we have the opportunity to replicate the experiment, we would find that the income figure will vary around its expected value of $8,000. Management would have some valuable information if they knew something about the potential magnitude of this variation and something about the chances of realizing the different values of the income variable.

In the literature, there are several models that provide analytical methods for calculating the properties of income when it is a function of several well-behaved random variables.[2] However, the approach to be discussed here may prove to be more practical and more general. If there is knowledge about the probability distributions for the random variables as just given, then it is possible to conduct a

---

[2]For example, see: R.K. Jaedicke and A.A. Robichek, "Cost-Volume-Profit Analysis Under Conditions of Uncertainty," *The Accounting Review* (October 1964), pp. 917–926; J.E. Hilliard and R.A. Leitch, "CVP Analysis Under Uncertainty: A Log Normal Approach," *The Accounting Review* (January 1975), pp. 69–80; and J.F. Kottas, A.H. Lau, and H. Lau, "A General Approach to Stochastic Management Planning Models: An Overview," *The Accounting Review* (April 1978) pp. 389–401.

simulation experiment to estimate various characteristics about income. Simulation allows us to model each of the random variables as they are predicted to behave. Then, we construct a relatively large sample of observations of the income figure. For each income observation draw a sample from the variable cost distribution, deduct this sampled cost from the $90 sales price, multiply the difference by a sample from the demand distribution, and reduce this result by a sample from the fixed cost distribution. After repeating this process many times examine the properties of the result.

Obviously, computational support is needed for conducting an experiment of this nature. The support could be in the form of a computer program written in a general computer programming language such as FORTRAN or BASIC. However, simulation languages such as GPSS, SIMSCRIPT, or SLAM make it easier to do some of the things that are common to simulations. The remainder of this section is an outline of an approach for simulating the preceding problem.

In the following experiment a sample size of 10,000 observations was selected. Define the random variables as V, Q, and F. Then income, I, is computed as:

$$I = (90 - V)Q - F$$

To obtain the first observation for I, it was necessary to draw a sample from each of the distributions for V, Q, and F and substitute them into the equation. This process was simply repeated a total of 10,000 times. The sample is larger than may be required, but the experiment took less than 50 seconds of computer time. It is common to refer to an experiment of this nature as **Monte Carlo simulation.** The name comes from the famous gambling capital of Monaco.

To illustrate the basics, let us consider how to simulate the random variable for demand *(Q)*. Most computer installations have a random number generator. Typically, these generators produce a series of numbers between 0 and 1. A good generator guarantees an *equal* chance of occurrence for every number in the 0 to 1 interval. Further, each member of the series is *statistically* independent of all other members of the series.

Given an appropriate generator, we can then arbitrarily define each random number to be representative of some possible outcome of the demand variable. For example, the chance of demand being in the range of 400 to 500⁻ is 2%. Let the random numbers in the range of 0.00 to 0.02⁻ be equivalent to this event. Then the random number of 0.02 to 0.15⁻ are equivalent to demand being in the second interval, 0.15 to 0.85⁻ to the third, 0.85 to 0.98⁻ to the fourth, and 0.98 to 1.00⁻ to the fifth. (Generally a value of 1.00 is never returned by a computerized random number generator.) A similar use of random numbers could be used for the variable and fixed costs.

To obtain a specific demand value, given these assignments, an interpolation must be made. Suppose the generator returned a random value of 0.43. This is associated with the third demand range, 600–800⁻. Range 3 is being simulated by the random numbers from 0.15 to, but not including, 0.85. The width of the range is 0.70. The value of 0.43 is 0.28 units from the leftmost point of the interval; a point whose distance from the leftmost point is 40% of the total interval. Since the third interval is 200 units in width, the point that is 40% from the left extreme of that interval is 680 (600 + 0.4 × 200). In short, a random number of 0.43 would equate to a demand of 680 units.

To complete the income computation, random numbers must be drawn for the variable and fixed cost components and equated to an observation. For simplicity, let us assume these numbers are 0.15 and 0.85, respectively. Thus, the variable cost per unit for this observation would be $45, the fixed costs would be $20,500, and the resulting income is:

$$I = (90 - 45)680 - 20,500 = 10,100$$

Exhibit 13.5 is a summary of the simulation for demand that resulted from the experiment of 10,000 observations. This summary is provided in order to demonstrate that the sampled demand actually occurred consistently with the population. Summary results could also be given for the variable cost per unit and the total fixed costs. As with the data on demand, they would confirm that the sample was consistent with the populations.

Finally, the results for the income variable are summarized in Exhibit 13.6. First, note that the sample mean was $7,904. The sample mean is 98.8% of the expected value of $8,000, a sampling error of 1.2%. The sample standard deviation was $5,568. A theoretical standard deviation for income has not been computed; thus there is no available standard for comparison. The sample standard deviation is an estimate of the population value but, unfortunately, contains sampling bias. Space does not permit an examination of the adjustment needed to remove this bias. However, for large sample sizes the unadjusted estimate can be used with a substantial amount of confidence.

To illustrate the way in which the data of Exhibit 13.6 can be used, suppose management is interested in the probability of being *above* the break-even point. As you can see from the simulation results in Exhibit 13.6, 6.93% of the cases had an income that was zero or below. Thus, the chances of being above break-even is

---

Exhibit 13.5   Eckel Company Summary of Simulation Results: The Demand Variable

Range	Number	Percent	Cumulative Percentage
400–499	189	1.89%	1.89%
500–699	1,343	13.43	15.32
600–799	6,961	69.61	84.93
800–899	1,297	12.97	97.90
900–1,000	210	2.10	100.00
Mean		698.979	
Standard deviation		105.062	

Exhibit 13.6   Eckel Company Summary of Simulation Results: The Income Variable

Range	Number	Percent	Cumulative Percentage
Up to −7,000	7	0.07%	0.07%
−6,999 to −5,000	34	0.34	0.41
−4,999 to −4,000	55	0.55	0.96
−3,999 to −3,000	74	0.74	1.70
−2,999 to −2,000	116	1.16	2.86
−1,999 to −1,000	161	1.61	4.47
−999 to 0	246	2.46	6.93
1 to 5,000	2,435	24.35	31.28
5,001 to 8,000	2,156	21.56	52.84
8,001 to 15,000	3,652	36.52	89.36
15,001 to 20,000	845	8.45	97.81
20,001 to 25,000	198	1.98	99.79
25,001 to 30,000	17	0.17	99.96
30,001 to 32,000	4	0.04	100.00
32,001 and above	0	0.00	100.00
Mean		7,904.203	
Standard deviation		5,568.000	

93.07% (100 − 6.93). As another representative question, assume the simulation was for a new product. Management requires products of this type to earn $8,000 or more with a minimum probability of 60%. Since 52.84% of the cases had an income of $8,000 or below, the probability of exceeding the income threshold is only 47.16%. The proposal does not meet management's criteria. These situations are sensitive to risk aversions that are difficult to express. By considering a distribution like the one in Exhibit 13.6, many managers may be better able to reflect these aversions than if they were requested to state them for the purpose of an input to an external decision model. If so, then a simulation approach has merit.

The discussion of this section has been elementary from the standpoint of simulation. The difficult issues involve such things as defining appropriate probability distributions, modeling the complex relationships (such as dependent variables), selecting appropriate sample sizes, and statistically interpreting the results.

⩾ CVP Analysis When the Relationships Are Nonlinear

In this section the concept of CVP analysis is extended to include **nonlinear analysis** situations—those where it is not reasonable to use linear revenue and cost relationships. If the demand for the product is dependent upon its price, then the revenue portion of the income function cannot be linear; linearity assumes the same price for all units.

In Chapter 23 the possibility of nonlinear cost relationships is explored. Thus, even if revenue is a linear function of volume, income may still be nonlinear. Obviously, both the revenue and cost functions could be nonlinear in the relevant operating range. These possibilities provide motivation for this section. It must be recognized that it may be a difficult task to specify the general form of a relationship (quadratic, cubic, and so forth). Further, the specification of the coefficients could also prove difficult, although regression analysis may be useful.

To illustrate this process as simply as possible, let us continue to assume that the Eckel Company's *cost* function is linear. However, assume that the sales price per unit, *S*, and the quantity demanded, *Q*, are dependent. Further, assume that the relationship *between S and Q* is linear (this is not the same as a linear revenue function). To make sense, the relationship should be such that demand, *Q*, goes down as the price, *S*, goes up and vice versa. Suppose that after some study management specifies the following relationship between price and demand:

$$S = -0.08Q + 146 \tag{13-15}$$

In (13-15) note that when *Q* is 700, *S* must be $90. Of course it has been assumed throughout the Eckel example that the sales price is $90. Further, in the last section it was assumed the demand was uncertain but with a mean of 700, given a $90 price. Thus, the function in (13-15) is consistent with earlier assumptions, but we hasten to point out that this function is not unique. There are many other linear functions similar to (13-15) that would be consistent with the assumptions.

Now, note that (13-15) is the sales price *per unit*. Thus the total revenue generated by a volume *Q*, is:

$$\text{Revenue} = SQ = (-0.08Q + 146)Q = -0.08Q^2 + 146Q \tag{13-16}$$

Equation (13-16) is plotted in Exhibit 13.7. The total cost function, $50Q + 20,000$, is also plotted in Exhibit 13.7. Deducting costs, $50Q + 20,000$, from the revenue yields the income:

$$I = -0.08Q^2 + 146Q - 50Q - 20,000 \tag{13-17}$$

$$I = -0.08Q^2 + 96Q - 20,000 \tag{13-18}$$

Now suppose management wants to know the break-even point. These are the points *a* and *c* as labeled in Exhibit 13.7. (Ignore point *b* for the moment.) That is, break-even would occur where revenue equals total cost or where the revenue and cost equations intersect. These points can be found by setting *I* equal to zero in equation (13-18) and solving. The result, of course, is a quadratic equation. Recall that when *x* is the variable the quadratic equation is:

$$x = \frac{-b \pm \sqrt{b^2 - 4ac}}{2a} \tag{13-19}$$

Exhibit 13.7   Plot of Nonlinear CVP Problem

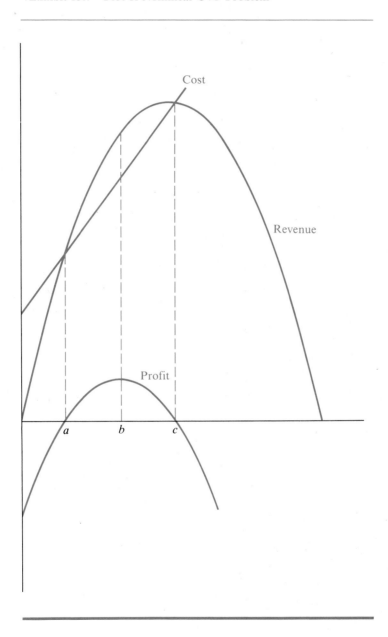

In equation (13-19), *a*, *b*, and *c* are, respectively, the coefficient on the squared term, the coefficient on *x*, and the fixed component. In our case Q is the variable. Thus:

$$Q = \frac{-96 \pm \sqrt{96^2 - 4(-0.08)(-20,000)}}{2(-0.08)}$$

$$Q = \frac{-96 \pm \sqrt{2,816}}{-0.16} = \frac{-96 \pm 53.066}{-0.16}$$

$$Q = 268.338 \text{ or } 931.662$$

To illustrate the validity of these solutions, income statements will be prepared. First determine the sale prices since the price and quantity were dependent. Using (13-15):

Case 1: $S = -0.08(268.338) + 146 = \$124.533$
Case 2: $S = -0.08(931.662) + 146 = \$ 71.467$

[handwritten annotation: at $71 they would sell 931 units]

Exhibit 13.8 contains the income statements for each of these break-even solutions.

For linear CVP problems it is trivial to consider optimal levels of volume unless there are some constraints. When unconstrained, the optimal point on a linear profit line is at an infinite volume. In contrast, the optimal solution to a nonlinear case is frequently finite even if there are no constraints.

In light of this, it would be legitimate to search for an optimal price-quantity strategy. Where will profits be maximized? In the graph of Exhibit 13.7 the optimal profits are at the point where the income curve is the highest. Also, this is the point where the *difference* between the revenue curve and the cost curve is the largest. This occurs at point *b*. To find the value of point *b*, calculus can be used. This

---

Exhibit 13.8   Eckel Company Income Statements for Break-Even Points in Nonlinear Case

	Case 1		Case 2	
Sales				
268.338 × $124.533		$33,417		
931.662 × $71.467				$66,583
Costs				
Variable				
268.338 × $50	$13,417			
931.662 × $50			$46,583	
Fixed	20,000	33,417	20,000	66,583
Net income		0		0

point would be at the maximum point on the *income* curve of equation (13-18). Such a point is found by first finding the points on the income curve that have a zero slope. These points are identified by determining the derivative, setting it equal to zero, and solving. The derivative of equation (13-18) with respect to Q is:

$$\frac{dI}{dQ} = -0.16Q + 96 \tag{13-20}$$

Setting the result in (13-20) equal to zero and solving:[3]

$$0.16Q = 96$$
$$Q = 600$$

The optimal price is found by evaluating (13-15) using the optimal Q of 600:

$$S = -0.08(600) + 146 = \$98$$

Thus, a price policy of \$90 is not optimal. Based on the assumed price-quantity relationship, a \$90 price produces a volume of 700 units (compared to 600) but also results in lower profits. The comparative profits are found by using (13-18).

$$\text{Income @ 700 units} = -0.08(700)^2 + 96(700) - 20,000$$
$$= \$8,000$$
$$\text{Income @ 600 units} = -0.08(600)^2 + 96(600) - 20,000$$
$$= \$8,800$$

In conclusion, if our analyses cover a range of volume such that linear approximations create excessive error, then this section is representative of the approach that can be used.

Summary

CVP analyses can be useful to decision makers in a variety of ways. In this chapter you should have acquired a sense of how to use this tool. The emphasis has not been on formula usage but on adaptation to the situation.

---

[3]Note that this result could also be derived by finding the point where marginal revenue equals marginal costs (as discussed in microeconomics). The marginal revenue is just the derivative of the revenue equation (13-16) with respect to Q:

$$\frac{dR}{dQ} = -0.16Q + 146$$

Likewise, the marginal cost is the derivative of the cost function:

$$C = 50Q + 20,000$$

$$\frac{dC}{dQ} = 50$$

Setting dR/dQ equal to dC/dQ:

$$-0.16Q + 146 = 50$$
$$\text{or} \quad 0.16Q = 96$$
$$Q = 600$$

In addition to the conventional type of analysis, this chapter introduced you to analyses when there are kinks in the cost functions, multiple products, uncertainty, and well-behaved nonlinear functions. Certainly these characteristics will be found in actual situations. If such is the case, you may be able to analyze the problem as if it were linear and not subject yourself to a great deal of error. The purpose of including these extensions is to provide you with an informed base for anticipating errors due to the assumptions of linearity and certainty. Further, the chapter provides you with a background that allows you to choose not to make the linearity and certainty assumptions.

The new key terms in this chapter with which you should be familiar include:

Cost-volume-profit analysis
Break-even
Margin of safety
Stochastic cost-volume-profit analysis
Random variables
Expected value
Simulation
Monte Carlo simulation
Nonlinear cost-volume-profit analysis

SELF-STUDY PROBLEM.   Remember the facts from the Eckel Company problem in the text:

Sales price per unit	$	90
Variable cost per unit		50
Fixed costs		20,000

Assume that Eckel's management is considering alternative wage plans. Currently the direct laborers are receiving a piece rate of $10 per unit (included in the variable manufacturing cost). The proposal under study would pay a flat monthly rate to each employee. In addition, the company would contribute to a pool an amount equal to $15 per unit for each unit in excess of 500 per month (the original break-even point). The pool would be divided according to a plan devised by the labor union. The fixed wage package would amount to $4,000 per month.

Required:

1. If this plan is adopted, how many units must be sold to break even?
2. Which wage plan, the existing or the proposed, would you suggest as preferable? Why?
3. Determine the volume (in units) that would be necessary to achieve a target after-tax income of $60,000. Note that this is the same target used for the original case on page 437. Assume the tax rate was and continues to be 40%. Compare the resulting volume with the volume necessary to achieve this target in the original case.
4. For what volume of sales will the proposed plan yield a higher income than the original plan?

5. With the existing wage plan, last year's achieved volume was 725 units. Assume last year's tax rate was 30%. If this year's tax rate is 40% what volume of sales must be achieved under the new plan to match last year's after-tax income?

Solution to Self-Study Problem

1. If the volume is less than or equal to 500, the costs are:

   Variable = 50 − 10 = 40 (the original $50 less the piece rate)
   Fixed = 20,000 + 4,000 = 24,000 (the original $20,000 plus the flat monthly rate in the proposal)

   If the volume is above 500, the costs are:

   Variable = 50 − 10 + 15 = 55 (same as for volume below 500 plus the contribution to the pool)

   Fixed = 24,000 (same as for volume below 500)

   Assume break-even is below 500 units. If so, then use (13-4) to find the volume:

   $$x_0 = \frac{24,000}{90 - 40} = 480$$

   Since this trial value is below 500 units (the assumption) it is feasible. Had it been above 500, the results would have been invalid because all of the costs used to find the volume are valid only for volumes below 500. In that case, another attempt would have to be made to find a break-even. (See part 3 for the approach.)

2. In comparison with the current wage plan, the proposal has a lower break-even point. However, this fact is not necessarily a relevant consideration. Assuming all other factors constant, a lower break-even point is preferred to a higher one. But all other factors are not constant in this case. The wage package is being changed and this could influence the behavior of the workers. Management must be concerned about the effects of the plan on productivity. If the new plan lowers motivation and productivity, then overall profits will ultimately decrease. It is the latter effect that will be of concern; not the effect on the break-even point.

3. The volume necessary to achieve this target would certainly be above 500 units. Thus, x_i would have to be such that:

   $$[(90 - 40)x_i - 15(x_i - 500) - 24,000]0.6 = 60,000$$

   The second term inside the parenthesis is the number of units above 500, $x_i - 500$, times the contribution that the company will make to the wage pool.
   Solving:

   $$50x_i - 15x_i + 7,500 - 24,000 = 60,000/0.6$$
   $$35x_i - 16,500 = 100,000$$
   $$35x_i = 116,500$$
   $$x_i = 3,328.57$$

   For the original wage plan, 3,000 units were needed to generate a $60,000 after-tax income. The wage proposal, therefore, would require 328.57 more units than the existing plan.

4. First, check to see if there are volumes below 500 units such that the new plan would have higher profits than the original plan. If pretax income from the proposed plan is greater than from the original plan, then after-tax income will also be greater. Thus taxes can be ignored. When is:

Profits from proposed plan > Profits from original plan
$(90 - 40)x - 24,000 > (90 - 50)x - 20,000$
$50x - 40x > 24,000 - 20,000$
$10x > 4,000$
$x > 400$

Profits from the proposed plan will exceed those from the original plan if $400 < x \leqslant 500$. (The 500 upper bound is necessary, at this point, since we have not yet considered volumes above 500.) Now check for volumes above 500 units. When is:

Profits from proposed plan > Profits from original plan
$(90 - 40)x - 15(x - 500) - 24,000 > (90 - 50)x - 20,000$
$50x - 15x + 7,500 - 24,000 > 40x - 20,000$
$3,500 > 5x$
$x < 700$

Now combining our two results, we conclude that if $400 < x < 700$ then the proposed plan's profits will exceed the original plan's.

5. Taxes will have to be incorporated in this case since it has been assumed that the current tax rate differs from last year's. First, compute last year's after-tax income so we know what the target is:

Contribution margin $(90 - 50)725$	$29,000
Fixed costs	20,000
Net income before tax	$ 9,000
Tax @ 30%	2,700
Net income after tax	$ 6,300

The volume necessary to earn $6,300 will certainly be above 500 units. Thus we will check only in the range such that $x \geqslant 500$:

$[50x - 15(x - 500) - 24,000]0.6 = 6,300$
$35x + 7,500 - 24,000 = 6,300/0.6$
$35x - 16,500 = 10,500$
$35x = 27,000$
$x = 771.43$

To verify, construct an income statement at the volume of 771.43 units.

Contribution margin	
First 500 units: $500(90 - 40)$	$25,000
Balance: $(771.43 - 500)(90 - 40 - 15)$	9,500
Total	$34,500
Fixed costs	24,000
Net income before tax	$10,500
Tax @ 40%	4,200
Net income after tax	$ 6,300

References

Charnes, A., Cooper, W.W., and Ijiri, Y. "Breakeven Budgeting and Programming to Goals," *Journal of Accounting Research* (Spring 1963): 16–41.

Given, H.R. "An Application of Curvilinear Break-Even Analysis," *The Accounting Review* (January 1966): 141–143.

Goggans, T.P. "Break-Even Analysis with Curvilinear Functions," *The Accounting Review* (October 1965): 867–871.

Hilliard, J.E., and Leitch, R.A. "CVP Analysis Under Uncertainty: A Log Normal Approach," *The Accounting Review* (January 1975): 69–80.

Jaedicke, R.K. "Improving B-E Analysis by Linear Programming Techniques," *NAA Bulletin* (March 1961): 5–12.

Jaedicke, R.K., and Robichek, A.A. "Cost-Volume-Profit Analysis Under Conditions of Uncertainty," *The Accounting Review* (October 1964): 917–926.

Kottas, J.F., Lau, A.H., and Lau, H. "A General Approach to Stochastic Management Planning Models: An Overview," *The Accounting Review* (April 1978): 389–401.

Liao, M. "Model Sampling: A Stochastic Cost-Volume-Profit Analysis," *The Accounting Review* (October 1975): 780–790.

Willson, J.D. "Practical Applications of Cost-Volume-Profit Analysis," *NAA Bulletin* (March 1960): 5–18.

Problems

13-1. Basic Problem on Break-Even Analysis. Complete the missing data for each of the following independent cases. Ignore income taxes.

	Case A	Case B	Case C
Selling price/unit	$ 2.00	_____	_____ *
Variable cost/unit	1.10	$ 1.00	_____ *
Fixed costs	18,000	_____	30,000
Contribution margin/unit	_____	2.00	_____
Break-even point (units)	_____	10,000	5,000
Profit if sales, in units, are 20% above break-even point	_____	_____	_____
Fixed cost if sales, in units, are 20% above break-even point	_____	_____	_____

*In Case C, variable costs are equal to 60% of sales.

13-2. Alternative to Problem 13-1. Following are three independent problems requiring CVP analysis. Ignore income taxes.

1. The variable costs to manufacture and sell a certain product amount to 80% of the revenue. The fixed costs for the year are $26,000, and each unit of product sells for $6.50. How many units must be sold in order to break even?

2. The fixed costs amount to $27,000 per year. Each unit of product is sold for $8.00. The variable costs per unit amount to $3.80. How many units must be sold in order to earn a net income equal to 15% of sales?

3. During January 19x6 the Ohio Company sold 12,000 units and incurred total costs of $340,000. During February the volume was 7,000 units, and total costs amounted to $215,000. The sales price is $30 per unit. Assuming that the cost behavior of the past will continue, how many units must be sold per month in order to break-even?

13-3. Adapted CMA Problem: CVP with Income Taxes. Siberian Ski Company recently expanded its manufacturing capacity, which will allow it to produce up to 15,000 pairs of cross-country skis of the mountaineering model or the touring model. The sales department assures management that it can sell between 9,000 and 13,000 of either product this year. Because the models are very similar, Siberian Ski will produce only one of the two models. The following information was compiled by the accounting department:

	Model	
	Mountaineering	*Touring*
Selling price per unit	$88.00	$80.00
Variable costs per unit	$52.80	$52.80

Fixed costs will total $369,600 if the mountaineering model is produced but will be only $316,800 if the touring model is produced. Siberian Ski Company is subject to a 40% income tax rate.

Required:

1. If Siberian Ski Company desires an after-tax net income of $24,000, how many pairs of touring model skis will the company have to sell?
2. What is the total sales revenue at which Siberian Ski would make the same profit or loss regardless of the ski model it decided to produce?
3. How much would the variable cost per unit of the touring model have to change before it had the same break-even point in units as the mountaineering model?
4. If the variable cost per unit of touring skis decreases by 10%, and the total fixed cost of touring skis increases by 10%, then what will be the new break-even point in units?

13-4. Adapted CMA Problem Involving Situational Cases with CVP Analysis. Laraby Company produces a single product. It sold 25,000 units last year with the following results:

Sales		$625,000
Variable costs	$375,000	
Fixed costs	150,000	525,000
Net income before taxes		$100,000
Income taxes		45,000
Net income		$ 55,000

In an attempt to improve the product, Laraby is considering replacing one of its component parts that has a cost of $2.50 with a new and better part costing $4.50 per unit in the coming year. A new machine would also be needed to increase plant capacity. The machine would cost $18,000 with a useful life of 6 years and no salvage value. The company uses straight line depreciation on all plant assets.

Required:

1. What was Laraby Company's break-even point in number of units last year?
2. How many units of product would Laraby Company have had to sell in the last year to earn $77,000 in net income after taxes?
3. If Laraby Company holds the sales price constant and makes the suggested changes, how many units of product must be sold in the coming year to break even?

4. If Laraby Company holds the sales price constant and makes the suggested changes, how many units of product will the company have to sell to make the same net income after taxes as last year?

5. If Laraby Company wishes to maintain the same contribution margin ratio, what selling price per unit of product must it charge next year to cover the increased material costs?

13-5. Adapted CMA Problem on Basic CVP Analysis. Pawnee Company operated at normal capacity during the current year producing 50,000 units of its single product. Sales total 40,000 units at an average price of $20 per unit. Variable manufacturing costs were $8 per unit, and variable marketing costs were $4 per unit sold. Fixed costs were incurred uniformly throughout the year and amounted to $188,000 for manufacturing and $64,000 for marketing. There was no year-end work-in-process inventory.

Required:

1. What is Pawnee's break-even point in sales dollars for the current year?
2. If Pawnee is subject to an income tax rate of 30%, what is the number of units required to be sold in the current year to earn an after-tax net income of $126,000?
3. Pawnee's variable manufacturing costs are expected to increase 10% in the coming year. What will be the break-even point in sales dollars for the coming year?

13-6. CVP Analyses with an Income Tax. The Duckworth Company produces a single product that sells at $10.00 per unit. The variable cost of producing the item is $3.00, and the variable selling expenses amount to $2.00 per unit. Fixed production costs amount to $30,000 per year, and fixed selling and administrative expenses total $10,000. The income tax rate is 40%.

Required:

1. At what unit volume must Duckworth operate in order to show an after-tax income equal to 10% of sales dollars?
2. Now assume that due to differences in the depreciation methods used, the factory depreciation for tax purposes is $4,000 less than that for financial accounting purposes, and depreciation classified as selling and administrative expense is $1,000 less than that for financial accounting purposes. What unit volume must Duckworth operate in order to show a reported after-tax income equal to $36,000?

13-7. CVP Analysis for a Decision on How To Schedule a New Order. Porter Company has been producing two products, A and B, at the rate of 20,000 and 10,000 units monthly. Direct-labor costs $10 per hour and products A and B need three hours and four hours, respectively. Material cost is $20 per unit for A and $40 per unit for B.

Using monthly data and a high-low analysis, production overhead costs *(OH)* have been found to be related with direct-labor hours *(DLH)* as follows:

$$OH = 500,000 + 5(DLH)$$

Variable selling costs average 10% of sales dollars. These costs are primarily delivery costs, which are always incurred by the Porter Company. Fixed selling and administrative costs total $100,000 per month.

The volume of A and B has been capable of being produced in one eight-hour shift. The maximum direct-labor time using one shift is 100,000 hours monthly. If a second shift is added it is estimated that additional fixed production costs equal to 20% of the current fixed costs would be needed to administer the second shift.

It is also possible to increase production to some extent by the use of overtime. Workers would earn the conventional 50% premium for overtime and managers would also earn one and a half times their equivalent hourly salary computed by assuming 1,840 hours per year. For each thirty hours of direct labor, one manager hour is required. Managers earn $36,800 per year.

Just recently a proposal was received to supply the Brewer Company with a customized version of product B. This would entail a long-term contract and Porter does not want to reduce the amount of regular production of products A and B. Thus, either a second shift or overtime is being considered.

The customized version of product B would require 25% more labor time than the regular version of B and 10% more material. Further, to monitor this contract, a special quality control inspector would have to be employed at an annual cost of $18,000.

Required:

1. Assuming a second shift is added to cover the increased labor time above 100,000 hours caused by this contract and that the sales price for the customized product B is $175 per unit, how many units must Brewer's contract per month be in order to break even on the contract?
2. Assuming overtime is used to provide for the increased labor time demands caused by this contract and the sales price of the customized product B is $175, how many units must Brewer's contract per month be in order to break even on the contract?
3. Determine the monthly volume of customized B above which a second shift would be preferred to overtime to cover a contract at a $175 price.
4. As a possible condition of adding a second shift Porter would like for the contract to earn an after-tax incremental income equal to 10% of the incremental sales volume. How many units are necessary to achieve this if a second shift is used? The marginal tax rate is 40% and the selling price is $175.
5. Suppose the Brewer Company wants 20,000 units monthly. What price should Porter set if it desires to have an after-tax incremental income of $498,300 on the contract and plans to add a second shift? The marginal tax rate is 40%.
6. Repeat part 5 but assume overtime will be used to generate the needed labor time

13-8. CMA Problem; Alternative to 13-7. The statement of income for Davann Co. presented below represents the operating results for the fiscal year just ended. Davann had sales of 1,800 tons of product during the current year. The manufacturing capacity of Davann's facilities is 3,000 tons of product.

Statement of Income
for the Year Ended December 31, 19x0

Sales	$900,000
Variable costs	
Manufacturing	$315,000
Selling costs	180,000
Total variable costs	$495,000
Contribution margin	$405,000

Fixed costs	
Manufacturing	$ 90,000
Selling	112,500
Administration	45,000
Total fixed costs	$247,500
Net income before income taxes	$157,500
Income taxes (40%)	63,000
Net income after income taxes	$ 94,500

Required:

1. What is the break-even, in tons, for 19x0?
2. If the sales volume is estimated to be 2,100 tons in the next year, and if the prices and costs stay at the same levels and amounts next year, what will be the after-tax net income Davann can expect for 19x1?
3. Davann has a potential foreign customer that has offered to buy 1,500 tons at $450 per ton. Assume that all of Davann's costs would be at the same levels and rates as in 19x0. What net income after taxes would Davann make if it took this order and rejected some business from regular customers so as not to exceed capacity?
4. Davann plans to market its product in a new territory. Davann estimates that an advertising and promotion program costing $61,500 annually would need to be undertaken for the next two or three years. In addition, a $25 per ton sales commission over and above the current commission to the sales force in the new territory would be required. How many tons would have to be sold in the new territory to maintain Davann's current after-tax income of $94,500?
5. Davann is considering replacing a highly labor-intensive process with an automatic machine. This would result in an increase of $58,500 annually in manufacturing fixed costs. The variable manufacturing costs would decrease $25 per ton. What would be the new break-even in tons?
6. Ignore the facts presented in requirement 5 and now assume that Davann estimates that the per-ton selling price would decline 10% next year. Variable costs would increase $40 per ton and the fixed costs would not change. What sales volume in dollars would be required to earn an after-tax income of $94,500 next year?

13-9. CVP Analyses for Financing Decisions. The Warner Company is considering the addition of a new product to its line. It would sell at $50 per unit. The addition of this new product would increase the fixed expenses by $4,000 per year. The engineering department indicates that the variable production costs would be $30 per unit.

Each product requires a certain amount of working capital to provide operational support. It is estimated that this new product would require an increase in working capital equal to $10 times the annual unit volume of sales. This increase in working capital can either be financed by issuing bonds, common stock, or a combination of bonds and stock.

Currently, Warner's bonds are selling at the face value of $500 per bond and they pay 6% interest. Its common stock is selling at $40 per share. The income tax rate is 40%.

Required:

1. Assume the company uses bonds to finance the increased working capital. What volume must the new product achieve in order to cover the additional costs (including bond interest) and add to total after-tax profits an amount equal to 10% of the new product's sales? (Interest is deductible for tax purposes.)

2. Assume the company uses common stock to finance the increased working capital. What volume must the new product achieve in order to cover the additional costs and generate an after-tax income of $2.00 per share of new common stock? (Common dividends are not deductible for tax purposes.)
3. Assume the company wants to finance half of the working capital by bond issue and half by stock issue. What volume must be achieved in order to cover the additional costs, the additional interest, and provide a dividend of $2.00 per share on the new common stock?

13-10. CVP Problem Based on Data from Conventional Income Statement under Inflationary Conditions. During 19x1 the Bakies Company presented the following income statement. A standard cost system is in use.

Sales (25,000 units)			$500,000
Cost of goods sold			
Beginning inventory (5,000 units)		$ 70,000	
Cost of producing 30,000 units:			
Material	$ 90,000		
Labor	150,000		
Variable overhead	120,000		
Fixed overhead applied	60,000	420,000	
Cost of goods available for sale		$490,000	
Less ending inventory (10,000 units)		140,000	350,000
Standard gross margin			$150,000
Variances			
Noncontrollable		(40,000)	
Variable cost variances		(1,000)	(41,000)
Actual gross margin			$109,000
Selling and administrative costs:			
Variable		$ 50,000	
Fixed		53,000	103,000
Net income before tax			$ 6,000
Less income tax @ 40%			2,400
Net income after tax			$ 3,600

Required:

1. Using the conventional assumptions of CVP analysis, compute Bakies's break-even point.
2. Compare your results in part 1 with the outcome for 19x1. Explain any differences.
3. Assume that inflation is expected to cause all revenue and cost items to increase by 10% during 19x2. Compute the break-even point for 19x2.
4. Continue the assumed inflation rate in part 3. However, assume that due to depreciation only 60% of the fixed costs are subject to the inflation. What is the break-even point for 19x2?
5. Assume the target after-tax income is $3,600.
   a. Using 19x1 cost and revenue data, what volume of sales is needed to achieve the target?
   b. Repeat part a using the inflation assumption in part 3. Compare your results with part a. Explain any differences.
   c. Repeat part a using the inflation assumption in part 4.

13-11. Adapted CMA Problem on CVP Analysis. The Barr Food Manufacturing Company is a medium-sized, publicly held corporation, producing a variety of consumer food and specialty products. Current year data were prepared as follows for the salad dressing product line using five months of actual expenses and a seven-month projection. These data were prepared for a preliminary 19x9 budget meeting between the specialty products division president, marketing vice-president, production vice-president, and the controller. The current year projection was accepted as being accurate, but it was agreed that the projected income was not at a satisfactory level.

Projected Income Statement
for the Year Ended December 31, 19x8
(5 months actual, 7 months projected)
(000 omitted)

Volume in gallons	5,000
Gross sales	$30,000
Freights, allowances, discounts	3,000
Net sales	$27,000
Less manufacturing costs	
Variable	$13,500
Fixed	2,100
Depreciation	700
Total manufacturing costs	$16,300
Gross profit	$10,700
Less expenses	
Marketing	$ 4,000
Brokerage	1,650
General and administrative	2,100
Research and development	500
Total expenses	$ 8,250
Income before taxes	$ 2,450

The division president stated she wanted, at a minimum, a 15% increase in gross sales dollars and not less than a 10% before-tax profit for 19x9. She also stated that she would be responsible for a $200,000 reduction in the general and administrative expenses to help achieve the profit goal.

Both the vice-president of marketing and the vice-president of production felt that the president's objectives would be difficult to achieve. However, they offered the following suggestions to reach the objectives:

1. *Sales volume*—The current share of the salad dressing market is 15%, and the total salad dressing market is expected to grow 5% for 19x9. Barr's current market share can be maintained by a marketing expenditure of $4,200,000. The two vice-presidents estimated that the market share could be increased by additional expenditures for advertising and sales promotion. For an additional expenditure of $525,000 the market share can be raised by one percentage point until the market share reaches 17%. To get further market penetration, an additional $875,000 must be spent for each percentage point until the market share reaches 20%. Any advertising and promotion expenditures beyond this level are not likely to increase the market share to more than 20%.

2. *Selling price*—The selling price will remain at $6.00 per gallon. The selling price is very closely related to the costs of the ingredients, which are not expected to change in 19x9 from the costs experienced in 19x8.
3. *Variable manufacturing costs*—Variable manufacturing costs are projected at 50% of the net sales dollar (gross sales less freight, allowances, and discounts).
4. *Fixed manufacturing costs*—An increase of $100,000 is projected for 19x9.
5. *Depreciation*—A projected increase in equipment will increase depreciation by $25,000 over the 19x8 projection.
6. *Freight, allowances and discounts*—The current rate of 10% of gross sales dollars is expected to continue in 19x9.
7. *Brokerage expense*—A rate of 5% of gross sales dollars is projected for 19x9.
8. *General and administrative expense*—A $200,000 decrease in general and administrative expense from the 19x8 forecast is projected; this is consistent with the president's commitment.
9. *Research and development expense*—A 5% increase from the absolute dollars in the 19x8 forecast will be necessary to meet divisional research targets.

Required:

1. The controller must put together a preliminary profit plan from the facts given. Can the president's objectives be achieved? If so, present the profit plan that best achieves them. If not, present the profit plan that most nearly meets the president's objectives.
2. The president's objectives, as described in the case, were stated in terms of a percentage increase in gross sales and the percentage return on sales.
   a. What other measures of performance (other than sales dollars and return on sales percentage) could be used in setting objectives?
   b. Discuss the advantages or disadvantages of the measures you present in relation to those in the case.

13-12. CVP Problems with Step-Fixed Costs. The Tricky-Tie-Tack Company sells one kind of tie tack at $8.00. The variable costs of producing and selling are $5.00. Fixed costs are as follows and depend on the number of tie tacks produced and sold:

Range:	0–20,000	20,001–40,000	40,001–70,000	70,001–100,000
Fixed costs:	$70,000	$90,000	$100,000	$110,000

The sales last year totaled 55,000 units. There is no expected change in the selling price or the behavior of the costs during the next year. The marginal income tax rate is 40%.

Required:

1. What is the break-even point in units?
2. What volume of sales (in units) is needed to earn a $96,000 after-tax income?
3. What volume of sales (in units) is needed to earn an after-tax income of 7.5% on sales?
4. The company is considering increasing its advertising by $60,000, which should increase its sales by 5,000 units over last year. What selling price would have to be adopted (for all units) if the company wanted to have an after-tax income that is $3,600 greater than last year?

13-13. Adapted CPA Problem on CVP Analysis with Step-Fixed Costs. The Columbus Hospital operates a general hospital but rents space and beds to separate entities for specialized areas such as pediatrics, maternity, psychiatry, and so on. Columbus charges each separate entity for common services to its patients such as meals and laundry and for administrative services such as billings, collections, and so on. All uncollectible accounts are charged directly to the entity. Space and bed rentals are fixed for the year.

For the entire year ended June 30, 19x3, the Pediatrics Department at Columbus Hospital charged each patient an average of $65 per day, had a capacity of 60 beds, operated 24 hours per day for 365 days, and had revenue of $1,138,800.

Expenses charged by the hospital to the Pediatrics Department for the year ended June 30, 19x3, were as follows:

	Basis of Allocation	
	Patient Days	*Bed Capacity*
Dietary	$ 42,952	
Janitorial		$ 12,800
Laundry	28,000	
Laboratory, other than direct		
charges to patients	47,800	
Pharmacy	33,800	
Repairs and maintenance	5,200	7,140
General administrative services		131,760
Rent		275,320
Billings and collections	40,000	
Bad debt expense	47,000	
Other	18,048	25,980
	$262,800	$453,000

The only personnel directly employed by the Pediatrics Department are supervising nurses, nurses, and aides. The hospital has minimum personnel requirements based on total annual patient days. Hospital requirements beginning at the minimum expected level of operation follow:

Annual Patient Days	*Aides*	*Nurses*	*Supervising Nurses*
10,000–14,000	21	11	4
14,001–17,000	22	12	4
17,001–23,725	22	13	4
23,726–25,550	25	14	5
25,551–27,375	26	14	5
27,376–29,200	29	16	6

These staffing levels represent full-time equivalents, and it should be assumed that the Pediatrics Department always employees only the minimum number of required full-time equivalent personnel.

Annual salaries for each class of employee follow: supervising nurses—$18,000, nurses—$13,000, and aides—$5,000. Salary expense for the year ended June 30, 19x3, for supervising nurses, nurses, and aides was $72,000, $169,000, and $110,000, respectively.

Required:

Calculate the *minimum* number of patient days required for the Pediatrics Department to break even for the year ending June 30, 19x4. Patient demand is unknown, but assume that revenue per patient day, cost per patient day, cost per bed, and employee salary rates will remain the same as for the year ended June 30, 19x3.

13-14. CVP Analysis with Nonlinear Variable Costs and Step-Fixed Costs. Patton Company sells a single product for $20 per unit. Fixed costs total $250,000. The variable cost per unit is $12. However, if the total volume produced in a year is between 20,001 and 40,000 units, then the variable cost is only $11 per unit for each unit in that range. The variable cost reduces to $10 per unit for each unit in excess of 40,000.

Required:

1. Find the break-even volume.
2. At what volume would the firm have to operate in order to earn an after-tax income of $120,000 if the tax rate is 40%?
3. Instead of the fixed costs being $250,000, suppose they behave as follows:

Volume:	0–10,000	10,001–30,000	30,001 and above
Fixed:	$250,000	$300,000	$320,000

Find the break-even point.

13-15. Continuation of Labor Productivity Problem from Chapter. Question 2 of the chapter case involving inflation and labor negotiations defined productivity strictly in terms of labor savings; that is, in solving for the labor reduction, the volume of output was held constant at 3,000 units (see page 442). Alternatively, we might let both the labor time per unit and volume of output change and search for the combination that still permits the firm to achieve an after-tax income of $60,000. (Recall that we determined 6,000 labor hours would yield 3,181.45 units of product if the labor time could be reduced to 1.885931559.) If we solve for productivity gains as suggested, less than 3,181.45 units will be needed to maintain profits and labor reductions will not need to be as great.

Required:

Assuming laborers still work a total of 6,000 hours, what labor time per unit must be achieved in order to still earn $60,000 on the resulting production volume? Compare your results with those of the previous approach.

13-16. Basic Multiple Product CVP Analysis. The Cassady Company has the ability to produce four products: A, B, C, and D. Some data about these products are in the following schdule:

	Product A	*Product B*	*Product C*	*Product D*
Sales price	$32	$14.00	$35	$27
Variable costs				
Material	$ 8	$ 4.00	$ 2	$ 4
Labor	10	2.50	15	10
Overhead	6	1.50	9	6
Selling expense	2	4.00	5	4

The annual fixed costs have been determined to be:

Manufacturing $3,000
Selling and administrative   1,750

Required:

1. Suppose that only product B is produced. What is the break-even point?
2. Continuing the assumption in question 1, assume that during its first year of operation, 3,000 units were produced and 2,000 units were sold. Ending inventory is carried at the average production cost. Compute the net income for the year. Compare the net income with your expectations based on question 1. Explain your results.
3. Now, assume that giving consideration to a variety of constraints, the firm has determined the optimal production to be:

   Product A   850 units
   Product B   1,000 units
   Product C   600 units

   Assuming the optimal production ratios, what is the break-even volume of A? of B? of C? of D?

13-17. CVP Problem with Multiple Products and Step Fixed Costs. The Napoleon Company produces three products, A, B, and C. Data about the three products follow:

	Selling Price/Unit	*Variable Cost/Unit*	*Direct-Labor Hours/Unit*	*Ratio*
A	$30	$20	2	1
B	40	10	1	4
C	50	30	4	5

The products are normally sold in the ratio A:B:C = 1:4:5.
   Napoleon's fixed costs behave in a step manner as follows:

Direct-Labor Hours	*Fixed Cost*
0–19,999	$230,000
20,000–39,999	276,000
40,000–59,999	345,000
60,000 and over	500,000

The firm's marginal tax rate is 40%.

Required:

1. Assuming the product mix ratio remains constant, how many units of A, B, and C must be sold to break-even?
2. Assume the firm has a goal to report an after-tax income equal to 10% of sales. How many units of A, B, and C must be sold to achieve this goal? Assume no change in the product mix.

13-18. CMA Problem with Multiple Products. Hewtex Electronics manufactures two products—tape recorders and electronic calculators—and sells them nationally to whole-salers and retailers. The Hewtex management is very pleased with the company's perfor-mance for the current fiscal year. Projected sales through December 31, 19x7, indicate that 70,000 tape recorders and 140,000 electronic calculators will be sold this year. The projected earnings statement, which follows, shows that Hewtex will exceed its earnings goal of 9% on sales after taxes.

	Tape Recorders		Electronic Calculators		
	Total Amount*	Per Unit	Total Amount*	Per Unit	Total*
Sales	$1,050	$15.00	$3,150	$22.50	$4,200.0
Production costs					
Materials	$ 280	$ 4.00	$ 630	$ 4.50	$ 910.0
Direct labor	140	2.00	420	3.00	560.0
Variable overhead	140	2.00	280	2.00	420.0
Fixed overhead	70	1.00	210	1.50	280.0
Total production costs	$ 630	$ 9.00	$1,540	$11.00	$2,170.0
Gross margin	$ 420	$ 6.00	$1,610	$11.50	$2,030.0
Fixed selling and administrative					1,040.0
Net income before income taxes					$ 990.0
Income taxes (55%)					544.5
Net Income					$ 445.5

*000 omitted; that is, in thousands.

The tape-recorder business has been fairly stable the last few years, and the company does not intend to change the tape recorder price. However, the competition among man-ufacturers of electronic calculators has been increasing. Hewtex's calculators have been very popular with consumers. In order to sustain interest in their calculators and to meet the price reductions expected from competitors, management has decided to reduce the wholesale price of its calculator from $22.50 to $20.00 per unit effective January 1, 19x8. At the same time the company plans to spend an additional $57,000 on advertising during fiscal year 19x8. As a consequence of these actions, management estimates that 80% of its total revenue will be derived from calculator sales as compared to 75% in 19x7. As in prior years, the sales mix is assumed to be the same at all volume levels.

The total fixed overhead costs will not change in 19x8, nor will the variable overhead cost rates (applied on a direct-labor hour base). However, the costs of material and direct labor are expected to change. The cost of solid state electronic components will be cheaper in 19x8. Hewtex estimates that material costs will drop 10% for the tape recorders and 20% for the calculators in 19x8. However, direct-labor costs for both products will increase 10% in the coming year.

Required:

1. How many tape-recorder and electronic calculator units did Hewtex Electronics have to sell in 19x7 to break-even?

2. What volume of sales is required if Hewtex Electronics is to earn a profit in 19x8 equal to 9% on sales after taxes?
3. How many tape-recorder and electronic calculator units will Hewtex have to sell in 19x8 to break even?

13-19. CVP Analysis with Joint Products. Reconsider the Illini Company in problem 10-3. Assume the $1,007,000 cost of processing 100,000 gallons of input consisted of $507,000 of fixed costs. The Department II and III costs are completely variable.

Required:

1. Determine Illini's break-even point.
2. Suppose Illini also had the opportunity to sell product A at the split-off point. What is the minimum total price the firm would have to receive in order to accept an order for 10,000 gallons?

13-20. Joint Products and CVP Analysis. Bibler Company processes peanuts into peanut butter and peanut oil. The normal volume of peanuts that can be processed per month is 30,000 pounds. Including the cost of peanuts, the variable cost per pound in the shelling, cleaning, and crushing (SCC) process is $0.60. The monthly fixed costs for the SCC department are $5,000.

The SCC process yields 70% paste, 20% oil, and 10% waste. The paste is mixed with butter in the mixing department to obtain peanut butter. A pound of paste is mixed with 0.2 pounds of butter to obtain 1.2 pounds of peanut butter. Including the butter, the variable cost of processing a pound of peanut butter in the mixing department is $0.25. (Note this is per pound of peanut butter, not per pound of paste.) The mixing department's fixed cost is $2,100 per month.

The oil must be pasteurized and bottled. The variable cost of bottling amounts to $0.45 per pound. Bottling's fixed costs are $700 per month.

Peanut butter sells for $1.40 per pound and peanut oil for $1.62 per pound.

Required:

1. Determine the number of pounds of peanuts that must be processed to break even.
2. Suppose there was an offer to purchase 5,000 pounds of paste at the split-off point. What is the minimum total sales price the Bibler Company should be willing to accept?

13-21. Basic CVP Problem with Simulation. Consider, again, the problem simulated in the section entitled CVP Analysis under Uncertainty (page 446). For each income observation, assume that the random variables are sampled in the following order:

1. Demand.
2. Variable cost.
3. Fixed cost.

Further assume that the first six numbers from a random number generator are:

1. 0.82   4. 0.40
2. 0.43   5. 0.77
3. 0.11   6. 0.86

Required:

Using these random numbers and the distributions stated in the text, determine the first two income values in a simulation.

13-22. CVP Simulation When Random Variables Are Dependent. Reconsider the simulated CVP problem on page 446. Now assume that the variable cost per unit is dependent upon the quantity. The quantity is distributed the same as in the chapter example. Given the quantity, the following schedule shows the dependence of variable cost.

Range of Quantity	Corresponding Range of Variable Cost
400–500	$60–65
500–600	55–60
600–800	45–55
800–900	40–45
900–1,000	35–40

That is, as volume increases, the manufacturing process becomes more efficient resulting in a lower unit cost. If demand is in the first range, then variable cost will be in the first range. However, the specific point within the first cost range will be independent of the value in the first quantity range. Thus, the relationships are dependent but not deterministic.

A simulation was run as follows:

1. Determine a quantity as per description in the text.
2. Based on the range in which the quantity falls, select the corresponding variable cost range for sampling.
3. Draw another random number between 0 and 1. Using this value, determine the variable cost by interpolating in the cost range selected in part 2.
4. Sample the fixed cost distribution and determine the income. The simulation reported in Exhibit 13.9 was controlled to ensure that the demand and fixed costs were observed in exactly the same sequence as the study reported in the text. For example, the demand variable had a sample distribution identical to that reported in Exhibit 13.5.

Using the same ranges as in Exhibit 13.6, Exhibit 13.9 is a summary of the distribution of the income.

Required:

1. Which situation, the text case or this case, has the greatest expectation? the greatest risk?
2. What are the chances of breaking even?
3. Explain why there is a higher standard deviation and probability of not breaking even in this case as compared to the case in the text.

13-23. CVP Problem with Uncertainty and Dependencies. The JR Company has found that certain variables affecting one of its cost-profit-volume analysis are random variables. That is, the values that these variables will be are subject to uncertainty. The sales price of the product is certain, $26 per unit. However, demand *(D)*, labor cost per unit *(L)*, material cost per unit *(M)*, and fixed cost *(F)* are uncertain.

Exhibit 13.9   Eckel Company Summary of Simulation
Results with Dependence: The Income Variable

Range	Number	Percent	Cumulative Percentage
Up to −7,000	133	1.33%	1.33%
−6,999 to −5,000	71	0.71	2.04
−4,999 to −4,000	97	0.97	3.01
−3,999 to −3,000	268	2.68	5.69
−2,999 to −2,000	372	3.72	9.41
−1,999 to −1,000	331	3.31	12.72
−999 to 0	164	1.64	14.36
1 to 5,000	1,368	13.68	28.04
5,001 to 8,000	2,349	23.49	51.53
8,001 to 15,000	3,283	32.83	84.36
15,001 to 20,000	632	6.32	90.68
20,001 to 25,000	715	7.15	97.83
25,001 to 30,000	121	1.21	99.04
30,001 to 32,000	65	0.65	99.69
32,001 and above	31	0.31	100.00
Mean		8,349.457	
Standard deviation		7,440.000	

It has been established that demand may take on any value in the range listed below. Each value within the given range is equally likely to occur.

Demand: 8,240 to 15,960

The other three variables, *L*, *M*, and *F*, are partially dependent on demand. These relationships are stated below where the *e* values represent the expected error around the value given by the first two terms of the respective functions:

$$L = 10 + 0.0002D + e_L$$
$$M = 6 + 0.0002D + e_M$$
$$F = 50,000 + 0.05D + e_F$$

Assume the error terms can be any value within the ranges that follows:

e_L: −0.10 to +0.10
e_M: −0.40 to +0.40
e_F: −300 to +300

It has been decided to simulate the case described above. Random numbers will be drawn and then used to pick values for *D*, e_L, e_M, and e_F. Assume the first eight numbers from a random number generator are as follows:

(1) 0.4   (5) 0.6
(2) 0.6   (6) 0.7
(3) 0.3   (7) 0.6
(4) 0.7   (8) 0.2

Required:

Determine the first two income values in the sample where the random numbers are used to determine the variables in the following order: D, e_L, e_M, and e_F.

13-24. Adapted CMA Problem on Nonlinear CVP Analysis. Hollis Company manufactures and markets a regulator that is used to maintain high levels of accuracy in timing clocks. The market for these regulators is limited and highly dependent upon the selling price. Consequently, Hollis Company employs a combination of differential calculus and economic concepts to determine the number of regulators to be produced and the selling price of each.

Based upon past relationships between the selling price and the resultant demand as well as an informal survey of customers, management has derived the following demand function, which is highly representative of the actual relationships:

$$D = 1,000 - 2P$$

where:

D = actual demand in units, and

P = price per unit.

The estimated manufacturing and selling costs for the coming year are as follows.

Variable costs	
Manufacturing	$75 per unit
Selling	$25 per unit
Traceable fixed costs	
Manufacturing	$24,000 per year
Selling	6,000 per year

Required:

Determine the number of regulators Hollis Company should produce and the selling price it should charge per regulator in order to maximize the company's profits from the regulator product line for the coming year.

13-25. Nonlinear CVP Problem. The Leathers Company produces a single product. It has found that its revenues and costs are *not* linear functions. Some careful statistical analyses have revealed the following:

1. If x is the quantity sold then the *per unit* selling price is: $34 - 0.025x$
2. The total cost function is a cubic equation:

$$\frac{0.0001}{3} x^3 - 0.05x^2 + 20x + 2,000$$

Required:

1. At what unit volume should Leathers operate in order to maximize profits?
2. What selling price should Leathers set in order to maximize profits?
3. What is the amount of the profit at the maximum point?

13-26. CMA Problem on Nonlinear CVP Analysis. SuperNut Company produces both chunky and smooth peanut butter from the same process. In the manufacturing process the quantity of chunky peanut butter produced increases as the quantity of smooth peanut butter decreases, and vice versa. The company's operations research staff has developed a production transformation equation to express the relationship between the two quantities of output which could be manufactured from a given batch of inputs (material, labor, overhead). The equation for producing chunky and smooth peanut butter is:

$$4c^2 + 9s^2 = 9,000,000$$

where:

c = chunky peanut butter

s = smooth peanut butter

All inputs are expressed in gallons.

Required:

1. What is the largest amount of chunky peanut butter that can be produced from the input level expressed in the transformation equation?
2. SuperNut Company sells twice as many gallons of chunky peanut butter as smooth peanut butter; that is, the demand for chunky is twice the demand for smooth. What amounts of chunky and smooth should be produced per batch in order to meet sales demand and also satisfy the constraints in the production transformation equation?

13-27. CMA Problem on Nonlinear CVP Analysis. Redler Company manufactures and sells an industrial-strength cleaning fluid. The equations presented below represent the revenue *(R)* and cost *(C)* functions for the company where x is equal to *thousands* of gallons of fluid.

$$R(x) = -100,000 + 26x - 0.05x^2$$

$$C(x) = 50,000 + 8x + 0.01x^2$$

Required:

1. Determine the function that represents the marginal cost to manufacture one gallon of cleaning fluid.
2. What quantity of cleaning fluid should be produced to maximize revenue?
3. What quantity of cleaning fluid should be produced to maximize profits?
4. What would the profit (loss) be if the company manufactured and sold 300,000 gallons of cleaning fluid?

CHAPTER 14

Concept of Relevant Data

*Chapter
Overview*

Several times in Chapters 3 through 11 it was suggested that cost data derived for purposes of inventory evaluation and income determination may not be useful for decision making. Now we want to consider this issue in more depth. The concepts discussed in this chapter are relatively simple but, in certain cases, their implementation may prove difficult. Following a section of definitions, we explore a variety of cases whose solutions require the consideration of data that may not be available in *conventional* cost accounting systems.

As future designers of accounting systems, you should be on the alert to recognize situations where managers unjustifiably use inappropriate data to make decisions. Perhaps they are aware of the limitations of the data they use and make adjustments when the data would cause errors. In other cases, managers may erroneously assume that the data are appropriate. In the latter event, large opportunity costs can result and accountants should assume the responsibility for preventing such a usage of the data.

Definitions

There are three terms that need to be understood before considering a set of cases that will illustrate the proper data considerations in decision making. Frequent reference will be made to **relevant data, sunk cost,** and **opportunity cost.** Each of these concepts will be briefly illustrated in this section.

RELEVANT DATA.   Relevant data are *future* data that *differ* from one alternative to another. In making decisions managers are selecting a future course of action. Thus, only *future* costs and revenues can be of importance. There is absolutely *nothing* managers can do now, or in the future, to change the costs of the past. Regardless of the future alternatives under consideration, none of their cash flow differentials will be due to past cash flows. Even if these past cash flows have not yet been assigned to projects, the selection of one alternative over another *would not change* the *total* amounts to be assigned. If the past cash flows are allocated (this is not saying that they should be allocated), the effect of the allocation on *total* income would be the same regardless of the alternative chosen. Thus, in effect, past data can be ignored and only future data need to be considered.

relevant data
* future oriented
* differs from one
*   alternative to*
*   the other*

In addition to being future-oriented, relevant data also differ from one alternative to another. If a future cash flow will be the same for *every* alternative under consideration, then it does not affect the choice among those alternatives and the item is therefore irrelevant. No harm is caused by including such data in the analyses so long as they are included for every alternative. However, inclusion creates a data overload and, as will be shown later, no information is lost by excluding the irrelevant items.

To illustrate these concepts, suppose that during 19x1 and 19x2 the Frazier Company had spent a total of $100,000 for the research and development (R & D) of a new product. The R & D efforts have not yet proven fruitful and no marketable product has materialized. On January 1, 19x3, the company faces the following decision:

A. Discontinue all efforts on this product, or
B. Invest an additional $20,000 for R & D with virtual certainty that the efforts will result in a product that will contribute a total of $30,000 over its variable manufacturing costs.

The engineers working on this project will earn $5,000 during the additional research and development time. These salaries are not included in the $20,000 or in the $30,000. The engineers will be retained by the firm regardless of the option chosen.

Based solely on the data available, the firm should choose alternative B. The $100,000 already expended for R & D is irrelevant. There is a temptation to say that the $100,000 has produced no results and that the project is not deserving of additional expenditures. But the expenditure is past history and is a recorded event regardless of the decision about alternative A or B. Further, the engineers' salaries are not relevant even though they are future expenditures. They will be incurred in either alternative and thus do not contribute to a difference between A and B.

The only data relevant to the decision are the future expenditure on research, $20,000, and the future revenue, $30,000. Since the relevant revenue of alternative B exceeds its relevant costs, alternative B will permit a positive net cash inflow of $10,000 in excess of the net incremental cash flow from alternative A. Thus, alternative B, subject to forecasting validity, will improve the firm's cash position.

To illustrate a possible misuse of the data consider the following analysis that might be prepared by someone not understanding the meaning of relevant data:

Revenue		$ 30,000
Costs:		
R & D: 19x1–19x2	$100,000	
R & D: 19x3:	20,000	
Engineers	5,000	125,000
Net loss		($ 95,000)

The implication of the above analysis is that the $100,000 and $5,000 amounts will not occur if alternative A is chosen. Of course, this is not true and, to be comparable with the foregoing analysis, alternative A's analysis must be made as follows:

Revenue		0
Costs		
R & D: 19x1–19x2	$100,000	
Engineers	5,000	105,000
Net loss		($105,000)

With this analysis you can see, as noted earlier, that the firm is $10,000 better off with alternative B.

SUNK COST. Sunk cost is a past cost. As explained in the previous subsection, past costs cannot be changed. Thus they are frequently referred to as sunk. Sunk costs are irrelevant costs but note that the converse is not true. Some irrelevant costs may be future costs. In the previous example, the $100,000 for research and development cost incurred in 19x1–19x2 is a sunk cost.

OPPORTUNITY COST. Opportunity cost was defined in Chapter 2 as a foregone profit of a rejected alternative. Care must be exercised not to overlook these costs since managers have the responsibility of maximizing the economic income of the firm. Opportunity costs may not be recorded as part of the accounting income computation, but nevertheless their occurrence may mean that the wealth of the firm has not been maximized.

In the preceding example there are some opportunity costs that, to this point, have been ignored. For example, what could be done with the $20,000 if alternative A is accepted? Implicitly, it was assumed that nothing would have been done with it since no return was included in A's analysis. Suppose the $20,000 could have been invested at 10%. Then there is a $2,000 opportunity cost of using it on additional research during 19x3. The economic advantage of alternative B over alternative A would be reduced from $10,000 to $8,000.

An alternative way of incorporating the 10% return would be to consider it as revenue associated with alternative A. The *final impact* of this treatment would have been identical to the previous result. It is not important how opportunity costs are included in the analyses but it is important to include them.

Another opportunity cost ignored in this case was the alternative use of the engineers' time. Certainly they would be engaged in some type of productive activity if alternative A is chosen. The return from this activity would be another opportunity cost charged against alternative B. Several of the following cases will further illustrate the measurement and usage of opportunity costs.

Illustrative Cases

In this section several cases are proposed and analyzed in order to provide you with an operational concept of good decision-making data. Frequently, data may be erroneously collected and used in such a way that the decision is right for the wrong reasons. In the following cases care is exercised to distinguish appropriate data even if they might not change the decision. There is more concern with valid analysis than with identification of the best decision.

The cases to be analyzed involve decisions about (1) replacement of productive equipment, (2) the sales price of an order from a new customer, (3) an advertising campaign under uncertainty, (4) the possible elimination of a segment of the business, (5) whether to make or buy a needed machine, (6) whether to make or buy where the opportunity cost is difficult to measure (an extension of case 5), and (7) the optimal marketing strategies when joint products are involved. Before considering the cases it is important to recognize that each of them will be analyzed from a *short-run point of view,* ignoring the time value of money. Analyses appropriate to long-term effects are considered in Chapters 15 and 16. This approach is taken so that the meaning of relevance can be emphasized. The concept of relevance is equally important to the capital budgeting topics in the next two chapters.

REPLACEMENT OF PRODUCTIVE EQUIPMENT. As our first example, let us assume that the Hamilton Company is considering whether one of its polishing machines should be replaced. Following are some data about the *existing machine:*

Book value (original cost less accumulated depreciation)	$21,000
Remaining useful life	3 years
Present salvage value	$10,000
Estimated salvage value at end of useful life	$ 2,000
Annual operating costs	$ 8,000

A proposal for a *replacement machine* has been carefully analyzed and the following data are considered to be reliable:

Acquisition cost	$26,000
Estimated useful life	3 years
Estimated salvage value at end of useful life	$ 5,000
Annual operating costs	$ 3,000

Based on these data, one staff member has prepared a schedule to support his recommendation *not* to replace the machine. You are to scrutinize his analysis for validity. The staff member's schedule follows:

Loss on disposal of old machine: (salvage value less book value = $10,000 − $21,000)	$(11,000)
Cost of new	(26,000)
Operating savings of new (3 years × annual operating savings = 3 × $5,000)	15,000
Salvage value of new machine in three years	5,000
Net disadvantage of new machine	$(17,000)

Does this analysis reflect economic realities? If not, how should the problem be analyzed? (Ignore income tax considerations and the time value of money until the next chapter.)

First, the analysis was made using an *incremental* approach. That is, there was a netting of the outcomes of one alternative against the outcomes of the other. In and of itself, this is not wrong, but such an approach can lead to unnecessary complexities for more involved problems. For example, it is difficult to do an incremental analysis when there are three or more options.

Second, and more important, the analysis has improperly accounted for some of the irrelevant costs. Note that the book value of the old machine was used to compute a loss in the event of its disposal. However, the book value of the machine is a sunk cost and irrelevant. The analysis implies that the effect of the book value would be avoided by not replacing the machine.

How, then, can the situation be better analyzed? It is suggested that you consider the *future* cash flow associated with each alternative and then compare the totals. This is done in Exhibit 14.1. Item 1 of the exhibit consists of each alternative's operating costs and is for the three years combined. In one sense, the first $9,000 of these costs is irrelevant in that an amount of this magnitude will be incurred regardless of the decision. However, as explained earlier, certain complexities will be avoided by initially considering each project in isolation of the others.

Item 2 is the net cash outflow that would be incurred now if the new machine is acquired. Note that the invoice price of the new machine is reduced by the present salvage value of the old machine. Finally, the anticipated salvage values at the end of three years are recognized as cash inflows (item 3).

As is indicated in Exhibit 14.1, the replacement alternative has a $2,000 advantage over the present machine. Implicitly, it has been assumed that there is no change in total revenue if the new machine is acquired. It may be impossible to

---

Exhibit 14.1   Hamilton Company Analysis of Polishing Machine Options* (Outflows in Parentheses)

	Alternative	
	Keep Old	*Buy New*
1. Operating costs		
Old: $8,000 × 3	$(24,000)	
New: $3,000 × 3		$(9,000)
2. Cost of new equipment (net)		
$26,000 − $10,000		(16,000)
3. Salvage Value at end of year 3	2,000	5,000
Total cash flow	$(22,000)	$(20,000)

*Ignoring income taxes and the time value of money.

attribute revenues to specific machines; revenue is the result of a combination of efforts. When revenues are constant they are irrelevant and, in such a case, the better alternative is the one with the smallest cash outflow.

As suggested earlier, the error of the original analysis was the failure to treat the $21,000 book value as an expense of either alternative. For the replacement option it is used to compute the loss on disposal as was done by the staff member preparing the original analysis. But to be comparable, it must be recognized that the book value would be used to compute depreciation if the old machine is retained. Since the old machine has an estimated salvage value of $2,000, the total depreciation for the three years would be $19,000. Thus, on an expense basis, the $17,000 loss in the original analysis should have been compared with the $19,000 loss of keeping the old machine. Again, there is a $2,000 advantage in favor of replacement. The analysis is much clearer, however, if the data are limited to those that are relevant.

EVALUATING SALES PRICE OF A SPECIAL ORDER. As a second example, assume the Cousins Company produces a single product that it regularly sells for $80 per unit. The following *attainable* standards have been in use:

Material: 4 units @ $5.00	$20.00
Direct labor: 2 hours @ $8.00	16.00
Variable overhead: 2 hours @ $4.00	8.00
Fixed overhead: 2 hours @ $5.00	10.00
Total manufacturing cost	$54.00

In addition to this, a cost analysis indicates that variable selling costs have been incurred at $3.00 per unit (including a sales commission of 1%). Based on normal volume, the fixed selling and administrative costs average $12.00 per unit. Since the total average cost is $69 ($54 + $3 + $12), a selling price of $80 generates an $11 per unit contribution toward profits. The $11 per unit is 13.75% of sales and this percentage is well within the range reported by the company's competitors.

Just recently, an offer was received from a foreign company for 2,500 units of the product at $70 per unit. Various export duties and special shipping requirements would cost the company $5,000 if the order is accepted. There would be no sales commissions paid on this order. As a representative of the company's accounting department you have been consulted for advice about accepting the contract.

At a fact-finding meeting you find one manager, Ms. Robin, arguing against accepting the contract. The essence of her argument is as follows: "The item costs $69 per unit to produce. With a $70 sales price, the 2,500 unit contract will produce profits of only $2,500 before considering the special costs of $5,000. Considering these costs, the contract would result in a $2,500 loss." How should you respond to Ms. Robin?

First, it is necessary to determine the relevant costs. What costs will be avoided if the contract is not accepted? In this case, the material, labor, and variable overhead will not be incurred if the contract is not accepted. However, the fixed factory overhead of $10 per unit is only an application rate. These costs would be incurred regardless of the contract decision and are not relevant. Variable selling costs would be incurred on this contract but not at $3.00 per unit. The sales commissions are not to be paid and constitute $0.80 of the $3.00 (0.01 × $80). Thus, the incremental variable selling cost is $2.20 per unit and would be avoided if the contract is refused. Fixed selling and administrative costs are not likely to change but the company would avoid the $5,000 special charges.

The following summarizes the potential effect of accepting the contract:

Revenue ($70 × 2,500)		$175,000
Less avoidable costs:		
Material ($20 × 2,500)	$50,000	
Labor ($16 × 2,500)	40,000	
Variable overhead ($8 × 2,500)	20,000	
Variable selling ($2.20 × 2,500)	5,500	
Special costs	5,000	120,500
Contribution of contract over		
avoidable costs		$ 54,500

From this, the issue can be more clearly analyzed.

Next it is necessary to determine if the firm is operating at capacity. If it is, then clearly it does not want to sell products at $70 that could otherwise be sold at $80. On the other hand, if there is idle capacity, then this contract could be accepted without interrupting regular sales, and the preceding analysis suggests the firm would be better off by $54,500. Further, will the sale at $70 have some domino effect on regular customers who have been paying $80? Since the new customer is in a foreign market, the risk of this effect may be minimal.

RELEVANT DATA AND UNCERTAINTY. In the previous cases the projected cash flows were assumed to occur with certainty. In practice this is rarely the case. The results of actions are uncertain. The following case illustrates a process that can be used when there is uncertainty about the data.

To illustrate, let us continue with the Cousins problem of the previous section. Assume the company has excess capacity and has not received the proposal from the foreign company. Further, the firm has $100,000 available and is considering two possible alternatives:

A. Invest in one-year securities currently returning 10%.
B. Conduct an advertising campaign with expected increases in product demand for the year as follows:

Unit Increase	Probability
2,000	10%
3,000	20
4,000	30
5,000	40

Currently, the idle capacity is 2,000 units: the equivalent of 4,000 labor hours. In the event that additional demand exceeds 2,000 units, it would be necessary to schedule production using overtime or to add a second shift. Overtime is paid at the usual time and one-half. A second shift would result in additional fixed costs amounting to $15,000 per year. An additional demand of 3,000 units could be met with an overtime cost of $8,000 (1,000 units over capacity × 2 hours × $4 overtime premium). This would be less expensive than scheduling a second shift. On the other hand, a demand in excess of 4,000 units can be more economically met by instituting the second shift.

To incorporate the uncertainty, it is necessary to compute the expected value of advertising. To explain and compute the expected value, it is first necessary to define conditional value. A *conditional value* is the return (or payoff) of an act, *given* that certain conditions have occurred. For our case, it is necessary to compute the returns of advertising, given the demand. The relevant conditional value of an outcome in this case is the volume times the contribution margin per unit less the *incremental* fixed costs (advertising and, if applicable, overtime premium or second-shift costs).

The contribution margin per unit is $33 ($80 − $20 − $16 − $8 − $3). In Exhibit 14.2 you will find a summary of the conditional payoffs for each possible outcome of advertising. The *expected value* of an action is the sum of the weighted conditional values where the weight is the probability of occurrence. This computation is also found in Exhibit 14.2.

As can be seen in Exhibit 14.2 the advertising expenditure is expected to return $19,900 over its cost ($119,900 − $100,000). In comparison, investment in the securities will return $10,000. It appears that an advertising campaign is a better

---

Exhibit 14.2   Cousins Company Expected Return of Advertising

Possible Outcome (additional units)	Conditional Value	Probability	Expected Value
2,000	$ 66,000[a]	0.1	$ 6,600
3,000	91,000[b]	0.2	18,200
4,000	117,000[c]	0.3	35,100
5,000	150,000[d]	0.4	60,000
			$119,900

[a] 2,000 × 33.
[b] 3,000 × 33 − 8,000 overtime.
[c] 4,000 × 33 − 15,000 shift cost.
[d] 5,000 × 33 − 15,000.

119900 - 100000 - 10000

cost of ad $ from the investment

use of the $100,000. However, there is more risk involved with an advertising campaign than with the investment. Risk is a condition where there is variability around the expected value of the action. For example, if demand is increased by only 2,000 units, the payoff will be $66,000, not $119,900. Decision makers have different aversions to risk, and normally they will require a compensation for accepting it. In the preceding case, the risk premium of accepting the advertising alternative over the short-term investment is $9,900. Whether or not this is adequate compensation for the risk is dependent upon the decision maker and the situation.

ELIMINATION OF A SEGMENT OF THE BUSINESS. As the next example involving the determination of relevant data, consider the Craig Steel Company, which has several plants located throughout the country. The one located in Oldsville is Craig's oldest and most inefficient plant and management has been considering its closing. The income statement in Exhibit 14.3 is reflective of the accounting results for the past several years.

At a semiannual review of operations, one of the corporate officers referred to the results in Exhibit 14.3 and stated that the evidence overwhelmingly supported the closing. Further, he states, "We cannot continue subsidizing a $7,000,000 loss at Oldsville; it is a millstone around our neck. We should have closed it three years ago." Is this conclusion fully justified?

As in the previous cases, you cannot completely answer this based on the facts that you have. However, it can be said that the results in Exhibit 14.3 are misleading for the decision being considered. To infer that company profits will increase

Exhibit 14.3   Craig Company Oldsville Plant Statement of Income for Year Ended December 31, 19x0 (000 omitted)

Sales			$21,000
Variable costs			
Manufacturing		$ 7,000	
Selling		1,000	8,000
Contribution margin			$13,000
Fixed costs			
Plant			
Supervision	$4,000		
Property taxes	2,000		
Depreciation	3,000		
Other	5,000	$14,000	
Allocated from corporate		6,000	20,000
Net Loss			$(7,000)

by $7,000,000 if the plant is closed assumes that all of the costs incurred and allocated to the Oldsville plant will be avoided if it is shut down. Even without additional knowledge, this result can be doubted.

If the plant is closed, then there is little doubt that the variable costs and the fixed supervision costs would be avoided. The property taxes will be avoided only if the property is sold. (Let us assume that this is possible in the relatively near future.) There is a temptation to say the same thing about the depreciation figure. But remember that it represents an allocation of a cash disbursement made in the past and is a sunk cost. This needs to be explored in more detail.

Suppose we are willing to limit the alternatives to (1) continue the plant as is, or (2) close the plant. Then the plant's exit value (that is, its salvage value) and the income from the best investment of this amount represent the relevant cost of the continued use of the plant, not its accounting depreciation. There is an operational problem, however, in that Exhibit 14.3 represents annualized data. A sale at salvage is a lump sum flow and is not directly comparable to an annual figure. Capital budgeting, discussed in the next two chapters, will provide a better way to deal with this problem.

For the time being, the annual cost of continued use of a long-lived asset can be roughly measured as the *yearly decline in exit (salvage)* value plus the annual income lost by not being able to invest the proceeds of the asset if it were sold now. Suppose the current exit value of the plant is $3,000,000 and continued use will cause an annual decline of $1,000,000 in that value. Further, the firm's best alternative use of available funds today would result in a 10% return. Then the cost of continuing the investment in the plant during the forthcoming year is $1,300,000 ($1,000,000 + 0.10 × $3,000,000).

Assume that other fixed plant costs represent annual cash outflows that would cease if the plant is closed. The final item in the income statement is an allocated share of the costs of operating corporate headquarters. If the Oldsville plant is closed, will corporate costs go down? Perhaps they will, and a careful analysis is needed. However, it is doubtful if they will be entirely eliminated. Let us assume they will not change at all. Then the relevant income from continued operations of the plant is:

Sales		$21,000
Avoidable costs		
Variable	$8,000	
Supervision	4,000	
Property taxes	2,000	
Long-lived asset cost	1,300	
Other	5,000	20,300
Plant's contribution to		
unavoidable cost and profits		$ 700

The problem is really more involved than assumed here. Many other questions must be raised. For example, do the results in Exhibit 14.3 reflect an optimal operating strategy for the Oldsville plant? If there are multiple products and a variety of limited resources, then has the plant been producing at the best feasible product mix? If not, what are the odds that it can efficiently adjust to the optimal? Given that an optimal can be achieved, what would be the relevant income?

Further, there may be other alternatives. For example, the plant could be modernized. If modernized, it is doubtful that the cost behavior and resource constraints would be as they are now. For the modernization alternative, the replacement costs become relevant and such an action can be justified only if the return on investment in the plant enables a better return than competing uses of the funds. All of this is much too complicated to include in the type of analysis presented here. Linear programming is a potential way of modeling all of these factors.

MAKE OR BUY.   The next case to be analyzed involves a make-or-buy decision. The Heiden Company's plant needs a new machine that would require some of the same technology and parts that are already available to the company. The machine could be purchased for $150,000. However, in the forthcoming year, the demand for the company's products can be met by operating at 75% of capacity. For this reason the company is considering the possibility of constructing the machine rather than buying it.

Should Heiden elect to build the machine, the job would require 30% of the year's capacity. The extra 5% would be generated by reducing the scheduled production (and sales) of product XYZ. The following additional data are available:

1. Fixed factory overhead amounts to $200,000 yearly, of which 30% would be allocated to the machine. This is consistent with the company's policy of full absorption costing.
2. The bill of materials for the machine is as follows:

   could be sold for

   Part A   1,000 units
   Part B   2,000 units
   Part C   3,000 units

3. Enough of part A is already on hand, having been acquired at a cost of $10.00 per unit. In anticipation of the possibility of building this machine, 1,000 units of the existing inventory have been put on a temporary hold status. Part A will continue to be needed in the production of the regular product lines. During the coming year the acquisition cost is estimated to be $11.00 per unit.
4. The present inventory of part B consists of 2,500 units acquired at a cost of $5.00 per unit. It is a high-technology part and has become obsolete for most purposes. However, it would be acceptable for the machine. The only other alternative is to sell the part at a scrap price of $0.50 per unit.
5. The 8,000 unit inventory of part C was acquired at $7.00 per unit. During the next year its unit price is expected to be $7.50.
6. The machine will require 15,000 labor hours. Of these hours, 10,000 will be provided by factory workers who are covered by guaranteed wage packages paying $6.00 per hour. The remaining hours would be generated by $5.00 per hour employees that would be laid

off if the machine is not produced. No idle time costs are included in the fixed costs mentioned in item 1.

7. Variable overhead is a function of direct-labor hours and is incurred at a $3.00 rate.
8. As indicated, product XYZ will be reduced if the machine is self-produced. This reduction would amount to 1,000 units. XYZ's net profit (based on a full cost allocation) is $2.00 per unit and its contribution margin is $3.00 per unit. Each of these figures are computed using a labor cost of $6.00 per hour.

Should the firm buy the machine on the market for $150,000 or build it? Exhibit 14.4 is a statement of the relevant cost of producing the machine and comparative costs at which the machine would be capitalized for accounting purposes if it is built. Following is an item-by-item analysis to support the data in Exhibit 14.4.

The items will be analyzed in the order given. First, the fixed overhead will not change regardless of the alternative selected. Since none of it can be attributed to the self-constructed machine, none of it is relevant. In contrast, $60,000 (0.30 × $200,000) would be allocated to the asset under full absorption accounting. The variable (direct) coster might object to this, but those arguments need not be considered again.

Exhibit 14.4   Heiden Company Relevant and Accounting Costs Proposed Machine Construction

	Relevant Cost	Accounting Cost
1. Fixed factory overhead	0	$ 60,000
2. Part A		
(1,000 × $11)	$ 11,000	
(1,000 × $10)		10,000
3. Part B		
(2,000 × $0.50)	1,000	
(2,000 × $5.00)		10,000
4. Part C		
(3,000 × $7.50)	22,500	
(3,000 × $7.00)		21,000
5. Labor		
First 10,000 hours	0	60,000
Remaining 5,000 hours @ $5.00	25,000	25,000
6. Variable overhead		
12,500 labor hours @ $3.00	37,500	45,000
7. Lost profits from decrease in product XYZ		
1,000 × $22.50	25,500	0
Total	$122,500	$231,000

Item 2 in Exhibit 14.4 is the cost of part A. The acquisition cost of $10.00 per unit is a sunk cost and irrelevant. But there is still a cost of using part A. If the machine is produced, 1,000 units of A will be taken from inventory and, in effect, diverted from regular production. It will cost $11.00 per unit to reinstate the inventory to the level that exists now.

Alternatively, suppose the entire existing inventory has already been designated for regular production. If so, then the parts for the machine would have to be acquired at the current market price of $11.00. In the final analysis, it is arbitrary as to which project (regular production or the machine) will use the existing inventory. Excepting other considerations, a coin flip could be used to make the decision. Will cost be dependent on a coin flip? Of course not. It is immaterial which units are physically used on the machine; the economic impact of their use is an outlay of $11.00 per unit. Thus, the future incremental cash outflow will be $11,000 ($11 × 1,000) if the parts are used on the machine. Of course, if the units for the machine come from existing inventory, there is no question about the capitalizable accounting cost; the historical cost is $10,000.

Part B (item 3 in the exhibit) is also in inventory and, like part A, the historical cost is irrelevant. If the 2,000 units are used for the construction of the machine, then alternative uses are prevented. Based on the available facts, sale at salvage appears to be the only other alternative use for the parts. Thus, sale at salvage value would be prohibited. Therefore, the future cash inflow would be reduced by $1,000 (2,000 × $0.50) if the parts are used on the machine.

The accounting cost of part B could be debated. Accounting principles require the lower of cost or market when there is obsolescence. Although this part is obsolete for regular production, it obviously has value for this machine. If the parts had not been recognized as obsolete before this time, it would be hard to argue for a write down now that a potential use has been identified. In this case, the capitalizable amount would be the original cost. On the other hand, if the obsolescence had been previously recognized and the inventory written down to $0.50 per unit, then the items could not be written up again. In this case, they would be assigned to the machine at $0.50 per unit.

The relevant cost of part C is $7.50. The situation for part C is analogous to part A.

Item 5 of Exhibit 14.4 is the direct-labor cost. Since the first 10,000 labor hours will be incurred regardless of the decision about the machine, the relevant cost is zero. Accounting principles, however, would assign the labor cost to the machine at $6.00 per hour. The remaining 5,000 hours would be avoided if the machine is not produced. Relevant and accounting cost would be the same in this case.

Before leaving the labor analysis it should be observed that some labor time must be shifted from the production of product XYZ to the machine. The impact of this shifting has been ignored at this point and will be considered under item 7 in Exhibit 14.4. This impact will also be ignored in the overhead analysis which follows.

Variable overhead, you should recall, was assumed to be a function of direct-labor hours. The question here involves a determination of the number of hours on which to base the overhead computation if the machine is produced. Although the first 10,000 hours had no relevant labor cost it cannot be assumed that variable overhead on the first 10,000 hours is irrelevant. It is not reasonable to assume that variable overhead continues to be incurred if the employees did not work. Granted, they will get paid even if the machine is not produced, but then they would not be doing anything that would cause variable overhead to increase. (There is a possible exception on this point depending upon how fringe benefits behave.) Thus, it is more reasonable to assume that variable overhead will be incurred if the machine is produced and avoided if it is not produced. However, some of the 15,000 labor hours will be incurred even if the machine is not produced. Since the 15,000 hours needed on the machine is 30% of capacity, capacity is 50,000 hours (15,000 ÷ 0.3). Product XYZ must be reduced in an amount equal to 5% of capacity or by 2,500 hours. Thus, only 12,500 of the 15,000 hours will be incurred if the machine is produced and, in turn, cause overhead to be incurred. As you can see in Exhibit 14.4, the relevant variable overhead cost is based on 12,500 hours.

Finally, consider the impact the machine will have on product XYZ. Of the alternative ways to get the extra 5% capacity to produce the machine, it has been assumed that reducing product XYZ represents the optimal or least costly way. In computing the opportunity cost of the reduction consider only those items that will actually change. The assigned fixed costs do not reflect costs that would be avoided by reducing XYZ's production. Therefore the net profit of $2.00 per unit is not relevant. The contribution margin of $3.00 is relevant because in this case the revenue would be lost and the variable cost would be avoided. The contribution margin is the net of these two items. However the $3 contribution margin includes some direct labor and variable overhead that will be incurred regardless of the decision. As discussed in the last paragraph, 2,500 hours of the needed labor will be generated by reducing product XYZ. This means XYZ requires 2.5 hours per unit, 2,500 ÷ 1,000. Since labor is $6 per hour and variable overhead is $3, the $3 per unit contribution margin includes $9 per hour that will not actually change in this case. This amounts to $22.50 per unit, 2.5 × $9. Therefore, the sacrifice of reducing XYZ by one unit is $25.50 ($22.50 + $3 contribution margin). In Exhibit 14.4, note the accounting cost of this item is zero. Accounting principles do not endorse the capitalization of opportunity costs. There is no exchange transaction that would establish this as a recordable event.

The decision about the machine should be based on the relevant cost data. The incremental cash flow of buying the machine is $150,000 which should be compared to the self-construction cost of $122,500. Obviously, the latter is the more favorable acquisition method. This suggests an interesting accounting problem. Can management justify the capitalization of $231,000 when the machine could have been acquired on the market at $150,000? Issues such as this are discussed more fully in intermediate financial accounting textbooks. Briefly, the difference in cost could be justified only if the self-constructed machine gave the firm some advantage over the purchased machine. The point that is desired to be made here, however, is that the

[handwritten marginal note: sacrifice should only equal $3 C.M.]

decision *should not* be made on the basis of the cost that might be assigned by the accounting system. For reporting purposes, accounting systems consider factors other than incremental economic advantages when establishing definitions of cost.

≥ EXTENSION OF MAKE OR BUY CASE. In order to illustrate the potential complexities of computing the relevant cost, consider one modificaiton to the preceding case. Part C, you will recall, had an historical cost of $7.00 and a replacement cost of $7.50. Consider the following additional facts.

This part is used only for one of the firm's products: the very popular PDQ model. Just last month the marketing research department determined that if PDQ were to be produced using part D, the product's profit rate would increase even though part D costs $9.00 per unit. The following comparative figures show why:

	Product PDQ			
	With Part C		*With Part D*	
Sales price per unit		$11.00		$12.75
Variable cost per unit				
Part C (part D)	$7.50		$9.00	
Labor and overhead	2.50	10.00	2.50	11.50
Contribution		$ 1.00		$ 1.25

The demand would not significantly decrease because of the proven increase in PDQ's reliability when part D is used. Part C could be salvaged at a price yielding $6.00 per unit net of selling expenses.

Now the relevant cost of part C will require a careful analysis. Immediately, the historical cost of $7.00 per unit can be ruled out. However, without question, $7.00 will be the accounting cost. In this situation the replacement cost ($7.50) of C is not relevant since the firm does not intend to actually replace part C in like-kind. Further, it is not clear, at this point, that the alternative use for part C is to sell it at salvage value. The concept of opportunity cost must be fine-tuned in this case.

When there are more than two alternative uses of resources, the opportunity cost of appropriating them for one alternative is the *larger* of the returns possible from the *remaining* alternatives. When a unit of part C is used on the machine, it is precluded from use in making the original model of PDQ as well as being sold at its salvage value of $6.00. Thus there must be a selection between the latter two uses of part C.

Setting aside for the moment the possibility of producing the machine, let us decide the optimal way to dispose of the existing inventory of part C. Within this context the two alternatives can be specifically stated as:

1. Continue producing the original PDQ model (call it PDQ1) until all of the parts are used. (Assume that a variety of constraints prevent producing both models of PDQ at the same time.)
2. Sell the parts at salvage and use the labor time that would have otherwise been used on product PDQ1 to produce the new PDQ model (call it PDQ2).

The incremental cash flow per *unit of part C,* depending upon the alternative, is:

	Alternative 1	*Alternative 2*
Incremental cash inflows:		
Sale price of PDQ1	$11.00	
Salvage value of part C plus sale price of PDQ2 ($6 + $12.75)		$18.75
Incremental cash outflow for materials	0	9.00
Net incremental cash inflows	$11.00	$ 9.75

Note in this analysis that there is no cash outflow for material in alternative 1. Part C has already been purchased and its cost is irrelevant. Although the labor and variable overhead to produce either model is a future cost, it does not differ between the alternatives and has been omitted in the preceding analysis. To produce model PDQ2, there would be a cash outflow for part D since there is no inventory on hand. Comparing the two alternatives, it can be seen that the Heiden Company would be better off continuing the production of PDQ1 until the supply of part C is exhausted. This alternative will now become the base for computing an opportunity cost if part C is used for the production of the machine.

Should 3,000 units be used in the production of the machine, there will be 3,000 fewer units available for alternative 1 as just described. As seen earlier, alternative A yields an incremental cash flow of $11.00 per unit. However, this must be adjusted to take into consideration that the firm could produce and sell 3,000 units of PDQ2 as a replacement for the lost 3,000 units of PDQ1. That is, the loss of $11.00 per unit from alternative 1 can be reduced by some gains from the use of the labor hours that would have otherwise been used for PDQ1. Since PDQ2 sells for $12.75, and since the firm would have to acquire a part D at $9.00, the relevant incremental cash inflow of this replacement activity is $3.75 per unit ($12.75 − $9.00). (Again note that the $2.50 labor and variable overhead cost will be incurred regardless of what is done in this case and can be ignored in computng incremental cash flows.) The net opportunity cost per unit of using part C for the proposed machine is $7.25 ($11.00 − $3.75). That is, the firm loses $11.00 from giving up alternative 1 but regains $3.75 of that loss through a replacement activity that becomes available when alternative 1 is foregone.

The $7.25 net opportunity cost can be derived in an alternative way. For convenience define two alternatives:

A. Use 3,000 units of part C to produce PDQ1.
B. Use 3,000 units of part C for the machine and utilize the labor scheduled for PDQ1 to produce 3,000 units of product PDQ2.

The total cash flows would be as follows:

	Alternative A		Alternative B	
Revenue:				
PDQ1 (3,000 × $11)		$33,000		
PDQ2 (3,000 × $12.75)				$38,250
Cash expenses:				
Material				
Part C	0			
Part D (3,000 × $9)			$27,000	
Labor and overhead				
(3,000 × $2.50)	$7,500	7,500	7,500	34,500
Net cash inflow		$25,500		$ 3,750

The cash flow from alternative B is $21,750 smaller than alternative A ($25,500 − $3,750). This reduction must be considered as a cost of the machine. On a per unit basis, this cost is $7.25 ($21,750 ÷ 3,000).

DECISIONS WHEN JOINT PRODUCTS ARE INVOLVED. As our final case let us consider a situation involving joint products. The case to be considered here is a modification of the Nevares Company problem in Chapter 10. With the modifications incorporated, the possible product flows are illustrated in Exhibit 14.5. The data given in this exhibit are for the normal monthly batch of 11,000 pounds. Note that each of the three products could either be sold at the split-off point or processed further.

There are a variety of decisions that might need to be made in cases such as the one described in Exhibit 14.5. A typical situation is deciding what should be done with the output of the joint process given that production has already been completed through the split-off point. For example, it can either be sold at the split-off point or processed further. What data are relevant to deciding between these two options?

Begin by assuming that the processing has been completed in the joint process (Department I). Then all costs incurred in that department (fixed and variable) are sunk and irrelevant to any subsequent decisions about the products. However, the fixed costs in the subsequent departments may be relevant or irrelevant. Fixed costs would be relevant when some or all of them will be eliminated if the department is discontinued.

Exhibit 14.6 is a schedule of relevant data assuming, unrealistically, that *all* of a department's fixed costs could be eliminated if it were discontinued. In contrast, Exhibit 14.7 contains results which assume that *none* of the fixed costs would be avoided if the department ceases to operate.

In comparing the two exhibits you should note that as we move from one extreme assumption to the other, only one decision about marketing strategy changed: product C's. This indicates that the decision about products A and B is fixed and independent of the amount of fixed costs which might be eliminated if Departments II and III cease to be used. Department IV's fixed costs would need

Exhibit 14.5   Description of Joint Products Problem

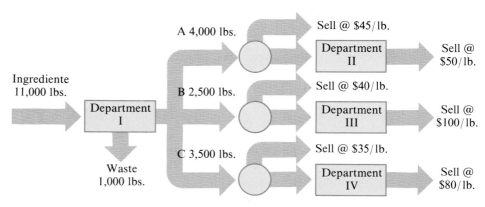

Estimated Monthly Costs if Each Department Operated at Normal Volume

	Department I	Department II	Department III	Department IV
Variable	$120,000	$ 80,000	$37,500	$140,000
Fixed	100,000	20,000	12,500	35,000
Total	$220,000	$100,000	$50,000	$175,000

Exhibit 14.6   Nevares Company Relevant Data Concerning Marketing Decisions about Joint Products with Assumption That All Fixed Costs Are Avoided

	Sell at Split-off	Process Further
Product A (4,000 lbs.)		
Sales	$180,000	$200,000
Relevant costs, Department II	0	100,000
Net relevant cash flow	$180,000*	$100,000
Product B (2,500 lbs.)		
Sales	$100,000	$250,000
Relevant costs, Department III	0	50,000
Net relevant cash flow	$100,000	$200,000*
Product C (3,500 lbs.)		
Sales	$122,500	$280,000
Relevant costs, Department IV	0	175,000
Net relevant cash flow	$122,500*	$105,000

*Optional action, given the assumption.

Exhibit 14.7   Nevares Company Relevant Data Concerning Marketing Decisions about Joint Products with Assumption of No Changes in Fixed Costs

	Sell at Split-off	*Process Further*
Product A (4,000 lbs.)		
Sales	$180,000	$200,000
Relevant costs, Department II	0	80,000
Net relevant cash flow	$180,000*	$120,000
Product B (2,500 lbs.)		
Sales	$100,000	$250,000
Relevant costs, Department III	0	37,500
Net relevant cash flow	$100,000	$212,500*
Product C (3,500 lbs.)		
Sales	$122,500	$280,000
Relevant costs, Department IV	0	140,000
Net relevant cash flow	$122,500	$140,000*

*Optimal action, given the assumption.

to be more carefully analyzed before management would be able to determine the optimal action about product C.

If there are alternative uses of the subsequent departments, then it is necessary to consider them. Even if an analysis such as the preceding one indicates a product should be processed further, such alternatives must be considered to measure the opportunity costs of using the department for the joint products. For example, if an alternative use of Department B enables a contribution margin of $112,500 per month or more, then the $112,500 from the alternative plus $100,000 from selling product B at the split-off point would match the $212,500 contribution of further processing product B (see Exhibit 14.7).

Another class of decisions is encountered if we drop the assumption that the production in the joint process is fixed. For example, there may be a variety of resource constraints that involve Department I as well as the other departments. If so, then there needs to be a consideration of the overall utilization of resources including the usage by Department I. It may not be desirable to assume that Department I is operated at capacity. If management wants the freedom to include Department I's activities in the decision set, then a way must be found to project the impact of its activities on profits. Given that the joint department's activity rate is to be considered a decision variable, then its variable costs become relevant. However, these costs still cannot be allocated to the final output for purposes of making decisions. They do not vary with the output of *individual* products. Instead, such costs are only a function of *input* to the department. This problem will be explored further in Chapter 22.

Summary

The concept of relevance is one of the most important concepts for an accountant. The concept is relatively simple but its implementation can prove difficult. A variety of situations were discussed in order to illustrate the multiple facets of this concept. There is no way to reduce relevance to a formula. You must analyze each case in an appropriate way. In the final analysis, you should be alert to determine the incremental cash flows. Also, be sure to consider lost opportunities that are attributable to a given decision.

You should now be familiar with the following new key terms introduced in this chapter:

Relevant data
Sunk cost
Opportunity cost
Conditional value
Expected value

SELF-STUDY PROBLEM (A CMA PROBLEM). Anchor Company manufactures several different styles of jewelry cases. Management estimates that during the third quarter of 19x6 the company will be operating at 80% of normal capacity. Because the company desires a higher utilization of plant capacity, the company will consider a special order.

Anchor has received special order inquiries from two companies. The first order is from JCP, Inc., which would like to market a jewelry case similar to one of Anchor's cases. The JCP jewelry case would be marketed under JCP's own label. JCP, Inc. has offered Anchor $5.75 per jewelry case for 20,000 cases to be shipped by October 1, 19x6. The cost data for the Anchor jewelry case, which would be similar to the specifications of the JCP special order, are as follows:

Regular selling price per unit	$9.00
Cost per unit	
Raw materials	$2.50
Direct labor 0.5 hour @ $6.00	3.00
Overhead 0.25 machine hour @ $4.00	1.00
Total costs	$6.50

According to the specifications provided by JCP Inc., the special order case requires less expensive raw materials. Consequently, the raw materials will only cost $2.25 per case. Management has estimated that the remaining costs, labor time, and machine time will be the same as those for the Anchor jewelry case.

The second special order was submitted by the Krage Co. for 7,500 jewelry cases at $7.50 per case. These jewelry cases, as with the JCP cases, would be marketed under the Krage label and have to be shipped by October 1, 19x6. However, the Krage jewelry case is different from any jewelry case in the Anchor line. The estimated costs of this case are as follows:

Raw materials	$3.25
Direct labor 0.5 hour @ $6.00	3.00
Overhead 0.5 machine hour @ $4.00	2.00
Total costs	$8.25

In addition, Anchor will incur $1,500 for additional setup costs and will have to purchase a $2,500 special device to manufacture these cases; this device will be discarded once the special order is completed.

The Anchor manufacturing capabilities are limited to the total machine hours available. The plant capacity under normal operations is 90,000 machine hours per year or 7,500 machine hours per month. The budgeted fixed overhead for 19x6 amounts to $216,000. All manufacturing overhead costs are applied to production on the basis of machine hours at $4.00 per hour.

Anchor will have the entire third quarter to work on the special orders. Management does not expect any repeat sales to be generated from either special order. Company practice precludes Anchor from subcontracting any portion of an order when special orders are not expected to generate repeat sales.

Required:

Should Anchor Company accept either special order? Justify your answer and show your calculations.

Solution to Self-Study Problem

First, determine the incremental income of accepting the JCP order. Note that this order can be worked on during the entire third quarter. Thus, there are 4,500 machine hours available that would otherwise be idle (3 × 7,500 × 0.2), because Anchor is presently only scheduled to operate at 80% of capacity. The order would require 5,000 machine hours (20,000 × 0.25). Thus, if the order is accepted, there will need to be 500 hours shifted from production already scheduled. This will create an opportunity cost and should be part of the incremental income computation.

Assuming that the only opportunity cost is the lost contribution of the reduced volume of regular jewelry cases, the opportunity cost can be computed as follows:

Additional machine hours needed for order	500
Machine hours/for one regular jewelry case	0.25
Total reduction needed in regular jewelry cases	2,000
Contribution margin per unit	
($9.00 − $2.50 − $3.00 − $0.40*)	$ 3.10
Total lost profits	$6,200

*Variable overhead rate = 0.25($4.00 − $216,000 fixed costs ÷ 90,000 normal machine hours)

= 0.25(4 − 2.40) = 0.25(1.60)

It might be argued that the variable overhead and labor costs will be incurred on these 500 hours under either condition (the regular cases or the special order). This is true and does make these costs irrelevant. See the alternative solution, below, where this is recognized.

The incremental income from the JCP order can now be computed:

Revenue 20,000 × $5.75		$115,000
Costs:		
Opportunity costs	$ 6,200	
Material 20,000 × 2.25	45,000	
Labor 20,000 × $3	60,000	
Variable overhead 20,000 × $0.4	8,000	119,200
Incremental loss		$(4,200)

An alternative way to compute the incremental loss on the JCP order is as follows. The opportunity cost on the 2,000 unit reduction of regular jewelry cases can be computed as $13,000, 2,000 units × ($9 − $2.50). This recognizes that the total labor and variable overhead are going to be the same regardless how the 500 machine hours are used. If this approach is used, then the direct-labor and variable overhead costs associated with the first 2,000 units of the special order must also be excluded. Thus, the incremental loss of the order can alternatively be derived as follows:

Revenue		$115,000
Costs		
Opportunity cost	$13,000	
Material	45,000	
Labor (20,000 − 2,000)3	54,000	
Variable overhead		
(20,000 − 2,000)0.4	7,200	119,200
Incremental loss		$(4,200)

Note then, that if irrelevant items are excluded in the computation of the incremental income of one alternative, they must be excluded in the computaiton of all alternatives' income.

Acceptance of the JCP order is not warranted. The losses and additional costs exceed the revenue. This is true even when the opportunity costs are computed from a short-run view. Failing to supply a regular customer now may lead to more than just an immediate loss. The customers may not place orders in the future as a result of being shorted this quarter. There are alternative actions Anchor could consider. For example, is it possible to employ some overtime labor to increase the machine capacity? If it is, that might be a less expensive way of generating the machine time for the special order than reducing the output of regular jewelry cases.

Now, compute the incremental income from the Krage order. This order requires 3,750 machine hours, $0.5 \times 7,500$. Since enough hours are free, this order will entail no opportunity cost. The incremental income from the Krage order is:

Revenue 7,500 × 7.50		$52,250
Costs		
Material 7,500 × 3.25	$24,375	
Labor 7,500 × 3.00	22,500	
Variable overhead		
7,500 × 0.5 × 1.60*	6,000	
Setup costs	1,500	
Special equipment	2,500	56,875
Incremental loss		($ 625)

This order, too, is not profitable to accept.

References

American Accounting Association. "Committee Report on Managerial Decision Models," *The Accounting Review Supplement* (1969): 42–76.

———. "Committee Report on Concepts and Standards—Internal Planning and Control," *The Accounting Review Supplement* (1974): 78–96.

Horngren, C.T. "Choosing Accounting Practices for Reporting to Management," *NAA Bulletin* (September 1962): 3–15.

McRae, T.W. "Opportunity and Incremental Costs: An Attempt to Define in Systems Terms," *The Accounting Review* (April 1970): 315–321.

Shwayder, K. "Relevance," *Journal of Accounting Research* (Spring 1968): 86–97.

Problems

14-1. Basic Problem Comparing Cash Flows and Income. The Carle Company is producing product R using a machine acquired three years ago (in 19x2) at a cost of $60,000. This machine has a three-year remaining useful life and is being depreciated using the straight-line method. Its salvage value on January 1, 19x5, is $55,000. Due to its age, the machine's production rate is declining and will be as follows:

19x5	10 per day
19x6	9 per day
19x7	8 per day

The company works 200 days per year.

Product R sells for $50 per unit. Exclusive of machine-related costs the variable cost of producing a unit of R is $20. The cost of operating the machine will be $20,000 per year regardless of the production volume.

At the beginning of 19x5 a proposal to replace the machine is being considered. The new machine will cost $105,000, have a useful life of three years and will be depreciated using the straight-line method. Regardless of production volume the new machine's operating cost will be $5,000 per year. Its production rate will be twenty per day in each year of its life.

The maximum demand for product R is 2,000 units annually. However this can be increased to 3,000 units if an advertising program is adopted. The effects of this program are estimated to last for three years and the program will cost $100,000. This cost will be amortized over three years.

Required:

1. For each possible decision combination, project the annual *income* and the three-year total.
2. For each possible decision combination, project the annual *cash flow* and the three-year total.

14-2. Alternative to 14-1 in Nonprofit Setting. The Darlene School District has recently purchased five school busses at a total cost of $100,000. However, the Darlene Area Transit Authority (DATA) has also just made a proposal whereby it would provide transportation for the students during the school travel times. Passcards would be issued to the eligible students and would be honored only on school days. The cost to the school district would be governed by the terms of a contract that is described as follows.

One school board member, Larry Musselman, is not in favor of any further discussions with DATA. He argues that the school busses have just been purchased. They have a five-year life and the board spent considerable time on that decision. He suggests that DATA be told to come back in about four years when the board will be considering the replacement of these busses.

A second member, Sarah Brickle, concurs with Musselman and adds that she has found out that the busses could only be sold for $80,000 even though they are virtually new. She points out that taking the $20,000 loss will be embarrassing, especially since most of the board members are up for reelection this year.

A third member, Harvey Kaufman, states that he is uncertain about what to do. "After all," he states, "the contract would provide some hedge against the anticipated inflation of 10% on gasoline, drivers' wages, maintenance, and insurance costs. The five-year contract offered by DATA would cost the school district $65,000 per year for the first two and a half years and $78,000 per year for the second two and a half years. With this contract we don't have to guess at what our transportation costs will be for the next five years."

The board treasurer, Bob Yoder, indicates that each bus would travel 100 miles per school day (180 school days are required) and that the buses average 10 miles per gallon of gas. The current gas price is $0.70 per gallon. Maintenance would total $4,400 and insurance $10,000 per year in terms of current costs. Currently each driver is earning $6,000 for the year. Yoder also indicates that straight line depreciation would be used in reporting the total cost of busing.

Required:

1. Assume the inflation rate does turn out to be 10%. Prepare a statement of busing costs for both of the alternatives showing costs for each of the five years and the five-year period.
2. Continuing the assumption about the inflation rate, prepare a statement of cash flows for both alternatives using the same format as in part 1.

3. Repeat part 2 but assume the inflation rate is zero.
4. How would you respond to Musselman's and Brickle's arguments?
5. If you were a member of the school board, how would you vote on this issue? Why?

14-3. CMA Problem—Pricing Decisions. Stac Industries is a multiproduct company with several manufacturing plants. The Clinton Plant manufactures and distributes two household cleaning and polishing compounds—regular and heavy-duty—under the Cleen-Brite label. The forecasted operating results for the first six months of 19x0 when 100,000 cases of each compound are expected to be manufactured and sold are presented in the following statement.

Forecasted Results of Operations
for the Six-Month Period
Ending June 30, 19x0
($000 omitted)

	Regular	Heavy-Duty	Total
Sales	$2,000	$3,000	$5,000
Cost of sales	1,600	1,900	3,500
Gross profit	$ 400	$1,100	$1,500
Selling and administrative expenses			
Variable	$ 400	$ 700	$1,100
Fixed*	240	360	600
Total	$ 640	$1,060	$1,700
Income (loss) before taxes	$ (240)	$ 40	$ (200)

*The fixed selling and administrative expenses are allocated between the two products on the basis of dollar sales volume on the internal reports.

The regular compound sold for $20 a case and the heavy-duty sold for $30 a case during the first six months of 19x0. The manufacturing costs by case of product are presented in the schedule below. Each product is manufactured on a separate production line. Annual normal manufacturing capacity is 200,000 cases of each product. However, the plant is capable of producing 250,000 cases of regular compound and 350,000 cases of heavy-duty compound annually.

The cost per case consists of the following:

	Regular	Heavy-Duty
Raw materials	$ 7.00	$ 8.00
Direct labor	4.00	4.00
Variable manufacturing overhead	1.00	2.00
Fixed manufacturing overhead*	4.00	5.00
Total	$16.00	$19.00
Variable selling and		
administrative cost	$ 4.00	$ 7.00

*Depreciation charges are 50% of the fixed manufacturing overhead of each line.

The schedule below reflects the consensus of top management regarding the price/volume alternatives for the Cleen-Brite products for the last six months of 19x0. These are essentially the same alternatives management had during the first six months of 19x0.

Regular Compound		Heavy-Duty Compound	
Alternative Prices (per case)	Sales Volume (in cases)	Alternative Prices (per case)	Sales Volume (in cases)
$18	120,000	$25	175,000
20	100,000	27	140,000
21	90,000	30	100,000
22	80,000	32	55,000
23	50,000	35	35,000

Top management believes the loss for the first six months reflects a tight profit margin caused by intense competition. Management also believes that many companies will be forced out of this market by next year and profits should improve.

Required:

1. What unit-selling price should Stac Industries select for each of the Cleen-Brite compounds (regular and heavy-duty) for the remaining six months of 19x0? Support your selection with appropriate calculations.
2. Without prejudice to your answer to requirement 1, assume the optimum price/volume alternatives for the last six months were a selling price of $23 and volume level of 50,000 cases for the regular compound and a selling price of $35 and volume of 35,000 cases for the heavy-duty compound.
   a. Should Stac Industries consider closing down its operations until 19x1 in order to minimize its losses? Support your answer with appropriate calculations.
   b. Identify and discuss the qualitative factors that should be considered in deciding whether the Clinton Plant should be closed down during the last six months of 19x0.

14-4. Adapted CMA Problem on Pricing Decision. Framar, Inc. manufactures automation machinery according to customer specifications. The company is relatively new and has grown each year. Framar operated at about 75% of practical capacity during the 19x7–x8 fiscal year. The operating results for the most recent fiscal year follow.

Framar Inc.
Income Statement
for the Year Ended September 30, 19x8
(000 omitted)

Sales	$25,000
Less sales commissions	2,500
Net sales	$22,500
Expenses	
Direct material	$ 6,000
Direct labor	7,500

Manufacturing overhead—variable		
Supplies	$ 625	
Indirect labor	1,500	
Power	125	2,250
Manufacturing overhead—fixed		
Supervision	$ 500	
Depreciation	1,000	1,500
Corporate administration		750
Total expenses		$18,000
Net income before taxes		$ 4,500
Income taxes (40%)		1,800
Net income		$ 2,700

Most of the management personnel had worked for firms in this type of business before joining Framar, but none of the top management had been responsible for overall corporate operations or for final decisions on prices. Nevertheless, the company has been successful.

The top management of Framar wants to have a more organized and formal pricing system to prepare quotes for potential customers. Therefore, it has developed the following pricing formula. The formula is based upon the company's operating results achieved during the 19x7–x8 fiscal year. The relationships used in the formula are expected to continue during the 19x8–x9 fiscal year. The company expects to operate at 75% of practical capacity during the current 19x8–x9 fiscal year.

APA, Inc. has asked Framar to submit a bid on some custom-designed machinery. Framar used the new formula to develop a price and submitted a bid of $165,000 to APA, Inc. The calculations to arrive at the bid price are given next to the following pricing formula.

Pricing Formula

Details of Formula		APA Bid Calculations
Estimated direct-material cost	$xx	$ 29,200
Estimated direct-labor cost	xx	56,000
Estimated manufacturing overhead calculated at 50% of direct labor	xx	28,000
Estimated corporate overhead calculated at 10% of direct labor	xx	5,600
Estimated total costs excluding sales commissions	xx	$118,800
Add 25% for profits and taxes	xx	29,700
Suggested price (with profits) before sales commissions	$xx	$148,500
Suggested total price equal to suggested price divided by 0.9 to adjust for 10% sales commission	$xx	$165,000

Required:

1. Calculate the impact the order from APA, Inc. would have on Framar, Inc.'s net income after taxes if Framar's bid of $165,000 were accepted by APA.
2. Assume APA, Inc. has rejected Framar's price but has stated it is willing to pay $127,000 for the machinery. Should Framar, Inc. manufacture the machinery for the counter offer of $127,000? Support your answer.
3. Calculate the lowest price Framar, Inc. can quote on this machinery without reducing its net income after taxes if it should manufacture the machinery.
4. Explain how the profit performance in 19x8–x9 would be affected if Framar, Inc. accepted all of its work at prices similar to the $127,000 counter offer of APA, Inc. described in part 2.

14-5. CMA Problem: Retailing Decision. Helene's, a high-fashion women's dress manufacturer, is planning to market a new cocktail dress for the coming season. Helene's supplies retailers in the East and Middle Atlantic states.

Four yards of material are required to lay out the dress pattern. Some material remains after cutting which can be sold as remnants.

The leftover material could also be used to manufacture a matching cape and handbag. However, if the leftover material is to be used for the cape and handbag, more care will be required in the cutting which will increase the cutting costs.

The company expected to sell 1,250 dresses if no matching cape or handbag was available. Helene's market research reveals that dress sales will be 20% higher if a matching cape and handbag are available. The market research indicates that the cape and/or handbag will not be sold individually but only as accessories with the dress. The various combinations of dresses, capes, and handbags that are expected to be sold by retailers are as follows:

	Percentage of Total
Complete sets of dress, cape, and handbag	70%
Dress and cape	6
Dress and handbag	15
Dress only	9
Total	100%

The material used in the dress costs $12.50 a yard or $50.00 for each dress. The cost of cutting the dress if the cape and handbag are not manufactured is estimated at $20.00 a dress, and the resulting remnants can be sold for $5.00 for each dress cut out. If the cape and handbag are to be manufactured, the cutting costs will be increased by $9.00 per dress. There will be no salable remnants if the capes and handbags are manufactured in the quantities estimated.

The selling prices and the costs to complete the three items once they are cut are presented below.

	Selling Price per Unit	*Unit Cost to Complete (excludes cost of material and cutting operation)*
Dress	$200.00	$80.00
Cape	27.50	19.50
Handbag	9.50	6.50

Required:

1. Calculate Helene's incremental profit or loss from manufacturing the capes and hand-bags in conjunction with the dresses.
2. Identify any nonquantitative factors that could influence Helene's management in its decision to manufacture the capes and handbags which match the dress.

14-6. Adapted CMA Problem Involving Uncertainty. The Unimat Company manufactures a unique thermostat that yields dramatic cost savings from effective climatic control of large buildings. The efficiency of the thermostat is dependent upon the quality of a specialized thermocouple. These thermocouples are purchased from Cosmic Company for $15 each.

Since early 19x6, an average of 10% of the thermocouples purchased from Cosmic have not met Unimat's quality requirements. The unusable thermocouples have ranged from 5 to 25% of the total number purchased and have resulted in failures to meet production schedules. In addition, Unimat has incurred additional costs to replace the defective units because the rejection rate of the units is within the range agreed upon in the contract.

Unimat is considering a proposal to manufacture the thermocouples. The company has the facilities and equipment to produce the components. The engineering department has designed a manufacturing system that will produce the thermocouples with a defective rate of 4% of the number of units produced. The schedule presents the engineers' estimates of the probabilities that different levels of variable manufacturing cost per thermocouple will be incurred under this system. The variable manufacturing cost per unit includes a cost adjustment for the defective units at the 4% rate. Additional annual fixed costs incurred by Unimat if it manufactures the thermocouple will amount to $32,500.

Estimated Variable Manufacturing Cost per Thermocouple Unit	Probability of Occurrence
$10.00	10%
12.00	30
14.00	40
16.00	20
	100%

Unimat Company will need 18,000 thermocouples to meet its annual demand requirements.

Required:

Prepare an expected value analysis to determine whether Unimat Company should manufacture the thermocouples.

14-7. Adapted CMA Problem: Elimination of a Segment. The Scio Division of George-town, Inc. manufactures and sells four related product lines. Each product is produced at one or more of the three manufacturing plants of the division. Following is a product-line profitability statement for the year ended December 31, 19x7, that shows a loss for the base-ball equipment line. A similar loss is projected for 19x8.

Product Line Profitability—19x7
(000 omitted)

	Football Equipment	Baseball Equipment	Hockey Equipment	Miscellaneous Sports Items	Total
Sales	$2,200	$1,000	$1,500	$500	$5,200
Cost of goods sold					
Material	$ 400	$ 175	$ 300	$ 90	$ 965
Labor and variable overhead	800	400	600	60	1,860
Fixed overhead	350	275	100	50	775
Total	$1,550	$ 850	$1,000	$200	$3,600
Gross profit	$ 650	$ 150	$ 500	$300	$1,600
Selling expense					
Variable	$ 440	$ 200	$ 300	$100	$1,040
Fixed	100	50	100	50	300
Corporate administration expenses	48	24	$ 36	12	120
Total	$ 588	$ 274	$ 436	$162	$1,460
Contribution to corporation	$ 62	$ (124)	$ 64	$138	$ 140

The baseball equipment is manufactured in the Evanston plant. Some football equipment and all miscellaneous sports items also are processed through this plant. A few of the miscellaneous items are manufactured, and the remainder are purchased for resale. The item purchased for resale is recorded as materials in the records. A separate production line is used to produce the products of each product line.

The following schedule presents the costs incurred at the Evanston plant in 19x7. Inventories at the end of the year were sustantially identical to those at the beginning of the year.

Evanston Plant Costs 19x7
(000 omitted)

	Football Equipment	Baseball Equipment	Miscellaneous Sports Items	Total
Material	$100	$175	$ 90	$ 365
Labor	$100	$200	$ 30	$ 330
Variable overhead				
Supplies	$ 85	$ 60	$ 12	$ 157
Power	50	110	7	167
Other	$ 15	$ 30	$ 11	$ 56
Subtotal	$150	$200	$ 30	$ 380
Fixed overhead				
Supervision[1]	$ 25	$ 30	$ 21	$ 76
Depreciation[2]	40	115	14	169
Plant rentals[3]	35	105	10	150
Other[4]	20	$ 25	$ 5	$ 50
Subtotal	$120	$275	$ 50	$ 445
Total costs	$470	$850	$200	$1,520

[1]The supervision costs represent salary and benefit costs of the supervisors in charge of each product line.
[2]Depreciation cost for machinery and equipment is charged to the product line on which the machinery is used.
[3]The plant is leased. The lease rentals are charged to the product lines on the basis of square feet occupied.
[4]Other fixed overhead costs are the cost of plant administration and are allocated arbitrarily by management decision.

The management of Georgetown, Inc. has requested a profitability study of the baseball equipment line to determine if the line should be discontinued. The marketing department of the Scio Division and the accounting department at the plant have developed the following additional data to be used in the study:

1. If the baseball equipment line is discontinued, the company will lose approximately 10% of its sales in each of the other lines.
2. The equipment now used in the manufacture of baseball equipment is quite specialized. It has a current salvage value of $105,000 and a remaining useful life of five years. This equipment cannot be used elsewhere in the company.
3. The plant space now occupied by the baseball equipment line could be closed off from the rest of the plant and rented for $175,000 per year.
4. If the line is discontinued, the supervisor of the baseball equipment line will be released. In keeping with company policy he would receive severance pay of $5,000.
5. The company has been able to invest excess funds at 10% per year.

Required:

Should Georgetown, Inc. discontinue the baseball equipment line? Support your answer with appropriate calculations and qualitative arguments.

14-8. CMA Problem: Relevant Cost for Special Order. Jenco, Inc., manufactures a combination fertilizer/weed-killer under the name Fertikil. This is the only product Jenco produces at the present time. Fertikil is sold nationwide through normal marketing channels to retail nurseries and garden stores.

Taylor Nursery plans to sell a similar fertilizer/weed-killer compound through its regional nursery chain under its own private label. Taylor has asked Jenco to submit a bid for a 25,000-pound order of the private brand compound. Although the chemical composition of the Taylor compound differs from Fertikil, the manufacturing process is very similar.

The Taylor compound would be produced in 1,000-pound lots. Each lot would require 60 direct-labor hours and the following chemicals:

Chemicals	Quantity in Pounds
CW-3	400
JX-6	300
MZ-8	200
BE-7	100

The first three chemicals (CW-3, JX-6, MZ-8) are all used in the production of Fertikil. BE-7 was used in a compound that Jenco has discontinued. This chemical was not sold or discarded because it does not deteriorate and there have been adequate storage facilities. Jenco could sell BE-7 at the prevailing market price less $0.10 per pound for selling/handling expenses.

Jenco also has on hand a chemical called CN-5, which was manufactured for use in another product that is no longer produced. CN-5, which cannot be used in Fertikil, can be substituted for CW-3 on a one-for-one basis without affecting the quality of the Taylor compound. The quantity of CN-5 in inventory has a salvage value of $500.

Inventory and cost data for the chemicals that can be used to produce the Taylor compound are as shown below:

Raw Material	Pounds in Inventory	Actual Price per Pound When Purchased	Current Market Price per Pound
CW-3	22,000	$0.80	$0.90
JX-6	5,000	0.55	0.60
MZ-8	8,000	1.40	1.60
BE-7	4,000	0.60	0.65
CN-5	5,500	0.75	(salvage)

The current direct-labor rate is $7.00 per hour. The manufacturing overhead rate is established at the beginning of the year and is applied consistently throughout the year using direct-labor hours (DLH) as the base. The predetermined overhead rate for the current year, based on a two-shift capacity of 400,000 total DLH with no overtime, is as follows:

Variable manufacturing overhead	$2.25 per DLH
Fixed manufacturing overhead	3.75 per DLH
Combined rate	$6.00 per DLH

Jenco's production manager reports that the present equipment and facilities are adequate to manufacture the Taylor compound. However, Jenco has been within 800 hours of its two-shift capacity each month for the past several months. If need be, the Taylor compound could be produced on regular time by shifting a portion of Fertikil production to overtime. Jenco's rate for overtime hours is one-and-one-half the regular pay rate of $10.50 per hour. There is no allowance for any overtime premium in the manufacturing overhead rate.

Jenco's standard markup policy for new products is 25% of full manufacturing cost.

Required:

1. Assume Jenco Inc. has decided to submit a bid for a 25,000-pound order of Taylor's new compound. The order must be delivered by the end of the current month. Taylor has indicated that this is a one-time order which will not be repeated. Calculate the lowest price Jenco should bid for the order and not reduce its net income.

2. Without prejudice to your answer to requirement 1, asssume that Taylor Nursery plans to place regular orders for 25,000 pound lots of the new compound during the coming year. Jenco expects the demand for Fertikil to remain about the same in the coming year. Therefore, the recurring orders from Taylor will put Jenco over its two-shift capacity. However, production can be scheduled so that 60% of each Taylor order can be completed during regular hours or Fertikil production could be shifted temporarily to overtime so that the Taylor orders could be produced on regular time. Jenco's production manager has estimated that the prices of all chemicals will stabilize at the current market rates for the coming year and that all other manufacturing costs are expected to be maintained at the same rates or amounts. Calculate the price Jenco Inc. should quote Taylor Nursery for each 25,000 pound lot of the new compound assuming that there will be recurring orders during the coming year.

14-9. CMA Problem: Selecting Best Option for Disposing of an Already Built Machine.
Auer Company had received an order for a piece of special machinery from Jay Company. Just as Auer Company completed the machine, Jay Company declared bankruptcy, defaulted on the order, and forfeited the 10% deposit paid on the selling price of $72,500.

Auer's manufacturing manager identified the costs already incurred in the production of the special machinery for Jay as follows:

Direct materials used		$16,600
Direct labor incurred		21,400
Overhead applied:		
Manufacturing:		
Variable	$10,700	
Fixed	5,350	16,050
Fixed selling and administrative		5,405
Total cost		$59,455

Another company, Kaytell Corp., would be interested in buying the special machinery if it is reworked to Kaytell's specifications. Auer offered to sell the reworked special machinery to Kaytell as a special order for a net price of $68,400. Kaytell has agreed to pay the net price when it takes delivery in two months. The additional identifiable costs to rework the machinery to the specifications of Kaytell are as follows:

Direct materials	$ 6,200
Direct labor	4,200
	$10,400

A second alternative available to Auer is to convert the special machinery to the standard model. The standard model lists for $62,500. The additional identifiable costs to convert the special machinery to the standard model are:

Direct materials	$ 2,850
Direct labor	3,300
	$ 6,150

A third alternative for the Auer Company is to sell, as a special order, the machine as is (e.g., without modification) for a net price of $52,000. However, the potential buyer of the unmodified machine does not want it for sixty days. The buyer offers a $7,000 down-payment with final payment upon delivery.

The following additional information is available regarding Auer's operations:

1. Sales commission rate on sales of standard models is 2%, whereas the sales commission rate on special orders is 3%. All sales commissions are calculated on net sales prices (i.e., list price less cash discount, if any).
2. Normal credit terms for sales of standard models are 2/10, net/30. Customers take the discounts except in rare instances. Credit terms for special orders are negotiated with the customer.
3. The application rates for manufacturing overhead and the fixed selling and administrative costs are as follows:

Manufacturing
    Variable   50% of direct-labor cost
    Fixed   25% of direct-labor cost
Selling and administrative
    Fixed   10% of the total of direct material, direct-labor, and manufacturing overhead costs.

4. Normal time required for rework is one month.
5. A surcharge of 5% of the sales price is placed on all customer requests for minor modifications of standard models.
6. Auer normally sells a sufficient number of standard models for the company to operate at a volume in excess of the break-even point.

Auer does not consider the time value of money in analyses of special orders and projects whenever the time period is less than one year because the effect is not significant.

Required:

1. Determine the dollar contribution each of the three alternatives will add to the Auer Company's before-tax profits.
2. If Kaytell makes Auer a counteroffer, what is the lowest price Auer Co. should accept for the reworked machinery from Kaytell? Explain your answer.
3. Discuss the influence fixed factory overhead cost should have on the sales prices quoted by Auer Company for special orders when:
   a. a firm is operating at or below the break-even point.
   b. a firm's special orders constitute efficient utilization of unused capacity above the break-even volume.

14-10. Bidding Problem Involving Opportunity Costs. The Shorthorn Company can produce two products, Bleus and Bonnets. Using the selling prices, the standard full absorption cost figures, and some standardized selling and administrative costs, the following per-unit profit figures have been estimated:

	Bleus		Bonnets	
Selling price		$20		$21.40
Direct material (at $2/unit of material)	$4.00		$6.00	
Direct labor (at $6/hour)	6.00		3.75	
Variable manufacturing overhead	2.00		1.25	
Fixed manufacturing overhead	1.60		1.00	
Variable selling expense	1.00		5.00	
Fixed selling and administrative	2.40	17	1.50	18.50
Net income		$ 3		$ 2.90

The variable and fixed manufacturing overhead rates were established on the basis of practical capacity of 100,000 direct-labor hours per year. (These rates are $2.00 and $1.60 per labor hour, respectively.) Likewise, the fixed selling and administrative costs were averaged over practical capacity for allocation purposes. The nature of the two products is such that the variable selling and administrative cost is a different rate for the two products.

The company has an opportunity to bid on a government contract that, if won, would be completed in the coming year. The contract is for a specialized product that requires some of the same technology as Bleus and Bonnets. The job would require the following resources:

Material	10,000 units
Labor	30,000 hours

Because of the special nature of this job, extra supervision would be needed. The actual supervision of the job would be done by an experienced supervisor who earns a salary of $20,000 annually. This project would require one-half of her time. The experienced supervisor would be released from one-half of her regular duties and these would be covered by a second-line supervisor earning $15,000 annually. Since the second-line supervisor would have learning involved, two-thirds of his time would be consumed in covering the experienced supervisor's duties. A new supervisor, at $12,000 annually, would be needed to cover the released duties of the second-line supervisor. This new supervisor would have no other duties.

Special tools, costing $8,000, would be needed. These tools normally have a two-year life. It is not likely that there would be any future need for the tools and they could be sold for $1,000 after the contract is finished.

The standard costs were revised at the beginning of the current year to reflect current prices. The actual direct material inventory contained 5,000 units, which were purchased at $1.95 per unit. Direct laborers would be laid off if not needed.

Required:

1. Assume that the market limits the sales of Bleus to 40,000 units yearly and Bonnets to 30,000 units. Prepare an itemized and supported schedule showing the minimum bid the company would have to submit on the government contract in order for total profits to be unaffected.
2. Now assume that there are no market constraints on either product and that the firm would make optimal use of its available labor time. What is the minimum bid the company would have to submit? Note that labor is the only constraint: 100,000 hours.
3. Again assume the market is limited to 40,000 units of Bleus and 30,000 units of Bonnets. Now assume that the government contract would require 50,000 labor hours. What is the minimum bid in this case?

14-11. Opportunity costs and Uncertainty. The HCF Company can produce three products: A, B, and Z. Currently the company is scheduled to produce only A and B. However, an invitation to bid on an order for 5,000 units of Z has been received. Since capacity is not being fully utilized HCF is trying to decide whether to bid and, if so, at what price. You are to prepare some analyses to help in making the decisions.

The following information about each of the products has been obtained:

	A	*B*	*Z*
Selling price/unit	$141	$84	Negotiated
Standards			
Material Q @ $10	3 units	2 units	4 units
Material T @ $4	2 units	2 units	1 unit
Labor @ $12/hour	4 hours	2 hours	5 hours

Variable overhead is applied at $5 per labor hour and fixed at $3.

The production capacity is 100,000 direct-labor hours per month. This represents the capacity for a three-shift schedule. Thus, overtime is not possible. The tentative production for the current month is for 20,000 units of A and 5,000 of B. Employees are not on a guaranteed annual wage and are laid off if production does not equal capacity.

At the beginning of the month 4,000 units of material Q are on hand having been acquired at the standard price of $10 per unit. The prices on Q have gone up to $11 per unit since the last purchase.

Required:

1. What is the minimum bid that HCF should make on the 5,000 units of Z?
2. In addition to the above assume that if products A and B are not supplied as planned in the current month then, in addition to losing the current sale, there is a risk of losing sales in later months to customers who are turned down in the current month. The probability of *additional* lost sales per unit of current sales not supplied depends on the product and is as follows:

Additional	Probability	
Lost Sales	If A	If B
1 unit	20%	50%
2 units	20	20
3 units	25	20
4 units	35	10

Considering this new data what is the minimum bid that HCF should submit?

14-12. Continuation of Chapter Case on Make or Buy. Reconisder the make-or-buy problem of the Heiden Company discussed in the text. The relevant cost of part C, as discussed in the modification of the situation, was rather involved, and this problem allows you to further explore that aspect of the case.

Required:

Determine the relevant cost of part C when the unit sales price of product PDQ2 (with part D) is:

1. $13.00	4. $12.50
2. $14.00	5. $12.00
3. $15.00	

14-13. Evaluating Segments When There Are Joint Products. The Crispy Potato Chip Company's cooking process is such that all chips produced are not of the same quality. Presently the chips are sorted into grade A, which is sold under their own label; grade B, which is sold to the Food City Stores and sold under their label; and grade C, which is sold as a casserole topping. Production statistics have indicated that of the total quantity of potatoes processed, 50% of the chips are grade A, 40% grade B, and 10% grade C. The sorting cannot be done until all production is complete. The results of operations for 19x1 follow:

	Grade A		Grade B		Grade C	
Sales		$150,000		$ 63,000		$ 17,000
Cost of potatoes[1]	$50,000		$40,000		$10,000	
Production costs[1]	30,000	80,000	24,000	64,000	6,000	16,000
Gross margin		$ 70,000		$ (1,000)		$ 1,000
Packing and distribution	$12,000		$10,000		$10,000	
Direct advertising	8,000		0		8,000	
President's salary[2]	7,000	27,000	7,000	17,000	7,000	25,000
Net income		$ 43,000		$(18,000)		$(24,000)

[1]Allocated on basis of production percentages.

[2]Allocated equally.

The company president is disturbed with the $1,000 total net income. Analysis reveals that the packing and distribution costs consisted primarily of the cost of bags and the cost of delivery. All products are delivered separately. The cooking process cannot be changed. Therefore, the production percentages cannot be changed. The results for 19x1 are considered to be typical for a considerable time into the future.

Required:

What action would you recommend with regard to keeping or discontinuing each grade in order to improve profits? Why? Support your answer with any detailed schedules you consider appropriate.

14-14. Adapted CMA Problem Involving Joint Products. The management of Bay Company is considering a proposal to install a third production department within its existing factory building. With the company's present production setup, raw material is passed through Department I to produce materials A and B in equal proportions. Material A is then passed through Department II to yield product C. Material B is presently being sold as is at a price of $20.25 per pound. Product C has a selling price of $100.00 per pound.

The per-pound standard costs currently being used by the Bay Company are as follows:

	Department I (Materials A and B)	Department II (Product C)	(Material B)
Prior department costs	$ 0	$53.03	$13.47
Direct material	20.00	0	0
Direct labor	7.00	12.00	0
Variable overhead	3.00	5.00	0
Fixed overhead:			
Attributable	2.25	2.25	0
Allocated (2/3, 1/3)	1.00	1.00	0
	$33.25	$73.28	$13.47

These standard costs were developed by using an estimated production volume of 200,000 pounds of raw material as the standard volume. The company assigns Department I costs to materials A and B in proportion to their net sales values at the point of separation, computed by deducting subsequent standard production costs from sales prices. The $300,000 of common fixed overhead costs are allocated to the two producing departments on the basis of the space used by the departments.

The proposed Department III would be used to process material B into product D. It is expected that any quantity of product D can be sold for $30.00 per pound. Standard costs per pound under this proposal were developed by using 200,000 pounds of raw material as the standard volume and are as follows:

	Department I (Materials A and B)	Department II (Product C)	Department III (Product D)
Prior department costs	0	$52.80	$13.20
Direct material	$20.00	0	0
Direct labor	7.00	12.00	5.50
Variable overhead	3.00	5.00	2.00
Fixed overhead:			
Attributable	2.25	2.25	1.75
Allocated (1/2, 1/4, 1/4)	0.75	0.75	0.75
	$33.00	$72.80	$23.20

Required:

1. Verify the prior department costs of $53.03 and $13.47 when two departments are in use.
2. Verify the prior department costs of $52.80 and $13.20 when three departments are proposed.
3. Comment on the allocation strategy evidently used to determine the joint cost allocation for the proposed situation. Your comments should be addressed from the view of cost determination for reporting purposes, not for decision-making purposes.
4. If (a) sales and product levels are expected to remain constant in the foreseeable future and (b) there are no foreseeable alternative uses for the available factory space, should the Bay Company install Department III and thereby produce product D? Show calculations to support your answer.

14-15. CMA Problem; Evaluating Payment Methods. Weldon's Bike Shop has been in business for five years. The shop buys medium-to-high-quality bicycles and related bike accessories for resale to customers.

The bike shop has shown profits for the past four years. The projected results for the current year are presented as follows:

Weldon's Bike Shop
Projected Statement of Income
for the Year Ended December 31, 19x8
(000 omitted)

	Dollars	Percent
Sales revenue	$300	100%
Cost of goods sold	180	60
Gross margin	$120	40%
Operating expenses		
Sales commissions	$ 15	5
Fixed expenses		
Advertising	9	3
Salaries	21	7
Rent	18	6
General administration	12	4
Total operating expenses	$ 75	25%
Net income before taxes	$ 45	15
Income taxes (40%)	18	6
Net income	$ 27	9%

The sales figure results from strict cash sales only. No personal checks are accepted, nor are credit or credit card sales made. Ann Weldon, the owner, is now considering accepting the following payment methods in addition to strict cash: (1) personal checks only, (2) bank credit cards only, and (3) both personal checks and bank credit cards. Ann believes that sales will increase if she accepts other payment methods in addition to strict cash. She also realizes that some cash customers will change to a different method of payment if alternative payment methods are available. The following schedule presents Ann Weldon's estimates of how sales will increase under each of the proposed three payment methods and how total sales will be collected under each of the three methods.

		Percentage of Total Sales Paid by		
Alternatives	*Percentage Increase in Sales*	*Cash*	*Check*	*Credit Card*
Payment by check	10%	60%	40%	0
Payment by bank credit card	20%	50%	0	50%
Payment by check and bank credit card	25%	20%	40%	40%

If checks are accepted as a method of payment, approximately 10% of all check sales can be expected to be returned for nonsufficient funds (NSF). One-half of the NSF checks (5% of check sales) would be collectible through a collection agency at a cost of 25% of the amount collected. The remaining one-half of the NSF checks would never be collected. In addition, the merchandise paid for by NSF checks would not be recovered.

Bank credit card sales can be deposited daily as if they were cash. However, the bank charges a 4% discount fee when credit card sales are deposited.

The cost behavior patterns of the existing costs and expenses are expected to be unchanged regardless of the payment method.

Required:

Prepare an analysis that shows the effect each of the proposed payment methods being considered by Weldon's Bike Shop would have on the shop's net income. Based upon your analysis, identify and explain whether Weldon's Bike Shop should accept any of the proposed payment methods in addition to strict cash, and if so, identify the method that should be selected.

14-16. CMA Problem on Selecting Optimal Travel Methods for Employees. G & H Real Estate Agency is a moderate-size company serving a metropolitan area of over one million people. G & H has twenty agents all of whom are free to list any kind of property from vacant land to commercial real estate anywhere in the greater metropolitan and surrounding three-county area. Each agent travels extensively to cover the area served by G & H.

G & H requires all agents to be willing to travel throughout the entire area to list and sell property. To subsidize this travel requirement, the company has a reimbursement policy of $0.25 per mile for all business connected travel. The agents are responsible for all costs associated with the operation of their own automobiles. Last year the average mileage claimed by an agent was 50,000 miles. The number of miles driven are approximatley the same each month, and the agents are reimbursed monthly.

The agents believe that $0.25 per mile reimbursement is not unreasonable. However, they think that it is not adequate considering the wear and tear on the car and the inconvenience of the excessive amount of travel. Many agents believe that the amount of business-related use is so great that two, and sometimes three, automobiles are required to meet their family needs. Further, the automobile used for business travel has to be traded in on an annual basis to avoid major repair costs.

Jack Golden, the president, believes that some of the arguments are legitimate. However, he also senses that some of the agents may have been claiming excess miles during the year. Golden is convinced that the annual mileage use would drop to 42,000 miles per year if the agents were not using their own cars. Therefore, he is considering an agency fleet of automobiles.

Golden asked both International Car Rental and a local automobile dealer, Aron Motor, to present proposals. The proposals are described below.

International Car Rental's Proposal

International presented a lease arrangement with the following requirements:

- G & H would rent twenty automobiles for an entire year at $66 per week per automobile and $0.14 per mile.
- When one of twenty automobiles is in for service, International would provide a replacement at $7 per day and $0.20 per mile. International would absorb all repair and maintenance costs. Normally, an automobile would be out of service only one day at a time, and each automobile can be expected to be out of service twelve days per year.
- Cost of insurance is included in the weekly rental rate.
- G & H would be required to purchase the gasoline for the automobiles at an average cost of $1.50 per gallon. International estimates that G & H should expect to get twenty one miles per gallon.
- International has agreed to collect the rental and mileage fees on a monthly basis.

Aron Motor's Proposal

Aron offered a purchase-buy back arrangement with the following requirements:

- G & H would buy twenty automobiles at $9,000 each. Aron would buy the automobiles back after one year at $4,000 each provided G & H subscribed to Aron's preferred customer maintenance and service plan.
- G & H would have to bring each automobile in once every two months for preventive maintenance and service. The cost to G & H for each service visit would be $50. Aron would provide a loaner automobile at no additional cost. Aron would accept responsibility for any additional repair and maintenance charges.
- G & H would have to purchase insurance at a cost of $200 for each automobile. This would be paid at the begining of the year.
- G & H would purchase a new set of tires after six months at $125 per set.
- G & H also would be responsible for the purchase of gasoline at an average cost of $1.50 per gallon. Aron states that because of proper maintenance, the automobiles will average twenty eight miles per gallon.
- Aron requires that the purchase price of the automobiles be paid in full at the beginning of the year. However, the preventive maintenance service fee would be paid monthly.

Golden is willing to make the decision on the basis of undiscounted cash flows. G & H's offices are open 300 days during the year.

Required:

Calculate an annual before-tax amount for:

1. the current reimbursement practice;
2. the proposal of International Car Rental; and
3. the proposal of Aron Motor

that Jack Golden can use to compare the three alternatives. Based upon the before-tax data, which alternative should Golden accept?

14-17. CMA Problem on Product Line Analysis. Valmar Products is a plumbing supply distributing company that carries the products of several manufacturers. Valmar sells its products to retail plumbing stores and to contractors over the counter. In addition, Valmar places orders for plumbing supplies and related materials for specific building and plumbing contractors directly with the manufacturers' factories. These special orders are sent directly to the contractors from the factories. Valmar bills the contractors for the direct orders and pays the manufacturer after the contractor has paid for the order. All customer orders except the direct shipment orders are filled from Valmar's inventories in its warehouse.

The income statement shown below presents the operating results for the past two fiscal years. In addition, the operating results by product line for the most recent fiscal year are presented below. For internal reporting purposes, the selling expenses, warehouse costs, and other operating expenses are allocated to the product lines on the basis of sales.

Valmar Products
Income Statement
for the Fiscal Years Ended May 31
($000 omitted)

	19x1	19x2
Revenue from sales	$12,000	$10,000
Cost of goods sold	9,810	8,300
Gross margin	$ 2,190	$ 1,700
Operating expenses		
Selling expenses	$ 250	$ 200
Warehouse costs	150	150
Other operating expenses	100	100
Total operating expenses	$ 500	$ 450
Net income from operations	$ 1,690	$ 1,250
Interest expense	250	300
Income before taxes	$ 1,440	$ 950
Income taxes (40%)	576	380
Net income	$ 864	$ 570

Valmar Products
Product-Line Operating Results
for the Fiscal Year Ended May 31,19x2

	Trims and Accessories	Valve and Pipe Fittings	Fixtures	Cash Counter Sales	Direct Shipments	Total
Sales	$2,000	$3,000	$1,000	$1,000	$3,000	$10,000
Cost of sales	1,480	2,445	705	865	2,805	8,300
Gross margin	$ 520	$ 555	$ 295	$ 135	$ 195	$ 1,700
Allocated operating expense	90	135	45	45	135	450
Operating income	$ 430	$ 420	$ 250	$ 90	$ 60	$1,250
Return on sales	21.5%	14.0%	25.0%	9.0%	2.0%	12.5%

Jeremy Lypor, president of Valmar is concerned because the current year's operating results are not up to expectations and have deteriorated from the prior year's results. The operating results by product line indicate that the cash counter sales are marginally profitable and the direct shipment business may not be worth the effort. However, Lypor does not have adequate information with which to make decisions concerning the separate product lines, nor does he have enough information to enable him to decide which lines should be promoted in order to improve the total results.

Statistics regarding the number of orders handled and the average book value of inventory carried in the warehouse were developed at the request of Lypor and are presented in the schedule shown below. In addition, the following information has been developed regarding Valmar's operations:

- Fifty percent of the selling expenses are commissions paid to salespersons on the basis of a flat percentage of sales billed; this same percentage is also paid on all cash counter sales.
- The other operating expenses and the balance of the selling expenses are directly related to the number of orders handled.
- Warehouse expenses are related to the value of inventory in the warehouse.
- Money is borrowed to carry inventory in the warehouse.

	Number of Orders Handled		Average Value of Inventory	
	Quantity	Percent	Amount ($000 omitted)	Percentage
Trims and accessories	1,008	12%	$ 160	10%
Valve and pipe fittings	6,048	72	1,248	78
Fixtures	756	9	160	10
Cash counter sales	—	—	32	2
Direct shipments	588	7	—	—
Totals	8,400	100	$1,600	100

Required:

1. President Lypor has requested that the present product-line statement be reviewed to determine if it can be revised to make it more useful in managing Valmar's business. Prepare a revised product-line statement for Valmar Products and explain all changes that were made in the revised statement.
2. Based upon your revised product-line statement for Valmar Products and the other facts presented in the problem, what advice would you give to President Lypor regarding:
   a. the direct shipment business?
   b. the cash counter sales business?
   c. the other three product lines?
   Explain your response in each case.

14-18. CMA Problem; Evaluating Employment Policies. Valbec Company manufactures and distributes doll houses. The toy industry is a seasonal business. Therefore, a large portion of Valbec's sales occur in the late summer and fall.

The projected sales in units for 19x8 are shown in the following schedule. With a sales price of $10 per unit, the total sales revenue for 19x8 is projected at $1.20 million. Valbec scheduled its production in the past so that finished goods inventory at the end of each month, exclusive of a safety stock of 4,000 doll houses, would equal the next month's sales.

One-half hour of direct-labor time is required to produce each doll house under normal operating conditions. Using the production schedule followed in the past, the total direct-labor hours by month that would be required to meet the 19x8 sales estimate are also shown in the schedule.

Valbec Company
Projected Sales and Planned Production
for the Year Ending December 31, 19x8

	Projected Sales (in units)	Direct-Labor Hours Required[a]
January	8,000	4,000
February	8,000	4,000
March	8,000	4,000
April	8,000	4,000
May	8,000	5,000
June	10,000	6,000
July	12,000	6,000
August	12,000	6,500
September	13,000	6,500
October	13,000	6,000
November	12,000	4,000
December	8,000	4,000[b]
Total	120,000 units	60,000 hours

[a]This schedule does not incorporate any additional direct-labor hours resulting from inefficiencies.

[b]Sales for January 19x9 are projected at 8,000 units.

The production schedule followed in the past requires the scheduling of overtime hours for any production over 8,000 units (4,000 direct labor hours) in one month. Although the use of overtime is feasible, the Valbec management has decided that it should consider two other possible alternatives: (1) hire temporary help from an agency during the peak months or (2) expand its labor force and adopt a level production schedule. The use of a second shift was not considered because management believed the community would not support this alternative.

Factory employees are paid $6.00 per hour for regular time; the fringe benefits average 20% of regular pay. For hours worked in excess of 4,000 hours per month, employees receive time and one-half; however, fringe benefits only average 10% on these additional wages. Past experience has shown that labor inefficiencies do occur during overtime at a rate equal to 5% of the overtime hours; this 5% inefficiency was not included in the direct-labor hour estimates presented in the schedule.

Rather than pay overtime to its regular labor force, Valbec could hire temporary employees when production exceeds 8,000 units per month. The temporary workers can be hired through an agency at the same labor rate of $6.00 per hour, but there would be no fringe-benefit costs. Management estimates that the temporary workers would require 25% more time than the regular employees to produce the doll houses.

If Valbec goes to a level production schedule, the labor force would be expanded. However, no overtime would be required. The same labor rate of $6.00 per hour and fringe-benefit rate of 20% would apply.

The manufacturing facilities have the capacity to produce 18,000 doll houses per month. On-site storage facilities for completed units are adequate. The estimated annual cost of carrying inventory is $1 per unit. Valbec is subject to a 40% income tax rate.

Required:

1. Prepare an analysis that compares the costs associated with each of Valbec Company's three alternatives:
   a. Schedule overtime hours.
   b. Hire temporary workers.
   c. Expand labor force and schedule level production.
2. Identify and discuss briefly the noncost factors and the factors that are difficult to cost that Valbec Company should consider in conjunction with the cost analysis prepared in part 1 before a final decision is made relative to the three alternatives.

14-19. CPA Problem on Evaluating Options for Using Excess Capacity. Marshall Manufacturing, Inc. has produced two products, Z and P, at its Richmond plant for several years. On March 31, 19x3, P was dropped from the product line. Marshall manufactures and sells 50,000 units of Z annually, and this is not expected to change. Unit material and direct labor costs are $12 and $7, respectively.

The Richmond plant is in a leased building; the lease expires June 30, 19x7. Annual rent is $75,000. The lease provides Marshall the right of sublet; all nonremovable leasehold improvements revert to the lessor. At the end of the lease, Marshall intends to close the plant and scrap all equipment.

P has been produced on two assembly lines which occupy 25% of the plant. The assembly lines will have a book value of $135,000 and a remaining useful life of seven years as of June 30, 19x3. This is the only portion of the plant available for alternative uses.

Marshall uses one unit of D to produce one unit of Z. D is purchased under a contract requiring a minimum annual purchase of 5,000 units. The contract expires June 30, 19x7. A list of D unit costs follows:

Annual Purchases (units)	Unit Cost
5,000– 7,499	$2.00
7,500– 19,499	1.95
20,000– 39,999	1.80
35,000– 99,999	1.65
100,000–250,000	1.35

Alternatives are available for using the space previously used to manufacture P. Some may be used in combination. All can be implemented by June 30, 19x3. Should no action be taken, the plant is expected to operate profitably, and manufacturing overhead is not expected to differ materially from past years when P was manufactured. Following are the alternatives:

1. Sell the two P assembly lines for $70,000. The purchaser will buy the equipment only if both lines can be acquired. The purchaser will pay all removal and transportation costs.
2. Sublet the floor space for an annual rate of $12,100. The lease will require that the equipment be removed (cost nominal) and leasehold improvements costing $38,000 be

installed. Indirect costs are expected to increase $3,500 annually as a result of the sublease.

3. Convert one or both P assembly lines to produce D at a cost of $45,500 for each line. The converted lines will have a remaining useful life of ten years. Each modified line can produce any number of units of D up to a maximum of 37,000 units at a unit direct material and direct labor cost of $0.10 and $0.25, respectively. Annual manufacturing overhead is expected to increase from $550,000 to $562,000 if one line is converted and to $566,000 if both lines are converted.

Required:

Prepare a schedule to analyze the best utilization of the following alternatives for the four years ended June 30, 19x7. *Ignore income taxes and the time value of money.*

1. Continue to purchase D; sell equipment; rent space.
2. Continue to purchase D; sell equipment.
3. Produce D on two assembly lines; purchase D as needed.
4. Produce D on one assembly line; purchase D as needed.

14-20. Continuation of Problem 13-13 (Step-Fixed Costs). In addition to the facts in problem 13-13, assume the Pediatrics Department operated at 100% capacity during 190 days for the past year. It is estimated that during 175 of these capacity days the demand averaged 37 patients more than capacity and even went as high as 40 patients more on some days. The hospital has an additional 40 beds available for rent for the year ending June 30, 19x4.

Required:

Assuming that patient demand, revenue per patient day, cost per patient day, cost per bed, and employee salary rates for the year ending June 30, 19x4 remain the same as for the year ended June 30, 19x3, should the Pediatrics Department rent the additional 40 beds?

CHAPTER 15

Capital Budgeting

In the last three chapters we examined some techniques that provide data which are useful in making short-run plans and decisions. A project that has a potential effect over several years requires a more complex analysis than a short-run project. **Capital budgeting** is the process of making decisions that would commit capital funds to long-lived projects. In this and the next chapter we will explore various approaches to making these decisions as well as the limitations and problems of the approaches, the data generation problems, and the role of the accountant in the implementation process.

As with any quantitative tool, capital budgeting methods *do not* have the capacity to consider *all* aspects of a decision. The methods to be discussed represent approaches to capturing those aspects of the decision that are capable of being measured in financial terms and reducing them to some index that can be used as *input* to the decision. Many important considerations may either be incapable of being measured or of being measured in financial terms. For example, the impact of a given project on employee morale may be important to the decision but not measurable. Thus, it must be emphasized that the methods to be discussed result in inputs to the decision and not in a decision itself.

In this chapter we will first examine the major differences between operating budgeting and capital budgeting. Then we will discuss some capital budgeting tools that do not consider the time value of money and some that do. Those that do not consider the time value of money include the accounting rate of return, the payback period, and the payback reciprocal. Those that do consider the time value of money include the discounted payback, the net present value index, the profitability index, and the internal rate of return. We will also discuss the influence of income taxes on capital allocation decisions.

Capital versus Operating Budgets

Operating budgets, as discussed in Chapter 12, are financial representations of the firm's plans for the year. Such budgets provide an early warning of problems that will result if the operations occur as forecasted and, thus, facilitate taking actions to prevent their occurrence. Operating budgets also provide standards against which the effectiveness and efficiency of management might be evaluated.

In contrast, capital budgeting tools provide some indexes that can be used when deciding whether to commit capital to long-run projects. Sometimes, there will be limited capital available and several projects may be competing for the limited funds. The capital constraint may be due to limited funds that are available for investment and/or a limited activity to generate new funds in the capital market. In these cases it is common to refer to the limited funds as the budget. However, it is also common to refer to the process of making these capital allocation decisions as capital budgeting even if the funds available are relatively unlimited. By relatively unlimited it is meant that the funds available exceed the sum of the capital required for all of the projects currently under consideration. In fact, it may even be found that decisions regarding project acceptance and project financing are made somewhat independently of each other.

Even though sufficient capital might be available, or can be generated, this does not mean that all projects should be accepted. To be accepted, a project should meet some criterion or criteria. As indicated earlier, there are many objectives that are being simultaneously sought by management and, therefore, there are several criteria that might be used. Now let us consider these criteria and the conditions under which they may prove to be useful.

Evaluation Models That Do Not Consider the Time Value of Money

In evaluating long-run projects, projects that extend through several time periods, it might be argued that consideration *must* given to the time value of money. That is, due to extreme time differences in the flow of cash there is no justification in adding the estimated cash flow in 19x1 to the estimated cash flow in 19x9. The concept of money having time value means that the receipts of $1,000 in each of the years 19x1 and 19x9 are not equivalent. This concept will be discussed more fully in a later section. In spite of this, several techniques are found in use that do not adjust for the time value of money. In this section these techniques will be discussed.

ACCOUNTING RATE OF RETURN. The first of the methods to be considered is the **accounting rate of return (ARR).** At best, ARR is a crude measure of the profitability of a project.[1] To compute the ARR it is necessary to first determine the average *income,* call it $\bar{y}$, that may be attributed to the project. Second, the incremental dollars invested in the project, denoted I, must be known. The ARR can be computed using either the original investment, I, or the *simple* average investment over the life of the project, $\bar{I}$. The latter, $\bar{I}$, would just be the initial investment plus the salvage value, if any, divided by two. Thus:

$$\text{ARR} = \frac{\bar{y}}{I} \text{ or } \frac{\bar{y}}{\bar{I}} \qquad (15\text{-}1)$$

[1] In a survey of large firms, it was found that 4% of them use accounting rate of return as their only capital budgeting method and 56% of the firms use it with one or more other methods. See: L.D. Schall, G.L. Sundem, and W.R. Geijsbeek, Jr. "Survey and Analysis of Capital Budgeting Methods," *The Journal of Finance* (March 1978), pp. 281–287.

To illustrate this and the other tools in this chapter, assume that the Orange Company is considering the purchase of a $100,000 machine that would increase production capacity by 10,000 units per year. Each unit of the product sells for $6.00 and the company is sure that the market is large enough to consume the additional 10,000 units during each year of the four-year life of the machine. It is estimated that there will be no salvage value of the machine at the end of its useful life. The variable costs total $2.00 per unit and the sum-of-years-digits depreciation method will be used.

The projected incremental income from this project is computed in Exhibit 15.1. The average income is $15,000, $60,000 ÷ 4, and the simple average investment is $50,000, $100,000 ÷ 2. Therefore, the ARR is:

$$\text{ARR} = \frac{\$\ 15,000}{\$100,000} = 15\% \text{ or } \frac{\$15,000}{\$50,000} = 30\%$$

Both methods of computing the ARR ignore the time value of money. Further, the first alternative completely ignores the recovery of the investment throughout the life of the project. That is, it assumes the $100,000 is invested in the project during each year. In reality, the investment is being recovered gradually throughout the project's life. The second method accounts for this recovery in a very simplistic manner.

PAYBACK PERIOD. A second evaluation method is the payback period. The **payback period (PB)** is the amount of time needed to recoup the initial incremental investment that is required for the project. If the incremental *cash flow* generated by the project is the *same* in each future period, call it C, then the payback period can be computed via a formula:

$$\text{PB} = \frac{I}{C} \qquad \text{\small investment} \atop \text{\small set payments} \tag{15-2}$$

Care must be exercised to divide by the cash flow, not the income, since the goal is to recoup the investment. For the project being considered by the Orange Company note that C is $40,000. This assumes that all revenues are collected in the period of recognition and all variable costs requiring cash are paid for in the period

---

Exhibit 15.1   Orange Company Incremental Income for Proposed Machine Purchase

	Year 1	Year 2	Year 3	Year 4	Total
Revenue	$60,000	$60,000	$60,000	$60,000	$240,000
Variable cost	20,000	20,000	20,000	20,000	80,000
Contribution margin	$40,000	$40,000	$40,000	$40,000	$160,000
Depreciation	40,000	30,000	20,000	10,000	100,000
Net income	$ 0	$10,000	$20,000	$30,000	$ 60,000

of recognition. Further, note that depreciation is not included in C. Depreciation is just the proration of the original investment over the periods benefiting from the machine. Then:

$$PB = \frac{\$100,000}{\$\ 40,000} = 2.5 \text{ years}$$

Should the period *cash flows be uneven*, then a formula cannot be applied. To illustrate the mechanics in such a case assume that the expenses in the Orange Company problem are to be paid for in the period of recognition, but that the revenues are collected as follows:

Year	Collections	Collections less Disbursements	Cumulative Cash Flow
1	$ 40,000	$ 20,000	$ 20,000
2	70,000	50,000	70,000
3	60,000	40,000	110,000
4	70,000	50,000	160,000
	$240,000	$160,000	

As you can see, the $100,000 investment is not fully recovered until sometime in the third year. If it is assumed that cash flows occur evenly throughout the year, then three-fourths of the third year will be needed to collect the remaining $30,000 needed to be recovered after the elapse of two years. Thus:

$$PB = 2 + \frac{\$30,000}{\$40,000} = 2\frac{3}{4}$$

In evaluating the usefulness of the payback period it should be noted that it is a valuable index when cash position is a critical concern. A manager's or a firm's utility function may be such that a project which returns its investment quicker than another project might be preferred, even if the latter might be expected to ultimately return a greater amount. The more distant a cash flow is from the present time, the smaller the chance that a manager may perceive of it materializing.

On the other hand, the payback period ignores the time value of money and the returns that occur *after* the payback time. To illustrate the latter point, note that the project in Exhibit 15.1 would have a payback of 2.5 years even if the cash flows would continue for another 6 years. That is, the payback periods for the original four-year project and the modified ten-year project would suggest indifference between them.

Nevertheless, the payback period is used frequently in making capital allocation decisions. It may be used in combination with the other tools to be discussed in this chapter rather than being used as a single-selection criterion.[2] For example, some maximum payback time may be set as an initial threshold. Any project that does not meet this criterion will be eliminated immediately. Those that do meet the criterion are then subjected to further analysis.

---

[2]In the survey mentioned in footnote 1, it was found that 2% of the firms used payback as their only capital budgeting method and 72% of the firms use it with one or more other methods.

PAYBACK RECIPROCAL. The final method of evaluation to be considered in the set of methods that ignore the time value of money is the **payback reciprocal.** The payback reciprocal (PR) is:

$$PR = \frac{1}{PB} \qquad\qquad (15\text{-}3)$$

For the original project of the Orange Company:

$$PR = \frac{1}{2.5} = 0.40$$

This index came into prominence prior to the existence of computer software that makes it possible to conveniently compute the internal rate of return (discussed later). Under certain conditions it has been shown that the payback reciprocal is a reasonably good estimator of the internal rate of return.

In fact, both the accounting rate of return and the payback reciprocal can be considered as crude estimates of the internal rate of return. However, when the life of the project is at least *double* the payback period, then the payback reciprocal is the better of the two as an estimate of the internal rate. Conversely, if the life is less than twice the payback period, then the accounting rate of return (using average investment) is the better of the two estimators.[3] In the Orange Company case, the project's life is four years, which is less than twice the payback period (2.5 years). Thus, the accounting rate of return of 30% will be a better estimate of the internal rate of return in this case.

Evaluation Methods That Do Consider the Time Value of Money

Before considering evaluation tools that incorporate the **time value of money,** there will be a review of what is meant by this concept. If you already feel comfortable with the meaning of the time value of money, then you may want to skip the review part of this section. Making use of this concept, there will be an examination of the discounted payback, the net present value index, the profitability index, and the internal rate of return. The section concludes with a case that illustrates some problems that can be encountered in using these tools to rank order the desirability of the projects.

REVIEW OF CONCEPT OF TIME VALUE OF MONEY.[4] Money has time value because of its ability to earn interest (either explicitly or implicitly). Suppose you can invest money to earn 10% compound annually (that is, once each year the interest is paid and becomes part of the principal for the next year). If you can invest now at 10% then you should *prefer* the immediate receipt of $1,000 to a receipt of $1,000 five years from now. If you have this preference, then it is inter-

---

[3]This conclusion was derived in M. Gordon, "Payoff Period and Rate of Profit," *Journal of Business* (October 1955), pp. 253–260.

[4]This subsection may be skipped if you already feel comfortable with the concept of the time value of money.

esting to ask how many dollars you would have to receive five years from now to cause you to be indifferent between that amount and an immediate receipt of $1,000. The so-called *future amount, F,* provides the answer. If you received the $1,000 now it would accumulate to $1,100 one year from now:

$$F_1 = \$1,000(1.10) = \$1,100$$

Then the $1,100 would become the principal for the second year and at the end of year 2 you would have $1,210:

$$F_2 = F_1(1.10) = [\$1,000(1.10)](1.10) = \$1,000(1.10)^2$$
$$= \$1,000(1.21) = \$1,210$$

Continuing this, the amount at the end of year 5 would be:

$$F_5 = \$1,000(1.10)^5 = \$1,000(1.61051) = \$1,610.51$$

Thus, with a 10% interest rate, you would be indifferent between the current receipt of $1,000 and the receipt of $1,610.51 five years from now. It should be noted that this conclusion only considers the value of interest and not other values you have. For example, if you would use the $1,000 to go to the current Olympic games, then no amount received five years from now would make you indifferent. It would be too late to go. In making these statements there is an assumption that it is not possible to borrow the money at 10% interest with a five year *delay* in making any payments.

To generalize this discussion, define:

P = Present amount
F = Future amount
i = Interest rate per period
n = Number of periods

Then:

$$F = P(1 + i)^n \tag{15-4}$$

Illustrating, suppose you were to invest $1,000 now in a two-year time certificate at 12% compounded quarterly. Then:

n = number of *quarters* = $2 \times 4 = 8$

i = *quarterly* interest rate = $0.12 \div 4 = 0.03$

F = $\$1,000(1 + 0.03)^8 = \$1,000(1.26677) = \$1,266.77$

Now, suppose you are told that you will receive F dollars at the end of period n and that your interest rate per period is i. How much would you be willing to accept now to be indifferent with the future receipt? Just solve equation (15-4) for P:

$$P = \frac{F}{(1 + i)^n} \tag{15-5}$$

Let

$$p_{i,n} = 1/(1 + i)^n$$

Then:

$$P = p_{i,n} \times F \tag{15-6}$$

Table A.2 in the appendix at the end of the book provides an assortment of **present value factors,** $p_{i,n}$. To illustrate the usage of the table and the present value concept, assume that interest can be earned at a 10% rate compounded semiannually. Then, $1,000 to be received five years from now would be equivalent to a current receipt of $613.90:

$$n = 2 \times 5 = 10; \ i = 0.10 \div 2 = 0.05$$

$$P = p_{0.05,10}(1,000) = 0.6139(\$1,000) = \$613.90$$

That is, if you had the $613.90 now and invested it for five years at 10% compounded semiannually you would have $1,000 five years from now.

Instead of single payments and receipts there may be recurring cash flows. If these recurring items have the *same* dollar amount and occur at the same point within the period, then the cash flow pattern is called an *annuity*. For example, if you are on a salary and if the deductions do not change, then your take-home pay represents an annuity. Suppose, then, that you have an insurance policy that will pay you $1,000 at the *end* of each year for five years. (This is called an annuity in arrears since the cash flow comes at the end of the period.) If your interest rate is 10% compounded annually, then what lump sum payment would you be willing to settle for now in lieu of such payments? You could discount each item as a single amount:

$$P = 1,000p_{0.1,1} + 1,000p_{0.1,2} + 1,000p_{0.1,3}$$

$$+ 1,000p_{0.1,4} + 1,000p_{0.1,5}$$

However, the problem can be solved in an easier way.

In general the present value of an n-period annuity of D dollars each period is:

$$P = \frac{D}{(1 + i)^1} + \frac{D}{(1 + i)^2} + \frac{D}{(1 + i)^3} + \cdots + \frac{D}{(1 + i)^n}$$

$$P = D\left[\frac{1}{(1 + i)^1} + \frac{1}{(1 + i)^2} + \frac{1}{(1 + i)^3} + \cdots + \frac{1}{(1 + i)^n}\right] \tag{15-7}$$

To find the sum inside the brackets of (15-7) you could just sum the first n entries of the appropriate column in Table A.2. This summing has already been done for you in Table A.3 in the end-of-book appendix.[5]

---

[5]So that we do not have to rely entirely on tables, we are motivated to look for some general way of expressing the sum. (Table storage for a computer program, for example, is not efficient. An easy way to obtain the sum can be derived by first multiplying both sides of equation (15-7) by $(1+i)$:

$$(1 + i)P = D\left[1 + \frac{1}{(1 + i)^1} + \frac{1}{(1 + i)^2} + \cdots + \frac{1}{(1 + i)^{n-1}}\right]$$

Then deducting (15-7) from this equation allows several terms to cancel out and we obtain:

$$(1 + i)P - P = D\left[1 - \frac{1}{(1 + i)^n}\right]$$

Simplifying, we obtain an easily evaluated equation for the sum:

$$P = D\frac{1}{i}\left[1 - \frac{1}{(1 + i)^n}\right] = Da_{i,n}; \text{ where } a_{i,n} = \frac{1}{i}\left[1 - \frac{1}{(1 + i)^n}\right]$$

Returning to our example, the present value of the $1,000 annuity is:

$$P = \$1,000 \times a_{0.1,5} = \$1,000(3.7908) = \$3,790.80 \qquad \text{Se pg 893}$$

That is, if you had the $3,790.80 now and invested it at 10% compounded annually, then you could withdraw $1,000 at the end of each of the five years before your fund would be exhausted. The following calculation verifies this:

Year	Beginning Investment	Interest @ 10%	Principal + Interest	Withdrawal	Ending Investment
1	$3,790.80	$379.08	$4,169.88	$1,000	$3,169.88
2	3,169.88	316.99	3,486.87	1,000	2,486.87
3	2,486.87	248.69	2,735.56	1,000	1,735.56
4	1,735.56	173.56	1,909.12	1,000	909.12
5	909.12	90.91	1,000.03	1,000	0.03

DISCOUNTED PAYBACK. As mentioned earlier, the payback period ignores the time value of money. Once it is recognized that money has a time value, it must be recognized there is an opportunity cost implicit in making an investment—the cost that would have been avoided if the capital had not been needed for the project. (If the capital or funds were already available and were used for the project, then the opportunity cost would be the interest that could have been earned via some alternative investment of the funds.) This recognition is the same as saying that you are *not* indifferent to choosing between receiving $1,000 now and $1,000 two years from now.

Such a recognition suggests that when the payback period is computed by using the actual cash flows then the measurements used are *not equivalent*. This can be adjusted for by discounting each of the cash flows back to the present, or by adjusting each period's beginning investment forward to be in dollars that are "time equivalent" to the recovered dollars. Either method converts the cash flows to common measurement units before accounting for the recovered amounts.

If a 10% discount rate is assumed, then the first method results in the following schedule for the Orange Company example introduced earlier:

Year	Cash Flow	$p_{0.1,n}$	Present Value	Cumulative Present Value
1	$40,000	0.9091	$36,364	$ 36,364
2	40,000	0.8264	33,056	69,420
3	40,000	0.7513	30,052	99,472
4	40,000	0.6830	27,320	126,792

As can be seen from examining the last column of this schedule, the recovery, in present value terms, occurs sometime during year 4. Although contradictory to the discounting procedure, assume that the cash flow for year 4 is received at a uniform rate. Then the remaining $528 ($100,000 − $99,472) is recovered after the elapse of 528/27,320 years. Thus, the discounted payback period (DPB) is:

[handwritten margin note: in this system pay is longer since the 100,000 initial investment could have been earning interest all along]

$$DPB = 3 + \frac{528}{27,320} = 3.0193 \text{ years}$$

In comparison with the payback period, the recovery time is increased because of the additional cash needed to recover the cost of the unrecovered investment which was ignored by the payback period. Like the payback, however, the discounted payback ignores what happens after the payback time.

NET PRESENT VALUE. A second analytical approach that considers the time value of money is a **net present value (NPV)** analysis.[6] It is similar to a revenue and expense analysis except that all items are adjusted to reflect equivalent cash flows at some chosen point in time (usually the time is the present although it does not have to be). A prerequisite for doing this is a discount rate. Possibilities include the rate of "interest" on the specific capital that will be used, the rate of return from some alternative investment, or the weighted cost of capital. The rate used may be adjusted for risk and/or inflation. The choice of the rate is an important issue and this will be discussed in the next chapter. For now, it will be assumed the rate is given.

If the present is picked as the point in time to which all cash flows will be adjusted, if it is assumed that all cash flows occur at year-end, and if a 10% discount rate is assumed, then the net present value of Orange's proposal is:

Present value of incremental contribution margin:

$40,000 \times a_{0.1,4} = \$40,000 \times 3.1699 =$	\$126,796
Incremental investment: $100,000 \times 1.0 =$	(100,000)
Net present value	\$ 26,796

Note, again, that depreciation was not included in the analysis. As stated earlier, depreciation does not represent a cash flow but an amortization of the original cost over the life of the asset. Using both the $100,000 investment and the depreciation would be a double counting.

What does the net present value represent? First, if this figure is positive, it indicates that the cash flow attributed to the project is *more than sufficient* to provide a return equal to the discount rate. In our example the minimum required, or the threshold, was 10%. It is now known that if the project in question has cash returns equal to the projections in Exhibit 15.1, then it has a better than a 10% return. If the net present value turned out to be negative, this would mean that the return on the project is below the discount rate. Assuming a relatively unlimited availability of capital, any project with a positive net present value would be accepted unless there were overriding nonfinancial considerations.

Second, the precise amount of the net present value represents the present value of the difference between the future cash flows and the sum of two items: the incremental investment and interest at the discount rate on the *unrecovered* portion of

---

[6]The survey referenced in footnote 1 found that 2% of the firms used NPV as their only capital budgeting method and 55% use it with one or more other methods.

[handwritten at bottom: PV of (future cash flows − (investment + interest]

that investment. Exhibit 15.2 illustrates this. The excess investment of $39,230 at the end of the project is in terms of year-4 dollars. However, the time point chosen for the net present value analysis was the beginning of year 1. Thus in Exhibit 15.2 it is shown that the present value of $39,230 is $26,794 which is essentially the same as the NPV just obtained.

In addition to determining the appropriate discount rate, another problem that will be encountered in using NPV is the lack of comparability of certain net present value amounts. This problem can arise when assessing the *relative* desirability of two projects that have different incremental investments and/or different lives. A possible tool in the case of different investment sizes is the profitability index discussed in the next section. Other considerations of these situations are deferred to the next chapter.

PROFITABILITY INDEX.   One way of adjusting for differences in the size of the incremental investment is to compute the **profitability index.** To illustrate the problem and the computation, assume that the Orange Company has a second project which is competing for the limited funds. Call the one in Exhibit 15.1 project A and the second one project B. Project B requires an incremental investment of $300,000, has a life of four years and an annual incremental cash flow of $110,000. The net present value, at 10%, is:

Present value of incremental cash flow:
$110,000 \times a_{0.10,4} = $110,000 \times 3.1699$ $348,689
Incremental investment   (300,000)
    Net present value $ 48,689

If the $48,689 net present value of project B is compared with the $26,796 of project A, then B appears to be better. However, doing this ignores the difference in the investment requirements. The profitability index, *PI,* relates the present value of the *future* net cash flows (excludes the inital investment and is denoted *PVF*) to the investment, *I:*

Exhibit 15.2   Demonstration of the Meaning of the NPV Figure

Year	Beginning Investment	Interest @ 10%	Investment plus Interest	Recovery	Ending Investment
1	($100,000)	($10,000)	($110,000)	$40,000	($70,000)
2	(70,000)	(7,000)	(77,000)	40,000	(37,000)
3	(37,000)	(3,700)	(40,700)	40,000	(700)
4	(700)	(70)	(770)	40,000	39,230*

*Present value of $39,230 = $39,230 \times p_{0.1, 4} = $39,230(0.683) = $26,794$. (The $2.00 difference between $26,794 and the NPV of $26,976 is due to rounding.)

$$PI = \frac{PVF}{I} \tag{15-8}$$

Then, the *PI* for projects *A* and *B* are:

$$PI_A = \frac{\$126,796}{\$100,000} = 1.26796; \quad PI_B = \frac{\$348,689}{\$300,000} = 1.1623$$

This comparison indicates that, on a dollar-for-dollar basis, project A is more profitable than project B. But, for reasons to be discussed later, let's stop short of saying that A should be preferred to B.

INTERNAL RATE OF RETURN. If an investment, or a project, enables cash to be recovered in excess of the original outlay, then it is said that the investment or project has earned a return. The internal rate of return is a rate of return computed on the *unrecovered* investment. To explain, think about this rate of return as the rate that you "pay" yourself as a dividend on your investment. If you invested $1,000 at the beginning of the year and received $1,150 back at the end of the year, then the excess return over the investment is $150 and the rate is 15% ($150 ÷ $1,000).

Consider another example. If interest is compounded annually and if an investment of $1,000 now returns $1,210 two years from now, the rate of interest is 10%. It is not 21% because this was a two-year investment and it is conventional to state interest rates at annual rates. Further, since interest is to be paid annually you must ask yourself what rate the $210 excess will permit you to pay yourself at the end of each year. Deferring for a moment how the 10% rate was determined, note that if you pay yourself 10% at the end of year one ($100), you start year 2 with a $1,100 investment (since you do not actually have the cash to permit this payment, it can be considered as an additional investment at the beginning of year 2). Then pay yourself another 10% ($110) for the second-year investment. Note that the $1,210 was just sufficient to recover the original investment and the self-paid interest ($1,000 + $100 + $110).

The **internal rate of return (IRR)** will be defined as the maximum "dividend" rate we can pay ourselves so that the future cash flows of a project will be just sufficient to cover the original investment and the self-paid dividends on the unrecovered portion of the investment.[7] Computationally, the IRR can be determined by finding the discount rate, *i*, that will cause the present value of the future cash flows to be exactly equal to the original investment.

For the preceding two-year example, there is a lump sum receipt at the end of year 2. Discount this receipt back at a rate *i* such that it is equal to the investment:

$$\$1,000 = \$1,210 \times p_{i,2}$$

$$p_{i,2} = \frac{\$1,000}{\$1,210} = 0.8264$$

Looking in Table A.2, you want to find the rate i that gives a $p_{i,2}$ value of 0.8264. It can be seen that this rate is 10% and, thus, is the IRR.

Next, consider the Orange Company's project in Exhibit 15.1. To find the IRR on that project you, again, will need to find the rate, i, that will set the present value of the $40,000 annuity equal to the investment:

$$\$100,000 = \$40,000 \times a_{i,4}$$

$$a_{i,4} = 2.5$$

Looking on line 4 in Table A.3 you will find that 2.5 implies an interest rate between 21% and 22%. Linear interpolation would result in a figure of 21.863%. Since the expression for $a_{i,n}$ is not linear, linear interpolation is not precise. A more precise return is 21.862%. (You need not be concerned about being this precise. A precise rate has been found because of the following illustration.) To illustrate the validity of this result consider Exhibit 15.3. Note that the estimated annual cash flow of $40,000 is sufficient to return the $100,000 investment and to pay a dividend of 21.862% on the unrecovered investment.

In general, projects will have fluctuating cash flows. In these cases, there is no general way to determine the IRR except by trial and error. That is, you pick a trial interest rate and if the present value of the cash flow using the chosen rate exceeds the investment, then you pick a higher rate and try again. Conversely, you pick a lower rate if the present value of the cash flows is lower than the investment. It is not too difficult to devise a computer algorithm to do this, however. Once the IRR is determined it would be compared with some critical value to determine if the project is desirable. This critical value should be the same rate that would be used for the NPV analysis. (Possibilities for critical rates are discussed in Chapter 16.)

ILLUSTRATION OF THE INVESTMENT RANKING PROBLEMS. None of these evaluation techniques are free from problems when used to rank order the "desirability" of two or more investments. In this section there is a demonstration of the care that must be used in interpreting the various capital budgeting methods. Data about the four projects that will be considered are in Exhibit 15.4.

Exhibit 15.3   Demonstration of the Meaning of the Internal Rate of Return

Year	Beginning Investment	Interest @ 0.21862	Beginning Investment + Interest	Recovery	Ending Investment
1	$100,000	$21,862	$121,862	$40,000	$81,862
2	81,862	17,897	99,759	40,000	59,759
3	59,759	13,065	72,824	40,000	32,824
4	32,824	7,176	40,000	40,000	0

Exhibit 15.4   Project Information

| | Required | Cash Returns | | |
Project	Investment	Year 1	Year 2	Year 3
A	$ 8,000	$4,000	$4,000	$4,000
B	10,000	5,200	5,200	2,600
C	4,000	2,100	2,100	2,100
D	8,000	2,000	2,000	8,000

Exhibit 15.5 displays the results of the payback (PB), discounted payback (DPB), net present value at 10% (NPV @ 10%), profitability index (PI @ 10%), and internal rate of return (IRR) computations. Note that, with one exception, each of the techniques yields a different ranking of the projects. The PI @ 10% and the IRR produced identical rankings in this case but it is not always true that these two tools will yield the same ranking.

To illustrate the significance of the problem created by the ranking differences, suppose that new investment capital is limited to $22,000. How will you allocate these funds? If you follow the rankings, your project selection will depend on the tool used. Following are the results using each of the five indexes:

PB: Adopt C, B, A (capital required = $22,000)
DPB: Adopt C, A, B (capital required = $22,000)
NPV @ 10%:   Adopt A, D, C (capital required = $20,000)
PI @ 10% and IRR: Adopt C, A, D (capital required = $20,000)

What is the correct set of projects to adopt? The answer to this depends on the decision maker's objectives. More will be said about this in the next chapter.

Exhibit 15.5   Project Evaluation Indexes* (Ranking in Parentheses)

Project	PB	DPB	NPV @ 10%	PI @ 10%	Approximate IRR
A	2.00 (3)	2.35 (2)	$1,947.60 (1)	1.243 (2)	23.4 (2)
B	1.92 (2)	2.50 (3)	977.98 (4)	1.098 (4)	16.1 (4)
C	1.90 (1)	2.23 (1)	1,222.49 (3)	1.306 (1)	26.7 (1)
D	2.50 (4)	2.75 (4)	1,481.40 (2)	1.185 (3)	18.0 (3)

*You are asked to verify some of these results in Problems 15-1 and 15-3.

Depending on the situation and on how the results of these tools are used, *the user* may be making some implicit assumptions. You should be aware of these so that you can do alternative analyses if your implicit assumptions are not justified. The *possible* assumptions are about what must be done with the cash flows (proceeds) that are generated by an investment. Some authors, for example, state that NPV assumes the proceeds are reinvested at the discount rate and that IRR assumes they are reinvested at the project's IRR. However, it is contended here that no assumption about proceed reinvestment is needed to state that the IRR on project A in Exhibit 15.5 is 23.4% or that its NPV using a 10% discount rate is $1,947.60. To illustrate the absence of an assumption consider, again, Exhibits 15.2 and 15.3. Note that the demonstrations in those exhibits never reinvested the proceeds. However, some assumptions are implicit if NPV and IRR are used as follows. Suppose it is stated that project A is preferred to project B because A's NPV is higher or because A's IRR is higher. The distinctions between the two uses of the indexes and the reasons for the difference in the assumptions are developed in the following paragraphs.

When alternatives are compared for purposes of finding an optimal investment portfolio there is no need to be concerned about what will be done with the total funds available. Note that when used as a factual statement about a project, both the NPV and the IRR are only meaningfully related to *unrecovered investment* in the project—not the original investment. For example, suppose that the choices are limited to projects A and D in Exhibit 15.4. Note that their investment requirements are the same, $8,000. Further, the total *undiscounted* future cash flows are the same, $12,000. When it is stated that A is preferred to D, presumably it is because the investment is recovered faster and some other returns can be gained that are not possible with D. When the NPV figures of the project are used to reflect the magnitude of this preference, there is, in effect, the assumption that the *proceeds* are invested so that they generate a NPV of zero. That is, the original project plus the reinvestment projects still yields a total NPV of $1,947.60. This can be the case only if the reinvestment projects have an NPV of zero. An NPV of zero implies a return equal to the discount rate. Likewise, a project's internal rate of return can be used as *the* criterion for portfolio selection decisions only if there is a willingness to assume that the proceeds of the project are reinvested at its IRR. If any of these assumptions are unlikely, then there is no justification in using the NPV or IRR without making an adjustment for the actual returns from the proceeds.

A similar assumption is implicit when there is a comparison of projects with unequal investment sizes, such as A and C in Exhibit 15.4. Note in Exhibit 15.5 that if the projects' NPV are used as the selection criterion, A is preferred to C. Again, if the NPV figures are not adjusted, there is an assumption that the $4,000 difference in the cost of the two projects can be invested at the discount rate and that the proceeds from either product are invested at the discount rate. Note that the NPV figures indicate A is preferred to C because investing $8,000 in A is better than investing $4,000 in C plus $4,000 at 10%. Also note that if the IRR is used as the selection criterion, C is preferred to A. Implicit in this is that the *difference* of

$4,000 can be invested at C's rate of return. Again, if any of these assumptions are not justified there would need to be an alternative analysis using adjusted cash flows.

To illustrate an adjustment technique, let us assume that the proceeds from Project A can be invested at 5%. Then the cash flows would be as follows:

	Current	*Year 1*	*Year 2*	*Year 3*
Original investment in project A	($8,000)	0	0	0
Proceeds from original investment	0	$4,000	$4,000	$ 4,000
Reinvestment of year one's proceeds	0	(4,000)	200	4,200[b]
Reinvestment of year two's proceeds	0	0	(4,200)[a]	4,410[b]
Net cash flow	($8,000)	0	0	$12,610

[a]Reinvestment of $4,000 from project A plus $200 from reinvestment income.

[b]There is no return until the principal is recovered. Since the analysis covers a three-year period, assume the principal of the reinvestment projects is returned at the end of year 3.

The adjusted NPV with this reinvestment assumption is:

Present value of cash flow: $12,610 × 0.7513	9,473.89
Original investment	(8,000.00)
NPV	$1,473.89

Compare this result with the NPV of project A in Exhibit 15.5 ($1,947.60). You can also find the internal rate of return on the portfolio of project A plus reinvestments via:

$$\$12,610 \times p_{i,3} = \$8,000$$

$$p_{i,3} = 0.6344$$

The value of i that would give the preceding $p_{i,3}$ value is 15.4% compared with 23.4% for project A. That is, the return on the portfolio is 15.4%. The portfolio includes project A, which earns 23.4%.

Effect of Income Taxes

One of the major expenses of a firm is the income tax. Obviously, it is necessary to include its effect in capital budgeting analyses. Often a decision hinges on the tax implications. In many cases, the tax laws themselves are created to provide the added incentive for organizations to expend the efforts to do some things that are considered to be in the best national interests. This expense must be treated differently than others because of the complexities of its determination. Tax laws generally follow accrual accounting principles rather than a system of cash receipts and disbursements.

Before considering the impact of income taxes on specific evaluation tools, let us consider the general effects. Except for the accounting rate of return, all of the tools discussed in this chapter make use of cash flows. Taxes are cash flows and the amounts are based on taxable income which is not based on cash flows of the current period. In capital budgeting it is frequently convenient to consider the after-tax cash flow on an item-by-item basis. The following general possibilities exist. If the tax rate is T and if the *pre*-tax cash flow is C (which may be either positive or negative), then the after-tax cash flow is $(1 - T)C$ so long as the timing and amount of C for tax purposes are essentially the same as the timing and amount of the related cash flow. For example, in the Orange Company case of Exhibit 15.1 the $60,000 cash received as revenue will yield $36,000 after taxes if the tax rate is 40% [$60,000(1 - 0.4)]. This is because there is a $60,000 cash inflow reduced by the increase in taxes due to that inflow. Likewise, the after-tax cash outflow for the variable costs of Exhibit 15.1 is $12,000 [$20,000(1 - 0.4)].

If C is not a direct input for the tax computation, then the after-tax cash flow is also equal to C. For example, if the $60,000 was a return from a tax-free bond, then its receipt would give rise to no taxes. Similarly, if the $20,000 of variable costs were not deductible for tax purposes, the after-tax cash outflow would be $20,000. Examples of cash outflows that are not *directly* deductible for tax purposes are expenditures that must be capitalized such as the $100,000 for the machine in the Orange Company case.

One other class of items exists. These are the items that are included for tax purposes but are not the result of an immediate cash flow. Depreciation is the major example of this type of item. Although depreciation reduces income and, in turn, reduces income taxes, there is no direct cash flow for the item itself. More generally, let N be a noncash, but reportable item for tax purposes. As with C, N can either be positive or negative, representing a taxable item or a deductible item, respectively. The after-tax cash flow is now $N(0 - T)$. Note that this expression has been set up in a manner parallel with the reportable cash items. That is, the zero inside the parenthesis indicates there was a direct cash flow equal to zero times N. Then there is the tax effect of $N(-T)$. Note that if N is negative, a tax-deductible item, then $N(-T)$ is positive, indicating a cash savings due to taxes.

Again, reconsider the proposed machine in the Orange Company case. In Exhibit 15.1, depreciation was computed using the sum-of-years-digits method and amounted to $40,000 in year 1. *If* that amount could be deducted for income tax purposes, then its deduction would reduce taxes by $16,000 [-$40,000(-0.4)]. However, this amount is determined as a result of applying accounting principles of depreciation. Effective October 1, 1981, the federal income tax law was modified. As a result of the modification it is less likely that acceptable accounting methods of depreciation will parallel acceptable methods for income tax purposes.

Let us briefly consider a taxpayer's options for "depreciation" under the tax code. It should be emphasized that these options are for tax purposes only and *do not dictate* what should be done for other reporting purposes. For tax purposes, the depreciation methods are limited to straight line (but over IRS specified recovery periods, not to be confused with useful life), units of production, and a specially defined accelerated method.[8] See Table A.4 in the appendix for details of the options.

The **Accelerated Cost Recovery System (ACRS)** requires assets (public utilities excepted) to be classified into one of three classes; three-year, five-year, or eighteen-year. The classification system is such that the useful life of an asset is usually longer than the class to which it must be assigned. Tax depreciation under ACRS enables the investment to be recovered over a period shorter than its actual life. Further, an accelerated method is applied using the tax life.

The three classes of assets are as follows:

- **Three-year property:** Autos, light trucks, and research and development equipment.
- **Five-year property:** Most other equipment.
- **Eighteen-year property:** Real property (buildings, for example).

Table A.4, in the appendix, contains the percentage of the original cost that can be recovered. Salvage value is ignored under tax law. For three-year and five-year property the deductions approximate the results of a 150% declining balance method. In effect one-half year's depreciation is allowed for the first year (regardless of time of purchase). There will be no recovery deduction for the year of disposal. The rates for eighteen-year property approximate the 175% declining balance rate.

To illustrate, the machine in the Orange Company case will be put into the five-year property class (it is equipment). The tax depreciation and tax reduction under the accelerated option of ACRS would be:

Recovery Year	Rate (from Table A.4)	Cost	Cost Recovery	Tax Reduction @ 40%
1	15%	$100,000	$15,000	$6,000
2	22	100,000	22,000	8,800
3	21	100,000	21,000	8,400
4	21	100,000	21,000	8,400
5	21	100,000	21,000	8,400

[8]Additional provisions in the tax code permit an investment tax credit for qualifying property. The rate is dependent on the recovery life. This is allowed in the year of acquisition and is subject to recapture depending on how long the asset is held. Also allowed in the tax code is an immediate write-off of up to $5,000 of certain assets that would otherwise have to be capitalized. The investment tax credit would not be allowed on the assets expensed under this provision. This text will not consider these two provisions, but you are advised to incorporate them into a capital investment analysis.

Summarizing the *after-tax* cash flow using the ACRS option:

	Year 1	Year 2	Year 3	Year 4
Revenue: $60,000(1 − 0.4)	$36,000	$36,000	$36,000	$36,000
Variable costs:				
− $20,000(1 − 0.4)	− 12,000	− 12,000	− 12,000	− 12,000
Contribution margin	$24,000	$24,000	$24,000	$24,000
Tax reduction due to				
depreciation	6,000	8,800	8,400	8,400
After-tax cash flow	$30,000	$32,800	$32,400	$32,400

Alternatively, income could have been converted to cash flows as follows:

	Year 1	Year 2	Year 3	Year 4
Contribution margin	$40,000	$40,000	$40,000	$40,000
Cost recovery (depreciation)	15,000	22,000	21,000	21,000
Net income before tax	$25,000	$18,000	$19,000	$19,000
Tax @ 40%	10,000	7,200	7,600	7,600
After-tax income	$15,000	$10,800	$11,400	$11,400
Add effect of depreciation				
(it was not a cash flow)	15,000	22,000	21,000	21,000
After-tax cash flow	$30,000	$32,800	$32,400	$32,400

Now let us consider the effect of the income tax on the specific capital budgeting methods.

ACCOUNTING RATE OF RETURN AFTER TAXES. The effect of the income tax on the ARR is rather simple. Now define $\bar{y}$ as the average accounting income *after* taxes. For accounting purposes, the depreciation method would still be SYD and the total depreciation for the four years would be $100,000. The pre-tax total income was computed in Exhibit 15.1 to be $60,000. The matching principle would require the income tax *expense* for the four years combined to be $24,000, 0.4 × $60,000. (Note from the preceding alternative computation that the actual cash outflow for taxes is more, $32,400 = $10,000 + $7,200 + $7,600 + $7,600. However, some of the tax paid would be deferred to a future period for expense purposes.) The average after-tax accounting income is $9,000 ($60,000 − $24,000) ÷ 4, and the after-tax ARR is:

$$\text{ARR (after taxes)} = \frac{\$9,000}{\$100,000} = 9\% \text{ or } \frac{\$9,000}{\$50,000} = 18\%$$

Note that these returns are just $(1 − T)$ times their pretax counterparts.

PAYBACK PERIOD AFTER TAXES. To compute the payback or discounted payback period, just use the after-tax cash flows in lieu of the pretax figures. Thus the after-tax payback period for the Orange project using the accelerated option of ACRS would be computed as follows:

Year	After-Tax Cash Flows	Cumulative
1	$30,000	$ 30,000
2	32,800	62,800
3	32,400	95,200
4	32,400	127,600

$$\text{PB (after tax)} = 3 + \frac{\$100,000 - \$95,200}{\$32,400} = 3.15 \text{ years}$$

Recall that the pretax payback was 2.5 years.

NPV AFTER TAXES. The after-tax NPV is also computed using the after-tax cash flows. There are many ways in which this can be implemented. With the organization of our data for the Orange example, the following is a natural way to derive the results:

	Amount	10% PVF	Present Value
Incremental after-tax cash flow in year 1	$ 30,000	0.9091	$ 27,273
Incremental after-tax cash flow in year 2	32,800	0.8264	27,106
Incremental after-tax cash flow in year 3	32,400	0.7513	24,342
Incremental after-tax cash flow in year 4	32,400	0.6830	22,129
Incremental after-tax cash flow in year 5*	8,400	0.6209	5,216
Investment	(100,000)	1.0000	(100,000)
Net present value			$ 6,066

*With the ACRS option, there is a depreciation deduction of $21,000 that can be taken in year 5 if the machine is not sold. This results in an $8,400 reduction in taxes.

Consideration of taxes reduced the NPV from a pretax amount of $26,796.

IRR AFTER TAXES. The after-tax IRR is just the interest rate, i, that will result in the following equality:

$$30,000p_{i,1} + 32,800p_{i,2} + 32,400 (p_{i,3} + p_{i,4}) + 8,400p_{i,5} = 100,000$$

By a trial-and-error procedure it is deduced that i must be 12.6 and, thus, is the IRR after taxes. This compares to a pretax IRR of 21.862%.

Case To Illustrate the Management of Data in an NPV Analysis

Now let's consider a somewhat more involved case than the previous ones in order to illustrate an efficient management of the analysis. Consider the Brown Company, which acquired a machine two years ago at a cost of $4,200. At that time the machine had an estimated useful life of seven years and no estimated salvage value. The original estimate of the useful life is still considered adequate. The machine is being depreciated using the accelerated option of ACRS for tax purposes, has an annual operating cost of $12,000, and a current disposal value of $2,000. If this machine is kept it is felt that three years from now it will need an overhaul costing $700. The overhaul could be expensed rather than capitalized.

An alternative to this machine is being considered. This new machine would cost $15,000, have a useful life of five years, and operating costs of $8,000 per year. If purchased, the company would use the accelerated option of ACRS for tax purposes. The machine has an estimated salvage value of $1,500 at the end of its useful life. However, the salvage value will be ignored in computing tax depreciation.

Given that the firm's marginal tax rate is 40% and its after-tax discount rate is 10%, what is the optimal course of action based on an NPV analysis? First, find the NPV of the cash flows associated with keeping the old machine. Then do a similar analysis for the new machine. Assume the revenues from either machine would be the same. If so, they are irrelevant to the analysis. Note that both of the NPV figures will be negative as a result of this exclusion. Consequently, the optimal alternative will be the one with the smaller negative amount.

The results are summarized in Exhibit 15.6. A few of the items need an explanation. First, consider the items under "Keep Old." Item 1 is the tax saving from the cost recovery on the old machine if it is kept. The current year would be recovery year number 3. From Table A.4, note that the cost recovery rate would equal 21% for each of the next three years. Since the tax rate is 40%, the tax savings is equal to 40% of the allowable cost recovery. (Note that this is a savings and, therefore, a positive figure.) The present value factor of a three-year annuity at 10% is 2.4868, and the present value of the future tax savings is $877. Operating costs and the overhaul are both tax deductible items. Note that the overhaul comes in year 3 and the present value factor is $p_{0,1,3}$. Of course, as discussed in the previous chapter, the original cost of the old machine is irrelevant to the decision since it is a sunk cost whose incurrence cannot be changed.

Under the "Buy New" option, items 1, 2, and 3 should be obvious. Remember that the salvage value is ignored for tax purposes. Item 4 recognizes that the old machine will be sold now if the new machine is purchased. The current market value would represent a cash flow that does not *directly* influence the income tax. There is a tax on sales of capital assets only to the extent the sales price exceeds the book value. The current book value of the old machine for tax purposes is:

Original cost	$4,200
Accumulated depreciation 4,200(0.15 + 0.22)	1,554
Book value	$2,646

Since the market value of $2,000 is less than the book value, there is a tax loss. The tax loss of $646, rather than the market value, is the *direct* input into the tax computation but it does not represent a cash flow. Therefore, the after-tax cash flow would be $-\$646(0 - 0.4)$. (This assumes that the total taxable income of the firm is still positive so that this item, in fact, reduces the tax liability.)

Exhibit 15.6   Comparative Analysis of Old and New Machines

Keep Old

Item	Amount	PVF	PV
1. Tax Effects of Depreciation			
(4,200 × 0.21)0.4	$ 353	2.4869	$ 877
2. Operating costs −$12,000(1−0.4)	(7,200)	3.7908	(27,294)
3. Overhaul in Year 3			
−700(1−0.4)	(420)	0.7513	(316)
Net Present Value			$(26,733)

Buy New

Item	Amount	PVF	PV
1. Cost	($15,000)	1.0000	($15,000)
2. Operating costs −$8,000(1−0.4)	(4,800)	3.7908	(18,196)
3. Tax Effects of Depreciation			

Year	Rate	Depreciation	Tax Rate			
1	15%	$2,250	0.4	900	0.9091	818
2	22	3,300	0.4	1,320	0.8264	1,091
3	21	3,150	0.4	1,260	0.7513	947
4	21	3,150	0.4	1,260	0.6830	861
5	21	3,150	0.4	1,260	0.6209	782

Item		Amount	PVF	PV
4. Sale of Old Machine				
a. Proceeds		2,000	1.0000	2,000
b. Tax Effects				
Current Market Value	$2,000			
Current Book Value	2,646			
Tax Loss	$ 646			
Tax Reduction at	0.4	258	1.0000	258
5. Salvage Value of New Machine				
a. Proceeds		1,500	0.6209	931
b. Tax Effects				
Year 5 Market Value	$1,500			
Year 5 Book Value	0			
Tax Gain	$1,500			
Tax Increase at	0.4	(600)	0.6209	(373)
Net Present Value				($25,881)*

---

*Optimal decision

Item 5 is similar to item 4. Again, the market value, itself, represents a cash flow with no direct tax effect. The book value for tax purposes would be zero if it is not provided for in the cost recovery method. Because the book value is zero, the tax gain is equal to the market value. The gain will cause the tax liability to be $600 higher at the end of year 5.

Summary

In this chapter we have surveyed some common tools that are used as aids in making capital allocation decisions. You should now be able to interpret, compute, and recognize the limitation of (1) the accounting rate of return, (2) the payback period, (3) the payback reciprocal, (4) the discounted payback period, (5) the NPV technique, and (6) the internal rate of return. Further, you should be able to perform these analyses with the existence of an income tax and to incorporate the relevant cost principles of the previous chapter. The problems that follow will introduce you to some different situations where these tools can be used but the principles of application will be the same as in the chapter.

In the next chapter we will explore, in more depth, some of the major problems of capital allocation. Included will be the issue of selecting a discount rate, how to deal with project comparisons when their lives are unequal, the effect of price level changes, the effects of uncertainty, and more on the method of project selection when there are limited funds available. Other topics will also be discussed.

Key terms of this chapter include:

Capital budgeting
Accounting rate of return
Payback period
Payback reciprocal
Time value of money
Annuity
Present value factor
Discounted payback period
Net present value
Profitability index
Internal rate of return
Accelerated Cost Recovery System (ACRS)

SELF-STUDY PROBLEM. The date is January 1, 19x5, and the Bowling Company is considering the replacement of an old machine that has a book value of $12,000 and a remaining useful life of five years. The remaining recovery life for tax purposes is four years. Annual operating expenses of this machine will be $2,500 per year and, due to various circumstances, will be disbursed as follows:

19x5—$2,500	19x7—$3,000	19x9—$2,000
19x6—$2,000	19x8—$3,000	

The old machine will require an immediate overhaul, which will cost $500 payable at the end of 19x5 and is tax deductible. It has a current scrap value of $8,000 and will have a scrap value of $1,000 at the end of five years. The scrap value is not being provided for in taking depreciation for tax purposes. The ACRS method of depreciation is being used for tax purposes.

The new machine will cost $12,000 and it will have a useful life of five years. Its annual operating expenses will be $500 per year, the disbursements being made in the year of expense. A scrap value of $2,000 is anticipated at the end of 19x9. Straight-line depreciation will be taken for tax purposes (five-year recovery period).

The company has been planning a rearrangement of the factory equipment during 19x7 requiring an estimated cost of $1,500 that would be paid for at the end of the year. If the new machine is purchased, the rearrangement will be done now. The cost would be $1,500 and would be paid at the end of 19x5. Assume that the rearrangement expense is fully deductible for tax purposes in the year in which the rearrangement takes place.

Assume that tax returns are filed on an accrual basis and that the tax rate is 40%. The minimum rate of return is 10% after taxes.

Required:

Prepare an analysis, using the NPV technique, to aid the company in making its decision.

Solution to Self-Study Problem

One of the keys to this problem is to remember that capital budgeting is based on cash flows, not on revenues and expenses. Since an accrual basis is used for tax purposes, the income tax is based on revenues and expenses. This is important only because the income tax is a cash flow.

Specifically, in 19x6 $2,000 is disbursed for operating expenses. However, $2,500 will be deducted for tax purposes. In 19x6, then, the cash outflow for operating expenses is $2,000 less a tax reduction of $1,000 (2,500 × 0.4). In fact, the tax reduction from operating expenses is $1,000 in each of the five years.

The NPV analysis is as follows. Additional explanatory notes are indicated below by reference to the schedule entry numbers.

Keep Old

	Amount	PVF	PV
1. Tax savings from depreciation			
12,000 ÷ 4 × 0.4	$ 1,200	3.1699	$ 3,804
2. Operating expenses			
19x5	(2,500)	0.9091	(2,273)
19x6	(2,000)	0.8264	(1,653)
19x7	(3,000)	0.7513	(2,254)
19x8	(3,000)	0.6830	(2,049)
19x9	(2,000)	0.6209	(1,242)
3. Tax savings from operating expense deduction			
2,500 × 0.4	1,000	3.7908	3,791
4. Overhaul (500) × 0.6	(300)	0.9091	(273)
5. Market value at end of year 5	1,000	0.6209	621
6. Tax on gain when disposed			
(1,000 − 0)0.4	(400)	0.6209	(248)
7. Plant rearrangement 1,500 (0.6)	(900)	0.7513	(676)
			($2,452)

Buy New

8. Cost	($12,000)	1.0000	($12,000)
9. Tax savings from depreciation			
$12,000 \div 5 \times 0.4$	960	3.7908	3,639
10. Operating expenses 500(0.6)	(300)	3.7908	(1,137)
11. Market value at end of year 5	2,000	0.6209	1,242
12. Tax on gain from disposal of new			
$(2,000 - 0)0.4$	(800)	0.6209	(497)
13. Plant rearrangement 1,500(0.6)	(900)	0.9091	(818)
14. Disposal of old machine	8,000	1.0000	8,000
15. Tax reduction due to loss on disposal			
$(8,000 - 12,000)0.4$	1,600	1.0000	1,600
			$ 29

1. Note the tax life of 4 years is the relevant time period for computing "depreciation." We are interested only in the tax effects of depreciation. Thus, it is necessary to use tax lives. Note that the PVF is at 10% for four years only.
2. See introductory discussion.
3. See introductory discussion. Note that the PVF is for five years.
5. The market value generates a cash inflow.
6. Since the book value for tax purposes is zero, there is a taxable income on the disposal and, thus, a tax increase (outflow).
7. The plant rearrangement will be relevant because it will come at a different time if the old machine is kept than if the new machine is purchased. The year 19x7 is three years from now and hence the PVF of 0.7513.
10. In the case of the new machine the cash outflow for operating expenses and the tax deduction are the same in each year. Thus the net cash flow is 500(1 − 0.4).
13. Note the PVF in comparison with item 7.
15. Since the current market value of the old machine is below the book value for tax purposes there will be a tax loss and, thus, a reduction in the total tax liability.

Based on the above analysis, the new machine should be purchased. Its NPV is higher than for the old machine.

References

Bierman, H., and Smidt, S. *The Capital Budgeting Decision*. 5th ed. New York: Macmillan, 1980.

Gordon, M.J. "Payoff Period and Rate of Profit," *Journal of Business* (October 1955): 253–262.

Klammar, T. "The Association of Capital Budgeting Techniques with Firm Performance," *The Accounting Review* (April 1973): 353–364.

Lorie, J.H., and Savage, L.J. "Three Problems in Rationing Capital," *Journal of Business* (October 1955): 229–239.

Rappaport, A. "The Discounted Payback Period," *Management Services* (July–August 1965): 30–35.

Weingartner, H.M. "The Excess Present Value Index—A Theoretical Basis and Critique," *Journal of Accounting Research* (Autumn 1963): 213–224.

_____. "Some New Views on the Payback Period and Capital Budgeting," *Management Science* (August 1969): B594–B607.

Problems

15-1. Application of Models That Do Not Consider the Time Value of Money. Consider project B in Exhibit 15.4.

Required:

1. Verify the payback period as indicated in Exhibit 15.5.
2. Compute the after-tax payback period assuming that the required investment is fully capitalizable, the marginal tax rate is 40%, and straight-line depreciation is taken. (This will be acceptable under the tax code as modifed October 1, 1981, if the assets are assumed to be three-year property.)
3. Compute the pretax payback reciprocal for project B.
4. Compute the after-tax payback reciprocal assuming a 40% tax rate and straight-line depreciation.

15-2. Review of Present Value Concepts. The following independent cases provide you with an avenue to review the concept of present values.

Required:

1. Suppose you invest $1,000 now in Bank A's time certificates at 8% interest compounded annually. What is the maximum amount you could withdraw ten years from now?
2. Suppose that Bank B is advertising time certificates at 7.8% compounded quarterly. Which plan, Bank B's or Bank A's in part 1, would result in the greatest amount at the end of ten years? [Some selected values may be useful to you: $(1.078)^{10} = 2.1193$, $(1.078)^{40} = 20.1721$, $(1.0195)^{10} = 1.2130$, $(1.0195)^{40} = 2.1652$.]
3. Assume your father is sixty years old and has a paid-up life insurance policy that is currently offering two options. Option 1 is a lump-sum payment of $100,000 to be made now. Option 2 is a yearly annuity of $11,700 to be paid starting one year from now and continuing for life.
   a. Which plan would you recommend if you expected your father to live fifteen more years and he could invest at 10%? In this part, and part b, assume that the maximization of the present value of the proceeds from the policy is the only objective your father has.
   b. Which plan would you recommend if your father could invest at 5% and his life expectancy was fifteen more years?
4. Suppose you had the option between declaring $100,000 as taxable income now, 12/31/x1, when your marginal tax rate was 30% or at 12/31/x6 when your marginal tax rate is expected to be 45%. You can invest to earn 10% after taxes. Assume that the present value of money is the only important factor in deciding when you would declare the $100,000 as income for tax purposes.

15-3. Application of Models That Consider the Time Value of Money. Reconsider project B in Exhibit 15.4. Assume that the required investment is fully capitalizable.

Required:

1. Verify the pretax discounted payback period as indicated in Exhibit 15.5.
2. Assume that the marginal tax rate is 40%. Compute the after-tax discounted payback period for project B assuming straight-line depreciation for tax purposes. This would be acceptable under the tax code as revised on October 1, 1981, if the assets are assumed to be three-year property.
3. Verify the net present value indicated in Exhibit 15.5.
4. Verify the IRR figure indicated in Exhibit 15.5 (Hint: Note that the return from project B can be viewed as two annuities—a two-year of $2,600 and a three-year of $2,600.)

15-4. Exploring the Meaning of NPV and IRR. Using project D from Exhibit 15.4, complete the following requirements.

Required:

1. Through an exhibit similar to Exhibit 15.2 show an alternative derivation of the net present value (at 10%) of $1,481.40.
2. Through an exhibit similar to Exhibit 15.3 show the IRR is 18%.

15-5. Detecting Error in Analysis. Professor Noitall gave the following question on an exam:

A new machine is being evaluated for acquisition that would cost $50,000, have a useful life of five years, and enable the production and sale of more units at a total contribution of $15,000 per year. The company requires a rate of return of 10% *before* taxes on projects of this nature, and it uses straight-line depreciation. Should the company purchase the machine?

One of the students, Kent Clark, gave the following answer:

	Amount	PVF	PV
Original Cost	($50,000)	1.0000	($50,000)
Increased Contribution	15,000	3.7908	56,862
Depreciation	(10,000)	3.7908	(31,046)
Net Present Value			($24,184)

Thus, the machine should not be purchased.
Kent received no points for his effort and is appealing.

Required:

As Professor Noitall's student assistant, explain what is wrong with Kent's solution *and why* it is wrong.

15-6. Applying Some of the Basic Tools. The Bee Gee Company is considering the replacement of an old machine that has a remaining life of five years but is fully depreciated for tax purposes. Machine A (a new one) will cost $5,000 and will reduce the company's cash operating costs before taxes by $1,713 per year for five years. The new machine would be depreciated on a straight-line basis over five years. This is acceptable under the October 1, 1981 revision of the tax code. The current salvage value of the old machine is zero. (That is, the old machine is useful only to the Bee Gee Company.) The tax rate is 30% and the firm's desired after-tax rate of return is 10%.

Required:

1. Compute the before-tax payback period.
2. Compute the after-tax payback period.
3. Compute the after-tax discounted payback period.
4. Find the net present value after taxes.
5. Find the profitability index.
6. Compute the after-tax internal rate of return
7. Machine B could be purchased for $2,000 and it would save $640 (after taxes) per year for five years. Its after-tax internal rate of return is 18%. Machine C could be purchased for $4,000 and would save $1,222 (after taxes) for five years. Its after-tax internal rate of return is 16%. Compute the IRR on the *incremental investment* in machine C (as compared to machine B).
8. Consider the two machines in part 7. Under what conditions, if any, would you recommend the purchase of machine C over machine B?

15-7. Alternative to 15-6; Two Projects. The Klekner Company is considering two projects that will compete for the same funds, which are limited to $70,848. The cash flows that are anticipated to be generated by each of the two projects are as follows:

	Year 0	Year 1	Year 2	Year 3	Year 4
Project A	($70,848)	$30,000	$30,000	$30,000	$30,000
Project B	($70,848)	-0-	15,000	30,000	98,025

Required:

1. Compute the pretax payback period for project A.
2. Compute the pretax payback period for project B.
3. Assume a discount rate of 10%
   a. Compute the net present value (NPV) of project A.
   b. Compute the NPV of project B.
4. Assume a discount rate of 20%.
   a. Compute the NPV of project A.
   b. Compute the NPV of project B.
   c. Compare your conclusions in part 4 with your conclusions in part 3. If they are different conclusions explain, in general terms, why they are different.
5. Determine the internal rate of return for project A.
6. Show that project B's internal rate of return is 22%. Note:

   If n = \qquad 1 \qquad 2 \qquad 3 \qquad 4

   $1/(1+0.22)^n$ = \quad 0.8197 \quad 0.6719 \quad 0.5507 \quad 0.4514

7. Based on the internal rate of return which project is preferred? If this preference differs from your preference in part 3, explain why.

15-8. Meaning of Discounting. Two other students in your class cannot agree on how to approach the following problem. A firm is going to buy a new machine for $100,000 that will enable the production of a new product. The $100,000 will have to be borrowed at an interest rate of 12% (the company's cost of capital). Because of the new product the firm's cash flow, net of out-of-pocket production expenses, will increase by $45,000. The life of the new machine will be five years. The firm will buy the new machine based on a NPV analysis.

Alan Trammel solves the problem by computing the net present value as follows:

NPV = 45,000 × 3.6048 − 100,000 = 62,216

Lance Parrish argues that Alan did not use the correct cash flow. He feels that since the firm will have to pay $12,000 in interest the cash flow is $33,000 ($45,000 − $12,000). Thus, Lance says the NPV is:

33,000 × 3.6048 − 100,000 = 18,958

They come to you for help.

Required:

1. Who do you think has solved the problem correctly? Why?
2. Using a schedule similar to Exhibit 15.3, test the validity of both of their NPVs.

15-9. CMA Problem; Basic. LeToy Company produces a wide variety of children's toys, most of which are manufactured from stamped parts. The Production Department recommended that a new stamping machine be acquired. The Production Department further recommended that the company only consider using the new stamping machine for five years. Top management has concurred with the recommendation and has assigned Ann Mitchum of the Budget and Planning Department to supervise the acquisition and to analyze the alternative financing available.

After careful analysis and review Mitchum has narrowed the financing of the project to two alternatives. The first alternative is a lease agreement with the manufacturer of the stamping machine. The manufacturer is willing to lease the equipment to LeToy for five years even though it has an economically useful life of ten years. The lease agreement calls for LeToy to make annual payments of $62,000 at the beginning of each year. The manufacturer (lessor) retains the title to the machine and there is no purchase option at the end of five years. Investment credit is claimed by the lessor and does not flow through to LeToy (lessee). This agreement would be considered a lease by the Internal Revenue Service.

The second alternative would be for LeToy to purchase the equipment outright from the manufacturer for $240,000. LeToy can claim an investment tax credit of $24,000 if it purchases the equipment. The investment tax credit is a direct reduction of the tax liability. Preliminary discussions with LeToy's bank indicate that the firm would be able to finance the asset acquisition with a 15% term loan.

LeToy would depreciate the equipment over five years using the ACRS method. The depreciable base must be reduced by an amount equal to one-half of the investment tax credit. The market value of the equipment at the end of five years would be $45,000.

All maintenance, taxes, and insurance are the same under both alternatives and are paid by LeToy. LeToy requires an after-tax cut-off return of 18% for investment decisions and is subject to a 40% corporate income tax rate on both operating income and capital gains and losses.

Required:

1. Calculate the relevant present value cost of the leasing alternative for LeToy Company.
2. Calculate the relevant present value cost of the purchase alternative for LeToy Company.

15-10. NPV Analysis When There is a Production Capacity Constraint. The Dauksewicz Company is considering the replacement of a machine that was acquired one year ago. The "old" machine cost $80,000 and has a present salvage value of $60,000. This decision is being considered because the machine only has an annual capacity of 30,000 units. Present estimates of the demand for the next four years are as follows:

Year 1	30,000 units	Year 3	40,000 units
Year 2	35,000 units	Year 4	50,000 units

The "old" machine had an original life of five years and is being depreciated on a straight-line basis for tax purposes. Four years from now this machine is estimated to have a market value of $10,000. Salvage value will not be provided for in tax depreciation accounting. The out-of-pocket cost of operating the machine is $20,000 per year plus $0.50 per unit produced.

The "new" machine under consideration has an annual capacity of 50,000 units and would cost $140,000. It also has a five-year life for tax purposes and would be depreciated using the straight-line method. It would be sold four years from now at an estimated value of $28,000. Its out-of-pocket operating costs have been reliably estimated to be $30,000 per year plus $0.40 per unit produced.

The product is sold for $20 per unit. Exclusive of machine operating costs and taxes, the variable cost per unit is $15. Dauksewicz uses a 14% discount rate and is subject to a marginal tax rate of 40%.

Required:

Prepare a net present value analysis to aid in this decision.

15-11. Applying the Basic Tools to a More Involved Situation. Reconsider the Brown Company problem in the last section of this chapter. In Exhibit 15.6 we have already done an NPV analysis using a 10% discount rate. In this problem you are asked to compute some of the other indexes discussed in the chapter. Remember that most of the tools make use of incremental data. In this case, this means the incremental flow of the new machine versus the old machine.

Required:

1. Assuming that the new machine is purchased, prepare a schedule showing the *incremental accounting income,* before and after taxes, attributable to the machine for each of the five years. For accounting purposes the old machine is being depreciated on a straight-line basis. The new machine will be depreciated using the SYD method. For tax purposes, the ACRS method will be used. Assume that the firm's *total* income, including this transaction, is greater than zero in each year.
2. Compute both the pretax and after-tax accounting rate of return. Remember that the investment is the incremental cash required to institute the project, not just the invoice price of the new machine.
3. Prepare a schedule showing the *incremental cash flows,* before and after taxes attributable to the machine for each of the five years.
4. Compute both the pretax and after-tax payback period.
5. Would the internal rate of return for the new machine be greater than or less than 10%? Why?

15-12. CMA Problem; Using NPV To Decide on Machine Acquisition. The WRL Company makes cookies for its chain of snack food stores. On January 2, 19x1, WRL Company purchased a special cookie-cutting machine; this machine has been used for three years. WRL

Company is considering the purchase of a newer, more efficient machine. If purchased, the new machine would be acquired on January 2, 19x4. WRL Company expects to sell 300,000 dozen cookies in each of the next four years. The selling price of the cookies is expected to average $0.50 per dozen.

WRL Company has two options: (1) continue to operate the old machine, or (2) sell the old machine and purchase the new machine. The following information has been assembled to help decide which option is more desirable.

	Old Machine	New Machine
Original cost of machine at acquisition	$80,000	$120,000
Salvage value at the end of useful life for depreciation purposes	$10,000	$ 20,000
Useful life from date of acquisition	7 years	4 years
Expected annual cash operating expenses:		
Variable cost per dozen	$0.20	$0.14
Total fixed costs	$15,000	$ 14,000
Depreciation method used for tax purposes	ACRS	ACRS
Estimated cash value of machines:		
January 2, 19x4	$40,000	$120,000
December 31, 19x7	$ 7,000	$ 20,000

WRL Company is subject to an overall income tax rate of 40%. Assume that all operating revenues and expenses occur at the end of the year. Assume that any gain or loss on the sale of machinery is treated as an ordinary tax item and will affect the taxes paid by WRL Company at the end of the year in which it is occurred.

Required:

1. Use the net present value method to determine whether WRL Company should retain the old machine or acquire the new machine. WRL requires an after-tax return of 16%.
2. Without prejudice to your answer to requirement 1, assume that the quantitative differences are so slight between the two alternatives that WRL Company is indifferent to the two proposals. Identify and discuss the nonquantitative factors that are important to this decision that WRL Company should consider.
3. Identify and discuss the advantages and disadvantages of using discounted cash flow techniques (e.g., the net present value method) for capital investment decisions.

15-13. CMA Problem; Using NPV to Make Warehouse Location Decision. U.S. Metal Corporation introduced in mid-19x2 a major product line to a new marketing area in southwestern Ohio. Public acceptance of the product line has exceeded original expectations. U.S. Metal's management believes this level of demand will continue through December 19x8.

The company had planned to serve the area directly from its Chicago plant where the customers would obtain the product f.o.b. Chicago. However, the high demand cannot be handled effectively in this manner. The management has identified two alternatives that could be initiated in January 19x3.

1. Continue to manufacture the product in Chicago but establish a warehouse 300 miles away in Dayton, Ohio, to distribute the product.
2. Provide a manufacturing, warehousing, and distribution facility in the Dayton area. This facility would not be operational until January 19x5. Consequently, a temporary warehouse would still have to be used during the first two years of the project.

Customers would obtain the product f.o.b. Dayton under both alternatives.

Bill Minnick, controller, has agreed to prepare an analysis to compare the two alternatives. He gathered the following facts for analysis.

1. The Chicago plant has sufficient capacity to manufacture the additional product volume expected to be demanded in the new marketing area. Only maintenance and insurance costs are expected to increase at the Chicago plant as a result of the additional manufacturing volume. These costs are expected to be $20,000 higher than normal in 19x3 and can be expected to increase by $3,000 annually as long as the product line is manufactured in Chicago.
2. U.S. Metal can lease sufficient warehouse space in Dayton for $24,000 annually. A lease agreement can be arranged in this amount for any period from two to six years. The annual lease payment would be due on December 31 for the following year.
3. Warehousing personnel would be hired to manage and operate the warehouse. The annual initial warehousing cost, excluding the lease payment, is estimated at $50,000. This amount is expected to increase by 10% annually.
4. Five truckloads of product per day, 250 days per year, would be shipped from Chicago to the Dayton warehouse by common carrier as long as the product is manufactured in Chicago. Each truckload would average 30,000 pounds. One common carrier has quoted U.S. Metal a freight rate of $1.00 per hundred weight for a 30,000-pound truckload ($300) plus a 20% fuel surcharge applied on the total freight charge for the one-way trip between Chicago and Dayton. The fuel surcharge is expected to continue at the same percentage through 19x8 but the freight rate per hundred weight for a 30,000-pound truckload is expected to increase each year as presented below:

19x4	$1.10
19x5	1.25
19x6	1.40
19x7	1.50
19x8	1.60

5. A building suitable for manufacturing, warehousing, and distributing the product line can be obtained in Dayton for $50,000 annually on a twenty-year lease. The lease would be signed December 31, 19x2, so that the equipment installation could be started on January 1, 19x3. The lease payments would be remitted on December 31, for the following year.
6. The Dayton warehousing operations and personnel would be transferred from the original leased warehouse to the combined facility in January 19x5. Because all functions would be in the same facility, annual warehousing personnel costs would be 10% lower than the cost of maintaining a separate warehouse as described in the first alternative.
7. The estimated total cost of the manufacturing equipment for the Dayton plant is $1.2 million. The equipment would be acquired and paid for as follows:

December 19x2	$ 510,000
December 19x3	450,000
December 19x4	240,000
	$1,200,000

The equipment would be fully operational in January 19x5.

8. The new equipment at the Dayton plant would be capable of manufacturing the product line at the same rate and costs, exclusive of maintenance and insurance, experienced at the Chicago plant. Annual maintenance and insurance costs for the Dayton equipment are expected to be $70,000 the first year the equipment is operational and increase $5,000 annually thereafter during the life of the project.

9. The new equipment would have a twenty-year estiamted economic life with no estimated salvage value at the end of twenty years. The company would use ACRS to write off the cost of the new manufacturing equipment for tax purposes. Once the equipment is placed in service, the new equipment would be written off over five years.

10. The new manufacturing equipment for the Dayton facility would qualify for the 10% investment tax credit. The credit would be claimed in the tax year the equipment becomes operational. Currently, the tax code requires the basis for depreciation to be reduced by one half of the investment tax credit taken.

11. If the market for the product line lasts only through 19x8 as forecast, the company could use the plant and equipment for other products. However, Minnick estimates U.S. Metal could sell the Dayton equipment in December 19x8 for $900,000 if the equipment is no longer needed. The building could be subleased for $50,000 per year for the remaining term of the lease when it is no longer needed.

12. U.S. Metal is subject to a 40% tax rate on operating income and on capital transactions. Assume that taxes are paid in the year in which the transactions occur.

Required:

Calculate the after-tax cash flows for the period 19x2 through 19x8 by year for each of the two alternatives being considered by U.S. Metal Corporation assuming that U.S. Metal will use discounted cash flow techniques in its decision process.

15-14. Evaluating Merits of Eliminating Segment of Business. Helen Hartburn owns two pizza shops. They both have been quite successful but Helen is ten years from retirement and in a rather comfortable financial position. Thus she is considering the sale of one of the shops in order to reduce some of the demands on her time. However, when Helen came to you for advice she stated that she did not want to sell unless it was a good deal.

Helen has provided you with the following data about the shop that might be sold:

Original cost of building and equipment	$210,000
Current book value	105,000
Current offer for shop	160,000
Expected market value ten years from now	30,000

The building and equipment were acquired fifteen years ago (before the tax modification of 1981) and is being depreciated on a straight-line basis with no salvage value being provided for at the end of their useful lives. Both the building and the equipment have the same useful life.

The income before taxes for this shop has been a constant $15,000 per year. The other shop has had an income before tax of $20,000 per year. Helen's *marginal* tax rates are as follows:

Taxable Income	Marginal Tax Rate
$14,001–$20,000	24%
20,001– 25,000	28
25,001– 30,000	32
30,001– 40,000	36
40,001–100,000	40

That is, the first $20,000 of income is taxed at 24% regardless of how much the total income is. If there is a current sale it will be consummated for tax purposes at the beginning of the tax year. Assume that a sale ten years from now will be consummated at the *end* of the last year of business.

Required:

Assuming Helen can earn 10% after taxes on her money, prepare an NPV analysis of her current alternatives for the shop.

15-15. Evaluating an Advertising Campaign. The Norbit Company produces and markets a toothpaste known as Kissing Breath. They already have a low-key advertising program but the marketing division has proposed a saturation campaign to run through the first six months of 19x1. The regular advertising would be discontinued during 19x1 and then resumed the following year. You have been asked to help evaluate the merits of this campaign.

The following data have been made available to you:

Campaign costs	
Preliminary research costs already incurred	$ 45,000
Additional costs to produce advertising	200,000
Total	$245,000

It is felt that this campaign will increase sales by 5,000 cases in 19x1. It is typical for the effects of such campaigns to vanish over time. Based on past experience it has been estimated that the incremental sales due to the campaign will be reduced in each year after the campaign year in an amount equal to 20% of the original increase.

Following is the product-line income statement for last year. The $45,000 preliminary research costs are not included.

Sales (10,000 cases @ $50)			$500,000
Cost of Goods Sold			
Material		$ 50,000	
Labor		100,000	
Variable overhead[1]		140,000	
Fixed overhead[2]		85,000	375,000
Gross Margin			$125,000
Selling Expenses			
Variable		$ 10,000	
Fixed		20,000	
Total		$ 30,000	
General and			
Administrative			
Salaries	$50,000		
Regular Advertising	10,000	60,000	90,000
Net Income			$ 35,000

[1]Includes depreciation (units of production method) at $1.00 per unit.

[2]Includes depreciation of $50,000.

The firm's after-tax discount rate is 12% and the marginal tax rate is 30%.

Required:

Prepare a net present value analysis to help in evaluating whether this campaign should be done.

15-16. Using NPV for a Municipal Decision. The city of Peaoreo is facing a decision about the purchase of a garbage truck. There are two models being considered. The larger model, Super Kan, has twice the capacity of the smaller model, Standard Kan. In order to service the city there will need to be twenty hours of pickup time per week. Using a driver and two assistants the Super Kan can be loaded in two hours. The Standard Kan could be loaded in one hour. The round trip to the landfill would be one hour for either truck.

The Super Kan costs $70,000. If purchased, the crew would do two loads per day and be responsible for the general maintenance and cleanup of the truck. The Standard Kan costs $25,000 and, if purchased, the crew would do four loads per day. Part-time help would be employed during the night hours for cleanup and general maintenance. The part-time help is estimated at four hours per day.

The regular crew will earn $8.00 per hour and will work forty hours per week. The part-time employees would be paid $4.00 per hour. Pickups will take place in each of the fifty-two weeks of the year.

Peaoreo's landfill is twenty miles outside the city. In order to complete the pickup a truck would travel forty miles per week within the city. The estimated gasoline consumptions are as follows:

	Super	*Standard*
In city	5 miles/gallon	7 miles/gallon
To and from landfill	10 miles/gallon	12 miles/gallon

Gasoline costs the city $1.30 per gallon. On the average either truck will require an overhaul every 5,000 miles costing an average of $200.

The Super Kan would be used for ten years. However, the Standard Kan would have to be replaced after five years. Assume it has no salvage value at that time. Also assume that the costs and operating characteristics would be the same as the current model.

The city would use a 10% discount rate.

Required:

Prepare a net present value analysis to provide information for the decision. Discount each year's operating costs as if they all took place at the end of the year.

15-17. Adapted CMA Problem on Product Addition Decision. The Baxter Company manufacturers toys and other short-lived fad items. The research and development department came up with an item that would make a good promotional gift for office equipment dealers. Aggressive and effective effort by Baxter's sales pesonnel has resulted in almost firm commitments for this product for the next three years. It is expected that the product's value will be exhausted by that time.

In order to produce the quantity demanded, Baxter will need to buy additional machinery and rent some additional space. It appears that about 25,000 square feet will be needed: 12,500 square feet of presently unused, but leased, space is available now. (Baxter's present lease, with ten years to run, costs $3.00 a foot.) There is another 12,500 square feet adjoining the Baxter facility, which Baxter will rent for three years at $4.00 per square foot per year if it decides to make this product.

The equipment will be purchased for about $900,000. It will require $30,000 in modifications, $60,000 for installation, and $90,000 for testing; all of these activitites will be done by a firm of engineers hired by Baxter. All of the expenditures will be paid for on January 1, 19x3, and capitalized.

The equipment should have a salvage value of about $180,000 at the end of the third year but it will be ignored for tax purposes. No additional general overhead costs are expected to be incurred.

The following estimates of revenues and expenses for this product for the three years have been developed:

	19x3	*19x4*	*19x5*
Sales	$1,000,000	$1,600,000	$900,000
Material, labor, and			
incurred overhead	400,000	750,000	350,000
Assigned general			
overhead	40,000	75,000	35,000
Rent	87,500	87,500	87,500
Depreciation	360,000	360,000	360,000
	$ 887,500	$1,272,500	$832,500
Income before tax	$ 112,500	$ 327,500	$ 67,500
Income tax (40%)	45,000	131,000	27,000
Income after tax	$ 67,500	$ 196,500	$ 40,500

Required:

1. Prepare a schedule that shows the incremental, after-tax cash flows for this project.
2. If the company requires a two-year payback period for its investment, would it undertake this project? Show your supporting calculations clearly.
3. Calculate the after-tax accounting rate of return for this project using the simple average of the beginning and ending book values as the denominator.
4. A newly hired business school graduate recommends that the company consider the use of net present value analysis to study this project. If the company sets a required rate of return of 20% after taxes, will this project be accepted? Show your supporting calculations clearly. (Assume all operating revenues and expenses occur at the end of the year.)

15-18. Adapted CMA Problem on New Product Decision and Optimal Equipment Acquisition Method. Edwards Corporation is a manufacturing concern that produces and sells a wide range of products. The company not only mass produces a number of products and equipment components but also is capable of producing special-purpose manufacturing equipment to customer specifications.

The firm is considering adding a new stapler to one of its product lines. More equipment will be required to produce the new stapler. There are three alternative ways to acquire the needed equipment: (1) purchase general-purpose equipment, (2) lease general-purpose equipment, (3) build special-purpose equipment. A fourth alternative, purchase of the special-purpose equipment, has been ruled out because it would be prohibitively expensive.

The general-purpose equipment can be purchased for $125,000. The equipment has an estimated salvage of $15,000 at the end of its useful life of ten years. At the end of five years the equipment can be used elsewhere in the plant or be sold for $40,000.

Alternatively, the general-purpose equipment can be acquired by a five-year lease for $40,000 annual rent. The lessor will assume all responsibility for taxes, insurance, and maintenance.

Finally, special-purpose equipment can be constructed by the Contract Equipment Department of the Edwards Corporation. Although the department is operating at a level that is normal for the time of year, it is below full capacity. The department could produce the equipment without interfering with its regular revenue-producing activities. Assume production time is nil and takes place at the beginning of year one.

The estimated departmental costs that would be capitalized if the special-purpose equipment is constructed amounts to:

Material and parts	$ 75,000
Direct labor	60,000
Variable overhead (50% of direct-labor dollars)	30,000
Fixed overhead (25% of direct-labor dollars)	15,000
Total	$180,000

Corporation general and administrative costs are fixed and average 20% of labor dollar content of factory production at normal activity.

Engineering and management studies provide the following yearly revenue and cost estimates (excluding lease payments and depreciation) for producing the new stapler depending upon the equipment used:

	General-Purpose Equipment		Self-Constructed Equipment
	Leased	*Purchased*	*Equipment*
Unit selling price	$5.00	$5.00	$5.00
Unit production costs			
Materials	$1.80	$1.80	$1.70
Variable conversion costs	1.60	1.60	1.40
Total unit production costs	$3.40	$3.40	$3.10
Unit contribution margin	$1.60	$1.60	$1.90
Estimated unit volume	40,000	40,000	40,000
Estimated total contribution			
margin	$64,000	64,000	$76,000
Other costs			
Supervision	$16,000	$16,000	$18,000
Taxes and insurance	——	3,000	5,000
Maintenance	——	3,000	2,000
Total	$16,000	$22,000	$25,000

The company will depreciate the general-purpose machine over five years using the ACRS method for tax purposes. The special-purpose machine will also be depreciated over five years using ACRS. Its salvage value at the end of that time is estimated to be $30,000 and will not be provided for.

The company uses an after-tax cost of capital of 10%. Its marginal tax rate is 40%.

Required:

1. Calculate the net present value for each of the three alternatives that Edwards Corporation has at its disposal.
2. Should Edwards Corporation select any of the three options, and if so, which one? Explain your answer.

15-19. NPV Analysis When There is Uncertainty. The CMA Company is contemplating adding a new product line that would require the purchase of a new machine to produce it. Complicating the decision is a lot of uncertainty about the demand for the new product and its selling price. Further, the total income of the firm is uncertain so that it is not known for sure what the marginal tax rate will be.

The new machine will cost $210,000 and will be depreciated for tax purposes over a three-year period using the straight-line method. Its capacity is 50,000 units per year.

The new product can be produced at a variable cost of $5 per unit. Except for the depreciation on the new machine there would be no incremental fixed production costs. Fixed costs would be allocated at $3 per unit including the depreciation on the new machine. There would be incremental selling and administrative costs of $80,000 per year.

The demand for the new product has been estimated as follows:

Years 1 and 2		Year 3	
Demand	*Probability*	*Demand*	*Probability*
30,000 units	30%	20,000 units	30%
40,000 units	40	30,000 units	50
50,000 units	30	40,000 units	20

Similarly, the sales price per unit has been estimated:

Years 1 and 2		Year 3	
Price	Probability	Price	Probability
$10	40%	$11	50%
$11	50%	$12	40%
$12	10%	$13	10%

Giving consideration to this new product, its potential sales and income, and to the potential income of other products, the tax accountant of the CMA company estimates the marginal tax rate (MTR) as follows:

Years 1 and 2		Year 3	
MTR	Probability	MTR	Probability
30%	10%	40%	20%
40	30	46	80
46	60		

CMA's discount rate is 12%.

Required:

Prepare an analysis to be used in deciding whether this product should be added to the product line.

CHAPTER 16 **Advanced Considerations in Capital Budgeting**

Chapter Overview

In the last chapter we explored the basic concepts of capital budgeting. However, there are some problem areas that were deferred to this chapter for discussion. In the first section of this chapter, we will consider ways to modify an analysis when there are two or more projects with different lives. In a second section we will consider the need for and the measurement of opportunity cost when a given proposal necessitates an increase in working capital. In a third section we will consider the impact of price level changes. A fourth section deals with capital budgeting and uncertainty.

The fifth section considers the possible conflicts between the NPV model and conventional performance evaluation methods. In practice we may find that long-term investments are commonly evaluated using criteria that are not consistent with the principles of capital budgeting. That is, evaluation measures may follow the accounting income model, whereas capital budgeting is cash-flow-oriented. A lack of consistency between desired decision models and control models may provide a strong, but undesired, motivation for managers to use wrong decision strategies.

In the sixth section we will deal with limitations on the available capital. Under these conditions there is a problem in making optimal project selections. We will consider some possible solution methods for such decisions. Next we will examine an approach to capital budgeting when leasing arrangements are involved.

At the end of the chapter we will consider different discount rate alternatives, including their measurement difficulties, and a procedure for incorporating the time value (cost) of money into CVP analyses. The latter topic was not considered in the CVP chapter because it involves an integration of capital budgeting concepts with CVP analysis.

Unequal-Lived Projects

All of the multiple-project examples that have been considered to this point assumed that each project in the analysis had the same life. Of course, it is too much to expect this to always be true. Suppose, for illustrative purposes, a firm can either invest in project A with a life of seven years *or* project B with a life of four years. If the life difference is not adjusted for and if we select between A and B on the basis of net present values, then we have assumed that the investment recovered from project B will be reinvested at the discount rate starting in year five. (Of course, if not adjusted for, we assume that recoveries during the life of each project and the difference between the initial investments are also invested at the discount rate.) If this assumption is not realistic, then what can be done?

There have been two basic proposals for dealing with unequal lives. One proposal involves selecting a given time period and then adjusting all proposals to be consistent with the time period selected. Time periods suggested for this approach include the shortest life, the longest life, or a time period that is divisible by all of the projects' lives. The second approach is called the "level payment" approach and will be explained after the first approach is illustrated.

If the shortest life is used as the common life, four years in our example, then project A will need to be adjusted to a shorter time period. One possible adjustment is to estimate A's bail-out value at the end of year 4 and treat this as an additional cash flow in year 4. Bail out means the net salvage or liquidation value of the project's assets at a given point in time. This value is used as a surrogate measure of the cash flows that would be realized by the longer lived project after the common life.

If the time period of the analysis is set equal to the life of the longer project, then there must be a determination of what will be done as a replacement for project B at the end of year 4. For example, if the project is an equipment acquisition, it might be assumed the equipment is replaced in like kind. Of course, in our example, the replacement would result in comparing an eight-year investment package with a seven-year package. Then it would be necessary to assume a bail-out value for the second four-year project.

To avoid the necessity of estimating bail-out values, the time period of the analysis could be chosen to be the smallest length of time divisible by both four and seven: twenty-eight. Using a life of twenty-eight assumes that project A is repeated four times and B, seven times. To illustrate, suppose projects A and B both require an investment of $10,000. Project A is expected to return $3,000 per year for seven years and B's annual expectation is $4,200 in each of four years.

Assuming the discount rate is 10% and *not* adjusting for the time difference, the present values are:

	Project A	*Project B*
Future cash flows		
$3,000 \times a_{0.10,7} = \$3,000 \times 4.8684$	$14,605.20	
$4,200 \times a_{0.10,4} = \$4,200 \times 3.1699$		$13,313.58
Investment	(10,000.00)	(10,000.00)
Net present value	$ 4,605.20	$ 3,313.58

Lacking an adjustment for time differences, project A is preferred to project B.

As indicated, when using this approach project A is assumed to be repeated a total of four times. The value of *each* replication *discounted to the time of its investment* is $4,605.20. To find the *present* value of the remaining three replications, just treat each of the $4,605.20 amounts as lump sum cash flows to be received at the beginning of the first year of the replication. Then discount these amounts back to the beginning of year 1 and add them to the NPV of the first investment.

For project A extended through twenty-eight years, the results are:

Replication	Present Value
First	$4,605.20
Second $4,605.20 × 0.5132[a]	2,363.39
Third $4,605.20 × 0.2633[b]	1,212.55
Fourth $4,605.20 × 0.1351[c]	622.16
Total	$8,803.30

[a]Investment occurs at beginning of year 8 (same as end of year7). The value of the project at the end of year 7 is $4,605.20. To discount to present, multiply by $p_{0.10,7}$ as found in Table A.2.

[b]The $4,605.20 is at the beginning of year 15 (end of year 14); multiply by $p_{0.10,14}$.

[c]Multiply by $p_{0.10,21} = 1/(1 + 0.1)^{21} = 0.1351$.

Performing a similar calculation for project B yields a result of $9,728. Now, with the implicit assumptions of these calculations, we can see that project B is preferred over A and is a reversal of the decision that would be reached without adjusting for the life differences.

A second major approach of analyzing projects with unequal lives is to use the **level payments approach.** This approach involves a simplification of the actual problem by converting all inflows and outflows to equivalent annual annuities. Then decisions are based on the magnitude of the differences between the annuities. The cash *inflows* of both projects in our example are already annuities. To determine an equivalent *outflow* annuity, call it F, for project A, determine the annual amount of a seven-year annuity at 10% (the discount rate) that is equal to a present outflow of $10,000:

$$10,000 = F \times a_{0.10,7}$$

$$10,000 = F \times 4.8684$$

$$F = 10,000 \div 4.8684 = 2.054$$

For project B, which had a four-year life, find F such that:

$$10,000 = F \times a_{0.10,4}$$

$$F = 10,000 \div 3.1699 = 3,155$$

For our example, the following schedule summarizes the level payment approach:

Project	Annual Inflow	Equivalent Level Outflow	Difference
A	$3,000	$2,054	$ 946
B	4,200	3,155	1,045

Again, we can see that project B is preferred over A since B's difference is greater than A's.

Projects Involving Increases in Working Capital

Another type of capital budgeting problem arises when there are proposals that require increases in working capital. For example, a certain type of machine may require a larger raw material inventory and/or result in larger average finished goods inventories. Other proposals may result in larger average account receivable balances. If so, there is an opportunity cost of having a larger working capital even though these increased assets may be fully recovered at some later point.

Investment in working capital requires equity, which has a cost. Suppose a five-year project requires working capital increases of $100,000 and that the cost of generating that capital is 10%. The increased working capital has an annual opportunity cost of $10,000. The present value of this annual cost is $37,908, $10,000 × 3.7908, and should be included in the determination of the project's net present value.

A short-cut way of including this opportunity cost in the analysis is to treat the increase in working capital as an additional investment. Then in order to derive the opportunity cost caused by the project it is necessary to assume that the increases are fully recoverable at the project's conclusion. In fact the firm may not reduce its working capital. However, the continued opportunity cost must be attributed to future projects, not to the current one. If the recovery is not assumed at the end of the current project, then it will be forced to recover costs that it did not cause. The recovery (or assumed recovery), however, is five years away. In present value terms, the cash flows are:

Increase in working capital	($100,000) × 1.00	($100,000)
Recovery of working capital		
at end of year 5	100,000 × 0.6209	62,090
Present value of working capital cost		$(37,910)

The $2 difference between this approach and the one in the last paragraph is due to rounding error.

Price Level Changes

Another problem of using capital budgeting is price level changes. Price level changes can affect capital budgeting models in very subtle ways. Thus, we need to give careful consideration to the problem. Two basic suggestions have been made to adjust for inflation in capital budgeting and both attempt to ensure that decisions are based on real or constant dollars.

The first method suggests that we (1) include an inflation factor in the discount rate and (2) forecast the future cash flows in terms of the price levels anticipated during the period of the cash flow. For example, if a particular machine will save 1,000 labor hours and if the current wage rate is $8.00 per hour, then in the current period the cash savings would be forecast at $8,000. If wage rates are expected to increase at 10% *per year,* then the dollar amount of the savings should be projected at $8,800 in year 2, $9,680 in the third year, and so forth. By including an inflation factor in the discount rate, the time value of money and the inflation would be simultaneously adjusted for by the discounting mechanism.

The other method suggested is one whereby (1) the future cash flows are stated in terms of the *current* price levels and (2) the discount rate *does not* include an inflation adjustment. Since the cash flows are in constant dollars, we need not, and *must not,* adjust for them through the discounting.

To illustrate these methods and their subtleties, consider the following situation. Assume a new machine costing $18,000 will enable a labor savings of 1,000 hours per year. The machine has a three-year life and no salvage value. Labor rates averaged $8.00 per hour in 19x0. This project is being considered at the beginning of 19x1, at which time the annual inflation rate for all products and services purchased (including wages) is anticipated to be 10% and the risk-adjusted-inflation-free discount rate is 12%. (For the moment, it is being assumed that the prices of all products and services are changing at identical rates.)

Method 1 would project the labor savings (assume all at year-end) to be $8,800 for year 1 ($8,000 × 1.10), $9,680 for year 2 ($8,800 × 1.10), and $10,648 for year 3 ($9,680 × 1.10). The first problem is determining the rate that simultaneously adjusts for time value and inflation. At first glance you might assume that the two rates, 12% and 10%, would just be added together and that the discounting would be done with a 22% rate. But this rate does not allow the additional dollars gained through inflation to be invested and earn interest.

In order to consider these effects, define i to be the risk-adjusted-inflation-free rate and f to be the inflation rate. Then r, the discount rate for method 1, should produce results that are identical to a process that adjusts for the time value of money separately from the inflation. If M_t is the actual money flow in period t, then method 2 referred to above would proceed as follows. First, inflation is adjusted out to obtain a real cash flow, R_t, as follows:

$$R_t = \frac{M_t}{(1 + f)^t} \tag{16-1}$$

Then, the present value, P_t, of the real cash flow, is:

$$P_t = \frac{R_t}{(1 + i)^t} \tag{16-2}$$

Substituting for R_t in (16-2) using the results in (16-1) we have:

$$P_t = \frac{M_t}{(1 + f)^t(1 + i)^t} = \frac{M_t}{[(1 + f)(1 + i)]^t} = \frac{M_t}{(1 + f + i + fi)^t} \tag{16-3}$$

To *simultaneously* adjust for time value and inflation (the first method) using a combined rate, r, we should use the following equation:

$$P_t = \frac{M_t}{(1 + r)^t} \tag{16-4}$$

To obtain the same results as in (16-3), we see that r must be such that:

$$(1 + r)^t = (1 + f + i + fi)^t \tag{16-5}$$

Thus:

$$r = f + i + fi \qquad\qquad\qquad (16\text{-}6)$$

Observe that r is the sum of the inflation rate, the risk-adjusted-inflation-free rate, and a cross-product. The latter term, in effect, allows for the increased earning power of the dollars obtained as a result of inflation.

For our example, the discount rate to be used in method 1 would be:

$$r = 0.10 + 0.12 + (0.10)(0.12) = 0.232$$

It can be shown that with a rate of 23.2% the present value factors for periods 1, 2, and 3 are 0.8117, 0.6588, and 0.5348, respectively. Then, the net present values of the real cash flows of the demonstration project are as follows:

Cash inflows:
Year 1 $ 8,800 × 0.8117		$ 7,143
Year 2 $ 9,680 × 0.6588		6,377
Year 3 $10,648 × 0.5348		5,695
Investment		(18,000)
Net present value		$ 1,215

Method 2 would treat the labor savings as an $8,000 annuity. That is, all resource savings would be stated at current price levels. The discount rate would be the risk-adjusted-inflation-free rate of 12%. Then:

"Real" cash inflows	$8,000 × 2.4018	$19,214
Investment		(18,000)
Net present value		$ 1,214

In the above example, it was assumed that the prices of all resources were changing at the same rate. Of course, this is not likely. If the prices of specific items are changing at a rate different than the average, then what should be done? Before suggesting an answer it will be helpful to consider "specific" and "general" price level changes and their relationship to each other.

If a firm regularly buys a product that is increasing in price *at a rate less than the average,* or general price levels, then in comparison with the average the firm is gaining purchasing power. To illustrate, suppose the firm uses material A to produce product Z, which it sells. Currently, material A can be purchased for $10 per unit and Z sells for $20 per unit. Thus, each sale of Z will currently permit the firm to buy two units of X. Suppose the price of material X goes up by 10% during the next year, to $11 per unit. Further, assume product Z increases in price at the average inflation rate (say 20%, so our computations are easy). This means that at year-end, Z sells for $24. Now, each sale of Z will enable the firm to purchase 2.1818 units of material X ($24 ÷ 11). That is, material X's prices have been such that with respect to the average change the firm has more purchasing power. A sale of one unit of Z will enable the firm to buy 0.1818 more units of material X at the end of the year then it would be able to at the beginning of the year.

Since decision making should be focused on maximizing the real wealth of the firm it will be necessary to adjust for price level changes in such a way as to capture phenomena like these described above. The first method of adjusting for price levels, as previously discussed, can be modified as follows:

1. Forecast the cash flows for each relevant item using its specific price level change.
2. Determine a discount rate, using equation (16-6), where i is the general, or average, change in prices.
3. Discount the cash flows as determined in step 1 using the discount rate determined in step 2.

Incorporating the differences between specific and general price levels into method 2 is not convenient. Thus, if it is desired to "account" for the difference in price level changes for several different resources associated with a capital budgeting project, it will be easier to use the first method.

The example above entailed the purchase of a depreciable asset. For tax purposes, the depreciation on assets must be based on original costs. This means the tax effect of $1.00 of depreciation, in real terms, will be less each year if general prices are increasing, or more if prices are decreasing. Depreciation is just a specific case of the situation cited above: specific price levels are changing at a different rate (zero) than the average. Obviously the procedural changes outlined above for method 1 will adjust for the differences in the relative rates of change. Of course, in forecasting the tax effects of depreciation, the specific price change is zero.

To illustrate, assume general prices are increasing at 10%, the risk-adjusted-inflation-free discount rate is 12%, and the firm's tax rate is 40%. The $18,000 machine purchased in the above example would generate a $6,000 tax deduction (straight-line depreciation was being used) and a $2,400 tax savings each year regardless of the inflation rate. To derive the present value of the tax savings stated in terms of the current year's price levels, use a 23.2% discount rate:

Year

1	2,400 × 0.8177	$1,948
2	2,400 × 0.6588	1,581
3	2,400 × 0.5348	1,284
		$4,813

If method 2 is used to adjust for the inflationary effects then one would proceed as follows. First, adjust out the impact of inflation on the tax savings resulting from the depreciation deduction. For example, with 10% inflation, a current tax reduction of $2,400 will have less purchasing power at the end of year 1. Specifically, the relative purchasing power is such that x, the current dollar equivalent, is:

$$\frac{x}{1.0} = \frac{2,400}{1.1} = 2,181.82$$

The current dollar equivalent of a deduction two years hence is:

$$\frac{x}{1.0} = \frac{2,400}{(1.1)^2} = 1,983.47$$

For the third year:

$$x = \frac{2,400}{(1.1)^3} = 1,803.15$$

The present value of the above amounts, at the inflation-free rate of 12%, is:

Year		
1	2,181.82 × 0.8929	$1,948
2	1,983.47 × 0.7972	1,581
3	1,803.15 × 0.7118	1,284
		$4,813

As you can see, with respect to the tax effects of the depreciation, both methods yield the same results. However, method 1 was easier to use.

Uncertainty

To this point it has either been assumed that all of the projected cash flows were known with certainty or that they represented the expected value of a random variable (defined in Chapter 13). In either case, the net present value analysis results in a point estimate with no measure of dispersion or distribution. One possibility is to increase the discount rate to require compensation for the perceived risk. Other possibilities are briefly discussed in this section.

Of course, one way to derive additional information when there is uncertainty is through simulation. The approach would be similar to what was done in the cost-volume-profit chapter. In this case, the random variables would be the cash flows in each year of the project. *If they are independent of each other,* then the simulation would entail the following steps:

1. Determine probability distributions for the cash flows in each year.
2. Randomly select an observation for each random variable; that is, the cash flow in each year.
3. Discount the selected values at an appropriate discount rate to determine the NPV of the sample.
4. Repeat steps 2 and 3 as often as necessary in order to derive a useful distribution of net present values.

The type of output derived from such a process is similar to that of a simulated CVP analysis. The probability associated with various magnitudes of net present values could be estimated and then let the decision maker react according to his or her aversion to risk. However, there are several things to consider before using this approach.

First, there is a question about what factors to include in the discount rate to be used in the simulation. If the decision maker is going to react to risk based upon the simulated distribution of NPV, then perhaps the discount rate *should not* include a risk factor. If it does, risk might be incorporated twice.

Second, it is not clear that the yearly cash flows will be independent random variables. For example, if year 1's cash flow is significantly below expectation, it may be a signal that the project is not going to be as successful as planned. If so, then the cash flows from later years will all be below the initial expectations rather than varying randomly around the mean. That is, they are dependent. Some types of dependent situations can be easily simulated; others cannot. Space does not permit expansion into this topic although it is an important consideration.

Problem of Project and Manager Evaluation When Capital Budgeting Is Employed

Like any other endeavors, capital projects need to be monitored, controlled, and evaluated. Unlike repetitive functions, it is difficult to establish a standard against which to measure effectiveness and efficiency. Capital projects are adopted on the basis of forecasts of relatively long periods of time. Thus, an evaluator must be less demanding as to the closeness of actual results to original estimates. But if there is no evaluation, project leaders may become more lax than desired. Just the knowledge of the requirement to prepare a report may induce the type of concern that management desires in project leaders.

Some general considerations need to be incorporated into an evaluation system for this type of decision. First, because of the increased uncertainties of long range projects, it is essential that project evaluation be considered as distinct from manager evaluation. The manager may not have control over all of the variables that will have an impact on the outcome of the project. Thus, just because a project yielded a return that was much less than anticipated, it does not necessarily follow that the manager failed. There is no formula that can be followed; judgment must be exercised and then only after all of the facts have been considered.

Second, one needs to be certain that evaluation criteria have *congruence* with good decision-making criteria. For example, if it is felt that NPV methods should be encouraged for decision making, then there is a question about whether net income should be used as an evaluative criterion. Remember that NPV is a model based on cash flows and net income is an accrual model. Are these models congruent? Lerner and Rappaport believe that congruence is lacking in this case and have suggested a way for managers to adapt to such a system.[1] This will be explored further in Chapter 19.

Finally, it is desirable to avoid evaluation systems that are based on short-run outcomes. This may be easier said than done. If managerial personnel never changed, then evaluations could be based on cumulative results over time. However, there are promotions, lateral movements, resignations, and retirements.

---

[1]Eugene M. Lerner and Alfred Rappaport, "Limit DCF in Capital Budgeting," *Harvard Business Review* (September–October 1968), pp. 133–139.

When these personnel changes occur the cumulative results are not relevant to evaluating the successor. Nevertheless, accountants must strive to design systems that will cause managers to be concerned about the long run. This, too, will be discussed at greater length in the control section of the book.

≥ Capital Budgeting When There Are Constraints

Occasionally, there are situations in which capital budgeting decisions are subject to constraints. For example, the set of projects with positive net present values may require more total capital than is available. Also, some projects may have to share a limited amount of research and development time. Third, some sets of projects may be such that not all could be accepted. For example, several machines under consideration may be competitors for the same place on the production line. If one is purchased, all others are precluded. Yet another example is the possibility of project dependence; that is, one project can be accepted only if others are accepted. In this section we will explore possible ways of incorporating constraints into the capital-budgeting decision model.

First, consider the case of limited capital. Some would argue that a firm should never allow limited capital to be the cause for rejecting projects with positive net present values. They reason that if a project's forecasted cash flows are sufficient to cover the cost of capital and an appropriate risk premium, then management should find some way of increasing the availability of capital. However, in the short run this may not be feasible and management will be forced to decide upon the optimal allocation of the limited capital.

To illustrate the problem of making this allocation decision by using the ranking process suggested in the previous chapter, assume that five projects with equal lives are being considered:

Project	Investment Requirement	Net Present Value
A	$22,000	$10,000
B	25,000	9,000
C	20,000	8,500
D	5,000	3,000
E	3,000	2,500

Note that these projects are ordered according to their net present values.

From previous discussions you should know that if adjustments are not made when using the IRR and NPV, then you are making certain assumptions about the usage of recovered capital and of investment differences. Without adjustment, IRR assumes the proceeds are invested at the project's return rate and NPV assumes reinvestment at the discount rate. If you are going to make one of these assumptions, it is more defensible to make the latter. With the latter you can at least argue that the recovered capital will be used to retire equity and that investment differences will also result in a smaller equity size. In either case, you are saving an equity cost equal to the discount rate.

Given that limited capital is going to be allocated on the basis of NPV, there is no guarantee that the ranking will lead to an optimal solution. Suppose capital is limited to $23,000 in the preceding case. Presumably, if the ranking is followed only project A (cost of $22,000) would be selected. The NPV of the solution would be $10,000. However, there is a better solution. If you skip down the ranking and pick the third project, C, and the fifth, E, then the entire $23,000 would be invested, resulting in an NPV of $11,000.

Next, assume the budget totaled $29,000. If you are careful to consider all possibilities, then you will find that the first two ranked projects should be skipped in favor of C, D, and E. With this selection the investment would total $28,000 and the projected NPV would be $14,000. The lesson of this example is that when there are constraints it is difficult to use "eyeball" methods in selecting the optimal set of projects. Remember there was only one constraint in this example. For more involved problems integer programming can be used to make an optimal project selection.

≥ Leases

Occasionally, assets needed for a given capital project may be considered for acquisition through a leasing arrangement. This can complicate the capital-budgeting analysis since leases are debt-financing tools. In effect, the lessor lends the needed capital to the lessee. Each lease payment implicitly contains a repayment of a portion of the loan and an interest charge.

When the possibility of a lease is involved, we should view the capital-budgeting decision as two-tiered. First, we must decide if the project should be adopted and, if so, then we must determine how the asset should be financed. The asset could be leased or the capital could be borrowed to buy the asset. After the first decision is made, the latter would be made on the basis of the financing arrangement with the smallest interest cost.

To illustrate the precautions that must be taken, assume the cash price of an asset is $100,000. If acquired, it is estimated that net cash inflows will be increased by $47,473 per year for the next three years. The company is currently using a discount rate of 25%. The firm from which the asset would be acquired has offered to lease it for three years at an annual rate of $43,798. These options are portrayed in frames A and B of Exhibit 16.1.

There is a temptation to analyze the alternatives by discounting the respective cash flow streams at the 25% discount rate as follows:

Lease

Present value of cash inflows 47,472 × 1.952	$ 92,667
Present value of cash outflows (43,798) × 1.952	(85,494)
Net present value	$ 7,173

Exhibit 16.1   Representation of Purchase and Lease Options

A. Purchase Ignoring Financing

Cash flow	(100,000)	47,473	47,473	47,473
Period:	1	2	3	4

B. Lease

Cash flow from asset		47,473	47,473	47,473
Cash flow for lease		(43,789)	(43,789)	(43,789)
Period:	1	2	3	4

C. Purchase Adjusted for Financing at 15%

Cash flow for/from asset	(100,000)	47,473	47,473	47,473
Cash flow for financing	100,000	(43,789)	(43,789)	(43,789)
Period:	1	2	3	4

D. Lease Using Cash Equivalent in Lieu of Lease Payments

Cash flow from asset	—	47,473	47,473	47,473
Adjusted cash flow for lease	(100,000)	—	—	—
Period:	1	2	3	4

Purchase		
Present value of cash inflows 47,473 × 1.952	$ 92,667
Outflow	(100,000)
Net present value	$ (7,333)

Based on this comparison (which may be erroneous) the asset would be acquired *only if leasing is used*. However, the analysis was not done in comparable terms. The leasing option included finance charges, and the purchase option (financed by borrowing from a third party) did not. We need to be consistent before we compare.

One way of achieving consistency is to include financing activities in the purchase option. This can be done by (1) assuming $100,000 is borrowed and (2) assuming that the loan and interest are paid in *equal installments* over the life of the project. At the beginning of year 1 the inflow from the loan and the cost of the asset offset each other resulting in a net cash flow of zero. The repayment schedule for this loan depends on the interest rate.

Before considering possible alternative borrowing rates, it is of interest to know the *implicit interest rate* incorporated in the lease. This rate would be such that the present value of the lease payments is equal to the cash equivalent price of $100,000 and is determined as follows:

$$100,000 = 43,798 \times a_{i,3}$$
$$a_{i,3} = 100,000 \div 43,798 = 2.2832$$

From Table A.3 note that for an n of 3, i would have to be between 14% ($a_{0.14,3} = 2.3216$) and 16% ($a_{0.16,3} = 2.2459$). Interpolation yields a rate of 15%.

Now consider possible loan interest rates to finance the purchase option. To establish a base point, first assume that the firm can independently borrow at the 15% rate implicit in the lease. With this rate, and ignoring taxes and differences in cash flows, the firm would be indifferent between the two financing alternatives. That is, at a 15% rate, the level annual payments needed to retire the debt and pay interest would be the same as the annual lease payment: $43,798. (The level payment is an assumption that will be changed later.) By including the financing activities in the purchase option, we have a beginning net investment of zero, annual cash inflows of $47,473, and annual cash outflows of $43,798. See frame C of Exhibit 16.1. These data are the same as in the original analysis of the lease (frame B of Exhibit 16.1). Given a discount rate of 25%, the NPV would be the same: $7,173. Note in either case, the original lease analysis or the *modified* purchase analysis, that the net cash flow each year is positive: $47,473 − $43,798. Therefore, the NPV would be positive for *any* positive discount rate.

Instead of including the financing arrangements in the purchase option, they could be removed from the lease option. This would be done by using the *cash equivalent* of the lease option instead of the lease payments. As discussed before, the lease is just a substitute for a loan. The cash equivalent of the lease obligations is the present value of the payments using the *implicit* interest rate. In our case, this amounts to $100,000. With this approach we obtain the same results as the original purchase analysis: that is, an equivalent original outlay of $100,000 and annual cash inflows of $47,473. (See frame D of Exhibit 16.1). At a 25% discount rate, the NPV is a negative $7,333. Now there are two ways of making the alternatives comparable but they do not lead to identical results.

Which of the two methods of obtaining comparability should be used? In defense of the first alternative it might be argued that so long as the annual cash inflows exceed the annual cash outflows, a project should be adopted. However, a firm could arrange the financing of *every* project so there would be annual installments to be paid in lieu of an up-front payment. Further, signing a lease does commit a firm to a future obligation. Perhaps this is viewed by the capital market in much the same way as a bank loan. If so, a lease is just as much a consumption of the firm's capacity to generate resources through debt securities as the issuance of bonds. This logic leads to the conclusion that we should cut through the form of the financing and look at the substance. To do this means that the preferred method of obtaining comparability excludes the financing transactions from the cash flows (the second method).

Stated alternatively, we must first decide if the project should be adopted by using the cash outlay or equivalent cash outlay as the initial investment. Then, if the result is favorable, the method of financing that should be selected is the one with the lowest marginal cost. In the preceding case, we cannot financially justify the project when using a 25% discount rate.

To further illustrate the preferred procedure, change the discount rate to 14%. Under these conditions, the project should be accepted since the NPV is positive:

Present value of cash inflows 47,473 × 2.3216	$110,213
Cash equivalent outflow	(100,000)
Net present value	$ 10,213

As the second decision we must select the debt method. Remember the lease has an implicit interest cost of 15%. If independent borrowing can be arranged for less than 15% then independent borrowing should be used. Otherwise, the lease should be accepted.

Let us summarize at this point. If a lease is one of the alternatives for financing a project, then an NPV analysis should first be done in order to determine if the project should be accepted. In doing this, the present value of the lease payments should be treated as the equivalent of an investment. (Usually this present value will equal the purchase price.) Although the present value of the lease payments is derived using the rate of interest implicit in the lease terms, the NPV analysis uses the firm's discount rate.

If this analysis results in a favorable decision, then the optimal financing strategy must be selected. This can be more complex than implied in the previous example. Let's now explore how the decision should be approached. The financing arrangements can involve a variety of cash flow patterns. These patterns may lead to situations where the best solution does not have the appearance of the best solution.

To illustrate, suppose a bank loan can be arranged for the $100,000 with the following repayment schedule:

End of Year	Payment
1	$ 16,000
2	16,000
3	116,000

It is obvious that this loan has a 16% interest rate. Recall the lease has an implicit rate of 15%. With a discount rate of 14%, we decided to accept the project. Now we must select between the loan and the lease. Apparently, the lease is the least expensive financing arrangement but we must be careful. The proceeds from the project will be used differently if the loan is taken instead of the lease.

The cash flows, net of all financing costs, are presented in Exhibit 16.2. Since the net figures in Exhibit 16.2 include the finance charges, they represent cash that

---

Exhibit 16.2   Net Cash Flows Lease versus Loan Problem

Year	*(1)* Proceeds from Project	*(2)* Loan Payment	*(3) = (1) − (2)* Net for Loan Option	*(4)* Lease Payment	*(5) = (1) − (4)* Net for Lease Option
1	$47,473	$16,000	$31,473	$43,473	$4,000
2	47,473	16,000	$31,473	43,473	4,000
3	47,473	116,000	(68,527)	43,473	4,000

---

can be used in alternative ways. Thus, the best financing alternative ultimately depends on how the excess cash will be used. If the alternative usage would yield less than 16% (the cost of the loan) the lease would automatically be preferred. But for higher yielding alternatives, the loan could prove better. This is because of the delayed repayment and trading on the equity. That is, if funds costing 16% can be used to earn more than 16%, the additional earnings will eventually offset the higher cost of the loan in comparison with the lease.

Consider some possibilities by first verifying the following calculations:

Rate of Earnings on Alternative	*NPV of Net Cash Flows of Loan Option Using Earnings Rate*	*NPV of Net Cash Flows of Lease Option Using Earnings Rate*
16%	$ 6,619	$8,984
18	7,568	8,697
20	8,427	8,425
25	10,235	7,808

Note that when the alternative earnings rate exceeds 20%, the loan becomes preferable even though its interest rate exceeds that of the lease.

Determining the Discount Rate

Several capital budgeting methods require a discount rate (discounted payback, net present value, and profitabiity index). Further, the internal rate of return method, when used as a project selection criterion, assumes there is a threshold, or hurdle, rate. That is, to be considered desirable from a financial standpoint, a project's IRR must exceed the threshold. Thus, all methods that incorporate the time value of money are dependent on a discount rate. In this section we will consider the problem of selecting an appropriate discount rate.

As a prerequisite to selecting a discount rate, we must agree upon a guiding concept. Should the marginal cost of capital be used, the return possible from alternative uses of the capital, or a weighted cost of capital?[2] In this section we will explore the meaning of each of these possibilities as well as their implementation. Additionally, the meaning of risk is explained, along with a discussion of how to incorporate aversions to risk into the capital budgeting model.

CONCEPTS.   One concept of a discount rate is the actual rate that must be paid on the funds used to finance the specific project. So, for example, if project A is to be financed with funds borrowed at 10%, then its discount rate is 10%. On the other hand, if project B uses funds from a preferred stock issue that cost 15%, then the discount rate will be 15%. A rate determined in this way is called the out-of-pocket cost of capital. This is not the real marginal cost because all opportunity costs are ignored.

In criticism of the out-of-pocket cost of capital, it can be argued that all projects should be subjected to the *same* discount rate. This is not the case if the out-of-pocket cost concept is used. If this concept is used and if project A, referred to above, generates a 12% return, then it would be acceptable. But if B earned 14%, it would not be acceptable. Further, as more and more of the least expensive capital is used, the firm will be forced to start using more expensive types of capital because of the forces at work in the market. This is one of the opportunity costs ignored by the out-of-pocket cost concept.

A second type of rate is based on the premise that projects should provide a return at least equal to the best alternative use of the funds. For example, this might be the return possible from a relatively risk-free government security. Such a rate may be defensible if (1) the capital was already available (idle cash) and (2) there are good reasons for not reducing the size of the total equity of the firm by retiring debt and stock.

Given conditions (1) and (2), a project that earns 12% would at least be better than an investment in 8% government securities. Further given condition (2), the actual cost of the capital would be irrelevant. Some would argue, however, that there is little reason to impose condition (2) on ourselves. If capital costs 14%, then they would argue that the firm might as well return it to the equity holders as

---

[2]A survey of large firms revealed the following relative usages as discount rates for capital budgeting:

17% Cost of debt
 9% Cost of equity
20% Measurement based on past experience
46% Weighted cost of capital
17% Expectation with respect to growth and dividend payout
 8% Risk-free rate plus premium for risk class
16% Other

See: L.D. Schall, G.L. Sundem, and W.R. Geigsbeck, Jr., "Survey and Analysis of Capital Budgeting Methods," *The Journal of Finance* (March 1978), pp. 281–287.

invest in anything earning less than 14%. Over the long run such a strategy might led to a decline in the size of the equity and of the firm.

Because of the aforementioned disadvantages of the first two concepts, a majority of analysts lean toward some type of **weighted cost of capital.** That is, capital is viewed as a pool that has many streams leading into it. When capital is used, it is viewed as coming from the pool, not from an individual stream. Thus, given a *mix* of debt, preferred stock, common stock, retained earnings, and recovered capital (assets protected from distribution through depreciation charges), a weighted cost can be computed. To do this, compute the cost of raising a dollar by each of the streams into the capital pool and then weight the cost of each individual stream by its proportion in the mix. Summing over all of the weighted costs gives a weighted cost of capital.

≥ COMPUTING THE WEIGHTED COST OF CAPITAL.   Before briefly illustrating how the weighted cost concept can be implemented, we should point out that the final result will be an estimate. Fortunately, the capital budgeting model is frequently insensitive to some degree of estimation error in the discount rate. Thus, it is not necessary to require perfection in measuring the cost of capital.

In measuring the cost of the individual streams, we are guided by what the firm would have to earn in order to maintain the value of the common share. The common shareholder is the owner and ultimate risk taker of the firm. Any action that would cause the value of the common share to decline should be avoided. A rate that results in no change in the value of the common share is the threshold or hurdle rate.

To measure the cost of the *debt* stream simply determine the *effective* rate of interest that would have to be paid to acquire capital by *new* debt incurrence. This rate, less any income tax effect, is the *minimum* that would have to be earned on debt-financed projects in order to maintain the value of the common share. The *contractual* rate on *existing* debt is not the appropriate rate. First, the contractual rate is applied to the face value of the debt. The latter is arbitrary and is no indication of the amount the market will be willing to pay for the security. If a bond with face value of $1,000 pays interest of 10% and can be sold for $900, then the annual interest paid is $100. The effective rate of interest is higher than the contractual rate because only $900 is received. Further, it is generally necessary to consider what it would cost to issue bonds now, not in the past. Frequently, the capital needed to finance a proposed project must come from *new sources.* Also, the existing debt will mature and if the size of the capital pool is to be maintained, then the maturing debt will have to be replaced. Future rates will determine the relevant cost of doing this.

The effective interest rate should also be net of income taxes. Since interest is deductible for tax purposes, the firm's after-tax cost of interest is smaller than the pretax cost. Defining the *pre*-tax interest rate as i, and the tax rate as T, then it follows that:

Cost of debt $= (1 - T)i$

To illustrate, assume the previously discussed bond is due in five years. Then, in return for a present receipt of $900, there is a promise to pay five annual installments of $100 plus $1,000 five years from now. The effective pretax interest, i, must be such that the present value of the future outflows is equal to $900:

$$900 = 100 \times a_{i,5} + 1,000 \times p_{i,5}$$

Using an iterative evaluation procedure, it can be shown that $i = 12.83\%$. Consequently, given a tax rate of 40%, the cost of debt is:[3]

Cost of debt = $(1 - 0.4)0.1283 = 0.07698 = 7.698\%$

A second component of the weighted average cost of capital is preferred stock. Unlike common stock, this type of stock generally has a contractual dividend rate. Thus, this rate can be used to compute an effective cost of acquiring capital by issuing preferred stock. However, unlike interest on debt, dividends are not deductible for tax purposes. Thus, the after-tax cost of preferred stock is equal to the pretax cost and the effective rate is just the annual contractual dividends per share divided by the price at which a share could be sold in the current market.

The logic of considering preferred dividends as a cost is the same as for interest on debt. If these dividends are not recovered by projects utilizing the capital, then the value of the common share will decline. To illustrate the computation, suppose a share of preferred stock with par value of $100 will sell for $120. If the stock pays a 12% dividend, then the effective cost is 10% ($12 ÷ $120).

The cost of the common equity component of capital is the most difficult to measure. Further, there is no agreement as to how it should be done. There is some agreement, however, that the cost of equity is the rate of earnings that must be achieved in order for the value of common shares to remain unchanged. Some would argue that this rate is the expected earnings per share divided by the current market value of the stock. Others would say that market values are the result of shareholders discounting the expected cash flows. If so, the cost of common equity is a function of expected dividends and expected per share prices.

The latter theory must allow for an expected growth in the dividend payments. For example, if we are willing to assume a very simple set of expectations, then the cost of common equity, k, would be the discount rate that sets the present value of the expected cash flows equal to the current price of the stock. Let P_0 be the current price, D_1 the expected dividend at the end of year 1, g the expected annual dividend growth percentage, and P_n the expected market value of the stock at the end of year n. Consequently, we wish to find k such that:

$$P_0 = \frac{D_1}{(1 + k)^1} + \frac{(1 + g)D_1}{(1 + k)^2} + \frac{(1 + g)^2 D_1}{(1 + k)^3} + \cdots$$
$$+ \frac{(1 + g)^{n-1} D_1}{(1 + k)^n} + \frac{P_n}{(1 + k)^n}$$

---

[3]This assumes that the discount is amortized for tax purposes using the compound-interest method.

For a large value of n (approaching infinity), it can be shown that the value of k needed to satisfy the above equation is given by:

$$k = \frac{D_1}{P_0} + g$$

Obviously, the determination of the growth rate, g, must be made with some subjectivity. Further, if it is necessary to determine the cost of *new* securities, then we must recognize that there would be some stock-issuance costs. Because of the issuance costs, the firm will have less cash than the shareholders paid. The usable cash will have to earn a rate in excess of k if the shareholders are to earn k percent on their original investment.

To extend this cost concept to capital resulting from earnings retention and capital recoveries (via depreciation policy), it must be recognized that the shareholders will not pay income tax on undistributed assets. Presumably, the shareholder will be willing to accept a smaller return on this kind of capital than on a direct investment. If such capital were distributed as dividends and if the shareholders desired it to remain in the business, then they would have to reinvest their dividends. But due to their own income taxes and brokerage costs, they would not be able to reinvest an amount equal to the corresponding undistributed assets. Thus, if k is the rate a firm must earn on direct investments, then it follows that the rate the firm must earn on retained earnings and capital recoveries would be less than k.

Assuming a cost has been determined for each of these components of the capital pool, then the next issue is determining the weighting factors. Usually, these are suggested to be the optimal proportions of each of the components to total equity. Space does not permit an elaboration of this determination.[4]

To illustrate the weighted average cost of capital computation, assume that the debt and preferred stock costs are as computed previously: 7.698% and 10%. Further, assume that the current dividend per share of common stock is $5.00, the current price is $60, and that dividends are expected to grow at an annual rate of 4%. Then:

$$k = \frac{D_1}{P_0} + g = \frac{(1 + g)D_0}{P_0} + g = \frac{(1.04)(5)}{60} + 0.04$$

$$k = 0.1267$$

As discussed earlier, giving consideration to the cost of issuing new stock increases the final cost of new common equity. In the example, assume that such a consideration increases the cost to 13%. Further, assume that the shareholders' tax and reinvestment cost adjustment reduces the rate on retained earnings and recovered capital to 11%. Finally, assume that column (1) of the following schedule represents the desired proportion of each source of capital.

[4]For an elaboration, see James C. Van Horne, *Financial Management and Policy,* 5th ed. (Englewood Cliffs, NJ: Prentice-Hall, 1980), pp. 232–234.

Weighted Cost of Capital Computation

	(1) Percentage	*(2)* Marginal Cost	*(3) = (1) × (2)* Weighted Cost
Debt	0.30	0.07698	0.023094
Preferred stock	0.10	0.10000	0.010000
Common stock	0.30	0.13000	0.039000
Retained earnings and recovered capital	0.30	0.11000	0.033000
Weighted cost			0.105094

This cost might be rounded to 10.5% when using it as a discount rate in NPV analyses.

SENSITIVITY.   As indicated earlier, it is not necessary to require complete accuracy in measuring the discount rate. Decision models are insensitive to measurement error *if* the error does not change the recommended course of action. The net present value model, as used to this point, results in an "accept" recommendation if the net present value is positive. Since the recommendation to accept a project occurs only when its NPV is positive, then any error in measuring the discount rate will cause a wrong recommendation only if the sign (positive or negative) of the project's NPV would be reversed from the results that would be obtained by using the correct rate.

To illustrate, reconsider the Brown Company problem of the previous chapter (summarized in Exhibit 15.6). In that problem a 10% discount rate was used and, based upon that rate, it was recommended that the new machine be purchased. However, it can be shown by trial and error that the recommendation would be to accept the machine if the discount rate was 12.412% or less. (The trial-and-error method was simply a process of trying different discount rates until the present value of the two alternatives were equal.) Obviously a rather significant variation around the original 10% discount rate can be tolerated before the wrong decision is made. Such a conclusion is context dependent and, in general, it cannot be concluded that an error of this magnitude can always be tolerated. Nevertheless, this demonstrates how to perform a *sensitivity analysis* of the NPV model with regard to the discount rate.

RISK FACTOR.   Very simply stated, **risk** is uncertainty about the outcome of an action. When a project is adopted, we can never be sure that the payoffs will turn out to be exactly as projected. Most decision makers are risk averse. That is, given two projects with unequal risk (a short-term government security and the development of a new product, for example), the risk avertor may subject the more risky investment to a higher threshold. Risk avertors require some type of compensation for accepting the more risky alternative. This compensation is frequently in the form of a requirement for a higher expected return.

One way to incorporate risk into the analysis is by increasing the discount rate used in discounting the cash flows from the more risky ventures. Thus, if the discount rate for riskless investments is 10%, then moderately risky projects might be discounted at 11%, average risky ones at 13%, and high risks at 16%. Because of the compounding nature of the NPV model, this method for risk adjustment implicitly assumes that risk increases over time. Obviously, a large amount of subjectivity must be exercised by management in selecting the amount by which the discount rate will be increased to allow for risk. But, in defense of this, a manager's attitude toward risk, is, itself, a subjective one. Thus, risk adjustment has an unavoidable appearance of subjectivity.

≥ Break-Even Analysis with Imputed Interest as a Cost

In Chapter 13 we discussed the CVP model but ignored a very real cost: the opportunity cost of the funds invested in long-lived assets. Since this cost is due to the time value of money, its consideration was delayed until the NPV model was introduced. Of course, the opportunity cost of invested funds is not recorded in the accounts and is not a factor in computing accounting income. But, decision makers and managerial accountants should be concerned with economic profits, not just reported profits. This section, then, is an enrichment section in which we discuss Rene Manes's proposal for using CVP analysis when it is desired to consider such a cost.[5]

To illustrate both the problem and the process, consider the following project. A machine with a five-year life can be acquired at a cost of $100,000. Straight-line depreciation will be used for tax purposes. The machine will enable the addition of a new product line which will yield a contribution margin of $8 per unit. Incremental fixed costs (excluding depreciation) will amount to $12,000 annually. The firm is subject to a marginal tax rate of 40% and uses an after-tax discount rate of 10%.

A conventional CVP analysis would add the annual depreciation ($20,000) to the other annual fixed costs and determine the break-even point as:

$$x_0 = \frac{20,000 + 12,000}{8} = 4,000$$

However, the cost of providing the $100,000 of capital is ignored. Implicitly, the conventional analysis assumes an interest rate of zero. This is not a sound economic assumption.

Let x be the annual unit volume of activity that is necessary in each year of the project's life to recover all costs. Assuming interest is compounded annually and that cash flows occur at year-end, we have:

$$[8x - 12,000 - 0.4(8x - 32,000)]a_{0.10,5} = 100,000 \tag{16-7}$$

The quantity, $8x - 12,000$, is the annual incremental cash flow exclusive of taxes. Since straight-line depreciation is being used for tax purposes, the incremental taxable income is $8x - 12,000 - 20,000$. The result inside the brackets is the annual

[5]Rene Manes, "A New Dimension to Breakeven Analysis," *Journal of Accounting Research* (Spring 1966), pp. 87–100.

after-tax cash flow. Multiplying by the present value factor of a five-year annuity at 10% and setting the result equal to the original investment permits the determination of the volume, x, that will just exactly recover all costs including the cost of capital.

From Table A.3, we find the $a_{0.10,5}$ value is 3.7908. Dividing both sides of (16-7) by this amount and combining similar terms yields:

$$4.8x + 800 = 26,379.66 \tag{16-8}$$

Deducting 800 from both sides and dividing by 4.8 solves for x:

$$x = 5,329$$

This figure can be compared with the conventional break-even volume of 4,000 units. In order for the volume of output to be sufficient to also recover the 10% interest on the unrecovered investment, it must be 1,329 units higher than if such costs were not considered relevant.

The Manes article generalized these results which we will not discuss. But this example indicates the basic idea of incorporating such costs into the analysis.

Summary

This chapter considered several problems that might be encountered when using capital budgeting. You should now be familiar with the problems of analyzing competing unequal-lived projects, determining the cost of working capital, adjusting for price level changes, and uncertainty. The chapter also alerted you to the problems of evaluating and controlling capital projects. Further, there was a discussion on how to analyze a problem that contains constraints, how to incorporate leases, and how to select a discount rate. Finally, there was an enrichment section incorporating the cost of capital into the CVP model.

Capital budgeting is a topic of interest to accountants, financial managers, and industrial engineers. The accountant, of course, will be a major provider of input data. This function is enhanced if the accountant has a strong background in the theory and concepts of this tool. In short, this has been the purpose of the last two chapters. With this background you should be able to be a major contributor to capital-budgeting analyses.

New key terms and concepts from this chapter with which you should be familiar include:

Level payment approach (of evaluating unequal lived projects)
Risk
Congruence
Weighted cost of capital
Sensitivity analysis

SELF-STUDY PROBLEM. The Sax Company is currently operating machine A at its full capacity of 25,000 units per year. However, orders are up to 50,000 units per year and a decision has already been made to increase the productive capacity of the plant. Two alternatives are being considered:

1. Buy a second machine A to double the capacity.
2. Sell machine A and replace it with machine B, which has a 60,000-unit capacity.

The existing machine A had a life of seven years when it was acquired three years ago. It cost $200,000 and is being depreciated over a five-year period for tax purposes using the straight-line method. The current salvage value of the machine is $60,000.

Inflation has been, and is expected to continue, at a 10% rate compounded annually on all items purchased. Thus, the current cost of machine A is $266,200. The expected life of a new machine A is also seven years and it will also be depreciated over five years for tax purposes using the straight-line method. If used for seven years a type-A machine will have no terminal salvage value.

A type-B machine currently costs $550,000. As with the other machines the useful life is seven years and it will be depreciated over five years using the straight-line method. There will be no terminal salvage value. A type-B machine will require $100,000 less in *non*cash working capital than two type-A machines.

In terms of beginning year-1 prices, the annual operating costs are $15,000 per machine for type A and $20,000 for type B. Inflation is expected to cause a 10% increase, compounded annually, in these costs.

The firm's inflation adjusted discount rate is 20%. Its marginal income tax rate is 40%.

Required:

Prepare a net present value analysis using a *seven-year period*.

Solution to Self-Study Problem

Note that the discount rate given is already adjusted to include the inflation rate. Thus, to use the discount rate, it is necessary to forecast all cash flows in terms of the price levels anticipated at the time of the flow. See the explanatory notes below, which are cross-referenced to the following solution.

Buy Second A	Amount	PVF	PV
1. Acquisition cost of second A	($266,200)	1.0000	($266,200)
2. Tax savings on depreciation			
266,200 ÷ 5 × 0.4	21,296	2.9906	63,688
3. Tax savings on existing machine			
200,000 ÷ 5 × 0.4	16,000	1.5278	24,445
4. Replacement of existing machine A at			
end of year 4 $266,200(1.10)^4$	(389,743)	0.4823	(187,973)
5. Tax savings from depreciation on replacement			
machine 389,743 ÷ 5 × 0.4	31,179	1.0159	31,675
Bail out on replacement machine			
at end of year 7			
6. Market value $60,000(1.10)^7$	116,923	0.2791	32,633

Buy Second A		Amount	PVF	PV
7. Decrease in taxes on assumed disposal				
Book value 389,743 ÷ 5 × 2	155,897			
Market value	116,923			
Loss	38,974			
Tax rate	0.4	15,590	0.2791	4,351
8. Operating costs				
Year 1 30,000(1.1)^1 × 0.6		(19,800)	0.8333	(16,499)
Year 2 30,000(1.1)^2 × 0.6		(21,780)	0.6944	(15,124)
Year 3 30,000(1.1)^3 × 0.6		(23,958)	0.5787	(13,864)
Year 4 30,000(1.1)^4 × 0.6		(26,354)	0.4823	(12,711)
Year 5 30,000(1.1)^5 × 0.6		(28,989)	0.4019	(11,651)
Year 6 30,000(1.1)^6 × 0.6		(31,888)	0.3349	(10,679)
Year 7 30,000(1.1)^7 × 0.6		(35,077)	0.2791	(9,790)
9. Working capital differential		(100,000)	1.0000	(100,000)
10. Recovery of working capital				
100,000(1.1)^7		194,872	0.2791	54,389
NPV				($433,310)

Buy Machine B

		Amount	PVF	PV
11. Cost		($550,000)	1.0000	($550,000)
12. Tax savings on depreciation				
550,000 ÷ 5 × 0.4		44,000	2.9906	131,586
Sale of old A				
13. Market value		60,000	1.0000	60,000
14. Tax savings from sale				
Book value 200,000 ÷ 5 × 2	80,000			
Market value	60,000			
Loss	20,000			
Tax rate	0.4	8,000	1.0000	8,000
15. Operating costs				
Year 1 20,000(1.10)^1 × 0.6		(13,200)	0.8333	(11,000)
Year 2 20,000(1.10)^2 × 0.6		(14,520)	0.6944	(10,083)
Year 3 20,000(1.10)^3 × 0.6		(15,972)	0.5787	(9,243)
Year 4 20,000(1.10)^4 × 0.6		(17,569)	0.4823	(8,474)
Year 5 20,000(1.10)^5 × 0.6		(19,326)	0.4019	(7,767)
Year 6 20,000(1.10)^6 × 0.6		(21,259)	0.3349	(7,120)
Year 7 20,000(1.10)^7 × 0.6		(23,385)	0.2791	(6,527)
NPV				($410,628)

EXPLANATORY NOTES (cross-referenced to the numbered items in the solution):

1. Should be obvious.
2. The second A will be depreciated over five years for tax purposes. The reduction of taxes through depreciation is what generates a cash flow. Therefore, the tax depreciation method is the relevant method. Note that the PVF is for a five-year annuity at 20%.
3. Should be obvious. The PVF is for two years.
4. Since the original machine A is three years old at decision time and since it has a total useful life of seven years it must be replaced at the end of year 4. Prices are going up at

10% per year. Thus the current purchase price of $266,200 must be projected for four years of inflations $(1.10)^4$. The PVF is for a single amount at the end of year 4.

5. The machine A purchased in year 4 will be depreciated for tax purposes using its acquisition cost. Since the analysis is over a seven-year period the tax savings from the depreciation is a three-year annuity (years 5, 6, and 7). A PVF can be arrived at as the PVF for a seven-year annuity (3.6046) less the PVF for a four-year annuity (2.5887). The difference, then, is the sum of the present-value factors for years 5, 6, and 7.

6. Because the replacement machine is still useful at the end of the planning horizon selected, seven years, you must derive its bail-out value as a surrogate for future cash flows. At the *beginning of year 1,* a three-year-old machine has a market value of $60,000. Since prices are increasing at 10% it would be reasonable to assume that a three-year-old machine will have a market value seven years from now of $60,000 $\times$ $(1.10)^7$. Obviously the PVF is for a single amount seven years hence.

7. If a bail-out is going to be assumed, a tax effect will have to be computed also. The second machine A will have two years of depreciation remaining to be taken for tax purposes at the end of year 7. Therefore, the book value is 2/5 of the original cost. The market value was derived in item 6 and is less than the book value. Thus, there is a tax loss and a decrease in the tax liability.

8. The $30,000 of operating costs are in terms of price levels at the beginning of year 1. Thus, in each year the $30,000 must first be adjusted for price levels. After taxes, the adjusted cash flow generates cash outflow equal to 60% of the original amount.

9. Since the two alternatives require different amounts of working capital there will be a difference between them with regard to the opportunity cost. Option A requires more working capital than option B, and this is shown as an incremental working capital of option A.

10. To properly compute the cost of working capital using the short-cut method, you must provide for a recovery of the working capital at the end of the planning horizon. Note that the working capital was of the *non*cash variety. If prices are increasing it is reasonable to expect the working capital items to also change in price. For example, 100 units of inventory would have a different dollar value at decision time than they will seven years later. Thus, in projecting the recovery, the dollar value has been inflated at $(1.10)^7$.

Items 11–15 should either be obvious or have explanations similar to those of option A. Since option B has the larger-price-level-adjusted NPV, it should be preferred to option A.

References

Hertz, D.B. "Risk Analysis in Capital Investment," *Harvard Business Review* (January–February 1964): 96–106.

Lerner, E.M., and Rappaport A., "Limit DCF in Capital Budgeting," *Harvard Business Review* (September–October 1968): 133–139.

Manes, R. "A New Dimension to Breakeven Analysis," *Journal of Accounting Research* (Spring 1966): 87–100.

Sharpe, W.F. *Portfolio Theory and Capital Markets,* New York: McGraw-Hill Book Co., 1970.

Vancil, R.F. "Lease or Borrow—New Method of Analysis," *Harvard Business Review* (September–October 1961): 122–136.

Van Horne, J.C. "A Note on Biases in Capital Budgeting Introduced by Inflation," *Journal of Financial and Quantitative Analysis* (January–February 1971): 653–658.

———. *Financial Management and Policy,* 5th ed. Englewood Cliffs, NJ: Prentice-Hall, Inc., 1980.

Weingartner, H.M. "Capital Budgeting of Interrelated Projects: Survey and Synthesis," *Management Science* (March 1966): 485–516.

Problems

16-1 Basic Problem on Unequal Lived Projects. The Paxton Company's production line will support one additional machine. Two machines are being considered: machine A and machine B. Machine A has an estimated useful life of three years and B five years. Following are the estimated pretax cash flows:

	Cost	Year 1	Year 2	Year 3	Year 4	Year 5
A	$15,000	$8,535	$8,535	$8,535	0	0
B	15,000	5,995	5,995	5,995	$5,995	$5,995

The marginal tax rate is 40%, the after-tax discount rate is 12%, and straight-line depreciation is used for tax purposes. Machine A will be considered three-year property and B five-year property for tax purposes.

Required:

1. Determine the after-tax internal rate of return for each machine.
2. Determine the net present values for each machine that would result if the time factor is not adjusted.
3. Determine the NPV using the shorter life. Assume machine B can be salvaged at its book value.
4. Determine the NPV using a time period that is divisible by both lives.
5. Do an NPV analysis using the level payment approach.
6. Comment on the results of your answers to the preceding questions

16-2. Problem To Show that Alternative Ways of Adjusting for Unequal-Lived Projects Yield Identical Results. A company is considering three projects whose estimated cash flows are as follows:

Project	Cost	Year 1	Year 2	Year 3	Year 4	Year 5	Year 6
A	$20,000	$12,459	$12,459	—	—	—	—
B	30,000	12,922	12,922	$12,922	—	—	—
C	40,000	9,729	9,729	9,729	$9,729	$9,729	$9,729

Present value factors for an interest rate of 8.6613% are:

Pd.	8.6613%
1	0.9203
2	0.8469
3	0.7794
4	0.7173
5	0.6601
6	0.6075

Required:

1. Show that the internal rates of return for projects A, B, and C are 16%, 14%, and 12%, respectively.
2. Without giving consideration to the life differences, rank the projects on the basis of an NPV analysis using a 10% discount rate.
3. Assume that the life differences will be adjusted for by replicating the projects over a time period that is divisible by all projects.
   a. Rank the projects when the discount rate is 10%.
   b. Rank the projects when the discount rate is 8.6613%.
   c. Rank the projects when the discount rate is 8%.
4. Now assume the level payments approach is to be used in comparing the projects.
   a. Rank the project when the discount rate is 10%.
   b. Rank the projects when the discount rate is 8.6613%.
   c. Rank the projects when the discount rate is 8%.

16-3. Adjusting for Life Differences When Cash Flows Are Not Annuities. The Hack Company is considering two projects whose cash flows are as follows:

	Investment	Year 1	Year 2	Year 3
A	($12,256)	$ 5,000	$10,000	—
B	($58,778)	40,000	20,000	$10,000

Only one of the projects can be adopted.

Required:

1. Assume the discount rate is 10%.
   a. Use the replication approach to decide which project should be adopted.
   b. Use the level payment approach to decide which project should be adopted.
2. Assume the discount rate is 11.519%. Then:

n	$p_{i,t}$	$a_{i,t}$
1	0.8967	0.8967
2	0.8041	1.7008
3	0.7210	2.4218
4	0.6466	3.0684
5	0.5798	3.6482

Repeat part 1.

3. Assume the discount rate is 11.8%. Then:

n	$p_{i,t}$	$a_{i,t}$
1	0.8945	0.8945
2	0.8000	1.6945
3	0.7156	2.4101
4	0.6401	3.0502
5	0.5725	3.6227

Repeat part 1.

16-4. Short Problem on Working Capital Cost. The Hahn Company is considering a six-year project that would require an immediate increase in working capital of $500,000. Its tax rate is 40% and its after-tax discount rate is 14%.

Required:

1. Using two different approaches, compute the cost of the increased capital.
2. Now show that, in general, the two approaches used in part 1 yield the same results. That is, assume the interest rate is i, the working capital requirement is W, and the life is n. The formulas for present-value computations are given in Tables A.2 and A.3.

16-5. Capital Budgeting and Inflation. The Avery Company has $100,000 available to help increase its sales. Two proposals are being considered.

1. Invest in an advertising campaign that will increase the pretax cash flows due to additional volume by $33,438 per year for each of five years. This increase is stated in terms of the 19x1 dollars (beginning of year). The advertising would be a tax-deductible expense in 19x1.
2. Invest in a new machine that would permit a new product to be added to the firm's line. The machine would have a five-year life and would increase cash flows before taxes by $40,000. Straight line depreciation would be used for tax purposes.

The firm's marginal tax rate is 40% and its risk-adjusted-inflation-free interest rate is 10%.

Required:

1. Ignore taxes. What is the NPV of the two alternatives? Assume that the 10% is a pretax rate.
2. What is the NPV of the two proposals after tax? Assume that the 10% is an after-tax rate.
3. Explain why the magnitude of the difference between the two proposals is smaller in part 2.
4. Now assume that the annual inflation rate is expected to be 8/110. Verify that the *pretax* cash flows are:

Proposal	Year 1	Year 2	Year 3	Year 4	Year 5
#1	35,870	38,479	41,277	44,279	47,499
#2	42,909	46,030	49,378	52,969	56,821

5. Assuming the inflation factor in part 4, what is the price level adjusted (real) NPV after taxes of each project?
6. If the preference between the two alternatives has changed from part 2 to part 5, explain why.

16-6. Integrative Problem. Ohio Monthly Publications, Inc. publishes a monthly magazine and is considering a promotion campaign to increase its sales. The promotion under consideration would cost $900,000 (payable and tax deductible at the beginning of the year). The three-year subscriptions would be received in one advanced payment (at the beginning of year 1) but would be reported for tax purposes as they are earned.

To support the increased sales, another production line would have to be installed. The equipment on this line would have a life of eighteen years and would be depreciated over the eighteen years on a straight line basis. It is estimated that the market value of this equipment would decline at the rate of $40,000 per year during the first three years of its life. In preparing the analysis it is to be assumed that the equipment will be sold at the end of three years (to compensate for the lack of a common time period). Also, to support the increased activity, working capital will have to be increased by $100,000 at the beginning of year 1.

The *incremental revenues* and *costs* (exclusive of gain and losses on asset disposals) are estimated as follows:

Item	Year 1	Year 2	Year 3
Incremental subscription revenue	$ 500,000	$500,000	$500,000
Incremental costs			
Campaign costs	900,000		
Other costs	200,000*	200,000*	200,000*
Total	$1,100,000	$200,000	$200,000
Incremental income	(600,000)#	300,000	300,000
Incremental tax @ 40%	(240,000)#	120,000	120,000
Incremental income after tax	$ (360,000)	$180,000	$180,000

*Includes depreciation on the new equipment amounting to $28,000.

#The estimated income from the current volume of subscriptions is greater than $600,000.

Required:

Assuming a discount rate of 10%, prepare a net present value analysis to be used in evaluating the merits of the proposal.

16-7. Comprehensive Problem on Chapters 15 and 16. The Sevigny Company is considering the replacement of an old machine that was purchased two years ago for $21,000. At that time, the estimated life was six years and it was set up to be depreciated for tax purposes as five-year property using the ACRS rates. Straight-line depreciation over six years was used for book purposes. On January 1, 19x1 (the current date), it is estimated that the old machine could be sold for $9,000. The estimate of the salvage value four years from now is $5,000.

The new machine under consideration would cost $12,000 and will have a useful life of six years. It also will be depreciated using the five-year property accelerated rates for tax purposes. For book purposes, sum-of-year-digits depreciation will be used. Defining n as the age of the machine at the time of disposal, the salvage value of the new machine can be estimated as follows:

$$0.10 \times (6 - n) \times \$12,000$$

The machines are to be compared over a common time period.

If the new machine is acquired, there would have to be a working capital increase amounting to $20,000. This is because of the larger inventories needed to support the machine. Further, the acquisition of this machine will enable the acceptance of a special order in 19x1. The incremental costs of producing the order will amount to $20,000 and would be incurred in 19x1. The contract sales price is $30,000 and would be received in three equal annual installments beginning December 31, 19x1. The tax code requires that the income on this contract be recognized in the year of the sale.

The company's weighted cost of capital is 10%, and its marginal tax rate is 40%.

Required:

Prepare an NPV analysis to be used in deciding whether the old machine should be replaced.

16-8. CMA Problem with Inflation. Catix Corporation is a divisionalized company, and each division has the authority to make capital expenditures up to $200,000 without approval of the corporate headquarters. The corporate controller has determined that the cost of capital for Catix Corporation is 12%. This rate does not include an allowance for inflation, which is expected to occur at an average rate of 8% over the next five years. Catix pays income taxes at the rate of 40%.

The Electronics Division of Catix is considering the purchase of an automated assembly and soldering machine for use in the manufacture of its printed circuit boards. The machine would be placed in service in early 19x1. The divisional controller estimates that if the machine is purchased, two positions will be eliminated yielding a cost savings for wages and employee benefits. However, the machine would require additional supplies and more power would be required to operate the machine. The cost savings and additional costs in current 19x0 prices are as follows:

Wages and employee benefits of the two positions eliminated ($25,000 each)	$50,000
Cost of additional supplies	$ 3,000
Cost of additional power	$10,000

The new machine would be purchased and installed at the end of 19x0 at a net cost of $100,000. If purchased, the machine would be depreciated on a straight-line basis for both book and tax purposes. The machine will become technologically obsolete in five years and will have no salvage value at that time.

The Electronics Division compensates for inflation in capital expenditure analyses by adjusting the expected cash flows by an estimated price level index. The adjusted after-tax cash flows are then discounted using the appropriate discount rate.

The Plastics Division of Catix compensates for inflation in capital expenditure analyses by adding the anticipated inflation rate to the cost of capital and then using the inflation adjusted cost of capital to discount the project cash flows. The Plastics Division recently rejected a project with cash flows and economic life similar to those associated with the machine under consideration by the Electronic Division. The Plastics Division's analysis of the rejected project was as follows:

Net pretax cost savings	$ 37,000
Less incremental depreciation expenses	20,000
Increase in taxable income	$ 17,000
Increase in income taxes (40%)	6,800
Increase in after-tax income	$ 10,200
Add back noncash expense (depreciation)	20,000
Net after-tax annual cash inflow (unadjusted for inflation)	$ 30,200
Present value of net cash inflows using the sum of the cost of capital (12%) and the inflation rate (8%) or a minimum required return of 20%	$ 89,996
Investment required	(100,000)
Net present value	($10,004)

All operating revenues and expenditures occur at the end of the year.

Required:

1. Calculate the net present value for the Electronic Division's project which will be meaningful to management.
2. Evaluate the methods used by the Plastics Division and the Electronics Division to compenste for expected inflation in capital expenditure analyses.

16-9. Capital Budgeting with General and Specific Price Changes. Moore Company has two divisions. Division A is located near a major metropolitan city and Division B in a rural midwestern community. Because of this Division A is expecting its material costs, which are currently the same as at Division B, to increase in price at a faster rate than B's.

Both divisions are considering an investment in a new machine that will enable the production of a new product, UFO. The company is unionized and the contract calls for wage adjustments in an amount equal to the national inflation rate. Inflation is expected to increase at 8% per year for the next five years.

The machine will cost either division $350,000 and have a five-year useful life. Straight-line depreciation will be used for tax purposes.

UFO will sell for $30 per unit in the first year. The selling price is expected to increase at average inflation rates. Both divisions estimate sales at 20,000 units per year. Variable overhead is also expected to increase at the average inflation rate. At current costs, the estimated costs of producing UFO are:

Material	$10 per unit
Labor	8 per unit
Variable overhead	5 per unit

You may assume there are no additional fixed costs except for the depreciation.

At Division A, the material costs are expected to increase at 14%, whereas at Division B, the material costs are expected to increase only at 2%. Both divisions use an inflation-free discount rate of 11.11%. Moore's tax rate is 40%.

Required:

1. Use an NPV analysis to decide what each division should do.
2. Comment on your results.

16-10. Capital Budgeting with Leases. The McElwain Company is considering the acquisition of a new machine. This machine would enable an increase in the *pretax* cash flows of $10,031 per year for the next five years. The machine could be purchased for $30,000 or leased at five annual payments of $7,514 beginning at the end of year 1. If purchased, the $30,000 would be borrowed from the bank at a rate of 10%.

Required:

1. Assume the pretax discount rate is 25%. Should the machine be acquired? If so, how?
2. Repeat part 1 but assume the discount rate is 14%.

16-11. Extension of Problem 16-10. In problem 16-10 it was indicated that the bank's interest rate was 10%. However, there are several possible loan arrangements where the cost would be 10%. For example, there might be a level repayment schedule, or a plan where interest is paid periodically and principal paid at the termination of the loan, or a plan where all interest and principal are paid at termination. Of course, this is not an exhaustive list. Suppose each of three banks quote a 10% interest rate but use a different plan. The specific terms are as follows.

		Payment at End of Year				
Bank	Loan	1	2	3	4	5
A	$30,000	$7,914	$7,914	$7,914	$7,914	$ 7,914
B	30,000	3,000	3,000	3,000	3,000	33,000
C	30,000	0	0	0	0	48,315

Required:

1. Verify that each of these plans bear interest at a cost of 10%.
2. Assuming the lease described in Problem 16-10, it will be of interest to select the best financing arrangement. Because of the difference in timing of the payments of the three loans, it is not automatic that a lease with implicit interest of 8% is better than a loan at 10%! Because of the difference in timing, the unpaid balances of the loans are not identical. The interest rate, of course, is based upon the unpaid balance. The key to the optimal selection of a financing plan is what will be done with recovered funds that are not needed to retire the loan or pay the lease.
   a. For each of the three plans (A, B, and C) and for the lease, prepare a schedule of annual *net* cash flows, that is, after loan and lease payments.
   b. Assume that recovered funds will earn 8%. Using 8% as a discount factor and the net cash flows from part a, find the NPV of each alternative. Rank the desirability of the four alternatives.
   c. Repeat part b assuming recovered funds will earn 10%.
   d. Repeat part b assuming recovered funds will earn 12%.
   e. Repeat part b assuming recovered funds will earn 14%.
3. Considering your results in part 2, explain what has happened and why.

16-12. Leases and Capital Budgeting. The Valenzuela Company is considering the acquisition of a computer that will save $28,590 in operating costs each year for the next four years. The computer can only be leased at an annual cost of $25,238.

Required:

1. Should the computer be acquired if the discount rate is 18%? Base your answer on net present value analyses.
2. Now assume the computer can either be purchased for $80,000 or leased as described above. The $80,000 would be borrowed from the bank and repaid by 4 annual installments of $27,456. Should the computer be acquired? If so, how? Assume the discount rate is 18% and that proceeds will be reinvested at 25%.
3. Assume the same facts as in question 2 but that the discount rate is 14%. Should the computer be acquired? If so, how?
4. Assume the same facts as in question 2 except that the bank loan of $80,000 will be repaid with three annual payments of $11,200 and a final one of $91,200 in the fourth period. Should the computer be acquired? If so, how?

16-13. CMA Problem on Cost of Capital. Timel Company is in the process of determining its capital budget for the coming fiscal year. Timel Company's balance sheet reflects five sources of long-term funds. The current outstanding amounts from these five sources are shown below and represent the company's historical sources of funds fairly accurately.

	Dollar Amount (in millions)	Percentage
Mortgage bonds ($1,000 par, 7.5%)	$135	15.0
Debentures ($1,000 par, 8%, due 19x5)	225	25.0
Preferred stock ($100 par, 7.5%)	90	10.0
Common stock ($10 par)	150	16.7
Retained earnings	300	33.3
	$900	100.0

Timel will raise the funds necessary to support the selected capital investment projects so as to maintain its historical distribution among the various sources of long-term funds. Thus, 15% will be obtained from additional mortgage bonds on new plant, 25% from debentures, 10% from preferred stock, and 50% from some common equity source. Timel's policy is to reinvest the funds derived from each year's earnings in new projects. Timel issues new common stock only after all funds provided from retained earnings have been exhausted.

Management estimates that its net income after taxes for the coming year will be $4.50 per common share. The dividend payout ratio will be 40% of earnings to common shareholders ($1.80 per share), the same ratio as in the prior four years. The preferred stockholders will receive $6.75 million. The earnings retained will be used as needed to support the capital investment program.

The capital budgeting staff, in conjunction with Timel's investment broker, has developed the following data regarding Timel's sources of funds if it were to raise funds in the current market.

	Par Value	Interest or Dividend Rate	Issue Price
Mortgage bonds	$1,000	14.0%	$1,000.00
Debentures	1,000	14.5	1,000.00
Preferred stock	100	13.5	99.25
Common stock	10	—	67.50

The estimated interest rates on the debt instruments and the dividend rate on the preferred stock are based upon the rates being experienced in the market by the firms that are of the same size and quality of Timel. The investment banker believes that Timel's price/earnings ratio of 15 is consistent with the 10% growth rate in earnings that the market is capitalizing in arriving at a price of $67.50 for the common stock.

Timel is subject to a 40% income tax rate.

Required:

1. Calculate the after-tax marginal cost of capital for each of the five sources of capital for Timel Company.

2. Calculate Timel Company's after-tax weighted average cost of capital.
3. Timel Company follows a practice that 50% of any funds raised will be derived from common equity sources. Determine the point of expansion at which Timel's source of common equity funds would switch from retained earnings to new common stock in the coming year.
4. If the basic business risks are similar for all firms in the industry in which Timel Company participates, would all firms in the industry have approximately the same weighted average cost of capital? Explain your answer.

16-14. CMA Problem on Weighted Cost of Capital. The Conner Company has the following capital structure:

Mortgage bonds 6%	$ 20,000,000
Common stock (one million shares)	25,000,000
Retained earnings	55,000,000
	$100,000,000

a. Mortgage bonds of similar quality could be sold at a net of 95 to yield 6.5%.
b. The common stock has been selling for $100 per share. The company has paid 50% of earnings in dividends for several years and intends to continue the policy. The current dividend is $4 per share. Earnings are growing at 5% per year.
c. If the company sold a new equity issue, it would expect to net $94 per share after all costs.
d. The marginal tax rate is 50%.

Conner wants to determine a cost of capital to use in capital budgeting. Additional projects would be financed to maintain the same relationship between debt and equity. Additional debt would consist of mortgage bonds and additional equity would consist of retained earnings.

Required:

1. Calculate the firm's weighted average cost of capital.
2. Explain why you used the weighting system you used.

16-15. Basic Sensitivity Analysis of Discount Rate. Reconsider machine A as described in problem 15-6. It was stated in 15-6 that the desired after-tax rate of return was 10%. Suppose the 10% is an estimate of the weighted cost of capital. How much error could be tolerated in measuring this cost before the decision using an NPV analysis would be different than resulted in problem 15-6?

16-16. Alternative to 16-15. Reconsider machine A as described in problem 15-6. Suppose the firm is uncertain about the estimate of cash savings in operating costs for machine A (the $1,713). Given the discount rate of 10%, by how much could the operating savings be reduced before the decision to acquire machine A is reversed?

16-17. CVP Problem with Cost of Capital. The Patton Company is considering the acquisition of a new machine that would cost $120,000 and have a useful life of five years. The new machine would be used to produce another product which the company cannot now produce. It would sell for $10 per unit and cost $6 per unit to produce exclusive of the estimated incremental $50,000 of fixed costs. The latter includes depreciation on the new machine computed on a straight-line basis. The marginal tax rate is 40% and the after-tax cost of capital is 14%.

Required:

1. Compute the annual break-even volume if the company ignores the cost of capital.
2. Compute the annual break-even volume if the cost of capital is to be considered.
3. Verify your answer in part 2 by finding the net present value of the after-tax cash flows that would result from the volume computed in part 2.

Part 4   Topics in Support of Control

CHAPTER 17

Control: Basic Concepts and Systems

Chapter Overview

Although there have been selected discussions of management control in previous chapters, this chapter initiates a more in-depth consideration of the accountant's role in this important activity. Control affects people and the way they behave in their jobs. Thus, the design of a control system is a very delicate assignment if it is done with a view toward enhancing the employees' ability to perform, their morale, and their attitude toward the firm. This chapter considers the general concepts, whereas subsequent chapters are devoted to some of the more technical issues of a control system.

The first section is a consideration of the nature of control and its various components. The second section covers responsibility accounting, which is basic to any type of control system. Another basic tool of accounting is internal control. Although it is explained more fully in auditing courses, the basic principles of internal control and its effect on cost/management accounting are examined in the third section. In the final section we discuss a variety of general considerations that are related to control.

The Nature and Components of Control

In this section we first define control and then consider the control process, including its components and the potential role of accounting. Increasingly, accountants and managers are recognizing that the behavioral impact of the control process is varied and complex. A discussion of the major behavioral issues will be woven throughout this section.

DEFINITION.   When we examine the literature, we find many definitions of control. Some of these definitions, especially those in the earlier literature, conceive of control as processes that strive to ensure adherence to plans. However, the current view of control is broader. As was mentioned earlier in the book, adherence to plans may not result in optimal strategies. Plans may have been optimal at the time they were made, but remember that they are usually formulated in an uncertain environment. With the passage of time comes the recognition that certain assumptions and predictions were not accurate, thus possibly justifying a change in those plans.

As a result of the previous discussion, **control** is defined as the *process used by a superior to deliberately influence a subordinate's actions with the purpose of causing actions to be taken which will minimize the deviation from the superior's objectives.*[1] A given superior's objectives may be influenced both by the person he or she reports to and by subordinates. But in the final analysis, control refers to the techniques used by a superior to gain adherence to chosen objectives. The design of a control system is, itself, a decision problem. What works in one case may not work in another. Factors influencing the selection of a system include the nature of the situation, the cognitive makeup of both the superior and the subordinates, the flexibility of the information system, and cost/benefit ratios.

COMPONENTS OF THE CONTROL PROCESS.   For accountants to best determine their potential contributions to the control process, they need to understand its component parts and their interrelationships. It is the purpose of this section to consider the elements of control.

One of the better descriptions of the control process is provided by Itami.[2] The following discussion is based on his description. As you read the discussion you can maintain perspective by also following the flowchart in Exhibit 17.1. Fundamental to control is **feedback information.** The necessity of feedback should be obvious. In order to control and to evaluate it is necessary to have some information about a subordinate's performance. The accountant, of course, will inevitably be involved in the feedback process. Decisions must be made about what should be collected and reported. This will be influenced by the superior's objective(s).

Further, there must be decisions about reports; their format, timing and distribution. How will the report be organized? How frequently should the data be reported? Who should get the reports? The section on responsibility accounting will provide some suggestions for format. Timing depends on the job being controlled. Reports on the performance of a machine operator may be daily, those on that of a foreman less frequent, and those on that of a plant supervisor even less frequent. In some systems, the distribution may be to the superior only. In others the subordinate will also receive a copy. Generally, the latter would be the preferred distribution. If the subordinate receives feedback, this creates the possibility that he/she will initiate the desired changes without intervention from the superior. It is probably safe to assume that fewer interventions will result in less conflict and better morale.

Feedback, by itself, is not sufficient for action on the part of either a subordinate or a superior. They need a **recognition criterion,** or a benchmark, against which to compare the results. Budgets and standards are examples of such criteria. Later

---

[1]For similar definitions see: A.S. Tannenbaum, "Control in Organizations: Individual Adjustment and Organization Performance," in C.P. Bonini, R.K. Jaedicke, and H.M. Wagner, eds., *Management Control: New Directions in Basic Research* (New York: McGraw-Hill, 1964), p. 299, and G.H. Hofstede, *The Game of Budget Control* (London: Tavistock Publications, 1968), p.11.

[2]See: Hiroyuki Itami, *Adaptive Behavior: Management Control and Information Analysis* (Sarasota, FL: American Accounting Association, 1977), pp. 12–17.

Exhibit 17.1   Flowchart of Control System

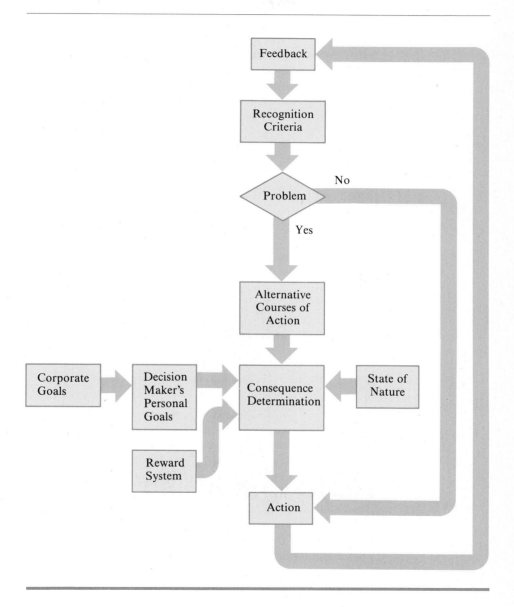

in the section we explore issues in establishing criteria, including their tightness and subordinate participation in setting them. Because of the definition of control, it may be necessary to adjust the criteria before evaluations are made. In the next chapter there is a discussion of a control system that incorporates such an adjustment. In short the control system is one whereby a subordinate's failure to react to changes in the environment appears as an unfavorable variance and is distinguished from the effects of environmental (noncontrollable) changes.

If a comparison of the feedback data with the criteria indicates a problem, then before any action can be taken there need to be **goals** that are used in selecting an action from a set of possible alternatives. For this purpose the goals will be personal rather than corporate. Obviously, it is desirable for personal and corporate goals to be congruent. However, this does not automatically occur. Management may have to devote major efforts to achieving goal congruence. But when achieved, it is one of the most effective means of control. This is not the place to explore the many avenues available to management for obtaining congruence. However, it should be remembered that achievement of employee internalization of corporate or institutional goals may be a more effective means of control than rules and regulations.

Next, the **consequences** to the subordinate of taking each of the alternatives will need to be forecasted. The consequences depend upon the reward system: merit pay, bonuses, promotions, and so forth. The accountant can make major contributions to this aspect of the control system by ensuring an appropriate objective data collection system and by anticipating whether there is sufficient congruence between employee rewards and accomplishment of corporate objectives. For example, sales commissions based on sales dollars will motivate salespersons to concentrate their effort on high-priced products. But this may not be desirable if the firm's objective is to maximize profits, and the high-priced items are not high-profit items.

Finally, when making decisions under uncertainty, the subordinate needs to specify his or her perception about the possible future **states of nature.** The subordinate's payoff of any given alternative may differ depending on the future state of nature. If so, the subordinate's decision about how to react to the feedback could be made only after giving consideration to the probabilities of state occurence.

Although the preceding discussion briefly describes the components of the control process, there are some other aspects which deserve to be mentioned. For example, the tightness of performance standards and the extent of subordinate participation in establishing them should be considered.

In previous chapters it was suggested that budgets and standards should be reasonably obtainable. But what does this mean? Unfortunately, no general answer can be given. Ultimately, the reasonableness and attainability of a standard depends on how the subordinate will react. There has been enough behavioral research to suggest that people react differently to identical stimuli. It is also unfortunate that a standard set to provide optimal motivation may not be in tune with the needs of a good planning system.

A person's reaction to the tightness of a particular performance measure is a function of several factors.[3] First, we all have certain innate desires to succeed and to avoid failure. Within the cognitive makeup of each individual, these will be competing desires. Further the relationship of these desires to each other will be different for each person. Also, for a given individual, the relationship among their many desires will vary with time and the task.

In addition to these innate desires, a subordinate's response to a given performance standard will depend on his or her assessment of the probability of success or failure. Thus, even if the subordinate has a very strong innate desire to succeed, a standard for which he or she perceives a low probability of achievement provides little motivation.

A third factor that influences the type of behavior expected of subordinates is the nature of the reward for success. Normally we would expect the probability of success and the amount of reward for achievement to vary inversely with each other. That is, the lower the probability of success, the higher the reward and vice versa.

When a person's desire to succeed is greater than his or her desire to avoid failure, their performance level is assumed to be a bell-shaped function of tightness. That is, for initial increases in tightness, *motivation* to achieve and *performance* levels increase. At some point, however, additional increases in the tightness will result in lower performance. There has been little research on how to operationally determine the optimal degree of tightness. As a rule of thumb, some suggest a level that has roughly a 50% chance of being achieved.

If optimal motivation is achieved as suggested, then standards, for example, might be set slightly higher than the reasonably expected performance level. If standards are set above expected performance levels, then they may not represent good assumptions for the budgetary process as illustrated in Chapter 12. That is, the *actual* consumption of resources would be expected to be higher than an estimate derived as the budgeted output multiplied by the standard. Depending on how tight the standards are set, the budget forecasts of profits, cash needs, purchasing needs, and so forth can be very misleading and result in bad decisions. This presents a dilemma that may be difficult to resolve. Two sets of standards, one for control purposes and one for planning purposes, is a possibility. Alternatively, the control-oriented standards could be used as a starting point and then include "planned inefficiencies" in the budget.

As a final point on this issue, let us consider the case where a person's desire to avoid failure exceeds their desire to succeed. In this case, it is plausible for the function relating performance to the degree of difficulty in meeting the standards to be U-shaped; that is, an inverted bell-shaped curve. Such an observation is made by Hopwood.[4] If this is the case, then the initial increases in the difficulty of meeting the standard will actually decrease the motivation to achieve them. But at

---

[3]For a more expanded discussion of this topic, see: Anthony Hopwood, *Accounting and Human Behaviour* (Englewood Cliffs, NJ: Prentice-Hall, 1976), pp. 39–69.

[4]Hopwood, *Accounting and Human Behaviour,* pp. 66–68.

some point on the difficulty scale, additional increases become effective in terms of increased motivation. As you can see, there is a dilemma about how to set standards in this case.

A second variable, the role of participation in setting performance measures, has been hotly debated in the literature. There are some who feel that participation increases the changes of achieving subordinate internalization of the final agreed-upon standards of performance. Many experimental studies have been conducted that purport this as a conclusion. Generalizations of the reported results are difficult, however, because of differences in situations and people.

Regarding participation, it should be noted that some people may have little desire to be independent and will readily accept an authoritarian style. Thus, participation may *not* lead to improved performance by such individuals. Also, there may be little to be gained by subordinate participation in setting standards of performance for highly programmed tasks. Routine simple tasks may have obvious rates of completion and will not be debated or questioned.

Finally, real participation will occur only when there is some reasonble chance the subordinates' views will be accepted as policy. In some companies, the subordinates may have a voice but the standards are always the superior's. This type of participation may still have some positive effects, however. For these cases the process would be viewed primarily as a communication process. The subordinates may better understand why certain positions are being taken. With increased understanding comes increased acceptance.

Responsibility Accounting

Responsibility accounting is one of the basic components of a good control system. The idea of responsibility accounting is that managers will be held accountable only for those items over which they can exercise a significant amount of control. The typical firm is organized so that the president delegates certain authority to his or her vice-presidents who, in turn, delegate a subset of their authority to various subordinates, and so forth.

Responsibility accounting begins with the lowest levels in the chain of command. At those levels careful consideration is given to budgeting the costs and, perhaps, revenues that are expected to be incurred or earned by the manager in charge. That is, the budgeting process as described in Chapter 12 may be used as a target, or goal, against which to evaluate the accomplishments for the period. Of course, the original budgets were constructed on a forecast of what the period's activity would be. However, the actual activity may not be as planned. If not, then the budget used in responsibility accounting should first be adjusted to the achieved output (a flexible budget). Actual costs and revenues are accumulated during the period and the performance report for the manager includes a comparison of the budgeted and the actual items. Variance analysis and explanatory narrative are also part of the performance evaluation.

For the next highest level of responsibility, the performance report is comprised of data from all units reporting to that manager and from data about his or her undelegated activities. This process continues by moving up through the management levels and terminates with the president's performance report.

To illustrate responsibility accounting, assume the simple organization chart as given in Exhibit 17.2. Exhibit 17.3 contains selected performance reports using hypothetical data for the assumed firm. Note the upward flow of the data. Even though the manager of the front axle division, for example, has delegated authority to the casting and assembly foremen, he is still responsible for all activities of the front axle plant.

Also note that the common costs of the front axle plant (office costs of $50,000) have not been allocated to the casting and assembly department. Likewise, the common costs of the manufacturing vice-president's office have not been allocated to the two plants nor have the president's office costs been allocated. This is in keeping with the concept of responsibility accounting. The subordinates below the person responsible for the common costs have no control over the incurrence. Thus, these subordinates should not be charged for any portion of the common costs.

Exhibit 17.2   Illustrative Organization Chart

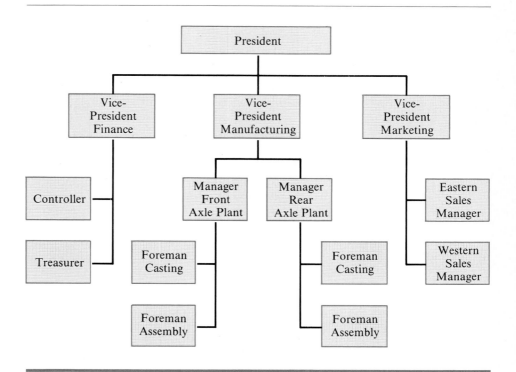

Exhibit 17.3   Responsibility Accounting: Selected Performance Reports (000 omitted)

	Budget	Actual	Variance
President			
President's office	$ 800	$ 810	$(10)
Finance	1,000	980	20
Manufacturing	3,200	3,000	200
Marketing	2,000	2,100	(100)
Total	$7,000	$6,890	$110
Vice-President—Manufacturing			
Vice-president's office	$ 200	$ 180	$ 20
Front axle	1,000	1,100	(100)
Rear axle	2,000	1,720	280
Total	$3,200	$3,000	$200
Front Axle			
Office	$ 50	$ 55	$ (5)
Casting	600	610	(10)
Assembly	350	435	(85)
Total	$1,000	$1,100	$(100)
Casting			
Material	$200	205	$(5)
Direct labor	300	303	(3)
Controllable overhead	100	102	(2)
Total	$600	$610	$(10)

A major problem to overcome in responsibility accounting is establishing controllability. In the strict sense, one might say that a particular item of cost is controllable by a given manager only if he or she, or a designate, has the sole authority to approve the invoice for payment. Many decisions, however, involve multiple decision makers. Because of this, some suggest that controllability should have a broader meaning. They would expand the definition to also include items over which a manager can exert significant influence. The reasoning for this is to create concern on the part of all possible participants in a decision. If the decision effects a manager's performance evaluation, then, presumably, he or she will do everything possible to ensure the decision is the best one possible. Of course, if this concept of controllability is adopted, then it is necessary to define "significant." This can be done only in the context of the specific situation.

Internal Control

Another facet of a control system is the set of procedures that provide reasonable insurance that the company's assets are used as intended and that collected data are reliable. Such procedures are referred to as **internal control.** A basic tenet of internal control is the appropriate separation of duties among the firm's employees. This section contains a brief discussion of these concepts as they affect a cost-management accounting system. Since internal controls must be incorporated into the accounting system, it is appropriate to consider them here.

The areas that are of concern include the internal control of material, labor, and overhead of a manufacturing firm. The basic concepts will be illustrated in the context of the material accounting system. For material, an appropriate assignment of duties should include the following *separately staffed* positions:

1. Storeroom clerk—responsible for managing the physical inventory of materials and supplies. Will receive all purchased items, through the receiving department, and only issue them to authorized persons.
2. Stores clerk—responsible for the maintenance of the inventory records and has no access to the storeroom.
3. Purchasing agent—responsible for the acquisition of materials and supplies including the selection of suppliers, transportation modes, follow-up, and so forth.
4. Receiving department—responsible for itemizing and inspecting the materials and supplies shipped from vendors.
5. Material handling—moves materials and supplies as needed within the firm.

In addition to these positions, there are others that are involved: the production supervisor, the accounting department, and the treasurer, for example. As the components of a good internal control system for material are discussed, the reasons for the separate positions will be explained.

To discuss the material accounting system in a logical sequence, first consider the ordering process, then the receiving and payment process, and finally the process of issuing materials to production. As is shown in Exhibit 17.4, the ordering process is initiated by the issue of a *purchase requisition*. The initiator of the requisition depends on the nature of the firm's activities and its system. If production is custom-order, then the production manager will likely be the one who makes the request. When the material is a regularly used item, inventory models might be used to determine the reorder point (defined as the quantity of inventory that, when reached, will signal the need for a reorder). Reorder points can either be monitored by a clerk or may be built into a computerized system that processes inventory data and, when reached, signals the computer to initiate a requisition.

Purchase requisitions flow to the purchasing agent who then order from a supplier using a *purchase order*. Copies of the purchase order would be transmitted back to the requestor (for his or her information and to avoid the possibility of a second requisition), and to the accounting department (to be used in approving a subsequent invoice for payment). Firms generally employ purchasing agents to (1) gain some efficiencies through centralized purchasing activities and (2) divide the workload so that each person's tasks are compatible.

The receiving and payment process is somewhat more complex. To understand the process, it is necessary to trace the flow of the physical units and of the supporting documents. In general, no person within the organization should be involved in *both* flows. This prevents employees from using the records to cover up unauthorized uses of material. A flowchart of this process is found in Exhibit 17.5.

Exhibit 17.4   Material Accounting: Ordering Process

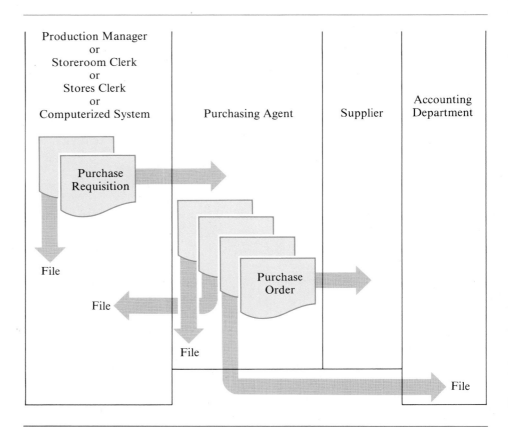

When received from the vendor, materials and supplies should be "blindly" counted by the receiving department. This means they are not told how many units were ordered or were billed to the firm. Not knowing how many units are expected will prevent unauthorized use of any unordered quantities. Further, this avoids the temptation to report the quantity received equal to the order amount without actually performing the count. The receiving and inspection report is then forwarded to accounting (to be used in the invoice payment approval process) and to the storeroom (so the storeroom clerk knows how many units for which he or she is accountable). Material handling would then physically transfer the goods from the receiving area to the storeroom. The storeroom clerk should match the physical quantities with those on the receiving report to ensure all of the units have been received.

The records flow is as follows. An invoice for the items purchased will go to the accounting department (perhaps via the purchasing agent). Payment is approved

---

Exhibit 17.5   Material Accounting: The Receiving and Payment Process

---

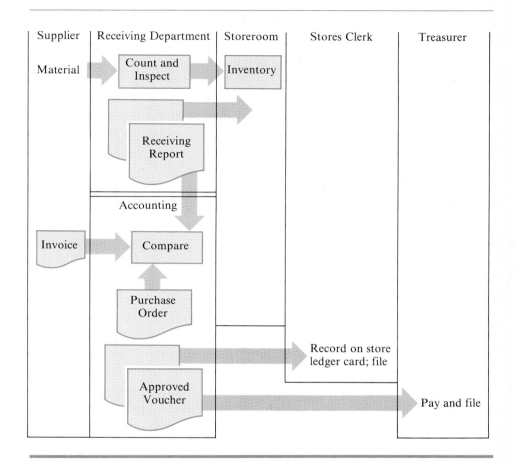

only after there is a comparison of the invoice with the receiving report and the purchase order. When all information is compared and verified, an approved invoice is sent to the stores clerk (to provide cost information for inventory accounting). The approved invoice would also be processed through a conventional cash disbursement process.

The transfer of material to production is as discussed in the job order chapter, Chapter 3. That is, the storeroom clerk should issue materials only upon the receipt of a properly executed materials requisition form (signed by a production supervisor). This form transfers the responsibility of the material from the storeroom clerk to the production department. The forms should be serially numbered, fully accounted for, and only available to production departments. In addition to its role in controlling material, the requisition is used for the collection of cost data by job and/or by department.

Internal control is more fully explained in auditing courses. Auditing, both internal and external, is very much concerned with these issues. However, the system designer must incorporate control features into the way job assignments are made, forms are designed, and form flows are developed.

Miscellaneous Considerations

In this final section several miscellaneous concepts related to control are discussed. First, there is a classification of management activities into classes known as strategic planning, management control, and operational control. The control and information system varies as a function of the type of activity, and it is useful to explore the differences. Second, the potential impact of accounting procedures on employee motivation will be considered. The third section is a consideration of alternative budget systems (the zero based budgeting and program planning and budgeting systems). Finally, there is a brief consideration of PERT (program evaluation and review technique).

DIFFERENCES IN CONTROL FOR VARIOUS LEVELS OF MANAGEMENT ACTIVITY.   It is not realistic to assume that all types of management activities can be controlled in the same way. Robert Anthony's classification of management activites has become widely accepted and is as follows:

Strategic planning—the process of deciding on objectives of the organization, changes in these objectives, the resources used to attain these objectives, and the policies that are to govern the acquisition, use and disposition of these resources.[5]

Management control—the process by which managers assure that resources are obtained and used effectively and efficiently in the accomplishment of the organization's objectives.[6]

Operational control—the process of ensuring that specific tasks are carried out effectively and efficiently.[7]

As you can see, Anthony chose not to classify activities according to the planning-control dichotomy. His feeling is that such a classification is not useful as a framework on which to construct either an information system or a control system. It is obvious, for example, that a vice-president's performance will not be evaluated using the same techniques as are used to evaluate the performance of a machine operator. Let us explore these classifications in greater detail.

Strategic planning activities are long run in nature, nonrepetitive, complex, and have major consequences. Performance evaluation in this area is very difficult and should be based on the results over a time span that is long enough for the outcome of the planning to come to fruition. For example, evaluating the decision to

---

[5]Robert N. Anthony, *Planning and Control System: A Framework for Analysis* (Boston: Harvard University Graduate School of Business Administration, 1965), p. 16.

[6]Anthony, *Planning and Control System*, p. 17.

[7]Anthony, *Planning and Control System*, p. 18.

research, develop, and market a new product line needs to be carried out over a relatively long period of time.

The management control process accepts, as a given, the policies and constraints established by the strategic planning activities. Planning is still involved in this process, and it is unfortunate that "control" is used in its designation. Responsibility accounting may be the primary tool of controlling management control activities. A significant portion of management control involves interpersonal activities of motivating people. Reducing these activities to a quantitative scale may be neither practical nor useful.

Operational control is associated with more routine activites. Evaluation is easier because the tasks are very well defined and performance measurements are very objective. Standards are appropriate control devices although it may not be necessary to convert variances to dollar amounts. Variation measured in units of material or hours of labor may be appropriate, or even preferable, when providing feedback to the managers and workers.

The information system designed to support the various managerial activities must take these differences into consideration. This, perhaps, is contrary to the often-proposed total systems approach. Basically, the concept of a total system can be compared to the upward flow concept of responsibility accounting. That is, with the "total systems approach" the output of the system for the second level of management would be a compilation of the data produced for the first, or lowest, level. But management control and strategic planning activities are not best served by simply aggregating the data for operational control.[8]

For strategic planning, decision-support data should consist of forecasts, not compilations of the past. It must include data about the firm's external environment as well as about the firm itself. It need not be so specific or so detailed as to permit exact predictions. For strategic planning purposes, it is sufficient just to be able to forecast the *approximate* impact of a particular strategy. However, the data requirements vary greatly from one strategic decision to another. Preplanning for these needs in an information collection system is difficult. Further, if the strategic planning process needs data about the operational activities, it may be more cost effective to sample the operational control data base rather than do a complete aggregation.

The system for strategic planning is not molded in the image that we typically have of a system. Rather than accounts and document flows, it consists of forecasting models, sampling models, regression models, econometric and operations research models, special cost studies, and so forth. To further improve their ability to serve management in this area, accountants need to be familiar with **data base management.** A basic concept of data base management is the storage of data in a disaggregated form. Conventional data collection systems are frequently designed to support a single purpose, that being financial reporting. As sales

---

[8]For an expanded discussion of this and the remaining ideas of this section, see: G. Anthony Gorry and Michael S. Scott Morton, "A Framework for Management Information Systems," *Sloan Management Review* (Fall 1971), pp. 55–70.

occur, the effect of each transaction is aggregated into the sales account and loses its separate identity. There may be another need for sales data, however, that should be a subset of total sales. Sorting for the subset with the appropriate characteristics could prove to be difficult unless the data base has been constructed properly.

In a data base file, each transaction is recorded as a separate event. Further, multiple characteristics are collected for each transaction such as customer, customer geographical location, amounts, and others. Then, various queries, or searches, can be performed on the raw data to generate aggregate results for given purposes, such as financial reports or special cost studies. That is, the data base file makes few assumptions about the possible uses of its contents. There is an increasing body of knowledge in the data management area, and accountants are going to have to become more knowledgeable about these systems.[9]

In terms of their data needs, the operational control activites are on the opposite end of the scale of strategic planning. Since these operational activities are routine, data collection can be standardized. Systems supporting these management activities are much more developed today than those for strategic planning. It may be an on-line system (entered directly into the computer) and an exhaustive collection rather than a sample. The system for the third activity, management control, will have characteristics that lie between the extremes represented by strategic planning and operational control.

ACCOUNTING AND MOTIVATION.   As long as accounting reports are used in the performance evaluation process, they will be a factor in motivating employees. It must be understood, however, that accounting data can provide both intended and unintended motivation.

People are influenced not only by the information they receive but also by the information they know they must supply to others. Prakash and Rappaport refer to this second influence as **information inductance**.[10] They define inductance as "the complex process through which the behavior of an information sender is influenced by the information he is required to communicate."[11]

Knowing that their actions must be reported may influence people in a variety of ways. First, there is the possibility that they will modify how they report their activities. These modifications could be sanctioned in the sense that there are generally agreed-upon alternatives for reporting various events. For example, LIFO might be used instead of FIFO. Nonsanctioned modifications could also be made. For example, a particular expense incurred late in the year may be delayed for reporting purposes until next year.

---

[9]For an expanded discussion of the nature of data-based management and its impact on accounting see: G.C. Everest and R. Weber, "A Relational Approach to Accounting Models," *The Accounting Review* (April 1977), pp. 340–359.

[10]Prem Prakash and Alfred Rappaport, "Information Inductance and Its Significance for Accounting," *Accounting Organizations and Society,* vol. 2, no. 1 (1977), pp. 29–38.

[11]Prakash and Rappaport, "Information Inductance," p. 29.

A second type of response is for the information sender to modify his or her behavior. For example, planned preventative maintenance may be postponed until a later period in order to improve the short-run performance report for the current period. Finally, an individual may actually change his or her objectives in response to the reporting and evaluation mechanism. Reporting on the contribution to profits of the products sold and determining bonuses thereon may cause a salesperson to shift his or her objective away from sales maximization.

The motivation attributable to acounting reports, whether reacting to them or in anticipation of them, can either be to the firm's advantage or disadvantage. The achieved motivation needs to be constantly monitored and evaluated by both accountants and managers. Undesired actions can be the fault of the system.

ALTERNATIVE BUDGET SYSTEM.   Rather than the budget systems discussed earlier in the book, we may find alternative budgeting systems used to aid the control function, especially in not-for-profit organizations. In this section, we very briefly describe the **program planning and budget system (PPBS)** and the **zero based budgeting system (ZBB).**

PPBS entails a process whereby, first, there is an identification of various programs, or plans of action, that can be taken to achieve the organization's objectives. The budget is oriented toward programs rather than toward departments or functions. That is, the budgeting emphasis is placed on forecasting the cost of the output rather than on the cost of operating a particular segment of the organization as was done in the type of budget system discussed in Chapter 12.

Such a budgeting format is useful when the resources of an organization are limited and there is a need to make decisions about which programs to support. By comparing the anticipated costs with the anticipated benefits on a program by program basis, better resource allocations will be made. The control inherent in such a process is more in the form of trying to prevent the adoption of wrong programs rather than in efficiently implementing selected programs.[12]

Another alternative budget system is zero based budgeting. Conventional budgeting within an organization typically is done in such a way that each year all components or divisions of the firm are given a maximum amount to accomplish their objectives. There is no requirement for the division to document or justify their need for these funds. (Maybe this is an amount equal to last year's budget or some percentage thereof.) The disadvantage of the typical system is that inefficiencies may be subsidized since there is no critical evaluation of the past uses of the funds. Only new requests and/or programs need to be justified when this approach is used.

In pure form, a ZBB system periodically rolls each division back to a zero budget. Although it is possible to do this annually, it is probably more feasible to roll back once every five years, for example, and use conventional budgeting in the

---

[12]For an expanded discussion of PPBS, see: David Novick, "What Program Budgeting Is and Is Not," *Contemporary Cost Accounting Control*, 2nd ed., ed. George J. Benston (Belmont, CA: Dickenson Publishing Co., 1977).

intervening years. In the year of the roll back, the organizational unit must be able to justify each dollar as a condition to it being included in their budget. Central management and the manager of the unit both benefit by being forced to evaluate the operations critically. However, there is a cost in the form of the time needed to defend ongoing activities.

In presenting a budget, each manager is asked to rank the unit's needs according to his or her perception of their necessity. Central management collectively considers the ranked requests of all units and then forms its own ranking scheme. Budget allocations are based on the available resources and the central rankings. Trade-offs will have to be made at both the divisional and central levels. Once the allocations are made, conventional budgeting methods are put into place for controlling the implementation of funded activities.[13]

A major advantage of a ZBB system is the increased possibility of eliminating **budget slack.** Budget slack represents allocated resources that are not really needed by a unit of the organization. Slack can become a significant problem when the firm's policy is to base next year's budget on last year's *actual* expenditures. Such a policy provides motivation of the unit manager to spend the budget even if all of the acquired resources and services are not needed. Over time, basing subsequent budgets on past expenditures will probably result in a slack that increases in amount. By periodically reviewing the entire request of a unit, slack could be reduced because it could not be defended.

PERT.   Budgets and standards are not the only quantitative tools available to help control the activities of an organization. The **Program Evaluation and Review Technique (PERT)** was developed for the Department of the Navy to help managers control the completion of large projects that consist of several interrelated subactivities. To use PERT, each of the subactivities must be defined and put into a precedence network. For any given activity, this network shows the preceding subactivities that must be completed before it can begin.

The supervisor of each subactivity is then asked to supply some estimates about the amount of time needed for its completion. Using these time estimates and the precedence relationships, PERT determines a critical path. The critical path is that set of activities such that if the completion of any activity in the set requires more time than estimated, then the completion of the project will be delayed beyond its original projected time. Operationally, we can find this by listing all possible paths through the network and summing the time of each component activity. The path with the *longest* completion time is the critical path. (There are shortcut ways for doing this but we need not discuss them here.)

The critical path activities would be "tagged" for more careful supervision than the noncritical activities. The latter activities have some slack time in the sense that

---

[13]A more detailed description of ZBB is found in: Peter A. Pyhrr, *Zero-Base Budgeting, A Practical Management Tool for Evaluating Expenses* (New York: John Wiley and Sons, 1973).

they could take more time than estimated and not delay the project's completion. Of course, for this to be true, the delay cannot exceed the slack time.[14]

To illustrate PERT, consider the following example. The Mag Company has to complete a project that has seven separate tasks that must be finished. The nature of the tasks are such that:

1. A and B may begin immediately.
2. C can begin when A is finished.
3. D can begin when B and C are finished.
4. E can begin when A is finished.
5. F can begin when B and C are finished.
6. G can begin when E and F are finished.

The estimated times to complete each of the tasks are as follows:

A — 2 weeks   E — 4 weeks
B — 3 weeks   F — 5 weeks
C — 3 weeks   G — 1 week
D — 7 weeks

The PERT network is found in Exhibit 17.6. Five paths can be identified. These paths are listed below with their times:

1. A → E → G   2 + 4 + 1 = 7
2. A → C → F → G   2 + 3 + 5 + 1 = 11
3. A → C → D   2 + 3 + 7 = 12
4. B → F → G   3 + 5 + 1 = 9
5. B → D   3 + 7 = 10

Since path 3 has the longest time, it is the critical path. If tasks A, C, or D take longer than their original times, then the project will be delayed beyond twelve weeks. Thus, these three tasks need to be carefully monitored. In contrast, if task B takes four weeks instead of three weeks the project will not take longer than estimated.

Summary

From this chapter you should have gained an increased understanding of the function of control and the accountant's role in it. Accountants and managers must carefully consider the messages created by a control system and work hard to prevent unintended results.

For any control system, consideration should be given to the desirability of subordinate participation in establishing the standards of performance. Further, the

---

[14]A complete discussion of PERT can be found in Ronald V. Hartley, *Operations Research: A Managerial Emphasis* (Santa Monica, Calif.: Goodyear Publishing Company, 1976), Chapter 11; or Frederick S. Hillier and Gerald J. Lieberman, *Introduction to Operations Research*, 3rd ed. (San Francisco: Holden-Day, Inc., 1980), Chapter 6.

Exhibit 17.6   PERT Relationships for Example Problem

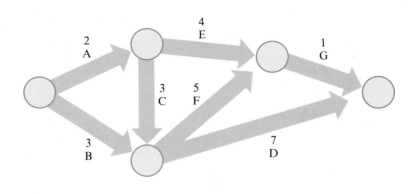

---

degree of difficulty that is used in setting the performance standards must be deliberated.

This chapter also contained a discussion of some of the mechanical aspects of control: responsibility accounting and the internal control mechanism. There was a discussion of the need of different systems for different types of management activities. Finally, there was an examination of the basics of the program planning and budgeting system, the zero based budget system, and PERT. In the remaining chapters there is a consideration of some specific ways in which the control process can be enhanced.

You should now be familiar with the following new key terms from this chapter:

Control
Feedback information
Recognition criterion
Responsibility accounting
Internal control
Strategic planning
Management control
Operational control
Data base management
Information inductance
Program planning and budget system
Zero based budgeting system
Budget slack
PERT

SELF-STUDY PROBLEM. The Twobig Company currently has two plants that manufacture product ZIP. One of these plants is located in Bigtown, the other in Littletown.

The Bigtown plant was constructed and equipped in 1960. Currently, the plant's workforce consists of 1,000 employees.

The Littletown plant was constructed in 1975. At that time it was equipped with the most technologically advanced equipment available. The managers of both plants agree that Littletown's equipment has the greatest productivity rate. Littletown employees 300 workers.

Twobig decided to construct the Littletown plant in 1975 because the availability of highly skilled employees in that area was greater than in the Bigtown area. Other companies had closed plants there in 1973 and the unemployment was relatively high. In fact, most of Littletown's employees are more highly skilled than many of Bigtown's and, in the opinion of some, are more highly motivated than the Bigtown employees.

In the interest of motivating the plants to be more efficient the vice-president of manufacturing is proposing a bonus plan for the plant managers. Specifically, his plan is to award a monthly bonus of $1,000 to a manager if his plant's monthly actual labor hours is at least 300 hours below the month's standard hours allowed.

Required:

The plan is to be discussed at the next staff meeting. As controller of the firm, prepare a statement of your concerns about the plan detailing any issues that need to be resolved in deciding whether or not to approve it.

Solution to Self-Study Problem:

There are several concerns and issues that need to be considered:

1. How have the standards been established at the two plants? If the standards are the same, then the plan unjustifiably favors Littletown. It is not Bigtown's fault that they do not have the more advanced equipment. The standards should reflect these differences.
2. Are we sure we want a bonus plan that gives the same reward regardless of the amount by which the standard is bettered? Is it possible this plan will encourage some manipulation in order to attempt to just "beat" the standard by 300 hours every month? Should the plan tie the bonus to the magnitude of the difference?
3. Since the plan calls for "beating" the standard by a set magnitude, 300 hours, it favors Bigtown. They operate at a larger volume than Littletown and they should not find it as hard to save 300 hours as Littletown. Should we be thinking in terms of "beating" the standard in percentages?
4. How much control do the plant managers have in establishing rewards for the workers? The plan calls for a bonus to the managers, not the workers. Efficiency can be achieved only through the workers. If the manager has no effective way to "share the wealth" he is likely to find resistance on the part of workers in achieving any efficiency. We must view the plant as a team.

5. Do we want to award bonuses on the basis of a "short period" of activity? This may further create an environment conducive to manipulation. Perhaps the bonuses should be tied to the performances over a longer period of time.

References

Benston, G.J. "The Role of the Firm's Accounting System for Motivation," *The Accounting Review* (April 1963): 347–354.

Caplan, E.H. "Behaviorial Assumptions of Management Accounting," *The Accounting Review* (July 1966): 496–509.

Ferrara, W.L. "Responsibility Accounting—A Basic Control Concept," *NAA Bulletin* (September 1964): 11–22.

Ridgway, V.F. "Dysfunctional Consequences of Performance Measurements," *Administrative Science Quarterly* (September 1956): 240–247.

Ronen, J., and Livingstone, J.G. "Expectancy Theory Approach to the Motivation Impacts of Budgets," *The Accounting Review* (October 1975): 671–685.

Schiff, M., and Lewin, A.Y. "The Impact of People on Budgets," *The Accounting Review* (April 1970): 259–268.

Swieringa, R.J. "A Behavioral Approach to Participative Budgeting," *Management Accounting* (February 1975): 35–39.

Problems

17-1. CMA Problem: Budgeting and Behavioral Considerations. The operating budget is a very common instrument used by many businesses. Although it usually is thought to be an important and necessary tool for management, it has been subject to some criticism from managers and researchers studying organizations and human behavior.

Required:

1. Describe and discuss the benefits of budgeting from the behavioral point of view.
2. Describe and discuss the criticisms leveled at the budgeting processes from the behavioral point of view.
3. What solutions are recommended to overcome the criticism described in part 2?

17-2. CMA Problem; the Budget Process. Springfield Corporation operates on a calendar-year basis. It begins the annual budgeting process in late August when the president established targets for the total dollar sales and net income before taxes for the next year.

The sales target is given to the marketing department where the marketing manager formulates a sales budget by product line in both units and dollars. From this budget, sales quotas by product line in units and dollars are established for each of the corporation's sales districts.

The marketing manager also estimates the cost of the marketing activities required to support the target sales volume and prepares a tentative marketing expense budget.

The executive vice-president uses the sales and profit targets, the sales budget by product line, and the tentative marketing expense budget to determine the dollar amounts that can be devoted to manufacturing and corporate office expense. The executive vice-president prepares the budget for corporate expenses and then forwards to the production department the product-line sales budget in units and the total dollar amount that can be devoted to manufacturing.

The production manager meets with the factory managers to develop a manufacturing plan that will produce the required units when needed within the cost constraints set by the executive vice-president. The budgeting process usually comes to a halt at this point because the production department does not consider the financial resources allocated to be adequate.

When this standstill occurs, the vice-president of finance, the executive vice-president, the marketing manager, and the production manager meet together to determine the final budgets for each of the areas. This normally results in a modest increase in the total amount available for manufacturing costs, while the marketing expense and corporate office expense budgets are cut. The total sales and net income figures proposed by the president are seldom changed. Although the participants are seldom pleased with the compromise, these budgets are final. Each executive then develops new detailed budgets for the operations in his or her area.

None of the areas has achieved its budget in recent years. Sales often run below the target. When budgeted sales are not achieved, each area is expected to cut costs so that the president's profit target can still be met. However, the profit target is seldom met because costs are not cut enough. In fact, costs often run above the original budget in all functional areas. The president is disturbed that Springfield has not been able to meet the sales and profit targets. He hired a consultant with considerable experience with companies in Springfield's industry. The consultant reviewed the budgets for the past four years. She concluded that the product-line sales budgets were reasonable and that the cost and expense budgets were adequate for the budgeted sales and production levels.

Required:

1. Discuss how the budgeting process as employed by Springfield Corporation contributes to the failure to achieve the president's sales and profit targets.
2. Suggest how Springfield Corporation's budgeting process could be revised to correct the problems.
3. Should the functional areas be expected to cut their costs when sales volume falls below budget? Explain your answer.

17-3. Changing Reporting Methods to Be More Behaviorally Sound. The Dirty Pool Table Company uses standard costs in evaluating its managers. It has established what were thought to be attainable standards for labor hours and then reduced the attainable standards by 10% in order to provide greater motivation. Overhead was applied on the basis of the adjusted labor standards, and based on this the following overhead report was prepared for use in evaluating one of the managers during the current month.

	Budget at Practical Capacity of 40,000 Labor Hours	Rate	Budget at Adjusted Standard Hours of 31,500	Actual Costs	Total Variance
Variable overhead	$120,000	$3.00	$ 94,500	$100,000	$(5,500)
Fixed overhead	80,000	2.00	63,000	79,000	(16,000)
Total	$200,000	$5.00	$157,500	$179,000	$(21,500)

As a new staff accountant you foresee some motivational problems with the company's performance evaluation.

Required:

Briefly discuss the problems and then revise the performance report so that it can be determined how close the manager came to attainable overhead costs.

17-4. Recasting a Performance Report to Improve Evaluations. The accountant for the Wretched Wrench Company prepared the following performance report for the foundry.

	Actual Cost	Variance
Direct labor	$440,000	$260,000 F
Indirect labor	6,100	3,900 F
Depreciation on factory building	5,000	0
Property taxes on factory	1,210	10 U
Depreciation on factory equipment[1]	1,200	800 F
Sales salaries	31,000	1,000 U
Factory supervision[2]	10,000	10,000 F
Raw ore used	130,000	70,000 F

[1]There were no acquisitions or sales of factory equipment during the year.

[2]Two supervisors are required when volume exceeds 70,000 units. The salary for each supervisor is the same.

You have discovered that the variances on the report represent deviations from a static (fixed) budget prepared for a volume of 100,000 units. The actual volume for the period was 60,000 units.

Required:

Prepare a revised performance report that is more in keeping with sound control concepts.

17-5. CMA Problem on Budgets Appropriate to Performance Evaluation. The Argo Co. has an extensive research program. The research activity is well organized. Each project is required to be broken down into its phases with the completion times and the cost of each phase estimated. The project descriptions and related estimates serve as the basis for the development of the annual research department budget.

The schedule below presents the costs for the approved research activities for a recent year. The actual costs incurred by projects or overhead category are compared to the approved activity and the variances noted on this same schedule.

Comparison of Actual with Budgeted Research Costs
(000 omitted)

	Approved Activity for the Year	Actual Costs for the Year	(Over) Under Budget
Projects in progress			
74-1	$ 23.2	$ 46.8	$(23.6)
75-3	464.0*	514.8	(50.8)
New projects			
78-1	348.0	351.0	(3.0)
78-2	232.0	257.4	(25.4)
78-3	92.8	0.0	92.8
Total research costs	$1,160.0	$1,170.0	$(10.0)

	Approved Activity for the Year	Actual Costs for the Year	(Over) Under Budget
General research			
Overhead costs (allocated to projects in proportion to their direct costs and included in the amounts shown above for each of the projects)			
Administration	$ 50.0	$ 52.0	$ (2.0)
Laboratory facilities	110.0	118.0	(8.0)
Total	$ 160.0	$ 170.0	$(10.0)
Allocated to projects	(160.0)	(170.0)	(10.0)
Balance	$ 0	$ 0	$ 0
Total research costs	$1,160.0	$1,170.0	$(10.0)

*Phases 3 and 4 only

The director of research prepared a narrative statement of research performance for the year to accompany the schedule. The director's statement follows.

"The year has been most successful. The two projects, 74-1 and 78-1, scheduled for completion in 19x8 were finished. Project 78-2 is progressing satisfactorily and should be completed in 19x9 as scheduled. The fourth phase of Project 75-3, with estimated direct research costs of $100,000, and the first phase of Project 78-3, both included in the approved activity for the year, could not be started because the principal researcher left our employment. They were resubmitted for approval in next year's activity plan."

Required:

1. From the information given, prepare an alternative schedule that will provide the management of Argo Co. with better information than the existing schedule by which to judge the research cost performance for the given year.
2. On the basis of the data in the problem, identify and explain an important weakness in Argo Co.'s system of controlling research costs.

17-6. CMA Problem on Establishing Responsibility. The Fillep Co. operates a standard cost system. The variances for each department are calculated and reported to the department manager. It is expected that the manager will use the information to improve operations and recognize that it is used by superiors when they are evaluating his or her performance.

Janet Smith was recently appointed manager of the assembly department of the company. She has complained that the system as designed is disadvantageous to her department. Included among the variances charged to the departments is one for rejected units. The inspection occurs at the end of the assembly department. The inspectors attempt to identify the cause of the rejection so that the department where the error occurred can be charged with it. Not all errors can be easily identified with a department. These are totalled and apportioned to the departments according to the number of identified errors. The variance for rejected units in each department is a combination of the errors caused by the department plus a portion of the unidentified causes of rejects.

Required:

1. Is Janet Smith's claim valid? Explain the reason(s) for your answer.
2. What would you recommend the company do to solve its problem with Janet Smith and her complaint?

17-7. Purpose of Internal Controls. Assuming a good material control system, explain how each of the following discrepancies would be detected and/or prevented.

1. Theft of material by the storeroom clerk.
2. Vendor sending more units than ordered.
3. Theft of material by the materials handler who moves the goods from the receiving room to the storeroom.
4. Theft of material by the store ledger clerk who intends to cover it by issuing a forged material requisition slip.
5. Vendor billing the company for more units than were shipped.
6. Vendor billing at a different price per unit than was indicated on the price list.
7. The collusion of the materials handler (who moves the goods from the receiving department to the storeroom) and the storeroom clerk in the theft of materials in transit to the storeroom.
8. The store ledger clerk misread an approved invoice and recorded the purchase of 100 units at $2,100 instead of $1,200.
9. The store ledger clerk posted a purchase of material X to the store ledger card of material Y.
10. The voucher clerk misread a voucher and recorded a purchase at $670 instead of $760.

17-8. CMA Problem; Obtaining Data for Strategic Planning. A regional governmental agency serves a nine-county area, with small offices located in each of the nine counties. Each office is responsible for the acquisition and storage of operating supplies used in the respective county. Therefore, each office has leased warehouse space and has one employee in charge of purchasing, warehousing, and record keeping for operating supplies.

The services provided by the governmental unit have increased substantially over the past ten years. Consequently, the use of supplies has increased greatly. Total acquisition cost of supplies reached $5.2 million during fiscal 19x5. Because the activity relating to operating supplies has become so large, the agency management is considering the establishment of a central purchasing and warehousing function for the nine-county area.

Currently, the total inventories for all nine county warehouses average $600,000 during a month. The offices pay from $2.10 to $3.25 per square foot for warehouse space. The total expenditures for warehouse facilities for fiscal 19x5 amounted to $275,000. Utilization of warehouse space averaged 60% of leased space for all offices and ranged from 45 to 70% in the individual cases.

The office in the extreme southwest portion of the nine-county region appears to be the most likely choice for the location of the central warehouse and purchasing function at this time. The greatest volume of operating supplies of all offices is used in this county. Warehouse space that should be adequate for the entire nine-county region is available because the present facility for this county, only partially leased at the present time, can be leased in its entirety. In addition, the rental fee would drop from $2.85 per square foot to $2.40 per square foot.

Required:

1. The agency is preparing a detailed analysis to be used to reach a decision on whether to continue with the present system or centralize the purchasing and warehousing function.

Identify and briefly justify the specific economic data the agency should accumulate for this analysis.
2. In addition to the economic data, what qualitative factors should the governmental unit consider before the decision is made?

17-9. CMA Problem Involving Motivation. The Parsons Co. compensates it field sales force on a commission and year-end bonus basis. The commission is 20% of standard gross margin (planned selling price less standard cost of goods sold on a full absorption basis) contingent upon collection of the account. Customer's credit is approved by the company's credit department. Price concessions are granted on occasion by the top sales management, but sales commissions are not reduced by the discount. A year-end bonus of 15% of commissions earned is paid to salespeople who equal or exceed their annual sales target. The annual sales target is usually established by applying approximately a 5% increase to the prior year's sales.

Required:

1. What features of this compensation plan would seem to be effective in motivating the salespeople to accomplish company goals of higher profits and return on investment? Explain why.
2. What features of this compensation plan would seem to be countereffective in motivating the salespeople to accomplish the company goals of higher profits and return on investment? Explain why.

17-10. CMA Problem; Setting Standards and Motivation. Harden Company has experienced increased production costs. The primary area of concern identified by management is direct labor. The company is considering adopting a standard cost system to help control labor and other costs. Useful historical data are not available because detailed production records have not been maintained.

Harden Company has retained Finch & Associates, an engineering consulting firm, to establish labor standards. After a complete study of the work process, the engineers recommended a labor standard of one unit of production every thirty minutes or sixteen units per day for each worker. Finch further advised that Harden's wage rates were below the prevailing rate of $10 per hour.

Harden's production vice-president thought this labor standard was too tight and the employees would be unable to attain it. From her experience with the labor force, she believed a labor standard of forty minutes per unit or twelve units per day for each worker would be more reasonable.

The president of Harden Company believed the standard should be set at a high level to motivate the workers, but he also recognized the standard should be set at a level to provide adequate information for control and reasonable cost comparisons. After much discussion, management decided to use a dual standard. The labor standard recommended by the engineering firm of one unit every thirty minutes would be employed in the plant as a motivation device, and a cost standard of forty minutes per unit would be used in reporting. Management also concluded that the workers would not be informed of the cost standard used for reporting purposes. The production vice-president conducted several sessions prior to implementation in the plant, informing the workers of the new standard cost system and answering questions. The new standards were not related to incentive pay but were introduced at the time wages were increased to $10 per hour.

The new standard cost system was implemented on January 1, 19x4. At the end of six months of operation, the following statistics on labor performance were presented to top management:

	Jan.	Feb.	Mar.	Apr.	May	June
Production (units)	5100	5000	4700	4500	4300	4400
Direct-labor hours	3000	2900	2900	3000	3000	3100
Variance from labor time standard	$1350 U	$1200 U	$1650 U	$2250 U	$2250 U	$2700 U
Variance from labor rate standard	$1200 F	$1300 F	$ 700 F	$ 0	$ 400 U	$ 500 U

Raw material quality, labor mix, and plant facilities and conditions have not changed to any great extent during the six-month period.

Required:

1. Discuss the impact of different types of standards on motivation, and specifically discuss the effect on motivation in Harden Company's plant of adopting the labor standard recommended by the engineering firm.
2. Evaluate Harden Company's decision to employ dual standards in their standard cost system.

17-11. CMA Problem; Compensation Plans and Motivation. Betterbuilt Corporation manufactures a full line of windows and doors including casement windows, bow windows, and patio doors. The bow windows and patio doors have a significantly higher profit margin per unit than casement windows as shown in the schedule below.

Unit Price and Cost Data

	Casement Windows	Bow Windows	Patio Doors
Sales price	$130	$250	$260
Manufacturing costs			
Direct Material	$ 25	$ 40	$ 50
Direct Labor	20	35	30
Variable overhead[1]	16	28	24
Fixed overhead[2]	24	42	$ 36
Total manufacturing costs	$ 85	$145	$140
Gross margin	$ 45	$105	$120

[1]Variable manufacturing overhead is applied at the rate of 80% of direct-labor cost.

[2]Fixed manufacturing overhead is applied at the rate of 120% of direct-labor cost.

The company sells almost entirely to general contractors of residential housing. Most of these contractors complete and sell fifteen to fifty houses per year. Each contractor builds tract houses that are similar, with some variations in exteriors and roof lines.

When contractors contact Betterbuilt, they are likely to seek bids for all the windows in the houses they plan to build in the next year. At this point, the Betterbuilt salespeople have an opportunity to influence the window configuration of these houses by suggesting patio doors or bow windows as variations for one or more casement windows for each of the several exteriors and roof lines built by the contractor.

The bow windows and patio doors are approximately twice as wide as the casement windows. A bow window or a patio door usually is substituted for two casement windows. Casement windows are usually ordered in pairs and placed side-by-side in those houses which could be modified to accept bow windows and patio doors.

Joseph Hite, president of Betterbuilt Corporation, is perplexed with the company's profit performance. In a conversation with his sales manager he declared, "Our total dollar sales volume is growing but our net income has not increased as it should. Our unit sales of casement windows have increased proportionately more than the sale of bow windows or patio doors. Why aren't our salespeople pushing our more profitable products?" The sales manager responded with a sense of frustration, "I don't know what else can be done. The salespeople have been told which type of windows we want sold due to the greater profit margin. Furthermore, they have the best compensation plan in the industry with $500 monthly draw against their commissions of 10% on sales dollars."

Required:

1. Identify the need(s) of the salespeople that would seem to be met by Betterbuilt's current compensation program.
2. Explain why Betterbuilt's present compensation program for its salespeople does not support the president's objectives to sell the more profitable units.
3. Identify and explain alternative compensation program(s) that may be more appropriate for motivating Betterbuilt Corporation's salespeple to sell the more profitable units.

17-12. Evaluating a Bonus System. At the Shafer Company sales representatives are assigned a specific geographical territory. Each representative markets several different products. One of the products, however, has been causing some problems. Product XC requires a substantial lead time to build and production has been relying heavily on sales forecasts to schedule its production. These forecasts have been primarily prepared by the sales representatives. Many of them have forecasted the sales of XC very optimistically. Their actual sales frequently turns out to be substantially below their forecasts. Manufacturing is getting increasingly upset because of the overproduction of a rather expensive product and the resulting increase in storage costs. Adjusting for the "optimistic" forecasts has not proven to work, at least to this point in time.

Each of the sales districts have different potentials and unique problems. Thus, each sales representative needs a different sized expense account for travel, entertainment and so forth. These expense account limitations are set as a percentage of budgeted sales volume. The percentage used in each district considers the special problems of that district.

The vice-president of marketing has continually argued against removing the sales representatives from the sales-forecasting process. He argues that no one else in the firm better understands the potential sales level and problems in the various territories.

In the opinion of some executives in the firm, sales are lagging behind the rest of the companies in the industry. Thus, among other proposals is one that would create a bonus system to provide added incentive to sales representatives.

The specific bonus plan under consideraton is as follows. Define *AS* as the year's actual sales for a sales representative and *SF* as their sales forecast for the year. The percentage, *P,* of the maximum annual bonus of $15,000 that can be earned is:

1. If $AS \geqslant SF$ then $P = 100 - 50\left(\dfrac{AS}{SF} - 1\right)$

2. If $AS < SF$ then $P = 100 - 100\left(1 - \dfrac{AS}{SF}\right)$

1. Assume the following hypothetical forecasts and sales data for five sales representatives:

Representative	Forecast	Actual
A	$150,000	$100,000
B	100,000	100,000
C	50,000	100,000
D	170,000	120,000
E	70,000	120,000

Compute the sales representative's bonus in each of the above cases.
2. Considering Shafer's situation, evaluate the strengths and weaknesses of the proposed bonus sytem.

17-13. CMA Problem; Performance Evaluation. Harold Small joined Morton Electric Company eight months ago as vice-president of personnel administration. Morton Electric Company is a small regional public utility serving 50,000 customers in three communities and the surrounding rural area. Electricity is generated at a central plant, but each community has a substation and its own work crew. The total labor force at the central plant and three substations, exclusive of administrative and clerical personnel, numbers 180 people.

Small designed and introduced a performance evaluation and review system (PERS) shortly after joining Morton. This system was based upon a similar system he had developed and administered in his prior position with a small company. He thought the system had worked well and that it could be easily adapted for use at Morton.

The purpose of PERS, as conceived by Small, is to provide a positive feedback system for evaluating employees that would be uniform for each class of employees. Thus, the system would indicate to employees how they were performing on the job and help them correct any shortcomings. The plant supervisors and field supervisors are responsible for administering the system for the plant workers and the substation crew workers, respectively. The general supervisors are responsible for the plant/field supervisors. Employees get personal PERS reports monthly informing them of their current status, and there is a review and evaluation every six months.

PERS is based on a point system in an attempt to make it uniform for all workers. There are eight categories for evaluation with a maximum number of points for each category and a total of 100 points for the system. The eight categories for the plant and crew workers and the maximum number of points in each category are as follows.

Categories	Points
1. *Quality of Work* Points are deducted if the job must be redone within forty-eight hours of completion.	15
2. *Productivity* Points are deducted if the work was not completed within the time specified for the type of job.	15
3. *Safety on the Job* Points are deducted if the employee does not use safe work habits on the job to protect himself or herself and others.	15

Categories	Points
4. *Neatness of work area or repair truck*	15
Points are deducted if the work area or truck is not clean and neat.	
5. *Cooperation with fellow workers*	10
Points are deducted if an employee does not work well with others.	
6. *Courtesy on the job and with the public*	10
Points are deducted if an employee is rude and unpleasant when there is contact with the public.	
7. *Appearance*	10
Points are deducted if an employee does not wear standard work clothing or if the clothing is sloppy and dirty at the beginning of each day	
8. *Tardiness/excess absenteeism*	10
Points are deducted if an employee arrives late or is absent for causes other than illness or death in the immediate family.	
Total points	100

The list of categories used to evelute the plant/field supervisors is slightly different.

Each employee begins the year with 100 points. If an infraction in any of the categories is observed, one to five penalty points can be assessed for each infraction. Notification is given to the employee indicating the infraction and the points to be deducted. A worker who is assessed twenty-five points in any one month or loses all the points in any category in one month is subject to immediate review. Likewise, anytime an employee drops below forty points, a review is scheduled. The general supervisor meets with the individual employee and the employee's plant/field supervisor at this review.

If an employee has no infractions during the month, up to twelve points can be restored to the employee's point total—two points each for categories 1–4 and one point each for categories 5–8. However, at no time can a worker have more than the maximum allowed in each category or more than 100 points in total.

When Small first introduced PERS to the general supervisors, they were not sure they liked the system. Small told them how well it had worked where he had used it before. Small's enthusiasm for the system and his likeable personality convinced the general supervisors that the system had merit.

There were a few isolated problems with the system in the first two months. Ray Meyers, a crew worker, is very unhappy with the new system as evidenced by his conversation with Dan Jenkins, a fellow crew worker:

Meyers: "Look at this notice of infraction—I have lost twenty-two points! I can't believe it!"
Jenkins: "How did your supervisor get you for that many points in such a short period?"
Meyers: "It's all related to that bad storm we had two weeks ago. He disagreed with me on the work at Elm and Wabash. It was dangerous and I probably did fly off the handle. It was late at night after I had been working fifteen to sixteen hours straight. Look what he got me for: five points for lack of cooperation, five points for a dirty uniform, five points for a messy truck including lunch bags and coffee cups in the cab, four points for slow work, and three points for being ten minutes late the next morning. Can you imagine that—being docked for ten minutes when I worked a double shift the day before—I didn't get home until 1:00 A.M. I even cleaned the truck up after he left that night—on my own time, no less!"

Jenkins: "At least you won't get reviewed."

Meyers: "Sure, but I bet he planned it to come out less than twenty-five points."

Jenkins: "Boy, we worked ourselves to a frazzle that night and the next two days. You know Mike's supervisor? Well, he recommended that his guys get positive points added back to their PERS reports over and above the normal monthly allowances."

Required:

1. Without regard to Ray Meyers's recent experience with the system, evaluate the performance evaluation and review system (PERS) in terms of its:
   a. design for a performance review and evaluation system.
   b. value as a motivation device.
2. What problems might occur in the administration of the performance evaluation and review system and how might these administrative problems affect employee motivation? Explain your answer.

17-14. CMA Problem; Effects of System on Motivation. Olim Corporation is a large manufacturing company in a heavily industrialized region of the northeast United States. The top management has indicated the need for production economy in its manufacturing processes because of declining profits. To encourage employees to work toward this goal, cost consciousness has been emphasized. A monetary incentive scheme has been developed to reward production managers who produce cost reductions that will be reflected immediately in the company's financial results.

The production managers have responded to this pressure in several ways. The rate at which products are being manufactured has been increased. Production managers are now rejecting greater quantities of raw materials and parts as they are received from the storeroom. They have postponed repair and maintenance work on machines where possible and have specified quick emergency repairs to avoid imminent breakdowns or to get machines back into production.

Each of these actions has increased friction among personnel in the plant. For example, the production managers' actions with respect to repair and maintenance have caused serious conflict between themselves and the maintenance department. The maintenance managers argue that the postponement of certain repairs in the short term and the use of emergency repair techniques will result in increased costs later and, in some instances, will reduce the life of the machine. They further argue that these practices reduce machine safety.

An even more serious matter is the growing bitterness between the production and maintenance managers and among the production managers due to the pressure placed upon the maintenance managers by individual production managers to obtain maintenance and repairs. The more aggressive production managers check upon the progress of the repair work in their department, have close friends in the maintenance department, or intimidate the maintenance department in order to have their repair work completed promptly. In several instances production departments whose production has been halted due to machine breakdowns have had to wait while another production department with an aggressive manager has received repair service on machines not needed in the current production run. Consequently, such managers are not popular with the other production managers.

The maintenance managers are upset at being subjected to the pressure and intimidation. They claim this makes it hard to determine which jobs are the most important. Further, the production departments' demands for immediate return to service of machines result in substandard repair work.

The production departments are charged with the actual costs of the repairs. A record of the repair work conducted in individual production departments is prepared by maintenance managers. This record, when completed in the accounting department, shows the repair hours, the rate of the maintenance worker who did the work, the maintenance overhead charge, and the cost of any parts. The record serves as the basis for the charges to the production department.

Production managers have complained about this charging system. They claim the charges to them depend upon which maintenance worker does the work (the hourly rate and efficiency), when the work is done (the production department is charged for the overtime premium), and how careful the worker is in recording the time on the job.

Required:

1. Identify and briefly explain the motivational factors that may promote friction between the production and maintenance managers of Olim Corporation.
2. Revise the system employed by Olim Corporation to charge production departments for repair costs so as to eliminate or reduce the production departments' complaints.

17-15. CMA Problem; Payroll Incentive System. Morac Industries is a rapidly growing ten-year-old company specializing in plumbing supplies. The company is relatively small, employing a total of 100 persons. There are twenty-five salaried employees in office and management positions. The remaining seventy-five employees perform various production-line functions and are paid on an hourly basis. Sales for 19x1 are forecast at $3 million.

Management has been so preoccupied with its goals of growth and financial stability that employee relations have been virtually ignored. Discontent among hourly paid employees has grown to the point that they are now considering unionization. Many employees do not believe their wage adjustments have kept pace either with industry standards or inflation. Additionally, these same employees do not believe they have been adequately rewarded for their contribution to the company's increase in productivity and performance.

Warren McMan, president of Morac, would like to avoid unionization. He believes this is possible if a suitable wage incentive/payment program can be developed. There has been good esprit de corps until recently and he believes strongly that most of the employees really do not want a union.

Mr. McMan, along with the company controller and manufacturing vice-president, developed a new payroll incentive system they hope will meet the hourly employees' concerns. This new system would apply to workers once they have completed the company's six-month training program. Currently, unskilled workers are hired at $5 per hour and immediately are put through the training program. At the end of the training program workers are assigned to a specific job and awarded wage increases of about $2 per hour. Under the proposed system subsequent merit wage increases would be approved by fellow employees. This new system would work as follows:

1. Employees who believe they deserve merit wage increases would file a wage increase request form (presented below). This form would indicate current wage rate, the amount of the requested pay increase, and the justification for the increase.
2. Each employee's request would be posted for one week giving the employee's peers ample time to study the request and observe performance. During this week, records of the employee's history, productivity, and job responsibilities would be available to the other employees.
3. Fellow employees would vote on each individual's merit wage request by secret ballot. If the majority vote is favorable, the request for a merit wage increase would be approved.

WAGE INCREASE REQUEST

Date of Request _____
Date of Vote _____

Name _____

Department _____ Job Title _____

Current wage rate $_____

Requested increase per hour $_____ to $_____

This will give me a total annual increase of $_____ which is a _____% increase.

I am requesting to increase because: _____

_____

_____

Voting results: Yes _____   No _____

Increase approved/denied   Effective date _____

Required:

Discuss the advantages and disadvantages to Morac Industries of the new payroll incentive system for approving merit wage increases. Your answer should specifically address the following issues.

1. Employee motivation.
2. Employee productivity.
3. Goal congruence between employee and company.
4. Administration of the system.

17-16. CMA Problem; Cases on Productivity. Improved productivity is considered an important way to reduce or control expenditures during periods of inflation. Productivity improvement can be obtained in a variety of ways including additional capital investment and more effective employee performance. The three cases presented below focus on attempts to increase employee productivity without added capital investment.

Case 1

The Customer Complaints Department is in charge of receiving, investigating, and responding to customer claims of poor service. The volume of paper work is very large and is growing because each complaint requires the processing of several forms and letters. A large staff is required for handling this processing. There is a wide span of control, with fifteen to twenty staff members reporting to each supervisor. The number of complaints processed per worker has shown a noticeable decline in recent months.

The department manager recommends that supervisors require increased performance. They should do this by setting performance objectives, making their presence more obvious, monitoring breaks and lunch hours, and seeing to it that talking among staff members is strictly curtailed. The supervisors should also make the staff aware that failure to achieve performance objectives will result in a negative evaluation of their performance.

Case 2

A department of an insurance company in charge of processing medical-related claims has had its budget reduced even though the number of claims has been increasing. This reduction comes after very small annual appropriation increases in prior years. Given the recent rate of inflation the actual resources available to do the work have decreased.

Top management recently has specified that certain claims be processed within forty-eight hours of receipt, a requirement that leads to special handling of such claims. Consequently, the budget reduction causes the processing of other claims to be delayed even further. The department manager complains that the budget cuts and the priority treatments of certain claims will reduce the department's overall productivity.

This manager recommends that top management allow all managers to participate more actively in the budget development and budget adjustments during the budget year. Further, once the general objectives for a department are established, the department manger should be allowed to set the priorities for the work to be accomplished.

Case 3

Investigative auditors within a welfare agency are responsible for detecting cases of welfare fraud. Because of the latest recession, the number of welfare fraud cases was expected to be significantly higher than in recent history. However, the number of cases discovered has not increased significantly. This may be due to the fact that investigators are becoming discourged because of the lack of follow-up action taken on their findings. Cases are backed up in legal processing. Even when the individuals are found guilty, the penalties are often very light. The investigators wonder if all their time and effort to uncover the fraudulent claims are justified.

The manager of the investigative Audit Department has recommended an annual performance incentive program for the investigators that is related only to the number of cases of fraud detected. The annual performance evaluation report would be filed in each investigator's personnel record and each investigator's annual salary adjustment would be based primarily upon the number of fraud cases detected. Currently, evaluations relate to the number of cases closed with conviction.

Required:

For each of the three cases presented, discuss whether or not the proposal of the department manager will improve productivity within the department. Explain, in detail, the reasons for your conclusion in each case.

17-17. CMA Problem on System Maintenance. Wright Company employs a computer-based data-processing system for maintaining all company records. The present system was developed in stages over the past five years and has been fully operational for the last two years.

When the system was being designed, all department heads were asked to specify the types of information and reports they would need for planning and controlling operations. The systems department attempted to meet the specifications of each department head. Company management specified that certain other reports be prepared for department heads. During the five years of systems development and operation there have been several changes in the department head positions due to attrition and promotions. The new department heads often made requests for additional reports according to their specifications. The systems department complied with all of these requests. Reports were discontinued only upon request by a department head, and then only if it was not a standard report required by top mangement. As a result, few reports were in fact discontinued. Consequently, the data-processing system was generating a large quantity of reports each reporting period.

Company mangement became concerned about the quantity of information that was being produced by the system. The internal audit department was asked to evaluate the effectiveness of the reports generated by the system. The audit staff determined early in the study that more information was being generated by the data-processing system than could be used effectively. They noted the following reactions to this information overload:

1. Many department heads would not act on certain reports during periods of peak activity. The department head would let these reports accumulate with the hope of catching up during a subsequent lull.
2. Some department heads had so many reports that they did not act at all upon the information or they made incorrect decisions because of misuse of information.
3. Frequently action required by the nature of the report data was not taken until the department head was reminded by someone who needed the decision. These department heads did not appear to have developed a priority system for acting on the information produced by the data processing system.
4. Department heads often developed the information they needed from alternative, independent sources, rather than from using the reports generated by the data-processing system. This was often easier than trying to search among the reports for the needed data.

Required:

1. Indicate, for each of the observed reactions, whether they are functional or dysfunctional behavioral responses. Explain your answer in each case.
2. Assuming one or more of these were dysfunctional, recommend procedures the company could employ to eliminate the dysfunctional behavior and to prevent its recurrence.

17-18. CMA Problem on Budgetary Slack. The Noton Company has operated a comprehensive budgeting system for many years. This system is a major component of the company's program to control operations and costs at its widely scattered plants. Periodically the plants' general mangers gather to discuss the overall company control system with the top management.

At this year's meeting the budgetary system was severely criticized by one of the most senior plant managers. He said that the system discriminated unfairly against the older, well-run, and established plants in favor of the newer plants. The impact was lower year-end bonuses and poor performance ratings. In addition, there were psychological consequences in the form of lower employee morale. In his judgment, revisions in the system were needed to make it more effective. The basic factors of Noton's budget include:

1. Announcement of an annual improvement percentage target established by top management.
2. Plant submission of budgets implementing the annual improvement target.
3. Management review and revision of the proposed budget.
4. Establishment and distribution of the final budget.

To support his arguments, he compared the budget revisions and performance results. The older plants were expected to achieve the improvement target but often were unable to meet it. On the other hand, the newer plants were often excused from meeting a portion of this target in their budgets. However, their performance was usually better than the final budget.

He further argued that the company did not recognize the operating differences that made attainment of the annual improvement factor difficult, if not impossible. His plant has been producing essentially the same product for its twenty years of existence. The machinery and equipment, which underwent many modifications in the first five years, have had no major changes in recent years. Because they are old, repair and maintenance costs have increased each year, and the machines are less reliable. The plant management team has been together for the last ten years and works well together. The labor force is mature, with many of the employees having the highest seniority in the company. In his judgment, significant improvements have been wrung out of the plant over the years and now merely keeping even is difficult.

For comparison he noted that one plant opened within the past four years will have an easier time meeting the company's expectations. The plant is new, containing modern equipment that is in some cases still experimental. Major modifications in equipment and operating systems have been made each year as the plant management has obtained a better understanding of the operations. The plant's management, although experienced, has been together only since its opening. The plant is located in a previously nonindustrial area and therefore has a relatively inexperienced work force.

Required:

1. Evaluate the manufacturing manager's views.
2. Equitable application of a budget system requires the ability of corporate management to remove budgetary slack in plant budgets. Discuss how each plant could conceal slack in its budget.

17-19. PERT Problem from CMA Exam. Ellen Jones is responsible for finding a suitable building and establishing a new convenience grocery store for Thrift-Mart, Inc. Jones enumerated the specific activities that have to be completed and the estimated time to establish each activity. In addition, she prepared the accompanying network diagram to aid in coordinating the activities. The list of activities to locate a building and establish a new store is as follows:

Activity Number	Description of Activity	Estimated Time Required (weeks)
1–2	Find building	4
2–3	Negotiate rental terms	2
3–4	Draft lease	4
2–5	Prepare store plants	4
5–6	Select and order fixtures	1
6–4	Delivery of fixtures	6
4–8	Install fixtures	3
5–7	Hire staff	5
7–8	Train staff	4
8–9	Receive inventory	2
9–10	Stock shelves	1

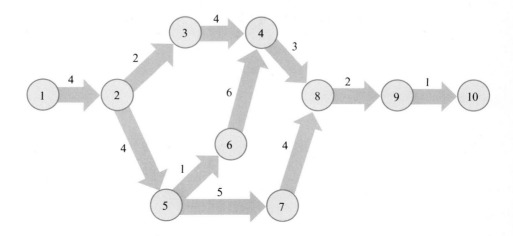

Required:

1. Identify the critical path for finding and establishing the new convenience store.
2. Ellen Jones would like to finish the store two weeks earlier than indicated by the schedule, and as a result, she is considering several alternatives. One such alternative is to convince the fixture manufacturer to deliver the fixtures in four weeks rather than in six weeks. Should Jones arrange for the manufacturer to deliver the fixtures in four weeks if the sole advantage of this schedule change is to open the store two weeks early? Justify your answer.
3. A program, such as the one illustrated by the network diagram for the new convenience store, cannot be implemented unless the required resources are available at the required dates. What additional information does Jones need to administer the proposed project properly?

CHAPTER 18

Variances from Standards: Alternatives and Significance

Chapter Overview

In Chapters 5 and 6 standard cost systems were discussed. The emphasis in those chapters was to explain the meaning of the variances and discuss the implications of standards for the accounting system. This chapter expands upon and enriches this important role of the management accountant.

Four alternative variance systems are considered. Some of these systems extend beyond the control of the production function to the control of profit centers. The first alternative discussed is a system of variances that can be used instead of the noncontrollable (volume) variance. The second system is one that can be used to analyze why actual profit differs from the budgeted profit and is applicable to profit center control. A third alternative is the ex-post variance system that is designed to encourage managers to adhere to optimal strategies rather than to beginning-of-the-period budgets. The last alternative discussed is a system of mix and yield variances when several different raw materials are needed to produce a single product.

Also considered in this chapter are some methods that can be used in assessing the significance of a variance. They help to answer how large a variance should be before resources are devoted to an investigative effort.

Alternative to Noncontrollable (Volume) Variance

The variance system to be discussed in this section is a substitute for the noncontrollable variance discussed in Chapter 5. In Chapter 5 it was observed that the noncontrollable variance has limited usefulness for short-term control. It only represents the overapplied or underapplied fixed overhead, not a *real economic consequence*. The noncontrollable variance results from the principle of maintaining relative stable unit costs in a full absorption cost system even when there are output fluctuations. If practical capacity is used as the divisor activity in determining the fixed overhead rate, then the noncontrollable variance will provide a *relative* measure of idle capacity when it is compared on a period-by-period basis. But the dollar value of the variance, as conventionally computed, provides no measure of the economic impact the idle capacity had on the firm.

Horngren has proposed an alternative to the noncontrollable variance that represents an attempt to avoid its shortcomings.[1] The basic idea of this alternative is to estimate the opportunity cost of having idle capacity rather than measuring the amount of fixed costs that are underapplied when it occurs. To implement the system, define four points on the measurement scale of capacity:

P = practical capacity
M = master budgeted sales (or standard units of capacity allowed for budgeted sales)
S = scheduled production (or standard units of capacity allowed for scheduled production)
A = actual production (or standard units of capacity allowed for actual production)

Exhibit 18.1 depicts the relationships. For the convenience of the figure it is assumed that $A < S < M$. One or more of these relationships could be reversed.

Assuming the divisor activity for the fixed overhead application rate is practical capacity, the conventional noncontrollable variance, in activity units, is the difference between P and A. Horngren's proposed system divides this unit variance into three components and converts the unit variances into dollars differently than the conventional system. Ignoring the conversion to dollars, for the moment, the three variances are:

1. **Expected idle capacity** = $P - M$. This represents planned idle capacity for the period.
2. **Marketing variance** = $M - S$. This variance results from the failure to achieve the budgeted level of sales. It should be explained by and possibly charged to the marketing staff. If S is greater than M, the variance would be favorable and might be due to greater-than-anticipated marketing efforts.
3. **Production variance** = $S - A$. There is no assurance than an acquired order will get scheduled for porduction in the same period. If not scheduled, this variance measures the effect. The production department is responsible for explaining the reasons that the orders were not produced.

Whether these unit variances should be converted into a dollar measure is an issue the analyst must resolve in the context of the situation. Depending on where the communication is being directed, physical measures may be preferable to dollar measures. However, if a dollar measure is desired, then this system will attempt to determine the *profit impact* of the unit variance rather than the resulting overapplied or underapplied fixed overhead.

One possibility for the dollar conversion is to assume the idle capacity could have been utilized by increasing the volume of the existing products. If the mix of those products can be agreed upon, then the profit impact would be determined by using the average contribution per unit of capacity devoted to the mix. If the market on existing products is already saturated, then it would be necessary to make some professional judgments about new uses of the idle capacity and the impact such uses would have on profits. As you can see, this system is more reflective of the economic impact of idle facilities than the noncontrollable variance.

---

[1]Charles Horngren, "A Contribution Approach to the Analysis of Capacity Utilization," *Accounting Review* (April 1967), pp. 254–262.

Exhibit 18.1   Representation of Capacity Utilization

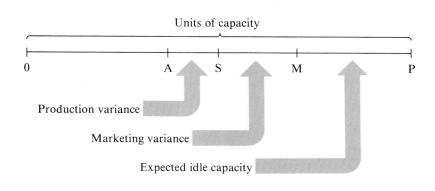

Consider the following example. At the start of the current period, the Kandler Company budgeted the following sales:

Product A: 10,000 units
Product B: 15,000 units

Product A requires four labor hours per unit and B requires two. Thus, the budgeted sales volume would require 70,000 hours ($10,000 \times 4 + 15,000 \times 2$). That is, $M = 70,000$. The practical capacity is 90,000 labor hours ($P = 90,000$).
During the period, orders were received as follows:

Product A: 9,000 units
Product B: 13,000 units

If all of the orders were scheduled for production, 62,000 labor hours would be required ($9,000 \times 4 + 13,000 \times 2$). In the notation, $S = 62,000$. The production department actually produced the following:

Product A: 8,500 units
Product B: 12,400 units

Thus, A, (the actual output in labor hours) = 58,800 ($8,500 \times 4 + 12,400 \times 2$).
In terms of labor hours:

Expected idle capacity =	90,000 − 70,000 =	20,000 hours
Market variance =	70,000 − 62,000 =	8,000 hours
Production variance =	62,000 − 58,800 =	3,200 hours

Now, what if it was desired to convert the above variances into the dollar impact on the firm? Suppose that the contribution margins(CM) were:

	Per Unit	Direct-Labor Hours per Unit	Per Direct-Labor Hour
Product A	$16.00	4	$4.00
Product B	$10.00	2	5.00

Then the dollar production variance could be computed as follows:

Product	Scheduled	Actual	Variance	Variance in Labor Hours	CM per Unit	Opportunity Cost
A	9,000	8,500	500	2,000	$4	$ 8,000
B	13,000	12,400	600	1,200	$5	6,000
				3,200		$14,000

Similarly, the dollar market variance is:

Product	Budget	Scheduled	Variance	Variance in Labor Hours	CM per Unit	Opportunity Cost
A	10,000	9,000	1,000	4,000	$4	$16,000
B	15,000	13,000	2,000	4,000	$5	20,000
				8,000		$36,000

In order to convert the expected idle capacity to a dollar measure, it will be necessary to make some assumptions and/or collect some additional information. For example, assume that the additional capacity could be utilized by increasing the sales of A and B. Further, assume the volume could be increased in the ratio that existed between the two products in the *master budget*. The mix in the budget was 10,000 units of A and 15,000 units of B, a 1-to-1.5 ratio. Then, the average contribution margin *per direct-labor hour* using the mix of one unit of A and 1.5 units of B is:

$$\frac{1.0(\$16.00) + 1.5(\$10.00)}{4(1) + 2(1.5)} = \frac{16 + 15}{4 + 3} = \frac{31}{7} = 4.4286$$

Thus, using this assumption:

Expected idle capacity variance = $(90,000 - 70,000)4.4286$
= $88,571 U

That is, if the idle capacity could be used as assumed, then the total contribution margin would be increased by $88,571 per year.

Profit Variance Analysis

We now turn our attention to the problems of controlling profit centers. These are organizational units within a firm that have control over both revenues and costs.

Because of this added dimension (in comparison with a cost center) additional types of variances from planned targets can occur.

Before the start of a period, it is conventional for profit centers, in consultation with central management, to establish a target income for the period. At the end of the period it would be natural to compare the actual income with the budget established at the beginning of the period. Inevitably, there will be variances between the budgeted and the actual income. Identifying the causes of these variances can be useful in controlling the operations of the profit center.

The **profit variance analysis** system is explained with the aid of the following case. The Dee Que Company has a Dairy Products Division that is managed as a profit center. The Dairy Products Division has three products it can produce and sell. Each of these products requires certain resources which are available in limited quantities: material X, material Y, and labor. Data about the products, including their resource requirements, are found in Exhibit 18.2.

Before the current period, assume that linear programming (discussed in Chapter 22) was used to determine the optimal use of the three limited resources. The LP solution indicated the following product mix:

A—100 units   B—0 units   C—200 units

All managers of the division participated in the review of the solution and agreed it represented a proper course of action. Based on this solution, a budgeted statement of contribution was prepared and is provided in Exhibit 18.3.

As data became available during the period, the Dairy Product's manager noted that the variable cost of product C was $28 instead of $27. This is due to the fact that it was taking four units of material Y to produce product C instead of three units. The unit cost of material Y is $1.00 and this accounts for the $1.00 increase in producing C. Further, all competitors were charging $31.50 for product C, and the division decided to follow the market. The cost of producing product C

**Exhibit 18.2   Dee Que Company Dairy Products Division
Product Information**

	Product				Cost per Unit
	A	*B*	*C*	*Availability*	
Sales price	$35	$25	$31	—	—
Variable cost	30	22	27	—	—
Contribution margin	$ 5	$ 5	$ 4		
Resource requirements					
Material X	3	1	2	800	$2
Material Y	4	5	3	1,000	1
Labor	4	3	4	1,200	5

Exhibit 18.3   Dee Que Company Dairy Products Division Budgeted Income Statement

Revenue			
Product A 100 × $35		$3,500	
Product C 200 × $31		6,200	$9,700
Variable costs			
Material X			
Product A 100 × 3 × $2	$ 600		
Product C 200 × 2 × $2	800	$1,400	
Material Y			
Product A 100 × 4 × $1	$ 400		
Product C 200 × 3 × $1	600	1,000	
Labor			
Product A 100 × 4 × $5	$2,000		
Product C 200 × 4 × $5	4,000	6,000	8,400
Contribution margin			$1,300

increased by a greater amount per unit than the per unit increase in the sales price. Thus management reacted to the reduced contribution margin by adopting a mix that resulted in the following sales for the period:

A—100 units   B—60 units   C—75 units

You can verify that this production schedule is feasible with respect to the availability of the three resources. That is, the schedule does not need more than 800 units of material X, 1,000 of material Y, and 1,200 hours of labor. The actual income for the period is presented in Exhibit 18.4. Note the actual contribution margin is $357.50 less than the budgeted contribution margin ($1,300 − $942.50).

Potentially, there are several reasons for a variance between the budgeted and actual income. A conventional profit variance analysis explains the variance using the following three components:

1. **Quantity variance**—the difference in income caused by a variation between the total budgeted unit volume of output and the actual volume.
2. **Mix variance**—the variance caused by the actual mix of the products being different from the planned mix. Each product contributes to profits at a different rate, and if there is a change in the mix there will be an effect on profits. As will be seen, this variance can be analyzed by product.
3. **Contribution margin variance**—this variance is due to the possibility that some, or all, of the products contribute to profits at a different rate than planned for in the budget. The contribution margin variance can be further analyzed into the effects due to sales prices being different than budgeted and the effects of variable cost differences. The latter variances may be further analyzed according to the standard cost variances discussed in Chapter 5.

Exhibit 18.4   Dee Que Company Dairy Product Division Actual Income Statement

---

Revenue			
Product A 100 × $35.00		$3,500.00	
Product B 60 × 25.00		1,500.00	
Product C 75 × 31.50		2,362.50	$7,362.50
Variable costs			
Material X			
Product A 100 × 3 × $2	$ 600		
Product B 60 × 1 × 2	120		
Product C 75 × 2 × 2	300	1,020.00	
Material Y			
Product A 100 × 4 × $1	$ 400		
Product B 60 × 5 × 1	300		
Product C 75 × 4 × 1	300*	1,000.00	
Labor			
Product A 100 × 4 × $5	$2,000		
Product B 60 × 3 × 5	900		
Product C 75 × 4 × 5	1,500	4,400.00	6,420.00
Contribution margin			$ 942.50

---

*This schedule assumes the increase in the cost of product C is due to inefficiency in material Y consumption. That is, four units of material Y per unit of product C were used instead of three.

Now consider the details of computing each of these variances. The quantity variance is determined by assuming the total actual volume of sales is composed of products in the same ratio as budgeted. (The effect of mix differences is to be isolated through the mix variance.) For purposes of this variance, the total volume is the sum of each product sold. In our case, the budgeted total volume is 300 units (100 of A + 200 of C) and the actual total volume is 235 (100 of A + 60 of B + 75 of C). The use of this sum is justified as follows. If, in fact, the product mix ratio remained constant as is assumed in the quantity variance, each unit of sales, *regardless of which product it is,* would contribute to profits at the average contribution margin rate. The average rate is the *budgeted* contribution margin of all products divided by the *budgeted* total volume of all products. The budgeted contribution margins are used because the contribution margin variance measures out the difference between the actual and budgeted rates. For the illustrative case:

$$\text{Average contribution margin} = \frac{\$1,300}{(100 + 200)} = \$4.33\tfrac{1}{3} = \tfrac{13}{3}$$

The total quantity variance is the difference in the *total* units actually sold and the *total* units budgeted multiplied by the average contribution margin. As in Chapter 5, the variances are computed so that a positive result is favorable and a negative is unfavorable. Thus:

$$\text{Quantity variance} = \left(\text{Total units actually sold} - \text{Total units budgeted}\right) \times \text{Average contribution margin} \tag{18-1}$$

For our example we have:

Quantity variance = (235 − 300) 13/3 = \$281.67 U

The \$281.67 variance is interpreted as follows. Assuming that the 235 units actually sold consisted of products *in the ratio of the budgeted product mix,* operating at this lower volume caused profits to be \$281.67 lower than anticipated. The quantity variance does not explain *why* the actual volume of sales differed from the budget, just the effect of the difference on income. As with any other variance, it may have been avoidable or unavoidable. For example, the variance could be due to changes in the market environment over which the division manager has no control. Follow-up investigations must be conducted before any decision is made about the meaning of the variance.

Next consider the mix variance. As indicated earlier, the mix variance isolates the effect of the difference between the actual mix and the budgeted mix. This variance is most easily computed on a product-by-product basis. The individual variances are summed to obtain the total mix variance. For a given product the mix variance is:

$$\text{Mix variance for a given product} = \left(\text{Actual quantity} - \text{Budget \%} \times \text{actual} \atop total \text{ volume}\right) \text{Product's budgeted contribution margin} \tag{18-2}$$

The second factor inside the parenthesis of (18-2) gives the volume of the specific product that would have been sold *if the mix had not changed.* The difference between this and the actual volume sold gives the mix differential in terms of units. Multiplying this difference by the contribution margin gives the dollar impact of the differential. For the example problem the budget percentages are:

A = 1/3   B = 0   C = 2/3

The mix variances (*MV*) are:

MV(A) = [100 − (1/3)235] × 5	\$108.33 F
MV(B) = [60 − (0)235] × 3	180.00 F
MV(C) = [75 − (2/3)235] × 4	326.66 U
Total mix variance	\$ 38.33 U

Again, the mix variance cannot really be declared favorable or unfavorable without further investigation. For example, if the actual profitability of product C declines, it may be desirable to reduce the volume of C. However, this reduction will result in an unfavorable mix variance due to product C. The variance system to be explored in the next section will examine this issue further and *may prove to be more useful* in the interpretation of a manager's performance.

The final component of the total profit variance is the contribution margin variance. Its computation is rather obvious:

$$\begin{array}{c} CM \text{ variance} \\ \text{for a given} \\ \text{product} \end{array} = \left(\begin{array}{cc} \text{Actual} & \text{Budgeted} \\ CM & CM \end{array} \right) \begin{array}{c} \text{Actual} \\ \text{quantity} \end{array} \tag{18-3}$$

For our case:

$CMV(A) = (5 - 5)100$	0
$CMV(B) = (3 - 3)60$	0
$CMV(C) = (3.50 - 4.00)75$	37.50 U
Total CM variance	$\underline{\underline{\$37.50}}$ U

It will be left as an exercise to further analyze the specific causes of the contribution margin variance. Finally, note that the sum of the three variances equals the total variance between the actual and budgeted income: $(-281.67 - 38.33 - 37.50) = -357.50$.

The three variances discussed in this section represent the conventional type of analyses that have been developed over the years for profit centers. However, the results are only an indication of the nature of the variance and are not suggestive of possible corrective actions that would be desirable in future planning. The next section introduces a system that may prove to be more useful as a control device.

Ex-Post Variance Analysis

The profit variance analysis system discussed in the previous subsection has the risk of not being supportive of the objective of control as defined in Chapter 17. That is, it may not encourage managers to adapt constantly to a changing environment. In response to this deficiency, Demski has proposed an alternative variance analysis system.[2] His system has been labeled the **ex-post variance analysis** system and is contingent upon the existence of a well-behaved model to determine an optimal use of limited resources given the conditions. Since it is not possible to develop such a model for every situation, the ex-post system will not always be operable. But when it is feasible, the system enables a significant improvement in the management control system and, thus, is worthy of our consideration.

The ex-post system is designed to motivate managers to use resources optimally rather than to merely adhere to the predetermined budget. The conventional profit variance system separates the difference between the actual and budgeted profit into the quantity, mix, and contribution margin variances. In contrast, the ex-post system classifies the total variance into a forecast variance and an opportunity cost. Let us now explore how this is accomplished and how the variances can be used.

---

[2]Joel Demski, "An Accounting System Structured on a Linear Programming Model," *Accounting Review* (October 1967), pp. 701–712. Also, see Demski, "Analyzing the Effectiveness of the Traditional Standard Cost Variance Model," *Management Accounting* (October 1967), pp. 9–19.

To facilitate the analysis, it is necessary to determine ex-post, or after the fact, what the optimal course of action should have been for the period. That is, after the actual facts become known, the ex-post optimal solution is determined by using the actual data and conditions as input to the formal decision model. There are some problems in implementing this system but before considering them the basic idea will be illustrated.

Reconsider the example in the previous section. You should recall that during the period the manager of the Dairy Products Division detected a change in product C's parameters. Using the actual data observed during the period, the ex-post optimal solution can be determined by deciding how the limited resources could have been best used. It can be shown that when product C is contributing $3.50 per unit instead of $4.00 and consuming four units of material Y instead of three, the best way to use the resources would have been as follows:[3]

A = 250;   B = C = 0;   Contribution margin = $1,250

In determining the ex-post solution it has been implicitly assumed that the differences between the original and the actual data were due to prediction or forecasting error. That is, the actual data represented the real relationships that existed at the beginning of the period and the information system was incorrect in its forecasts. In short, the solution to the ex-post model assumes that its data were in effect *during the entire period* covered by the model. Of course, the differences might have been due to an environmental change that occurred after the period began. If so, the optimal strategy would change only at the time of the environmental change. Then the ex-post optimal solution for the period would be a combination of the optimal strategies for the various conditions that existed during the period.

Given the assumption that the observed values of the parameters were in effect during the entire period, the ex-post optimal solution would have yielded a contribution margin (*CM*) of $1,250. Thus:

Budgeted contribution margin = $1,300 (see Exhibit 18.3)
Ex-post optimal contribution margin = $1,250 (from ex-post analysis)
Actual contribution margin = $942.50 (see Exhibit 18.4)

The *forecast variance* and the *opportunity cost* components of the ex-post system are computed as follows:

Forecast variance = (Ex-post *CM* − Budgeted *CM*)   (18-4)
Opportunity cost = (Actual *CM* − Ex-post *CM*)   (18-5)

For the illustrative case:

---

[3]The solution stated above is the optimal solution to the following linear programming model:
Maximize: 5A + 3B + 3.5C
Subject to: 3A + B + 2.0C ≤   800
             4A + 5B + 4.0C ≤ 1,000
             4A + 3B + 4.0C ≤ 1,200

Forecast variance = 1,250 − 1,300 = $ 50.00 U
Opportunity cost = 942.50 − 1,250 =   307.50 U
    Total $357.50 U

Note that the sum of the two variances is equal to the difference between actual *CM* and budgeted *CM*. The forecast variance component recognizes that portion of the total *CM* variance that was not really capable of being earned anyway based on the actual conditions that were assumed to exist. The opportunity cost, as indicated, is the difference between the actual *CM* and the ex-post optimal *CM*. Holding managers responsible for this difference should motivate them to constantly monitor the data and their strategies. As you can see, this variance is controllable only by changing the plans to adapt to the conditions, not by adhering to the original plans.

Caution must be used in interpreting the opportunity cost variance. Even a competent manager will need some time to detect that the forecast was wrong and to adjust his or her plans. Thus, there should be no expectation that the opportunity cost can be entirely avoided by the operating manager. That is, a portion of the opportunity cost might be attributed to the forecasting system. Based on a forecast, certain plans are made and put into effect. To adapt to changed perceptions of the environment or to actual changes, some reasonable transition period must be anticipated. If the forecasting system misread the environment, as opposed to the environment changing, then the forecasting system is responsible for the opportunity cost that occurs during the transition period. The opportunity cost incurred while reacting to changes is uncontrollable. In summary, not all of the opportunity cost will necessarily be attributed to the operating manager nor can all of it be considered as controllable. The uncontrollable portion can be isolated in the variance investigation phase.

In addition to the above considerations, it should be noted that the parameter changes that occurred may have been controllable. In our example, the fact that product C required four units of material Y instead of three may be due to production inefficiencies that could have been avoided. If so, then there must be a decision made as to how the ex-post optimum will be determined. The options are to use achievable standards or actual performance rates. Presumably, the former would be more in line with the concept of control. If such a variance is actually avoidable, then its incurrence leads to an opportunity cost.

Should it be determined that the material Y usage rate was controllable, then the ex-post analysis of the best use of the resources would be done using only one change in the data. The sales price of product C would be $31.50 instead of $31.00. Since it is being assumed that the material Y usage variance is controllable, the ex-post analysis would continue to assume that product C would need three units of Y and that its total variable production cost was $27:

Material X	2 units @ $2.00	$ 4.00
Material Y	3 units @ $1.00	3.00
Labor	4 hours @ $5.00	20.00
		$27.00

To use the ex-post system it is not necessary that the formal decision process be a linear programming model. Inventory models, queueing models, and so forth, could also be used. In the end-of-chapter exercises, you will be asked to expand upon the ideas of this system using an inventory model.

Yield and Mix Variance

In Chapters 5 and 6 it was basically assumed that a firm's products required a constant set of *nonsubstitutable* resources. That is, in the manufacture of a parlor game, paper could not be substituted for cardboard and vice versa. In some situations, however, substitution may be feasible and even desirable. For example, a public accounting firm may be able to have a senior staff person do a junior's job on an engagement that is running at a time when all juniors are assigned to other jobs. Or a processed meat company may be able to use pork instead of beef in the production of summer sausage.

If substitutions occur in a standard cost system, then variances from the standard may result from the substitution. It may be useful to measure the effect of the substitution as a further analysis of the variances as computed in Chapter 5. If materials and/or labor are substituted and if the items involved each have different costs, then the substitution will at least cause a *mix variance*. In addition, there may also be a *yield variance* if the new combination of inputs generates a different rate of output than the mix of inputs used in setting the standards. For example, the substitution of pork for beef may result in more shrinkage in the cooking process than was planned for when the standards were established. This could be attributed to pork having a higher fat content than beef.

To illustrate consider the Oscar Mayo Company that produces a variety of processed meats including summer sausage. They have established standards for summer sausage based on the costs of pork and beef, the availability of each, quality requirements, the demand for the products, and so forth, as follows:

For 1,000 pounds of summer sausage

Pork	500* pounds @ $1.00	$ 500
Beef	722* pounds @ $1.50	1,083
Total meat cost		$1,583

*There is shrinkage in the cooking process due to fat content.

The standard meat cost per pound of summer sausage is $1.583 ($1,583 ÷ 1,000). The anticipated yield is 81.83%, output ÷ input or 1,000 ÷ (500 + 722).

During the current period, beef was somewhat more scarce than normal. Thus, pork was substituted for beef. One 1,000-pound batch of summer sausage was made. Meat purchased and used for this batch was:

Pork	600 pounds @ $1.00	$ 600
Beef	644 pounds @ $1.50	966
		$1,566

The conventional material price (*MPV*) and quantity variances (*MQV*) are as follows:

$$MPV \text{ (pork)} = (1.00 - 1.00)600 = \text{-0-}$$
$$MPV \text{ (beef)} = (1.50 - 1.50)644 = \text{-0-} \qquad \underline{\text{-0-}}$$
$$MQV \text{ (pork)} = (500 - 600)1.00 = 100 \text{ U}$$
$$MQV \text{ (beef)} = (722 - 644)1.50 = \underline{117} \text{ F} \qquad \underline{\underline{17}} \text{ F}$$

The $17.00 quantity variance can be further analyzed as to mix and yield variances. This process parallels the mix and quantity variance of the profit variance analysis of a previous section. The mix variance is:

$$\begin{matrix} \text{Mix variance} \\ \text{for a given} \\ \text{input} \end{matrix} = \begin{pmatrix} \text{Budget \%} \\ \times \text{ actual} \\ \textit{total } \text{input} \end{pmatrix} \begin{matrix} \text{Actual} \\ \text{quantity} \end{matrix} \begin{pmatrix} \text{Input's} \\ \text{standard} \\ \text{cost} \end{pmatrix} \qquad (18\text{-}6)$$

Because this is an analysis of a cost variance instead of a profit variance, the relationship within the parentheses of equation (18-6) is reversed in comparison with equation (18-2). The first term inside the parenthesis computes the amount of a given material that would have been used if the budget mixes had been adhered to. It is based on the total of *all* material used during the period (600 pounds of pork plus 644 pounds of beef, or 1,244 pounds in our case). Thus, the mix variances (*MV*) are:

$$MV \text{ (pork)} = \left(\frac{500^*}{1,222} \times 1,244 - 600 \right)\$1.00 = (509 - 600)\$1.00 = \$ \; 91.00 \text{ U}$$

$$MV \text{ (beef)} = \left(\frac{722^*}{1,222} \times 1,244 - 644 \right)\$1.50 = (735 - 644)\$1.50 = \underline{136.50} \text{ F}$$

$$\underline{\underline{\$ \; 45.50}} \text{ F}$$

*The amount of pork and beef budgeted for one 1,000-pound batch.

The second variance, yield, reflects the fact that the relationship between the output and input was not the same as planned for in the budgeting process. The anticipated yield was 0.8183 pounds of summer sausage per pound of meat used and the actual yield this period was 0.8039, 1,000 ÷ 1,244. In general, the yield variance is:

Yield variance = (Actual yield % × Actual input − Standard   (18-7)
   yield % × Actual input) × (Standard material cost per unit)

For our problem:

$$\begin{aligned} \text{Yield variance} &= (0.8039 \times 1,244 - 0.8183 \times 1,244)1.583 \\ &= (1,000 - 1,018) \; 1.583 = \qquad \$28.50 \text{ U} \end{aligned}$$

The logic of equation (18-7) is as follows. If the actual input had been yielding summer sausage at the expected yield rate of 81.83%, 1,244 pounds of input would have yielded 1,019 pounds of summer sausage (0.8183 × 1,244) instead of 1,000 pounds. In general, this is the standard yield times the actual input. The difference between the actual yield and the expected yield is converted to dollars using the standard *total* material cost of one pound of summer sausage. That is, since we are analyzing material quantity variance, the yield variance is the material cost of the "lost" output.

Note that the $17.00 favorable material quantity variance, as computed with the conventional variance system, is now divided into two components:

Mix variance	$45.50 F
Yield variance	28.50 U
Total variance	$17.00 F

This will be explored further in the end-of-chapter problems. The ideas of this section can also be applied to labor analyses, if there are multiple classes of labor, and to nonproduction situations such as consulting and public accounting engagements where different types of personnel are used on the assignment. Of course all of these applications assume standard labor and professional time can be established.

Deciding When to Investigate a Variance

In this section we will examine two approaches that can be used to decide if variances are significant enough to investigate. One approach is based on sampling concepts and includes $\bar{x}$ and R (mean and range) limits. The other approach bases the variance investigation decisions on an expected payoff criterion.

CONTROL LIMITS BASED ON SAMPLING CONCEPTS. Variance investigative **control limits** can be established through the idea of sampling procedures that have been developed by the quality control profession. A very naive form of such a control limit is to establish it as an arbitrary percentage of the mean quantity of material and/or labor that should be used in completing a given number of units. Then an investigation would be conducted only if the actual quantity is more, or possibly less, than this percentage.

Should there be a desire to establish limits that have more valid statistical properties, then the following approach should be followed. First, when the production process is known to be in control, there should be a sampling of the outcomes in order to estimate a mean and a standard deviation of the "in control" population. These estimates are then used to establish a control range such that the chances are small of an observation falling outside of it when *only* random causes are at work. Then, when an observation does fall outside the range there would be a very high probability the process is out of control.

One way to estimate the mean of a population (such as the labor time needed to complete a unit when the process is in control) is to draw a sample and use the mean of the sample as the estimator of the population's mean. Another way is to draw several samples and use the mean of the sample means as the estimator.

Define:

n = Number of observations in a sample

m = Number of samples

$x_{i,j}$ = Observation i of sample j

Then, the jth sample's mean, $\bar{x}_j$, and the mean of the means, $\bar{\bar{x}}$, are:

$$\bar{x}_j = \frac{1}{n}\left(\sum_{i=1}^{n} x_{i,j}\right) \tag{18-8}$$

$$\bar{\bar{x}} = \frac{1}{m}\left(\sum_{j=1}^{m} \bar{x}_j\right) \tag{18-9}$$

The population's standard deviation can either be estimated by the sample's standard deviation or, preferably, by the standard deviation of all of the observations, that is, using all m samples of n observations each. Defining this estimate as $\hat{\sigma}$ and using the second method, the standard deviation is computed as:

$$\hat{\sigma} = \sqrt{\frac{\sum_{i=1}^{n}\sum_{j=1}^{m}(x_{i,j} - \bar{\bar{x}})^2}{n(m) - 1}} \tag{18-10}$$

Control is then implemented as follows. First, the output of a given period is examined to determine the average resources consumed in its production. In effect, this average is the mean of a sample. Then, determine if the observation is within the range of normal variation when the process is in control. To establish such a range, we need the standard deviation of the sample means, not the standard deviation of individual observations. The first standard deviation is called $\hat{\sigma}_{\bar{x}}$ the latter $\hat{\sigma}$. This is due to the fact that the observation is the mean amount of labor needed for this week's production. An estimate of the standard deviation of sample means, $\hat{\sigma}_{\bar{x}}$, is computed in most basic statistics books as:

$$\hat{\sigma}_{\bar{x}} = \frac{\hat{\sigma}}{\sqrt{n}} \tag{18-11}$$

The central limit theorem of statistics ensures us that the distribution of sample means is normally distributed even if the population is not normal. Thus, the normal distribution can be used to construct the control limits. (If the sample size is small, then the t-distribution should be used.) Let p be the probability that an observation will be outside the range as a result of chance causes. Then the control range will have a $(1 - p)$ chance of including observations from an in-control process. Supppose we want p to be 95%. This means that for a 95% confidence interval we must move either direction from the mean so that a 2.5% chance is left in each tail. The subscript on the *t*-value in Table A.1 (in the Appendix) indicates the percentage in *one* tail and the entry in the table indicates the number of standard deviations ($\hat{\sigma}_{\bar{x}}$) to move in either direction from the mean $\bar{\bar{x}}$, in order to establish the desired control range. Thus we would use the $t_{0.025}$ column and the row appropriate to our sample size. In general, denote the value $t_{p/2}$. Then:

$$(1 - p) \text{ control range} = \bar{\bar{x}} \pm t_{p/2} (\hat{\sigma}_{\bar{x}}) \tag{18-12}$$

To illustrate, suppose for a given process the average labor hours per unit when the process is in control is twenty ($\bar{\bar{x}}$) and the population's standard deviation is estimated to be two ($\hat{\sigma}$). A 95% control range for the mean of a sample of twenty five items is computed using a t-value for twenty four degrees of freedom. (See Table A.1.) Thus:

$$\hat{\sigma}_{\bar{x}} = \frac{2}{\sqrt{25}} = 0.4$$

and:

$$
\begin{aligned}
95\% &= 20 \pm t_{0.025} \times 0.4 \\
&= 20 \pm 2.06 \times 0.4 \\
&= [19.176 \quad 20.824]
\end{aligned}
$$

Suppose now that in the current week twenty five units had been produced at an average labor consumption of twenty one hours per unit. The above range indicates there is a high probability that *non*random causes account for this week's observation being outside the control range. Exhibit 18.5 is a visualization of the range. Since the process has a high probability of being out of control, it should be investigated unless it is felt that the investigative costs would exceed the benefits.

To supplement the $\bar{x}$ range, another factor should be considered. In computing the average of the observations for the week, high and low values will cancel out against each other and potentially disguise an erratic behavior. To compensate for this, the quality control profession has developed another test called an *R (range) control chart*. An *R*-chart is developed as follows. First, several samples are drawn

Exhibit 18.5   Control Range

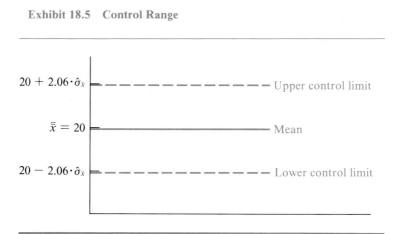

when the process is in control. For each sample, a range (high minus low) is computed. Using the average range, $\overline{R}$ and some factors that have been specially developed for this purpose (called D_3 and D_4) the R-limits for 99% confidence (3σ) are:

$$3\sigma \ R\text{-limit} = D_3(\overline{R}) \text{ to } D_4(\overline{R})$$

The selected D_3 and D_4 values found in Exhibit 18.6 are those needed to develop a 3σ interval. The 3σ interval gives virtual assurance of encompassing the sample range *if the process is in control.* Thus, a sample with a range outside the control interval is a signal that the process might be out of control.

MAKING VARIANCE INVESTIGATION DECISIONS USING THE EXPECTED VALUE CRITERION. None of the previously discussed models for assessing the significance of a variance considered investigative costs as a factor. If the cost-benefit relationship is important to the decision maker, then an expected value approach can be applied to the investigation decision. That is, an investigation is not warranted if the expected cost savings resulting from correcting an out-of-control process do not exceed the cost of making the investigation. In its simplest form, this decision problem has two alternatives (do not investigate or

Exhibit 18.6   Factors for R Control Chart
Three σ Control Limits

Number of Observations in Sample	Lower Control Limit (D_3)	Upper Control Limit (D_4)
2	0	3.267
3	0	2.575
4	0	2.282
5	0	2.115
6	0	2.004
7	0.076	1.924
8	0.136	1.864
9	0.184	1.816
10	0.223	1.777
11	0.256	1.744
12	0.284	1.716
13	0.308	1.671
14	0.329	1.671
15	0.348	1.652

(Source: Adapted with permission from Eugene L. Grant and Richard S. Leavenworth, *Statistical Quality Control,* 4th ed. (New York: McGraw-Hill Book Co., 1972), Table C, p. 645.)

investigate) and two states of nature (in control and not in control). Define the following:

C = Cost of conducting an investigation

R = Cost of correcting an out-of-control process

L = Opportunity cost of not correcting an out-of-control process

p = Probability of the state of nature being in control

The payoff table for this decision is found in Exhibit 18.7. If there is no investigation when the state of nature is in control, then no costs are incurred. On the other hand, if there is no investigation when the process is out of control, then the opportunity cost, L, is incurred. This opportunity cost is the savings in the operating costs that could be realized if the investigation was done. Determining L will not be easy. The savings is a function of the excess costs attributable to the causal factor and of the length of time the process would remain in control after it is corrected. That is, an investigation and correction will not permanently prevent the process from going out of control. Thus, the opportunity cost of not investigating should be a function only of the length of time for which the correction is effective. Since the length of the effect of a correction is uncertain, the computation of L would, itself, be an expected value.[4] Further, if the effect of a correction covers several periods it is desirable to discount the savings and use their expected present value as the L value.

Next, consider the conditional payoffs of the decision to investigate. If the process is in control, then the cost of investigation, C, is the only cost incurred. Should the process be out of control, then the cost of correction is incurred in addition to the cost of investigation, a total of $C + R$.

The probability of being in control would be a professional judgment and could be better made if some of the previously discussed statistical data were available. Also, the manager receives periodic cost reports about the process and, based on these reports, may want to revise his or her probability estimate.[5]

It should be noted that certain assumptions have been made in formulating the problem. First, it is assumed there are only two states of nature. In reality there could be multiple states representing a continuum of out-of-control conditions. At some cost, additional states of nature should be considered in the analysis. Further, it is assumed that if the process is out of control and an investigation is conducted, it will positively detect the cause of the problem. Further, it is assumed that any corrective action taken will be effective. It is also possible to include alternative investigative strategies in the set of available actions. Presumably, they would be less costly than a complete investigation and have smaller chances of detecting the cause of the variance.

[4]For an expanded discussion of this measurement problem see Robert Magee, "A Simulation Analysis of Alternative Cost Variance Investigation Models," *Accounting Review* (July 1976), pp. 529–544.

[5]For additional discussion of probability revision in this context, see Thomas Dyckman, "The Investigation of Cost Variances," *Journal of Accounting Research* (Autumn 1969), pp. 215–244.

Exhibit 18.7   Payoff Table Variance Investigation Decision

	State of Nature	
	In Control	*Out of Control*
Do not investigate (DI)	0	L
Investigate (I)	C	C + R
Probability	p	1 − p

Given the assumptions and the resulting payoff table, an investigation could be justified only if the expected cost of the investigation is less than the expected cost of not investigating. That is,

Investigate if: EV(I) < EV(NI)

Using the payoffs in Exhibit 18.7, investigation would be preferred if:

$$pC + (1 - p)(C + R) < (1 - p)L$$

Expanding:

$$pC + C + R - pC - pR < L - pL$$

Simplifying:

$$pL - pR < L - C - R$$

or

$$p < \frac{L - C - R}{L - R} \qquad (18\text{-}13)$$

To illustrate, suppose the cost of performing an investigation is $100, the cost of making corrections is $150, and the present value of the expected savings of making a correction is $800. Then, an investigation should be made if the probability of being in control is less than 84.6%:

$$p < \frac{800 - 100 - 150}{800 - 150} = 0.846$$

Even if rough estimates of the parameters must be used, the application of the criterion given in (18-13) permits better investigation decisions than some ad hoc rule.

Summary

This chapter examined ways of extending control to a profit center. To facilitate the analysis of a variance from a profit center's budget, two systems were discussed: the profit variance system and the ex-post variance system. An alternative to the noncontrollable (volume) variance was also explained as was a mix-and-yield analysis of the material quantity variance.

Another purpose of this chapter was to enhance a better understanding of control systems. Various factors must be considered when interpreting the variances of a standard cost system. It is important to remember that random variation must be expected even when the process is in control. A variety of methods can be used to account for these influences. Among the methods that can aid in assessing the significance of variances are control charts and decision rules based on an expected value criterion. If used wisely, the various tools introduced in this chapter can help accountants to minimize an image of being financial police officers.

New terms and concepts introduced in this chapter include:

Production variance
Marketing variance
Expected idle capacity
Profit variance analysis
Quantity variance
Mix variance
Contribution margin variance
Ex-post variance analysis
Forecast variance
Opportunity cost variance
Yield variance
Control limit
R (range) control chart

SELF-STUDY PROBLEM. The Simple Products Company produces four products whose planned class I and class II labor requirements and contribution margins are as follows:

	A	*B*	*C*	*D*
Class I labor per unit	2	1/2	3	2
Class II labor per unit	4	2	1	2
Contribution margin per unit	$6	$2	$4	$3

At the beginning of the current period the amount of class I labor available was forecast at 4,000 hours and the availability of class II was estimated to be 6,000 hours. The markets for products A and B are limited to 1,000 and 2,000 units per period, respectively. A contract has been signed to deliver 600 units of product C to the Complex Products Company.

Based on the above forecasts, the optimal product mix and resulting contribution margins were set as:

Product	*Units*	*Contribution per Unit*	*Total Contribution*
A	850	$6	$5,100
B	1,000	$2	2,000
C	600	$4	2,400
D	–0–	$3	–0–
Total			$9,500

The second day of the period the manager discovered the cost of producing product A was actually $1.00 higher than had been originally estimated. On an ad hoc basis the manager changed the mix to:

A—350   B—2,000   C—600   D—0

This resulted in an actual contribution margin of $8,150.

At the end of the period it was determined that the best solution, given the actual cost of product A, would have been:

A—300   B—2,000   C—800   D—0   CM = $8,700

Required:

1. Use the profit variance analysis to reconcile the difference between the budgeted and actual contribution margin for the period.
2. Use the ex-post variance analysis to explain the difference between the actual and budgeted contribution margin for the period.
3. The complete labor standards for product A are:

Class I labor	2 hours @ $10	$20
Class II labor	4 hours @ $ 8	32
		$52

During the above period, the following actual labor was incurred for product A:

Class I labor	875 hours @ $10	$ 8,750
Class II labor	1,225 hours @ $ 8	9,800
		$18,550

  a. Further analyze the contribution margin variance to determine the portion due to labor rate variance and labor efficiency variance.
  b. Analyze the labor efficiency variance in part 3-a into mix and yield variances.

Solution to Self-Study Problem

1. First, note that the total variance between the budgeted and actual profit is $1,350 U ($8,150 − $9,500). The profit variance analysis would separate this variance into three components:
   a. Quantity variance = (Total units sold − Total units budgeted) × Average CM per unit in the budget

$$\text{Average } CM = \frac{\$5,100 + \$2,000 + \$2,400}{850 + 1,000 + 600} = \$3.87755$$

$$QV = ([350 + 2,000 + 600] - [850 + 1,000 + 600])3.87755$$

$$= (2,950 - 2,450)\,3.87755$$

$$= \$1,939 \; F$$

b. Mix variance = (Actual quantity of a product − Budget % × Actual total volume)
   × Product's *CM*

$$MV(A) = (350 - \frac{850}{2,450} \times 2,950)6 = \quad \$4,041 \text{ U}$$

$$MV(B) = (2,000 - \frac{1,000}{2,450} \times 2,950)2 = \quad 1,592 \text{ F}$$

$$MV(C) = (600 - \frac{600}{2,450} \times 2,950)4 = \quad \underline{490} \text{ U}$$

$$\underline{\underline{\$2,939}} \text{ U}$$

c. *CM* variance = (Standard *CM* − Actual *CM*)Actual quantity sold
   This exists only for product A:
   $CM(A) = (5 - 6)350 = 350$ U

In summary:

Quantity variance	$1,939 U
Mix variance	2,939 U
Contribution margin variance	350 U
	$1,350 U

2. For the ex-post system:

Budgeted contribution margin =	$9,500
Ex-post optimal contribution margin =	$8,700
Actual contribution margin =	$8,150

This system would divide the total variance of $1,350 into:
a. Forecast variance = Ex-post − Budgeted
   = $8,700 − $9,500 = $ 800 U
b. Opportunity cost = Actual − Ex-post
   = $8,150 − $8,700 = 550 U
   Total $1,350

3. a. The contribution margin variance due to the labor rate variances are zero since both
   classes of labor were paid at the standard rate. However, for labor efficiency variance:

   Standard labor allowed:

   Class I 350 × 2 =   700 hours
   Class II 350 × 4 = 1,400 hours

   Thus:

   LEV (Class I) = (700 − 875)10   = $1,750 U
   LEV (Class II) = (1,400 − 1,225)8 =   1,400 F
       Total labor efficiency $ 350 U

   In this case, the entire contribution margin variance on product A is explained by the
   labor efficiency variance.

b. The $350 labor efficiency variance can be further analyzed, in this case, into mix and yield variances. For the mix variance the total input for the period was 2,100 hours (875 + 1,225). The budget mix ratios of class I and class II labor are 1/3 and 2/3. Thus:

$$MV(\text{Class I}) = [(1/3 \times 2,100) - 875]10 = \$1,750 \text{ U}$$
$$MV(\text{Class II}) = [(2/3 \times 2,100) - 1,225]8 = \underline{1,400} \text{ F}$$
$$\text{Total mix variance} \qquad\qquad\qquad \$\underline{\underline{\ 350}} \text{ U}$$

Since this is equal to the total labor efficiency variance, there would be no yield variance. This can be verified as follows. The standard yield percentage is one A for each six labor hours: 1/6. The actual is 350 units ÷ 2,100 total hours or 1/6. Thus, the substitution of class I labor for class II labor did not affect the yield in this case.

References

Bierman, H., Fouraker, L.E., and Jaedicke, R.K. "A Use of Probability and Statistics in Performance Evaluation," *The Accounting Review* (July 1961): 409–417.

Demski, J. "An Accounting System Structured on a Linear Programming Model," *The Accounting Review* (October 1976): 701–712.

Duncan, A.J. "The Economic Design of $\bar{x}$ Charts Used to Maintain Current Control of a Process," *Journal of the American Statistical Association* (June 1956): 228–242

Dyckman, T. "The Investigation of Cost Variances," *Journal of Accounting Research* (Autumn 1969): 215–244.

Kaplan, R.S. "Optimal Investigation Strategies with Imperfect Information," *Journal of Accounting Research* (Spring 1969): 32–43.

Stallman, J. "A Framework for Evaluating Cost Control Procedures for a Process," *The Accounting Review* (October 1972): 774–790.

Problems

18-1. Alternative to Noncontrollable (Volume) Variance. The Perry Company has a practical capacity of 20,000 units per month and uses a standard cost accounting system. During June 19x6, they produced and sold 15,000 units while incurring $60,000 of manufacturing expenses (including $20,000 fixed) and $10,000 of selling and administrative expenses (including $3,000 fixed). The total standard variable cost was $3.00 per unit ($0.30 of which represents selling and administrative cost). During June the company received orders equal to 90% of the amount budgeted. The budget was based on 90% of practical capacity and showed an income of $13,000. The selling price was fixed at $5.00 per unit and fixed costs totaling $23,000 were budgeted for June. Inventories did not change during June.

Required:

1. Prepare a statement of actual income using the variable (direct) cost concept.
2. Analyze the variance between the budgeted and actual income using appropriate variances from the standard cost system and from the system proposed as an alternative to the noncontrollable variance.

18-2. Alternative to Noncontrollable Variance. The Brooks Company produces two products, A and B. The fixed manufacturing cost has been budgeted at $400,000 per year and will be assigned on the basis of a practical capacity of 200,000 direct-labor hours per year.

The budgeted production for the current year, the standard direct-labor hours, sales prices, and variable costs per unit are:

Product	Budgeted Units	Direct-Labor Hours per Unit	Sales Price	Variable Cost
A	30,000	2	$ 40	$30.00
B	40,000	3	100	80.50

During the current year the orders received and production accomplished were:

Product	Orders	Production
A	27,000	21,600
B	36,000	28,800

The actual direct-labor hours incurred during the current period totaled 131,000.

Required:

1. What is the noncontrollable (volume) variance for the current year?
2. Assuming the variances are converted to dollars using the fixed overhead rate, provide an alternative analysis of the "volume" variance. That is divide the variance into three components that will better reflect the reasons for unused capacity.
3. Now assume the orders received and production scheduled for the period were:

Product	Orders	Production
A	28,000	28,000
B	44,000	42,000

The actual hours incurred totaled 183,000. Repeat parts 1 and 2 using these data.
4. Assume the three components of volume variance referred to above will be converted to dollars using opportunity cost. Further, assume idle capacity can be filled using an A to B mix of three to four. Using the actual orders and production in part 3 recompute the three "volume" variances.

18-3. Basic Problem on Profit Variance Analysis. The Bedford Company had prepared the following budget for January 19x1:

	Product A	Product B	Total
Sales (in units)	4,000	6,000	
Sales revenue	$40,000	$30,000	$70,000
Variable cost	24,000	18,000	42,000
Contribution margin	$16,000	$12,000	$28,000
Fixed costs			15,000
Net income before tax			$13,000
Income tax @ 50%			6,500
Net income			$ 6,500

The actual results for January 19x1 are as follows:

	Product A	Product B	Total
Sales (in units)	6,000	6,000	
Sales revenue	$60,600	$29,000	$89,600
Variable cost	35,400	20,000	55,400
Contribution margin	$25,200	$ 9,000	$34,200
Fixed cost			16,000
Net income before tax			$18,200
Income tax @ 50%			9,100
Net income			$ 9,100

Required:

Prepare an analysis of the variance between actual and budgeted contribution margin. Consider the mix, quantity, and contribution margin variances.

18-4. Continuation of Problem Studied in Chapter. Reconsider the Dee Que Company from this chapter. The contribution margin variance was computed to be $37.50 U.

Required:

To the extent permitted by the data given in the chapter, further analyze the contribution margin variance.

18-5. CMA Problem on Profit Variance Analysis. The Arsco Co. makes three grades of indoor-outdoor carpets. The sales volume for the annual budget is determined by estimating the total market volume for the indoor-outdoor carpet and then applying the company's prior year market share, adjusted for planned changes due to company programs for the coming year. The volume is apportioned between the three grades, based upon the prior year's product mix, again adjusted for planned changes due to company programs for the coming year.

The company budget for 19x3 and the results of operations for 19x3 follow.

	Budget			
	Grade 1	Grade 2	Grade 3	Total
Sales (rolls)	1,000	1,000	2,000	4,000
Sales dollars (000 omitted)	$1,000	$2,000	$3,000	$6,000
Variable expense	700	1,600	2,300	4,600
Variable margin	$ 300	$ 400	$ 700	$1,400
Traceable fixed expense	200	200	300	700
Traceable margin	$ 100	$ 200	$ 400	$ 700
Selling and administrative expense				$ 250
Net income				$ 450

| | | Actual | | |
	Grade 1	Grade 2	Grade 3	Total
Sales (rolls)	800	1,000	2,100	3,900
Sales dollars (000 omitted)	$ 810	$2,000	$3,000	$5,810
Variable expense	560	1,610	2,320	4,490
Variable margin	$ 250	$ 390	$ 680	$1,320
Traceable fixed expense	210	220	315	745
Traceable margin	$ 40	$ 170	$ 365	$ 575
Selling and administrative expense				$ 275
Net income				$ 300

Industry volume was estimated at 40,000 rolls for budgeting purposes. Actual industry volume for 19x3 was 38,000 rolls.

Required:

1. Calculate the profit impact of the unit sales volume variance for 19x3 using budgeted variable margins.
2. What portion of the variance, if any, can be attributed to the state of the carpet market?
3. What is the dollar impact on profits (using budgeted variable margins) of the shift in product mix from the budgeted mix?

18-6. Comprehensive Problem on Profit Variance Analysis. The Schoenfeld Company produces two products, X and Y. It reports on a *full absorption cost basis* using the following standards:

	Product X	Product Y
Material @ $2	$10	$ 6
Labor @ $5	10	20
Variable overhead @ $1 per DLH	2	4
Fixed overhead @ $2 per DLH*	4	8
Total	$26	$38

*Fixed overhead rate:

Budgeted fixed costs	$400,000
DLH at practical capacity	200,000
Rate per DLH	$ 2

Product X sells at $40 per unit and Y at $50. The following summarizes Schoenfeld's plan for 19x1:

	Product X (in units)	Product Y (in units)
Beginning inventory	10,000	5,000
Budgeted sales	80,000	15,000
Budgeted production	75,000	12,500

The actual results for 19x1 were as follows:

	Product X (in units)	Product Y (in units)
Sales	75,000 @ $40	16,000 @ $51
Production	70,000	13,500

Actual costs recorded for 19x1 include:

Materials purchased and used	390,000 units @ $2.02
Labor	195,000 hours @ $5.00
Variable overhead	$204,750
Fixed overhead	$402,000

All variances, including the noncontrollable (volume) variance, are closed to cost of goods sold. Ignore selling and administrative expenses.

Required:

1. Prepare the 19x1 budgeted statement of income.
2. Prepare the 19x1 statement of actual income.
3. In as much detail as the data permits, prepare a conventional profit variance analysis of the difference between budgeted and actual income.

18-7. Variation of Problem 18-6. Reconsider problem 18-6 but assume the actual results for 19x1 are as follows:

	Product X (in units)	Product Y (in units)
Sales	75,000 @ $40	16,000 @ $51
Production	72,000	13,000

Actual costs recorded for 19x1 include:

Materials purchased and used	399,000 units @ $2.00
Labor	196,000 hours @ $5.00
Variable overhead	$196,000
Fixed overhead	$400,000

Required:

1. Prepare the 19x1 budgeted statement of income if you did not do problem 18-6.
2. Prepare the 19x1 statement of actual income.
3. In as much detail as the data permits, prepare a conventional profit variance analysis of the difference between budgeted and actual income.

18-8. Adapted CMA Problem on Gross Profit Variance Analysis. The Markley Division of Rosette Industries manufactures and sells patio chairs. The chairs are manufactured in two versions—a metal model and a plastic model of a lesser quality. The company uses its own sales force to sell the chairs to retail stores and to catalog outlets. Generally, customers purchase both the metal and plastic versions.

The chairs are manufactured on two different assembly lines located in adjoining buildings. Division management and the sales department occupy the third building on the property. The division management includes a division controller responsible for the divisional financial activities and the preparation of reports explaining the differences between actual and budgeted performance. The controller structures these reports such that the sales activities are distinguished from cost factors so that each can be analyzed separately.

Operating results for the first three months of the fiscal year as compared to the budget are presented below. The budget for the current year was based upon the assumption that Markley Division would maintain its present market share of the estimated total patio chair market (plastic and metal combined). A status report had been sent to corporate management toward the end of the second month indicating that divisional operating income for the first quarter would probably be about 45% below budget; this estimate was just about on target. The division's operating income was below budget even though industry volume for patio chairs increased by 10% more than was expected at the time the budget was developed.

Markley Division
Operating Results for the First Quarter

	Actual	Budget	Favorable (unfavorable) relative to the budget
Sales in units			
Plastic model	60,000	50,000	10,000
Metal model	20,000	25,000	(5,000)
Sales revenue			
Plastic model	$630,000	$500,000	$130,000
Metal model	300,000	375,000	(75,000)
Total sales	$930,000	$875,000	$ 55,000
Less variable costs			
Manufacturing (at standard)			
Plastic model	$480,000	$400,000	$(80,000)
Metal model	200,000	250,000	50,000
Selling			
Commissions	46,500	43,750	(2,750)
Bad debts	9,300	8,750	(550)
Total variable costs (before variances)	$735,800	$702,500	$(33,300)
Contribution margin (before variances)	$194,200	$172,500	$ 21,700
Variable cost variances	49,600	——	(49,600)
Contribution margin	$144,600	$172,500	$(27,900)
Fixed costs			
Manufacturing costs	$ 49,200	$ 48,000	$ (1,200)
Selling & administrative	38,500	36,000	(2,500)
Corporation offices	18,500	17,500	(1,000)
Total	$106,200	$101,500	$ (4,700)
Divisional income	$ 38,400	$ 71,000	$(32,600)

The manufacturing activities for the quarter resulted in the production of 55,000 plastic chairs and 22,500 metal chairs. The costs incurred by each manufacturing unit are presented below.

	Plastic Model	Metal Model
Raw material (stated in equivalent finished chairs)		
Purchases		
Plastic 60,000 @ $5.65	$339,000	
Metal 30,000 @ $6.00		$180,000
Usage		
Plastic 56,000 @ $5.00	280,000	
Metal 23,000 @ $6.00		138,000
Direct labor		
9,300 hours @ $6.00 per hour	55,800	
5,600 hours @ $8.00 per hour		44,800
Manufacturing overhead		
Variable		
Supplies	43,000	18,000
Power	50,000	15,000
Employee benefits	19,000	12,000
Fixed		
Supervision	14,000	11,000
Depreciation	12,000	9,000
Property taxes and other items	1,900	1,300

The standard variable manufacturing costs per unit and the budgeted monthly fixed manufacturing costs established for the current year are presented below.

	Plastic Model	Metal Model
Raw material	$ 5.00	$ 6.00
Direct labor		
1/6 hour @ $6.00 per DLH	1.00	
1/4 hour @ $8.00 per DLH		2.00
Variable overhead		
1/6 hour @ $12.00 per DLH	2.00	
1/4 hour @ $8.00 per DLH		2.00
Standard variable manufacturing cost per unit	$ 8.00	$10.00
Budgeted fixed cost per month		
Supervision	$4,500	$3,500
Depreciation	4,000	3,000
Property taxes and other items	600	400
Total budgeted fixed manufacturing costs	$9,100	$6,900

Required:

1. Explain the $27,900 variance in Markley Division's contribution margin attributable to:
   a. Sales volume variance
   b. Sales mix variance.
   c. Contribution margin variance. Hint: Do not use equation 18-3. Contribution margin variance is a combination of sales price variances and variances from standard variable costs.
2. What portion of sales volume variance, if any, can be attributed to a change in Markley Division's market share?
3. Analyze the variance in Markley Division's variable manufacturing costs ($49,600) in as much detail as the data permit.

18-9. Basic Problem on Ex-Post Variance Analysis. The Zimmerman Company produces three products: A, B, and C. Material and labor are available in limited quantities. At the beginning of the period the resource requirements for each product, the resource availabilities, and the products' contribution margins were estimated:

	Product A	Product B	Product C	Availability
Labor	2.7 hours	2 hours	0.8 hours	2,600 hours
Material	0.9 pounds	2 pounds	3.2 pounds	3,800 pounds
Contribution margin per unit	$90	$100	$80	

It can be shown that the optimal use of the resources is to produce as follows:

$$A = 0 \qquad B = 1,100 \qquad C = 500$$

In reality, the contribution margin per unit for product B was $90 at January 2, 19x1, instead of $100. Using this value for B's contribution margin, the following production quantities would be the optimal use of Zimmerman's resources:

$$A = 666\tfrac{2}{3} \qquad B = 0 \qquad C = 1,000$$

Required:

1. Assume the firm produced and sold 1,100 units of B and 500 units of C during January. Compute the forecasting variance and the opportunity cost.
2. Now assume that exactly halfway through January, management detected the forecast error. Production had finished 550 units of B and 250 units of C. During the last half of the month, a proportional amount of the optimal mix was used. Compute the forecasting variance and the opportunity cost. Did they turn out as you would expect given the adjustment made by management?
3. Assume that B's contribution changed from $100 to $90 at the middle of January because of environmental factors. Further, assume that management observed this and reacted immediately. That is, the output for January was exactly the same as in part 2. Compute the forecasting variance and the opportunity cost.

4. Finally, assume that on January 2 product A's contribution was really $106 per unit instead of $90 as indicated by the information system. The optimal use of the resources in this case is to produce as follows:

$$A = 666\tfrac{2}{3} \qquad B = 0 \qquad C = 1,000$$

The company produced and sold 1,100 units of B and 500 of C during January.
   a. Using the profit variance system, compute the variances.
   b. Using the ex-post system, compute the variances.

18-10. Continuation of Chapter Problem on Ex-Post Variance Analysis. Reconsider the chapter illustrative problem on ex-post variance analysis. At the end of the discussion of that problem a question was raised about whether the extra consumption of material Y in producing product C was a controllable variance. Suppose, now, that when the manager recognized that product C was requiring four units of material Y instead of three, that he quickly reformulated his problem and determined an optimal use of the resources based on this observation. That is, he did not question the consumption of material Y but accepted it. Further, assume that he was able to immediately change the production schedule to the one stated on page 644:

$$A = 250; \qquad B = C = 0; \qquad \text{Actual } CM = \$1,250$$

Given that the material Y consumption is controllable, the optimal ex-post production would be based on product C's contribution margin being $31.50, its material Y consumption being three units, and its variable cost being $27. If so, the optimal production volume would be:

$$A = 100; \qquad B = 0; \qquad C = 200; \qquad \text{Contribution margin} = \$1,400$$

Required:

1. Given the above facts, compute the forecast and opportunity cost variances.
2. Given the above facts, analyze the variance using the profit variance analysis method.
3. Suppose the manager had used the product mix of Exhibit 18.4. Given that the material Y consumption is controllable, compute the forecast and opportunity cost variance.

18-11. Ex-Post Variance System with EOQ Model. The Wyatt Company uses the economical order quantity (EOQ) model to make decisions about the purchase order sizes for its only product. When the EOQ model is applicable, the inventory cost and optimal order quantity are given, respectively, by:

$$C = \frac{DK}{q} + \frac{qH}{2}$$

$$q^* = \sqrt{\frac{2DK}{H}}$$

where:

C = total cost,
D = annual demand,
K = order cost per order,
H = holding cost per unit per year, and
q^* = optimal order size.

At the beginning of 19x1 the following data were estimated:

D = 104,000 units for the year
K = \$15 per order
H = \$0.195 per unit per year

Using these data, a solution was derived and used the entire year. However, the actual holding cost in effect during 19x1 was \$0.1248 per unit instead of \$0.195.

Required:

Determine the forecasting variance and opportunity cost incurred in 19x1.

18-12. Extension of Ex-Post Variance System. The Mautz Company produces three products: A, B, and C. The products, contribution margins, material and labor requirements, and the total availability of resources are as follows:

	Product A	*Product B*	*Product C*	*Availability*
Contribution margin per unit	\$40	\$45	\$24	
Material	2 pounds	3 pounds	1 pound	100/four months
Labor	3 hours	3 hours	2 hours	30/week

It can be shown that the optimal production for a *four-week* period is:

A = 20;   B = 20;   C = 0

The production manager scheduled the production over the four-week period as follows:

Week	*A*	*B*
1	10	0
2	10	0
3	0	10
4	0	10

After week 1 was implemented it was discovered that the contribution on product A had actually been \$35 per unit instead of \$40. The optimal use of the resources considering this change, is:

A = 0   B = $26\frac{2}{3}$ C = 20

Required:

1. Assuming that the manager does not change the production schedule, then:
    a. What is the forecasting variance using the ex-post variance analysis?
    b. What is the opportunity cost?

2. Assume that the manager uses the following schedule during the last three weeks

Week	A	B	C
2	0	$6\frac{2}{3}$	5
3	0	$6\frac{2}{3}$	5
4	0	$6\frac{2}{3}$	5

(Note that this would be the average weekly schedule if the monthly solution was B = $26\frac{2}{3}$ and C = 20.) What is the opportunity cost variance for the entire month?

3. An analyst suggested that the schedule proposed in part 2 is not the optimal. The correct optimal solution, considering the resources consumed in the first week and the amount remaining for the last three weeks, is:

$$B = 23\frac{1}{3} = 10$$

a. What is the forecasting variance for the month if this solution is used for the last three weeks?

b. What is the opportunity cost for the month if this solution is used for the last three weeks?

4. Suppose at the *beginning* of week 1 the manager scheduled the production as:

Week	A	B
1	0	10
2	0	10
3	10	0
4	10	0

Further, suppose at the end of week 1 the contribution margin of product A was found to be $35 (as before). Could the production manager avoid an opportunity cost? How?

5. Return to the original problem with A's contribution at $40. Due to labor inefficiency the actual production achieved was as follows:

Week	A	B
1	9	0
2	9	0
3	2	7
4	0	9

That is, it was taking $3\frac{1}{3}$ hours per unit for both A and B.

a. What is the opportunity cost?

b. The conventional labor efficiency variance (LEV) would be:

LEV = (Standard hours allowed − Actual hours)Standard wage rate

For this case:

Standard hours = 20 A's @ 3 + 16 B's @ 3 = 108

and:

LEV = (108 − 120)standard wage rate

Comment on the implications of the results in part a for "conventional variance analysis." In your comments also consider the case where labor is unlimited (or, at least, relatively unlimited).

18-13. Basic Problem on Mix and Yield Variance. The General Hills Company produces flour. Two types of wheat can be used, red and white. Following is the standard per 100 pounds of flour:

Red wheat	60.00 pounds @ $3.00	$180
White wheat	57.50 pounds @ $4.00	230
Total material cost		$410

During the current period 10,000 pounds of flour were produced. The actual wheat purchased and used was:

Red wheat	5,000 pounds @ $3.10	$15,500.00
White wheat	6,875 pounds @ $4.05	27,843.75
		$43,343.75

Required:

1. Compute the conventional material price and material quantity variances.
2. Analyze the material quantity variance into mix and yield components.

18-14. CMA Problem on Material Mix and Yield Variance. Energy Products Company produces a gasoline additive, Gas Gain. This product increases engine efficiency and improves gasoline mileage by creating a more complete burn in the combustion process.

Careful controls are required during the production process to ensure that the proper mix of input chemicals is achieved and that evaporation is controlled. If the controls are not effective, there can be loss of output and efficiency.

The standard cost of producing a 500-liter batch of Gas Gain is $135. The standard materials mix and related standard cost of each chemical used in a 500-liter batch are as follows.

Chemical	Standard Input Quantity in Liters	Standard Cost per Liter	Total Cost
Echol	200	$0.200	$ 40.00
Protex	100	0.425	42.50
Benz	250	0.150	37.50
CT-40	50	0.300	15.00
	600		$135.00

The quantities of chemicals purchased and used during the current production period are shown in the schedule below. A total of 140 batches of Gas Gain were manufactured during the current production period. Energy products determines its cost and chemical usage variations at the end of each production period.

Chemical	Quantity Purchased	Total Purchase Price	Quantity Used
Echol	25,000 liters	$ 5,365	26,600 liters
Protex	13,000 liters	6,240	12,880 liters
Benz	40,000 liters	5,840	37,800 liters
CT-40	7,500 liters	2,220	7,140 liters
Total	85,500 liters	$19,665	84,420 liters

Required:

1. Calculate the purchase price variances by chemical for Energy Products Company.
2. Calculate the total material usage variance related to Gas Gain for Energy Products Company and then analyze this total usage variance into the following two components:
   a. Total mix variance
   b. Total yield variance

18-15. Extension of Chapter Demonstration Problem on Mix and Yield Variance. Reconsider the Oscar Mayo problem in the section on Yield and Mix Variance. During the second and third months, the following production and cost data were recorded:

	Month 2	Month 3
Pounds of summer sausage produced	3,000	4,000
Pork purchased and used (pounds)	1,400	2,200
Beef purchased and used (pounds)	2,266	2,733
Cost per pound		
Pork	$1.00	$1.05
Beef	$1.50	$1.45

Required:

1. Compute the material price and quantity variances for month 2.
2. Analyze the material quantity variance for month 2 into mix and yield components.
3. Explain what must have happened in month 2 to obtain the results you obtained above.
4. Compute the material price and quantity variances for month 3.
5. Analyze the material quantity variance for month 3 into mix and yield components.

18-16. Setting and Using Control Limits. The Littleton Company sampled the labor time needed to produce one of its products when there was some reasonable assurance the production process was in control. Following are the samples that were collected. Each entry in the schedule represents the number of hours needed to complete the unit represented by the observation.

Observation	Sample Number				
	1	*2*	*3*	*4*	*5*
1	46.0	53.5	44.7	50.2	55.1
2	46.7	54.1	44.3	45.3	45.4
3	51.7	52.0	45.5	58.6	49.8
4	54.1	49.2	47.4	56.2	44.2
5	54.3	49.4	51.0	52.3	48.8
6	46.1	56.0	48.0	43.3	49.3
7	54.1	49.5	49.6	47.1	53.7
8	57.0	53.2	48.8	48.5	55.5
Sum	410.0	416.7	379.3	401.5	401.8

It can be shown that the sum of the squared variances around the grand mean, $\bar{\bar{x}}$ is 639.40775.

Required:

1. Establish a 95% control range for the mean of a sample size of eight.
2. Establish a 3σ R-chart.
3. Sometime later, the following times were reported for a group of eight units: 48.0, 49.3, 57.9, 62.1, 62.4, 48.2, 62.1, 67.2. What conclusions would you draw about the likely status of the process? Why?
4. Repeat part 3 but assume the following times were reported: 40.0, 41.8, 54.2, 60.2, 60.6, 40.4, 60.2, 67.4.

18-17. Considering Cost in Variance Investigation. Note that equation (18-13) can be stated as:

$$p < 1 - \frac{C}{L - R}$$

That is, when p, the probability of being in control, is less than the right-hand side of (18-13), then an investigation can be justified on a cost-benefit basis.

Required:

1. Demonstrate the behavior of the critical p value by computing it for the cases represented by the cells in the following table.

C	L − R			
	3,000	4,000	5,000	6,000
500				
1,000				
1,500				
2,000				

2. Suppose the probability that the process is in control has been estimated to be 70%. The cost of investigating is $1,000. Under what conditions could you justify doing a variance investigation?

18-18. Investigation of Cost Variances. The Wagner Company decides whether or not to investigate labor efficiency variances using the rule from cost-benefit analysis. That is, an investigation should be made only if the probability, *p,* of the process being in control is as follows:

$$p < \frac{L - C - R}{L - R}$$

where: L = the cost savings that will result by returning an out-of-control process back into control.

C = cost of doing an investigation.

R = cost of correcting the process if it is found to be out of control.

When in control it is felt that the labor hours per unit produced will be found in the range of 2.5 to 3.5 with an average of 3. When out of control the labor hours per unit are expected to be in the range of 3.2 to 5.2 with an average of 4.2. Wage rates average $8 per hour and variable overhead, as a function of labor hours, is $2.

The manager receives a labor report every two weeks and, at that time, decides whether or not to investigate the process. If the process is out of control and not investigated, then the loss is equal to the increase in costs due to operating inefficiently. There will be no reduction in output; it will just take longer to accomplish it. Production volume per week averages 1,200 units. For simplicity, assume that if the process goes out of control it will do so during the last day of the reporting period. Thus the manager asks that the last day's production data be reported separately.

The cost of doing an investigation is $5,000. If the process is out of control then it will cost an average of $2,400 to correct it.

Required:

1. Before the start of a given reporting period the manager assesses the probability that the process is in control at 95%. Should an investigation be made? Why?
2. At the end of the second week it is reported that the average labor hours was 3.1 and, for the last day of the period, 3.3. The manager subjectively revises his probability of the process being in control at 85%. Should he investigate?
3. At the end of the fourth week it is reported that the average labor for the period was 3.3 and, for the last day, 3.9. The manager revises his probability of the process being in control at 70%. Should he investigate?
4. Return to the situation in question 2. Given the facts, how low would the cost of investigating have to be in order to justify doing an investigation at this point in time?

CHAPTER 19

Evaluating Performance in A Decentralized Organization

Most large firms are organized according to a divisional structure such that the decision-making responsibility is distributed among several managers. When decisions are delegated, there are a variety of problems of accounting to the superior for the purpose of controlling the subordinate. This and the next chapter are devoted to identifying these problems and exploring some possible solutions.

The discussion begins by considering the characteristics of and reasons for decentralization. Then, three forms of decentralization are identified. The remainder of the chapter considers the problems of evaluating one form of a decentralized unit—the investment center.

In the third section there is a discussion of the various measurements that have been proposed for controlling investment centers. These include return on investment and residual income. The fourth section investigates some issues concerning the measurement of income and investment when they are used to compute return on investment and residual income.

Characteristics of and Reasons for Decentralization

With respect to decision making, organizations can be classified on a scale of "centralized" to "decentralized." A completely **centralized organization** is one where all decisions are made by the top echelon of management. Obviously, a one-person business is centralized with respect to decision making. In multiperson organizations, centralization may exist in degrees. Some minor decisions may be delegated but all of the major decisions are made by top management.

Decentralization is at the opposite end of the scale. In a **decentralized organization** the major decison-making authority is widely diffused among several managers. Managers at levels below the top (or central) echelon have the authority to make certain major decisions without first clearing them through central headquarters. The centralized-decentralized scale is continuous, and it is not possible to define precisely the point at which an organization would be declared as centralized or decentralized.

There are several possible reasons that may contribute to the decision to decentralize. One reason is the *growth* of the firm to a point that the volume of decisions is too large to be administered efficiently by top management. Decentralization may be the only practical way of coping with the volume of decisions that must be made.

A second reason for decentralization is that *division managers are closer to the activities of their division* than is possible for central management. Thus, the division managers should be able to make quicker decisions. It can be reasoned that constant contact with the situation not only makes possible faster decisions, but also improves the quality, or optimality, of the decisions.

A third motivation is that a decentralized structure creates a *training ground for future top-level administrators*. Further, highly skilled people probably will react negatively to the prospects of lengthy service in a position of little responsibility. Thus, the existence of positions of responsibility into which such people may move can be a major factor in a firm's ability to retain quality personnel.

The widespread trend toward *diversification* is another motivation for decentralization. If a firm's activities are extremely diverse, it is nearly impossible for its affairs to be managed by a relatively small group. The factors to be considered by a manager in the soft-drink industry, for example, will be much different from the factors to be considered in the soap industry. Thus, if a firm has diversified into several product lines, it might be decentralized according to those lines.

Fifth, a decentralized structure may result in *greater creativity* on the part of the personnel. If fewer levels of approval are needed to take some action, there may be a greater chance that some new idea will be attempted.

Finally, it may be *easier to evaluate managers* in a decentralized organization. If managers have a significant degree of authority over all functions of their area (production, selling, and so forth), it is much more difficult for them to attempt to shift the blame for failure to someone else. As a by-product, knowledge that they will be evaluated probably increases managers' incentives to succeed and, thus, improves corporate profits.

There may be other reasons why firms choose a decentralized organization, but these are the major ones. Of course, there are some disadvantages of this form of organization. For example, there may not be complete congruence among the goals of all of the decision makers. Some problems of this nature will be specifically identified as we progress through this and the next chapter. Also, there may be some dysfunctional competition and/or friction among the managers. Further, central management will have to make certain decisions that require first hand knowledge that may be lacking in a decentralized firm. However, for firms that decentralize, it is presumed that the advantages outweigh the disadvantages.

Forms of Decentralization

It was suggested in the last section that decentralization may exist in various degrees or forms. This section considers a classification of these forms and identifies the reasons for singling out one of these forms for further discussion.

The classification scheme proposed here is based on the scope of the decision-making authority given to a particular manager. The forms in the classification scheme are frequently referred to as cost centers, profit centers, and investment centers. As each form is defined we also explore the general nature of the control system which is necessary.

In **cost centers** the manager has the authority to make decisions that only affect the firm's cost. Cost center managers have no authority to make decisions about what will be done with the output of their unit or about the resources at the disposal of the center. A production department, for example, has no control of what is done with its output; therefore, it is a cost center. Likewise, a service department is a cost center. Further, the research and development unit of a firm is a cost center, as is the strategic planning unit and the controller's unit.

Managers of cost centers have their authority delegated by a superior. The superior holds managers accountable and will desire to make periodic evaluations of them. The tools appropriate for this accounting and evaluation consist of standards, budgets, and responsibility accounting. These tools have been thoroughly discussed in previous chapters. Thus, additional discussion of cost center control is not necessary here.

A **profit center** manager has authority to make decisions which affect the costs and revenues of the center but not its productive assets. In a sense, it may be contradictory to infer that a unit has control of its profits if it has no control of its investment. Certainly, such a unit does not have complete control of its profits because it cannot consider alternative uses of the assets.

Profit center control can be exercised through the construction of profit targets and the analysis of the variances therefrom. These methods were discussed in the previous chapter.

The manager of an **investment center** has more autonomy than either the manger of a cost or profit center. The manager of such a center is given control of costs, revenues, and investment. This control may not be as complete as in a one-person business, but it is relatively free from constraints.

To control an investment center, a manager needs to monitor the relationship between the unit's income and the investment used to generate the income. This gives rise to control devices that have not been considered earlier. Three basic issues must be resolved in implementing any type of investment center control:

1. How should income be measured?
2. How should investment be measured?
3. What is the best way to measure the relationship between income and investment?

The remainder of the chapter considers possible resolutions of these three issues.

Controlling Investment Centers

In controlling investment centers it is essential to distinguish between the need to evaluate the *manager* of the center and the need to evaluate the *return on the assets* at the center's command. Evaluations of the first type will be input for personnel decisions. The second type will be input for decisions about the allocation of additional resources to the investment center. For these two purposes, the way income and investment are measured and the relationship between them will not necessarily be the same.

For example, a poor investment center performance may be due to circumstances beyond its manager's control. If these circumstances are permanent, then the evidence may justify a decision not to invest additional resources or to divest existing resources. It does not necessarily follow that the manager should be judged as doing a poor job. The reasons for maintaining these separate views will be amplified in the discussion that follows.

The remainder of this section is an explanation of two performance indexes that are frequently used for either manager or asset evaluation: return on investment and residual income. The initial discussion of these indexes concentrates on the fundamentals. No attention will be given to the modifications that are needed for the two separate uses. These are considered later.

RETURN ON INVESTMENT. **Return on Investment (ROI)** is the ratio of income to investment:

$$\text{ROI} = \frac{\text{Income}}{\text{Investment}} \tag{19-1}$$

The higher the ROI, the more effective the assets have been used. Sometimes this ratio is expressed as the product of two other ratios: the asset turnover ratio and the ratio of income to sales. The *asset turnover ratio* is sales divided by investment and indicates the number of times the investment was turned over during the period. The *income to sales* ratio is income divided by sales. Thus:

$$\text{ROI} = \frac{\text{Asset turnover}}{\text{ratio}} \times \frac{\text{Income-to-}}{\text{sales ratio}} = \frac{\text{Sales}}{\text{Investment}} \times \frac{\text{Income}}{\text{Sales}} \tag{19-2}$$

Obviously, the result in (19-2) is the same as the one in (19-1) since sales cancel out. The advantage of using the form in (19-2) is the ability to emphasize the ways ROI can be improved. The first term, asset turnover, indicates that even if it is impossible to change the percentage of profits to sales, ROI can be increased by (1) increasing sales volume or (2) decreasing investment. The second component highlights that ROI can be increased by being more efficient, that is, by reducing the cost rate and, therefore, increasing the ratio of income to sales. ROI would also increase if the sales price is increased and all other factors are constant.

Naturally, there will be some dependencies among the variables of the ROI computation. For example, it may not be possible to increase total sales volume without lowering the sales prices. Lower prices, of course, will decrease the income-to-sales ratio. Also, increased sales may be possible only if there is increased investment. For example, if the center is already operating at full capacity, then increased sales would be impossible without an investment in additional facilities. Nevertheless, (19-2) is a general indication of the way ROI can be increased.

For control purposes, it is legitimate to ask what the ROI should be in order to consider the manager's performance acceptable. Of course there is no obvious answer to this question. An acceptable ROI depends on the nature of the industry, the state of the economy, the goals of the firm, the way income and investment are measured, and other factors. Frequently, acceptability is not judged against a standard, but against previous performance. That is, if there is some year-to-year increase in ROI, performance may be considered acceptable. This concept is not necessarily endorsed, but its possibility in practice certainly must be recognized.

A concept of acceptability based on comparison with previous years is one of the major problems of ROI. To illustrate the problem, suppose that in 19x1 Division A (an investment center) reported an ROI of 26%. For 19x2 Division A has established a goal of increasing its ROI to 27%. During 19x2 the division has the opportunity to invest in a project that requires additional funds of $10,000. The projected net income attributable to the project in year 1 is $2,500. Obviously, the estimated ROI for the new project in year 1 is 25%. Assume the company's cost of capital is 20%. Given that Division A's 19x1 investment will be kept intact during 19x2 and that its earning power will not change, should it accept the proposed project?

Divison A's decision will depend, in part, on how central headquarters evaluates the divisional manager. If the manager knows that growth in the ROI is expected, then, as is shown in Exhibit 19.1, the project should be rejected because of the expected decrease in ROI attributable to its acceptance. Observe the possible lack of goal congruence. The new project is expected to return an amount in excess of the firm's cost of capital. Yet, the use of ROI provides Divison A a very good reason for rejecting the project.

It might be argued that the Division A manager is taking a short-run point of view by only considering the proposed project's impact on the 19x2 ROI. However, the way ROI is used by a superior can be the reason the manager takes a short-run view. If control devices are geared to the short run, can any other type of reaction really be expected? In designing control systems accountants and managers must take precautions if they expect personnel to internalize goals and policies that are to the long-run advantage of the firm.

Another problem with ROI is that all of an investment center's assets are usually subjected to a single criteria. It is normal for central management to have some lower bound on a center's ROI which, if it is not achieved, signals the need for a critical evaluation. All assets are included in the divisor of the ROI even though they will likely have dissimilar earning expectations. This may not be desirable. For

---

Exhibit 19.1   Division A ROI Comparisons

	19x1	*Proposal*	*19x2 with Proposal Included*
Income	$ 26,000*	$ 2,500	$ 28,500
Investment	100,000*	10,000	110,000
ROI	26%	25%	25.9%

*Arbitrarily selected to give an ROI of 26%.

example, highly specialized equipment probably has different expectations than a general-purpose warehouse. Of course, it would be possible to avoid this problem by setting the minimum ROI as a weighted average of the respective earning expectations.

ROI also does not consider the time value of money. It is computed using only the results of a given period. Incorporating the long-run implications of a manager's decision into a single index is not easy. Because of the problems, it is recommended that ROI not be used alone.

A well-documented response to the need for considering multiple aspects in the evaluation process is that of General Electric Company. It is based on "key result areas" that are listed below along with a brief indication of ways of measuring them.[1]

1. Profitability—ROI, perhaps, is an adequate measurement of this.
2. Productivity—This is the relationship between input and output. Input would include materials and all forms of labor, production, and administrative functions. Output, in general, would be the goods and services provided for societal consumption. Obviously, there would be many problems in measuring the two components. However, some of these problems would be mitigated by following consistent measurement rules over time and using the results as a comparative rather than as an absolute index.
3. Marketing effectiveness—This might be measured by the firm's market position. To assess the position, consideration must be given to how to define the market and how to measure the division's share of the market. Again some of the measurement problems are mitigated by considering the trend of the ratio as measured in a consistent way over time.
4. Product leadership—In general, this would be measured by the trend of the consuming market's view of the firm's products. Product quality and innovations introduced by the division are factors to be considered in the measurement of this element.
5. Personnel development—This would be some measurement of the success of efforts directed toward training personnel to advance up the organizational ladder and assume greater responsibilities.
6. Employee attitudes—Basically, this is the state of employee morale. Measurements might include employee turnover rates, absenteeism, grievance cases, and so forth.
7. Public responsibility—This needs a measurement of the division's contribution to society. Obviously, such a measurement cannot be very objective.
8. Balance between short-run and long-run goals—Measurement problems would include the determination of the relative weight on each goal and how to evaluate tradeoffs between goals that have dissimilar measurements.

RESIDUAL INCOME. One of the major problems of using ROI is the potential dysfunctional consequences caused by it being a ratio (the problem that was encountered by Division A in the preceding case). In response to this problem, **residual income (RI)** has been proposed as an alternative. RI is not a ratio of income to investment but the amount of income earned in excess of a charge for

---

[1]See E. Kirby Warren, *Long-Range Planning: The Executive Viewpoint* (Englewood Cliffs, NJ: Prentice-Hall, Inc., 1966).

the investment used by the center. In short, the cost of the investment center's capital is considered as another expense.

To illustrate the RI computation, reconsider the example of the previous section. Recall that the company's cost of capital was 20%. Like ROI, RI relates income to investment, but the relationship is in the form of an interest charge rather than a ratio. Exhibit 19.2 contains the RI computation for the illustrative example.

Note in Exhibit 19.2 that the proposal, if accepted, will increase RI. Remember that it lowered ROI. Thus, in comparison with ROI, RI may lead to greater goal congruence. As long as any proposal is expected to return more than the firm's cost of capital, the investment center's RI will increase. As was shown in the last section, ROI may not increase in such a case. Because of this, RI must be given serious consideration as an improvement over ROI.

In addition to avoiding the goal congruence problems of ROI, RI is also flexible enough to permit different cost-of-capital rates to be applied to different kinds of investments. It is easy to see how this would be done by reviewing the computation in Exhibit 19.2. That is, in computing the cost of investment just use as many classes of investment as are needed multiplying each by a different rate. Like ROI, however, RI ignores the time value of money, is a short-run index, measures only one component of success, and is plagued by the problem of how to measure income and investment.

Measuring Income and Investment for Evaluation of Investment Centers

Regardless of whether ROI or RI is to be used for investment center evaluation, there are problems involved in measuring income and investment. Of course, such measurements already exist to support financial accounting requirements and, if used, would require no additional effort. For evaluation purposes, however, these conventional financial accounting measurements of income and investment may not be the best. This section considers why and suggests some alternatives.

Exhibit 19.2   Division A RI Computation

	19x1	*Proposal*	*19x2 with Proposal Included*
Income not including cost of capital	$ 26,000	$ 2,500	$ 28,500
Investment	100,000	10,000	110,000
Cost of capital rate	0.20	0.20	0.20
Cost of capital	20,000	2,000	22,000
Residual income	$ 6,000	$ 500	$ 6,500

First we consider some basic concepts of income and investment measurement for this purpose. This is followed by a consideration of some specific measurement problems. Among the specific problems to be considered are those created by depreciation accounting and asset evaluation. Also considered is the question of whether to include long-term assets at their gross or net values and the question of how to compensate for price level changes.

BASIC CONCEPTS OF INCOME. Throughout the book we have emphasized the need to give careful consideration to how cost and income are measured for various purposes. Caution must also be exercised when evaluating managers and assets using ROI and RI. This section is a brief summary of these considerations as they apply to divisional performance evaluation.

First, a general concept of income should be selected: full absorption, variable (direct) costing, or some alternative concept. The contrasts among the concepts were drawn in Chapter 7.

In selecting an item to include in the income for the manager's ROI or RI computation, the criterion is for the manager to have a significant amount of control over its incurrence. For control purposes, the fixed-variable dichotomy is not a satisfactory criterion for item selection. Furthermore, the fact that an item benefits a given investment center is not prima facie evidence of controllability by the manager. Control over that item may have been retained by central management. If so it should not affect the evaluation of the center's manager. When ROI and RI are being used to evaluate the investment of assets, instead of the manager, then the criterion for inclusion is for the item to be attributable to the center.

In summary, it is recommended that regardless of which concept of income is used, it should be modified for the ROI and RI computation. For manager evaluation, income should be adjusted by removing all items that are not controllable by the manager, both variable and fixed. The remaining items should be accounted for in such a way as to reflect the impact that the decisions of the period had on the corporate well-being. If the alternative income concept discussed in Chapter 7 is impractical, then a modified variable (direct) costing income will generally be the next best approach.

Independent of the general concept of income to be used, there are other issues. For example, the income measurement of one investment center should be relatively free of inefficiencies and efficiencies of other centers. This is a problem only when the output of one center becomes an input for other centers. If such products and services are transferred at *actual* production costs, then this rule could be violated. A similar requirement was discussed in Chapter 9 with respect to service department accounting.

Now consider the question as to whether an investment center's performance index should be allowed to increase by any action that reduced the *firm's* income. For example, suppose that Division X has been purchasing one of its raw materials from Company A. The purchasing agent finds that the raw material can be acquired at a marginally lower price from Company B and changes suppliers.

Company A is a customer of Division Y. In response to the loss of business from Division X, Company A ceases doing business with Division Y. Assume the profits lost at Division Y are greater than the cost savings at Division X.

What are the accounting implications of this situation? Should Division X be accountable for the opportunity cost incurred by Division Y? This is not an easy question to answer. The rule says yes, but to do so will cause Division X to feel that they have been stripped of some of their autonomy. That is, knowing that such costs might be charged to it encroaches on Division X's freedom to operate independently of other divisions. In defense of the rule, this is exactly the type of consideration that central headquarters would encourage. From their view, the manager of Division X should consider the effects of his or her actions on the other divisions of the firm.

Given that Division X should be charged with the opportunity cost, the next problem is its measurement. Presumably, it is necessary to determine the amount of profit from sales that will be lost by Division Y during the interval needed to restore its volume back to the original level. Obviously, this will not be easy to measure. Further, the entire effect may not occur in the same period in which the decision was made. Several future periods may experience reduced sales. In spite of the problems, a good evaluation system must incorporate these considerations into its measurements.

BASIC CONCEPTS OF INVESTMENT. The second component of the ROI and RI indexes is the investment. In measuring investment, two questions must be answered:

1. Which assets should be included?
2. What dollar amounts should be attached to the included assets?

In practice, we find that these questions have a variety of solutions. Possible asset combinations include:

1. All assets that are included on the conventional balance sheet.
2. Long-term assets plus *net* current assets.
3. Long-term assets, receivables, and inventory.
4. Any of the above plus economic assets that are not included on the conventional balance sheet.

For measurement purposes, it is possible to use:

A. Historical cost.
B. Price-level adjusted costs (also called constant dollars).[2]
C. Replacement cost (also called current cost).[3]
D. Disposal values (also called exit prices).

---

[2]See FASB Statement No. 33, *Financial Reporting and Changing Prices* (September 1979), p. 9.

[3]FASB Statement No. 33, p. 9.

First, consider a criterion for asset selection. In practice, a variety of approaches for selecting an investment base will be found.[4] The variety, in part, might be attributable to the practice of including only those assets over which the manager has control. In some decentralized firms, central headquarters manages the cash and short-term investments of *the firm*. If this is the case, investment center managers would not control cash and option 3 would be appropriate. Option 1 should be used if the managers had control of all assets. Option 2 suggests the managers also control the short-term liabilities. Other options might be used. For example, in addition to managing cash, central headquarters might also maintain control over credit and collections. Then it would be appropriate to omit receivables from the asset base.

A second contributing factor to the variety of bases found in practice is the possibility that firms use ROI and RI for multiple purposes (for example, both manager control and asset profitability analysis). If so, then compromises may be needed in selecting the investment base. Also, firms may be at different stages of maturity with respect to their view of control. A more mature firm shows greater sensitivity for what is included in the computations.

Surveys of accounting practice indicate that for ROI and RI purposes, asset pools are sometimes allocated among investment centers.[5] That is, certain assets may be controlled by central headquarters but allocated to the centers for inclusion in their investment bases. Such a practice can be defended as follows. Even though investment center managers do not have control over the centrally managed assets, the centers still receive the benefits. These benefits are reflected in each center's income. Further, it may not be possible to measure the amount of the income attributable to the centrally managed assets so that it can be removed from the income figure. If the benefits are left in the divisional income, it somewhat logically follows that the assets should be included in the investment base. When the centrally managed assets are shared by other divisions, then they will have to be allocated among the divisions. Selecting proper allocation bases for assets is the same type of problem as for the allocation of costs. The base should reflect the relationship between the investment center's activities and the level of centrally controlled assets needed to support the activities. For example, the corporate cash account might be allocated using budgeted cash needs as the base.

The fourth concept of an investment base listed above has not yet been discussed. Many firms and investment centers have significant economic resources that do not qualify as "*accounting assets*." Human resources represent one of the most significant of the "off-balance-sheet" assets. Certainly it makes no sense to use ROI as a performance index of a service-oriented organization if the investment base is the one given by conventional financial accounting. The physical assets of a consulting firm (office furniture and equipment for example) are insignificant to its function. The cadre of executives and employees represent a stream

---

[4]See: Richard Vancil, *Decentralization: Managerial Ambiguity by Design* (Homewood, Ill: Dow Jones-Irwin, 1979), pp. 337–360.

[5]See Vancil, *Decentralization,* p. 341.

of future benefits to the firm. However, due to the lack of an objective way to measure these benefits, the accounting profession has elected not to formally include them among the firm's *recorded* assets. Executive salaries, in a sense, can be viewed as the current cost of the benefits, but unlike tangible assets, there is no acknowledgment of the asset's existence in the conventional financial statements. All firms have such resources; using a service organization as an example merely dramatizes the problem.

Another example of an unrecorded asset is the operating lease (as opposed to a capital lease). To be an operating lease, certain criteria must be met.[6] In effect, the criteria guarantee there is no resemblance of or actual ownership of the physical asset. Nevertheless, an investment center still enjoys the earning potential of leased assets even if they are not included in the balance sheet. Human resources and operating leases both represent ways for a manager to increase the center's income without increasing the *recorded accounting investment.* (This is not to say that in their internal reporting firms should or will record leases according to Financial Accounting Standards.)

Regardless of which assets are selected for the investment base, we still face the question of how to assign dollar values to them. Historical costs are objective and readily available. But historical costs may be irrelevant as the measure of investment for purposes of ROI and RI. If managers are to be evaluated via some index, then it is somewhat certain that they will consider the effects of their decisions on that index as an input to their decision. Historical cost does not necessarily reflect the relative economic value of the assets involved. Decisions should be a function only of factors that do reflect economic realities.

Alternatives to historical cost include price-level adjusted costs (constant dollar costs), current cost of the asset's remaining service potential (replacement costs), and exit prices (the amount for which the asset could be sold). Again, remember the purpose here is to derive measures appropriate for a managerial control system, not a financial reporting system. A single measurement scheme is not necessarily appropriate for all purposes. It should also be noted that since FASB Statement 33 went into effect,[7] many companies have had to generate some of these data for external reporting purposes. Thus, the cost of obtaining the data for internal uses may be very small.

Price-level adjusted costs would state all expenses and investments in dollars that have a common purchasing power. Although price-level adjusted data are better for control purposes than original dollars, they, too, are not necessarily appropriate for ROI and RI.

Current cost is the amount that would have to be sacrificed to acquire the *equivalent* asset now. It is interesting to debate whether current cost is the appropriate measurement concept for control purposes. Current cost is not necessarily equivalent to the amount of cash that can be made available by the disposal of the asset.

---

[6]For the specific criteria see FASB Statement No. 13, *Accounting for Leases* (November 1976).

[7]As mentioned earlier, FASB Statement No. 33, *Financial Reporting and Changing Prices,* was issued in September 1979.

In evaluating the adequacy of a base, it is necessary to consider whether the evaluation indexes can be improved *without* improving the wealth of the firm or the investment center. Before discussing this issue, consider the meaning of exit value.

Exit, or *disposal value,* represents the amount of cash that would be generated by selling the asset now. This amount, then, represents the resources that could be made available for an alternative use. However, it must be recognized that the realization of the disposal value may entail an opportunity cost. That is, the earning power of the disposed asset is lost. To help clarify the issue of whether to use current cost or exit value in measuring the investment base for ROI and RI, consider the following example.

Suppose Division Z of the Kowalski Company has a single asset that will earn $100 next year. The asset's current replacement cost is $1,000 and its present disposal (exit) value is $400. Following are the ROI and RI data where investment is measured using current cost and exit value, respectively:

	Investment Base Measurement	
	Current Cost of $1,000	*Exit Value of $400*
ROI ($100 ÷ investment)	10%	25%
RI (assuming a 5% cost of capital ; $100 − 0.05 × investment)	$50	$80

Now, suppose the division manager is considering an alternative that would require an investment of $400. The alternative investment's first year income is forecasted to be $80. However, the only way the manager can take advantage of this opportunity is to dispose of the divisions's existing assets. Ignoring any losses on the disposal of the existing assets, the ROI on the new alternative is 20% ($80 ÷ $400) and the RI is $60 ($80 − 0.05 × $400).

Note that both of these figures fall between their counterparts computed above. Thus, if ROI and RI are based on current costs, then the manager would be prudent to sell the existing assets and accept the alternative. Both the ROI and RI would increase. On the other hand, if ROI and RI are based on exit values, the manager would be prudent to reject the alternative and keep the existing assets. Both the ROI and RI would decrease from their present levels if the alternative is adopted.

Apart from the indexes, should the manager shift his investment to the alternative? If the lost profits from the disposed asset are considered, the alternative is not *economically* desirable (the manager would be giving up $100 to earn $80). Only if the ROI and RI for the existing asset are *based on exit values,* will the manager pick the alternative that maximizes the well-being of the firm. The exit-value-based ROI and RI indexes are indicating the return on the cash equivalent of the existing assets. If the cash equivalent cannot earn more in the alternative use, then there is no merit of selling the existing assets so that the alternative can be selected. It should be carefully noted, however, that this analysis did not consider the impact beyond year 1.

Will the ROI and RI give correct messages when they are based on current costs? If current costs are used to evaluate the ROI and RI investment component, the analysis becomes a bit more complicated. It is not appropriate to compare a replacement cost based on ROI of 10% with a projection from the new asset of 20%. The replacement cost does not measure the cash equivalent that could be generated for an alternative use. That is, the existing assets will not yield $1,000 that can be used for an alternative, only $400.

The "strong" case made above for exit values as the appropriate way to measure assets for ROI and RI purposes needs to be tempered somewhat. The case was made under the assumption that a division manager has total and complete autonomy over the divisional operations. This means, for example, that the division manager has total authority to drastically change the nature of the division. At the extreme this means that the division may even change its activities so that it is operating in a different industry. In reality a manager's autonomy will not likely be that great. Most likely, a drastic change of purpose will need approval by central management. In this sense, then, there may be no *true* investment centers in practice. To the extent that this is correct, the case for exit values is not as strong as was made in the previous paragraphs.

Another problem with any measurement approach other than exit value is what to do with the gain or loss when the asset is sold. In the above case, the manager can anticipate a $600 loss to be reflected in his first year's income if the existing assets are valued at replacement cost and then sold for $400. Of course, this is a one-time event and should not be considered as reflective of the entire project. But in this particular case, any signal a manager might receive that would discourage his selection of the new alternative is appropriate because the alternative was not economically advantageous. In other cases, we might not be as fortunate. (Problem 19-14 explores this in more detail.) These types of problems, however, are not due to the way income and investment are measured, but to the limitations of ROI and RI as evaluation devices. Thus, *it is impossible to achieve a completely satisfactory control system by using only these tools.*

In many cases, an asset's current cost and exit price may be approximately the same. But this is not always the case. For example, a very special-purpose machine constructed especially for one firm may have a nominal disposal value. If disposal value is used as the asset base, the ROI on such an investment would be very high (approaching infinity). Whether or not such a message is valid is dependent on the usage of the ROI figure. This might be an appropriate message for decision making but inappropriate for personnel evaluation. Finally, the measurement of either the current cost or exit value may be difficult. In this event, an adjustment of historical costs for price level changes may be a feasible alternative that will reduce the opportunity cost of incorrect decisions.

PROBLEMS CAUSED BY DEPRECIATION POLICY AND ASSET EVALU-
ATION. A major portion of an investment center's asset base is normally
accounted for by long-term assets. Therefore, it is important to give careful consideration to how these assets and their related depreciation can affect the ROI
and RI computation. This section will further demonstrate how the accounting for
these assets in conventional ways may result in unwanted actions on the part of
managers.

First, consider the potential impact of the depreciation policy on managerial
actions. This will be explained via an illustration. At the beginning of 19x1, the
Eastern Division of the American Company projected their position at the end of
the year to be as follows:

Net income	$ 150,000
Assets	$1,000,000
ROI	15%

Very early in January a new project was proposed. The following data were submitted in support of its acceptance:

Cost	$120,000
Projected cash flows in 19x1, 19x2, and 19x3	56,967
Internal rate of return on the project	20%
Company cost of capital	12%

At the meeting of the Eastern Division executive committee, a debate ensued
as to whether the project should be adopted. The project manager noted that the
internal rate of return was forecasted to be higher than either the company's cost
of capital or the division's forecasted ROI for the year and, therefore, should be
adopted. On the other side of the case, the divisional controller presents the results
of his calculations found in Exhibit 19.3. The controller asks the managers if they
really want to adopt a project that reduces the forecasted ROI.

This case dramatizes the lack of goal congruence between the ROI control technique and good decision-making techniques. Using residual income *will not overcome* this. Following are the forecasted RI figures with and without the project:

	Without Project	*With Project*
Net income (per Exhibit 19.3)	$150,000	$146,967
Cost of capital		
0.12 × $1,000,000	120,000	
0.12 × $1,120,000		134,000
Residual income	$ 30,000	$ 12,567

The reason both ROI and RI make the proposed project look unacceptable, in
spite of its internal rate of return, is the method of valuing and depreciating the

---

Exhibit 19.3   American Company Eastern Division Forecasted 19x1 ROI with Proposed Project Included

Net Income		
Without project		$ 150,000
From project		
Cash flow	$56,967	
Additional depreciation using sum-of-years digits	(60,000)	(3,033)
Total		$ 146,967
Assets ($1,000,000 + $120,000)		$1,120,000
ROI		13.12%

---

asset. The *only* depreciation method that will always cause ROI and RI to be congruent with the net present value criterion is the **compound interest depreciation method.** Compound interest depreciation is the amount of principal recovered from each year's cash flow. That is, the annual depreciation is the amount of the year's cash flow in excess of the interest on the unrecovered investment computed by *using the project's internal rate of return.* Exhibit 19.4 contains the compound interest depreciation calculations for the proposed project. Note that interest is computed using the project's internal rate of return. The interest is then deducted from the cash flow to arrive at the portion of the investment recovered in a given year. The latter is equal to the depreciation to be recognized under this method. Exhibit 19.5 contains the ROI and RI calculations using the compound interest depreciation figures.

Note that when computed using compound interest depreciation, both the ROI and RI forecasts are increased by adopting the project (15.54% vs. 15% and $39,600 vs. $30,000). Since the project's return exceeds the cost of capital and the

---

Exhibit 19.4   American Company Eastern Division Compound Interest Depreciation for Proposed Project

Year	Investment at Beginning of Year	Cash Flow	20% Interest on Beginning Investment	Depreciation Cash Flow less Interest
1	$120,000	$56,967	$24,000	$32,967
2	87,033	56,967	17,407	39,560
3	47,473	56,967	9,495	47,472

Exhibit 19.5   American Company Eastern Division Forecasted 19x1 ROI and RI with Compound Interest

Net Income		
Without project		$150,000
From project		
Cash flow	$56,967	
Less compound interest		
depreciation (per Exhibit 19.4)	32,967	24,000
Total		$174,000
Cost of capital (0.12 × $1,120,000)		134,400
Residual income		$ 39,600
ROI ($174,000 ÷ $1,120,000)		15.54%

---

original forecast of ROI, these indexes should be expected to increase. Two additional comments are in order. First, the depreciation charges under the compound interest method are increasing over time. This is the exact opposite of what managers have learned to expect. Further, such a behavior most likely does not correspond to the rate at which the assets are expected to benefit the firm. That is, it is not expected that an asset will benefit the later periods of its life more than the earlier years. Thus, a proposal to use this depreciation method may be met with resistance in practice.

A second problem occurs because the depreciation is to be computed by using the internal rate of return. The previous example used a specific project with identifiable cash flows. However, it is not likely that it will be possible to identify the portion of the firm's cash flow that is attributable to each of its assets. Even if such an assignment of cash flows could be made, it is not likely the forecasted and actual results will be the same. If not, the true internal rate of return will not be known until the project's life is terminated. It is not clear what should be done for depreciation calculations when it becomes known that actual cash flows are different from those anticipated when the internal rate of return was forecasted. These issues are further examined in problem 19-13.

GROSS VERSUS NET ASSET VALUES.   Although current cost and exit values were discussed as being preferable to historical cost as an investment measurement base, historical costs dominate practice. When historical costs or current costs are used, there must be a decision about using the gross or net book value of long-term assets. That is, should the accumulated depreciation be deducted in arriving at the amount to be included? In financial accounting, of course, long-term assets are carried at net. Because of this convention, it is not surprising to find that a majority of companies use net book value in their ROI and RI computations. The study by Vancil indicates that 85% of his sample used net, 15% gross.[8]

Holding all other factors constant, the use of net book values for long-term assets results in a smaller investment base in each year of the life of a specific asset. Assuming there is no significant change in the income produced by the asset, the numerator of the ROI computation remains relatively constant. Thus, for a given asset, ROI increases merely as a result of the accounting procedures. That is, the numerator remains constant and the denominator decreases. There would be a similar impact on RI. Some companies consider this behavior of ROI and RI to be an undesirable reflection of economic realities and use gross values instead of net. Obviously, holding all other factors constant, this practice would result in a level investment base over time.

As appealing as this argument for using gross values might appear, let us further consider the issues before taking a stance. Holding all other factors constant is not really legitimate. Remember that depreciation is an expense that does not require an outlay of assets during the period of recognition. Thus, for a given accounting period, the increase in assets due to operations will be greater than the increase in retained earnings. Those assets protected by the depreciation policy become available for the firm's use and would also be included in the investment base. Thus, when we consider the total investment, we see that using gross values for long-term assets results in a double counting. The long-term assets are included at their original cost, and the portion of the original cost recovered during the period is included in some other category (cash, receivables, inventory, or some other asset).

To illustrate these ideas, the proposed project of the Eastern Division (summarized in Exhibit 19.4) will be used. So that other factors do not interfere with the results, three factors will be assumed:

1. The compound interest depreciation method is used.
2. Dividends will be paid in an amount equal to the net income.
3. Assets recovered through the project's earnings, and not declared as dividends, will be invested in a nondepreciable asset and earn income at a rate equal to the project's internal return, 20%.

Exhibit 19.6 computes the divisional income and investment for this case. The line 1 amounts are obvious. At the beginning of year 1, there are no other assets and, therefore, no other cash flows during the year. For the moment, ignore the remaining items on line 2. Line 4 is also obvious. Line 5 is the book value of the original assets at the beginning of the year (the original investment less the accumulated depreciation). Line 6 is the accumulated other assets at the beginning of the year. For year 2, the accumulation is equal to the cash inflows of year 1 reduced by the cash dividends in year 1. (Dividends are to equal net income.)

The amount of other assets accumulated at the beginning of year 2 (from line 6) becomes the base for year 2's other cash flow computation on line 2. The earning

---

[8]Vancil, *Decentralization,* p. 351.

Exhibit 19.6   American Company Eastern Division Illustration of Gross versus Book in Asset Evaluation

	Year		
	1	*2*	*3*
1. Project's cash flow	$ 56,967	$ 56,967	$ 56,967
2. Other cash flow: 20% of other assets at beginning of year (from line 6)	0		
$32,967 × 0.20		6,593	
$72,527 × 0.20			14,505
3. Total	$ 56,967	$ 63,560	$ 71,472
4. Compound interest depreciation on project (from Exhibit 19.4)	32,967	39,560	47,472
Net income	$ 24,000	$ 24,000	$ 24,000
5. Book value of long term assets at *beginning* of year	$120,000		
$120,000 − $32,967		87,033	
$ 87,033 − $39,560			47,473
6. Other assets accumulated through *beginning* of year:	0		
$56,967 − $24,000[a]		$ 32,967	
$32,967 + ($63,560 − $24,000)[a]			$ 72,527
7. Total assets at *beginning* of year	$120,000	$120,000	$120,000

[a]Each year's dividend is equal to the year's net income.

rate for the other assets was assumed equal to the project's rate so that it would be obvious what the entire asset package was earning: 20%. The *accumulated* other assets at the beginning of year 3 is the amount accumulated through year 1 plus year 2's layer. The latter, again, is the cash inflows reduced by the dividend payment.

Now, return to the gross versus net question. If long-term assets are valued at gross, then the *beginning of year investment base* and ROI are as follows:

	Year 1	Year 2	Year 3
Long-term assets (gross)	$120,000	$120,000	$120,000
Other (from Exhibit 19.6)	0	32,967	72,527
Total	$120,000	$152,967	$192,527
ROI $24,000 ÷ Total	20%	15.69%	12.47%

Alternatively, if the long-term assets are included at net, then, as indicated on line 7 of Exhibit 19.6, the beginning of year investment base is $120,000 in each year, and each year's ROI is 20%. When the recovered assets are reinvested, it seems clear that depreciable assets should be included at their net value rather than their gross value. With the assumptions, all assets were earning 20% and the ROI should be 20% in each year.

There is one final consideration in this issue. The preceding example implicitly assumed that the recovered assets were under the control of the investment center. As indicated earlier, some firms retain cash management as a responsibility of central headquarters. Then a case can be made for excluding the recovered assets from the investment base of the division. If the recovered assets are excluded and if compound interest depreciation is not used, then valuing long-term assets at net book values will result in an increasing ROI over time. To mitigate this, long-term assets could be included at gross as was originally suggested.

We have not come to a firm conclusion on the net versus gross issue, but this was not our purpose. Instead, our goal was to explore the issues so that you have a strong base from which to reason when you encounter an actual situation.

PROBLEMS CAUSED BY PRICE LEVEL CHANGES. As has been indicated earlier, price level changes can cause some subtle problems with respect to the usage of ROI and RI. In this section, we will explore these problems in more detail. Two types of problems are caused by the failure to adjust for changes in prices. First, the manager of an investment center may make inappropriate decisions. Second, when there are two or more centers being evaluated on a comparative basis, failure to adjust for changes in price levels can cause a lack of comparability.

With respect to the first problem, it should be obvious how ROI and RI computed on an historical cost basis can be dysfunctional. A "profitable" sale of one noncash asset to enable the acquisition of another could be refused in a period of rising price levels simply because the new assets will be measured in different dollars. That is, in comparison with an unadjusted cost of the old assets, the exchange could cause the ROI investment base to go up at a greater rate than the income. This would lower ROI but this, in part, is a function of the change to dollars with different purchasing power.

The second problem of not adjusting for changes in price levels is the distortion of the comparative data among investment centers. That is, if comparable assets are acquired by divisions in different years, they will be shown at different costs. If investment center comparisons are a major use of ROI and RI and if the use of exit values is not practical, then the following adjustments should be made:

1. When inventory methods differ from center to center, a common method should be selected. All centers that are *not* using the selected method should adjust their income and investment to amounts that would have resulted if the selected inventory method was used.
2. When depreciation methods vary from center to center, then all of the centers' income and accumulated depreciation amounts should be adjusted to a common method. An exception could be justified if the difference in the methods is attributable to the need for reflecting differences in the rate of economic depreciation.
3. Depreciation and the book value of assets need to be adjusted to a common price level, preferably, the current price level.

These adjustments are needed to help central management make proper evaluations of the divisions and the managers rather than helping the investment center manager. Thus, the issue is more one of comparability than a proper reflection of economic consequences. For this purpose it is not as important to choose the correct method as it is to use the same method.

Summary

The control of decentralized units is a complex process. Managers of these units frequently commit the investment centers to long-run courses of action. The outcome and wisdom of these actions may not be known until several periods have passed. Yet periodic feedback about progress is needed. The system of providing and using periodic feedback may instill managers with goals that are short run.

Return on investment and residual income are the most widely used criteria for the evalution of decentralized operations. Despite their limitations, they are perhaps the best that are yet available. The major purpose of this chapter was to evaluate these criteria and highlight their limitations. Awareness of the problems that ROI and RI can cause will enable more intelligent and mature usage.

This chapter has established the possibility of incongruence when ROI is used. Projects might be rejected even if their return exceeds the cost of capital. Further, there is the problem of defining controllable income and investment for use in the computations. Also causing problems are the conventional accounting practices for long-term assets and price level changes. Some of these problems are easily correctable, others are not.

The new key terms and concepts with which you should be familiar from this chapter include:

Centralized organization
Decentralized organization
Cost center
Profit center
Investment center
Return on investment
Asset turnover ratio
Residual income
Exit value
Compound interest depreciation method

SELF-STUDY PROBLEM NUMBER ONE. Self-study problem one is an adapted CMA problem. Peterdonn Corporation made a capital investment of $100,000 in new equipment two years ago. The analysis made at that time indicated the equipment would save $36,425 in operating expenses per year over a five-year period, or a 24% return on capital before taxes per year based upon the internal rate-of-return analysis.

The department manager believed that the equipment had "lived up" to its expectations. However, the departmental report showing the overall return on investment (ROI) rate for the first year in which this equipment was used did not reflect as much improvement as had been expected. The department manager asked the accounting section to "break out" the figures related to this investment to find out why it did not contribute more to the department's ROI.

The accounting section was able to identify the equipment and its contribution to the department's operations. The report presented to the department manager at the end of the first year is shown below.

Reduced operating expenses due to new equipment	$ 36,425
Less: Depreciation at 20% of cost	20,000
Contribution before taxes	$ 16,425
Investment at beginning of year	$100,000
Investment at end of year	$ 80,000

$$\text{ROI} = \frac{16,425}{100,000} = 16.4\%$$

The department manager was surprised that the ROI was less than 24% because the new equipment performed as expected. The staff analyst in the accounting section replied that the company ROI for performance evaluation differed from that used for capital investment analysis. The analyst commented that the discrepancy could be solved if the company used the compound interest method of depreciation for its performance evaluation reports.

Required:

1. Discuss the reasons why the ROI of 16.4% for the new equipment as calculated in the department's report by the accounting section differs from the 24% internal rate of return calculated at the time the machine was approved for purchase.
2. Restructure the data from the discounted cash flow analysis so that the expected performance of the new equipment is consistent with the operating reports received by the department manager.

Solution to Self-Study Problem One

1. The IRR implicitly assumes that depreciation will be computed by the compound interest method. It was not computed this way for purposes of ROI and therefore, the reported income will not be the same as the income using compound interest depreciation. The measurement of the investment (the divisor for ROI) will also be affected by the depreciation method used. For year 2 and beyond, the ROI divisor will be different than is implicitly assumed by IRR.
2. For this project the compound interest depreciation will be:

Year	Beginning Investment	Interest at IRR of 24%	Cash Inflow	Depreciation	Ending Investment
1	$100,000	$24,000	$36,425	$12,425	$87,575
2	87,575	21,018	36,425	15,407	72,168
3	72,168	17,320	36,425	19,105	53,063
4	53,063	12,735	36,425	23,690	29,373
5	29,373	7,050	36,425	29,373	0

Thus, the ROI for year 1 is:

$$ROI = \frac{36,425 - 12,425}{100,000} = 24\%$$

SELF-STUDY PROBLEM TWO. The TI Company is considering the use of either ROI or RI in evaluating the performance of its several divisional managers. You have been asked to do a trial analysis using the Typewriter Division. Following is its statement of assets at the beginning of 19x1 and its income for 19x1 (based on historical costs).

Assets	
Cash	$ 10,000
Accounts receivable	20,000
Raw material inventory	40,000
Operating assets (cost)	100,000
Accumulated depreciation	(50,000)
Total	$120,000
Income	
Sales	$109,000
Cost of goods sold	80,000
Gross margin	$ 29,000
Depreciation (straight line)	$ 5,000
Net income	$ 24,000

At the beginning of 19x1 the raw material inventory could have been replaced at a cost of $50,000. It could also have been sold by TI in the market for $50,000. The operating assets could have been replaced at a cost of $250,000 but only had a disposal value of $90,000 at 1/1/x1. At 12/31/x1 the disposal value of the operating assets is $80,000. If either the current cost or exit value concept is used, the 19x1 cost of goods sold would be $85,000. The divisions are to be charged 5% on their investments if RI is used.

Required:

1. Assume that all of the items reported above are controllable by the division manager. If investment is measured at the beginning of the year, compute the ROI and RI under:
   a. Historical costing concepts.
   b. Current cost concepts
   c. Exit value concepts.
2. Assume that the division is considering an investment in nondepreciable assets that would cost $160,000 and yield 7% income per year. What would you expect the manager to do if (1) the amount of cash, receivables, and inventory did not change during 19x1; (2) he had to sell all existing assets to generate the $160,000; (3) if the replacement cost of the assets did not change during 19x1; (4) if it is expected the disposal value of the operating assets would decline to $70,000 by the end of 19x2; and

a. ROI is used with historical cost?

b. RI is used with historical cost?

c. ROI is used with current cost?

d. RI is used with current cost?

e. ROI is used with exit values?

f. RI is used with exit values?

3. Repeat part 2 but assume that the $160,000 can be acquired through new funds available from central headquarters. That is the division can expand its total investment.

Solution to Self-Study Problem Two

1. a.
$$\text{ROI} = \frac{24,000}{120,000} = 20\%$$

$$\text{RI} = \$24,000 - 0.05(\$120,000) = \$18,000$$

b. Beginning assets and income for parts 1-b and 1-c:

	Current Cost	*Exit Value*
Assets		
Cash	$ 10,000	$ 10,000
Accounts receivable	20,000	20,000
Raw material inventory	50,000	50,000
Operating assets	250,000	90,000
Accumulated depreciation	(125,000)	
Total	$205,000	$170,000
Income		
Sales	$109,000	$109,000
Cost of goods sold	85,000	85,000
Gross margin	$ 24,000	$ 24,000
Depreciation	12,500[a]	10,000[b]
Net income	$ 11,500	$ 14,000

[a]The straight-line rate can be determined from the historical cost statements as 5% (5,000 depreciation expense ÷ $100,000 cost). For current cost: 0.05 × $250,000.

[b]The exit value has declined by $10,000 during the year: $90,000 − $80,000.

$$\text{ROI} = \frac{11,500}{205,000} = 5.61\%$$

$$\text{RI} = \$11,500 - 0.05(\$205,000) = \$1,250$$

c. Using figures from 1-b:

$$\text{ROI} = \frac{14,000}{170,000} = 8.24\%$$

$$RI = \$14,000 - 0.05(\$170,000) = \$5,000$$

2. Note that all of the existing assets would have to be sold at their exit values in order to invest in the new alternative. With assumptions (3) and (4) the net income (under all three concepts) would be projected to be the same as for 19x1 if the existing assets are kept. With the assumptions, the total investment at the end of 19x1 would just be the beginning assets less the 19x1 depreciation.

    a. If the alternative investment is selected, then the ROI would go from 20.87% [$24,000 ÷ (120,000 − 5,000)] to 7%. Therefore, the alternative would probably be rejected.

    b. The RI would go from $18,250 [$24,000 − 0.05($115,000)] to $3,200 [0.07(160,000) − 0.05(160,000)]. Reject.

    c. The ROI would go from 5.97% [$11,500 ÷ (205,000 − 12,500)] to 7%. Accept.

    d. The RI would go from $1,875 [$11,500 − 0.05(192,500)] to $3,200. Accept.

    e. The ROI would go from 8.75% [$14,000 ÷ (170,000 − 10,000)] to 7%. Reject.

    f. The RI would go from $6,000 [$14,000 − 0.05(160,000)] to $3,200. Reject.

3. In this situation, the manager will not have to dispose of his existing assets in order to take advantage of the new project. In each case the net income will be the projected income for 19x2 plus the projected income from the new alternative of $11,200 (160,000 × 0.07). The investment will just be $160,000 higher than in part 2.

    a. If the alternative is added, the ROI would go from 20.87% (computed in part 2) to 12.8%, (24,000 + 11,200) ÷ (115,000 + 160,000). Reject.

    b. The RI would go from $18,250 (computed in part 2) to $21,450, (35,200 − 0.05 × 275,000). Accept.

    c. The ROI would go from 5.97% (computed in part 2) to 6.44%, (11,500 + 11,200) ÷ (192,500 + 160,000). Accept.

    d. The RI would go from $1,875 (computed in part 2) to $5,075, (22,700 − 0.05 × 352,500). Accept.

    e. The ROI would go from 8.75% (computed in part 2) to 7.88%, (14,000 + 11,200) ÷ (160,000 + 160,000). Reject.

    f. The RI would go from $6,000 (computed in part 2) to $9,200, (25,200 − 0.05 × 320,000). Accept.

References

Bierman, H. "ROI as a Measure of Managerial Performance," *Financial Executive* (March 1973): 40–46.

Ferrara, W. "Probabilistic Approaches to ROI and RI," *The Accounting Review* (July 1977): 597–604.

Henderson, B.D., and Dearden, J. "New System for Divisional Control," *Harvard Business Review* (September–October 1966): 144–160.

Shillinglaw, G. "Toward a Theory of Divisional Income Measurement," *The Accounting Review* (April 1962): 208–216.

Shwadyer, K. "A Proposed Modification to Residual Income," *The Accounting Review* (April 1970): 299–307.

Solomons, D. *Divisional Performance: Measurement and Control.* New York: Financial Executives Research Foundation, 1965.

Problems

19-1. Basic Problems on ROI and RI. The Royal Company has three divisions, K, C, and R. For a recent period, the following data were reported.

	Division K	Division C	Division R
Sales	$20,000	320,000	670,000
Income	2,000	$16,000	10,000
Investment	10,000	80 ? m	$50,000
Asset turnover	? 2	4.0	? 1.34
Income to sales	? .10	? .05	0.15
ROI	? .20	0.2	? 20
RI using 10% cost of capital	1000 ?	16,000 ?	$ 5,000

Required:

1. Complete the missing data in this schedule.
2. Rank the divisions in terms of efficiency. How did you arrive at your rankings?
3. Rank the divisions in terms of their effective use of resources in capturing the market. How did you arrive at your rankings?
4. Discuss any shortcomings you see in using these data for evaluating the managers of the three divisions.

19-2. Improving ROI and RI. The White Company has two divisions, A and Z. Following are some recent data:

	Division A	Division Z
Asset turnover	10.00	2.00
Income to sales	0.01	0.05
ROI	0.10	0.10
RI using an 8% cost of capital	$ 2,000	$ 2,000
Sales	$1,000,000	$ 200,000
Income	$ 10,000	$ 10,000
Investment	$ 100,000	$ 100,000

Required:

1. Assume each division could reduce costs in an amount equal to 1% of its sales. What would the new ROI be for each division? What would the new RI be?
2. Assume each division could turn over its assets one additional time. What would the new ROI be for each division? What would the new RI be?
3. Division A can increase sales from 100,000 units to 140,000 units if the sales price on all units is reduced by $1. The increased sales will require additional plant and equipment. What is the maximum amount the division would be willing to invest in plant and equipment if it wanted to increase its ROI to 12%? Assume that at the volume reported the costs consisted of 60% variable and 40% fixed.
4. Repeat part 3, but assume the division wanted to increase its RI to $10,000.

19-3. CMA Problem on ROI and Goal Congruence. The Notewon Corporation is a highly diversified company that grants its divisional executives a significant amount of authority in operating the divisions. Each division is responsible for its own sales, pricing, production, costs of operations, and the management of accounts receivable, inventories, accounts payable, and use of existing facilities. Cash is managed by corporate headquarters; all cash in excess of normal operating needs of the divisions is transferred periodically to corporate headquarters for redistribution or investment.

Divisional executives are responsible for presenting requests to corporate management for investment projects. Proposals are analyzed and documented at corporate headquarters. The final decision to commit funds to acquire equipment, to expand existing facilities, or for other investment purposes rests with corporate management. This procedure for investment projects is necessitated by Notewon's capital allocation policy.

Notewon evaluates the performance of division executives by ROI. The asset base is composed of fixed assets employed plus working capital exclusive of cash.

The ROI performance of a divisional executive is the most important appraisal factor for salary changes. In addition, the annual performance bonus is based on the ROI results with increases in ROI having a significant impact on the amount of the bonus.

Notewon Corporation adopted the ROI performance measure and related compensation procedures about ten years ago. The corporation did so to increase the awareness of divisional management of the importance of the profit/asset relationship and to provide additional incentive to the divisional executives to seek investment opportunities.

The corporation seems to have benefited from the program. The ROI for the corporation, as a whole, increased during the first years of the program. Although the ROI has continued to grow in each division, the corporate ROI has declined in recent years. The corporation has accumulated a sizeable amount of cash and short-term marketable securities in the past three years.

The corporation management is concerned about the increase in the short-term marketable securities. A recent article in a financial publication suggested that the use of ROI was overemphasized by some companies with results similar to those experienced by Notewon.

Required:

1. Describe the specific actions division managers might have taken to cause the ROI to grow in each division but decline for the corporation. Illustrate your explanation with appropriate examples.
2. Explain, using the concepts of goal congruence and motivation of divisional executives, how Notewon Corporation's overemphasis on the use of ROI might result in the recent decline in the corporation's return on investment and the increase in cash and short-term marketable securities.
3. What changes could be made in Notewon Corporation's compensation policy to avoid this problem? Explain your answer.

19-4. CMA Problem on Evaluating a Responsibility Center. The ATCO Co. purchased the Dexter Co. three years ago. Before the acquisition Dexter manufactured and sold plastic products to a wide variety of customers. Dexter has since become a division of ATCO and now only manufactures plastic components for products made by ATCO's Macon Division. Macon sells its products to hardware wholesalers.

ATCO's corporate management gives the Dexter Division management a considerable amount of authority in running the division's operations. However, corporate management retains authority for decisions regarding capital investments, price setting of all products, and the quantity of each product to be produced by the Dexter Division.

ATCO has a formal performance evaluation program for the management of all of its divisions. The performance evaluation program relies heavily on each division's return on investment. The income statement of Dexter Division presented below provides the basis for the evaluation of Dexter's divisional management.

Sales (000 omitted)		$4,000
Cost and expenses		
Product costs		
Direct materials	$ 500	
Direct labor	1,100	
Factory overhead	1,300	
Total	$2,900	
Less: increase in inventory	350	$2,550
Engineering and research		120
Shipping and receiving		240
Division administration		
Manager's office	$ 210	
Cost accounting	40	
Personnel	82	332
Corporate costs		
Computer	$ 48	
General services	230	278
Total costs and expenses		$3,520
Divisional operating income		$ 480
Net plant investment		$1,600
Return on investment		30%

Financial statements for the divisions are prepared by the corporate accounting staff. Corporate general services costs are allocated on the basis of sales dollars and the computer department's actual costs are apportioned among the divisions on the basis of use. The net division investment includes division fixed assets at net book value (cost less depreciation), division inventory, and corporate working capital apportioned to the divisions on the basis of sales dollars.

Required:

1. Discuss the financial reporting and performance evaluation program of ATCO Co. as it relates to the responsibilities of the Dexter Division.
2. Based upon your response to requirement 1, recommend appropriate revisions of the financial information and reports used to evaluate the performance of Dexter's divisional management. If revisions are not necessary, explain why.

19-5. CMA Problem on Evaluating Managers. The Texon Co. is organized into autonomous divisions along regional market lines. Each division manager is responsible for sales, cost of operations, acquisition and financing of divisional assets, and working capital management.

The vice-president of general operations for the company will retire in September 19x5. A review of the performance, attitudes, and skills of several management employees has been undertaken to find a replacement. Interviews with qualified outside candidates also have been held. The selection committee has narrowed the choice to the managers of Divisions A and F.

Both candidates were appointed division managers in late 19x1. The manager of Division A had been the assistant manager of that division for the prior five years. The manager of Division F had served as assistant division manager of Division B before being appointed to her present post. She took over Division F, a division newly formed in 19x0, when its first manager left to join a competitor. The financial results of their performance in the past three years is reported in the accompanying schedule.

	Division A			Division F		
	19x2	*19x3*	*19x4*	*19x2*	*19x3*	*19x4*
			(000 omitted)			
Estimated industry sales —market area	$10,000	$12,000	$13,000	$5,000	$6,000	$6,500
Division sales	$ 1,000	$ 1,100	$ 1,210	$ 450	$ 600	$ 750
Variable costs	$ 300	$ 320	$ 345	$ 135	$ 175	$ 210
Managed costs	400	405	420	170	200	230
Committed costs	275	325	350	140	200	250
Total costs	$ 975	$ 1,050	$ 1,115	$ 445	$ 575	$ 690
Net income	$ 25	$ 50	$ 95	$ 5	$ 25	$ 60
Assets employed	$ 330	$ 340	$ 360	$ 170	$ 240	$ 300
Liabilities incurred	103	105	115	47	100	130
Net investment	227	235	245	123	140	170
Return on investment	11%	21%	39%	4%	18%	35%

Required:

1. Texon Co. measures the performance of the divisions and the division managers on the basis of their return on investment (ROI). Is this an appropriate measurement for the division managers? Explain.
2. Many believe that a single measure, such as ROI, is inadequate to fully evaluate performance. What additional measure(s) could be used for performance evaluation? Give reasons for each measure listed.
3. On the basis of the information given, which manager would you recommend for vice-president of general operations? Present reasons to support your answer.

19-6. CMA Problem on Using Responsibility Accounting to Evaluate Performance. George Johnson was hired on July 1, 19x1, as assistant general manager of the Botel Division of Staple, Inc. It was understood that he would be elevated to general manager of the division on January 1, 19x3, when the then current general manager retired, and this was duly done. In addition to becoming acquainted with the division and the general manager's duties, Mr. Johnson was specifically charged with the responsibility for development of the 19x2 and 19x3 budgets. As general manager in 19x3, he was, obviously, responsible for the 19x4 budget.

The Staple Company is a multiproduct company that is highly decentralized. Each division is quite autonomous. The corporation staff approves division-prepared operating budgets but seldom makes major changes in them. The corporate staff actively participates in decisions requiring capital investment (for expansion or replacement) and makes the final decisions. The division management is responsible for implementing the capital program. The major method used by the Staple Company to measure division performance is contribution return on division net investment. The following budgets were approved by the corporation. Revision of the 19x4 budget is not considered necessary even though 19x3 actual departed from the approved 19x3 budget.

	Actual			Budget	
	19x1	*19x2*	*19x3*	*19x3*	*19x4*
			(000 omitted)		
Sales	$1,000	$1,500	$1,800	$2,000	$2,400
Less division variable costs:					
Material and labor	250	375	450	500	600
Repairs	50	75	50	100	120
Supplies	20	30	36	40	48
Less division managed costs:					
Employee training	30	35	25	40	45
Maintenance	50	55	40	60	70
Less division committed costs:					
Depreciation	120	160	160	200	200
Rent	80	100	110	140	140
Total	600	830	871	1,080	1,223
Division net contribution	400	670	929	920	1,177
Division investment:					
Accounts receivable	100	150	180	200	240
Inventory	200	300	270	400	480
Fixed assets	1,590	2,565	2,800	3,380	4,000
Less: accounts and wages payable	(150)	(225)	(350)	(300)	(360)
Net investment	1,740	2,790	2,900	3,680	4,360
Contribution return on net investment	23%	24%	32%	25%	27%

Required:

1. Identify Mr. Johnson's responsibilities under the management and measurement program described.
2. Appraise the performance of Mr. Johnson in 19x3.
3. Recommend to the president any changes in the responsibilities assigned to managers or in the measurement methods used to evaluate division management based upon your analysis.

19-7. Dysfunctional Problems with ROI and RI. The general manager of one of the Brett Company's divisions has been requested to submit her proposed capital budget for inclusion in the company's 19x1 budget. The manager has been considering all of the following projects. Assume they have equal risk.

Project	Investment Required	First-Year Return
1	$300,000	$69,000
2	120,000	38,400
3	87,500	12,250
4	60,000	10,800
5	40,000	8,400
6	17,500	4,900

The division is limited to $750,000 of capital. The firm has a 15% cost of capital.

Required:

1. The manager of the division will be evaluated using ROI. Assume the division is a *new* one with no capital invested at the time of selecting from among the six projects. Which projects should be selected if the division wants to maximize its ROI? Why?
2. Assume the same as part 1 except that the division is one year old and had reported an ROI of 20% on a capital investment of $500,000 during year 1. You may assume that the investment before additional projects is still $500,000 and will continue to earn 20% in year 2. The division still has $750,000 of capital available for the special projects. What projects should it elect given the evaluation criterion? Why?
3. Again, assume the same as in part 1 except that the manager will be evaluated using RI. What should be done? Why?
4. Comment on the reason(s) for the differences in actions, if any, that might be expected if ROI is used instead of RI.

19-8. Problems of ROI. The Kauber Company is organized into three divisions: A, B, and C. Prior to the consideration of new projects these divisions have projected their 19x3 net incomes and investments as follows:

	A	B	C
Projected Income	$ 20,000	$ 5,000	$ 38,000
Current Investment	$200,000	$50,000	$200,000

Suppose each of the three divisions is presently considering three projects. The estimated rates of return and investments are:

Project	Rate of Return	Investment
I	20%	$40,000
II	15	20,000
III	13	10,000

All three projects are available, without constraint, to each of the divisions. Each may adopt any or all of the projects. Kauber Company's cost of capital is estimated at 14%.

Required:

1. Assume that the divisions will be evaluated using return on investment (ROI) as the primary index. What action should each division manager take with respect to the three projects? Explain.
2. Evaluate the results you obtained in part 1 from the perspective of the firm.
3. Now assume the divisions will be evaluated using residual income (RI) as the primary index. What action should each division manager take with respect to the three projects? Explain.
4. Evaluate the results you obtained in part 3 from the perspective of the firm.

19-9. Measuring Income and Investment for ROI. The Leonard Company has two divisions that, for purposes of this problem, are virtually identical. Using standard full absorption costing, the following income statements were prepared for 19x2:

	Division A	Division B
Sales @ $80 per unit	$3,200,000	$3,200,000
Cost of goods sold		
Beginning inventory	$ 200,000	$ 200,000
Cost of production	2,000,000	1,600,000
Cost of goods available	$2,200,000	$1,800,000
Ending inventory	600,000	200,000
Standard cost of sales	$1,600,000	$1,600,000
Variances		
Variable cost	30,000 U	30,000 U
Noncontrollable	0	100,000 U
Total	$1,630,000	$1,730,000
Gross margin	$1,570,000	$1,470,000
Selling and administrative		
Variable (controllable)	$ 200,000	$ 200,000
Variable (allocated from		
central headquarters)	120,000	200,000
Fixed (controllable)	500,000	500,000
Fixed (noncontrollable)	380,000	400,000
Total	$1,200,000	$1,300,000
Net income	$ 370,000	$ 170,000

The standards, for either division, are as follows:

Material (3 units @ $4)	$12
Labor (2 hours @ $6)	12
Variable overhead (2 hours @ $3)	6
Fixed overhead (2 hours @ $5)	10
Total	$40

The budgeted fixed overhead and labor capacity are the same at both divisions:

Factory supervision	$100,000
Equipment depreciation	150,000
Building depreciation	180,000

Property taxes (equipment and building)	50,000
Other—controllable	20,000
Total	$500,000
Direct-labor hours at capacity	100,000
Fixed overhead rate	$5.00

Following are the asset balances at January 1, 19x2:

	Corporate Headquarters	Division A	Division B
Cash	$ 400,000	0	0
Accounts receivable	960,000	0	0
Inventory	0	$ 200,000	$ 200,000
Building	400,000	1,200,000	1,200,000
Equipment	100,000	1,800,000	1,800,000
Total	$1,860,000	$3,200,000	$3,200,000

Additional information is as follows:

1. The division managers have complete control over equipment decisions.
2. Corporate headquarters retains control of cash and building decisions.
3. The accounts receivable records are maintained at corporate headquarters, but the division managers set credit policy. During 19x2, the Division A manager estimated that 90% of their sales were on account. Division B's manager estimates 60% of their sales were on account.
4. The forecasted demand for the product in 19x3 is 45,000 units.

Preliminary ROI calculations have been made. In doing this, the central headquarter's assets were allocated equally, based on sales. Thus:

$$\text{For A: ROI} = \frac{370,000}{3,200,000 + 930,000} = 8.96\%$$

$$\text{For B: ROI} = \frac{170,000}{3,200,000 + 930,000} = 4.12\%$$

Required:

1. Evaluate the merits of these ROI values. If necessary, revise the calculations, providing reasons for the changes you make.
2. Assume the forecasted demand in assumption 4 is 70,000 units instead of 45,000 units. Revise the ROI calculations and comment on your results.

19-10. CVP Analysis, ROI, and RI. The Gregory Company's XYZ Division is autonomous and evaluated by a variety of ways including return on investment (ROI) and residual income (RI). Data concerning the only product handled by XYZ include the following:

Sales price per unit	$80
Total variable cost per unit	$50
Total fixed costs	$ 70,000
Long-term assets	$800,000

The investment base for both the ROI and RI is long-term assets plus working capital. The working capital will increase as total volume increases. As an approximation of the working-capital needs, XYZ estimates $2 of working capital for every unit of product produced. The firms cost of capital is 10%.

Required:

1. Suppose XYZ has a target ROI of 15%. At what volume would it have to operate in order to achieve this goal?
2. Suppose XYZ has a target RI of $50,000. At what volume would it have to operate in order to achieve this goal?
3. Now suppose two products are sold, the one described above, call it A, and a second, call it B. Data about B include:

Sales price per unit	$50
Variable cost per unit	$35
Working capital per unit	$ 3
Ratio of A to B	3 to 2

There would be no added fixed costs of including B in the product line. Given the 3-to-2 ratio, what would the volume of A and B have to be to yield an ROI of 15%?

19-11. Comparing Divisions When There Is Inflation. The Porter Company is divisionalized, with the Rear Axle Division located in Backwoods and the Front Axle Division in Uptown. One of the indexes used for evaluation purposes is residual income (RI). The two division managers are, to some extent, in competition with each other for resources. An appropriate measure of income will be reduced by an interest factor of 10%. The assets will be measured in a way that is most appropriate for the situation. That is, a measure should be used that will result in the most comparability between the managers. The following data are available at December 31, 19x9:

	Front Axle Division	Rear Axle Division
Sales	$200,000	$400,000
Variable costs	60,000	160,000
Contribution margin	$140,000	$240,000
Separable controllable fixed costs	60,000	70,000
Controllable margin	$ 80,000	$170,000
Separable noncontrollable fixed costs	30,000	50,000
Division margin	$ 50,000	$120,000
Allocated fixed costs	40,000	80,000
Net income	$ 10,000	$ 40,000
Balances at 1/1/x9 included		
Cash	$ 10,000	$ 15,000
Accounts receivable	18,000	25,000
Inventory	30,000	20,000
Fixed assets—acquired in 19x0 less accumulated depreciation of $45,000	55,000	
Fixed assets—acquired in 19x8 less accumulated depreciation of $10,000		190,000
Total assets	$113,000	$250,000

Other information includes the following:

1. The home office of the firm controls the cash and accounts receivable.
2. The straight-line depreciation method is used.
3. The Front Axle Division uses FIFO, and the Rear Axle Division uses LIFO. If the Front Axle Division had used LIFO, the beginning inventory would have been $21,000. The variable costs in 19x9 would have been $2,000 higher. If the Rear Axle Division used FIFO, the beginning inventory would have been $32,000. Its variable cost would also be $1,000 lower.
4. The price levels in 19x8 and 19x9 were 100% higher than in 19x0.

Required:

Compute the residual income for each division. Explain your assumptions.

19-12. ROI and RI with Compound Interest Depreciation. The Aikens Division of the Gura Company has compiled the following figures in preparation for planning the 19x9 operations:

	Actual 19x8	Estimated 19x9
Net income	$ 210,000	$ 210,000
Beginning assets (book value)*	1,000,000	1,000,000
ROI	21%	21%
Residual income (using the company cost of capital at 15%)	60,000	60,000

*The estimated figures do not include the effects of any new projects. The divisions use book value because they have been given control of the working capital.

One new project under consideration for 19x9 would entail the purchase of equipment at $47,683. The estimated cash inflows for the project are $10,000, $40,000, and $20,000 for years 1, 2, and 3, respectively. If the equipment is purchased, it can be shown that the cash flows imply a 20% internal rate of return.

Required:

1. Using the company's cost of capital as the discount rate, find the net present value of the cash flow if the new equipment is purchased. Should the project be acquired?
2. Assume the new equipment is purchased and that compound interest depreciation is used. Prepare a schedule of depreciation expense to be recognized in each year of the life of the new machine.
3. Determine the divisional ROI for 19x9 assuming the project is adopted at the beginning of the year and that the divisor for ROI is the beginning-of-year assets. Assume the compound interest depreciation method is used. Based on the ROI for 19x9, would the division acquire the machine? Why?
4. Assume the same facts as in part 3. Determine the RI. Based on RI in 19x9, would the division acquire the machine? Why?
5. Now assume that depreciation is determined by the sum-of-year-digits method. Find the 19x9 RI if the new machine is acquired. Based on 19x9 RI, should the new equipment be acquired? Why?
6. Summarize your observations in this problem.

19-13. Problems of Using Compound Interest Depreciation. The Otis Company has two divisions, A and B. In January of 19x1, Division A proposed an investment costing $10,000. The project had estimated annual returns of $4,747 over its three-year life. At that time, the firm's performance evaluation committee decided to use a compound interest depreciation based ROI in order to be congruent with decision making tools.

The internal rate of return for the project was correctly estimated at 20%. Based on this, the depreciation schedule is as follows:

Year	Beginning Investment	Estimated Return	20% Interest on Beginning Investment	Depreciation
1	$10,000	$4,747	$2,000	$2,747
2	7,253	4,747	1,450	3,297
3	3,956	4,747	791	3,956
4	0			

Now there is a problem. Division A's return in year 1 turned out to be $4,021 instead of $4,747. Using the preceding schedule and assuming the returns continue to be $4,021, a committee staff member prepared the following schedule:

Year	Return	Depreciation	Income	Beginning Investment	ROI
1	$4,021	$2,747	$1,274	$10,000	12.74
2	4,021	3,297	724	7,253	9.98
3	4,021	3,956	65	3,956	1.16

Required:

Continuing the assumption of the returns being $4,021 in years 2 and 3, evaluate the ROI computations for Division A. Prepare any revised three-year schedule you think might be needed to better implement the intentions of the evaluation committee.

19-14. Current (Replacement) Cost versus Disposal Value. Reconsider the Kowalski Company case introduced in the section entitled Basic Concepts of Investment. Assume the assets already owned are forecast to generate a cash flow of $263.80 per year for five years. The alternative investment, costing $400, will return a cash flow of $133.75 per year for five years. Continue to assume the existing assets have a replacement cost of $1,000 and a disposal value of $400.

Required:

1. Determine the internal rate of return on the existing assets, assuming replacement cost as the measure of the present value.
2. Ignoring opportunity cost, determine the internal rate of return for the alternative being considered.
3. Which of the two alternatives will maximize wealth? Why?
4. For each alternative, prepare a schedule computing compound interest depreciation. (Assume existing assets are carried at replacement cost. Ignore the opportunity cost of selecting the new alternative. Note: It would also be ignored for conventional accounting purposes.)

5. Assuming compound interest depreciation is used and that income is to be computed excluding gains and losses of asset disposals, compute the projected first-year ROI for each alternative. What are the implications of your results?

6. Assume gains and losses on asset disposals are included in the income figure. Based on the first-year ROI, what would you expect the manager to do if replacement cost is used in measuring the ROI investment base? If disposal values are used?

7. Now assume the alternative is projected to return cash flows of $265.30 per year instead of $133.75. It can be shown that this investment (cost of $400) has an internal rate of return of 60%.
   a. To maximize wealth, what should the firm do?
   b. Assume gains and losses on asset disposals are used in computing income and that compound interest depreciation is used. Based on the first-year ROI, what would you expect the manager to do if replacement cost is used in measuring the ROI investment base? If disposal values are used? Comment on the results.

19-15. Gross versus Net in Measuring Investment. Reconsider the Otis Company in problem 19-13. Assume Division B made a proposal identical to that of Division A. Unlike A, however, the actual cash flows turned out to be equal to the estimate. For simplicity, assume the project in question was the total investment at the beginning of 19x1.

Required:

1. Assume that straight-line depreciation is taken and that the division has no control over the cash proceeds of the project.
   a. Compute the ROI for each of the three years, using net book values.
   b. Compute the ROI for each of the three years, using gross book values.
   c. Compare the results of parts a and b.

2. Assume the same as in part 1 except that all proceeds will be invested by the division in nondepreciable assets to earn 20% per year.
   a. Compute the ROI for each of the three years, using net book values for the depreciable assets.
   b. Compute the ROI for each of the three years, using gross book values for the depreciable assets.

3. Assume the same as in part 1 except that compound interest depreciation is used. The compound interest depreciation is computed in problem 19-13.
   a. Compute the ROI for each of the three years, using net book values.
   b. Compute the ROI for each of the three years, using gross book values.
   c. Compare the results of parts a and b.
   d. Compare the results with those in part 1.

4. Now assume that all proceeds will be invested by the division in nondepreciable assets to earn 10%. Further, the compound interest depreciation method is used. Compute the ROI for each of the three years, using net book values for the depreciable assets. Comment on the results.

19-16. Making Decisions When ROI Is Affected by Price Level Changes. Assume the following information for Division Q of the McRae Company:

1. In 19x1 a machine costing $100,000 was acquired by Division Q. It had an estimated life of ten years.
2. The straight-line depreciation method is used.

3. It is now early 19x6 and the division is considering the replacement of the machine.
4. Price levels have doubled since 19x1 and a new machine would cost $200,000. Its life also would be ten years.
5. For simplicity, the division has only two assets at January 1, 19x6:

Short-term securities	$500,000
Machine (net)	50,000
Total	$550,000

6. The short-term securites are earning 5%.
7. The projected income for 19x6 using unadjusted data is:

From sale of product		
Revenue		$60,000
Cash operating expenses	$20,000	
Depreciation	10,000	30,000
Total		30,000
Interest income 500,000 × 0.05		25,000
Total income		$55,000

8. The new machine being considered will reduce the forecasted cash operating expenses by $15,000: from $20,000 to $5,000.
9. The old machine can be sold at an amount equal to its price-level adjusted book value: ($50,000 × 2) or $100,000. Implicitly, this assumption equates disposal value with price-level adjusted book values and with current cost. In reality, the disposal value may not be equal to either of these values. To assume anything different, however, complicates the problem to a greater extent than desired.

Required:

1. Compute the projected ROI if the machine is not replaced. Use unadjusted net book values.
2. Assume the machine is replaced. Compute the projected ROI.
3. Based on your results in parts 1 and 2, what would the Division Q manager do? Why? What should the manager do if the goal is to maximize the economic resources of the firm? Why?
4. Repeat part 1 using price level adjusted data.
5. Comparing part 2 with part 4, what would the division manager do?

19-17. Operating Leases and Performance Evaluation. The Wilson Company is organized into two division, A and B. Assume, for simplicity, that at January 1, 19x1, they both have total assets of $1,200,000, all of which are short-term securities. On this same date, both divisions acquire selected assets from the same vendor. Optional acquisition methods are:

a. Buy assets at $200,000. Estimated life is five years.
b. Lease the assets for a two-year period, with lease payments being $52,759 payable at the *end* of each year. The owner can lease the asset for a total of five years. This lease payment implies an interest rate of 10%. If used, this lease would qualify as an operating lease according to FASB Statement 13 and would not be capitalized.

If acquired, Division A would use acquisition method A and Division B, method B. Division A would convert short-term investments to raise the needed cash for an acquisition. Compound interest depreciation will be used for long-term assets.

Required:

1. Assume the short-term investments are earning 10% for either division and that the new assets would generate an annual cash flow of $52,759 whether purchased or leased. Compute the ROI for both divisions assuming the new assets are acquired as previously indicated.
2. Now assume the short-term investments are earning 15% and that the new assets would generate an annual cash flow of $59,663. (For the purchase option, this results in an internal rate of return of 15%). Compute the ROI for both divisions.
3. Repeat part 2 but assume the short-term investments are earning 10%.
4. Explain any differences between the ROI results for the two divisions. Are they defensible in the sense of representing economic differences?

19-18. ROI, RI, and Leases. The Asman Company is divisionalized and one of its divisions, M, has been faced with a variety of problems involving capital investments. The problems center on valuing assets and the use of these values in ROI and RI computations.

Following is a representative case illustrating some of M's problems. Assume the following initial asset base for Division M:

	Assets	Projected Annual Income
Short-Term Investments (earning 16%)	$ 30,000	$ 4,800
Long-Term Nondepreciable Investments (earning 19%)	200,000	38,000
	$230,000	$42,800

Proposal A would entail the division engaging in a small manufacturing operation that would require the acquisition of $30,000 of depreciable assets. The projected cash flows on this venture are $14,242 per year for three years, an internal rate of return of 20%. If the compound interest depreciation method is used for this project the annual depreciation figures would be $8,242, $9,890, and $11,868. If adopted the division would convert its short-term investments.

As an alternative to purchasing the assets Division M is considering a leasing arrangement. The machine manufacturer has offered a three-year lease with annual payments of $13,139. The interest implicit in the lease is 15%. That is, the interest rate, i, that causes equality of the following expression is 15%:

$$13,139a_{3,i} = 30,000$$

Required:

1. One manager at Division M reasons that the purchase option is costing them 16% (since the short-term investments would be used to finance the purchase) and leasing is costing 15%. Thus, leasing should be used. Assume the division will retain control over the cash protected by the depreciation policy and will reinvest it in 16% short-term investments.

That is, the division will transfer cash to central headquarters in an amount equal to the net income. Using the compound interest depreciation method, compute M's ROI figures over the next three years (a) assuming a purchase of the machine and (b) assuming a lease. Assume the firm does not capitalize leases into the investment base of the division.

2. In discussing the solution in part 1, one of the corporate officials questions two things:
   a. Why not include the lease in the investment base? It does provide resources to work with and the division benefits from the return the leased assets enable. Further, for external reporting, the lease, in this case, must be reported as an asset.
   b. If the lease is included in the investment base, then lease amortization should be taken as an expense instead of the lease payments. The compound interest amortization of the lease if $8,639, $9,935, and $11,426.

   Do part b from question 1 in line with these suggestions. Lease amortization is treated like depreciation with respect to divisional control of the proceeds.

3. What would the residual income be in question 1 if the division is charged 10% on its investment base?

4. What would be the residual income for the lease option using the suggestions in question 2?

5. Based on the above results what would you recommend as policy with respect to lease accounting and with respect to performance indexes?

19-19. ROI, RI, and Goal Congruence. The S Division of the Killer Bee Company currently has the following asset structure:

Short-Term Investments (earning 6%)	$ 60,000
Other Assets (replacement value)	140,000
	$200,000

The other assets have a three-year life and are projected to generate a cash flow of $56,296 each year of their remaining life.

At the beginning of the current year Division S is considering two projects, I and II. Either I or II can be adopted but not both. Their respective cash flows are projected as follows:

	I	II
Cost	($60,000)	($60,000)
Cash flow at end of		
Year 1	$48,000	$30,000
Year 2	30,000	30,000
Year 3	8,000	30,000

The firm's cost of capital is 10%. The internal rates of return and NPVs (at 10%) for the two projects are as follows:

	I	II
IRR	27.443%	23.3752%
NPV (at 10%)	$14,440	$14,606

Knowing the problems that can be caused by ROI, the company decided several years ago to evaluate and motivate managers with residual income. In fact, managers earn a bonus equal to 10% of the annual residual income (if it is positive).

In evaluating proposals I and II the manager of Division S makes the following computations. (Straight-line depreciation is company policy.)

	Year 1	Year 2	Year 3
Project I			
Balance Sheet			
Other Assets	$140,000	$ 93,334	$46,668
Project Assets	60,000	40,000	20,000
Total Assets	$200,000	$133,334	$66,668
RI Computations			
Cash flow on other	$ 56,296	$ 56,296	$56,296
Cash flow on project	48,000	30,000	8,000
Total cash flow	$104,296	$ 86,296	$64,296
Depreciation on other	46,666	46,666	46,666
Depreciation on project	20,000	20,000	20,000
Net income	$ 37,630	$ 19,630	$(2,370)
Cost of capital	20,000	13,333	6,667
RI	$ 17,630	$ 6,297	$(9,037)
Bonus	$ 1,763	$ 630	-0-

	Year 1	Year 2	Year 3
Project II			
Balance Sheet			
Other Assets	$140,000	$ 93,334	$46,668
Project Assets	60,000	40,000	20,000
Total Assets	$200,000	$133,334	$66,668
RI Computations			
Cash flow on other	$ 56,296	$ 56,296	$56,296
Cash flow on project	30,000	30,000	30,000
Total cash flow	86,296	86,296	86,296
Depreciation on other	46,666	46,666	46,666
Depreciation on project	20,000	20,000	20,000
Net income	$ 19,630	$ 19,630	$19,630
Cost of capital	20,000	13,333	6,667
RI	$ (370)	$ 6,297	$12,963
Bonus	-0-	630	1,296

The present value of the manager's total bonus is going to be higher for project 1 than for project II regardless of his personal discount rate. Thus, he plans to adopt project I.

Required:

1. In reviewing the manager's plan one executive, who had been instrumental in converting from ROI to RI, commented that he didn't understand why RI was leading to a different course of action than is implied by the NPV figures. Explain.

2. It can be shown that the internal rate of return on the other assets is 10% and that the compound interest depreciation figures are as follows:

	Year 1	*Year 2*	*Year 3*
Other Assets	$42,296	$46,526	$51,178
Project I Assets	31,536	22,188	6,278
Project II Assets	15,975	19,709	24,316

Confirm the depreciation on other assets.

3. Assume that compound interest depreciation is required to be used in computing RI. What should the Division S manager do if his personal interest rate is 8%. Why?

4. At a second meeting, after digesting the information you computed in the previous questions, a vice-president asks why the recovered investments are not showing up in years 2 and 3. She reminds the group that the divisions only remit cash to central headquarters in an amount equal to residual income. Thus, in effect, the divisions control the cash protected by the depreciation policy. Assume this cash will be invested in short-term investments at 6%. Now what should the division manager do? (Continue the assumption of compound interest depreciation.)

CHAPTER 20 — Transfer Pricing

CHAPTER 20 **Transfer Pricing**

Chapter Overview

Although not always the case in decentralized firms, there are many situations where the output of one investment center of the firm is used as an input by one or more of the firm's other centers. In such cases, managers face the interesting and complex problem of establishing the price at which the product or service will be transferred between the centers. Accountants become involved in this issue as advisors on the potential consequences of the price with regard to its effect on decision making and performance evaluations.

The chapter starts by considering a classification of the types of situations for which a transfer price is needed. In the next section, we introduce the various concepts that have been proposed for establishing such a price. The major intent of the second section is to critically evaluate the proposals as they affect decision making and control. Throughout the section, it will become obvious that a single transfer price probably will not serve all purposes equally well. The final section addresses the question of whether it is possible to resolve the conflict created by these multiple needs.

Classification of Possible Situations

As background for the discussion of transfer pricing, a situational classification scheme is introduced in this section. There are several dimensions that contribute to the problem, including different types of supplier divisions, consumer divisions, competition, and potential uses of a transfer price. (Throughout the remainder of this chapter, a division will be assumed to be a profit or investment center.)

First, consider the classification of *supplier divisions*. With respect to the product for which a transfer price is desired, a division might:

1. Be the only supplier. That is, no other firm or no other division in the parent firm manufactures the product.
2. Be one of several divisions within the firm to produce the product but has no competition from outside the firm.
3. Be one of several possible suppliers of the product, including some outside suppliers.

Continuing to concentrate on the product for which the transfer price is needed, consider the classification of potential *consumer divisions,* that is, a division on the receiving end of the transfer. Such a division may:

1. Be the only possible consumer of the product. That is, no other firm or no other division within the parent firm uses the product.
2. Be one of several divisions within the firm to use the product, but the firm is the only consumer.
3. Be one of multiple consumers of the product, including other firms. Exhibit 20.1 summarizes the classification schemes of suppliers and consumers of a given product and shows the resulting combinations.

Some of the combinations in Exhibit 20.1 are more likely to be found than others. With enough digging, examples could be found for each case. That will not be done here, however. As will be seen later, a transfer pricing system, in part, is a function of where the situation fits in the classification of Exhibit 20.1.

A third factor affecting the transfer price is the product structure of the supplying division. The product for which a transfer price is needed may be the only product of the division or it may be one of several outputs. If the supplying division is a multiple-product division, then a fourth variable is whether the other products are marketed outside the firm. Fifth, the type of competition experienced by the divisions (pure, oligopolistic, and so forth) will be a variable. All of these factors must be considered in selecting a transfer pricing rule.

A final classification is that of possible uses of a transfer price. These include:

1. Input to decision making.
2. Input to an index or indexes for evaluating the *manager* of the division.
3. Input to an index or indexes for evaluating the *division*.
4. Input to a variety of financial accounting requirements including local and state tax returns. Could also be input to cost determination of CASB-covered contracts.

It would be ideal if a single transfer price could be optimal for all uses. But by now you should anticipate that this is unlikely.

Exhibit 20.1   Situation Classification of Possible Relationships between Supplier and Consumer

	Sole Consumer	One of Multiple Internal Consumers	One of Multiple Consumers from Inside or Outside the firm
Sole Supplier	1*	2	3
One of Multiple Internal Suppliers	4	5	6
One of Multiple Suppliers from Inside or Outside the firm	7	8	9

*Case Number

Transfer Pricing Methods

In this section we describe the various methods that have been proposed in practice and in the literature for establishing a transfer price. The methods to be discussed are listed here and should not be considered equally desirable. Thus, in addition to the descriptions, the effectiveness of each method is evaluated from the viewpoint of decision making and control. Some conclusions are reached with respect to the desirability of each. The pricing methods to be discussed include:

1. Variable cost of manufacturing in supplier division.
2. Full cost of manufacturing in supplier division.
3. Market price of the product (if it exists).
4. Variable cost plus an appropriate markup.
5. Negotiated price.

Before discussing the details of the various methods, it is interesting to consider their relative popularity. Vancil's survey consisted of 239 companies that need a transfer pricing policy. Following are the percentages reporting the usage of each of these methods:[1]

4.6%	Variable cost
25.5%	Full Cost
31.0%	Market price
16.7%	Cost plus
22.0%	Negotiation

In evaluating a *transfer price,* two criteria should be used:

1. *Does the pricing system encourage goal congruence? Congruence occurs when divisions optimize their own objectives and, at the same time, those of the firm.*
2. *When used in performance evaluation, does the transfer price permit a fair evaluation both in an absolute and a relative sense?*

With these criteria in mind, let us now examine the proposed methods.

VARIABLE COST. A variable cost-based transfer price could be in terms of either actual or standard costs. Of the two variations, standard cost is preferred. An actual cost transfer price causes the performance evaluation of the buying division to be a function of the supplying division's performance.

Regardless of the variation, such a transfer price would not yield any profit to the supplier division. For evaluation purposes, it is seldom possible to demonstrate that the profit of a successful effort is entirely attributable to the division that markets the final product. For this reason, the variable cost method does not meet the second criterion for an acceptable transfer price. If the product represents a very small percentage of the supplier's total activity, then this method might not be opposed because of immateriality. Further, if the situation is such that none of the

---

[1]Richard F. Vancil, *Decentralization: Managerial Ambiguity by Design* (Homewood, Ill.: Dow-Jones Irwin, 1979), p. 180.

supplier's products have an external market, then it may not be important, or desirable, to control the division by profit performance measurements. In these cases, the supplying units are not profit or investment centers and should be controlled in other ways.

The variable cost transfer price also does not satisfy the goal congruence criterion. If a product is transferred from one division to another at its variable cost, then the division that markets the product will have incomplete knowledge of the cost structure of the firm (as opposed to the division). Fixed costs are totally ignored in this system. Obviously, long-run pricing strategies and/or decisions to compete at the price established by the market cannot be made properly without this knowledge. Since a variable cost system does not acceptably serve either of the major uses of a transfer price, there is little merit in using it. Of course, the previously cited statistics indicate that few firms use this method.

FULL COST. The second transfer policy listed was full cost, variable plus fixed. Although there are many ways in which fixed costs might be allocated to the transferred product, the full cost method is one that transfers all costs of the supplying division to the consuming division. This method has some of the deficiencies of a variable cost price. That is, no profits would be recognized by the supplying division since their "sales" price is equal to their total cost.

For decision-making purposes, this system transfers fixed costs but they will likely be considered by the purchasing division as if they are variable costs. The receiving division would just treat the transfer price as an equivalent of a purchase price from an outside supplier. Thus, when making decisions that require marginal cost data, the receiving division could suboptimize the achievement of the firm's goals.

To illustrate, consider a case that will be continued throughout the remainder of the chapter. The National Company has two divisions: the Northern and the Southern. One of the Northern Division's products, part ND-11, is used in the production of the Southern Division's product, SD-22. Cost accounting data regarding the products are summarized in Exhibit 20.2. Assume a full cost transfer price is used for part ND-11.

Now assume the Southern Division has excess capacity and is reviewing an offer from a foreign company for product SD-22. The foreign company offer was at $90 per unit. Southern rejected the offer, reasoning that their variable costs are $100 per unit. This was the correct decision for the *division*, but not for the firm. The firm's variable costs total $70 ($50 + $20), and the $90 offer would have enabled a $20 per unit contribution to the firm's fixed costs and profits. Thus, it is concluded that the full cost system is not generally acceptable for either decision making or control.

MARKET PRICES. Market price is a third possible transfer price method. If the supplying division has an external market for its product (cases 3, 6, and 9 in Exhibit 20.1), then a relatively strong case can be made for using the external market price as the transfer price. It is reasoned that the market price measures the

Exhibit 20.2   National Company Cost Accounting Data

	Northern Division Part ND-11	Southern Division Product SD-22
Direct variable cost	$50.00	$20.00
Part ND-11 (transfer)	—	80.00
Fixed costs (from below)	30.00	50.00
Total	$80.00	$150.00
Budgeted fixed costs	$750,000	$2,000,000
Direct-labor hours (DLH) at normal activity	100,000	200,000
Fixed overhead rate per DLH	$7.50	$10.00
Standard DLH allowed:		
Part ND-11	4	
Product SD-22		5
Fixed cost per unit	$30.00	$50.00

economic value of the product being transferred and is an objective way to price the exchange between two divisions. For either division, the alternative to an internal transfer is the external market.

If used, the market price would permit the recognition of profits at the supplying division and, for control purposes, would be a significant improvement over either of the two previously discussed methods. This reflects each division's contribution to company profits as measured by the market, and is the type of measurement needed for control purposes. However, as a general rule for a transfer price, the market price system is also deficient.

The method's first problem is that all products do not have an intermediate market. Second, even if an outside market exists, the use of the market price may not ensure optimal decisions. The use of such prices implies a perfect market. That is, there is an assumption that the supplying division could utilize its entire capacity by selling in the external market at the existing price. Further, there is an assumption that the product in question represents the optimal use of the supplier's capacity. By extending the previous example, we demonstrate the problems of using the market price even when it is available.

In addition to the data of Exhibit 20.2, assume the following:

Market price of ND-11	$100
Market price of SD-22	
Case A	$200
Case B	$120
Case C	$110

First, assume there is no market limitation on the amount of product ND-11 that could be sold in the intermediate market. Further, assume there is no better usage of Northern's capacity than the production of ND-11. Exhibit 20.3 shows the effect of the firm's profits for each case (A, B, and C). Assuming the transfer price is equal to the market price of $100, Exhibit 20.3 also projects the Southern Division's reported profits in each case.

Examination of the first schedule in Exhibit 20.3 reveals the preferences of the *firm* to be as follows:

Case A—Use ND-11 to produce SD-22
Case B—Indifferent between the uses of ND-11
Case C—Sell ND-11 in the external market

Using the market price as the transfer price leads to perfect congruence in each case of this situation. As the second schedule of Exhibit 20.3 reveals, the Southern Division would be motivated to buy in Case A, indifferent in Case B, and discouraged to buy in Case C.

Now consider a situation where the use of the market price does not permit goal congruence. Assume the Northern Division only produces part ND-11. Also assume that the division's normal activity has been at practical capacity. Thus, capacity is 25,000 units of ND-11 (100,000 direct-labor hours ÷ 4 hours per unit;

Exhibit 20.3   National Company Analysis of Marketing Alternatives

Contribution to Firm's Profits

	Case A		Case B		Case C	
	Sell*	Transfer*	Sell	Transfer	Sell	Transfer
Sales price	$100	$200	$100	$120	$100	$110
Variable costs						
Northern Division	$ 50	$ 50	$ 50	$ 50	$ 50	$ 50
Southern Division	—	20	—	20	—	20
Total	$ 50	$ 70	$ 50	$ 70	$ 50	$ 70
Contribution	$ 50	$130	$ 50	$ 50	$ 50	$ 40

Reported Contribution at Southern if Transferred

	Case A	Case B	Case C
Sales price	$200	$120	$110
Variable costs			
Transfer price	$100	$100	$100
Direct variable cost	20	20	20
Total	$120	$120	$120
Contribution	$ 80	$ 0	$(10)

*"Sell" means Northern sells in the outside market. "Transfer" means ND-11 is transferred to Southern for conversion into SD-22.

see Exhibit 20.2). Further, assume that at a price of $100, the Northern Division will be able to sell a maximum of 15,000 units in the external market. However, by lowering its price to $92 the external market demand could be increased to 25,000 units.

It is not clear in this situation which market price should be used, $100 or $92. However, it makes no difference which one is used in Case C (a $110 sales price for SD-22). Either of the values as a transfer price for ND-11 would result in a negative contribution to the Southern Division and discourage them from demanding the part. Is this the optimal strategy that central headquarters would want?

To answer this question, consider the alternatives from the firm's perspective. It can:

1. Keep the price of ND-11 at $100 and use the remaining 10,000-unit capacity at Northern to support production of SD-22 at Southern.
2. Lower the price of ND-11 to $92 and use all of Northern's capacity to produce for the external market.

The contribution of each of the alternatives is computed in Exhibit 20.4. As can be seen, alternative 1 is preferred by the firm. However, for Case C a market-based transfer of either $100 or $92 is not going to induce the Southern Division to elect an action that is congruent with the firm's best interests. That is, Southern's total cost would be $120 or $112 which would generate a loss if the sales price of SD-22 is $110. A system that overcomes this problem is discussed in the next section.

VARIABLE COST PLUS "APPROPRIATE" MARKUP. Another class of pricing systems is variable cost plus a markup. In practice, there is a variety of ways to determine the markup. One option computes the markup as allocated fixed costs plus a profit allowance. The profit allowance might be the amount needed for the

---

Exhibit 20.4   National Company Analysis of Second Situation

	Alternative 1	*Alternative 2*
Revenue		
ND-11: 15,000 × $100	$1,500,000	
SD-22: 10,000 × $110	1,100,000	
ND-11: 25,000 × $92		$2,300,000
Total	$2,600,000	$2,300,000
Variable costs		
Northern Division 25,000 × $50	$1,250,000	$1,250,000
Southern Division 10,000 × $20	200,000	
Total	$1,450,000	$1,250,000
Contribution margin	$1,150,000	$1,050,000

supplying division to report a fair return on sales or on assets. This concept of a markup is reasonably satisfactory for control purposes because there is an attempt to recognize the contribution that each participating division made toward the total earned profits. However, for decision-making purposes, the system is not satisfactory.

The flaw for decision-making purposes is the same as the full cost pricing system. Not only is there a chance that the selling division's fixed costs will be misused by the buying division in making marginal decisions, but the profit allowance may also be treated as if it is an out-of-pocket cost for the firm. Because of the profit allowance, the divisions making the marketing decisions will not even have correct knowledge of the normalized, or average, production costs. Thus, nonoptimal long-run strategies may be selected.

Another variation of this system is a price equal to variable cost plus the opportunity cost incurred *by the selling division* in accepting the intracompany business. The rationale for this price is that a potential buying division should be discouraged from using another division's output if the buying division cannot earn a return in excess of what the selling division could earn through an alternative use of its capacity. Using previous examples, the acceptability of this method for decision-making purposes is now demonstrated.

Reconsider the previous problem involving the Northern and Southern divisions of the National Company. Return to the assumption that the Northern Division could sell at $100 as much of part ND-11 in the external market as is permitted by the division's capacity. Thus, sale to an internal division is feasible only if external sales are reduced. The reduction in external sales represents Northern's opportunity cost. Foregoing an outside sale results in a lost contribution of $50 ($100 sales price less $50 variable cost). Thus, the transfer price system being explored in this section is:

$$\text{Transfer price} = \text{Variable cost} + \text{Opportunity cost}$$
$$= \$50 + \$50$$
$$= \$100$$

Since the transfer price is $100, the results for cases A, B, and C are the same as in Exhibit 20.3. It was demonstrated in Exhibit 20.3 that a $100 transfer price resulted in goal congruence. The transfer price in this situation equals the external market price, but it cannot be assumed that the system of this section always yields this as the result. A different result is illustrated in the next example.

The modified situation of the National Company problem, as discussed in the previous section, illustrated a failure of the market price scheme. Let us now use the system of this section to determine a transfer price for the modified problem. When there is a market constraint on the seller's product, it is more difficult to determine the opportunity cost. For the first 10,000 units sold to Southern, Northern's opportunity cost is the difference between the payoff earned by using the 25,000-unit capacity for external sales and using only 15,000 units of capacity for external sales. Northern can sell 25,000 units in the external market *only if the sales price is reduced to $92*. Thus, the opportunity cost is:

Payoff of selling 25,000 units of
 ND-11 in external market (92 − 50)25,000 $1,050,000
Payoff of selling 15,000 units of
 ND-11 in external market (100 − 50)15,000   750,000
Opportunity cost of selling 10,000 units
 of ND-11 to Southern $ 300,000

The opportunity cost per unit sold to Southern is $30 ($300,000 ÷ 10,000). Thus, the transfer price is:

Transfer price = Variable cost + Opporunity cost
              = $50 + $30
              = $80

If Southern is charged $80 for ND-11, then its total variable cost is $100 ($20 + $80). Thus, in case C (market price of SD-22 equal to $110; see page 719) Southern could earn a contribution of $10 per unit by accepting the transfer and would be motivated to do so. As was shown in Exhibit 20.4, Northern should use 10,000 units of its capacity to produce for Southern. Thus, the $80 price achieves congruence.

An $80 transfer price is only correct for the first 10,000 units of ND-11 transferred, however. Since Northern can sell up to 15,000 units by keeping its sales price at $100, the opportunity cost for transferring units in excess of 10,000 is $50 ($100 − $50). Thus, in order to achieve proper decision making through the pricing mechanism, the following schedule for transfers would have to be in effect:

Units	Price
0–10,000	$ 80
10,001–25,000	100

To further illustrate the adequacy of the pricing mechanism proposed in this section, assume the price of Southern's product, SD-22, is $100, rather than $110. Then, the *firm's* per unit contribution of transferring part ND-11 to the Southern Division for the production of SD-22 is $30 ($100 − $50 − $20). This is the same as the per unit contribution that Northern would earn if the external sales price of ND-11 is lowered to $92. That is, as shown previously, lowering the price to $92 so that the additional 10,000 units could be externally sold results in a $300,000 increase in the total contribution, an average of $30. Since the per-unit contribution margins are the same for each alternative action for the 10,000 units, the firm is indifferent as to which course of action is taken. The advantage of the proposed system is demonstrated by noting that the Southern Division is *also* indifferent with a transfer price of $80. That is, its per unit contribution is $0 ($100 − $80 − $20).

Further examination of the proposal in this section is warranted. Suppose the product being transferred has no external market. Is it possible for the supplying division to incur an opportunity cost? Two possibilities are considered. If the selling division produces several products, then the capacity needed for the transferred product may have to be generated by reducing the output of one or more other products. The opportunity costs incurred as a result of transferring the product internally would be equal to the sacrificed profits caused by the diversion of resources from the production of other products to the production of the transferred product.

If the supplying division produces a single product that has no external market, then opportunity costs could be measured by the cash flows forgone by having funds invested in the facilities. That is, the alternative to using the capacity for internally consumed output is to spinoff the investment in facilities and use the funds in an alternative way.

Another difficulty in measuring opportunity costs arises if the supplying division has multiple limited resources. If, for example, labor time, machine time, and material are all available in limited quantities, then what does it cost to shift some combination of these resources to produce a product that is transferred to another division? Each of the products at the supplying division will most likely require a different mix of the three resources. Thus, the measurement of the opportunity cost is more involved than computing the impact of trading a unit of one product for a unit of another. (Linear programming is a possible approach to measuring opportunity costs in these cases.)

If there are multiple internal consuming divisions, then even more measurement difficulties arise. For example, the alternative of Division A selling to Division B might be selling to Division C. How would Division A's opportunity cost be measured? Its computation would depend on a transfer price to Division C. The transfer price to Division C might, in turn, be a function of the transfer price to Division B. Thus, we are caught in a vicious circle.

Finally, when there are multiple consuming divisions, an optimal pricing system may be one that charges each division a different price for the same product. Although it may be possible to defend such a structure economically, it probably will be difficult for the system to gain any degree of understanding and acceptance on the part of the various division managers.

In summary of the decision-making implications, the concept of a transfer price being variable cost plus an opportunity cost is very appealing. The major problem is measuring the opportunity cost. Except for the measurement problem, however, there appear to be few valid objections to this system.

Not yet mentioned is the adequacy of this system for evaluation purposes. Assuming it is workable, the objections for control purposes are minimal. The revenue recognizable by the supplying division is such that its income would be *no lower* than if it used its resources in an alternative way. This is a reasonably fair way of measuring the worth of the division's contribution to the total effort of all participating divisions. One potential problem, however, would arise if the supplying division actually had no alternative use of its resources and, therefore, no opportunity cost. No profits would accrue to such a division if the proposed transfer price is used, and it might be hard to defend a position that the division did not contribute to the total accomplishment. On the other hand, it might be hard to find a case where there is no alternative use of the resources. Alternatively, we might argue that the division is not a profit center. Perhaps it should be evaluated as a cost center rather than a profit center.

NEGOTIATED PRICES. A fifth approach to transfer pricing is negotiation. Rather than central headquarters trying to establish a price, they could, in the spirit of total autonomy, let the two divisional managers involved in a potential transfer reach a mutually acceptable *negotiated transfer price*. In a sense, this parallels the activity in an open market. The product's value to the consumer is not based on its cost, but on what the consumer is willing to pay after all bargaining is completed.

A negotiation system will work only if all divisional managers *are truly free to bargain* and are allowed complete autonomy. If there is no other market for the product and no alternative use for the facilities, then the manager of the supplying unit is *not free* to bargain. The manager of the supplying division has no alternative in this case and must meet all of the buyer's demands. Also, a consuming division must be able to acquire the product or an acceptable substitute from an outside supplier or have the ability to use its facilities in a way that would be independent of the supplying division. Otherwise, the manager would have to meet all of the demands of the seller.

The firm may have to be willing to incur some short-term losses while the bargaining process converges to an optimal price. If central headquarters observes that agreed-upon prices are not optimal, it must refrain from interfering or the managers may perceive they have no real bargaining power. Subject to these conditions, a system of negotiation may be acceptable from the viewpoint of both decision making and control.

Is It Possible To Resolve the Conflicts?

Decentralization creates several problems. Some decisions that are made by managers of a decentralized unit are suboptimal from the firm's point of view. Single transfer prices for each product are the norm and contribute to suboptimization. A single price may not be the correct price for all buying divisions or for both decision making and control. But there are some practical reasons for having only one price for each product. Of course, as pointed out earlier, the cost of the suboptimal decisions is presumably recovered through other advantages. In this section there is a discussion of possible ways to minimize the conflicts.

Except for the variable cost plus opportunity cost system, no other adequately serves the two major uses of a transfer price, decision making and control. When it becomes impractical to measure the opportunity cost, what can be done? One solution is to deliberately select one of the purposes to serve adequately and recognize the limitations when used for the other purpose. For example, it might be decided to design a transfer pricing system that primarily serves decision-making needs and then make some adjustments for the unfavorable consequences in performance evaluation. On the other hand, if the decisions to be made are relatively insensitive to the transfer price, then a system should be selected that best measures a division's contribution toward the total accomplishment. That is, concentrate on constructing a good control system.

Some authors have gone so far as to propose a dual pricing system. That is, one price should be used for decision-making purposes and another for control. This can be implemented by charging the purchasing division with a decision-making-oriented price and crediting the selling division with a control-oriented price. The difference would be charged to central headquarters.

Several versions of a dual price system may be possible. Space permits only a sampling of the schemes. One possibility is to credit the selling division with full cost plus an allocated share of the total profits realized by the firm. For example, assume that three divisions are involved in the production of one of the firm's products. The following data have been compiled for a product that is sold for $180:

	Division A	Division B	Division C	Total
Variable cost	$30	$40	$50	$120
Normalized fixed cost	$20	$30	$40	$ 90

Some firms, in response to this situation, will allocate the total contribution margin among the divisions using a variable cost base. Thus, the contribution margin of $60 ($180 − $120) would be divided as follows:

$$\text{To A: } \$60 \times \frac{\$30}{\$120} = \$15$$

$$\text{To B: } \$60 \times \frac{\$40}{\$120} = \$20$$

$$\text{To C: } \$60 \times \frac{\$50}{\$120} = \$25$$

When the transfer is made from Division A to Division B, the dual price version proposed here results in a $65 sale for A ($30 variable cost + $20 fixed cost + $15 allocated contribution margin). Similarly, when the transfer is made from B to C, B's sales would be credited for $90, $40 variable cost + $30 fixed cost + $20 allocated contribution margin, *plus* an allowance for A's costs depending upon the accounting methods being used for prior divisions' costs.

The advantage of the dual system is that A's sales price does not have to be B's purchase price. In this example it is not necessary to charge Division B $65 for the product they purchase from A. Instead, B could be charged with A's standard variable cost plus some fixed cost. Further, the fixed cost would not have to be charged on a unit basis. Charging fixed costs by the unit cost method would cause them to be viewed as a variable cost by Division B. Instead, B could be charged with a lump sum amount of A's fixed cost commensurate with the benefit these costs contribute to the buying division. This is similar to the dual-based distribution system discussed in the service department accounting of Chapter 9. Such a method would enable receiving departments to have correct knowledge of the *firm's* cost behavior patterns. However, the method of incorporating prior divisions' costs into the price to be credited to the selling division remains a dilemma. One possibility is to average the fixed costs transferred into a division over the division's normal output, just as is done with the indirect fixed costs. One of the end-of-chapter problems requires consideration of the details of this proposal.

It is not possible to expect the solution of the transfer pricing problem to be an easy one. All that can be suggested is that fairness of evaluation and proper decision-making support be kept in mind. If one of these objectives is given more emphasis than the other, then some allowance may be needed when using the price for other purposes.

Summary

Transfer prices can be dysfunctional if they are not established by a reasoned approach. This chapter demonstrated the various approaches that are used and highlighted the problems of each. If feasible, the transfer price should be variable cost plus the opportunity cost attributable to the use of the resources for the transferred product. If an intermediate market exists for the product, the market price will be appropriate unless the market is imperfect. Then, the market price transfer may not lead to the desired congruence.

In some cases it is not appropriate to use a single price for all purposes requiring a transfer price. Yet, it may not be practical to have multiple prices. Thus, the accountant must work carefully with management to ensure the overall appropriateness of the price that is used.

The new key terms and concepts in this chapter include:

Transfer price
Negotiated transfer price

SELF-STUDY PROBLEM. The Virdon Company has two divisions, Left and Right. The Left Division has a practical capacity of 100,000 direct-labor hours per period. Its fixed costs amount to $500,000 and its variable labor and overhead costs are expected to be $10 per labor hour.

For the past several periods the Right Division has had an idle capacity of 50,000 machine hours. To use the capacity, Right is considering the production of product R2D2. A unit of R2D2 would need one pound of a special metal, L-1, *which can only be acquired from the Left Division.* In addition to L-1, product R2D2 would require $10 of other materials and two machine hours in order to produce it in the Right Division. Overhead costs are expected to be $15 per machine hour. There is no direct labor in the Right Division. The division's fixed costs are assigned at a rate of $8 per machine hour.

The specifications for a pound of metal L-1 in the Left Division are:

Labor hours   4
Materials $10 total

Required:

1. Assume R2D2 can be sold at $120 and that the Left Division has no other use for its capacity other than the production of L-1. At what price would you transfer L-1 to the Right Division? Why?
2. Now assume that the Right Division has the same situation as described above including the facts in part 1. Further, assume that the Left Division can produce product L-200 in addition to L-1. L-200 would be sold at $100 per pound in the external market. Its requirements per pound are:

   Materials $20
   Labor time   5 hours

   Both R2D2 and L-200 have market demands that would consume all of the available capacity at Virdon. What is the optimal way for Virdon to use the capacity of the Left Division?
3. Continue part 2. Assume that the transfer price for L-1 will be variable cost plus opportunity cost. Determine the per-pound transfer price for L-1.
4. Will the transfer price determined in part 3 cause the divisional managers to select actions in keeping with the optimal solution identified in part 2?
5. What price must the Right Division be able to get for product R2D2 so that the company would be indifferent to whether the Left Division's capacity was used to produce L-1 or L-200?
6. Given the minimum price for R2D2 determined in part 5, what would the Left Division's reaction be to the transfer price determined in part 3?

Solution to Self-Study Problem

1. In order to send proper "messages" for short-run decision making, a transfer price should be variable cost plus opportunity cost. In this case, the Left Division has no other alternative use for its capacity and, therefore, no opportunity cost. Thus:

   Transfer price for L-1 = Variable cost + $0
   $$= [\$10 + 4(\$10)] + 0 = \$50$$

2. There are two alternatives:
   A. Use Left's capacity for L-1. The capacity at Left will enable 25,000 pounds of L-1 to be produced (100,000 labor hours ÷ 4 labor hours per pound). A production of 25,000 pounds of L-1 will enable 25,000 units of R2D2 to be produced in the Right Division. This would require 50,000 machine hours (25,000 × 2) and would use the remainder of Right's capacity.
   B. Use Left's capacity for L-200. The capacity at Left will enable 20,000 pounds of L-200 to be produced (100,000 labor hours ÷ 5 labor hours per pound).
   The contribution of each of these alternatives is:

	A	B
Sales		
R2D2 25,000 × $120	$3,000,000	
L-200 20,000 × $100		$2,000,000
Variable cost		
Left Division		
L-1: 25,000($10 + 4 × $10)	$1,250,000	
L-200: 20,000($20 + 5 × $10)		$1,400,000
Right Division		
R2D2: 25,000($10 + 2 × $15)	1,000,000	
Total	$2,250,000	$1,400,000
Contribution	$ 750,000	$ 600,000

The firm, therefore, would prefer the Left Division to use all of its capacity in producing L-1 (alternative A).

3. Now, the Left Division has an alternative use of its capacity. It can use it to produce 20,000 pounds of L-200. If, instead, the labor capacity is used to produce L-1, then Left cannot produce L-200. As can be seen from alternative B in part 2, L-200 will contribute $600,000 toward profits at the Left Division. Therefore, the opportunity cost of using all of its capacity to produce L-1 is $600,000. This averages $24 per pound of L-1 ($600,000 ÷ 25,000). Thus:

Transfer price of L-1 = Variable cost + Opportunity cost
                     = $50 + $24
                     = $74

4. A transfer price of $74 will result in a per unit variable cost for R2D2 of $114:

L-1	$ 74.00
Other material	10.00
Overhead cost 2 × $15	30.00
	$114.00

Right can still earn a contribution toward fixed costs and profits of $6.00 per unit ($120 − $114). Thus, they should still demand L-1 from the Left Division. This is congruent with the results in part 2.

5. To answer this, use the results in part 2. The price of R2D2 that would cause indifference is the one that would generate an income of $600,000 (the same as alternative B). Let p be that price. Then:

25,000p − 2,250,000 = 600,000
25,000p = 2,850,000
      p = 114

6. The Right Division would also be indifferent. It was shown in part 4 that their variable cost per unit would be $114 if the transfer price of L-1 was $74. If R2D2 sold for $114, then the Right Division would have no contribution to their own profits considering the

transfer price of L-1 is $74. Again, there is goal congruence. Both the firm and the Right Division are indifferent.

References

Abdel-khalik, A.R., and Lusk, E.J. "Transfer Pricing—A Synthesis," *The Accounting Review* (January 1974): 8–23.

Dopuch, N., and Drake, D.F. "Accounting Implications of a Mathematical Programming Approach to the Transfer Price Problem," *Journal of Accounting Research* (Spring 1964): 10–24.

Godfrey, J. "Short-Run Planning in a Decentralized Firm," *The Accounting Review* (April 1971): 286–297.

Hirshleifer, J. "On the Economics of Transfer Pricing," *The Journal of Business* (July 1956): 172–184.

Solomons, D. *Divisional Performance: Measurement and Control.* New York: Financial Executives Research Foundation, 1965.

Watson, D.J.H., and Baumler, J.V. "Transfer Pricing: A Behavioral Context," *The Accounting Review* (July 1975): 466–474.

Problems

20-1. Adapted CMA Problem on Basics of Transfer Pricing. MBR Inc. consists of three divisions that formerly were three independent manufacturing companies. The three divisions have operated as if they were still independent companies. Each division has its own sales force and production facilities. Each division management is responsible for sales, cost of operations, acquisition and financing of divisional assets, and working capital management. The corporate management of MBR evaluates the performance of the divisions and division managements on the basis of return on investment.

Mitchell Division has just been awarded a contract for a product that uses a component manufactured by the Roach Division as well as by outside suppliers. Mitchell used a cost figure of $3.80 for the component manufactured by Roach in preparing its bid for the new product. This cost figure was supplied by Roach in response to Mitchell's request for the average variable cost of the component and represents the standard variable manufacturing cost and variable selling and distribution expense.

Roach has an active sales force that is continually soliciting new prospects. Roach's regular selling price for the component Mitchell needs for the new product is $6.50. Sales of this component are expected to increase. However, the Roach management has indicated that it could supply Mitchell with the required quantities of the component at the regular selling price less variable selling and distribution expenses. Mitchell's management has responded by offering to pay standard variable manufacturing cost plus 20%.

The two divisions have been unable to agree on a transfer price. Corporate management has never established a transfer price policy because interdivisional transactions have never occurred. As a compromise, the corporate vice-president of finance has suggested a price equal to the standard full manufacturing cost (that is, no selling and distribution expenses) plus a 15% markup. This price has also been rejected by the two division managers, because each considered it grossly unfair.

The unit cost structure for the Roach component, and the three suggested prices are as follows:

Regular selling price	$6.50
Standard variable manufacturing cost	$3.20
Standard fixed manufacturing cost	1.20
Variable selling and distribution expenses	0.60
Total	$5.00
Regular selling price less variable selling and distribution expense ($6.50 − $0.60)	$5.90
Variable manufacturing cost plus 20% ($3.20 × 1.20)	$3.84
Standard full manufacturing cost plus 15% ($4.40 × 1.15)	$5.06

Required:

1. Discuss the effect each of the three proposed prices might have on the Roach division management's attitude toward intracompany business.
2. Is the negotiation of a price between the Mitchell and Roach divisions a satisfactory method to solve the transfer price problem? Explain your answer.
3. Should the corporate management of MBR Inc. become involved in this transfer price controversy? Explain your answer.

20-2. Adapted CMA Problem on Selecting Proper Transfer Price. The Lorax Electric Company manufactures a large variety of systems and individual components for the electronics industry. The firm is organized into several divisions, with division managers given the authority to make virtually all operating decisions. Management control over divisional operations is maintained by a system of divisional profit and return-on-investment measures that are reviewed regularly by top management. The top management of Lorax has been quite pleased with the effectiveness of the system they have been using and believe that it is responsible for the company's improved profitability over the last few years.

The Devices Division manufactures solid-state devices and is operating at capacity. The Systems Division has asked the Devices Division to supply a large quantity of integrated circuit IC378. The Devices Division currently is selling this component to its regular customers at $40 per hundred.

The Systems Division, which is operating at about 60% capacity, wants this particular component for a digital clock system. It has an opportunity to supply large quantities of these digital clock systems to Centonic Electric, a major producer of clock radios and other popular electronic home entertainment equipment. This is the first opportunity any of the Lorax divisions have had to do business with Centonic Electric. Centonic Electric has offered to pay $7.50 per clock system.

The Systems Division prepared an analysis of the probable costs to produce the clock systems. The amount that could be paid to the Devices Division for the integrated circuits was determined by working backward from the selling price. The cost estimates employed by the division reflected the highest per unit cost the Systems Division could incur for each cost component and still leave a sufficient margin so that the division's income statement could show reasonable improvement. The cost estimates are summarized here.

Proposed selling price		$7.50
Costs excluding required integrated circuits (IC378)		
Components purchased from outside suppliers	$2.75	
Circuit board etching—labor and variable overhead	0.40	
Assembly, testing, packaging—labor and variable overhead	1.35	
Fixed overhead allocations	1.50	
Profit margin	0.50	6.50
Amount that can be paid for integrated circuits IC378 (5 @ $20 per hundred)		$1.00

As a result of this analysis, the Systems Division offered the Devices Division a price of $20 per hundred for the integrated circuit. This bid was refused by the manager of the Devices Division because he felt the Systems Division should at least meet the price of $40 per hundred that regular customers pay. When the Systems Division found that it could not obtain a comparable integrated circuit from outside vendors, the situation was brought to an arbitration committee that had been set up to review such problems.

The arbitration committee prepared an analysis that showed that $0.15 would cover variable costs of producing the integrated circuit, $0.28 would cover the full cost including fixed overhead, and $0.35 would provide a gross margin equal to the average gross margin on all of the products sold by the Devices Division. The manager of the Systems Division reacted by stating, "They could sell us that integrated circuit for $0.20 and still earn a positive contribution toward profit. In fact, they should be required to sell at their variable cost—$0.15, and not be allowed to take advantage of us."

Lou Belcher, manager of Devices, countered by arguing that, "It doesn't make sense to sell to the Systems Division at $20 per hundred when we can get $40 per hundred outside on all we can produce. In fact, Systems could pay us up to almost $60 per hundred and they would still have a positive contribution to profit."

The recommendation of the committee, to set the price at $0.35 per unit ($35 per hundred), so that Devices could earn a fair gross margin, was rejected by both division managers. Consequently, the problem was brought to the attention of the vice-president of operations.

Required:

1. What is the immediate economic effect on the Lorax Company as a whole if the Devices Division were required to supply IC378 to the Systems Division at $0.35 per unit—the price recommended by the arbitration committee? Explain your answer.
2. Discuss the advisability of intervention by top management as a solution to transfer pricing disputes between division managers such as the one experienced by Lorax Electric Company.
3. Suppose that Lorax adopted a policy of requiring that the price to be paid in all internal transfers by the buying division be equal to the variable costs per unit of the selling division for that product and that the supplying division be required to sell if the buying divi-

sion decided to buy the item. Discuss the consequences of adopting such a policy as a way of avoiding the need for the arbitration committee or for intervention by the vice-president.
4. Suggest an alternative transfer price that would overcome some of the problems mentioned. Show how it would result in goal congruence.

20-3. Adapted CMA Problem on Using Transfer Prices to Achieve Goal Congruence. The Ajax division of Gunnco, operating at capacity, has been asked by the Defco division of Gunnco Corp. to supply it with electrical fitting 1726. Ajax sells this part to its regular customers for $7.50 each. Defco, which is operating at 50% capacity, is willing to pay $5.00 each for the fitting. This is the full absorption cost per unit at Ajax. Defco will put the fitting into a brake unit it is manufacturing for a commercial airplane manufacturer. The contract with the airplane manufacturer calls for reimbursement of full cost to Gunnco plus 10%.

Ajax has a variable cost of producing fitting 1726 of $4.25. The cost of the brake unit as being built by Defco is as follows:

Purchased parts—outside vendors	$22.50
Ajax fitting—1726	5.00
Other variable costs	14.00
Fixed overhead and administration	8.00
	$49.50

The company uses return on investment and dollar profits in the measurement of division and divisional manager performance.

Required:

1. Consider that you are the division controller of Ajax. Would you recommend that Ajax supply fitting 1726 to Defco? (Ignore any income tax issues.) Why or why not?
2. Would it be to the short-run economic advantage of the Gunnco Corporation for the Ajax division to supply Defco division with fitting 1726 at $5.00 each? (Ignore any income tax issues.) Explain your answer.
3. Suggest an alternative transfer price and show how it could lead to goal congruence.

20-4. Negotiating Transfer Prices When ROI is Used. The UI Company has two divisions, U and I. Division U produces product X, which it sells in an outside market as well as to Division I, which processes it to produce product Z. The manager of Division I has expressed her opinion that the transfer price is too high. The two division managers are about to enter into discussions to resolve the conflict, and the manager of Division U wants you to supply him with some information before the discussions. Division U has been selling 80,000 units to outsiders and 20,000 units to Division I, all at $10.00 per unit. It is not anticipated that these demands will change. The variable cost is $6.00 per unit, and the fixed costs are $195,000. The average available assets have been $1,000,000.

The Division U manager anticipates that Division I will want a transfer price of $9.00. If he does not sell to Division I, $15,000 of fixed cost and $300,000 of assets can be eliminated. The manager of Division U would have no control over the proceeds from the sale of the assets and is judged primarily on his rate of return.

Required:

1. Should he sell to Division I at $9.00? Support your decision with detailed calculations.
2. What is the lowest price that the Division U manager should accept? Support your decision with detailed calculations.

20-5. CMA Problem: Decision Making When There Is a Transfer Price. National Industries is a diversified corporation with separate and distinct operating divisions. Each division's performance is evaluated on the basis of total dollar profits and return-on-division investment.

The WindAir Division manufactures and sells air-conditioner units. The coming year's budgeted income statement, based upon a sales volume of 15,000 units, follows.

	Per Unit	Total (000 omitted)
Sales revenue	$400	$6,000
Manufacturing costs		
Compressor	$ 70	$1,050
Other raw materials	37	555
Direct labor	30	450
Variable overhead	45	675
Fixed overhead	32	480
Total manufacturing costs	$214	$3,210
Gross margin	$186	$2,790
Operating expenses		
Variable selling	$ 18	$ 270
Fixed selling	19	285
Fixed administrative	38	570
Total operating expenses	$ 75	$1,125
Net income before taxes	$111	$1,665

WindAir's division manager believes sales can be increased if the unit selling price of air conditioners is reduced. A market research study conducted by an independent firm at the request of the manager indicates that a 5% reduction in the selling price ($20) would increase sales volume 16% or 2,400 units. WindAir has sufficient production capacity to manage this increased volume with no increase in fixed costs.

At the present time WindAir uses a compressor in its units which it purchases from an outside supplier at a cost of $70 per compressor. The division manager of WindAir has approached the manager of the Compressor Division regarding the sale of a compressor unit to WindAir. The Compressor Division currently manufactures and sells a unit exclusively to outside firms that is similar to the unit used by WindAir. The specifications of the WindAir compressor are slightly different which would reduce the Compressor Division's raw material cost by $1.50 per unit. In addition, the Compressor Division would not incur any variable selling costs for the units sold to WindAir. The manager of WindAir wants all of the compressors it uses to come from one supplier and has offered to pay $50 for each compressor unit.

The Compressor Division has the capacity to produce 75,000 units. The coming year's budgeted income statement for the Compressor Division follows and is based upon a sales volume of 64,000 units without considering WindAir's proposal.

	Per Unit	Total (000 omitted)
Sales revenue	$100	$6,400
Manufacturing costs		
Raw materials	$ 12	$ 768
Direct labor	8	512
Variable overhead	10	640
Fixed overhead	11	704
Total manufacturing costs	$ 41	$2,624
Gross margin	$ 59	$3,776
Operating expenses		
Variable selling	$ 6	$ 384
Fixed selling	4	256
Fixed administrative	7	448
Total operating expenses	$ 17	$1,088
Net income before taxes	$ 42	$2,688

Required:

1. Should WindAir Division institute the 5% price reduction on its air-conditioner units even if it cannot acquire the compressors internally for $50 each? Support your conclusion with appropriate calculations.

2. Without prejudice to your answer to part 1, assume WindAir needs 17,400 units. Should the Compressor Division be willing to supply the compressor units for $50 each? Support your conclusions with appropriate calculations.

3. Without prejudice to your answer to part 1, assume WindAir needs 17,400 units. Would it be in the best interest of National Industries for the Compressor Division to supply the compressor units at $50 each to the WindAir Division? Support your conclusions with appropriate calculations.

20-6. CMA Problem: Transfer Pricing and Nonlinear Profit Function. A.R. Oma, Inc. manufactures a line of men's perfumes and after-shaving lotions. The manufacturing process is basically a series of mixing operations with the addition of certain aromatic and coloring ingredients; the finished product is packaged in a company-produced glass bottle and packed in cases containing six bottles.

A.R. Oma feels that the sale of its product is heavily influenced by the appearance and appeal of the bottle and has, therefore, devoted considerable managerial effort to the bottle production process. This has resulted in the development of certain unique bottle production processes in which management takes considerable pride.

The two areas (perfume production and bottle manufacture) have evolved over the years in an almost independent manner; in fact, a rivalry has developed between management personnel over which division is the more important to A.R. Oma. This attitude is probably intensified because the bottle manufacturing plant was purchased intact ten years ago, and no real interchange of management personnel or ideas (except at the top corporate level) has taken place.

Since the acquisition, all bottle production has been absorbed by the perfume manufacturing plant. Each area is considered a separate profit center and evaluated as such. As the new corporate controller, you are responsible for the definition of a proper transfer value to use in crediting the bottle production profit center and in debiting the packaging profit center.

At your request, the bottle division general manager has asked certain other bottle manufacturers to quote a price for the quantity and sizes demanded by the perfume division. These competitive prices are:

Volume	Total Price	Price per Case
2,000,000 equivalent cases*	$ 4,000,000	$2.00
4,000,000	$ 7,000,000	$1.75
6,000,000	$10,000,000	$1.67

*An equivalent case represents six bottles each.

A cost analysis of the internal bottle plant indicates that they can produce bottles at these costs.

Volume	Total Price	Cost per Case
2,000,000 equivalent cases	$ 3,200,000	$1.60
4,000,000	$ 5,200,000	$1.30
6,000,000	$ 7,200,000	$1.20

(Your cost analysts point out that these costs represent fixed costs of $1,200,000 and variable costs of $1.00 per equivalent case.)

These figures have given rise to considerable corporate discussion as to the proper value to use in the transfer of bottles to the perfume division. This interest is heightened because a significant portion of a division manager's income is an incentive bonus based on profit center results.

The perfume production division has the following costs in addition to the bottle costs:

Volume	Total Cost	Cost per Case
2,000,000 cases	$16,400,000	$8.20
4,000,000	$32,400,000	$8.10
6,000,000	$48,400,000	$8.07

After considerable analysis, the marketing research department furnished you with the following price-demand relationship for the finished product:

Sales Volume	Total Sales Revenue	Sales Price per Unit
2,000,000 cases	$25,000,000	$12.50
4,000,000	$45,600,000	$11.40
6,000,000	$63,900,000	$10.65

Required:

1. The A.R. Oma Company has used market prices as transfer prices in the past. Using the current market prices and costs, and assuming a volume of 6,000,000 cases, calculate the income for
   a. The bottle division.
   b. The perfume division.
   c. The corporation.
2. Is this production and sales level the most profitable volume for
   a. The bottle division?
   b. The perfume division?
   c. The corporation?
   Explain your answer.

20-7. Transfer Pricing in a Nonlinear Situation. The Laskey Company has two divisions, Toledo and San Francisco. The Toledo Division produces product G, which it can sell externally and/or transfer to the San Francisco Division for use in producing product B. (One G is needed for each B.) The revenue function for both products G and B are "nonlinear" in that higher demands can be achieved only with lower sales prices. Likewise, both divisions' cost functions are nonlinear.

Following are estimates of total sales and costs for various levels of product activity. For puposes of this problem it is appropriate to consider only the levels included in these estimates.

Toledo Division:

G Sales (units)	Total G Sales	Production Volume	Total Toledo Costs
10,000	$290,000	10,000	$ 250,000
20,000	480,000	20,000	490,000
30,000	690,000	30,000	750,000
40,000	880,000	40,000	1,040,000

San Francisco Division:

B Volume (units)	Total B Sales	San Francisco Costs (excluding transfer cost)
10,000	$ 400,000	$100,000
20,000	760,000	180,000
30,000	960,000	250,000
40,000	1,240,000	330,000

Required:

1. From the viewpoint of the firm how should the capacity of the Toledo Division be used? That is, how many units should Toledo sell externally and how many should it transfer to the San Francisco Division? Support your answer.
2. Suppose the transfer price on product G was set at $29 ($290,000 ÷ 10,000) which is the going market price. Would it be reasonable to expect the two divisions to "settle" on the solution you found in part 1? Why?
3. Now consider a proposal to set the transfer price as variable cost plus opportunity cost. Your assistant at the Toledo Division is having trouble implementing this. He reasons

that if the cost structure was linear, then the transfer price would be variable cost until the idle capacity is exhausted. Then the transfer price would be variable cost plus opportunity cost. However, he is not sure what variable cost to use. He presents the following schedule:

First 10,000 units transferred, transfer price = ?
Second 10,000 units transferred, transfer price = ?
Third 10,000 units transferred, transfer price = ?
Fourth 10,000 units transferred, transfer price = 29
    29 = (250,000/10,000) + 40,000/10,000

How would you recommend completing the schedule?

4. Show that your transfer price system in part 3 will cause the San Francisco Division to order the proper amount from the Toledo Division.

5. Another proposal from the Toledo Division is for a $30 transfer price on product G. It was derived as follows. Let's assume we use the second 10,000 units produced as those we sell externally. This would give us a $50,000 profit [290,000 − (490,000 − 250,000)]. Then send the first 10,000 units of G to the San Francisco Division. The variable cost is $25 per unit and the transfer price is $25 plus a $5 opportunity cost per unit. Evaluate the price in terms of goal congruence.

20-8. Situational Cases on Transfer Pricing. The ZAP Company has two divisions, Atlanta and Boston. One of the parts produced by the Atlanta division is used in the production of a product that is assembled at the Boston division. This part is not unique, and there is a readily defined market such that Atlanta can sell outside the firm and Boston can buy outside.

The following information is descriptive of the normal expectations for the Atlanta division:

Capacity to produce the part	12,500 units
External sales at $50 per unit	10,000 units
Sales to Boston	2,500 units
Costs:	
Variable manufacturing per unit	$42.00
Variable selling costs (if external; not incurred on internal transfers)	1.00
Fixed manufacturing (based on 12,500 units)	3.00
Fixed selling (based on 10,000 units)	0.50

The Boston division presents the following data based on the assumption of a volume of 2,500 units (one part is needed for each unit of B's output):

Variable manufacturing cost per unit (exclusive of transfer price or outside purchase price)	$ 40.00
Variable selling expense per unit	13.00

Fixed manufacturing cost	5.00
Fixed selling expense	2.00
Selling price of finished product	120.00

Required:

1. If Atlanta could sell 12,500 units at $50 each in the outside market, what transfer price would central management prefer in order to have proper motivation on the part of the Boston division?
2. As controller of the Boston division, would you advise buying at the transfer price determined in part 1? Show why or why not.
3. Assume the situation and the transfer price determined in part 1. If Boston's selling price dropped to $100, would Boston buy at that price? Would this be the proper act from the standpoint of the firm? Why?
4. Assume that Atlanta did not have an outside demand in excess of 10,000 units and could reduce its total fixed manufacturing cost by 10% if the volume were reduced to 10,000 units. What is the appropriate transfer price for motivation purposes?
5. Suppose that Atlanta's maximum outside market is 11,000 units at the $50 price, and there is no other usage for the capacity and no way to increase the demand for the product. What transfer price(s) would central management prefer for motivational purposes?
6. Suppose Boston's selling price is $90 instead of $120. Further, assume that one of Boston's customers is also a customer of the Atlanta division. Boston refuses to buy the part on the outside market at $50 since the selling price of $90 would not be high enough to even cover the variable costs. If Atlanta does not lower the transfer price, then Boston will not sell to this customer, who, in turn, will probably cancel the usual order of 5,000 units from Atlanta. There is no other demand for the product and no other usage of Atlanta's capacity. Fixed costs would not change at either division. What would you advise the Atlanta management to accept as the lowest transfer price? Support your recommendation with computations.

20-9. Continuation of Self-Study Problem. Reconsider the Virdon Company in the self-study problem. Continue the assumption that the Left Division can produce both L-1 and L-200. Now, assume that the external market for L-200 is limited to 10,000 pounds. The Right Division can sell all the R2D2 it can manufacture at $120. What transfer price(s) should be used for L-1? What might be the reaction to these prices?

20-10. Additional Situations Using Case in Self-Study Problem. Reconsider the self-study problem but assume that product L-1 can be sold externally as well as internally. Initially, assume the intermediate market price of product L-1 is $70 per pound.

Required:

1. Assume there are no market constraints for products L-1, L-200, and R2D2. What is the optimal way for the Virdon Company to use the capacity of the Left Division? Support your answer.
2. Assume that the transfer price for L-1 is to be variable cost plus opportunity cost. Determine the per-pound transfer price. Will it cause the divisional managers to select solutions in keeping with your solution to part 1?
3. Now suppose that the market price for L-1 is $75 per pound. What transfer price would you recommend? Will it induce optimal actions? Why? Assume that R2D2 still sells at $120 per unit.

4. Repeat part 3, but assume the market price for L-1 is $80 per pound.
5. Assume again that the market price for L-1 is $70 per pound. Further, assume the external sales of L-1 are limited to 5,000 pounds and that the market for L-200 is limited to 10,000 pounds. What transfer price would you recommend? Why?
6. Repeat part 5, but assume that the market price of L-1 is $75 per pound.

20-11. Transfer Pricing When There Are Multiple Internal Users. The J.R. Company is organized into three divisions: A, B, and C. Division A produces product X, which can be sold externally at $23 per ton or transferred either to Division B or C for use in their products.

Division A has an annual capacity to produce 60,000 tons of product X. The variable production and selling costs are $20 per ton, and the yearly fixed costs are $120,000. Division B could use product X to produce product Y. Each unit of Y requires two tons of X. Other variable costs of producing Y would amount to $10 per unit. The market for product Y is estimated to be in excess of Division B's capacity of 30,000 units. Fixed costs would be assigned to product Y at a rate of $15 per unit. Product Y can be sold at $65 per unit.

Division C needs product X in the manufacture of product Z. In addition to three tons of X, other production costs per barrel of Z total $5. The market for Z also exceeds Division C's capacity of 20,000 barrels. Fixed costs are assigned at a rate of $10 per barrel. Product Z's selling price is $77.

All divisions are evaluated on the basis of their profit performance. Currently, the manager of Division A is discussing with the other two managers the price to be charged for product X.

Required:

1. Suppose the transfer price on product X is set at its intermediate market price less selling costs of $2 that Division A would not incur on internal transfers. If a transfer price of $21 per ton is used, what would you expect to happen with respect to the demand for A's output? Why?
2. What is the optimal strategy from the firm's point of view? That is, at what levels of volume should each of the three divisions operate? Note that it is possible to acquire X on the external market at $23 per ton.
3. The Division A manager has made the calculations required in part 2 and knows that if she sells internally the firm's profits would be greater than if she sold externally. Thus, she reasons that even though her profits would be the same from an internal sale at $21 per ton and an external sale at $23 per ton, she should *not* be indifferent. Since a decision to sell internally leads to greater company profits, she reasons her profits should be higher and thus is not inclined to settle for a $21 per ton transfer price. What suggestions can you make for an acceptable transfer price? You might want to consider the maximum amount each division would be willing to pay to Division A in the process of making your recommendation.

20-12. Problems of a Transfer Price Based on an Allocation of the Contribution Margin. The Puhl Company produces earth-moving equipment that requires input by three divisions. Motors are built by Division A. The motors are then transferred to Division B, which constructs a chassis and installs the motor. Finally, the motorized chassis is transferred to Division C, which builds the body.

Central management feels that all divisions should be evaluated as investment centers and that they should be credited with an equitable share of the profits from the earth-moving equipment. They have reasoned that proportional efforts can be measured by the ratio of the division's variable cost to the total variable cost of the equipment.

One type of equipment sells for $180,000. Total variable costs are $100,000: $20,000 at A, $30,000 at B, and $50,000 at C. Transfer prices are set at variable cost plus a proportional share of the total contribution margin.

Required:

1. Determine the transfer prices using management's method.
2. Division C is considering some cost saving proposals that would reduce the variable cost of their production from $50,000 to $45,000. There would be no effect on other costs or on the sales price. Using the revised cost data, determine the transfer prices.
3. Return to the original situation and assume Division B is evaluating a cost-saving proposal. The estimates are that the plan would reduce the variable cost from $30,000 to $25,000. Determine the transfer prices.
4. Compare the per unit profits that resulted in parts 2 and 3 with the original profits. What response might you anticipate from the various managers? Why?
5. Return to the original situation and compute the per-unit profit that would result if Division B deliberately increased their cost to $35,000. Evaluate your results.

20-13. Devising an Accounting System with Transfer Prices. The Forsch Company has three divisions, with frequent transfers from one division to another. A particular product requires the efforts of all three divisions. The transfer prices have been formulated so that there is an equitable sharing of the contribution margin for the final product. The contribution margin was prorated on the ratio of variable costs.

Following are the expected per-unit contributions of using the transfer price system:

	Division A		Division B		Division C		Firm
Transfer or sales price (forced)		$200		$500		$1,000	$1,000
Direct variable cost	$120		$180		$300		600
Transfer price	—	120	200	380	500	800	—
Contribution margin		$ 80		$120		$ 200	$ 400

Corporate headquarters maintains control over cash so that when a transfer is made there is no exchange of cash between divisions. As a result, the books of each division should have an account called "Corporate Headquarters," and corporate headquarters would have an account for each division. In consolidating the records, these accounts would offset each other.

Required:

Assume one unit of product is manufactured and sold. Prepare the entries for each division and for corporate headquarters.

20-14. Continuation of Problem 20-13 with a Dual Pricing System. Reconsider problem 20-13 but assume the firm wants to use a dual pricing system. That is, each division's sales will be equal to the accumulated variable cost plus the profit margin computed in problem 20-13. The purchase price to the buying division will be the accumulated variable costs. The motivation for this is to facilitate accurate knowledge of the firm's cost structure. (Ignore fixed costs for this problem.) Thus, the following prices are in effect:

	Transfer In Price	Transfer Out Price
Division A	——	$200
Division B	$120	420[a]
Division C	300[b]	800[c]

[a]Division A's variable cost + Division B's variable cost plus $120 contribution margin.

[b]Division A's variable cost + Division B's variable cost.

[c]Variable costs of all three divisions + $200 contribution margin.

When a transfer occurs, the difference between the sales price and the purchase price will be charged to an intercompany profit account at corporate headquarters. The accounting for a sale at Division C will be as though they sold it to corporate headquarters. The actual sale will be accounted for at the corporate office.

Required:

Assume one unit of product is manufactured and sold. Prepare the entries for each division and for corporate headquarters. Also make the closing entries on all books.

20-15. Comprehensive Transfer Pricing Problem. The Finish Company is divisionalized. Two of the divisions, I and II, have been at odds over the pricing of intracompany transfers. Several years ago Finish's management decided upon a policy of setting the transfer price of product A, which is produced by Division I and can be used by Division II in the production of product Y. Although management periodically reviews and changes this price, neither division has had any input to its determination. Furthermore, because of past refusals by Division I to transfer to II, central management made it policy that Division I had to supply II's requests up to at least 1,000 units of Product A per period.

Both managers are evaluated by residual income and they are constantly at "war" as to how the other is taking advantage of the "system" at their expense. Both argue that they are suboptimizing profits. To date central management's attitude has been that since both are "unhappy" the system must be working. As the new controller, you come into the firm with an "objective" point of view and decide to explore the issues on your own.

You have discovered the following facts. The costs of producing products A and B at Division I are:

	Product A	Product B
Material	$20	$10
Labor at $5 per hour	25	40
Overhead at $6 per machine hour	24	36
	$69	$86

The $6 overhead rate includes fixed costs that are $16,000 per period. The rate is based on practical capacity of 8,000 machine hours. Product A can either be sold externally or transferred to Division II. Product B can only be sold externally.

The costs of producing products Y and Z at Division II are:

	Product Y	Product Z
Material	$ 5	$21
Labor at $5 per hour	25	15
Overhead at $3 per		
labor hour	15	9
Product A @ $80	80	0
	$125	$45

Division II's fixed costs per period are $15,000 and the fixed overhead rate is based on 10,000 labor hours at practical capacity.

Variable selling costs on *external sales* average = 5% of the sales price at either division.

Required:

1. Assume the sales prices of the four products are:
   A: $ 90.00
   B: 110.00
   Y: 138.00
   Z: 52.50
   The transfer price of $80 was picked to "split the profits" on product A between Divisions I and II. "With a market of $90 and costs of $69, an $80 transfer price yields about a $10 profit to each division," according to one manager.
   a. Analyze the adequacy of management's transfer policies.
   b. If you were the manager of Division I and had no policies imposed by central headquarters, how many units of product A and product B would you produce to maximize your profits? (Remember that you have a machine-hour constraint of 8,000 hours.)
   c. Assume for this question that Division II cannot sell any product Z. Division II can buy product A on the external market for $90. What is the optimal product mix at Division I from the perspective of the firm? Explain.
   d. Continuing part c, what is the transfer price that would result if it is based on variable cost plus opportunity cost? Would Division II buy at this price? Is the result congruent with your recommendation in part c?
   e. Now drop the assumption that product Z cannot be sold by Division II. Will Division II purchase product A and make product Y if the transfer price in part d is used? Why? Remember that Division II's labor hours are limited to 10,000.
   f. Continue part e. Will the course of action taken by the Division II manager be the same as the plan considered optimal from the firm's perspective?

2. Suppose the sales price of the four products are:
   A: $ 90.00
   B: 110.00
   Y: 145.92
   Z: 52.50
   a. Since the sales prices have not changed at Division I the transfer price, based on variable cost plus opportunity cost, for product A is the same as in part 1-d. Given that Division II can sell both Y and Z, what would be its preference with this transfer price?
   b. Would the firm have the same preference as Division II?

Part 5   Quantitative Support Topics

CHAPTER 21

Planning Aids—Spreadsheets and Decision Support Systems

In this chapter we will discuss some enrichment topics related to planning. These include computer spreadsheets and decision support systems (DSS). These tools have become very important to both accountants and managers and are used extensively. In spite of its importance, the topic is included in an enrichment chapter since the available packages differ from each other in terms of their specific commands. Three representative packages have been chosen to illustrate what most of these packages can do for the accountant and the decision maker. Since the chosen packages are representative and are not the only software that can be used, it was felt that the topic should be considered in an enrichment chapter.

The chapter will be of maximum usefulness if you read it while working with the particular computer package. In the event that you do not have access to any of the three packages discussed in this chapter, you can still gain some appreciation for what they will do by scanning the chapter. Obviously, in this case, you will not want to give any attention to the details of using the package.

Spreadsheets

As you might suspect, there are possible alternative strategies that might be assumed at the beginning of a budget period. Management may want to have the master budget projected for several of them. If so, the accountant needs some computational help because a complete master budget is imposing, even to do it once. The area of computer spreadsheets and decision support systems have been developed and offers this needed help.

Spreadsheets are computer packages that provide you with an empty worksheet and enable you to conveniently use and manipulate it. Following are some of the more prominent ones:

1. Lotus 1-2-3
2. Lotus Symphony
3. Multiplan
4. SuperCalc
5. VisiCalc

Today's management accountant must be knowledgeable about computer spreadsheets. Computer spreadsheets certainly remove much of the drudgery in the use of planning tools and allow the accountant to give more attention to the important issues. In this section there is an examination of the basics of one spreadsheet package—Lotus 1-2-3. It is representative of all such computer aids.

To illustrate financial spreadsheets, let's use part of the comprehensive budgeting example of Chapter 12. Specifically the production budget for Oakes will be used as an illustration. You may need to review the information in numbers 1 and 4 of Exhibit 12.3. Although budgeting is the application that will be used to illustrate spreadsheets and decision support systems, it is important to note that they may be used in many other ways. Some of the end-of-chapter problems will direct you to other applications.

When you are successful in bringing up Lotus 1-2-3, the screen will show a portion of a blank worksheet with 2,048 rows (numbered 1 to 2,048) and 256 columns (labeled A, B, . . . , Z, AA, . . . , AZ, . . . IV). You can move around the worksheet with the cursor keys. In addition to the worksheet, there is a message code in the upper right corner of the screen and a cell address in the upper left corner. The cell address indicates where the cursor (pointer) is presently located. Move the cursor (the highlighted box) and watch the address change.

To define a model in 1-2-3, move the cursor to the cell that you wish to define and type your entry. What you type will initially appear in the blank line just below the cell address. The cells of the worksheet can be used for labels, numbers, or formulas. At your option, groups of cells can be treated as one entity. Lotus calls these "ranges." Each cell initially starts with a predefined width of nine characters but you can change that to suit your own needs. (Note that you can get on-line help by pressing the appropriate keys; F1 on the IBM PC version of 1-2-3. Pressing ESC will return you to the worksheet.)

Now consider the Oakes Company production budget. Use column A to enter row names. Since all columns are initially nine characters long, change the width before you start. Place the cursor in cell A1. Press the slash (/) key at the lower right corner of the key board. A menu will appear at the top of the screen. The line below the menu is a short description of what the highlighted selection of the menu will do. (The highlighted selection is represented in **boldface** below.)

Worksheet   Range   Copy   Move   File   Print   Graph   Data   Quit
Global, Insert, Delete, Column-Width, Erase, Titles, Window, Status

Move the cursor to Worksheet and press enter (or press W). A new menu line appears:

Global   Insert   Delete   Column-Width   Erase   Titles   Window   Status
Set worksheet settings

Press C for column width. Now press S for set current column width (the column in which the cursor is located). You can now see the default column width of 9.

Type 30 to allow room for the variable names and press enter. The worksheet's column A is now wider.

Columns B, C, D, E, and F will be used in this model for January through April and a Total column. Let's use row one for column labels. Move the cursor to cell B1, type "JAN, and press enter. The quote (") tells 1-2-3 to right justify the entry. (A single quote (') tells it to left justify and a hat (^) tells it to center.) Move the cursor to C1, type "FEB and so forth.

Next, supply the row labels. Move the cursor to cell A2, type PRODUCTION OF WALL CABINETS, and press enter. Note that 1-2-3 reads your intentions. As soon as a letter is typed, 1-2-3 assumes your entry is going to be a label. Then move the cursor to A3, type SALES OF WALL CABINETS and so forth until labels similar to Exhibit 21.2 are entered. Pressing the down cursor (↓) will simultaneously enter your selection and move to the next cell. (You can leave row 8 blank in order to separate the two budgets.)

To keep your row and column labels from scrolling off the screen, move the cursor to cell B2, enter /, then W, then T (for Titles), and then B (for Both). You will now note that when you move out to the total column, the variable names do not disappear from the screen.

The next task is to define the entries for the four months and the total column. Move the cursor to cell B3 in preparation of defining January's sales needs. (Pressing F5 on the IBM version of Lotus is a "go to" command. When prompted, enter the cell address and press enter. This permits fast "travel" to a cell.) When in cell B3, type 10000 (no commas). Move to cell C3, type 20000, and so forth. At cell F3 (the Total) it is recommended that you enter a formula. Then, if it is desired to do some what-ifs on wall cabinet sales, the total column will automatically adjust itself. The SUM function can be used. Type @SUM(B3..D3). This tells 1-2-3 to add columns B3 through D3 (January through March). Check the results in cell F3 after you press enter.

Move to cell B4. The desired ending inventory is 50% of next month sales. Type 0.5*C3. Confirm the results after pressing enter. February's ending inventory has the same *relationship*. Although it would be easy to move to cell C4 and type 0.5*D3, this will not be done in order to illustrate a powerful feature of 1-2-3. Instead, the /Copy command will be used. Enter /C. Note the upper left corner of the screen. The message "Enter range to copy FROM: B4..B4" indicates the cells 1-2-3 is prepared to copy. You can either edit the string "B4..B4," by typing over it, or use the "point" feature. The latter is invoked by moving the cursor. Try it by moving to the right. Watch the right-most point of the range as you do.

Move the cursor back to B4 since cell B4 is the only cell desired to be copied here. Once you have the range as desired, press enter. A second message appears. This requests the range in*to* which you wish to copy. Move the cursor to C4. The point feature can be used to select a range. Press the period (.) and then the cursor can be moved to establish the right-most point of the range, cell E4. Press enter. Move the cursor back to cell C4 and note the formula in the upper left corner. Even though you copied from cell B4 with a formula of 0.5*C3, note that C4's entry is

0.5*D3. That is, 1-2-3 maintained the relationship of the previous column. Similar results can be noted in the other cells.

Move to cell F4. The quarter's ending inventory is the same as March's. A simple way to tell 1-2-3 this is to type +D4. (Typing D4 would be interpreted as a label since it would start with a letter.)

Now move to cell B5. This value is equal to the sum of B3 and B4. Type this: @SUM(B3,B4). (The SUM function can be used to sum across rows or down columns. Further, it can be used to sum a range, xx..yy, or a list of cells, xx,yy, . . . ,zz.) Copy this relationship to all other cells in row 5 as follows (do not type the commas): /, C, (press enter), move cursor to cell C5, . (type the period), move cursor to F5, and press enter. To verify the relationship has been maintained, move to cell C5 and observe the formula is @SUM(C3,C4). Move to B6. Type 8000 (the beginning inventory of wall cabinets). Move to C6. Cell C6 should be equal to cell B4. Type +B4. Copy the relationship to cells D6 and E6: /, C (press enter), move cursor to D6, . (type period), move cursor to E6, (press enter). For cell F6, type +B6 (January's beginning inventory).

All of the entries in row 7 would be row 5 − row 6. Type +B5 − B6 for cell B7 and then use the copy feature for the other cells in row 7.

The above process would be repeated for base cabinets. To save your file on a disk (in drive B), type /, select File, and then select Save. Enter a file name, such as PRODBGT, when prompted. Exhibit 21.1 is a listing of the cell formulas for this model and Exhibit 21.2 is the solution. Note that April is printed but that the figures are meaningless. We will not discuss how the April column could be omitted on printouts.

Exhibit 21.1   Lotus 1-2-3 Model for Oakes Production Budget

```
              A                   B             C            D            E            F
1                             !     JAN!        FEB!         MAR!         APR!     TOTAL
2 PRODUCTION OF WALL CABINETS  !        !           !            !            !
3 SALES OF WALL CABINETS       !   10000!     20000!       20000!       20000!@SUM(B3..D3)
4 DESIRED ENDING INVENTORY OF WC!0.5*C3  !0.5*D3    !0.5*E3    !0.5*F3    !+D4
5 TOTAL WALL CABINETS NEEDED   !@SUM(B3,B4)  !@SUM(C3,C4)  !@SUM(D3,D4)  !@SUM(E3,E4)  !@SUM(F3,F4)
6 BEGINNING INVENTORY OF WALL CA!  8000!+B4   !+C4   !+D4   !+B6
7 PRODUCTION OF WALL CABINETS   !+B5-B6   !+C5-C6   !+D5-D6   !+E5-E6   !+F5-F6
8                              !        !           !            !            !
9 PRODUCTION OF BASE CABINETS   !        !           !            !            !
10 SALES OF BASE CABINETS       !   20000!     30000!       10000!       20000!@SUM(B10..D10)
11 DESIRED ENDING INVENTORY OF BC!0.25*C10 !0.25*D10  !0.25*E10  !0.25*F10  !+D11
12 TOTAL BASE CABINETS NEEDED   !@SUM(B10,B11)!@SUM(C10,C11)!@SUM(D10,D11)!@SUM(E10,E11)!@SUM(F10,F11)
13 BEGINNING INVENTORY OF BASE CA!  5000!+B11  !+C11  !+D11  !+B13
14 PRODUCTION OF BASE CABINETS  !+B12-B13   !+C12-C13   !+D12-D13   !+E12-E13   !+F12-F13
```

Exhibit 21.2   Solution to Lotus Model in Exhibit 21.1

	JAN	FEB	MAR	APR	TOTAL
PRODUCTION OF WALL CABINETS					
SALES OF WALL CABINETS	10000	20000	20000	20000	50000
DESIRED ENDING INVENTORY OF WC	10000	10000	10000	25000	10000
TOTAL WALL CABINETS NEEDED	20000	30000	30000	45000	60000
BEGINNING INVENTORY OF WALL CA	8000	10000	10000	10000	8000
PRODUCTION OF WALL CABINETS	12000	20000	20000	35000	52000
PRODUCTION OF BASE CABINETS					
SALES OF BASE CABINETS	20000	30000	10000	20000	60000
DESIRED ENDING INVENTORY OF BC	7500	2500	5000	15000	5000
TOTAL BASE CABINETS NEEDED	27500	32500	15000	35000	65000
BEGINNING INVENTORY OF BASE CA	5000	7500	2500	5000	5000
PRODUCTION OF WALL CABINETS	22500	25000	12500	30000	60000

Now suppose the following what-if questions wanted to be asked.

1. The sales of wall cabinets is 12,000 in the first month and then grows by 10% per month thereafter?
2. The desired ending inventory of base cabinets is 40% of next month's sales instead of 25%?
3. Both of the above changes occur together?
4. The raw material needed for wall cabinets and base cabinets is two units and three units, respectively, the sales are as given in what-if question 1, and it is desired to know how much total material is needed to support the production?

In Lotus, to pose these questions, just go to the cells in which the changes are desired and enter the new values. Thus for case 1, make the following changes:

Cell	New Entry
B3	12000
C3	1.1*B3
D3	1.1*C3
E3	1.1*D3

The results are in Exhibit 21.3.

In order to do the second what-if, just retrieve the original model by entering /
FR and selecting PRODBGT (if that is the name you gave this model). Change the
values on row 11 to 0.4*(the appropriate cell). The results are in Exhibit 21.4. To
do what-if 3 keep the last version and change the values on row 3 to be the same
as in what-if 1. The results are in Exhibit 21.5.

Exhibit 21.3   Lotus 1-2-3 Solution to First What If

	JAN	FEB	MAR	APR	TOTAL
PRODUCTION OF WALL CABINETS					
SALES OF WALL CABINETS	12000	13200	14520	15972	39720
DESIRED ENDING INVENTORY OF WC	6600	7260	7986	19860	7986
TOTAL WALL CABINETS NEEDED	18600	20460	22506	35832	47706
BEGINNING INVENTORY OF WALL CA	8000	6600	7260	7986	8000
PRODUCTION OF WALL CABINETS	10600	13860	15246	27846	39706
PRODUCTION OF BASE CABINETS					
SALES OF BASE CABINETS	20000	30000	10000	20000	60000
DESIRED ENDING INVENTORY OF BC	7500	2500	5000	15000	5000
TOTAL BASE CABINETS NEEDED	27500	32500	15000	35000	65000
BEGINNING INVENTORY OF BASE CA	5000	7500	2500	5000	5000
PRODUCTION OF ·BASE CABINETS	22500	25000	12500	30000	60000

Exhibit 21.4   Lotus 1-2-3 Solution to Second What If

	JAN	FEB	MAR	APR	TOTAL
PRODUCTION OF WALL CABINETS					
SALES OF WALL CABINETS	10000	20000	20000	20000	50000
DESIRED ENDING INVENTORY OF WC	10000	10000	10000	25000	10000
TOTAL WALL CABINETS NEEDED	20000	30000	30000	45000	60000
BEGINNING INVENTORY OF WALL CA	8000	10000	10000	10000	8000
PRODUCTION OF WALL CABINETS	12000	20000	20000	35000	52000
PRODUCTION OF BASE CABINETS					
SALES OF BASE CABINETS	20000	30000	10000	20000	60000
DESIRED ENDING INVENTORY OF BC	12000	4000	8000	24000	8000
TOTAL BASE CABINETS NEEDED	32000	34000	18000	44000	68000
BEGINNING INVENTORY OF BASE CA	5000	12000	4000	8000	5000
PRODUCTION OF BASE CABINETS	27000	22000	14000	36000	63000

Exhibit 21.5   Lotus 1-2-3 Solution to Third What If

	JAN	FEB	MAR	APR	TOTAL
PRODUCTION OF WALL CABINETS					
SALES OF WALL CABINETS	12000	13200	14520	15972	39720
DESIRED ENDING INVENTORY OF WC	6600	7260	7986	19860	7986
TOTAL WALL CABINETS NEEDED	18600	20460	22506	35832	47706
BEGINNING INVENTORY OF WALL CA	8000	6600	7260	7986	8000
PRODUCTION OF WALL CABINETS	10600	13860	15246	27846	39706
PRODUCTION OF BASE CABINETS					
SALES OF BASE CABINETS	20000	30000	10000	20000	60000
DESIRED ENDING INVENTORY OF BC	12000	4000	8000	24000	8000
TOTAL BASE CABINETS NEEDED	32000	34000	18000	44000	68000
BEGINNING INVENTORY OF BASE CA	5000	12000	4000	8000	5000
PRODUCTION OF BASE CABINETS	27000	22000	14000	36000	63000

For what-if case 4 it will be necessary to add a line to the model. Retrieve the original model and change row 3. Then, go to cell A16 and type MATERIAL NEEDS. Next, go to cell B16 and enter: 2*B7 + 3*B14. Copy the results to cell C16 and D16. If a total is desired, cell F16 should be @SUM(B16..D16). The results are in Exhibit 21.6.

Now consider a "goal-seeking problem." What would the sales of wall cabinets in period 2 have to be in order to reduce the production of wall cabinets in period 1 from 12,000 to 10,000? It will be necessary for you to continually enter different values for the change variable until the goal variable achieves its desired value. Retrieve the original model and move the cursor to cell C3. Reduce it to 18000. The January production of wall cabinets (cell B7) changes to 11000. Try 16000 in cell C3 and B7 goes to 10000 (the desired value).

Decision Support Systems

Decision Support Systems (DSS) differ from spreadsheets in that they will do more things for the user. For example, the goal seeking question posed in the last section can be accomplished directly instead of by a trial and error procedure. DSS will also have the capability of handling larger models, extensive report writing features, the ability to consolidate several models, and the ability to handle certain types of simultaneous equations. With a DSS you will also have the ability to create and use datafiles. This means that a generalized model can be built and then run using a different data file each time. When there are several divisions within a

Exhibit 21.6   Lotus 1-2-3 Solution to Fourth What If

		JAN	FEB	MAR	APR	TOTAL
PRODUCTION OF WALL CABINETS						
SALES OF WALL CABINETS		12000	13200	14520	15972	39720
DESIRED ENDING INVENTORY OF	WC	6600	7260	7986	19860	7986
TOTAL WALL CABINETS NEEDED		18600	20460	22506	35832	47706
BEGINNING INVENTORY OF WALL	CA	8000	6600	7260	7986	8000
PRODUCTION OF WALL CABINETS		10600	13860	15246	27846	39706
PRODUCTION OF BASE CABINETS						
SALES OF BASE CABINETS		20000	30000	10000	20000	60000
DESIRED ENDING INVENTORY OF	BC	7500	2500	5000	15000	5000
TOTAL BASE CABINETS NEEDED		27500	32500	15000	35000	65000
BEGINNING INVENTORY OF BASE	CA	5000	7500	2500	5000	5000
PRODUCTION OF BASE CABINETS		22500	25000	12500	30000	60000
MATERIAL NEEDS		88700	102720	67992		259412

firm this is a convenient feature because one model can be used with each division's data. Commercially marketed main frame DSS packages include IFPS, COMOS, PLANCODE, PROPHIT II, SIMPLAN, APL∗PLUS, and PSG. At the microcomputer level, there is IFPS/Personal.

IFPS.   The package to be explored in this section is one of the fourth generation of computer languages. Never before has it been so easy to "talk" with the computer. Only a very few commands have to be learned in order to use the basic ideas of a package like IFPS (Interactive Financial Planning System). Such systems have more sophisticated ability than will be discussed here since space does not permit a complete examination.

To illustrate IFPS, let's use the same example used to illustrate Lotus 1-2-3. It will first be necessary to bring IFPS up on your time sharing computer. The procedures for doing this are dependent on the computer you are using and the protocol established by the installation. Assuming you have interfaced with IFPS successfully, it will first ask you for the name of the file containing your models and reports. A model is designed by the user and is the set of relationships that define the situation the user wishes to represent. Reports are elaborate "formating" devices that allow the user to select the portion of the model to output (either on the monitor or the printer) and the form in which it will be shown. IFPS's report feature will not be examined in this book.

Suppose we call our file OAKES and our model on the file PRODBGT for production budget. (See Exhibit 21.7 for the complete computer session and follow along as it is discussed.) Having searched for the file OAKES and not finding it, the IFPS system assumes you want to create a new file and responds with the message you find in Exhibit 21.7. There are many executive commands that can be issued in IFPS, including the request to build a model. Thus in response to the request for an executive command, the command MODEL PRODBGT has been entered. IFPS recognizes that a model by this name is not on the file called OAKES and instructs you to start entering a new model. The next command you find in Exhibit 21.7 is the AUTO command. This asks IFPS to automatically generate line numbers so that it is not necessary to type them in or accept the default line numbering system of IFPS. "AUTO 10 10" asks for the line numbers to start at 10 and to be increased by increments of 10.

Since IFPS starts with an empty worksheet it is necessary to declare the columns and the rows. The columns must be defined first. This is done in statement 10. Five columns are defined, one for each of the first four months and one for the quarterly total. The latter is what IFPS calls a special column and will be discussed later. Statement 20 begins with an asterisk ($*$) and is the way IFPS identifies a comment.

In statement 30 a variable, SALES OF WALL CABINETS, is declared and its value for each regular column is defined. Perhaps it appears that the values for only two columns were defined. However, it is a convention of IFPS that the default value for a column (value used if not specifically declared) is the value in the column to its immediate left. In the case of the sales of wall cabinets, this is exactly what is wanted—a value of 20,000 in each of the last three months. (Until defined as a special column, the Total column will be treated as a regular column and would have a value of 20,000 also. This is not desired.) An alternative way of defining the sales of wall cabinets would be to use the FOR command. "FOR n" says to use the expression for the next n columns. Thus, the following would be acceptable:

SALES OF WALL CABINETS = 10000, 20000 FOR 3

Line 40 defines how the ending inventory of wall cabinets is to be computed. It uses another of the special commands of IFPS, FUTURE. The FUTURE command causes IFPS to look to the right in the worksheet. For this case it is desired to look to the right in the row representing SALES OF WALL CABINETS and multiply the amount found there by 0.50. This, of course, is appropriate since the ending inventory of wall cabinets is desired to be 50% of next month's sales.

Line 50 defines the total needs to be the sum of L30 (SALES OF WALL CABINETS) and L40 (DESIRED EI OF WALL CABINETS). Variables can be referred to either by name or by line number (L30, or LINE 30, for example). Line 60 defines the BI OF WALL CABINETS. The January beginning inventory of wall cabinets is given. Thereafter, it is equal to the previous period's ending inventory. PREVIOUS is another IFPS command instructing it to look to the left; in this case, to the left in the row representing DESIRED EI OF WALL CABINETS. That is, the current period's beginning inventory is equal to the previous period's ending inventory. Line 70 should be obvious.

Line 80 through 120 defines the TOTAL column as a special column. When the command COLUMN appears, it serves notice that the column named after it is a

Exhibit 21.7   IFPS Model for Oakes Production Budget[*]

```
@IFPS                    (@ or some other symbol will be your system's prompt)
ENTER NAME OF THE FILE CONTAINING MODELS AND REPORTS
? OAKES                  (? is IFPS's prompt)
FILE OAKES NOT FOUND - NEW FILE WILL BE CREATED
READY FOR EXECUTIVE COMMAND
? MODEL PRODBGT
BEGIN ENTERING NEW MODEL
? AUTO 10 10
10 ? COLUMNS 1, 2, 3, 4, TOTAL
20 ? *PRODUCTION OF WALL CABINETS
30 ? SALES OF WALL CABINETS = 10000, 20000
40 ? DESIRED EI OF WALL CABINETS = 0.5*FUTURE SALES OF WALL CABINETS
50 ? TOTAL WALL CABINETS NEEDED = L30 + L40
60 ? BI OF WALL CABINETS = 8000, PREVIOUS L40
70 ? PRODUCTION OF WALL CABINETS = L50 - L60
80 ? COLUMN TOTAL FOR SALES OF WALL CABINETS = SUM (C1 THRU C3)
90 ? COLUMN TOTAL FOR L40 = C3
100 ? COLUMN TOTAL FOR L50 = L30 + L40
110 ? COLUMN TOTAL FOR L60 = C1
120 ? COLUMN TOTAL FOR L70 = L50 - L60
130 ? *
140 ? *PRODUCTION OF BASE CABINETS
150 ? SALES OF BASE CABINETS = 20000, 30000, 10000, 20000
160 ? DESIRED EI OF BASE CABINETS = 0.25*FUTURE SALES OF BASE CABINETS
170 ? TOTAL BASE CABINETS NEEDED = L150 + L160
180 ? BI OF BASE CABINETS = 5000, PREVIOUS L160
190 ? PRODUCTION OF BASE CABINETS = L170 - L180
200 ? COLUMN TOTAL FOR SALES OF BASE CABINETS = SUM (C1 THRU C3)
210 ? COLUMN TOTAL FOR L160 = C3
220 ? COLUMN TOTAL FOR L170 = L150 + L160
230 ? COLUMN TOTAL FOR L180 = C1
240 ? COLUMN TOTAL FOR L190 = L170 - L180
250 ? END
READY FOR EDIT
? SOLVE
MODEL PRODBGT  VERSION OF   02/03/84   13:43 -- 5 COLUMNS 10 VARIABLES
ENTER SOLVE OPTIONS
? COLUMNS 1,2,3, TOTAL
? COMMAS
? ALL
```

*See Exhibit 21.8 for the output resulting from the above session.

special column. Line 80 defines the TOTAL SALES OF WALL CABINETS for the quarter. SUM is another IFPS command that can be used either to add down a column or add across columns (when used in special column definitions). In this case it is to add across columns. To do this, it is necessary to indicate with a C that the entries inside the parenthesis are column names. As you can see in line 80, columns 1 through 3 are being added. (THRU is an IFPS command that means what it says.)

Line 90 defines the special column entry for L40 (the DESIRED EI OF WALL CABINETS). This would be the same as the month 3 ending inventory (column 3). Line 100 defines the TOTAL WALL CABINETS NEEDED for the quarter. Line 110 indicates that the beginning inventory for the quarter is the same as month one's beginning inventory. Line 120 is obvious.

The effect of L130 is to insert a blank line between the budget for wall cabinets and the budget for base cabinets. Lines 140 through 240 define the relationships for base cabinets in a manner similar to what was done for wall cabinets. Note that since the forecasted demand was different for each of the first four months, each value had to be separately declared in line 150. When prompted for line 250 the response was END. This "turns off" the AUTO command. The computer responds by asking if you want to edit the model. Changes could be made in the model at this point using the IFPS edit commands. However, it is not necessary to wait until this point to make changes. The edit commands are available to the user while the model is being built so that errors can be corrected as soon as they are detected. Space does not permit a discussion of the edit commands, however.

Let's assume that the model has been entered exactly as wanted. Then the next logical thing to do is "solve" the model. Note that immediately after the request to edit, SOLVE has been entered. If the model has no syntax errors it will be solved and you will be notified of the completion of the solution process with a statement similar to: MODEL PRODBGT VERSION OF . . . 5 COLUMNS 10 VARIABLES.

Further, you will be asked for solve options. There are many solve options that can be entered at this point but only three are discussed here. First, column 4 is not wanted in the output. It was included in the model so that the month 3 ending inventory could be computed. However, there was not enough information provided to do a complete budget for month 4. Thus the results in column 4 will not be of any value. The solve option, COLUMNS 1, 2, 3, TOTAL indicates that these are the only columns desired in the output. The next option, COMMAS, asks IFPS to insert commas in our numerical output. The final option instructs IFPS to include all rows in the output. (It is possible to be selective about which rows are displayed.) Exhibit 21.8 contains the output from these commands. (With Lotus 1-2-3 it is not as easy to be selective about what the output will be. It can be done, but it takes a lot of file manipulation.)

A major advantage of a computer spreadsheet is the ability to make changes and quickly see the results. To illustrate, the session with PRODBGT is continued in Exhibit 21.9. After the output of Exhibit 21.8 is given, IFPS will again ask for SOLVE OPTIONS. Another option that can be requested at this point is a WHAT IF.

Exhibit 21.8   IFPS Solution to MODEL PRODBGT

```
                                      1        2        3       TOTAL

PRODUCTION OF WALL CABINETS
SALES OF WALL CABINETS             10,000   20,000   20,000    50,000
DESIRED EI OF WALL CABINETS        10,000   10,000   10,000    10,000
TOTAL WALL CABINETS NEEDED         20,000   30,000   30,000    60,000
BI OF WALL CABINETS                 8,000   10,000   10,000     8,000
PRODUCTION OF WALL CABINETS        12,000   20,000   20,000    52,000

PRODUCTION OF BASE CABINETS
SALES OF BASE CABINETS             20,000   30,000   10,000    60,000
DESIRED EI OF BASE CABINETS         7,500    2,500    5,000     5,000
TOTAL BASE CABINETS NEEDED         27,500   32,500   15,000    65,000
BI OF BASE CABINETS                 5,000    7,500    2,500     5,000
PRODUCTION OF BASE CABINETS        22,500   25,000   12,500    60,000
```

WHAT IFs, in IFPS, are temporary changes to the basic model. For example, consider the four WHAT IFs used in the last section. As you can see in Exhibit 21.9, WHAT IF is invoked by entering WHAT IF. IFPS will respond asking you to enter statements. To perform the first what if, it is necessary to respond as follows:

SALES OF WALL CABINETS = 12000, 1.1 * PREVIOUS

This will cause a temporary change in wall cabinet sales and resolves the entire model based on the change. To indicate that you have entered all of your desired changes just enter SOLVE when prompted with the question mark. Further, it is possible to temporarily create new variables (see what if case 4).

After entering SOLVE you will again be asked for solve options. Since it was indicated earlier that only Columns 1-3 and TOTAL were wanted and that commas were to be inserted, these options remain in effect. Further, the production of base cabinets will not be affected by this what if so let's ask for L20 THRU L70. The results are contained in Exhibit 21.9

The session continues in Exhibit 21.10. After printing our request, IFPS again asks for solve options. Let's now consider the second what if. Indicate that another what if is desired. The computer responds as indicated in Exhibit 21.10. Enter the statement which will temporarily redefine the ending inventory relationship and tell IFPS to solve. To show that the changes are temporary let's repond with ALL. Note that the sales of wall cabinets have been returned to the original status and that base cabinet ending inventory is at the new level.

Exhibit 21.9   IFPS Solution First What If

```
ENTER SOLVE OPTIONS
? WHAT IF
WHAT IF CASE 1
ENTER STATEMENTS
? SALES OF WALL CABINETS = 12000, 1.1 * PREVIOUS
? SOLVE
ENTER SOLVE OPTIONS
L20 THRU L70


***** WHAT IF CASE 1 *****
1 WHAT IF STATEMENT PROCESSED

                                 1        2        3     TOTAL

PRODUCTION OF WALL CABINETS
SALES OF WALL CABINETS        12,000   13,200   14,520   39,720
DESIRED EI OF WALL CABINETS    6,600    7,260    7,986    7,986
TOTAL WALL CABINETS NEEDED    18,600   20,460   22,506   47,706
BI OF WALL CABINETS            8,000    6,600    7,260    8,000
PRODUCTION OF WALL CABINETS   10,600   13,860   15,246   39,706
```

The third what if case is considered in Exhibit 21.11. Since the third case is a combination of the first two, it permits an illustration of the WHAT IF CONTINUE command. When this commnd is used, the temporary statements in the last what-if case are retained while allowing additional statements. Note in Exhibit 21.11 that WHAT IF CONTINUE has been entered. Now just add the first what if statement to the one retained from case 2. When responding to the SOLVE command, IFPS verifies that two statements have been processed. All variables have been asked for in the output so you can see both statements were in effect.

The final what if case is contained in Exhibit 21.12. Note that WHAT IF was entered as the solve option. This clears all statements and allows us to start with the original model. The second what if statement entered in Exhibit 21.12 defines a new variable which is accepted with a warning. Note in Exhibit 21.12 that ALL was entered as the solve option. Examination of the output reveals that MATERIALS NEEDS was not printed. This is because it is a new variable. Its solution is contained in the model but it will be necessary to ask for it separately. As the next solve option, request MATERIAL NEEDS. It is then provided for the three regular columns but not for the special column.

Exhibit 21.10   IFPS Solution Second What If

```
ENTER SOLVE OPTIONS
? WHAT IF
WHAT IF CASE 2
ENTER STATEMENTS
? DESIRED EI OF BASE CABINETS = 0.4 * FUTURE SALES OF BASE CABINETS
? SOLVE
ENTER SOLVE OPTIONS
? ALL


***** WHAT IF CASE 2 *****
1 WHAT IF STATEMENT PROCESSED

                                    1        2        3     TOTAL

PRODUCTION OF WALL CABINETS
SALES OF WALL CABINETS           10,000   20,000   20,000   50,000
DESIRED EI OF WALL CABINETS      10,000   10,000   10,000   10,000
TOTAL WALL CABINETS NEEDED       20,000   30,000   30,000   60,000
BI OF WALL CABINETS               8,000   10,000   10,000    8,000
PRODUCTION OF WALL CABINETS      12,000   20,000   20,000   52,000

PRODUCTION OF BASE CABINETS
SALES OF BASE CABINETS           20,000   30,000   10,000   60,000
DESIRED EI OF BASE CABINETS      12,000    4,000    8,000    8,000
TOTAL BASE CABINETS NEEDED       32,000   34,000   18,000   68,000
BI OF BASE CABINETS               5,000   12,000    4,000    5,000
PRODUCTION OF BASE CABINETS      27,000   22,000   14,000   63,000
```

Goal seeking is another powerful feature of IFPS. Goal seeking can be used to determine ways of achieving some target. To achieve a target value of one variable, another variable has to be changed. So, for example:

1. What would the sales of wall cabinets in period 1 have to be in order to reduce the production of wall cabinets in period 1 from 12,000 in the original case to 10,000? Perhaps this is a relevant question if there is a limited production capacity.
2. What would the sales of wall cabinets in period 2 have to be in order to reduce the production of wall cabinets in period 1 from 12,000 to 10,000? This is another way to meet a production limitation in period 1 since changing the sales in period 2 will change the ending inventory needed in period 1 and, therefore, the production in period 1. (Note that this is the same goal that was used in the Lotus 1-2-3 session.)

Exhibit 21.11   IFPS Solution Third What If

```
ENTER SOLVE OPTIONS
? WHAT IF CONTINUE
WHAT IF CASE 3
ENTER STATEMENTS
? SALES OF WALL CABINETS = 12000, 1.1 * PREVIOUS
? SOLVE
ENTER SOLVE OPTIONS
? ALL


***** WHAT IF CASE 3 *****
2 WHAT IF STATEMENTS PROCESSED
```

	1	2	3	TOTAL
PRODUCTION OF WALL CABINETS				
SALES OF WALL CABINETS	12,000	13,200	14,520	39,720
DESIRED EI OF WALL CABINETS	6,600	7,260	7,986	7,986
TOTAL WALL CABINETS NEEDED	18,600	20,460	22,506	47,706
BI OF WALL CABINETS	8,000	6,600	7,260	8,000
PRODUCTION OF WALL CABINETS	10,600	13,860	15,246	39,706
PRODUCTION OF BASE CABINETS				
SALES OF BASE CABINETS	20,000	30,000	10,000	60,000
DESIRED EI OF BASE CABINETS	12,000	4,000	8,000	8,000
TOTAL BASE CABINETS NEEDED	32,000	34,000	18,000	68,000
BI OF BASE CABINETS	5,000	12,000	4,000	5,000
PRODUCTION OF BASE CABINETS	27,000	22,000	14,000	63,000

Exhibit 21.13 continues the session. In order to return to the original model the command BASE MODEL has been entered as the first solve option. (It is possible to do goal seeks with the temporary what if statements. If it is not desired to do this, BASE MODEL erases the temporary statements.) To engage the goal-seeking routine enter GOAL SEEKING in response to the next prompt.

The goal-seeking routine will first ask for the variable to be changed to achieve the desired goal. In goal-seeking case 1, this is SALES OF WALL CABINETS(1). To indicate column 1, it was necessary to enter (1) after the name of the variable. Next the user will be asked for the computational statement(s) for performance. In case 1 this is:

PRODUCTION OF WALL CABINETS(1) = 10000

Exhibit 21.12   IFPS Solution Fourth What If

```
ENTER SOLVE OPTIONS
? WHAT IF
WHAT IF CASE 4
ENTER STATEMENTS
? SALES OF WALL CABINETS = 12000, 1.1 * PREVIOUS
? MATERIAL NEEDS = 2 * L70 + 3 * L190
WARNING - NEW VARIABLE WAS CREATED
? SOLVE
ENTER SOLVE OPTIONS
? ALL


***** WHAT IF CASE 4 *****
2 WHAT IF STATEMENTS PROCESSED

                                    1         2         3      TOTAL


PRODUCTION OF WALL CABINETS
SALES OF WALL CABINETS          12,000    13,200    14,520    39,720
DESIRED EI OF WALL CABINETS      6,600     7,260     7,986     7,986
TOTAL WALL CABINETS NEEDED      18,600    20,460    22,506    47,706
BI OF WALL CABINETS              8,000     6,600     7,260     8,000
PRODUCTION OF WALL CABINETS     10,600    13,860    15,246    39,706

PRODUCTION OF BASE CABINETS
SALES OF BASE CABINETS          20,000    30,000    10,000    60,000
DESIRED EI OF BASE CABINETS      7,500     2,500     5,000     5,000
TOTAL BASE CABINETS NEEDED      27,500    32,500    15,000    65,000
BI OF BASE CABINETS              5,000     7,500     2,500     5,000
PRODUCTION OF BASE CABINETS     22,500    25,000    12,500    60,000

ENTER SOLVE OPTIONS
? MATERIAL NEEDS

                                    1         2         3      TOTAL

MATERIAL NEEDS                  88,700   102,720    67,992
```

Exhibit 21.13   IFPS Solution First Goal-Seeking Case

```
ENTER SOLVE OPTIONS
? BASE MODEL
? GOAL SEEKING
GOAL SEEKING CASE 1
ENTER NAME OF VARIABLE(S) TO BE ADJUSTED TO ACHIEVE PERFORMANCE
? SALES NEEDS OF WALL CABINETS(1)
ENTER 1 COMPUTATIONAL STATEMENT(S) FOR PERFORMANCE
? PRODUCTION OF WALL CABINETS(1) = 10000


***** GOAL SEEKING CASE 1 *****

                                    1        2        3     TOTAL

SALES OF WALL CABINETS           8,000   20,000   20,000   48,000

ENTER SOLVE OPTIONS
? L20 THRU L70

                                    1        2        3     TOTAL


PRODUCTION OF WALL CABINETS
SALES OF WALL CABINETS           8,000   20,000   20,000   48,000
DESIRED EI OF WALL CABINETS     10,000   10,000   10,000   10,000
TOTAL WALL CABINETS NEEDED      18,000   30,000   30,000   58,000
BI OF WALL CABINETS              8,000   10,000   10,000    8,000
PRODUCTION OF WALL CABINETS     10,000   20,000   20,000   50,000
```

As can be seen in Exhibit 21.13, the sales of wall cabinets must be reduced to 8,000 to cause the production of wall cabinets to be reduced to 10,000. Of course, this is reasonable. To see the affected portion of the model at this point, respond L20 THRU L70 when asked to enter solve options.

Exhibit 21.14 contains the portion of the session for goal-seeking case number 2. This time the variable to be adjusted is SALES OF WALL CABINETS(2). The computational statement is the same as in case 1. As indicated in Exhibit 21.14, the sales in period 2 must be reduced to 16,000 units in order to accomplish the goal. These two goal-seeking cases are not complex but they show the potential of this IFPS feature. In order to have "more interesting" cases, it is necessary to have a more complete model.

Exhibit 21.14   IFPS Solution Second Goal-Seeking Case

```
ENTER SOLVE OPTIONS
? GOAL SEEKING
GOAL SEEKING CASE 2
ENTER NAME OF VARIABLE(S) TO BE ADJUSTED TO ACHIEVE PERFORMANCE
? SALES NEEDS OF WALL CABINETS(2)
ENTER 1 COMPUTATIONAL STATEMENT(S) FOR PERFORMANCE
? PRODUCTION OF WALL CABINETS(1) = 10000


***** GOAL SEEKING CASE 2 *****

                                  1        2        3      TOTAL

SALES OF WALL CABINETS         10,000   16,000   20,000   46,000

ENTER SOLVE OPTIONS
L20 THRU L70

                                  1        2        3      TOTAL


PRODUCTION OF WALL CABINETS
SALES OF WALL CABINETS         10,000   16,000   20,000   46,000
DESIRED EI OF WALL CABINETS     8,000   10,000   10,000   10,000
TOTAL WALL CABINETS NEEDED     18,000   26,000   30,000   56,000
BI OF WALL CABINETS             8,000    8,000   10,000    8,000
PRODUCTION OF WALL CABINETS    10,000   18,000   20,000   48,000
```

IFPS/PERSONAL.   IFPS/Personal is a DSS package for the microcomputer. It does not have all the power of the mainframe version. Further, even though IFPS/Personal is a companion product of IFPS, the two products accomplish their objectives differently. Some of the differences will be illustrated by solving the same example used above.

Exhibit 21.15 is a listing of the model necessary to solve the Oakes Company production budget using IFPS/Personal. There are four notable differences described below.

1. Remarks are noted with a \ instead of a ∗.
2. Rather than having line numbers, IFPS/Personal allows (but does not require) statement labels. These labels can be letters and/or numbers, followed by a colon. For example, the SALES OF WALL CABINETS variable in Exhibit 21.15 has been labeled WS:. Later in the model it is possible to refer to the variable by name or by its label.

Exhibit 21.15   IFPS/Personal Version of Production Budget

```
COLUMNS JAN THRU APR, TOTAL
\PRODUCTION OF WALL CABINETS
WS: SALES OF WALL CABINETS = 10000, 20000
EIW: DESIRED EI OF WALL CABINETS = 0.5*FUTURE WS: FOR 4, EIW:[MAR]
TW: TOTAL WALL CABINETS NEEDED = WS: + EIW:
BIW: BI OF WALL CABINETS = 8000, PREVIOUS EIW: FOR 3, BIW:[JAN]
PW: PRODUCTION OF WALL CABINETS = TW: - BIW:
\
\PRODUCTION OF BASE CABINETS
BS: SALES OF BASE CABINETS = 20000, 30000, 10000, 20000
EIB: DESIRED EI OF BASE CABINETS=0.25*FUTURE BS: FOR 4, EIB:[MAR]
TB: TOTAL BASE CABINETS NEEDED = BS: + EIB:
BIB: BI OF BASE CABINETS = 5000, PREVIOUS EIB: FOR 3, BIB:[JAN]
PB: PRODUCTION OF BASE CABINETS = TB: - BIB:
\
REDEFINE TOTAL FOR WS:,BS:=SUM([JAN] THRU [MAR])
```

3. IFPS/Personal defines special columns using the command REDEFINE instead of COL-UMNS. Column references are included in brackets, [ ]. Unlike IFPS, if the "special column" is not redefined for a selected variable, the logic of that variable will continue into (and through) the special column. In our example it is necessary to redefine the Total column for each of the sales variables. For the other variables the "normal logic" will also work in the special column.
4. The final difference to be noted here is the possibility of subscripting a variable name, or its label, and using the subscripted variable in expressions. For example, note the line labeled EIW: in Exhibit 21.15. The fifth column of DESIRED EI OF WALL CABINETS is defined EIW:[MAR]. What EIW:[MAR] says is to set the Total column equal to the value in the March column of the variable labeled EIW:. This causes the ending inventory for the quarter to be equal to the ending inventory of March.

In addition to the modeling language of IFPS and IFPS/Personal being different, the user accesses the software differently. IFPS/Personal is menu driven. When you are successful in bringing up the system, there will be a menu line at the bottom of the screen as follows:

IFPS: **Model**   Edit   Files   Profile Interface Log
         eXecute Consolidate Datafile Quit   Help

To enter a new model, the user places the cursor on Edit and presses enter. (Pressing the space bar will move the cursor.) IFPS/Personal will then ask for a file specification. For the Oakes problem, answer MODEL PRODBGT. IFPS/Personal will respond that PRODBGT is a new file and instructs you to begin entering. Then the following menu line appears:

Edit: **Append** Copy   Delete   Get   Include
         Locate   Move   Name   Replace Save   Undo   Visual

Place the cursor on Append and press enter. The cursor moves to the top of the screen and the model can be entered. IFPS/Personal has its own editing commands, which will not be discussed here. When your model is entered, toggle back to the menu line (press F10) place the cursor on Save and press enter.

To solve the model, move back to the IFPS menu line (hitting ESC, for "escape," moves up the ring of menu lines). Move the cursor to Model and press enter. A new menu will appear as follows:

Model: View   Plot Report   Edit   **Get**   reset   Data_edit
         Files   lisT Log   Create   cOmpile Invert Using

Place the cursor on Get and press enter. IFPS will ask for a model name. Type PRODBGT. You will be returned to the above menu line. To look at the model again, move the cursor to List and hit enter. The model will be solved if you move the cursor to View and hit enter. After a lapse of time the solved model will appear at the top of the screen and the model listing in the middle. A new menu will be at the bottom of the screen:

View: **What_If** wIndows   Variables Columns
         Set   Format   Analyze

If you would like to remove the April column, move the cursor to Columns, hit enter and then answer JAN,FEB,MAR,TOTAL when asked for the column list. Upon hitting enter, the solution at the top of the screen will delete the April column.

To do what ifs and goal seeks move the cursor to the What_if option in the View menu and press enter. A third window, the case window, will now appear on the screen along with a new menu line:

What_If: **Base**   Get   Name   Save
           solVe   gOal_seek Edit_case Update

New statements can be entered in the case window that will be temporary lines to the base model. To do this, select Edit_case. After entering the new statements in the case window, toggle back to the menu line by pressing F10. When solved (solVe), the temporary lines will be used. Space does not permit a detailed description of the protocol of doing what ifs and goal seeking but the results would be the same as previously discussed.

Another nice feature of IFPS/Personal is the ability to do graphics. One will be illustrated. Suppose you want to display the comparative production requirements on a month-to-month basis. After the model is solved, move to the Model menu. Place the cursor on Plot and press enter. The following menu will appear:

Plot: **Variables** Columns   shoW   scAle
         Save   Get   Options

Select Variables and enter PRODUCTION OF WALL CABINETS, PRODUC-TION OF BASE CABINETS when asked for the variable list. Return to the menu and select Columns. Enter JAN,FEB,MAR when asked for the list. Return to the Plot menu (using esc), select shoW and enter. IFPS/Personal will produce a graph similar to the one shown in Exhibit 21.16.

Summary

This chapter introduced you to computer spreadsheets and Decision Support Systems. Lotus 1-2-3, the Interactive Financial Planning System, and IFPS/Personal were used as examples of this type of computer software. Many other packages do operations similar to those illustrated using these three packages. You are encouraged to determine what is available at your university and use it to solve some of the problems in this and other chapters. It is an exciting new way to use computers.

  Key terms introduced in this chapter include:

Selected Lotus 1-2-3 commands
Selected IFPS commands

Exhibit 21.16   Graph Showing Production Volumes as Produced by IFPS/Personal

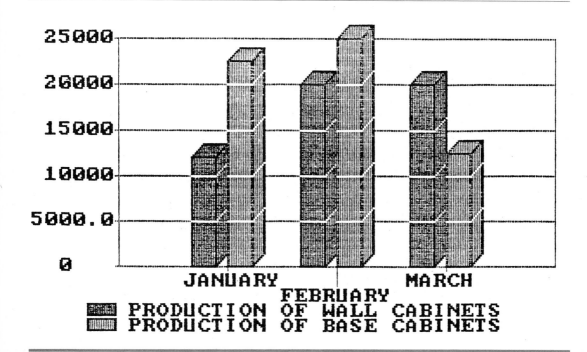

SELF-STUDY PROBLEM. The Oakes Company production budget developed in Chapter 12 was used in this chapter to demonstrate a computer spreadsheet. If you have access to another spreadsheet, such as Multiplan or VisaCalc, you should create a similar model using that package. If you have access to Lotus 1-2-3 or IFPS, then extend the model of Exhibit 21.1 to model the material purchasing budget for Oakes. Compare your results with those in Exhibit 12.5.

Solution to Self-Study Problem

The following contains the new cell entries that would have to be added to those of Exhibit 21.1 in order to do this problem with Lotus 1-2-3. The solution allows for skipping one row after row 14 of Exhibit 21.1 and starts in row 16.

A	B	C	D	E	F
	"JAN	"FEB	"MAR	"APR	"TOTAL
16 PURCHASING REQUIREMENTS					
17 FOR WALL CABINETS	2*B7	2*C7	2*D7	2*E7	@SUM(B17..D17)
18 FOR BASE CABINETS	3*B14	3*C14	3*D14	3*E14	@SUM(B18..D18)
19 TOTAL	+B17+B18	+C17+C18	+D17+D18	+E17+E18	@SUM(B19..D19)
20 DESIRED ENDING INVENTORY	@ROUND(C19/3,0)	@ROUND(D19/3,0)	40000	@ROUND(F19/3,0)	+D20
21 TOTAL NEEDS	+B19+B20	+C19+C20	+D19+D20	+E19+E20	+F19+F20
22 BEGINNING INVENTORY	35000	+B20	+C20	+D20	+B22
23 PURCHASING REQS (FEET)	+B21-B22	+C21-C22	+D21-D22	+E21-E22	+F21-F22
24 COST PER FOOT	5	5	5	5	5
25 PURCHASING REQS (DOLLARS)	+B24*B23	+C24*C23	+D24*D23	+E24*E23	+F24*F23

The @ROUND function used in row 20 rounds the results of the computation within the parentheses to a precision governed by the number of decimals entered after the comma. In this case, 0 decimals were selected.

References

Gray, P. *Student Guide to IFPS*. New York: McGraw-Hill Book Company, 1983.

Mayo, R.B. *Corporate Planning and Modeling with SIMPLAN*. Reading, Mass: Addison-Wesley, 1979.

Naylor, T.H. (ed.). *Simulation Models in Corporate Planning*. New York: Praeger Publishers, 1979.

Shaffer, D. *1-2-3 Revealed*. Reston, Va.: Reston Publishing Company, Inc., 1984.

Problems

21-1. Basic Problem Using Spreadsheet. Reconsider the Oakes Company's production and purchasing budget.

Required:

1. If you have access to Lotus 1-2-3, IFPS, or IFPS/Personal, copy the program listed in Exhibit 21.1, 21.7, or 21.15 and run it to verify the results. If you have access to some other

spreadsheet package, develop and run an equivalent model for Oakes's production and purchasing.
2. What if wall cabinet sales are projected at 50,000, 60,000, 30,000, and 70,000 units for the first four months? Use your model in part 1 to find the projected production requirements.

21-2. Continuation of Spreadsheet Problem. This problem assumes you have done part 1 of problem 21-1.

Required:

1. Add to the Oakes's purchasing and production model in order to do the labor budget. Compare your results with Exhibit 12.6.
2. What if Oakes has a goal of increasing the direct labor needed in January to 120,000 hours by adjusting the desired ending inventory of base cabinets for January? That is, management desires to work at capacity in January since February is scheduled to use overtime.

21-3. Addition to Spreadsheet Problem of 21-2. This problem assumes you were successful in incorporating the labor budget for the Oakes Company into the spreadsheet model started in the chapter.

Required:

1. Add the overhead budget displayed in Exhibit 12.7. You may omit the rate column. Also add the selling and administrative budget (Exhibit 12.8).
2. Add the schedule of accounts collection (Exhibit 12.9). Make the total column the total cash collections and put it on the right. Omit the "Collectible" and "Bad Debts" column. Just provide a variable for Beginning Accounts Receivable and provide the January and February figures. Then provide a second variable for collections on new accounts. Do not provide separate lines for each month. Be sure to include sales discounts.
3. Add the cash payments schedule (Exhibit 12.10). You need not include separate rows under the major entries for materials, supplies, labor, and so forth. That is, just have one row for cash payments for materials, for supplies, and so forth. Idle time and overtime premium will be difficult. Let the model compute it. Thus you will need to let the model:
   a. Determine the difference between labor hours needed (DL) and the normal capacity (NC). If DL − NC is negative, you have idle time. If positive, you have overtime.
   b. Use the IF-THEN-ELSE feature (@IF in 1-2-3) to compute the idle time cost or overtime premium. The IF-THEN-ELSE feature in IFPS works as follows:

   variable = IF "test" THEN "true expression" ELSE "false expression"

   where "test" is a comparison between two or more expressions, "true expression" is an expression that assigns the value if the test is valid, and "false expression" is an expression that assigns the value if the test is invalid.
   Operators that can be used in IFPS include .EQ. for equal to, .NE. for not equal to, .LE. for less than or equal to, .LT. for less than, .GE. for greater than or equal to, and .GT. for greater than.
   The @IF function in 1-2-3 is of the form @IF (a,vtrue,vfalse) where "a," "vtrue," and "vfalse" are the same as the three arguments of IFPS. The operators in 1-2-3 are =, <> for not equal to <=, <, >=, and >.

21-4. Spreadsheet for Self-Study Problem. If you have access to any type of spreadsheet software, formulate a model to solve the self-study problem in Chapter 12.

21-5. Spreadsheet Model for Problem 12-4. If you have access to any type of spreadsheet software, formulate a model to solve the Simmons Company problem in problem 12-4.

21-6. Spreadsheet Model for Problem 12-6. If you have access to any type of spreadsheet software, formulate a model to solve the Fremont Company problem in problem 12-6.

21-7. Spreadsheet Model for Problem 12-10. If you have access to any type of spreadsheet software, formulate a model to solve the Ace Company problem in problem 12-10.

21-8. Spreadsheet Model for Problem 12-13. If you have access to any type of spreadsheet software, formulate a model to solve the UBE problem in problem 12-13.

21-9. Spreadsheets and Process Costing. Consider problem 4-7. Formulate a generalized spreadsheet to solve this problem. For example devote a cell each to the percentage completion of the beginning inventory with respect to material and with respect to conversion costs. Compute the equivalent units by reference to the cells containing the percentage completion. That is, write the model in such a way that a minimum number of cells have to be changed when the data changes. See problem 21-11.

21-10. Alternative to 21-9. Consider problem 4-8 and build a generalized model. As in problem 21-9, make the model general enough so that it can be easily used as the data changes from month to month.

21-11. Using Spreadsheet in Problem 21-9. Consider the following new situations for the Rice Company of problem 4-7. For each situation use your model from problem 21-9 to complete the following table:

	Case 1	Case 2	Case 3	Case 4
Beginning inventory (units)	3,000*	3,000*	3,000*	4,000*
Percentage completion of beginning inventory	80%	1/3	1/3	25%
Started (units)	11,000	11,000	11,000	20,000
To finished goods (units)	10,000	10,000	10,000	18,000
Ending inventory (units)	4,000	4,000	4,000	6,000
Percentage completion of ending inventory	25%	60%	80%	40%
Current material cost	22,050	22,050	22,050	35,000
Current conversion cost	30,000	30,000	30,000	46,000
Cost assigned to finished goods	?	?	?	?
Cost assigned to ending work-in-process inventory	?	?	?	?

*In Cases 1–3, assume the cost of the inventory is the same as in the orignal problem. In case 4 assume the cost is $4,180 for material and $2,980 for conversion cost.

21-12. Alternative to 21-11 Using Spreadsheet in 21-10. Repeat problem 21-11 but assume the Rice Company uses modified FIFO for which a model was developed in 21-10.

21-13. Spreadsheets and Standard Costing. Consider the demonstration problem in Chapter 5 (E.E. Ray Company). It is desired to setup a generalized spreadsheet to compute the company's *overhead variances*. The spreadsheet should have columns similar to Exhibit 5.9 with rows for:

1. Labor hours.
2. Fixed cost.
3. Variable cost.

Further, the spreadsheet should contain entries for each of the four overhead variances:

1. Fixed overhead spending variance.
2. Noncontrollable variance.
3. Variable overhead spending variance.
4. Variable overhead efficiency variance.

Required:

1. Prepare a spreadsheet that is general in nature. That is, E.E. Ray wants to use it each month and wants to change a minimum number of entries each time.
2. Using the data in problem 5-6 employ the spreadsheet to compute February's variances.

21-14. Spreadsheets and CVP Analysis. Using the Eckel case in Chapter 13, write a one-column model that contains the following:

Sales volume
Sales revenue
Variable cost
Fixed costs
Net income before tax
Income tax
Net income after tax
Ratio of net income to sales

Manipulate the sales volume in order to find (a) the break-even volume, (b) a net income of $5,000 after taxes, and (c) an after-tax income equal to 12% of sales.

21-15. Addition to 21-14. Add a second column to your model in 21-14 to do the Ritts problem of Chapter 13. To model the step-fixed costs you can use the @IF function of Lotus 1-2-3 or the STEP function of IFPS. Use the help function to get the details. Repeat the goal searches mentioned in problem 21-14 for the Ritts Company.

21-16. Spreadsheets and Capital Budgeting. Write a spreadsheet that will compute the NPV and IRR for the four cases of Exhibit 15.4. In Lotus consult help about @NPV and @IRR. For IFPS consult help about NPVC and IRR.

CHAPTER 22

Planning Aids—Linear Programming and Inventory Models

*Chapter
Overview*

In this chapter there is an introduction to two quantitative tools that can be of benefit to managerial planning and decision making. These tools are linear programming and inventory models. The discussion of the models, themselves, is kept relatively simple since they are topics of most courses in quantitative methods. The major emphasis is on what the accountant will have to do to provide proper data for the models. The models will require a variety of cost and revenue data and if the data are not in keeping with the purpose of the model, the decision maker can be led astray. There will be a section devoted to each of the two models.

Linear Programming

The planning process (either budgeting, decision making, or cost-volume-profit analysis) may reveal that certain resources are demanded in an amount that exceeds their availability. For example, the Oakes Company in Chapter 12 was scheduled to use more labor during February than is normally available. In the budget of Chapter 12 it was assumed that overtime would and could be utilized. However, there was no attempt to schedule Oakes's resources in the most efficient manner. For example, rather than allow January to incur idle time followed by overtime in February management should consider shifting some of February's production requirements to January. This would reduce both idle time and overtime. Of course there would be added costs of carrying a larger inventory that would have to be considered.

GENERAL INTRODUCTION TO LINEAR PROGRAMMING.   Even in relatively simple cases it becomes difficult to determine the optimal allocation of resources. Help is needed, and an operations research model may at times be useful. **Linear programming (LP)**, for example, is one such mathematical technique for selecting optimal allocations of resources when all of the relationships can be represented by linear equations. To illustrate the general form of LP, assume that two products, A and B, can be produced. Product A contributes $6 toward fixed costs and profits and product B, $4. Each day there are ten hours of labor available and eight units of material. Product A requires two hours of labor and one unit of material. Product B requires one hour of labor and one unit of material. Product B's market is limited to seven units per day.

Define A and B to be variables representing the quantity of each product produced. The objective equation of the LP model is constructed to maximize the total contribution margin subject to the constraints on labor, material, and B's market. That is:

Maximize $6A + 4B$	(objective function)	(22-1)
Subject to: $2A + 1B \leq 10$	(labor)	(22-2)
$A + B \leq 8$	(material)	(22-3)
$B \leq 7$	(market constraint on B)	(22-4)
$A, \ B \geq 0$	(nonnegativity constraints)	(22-5)

Although it is not practical to solve large-scale LP problems graphically, one can sense the essence of a solution procedure by considering a graphical method. Exhibit 22.1 is a graph of the constraints. Each line represents a boundary of the area of possible solutions permitted by the associated constraint. For example, the nonnegativity constraint on product A limits the solutions to all positive values of A: the area above the A axis. Similarly, the nonnegativity constraint on B limits the solutions to all positive values of B: the area to the right of the B axis. Together, the two nonnegativity constraints limit the solution to the first quadrant (the upper right area).

The remaining three constraints (labor, material, and B's market) eliminate other possible solutions from the first quadrant. The labor constraint *at its boundary* is linear and is:

$2A + 1B = 10$ (boundary is where there is equality)

The boundary can be plotted by selecting two points which satisfy the preceding equality. One point on the labor constraint boundary is where $A = 0$. If $A = 0$, then B must equal 10. A second point is where $B = 0$. If $B = 0$, then $A = 5$. Locating the points $(0, 10)$ and $(5, 0)$ on the graph and connecting them with a straight line yields a boundary of the solutions that will not violate the labor constraint. Likewise, plot the material and market constraint. The combined result of the five constraints is called the area of feasible solutions and is the shaded area in Exhibit 22.1.

An entire family of objective functions can be plotted by selecting several values of P and finding, for each P, the A and B that satisfy:

$P = 6A + 4B$

For example, consider $P = 12$ and $P = 24$. To have a profit of \$12, the solution of A and B would have to be such that:

$12 = 6A + 4B$

A \$12 profit curve can be plotted in the same way as the constraint boundaries were plotted. That is, if $B = 0$ then $A = 2$ and if $A = 0$ then $B = 3$. Two points on the \$12 profit curve are $(2, 0)$ and $(0, 3)$. All points on the line passing through $(2, 0)$ and $(0, 3)$ have a \$12 profit. This line is plotted in Exhibit 22.2. Likewise, for a \$24 profit:

$24 = 6A + 4B$

Exhibit 22.1   Graph of Illustrative LP Problem

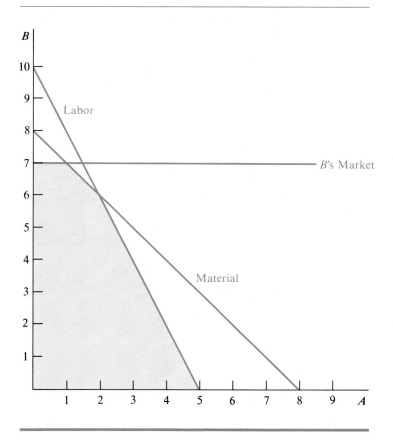

Two points on the $24 curve are (4, 0) and (0, 6). The $24 profit line is also plotted in Exhibit 22.2. Each member of the family of profit curves would have distinct lines and they would be parallel to each other. Thus to maximize P it would be necessary to find the line that is as far from the origin, (0, 0), as possible and yet be in the area of feasible solutions.

Since each member of the family is linear, the line representing the maximum value of P will pass through one of the corner points of the feasible area. A corner point is one where the perimeter of the feasible area changes directions. For this problem the corner points are (0, 0), (0, 7), (1, 7), (2, 6), and (5, 0). Thus, to identify the optimal solution, just compute the value of the objective equation at each corner point and select the largest result. Since the contribution margins per unit are $6 and $4, you should verify that the total contribution margin at the corner points are $0, $28, $34, $36, and $30, respectively. The point (2, 6) yields the largest value and thus the optimal solution is to produce 2 units of A and 6 of B.

Exhibit 22.2   Illustrative LP Problem with Profit Lines Added

---

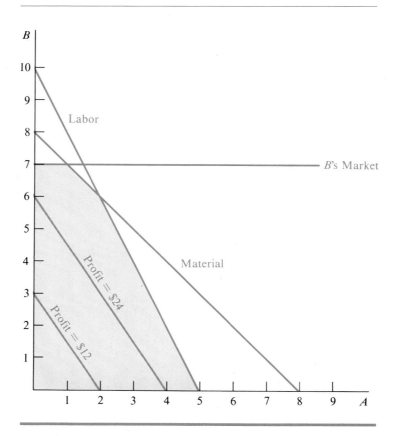

Although the budget situation of Chapter 12 is more complicated than this example, LP can still be used to help select an optimal strategy for the use of limited resources and scheduling production. To do this is somewhat more involved.

GENERAL DATA CONCEPTS.   A specific linear programming (LP) problem was illustrated in equations (22-1) through (22-5). Note that in this specific example the model requires a set of decision variables to be defined (A and B). That is, A is a variable representing the number of units of product A produced, etc. When you encounter general statements of LP problems you will find the variables referred to as $x_1, x_2, \ldots , x_n$. That is, in general there are n variables where x_1 is the variable representing the number of times to use activity 1, x_2 the variable representing the number of times to use activity 2, and so forth.

Also note there are three types of data requirements for an LP model:

1. The effect that each variable has on the objective equation (the $6 and $4 in equation (22-1)). In general, the effect of variable x_j on the objective equation is referred to as c_j. In implementing the model, the c_j notation is replaced by a specific number and is used in the model as a general reference to these data.
2. A set of values representing the maximum availability of resources or the minimum levels of requirements, depending on the nature of the constraints. The constraints in (22-2), (22-3), and (22-4), for example, limited the labor consumption to 10, the material consumption to 8, and the sales of product B to 7. These values are called the right-hand sides of the constraints and are generally referred to as b_i. That is, b_i is the right-hand side of the ith constraint.
3. A set of values that represent the rate at which a variable consumes resources or contributes to requirements, depending on the nature of the constraint. For example, product A in the preceding problem requires two hours of labor, one unit of material, and zero units of product B's market potential. In general these values are denoted as $a_{i,j}$ where i refers to the constraint and j the variable.

Using the notation explained above, the general LP model is as follows:

Maximize or minimize: $$c_1x_1 + c_2x_2 + \ldots + c_nx_n \qquad (22\text{-}6)$$
Subject to:
$$\left. \begin{array}{l} a_{1,1}x_1 + a_{1,2}x_2 + \ldots + a_{1,n}x_n \leq \text{ or } \geq \text{ or } = b_1 \\ a_{2,1}x_1 + a_{2,2}x_2 + \ldots + a_{2,n}x_n \leq \text{ or } \geq \text{ or } = b_2 \\ \vdots \qquad \vdots \qquad\qquad \vdots \qquad\qquad \vdots \\ a_{m,1}x_1 + a_{m,2}x_2 + \ldots + a_{m,n}x_n \leq \text{ or } \geq \text{ or } = b_m \end{array} \right\} \qquad (22\text{-}7)$$
$$x_j \geq 0 \text{ for all } j \qquad (22\text{-}8)$$

The LP model assumes the c_j and $a_{i,j}$ coefficients are marginal values. That is, they represent the effect (either on the objective or the constraint) of changing variable x_j by *one* unit. This means, for example, that allocated fixed costs musts be excluded from the unit cost data used in LP models. Of course, any of the cost behavior analyses used for standard cost setting would be a useful way of obtaining these data. It also means the data should represent actual economic phenomena and not accounting representations of the phenomena. For example, accounting depreciation is not, in most cases, a good representation of economic depreciation and, therefore, would not be appropriate for an LP model.

In short, when LP models require financial data, they must reflect *future* financial impacts. Because of this, any data that might be provided by accountants are subject to estimation error. Fortunately, however, the LP model may be insensitive to some errors. Computer LP algorithms provide some sensitivity results as a standard output.

In order to demonstrate that accountants' data do not have to be "perfectly" accurate, let's consider, in a nontechnical way, the **sensitivity** of an LP model. It can be shown, for example, that the contribution margin on product A, c_A of the LP model in (22-1) through (22-5), can be anywhere in the range from $4 per unit to $8 per unit and not cause a change in the optimal solution to the model. That is:

$$4 \leq c_A \leq 8$$

The above range assumes that all other factors are constant. That is, in computing the range it is assumed that B's contribution does not change and that the constraints do not change in *any* way (either the $a_{i,j}$ or b_i values).

The validity of this range can be illustrated by evaluating the objective function at each of the corner points of the feasible area as originally shown in Exhibit 22.1. First use the value at the lower extreme of the range on c_A and then at the upper extreme. In the following schedule the results for each of these extremes are shown along with the results for the original objective equation.

Corner Point		Results Using Lower Extreme for c_A	Results for Original Objective	Results Using Upper Extreme for c_A
A	*B*	$4A + 4B$	$6A + 4B$	$8A + 4B$
0	0	0	0	0
0	7	28	28	28
1	7	32	34	36
2	6	32	36	40
5	0	20	30	40

As can be seen, the point (2, 6) is optimal for all three of the above objective equations. Granted, other points are also optimal: point (1, 7) at the lower extreme and (5, 0) at the upper. However (2, 6) did remain optimal for a c_A of $4, $6, or $8.

Knowledge of sensitivity ranges benefits accountants in the following way. It may be impossible to say that product A's contribution margin is exactly $6 as was implicitly assumed in the original problem. But it is now known that it is not always necessary to be exact in measuring a variable's contribution margin for usage in linear programming models.

Computer algorithms also provide sensitivity ranges for the b_i parameters and the $a_{i,j}$ values.[1] In addition to analyses of the sensitivity of the c_j, b_i, and $a_{i,j}$ values, other types of sensitivity can be performed. For example, the accountant may be asked to estimate the cost of some resource that is used in producing several of the products in an LP model. It there is uncertainty about this estimate and if, in fact, it may be different from the original estimate, then the c_j values of several variables may change simultaneously. Sensitivity analyses have been developed to find the range in which the cost of such a resource can vary without causing a change in the optimal solution.[2]

---

[1] For example, see David R. Anderson, Dennis J. Sweeney, and Thomas A. Williams, *An Introduction to Management Science,* 4th ed. (St. Paul, MN: West Publishing Company, 1985), Chapter 4.

[2] See: Ronald V. Hartley, "Some Extensions of Sensitivity Analysis," *The Accounting Review* (April 1970), pp. 223– 234.

To illustrate, it can be shown that the cost of labor in constraint (22-2) may increase by as much as $2 and not cause the original optimal solution to change from A = 2 and B = 6. If labor did increase by $2, then the contribution margin on product A would decrease by $4 ($2 per hour × 2 hours per unit) down to $2 ($6 − $4). Product B's contribution would decrease by $2 ($2 per hour × 1 hour per unit) down to $2 ($4 − $2). The following verifies that the original solution is still optimal although the point (1, 7) is also optimal.

Corner Point		Results for an Equation of
A	B	2A + 2B
0	0	0
0	7	14
1	7	16
2	**6**	**16**
5	0	10

Another type of sensitivity that should be of concern to accountants is one whereby there is a change in an $a_{i,j}$ value and a simultaneous and related change in the c_j value. For example, if labor costs $2 per hour and if product A turns out to require three hours instead of two, then $a_{1,A}$ becomes three and *at the same time* c_A becomes $4 ($6 − $2). The $2 decrease represents the additional labor hour. Sensitivity ranges on these kinds of changes can also be computed but we will not pursue this further.[3]

As the final consideration, accountants need to ensure that the data represent *future* economic sacrifices. The principles of Chapter 14 (Relevant Data) are applicable. Historical costs are a starting point, but it is necessary to make sure they are representative of future economic costs. A major difficulty in implementing this concept is to find an appropriate way to account for the cost of depreciable facilities. Let's consider this issue further.

It may be conventional to treat depreciation as a fixed cost and, therefore, exclude it from the cost coefficients of a mathematical programming model. This is appropriate when the replacement of such facilities is only dependent on *time*. However, if replacement is a function of *usage,* then treating the asset's cost as irrelevant may lead to a nonoptimal decision. When replacement is a function of usage, increased consumption results in more frequent replacements. By ignoring the depreciation, the model will tend to "use" the asset more intensely than it would if the depreciation is considered. The more intense use may not be an optimal strategy.

To adjust for this problem is difficult. Perhaps the replacement cost of the asset can be estimated and then divided by the estimated hours of usage to obtain a "variable" usage cost. This cost could then be incorporated into the parameters of

---

[3]See: William F. Bentz, Lawrence A. Sherr, and Robert E. Miller, "Sensitivity Analysis with Interaction Effects," *Decision Sciences* (July 1976), pp. 432–446.

the objective function. Such a treatment can create difficulty, however, if the problem is to be solved using a multiperiod model with discounted *cash* flows for the objective equation. The problem is that the cash flow for replacement comes in bundles rather than uniformly with usage. To properly model this case, it may be necessary to use integer programming and this goes beyond the scope of this chapter.

≥ CONTINUATION OF JOINT-PRODUCTS PROBLEM FROM CHAPTER 14.   To further illustrate the problem of providing data for an LP model, let's consider a case introduced earlier. As a result of a case in Chapter 14 it is known that joint costs can be difficult to account for in making decisions. The case studied there could be solved by treating the joint costs as irrelevant. But in other situations, they may be relevant.

To illustrate an accounting for variable costs of the joint process in the latter case, reconsider the situation originally depicted in Exhibit 14.5 and reproduced in Exhibit 22.3. Suppose management is trying to determine the optimal quantities of each of the products to sell. The maximum quantity of the raw material, Ingrediente, that can be made available per month is 11,000 pounds. Management is not sure that Department I should be operated at the full 11,000-pound capacity and wants to consider its utilization as a variable.

Define the following variables:

$$A_1 = \text{quantity of product A sold at the split-off point}$$
$$A_2 = \text{quantity of product A sold after additional processing}$$
$$B_1, B_2, C_1, \text{and } C_2 = \text{similar to the preceding except they are for products B and C}$$

Since the objective equation coefficients must be such that they indicate the impact of changing the decision variable by one unit, all fixed costs *and the variable costs in Department I* must be excluded in determining the coefficients for the variables just defined. To account for Department I's cost, another variable needs to be defined. Let:

M = the number of pounds of material processed by Department I during the month

With these variables the model can be specified. The only factors that *change directly* with the variables A_1, B_1, and C_1 are their respective sales prices. For products A_2, B_2, and C_2 the directly traceable factors include both the sales prices and the variable costs of the appropriate departments beyond the split-off point. Thus, the coefficients for these variables are determined from the data in Exhibit 22.3 as follows:

A_1: Sales price of A at the split-off point = $45
A_2: Sales price of A after additional processing − *variable* cost in Department II

Exhibit 22.3   Joint-Products Problem

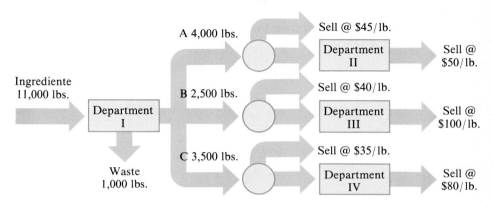

Estimated Monthly Costs if Each Department Operated at Normal Volume

	Department I	Department II	Department III	Department IV
Variable	$120,000	$ 80,000	$37,500	$140,000
Fixed	100,000	20,000	12,500	35,000
Total	$220,000	$100,000	$50,000	$175,000

$$\$50 - \frac{\$80,000}{4,000} = \$30$$

B_1: Sales price of B at the split-off point $= \$40$

B_2: Sales price of B after additional processing $-$ *variable* cost in Department III

$$\$100 - \frac{\$37,500}{2,500} = \$85$$

C_1: Sales price of C at the split-off point $= \$35$

C_2: Sales price of C after additional processing $-$ *variable* cost in Department IV

$$\$80 - \frac{\$140,000}{3,500} = \$45$$

The coefficient for variable M will be the unit variable cost of Department I ($120,000 \div 11,000 = \$10.91$). Thus, the objective equation for our problem is:

Maximize: $45A_1 + 30A_2 + 40B_1 + 85B_2 + 35C_1 + 40C_2 - 10.91M$ **(22-9)**

In order to further explain, let's consider the constraints for this problem. First, the amount of material that can be used is limited to 11,000 pounds. In terms of the above variables, this can be constrained as:

$$M \leq 11,000 \tag{22-10}$$

A second general type of constraint needed is one to ensure that the sales of a product do not exceed the production of the product. There would be three constraints of this type, one for the A product group as well as for the B and C groups. The amount of the A group produced is a function of variable M. From Exhibit 22.3 you can see that every pound of M is expected to yield 4/11 pounds of A. In terms of the variables, A can either be sold as A_1 or A_2 but the sum of A_1 and A_2 cannot exceed the production:

$$A_1 + A_2 \leq 4/11M \tag{22-11}$$

Similarly:

$$B_1 + B_2 \leq 25/110M \tag{22-12}$$

$$C_1 + C_2 \leq 35/110M \tag{22-13}$$

Now, before any of the products can be sold, constraints (22-11), (22-12), and (22-13) force some production in the joint process. When M takes on a nonzero value, this causes an increase in Department I's cost at the rate of $10.91 per pound as reflected in the objective equation, (22-9).[4]

Inventory Models

Inventory models (Economical Order Quantity or EOQ models) constitute another class of models that requires data from an accounting system. After considering the nature and purpose of these models, this section will consider those data requirements.

NATURE OF INVENTORY MODELS.   The purpose of an inventory model is to select the order size, or production run size, that will minimize the inventory related costs. That is, such models assume the total demand over a given period of time, say a year, is known and it is desired to determine the quantity to purchase on each order, or the quantity to produce in each production run, in order to minimize costs. These costs include ordering and/or setup costs, holding costs, stockout costs, and purchase or production costs. Each of these costs will be defined. When items are being purchased, *ordering costs* are incurred and include such expenses as the purchasing agents' salaries, clerical wages, forms, telephone, and receiving costs. If the situation is a production decision rather than a purchasing decision, then setup costs are incurred in addition to ordering costs. *Setup costs* consist of the costs of preparing the production line for the job and the cost of testing, including any spoilage that is expected during the test period.

---

[4]For an expanded discussion of this type of problem, see: Ronald V. Hartley, "Decision Making When Joint Products Are Involved," *The Accounting Review* (October 1971), pp. 746–755.

Holding costs consist of warehousing costs, property taxes, insurance, handling costs, deterioration, and the opportunity cost of investing funds in inventory. The latter cost is typically significant and also one for which there is no accounting record of past amounts. Special attention will be given to opportunity costs later in the section.

Stockout costs are incurred when the demand for the product exceeds its supply. They include out-of-pocket costs of notifying the customer and of making special attempts to retain the order. Order retention efforts are not always successful and the lost profits must also be included in the stockout costs. Perhaps the customer's business will just be lost on this transaction but there is also a chance of losing their continuing business. Conceptually, then, the opportunity cost should be measured as the present value of the expected losses resulting from the shortage.

The meaning of purchase (invoice) and production costs should be obvious. *If these costs are not a function of the order or production size, they are irrelevant.* In such a case the *total* invoice or production cost for the year would be the same regardless of the order or production run size. However, if there are quantity discounts, then the total invoice costs for the year could differ depending on the order size. There is a class of inventory models that incorporates quantity discount schemes into its solution algorithm. Space does not permit an examination of those algorithms, however.[5]

The cost equation for inventory models is expressed as a function of the order size. Define the variable q to represent this quantity. Also define:

K = ordering cost per order
H = holding cost per unit of inventory per period
D = total expected demand for product during the period

Stockout costs will be ignored for the model discussed here.

Because the costs must be a function of q, it is necessary to define the number of orders and the average inventory as functions of q. Since D is the expected yearly demand, and a known constant, the number of orders in the year is simply $D \div q$. Thus, the yearly ordering cost is the number of orders times the cost per order $(D/q)K$. Further, if a constant linear demand for the product is assumed, then the inventory level starts at q when the order is received and reduces to zero at the point in time just prior to the receipt of the next order. Consequently, the average inventory is just $q \div 2$. The cost of holding inventory is $(q/2)H$. C, the total cost function, is the sum of the ordering and holding costs:

$$C = \frac{DK}{q} + \frac{Hq}{2} \qquad\qquad (22\text{-}14)$$

Each term of (22-14) is plotted in Exhibit 22.4 along with the total cost. As you can see, the behavior of the first term, DK/q, is one that starts high when q is low and then decreases as q increases. The second term is just a linear function of q.

---

[5]For a discussion of quantity discount models see: G. Hadley and T.M. Whitin, *Analysis of Inventory Systems* (Englewood Cliffs, NJ: Prentice-Hall, 1963), pp. 62–68.

Adding the two gives the bowl-shaped curve in Exhibit 22.4. Note that the minimum point on the total cost curve, C, is found at the q where the ordering cost curve, DK/q, intersects the holding cost curve, Hq/2. Define the optimal q to be q*. Then, the above observation says that at q*:

$$\frac{DK}{q^*} = \frac{H}{2}q^*$$

Solving:

$$DK = \frac{H}{2}(q^*)^2$$

$$(q^*)^2 = \frac{2DK}{H}$$

and:

$$q^* = \sqrt{\frac{2DK}{H}} \qquad\qquad (22\text{-}15)$$

To illustrate, suppose:

D = 30,000 per year
K = $20 per order
H = $7.50 per unit per year

Then:

$$q^* = \sqrt{\frac{2(30,000)(20)}{7.50}} = \sqrt{160,000} = 400$$

Note that as K, the order cost, becomes higher, the order quantity becomes higher. Likewise, as H, the holding cost, becomes higher, the order quantity becomes lower. Both of these results are reasonable.

DATA REQUIREMENTS. As a general rule, the data for inventory models have characteristics that are similar to linear programming models. That is, the values of K and H in the preceding model must be *marginal* costs with respect to the number of orders and the size of the inventory, respectively. Again, as might be expected, the real world is frequently not divisible into perfectly fixed and variable relationships. Let us briefly consider each type of cost and some of the measurement problems.

   Ordering costs may be dominated by step costs. Purchasing agents, for example, must be employed in integer quantities. The question arises, then, whether these costs should be treated as fixed with respect to the order quantity decision or as some other function. If they are treated as fixed then there is an implicit assumption that:

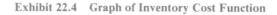

Exhibit 22.4   Graph of Inventory Cost Function

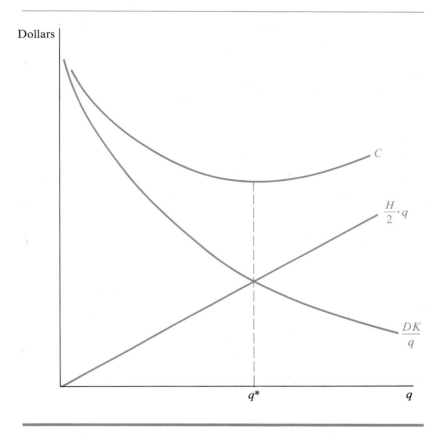

1. The number of purchasing agents is fixed and they will always be able to process all orders.
2. The agents will not be doing anything except processing orders.

Ignoring the agents' salaries lowers K in equation (22-15), lowers q^*, and increases the number of orders. Thus, excluding these costs from the model, especially for a firm that needs many different inventory items, increases the risk that the solution will require more agents than originally assumed. Instead of employing additional agents, it may be less costly to increase order sizes and carry a higher average inventory.

Even if the existing group of agents could process the number of orders that represent realistic solutions to the problem it may not be desirable to make the second assumption. If purchasing agents have other duties, then an increase in the number of orders to be processed decreases the amount of time the agents can spend on nonordering activities. Thus, there would still be a cost represented by the outlay needed to have the nonordering services covered in some alternative way.

Should these possibilities be of major concern, what can be done? One possibility is to linearize the step costs. Linearization is done by averaging an agent's salary over the expected number of orders that could be processed if the agent devoted his or her entire time to ordering activities. This amount plus the other relevant ordering costs gives the K parameter. The model would then minimize those costs than can be *attributed* to the ordering function.

Another useful aid for generating the inventory model's data is regression analysis (see Chapter 23). For such an analysis, the dependent variable would be total ordering costs, with the independent variable being the number of orders. Before using the regression model, cost data would need to be scrutinized carefully to ensure they represent ordering activities and that they have been assigned to the period in which they were actually incurred.

In measuring holding costs, you will face some of the same problems mentioned previously. Further there are problems in measuring the opportunity cost of the investment in inventory. The theory behind such a cost is that inventory is a type of "fixed" asset. Even though the inventory may frequently turn over, there is still a relatively constant number of dollars invested. The larger the inventory, the more dollars there are invested and the greater the need to secure additional capital for other purposes. Ignoring the cost will result in a more intense use of capital for inventory than can be justified.

Although it is relatively easy to construct a convincing argument for including the opportunity cost, it is difficult to measure. Several would argue that the weighted cost of capital should be used. The basis for such an argument is similar to that advanced in Chapter 16 when discussing the appropriate discount rate for a capital budgeting model. There is merit in this view since inventory requires capital from the total pool of capital just the same as major long-run projects.

In many cases some of the costs needed for inventory models may have to be *subjectively* estimated. Estimates increase the risk of measurement error, but the errors may not result in as much displacement from the optimal cost as you might suspect. As with linear programming, sensitivity analysis can prove useful.

To briefly introduce sensitivity analysis, let us reconsider the numerical example introduced in the previous subsection. Assuming the actual order costs and holding costs were as estimated, $20 and $7.50, the total cost of using an order size of 400 can be found by using equation (22-14):

$$C = \frac{D}{q}(K) + \frac{q}{2}(H) = \frac{30,000}{400}(20) + \frac{400}{2}(7.50) = \$3,000$$

Now suppose the holding cost actually was $13.33\frac{1}{3}$ per unit per year insted of $7.50. However the order size of 400, representing the optimal q for the original data, was actually used during the year. The actual inventory related cost per year would be:

$$C(400) = \frac{30,000}{400}(20) + \frac{400}{2}(13.33\tfrac{1}{3}) = \$4,166.67$$

If it had been known that H was $13.33\frac{1}{3}$ instead of $7.50 q* would have been as follows:

$$q_* = \sqrt{\frac{2(30,000)(20)}{(13.33\frac{1}{3})}} = 300$$

The yearly inventory related costs incurred by using the optimal quantity is:

$$C(300) = \frac{30,000}{300}(20) + \frac{300}{2}(13.33\frac{1}{3}) = \$4,000$$

Thus, even though the ratio of the actual holding cost to the one originally used is 1.77 ($13.33\frac{1}{3} \div 7.50$), the ratio of the actual cost to the optimal cost is 1.04^+ ($4,166.67 \div 4,000$). There was significant error in the measurement of holding costs but not that great of a displacement from the optimal cost. Thus, the accountant can feel somewhat more confident about cost estimates in that small errors will not materially increase costs.

Summary

Quantitative methods have been increasingly accepted by decision makers. Inappropriate or unavailable data may be a deterrent to their use. This chapter is, in part, a response to this need. Even though an incomplete treatise, it does provide accountants a base upon which to develop an improved ability to serve the quantitative disciplines.

From this chapter you should have gained additional understandings about using the marginal cost concept in providing data for linear programming and inventory models. Practical problems of measuring costs were discussed. That is, cost functions and decision models may have to be approximate rather than exact. You are encouraged to continue studying quantitative models. Increased understanding of the models will substantially increase your ability to serve their data needs.

Key terms for this chapter include:

Linear programming
Sensitivity analysis
Inventory models

SELF-STUDY PROBLEM ONE. This self-study problem is a CMA Exam question. Leastan Company manufactures a line of carpeting that includes a commercial carpet and a residential carpet. Two grades of fiber, heavy-duty and regular, are used in manufacturing both types of carpeting. The mix of the two grades of fiber differs in each type of carpeting with the commercial grade using a greater amount of heavy-duty fiber.

Leastan will introduce a new line of carpeting in two months to replace the current line. The present fiber in stock will not be used in the new line. Management wants to exhaust the present stock of regular and heavy duty fiber during the last month of production.

Data regarding the current line of commercial and residential carpeting are presented below:

	Commercial	Residential
Selling price per roll	$1,000	$800
Production specifications per roll of carpet		
Heavy-duty fiber	80 pounds	40 pounds
Regular fiber	20 pounds	40 pounds
Direct-labor hours	15 hours	15 hours
Standard cost per roll of carpet		
Heavy-duty fiber ($3/pound)	$ 240	$120
Regular fiber ($2/pound)	40	80
Direct labor ($10/DLH)	150	150
Variable manufacturing overhead		
(60% of direct labor cost)	90	90
Fixed manufacturing overhead		
(120% of direct-labor cost)	180	180
Total standard cost per roll	$ 700	$620

Leaston has 42,000 pounds of heavy-duty fiber and 24,000 pounds of regular fiber in stock. All fiber not used in the manufacture of the present types of carpeting during the last month of production can be sold as scrap at $0.25 a pound.

There are a maximum of 10,500 direct-labor hours available during the month. The labor force can work on either type of carpeting.

Sufficient demand exists for the present line of carpeting so that all quantities produced can be sold.

Required:

Formulate the objective and constraint functions so that Leastan's problem can be solved by linear programming.

Solution to Self-Study Problem One

Because the stock of regular and heavy-duty fiber is not to be used in the new line of carpets, the standard costs of the fibers are not relevant to the decision. The cost of the existing fiber is a sunk cost. The scrap value of the fiber is relevant because when it is used in producing carpet the firm must forego this scrap revenue. To incorporate this into the model, define S_1 and S_2 as the number of pounds of heavy-duty and regular fiber not used this month and, therefore, sold for scrap. The opportunity cost of using the fiber in the production of carpet will be implicitly considered as follows. When used in production the slack variable will be lower and, therefore, scrap revenue will be lower. Thus, fiber will incur a zero out-of-pocket cost when used in carpet. Further, the fixed overhead is not relevant. Thus the relevant contribution margins are as follows.

	Commercial		Residential	
Sales price	$1000		$800	
Variable cost				
Heavy duty fiber	$ 0		$ 0	
Regular fiber	0	0		
Direct labor	150		150	
Variable overhead	90	240	90	240
Contribution margin		$ 760		$560

Define C to be the number of rolls of commercial carpet and R as the number of rolls of residential carpet. Then:

Maximize: $760C + 560R + 0.25S_1 + 0.25S_2$

Subject to:

$$80C + 40R + S_1 \qquad\qquad = 42{,}000 \text{ (Heavy-duty)}$$

$$20C + 40R \qquad\quad + \quad S_2 = 24{,}000 \text{ (Regular)}$$

$$15C + 15R \qquad\qquad\qquad \leqslant 10{,}500 \text{ (Labor)}$$

SELF-STUDY PROBLEM TWO. The Feller Company has a yearly demand for 100,000 units of one of its products. It costs $80 per order to place an order. The item has an invoice price of $100 per unit and sells for $175. Warehousing costs, property taxes, and other out-of-pocket costs average $0.50/unit/year. At the present time the company would use any available funds to retire bonds that are earning 10% per year. The company is also earning 15% on its present assets, and its weighted cost of capital is 12%. What is the optimal order quantity?

Solution to Self-Study Problem Two

The parameters needed for the inventory model, as described in equation (22-15), are as follows:

$D = 100{,}000$
$K = 80$
$H = 0.50 + (0.12)100 = \$1.70$

Parameter H includes the out-of-pocket cost of $0.50 plus an opportunity cost on the investment in inventory. The inventory costs $100 per unit and every unit in inventory ties up $100 (on the average) that would require capital. Since the weighted cost of capital is 12%, this investment costs $1.20 per year for each item carried in the inventory. The EOQ formula, itself, factors into consideration the average inventory. It is instructive to compare the treatment of opportunity cost in this problem with the treatment in self-study problem one. The opportunity cost is included as a function of the inventory order quantity because of the scope of the inventory model. The inventory model does not include the act of borrowing capital and, therefore, if the cost of capital is not included then it is ignored. In contrast, the LP model in self-study problem one included the act of selling the excess fiber or scrap. Because of this, the opportunity cost did not have to be explicitly included in the coefficients for C and R. Thus:

$$q_* = \sqrt{\frac{2(100,000)(80)}{1.70}} = \sqrt{9,411,764.706} = 3,068$$

References

Jensen, D. "Hartley's Demand-Price Analysis in a Case of Joint Production: A Comment," *The Accounting Review* (October 1973): 768–770.
Lea, R. "A Note on the Definition of Cost Coefficients in a Linear Programming Model," *The Accounting Review* (April 1972): 346–350.
Monden, Y. *Toyota Production System.* Norcross, GA: Institute of Industrial Engineers, 1983.
Schroeder, R.G., and Krishnan, R. "Return on Investment as a Criterion for Inventory Models," *Decision Sciences* (October 1976): 697–704.

Problems

22-1. Continuation of Basic LP Problem in Text. Instead of the objective equation used in the illustrative LP problem in the text, assume the contribution margins for products A and B are $10 and $3, respectively.

Required:

1. What would be the optimal quantities to budget for products A and B?
2. Suppose the contribution margins for A and B were −$2 (negative) and $4. What would be the optimal quantities to budget?

22-2. Basic LP Problem. The Biplane Company manufactures two products, A and B. Product A sells for $30 per unit and B for $51. Both products require a raw material that costs $2 per unit and whose supply is limited to eighteen units per week. Direct laborers earn $8 per hour and can work up to fifteen hours per week.

Product A requires two units of material and one hour of labor. Its maximum market potential per week is six units. Product B requires three units of material and three hours of labor. There is a contract with one of Biplane's customers to supply them with one unit of B per week. Thus, the production of B must be at least one unit per week.

Variable overhead is applied at $6 per labor hour and fixed overhead at $4 per hour.

Required:

1. Construct the LP model that can be solved for the optimal amounts to budget for Products A and B.
2. Graphically solve the model you formulated in part 1.

22-3. LP as Input to Budgeting Process. The Carew Company produces two products A and B. Linear programming is used to determine the optimal number of units to produce each month. There are four constraints on the production:

1. A special material (CA-29) can only be acquired at a maximum rate of 2,500 pounds per month.
2. The maximum market potential for product A is 1,000 units per month.
3. The maximum market potential for product B is 300 units per month.

4. Carew has a contract with the Foli Company such that any combination of A and B totaling 600 units must be provided.

Product A requires two pounds of the special material per unit and B five pounds. The contribution margins per unit are expected to be as follows:

	January	*February*
Product A	$ 5	$ 7
Product B	15	15

Any unit produced in a month can be sold in the same month at the prices listed above.

Both products also require material CA-44, which can be purchased in relatively unlimited quantities. However there is a lead time of three fourths of a month that must be planned for. Product A requires three units of CA-44 and B four units.

Required:

Determine the optimal production schedules and a schedule of the amount of material CA-44 to purchase during January. Assume that January's beginning inventory of CA-44 is equal to the amount that would have been budgeted in the prior month. (Hint: You probably should define A as the hundreds of A to produce and B as the hundreds of B.)

22-4. Adapted CMA Problem on Linear Programming Formulation for Product Mix Decision. The Witchell Corporation manufactures and sells three grades of a single wood product, A, B, and C. Each grade must be processed through three phases—cutting, fitting, and finishing—before it is sold.

The following unit information is provided:

	A	*B*	*C*
Selling price	$10.00	$15.00	$20.00
Material requirements in board feet	7	7	10
Labor requirements in hours			
Cutting	3/6	3/6	4/6
Fitting	1/6	1/6	2/6
Finishing	1/6	2/6	3/6

Only 5,000 board feet per week can be obtained. The cutting department has 180 hours of labor available each week. The fitting and finishing departments each have 120 hours of labor available each week. No overtime is allowed.

Contract commitments require the company to make fifty units of A per week. In addition, company policy is to produce at least fifty additional units of each of the three products each week to actively remain in each of the three markets. Because of competition only 130 units of C can be sold each week.

The material cost is $0.10 per foot. Labor is paid at $10 per hour, variable overhead is applied at $0.20 per direct-labor hour, and fixed overhead at $0.12 per direct-labor hour.

Required:

Formulate and label the linear objective function and the constraint functions necessary to maximize Witchell's profits.

22-5. Adapted CMA Problem on LP. Excelsion Corporation manufactures and sells two kinds of containers—paperboard and plastic. The company produced and sold 100,000 paperboard containers and 75,000 plastic containers during the month of April. A total of 4,000 and 6,000 direct-labor hours were used in producing the paperboard and plastic containers, respectively.

The company has not been able to maintain an inventory of either product, due to the high demand; this situation is expected to continue in the future. Workers can be shifted from the production of paperboard to plastic containers and vice versa, but additional labor is not available in the community. In addition, there will be a shortage of plastic material used in the manufacture of the plastic container in the coming months due to a labor strike at the facilities of a key supplier. Management has estimated there will be only enough raw material to produce 60,000 plastic containers during June.

The income statement for Excelsion Corporation for the month of April follows. The costs presented in the statement are representative of prior periods and are expected to continue at the same rates or levels in the future.

	Paperboard Containers	Plastic Containers
Sales	$220,800	$222,900
Less: Returns and allowances	$ 6,360	$ 7,200
Discounts	2,440	3,450
	$ 8,800	$ 10,650
Net sales	$212,000	$212,250
Cost of sales		
Raw material cost	$123,000	$120,750
Direct labor	26,000	28,500
Indirect labor (variable with direct-labor hours)	4,000	4,500
Depreciation—machinery	14,000	12,250
Depreciation—building	10,000	10,000
Cost of sales	$177,000	$176,000
Gross profit	$ 35,000	$ 36,250
Selling and general expenses		
General expenses—variable	$ 8,000	$ 7,500
General expenses—fixed	1,000	1,000
Commissions	11,000	15,750
Total operating expenses	$ 20,000	$ 24,250
Income before tax	$ 15,000	$ 12,000
Income taxes (40%)	6,000	$ 4,800
Net income	$ 9,000	$ 7,200

Required:

1. The management of Excelsion Corporation plans to use linear programming to determine the optimal mix of paperboard and plastic containers for the month of June to achieve maximum profits. Using data presented in the April income statement, formulate and label:
   a. The objective function.
   b. The constraint functions.

2. What contribution would the management accountant normally make to a team established to develop the linear programming model and apply it to a decision problem?

22-6. Adapted CMA Problem on LP Formulation and Solution. Girth, Inc. makes two kinds of men's suede leather belts. Belt A is a high quality belt, whereas belt B is of somewhat lower quality. The company earns $7.00 for each unit of belt A that is sold, and $2.00 for each unit sold of belt B. Each unit (belt) of type A requires twice as much manufacturing time as is required for a unit of type B. Further, if only belt B is made, Girth has the capacity to manufacture 1,000 units per day. Suede leather is purchased by Girth under a long-term contract that makes available to Girth enough leather to make 800 belts per day (A and B combined). Belt A requires a fancy buckle, of which only 400 per day are available. Belt B requires a different (plain) buckle, of which 700 per day are available. The demand for the suede leather belts (A or B) is such that Girth can sell all that it produces.

Required:

1. Formulate and graph Girth's linear programming model to maximize its profits.
2. Using the graph solve the model.
3. Assume the same facts above except that the sole supplier of buckles for belt A informs Girth Inc. that it will be unable to supply more than 100 fancy buckles per day. How many units of each of the two belts should be produced each day to maximize profits.
4. Assume the same facts as in part 3 except that Texas Buckles, Inc. could supply Girth with the additional fancy buckles it needs. The price would be $3.50 more than Girth, Inc. is paying for such buckles. How many, if any, fancy buckles should Girth Inc. buy from Texas Buckles, Inc? Explain how you determined your answer.

22-7. CMA Problems; Correcting and Solving LP Problem. The Elon Co. manufactures two industrial products: X-10, which sells for $90 a unit, and Y-12, which sells for $85 a unit. Each product is processed through both of the company's manufacturing departments. The limited availability of labor, material, and equipment capacity has restricted the ability of the firm to meet the demand for its products. The production department believes that linear programming can be used to routinize the production schedule for the two products.

The following data are available to the production department.

	Amount Required Per Unit	
	X-10	Y-12
Direct material: Weekly supply is limited to 1800 pounds at $12.00 per pound	4 pounds	2 pounds
Direct labor:		
Department 1—Weekly supply limited to 10 people at 40 hours each at an hourly rate of $6	$\frac{2}{3}$ hour	1 hour
Department 2—Weekly supply limited to 15 people at 40 hours each at an hourly rate of $8	1.25 hours	1 hour
Machine Time:		
Department 1—Weekly capacity limited to 250 hours	$\frac{1}{2}$ hour	$\frac{1}{2}$ hour
Department 2—Weekly capacity limited to 300 hours	0 hours	1 hour

The overhead costs for Elon are accumulated on a plantwide basis. The overhead is assigned to products on the basis of the number of direct-labor hours required to manufacture the product. This base is appropriate for overhead assignment because most of the variable overhead costs vary as a function of labor time. The estimated overhead cost per direct-labor hour is:

Variable overhead cost	$ 6.00
Fixed overhead cost	6.00
Total overhead cost per direct-labor hour	$12.00

The production department formulated the following equations for the linear programming statement of the problem.

A = number of units of X-10 to be produced
B = number of units of Y-12 to be produced

Objective function to minimize costs:
Minimize Z = 85A + 62B

Constraints
Material:	4A + 2B ≤ 1,800 pounds
Department 1 labor:	($\frac{2}{3}$)A + 1B ≤ 400 hours
Department 2 labor:	1.25A + 1B ≤ 600 hours
Nonnegativity:	A ≥ 0; B ≥ 0

Required:

1. The formulation of the linear programming equations as prepared by Elon Co.'s production department is incorrect. Explain what errors have been made in the formulation prepared by the production department.
2. Formulate and label the proper equations for the linear programming statement of Elon Co.'s production problem.

22-8. Linear Programming and Data Requirements. The Aaron Company is faced with the problem of scheduling production of three products and subcontracting certain casting operations. The company is anxious to supply the products in quantities that will be most profitable.

Each of the products require casting, machining, and assembly and packaging. Casting operations for products A and B can be subcontracted, but the castings for product C require special equipment that precludes the use of subcontractors. Aaron has capacities of 8,000 minutes of casting time, 12,000 minutes of machining time, and 10,000 minutes of assembly and packaging time per week. Other relevant data are:

	Product		
	A	B	C
Casting time requirement (minutes/unit)	6	10	8
Machining time requirement (minutes/unit)	6	3	8
Assembly and packaging time (minutes/unit)	3	2	2

| | Product | | |
	A	B	C
Variable costs			
Cost of castings:			
Produced at Aaron	$0.30	$0.50	$0.40
Subcontracted	0.50	0.60	——
Cost of machining	0.20	0.10	0.27
Cost of assembly and packaging	0.30	0.20	0.20
Plant fixed cost/unit (allocation based on last year's actual production):			
Produced at Aaron	0.20	0.30	0.40
Subcontracted	0.15	0.15	——
Selling price	1.50	1.80	1.97

Required:

Define the following variables:

A_1 = units of product A; casting self-produced

A_2 = units of product B; casting subcontracted

B_1 and B_2 = similar to A

C = units of product C

Set up the complete LP problem.

22-9. LP Set Up Problem when there is Overtime. The Ripken Company produces three products, A, B, and C. Following is a schedule of labor time required in Department I and II and material required:

	A	B	C	Available at Normal Levels	Normal Cost/Unit
Department I labor	2	6	5	4,000 hours	$4
Department II labor	3	3	8	2,000 hours	$6
Material	4	3	6	3,000 units	$6

Products A, B, and C sell at unit prices of $100, $150, and $300, respectively. An analysis reveals that variable overhead is $2.00 per labor hour. Overtime premiums are the usual 50% of base wages. Additional material can be acquired at a premium of $2.00 per unit.

Overtime should not exceed 100 hours in Department I nor 300 hours in Department II.

Define A, B, and C as the units of each of the products to be produced. Further, define T_1 and T_2 as the overtime hours employed in Department I and Department II, respectively. Define M as the material purchased in excess of the normal amount available.

Required:

Formulate the linear programming model to solve for the optimal quantities of A, B, and C to produce and for the optimal levels of resources in excess of normal amounts to acquire.

22-10. LP and Fixed Costs. The Watch-It Company has a problem of determining how much of each of its two products to produce. Based on the facts given the analyst, the following LP model was used to solve it.

Maximize: $1A + 2.5B$
Subject to:
$$A + B \leq 80 \qquad \text{(Material)}$$
$$2A + B \leq 100 \qquad \text{(Labor)}$$
$$B \leq 70 \qquad \text{(Market on B)}$$

Required:

1. Show that the optimal solution is:

$$A = 10 \quad \text{and} \quad B = 70$$

and that the optimal profit is $185.
2. Mr. Astute had asked for a cost behavior analysis and was told that the $1.00 per unit profit on A and $2.50 per unit profit on B included an allocation of $250 fixed cost based on practical capacity of 100 direct-labor hours. Based on this, what LP model should be used to solve the company's product mix problem?
3. Resolve the problem using your model in part 2.
4. Comment on the implications of the results of this problem.

22-11. Sensitivity Analysis Using Chapter Problem. Reconsider the LP problem used as a demonstration in this chapter (stated on page 774). The sensitivity analysis of product B's contribution margin indicates the following range of values within which it could vary without changing the optimal solution:

$$3 \leq c_B \leq 6$$

Required:

1. Show that the solution $(A, B) = (2, 6)$ is still optimal if c_B is $3.
2. Show that the solution $(A, B) = (2, 6)$ is still optimal if c_B is $6.
3. Show that the solution $(A, B) = (2, 6)$ is *not* optimal if c_B is $7.
4. Remember in the text it was stated that the sensitivity range on c_A was:

$$4 \leq c_A \leq 8$$

Now, suppose c_A is $7 (within c_A's sensitivity range) and c_B is $3 (within c_B's sensitivity range). Show that the solution $(A, B) = (2, 6)$ is not the optimal solution for these objective equation values.
5. Explain why, in part 4, the solution $(A, B) = (2, 6)$ did not remain optimal even though both products' contribution margins were within the ranges where it was stated the optimal solution would not change.

22-12. Sensitivity Analysis of Linear Programming Problem. Consider the following linear programming problem:

Maximize: $-8x_1 + 12x_2$
Subject to:
$$2x_1 + 3x_2 \leq 18$$
$$3x_1 + x_2 \geq 3$$
$$x_1 - x_2 \leq 4$$
$$-2x_1 + x_2 \leq 4$$

Required:

1. Using graphical techniques solve this problem for the optimal product mix.
2. A sensitivity analysis of the objective equation coefficients has been done the results of which are as follows:

$$-24 \leqslant c_1 \leqslant 8 \qquad 4 \leqslant c_2 \leqslant \infty$$

   Show that c_1 can be increased from -8 to $+8$ and not cause the solution you found in part 1 to be nonoptimal.
3. What are the implications for accounting of the sensitivity results given in part 2?
4. Assume the first constraint in this model is for labor. The sensitivity analysis indicates that labor cost may increase by as much as $2 per hour and not affect the optimality of the solution found in part 1. Show that this analysis is valid.

22-13. CMA Problem on Basic Inventory Modeling. The Robney Company is a restaurant supplier that sells a number of products to various restaurants in the area. One of their products is a special meat cutter with a disposable blade.

The blades are sold in packages of twelve blades for $20.00 per package. After a number of years, it has been determined that the demand for the replacement blades is at a constant rate of 2,000 packages per month. The packages cost the Robney Company $10.00 each from the manufacturer and require a three-day lead time from date of order to date of delivery. The ordering cost is $1.20 per order and the carrying cost is 10% per year.

Robney is going to use the economic order quantity formula:

$$\text{EOQ} = \sqrt{\frac{2(\text{Annual requirements}) (\text{Cost per order})}{(\text{Price per unit}) (\text{Carrying cost})}}$$

Required:

1. Calculate:
   a. The economic order quantity.
   b. The number of orders needed per year.
   c. The total cost of buying and carrying blades for the year.
2. Assuming there is no reserve (safety stock) and that the present inventory level is 200 packages, when should the next order be placed? (360 days equal one year.)
3. Discuss the problems that most firms would have in attempting to apply this formula to their inventory problems.

22-14. CMA Problem on Providing Data for Inventory Model. Pointer Furniture Company manufactures and sells office furniture. In order to compete effectively in different quality and price markets it produces several brands of office furniture. The manufacturing operations is organized by the item produced rather than by the furniture line. Thus, the desks for all brands are manufactured on the same production line. For efficiency and quality control reasons the desks are manufactured in batches. For example, ten high-quality desks might be manufactured during the first two weeks in October and fifty units of a lower-quality desk during the last two weeks. Because each model has its own unique manufacturing requirement, the change from one model to another requires the factory's equipment to be adjusted.

The management of Pointer wants to determine the most economical production run for each of the items in its product lines. The manager of the cost accounting department is going to adapt the economic order quantity (EOQ) inventory model for this analysis.

One of the cost parameters that must be determined before the model can be employed is the setup cost incurred when there is a change to a different furniture model. The cost accounting department has been asked to determine the setup cost for the desk (Model JE 40) in its junior executive line as an example.

The equipment maintenance department is responsible for all of the changeover adjustments on production lines in addition to the preventive and regular maintenance of all the production equipment. The equipment maintenance staff has a forty-hour work week; the size of the staff is changed only if there is a change in the workload that is expected to persist for an extended period of time. The Equipment Maintenance Department had ten employees last year, and they each averaged 2,000 hours for the year. They are paid $9.00 an hour, and employee benefits average 20% of wage costs. The other departmental costs, which include such items as supervision, depreciation, insurance, etc., total $50,000 per year.

Two workers from the equipment maintenance department are required to make the change on the desk line for model JE 40. They spend an estimated five hours in setting up the equipment as follows:

Machinery changes	3 hours
Testing	1 hour
Machinery readjustments	1 hour
Total	5 hours

The desk production line on which Model JE 40 is manufactured is operated by five workers. During the changeover these workers assist the maintenance workers when needed and operate the line during the test run. However, they are idle for approximately 40% of the time required for the changeover.

The production workers are paid a basic wage rate of $7.50 an hour. Two overhead bases are used to apply the indirect costs of this production line because some of the costs vary in proportion to direct-labor hours, whereas others vary with machine hours. The overhead rates applicable for the current year are as follows:

	Based on Direct-Labor Hours	*Based on Machine Hours*
Variable	$2.75	$ 5.00
Fixed	2.25	$15.00
	$5.00	$20.00

These department overhead rates are based upon an expected activity of 10,000 direct-labor hours and 1,500 machine hours for the current year. This department is not scheduled to operate at full capacity because production capability currently exceeds sales potential.

The estimated cost of the direct materials used in the test run totals $200. Salvage material from the test run should total $50.

Required:

1. Prepare an estimate of Pointer Furniture Company's setup cost for desk Model JE 40 for use in the economic production run model. For each cost item identified in the problem, justify the amount and the reason for including the cost item in your estimate. Explain the reason for excluding any cost item from your estimate.

2. Identify the cost items that would be included in an estimate of Pointer Furniture Company's cost of carrying the desks in inventory.

22-15. CMA Problem on Providing Data for Inventory Model. Evans Inc. is a large wholesale distributor that deals exclusively in baby shoes. Due to the substantial costs related to ordering and storing the shoes, the company has decided to employ the economic order quantity (EOQ) method to help determine the optimum quantities of shoes to order from the different manufacturers. The EOQ formula is:

$$EOQ = \sqrt{\frac{2C_o D}{PC_s}}$$

where:

EOQ = optimum number of units per purchase order

D = annual demand

P = purchase price per unit

C_o = cost of placing an order

C_s = the annual cost of storage per dollar of investment in inventory

Before Evans Inc. can employ the EOQ model, they need to develop values for the two cost parameters by using cost data from the most recent fiscal year, 19x5.

The company placed 4,000 purchase orders during 19x5. The largest number of orders placed during any one month was 400 orders in June, and the smallest number of orders placed was 250 in December. Selected cost data for these two months and the year for the purchasing, accounts payable, and warehousing operations are as follows.

	Costs of High-Activity Month (June: 400 orders)	Costs for Low-Activity Month (December: 250 orders)	Annual Costs
Purchasing Department			
Purchasing manager	$ 1,750	$ 1,750	$ 21,000
Buyers	2,500	$ 1,900	28,500
Clerks	2,000	$ 1,100	20,600
Supplies	275	150	2,500
Accounts Payable Department			
Clerks	2,000	1,500	21,500
Supplies	125	75	1,100
Data processing	2,600	2,300	30,000
Warehouse			
Foreman	1,250	1,250	15,000
Receiving clerks	2,300	1,800	23,300
Receiving supplies	50	25	500
Shipping clerks	3,800	3,500	44,000
Shipping supplies	1,350	1,200	15,200
Freight out	1,600	1,300	16,800
	$21,600	$17,850	$240,000

The purchasing department is responsible for placing all orders. The costs listed for the accounts payable department relate only to the processing of purchase orders for payment. The warehouse costs reflect two operations—receiving and shipping. The receiving clerks inspect all incoming shipments and place the orders in storage. The shipping clerks are responsible for processing all sales orders to retailers.

The company leases space in a public warehouse. The rental fee is priced according to the square feet occupied during a month. The annual charges during 19x5 totaled $34,500. Annual insurance and property taxes on the shoes stored in the warehouse amounted to $5,700 and $7,300, respectively. The company pays 8% a year for a small amount of short-term, seasonal bank debt. Long-term capital investments are expected to produce a rate of return of 12% after taxes. The effective tax rate is 40%.

Inventory balances tend to fluctuate during the year depending upon the demand for baby shoes. Selected data on inventory balances are as follows.

Inventory January 1, 19x5	$160,000
Inventory December 31, 19x5	120,000
Highest inventory balance (June)	220,000
Lowest inventory balance (December)	120,000
Average monthly inventory	190,000

The boxes in which the baby shoes are stored are all approximately the same size. Consequently, the shoes all occupy about the same amount of storage space in the warehouse.

Required:

1. Using the 19x5 data, determine estimated values appropriate for:
   a. C_O—cost of placing an order.
   b. C_S—the annual cost of storage per dollar of investment in inventory.
2. Should Evans Inc. use the cost parameters developed solely from the historical data in the employment of the EOQ model? Explain your answer.

22-16. Data for EOQ Model. The Ray Company uses the EOQ model to determine the optimal order size of its product. Remember that the order cost is a cost per order and holding cost is the annual cost *per unit in inventory.*

You have researched the situation and discovered the following facts:

1. The annual demand for the product is expected to be 200,000 units.
2. The invoice cost of the product is $10 per unit.
3. Purchasing agents are paid $20,000 per year. If they spent their entire time on the purchasing of this product an agent could do 2,000 orders per year. When not working on this product, agents do other essential tasks for the firm.
4. A warehouse will be rented exclusively for this product at $0.75 per year per unit of warehouse capacity. The capacity will be equal to the optimal order size.
5. The cost of capital is 10%.
6. The secretarial cost and supplies per order will be $7.50.
7. The cost of receiving and processing an order at the warehouse dock is $50.
8. Insurance cost of storing inventory is $0.50 per unit of inventory per year.

Required:

Determine the optimal order quantity.

22-17. CMA Problem: Relevant Data for EOQ Model. SaPane Company is a regional distributor of automobile window glass. With the introduction of the new subcompact car models and the expected high level of consumer demand, management recognizes a need to determine the total inventory cost associated with maintaining an optimal supply of replacement windshields for the new subcompact cars introduced by each of the three major manufacturers. SaPane is expecting a daily demand for thirty-six windshields. The purchase price of each windshield is $50.

Other costs associated with ordering and maintaining an inventory of these windshields are as follows:

1. The historical ordering costs incurred in the Purchase Order Department for placing and processing orders is shown below:

Year	Orders Placed and Processed	Total Ordering Costs
19x1	20	$12,300
19x2	55	12,475
19x3	100	12,700

   Management expects the ordering costs to increase 16% over the amounts and rates experienced the last three years.
2. The windshield manufacturer charges SaPane a $75 shipping fee per order.
3. A clerk in the Receiving Department receives, inspects, and secures the windshields as they arrive from the manufacturer. This activity requires eight hours per order received. This clerk has no other responsibilities and is paid at the rate of $9 per hour. Related variable overhead costs in this department are applied at the rate of $2.50 per hour.
4. Additional warehouse space will have to be rented to store the new windshields. Space can be rented as needed in a public warehouse at an estimated cost of $2,500 per year plus $5.35 per windshield.
5. Breakage cost is estimated to be 6% of the average inventory value.
6. Taxes and fire insurance on the inventory are $1.15 per windshield.
7. The desired rate of return on the investment in inventory is 21% of the purchase price.

Six working days are required from the time the order is placed with the manufacturer until it is received. SaPane uses a 300-day work year when making economic order quantity computations.

Required:

1. Calculate the following values for SaPane Company.
   a. The value for ordering cost that should be used in the EOQ formula.
   b. The value for storage cost that should be used in the EOQ formula.
   c. The economic order quantity.

CHAPTER 23 **Regression Analysis**

Several problems discussed in this book needed to have costs analyzed as to their fixed and variable components. Until this point it was assumed that the simple analytical techniques for analyzing costs were adequate. In this chapter regression analysis is introduced as an alternative procedure for those situations that might require more sophisticated methods in order to have acceptable results.

The discussion proceeds as follows. First, the basic idea of regression is explained through a single independent variable model. Such a model is sometimes called the least squares model. Then there is a discussion of a variety of statistics related to the regression model. The purpose is to help you understand how to use the model. Finally, the idea of the basic regression model is extended to more advanced situations, including multiple explanatory variable models and nonlinear models.

Simple Linear Regression

Simple linear regression, like the high-low method, assumes that the estimating line is of the form in equation (23-1):

$$y = a + bx$$

That is, it is assumed there is a *single* independent variable and that the relationship between it and the dependent variable is *linear.* The basic idea of regression is very simple. The objective is to construct a good fitting line through all of the data that are available. However, unlike the other methods discussed elsewhere in the book, regression is based on some mathematical principles that ensure a best fitting line. To further understand the method, it is necessary to consider how "best" is operationally defined.

To explain "best," consider the two graphs in Exhibit 23.1. For simplicity, only three hypothetical actual data points have been plotted. Assume that we are interested in finding the function that best relates overhead cost to direct labor hours. In both graphs, the actual overhead cost associated with direct-labor hours (DLH) of x_1, x_2, and x_3 are the same and plotted as the open circles. That is, a cost of y_1 dollars was incurred when DLH was x_1, y_2 dollars when DLH was x_2, and so forth. The two graphs represent two possible estimating equations. There are an infinite

Exhibit 23.1   Trial-Estimating Lines through Data

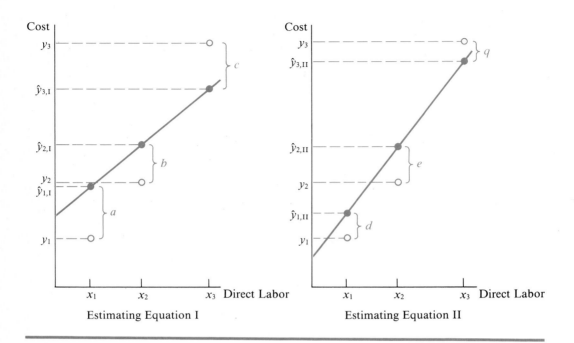

Estimating Equation I   Estimating Equation II

number of lines that could be constructed through the data. Two have been arbitrarily selected to facilitate the discussion of the way the regression model selects
the best fitting line. In regression analysis it is conventional to denote the estimate
of the dependent variable, y, as $\hat{y}$ (read "y hat"). Thus, at a volume of x_1, equation
I estimates overhead cost to be $\hat{y}_{1,I}$. The estimates are represented as the dots on
the estimating lines. At volumes of x_2 and x_3, the estimates are $\hat{y}_{2,I}$ and $\hat{y}_{3,I}$, respectively. For these three volumes of DLH, equation II estimates overhead costs to be
$\hat{y}_{1,II}$, $\hat{y}_{2,II}$, and $\hat{y}_{3,II}$.

The *best* fitting equation is defined as the one that has the smallest sum of
squared vertical distances between the actual observation of the dependent variable and the estimate given by the equation. The differences (or deviations) for
equation I are denoted as the intervals a, b, and c in Exhibit 23.1. For equation II,
the differences are d, e, and f. Some of the deviations are positive (c and f) and
some are negative (a, b, d, and e). Since some of the deviations are positive and
some negative, just adding the vertical deviations may be misleading as a measure
of the goodness of fit since the negative deviations will net out against the positive
deviations. Thus, conventional regression analysis uses *squared* deviations which
will all be positive. Calculus and these definitions are used to determine values for
the a and b parameters that specify the particular line that should be employed.

That is, different lines can be specified by using different intercepts (the "a" parameter) and slopes (the "b" parameter). Since the "a" and "b" values can be changed to represent different lines they become the variables of the regression analysis (as opposed to the situational variables, x and y).

Actually, the values resulting from a regression analysis are *estimates* of the true relationships. Denoting the estimates of a and b as â and $\hat{b}$, the estimate of the value of the dependent variable, $\hat{y}_i$, given a value of the independent variable, x_i, can be generalized as follows:

$$\hat{y}_i = \hat{a} + \hat{b}x_i \tag{23-2}$$

There are many statistical computer packages[1] and hand-held calculators that will process the sample data to provide you with â and $\hat{b}$. The values are determined by these packages (and calculators) as described in the following paragraphs.

Define e_i as the difference between the *actual* value of the dependent variable for case i of the sample and the *estimated* value using the ith value of the independent variable. The e_i values are the vertical differences between the estimates and actuals as shown in Exhibit 23.1 (a, b, and c or d, e, and f). Thus:

$$e_i = y_i - \hat{y}_i \tag{23-3}$$

The square of the difference for observation i is:

$$e_i^2 = (y_i - \hat{y}_i)^2 \tag{23-4}$$

Since $\hat{y}_i$ is given by equation (23-2), equation (23-4) expands to:

$$e_i^2 = (y_i - \hat{a} - \hat{b}x_i)^2 \tag{23-5}$$

The overall error resulting from using a given line as a fit to the n observations in the sample is represented by adding all of the above errors:

$$\sum_{i=1}^{n} e_i^2 = \sum_{i=1}^{n} (y_i - \hat{a} - \hat{b}x_i)^2 \tag{23-6}$$

$$(n = \text{number of observations in sample})$$

The best fitting line is the one that minimizes the sum in (23-6). Different lines can be selected by selecting different values for the intercept, â, and the slope, $\hat{b}$. As indicated earlier, these become the regression variables.

Since equation (23-6) contains two variables, â and $\hat{b}$, its minimum value is found by determining the values of â and $\hat{b}$ that cause the two partial derivatives (one with respect to â and the other with respect to $\hat{b}$) to simultaneously equal zero. Taking these derivatives, setting the results equal to zero, and solving yields equations (23-7) and (23-8). In the notation of these two equations, Σx means the sum of all of the x observations; Σy, the sum of all y values; Σx^2, sum of the squared x values; and Σxy, the sum of the cross-products of x and y. When all of the above is done, the values of $\hat{b}$ and â for the best fitting equation are:

---

[1] For example, there is SPSS (Statistical Package for the Social Sciences), SAS (Statistical Analysis System), and BMDP (Biomedical Package).

$$\hat{b} = \frac{n(\Sigma xy) - (\Sigma x)(\Sigma y)}{n(\Sigma x^2) - (\Sigma x)^2} \qquad \text{Sum of observations}$$

(23-7)

$$\hat{a} = \frac{(\Sigma y)(\Sigma x^2) - (\Sigma x)(\Sigma xy)}{n(\Sigma x^2) - (\Sigma x)^2}$$

(23-8)

An alternative to (23-8) can be used if $\hat{b}$ is solved first:

$$\hat{a} = \bar{y} - \hat{b}\bar{x}$$

(23-9)

where $\bar{y}$ and $\bar{x}$ are the average y and x observations in the sample.

To illustrate the regression model, the example of Chapter 2 will be used. The data of that problem are reproduced in Exhibit 23.2. Also shown in Exhibit 23.2 are the various values needed to use equations (23-7) and (23-9). From Exhibit 23.2 you can see that:

$$\Sigma y = 147{,}322 \qquad \Sigma x = 10{,}826 \qquad n = 5$$
$$\Sigma xy = 320{,}988{,}114 \qquad \bar{y} = 29{,}464.4$$
$$\Sigma x^2 = 23{,}744{,}612 \qquad \bar{x} = 2{,}165.2$$

Thus:

$$\hat{b} = \frac{5(320{,}988{,}114) - (10{,}826)(147{,}322)}{5(23{,}744{,}612) - (10{,}826)^2}$$

$$= \frac{10{,}032{,}598}{1{,}520{,}784} = 6.59699$$

and using (23-9):

$$\hat{a} = 29{,}464.4 - 6.59699(2{,}165.2) = 15{,}180.60$$

The regression equation, then, is:

$$\hat{y} = 15{,}180.6 + 6.59699x$$

(23-10)

Exhibit 23.2   Delaware Drill Company Illustrative Data

Month	Overhead Costs (y)	Direct Labor Hours (x)	xy	x^2
1	$ 32,457	2,416	78,416,112	5,837,056
2	29,570	2,324	68,720,680	5,400,976
3	30,057	2,354	70,754,178	5,541,316
4	27,176	1,840	50,003,840	3,385,600
5	28,062	1,892	53,093,304	3,579,664
Sum	$147,322	10,826	320,988,114	23,744,612
Average	29,464.4	2,165.2		

Coefficient of Determination (r^2)

Regression identifies the best fitting line using a given variable and a given data set. This *does not* ensure that the equation is useful. There is a burden on the user to select appropriate variables for the analysis. If you want to estimate overhead costs in the assembly department as a function of the total number of points scored in the National Football League last week, the regression model will provide you with an equation. But will the estimating equation be of any value? This will now be considered.

The **coefficient of determination, r^2,** is one indicator of the potential usefulness of a regression equation. This value will range between 0 and 1 and is the percentage of the sample variance of the dependent variable explained by having knowledge of the independent variable. In short, it is a measure of the goodness of the fit of the line to the sample data.

How is r^2 determined? Basically it is necessary to determine the effect that knowledge of the independent variable has on the ability to estimate the dependent variable. For example, what is the effect of having knowledge of direct-labor hours when trying to estimate overhead costs? To measure this effect there must be a base for comparison. What if information *had not* been collected about direct-labor hours? Then how would the overhead costs be estimated? Under these conditions the most reasonable estimate would be given by the average of all past cost observations, $\bar{y}$. That is, estimate the monthly overhead costs at $\bar{y}$ or at \$29,464.40 in the Delaware Drill example.

The sum of the squares of the actual y_i values around the mean value of y is used as the reference point for judging other estimating equations. Using $\bar{y}$ as the estimator, compute the sum of the squares (SS) of the differences between the actual observations in the sample and y. Call this $SS_{\bar{y}}$ (sum of squares around $\bar{y}$) and compute it as:

$$SS_{\bar{y}} = \sum_{i=1}^{n} (y_i - \bar{y})^2$$

With knowledge of the independent variable, the overhead costs are estimated via the regression equation, $\hat{y}_i$. The sum of squares of the differences between the actual, y_i, and the regression estimate is $SS_{\hat{y}}$ (sum of the squares around $\hat{y}$):

$$SS_{\hat{y}} = \sum_{i=1}^{n} (y_i - \hat{y}_i)^2$$

Dividing the second sum, $SS_{\hat{y}}$, by the first sum, $SS_{\bar{y}}$, gives the percentage of the sample variance that is *unexplained* by having knowledge of the independent variable. This percentage is subtracted from 1 to give the percentage of the variance *explained* and the r^2 value:

$$r^2 = 1 - \frac{SS_{\hat{y}}}{SS_{\bar{y}}} \tag{23-11}$$

Exhibit 23.3 derives the data needed for the Delaware Drill example. Note column 6. This column contains the $\hat{y}_i$ values or the regression estimates for the values of

Exhibit 23.3   Input for r^2 Computation

(1)	(2)	(3)	(4)	(5)	(6)*	(7)
i	y_i	x_i	$\bar{y}$	$(y_i - \bar{y})^2$	$\hat{y}_i$	$(y_i - \hat{y}_i)^2$
1	32,457	2,416	29,464.4	8,955,654.76	31,119	1,790,244
2	29,570	2,324	29,464.4	11,151.36	30,512	887,364
3	30,057	2,354	29,464.4	351,174.76	30,710	426,409
4	27,176	1,840	29,464.4	5,236,774.56	27,319	20,449
5	28,062	1,892	29,464.4	1,966,725.76	27,662	160,000
Sum				16,521,481.20		3,284,466
				$= SS_{\bar{y}}$		$= SS_{\hat{y}}$

*$\hat{y}_i = 15{,}180.60 + 6.59699x_i$

x_i in the sample. Just substitute the actual x_i values of column 3 into the regression equation. The regression equation is reprinted in the table footnote. Thus:

$$r^2 = 1 - \frac{3{,}284{,}466.0}{16{,}521{,}481.2} = 0.8012$$

What value should r^2 be before an equation is declared to be acceptable? This depends on the situation. The r^2 of 0.8012 in our example is reasonably high for the type of situation to which the regression model was applied. Of course, the higher the r^2 the better, but it is not possible to be much more definitive than this. Obviously r^2 is not going to be high unless the dependent variable is highly correlated with the independent variable. But correlation does not imply causality. Two variables can be highly correlated but not be a causal factor in the occurrences of each. Thus, professional judgment also needs to be exercised in selecting independent variables.

The r^2 statistic can be used in deciding which of several possible regression equations should be selected. For example, suppose overhead costs have been regressed with (1) direct-labor hours, (2) machine hours, and (3) both labor hours and machine hours. Which of the three results, if any, should be used? The equation with the highest r^2 value would be a favored candidate assuming that the r^2 is significant and that other statistics for the regression model are not in conflict with this conclusion.

Standard Error of the Estimate (s_e)

As discussed in the preceding paragraphs, a regression equation, in general, will not result in a perfect fit to the sample data. Compare columns 6 and 2 of Exhibit 23.3. The **standard error of the estimate (s_e)** is a measure of the "average" difference between the actual observations of the dependent variable in the sample and the values predicted by the regression equation. When the regression equation is used to predict future overhead costs, s_e provides an estimate of the amount by which the actual outcome *might* differ from the estimate. These errors can be standardized and then used to estimate the prediction error that will result when the equation is applied in a forecasting situation.

Using the data from the sample, the sum of squares around the prediction, $SS_{\hat{y}}$, will be "averaged" in order to estimate the error that can be expected when forecasting for the population. So that this average satisfies some desirable statistical properties, the sum of squares around $\hat{y}_i$, $\Sigma(y_i - \hat{y}_i)^2$, is divided by the number of degrees of freedom instead of n. The **degrees of freedom** are the number of observations in the sample reduced by the number of parameters that must be determined in the regression equation (two in our example; a and b). To explain this, note that to find a solution for the parameters there must be at least as many observations as parameters. If the equation is of the form $y = a + bx$ and if there were only two observations, then the best fitting line would pass through both observations. Thus, before there can be any estimation error there must be more observations than there are parameters in the equation. The number of observations in excess of the number of parameters is called the degrees of freedom (df). This is $(n - 2)$ in a regression model using one independent variable, $(n - 3)$ in a model using two independent variables, and so forth. In the latter case the three parameters to be determined are the intercept and the slope of each of the two variables, $(1 + 2)$. The sum of the squared error is averaged over the degrees of freedom. To convert the average squared error to the average error, take the square root since all of the deviations have originally been squared:

$$s_e = \sqrt{\frac{\Sigma(y_i - \hat{y}_i)^2}{df}} \qquad \text{(23-12)}$$

For the Delaware Drill case the number of observations was 5. Thus:

$$s_e = \sqrt{\frac{3,284,466}{5 - 2}} = \sqrt{1,094,822} = 1,046.34$$

Estimation error is due to several factors. There will be estimation error if relevant variables have been excluded, and/or there are elements that behave in a completely unpredictable manner, and/or there is measurement error. It is usually safe to assume that these factors will not "gang up" on us and that there will be as many that cause us to overestimate as there are to cause us to underestimate. In particular, it is assumed that the errors behave according to the normal distribution with a mean error of zero and a standard deviation that can be estimated by s_e or the standard error of the estimate. This will not be justified if additional analysis indicates the existence of heteroscedasticity as defined on page 814.

Standard Error for the Parameters

The next regression statistic to be discussed is the **standard error of the estimate for the parameter b (s_b).** This statistic is a measure of the sampling error that results from estimating the true coefficient that exists in the population. One usage of s_b is to test the hypothesis that there is no linear relationship in the population between the dependent variable and the independent variable. If the hypothesis is accepted, then the independent variable should be rejected as an explainer of the dependent variable. This is illustrated below.

For the b of a single variable equation, this statistic is:

$$s_b = \frac{s_e}{\sqrt{\Sigma(x_i - \bar{x})^2}}$$ (23-13)

In the Delaware Drill case, $\bar{x}$ is 2,165.2 (see Exhibit 23.2). Thus:

i	x_i	$(x_i - \bar{x})^2$
1	2,416	62,900.64
2	2,324	25,217.44
3	2,354	35,645.44
4	1,840	105,755.04
5	1,892	74,638.24
	Sum	304,156.80

Then:

$$s_b = \frac{1,046.34}{\sqrt{304,156.8}} = 1.89725$$

As with any other standard error, s_b can be used to establish a confidence interval for the b parameter. A **confidence interval** is a range of values that would provide a selected chance, or probability, of including the actual value of the parameter. To graphically illustrate the problem, assume management is interested in establishing an interval such that the probability of including the actual value of b is equal to p. The estimate of b, 6.59699, can be viewed as a "mean" of the distribution. If, for the moment, it is assumed the distribution is normal with mean zero and standard deviation σ, then Exhibit 23.4 depicts the problem. To obtain the confidene of p it is necessary to make the range equal to the mean plus-and-minus z standard deviations.

For σ use s_b. If the sample size is large (say, greater than 30) and the distribution is normal, then a normal distribution table can be used to select a z-value that will give the probability of p. For smaller samples, it is recommended that a t-distribution be used in selecting the z-value. Table A.1 (found in the appendix at the back of the book) is an abridged t-table. It should be used as follows. For a 90% p value (see Exhibit 23.4), it is necessary to have 5% in *each* tail (a tail is the extreme left or right portion of Exhibit 23.4). The subscript on the t-values in Table A.1 indicates the percentage in *one* tail. Thus, to ensure a p of 90%, use the column labeled $t_{0.05}$. For a p of 95%, use the column labeled $t_{0.025}$, and so forth. The "df" column means degrees of freedom which were defined in the previous section.

For the illustrative case, assume management wants a 95% confidence interval on the b parameter. There are three degrees of freedom, 5 - 2, and the $t_{0.025}$ value for three degrees of freedom is 3.18. Thus:

Exhibit 23.4   Illustration of Confidence Interval Problem

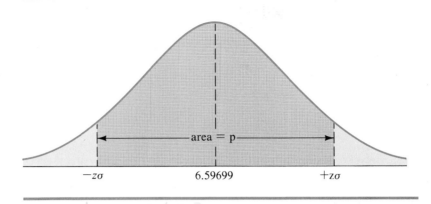

$$\text{CI}_{0.95} = 6.59699 \pm 3.18(1.89725) = [0.5637\ 12.6300]$$

Thus, you can state that b is between 0.5637 and 12.6300 and be 95% sure you will be right.

The standard error of b can also be used to test a hypothesis which is stated as follows: "There is no linear relationship in the population between the independent variable and the dependent variable." Remember that $\hat{b}$ is an estimate of the slope of this relationship. If it is hypothesized that overhead is *not* linearly related with direct labor hours, then b would be zero. That is, overhead would not change with direct labor hours meaning that the equation is of the form $\hat{y} = a + 0x$. What are the odds, in our example, that the actual slope is zero and the estimate, $\hat{b}$, turned out to be 6.59699 strictly by chance? In testing this hypothesis first compute the **t-ratio** as:

$$\text{t-ratio} = \frac{\hat{b}}{s_b}$$

This ratio represents the number of standard deviations that the estimate varies from the hypothesized value of zero.

For the example, the t-ratio is 3.48 (6.59699 ÷ 1.89725). To interpret this value use the t-distribution in Table A.1 since the sample size is small. For three degrees of freedom, look across the row until a value of 3.48 is found. Notice that it is between $t_{0.025}$ and $t_{0.005}$. Thus, there is a 1% to 5% chance that the real value of b is 0 and turned out to be 6.59699 strictly due to random causes. (Remember that a $t_{0.025}$ value puts 2.5% in each tail.) Thus, with virtual certainty, the hypothesis can be rejected. The estimate of b is so many standard deviations from the hypothesized value of zero that it is virtually impossible to have gotten it as a result of sampling error. Thus the population has a large chance of having a b value different from zero.

For a large sample, the hypothesis that there is no linear relationship between the dependent variable and the independent variable can be rejected if the t-ratio is greater than $+2$ or lower than -2. This is comparable to a 95% confidence interval. That is, if the value of b is 0 (zero), then a sampling procedure that generates a $\hat{b}$ value that is outside of a 95% confidence interval is highly unlikely. The fact that a $\hat{y}$ is outside the 95% confidence range cannot be ignored. If this happens, then it is "safe" to conclude the hypothesis is wrong and that the b value is not zero.

Establishing Confidence Intervals around a Regression Estimate

When using the regression equation to predict the value of the dependent variable for a given value of the independent variable, it is certain that the actual observations will differ from the estimate. An estimate just indicates the *average* value that could be expected for the dependent variable if there was the chance to experience the given activity level many times. To describe the uncertainty associated with the regression estimate, it is desirable to establish some confidence intervals just as has been done for other types of estimates.

Now the problem can be stated more succinctly. Define x_k as the given value of the independent variable for which there will be a prediction. In general, the actual cost, y_k, will be given by equation (23-15):

$$y_k = \hat{y}_k + e_k = (\hat{a} + \hat{b}x_k) + e_k \tag{23-15}$$

An estimate of the standard deviation can be obtained for use in the interval construction problem by first estimating the variance of y_k:

$$V(y_k) = V(\hat{a} + \hat{b}x + e_k) \tag{23-16}$$

It can be shown[2] that this results in:

$$V(y_k) = s_e^2 \left[1 + \frac{1}{n} + \frac{(x_k - \bar{x})^2}{\Sigma(x_i - \bar{x})^2} \right] \tag{23-17}$$

Taking the square root of $V(y_k)$ will give the estimated standard deviation to use in establishing the confidence interval.

For small samples (say 30 or less) the student's t-distribution should be used instead of the normal distribution in order to obtain the number of standard deviations for establishing the confidence interval. The example has 3 degrees of freedom and the t-value for a 95% confidence interval ($CI_{0.95}$) is 3.18. Then:

$$\hat{y}_k = \hat{a} + \hat{b}x$$

and the $CI_{0.95}$ is:

---

[2]N.R. Draper and H. Smith, *Applied Regression Analysis*, 2nd ed. (New York: John Wiley & Co., 1981), pp. 28–31.

$$CI_{0.95} = \hat{y}_k \pm 3.18(s_e) \sqrt{1 + \frac{1}{n} + \frac{(x_k - \bar{x})^2}{\Sigma(x_i - \bar{x})^2}} \qquad (23\text{-}18)$$

If equation (23-10) were used to estimate the overhead costs at 2,000 direct labor hours, the results are:

$$\hat{y} = 15{,}180.60 + 6.59699(2{,}000) = 28{,}374.58$$

Previously, s_e was computed to be 1,046.34, $\bar{x}$ as 2,165.2, and $\Sigma(x_i - \bar{x})^2$ as 304,156.80. Thus:

$$CI_{0.95} = 28{,}374.58 \pm 3.18(1{,}046.34) \sqrt{1 + \frac{1}{5} + \frac{(2{,}000 - 2{,}165.2)^2}{304{,}156.80}}$$

$$= 28{,}374.58 \pm 3.18(1{,}188.29) = [24{,}596 \quad 32{,}153]$$

When n is large, use the normal distribution to determine the number of standard deviations for the confidence interval. This is the reason a t-value for df $= \infty$ has been included in Table A.1. It can be shown that as n approaches infinity the t-distribution approaches the normal distribution. Also, when n is large some analysts will approximate the confidence interval by ignoring the term under the radical in (23-18). The rationale for this is that:

1. limit $\frac{1}{n} = 0$
   $n \to \infty$

2. For a large n, $\Sigma(x_i - \bar{x})^2$ is going to be large so that the last term under the radical in (23-18) will not be significant unless x_k differs from the mean, $\bar{x}$, by a large amount. Thus, assuming n is large, such an approximation of a 95% confidence interval would be as follows:

   $$\text{Approximate } CI_{0.95} = \hat{y}_k \pm 1.96(s_e)$$

Assumptions and Limitations of Regression Analysis

Also important to using regression analysis is an understanding of the assumptions and limitations. This section is a brief consideration of the important assumptions.

One limitation is the range of values for which the equation should be used. The results can be misleading when used to estimate costs for values of the independent variable that are *outside* the range observed in the sample. For example, in Exhibit 23.2, direct-labor hours ranged from 1,840 to 2,416. Attempting to extrapolate outside this range has its problems in that the real relationship may be very different than that within the range. For example, the relationship in the population may really be nonlinear, and if the sample came entirely from a relatively linear segment of the population, extreme estimating error could occur for the values of the independent variable outside the bounds of the sample. Thus, there should be very strong reservations about using the model for these levels of activity unless there is convincing nonstatistical evidence the model should still apply.

Remember that simple regression assumes there is a *linear relationship* between the two variables in the population. The model will fit a linear line to the data *even if* the actual relationship is not linear. The burden is on the user to examine the process and the data. A scattergraph may indicate the behavior is nonlinear and, in turn, suggest an alternative form whereby, with some adjustments, the regression model can be used to determine its parameters. Some possibilities are explored later.

A second assumption is that the variance of the error term is constant across all values of x or, in other words, is independent of x. This is known as **homoscedasticity.** Lack of this property is known as **heteroscedasticity.** Exhibit 23.5 contains examples of each of these conditions. The figure on the left is the case of perfect homoscedasticity. That is, the observations at any given direct-labor value are constantly distributed. In contrast, the relationship on the right has a larger variance for high values of direct-labor hours than for low values of direct-labor hours. Without this assumption it is not possible to use the previously discussed method for establishing confidence intervals around the estimated costs at given values of the independent variable.

If it is assumed that the variance is constant for all direct labor hours when, in fact, it is larger for some and smaller for others, there will be errors in computing the confidence interval for the cost at some values of the independent variable. For example, the error in the nonconstant variance illustration of Exhibit 23.5 would be "averaged" in computing the standard error of the estimate. If the standard error was then used to construct a confidence interval around the estimate of a small direct labor hour amount, the interval would be too large. Conversely, the interval would be too small for an estimate at a larger direct labor hour figure. A method known as weighted least squares might be appropriate for use in the case of heteroscedasticity.

Third, it is assumed that successive observations of the dependent variable are independent of each other. When successive observations of the dependent variable are not independent, the condition is known as **autocorrelation.** An example of autocorrelation follows. In the manufacturing of a certain chemical assume it is necessary to maintain a controlled environment with regard to temperature, humidity and other weather related factors. These factors, of course, depend on the month of the year. In Exhibit 23.6 (Graph A) you will find a plot of the weekly costs versus direct-labor hours for a period of two months, April and August. With no identification of which points represent which weeks, the results look typical and free of problems.

In Graph B, the data are labeled 1 through 8 where 1 through 4 represent weeks from April and 5 through 8, August. Suppose the line in Graph B represents the regression line fit through the eight observations. Note that the August observations tend to all be above the line (except #6) and the April observations below the line. This suggests the cost observations are *not* independent of each other.

Exhibit 23.5   Examples of Constant Variance (Homoscedasticity) and Nonconstant Variance (Heteroscedasticity)

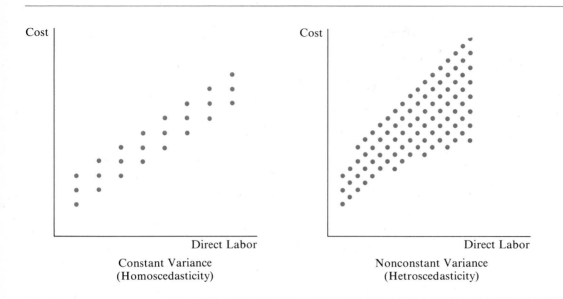

Constant Variance
(Homoscedasticity)

Nonconstant Variance
(Hetroscedasticity)

A test, known as the Durbin-Watson test, can be used to detect autocorrelation. Space does not permit an elaboration on how to use this test. When autocorrelation is present there are several possible courses of action that can be taken to deal with it.[3] In this example, the solution may be as simple as adding a set of dummy variables to the model. These variables would be used to identify the month in which the observation is taken. If D_4 is the dummy variable for April, it would be set equal to 1 if the weekly observation is from April and 0 otherwise. The coefficient for the dummy variable in the resulting regression equation would represent an adjustment to reflect the cost differential due to seasonal effects.

Fourth, it is assumed that the error term has a mean of zero and is normally distributed. That is, if it is possible to have several observations of each value of the independent variable, then this assumption is that the error terms, $y_i - \hat{y}_i$, are normally distributed around $\hat{y}_i$. The latter can be tested by plotting the errors (the residuals). Some computer packages will do this for you. If this assumption is not justified, then obviously it is not advisable to use the method suggested earlier to construct meaningful confidence intervals.

[3]For example, see R.S. Pendyck and D.L. Rubenfeld, *Econometric Models and Economic Forecasts* (New York: McGraw-Hill Book Co., 1976), pp. 108–113.

Exhibit 23.6   Illustration of Autocorrelation

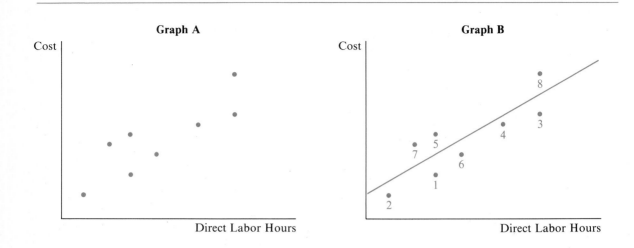

Finally the sample data should be scrutinized carefully before applying the regression model. Inflation, technology changes, and recording practices within the accounting system can all induce undesirable "shocks" in the data. Let us briefly consider each of these factors.

Inflation is always a potential problem when financial data are involved in a regression analysis. For example, suppose an analysis of overhead cost behavior is to be done using the last twenty four months of data. Further, suppose it is known that inflation has been roughly 1% per month. Then, as one approach, the cost data could be adjusted forward to current price levels. Selecting the last month, month 24, as the base period, month 23's costs, C_{23}, should be adjusted to $(1.01)^1 C_{23}$, month 22's to $(1.01)^2 C_{22}$, and so forth. Month 1's cost would be adjusted as $(1.01)^{23} C_1$.

With this adjustment, the regression equation's coefficients will be in terms of month 24's price levels. When using the results to forecast months 25, 26, and so forth, it is necessary to account for the anticipated inflation of future periods. For example, if it is reasonable to assume a continuation of the 1% inflation, then the results of using the preceding regression equation for month 26, call it R_{26}, will have to be adjusted forward by two months (26 - 24) as follows: $(1.01)^2 R_{26}$.

In addition to the adjustment just suggested, it is also necessary to recognize the possibility that not all components of total overhead will be subject to the same rate of inflation. In this case it perhaps would be necessary to classify costs into separate pools according to their inflation rates and then apply regression analysis to the separate pools. Further, some costs, such as depreciation, will not be subject to any inflation.

Another approach to dealing with inflation is to include a time variable in the regression equation (multiple regression is discussed later). This technique might be particularly useful when the actual rate of inflation is not known. In effect, this method lets the regression model do the adjustment. The mechanics in this case are as follows. If T is defined as the time variable, then T for the first month can be set equal to 1. For the second month, T would equal 2, and so forth. The regression model will return a coefficient for the T variable just as it returns a coefficient for the other variables. This coefficient would represent a monthly lump-sum adjustment for inflation. To use the results of the regression in forecasting month 26's costs, T would be set equal to 26.

This method is also not without its problems. The adjustment for inflation is a fixed amount per period. In effect, it assumes that resource consumptions will remain at approximately the same levels each period. For example, the total supplies purchased is assumed to remain constant. In fact, with respect to variable costs the inflation rate is affecting only the cost per unit at a constant rate. A 1% increase in the unit cost of supplies will have a larger impact if 10,000 units are purchased than if 5,000 units are acquired. Thus, a lump-sum adjustment during periods of high fluctuating volume may result in substantial estimation error.

A second factor affecting data is the possibility of changes in technology. Factory equipment may have been replaced during the sample time period. If so, the portion of the sample before the change is not representative of current conditions and should be omitted.

A final consideration is the possibility of incorrect data as a result of the accounting procedures. The problem is associated with choosing the length of the time period that constitutes one observation in the sample. For example, it is possible to choose weekly, monthly, or yearly time periods. If short time periods are chosen, then the accounting system may not record all of the costs caused by the activity of that period as a cost of the period. That is, the recording of certain costs may lag behind their actual incurrence. On the other hand, long time periods may result in the averaging of high and low periods of activity. If so, some information about cost behavior may be lost or disguised.

Topics in Multiple Regression

Multiple regression is just an extension of simple regression. When it is felt that several variables contribute significantly to the incurrence of cost, then different equations can be tested by considering the goodness of fit statistics. Extending the model to several variables gives rise to some additional considerations that will be examined in this section.

The basic form of the multiple regression model is:

$$\hat{y} = \hat{a} + \hat{b}_A x_A + \hat{b}_B x_B + \ldots + \hat{b}_M x_M \tag{23-19}$$

where the multiple variables are denoted as x_A, x_B, ... x_M. Each variable would have a coefficient, b_A, b_B, ..., b_M, which would be estimated as $\hat{b}_A$, $\hat{b}_B$, ..., $\hat{b}_M$.

For example in the Delaware Drill case, if it was felt that overhead was a function of direct-labor hours and machine hours, both could be used as explanatory variables in a regression analysis. Of course it would be necessary to have data on machine hours for each case in the sample. Thus, each case submitted to a computer package would be of the form:

[Overhead cost   Direct-labor hours   Machine hours]

When using multiple regression there are two more problems in addition to those mentioned in the previous section. These are the problems of multicollinearity and the meaning of r^2 in evaluating a multiple variable equation. **Multicollinearity** is the existence of significant correlation between one explanatory variable and another. Note that this is correlation among the explanatory variables—not between an explanatory variable and the dependent variable.

The existence of multicollinearity *does not* necessarily make it improper to include the correlated explanatory variables in the regression equation, but it does create a restriction on the usage of the results. In an equation of the form of (23-19) there would be a tendency to say that the b values represent marginal costs. That is, it might be desired to say that b_A represents the increase in y that results from a one-unit increase in x_A. To be able to say this it is necessary to assume x_A can be increased while holding x_B, x_C, ..., x_M constant. If there is correlation between x_A and x_B, for example, then it is not possible to really hold x_B constant while x_A is changed. Correlation implies that x_B will also change, and thus changing x_A by one unit will have an effect on y that is not equal to b_A. If marginal cost data are needed then there is difficulty when there is multicollinearity. Further, there may be no way to solve the problem; the way the world behaves cannot be changed. However, the multiple variable equation would still be useful in estimating the total costs. The limitation occurs only when marginal cost data are needed.

The second problem is the interpretation of the r^2 statistic when using multiple explanatory variables. To illustrate, suppose overhead has been regressed with labor hours resulting in an equation with an r^2 of 0.60. Thinking that r^2 was too low the analyst decides to do a regression with two explanatory variables: labor and machine hours. If the r^2 of the second equation is compared with the first it will most likely be found to be higher. Even if machine hours were not related at all to overhead, the r^2 of the second equation would not be lower. Remember that regression finds the line that minimizes the sum of the squared error around the estimate. The model would not fit a line that is worse than the one using only direct-labor hours. Before it would do that, a coefficient of zero would be assigned to the machine-hour variable so that the sum of the squared error around the mean would be no larger than in the labor model. *Small* increases in the r^2 values do not imply a better model. To compensate for this, there is an adjusted r^2 statistic.

The **adjusted r^2** is computed as follows:

$$\text{Adjusted } r^2 = 1 - \frac{SS_y/df}{SS_{\bar{y}}/(n-1)} \qquad \text{(23-20)}$$

Following is a rationale of the above equation. Each of the sum of squares is divided by the number of degrees of freedom. For $SS_{\bar{y}}$, the degrees of freedom equal the number of observations less the number of parameters in the regression equation. As the number of variables in a regression equation increases, the degrees of freedom become smaller and the numerator of equation (23-20) can become larger if there is not a significant decrease in $SS_{\hat{y}}$ when additional variables are used in the equation. Conversely, the degrees of freedom of $SS_{\bar{y}}$ are (n-1). Before there can be a variance around the mean there has to be more than one observation. Thus the average sum of squares around the mean is computed by dividing by (n-1). As additional variables are added to a regression model, the denominator of (23-20) does not change. The net effect is as follows. Suppose the additional variables added do not decrease $SS_{\hat{y}}$ by a significant amount. Then the new sum of squares around the estimate divided by the lower degrees of freedom may result in an increase in the numerator of (23-20) when compared to a model with fewer explanatory variables. If so, the right-most term of (23-20) becomes larger and the adjusted r^2 becomes smaller.

The adjusted r^2, then, is a better statistic to compare alternative models that use the same sample data. If a model with a larger number of explanatory variables produces a lower adjusted r^2, then it would be necessary to conclude that the larger model is not as satisfactory even if the r^2 value did increase. In the example problem the adjusted r^2 is:

$$\text{Adjusted } r^2 = 1 - \frac{3{,}284{,}466.00/(5\text{-}2)}{16{,}521{,}481.20/(5\text{-}1)} = 0.735$$

Nonlinear Regression

In addition to being able to deal with multiple explanatory variables as suggested previously, multiple regression also permits the fitting of certain nonlinear functions to sample data. For example, if a plot of the data indicates the cost curve is S-shaped (as in Exhibit 23.7), then such a behavior can be modeled by a cubic equation; that is:

$$y = b_A x^3 + b_B x^2 + b_C x + a \tag{23-21}$$

If it was thought (23-21) was an appropriate form, then an equation can be constructed with three explanatory variables, x^3, x^2, and x. Although equation (23-21) is a nonlinear function of the environmental variables (y and x) it is a linear function of the regression variables (b_A, b_B, and b_C). Thus, the linear regression model can still be used. Suppose one observation from such a situation had 100 direct-labor hours and a cost of \$20,000. Then the input for this case would be:

$$[y, x^3, x^2, x] = [20{,}000, 1{,}000{,}000, 10{,}000, 100]$$

As another example of a nonlinear form, suppose an analysis reveals the relationship is:

$$y = ax^b \tag{23-22}$$

As in previous expressions, y and x are the environmental variables. Again, suppose y is cost and x is direct-labor hours. The regression variables are "a" and "b." However, "b" is an exponent in the relational form being hypothesized. Equations

Exhibit 23.7   S-Shaped Curve

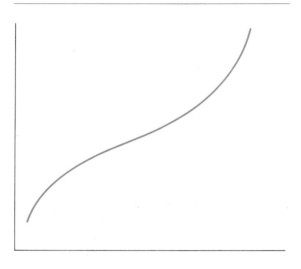

of the form in (23-22) are frequently used when learning curves are needed (see Chapter 24). In order to use the regression model to find the "a" and "b" parameters that yield the best-fitting equation of this form it will be necessary to do some transformations.

By taking logs, a linear form is obtained:

$$\log y = \log a + b \cdot \log x \tag{23-23}$$

That is, log a replaces "a" and b is multiplied by log x (instead of x) in comparison to the standard linear equation that has been used to this point. Thus, by inputting the log of y (instead of y) and the log of x (instead of x) into a regression model, it would return *log a* as its constant and b as its slope. Taking the antilog of the returned constant would give the "a" value and the best fitting curve of the form $y = ax^b$.

To illustrate, suppose the first two observations from a situation where there is a possibility that equation (23-22) has a good chance of representing the relationships is:

Cost	Direct-Labor Hours
$707	50
$894	80

The input would be of the form:

[log y   log x]

The specific values for the two items in the sample are:

[log 707   log 50] = [2.84   1.699]
[log 894   log 80] = [2.95   1.903]

Now, suppose the regression package returned values as follows:

Intercept: 2.00
Coefficient on x: 0.50

Because of the transformation made to have a linear equation it should be remembered that the model is returning the *log* of "a," not "a." To determine "a," take the antilog of 2.00. (This would be the number that is equal to 10 raised to the second power.) The antilog of 2.00 is 100. Thus the best-fitting equation of the form given in equation (23-22) is:

$$y = 100x^{0.5}$$

Implications of Regression Analysis for Accounting

The premise made at the beginning of this chapter was that regression analysis might be useful to accountants in analyzing cost behavior. Let's consider some specific ways the results might be used.

It should be obvious that regression results can be useful in predicting, or budgeting, costs. Given the equation and the anticipated level for the independent variable, just substitute the latter in order to predict the cost. As discussed earlier, it might be desirable to use the standard error of the estimate to establish a confidence interval around the resulting prediction. This interval might be used by management in a variety of what-if questions.

A further use of regression results is in the determination of overhead rates. The "b" coefficient in a regression equation represents the anticipate rate of variable cost incurrence per unit of change in the independent variable. Because of this, the value of "b" may represent an appropriate rate at which to assign variable overhead cost to production. If it turns out that two or more variables are needed in a regression equation in order to have acceptable predictability, then it would be necessary to apply variable overhead on the basis of each of the measures of activity using the respective coefficients. For example, suppose the best fitting equation is a function of direct-labor hours (DLH) and machine hours (MH):

$$y = 90,000 + 3.5(DLH) + 2.34(MH)$$

Then, apply variable overhead at the rate of $3.50 per direct-labor hour and $2.34 per machine hour. If a particular unit of the finished product requires two labor hours and three machine hours, then it should be assigned $14.02 of variable overhead cost (2 × $3.50 + 3 × $2.34).

Also observe the implications of the last example for standard costing. Since variable overhead is being applied on the basis of two activity measures, there would be need for two overhead efficiency variances. Overhead efficiency variance would occur if labor hours were not at standard and/or if machine hours varied. Thus:

VOHE (based on labor) = (standard labor hours − actual labor hours)$3.50
VOHE (based on machine time = (standard machine hours − actual machine hours)$2.34

The intercept, $90,000 in the above example, would be included in the fixed overhead rate. By definition, fixed costs do not vary with the measure of activity. If there is only one measure of activity, labor hours for example, then it is conventional to apply fixed costs over that activity. If multiple independent variables are used in the regression equation, then it will be necessary to arbitrarily choose *one* of the activities for purposes of determining a fixed overhead application rate. Then a specific value of the chosen activity (practical capacity or normal activity, for example) would be used as the divisor. In the above case suppose machine hours are chosen and that machine hours average 30,000 under normal conditions. The fixed overhead application rate would be $3.00 per machine hour ($90,000 ÷ 30,000).

Summary

The purpose of this chapter was to introduce you to the topic of regression analysis. You may find that the "conventional" methods of cost analyses will not always be appropriate. If not, regression analysis may be worth considering. You were introduced to the model, to how to use the model, and to how to interpret the results. Key terms include:

Regression analysis
Coefficient of determination (r^2)
Standard error of estimate (s_e)
Degrees of freedom
Standard error for the parameters
t-ratio
Confidence intervals
Homoscedasticity
Heteroscedasticity
Autocorrelation
Multicollinearity

SELF-STUDY PROBLEM ONE. The Leaky Roofing Company produces roofing supplies. Extensive use is made of regression studies in projecting its financial plans. First, the company has found that its unit sales in a given month (S_j) is a function of the housing starts (H) in month (j-2) *and* month (j-3). That is, there is a two-month to three-month lag between the start of construction and the need for roofing. Specifically, the regression equation is:

$$S_j = 2,000 + 3H_{j-2} + 1H_{j-3}; \quad r^2 = 0.796; \quad s_e = 100$$

Standard errors for the coefficients are:

$$s_a = 50; \quad s_{b(1)} = 0.5; \quad s_{b(2)} = 0.1$$

Because of shipping time the production for the anticipated sales in month j is completed in the preceding month (month j-1). Of course, the actual results vary around the predicted amounts, but the firm has found this variance to be small and normally distributed around the prediction. Thus, they continue to use regression in planning for production and sales.

The manufacturing cost (M_j) as a function of production (P_j) are to be estimated by:

$$M_j = 40,000 + 6P_j; \quad r^2 = 0.89 \quad s_e = 1,000$$

Standard errors for the coefficients:

$$s_a = 200; \quad s_b = 1$$

The administrative costs (A_j) are a function of both sales units and production units:

$$A_j = 20,000 + 2S_j + 1P_j; \quad r^2 = 0.85; \quad s_e = 1,100$$

Standard errors for the coefficients are:

$$s_a = 100; \quad s_{b(1)} = 0.2; \quad s_{b(2)} = 0.25$$

The housing starts for the last four months were:

April—1,000;   May—1,000;   June—2,000;   July—3,000

Required:

1. Evaluate the statistical acceptability of the regression equations being used by the firm.
2. Estimate the unit sales for August.
3. Estimate the manufacturing costs for August.
4. Estimate the administrative cost for August.
5. It has been several months since the above results were derived. The controller would like to have an update based on the additional data that are now available. Among the data collected since the last study are the following:

Month	Housing Starts	Production	Sales	Manufacturing Costs	Administrative Costs
19x1					
August	1,100	10,000	11,000	$100,140	$53,259
September	525	8,000	10,139	88,463	57,523
October	475	4,675	8,225	68,914	43,857
November	350	3,950	4,649	63,801	33,560
December	250	3,525	3,897	60,310	34,200
19x2					
January	200	3,100	3,636	59,387	30,700
February	400	2,850	3,089	57,125	28,367
March	500	3,400	2,894	59,600	30,239
April	1,000	3,900	3,250	63,280	31,596
May	1,000	5,500	3,974	72,960	33,000
June	2,000	6,000	5,912	74,521	37,264
July	3,000	9,000	8,895	94,192	47,216

a. Using the above data what would be the first two complete sets of input to a regression model in order to find a regression equation in the form of the one currently being used to estimate production costs?

b. Using the above data what would be the first two complete sets of input to a regression model in order to find a regression equation in the form of the one currently being used to estimate administrative costs?

c. Using the above data what would be the first two complete sets of input to a regression model in order to find a regression equation in the form of the one currently being used to estimate sales volume?

Solution to Self-Study Problem One

1. All of the r^2 values are reasonably high and would indicate acceptability. Further each of the t-ratios are above 2.0. For example, in the sales regression equation they are 6 (3 ÷ 0.5) and 10, (1 ÷ 0.1). (These are the coefficients divided by the s_b values.) Since all are above 2.0, the hypothesis of no linear relationship between the dependent variable and the various independent variables can be rejected.

2. For August, $j = 8$ and

$$S_8 = 2,000 + 3H_{8\text{-}2} + 1H_{8\text{-}3} = 2,000 + 3H_6 + H_5$$
$$= 2,000 + 3(2,000) + 1(1,000) = 9,000$$

3. In August the firm will need to produce a volume sufficient to meet September's sales. (The lead time for shipping is one month.) September sales can be estimated as:

$$S_9 = 2,000 + 3H_7 + 1H_6 = 2,000 + 3(3,000) + 1(2,000) = 13,000$$
Thus:

$$P_8 = S_9 = 13,000 \text{ and}$$
$$M_8 = 40,000 + 6(13,000) = 118,000$$

4. $A_8 = 20,000 + 2S_8 + 1P_8$
   $= 20,000 + 2(9,000) + 1(13,000) = 51,000$

5. a. The equation currently used relates production costs with production volume. Thus, the input would be of the form:

   [Production costs   Production volume]

   The first two complete input pairs are from August and September of 19x1:

   [100,140   10,000]
   [88,463   8,000]

   b. For administrative costs, the equation needs data of the form:

   [Administrative cost   Sales volume   Production volume]

   From August and September 19x1:

[53,259   11,000   10,000]
[57,523   10,139   8,000]

c. Sales volume was being related to the housing starts two months removed and three months removed. The data would be of the form:

[S_j   H_{j-2}   H_{j-3}

The first complete observations from the data given would be November and December 19x1:

[4,649   525   1,100]
[3,897   475   525]

Note in the above two cases that September sales are an input in each. For November, September is two months removed, whereas it is three months removed for the December observation.

SELF-STUDY PROBLEM TWO. The REG Company has produced the same five products for the last two years. Currently they are in need of some overhead cost analyses for a variety of purposes. The following data are available:
Production Volumes:

Month	Rear Axles	Front Axles	Transmissions	Chassis	Motors
1	1,000	1,500	0	6,000	0
2	0	2,385	2,641	0	0
3	2,817	0	1,972	0	0
4	0	2,654	1,590	0	0
5	2,000	0	1,000	10,500	1,833
6	5,118	1,676	0	0	0
7	2,000	0	1,517	11,724	0
8	0	1,785	2,241	0	0
9	4,318	176	0	0	0
10	3,616	0	2,639	0	0
11	0	1,908	2,579	0	0
12	0	4,054	1,190	0	0
13	3,000	800	0	300	2,533
14	2,500	0	1,200	9,450	600
15	4,118	1,176	0	0	0
16	0	3,031	1,585	0	0
17	3,500	0	1,300	10,800	200
18	0	2,892	2,954	0	0
19	3,541	1,411	0	0	0
20	0	3,769	949	0	0
21	3,530	0	450	0	1,293
22	0	2,969	1,082	0	0
23	1,176	3,765	0	0	0

Month	Overhead Cost	Labor Hours	Machine Hours
1	$374,731	29,951	8,583
2	567,960	27,059	23,051
3	498,822	19,237	23,120
4	470,404	26,159	17,460
5	564,317	34,817	19,558
6	658,974	39,845	25,697
7	514,972	38,125	17,192
8	449,191	21,677	18,875
9	468,342	23,830	17,828
10	559,355	26,170	30,371
11	479,391	23,276	21,291
12	536,747	36,232	19,330
13	484,983	21,598	22,162
14	595,345	35,262	19,068
15	503,317	30,275	20,041
16	545,742	27,795	18,609
17	582,362	43,472	22,410
18	622,231	33,932	26,427
19	467,616	28,541	18,474
20	514,168	33,948	16,925
21	484,296	19,415	20,705
22	424,717	26,919	15,519
23	475,186	26,544	16,341

Since you have these data and are reasonably sure they are relatively free of measurement error, you decide to do some regression studies. At your previous company you used direct-labor hours (L) as the independent variable in a regression study. For the given data, your study results in the following:

$$\hat{y} = 345,116 + 5.7938L; \qquad r^2 = 0.342 \qquad \text{Adjusted } r^2 = 0.310$$
$$s_e = 54,722 \qquad\qquad\qquad s_a = 52,697 \qquad s_b = 1.755$$

Required:

1. Evaluate the merits of using the preceding function with labor as the independent variable.
2. Suggest alternative regression studies that might be done in this case.
3. Assume that you want to try to keep the results simple. Use a regression package to do another study using a *single* independent variable and compare your results with the preceding results.
4. Using multiple regression, see if you can find a better estimating equation.

Solution to Self-Study Problem Two

1. The regression of overhead costs with direct-labor hours has a very low r^2 value. It certainly is not strong enough to merit the use of the equation as a method of estimating

overhead costs. The t-ratio for labor is 3.30 (5.7938 ÷ 1.755). Thus a hypothesis of no linear relationship between overhead and labor hours can be rejected.

2. Overhead could be a nonlinear function of labor hours, a linear function of machine hours, or of labor and machine hours, or of the five different products.

3. Try machine hours as the independent variable. See Exhibit 23.8 for the results using the SAS package. The equation, r^2, adjusted r^2, s_e (ROOT MSE), and s_b values are highlighted in the computer output. The r^2 and adjusted r^2 are higher than for labor but still not outstanding. The s_e value is lower and the t-ratio on machine hours is 4.65, indicating that the hypothesis of no linear relationship with machine hours can also be rejected.

4. Two multiple variable regression models are tried: one with labor and machine hours as the explanatory variables and one with the five products as the variables. The results are in Exhibits 23.9 and 23.10. Again, the significant statistics are highlighted. They indicate that both models have approximately the same validity. The r^2 and adjusted r^2 values are close to each other. This might be expected so long as there is little variation of actual labor and machine hours per unit of product in comparison with the average values per unit. Should there be significant variation of these values around the average and *if* labor and machine hours are the most important causal variables, then the labor-and-machine hour model would turn out to be the best. In such a case, the units of production model would not pick up the costs caused by the extreme variation of labor and machine hours. If such an outcome is possible, then it would be best to use the model based on labor and machine hours. Otherwise, it would not make much difference which model is used. Do

---

Exhibit 23.8   Results of Regression Overhead with Machine Hours

---

MOH WITH MH

DEP VARIABLE: MOH

SOURCE	*DF*	*SUM OF SQUARES*	*MEAN SQUARE*	*F VALUE*	*PROB > F*
MODEL	1	48480382830	48480382830	21.650	0.0001
ERROR	21	47025803329	2239323968		
C TOTAL	22	95506186159			

ROOT MSE	47321.496	R-SQUARE	0.5076	
DEP MEAN	514920	ADJ R-SQ	0.4842	
C.V.	9.190061			

VARIABLE	*DF*	*PARAMETER ESTIMATE*	*STANDARD ERROR*	*T FOR HO: PARAMETER = 0*	*PROB > !T!*
INTERCEP	1	298511	47545.743	6.278	0.0001
MH	1	10.843179	2.330409	4.653	0.0001

Exhibit 23.9   Results of Regression Overhead with Labor Hours and Machine Hours

MOH WITH DLH AND MH

DEP VARIABLE: MOH

SOURCE	DF	SUM OF SQUARES	MEAN SQUARE	F VALUE	PROB > F
MODEL	2	79232168747	39616084373	48.686	0.0001
ERROR	20	16274017413	813700871		
C TOTAL	22	95506186159			

ROOT MSE	28525.443	R-SQUARE	0.8296
DEP MEAN	514920	ADJ R-SQ	0.8126
C.V.	5.539777		

VARIABLE	DF	PARAMETER ESTIMATE	STANDARD ERROR	T FOR H0: PARAMETER = 0	PROB > !T!
INTERCEP	1	137751	38797.768	3.550	0.0020
DLH	1	5.626949	0.915314	6.148	0.0001
MH	1	10.635087	1.405180	7.568	0.0001

note, however, that the adjusted r^2 of the five-product model is lower than the adjusted r^2 of the labor-and-machine-hour model. This statistic suggests that the latter model is marginally better.

References

Benston, G.J. "Multiple Regression Analysis of Cost Behavior," *The Accounting Review* (October 1966): 657–672.

Comiskey, E. "Cost Control by Regression Analysis," *The Accounting Review* (April 1966): 235–238.

Draper, N.R., and Smith, H. *Applied Regression Analysis*, 2nd ed. New York: John Wiley and Sons, 1981.

Jensen, R. "Multiple Regression Models for Cost Control—Assumptions and Limitations," *The Accounting Review* (April 1967): 265–273.

Johnston, J. *Statistical Cost Analysis*. New York: McGraw-Hill Book Co., 1960.

Pendyck, R.S., and Rubenfeld, D.L. *Econometric Models and Economic Forecasts*. New York: McGraw-Hill Book Co., 1976.

Problems

23-1. Basic Regression. The Reggie Company produces a delectable candy bar that is especially popular in California. The company has been in operation for six months and realizes that there is a problem in estimating the overhead costs. The data, to date, are:

Exhibit 23.10   Results of Regression Overhead with the Five-Product Volumes

MOH WITH THE PRODUCTS

DEP VARIABLE: MOH

SOURCE	DF	SUM OF SQUARES	MEAN SQUARE	F VALUE	PROB > F
MODEL	5	79447418089	15889483618	16.821	0.0001
ERROR	17	16058768071	944633416		
C TOTAL	22	95506186159			

ROOT MSE	30734.889	R-SQUARE	0.8319
DEP MEAN	514920	ADJ R-SQ	0.7824
C.V.	5.968862		

VARIABLE	DF	PARAMETER ESTIMATE	STANDARD ERROR	T FOR HO: PARAMETER = 0	PROB > !T!
INTERCEP	1	119672	45971.564	2.603	0.0186
REAR	1	71.574886	8.530069	8.391	0.0001
FRONT	1	80.314866	11.073614	7.253	0.0001
TRANS	1	86.461318	10.316650	8.381	0.0001
CHASSIS	1	11.785193	2.105723	5.597	0.0001
MOTORS	1	43.467410	11.679044	3.722	0.0017

Month	Production	Overhead Cost
1	100	$ 1,200
2	200	1,500
3	300	2,250
4	200	1,750
5	300	2,300
6	400	2,700
Total	1,500	$11,700

As a staff accountant in the controller's office you are trying to determine how best to estimate the costs and are considering the regression method.

Required:

1. Determine the regression equation.
2. Compute the r^2 statistic.
3. Compute the s_e statistic.
4. Compute the s_b statistic.
5. Compute the adjusted r^2.

6. Establish the 95% confidence interval for the cost estimate at 350 units.
7. Is it reasonable, in this case, to assume that there is a linear relationship between production and overhead costs? Why?

23-2. Selecting and Defending a Regression Equation. The TWO Company has the following data available for purposes of estimating its overhead costs:

Period	Overhead Cost	Direct-Labor Hours	Machine Hours
1	249,330	11,319	2,580
2	348,840	11,616	13,470
3	444,820	13,436	23,623
4	291,880	13,127	4,884
5	274,095	9,327	9,029
6	332,435	10,993	12,112
7	287,755	7,272	15,498
8	288,395	7,335	11,874
9	434,760	13,713	26,461
10	429,650	12,204	18,842

Several regressions have been done:

I—Overhead cost with direct-labor hours (DLH).
II—Overhead cost with direct-labor hours (DLH) and time (T); T = 1, 2, ..., 10.
III—Overhead cost with machine hours (MH).
IV—Overhead cost with direct-labor hours (DLH) and machine hours (MH).
V—Overhead cost with direct-labor hours (DLH), machine hours (MH), and time (T); T = 1, 2, ..., 10.

The results are summarized as follows:

	I	II	III	IV	V
Intercept	119,276	19,309	219,400	99,298	83,870
Standard error	95,571	89,680	24,267	33,947	42,440
t-ratio	1.25	0.22	9.04	2.93	1.98
DLH coefficient	19.84	22.77	—	12.39	13.41
Standard error	8.49	7.04	—	3.16	3.64
t-ratio	2.34	3.23	—	3.91	3.68
MH coefficient	—	—	8.59	7.38	6.86
Standard error	—	—	1.56	0.98	1.30
t-ratio	—	—	5.52	7.54	5.30
T coefficient	—	12,298	—	—	2,072
Standard error	—	5,472	—	—	3,143
t-ratio	—	2.25	—	—	0.66
r^2	0.406	0.655	0.792	0.935	0.939
s_e	59,948	48,844	35,461	21,229	22,141

In period 12 the firm is forecasting an activity of 10,000 labor hours and 11,000 machine hours.

Required:

1. Provide an estimate of the firm's overhead cost for period 12.
2. Justify what you did in part 1.
3. For confidence interval construction you need a t-value from the t-table. Remember that you need degrees of freedom and one of the t-columns, $t_{0.05}$, $t_{0.025}$, $t_{0.005}$, and so forth. Considering your results in part 1, indicate which t-value you would use for a 90% confidence interval construction. (Be sure to indicate both the row and column.)
4. Assume the proper t-value from part 3 is 2.00. Provide an estimate (not the precise value) of the 90% confidence interval for your estimate in part 1.

23-3. Adapted CMA Problem on Evaluation of Estimating Tools. The Ramon Co. manufactures a wide range of products at several different plant locations. The Franklin plant, which manufactures electrical components, has been experiencing some difficulties with fluctuating monthly overhead costs. The fluctuations have made it difficult to estimate the level of overhead that will be incurred for any one month.

Management wants to be able to estimate overhead costs accurately in order to plan its operating and financial needs better. A trade association publication to which Ramon Co. subscribes indicates that, for companies manufacturing electrical components, overhead tends to vary with direct-labor hours.

One member of the accounting staff has proposed that the cost behavior pattern of the overhead costs be determined. Then overhead costs could be predicted from the budgeted direct-labor hours.

Another member of the accounting staff suggested that a good starting place for determining the cost behavior pattern of overhead costs would be an analysis of historical data. The historical cost behavior pattern would provide a basis for estimating future overhead costs. The methods proposed for determining the cost behavior pattern included the high-low method, the scattergraph method, simple linear regression, and multiple regression. Of these methods Ramon Co. decided to employ the high-low method, the scattergraph method, and simple linear regression. Data on direct-labor hours and the respective overhead costs incurred were collected for the previous two years. The raw data are as follows:

	19x3 Direct-Labor Hours	19x3 Overhead Costs	19x4 Direct-Labor Hours	19x4 Overhead Costs
January	20,000	$84,000	21,000	$86,000
February	25,000	99,000	24,000	93,000
March	22,000	89,500	23,000	93,000
April	23,000	90,000	22,000	87,000
May	20,000	81,500	20,000	80,000
June	19,000	75,500	18,000	76,500
July	14,000	70,500	12,000	67,500
August	10,000	64,500	13,000	71,000
September	12,000	69,000	15,000	73,500
October	17,000	75,000	17,000	72,500
November	16,000	71,500	15,000	71,000
December	19,000	78,000	18,000	75,000

Using linear regression, the following data were obtained:

Coefficient of determination	0.9109
Coefficient of correlation	0.9544
Coefficients of regression equation:	
Constant	39,859
Independent variable	2.1549
Standard error of the estimate	2,840
Standard error of the regression coefficient for the independent variable	0.1437

Required:

1. Construct a scattergraph.
2. Using the high-low method, determine the cost behavior pattern of the overhead costs for the Franklin plant.
3. Using the results of the regression analysis, calculate the estimate of overhead costs for 22,500 direct-labor hours.
4. Of the three proposed methods (high-low, scattergraph, linear regression), which one should Ramon Co. employ to determine the historical cost behavior pattern of Franklin plant's overhead costs? Explain your answer completely, indicating the reasons why the other methods should not be used.

23-4. Exploring Various Concepts of Estimating Tools: Using the five months of data in the Delaware Drill Company case from Chapter 2, a high-low estimating equation was derived as:

$$\hat{y} = 10,306.14 + 9.1684x \quad \text{(see (2-5))}$$

The average y, $\bar{y}$, was 29,464.4   (see Exhibit 23.2).

Required:

1. In the accompanying table, the sum of squares of y around its mean has been computed. Finish the table to compute the sum of squares around the high-low estimate, $\hat{y}$.

(1)	(2)	(3)	(4)	(5)	(6)
i	x_i	y_i	$(y_i - \bar{y})^2$	$\hat{y}_i$	$(y_i - \hat{y}_i)^2$
1	2,416	32,457	8,955,654.76		
2	2,324	29,570	11,151.36		
3	2,354	30,057	351,174.76		
4	1,840	27,176	5,236,774.56		
5	1,892	28,062	1,966,725.75		
			16,521,481.20		

2. What percentage of the sample sum of squares around the mean has been explained by using the high-low equation? Compare this with the r^2 of the regression equation computed in this chapter. Is the relationship what you would expect?
3. Could there be any *linear function* of direct-labor hours that would have a larger r^2 than the regression equation in (23-10)? Why?

4. Could there be any other function of *direct-labor hours* that would have a larger r^2 than the regression equation in (23-10)? Why?

23-5. Regression for Cash Forecasting. The Jennings Company has experienced the following sales and cash collection of sales for the past twenty-four months:

Month	Sales	Cash Collections
1	$100,000	$120,000
2	150,000	134,500
3	130,000	141,000
4	180,000	158,000
•	•	•
•	•	•
•	•	•
24	200,000	175,000

It is known that the sales are collected during the month of sales and the following two months. The company desires to use regression to estimate the collection percentages. That is C_j (cash collections in month j) is a function of S_j, S_{j-1}, and S_{j-2} (the sales in month j and the two preceding months).

Required:

1. Write the general form of the regression equation implied by the situation.
2. Provide the specific input to a regression package for the first two observations that are possible given the sample. That is, give the input for the dependent variable and the independent variable(s).

23-6. Nonlinear Cost Behavior. The Guidry Company produces several products and is quite confident that its overhead costs are a function of direct-labor hours. They have experienced a very wide fluctuation in volume and when a scattergraph was prepared, the data did not seem to be a linear function of direct-labor hours. Representative data (in thousands) for nine months are as follows:

Month	Overhead Costs	Direct-Labor Hours	Month	Overhead Costs	Direct-Labor Hours
1	200.00	10	6	118.55	1
2	134.40	2	7	210.40	12
3	159.20	4	8	265.60	18
4	300.00	20	9	189.60	8
5	231.25	15			

Required:

1. Plot the data to see if you concur that the behavior is nonlinear.
2. Using months 4 and 6 as the high and low observations, construct the high-low estimating equation. Evaluate its usefulness if the usual range of activity is from four to fifteen direct-labor hours.

3. Using months 5 and 3 as the high and low observations, construct the high-low estimating equation. Evaluate its usefulness if the usual range of activity is from four to fifteen direct-labor hours.

4. In month 10, the firm has estimated a demand for its products that would require 1,000 labor hours. After this forecast was made, an offer was received from a new customer located outside the regular market area that would entail another 1,000 labor hours of work. The material and labor for this order would amount to $10,000, and, based on the cost figures implied by the equation in part 3, a manager proposes the acceptance of this new contract at the offer of $20,000. This contract is not likely to lead to a permanent increase in demand. Would you advise its acceptance? Why?

5. B. Martin, a new member of the accounting staff, conjectured that the cost function was really a cubic function. He did a regression using the cubic form and found:

$$\hat{y} = 0.05x^3 - 1.5x^2 + 20x + 100$$

To confirm his results you decide to do a similar study. What data would you submit to a regression package for month 1? For month 2?

6. You confirm Martin's results. How would you compute the increased overhead cost resulting from working the x thousandth hour (that is, the marginal cost of the x thousandth hour)? As a function of x, show how to compute the *average* overhead cost of working x thousand hours.

23-7. CMA Problem on Accountant's Responsibility in Regression Analysis. The Alma plant manufactures the industrial product line of CJS Industries. Plant management wants to be able to get a good, yet quick, estimate of the manufacturing overhead costs that can be expected to be incurred each month. The easiest and simplest method to accomplish this task appears to be to develop a flexible budget formula for the manufacturing overhead costs.

The plant's accounting staff suggested that simple linear regression be used to determine the cost behavior pattern of the overhead costs. The regression data can provide the basis for the flexible budget formula. Sufficient evidence is available to conclude that manufacturing overhead costs vary with direct-labor hours. The actual direct-labor hours and the corresponding manufacturing overhead costs for each month of the last three years were used in the linear regression analysis.

The three-year period contained various occurrences not uncommon to many businesses. During the first year production was severely curtailed during two months due to wildcat strikes. In the second year production was reduced in one month because of material shortages and materially increased (overtime scheduled) during two months to meet the units required for a one-time sales order. At the end of the second year employee benefits were raised significantly as the result of a labor agreement. Production during the third year was not affected by any special circumstances.

Various members of Alma's accounting staff raised some issues regarding the historical data collected for the regression analysis. These issues were as follows.

1. Some members of the accounting staff believed that the use of data from all thirty-six months would provide a more accurate portrayal of the cost behavior. Although they recognized that any of the monthly data could include efficiencies and inefficiencies, they believed these efficiencies and inefficiencies would tend to balance out over a longer period of time.

looked good [handwritten]

2. Other members of the accounting staff suggested that only those months that were considered normal should be used so that the regression would not be distorted.
3. Still other members felt that only the most recent twelve months should be used because they were the most current. *← current is not always good* [handwritten]
4. Some members questioned whether historical data should be used at all to form the basis for a flexible budget formula.

The accounting department ran two regression analyses of the data—one using the data from all thirty-six months and the other using only the data from the last twelve months. The information derived from the two linear regressions is shown in the accompanying table.

considered normal [handwritten]

Least Squares Regression Analyses

	Data from All Thirty-six Months	Data from Most Recent Twelve Months
Coefficients of the regression equation:		
Constant	$123,810	$109,020
Independent variable (DLH)	$ 1.6003	$ 4.1977
Coefficient of correlation *higher the better (r)*	0.4710	0.6891
Standard error of the estimate *Se*	13,003	7,473
Standard error of the regression coefficient for the independent variable *or Sb*	0.9744	1.3959
Calculated t-statistic for the regression coefficient	1.6423	3.0072
t-statistic required for a 95% confidence internal		
34 degrees of freedom (36 - 2)	1.960	
10 degrees of freedom (12 - 2)		2.228

lower the better [handwritten, next to coefficient of correlation / standard error rows]

Required:

1. From the results of Alma plant's regression analyses that used the data from all thirty-six months:
   a. Formulate the flexible budget equation that can be employed to estimate monthly manufacturing overhead costs.
   b. Calculate the estimate of overhead costs for a month when 25,000 direct-labor hours are worked.
2. Using only the results of the two regression analyses, explain which of the two results (twelve months versus thirty-six months) you would use as a basis for the flexible budget formula.
3. How would the four specific issues raised by the members of Alma's accounting staff influence your willingness to use the results of the statistical analyses as the basis for the flexible budget formula? Explain your answer.

23-8. Cost Behavior Determination When There Is Inflation. Consider the following six observations concerning the overhead cost of the Collins Company:

Month	Overhead Cost	Direct-Labor Hours
1	$130,000	10,000
2	234,600	20,000
3	187,272	15,000
4	159,181	12,000
5	357,203	30,000
6	309,142	25,000

Required:

1. Using the data as given here, what is the cost-estimating equation using the high-low method?
2. Now suppose you are told that inflation has been averaging 2% per month. Repeat part 1 using month 6 as the base period.
3. Assume you wanted to do a regression analysis using month 7 as the base period. (The inflation rate is projected to continue at the rate stated in part 2.) What data would be submitted to the regression model?
4. Assume the regression in part 3 resulted in:

$$\hat{y} = 33,784 + 11.26x$$

Estimate the costs for month 8 if direct-labor hours are budgeted at 22,000 hours. Assume the inflation is expected to continue at 2% per month.
5. Now assume you have no knowledge of a specific inflation rate but suspect that it is present. Define T as a time variable. What data should be submitted to a multiple regression model?
6. Now assume the regression in part 5 resulted in:

$$\hat{y} = 16,036 + 10.63x + 4,324T$$

Estimate the costs in month 8 if direct labor is budgeted at 22,000 hours.

23-9. Regression Input, Evaluation, and Use. The Yount Company has the following cost and statistical data available for use in predicting its overhead cost. Monthly data for 19x6 and 19x7:

Month	Budgeted Overhead	Actual Overhead	Budgeted Labor Hours	Actual Labor Hours	Budgeted Machine Hours	Actual Machine Hours
1	$150,000	$179,860	5,000	6,650	3,000	3,060
2	75,000	96,740	2,000	3,180	1,500	1,990
3	105,000	161,200	3,000	5,960	2,500	2,880
·	·	·	·	·	·	·
·	·	·	·	·	·	·
·	·	·	·	·	·	·
24	180,000	137,270	6,000	6,365	4,000	3,530

The plant and equipment was purchased at a cost of $720,000 in 19x1. It is being depreciated on a straight-line basis over a twenty-year life.

A single labor contract has been in force during 19x6 and 19x7. The average wage rate was $9 per hour. Some employees, however, are on a guaranteed wage plan. Thus, there is occasionally some idle time. This occurred in month 2, for example, when 1,000 hours were paid for but not used. The idle-time hours are not included in the budgeted or actual labor hours above. Idle-labor cost is included in the budgeted and actual overhead.

Required:

1. One manager suggests overhead is a function of labor and machine hours. What are the first two complete data observations that would be needed by a regression package in this case to find the regression equation suggested by this manager? *Support your answer.*
2. Suppose the results of your study in question 1 turned out as follows where OH = overhead, L = labor hours, and M = machine hours.

$$OH = 20,000 + 20L + 10M$$
$$r^2 = 0.78 \quad s_e = 500 \quad s_{b(L)} = 8 \quad s_{b(M)} = 9$$

   a. Evaluate these results.
   b. Regardless of your evaluation, use the results to determine a 95% confidence range for the budgeted overhead in January of 19x8 when the budgeted labor hours are 4,000 and the budgeted machine hours are 2,000. You need not use the complex confidence interval equation but you should still adjust for the sample size by using the appropriate number of deviations from the t-table.
3. A second manager thinks overhead might be a cubic function of labor hours. What are the first two complete data observations that would be needed by a regression package in this case to find the suggested equation?
4. Now assume inflation occurred at a monthly compound rate of 1% during 19x6 and 19x7. This rate is considered applicable only to items *purchased* during 19x6 and 19x7 except for idle-time costs whose rate per hour is fixed by the contract. Assume the data are to be submitted to a regression package in terms of month 24's price levels and that overhead is hypothesized to be a linear function of direct-labor hours. What are the first two complete data observations that would be needed by a regression package in this case to find the suggested equation?
5. Assume your results in part 4 are:

$$OH = 20,000 + 25L$$

   In 19x8 the average inflation rate across all items in overhead is projected to be 0.50%. Assuming the budget data in question 2-b, what is your forecast of overhead for January of 19x8?
6. Another manager thinks the overhead cost is of the functional form:

$$OH = a + b_1L + b_2M + b_3(L)(M)$$

   What is the first complete data observation that would be needed by a regression package in this case to find the suggested equation?

23-10. Regression Where There is Inflation. The Munson Company, in an attempt to better forecast its overhead costs, is trying to apply regression analysis. After much study they have concluded that direct-labor hours represent a good independent variable, but there is still some dissatisfaction with the results. The data that are being used were collected over the last two years and are as follows:

| | 19x1 | | 19x2 | |
| | *Overhead* | *Direct-Labor* | *Overhead* | *Direct-Labor* |
Month	*Costs*	*Hours*	*Costs*	*Hours*
1	$14,185	1,837	$13,425	1,485
2	15,610	2,101	15,237	1,798
3	15,011	1,961	14,626	1,672
4	15,491	2,031	14,393	1,611
5	14,972	1,908	14,996	1,703
6	16,695	2,221	16,085	1,882
7	15,939	2,054	17,324	2,076
8	14,767	1,816	18,023	2,171
9	15,532	1,946	16,627	1,905
10	15,992	2,011	17,942	2,111
11	16,186	2,023	19,151	2,294
12	14,350	1,668	17,409	1,975

The regression of overhead with direct-labor hours did not result in an exceptionally high r^2 and the standard error was relatively large. One day the company economist joins you at lunch and mentions that the company is experiencing a rather significant problem with inflation. You wonder if that might be a cause of the problem in obtaining satisfactory results in your cost studies.

Required:

1. Using a computer package, find the regression equation using direct-labor hours as your only variable. (If a package is not available, your instructor may elect to provide you some additional data for this question.)
2. Since inflation may be a function of time, suggest a variable(s) that might be included in the analysis to account for it. What value would this variable(s) have for each of the observations noted above?
3. Using your new variable(s) from part 2 and a computer package do another regression study. (Again, if a package is not available, your instructor may provide you some data and with some additional equations.) Compare your results with part 1. Is there an improvement? Why?
4. How would you interpret the coefficients for each of your variables in part 3?
5. Using your results from part 3, estimate the costs for February of 19x3 assuming a budgeted direct-labor volume of 2,000 hours.
6. Suggest another way this problem might be approached whereby you would only use one independent variable. What are the probable problems in implementing your suggestion.

23-11. Comprehensive Case with Nonlinear Cost Behavior. The Lemon and Orange Company is a rather progressive company and two years ago established a regression equation to estimate the behavior of one of its major costs. The independent variable was direct-labor (DL) hours. This was done at the end of 19x2 using the monthly data of 19x1 and 19x2. The results have been used to estimate this cost during 19x3 and 19x4, and the manager is upset with the inaccuracy of the equation. As a result of the prediction errors, he has made some bad decisions with regard to cash management.

Below are the data for 19x1 through 19x4:

	19x1		19x2		19x3		19x4	
	DL		DL		DL		DL	
Month	Hours	Cost	Hours	Cost	Hours	Cost	Hours	Cost
1	727	$10,589	901	$13,403	1,900	$109,661	2,026	$137,565
2	899	13,360	886	13,081	927	14,952	1,852	100,447
3	772	11,151	834	12,093	2,305	216,738	1,337	34,525
4	766	11,072	947	14,490	1,785	88,321	1,695	73,814
5	639	9,772	943	14,387	1,825	95,224	1,249	28,261
6	785	11,370	965	14,985	1,619	63,154	2,059	145,547
7	743	10,825	944	14,425	1,529	52,226	2,506	291,155
8	864	12,652	689	10,203	1,632	64,819	397	9,391
9	936	14,214	797	11,555	2,763	410,020	2,386	244,936
10	794	11,446	864	12,669	1,311	32,782	2,050	143,433
11	925	13,948	761	11,036	1,246	28,450	1,718	77,543
12	824	11,917	944	14,432	2,253	200,040	706	11,531

When a regression package was applied using the data from 19x1 and 19x2 the following results were obtained:

	Coefficient	Standard Error	t-ratio
Constant	− 1,713.48	480.10	− 3.57
Labor Variable	16.8841	0.5686	29.7
$r^2 = 0.9757$	$s_e = 251.22$		

Required:

1. Explain why this regression equation generated so much estimation error during 19x3 and 19x4.
2. Suppose as a result of your reasons in part 1 you decide to do a regression using only the 19x3 and 19x4 data. The results are as follows:

	Coefficient	Standard Error	t-ratio
Constant	− 155,244.17	31,263.93	− 4.97
Labor Variable	155.82	17.38	8.97
$r^2 = 0.7852$	$s_e = 47,206.06$		

Provide an explanation for why this fit was not as good as the fit to the 19x1 and 19x2 data.
3. Another staff accountant plotted the data and said it looked S-shaped. With this knowledge, use a computer code to obtain another equation for the 19x3 and 19x4 data.

23-12. Comprehensive Job Cost Problem Requiring Use of Regression Analysis. The Oak Company manufactures a variety of products according to customer specification. Thus, a job order system is used. The manufacturing area is organized into two departments for control purposes, Department A and Department B. Each job requires processing in both departments and it is always done in sequence: first A, then B.

Both departments maintain a manufacturing overhead account and use a predetermined overhead rate. Department A's rate has been established at $10 per direct-labor hour. The accounting process has been delayed during January and February of 19x1 because the rate for Department B has not yet been established.

Following are some *annual* data about Department B at various activity levels:

	Theoretical Capacity	Practical Capacity	Normal Activity	Expected Activity—19x1
Direct-labor hours (DLH)	100,000	80,000	75,000	57,000
Direct-labor dollars (DL$)	$ 800,000	$650,000	$620,000	$450,000
Machine hours (MH)	200,000	190,000	152,000	114,000
Budgeted manufacturing overhead (MOH)				
Fixed	$ 456,000	$456,000	$456,000	$456,000
Variable	1,000,000	950,000	760,000	570,000

A statistical correlation study has been done using price-level adjusted historical data. The following correlation matrix was made available to you:

	MOH	DL$	DLH	MH
MOH	1.00	0.75	0.79	0.89
DL$		1.00	0.91	0.20
DLH			1.00	0.32
MH				1.00

At January 31, 19x1, two partially completed jobs (1 and 2) were still in process. These jobs were completed during February as well as job 3. At February 28, two jobs (4 and 5) were still in process. Job 5 was not yet finished in Department A. Production data from *Department B* for the five jobs are as follows:

Department B:	Job 1	Job 2	Job 3	Job 4	Job 5	Total
January 19x1						
Direct-labor hours	300	——	——	——	——	300
Machine hours	500	——	——	——	——	500
February 19x1						
Direct-labor hours	200	1,400	2,500	600	——	4,700
Machine hours	800	3,000	4,000	2,200	——	10,000

To the extent possible, the job cost sheets for jobs 1, 2, 3, 4, and 5 have been completed and are given below. The bracketed spaces, [ ], require your attention.

	Job 1	Job 2	Job 3	Job 4	Job 5	Total
January						
Department A						
Material	$10,000	$20,000	—	—	—	$30,000
Direct labor @ $5	7,500	12,000	—	—	—	19,500
Manufacturing OH @ $10/DLH	15,000	24,000	—	—	—	39,000
Department B						
Material	20,000	—	—	—	—	20,000
Direct labor	2,500	—	—	—	—	2,500
Manufacturing OH	[ ]	—	—	—	—	[ ]
Total—January	[ ]	56,000	—	—	—	[ ]
February						
Department A						
Material	—	-0-	$10,000	$ 8,000	$ 3,000	$21,000
Direct labor	—	8,000	7,000	10,000	5,000	30,000
Manufacturing OH	—	16,000	14,000	20,000	10,000	60,000
Department B						
Material	-0-	5,000	15,000	9,000	—	29,000
Direct labor	1,700	11,000	20,000	5,000	—	37,700
Manufacturing OH	[ ]	[ ]	[ ]	[ ]	—	[ ]
Total—February	[ ]	[ ]	[ ]	[ ]	18,000	[ ]
Total	[ ]	[ ]	[ ]	[ ]	18,000	[ ]

Required:

1. Complete the job cost sheets provided above.
2. Explain and justify your reasoning in part 1.
3. Prepare the journal entry recording all direct material issued to production during February, 19x1.
4. Prepare the journal entry recording and distributing all direct labor incurred in February 19x1 and the employer's social security tax. The social security tax is 7% for both the employee and the employer, and other withholdings average 13%.
5. Several production workers from Department A took vacations during February. Their gross vacation pay totaled $3,000. Prepare the entry(s) to record this. You may assume the same rates as stated in part 4.
6. Other actual overhead (not including any mentioned elsewhere) totaled $62,000 in Department A for February. Prepare *all* journal entries for overhead in Department A for February.
7. Prepare the entry transferring the appropriate amount of costs from Department A to Department B during February. Be sure to completely support your amount.
8. Prepare the entry transferring the appropriate amount of costs from Department B to Finished Goods during February. Be sure to completely support your amount.

23-13. Data for Regression: From Job Cost System. The Fabulous Fabric Company produces a variety of grades of cloth in a variety of colors and widths. Because of the noncontinuous nature of its production, a job order system is used to account for the output. A predetermined overhead rate based on direct-labor hours at normal activity was established at the beginning of 19x1. This rate has not been changed since then. Overhead is charged to the jobs on the basis of this rate multiplied by the actual direct-labor hours incurred. At that time the budget was estimated assuming a normal volume of activity but no special cost studies were done. The overhead rate was established at $18 per direct-labor hour. The $18 rate has been used both for budgeting and costing purposes. The results have been of mixed accuracy and the controller is looking for improved techniques.

You are to help with some regression studies that were authorized to improve the accounting methods for overhead. You know that each job requires different types of labor skills as well as different types of material. Following are the job-cost cards for *all* jobs worked on during November and December of 19x2.

Job 109 (3,500 bolts—Completed: 11/13/x2)

Date	Material	Direct Labor	Applied Overhead
October	$50,000	$36,000	$72,000
November	–0–	30,000	54,000

Job 110 (1,000 bolts—Completed: 11/29/x2)

Date	Material	Direct Labor	Applied Overhead
November	$15,000	$22,000	$36,000

Job 111 (3,900 bolts—Completed: 12/23/x2)

Date	Material	Direct Labor	Applied Overhead
November	$55,000	$21,000	$54,000
December	–0–	55,000	90,000

Job 112 (6,100 bolts—Completed: 1/30/x3)

Date	Material	Direct Labor	Applied Overhead
December	$87,000	$63,000	$126,000
January	–0–	50,000	90,000

The manufacturing overhead account for November and December of 19x2 is as follows:

Manufacturing Overhead

November 1 Balance	2,000	Applied—November	144,000
Actual—November	156,000	November 30 Balance	14,000
	15,8000		158,000
December 1 Balance	14,000	Applied—December	216,000
Actual—December	200,000		
December 31 Balance	2,000		
	216,000		216,000
		December 31 Balance	2,000

At yearly normal activity the firm would incur 120,000 direct-labor hours and 240,000 machine hours. The machine hours incurred in November 19x2 totaled 16,000 hours and December's total was 22,000 hours.

Required:

1. Assume you want to run a regression on overhead cost using labor hours as the only independent variable. What specific amounts would you submit to a regression package for November and December 19x2? For each month provide the observed y and x values.

2. Assume that you did an analysis similar to part 1 for each of twenty-four months in 19x1 and 19x2 and the regression equation was as follows:

$$\hat{y} = 38,600 + 7.20x; \quad r^2 = 0.70;$$
$$s_e = 1,500; \quad s_b = 1.00$$

   Suppose the firm is budgeting 11,000 labor hours for February 19x3. What is the budgeted overhead cost for February?

3. What range of costs would you provide in order to be 95% confident of including the actual costs in February if 11,000 hours were incurred. Assume that the sample size is relatively large and that labor hours averaged close to 11,000 in the sample. The appropriate t-value is 1.96.

4. Using the result in part 2, determine the fixed and variable overhead application rate.

5. How much overhead cost would be applied for February if the firm operated at 11,000 hours (that is, the same as the labor hours budgeted in part 2)?

6. Suppose the actual overhead cost for February turned out to be $119,000 when the actual hours were 11,000. How would you judge the efficiency of the manager with respect to overhead? Explain your reasoning.

7. Assume that you want to run a regression on overhead cost using two independent variables: labor hours and machine hours. What specific amounts would you submit to a regression package for November and December 19x2? Provide the values of the dependent variable and independent variables.

8. Suppose you believe that overhead cost may be a *cubic* function of labor hours. What specific amounts would you submit to a regression package for November 19x2 in order to test this hypothesis?

9. Suppose that inflation had been significant during 19x1 and 19x2. An analyst had decided to account for this by including a time index variable, T, as one of the independent variables in a regression package in addition to labor (L) and machine hours (M). November and December 19x2 were considered as months 23 and 24. The following result was obtained:

$$\hat{y} = 50,000 + 5L + 4M + 100T$$

   Estimate the overhead costs for February 19x3 assuming a budget of 11,000 labor hours and 20,000 machine hours.

23-14. Overhead Accounting under Standard Costing and Using Regression Analysis. The BG Company has done a regression of its total overhead (MOH) and found it to be best related with machine hours (MH). Results were:

$$MOH = 800,000 + 4(MH)$$
$$r^2 = 0.832 \quad s_b = 0.69$$

BG's normal activity level amounts to 400,000 machine hours annually. For the current year's production the standard machine hours allowed were 375,000 and the actual machine hours used was 380,000. Actual overhead costs consisted of $798,000 fixed and $1,600,000 variable.

Required:

1. How much *total* overhead would have been applied?
2. What is the variable overhead efficiency variance?
3. What is the variable overhead spending variance?
4. What is the fixed overhead spending variance?
5. What is the noncontrollable (volume) variance?

23-15. Regression and Standards. The T. Blue Lasorta Company is trying to improve its budgeting and standard cost system. In the past it assumed that total overhead was a function only of direct-labor hours. The company has suspected, however, that it was a function of both direct-labor hours and machine hours. A regression study confirmed the suspicions. The study was accomplished using the *monthly* data for the last five years. The regression equation using direct-labor hours (x_1) and machine hours (x_2) had an r^2 of 0.91, whereas the one using only direct-labor hours had an r^2 of 0.68. The regression equation based on the five-year history is:

$$\hat{y} = 1,000 + 8x_1 + 5x_2$$

The standard errors of the estimate (s_e) is 1,000, and the standard error of the coefficients on the variables are:

$$s(b_1) = 1.2; \quad s(b_2) = 0.8$$

Fixed overhead is to be assigned on the basis of direct-labor hours at practical capacity. The capacity totals 60,000 labor hours per year. Two products are produced, A and B. A unit of product A requires four direct-labor hours and two machine hours, whereas product B requires three hours of each.

Required:

1. Assuming that 500 units of A and 400 units of B are budgeted for production during January of the coming year, what is the amount that should be budgeted for overhead?
2. What is the standard overhead cost to be assigned to each unit of product A under a full absorption standard cost system?
3. What overhead variances would you need in addition to the spending and noncontrollable variances? How would you compute them?

23-16. Standard Costing and Regression. The Goodman Company produces three products. Two of them, clarinets and saxophones, require processing both in Departments I and II. *Department II transfers its completed production to finished goods inventory.* The Engineering Department provided the following standards for Department II:

	Clarinets	Saxophones
Department I output	2 parts	1 part
Labor	3 hours	4 hours
Machine time	5 hours	2 hours

Department I's output has a standard cost of $10 per part ($2 for material, $5 for labor, and $3 for overhead). During the current period it completed 50,000 parts at a total actual cost of $525,000. All 50,000 parts were transferred to Department II.

Department II adds the parts from Department I at the beginning of the production of clarinets and saxophones. The standard cost of labor in Department II is $8 per hour. Exclusive of supervision costs, a regression of Department II's *monthly* overhead, y, with labor, L, and machine time, M, gave the best results:

$$\hat{y} = 90,000 + 3L + 6M$$

Supervision costs in Department II are a step-function of its monthly direct-labor hours:

Hours	Total Supervision
0 to 75,000	$ 60,000
75,001 to 150,000	130,000
150,001 to 225,000	210,000

For the past five years standard-labor hours in Department II have averaged 100,000 per month. During the next few years it is estimated that the demand for products will increase such that 10% more labor hours can reasonably be expected to be needed in Department II.
Sales and inventory data of Department II for the current period include:

	Clarinets	Saxophones
Sales (units)	19,000	7,600
Beginning finished goods inventory (units)	2,000	500
Ending finished goods inventory (units)	4,000	900
Beginning WIP—Department II inventory (units)	1,000	0
Percentage completion		
Labor	25%	——
Machine time	75%	——
Ending WIP—Department II inventory (units)	0	2,000
Percentage completion		
Labor	——	30%
Machine time	——	60%

Other actual costs incurred in Department II during the current period include:

Direct labor (109,000 hours @ $8)	$ 872,000
Total manufacturing overhead	$1,250,000
Actual machine hours worked	115,000

Required:

1. Prepare a schedule of the total full absorption standard cost *per unit* for clarinets and saxophones to be used in the accounting process for Department II.
2. For the current month determine the standard quantities allowed in Department II for (a) Department I's output, (b) labor time, and (c) machine time.

3. Assume the answers to the three questions in part 2 are (a) 50,000 pounds, (b) 98,000 hours, and (c) 120,000 hours. Further, assume that the following entries have already been made:

WIP—Department II (109,000 × $8)	872,000	
Payroll		872,000
MOH—Department II	1,250,000	
Miscellaneous		1,250,000

The company uses standard costs in their accounts.
   a. Prepare the entry to transfer Department I's output to Department II for the current period.
   b. Prepare the entry to apply Department II's total overhead (fixed and variable) for the period. (This is done at the end of the period after the output is known.)
   c. Prepare the entry to record Department II's labor efficiency variance for the period.
   d. Prepare the entry to record *all* overhead variances for the period in as much detail as permitted by the data.

23-17. Using Regression Results to Examine Significance of Variable Overhead Spending Variance. In establishing overhead standards, the DeMaris Company used regression analysis. Based on a twenty-four-month sample, the following data were derived using direct-labor hours as the independent variable:

$$\hat{y} = 12,000 + 7.5x$$
$$r^2 = 0.88 \quad s_e = 750 \quad s_b = 0.55$$

Thus, variable overhead was applied at the rate of $7.50 per labor hour. During the current month, 2,000 direct-labor hours were incurred and a $2,000 unfavorable variable overhead spending variance was reported.

Required:

Based on a 95% confidence interval, is the variance significant enough to investigate?

23-18. Regression Analysis and Variable Costing. At the end of January 19x2, the Pitt Company's accountant prepared the following monthly income statement based on *actual, full-cost* principles:

Sales (100,000 units)			$1,000,000
Cost of sales			
Beginning inventory (5,000 units)		$ 37,500	
Cost of current production			
(110,000 units)			
Direct material	$220,000		
Direct labor	330,000		
Total manufacturing			
overhead	269,500	819,500	
Cost of goods available		$857,000	
Ending inventory		111,750	745,250
Gross margin			$ 254,750
Selling and general expenses			180,000
Net income			$ 74,750

You just returned from an executive training seminar that discussed variable costing and regression analysis as tools from which an executive could benefit. The company produces several products but during January 19x2 its production and sales were limited to a single product. Fortunately the accountant kept a lot of production and other statistics on file and you had a staff member do some regression analyses. Define:

H = total manufacturing overhead
G = total selling and general expenses
S = sales dollars
L = total direct-labor hours
M = total machine hours

Your staff person reported that using the last twenty-four months of data (during which several products were produced) the following regressions were done:

	r^2	s_e
$\hat{H} = 100,000 + 3\,L$	0.89	4,000
$\hat{H} = 75,000 + 2M$	0.75	4,200
$\hat{G} = 80,000 + 0.10S$	0.50	1,000
$\hat{G} = 75,000 + 2L$	0.60	900
$\hat{G} = 63,000 + 0.05S + 1.2L$	0.86	500

You know that each unit of the product produced in January required 1/2 labor hour per unit and 1 machine hour. Also, there is no significant correlation among S, L, and M in the data because the firm experiences a constantly changing product mix.

Required:

1. Recast the preceding statement into a variable costing format. You need not include inventories in the variable costing statement. Any *error* (difference between the estimate and the actual) of using the regression equation is to be considered as an adjustment to the *fixed* element.
2. Determine the total cost at which the total ending inventory would be carried under variable costing principles.
3. Suppose you were using the preceding regression equations to forecast the total overhead cost for a production of 110,000 units. What is the range of costs for which you are 95% confident of including the actual cost if the sample size were large and if the value of the independent variable were close to the sample mean of the independent variable?

23-19. Projected Income Statement Using Regression Analysis. The Leaky Roofing Company produces roofing supplies. Extensive use is made of regression studies in projecting its financial plans. First, the company has found that its sales in a given month (S_j) are a function of the housing starts in month (j - 2) and month (j - 3). That is, there is a two-month to three-month lag between the start of construction and the need for roofing. Specifically the regression equation is:

$$S_j = 2,000 + 3H_{j-2} + 1H_{j-3} \quad \text{(where } H_j = \text{housing starts in month j)}$$

Because of shipping time, the production for the anticipated sales in month j is completed in the preceding month (month j-1). Of course, the actual results vary around the predicted amounts, but the firm has found this variance to be small and normally distributed on either side of the prediction. Thus, they continue to use the regression in planning for production and sales.

Following is the actual income statement for July. The inventory is evaluated at the average production cost during July.

Sales ($7,000 @ $16)		$112,000
Cost of sales		
Beginning finished goods inventory		
(6,000 units)	$ 60,000	
Production costs added		
Material (see note)	31,500	
Labor (see note)	37,800	
Overhead (see note)	18,900	
Cost of goods available	$148,200	
Ending finished goods inventory		
(8,000 units)	78,400	69,800
Gross margin		$ 42,200
Selling and administrative expenses		
Variable selling	$ 12,600	
Fixed selling and administrative	7,400	20,000
Net income before tax		$ 22,200

Note: The material and labor cost per unit remains constant. The $18,900 of overhead (OH) is an actual amount incurred. For projections, the firm uses the following regression equation (P = production):

$$OH = 9,100 + 0.1P$$

The housing starts for the last four months are known to be:

April	1,000
May	1,000
June	2,000
July	3,000

Required:

Prepare a statement of projected income for August.

23-20. CMA Problem on LP and Regression Analysis. The Tripro Company produces and sells three products hereafter referred to as products A, B, and C. The company is currently changing its short-range planning approach in an attempt to incorporate some of the newer planning techniques. The controller and some of her staff have been conferring with a consultant on the feasibility of using a linear programming model for determining the optimum product mix.

Information for short-range planning has been developed in the same format as in prior years. This information includes expected sales prices and expected direct labor and material costs for each product. In addition, variable and fixed overhead costs were assumed to be the same for each product because approximately equal quantities of the products were produced and sold.

Price and Cost Information (per unit)

	A	B	C
Selling price	$25.00	$30.00	$40.00
Direct labor	7.50	10.00	12.50
Direct materials	9.00	6.00	10.50
Variable overhead	6.00	6.00	6.00
Fixed overhead	6.00	6.00	6.00

All three products use the same type of direct material, which costs $1.50 per pound of material. Direct labor is paid at the rate of $5.00 per hour. There are 2,000 direct-labor hours and 20,000 pounds of direct materials available in a month.

Required:

1. Formulate and label the linear programming objective function and constraint functions necessary to maximize Tripro's contribution margin. Use A, B, and C to represent units of the three products.
2. The consultant, upon reviewing the data presented and the linear programming functions developed, performed further analysis of overhead costs. He used a multiple linear regression model to analyze the overhead cost behavior. The regression model incorporated observations from the past forty-eight months of total overhead costs and the direct-labor hours for each product. The following equation was the result:

$$Y = \$5,000 + 2x_a + 4x_b + 3x_c$$

where: Y = monthly total overhead in dollars, x_a = monthly direct-labor hours for product A, x_b = monthly direct-labor hours for product B, and x_c = monthly direct-labor hours for product C. The total regression has been determined to be statistically significant as has each of the individual regression coefficients. Reformulate the objective function for Tripro Company using the results of this analysis.

Learning Curves

Situations may be encountered where people are still learning how to perform a task. That is, with experience, workers perform a task much more quickly. For example, the second time you do a problem on a particular accounting topic you have probably noted that you did it faster than the first problem assigned. When accountants are involved with a process where there is learning, several implications arise.

This chapter begins with an introduction to the mechanics of the learning phenomena. This includes the discussion of a variety of learning curve models. Then there is a discussion of the use of these models in the budgeting process. That is, if learning is occurring then how are resource needs estimated and budgeted? A third section is devoted to the implication for standard cost systems. The last section considers the problems and some solutions of establishing an appropriate learning curve.

Basics of Learning Curves

In industries such as airplane construction, the learning phenomenon is easily noticeable. Let's suppose it took 10,000 labor hours to assemble the first airplane of a particular model. After one airplane, the average assembly time is 10,000 hours (10,000 ÷ 1). Now, suppose that the average assembly time after constructing two airplanes is noted to be 8,500. Observe that this is 85% of the average after one airplane. This means that the time needed for the second airplane had to be less than 10,000 hours in order to have an average of 8,500. Specifically:

Total time for first two airplanes	2 × 8,500	17,000
Total time for first airplane		10,000
Total time for second airplane		7,000

Continuing further, suppose it was noted that the average assembly time for the first *four* airplanes was 7,225. This average is 85% of the average after two airplanes (7,225 ÷ 8,500). After the construction of eight airplanes, the average assembly time was 6,141.25 hours. Again note that this average is 85% of the average after four airplanes (6,141.25 ÷ 7,225). The noted behavior can be described as follows:

After each *doubling* of experience, the cumulative *average* resource consumption is equal to a constant percentage of the previous average resource consumption.

Exhibit 24.1 summarizes the data for the first eight airplanes and projects the labor hours through the next three doublings of experience.

The above phenomenon is an **average-consumption-based learning curve model** with an 85% learning factor. (Later in this chapter the marginal-contribution-based learning curve model will be introduced.) That is, for each doubling of experience, the cumulative average is 85% of the previous average. These data are plotted in Exhibit 24.2. The graph at the left in Exhibit 24.2 is for the *average* labor hours and the right graph is for the *total* labor hours. Notice in the right graph that total labor hours is increasing at a decreasing rate (a nonlinear behavior).

The procedure used in Exhibit 24.1 is sufficient to estimate labor hours if it is only necessary to do so at one of the "doubled" values. But what if it is necessary to know the average after ten airplanes or forty airplanes, for example? Or, what if it is necessary to know the estimated time to produce the tenth or the fortieth airplane? In order to answer these kinds of questions it is necessary to convert the observed phenomena into a summarizing equation.

THE DOUBLING LEARNING CURVE MODEL. We now consider how to arrive at the equations represented by the curves in Exhibit 24.2. Define:

x = cumulative number of units produced.
$\overline{Y}_x$ = average labor time after x units have been produced.
a = labor time required for *first* unit.
b = a "learning factor" computed via equation (24-2) below.
k = learning curve percentage; the ratio of the average labor time consumed *after* doubling to the average labor time consumed *before* doubling.

Exhibit 24.1   Learning Phenomena Based on Doubling of Experience (The Model Based on Average Consumption)

Cumulative Units	Cumulative Average (0.85 × Previous Average)	Total Hours (Units × Average)
1	10,000.0000	10,000
2	8,500.0000	17,000
4	7,225.0000	28,900
8	6,141.2500	49,130
16	5,220.0625	83,521
32	4,437.0531	141,986
64	3,771.4952	241,376

Exhibit 24.2   Graphs of Labor Hours When There Is Learning

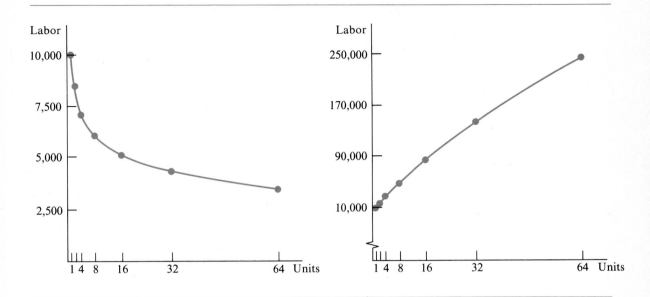

Then, it can be shown that the equation for the left graph, the average labor time, of Exhibit 24.2 is:

$$\overline{Y}_x = ax^b \qquad\qquad\qquad\qquad\qquad (24\text{-}1)$$

where:

$$b = \frac{\log k}{\log 2} \qquad\qquad\qquad\qquad\qquad (24\text{-}2)$$

and:

$\log k$ = the common logarithm of k

$\log 2$ = the common logarithm of 2

For the example in the previous section:

a = 10,000

k = 0.85

$$b = \frac{\log (0.85)}{\log 2} = \frac{-0.07058}{0.30103} = -0.23447$$

(A calculator having a log function was used to find the above values.) Thus:

$$\overline{Y}_x = 10,000x^{-0.23447} \tag{24-1'}$$

If your calculator has a y^x key (indicating, raise the first entry keyed in, y, to the x power, the second number keyed in), then you can verify the following representative values:

x	$x^{-0.23447}$	$\overline{Y}_x = 10,000x^{-0.23447}$
1	1.000000	10,000.00
2	0.850000	8,500.00
3	0.772900	7,729.00
4	0.722500	7,225.00
8	0.614125	6,141.25
10	0.582820	5,828.20
40	0.421088	4,210.88
64	0.377149	3,771.49

Note that the $\overline{Y}_x$ values at 1, 2, 4, 8, and 64 are the same as in Exhibit 24.1. In addition, we now have the ability to compute the average after any cumulative production (3, 10, or 40, for example).

To compute the total labor needed for the first x units, T_x, just multiply the cumulative production, x, by the average after x units, $\overline{Y}_x$:

$$T_x = x(\overline{Y}_x) \tag{24-3}$$

You can verify that for x equal to 1, 2, 4, 8, or 64 that the total labor, $x(\overline{Y}_x)$ computed from the above schedule, is the same as in Exhibit 24.1. Another form of (24-3) can be derived by substituting (24-1) into (24-3):

$$T_x = x(\overline{Y}_x) = x(ax^b)$$
$$T_x = ax^{b+1} \tag{24-4}$$

For the above example:

$$T_x = 10,000x^{0.76553} \tag{24-4'}$$

GENERAL LOG-LINEAR MODEL.   It is not necessary to develop the learning curve model in the way discussed in the previous section. It is only necessary to determine the "a" and "b" shape parameters for equation (24-4). That is, use the same notation of the previous section and define:

$$b' = b + 1$$

Then, a general form is:

$$T_x = ax^{b'} \tag{24-5}$$

There is a whole family of curves of this form.

The two curves in Exhibit 24.3 both have "a" values of 100. To show the effect of the b' parameter, curves for b' equal to 0.7 and 0.5 have been plotted. Note that for the initial increases in volume the curve bends and then straightens out as the learning effect vanishes. It should also be noted that when b' equals 1, the curve $T_x = ax^{b'}$ generates the conventional variable cost curve. If b' were equal to 0, the curve would be equivalent to a fixed cost behavior. Should b' exceed 1, then the curve would increase at an increasing rate. Such behavior would not be expected in a learning situation. Thus, b' can be expected to be between 0 and 1. In the last section of this chapter there is a discussion of some methods of determining the shape parameters.

The above model is sometimes called the log-linear model. It is so named because when a log transformation is done, the results are linear:

$\log T_x = \log[ax^{b'}]$
$\log T_x = \log a + \log [x^{b'}]$
$\log T_x = \log a + b'(\log x)$

Exhibit 24.3   Family of Curves That Represent Learning Behavior

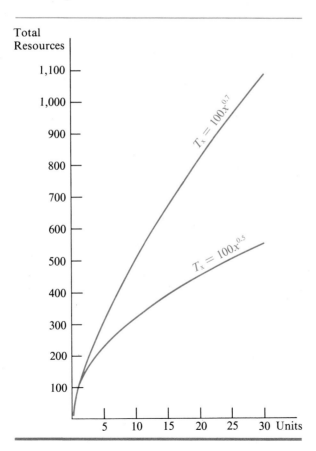

If the observations are plotted on log-log graph paper, both the average labor curve and the total labor curve would be linear. This observation will be used in a later section.

Sometimes you will find reference to an alternative log-linear model. The previous model is based on the observation that the *average* labor reduced by a constant percentage as experience doubled. The **marginal-consumption-based learning curve** is as follows:

> After each *doubling* of experience the *marginal* (incremental) resource consumption is equal to a constant percentage of the previous marginal resource consumption.

To illustrate, suppose the *marginal* labor consumption for the first airplane is 10,000 hours. Then, suppose the marginal consumption for the second airplane is 8,000 hours; for the fourth, 6,400 hours; the eighth, 5,120 hours; and so forth. Note this is different than our first example and that the marginal consumption is 80% of that for the unit resulting from the previous doubling of experience. Following is a summary:

Cumulative Unit	Marginal Consumption (0.8 × Previous Marginal Consumption)
1	10,000.0
2	8,000.0
4	6,400.0
8	5,120.0
16	4,096.0
32	3,276.8

This model can also be generalized. Define:

x = cumulative number of units produced.
M_x = marginal (incremental) resource consumption for the xth unit.
r = marginal learning curve percentage; the ratio of the marginal labor time consumed after doubling to the marginal labor time consumed before doubling.
a = time for the *first* unit.
c = learning factor for the marginal learning curve model.

Then:

$$c = \frac{\log r}{\log 2} \tag{24-6}$$

and:

$$M_x = ax^c \tag{24-7}$$

In the above example:

$a = 10{,}000$

$$c = \frac{\log (0.80)}{\log 2} = \frac{-0.09691}{0.30103} = -0.3219$$

Thus:

$$M_x = 10,000x^{-0.3219} \qquad\qquad (24\text{-}7')$$

Following are some representative values from (24-7′):

x	$x^{-0.3219}$	$M_x = 10,000x^{-0.3219}$
1	1.0000	10,000
2	0.8000	8,000
3	0.7021	7,021
4	0.6400	6,400
5	0.5956	5,956
8	0.5120	5,120

When this learning curve model is used, it is not as easy to determine the total resources required for, say, the first four units. The total would have to be derived as follows:

Resources needed for first four units $= M_1 + M_2 + M_3 + M_4$

$$= 10,000 + 8,000 + 7,021 + 6,400 = 31,421 \text{ hours}$$

On the other hand, when using the "marginal" learning curve model it is easy to determine the labor needed for a particular unit. Such an estimate is not easy to determine from the "average" learning curve model. Thus, both models have their advantages. In the accounting literature, the "average" model is the more popular of the two, however.

OTHER MODELS. Log-linear learning curve models are not the only ones that have been proposed. As a preface to a general, nontechnical discussion of some other options, equation (24-7) will be plotted. That is, the other models will be related to the "marginal" model. Further, the plot will be done in log-log form. Taking logs of (24-7):

$$\log M_x = \log a + c(\log x) \qquad\qquad (24\text{-}8)$$

Since c will normally be negative, the log-linear marginal model will be as shown in Exhibit 24.4.

Other models that have been used in practice include:

1. The plateau model,
2. The asymptotic model,
3. The Stanford-B model, and
4. The S-model.

A brief, general discussion of each follows.

The **plateau model** is perhaps more representative of real-world situations than the log-linear model. It presumes that learning will eventually cease. That is, the marginal consumption of labor per unit will eventually level out and remain the same after a certain number of units have been produced. If the log-linear line in Exhibit 24.4 is extended to the right it must eventually reach zero. This says that

Exhibit 24.4   Log-Linear Marginal Learning Curve Model

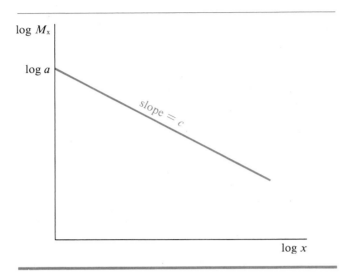

at some point no labor hours are being consumed and, of course, is unrealistic. Plotted in log-log form, the plateau model is represented in Exhibit 24.5.

The **asymptotic model** is a variaton of the plateau model. It assumes that the marginal labor required per unit is decreasing at a *decreasing* rate (rather than at a constant rate as in the log-linear model) and approaches some plateau level. In log-log form, this model is plotted in Exhibit 24.6.

The **Stanford-B model** has been used by the Boeing Corporation to model the learning phenomenon it noted in the construction of airplanes. In effect, this model assumes that learning is somewhat "slow" at the outset. Then after some amount of experience, the behavior is similar to the log-linear model. Exhibit 24.7 depicts the Stanford-B model.

The **S-model** is a combination of the Stanford-B model, in terms of initial behavior, the log-linear model, in terms of the "mid-x range," and the plateau model at the "high-x range." Exhibit 24.8 depicts its form. (Note the "S" is a "backward-S.")

It is beyond the scope of this chapter to get into the mathematical details of these alternative models. This is a topic for industrial engineering.

Budgeting and Learning Curves

In this section we consider one potential use of learning curves. We discuss how learning curves may be used in the planning and estimating of resources for future periods when learning is still occurring. The specific models (both the "average"

Exhibit 24.5   Plot of Plateau Model

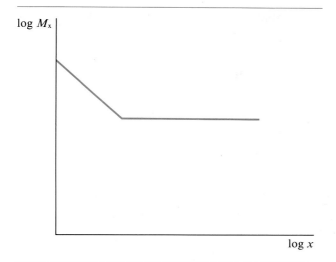

Exhibit 24.6   Plot of Asymptotic Model

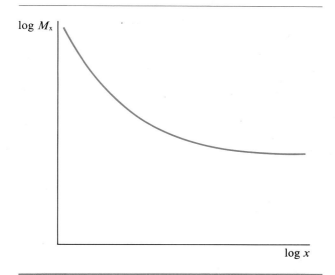

Exhibit 24.7   Plot of Stanford-B Model

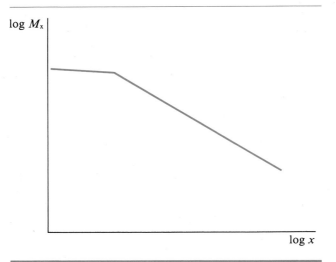

Exhibit 24.8   Plot of S-Model

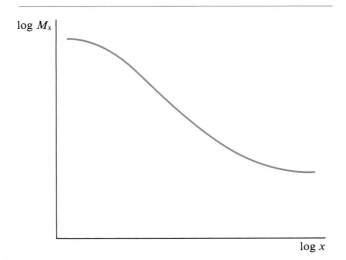

and the "marginal") of the previous section will be used to demonstrate the application.

Suppose the learning curve in effect is the one based on "average" consumption in (24-4′):

$$T_x = 10,000x^{0.76553}$$

Now, suppose we have the following:

Month	Production
1	8 units (actual)
2	24 units (budgeted)
3	20 units (budgeted)

Further, it is desired to budget the labor needs and labor cost for months 2 and 3.

To proceed, note that x in (24-4′) is the *cumulative* x. Thus:

Month	Cumulative Production
1	8
2	32
3	52

The budget for month 2 can be derived from Exhibit 24.1 or via "formula." From Exhibit 24.1:

Estimated labor for first 32 airplanes	141,986
Estimated labor for first 8 airplanes	49,130
Estimated labor for 24 airplanes in month 2	92,856

Using a formula:

Labor for month 2 $= T_{32} - T_8$

Note that the x in T_x is the cumulative production at the end of month 2 and month 1, respectively. Use (24-4′) to evaluate the two T_x values:

$$\begin{aligned}
\text{Labor for month 2} &= 10,000(32)^{0.76553} - 10,000\,(8)^{0.76553} \\
&= 10,000(14.1986) - 10,000(4.913) \\
&= 141,986 - 49,130 \\
&= 92,856 \text{ hours}
\end{aligned}$$

Since the cumulative production through the end of month 3 does not fall at one of the "doubling points," it will be necessary to budget month 3's labor via "formula."

Labor for month 3 $= T_{52} - T_{32}$

Again, note the x in T_x is the cumulative production at the end of month 3 and month 2, respectively. Using (24-4′) for the T_x value:

Labor for month 3 $= 10,000(52)^{0.76553} - 10,000\,(32)^{0.76553}$
$= 10,000(20.5898) - 10,000(14.198)$
$= 205,898 - 141,980$
$= 63,918$ hours

Next, consider how the budgeting would work if it had been decided to use the "marginal" model in equation (24-7'):

$$M_x = 10,000x^{-0.3219}$$

Further, suppose we have the following:

Month	Production
1	2 (actual)
2	4 (budgeted)
3	3 (budgeted)

Since M_x gives the incremental labor for the xth unit, it will be necessary to add the four marginal values. Thus the budget for month 2 is:

Labor for month 2 $= M_3 + M_4 + M_5 + M_6$

Again, note that the x in M_x is the cumulative production. Thus, the four units produced in month 2 would be units 3, 4, 5, and 6. Therefore from (24-7'):

Labor for month 2 $= 10,000[3^{-0.3219} + 4^{-0.3219} + 5^{-0.3219} + 6^{-0.3219}]$
$= 10,000[0.7201 + 0.6400 + 0.5957 + 0.5617]$
$= 10,000[2.4995]$
$= 24,995$ hours

In month 3 the firm is scheduled to produce units 7, 8, and 9. Thus:

Labor for month 3 $= M_7 + M_8 + M_9$
$= 10,000[7^{-0.3219} + 8^{-0.3219} + 9^{-0.3219}]$
$= 10,000[0.5345 + 0.5120 + 0.4930]$
$= 10,000[1.5395]$
$= 15,395$ hours

Obviously, the above estimating method will be laborious if the number of units to be produced is large. Through integral calculus an alternative approach can be derived. Define:

E = cumulative experience through the *end* of the period for which the estimate is needed.
B = cumulative experience before the period for which the estimate is needed.
a and c as in equation (24-7).

Then it can be shown that the sum, S, of the resources needed for unit (B + 1) through unit E is:

$$S = \frac{a}{1 + c}[E^{1+c} - B^{1+c}] \tag{24-9}$$

To illustrate, use month 3 from the previous example:

$E = 9; \quad B = 6; \quad a = 10,000; \quad c = -0.3219$

$$S = \frac{10,000}{1 - 0.3219}[9^{(1 - 0.3219)} - 6^{(1 - 0.3219)}] \qquad\qquad (24\text{-}9')$$

$S = 14,747[4.4368 - 3.3702]$

$S = 15,729$

The result does not agree exactly with the previous calculation of 15,395 because equation (24-9) assumes a continuous learning curve rather than a discrete set of points as was assumed in the original calculation. For larger values of x, the difference between the two methods becomes much smaller.

Standard Costing and Learning Curves

Now consider the problem of controlling and evaluating performance in an environment where learning is still taking place. If a standard cost system is considered for this purpose, then extreme care must be exercised. Obviously, the standards would have to be revised frequently. The output per labor hour, for example, would be expected to increase with experience. If the standards are based on initial expectations, then they will be too loose after experience has been gained. Conversely, if they are based on an experienced work force, then they will be too tight during the early experiences.

To illustrate, reconsider the situation used to explain the "average" consumption model earlier in the chapter. That is, the average and total consumption of labor is modeled as:

$\bar{y}_x = 10,000x^{-0.23447}$
$T_x = 10,000x^{0.76553}$

How could we set standard allowances in this case?

To set standards for the forthcoming period it would be necessary to estimate the total production for the period. Let us assume that the budget for the forthcoming period is to produce twenty-four airplanes. Further, assume that eight airplanes have been produced to date. That is, the situation is the same as described in the last section except we are assuming the period is a year rather than a month. It was shown in the last section that the budgeted labor for this situation is 92,856 hours. A standard labor allowance per airplane for the current period can be set at 3,869 (92,856 ÷ 24). Let's explore the problems that might be encountered with this standard.

Assume that actual production for the year turned out be be twenty airplanes instead of twenty-four. Using the predetermined standard the labor allowance for the period would be 77,380 (3,869 × 20). Suppose the actual labor used during the year was 80,000 hours. Can it be said that the labor efficiency variance is 2,620 (77,380 − 80,000)? Because of the way the standard was constructed the variance will be contaminated with calculation error. An average labor time demand of 3,869 hours per airplane is valid only if the production is twenty-four airplanes during the year. The learning curve model would imply that the labor time should be 79,058 hours for the year:

$$\text{Labor} = T_{28} - T_8 = 10,000(28)^{0.76557} - 10,000(8)^{0.76557}$$
$$= 128,189 - 49,130$$
$$= 79,058$$

Thus the variance from expectation is only 942 hours ($79,058 - 80,000$) instead of 2,620.

The only way to overcome the problem illustrated above is to evaluate performance using a flexible budget approach. That is, a labor budget for a variety of output levels should be constructed and presented to the production manager prior to the start of production. Using only three levels the following illustrates.

	Labor Budget for		
	Twenty-three Airplanes	*Twenty-four Airplanes*	*Twenty-five Airplanes*
$T_{31} - T_8 = 138,576 - 49,130$	89,446		
$T_{32} - T_8 = 141,986 - 49,130$		92,856	
$T_{33} - T_8 = 145,370 - 49,130$			96,240

When learning is still significant the latter approach will be preferable to the former. If the first approach is used, then some of the resulting variance will not be attributable to production efforts and will have to be accounted for in the variance explanation process.

Establishing a Learning Curve

It was indicated earlier in the chapter that there would be a discussion of how to determine a learning curve. Both types of learning curves discussed are of the following general form:

$$y = ax^b \tag{24-10}$$

If there has already been some accumulated experience then it is possible to use regression analysis in order to find the general shape parameters (the a and b values) for the best fitting model of the form in (24-10). As was indicated earlier, a log transformation of equation (24-10) will result in a linear equation:

$$\log y = \log a + b(\log x) \tag{24-11}$$

That is, in comparison with a pure linear model of the form $y = a + bx$, the above model replaces a with log a and b is multiplied by log x (instead of x). Thus, by inputting the log of y (instead of y) and the log of x (instead of x) into a regression of model, it would return *log a* as its constant and b as its slope. Taking the antilog of the returned constant would give the "a" value and the best fitting curve of the form $y = ax^b$.

To illustrate, suppose the first eight units produced required the following labor hours:

x Unit	Hours	y Cumulative Hours
1	195	195
2	183	378
3	150	528
4	155	683
5	163	846
6	122	968
7	141	1,109
8	143	1,252

It is obvious that some type of learning is occurring although it is not following a "smooth" curve (the fifth unit required more time than the fourth, for example). Assume the learning is following the "average" consumption model. As defined in (24-4), T_x, or the dependent variable y as used above, is the cumulative resources needed to produce the cumulative volume, x. Thus, the input would be as follows:

Case 1: $[\log y_1 \quad \log x_1] = [\log 195 \quad \log 1] = [2.290 \quad 0.000]$

Case 2: $[\log y_2 \quad \log x_2] = [\log 378 \quad \log 2] = [2.577 \quad 0.301]$

Case 3: $[\log y_3 \quad \log x_3] = [\log 528 \quad \log 3] = [2.723 \quad 0.477]$

.   .   .

.   .   .

.   .   .

Case 8: $[\log y_8 \quad \log x_8] = [\log 1,252 \quad \log 8] = [3.098 \quad 0.903]$

A regression model of the above form would have an intercept of 2.2989 and a slope of 0.8879 for the above data. These values are log â and b̂, respectively. The antilog of 2.2989 is 199.02. That is, $10^{2.2989} = 199.02$. Thus, the results suggest the equation should be:

$$y = 199.02x^{0.8879}$$

One of the end-of-chapter problems will require you to find the best equation assuming the above data are to be modeled using the "marginal" consumption model.

Summary

This chapter has introduced you to the topic of learning curves. Occasionally you will encounter situations when the learning process is significant. If so, there are many implications for the accounting function. This chapter exposed you to the general nature of learning curves and went into detail concerning two major variations: the "average" consumption and "marginal" consumption model. Also discussed were the problems of budgeting resources and controlling performance in a learning environment. There was exposure to alternative learning curve models from the area of industrial engineering. Finally, there was a discussion of how regression analysis might be used in the process of establishing a learning curve.

New key terms from the chapter are:

Learning curve
Average consumption learning curve model
Marginal consumption learning curve model
Plateau model
Asymptotic model
Stanford-B model
S-model

SELF-STUDY PROBLEM. Assume a firm is about to start production on a new product. Based on experiences with similar products the firm expects labor consumption to follow an 86% average learning curve model. The first batch of this product is estimated to require 1,000 labor hours.

Required:

1. How many labor hours would be expected to be incurred for the second batch? For the third?
2. Complete a schedule showing the expected labor for the fourth through the eighth batch.
3. Assuming ten batches have already been produced prior to 19x5, what would be the budgeted labor hours for 19x5 if the production volume is scheduled at fifteen batches?
4. What would be the standard labor allowance per batch for 19x5?
5. What if the actual production in 19x5 was twenty batches and the actual labor consumed was 8,300 hours? What is the labor efficiency variance if the standard labor rate is $12.00 per hour?
6. Evaluate the significance of the labor efficiency variance computed in part 5 for evaluating the performance of the production department.

Solution to Self-Study Problem

1. If the learning curve is 86%, then:

$$k = \frac{\log 0.86}{\log 2} = -0.21759$$

and

$$\overline{Y}_x = 1,000x^{-0.21759}$$

For x = 2:
$$\overline{Y}_2 = 1,000(2)^{-0.21759} = 860$$
$$T_2 = 860(2) = 1,720$$

The labor for batch number 2 is:
$$T_2 - T_1 = 1,720 - 1,000 = 720$$

For x = 3:

$$\overline{Y}_3 = 1,000(3)^{-0.21759} = 787.38$$
$$T_3 = 787.38(3) = 2,362.13$$

The labor for batch number 3 is:

$$T_3 - T_2 = 2,362.13 - 1,720 = 642.13$$

2.

Unit	Cumulative Average	Total	Marginal Consumption
3	787.38	2,362.13	642.13
4	739.60	2,958.40	596.27
5	704.55	3,522.75	564.35
6	677.14	4,062.84	540.09
7	654.81	4,583.67	520.83
8	636.06	5,088.48	504.81

3. $T_x = 1,000x^{(1-0.21759)} = 1,000x^{0.78241}$

   Budget $= T_{25} - T_{10}$

$$= 1,000(25)^{0.78241} - 1,000(10)^{0.78241}$$
$$= 12,410 - 6,059 = 6,351 \text{ hours}$$

4. Standard per batch $= 6,351 \div 15 = 423.4$

5. Standard allowance $= 20(423.4) = 8,468$
   Labor efficiency variance $= (8,468 - 8,300)12 = 2,016 \text{ F}$

6. Because of the learning factor and the production for the year exceeding the budget, the standard allowance will not be what was really expected. The allowance would really be:

$$T_{30} - T_{10} = 1,000(30)^{0.78241} - 1,000(10)^{0.78241}$$
$$= 14,312 - 6,059 = 8,253$$

Thus, the "true" labor efficiency variance is:

$$(8,253 - 8,300)12 = 564 \text{ U}$$

References

Summers, E.L., and Welsch, G.A. "How Learning Curve Models Can Be Applied to Profit Planning," *Management Services* (March/April 1970): 45–50.

Yelle, L.E. "The Learning Curve: Historical Review and Comprehensive Survey," *Decision Sciences* (April 1979): 302–328.

Problems

24-1. Basic Learning Curve Calculations. The Phony Company produces portable tape players. A new ultracompact model has just been introduced. It is estimated that the first unit will require fifty hours to assemble but that labor time will follow a 75% *average* learning curve model. Complete the following table.

Cumulative Output	Cumulative Average Time	Total Time	Marginal Time
1			
2			
3			
4			
5			

24-2. Continuation of 24-1. Assume the same facts as in 24-1 except that the learning curve will follow a 75% *marginal* model. Complete a table similar to that in problem 24-1.

24-3. Deducing Relationships in a Learning Curve Model. Assume that for a particular product, the Tiger Company is experiencing a constant rate of learning (based on the *average* time model). Complete the following table.

Cumulative Output	Cumulative Average Time	Total Time	Marginal Time
1	100	100	100
2	82	164	64
3			
4			

24-4. Alternative to 24-3. For a particular product the ZYX Company is experiencing a constant rate of learning (based on the *marginal* time model). Complete the following table.

Cumulative Output	Cumulative Average Time	Total Time	Marginal Time
1	200	200	200
2	188	376	176
3			
4			

24-5. Basic Problem on Learning Phenomena. The Oester Company started producing product 2B during 19x1. The 19x1 records show that three units were produced and that 2,408 labor hours were incurred. The production budget for 19x2 includes five units of product 2B.

Required:

1. Based on this information, how many labor hours would you budget for product 2B during 19x2?
2. A recently hired staff accountant has analyzed the experience with product 2B and feels there is a learning phenomenon involved. She suggests that cumulative labor, T_x, as a function of cumulative production, x, is:

$$T_x = 1000x^{0.8}$$

Estimate the 19x2 labor requirement given that the analyst's equation is correct. The following values may be of help:

x: 1.0 2.000 3.000 4.000 5.000 6.000 7.000 8.000
$x^{0.8}$: 1.0 1.741 2.408 3.031 3.624 4.193 4.743 5.278

3. What are the implications of using your result in part 1 when the actual behavior is according to the equation in part 2?

24-6. Learning Effects. The Nettles Company is bidding on a contract for one of its specialty products. They have previously produced four batches of this product incurring the following costs:

Material @ $10,000 per batch	$ 40,000
Labor 25,600 hours @ $6.00	153,600
Variable overhead as a function of labor hours	
25,600 @ $2.00	51,200
Fixed overhead costs assigned on basis of labor	
hours 25,600 @ $1.00	25,600
Total cost	$270,400

You feel certain that labor time is a nonlinear function of cumulative production because of learning. The estimated equation for this is $T_x = 10,000x^{0.6781}$ where

x = cumulative batches of the product
T_x = cumulative labor needed for cumulative production

The contract on which we are now bidding would call for twelve batches. In determining the costs in preparation for the bid, one of the other staff members suggests that we add our usual profit to an estimated cost of $811,200 ($270,400 × 3) since this contract is three times as large as the previous one.

Required:

What would be your estimate of the *incremental* costs on this contract? That is, what is the increase in costs that would be incurred if we win the bid?

24-7. Learning Curves and Standards. Suppose you are a staff accountant for the Nettles Company of problem 24-6. Now your task is to develop labor standards for the specialty product discussed in that problem. Rather than the bidding situation discussed there, assume that production is planned on a regular basis at a normal rate of four batches per year. It is company policy to establish one standard for use the entire year and to make annual revisions.

Required:

1. What would you have established as the standard labor per batch in year 1?
2. At what value would you establish the standard per batch in year 2? (Note: $(8)^{0.6781} = 4.0962$.)

3. Assuming that actual production was four batches in both years 1 and 2, what would be the standard per batch in year 3? (Note: $(12)^{0.6781} = 5.3925$.)
4. In year 3 the actual production was three batches and the actual labor was 9,900 hours. What would be the labor efficiency variance for year 3? Comment on its usefulness in evaluating the production manager.

24-8. Using a Marginal Learning Curve Model. Assume the marginal learning curve model on page 857 of the chapter:

$$M_x = 10,000x^{-0.3219}$$

Further, assume that fifty airplanes were produced in the first three months. Five airplanes are budgeted for month 4.

Required:

1. Estimate the labor needed for these five airplanes using the sum of the appropriate M values.
2. Estimate the labor needed for these five airplanes using equation (24-9). Compare your results.

24-9. Using Regression to Determine Learning Curve. Reconsider the problem from the section on Establishing Learning Curves. Information for the first eight units is provided on page 865. Now, assume there is a hypothesis that the learning follows the marginal learning curve model rather than the average model.

Required:

1. What data must be submitted to a regression model in order to find the best fit of the form:

$$M_x = ax^c$$

2. If you have access to a computer regression package, determine the specific model of the above form.

24-10. Regression When There Is Learning. The LCF Company produces a product that is subject to significant technology changes. With each change there is a lot of learning that occurs in the production process. The latest change took place at the beginning of period 1. Eight units were produced in period 1 and the following data were recorded:

Unit	Incremental Labor	Cumulative Labor
1	300	300
2	205	505
3	179	684
4	165	849
5	154	1,003
6	147	1,150
7	141	1,291
8	136	1,427

The firm uses a learning curve of the form:

$$T_x = ax^b$$

No technology changes are scheduled for period 2 during which five units are scheduled for production. You are to estimate the direct labor required for period 2.

Required:

Use a regression package to find the best regression equation and then estimate the labor needed in period 2.

24-11. Using Regression to Find Learning Curve. As a staff accountant for the Rivers Company you have the task of preparing cost estimates for a variety of purposes. The case you are now working on involves estimates for a new product that was recently added to the company's line. To date, six batches of this product have been produced and the following data are available.

Batch	Labor Consumed (hours)
1	5,020
2	3,740
3	3,480
4	3,240
5	3,120
6	2,880

Based on past experience you feel that a learning effect is present, and the six observations confirm this.

Required:

1. Prepare the input to a regression package to find the parameters of the best-fitting learning curve of the form in equation (24-4). That is, list the values of the dependent and independent variables for each case.
2. Suppose that, based on common logs, the results were as follows:

   $$T_x = 3.69966 + 0.81346x$$

   Given these results, what would be the equation for T_x?

24-12. CMA Problem on Learning Curves. The Xyon Company has purchased 80,000 pumps annually from Kobec Inc. The price has increased each year and reached $68.00 per unit last year. Because the purchase price has increased significantly, Xyon management has asked that an estimate be made of the cost to manufacture it in its own facilities. Xyon's products consist of stamping and castings. The company has little experience with products requiring assembly.

The engineering, manufacturing, and accounting departments have prepared a report for management that included the estimate shown below for an assembly run of 10,000 units. Additional production employees would be hired to manufacture the subassembly. However, no additional equipment, space, or supervision would be needed.

Components (outside purchases)	$120,000
Assembly labor[1]	300,000
Factory overhead[2]	450,000
General and administrative overhead[3]	87,000
Total costs	$957,000

[1]Assembly labor consists of hourly production workers.

[2]Factory overhead is applied to products on a direct-labor-dollar basis. Variable overhead costs vary closely with direct-labor dollars.

Factory overhead rate	50% of direct-labor dollars
Variable overhead	100% of direct-labor dollars
Factory overhead rate	150% of direct-labor dollars

[3]General and administrative overhead is applied at 10% of the total cost of material (or components), assembly labor, and factory overhead.

The report states that total costs for 10,000 units are estimated at $957,000 or $95.70 a unit. The current purchase price is $68.00 a unit so the report recommends a continued purchase of the product.

Required:

1. Was the analysis prepared by the engineering, manufacturing, and accounting departments of Xyon Company and the recommendation to continue purchasing the pumps that followed from the analysis correct? Explain your answer and include any supportive calculations you consider necessary.
2. Assume Xyon Company could experience labor cost improvements on the pump assembly consistent with an 80% average learning curve. An assembly run of 10,000 units represents the initial lot or batch for measurement purposes. Should Xyon produce the 80,000 pumps in this situation? Explain your answer.

24-13. CMA Problem on Learning Curves. The Kelly Company plans to manufacture a product, called Electrocal, that requires a substantial amount of direct labor on each unit. Based on the company's experience with other products that required similar amounts of direct labor, management believes that there is a learning factor in the production process used to manufacture Electrocal.

Each unit of Electrocal requires fifty square feet of raw material at a cost of $30 per square foot for a total material cost of $1,500. The standard direct-labor rate is $25 per direct-labor hour. Variable manufacturing overhead is assigned to products at a rate of $40 per direct-labor hour. The company adds a markup of 30% on variable manufacturing cost in determining an initial bid price for all products.

Data on the product of the first two lots (sixteen units) of Electrocal is as follows:

- The first lot of eight units required a total of 3,200 direct-labor hours.
- The second lot of eight units required a total of 2,240 direct-labor hours.

Based on prior production experience, Kelly anticipates that there will be no significant improvement in production time after the first thirty-two units. Therefore a standard for direct-labor hours will be established based on the average hours per unit of units 17 through 32.

Required:

1. Based upon the data presented for the first sixteen units, what learning rate appears to be applicable to the direct labor required to produce Electrocal? Support your answer with appropriate calculations.
2. Calculate the standard for direct-labor hours that Kelly Company should establish for each unit of Electrocal.
3. After the first thirty-two units have been manufactured, Kelly Company was asked to submit a bid on an additional ninety-six units. What price should Kelly bid on this order of ninety-six units? Explain your answer.
4. Knowledge of the learning curve phenomenon can be a valuable management tool. Explain how management can apply the learning curve in the planning and controlling of business operations.

24-14. Learning Curves and Capital Budgeting. The BYU Company is considering two new products, A and B. For comparative purposes, assume the two products are identical except for one item. There is expected to be learning involved in producing product B but not in producing product A.

The common data for the two projects are:

1. It will cost $50,000 at the beginning of the first year to enable the production of either product.
2. The demand for either product is projected at fifteen units per year for the next five years.
3. The sales price of either product is $2,000 per unit.
4. Material cost is estimated to be $200 per unit for either product.
5. Labor and variable overhead cost will total $10 per labor hour.
6. BYU's discount rate is 10%.
7. All cash flows can be assumed to occur at the end of the year.

The labor for product A is expected to be 100 hours per unit. For product B, labor is expected to follow an 80% average learning curve model where the first unit requires 100 labor hours.

Required:

Determine the net present value of adopting each of the products. You may ignore income taxes. Compare your results.

24-15. Learning Curves and CVP Analysis. The Noname Company is considering the production of a new product which will sell at $1,700 per unit. The engineering specifications call for material at $100 per unit of that product. Labor is expected to behave according to the average learning curve model with a factor of 80%. The first unit of the product is expected to require 100 labor hours. Labor will cost $10 per hour and variable factory overhead is expected to be $4 per labor hour. The incremental fixed factory overhead expected to result from the introduction of this new product is $5,000 per year.

Required:

1. Assuming there is no constraint on the available labor time during the year, how many units of the new product would have to be produced and sold in order to break-even on

this proposal? (Hint: You will need to use a trial-and-error procedure in order to answer this and the next question.)

2. Now assume that the maximum labor available is 280 hours per year. How many units of the new product would have to be produced and sold in order to break-even on this proposal?

CHAPTER 25

Decision Making under Uncertainty And Information Economics

The final topic considered in this book is decision making under uncertainty. An uncertain decision making situation is one whereby:

1. There are two or more actions, or alternatives, available to the decision maker, and
2. The decision maker does not have exact values for all of the external (noncontrollable) variables that would influence his or her selection among the alternatives.

For example, if the decision concerns the volume of a particular product to schedule for a given period, the decision maker would generally be influenced by the anticipated *demand* for the product and by its *rate of contribution to profits*. It is not likely that either of these factors will be known with certainty. The former will be affected by economic conditions, by the firm's marketing and pricing policies, and by the actions of competitors, just to name a few. The latter will be a function of actual incremental costs which also may not be known with certainty.

Some of the basic concepts of making decisions in an uncertain environment were discussed in Chapters 13 and 14. In this chapter we will explore these concepts in more depth. Also we will consider the value of information.

A Basic Example

To illustrate a basic approach for decision making under uncertainty, suppose the Mantle Company must decide which sales price to charge for its product. For simplicity, assume that only two prices are being considered: $5 per unit and $6 per unit. The demand for the product *and* the variable production costs are both uncertain quantities. As reflected in Exhibit 25.1, management believes that, regardless of production volume, there is a 70% chance of the variable manufacturing cost being $2.00 per unit and a 30% chance of it being $3.00. That is, for purposes of this example, it is assumed that the variable production cost per unit is independent of the production volume.

The demand function is dependent upon which sales price is selected and is also shown in Exhibit 25.1. This function should be read as follows: "If the sales price is $5, then there is a 30% chance the demand will be 5,000 units, a 50% chance it will be 6,000 units, a 20% chance it will be 7,000 units and 0% chance it will be any other volume." Further, assume that the actual demand is determined immediately after the price is announced, thus permitting production to be scheduled in

Exhibit 25.1   Probability Functions

Probability of Variable Cost

Variable Cost	Probability
$2	0.70
$3	0.30
	1.00

Probabilities of Demand Given Sales Price

Demand (units)	Probability of Demand if Selling Price = $5	Probability of Demand if Selling Price = $6
3,000	0.0	0.1
4,000	0.0	0.5
5,000	0.3	0.4
6,000	0.5	0.0
7,000	0.2	0.0
	1.0	1.0

an amount equal to demand. (The latter assumption will be relaxed in the self-study problem.

For situations such as this, it is helpful to construct a payoff table. A **payoff table** is a schedule of conditional values. In Chapter 14, a **conditional value** was defined as the payoff of an action *given* that certain conditions have occurred. The actions in this problem are as follows. Define A_1 as the action of setting the sales price at $5 and A_2 as selecting the $6 price.

The conditions that might occur are collectively referred to as the **state of nature.** In the Mantle Company problem, the state of nature can be influenced by the decision maker's action. That is, demand is a function of the sales price. The state of nature in this case contains two elements: the demand and the variable cost. To completely describe a state of nature, both elements must be stated. For example, one state of nature is a demand of 3,000 units and a variable cost of $2. Denote this as (3K, 2). The complete set of states is specified in Exhibit 25.2.

Each entry in the payoff table of Exhibit 25.2 is the contribution to profits given the action and the state of nature. For example, the conditional value of action A_1 and state (3K, 2), demand of 3,000, and a variable cost of $2.00 is:

(Sales price $-$ Variable cost) $\times$ Demand $= (5 - 2)3,000 = 9,000$

The payoff of action A_2 given state (4K, 3) is:

($6 $-$ $3)4,000 = 12,000$

All other payoff values are similarly derived.

Exhibit 25.2   Mantle Company Payoff Table and Probability of States of Nature

Payoff Table*

State of Nature

Act	(3K, 2)	(4K, 2)	(5K, 2)	(6K, 2)	(7K, 2)	(3K, 3)	(4K, 3)	(5K, 3)	(6K, 3)	(7K, 3)
A_1 = \$5	9,000	12,000	15,000	18,000	21,000	6,000	8,000	10,000	12,000	14,000
A_2 = \$6	12,000	16,000	20,000	24,000	28,000	9,000	12,000	15,000	18,000	21,000

Probability of Occurrence[+]

State of Nature

Act	(3K, 2)	(4K, 2)	(5K, 2)	(6K, 2)	(7K, 2)	(3K, 3)	(4K, 3)	(5K, 3)	(6K, 3)	(7K, 3)
A_1 = \$5	0.00	0.00	0.21	0.35	0.14	0.00	0.00	0.09	0.15	0.06
A_2 = \$6	0.07	0.35	0.28	0.00	0.00	0.03	0.15	0.12	0.00	0.00

*Given as (Sales price − Variable cost) × Demand

[+]Determined as follows:

(Probability of variable cost) × (Probability of demand given the sales price)

Also in Exhibit 25.2 you will find a table of probabilities of the various states of nature, given the sales price. Since demand is dependent upon sales price, the states of nature have probabilities that depend upon the action taken. Unit variable cost and demand were assumed to be independent; therefore, the probability that they will occur jointly is the product of their individual, or marginal probabilities. For example, assume the sales price is selected to be \$5. Then there is no chance of demand being 3,000 or 4,000 units (see Exhibit 25.1). Therefore, given a sales price of \$5, the chance of a 3,000 or a 4,000 unit demand occurring simultaneously with either the \$2 or \$3 variable cost is zero. With a \$5 sales price there is a 30% chance of demand being 5,000 units. Since there is a 70% chance of the unit variable cost being \$2, the probability of these two events occurring together, given the sales price, is 21% (0.3 × 0.7). As a final illustration, the probability of state (3K, 3), given action A_2, is 3% (0.1 × 0.3). You should verify the remaining entries in the probability table.

As defined in Chapter 14, the **expected value** (EV) of an action is the sum of the weighted conditional values. For this case, the expected value of action A_1 is the sum of the conditional values on the first row of the payoff table in Exhibit 25.2 weighted by the corresponding value from row 1 in the probability table:

$$EV(A_1) = 9,000(0.0) + 12,000(0.0) + 15,000(0.21)$$
$$+ 18,000(0.35) + 21,000(0.14) + 6,000(0.0)$$
$$+ 8,000(0.0) + 10,000(0.09) + 12,000(0.15)$$
$$+ 14,000(0.06)$$
$$EV(A_1) = \$15,930$$

For action A_2, use the corresponding values from the second rows of the two tables:

$$EV(A_2) = 12,000(0.07) + 16,000(0.35) + 20,000(0.28)$$
$$+ 9,000(0.03) + 12,000(0.15) + 15,000(0.12)$$
$$EV(A_2) = \$15,910$$

In terms of expected dollar values, the optimal decision is to set the sales price at \$5, $[EV(A_1) > EV(A_2)]$. This assumes several things. First, the preceding criterion assumes that the decision maker has no aversion to risk and is willing to make decisions based on an expected *dollar* payoff. If there is aversion to risk, then action A_2 might be preferred to action A_1 even though its expected dollar payoff is lower. This preference would exist if the decision maker perceived action A_1 to have greater risk than action A_2 and considered the \$20 difference in expected values to be inadequate compensation for the risk.

If it is suspected that the decision maker has an aversion to risk, then an alternative approach would have to be taken. This will not be explored here.

Another assumption of the expected value criterion is that the data are free of measurement error. If it is possible that there are measurement errors, then sensitivity analyses can be done. This would be accomplished by computing the expected values using different assumed amounts for the payoffs and/or the state of nature probabilities. If the decision remains the same for another set of data, then it is said the decision is insensitive to the changes.

Value of Information

Increasingly, accountants and decision makers are viewing information as a scarce commodity that has a value and a cost. As with any other commodity, consideration should be given to the cost-benefit relationships before there is an expenditure of resources to acquire the information. In this section there is an examination of a process of determining the value, or benefit, of information and, in turn, a process of making decisions about acquiring data.

Since the Mantle Company problem of the previous section is relatively complex for this purpose, another example will be used to introduce the nature of information evaluation. Then the concepts will be applied to the Mantle Company problem.

Suppose the Rosen Company must choose one of three alternatives in an environment that has only two states of nature, good economic conditions or poor economic conditions. The company is willing to make decisions using an expected dollar criterion. Following is the payoff table:

	Bad	*Good*
A_1	10,000	12,000
A_2	8,000	14,000
A_3	6,000	16,000
Probability	0.6	0.4

The expected values of each of the acts are:

EV(A_1) = 0.6(10,000) + 0.4(12,000) = 10,800 (optimal)
EV(A_2) = 0.6(8,000) + 0.4(14,000) = 10,400
EV(A_3) = 0.6(6,000) + 0.4(16,000) = 10,000

Now suppose it is possible to acquire some additional information about the likelihood of occurrence of the two states. Further, assume that the information source is perfectly reliable. That is, if the source predicts the state of nature is likely to be good economic conditions, then, in fact, it will be good. What is the value of this information?

To determine the value, it is necessary to find the maximum number of dollars the decision maker would be willing to pay to acquire the data. First, compute the expected value of the course of action that would be taken *after* the information is acquired. What will be done, for example, if it is known for sure that economic conditions will be bad? Obviously, alternative A_1 will be picked. It has the highest payoff for bad economic conditions. Likewise, if it is known that good conditions will occur, A_3 will be elected. A_3 has the highest payoff when the state of nature is good economic conditions. The following summarizes the expected value of the course of action to be taken, given perfect information:

Information Indicates That State of Nature Will Be	Optimal Action	Payoff	Probability That Information Will Predict Listed State of Nature	Expected Value
Bad	A_1	$10,000	0.6	$ 6,000
Good	A_3	16,000	0.4	6,400
				$12,400

Note the probabilities that have been used. The probabilities of *obtaining information* that economic conditions will be bad or good are equal to the decision maker's prior probabilities about the state of nature. The decision maker should view the chances of these two possible information events to be the same. That is, if a decision maker thinks bad conditions has a 60% chance of occurring, he or she should also feel there is a 60% chance of receiving information to that effect.

The expected value of the course of action that will be taken, given perfect information, is $12,400. Recall that the best course of action given no additional information is A_1 with an expected value of $10,800. (See above.) Thus, the expected return would be increased by $1,600 ($12,400 − $10,800) if the perfect information is acquired. The increase in this expectation is the **expected value of perfect information.**

Obviously, few sources of information are perfectly reliable. To determine the value of imperfect information, it is necessary to employ a similar but more involved process. With perfect information, it is known exactly which state of nature will occur once the information is received. That is, the probability of the state indicated by the information is revised to be equal to one and the probability of all other states are revised to zero. If the information source is imperfect, then the process of revising the state probabilities is more complex and uses Bayesian probability procedures.[1] The value of imperfect information will not exceed the value of perfect information.

With this basic idea about the value of information, let us return to the Mantle Company problem. Recall that two components were necessary to completely define the state of nature: the variable cost per unit and the demand. Therefore, it is possible to acquire additional information about either or both of these components. Let us suppose that management is only going to consider a cost investigation that will positively identify which variable cost rate is actually in effect. That is, the information is perfect information.

In the event the investigation reaches the conclusion that the cost rate is $2.00, then the probability table in Exhibit 25.2 would change. Since the information is perfect, the probability of a $2 cost should be revised to 1.00 and the probability of a $3 cost to 0. All of the entries in the *last five* columns of the probability table in Exhibit 25.2 would be zero because the probability of a $3 cost is zero. The remaining probabilities are just those for the demand, given a selling price and are revised in Exhibit 25.3. To choose the optimal act, *given a variable cost of $2,* just use the payoffs from Exhibit 25.2 and the appropriate revised probabilities from Exhibit 25.3 to compute the expected values:

$$EV(A_1) = 0.0(9,000) + 0.0(12,000) + 0.3(15,000) + 0.5(18,000)$$
$$+ 0.2(21,000) + 0.0(6,000) + 0.0(8,000) +$$
$$+ 0.0(10,000) + 0.0(12,000) + 0.0(14,000)$$
$$\underline{\$17,700} \text{ (optimal)}$$

$$EV(A_2) = 0.1(12,000) + 0.5(16,000) + 0.4(20,000)$$
$$+ 0.0(24,000) + 0.0(28,000) + 0.0(9,000)$$
$$+ 0.0(12,000) + 0.0(15,000) + 0.0(18,000)$$
$$+ 0.0(21,000)$$
$$\underline{\$17,200}$$

If the investigation indicates the variable cost is $2 per unit, then action A_1 (sales price = $5) should be selected to optimize the expected return at a value of $17,700.

Now, if the investigation indicates the unit cost is $3, then the probabilities in the first five columns of Exhibit 25.2 would be revised to be 0.0 and the last five columns to be equal to those in Exhibit 25.1. That is, the probability of a $3 cost is 1.0 and the probability of a $2 cost is zero. See the second schedule in Exhibit 25.3 for a complete revision. You should verify that:

$$EV(A_1) = \$11,800$$
$$EV(A_2) = \$12,900 \text{ (optimal)}$$

---

[1] For a discussion of this, you are referred to a basic statistics book such as John Neter, William Wasserman, and G.A. Whitmore, *Applied Statistics* (Boston: Allyn and Bacon, Inc., 1978), Chapters 22 and 23.

Exhibit 25.3   Revised Probabilities Given Perfect Information That Variable Cost Is $2.00

					State of Nature					
Act	(3K, 2)	(4K, 2)	(5K, 2)	(6K, 2)	(7K, 2)	(3K, 3)	(4K, 3)	(5K, 3)	(6K, 3)	(7K, 3)
$A_1 = \$5$	0.00	0.00	0.30	0.50	0.20	0.00	0.00	0.00	0.00	0.00
$A_2 = \$6$	0.10	0.50	0.40	0.00	0.00	0.00	0.00	0.00	0.00	0.00

Revised Probabilities Given Perfect Information That Variable Cost Is $3.00

					State of Nature					
Act	(3K, 2)	(4K, 2)	(5K, 2)	(6K, 2)	(7K, 2)	(3K, 3)	(4K, 3)	(5K, 3)	(6K, 3)	(7K, 3)
$A_1 = \$5$	0.00	0.00	0.00	0.00	0.00	0.00	0.00	0.30	0.50	0.20
$A_2 = \$6$	0.00	0.00	0.00	0.00	0.00	0.10	0.50	0.40	0.00	0.00

Thus, given a variable cost of $3 per unit, the best decision is to set the sales price at $6.

Before the cost investigation, the decision maker believed there was a 70% chance of a message to the effect that the unit cost was $2 and a 30% chance of a message of $3. Thus, the expected value of the best strategy, given the cost investigation, is:

$$EV = 0.7(\text{EV of optimal act given \$2 variable cost}) +$$
$$0.3(\text{EV of optimal act given \$3 variable cost})$$
$$EV = 0.7(17,700) + 0.3(12,900) = \$16,260$$

Without the cost investigation, the expected value was $15,930 (see computation on page 877). Therefore, the expected benefit of the investigation is $330 ($16,260 − $15,930). If the investigation can be done for less than $330, then it can be justified.

In addition to a cost investigation, it might also be possible to "purchase" information about the demand component of the state of nature. Of course, demand is a function of the selected sales price and such information might be more difficult to acquire. This aspect of the problem will be explored in a self-study problem, problem 25-5, and problem 25-6.

In closing this section it should be noted that measuring the value of information in a real situation will be challenging. Nevertheless, information is constantly being "purchased" in the day-to-day operation of organizations. It is essential that the worth of information be considered in making the decision about its acquisition. The accounting profession has reached the point where it is irresponsible to assume that all information is worth more than its cost. It has been the purpose of this section to establish a framework for considering this issue. There needs to be significant application research, however, before this area of management accounting will be of major significance to practitioners.

Summary

From this chapter you should have a better appreciation of the need to consider the relationship between benefits and costs before making decisions about acquiring data. Increased accuracy may not be justified when costs are considered.
    Key terms for this chapter include:

Payoff table
Conditional value
State of nature
Expected value
Information
Expected value of perfect information

SELF-STUDY PROBLEM. Reconsider the Mantle Company problem but now assume it is not feasible to determine the demand before the production size is selected. Further, assume the product is perishable so that it is not possible to store any production that exceeds demand. Also, it is not possible to acquire additional units if demand exceeds production; thus, the demand is lost. At the beginning of the period two decisions must be made: the sales price to set and the production quantity to schedule. Considering all of the combinations, there are six possible alternatives, three production quantities for each of the two sales prices.
    The probabilities are the same as in the chapter: 0.7 of a $2 variable cost, 0.3 of a $3 cost, and demand as in Exhibit 25.1.

Required:

1. Construct a payoff table, a table of state probabilities, and compute the expected payoff of each of the six actions. Compare the payoff of the optimal strategy with that of the original problem. Why is it different?
2. Now assume it is possible to perform a perfectly reliable cost study to determine which variable cost will be incurred. How much would it be worth? Compare your results with the value of the cost study in the original problem.

Solution to Self-Study Problem

Part 1. To answer part 1 it is necessary to determine the following three elements for the payoff table:

a. Identify the possible alternatives.
b. Identify the possible states of nature.
c. Compute the conditional values of each alternative given a state of nature.

The possible alternatives are:

A_1 = Set sales price equal to $5 and produce 5,000 units.
A_2 = Set sales price equal to $5 and produce 6,000 units.

A_3 = Set sales price equal to $5 and produce 7,000 units.
A_4 = Set sales price equal to $6 and produce 3,000 units.
A_5 = Set sales price equal to $6 and produce 4,000 units.
A_6 = Set sales price equal to $6 and produce 5,000 units.

The states of nature are same as in the chapter example. Exhibit 25.4 is the payoff table.

Selected conditional values will be derived. Consider alternative A_1, which has a sales price of $5, and, if selected, the sales volume will either be 5,000, 6,000, or 7,000 units. If the state of nature turns out to be a demand of 5,000 units and a variable cost of $2, (5K, 2), then the profit will be computed using the first equation in Exhibit 25.4:

$$(\$5)5,000 - (\$2)5,000 = 15,000$$

If the state is (6K, 2) then the sales are limited to 5,000 units (the production volume of alternative A_1). If it can be assumed that the only opportunity cost of the lost sale is the profit of the sales loss of the current period (no longer term losses), then the payoff is computed using the second equation in Exhibit 25.4:

$$(\$5)5,000 - (\$2)5,000 = 15,000$$

Now consider alternative 2, where 6,000 units are produced and sold at $5. If the state turns out to be (5K, 2) then 1,000 more units than needed have been produced. The payoff, via the first equation in Exhibit 25.4, is:

$$(\$5)5,000 - (\$2)6,000 = 13,000$$

Finally, consider A_3 and state (6K, 2). A_3 entails a production of 7,000 units but, in this case, only 6,000 units are demanded. The payoff is:

$$(\$5)6,000 - (\$2)7,000 = 16,000$$

You should verify the remaining entries of Exhibit 25.4.

Exhibit 25.5 contains the relevant probabilities. Since alternatives A_1, A_2, and A_3 all entail a $5 price, the probability of the states of nature would be the same and also the

**Exhibit 25.4   Self-Study Problem Payoff Table (000 omitted)
Entries Determined via Equations Listed Below***

					State of Nature = (demand, variable cost)					
Act	*(3K, 2)*	*(4K, 2)*	*(5K, 2)*	*(6K, 2)*	*(7K, 2)*	*(3K, 3)*	*(4K, 3)*	*(5K, 3)*	*(6K, 3)*	*(7K, 3)*
A_1	n/a	n/a	15	15	15	n/a	n/a	10	10	10
A_2	n/a	n/a	13	18	18	n/a	n/a	7	12	12
A_3	n/a	n/a	11	16	21	n/a	n/a	4	9	14
A_4	12	12	12	n/a	n/a	9	9	9	n/a	n/a
A_5	10	16	16	n/a	n/a	6	12	12	n/a	n/a
A_6	8	14	20	n/a	n/a	3	9	15	n/a	n/a

n/a = not applicable
*If Demand ≤ Production:
    (Sales price)(Demand) − (Variable cost)(Production)
If Demand > Production:
    (Sales price)(Production) − (Variable cost)(Production)

Exhibit 25.5   Self-Study Problem
State Probabilities Computed by Equation Below*

					State of Nature					
Act	*(3K, 2)*	*(4K, 2)*	*(5K, 2)*	*(6K, 2)*	*(7K, 2)*	*(3K, 3)*	*(4K, 3)*	*(5K, 3)*	*(6K, 3)*	*(7K, 3)*
A_1 or A_2 or A_3	0.00	0.00	0.21	0.35	0.14	0.00	0.00	0.09	0.15	0.06
A_4 or A_5 or A_6	0.07	0.35	0.28	0.00	0.00	0.03	0.15	0.12	0.00	0.00

*(Probability of variable cost) × (Probability of demand given the sale price)

same as alternative A_1 in Exhibit 25.2. Likewise, alternatives A_4, A_5, and A_6 have a $6 sales price and the state probabilities would be the same as alternative A_2 in Exhibit 25.2.

To compute the expected value (EV) of each alternative just add the sum of the weighted conditional values:

$EV(A_1) = 13,500$ $EV(A_4) = 11,100$
$EV(A_2) = 14,700$ (Optimal) $EV(A_5) = 14,200$
$EV(A_3) = 13,400$ $EV(A_6) = 14,300$

As can be seen, A_2 is the optimal act. The payoff will average $14,700 in comparison with the payoff of the original situation of $15,930. This payoff is lower because there is more risk; the demand is not known at the time the production must be set.

Part 2. Now consider quesiton 2. If it is possible to perform a cost study that will predict, with certainty, which variable costs will be incurred, then the probability table in Exhibit 25.5 changes to be the same as for the $5 and $6 price in the first schedule in Exhibit 25.3. Then, if the variable cost is $2, the expected values are determined using the payoffs in Exhibit 25.4 and the revised probabilities:

$EV(A_1) = 15,000(0.3) + 15,000(0.5) + 15,000(0.2) = 15,000$
$EV(A_2) = 13,000(0.3) + 18,000(0.5) + 18,000(0.2) = 16,500$ (Optimal)
$EV(A_3) = 11,000(0.3) + 16,000(0.5) + 21,000(0.2) = 15,500$
$EV(A_4) = 12,000(0.1) + 12,000(0.5) + 12,000(0.4) = 12,000$
$EV(A_5) = 10,000(0.1) + 16,000(0.5) + 16,000(0.4) = 15,400$
$EV(A_6) = 8,000(0.1) + 14,000(0.5) + 20,000(0.4) = 15,800$

Thus, if told the variable cost is $2, management should select A_2 as its strategy.

Similarly, if the variable cost is $3, the revised probabilities are those for the $5 and $6 price in the second schedule of Exhibit 25.3. The expected values are determined using the payoffs in Exhibit 25.4 and the revised probabilities:

$EV(A_1) = 10,000(0.3) + 10,000(0.5) + 10,000(0.2) = 10,000$
$EV(A_2) = 7,000(0.3) + 12,000(0.5) + 12,000(0.2) = 10,500$
$EV(A_3) = 4,000(0.3) + 9,000(0.5) + 13,000(0.2) = 8,500$
$EV(A_4) = 9,000(0.1) + 9,000(0.5) + 9,000(0.4) = 9,000$
$EV(A_5) = 6,000(0.1) + 12,000(0.5) + 12,000(0.4) = 11,400$ (Optimal)
$EV(A_6) = 3,000(0.1) + 9,000(0.5) + 15,000(0.4) = 10,800$

In this case, A_5 should be chosen. Since the probability of the two respective variable costs are 0.7 and 0.3, respectively, the expected value with perfect information about variable cost is:

EV = 0.7(EV of optimal act given variable cost = $2)
      + 0.3(EV of optimal act given variable cost = $3)
   = (0.7)16,500 + (0.3)11,400 = 14,970

In comparison with the EV of the optimal act without this information (see page 883), the above EV is $270 higher ($14,970 − $14,700) and, therefore, is the worth of this information.

References

Demski, J., and Feltham, G. *Cost Determination: A Conceptual Approach.* Ames, IA: Iowa State University Press, 1976.

Problems

25-1. CMA Problem with a Payoff Table. The Jon Co. has just agreed to supply Arom Chemical Inc. with a substance critical to one of Arom's manufacturing processes. Due to the critical nature of the substance, Jon Co. has agreed to pay Arom $1,000 for any shipment that is not received by Arom on the day it is required.

Arom establishes a production schedule that enables it to notify Jon Co. of the necessary quantity fifteen days in advance of the required date. Jon can produce the substance in five days. However, capacity is not always readily available, which means that Jon may not be able to produce the substance for several days. Therefore, there may be occasions when there are only one or two days available to deliver the substance. When the substance is completed by Jon Co.'s manufacturing department and released to its shipping department, the number of days remaining before Arom Chemical Inc. needs the substance will be known.

Jon Co. has undertaken a review of delivery reliability and costs of alternative shipping methods. The results are presented in the following table.

Shipping Method	Cost per Shipment	Probability that the shipment will take ___ days					
		1	2	3	4	5	6
Motor freight	$100	—	—	0.10	0.20	0.40	0.30
Air freight	$200	—	0.30	0.60	0.10	—	—
Air express	$400	0.80	0.20	—	—	—	—

Required:

Prepare a decision table that can be used by Jon Co.'s shipping clerk to decide which delivery alternative to select. Use the expected monetary value decision criteria as the basis for constructing the table.

25-2. CMA Problem: Basic Analysis with Uncertainty. Vendo, Inc. has been operating the concession stands at the university football stadium. The university has had successful football teams for many years; as a result the stadium is always full. The university is located in an area that suffers no rain during the football season. From time to time, Vendo has found itself very short of hot dogs and at other times it has had many left over. A review of the records of sales of the past five seasons revealed the following frequency of hot dogs sold.

10,000 hot dogs	5 times	30,000 hot dogs	20 times
20,000 hot dogs	10 times	40,000 hot dogs	15 times

Hot dogs sell for $0.50 each and cost Vendo $0.30 each. Unsold hot dogs are given to a local orphanage without charge.

Required:

1. Assuming that only the four quantities listed were ever sold and that the occurrences were random events, prepare a payoff table (ignore income taxes) to represent the four possible strategies of ordering 10,000, 20,000, 30,000, or 40,000 hot dogs.
2. Using the expected value decision rule, determine the best strategy.
3. What is the dollar value of perfect information in this problem?

25-3. Adapted CMA Problem with Uncertainty (Basic). The Jessica Co. has been searching for more formal ways to analyze its alternative courses of action. The expected value decision model was among those considered. In order to test the effectiveness of the expected value model a one-year trial in a small department was authorized.

This department buys and resells a perishable product. A large purchase at the beginning of each month provides a lower cost than more frequent purchases and also assures that Jessica Co. can buy all of the items it wants. Unfortunately, if too much is purchased the product unsold at the end of the month is worthless and must be discarded.

If an inadequate quantity is purchased, additional quantities probably cannot be purchased. If any should be available, they would probably be of poor quality and be overpriced. Jessica chooses to lose the potential sales rather than furnish a poor quality product. The standard purchase arrangement is $50,000 plus $0.50 for each unit purchased for orders of 100,000 units or more. Jessica is paid $1.25 per unit by its customers.

The needs of Jessica's customers limit the possible sales volumes to only four quantities per month—100,000, 120,000, 140,000, or 180,000 units. However, the total quantity needed for a given month cannot be determined before the date Jessica must make its purchases. The sales managers are willing to place a probability estimate on each of the four possible sales volumes each month. They noted that the probabilities for the four sales volumes change from month to month because of the seasonal nature of the customers' business. Their probability estimates for December 19x8 sales units are 10% for 100,000, 30% for 120,000, 40% for 140,000, and 20% for 180,000.

The following schedule shows the quantity purchased each month based upon the expected value decision model. The actual units sold and product discarded or sales lost are shown also.

	Quantity (in units)			Sales Units
	Purchased	Sold	Discarded	Lost
January	100,000	100,000	——	20,000
February	120,000	100,000	20,000	——
March	180,000	140,000	40,000	——
April	100,000	100,000	——	80,000
May	100,000	100,000	——	——
June	140,000	140,000	——	——
July	140,000	100,000	40,000	——
August	140,000	120,000	20,000	——
September	120,000	100,000	20,000	——
October	120,000	120,000	——	20,000
November	180,000	140,000	40,000	——

Required:

1. What quantity should be ordered for December 19x8 if the expected value decision model is used?
2. Suppose Jessica could ascertain its customers' needs before placing its purchase order rather than relying on the expected value decision model. How much would it pay to obtain this information for December?

25-4. CMA Problem with Uncertainty.

Part a. The Wing Manufacturing Corporation produces a chemical compound, product X, which deteriorates and must be discarded if it is not sold by the end of the month during which it is produced. The total variable cost of the manufactured compound, product X, is $50 per unit and its selling price is $80 per unit. Wing can purchase the same compound from a competing company at $80 per unit plus $10 freight per unit. Management has estimated that failure to fill orders would result in the loss of 80% of customers placing orders for the compound. Wing has manufactured and sold product X for the past twenty months. Demand for product X has been irregular and at present there is no consistent sales trend. During this period monthly sales have been as follows:

Units Sold per Month	Number of Months
8,000	5
9,000	12
10,000	3

Required:

1. Compute the probability of sales of product X of 8,000, 9,000, or 10,000 units in any month.
2. Compute what the contribution margin would be if 9,000 units of product X were ordered and either 8,000, 9,000, or 10,000 units were manufactured in that same month (with additional units, if necessary, being purchased).
3. Compute the average monthly contribution margin that Wing can expect if 9,000 units of product X are manufactured every month and all sales orders are filled.

Part b. In the production of product X, Wing uses a primary ingredient, K-1. This ingredient is purchased from an outside supplier at a cost of $24 per unit of compound. It is estimated that there is a 70% chance that the supplier of K-1 may be shut down by a strike for an indefinite period. A substitute ingredient, K-2, is available at $36 per unit of compound but Wing must contact this alternative source immediately to secure sufficient quantities. A firm purchase contract for either material must now be made for production of the primary ingredient next month. If an order were placed for K-1 and a strike occurred, Wing would be released from the contract and management would purchase the chemical compound from its competitor. Assume that 9,000 units are to be manufactured and all sales orders are to be filled.

Required:

1. Compute the monthly contribution margin from sales of 8,000, 9,000, and 10,000 units if the substitute ingredient K-2 is ordered.

2. Prepare a schedule computing the average monthly contribution margin that Wing should expect if the primary ingredient K-1 is ordered with the existing probability of a strike at the supplier. Assume that the expected average monthly contribution margin from manufacturing will be $130,000 using the primary ingredient, and the expected average monthly loss from purchasing product X from the competitor (in case of a strike) will be $45,000.

25-5. Value of Information. Reconsider the Mantle Company problem introduced in the chapter. Now, assume that it is possible to purchase information about *all* aspects of the state of nature before a decision about the price has to be made. The information would include a cost prediction, a demand prediction given a $5 price, and a demand prediction given a $6 price. Continue the assumption about the independence among these three components of a state and the estimates of the prior probabilities. (Remember it was felt there was a 70% chance the variable cost would be $2 and a 30% chance of a $3 cost. The demand probabilities are in Exhibit 25.1.)

Required:

1. Determine the value of the information referred to, assuming it is a perfect predictor of all aspects of the state of nature. Recognize that there are eighteen possible states (2 × 3 × 3: two outcomes for variable cost, three outcomes given a price of $5, and three outcomes given a price of $6).
2. Compare the value found in part 1 with the value of the information described in the text; that is, the cost study done by itself.

25-6. Extension of Self-Study Problem. Reconsider the self-study problem. Assume it is possible to purchase perfectly reliable information about all aspects of the state of nature before making any decisions. This would include a cost prediction, a demand prediction given a $5 price, and demand prediction given a $6 price. What is the value of this information?

25-7. Selecting a Selling Price and Production Level under Uncertainty. A firm is trying to determine the best selling price to set for one of its products. The decision is complicated in that the yearly *demand* function is not known with certainty. The firm is confident, however, that the unit demand is a function of the sales price and is either D_1 or D_2 where:

$$D_1 = 200,000 - 25,000s \qquad \text{and} \qquad D_2 = 240,000 - 20,000s$$
$$s = \text{selling price}$$

The firm believes that the demand function is somewhat more likely to be D_1 than D_2 and has established the prior probabilities as:

$$p(D_1) = 0.55 \qquad \text{and} \qquad p(D_2) = 0.45$$

In addition to selecting a sales price, the firm has to determine the production quantity. Because of a substantial production lead time this quantity must be selected before it is known what the demand level will be. If production turns out to exceed demand the excess quantity will be carried forward in inventory at a cost of $1 per unit. If demand exceeds production then the firm feels the long-run optimal strategy is still to supply the demand. To do this they will buy the item from a competitor at $3 per unit and ship it to their own customers.

The production cost of the product is $1.50 per unit plus fixed costs of $50,000 per period. The following six sales-price-production-quantity combinations are under consideration:

1. $4.75, 81,250 units
2. $4.75, 145,000 units
3. $5.50, 62,500 units
4. $5.50, 130,000 units
5. $7.25, 18,750 units
6. $7.25, 95,000 units

For a given sales price the two production quantities are equal to the demands that will result if the first or second function turns out to be the actual demand function.

Required:

1. From the six alternatives listed above determine the optimal. (Variable costing will be used to report income.)
2. The price of $4.75 is the one that would optimize profits given that the demand function is D_1. Verify this using optimization techniques from calculus.
3. Suppose some market research can be done before making the price and production decision in order to determine what the demand function is. What is the maximum cost the firm could pay for this market research assuming it would reveal, with certainty, which demand function is valid?

25-8. CMA Problem: Inventory Modeling and Uncertainty. The Starr Company manufactures several products. One of its main products requires an electric motor. The management of Starr Company uses the economic order quantity formula (EOQ) to determine the optimum number of motors to order. Management now wants to determine how much safety stock to order.

Starr Company uses 30,000 electric motors annually (300 working days). Using the EOQ formula, the company orders 3,000 motors at a time. The lead time for an order is five days. The annual cost of carrying one motor in safety stock is $10. Management has also estimated that the cost of being out of stock is $20 for each motor they are short.

Starr Company has analyzed the usage during past reorder periods by examining the inventory records. The records indicate the following usage patterns during the past reorder periods:

Usage During Lead Time	Number of Times Quantity Was Used
440	6
460	12
480	16
500	130
520	20
540	10
560	6
	200

Required:

1. Using an expected value approach, determine the level of safety stock for electric motors that Starr Company should maintain in order to minimize costs.
2. What would be Starr Company's new reorder point?

Appendix

Table A.1   Student's t Distribution

df	$t_{0.05}$	$t_{0.025}$	$t_{0.005}$	df	$t_{0.05}$	$t_{0.025}$	$t_{0.005}$
1	6.31	12.71	63.66	16	1.75	2.12	2.92
2	2.92	4.30	9.92	17	1.74	2.11	2.90
3	2.35	3.18	5.84	18	1.73	2.10	2.88
4	2.13	2.78	4.60	19	1.73	2.09	2.86
5	2.02	2.57	4.03	20	1.72	2.09	2.84
6	1.94	2.45	3.71	21	1.72	2.08	2.83
7	1.90	2.36	3.50	22	1.72	2.07	2.82
8	1.86	2.31	3.36	23	1.71	2.07	2.81
9	1.83	2.26	3.25	24	1.71	2.06	2.80
10	1.81	2.23	3.17	25	1.71	2.06	2.79
11	1.80	2.20	3.11	26	1.71	2.06	2.78
12	1.78	2.18	3.06	27	1.70	2.05	2.77
13	1.77	2.16	3.01	28	1.70	2.05	2.76
14	1.76	2.14	2.98	29	1.70	2.05	2.76
15	1.75	2.13	2.95	30	1.70	2.04	2.75
				∞	1.65	1.96	2.58

Abridged from Table III, Fisher and Yates, *Statistical Tables for Biological, Agricultural and Medical Research* (6th edition, Longman 1974). Edinburgh: Oliver and Boyd, Ltd. Reprinted with permission of the publisher.

Table A.2   Present Value of $1.00 Received at End of Period n

$p_{i,n} = 1/(1 + i)^n$

n	5.000	8.000	10.000	12.000	14.000	15.000	16.000	18.000	20.000	21.000	22.000	25.000	30.000
1	0.9524	0.9259	0.9091	0.8929	0.8772	0.8696	0.8621	0.8475	0.8333	0.8264	0.8197	0.8000	0.7692
2	0.9070	0.8573	0.8264	0.7972	0.7695	0.7561	0.7432	0.7182	0.6944	0.6830	0.6719	0.6400	0.5917
3	0.8638	0.7938	0.7513	0.7118	0.6750	0.6575	0.6407	0.6086	0.5787	0.5645	0.5507	0.5120	0.4552
4	0.8227	0.7350	0.6830	0.6355	0.5921	0.5718	0.5523	0.5158	0.4823	0.4665	0.4514	0.4096	0.3501
5	0.7835	0.6806	0.6209	0.5674	0.5194	0.4972	0.4761	0.4371	0.4019	0.3855	0.3700	0.3277	0.2693
6	0.7462	0.6302	0.5645	0.5066	0.4556	0.4323	0.4104	0.3704	0.3349	0.3186	0.3033	0.2621	0.2072
7	0.7107	0.5835	0.5132	0.4523	0.3996	0.3759	0.3538	0.3139	0.2791	0.2633	0.2486	0.2097	0.1594
8	0.6768	0.5403	0.4665	0.4039	0.3506	0.3269	0.3050	0.2660	0.2326	0.2176	0.2038	0.1678	0.1226
9	0.6446	0.5002	0.4241	0.3606	0.3075	0.2843	0.2630	0.2255	0.1938	0.1799	0.1670	0.1342	0.0943
10	0.6139	0.4632	0.3855	0.3220	0.2697	0.2472	0.2267	0.1911	0.1615	0.1486	0.1369	0.1074	0.0725
11	0.5847	0.4289	0.3505	0.2875	0.2366	0.2149	0.1954	0.1619	0.1346	0.1228	0.1122	0.0859	0.0558
12	0.5568	0.3971	0.3186	0.2567	0.2076	0.1869	0.1685	0.1372	0.1122	0.1015	0.0920	0.0687	0.0429
13	0.5303	0.3677	0.2897	0.2292	0.1821	0.1625	0.1452	0.1163	0.0935	0.0839	0.0754	0.0550	0.0330
14	0.5051	0.3405	0.2633	0.2046	0.1597	0.1413	0.1252	0.0985	0.0779	0.0693	0.0618	0.0440	0.0254
15	0.4810	0.3152	0.2394	0.1827	0.1401	0.1229	0.1079	0.0835	0.0649	0.0573	0.0507	0.0352	0.0195
16	0.4581	0.2919	0.2176	0.1631	0.1229	0.1069	0.0930	0.0708	0.0541	0.0474	0.0415	0.0281	0.0150
17	0.4363	0.2703	0.1978	0.1456	0.1078	0.0929	0.0802	0.0600	0.0451	0.0391	0.0340	0.0225	0.0116
18	0.4155	0.2502	0.1799	0.1300	0.0946	0.0808	0.0691	0.0508	0.0376	0.0323	0.0279	0.0180	0.0089
19	0.3957	0.2317	0.1635	0.1161	0.0829	0.0703	0.0596	0.0431	0.0313	0.0267	0.0229	0.0144	0.0068
20	0.3769	0.2145	0.1486	0.1037	0.0728	0.0611	0.0514	0.0365	0.0261	0.0221	0.0187	0.0115	0.0053

Table A.3   Present Value of a \$1.00 Annuity Received at End of Each of n Periods

$$a_{i,n} = \frac{1}{i}\left[1 - \frac{1}{(1+i)^n}\right]$$ *PV of a = $a_{i,n}$ see pg 530*

n	5.0000	8.0000	10.0000	12.0000	14.0000	15.0000	16.0000	18.0000	20.0000	21.0000	22.0000	25.0000	30.0000
1	0.9524	0.9259	0.9091	0.8929	0.8772	0.8696	0.8621	0.8475	0.8333	0.8264	0.8197	0.8000	0.7692
2	1.8594	1.7833	1.7355	1.6901	1.6467	1.6257	1.6052	1.5656	1.5278	1.5095	1.4915	1.4400	1.3609
3	2.7232	2.5771	2.4869	2.4018	2.3216	2.2832	2.2459	2.1743	2.1065	2.0739	2.0422	1.9520	1.8161
4	3.5459	3.3121	3.1699	3.0373	2.9137	2.8550	2.7982	2.6901	2.5887	2.5404	2.4936	2.3616	2.1662
5	4.3295	3.9927	3.7908	3.6048	3.4331	3.3522	3.2743	3.1272	2.9906	2.9260	2.8636	2.6893	2.4356
6	5.0757	4.6229	4.3553	4.1114	3.8887	3.7845	3.6847	3.4976	3.3255	3.2446	3.1669	2.9514	2.6427
7	5.7864	5.2064	4.8684	4.5638	4.2883	4.1604	4.0386	3.8115	3.6046	3.5079	3.4155	3.1611	2.8021
8	6.4632	5.7466	5.3349	4.9676	4.6389	4.4873	4.3436	4.0776	3.8372	3.7256	3.6193	3.3289	2.9247
9	7.1078	6.2469	5.7590	5.3283	4.9464	4.7716	4.6065	4.3030	4.0310	3.9054	3.7863	3.4631	3.0190
10	7.7217	6.7101	6.1446	5.6502	5.2161	5.0188	4.8332	4.4941	4.1925	4.0541	3.9232	3.5705	3.0915
11	8.3064	7.1390	6.4951	5.9377	5.4527	5.2337	5.0286	4.6560	4.3271	4.1769	4.0354	3.6564	3.1473
12	8.8632	7.5361	6.8137	6.1944	5.6603	5.4206	5.1971	4.7932	4.4392	4.2785	4.1274	3.7251	3.1903
13	9.3936	7.9038	7.1034	6.4235	5.8424	5.5831	5.3423	4.9095	4.5327	4.3624	4.2028	3.7801	3.2233
14	9.8986	8.2442	7.3667	6.6282	6.0021	5.7245	5.4675	5.0081	4.6106	4.4317	4.2646	3.8241	3.2487
15	10.3796	8.5595	7.6061	6.8109	6.1422	5.8474	5.5755	5.0916	4.6755	4.4890	4.3152	3.8593	3.2682
16	10.8378	8.8514	7.8237	6.9740	6.2651	5.9542	5.6685	5.1624	4.7296	4.5364	4.3567	3.8874	3.2832
17	11.2741	9.1216	8.0216	7.1196	6.3729	6.0472	5.7487	5.2223	4.7746	4.5755	4.3908	3.9099	3.2948
18	11.6896	9.3719	8.2014	7.2497	6.4674	6.1280	5.8178	5.2732	4.8122	4.6079	4.4187	3.9279	3.3037
19	12.0853	9.6036	8.3649	7.3658	6.5504	6.1982	5.8775	5.3162	4.8435	4.6346	4.4415	3.9424	3.3105
20	12.4622	9.8181	8.5136	7.4694	6.6231	6.2593	5.9288	5.3527	4.8696	4.6567	4.4603	3.9539	3.3158

Table A.4   Accelerated Recovery Tables for Three-Year and Five-Year Property

Recovery Year	Three-year	Five-year
1	25%	15%
2	38	22
3	37	21
4		21
5		21

Eighteen-Year Property (use column for the month of acquisition)

Recovery Year	1	2	3	4	5	6	7	8	9	10	11	12
1	9	9	8	7	6	5	4	4	3	2	1	0.4
2	9	9	9	9	9	9	9	9	9	10	10	10.0
3	8	8	8	8	8	8	8	8	9	9	9	9.0
4	7	7	7	7	7	8	8	8	8	8	8	8.0
5	7	7	7	7	7	7	7	7	7	7	7	7.0
6	6	6	6	6	6	6	6	6	6	6	6	6.0
7	5	5	5	5	6	6	6	6	6	6	6	6.0
8	5	5	5	5	5	5	5	5	5	5	5	5.0
9	5	5	5	5	5	5	5	5	5	5	5	5.0
10	5	5	5	5	5	5	5	5	5	5	5	5.0
11	5	5	5	5	5	5	5	5	5	5	5	5.0
12	5	5	5	5	5	5	5	5	5	5	5	5.0
13	4	4	4	5	4	4	5	4	4	4	5	5.0
14	4	4	4	4	4	4	4	4	4	4	4	4.0
15	4	4	4	4	4	4	4	4	4	4	4	4.0
16	4	4	4	4	4	4	4	4	4	4	4	4.0
17	4	4	4	4	4	4	4	4	4	4	4	4.0
18	4	3	4	4	4	4	4	4	4	4	4	4.0
19		1	1	1	2	2	2	3	3	3	3	3.6

Glossary

Abnormal spoilage Spoilage that would have been avoidable with better performance.

Absorption costing An accounting method that includes fixed production costs as a cost of the product (rather than of the period).

Accelerated Cost Recovery System A system introduced in the Economic Recovery Tax Act of 1981 that permits the accelerated recovery of an investment over a life that is usually shorter than the useful life.

Accounting rate of return The average income per year resulting from a project divided by the investment needed to adopt the project (or by the average investment).

Accretion An increase in the volume of the product during the production process.

Actual costing A system that prorates all of the manufacturing costs incurred during a period according to the production of the period.

Adjusted r^2 A statistic similar to r^2 computed with consideration given to the degrees of freedom in the sample. Useful in comparing regression models when additional explanatory variables are added.

Allocation The process of prorating indirect costs among the several benefited cost objectives.

Annuity Cash flows that occur at regular intervals and in an equal amount at each occurrence.

Applied overhead The amount of overhead actually charged (assigned) to the current period's production.

Asset turnover ratio Sales divided by investment; the number of times the investment was turned over during the period.

Asymptotic learning curve model A learning curve model that assumes that resource consumption per unit is decreasing at a decreasing rate.

Attributable costs Costs that would be eliminated if the service, or product, were eliminated and if enough time were allowed to make the necessary adjustments.

Authoritarian budget style The input and assumptions of the budget process are originated by top-level management and then communicated to subordinates.

Autocorrelation A condition whereby an observation taken at time t is related to previous observations; that is, an observation is not independent of previous observations.

Average-consumption-based learning curve Assumes that after each doubling of experience, the cumulative average resource consumption is equal to a constant percentage of the previous average resource consumption.

Avoidable costs   See attributable costs.

Basic standards   Standards that are not frequently revised.

Break-even   The volume that must be achieved so there is zero profit.

Budget   A financial statement of the projected results of a plan of action.

Budget assumptions   The assumed conditions under which a budget is constructed. Includes predictions of sales, collection patterns, expansion plans, inventory needs, and so forth.

Budget slack   Allocated resources that are not really needed by the unit of the organization.

By-products   Products that are produced jointly with other products but that are of relatively minor value.

Capital budgeting   Tools, or indexes, that can be used in deciding whether to commit capital to long-run projects.

Cash budget   Schedule of cash flows projected to result from the various plans of management.

Centralized organization   An organization in which all major decisions are channeled through the top echelon of management.

Chain joint processes   Situations in which there are multiple split-off points. One of the products of a joint process becomes an input into another joint process which, in turn, has multiple products as an output.

Clock card   A document used to record the total elapsed time that an employee spent on the job.

Coefficient of determination (r^2)   The percentage of the sample variance of the dependent variable explained by having knowledge of the independent variable.

Committed costs   Fixed costs that cannot be avoided in the short run.

Compound interest depreciation method   A method whereby the depreciation is equal to the principal recovered during the current period; that is, the excess of the cash flow over the interest on the unrecovered investment using the internal rate of return as the interest rate.

Conditional value   The return (or payoff) of an act, given that certain conditions have occurred.

Confidence interval   A range of values so there is a given probability that the actual outcome of the action will be included.

Contribution margin   The difference between the selling price and the total variable costs (manufacturing, selling, and administrative).

Contribution margin reporting format   A form of income statement that deducts variable costs from revenues to obtain the total contribution margin and then deducts fixed costs to derive income.

Contribution margin variance (in profit variance analysis)   Variance due to changes in sales prices and/or variable costs.

Control   The system used by a superior to deliberately influence a subordinate to act according to the superior's objectives. The process of ensuring that objectives are achieved.

Controllable costs   Costs for which a manager can exert a significant amount of influence.

Control limit   A statistical range within which a cost can reasonably be expected to fall if the process is in control. An observation outside this range is probably an indicator that the process is out of control.

Controller   The officer of an organization responsible for designing, installing, and operating the accounting system.

Conversion costs   Direct labor plus manufacturing overhead: the costs needed to convert material to finished production.

Correlation   The existence of a strong linear relationship between two variables.

Cost   The sum of the necessary outlays made in order to acquire an asset and to make it ready for its intended use. The value of the assets given in exchange at the time of an asset's acquisition.

Cost Accounting Standards Board   A board created by the U.S. Congress to establish accounting rules to be used in costing certain government contracts.

Cost attachment   The process of assigning costs to a product so that they may be held in inventory until a sale is completed. Permits the matching of efforts and accomplishments.

Cost center   Responsibility center wherein the manager only has the authority to make decisions that affect costs.

Cost objective   Some entity for which it is desired to collect cost data.

Cost-volume-profit analysis   A tool that incorporates the relationships between volume, costs, and revenues in order to project the impact of various courses of action.

Currently attainable standards   Standards that can be achieved with an acceptable level of performance, allowing for normal and unavoidable material wastage and for work breaks and machine repairs.

Current expected activity   The level at which a firm can reasonably expect to operate during the next period.

Data base management   A data storage concept whereby information is maintained in a disaggregative form in order to permit a varied and widespread use of the common file.

Decentralized organization   An organization in which the decision-making responsibility is distributed among several managers.

Decision making   The process of determining whether to commit resources to a given purpose.

Degrees of freedom   The number of observations in the sample reduced by the number of parameters that must be determined for the regression equation.

Department overhead rate   Each of several production departments uses an overhead application rate developed to give consideration to the department's operating characteristics.

Dependent variable   A variable whose value is a function of some other variable(s).

Differential costs   See incremental costs.

Direct allocation method   A method of allocating costs of reciprocal services whereby the services rendered to other service departments are ignored and the assignment is made directly to the production departments.

Direct costs   Costs that can be conveniently traced to a given cost objective.

Direct costing   See variable costing.

Direct labor   Wages paid to those employees for time that they are physically engaged in the actual production process as opposed to support activities such as supervision, cleanup, and production accounting.

Direct material   Material that becomes a physical part of the finished products and can be conveniently traced to them.

Discounted payback   The period of time needed to recover the original investment in a project plus the interest on the unrecovered investment.

Discretionary costs   See programmed costs.

Divisor activity   The volume of activity (practical capacity, normal activity, or expected activity) used as the denominator in determining the fixed overhead rate.

Dual distribution base   A system that allocates the fixed costs of a service department on the basis of the user departments' outputs when they are operating at full capacity and the variable cost on the basis of actual consumption of the output.

Effectiveness   A measure of the extent to which a goal is accomplished.

Efficiency   A measure of the relationship between the resources used (the input) and the accomplishment achieved (the output).

Equivalent unit   The fractional part of a whole unit that would result from the total effort expended on the partially finished unit.

Expected idle capacity   Unutilized capacity that would result even if the sales budget were achieved.

Expected value   The average value that would result from repeated observations of the distribution of some random variable. Also, the sum of the weighted conditional values where the weight is the probability of occurrence of the event giving the conditional value.

Expected value of perfect information   The difference between the expected value with perfect information about the occurrence of the states of nature and the expected value that would result in the absence of such information.

Expense   The expired cost resulting from a productive usage of an asset.

Exploratory variable   See independent variable.

Exit value   The amount of cash that would be generated by selling an asset now.

Ex-post variance analysis   A variance system that is designed with the purpose of motivating managers to have as their goal the optimal use of resources rather than mere adherence to the predetermined budget.

Feedback information   Information about a subordinate's performance that is communicated both to the superior and to the subordinate.

Financial Accounting Standards Board   A private, independent board created by the American Institute of Certified Public Accountants and given the responsibility of determining the standards to be used by firms when reporting to the public.

Financial Executives Institute   A professional organization of corporate vice-presidents of finance and controllers.

Finished goods   The (cost of) units that have been finished but not sold.

Fixed costs Costs that do not change in direct proportion to some given measure of activity.

Fixed overhead spending variance The difference between the budgeted and actual fixed overhead.

Flexible budget A budget that estimates costs according to their behavior: fixed approximately the same for all activity levels and variable according to the activity level.

Forecast variance (in ex-post variance system) The difference between the ex-post optimal income and the budgeted income. The portion of the income variance that could not have been achieved with better performance, given the circumstances that actually resulted during implementation.

Full absorption cost A system that assigns a share of the fixed manufacturing overhead to the units produced.

General factory overhead Costs that benefit all departments within the production area.

Goals Desired achievements; normally accompanied with a plan of action for their fulfillment.

Heteroscedasticity A condition of regression analysis whereby the variance of the error term is *not* constant for all values of the independent variable.

High-low method A method of estimating costs using an equation that is obtained by constructing a straight line passing through two points representing a relatively low and a relatively high volume of activity.

Historical communication approach A systems design approach with a goal of producing a single set of summary data which can be used reasonably well by all interested parties.

Historical cost The actual outlay made at the time that an asset is acquired.

Homoscedasticity A condition of regression analysis whereby the variance of the error term is constant for all values of the independent variable.

Hypothetical market value method Refers to the net realizable value method of allocating joint costs, especially when the market value of the products at the split-off point must be deduced (that is, they do not exist).

Incremental costs Additional costs that will be incurred as a result of making the decision to accept some course of action.

Independent variable A causal variable; partly responsible for the value taken on by some other variable(s).

Indirect costs Costs that cannot be traced to a single cost objective.

Indirect cost pool A group of costs identified with two or more cost objectives but not identified specifically with any final cost objective.

Information Data that change the decision maker's perception of some component of the decision process.

Information evaluation approach A system design approach that is based on the principle that the benefit of generated information should exceed the cost of providing it.

Information inductance The complex process through which the behavior of an information sender is influenced by the information he or she is required to communicate.

Institute of Internal Auditing A professional organization open to those interested in internal auditing.

Internal auditing director   The officer of a firm who has the responsibility of developing and maintaining the internal control system to aid in protecting the firm's assets.

Internal control   The set of procedures that provides reasonable assurance that the company's assets are used as intended and that collected data are reliable.

Internal rate of return   The maximum "dividend" rate that can be self-paid so that the future cash flows of a project will be just sufficient to cover the original investment and the self-paid dividends on the unrecovered portion of the investment. (Alternatively, the discount rate which, if used in the net present value method, will result in a net present value of zero.)

Internal Revenue Service   The branch of government given the responsibility for tax collection.

Inventory models   A set of techniques helpful in deciding how to optimally set the order size or production run in order to minimize the inventory-related costs of ordering, storage, and stockout.

Investment center   A responsibility center wherein the manager has decision-making authority and control over costs, revenues, and the investment base.

Job card   An accounting document used to accumulate the cost of completing a specific job.

Job order system   A system that accumulates cost by lots (or jobs).

Joint costs   Costs incurred in a single manufacturing process for the joint benefit of two or more products.

Joint price-quantity variance   The difference between the standard cost and actual cost of material multiplied by the difference between the actual quantity used and the standard allowed.

Joint products   Products that must be produced in part with other products. They may be converted to main products or by-products.

Labor efficiency variance   The difference between the standard labor hours allowed and the actual hours multiplied by the standard labor rate.

Labor rate variance   The difference between the standard labor rate and the actual labor rate multiplied by the actual labor hours.

Learning curve   A curve that represents the consumption of resources as a function of experience when the amount of resources needed declines with experience.

Least squares analysis   A term referring to regression analysis when there is only one explanatory variable.

Linear programming   A mathematical method of selecting the optimal uses of limited resources. Contains a linear objective function and one or more linear constraints.

Loss   The expired cost resulting from a decline in the service potential of an asset that generated no benefit.

Management control   The process by which managers assure that resources are obtained and used effectively and efficiently in the accomplishment of the organization's objectives.

Manufacturing costs   Those costs directly identified with the production function.

Manufacturing overhead All production costs except direct material and direct labor; costs that cannot be conveniently traced to the product.

Margin of safety The difference between some planned-for (budgeted) volume and the break-even point. The amount by which actual sales can fall below projected sales and still avoid incurring a loss.

Marginal-consumption-based learning curve A model that assumes that after each doubling of experience the marginal (incremental) resource consumption will equal a constant percentage of the previous marginal resource consumption.

Marginal costs See incremental costs.

Marketing variance The unutilized capacity resulting from the failure to obtain orders equal to the budgeted level of sales.

Master budget A set of departmental and functional budgets that projects the financial impact of management's plan(s).

Material inventory As asset representing raw materials on hand and available for use in producing the firm's product.

Material price variance The difference between the standard cost and the actual cost of material multiplied by the actual quantity purchased (or used).

Material quantity variance The difference between the standard material allowed for the output and the actual material used multiplied by the standard cost of material.

Materials budget A schedule of raw material purchase requirements that is necessary to meet the various objectives.

Materials requisition A document that transfers responsibility for issued materials from the storeroom clerk to some production entity.

Materials requisition summary An accounting document used to collect the sum of the materials issued during a given accounting period.

Mixed costs Costs that have both fixed and variable behavior charcteristics.

Mix variance (in profit variance analysis) The variance caused by the actual mix of the products being different from the planned mix.

Modified FIFO equivalent unit method Allocates the current production costs over the current work effort; the cost assigned to the beginning inventory last period remains attached to that layer.

Monte Carlo simulation See simulation.

Multicollinearity The existence of a significant correlation between one explanatory variable and another.

Multiple regression A regression using two or more explanatory variables.

National Association of Accountants A professional organization open to all managerial accountants and others with an interest in management accounting.

Negotiated transfer price A transfer price determined as a result of the bargaining between managers of the divisions affected by the inter-company transfer of products or services.

New present value The difference between the present value of all the cash inflows attributable to a project and the present value of all the cash outflows.

Net realizable value less normal profit method   Method whereby joint costs are assigned so that the total profit earned from all production is prorated according to each dollar of cost incurred regardless of where it is incurred.

Net realizable value method of allocating joint costs   A weighted average method of allocating joint costs whereby the weights are equal to the market value of the products at the split-off point.

Noncontrollable costs   Costs for which a manager cannot exert a significant amount of influence.

Noncontrollable variance   The difference between the applied fixed overhead and the budgeted fixed overhead.

Nonlinear cost-volume-profit analysis   CVP when the cost and/or revenue functions are not linear functions of volume.

Normal activity   The level at which the firm must typically operate in order to support the actual demand for the products.

Normal costing   A cost accounting system that assigns fixed overhead at a predetermined rate while accounting for other costs at the actual rate.

Normal spoilage   Expected and unavoidable damage.

Omission method of accounting for normal spoilage   A process cost method whereby the normally spoiled units are excluded from the equivalent unit computation, thereby increasing the cost per equivalent unit that is used in assigning the cost of normally spoiled units.

Operating budget   See master budget.

Operational control   The process of assuring that specific tasks are carried out effectively and efficiently.

Opportunity cost   The satisfaction, or gain, foregone as a result of taking a given course of action.

Opportunity cost variance (in ex-post variance system)   The difference between the actual income and the ex-post income. The variance that could have been eliminated if the managers were better able to make optimal uses of resources.

Order-filling costs   Costs incurred to fulfill the sale of the products: warehousing, transportation, delivery, and order processing costs.

Order-getting costs   The costs of generating demand for the products: advertising, sales salaries and commissions, sales promotions, and marketing research costs.

Overapplied overhead   The amount by which the applied overhead exceeds the actual overhead.

Participatory budget style   Input and assumptions of budget process come from all levels within the organization, with some give-and-take to reach a mutually agreed-upon base for constructing the budget.

Payback period   The amount of time needed to recoup the initial investment that is required for the project.

Payback reciprocal   The inverse of the payback period: $1/PB$. Under some conditions, it may be a good approximation of a project's internal rate of return.

Payoff table A schedule of conditional values; that is, the results that are expected to occur for each action that can be taken, given a specific state of nature.

Payroll sheet An accounting document used to compute employees' gross wages and withholdings and to summarize them for purposes of an accounting entry.

Period cost An expense that is completely charged off in the period of occurrence as opposed to being assigned to the production.

PERT—Program Evaluation and Review Technique Planning and control of a large-scaled project through the use of a network that shows the precedence relationships between the tasks. A critical path can be identified such that if any of the events on the path are delayed, then the whole project is delayed.

Planning The process of implementing managers' decisions.

Planning Executives Institute A professional organization for those who are involved in a firm's planning activities.

Plant-wide overhead rate A rate of overhead application that is used by all departments.

Plateau learning curve model A model that presumes learning will eventually cease (or reach a plateau).

Practical capacity Theoretical capacity reduced by an allowance for a reasonable amount of nonproductive time.

Predetermined overhead rate A rate of applying overhead to production. Established at the beginning of an accounting period, it facilitates the averaging of costs over all production.

Present value factor A multiplier to convert a dollar flow to its present value. The multiplier depends on the interest rate, the timing of the cash flow, and whether the flow is a single amount or an annuity.

Probability The chance that an event will occur.

Probability distribution A complete specification of all possible events along with their chances of occurrence.

Process cost system A system that accumulates production costs according to responsibility centers and assigns the cost of each center to the products processed by that center.

Product costs The set of the firm's costs that will be assigned to the units produced and released against revenue only when the product is sold.

Production budget Schedule of units needed to be produced in order to meet the various objectives.

Production variance The unutilized capacity resulting from the failure to schedule acquired orders for production.

Profitability index The ratio of the present value of the future net cash flows (excluding the initial investment) to the initial investment.

Profit center A responsibility center wherein the manager has the authority to make decisions that affect the costs and revenues of the center.

Profit variance analysis   A system of variances that explains the reasons why actual profit differed from the projected profit.

Programmed costs   Discretionary costs that, though fixed in nature, can be avoided even in the short run.

Program Planning and Budget System   A process whereby various plans are identified and then a budget developed in support of each plan. The budget is plan oriented rather than responsibility center oriented.

Pure price variance   The difference between the standard material cost and the actual cost multiplied by the standard quantity of material allowed for the output.

Quantity variance (in profit variance analysis)   Difference in income caused by a variation between the total budgeted unit volume of output and the actual volume.

r^2 See coefficient of determination.

R (range) control chart   The interval in which the range (high observation less low observation) of cost observations will probably fall if the process is in control.

Random variables   Variables that can assume any of several possible values.

Reciprocal equation method   A set of equations formulated to find the total cost of operating each of several reciprocally related service departments after all allocations have been made. These equations are then solved simultaneously using algebra or matrix algebra.

Reciprocal services   A situation in which two or more service departments provide output to each other.

Recognition and reassignment method   A process cost method that separately computes the cost of normally spoiled units and then allocates the resulting cost only to those good units that passed the inspection point during the current period.

Recognition criterion   A benchmark, or target, against which performance can be compared.

Recycling   The reuse of spoiled products in a production process.

Regression analysis   A method of constructing an estimating line through sample data such that the line is the best possible fit of the form selected. The squared differences around the line are minimized.

Relative sales value method   See net realizable value method.

Relevant data   Future data that differ from one alternative to another.

Relevant range   The interval of activity for which a given cost behavior is relatively accurate.

Replacement cost   The current cost; the outlay that would have to be made if an asset were to be replaced at the current time.

Residual income   The amount of income earned in excess of a "charge" for the investment used by the responsibility center.

Responsibility accounting   A control system whereby managers are held accountable only for those items over which they can exercise a significant amount of control.

Responsibility center   A subunit of personnel, having a designated supervisor, that is formed as a means of controlling performance.

Return on investment The ratio of income to investment. Both income and investment should be controllable and can be measured in a variety of ways.

Rework The process of correcting damage done to a product.

Risk Uncertainty about the outcome of an action.

Scattergraph A graph of costs as they relate to some measure of activity.

Scrap value The sales value of spoiled production.

s_e See standard error of the estimate.

Securities and Exchange Commission The branch of the U.S. Government responsible for ensuring that individuals who trade in the stock of publicly held companies have access to neutral and fair financial data.

Segment reporting The reporting of the income and asset position for each major product or geographical segment of an organization.

Sensitivity analysis An examination of the influence of change(s) in a specific parameter(s) on the results of a given model.

Separable costs See direct costs.

Service department A responsibility center that provides products and services that are used entirely within the firm.

Shrinkage The evaporation or other disappearance of materials during the production process.

Simulation An "experiment," usually done on the computer, whereby the various random variables are caused to behave according to their respective probability distributions in order to collect data about the expected behavior of the system within which they all react.

Spending variance See either variable or fixed overhead spending variance.

Split-off point The point in the manufacturing process where main or by-products become separately identifiable.

S- model learning curve A model that is a combination of the Stanford-B model and the plateau model.

Spoilage The portion of the firm's finished or partially finished production that is damaged or defective.

Standard error of the estimate A measure of the dispersion of the sample values of the dependent variable around the regression estimate.

Standard error of the parameter A measure of the sampling error that results from using an estimate of the population's parameter.

Standards Carefully predetermined amounts of resources that are expected to be consumed in accomplishing some objective.

Stanford-B learning curve A model that assumes that learning is somewhat slow at the outset.

Started and finished Units placed into production during the current period and transferred out prior to the end of the same period.

States of nature The set of possible conditions that might occur; they are not controllable by the decision maker.

Step-fixed costs   Costs that change in a stair-step manner with respect to some measure of activity.

Step method   A system of allocating reciprocal services whereby one of the service departments is selected to be the first one allocated. After the chosen department's costs are allocated, a second department is chosen and its costs, including the costs allocated from the first department, are allocated to all but the first department allocated. Then these two departments are ignored in making the allocations to the remaining departments (and so forth.)

Stochastic cost-volume-profit analysis   CVP that gives consideration to the uncertainty about the value of relevant random variables: the sales price, quantity demanded, variable cost, and fixed cost, for example.

Stores   Another term for *materials,* especially if it refers to both direct and indirect materials.

Strategic planning   The process of deciding on the objectives of the organization, on changes in these objectives, on the resources used to attain these objectives, and on the policies that are to govern the acquisition, use, and disposition of these resources.

Sunk cost   A past cost; irrelevant to decision making.

Theoretical capacity   The volume of activity that is possible if both people and machines worked continuously.

Theoretical standards   Standards that are set assuming that both people and machinery work at peak efficiency 100% of the time.

Time ticket   An accounting document used to analyze the type of work done by an employee—via department served, or as direct or indirect, for example.

Time value of money   The value attributed to money as a result of its ability to earn interest over time.

Transfer price   The price at which the output of one division of the firm is "sold" to another division of the same firm.

t-ratio ($\hat{b}/s_b$)   The number of standard deviations by which the estimated b value varies from zero.

Treasurer   The officer of the organization responsible for managing the money.

Underapplied overhead   The amount by which the actual overhead exceeds the applied overhead.

Units method of allocating joint costs   The total costs incurred in a joint process are allocated to the various products according to the ratios of a physical measurement of the output.

User decision model   A systems design approach that attempts to provide data that are appropriate for the intended use.

Variable cost   Cost that changes in direct proportion to the measure of activity.

Variable costing   A cost accounting system that does not assign any fixed manufacturing cost to production. Fixed overhead is a period cost.

Variable overhead efficiency variance   The difference between the standard activity level allowed and the actual activity level multiplied by the standard variable overhead rate.

Variable overhead spending variance The difference between the variable overhead budgeted at actual activity levels and the actual variable overhead.

Volume variance See noncontrollable variance.

Waste The loss of a resource (input) during the process of production or the loss of an input before it becomes part of the potential output.

Weighted average equivalent unit method A method that adds the cost of the beginning inventory to a pool of current costs and then allocates the resulting pool of costs to the work effort represented by the beginning inventory plus the current work.

Weighted average method of allocating joint costs The total costs incurred in a joint process are allocated to the various products according to a weighting scheme that reflects the collective differences among the products.

Weighted cost of capital A sum of weighted costs whereby the cost of raising each pool of capital (debt, preferred stock, and common stock) is weighted by the proportion of each pool in comparison to the total capital pool.

Work-in-process The (cost of) units that are not entirely completed at the date of the inventory.

Zero-based budgeting system A budget system whereby each budget is periodically rolled back to zero, requiring the complete justification of every dollar that is returned to the budget.

Index